International Human Rights Law and Practice

Ilias Bantekas is Professor of International Law and Arbitration, Hamad bin Khalifa University (Qatar Foundation), College of Law. He has advised governments, international organisations and NGOs in most fields of human rights and international law, and was a member of the Greek Truth Committee on Debt. His recent books include: *Sovereign Debt and Human Rights* (with C. Lumina, Oxford 2018), and *Commentary on the UN Convention on the Rights of Persons with Disability* (jointly edited with M. A. Stein and D. Anastasiou, Oxford 2018).

Lutz Oette is a Reader in International Law at SOAS, University of London and Director of the SOAS Centre for Human Rights Law. He has pursued human rights cases before several regional and international bodies, and engaged with a range of actors in comparative research, advocacy and reform projects aimed at developing and implementing international human rights standards.

International Human Rights Law and Practice

Third Edition

Ilias Bantekas

Hamad bin Khalifa University (Qatar Foundation)

Lutz Oette

SOAS, University of London

CAMBRIDGE
UNIVERSITY PRESS

CAMBRIDGE
UNIVERSITY PRESS

Shaftesbury Road, Cambridge CB2 8EA, United Kingdom

One Liberty Plaza, 20th Floor, New York, NY 10006, USA

477 Williamstown Road, Port Melbourne, VIC 3207, Australia

314–321, 3rd Floor, Plot 3, Splendor Forum, Jasola District Centre, New Delhi – 110025, India

103 Penang Road, #05–06/07, Visioncrest Commercial, Singapore 238467

Cambridge University Press is part of Cambridge University Press & Assessment, a department of the University of Cambridge.

We share the University's mission to contribute to society through the pursuit of education, learning and research at the highest international levels of excellence.

www.cambridge.org
Information on this title: www.cambridge.org/9781108711753

DOI: 10.1017/9781108612524

First edition Cambridge University Press & Assessment 2013
Second edition 2016
Third edition 2020

A catalogue record for this publication is available from the British Library

Library of Congress Cataloging-in-Publication data
Names: Bantekas, Ilias, author. | Oette, Lutz, author.
Title: International human rights law and practice / Ilias Bantekas, Brunel University; Lutz Oette, School of Oriental and African Studies, University of London.
Description: Third edition. | Cambridge, United Kingdom ; New York, NY : Cambridge University Press, 2020. | Includes bibliographical references and index.
Identifiers: LCCN 2020004146 (print) | LCCN 2020004147 (ebook) |
ISBN 9781108711753 (paperback) | ISBN 9781108612524 (ebook)
Subjects: LCSH: Human rights. | International law and human rights.
Classification: LCC K3240 .B36 2020 (print) | LCC K3240 (ebook) | DDC 341.4/8–dc23
LC record available at https://lccn.loc.gov/2020004146
LC ebook record available at https://lccn.loc.gov/2020004147

ISBN 978-1-108-71175-3 Paperback

This book is dedicated to the late Rupa Reddy,
a dear colleague and talented scholar whose passion for,
and commitment to the human rights of women will be an
abiding memory and a lasting inspiration.

The cover image by Safia Ishaq Mohamed is a painting and artistic reflection of the arrest of members of the No to Women Oppression Group in Sudan. Safia Ishaq Mohamed graduated as a student of the Fine Arts College in Khartoum in 2010, and used her art to speak to the role of women in society. When she took part in demonstrations in 2011 as a member of the pro-democracy Girifna protest movement, she was abducted and raped by three Sudanese security officers. She was widely admired for her subsequent courage to speak out about her ordeal, posting her testimony on YouTube.

Safia Ishaq Mohamed brought her case against Sudan before the African Commission on Human and Peoples' Rights, which is still pending (it was declared admissible in 2014). She subsequently had to flee the country and now lives in France where she has participated in several art exhibitions. She strongly believes in the powerful role of art in addressing human rights issues, which was particularly prominent in the paintings by women during the Sudanese revolution in 2019.

CONTENTS

TABLE OF CASES

Arbitration Tribunals

Harry Roberts (USA) *v.* United Mexican States, General Claims Commission
 (Mexico and United States) (1926) 4 RIAA 77
Methanex Corp *v.* USA (UNCITRAL Rules) Merits (3 August 2005)
Netherlands *v.* United States (Island of Palmas case) (1928) 2 UNRIAA 831
Tinoco Arbitration (Great Britain *v.* Costa Rica) AJIL 18 (1923)
USA–UK Cayuga Indians Arbitral Award (1926) 6 UNRIAA 173

International Centre for the Settlement of Investment Disputes (ICSID)

CMS Gas Transmission Company *v.* Argentine Republic (12 May 2005)
Compãnia del Desarrollo de Santa Elena SA *v.* Costa Rica, Merits
 (17 February 2000)
Continental Casualty Co *v.* Argentine Republic, Merits (15 September 2008)
El Paso Energy International Company *v.* Argentine Republic, Merits
 (31 October 2011)
LG & E *v.* Argentine Republic, Merits (3 October 2006)
Malaysian Historical Salvors *v.* Malaysia, Decision on Annulment
 (16 April 2009)
Mamidoil *v.* Albania, Merits (30 March 2015)
Postova Banka AS and Istrokapital SE *v.* Greece, Merits (9 April 2015)
Saipem *v.* Bangladesh, Decision on Jurisdiction (21 March 2007)
Salini Construttori SpA Italstrade SpA *v.* Morocco, Jurisdiction (23 July 2001)
Saluka Investments BV *v.* Czech Republic, Partial Award on Merits
 (17 March 2006)
Société Générale de Surveillance (SGS) *v.* Pakistan, Decision on Jurisdiction
 (6 August 2003)
Técnicas Medioambientales Tecmed SA *v.* Mexico, Merits (29 May 2003)
Urbaser S.A. and Consorcio de Aguas Bilbao Bizkaia *v.* Argentine Republic
 Award (6 December 2016)
Wena Hotels Ltd *v.* Egypt, Annulment (5 February 2002)

Permanent Court of Arbitration (PCA)

International Courts, Tribunals and Treaty Bodies

African Commission on Human and Peoples' Rights (ACmHPR)

African Committee of Experts on the Rights and Welfare of the Child (ACtERWC)

African Court on Human and Peoples' Rights (ACtHPR)

Caribbean Court of Justice (CCJ)

Committee against Torture (CtAT)

Committee on Economic, Social and Cultural Rights (CESCR)

Committee on the Elimination of Discrimination against Women (CtEDAW)

Committee on the Elimination of Racial Discrimination (CERD)

Committee on the Rights of Persons with Disabilities (CtRPD)

Committee on the Rights of the Child

East African Court of Justice

ECOWAS Community Court of Justice

European Commission and Court of Human Rights (ECtHR)

European Committee of Social Rights (ECSR)

European Court of Justice/Court of Justice of the European Union (CJEU)

Extraordinary African Chamber in the Senegalese Courts

Human Rights Chamber for Bosnia and Herzegovina

Human Rights Committee (HRCtee)

Inter-American Commission on Human Rights (IACHR)

Inter-American Court of Human Rights (IACtHR)

International Court of Justice (ICJ)

International Criminal Court (ICC)

International Criminal Tribunal for Rwanda (ICTR)

International Criminal Tribunal for the former Yugoslavia (ICTY)

Nuremberg International Military Tribunal

Permanent Court of International Justice (PCIJ)

Sierra Leone Special Court (SLSC)

South African Development Community (SADC) Tribunal

Special Tribunal for Lebanon (STL)

UNMIK Advisory Panel

World Trade Organization Dispute Settlement Body

United States – Import prohibition of certain Shrimp and Shrimp Products (20 September 1999) WT/DS58/AV/R (Appellate Body Report), WT/DS58/R (Panel Report)

World War II Military Commissions

Re Dostler, 13 AD 281 (1945)
USA *v.* Carl Krauch et al. (IG Farben case) 15 ILR 668 (1948)
USA *v.* Flick, 14 ILR 266 (1947)
USA *v.* Krupp, 15 ILR 620 (1948)

National Cases

Argentina

Asociación Benghalensis and Others *v.* Ministerio de Salud y Acción Social, Judgment (1 June 2000)
Asociación de Esclerosis Múltiple de Salta *v.* Ministerio de Salud-Estato Nacional (Multiple Sclerosis case) Judgment (18 December 2003)
Campodónico de Beviacqua, Ana Carina *v.* Ministerio de Salud y Banco Drogas Neoplásicas, Judgment (24 October 2000)
Etcheverry *v.* Omint Sociedad Anónima y Servicios, Judgment (13 March 2001)
Settlement Agreement between AJIC and the City of Buenos Aires concerning case 23360/0 (2008) (2 September 2011)
Viceconti *v.* Ministry of Health and Social Welfare, case no. 31, 777/96, Judgment (2 June 1998)

Australia

A *v.* Minister for Immigration and Ethnic Affairs [1997] 190 CLR 225
BGP Properties Pty Limited *v.* Lake Macquarie City Council [2004] NSWLEC 399
Chen Shi Hai *v.* Minister for Immigration and Multicultural Affairs [2000] 201 CLR 293
Gibbs *v.* Capewell (1995) 128 ALR 515
Kruger *v.* The Commonwealth (1997) 190 CLR 1
Minister for Immigration and Multicultural Affairs *v.* Abdi [1999] FCA 299
Re Minister for Immigration and Multicultural Affairs, ex parte Miah [2001] HCA 22
X *v.* Commonwealth [1999] HCA 63
Watson's Bay and South Shore Ferry Co. Ltd *v.* Whitfield [1919] 27 CLR 268

Pakistan

Zia, Shehla *v.* WAPDA, PLD (1994) SC 693

Peru

Azanca Alhelí Meza García, case no. 2945-2003-AA/TC (20 April 2004)
  (Constitutional Tribunal of Peru)

Philippines

Minors Oposa *v.* Secretary of the Dept of Environmental and Natural Resources,
  Philippines Supreme Court judgment (1994) 33 ILM 173

Romania

Constitutional Court judgment no. 872 (25 June 2010)

South Africa

Governing Body of Juma Musjid Primary School and Others *v.* Essay NO. and
  Others [2011] ZACC 13
Government of the Republic of South Africa and Others *v.* Grootboom and
  Others [2000] ZACC 19
Hoffman *v.* South African Airways [2000] ZACC 17
Khosa and Others *v.* Minister of Social Development [2004] 6 BCLR 569
Madzodzo and Others *v.* Minister of Basic Education, Order (20 February 2014)
Mazibuko and Others *v.* City of Johannesburg [2009] ZACC 28
Pharmaceutical Manufacturers' Association of South Africa et al. *v.* President
  of the Republic of South Africa, case no. 4183/98 (RSA High Court,
  Transvaal provincial division)
S *v.* Petane [1988] 3 SARL 51
Soobramoney *v.* Minister of Health, KwaZulu-Natal, 1998 (1) SA 765
South African Minister of Health *v.* Treatment Action Campaign, 2002 (5) SA 721

Spain

Guatemalan Generals case, Constitutional Tribunal (26 September 2005)
Judgment No. 1263/2018, Spanish Supreme Court (17 July 2018)

Sri Lanka

Bulankulama and Others *v.* Secretary, Ministry of Industrial Development and
  Others (Eppawela Case) (Sri Lanka) (2000) 3 Sri LR 243
Singarasa *v.* Attorney General, S.C. SPL (LA) No.182/99 (2006)

United States (US)

ABBREVIATIONS

AC	Appeal Cases law reports (England)
ACHPR	African Charter on Human and Peoples' Rights
ACHR	American Convention on Human Rights
ACJ	African Court of Justice
ACmHPR	African Commission on Human and Peoples' Rights
ACtERWC	African Committee of Experts on the Rights and Welfare of the Child
ACtHPR	African Court on Human and Peoples' Rights
AD	Annual Digest
AHRLR	African Human Rights Law Reports
AI	Amnesty International
AICHR	ASEAN Intergovernmental Commission on Human Rights
AIR	All India Reports
All ER	All England Reports
ALR	Australian Law Reports
ARIO	ILC Articles on the Responsibility of International Organisations
ARSIWA	Articles on Responsibility of States for Internationally Wrongful Acts
ASEAN	Association of Southeast Asian Nations
AU	African Union
BCLR	Butterworth's Constitutional Law Reports (RSA)
BGH	*Bundesgerichtshof* (German Federal Court of Justice)
BHRC	Butterworth's Human Rights Cases
BiH	Bosnia and Herzegovina
BIT	bilateral investment treaty
BLD	Bangladesh Legal Decision (reports)
BLR	Botswana Law Reports
BOP	balance of payments
BVerfG	*Bundesverfassungsgericht* (German Constitutional Court)
BVerwG	*Bundesverwaltungsgericht* (Federal Administrative Court of Germany)
CAT	Convention against Torture and Other Cruel, Inhuman or Degrading Treatment or Punishment

CCJ	Caribbean Court of Justice
CDO	collateral debt obligations
CDS	credit default swaps
CED	Committee on Enforced Disappearances
CEDAW	Convention on the Elimination of All Forms of Discrimination against Women
CEJIL	Centre for Justice and International Law
CERD	Committee on the Elimination of Racial Discrimination
CESCR	Committee on Economic, Social and Cultural Rights
CETS	Council of Europe Treaty Series
CIA	Central Intelligence Agency
CIF	Commodity Investment Fund
CJEU	Court of Justice of the European Union
CLR	Commonwealth Law Reports
Cm.	Command Paper (UK)
CMW	Committee on Migrant Workers
CoE	Council of Europe
COHRE	Centre on Housing Rights and Evictions
CoM	Committee of Ministers (Europe)
CommHR	Commission on Human Rights (UN)
CPED	International Convention for the Protection of All Persons from Enforced Disappearance
CPP-NPA	Communist Party of the Philippines – New People's Army
CPT	European Committee for the Prevention of Torture and Inhuman or Degrading Treatment or Punishment
CRC	Convention on the Rights of the Child
CRPD	Convention on the Rights of Persons with Disabilities
CSCE	Conference on Security and Cooperation in Europe
CSOs	civil society organisations
CtAT	Committee against Torture
CtEDAW	Committee on the Elimination of Discrimination against Women
CtRC	Committee on the Rights of the Child
CtRPD	Committee on the Rights of Persons with Disabilities
DAC	Development Assistance Committee (OECD)
DEVAW	Declaration on the Elimination of Violence Against Women (1994)
DLR	Dominion Law Reports
D & R	Decisions and Reports of the European Committee on Human Rights
DTA	Detainee Treatment Act (USA)
EAC	East African Community

EC	European Community
ECB	European Central Bank
ECCC	Extraordinary Chambers in the Courts of Cambodia
ECHR	European Convention on Human Rights
ECJ	European Court of Justice
ECOSOC	Economic and Social Council (UN)
ECOWAS	Economic Community of West African States
ECOWAS CCJ	ECOWAS Community Court of Justice
ECR	European Court Reports (ECJ)
ECSR	European Committee of Social Rights
ECtHR	European Court of Human Rights
EFSF	European Financial Stability Facility
EHRAC	European Human Rights Advocacy Centre
EHRR	European Human Rights Reports
EOHR	Egyptian Organization for Human Rights
ESC	economic, social and cultural rights
ESM	European Stability Mechanism
EU	European Union
EULEX	EU Rule of Law Mission in Kosovo
EWHC	High Court of England and Wales
F.	Federal reporter (USA)
FAO	Food and Agriculture Organization
FCO	Foreign and Commonwealth Office (UK)
FDI	foreign direct investment
FGC	female genital cutting
FGM	female genital mutilation
FIDH	International Federation of Human Rights
FIDIC	International Federation of Consulting Engineers
FPIC	free, prior and informed consent
FRONTEX	Frontières Extérieures (European Border and Coast Guard Agency)
FRY	Federal Republic of Yugoslavia
G-77	Group of 77 (nations)
GATT	General Agreement on Tariffs and Trade
GC	Grand Chamber (of the ECtHR)
GDP	gross domestic product
GDR	German Democratic Republic (East Germany)
GEF	global environmental facility
GRI	Global Reporting Initiative
GSP	Generalised System of Preferences
HCJ	High Court of Justice (Israel)
HDI	Human Development Index

HIPC	highly indebted poor countries
HPG	Humanitarian Policy Group
HRAP	Human Rights Advisory Panel
HRBA	human rights-based approach
HRC	Human Rights Council
HRCtee	Human Rights Committee
HRIA	human rights impact assessment
HRRP	Human Rights Review Panel
HRW	Human Rights Watch
IACHR	Inter-American Commission on Human Rights
IACtHR	Inter-American Court of Human Rights
IBA	International Bar Association
IBP	International Budget Partnerships
IBRD	International Bank for Reconstruction and Development
ICC	International Criminal Court
ICCPR	International Covenant on Civil and Political Rights
ICERD	International Convention on the Elimination of All Forms of Racial Discrimination
ICESCR	International Covenant on Economic, Social and Cultural Rights
ICHRP	International Council on Human Rights Policy
ICJ	International Court of Justice
ICRC	International Committee of the Red Cross
ICRMW	International Convention on the Protection of the Rights of All Migrant Workers and Members of Their Families
ICSID	International Centre for the Settlement of Investment Disputes
ICSPCA	International Convention on the Suppression and Punishment of the Crime of Apartheid
ICTR	International Criminal Tribunal for Rwanda
ICTY	International Criminal Tribunal for the former Yugoslavia
IDB	International Development Bank
IDP	internally displaced person
IFI	international financial institution
IGO	intergovernmental organisation
IHL	international humanitarian law
ILA	International Law Association
ILC	International Law Commission
ILM	International Legal Materials
ILO	International Labour Organization
ILP	international legal personality
ILR	International Law Reports

IMF	International Monetary Fund
IMT	International Military Tribunal at Nuremberg
INSC	Supreme Court of India Judgments
IP	intellectual property
IPCC	Independent Police Complaints Commission (England and Wales)
IPP	indigenous peoples plan
IPPF	indigenous peoples planning framework
IRA	Irish Republican Army
IRCT	International Rehabilitation Council for Torture Victims
IS	Islamic State
ISC	Intelligence and Security Committee (UK)
IVF	in-vitro fertilization
KB	King's Bench
KFOR	Kosovo Force
LAS	League of Arab States
LDCs	least developed countries
LFJL	Lawyers for Justice in Libya
LGBTI	lesbian, gay, bisexual, transgender and intersex
LNTS	League of Nations Treaty Series
LRA	Lord's Resistance Army
LTTE	Liberation Tigers of Tamil Eelam
MDER	minimum dietary energy requirements
MDGs	Millennium Development Goals
MFI	microfinancing institution
MFN	most favoured nation
MI5	Military Intelligence, Section 5 (UK)
MICS	Multiple Indicator Cluster Survey
MIGA	Multilateral Investment Guarantee Agency
MLA	mutual legal assistance
MMDA	Model Mine Development Agreement
MNC	multinational corporation
MoU	memorandum of understanding
MRM	monitoring and reporting mechanism
NATO	North Atlantic Treaty Organization
NBC	nuclear, biological and chemical first aid kit
NgHC	Nigerian High Court
NGO	non-governmental organisation
NHRI	national human rights institution
NLM	national liberation movement
NSAs	non-state actors
NTC	National Transitional Council (Libya)

OAS	Organization of American States
OAU	Organisation of African Unity
ODA	overseas development assistance
OECD	Organisation for Economic Cooperation and Development
OHCHR	Office of the High Commissioner for Human Rights
OJ	Official Journal (EC)
OLC	Office of the Legal Counsel (US Dept of Justice)
OP	Operational Policy (World Bank)
OPCAT	Optional Protocol to the Convention against Torture
OSCE	Organization for Security and Cooperation in Europe
PAT	poverty assessment tool
PB	participatory budgeting
PCA	Permanent Court of Arbitration
PCIJ	Permanent Court of International Justice
PII	public interest immunity
PKK	Kurdistan Workers' Party
PLD	All Pakistan Legal Decisions
PLO	Palestine Liberation Organization
PNS	parasympathetic nervous system
POW	prisoner of war
PRGF	poverty reduction growth facility
PRSP	poverty reduction strategy paper
QB	Queen's Bench
R 61	Rule 61 decision (ICTY)
R2P	responsibility to protect
ROE	rules of engagement
RSA	Republic of South Africa
RSLR	River State Law Reports (Nigeria)
RTD	right to development
RTHE	right to a healthy environment
SA	South African (law reports)
SADC	South African Development Community
SAP	structural adjustment programme
SCC	Supreme Court Cases (India)
SCR	Supreme Court Reports (India)
SCR	Supreme Court Reports (Canada)
S. Ct.	Supreme Court Reports (USA)
SERAC	Social and Economic Rights Action Centre
SIA	social impact assessment
SLSC	Sierra Leone Special Court
SMEs	small and medium-sized enterprises
SNS	sympathetic nervous system

SPLM	Sudan People's Liberation Movement
SPT	Subcommittee on Prevention of Torture
Stat.	US Statutes at large
STL	Special Tribunal for Lebanon
TEU	Treaty on the European Union
TFEU	Treaty on the Functioning of the European Union
TRIPS	Agreement on Trade-Related Aspects of Intellectual Property Rights
TRNC	Turkish Republic of Northern Cyprus
UDHR	Universal Declaration of Human Rights
UHRC	Uganda Human Rights Commission
UK	United Kingdom
UKHL	UK House of Lords
UKSC	UK Supreme Court
UN	United Nations
UNAMID	AU/UN Hybrid Operation in Darfur
UNCAC	UN Convention against Corruption
UNCITRAL	UN Commission on International Trade Law
UNCLOS	UN Convention on the Law of the Sea
UNCTAD	UN Conference on Trade and Development
UNDP	UN Development Programme
UNDRIP	UN Declaration on the Rights of Indigenous Peoples
UNEP	United Nations Environment Programme
UNESCO	United Nations Educational, Scientific and Cultural Organization
UNGA	UN General Assembly
UNHCR	UN High Commissioner for Refugees
UNICEF	UN International Children's (Emergency) Fund
UNMIK	UN Mission in Kosovo
UNMIS	UN Mission in Sudan
UNOSAT	UN Operational Satellite Applications Program
UNOSOM	UN Operation in Somalia
UNRIAA	UN Reports of International Arbitral Awards
UNSC	UN Security Council
UNTS	UN Treaty Series
UPR	universal periodic review
US	US Supreme Court [reporter]
US(A)	United States (of America)
USC	United States Codes
VAT	value added tax
VCLT	Vienna Convention on the Law of Treaties
WAF	Women's Action Forum (Pakistan)

WFS	World Food Summits
WGEID	Working Group on Enforced or Involuntary Disappearances
WHO	World Health Organization
WLR	Weekly Law Reports (England)
WMA	World Medical Association
WTO	World Trade Organization
ZACC	Constitutional Court of South Africa (reports)

Introduction

The gap between the promise embodied in international human rights law and actual practice is frustrating, as those working in the field know only too well. A critical observer may well turn round saying, 'I told you so, your belief in the power of law was mistaken in the first place'. Yet a believer in the system may counter, 'Yes, we are facing some problems, but we're still just at the beginning; we need more human rights law and things will improve'. These opposing strands point to broader questions, namely whether human rights provide the best language to safeguard core values and, if so, whether law is a suitable vehicle to promote, protect and vindicate them. Posing the very question suggests that human rights law has somehow lost its innocence – or naivety – in the sense that it is no longer self-evidently good or considered able to provide solutions to the myriad contemporary challenges. This is not a bad thing: on the contrary. Human rights are born out of intense struggles and develop in constant contestation with power and power relations. The law on human rights is therefore at any given time a temporary reflection of an understanding that is already pregnant with future developments and challenges. Being aware of the contentious nature of human rights protects from developing self-congratulatory attitudes and guards against their misappropriation by elites. Ultimately, human rights are not something fragile out there that need protection. Instead, they are constantly claimed and developed, if not made anew, by multiple actors, all of us, who engage with them in one way or another, as rights-holders, advocates or otherwise, if only by reading this book.

The book is based on this premise, which it seeks to mainstream into the format of a textbook. As this is primarily an international human rights *law* textbook, it seeks to do justice to both the law and the struggle for human rights, and how they interact in practice. With these considerations in mind, the book aims to offer both a sound exposition of the law and a contextual perspective of the realities in which the law is set and how various actors use it. Our intention is to go beyond theory and human rights jurisprudence, and to bring out and reflect on the thinking, challenges and dilemmas faced by the various actors making up the system. To this end each chapter includes a substantial part on practical application, including a series of case studies that seek to capture the complex realities of international human rights law in action. This approach provides unique insights into the global endeavour for human rights protection and how human rights and international human rights law are constructed in the process. We hope that this will encourage critical contextual thinking and provide a good sense of what international human rights law means in practice.

Being true to the importance of discourse in human rights, the book is enriched by a plurality of voices. Twenty-five practitioners speak to us through a series of interviews. These practitioners are directly concerned with human rights and many of them have been at the forefront of critical developments. Indeed, several interviewees have suffered violations of human rights and/ or faced repercussions on account of their work. The interviewees have been selected so as to share a range of different perspectives. They include grass-roots activists using multiple strategies to advocate human rights protection and changes to the system; representatives of non-governmental organisations (NGOs) known for innovative approaches; lawyers who have litigated human rights cases at the national, regional and international level; doctors who have been at the heart of documenting violations; academics combining theory and practice; those working for and with human rights bodies at the national, regional and international levels; and military legal advisors reflecting on the issue of battlefield compliance.

The book covers the foundations of human rights and international human rights law, institutional protection, a number of individual and collective rights, and a series of cross-cutting issues posing particular challenges for the effective protection of human rights in various contexts. It comprises twenty chapters. The first three chapters address foundational questions of international human rights, including its law and practice. In Chapters 4 to 6 we set out the institutional framework of human rights protection at the international and regional level; these are complemented by Chapter 7, which focuses specifically on individual complaints procedures. Chapters 8 to 15 focus on the various types of rights: civil and political rights; economic, social and cultural rights; group rights; the human rights of women; the rights of the child; the rights of vulnerable groups and persons; the right to development; and victims' rights and reparation. In Chapters 16 to 20 we examine human rights in the broader context, discussing both promises and challenges that have become apparent in addressing pressing issues. These include protection during times of armed conflict; individual criminal accountability; counter-terrorism and human rights; the difficulties posed by non-state actors (NSAs) for the system of human rights protection; and the detrimental impact of the process of globalisation. Chapters 1 to 3, 5 to 8 and 15 were written by Lutz Oette (15.9.3 by Ilias Bantekas), Chapters 4, 9, 10, 13, 16 to 20 by Ilias Bantekas, Chapters 12 and 13 jointly (12.1 to 12.4.1, 13.3.3,

13.3.5 and 13.3.6 by Ilias Bantekas; 12.5 to Case Study 12.2, and 13.1–13.3.2 and 13.3.4 by Lutz Oette), and Chapter 11 by the late Rupa Reddy.

Given the inherent limitations of a textbook, each chapter provides a list of further reading, comprising literature and key websites, for the reader wishing to engage in depth with the issues raised and to undertake further research. For the sake of brevity in the text itself, we provide full case citations in the Table of Cases only. The footnotes cite the case name, and human rights court or treaty body (as abbreviated) and year, for example *Rajapakse v. Sri Lanka* (HRCtee) (2006). For national cases, the case name is followed by the country and the year, for example, *Boumediene v. Bush* (US) (2008).

The text was completed in May 2019, and we have endeavoured to include developments up to that date as much as possible. Every effort has been made to ensure that all website links were live as of that date.

While writing a book can be a rather solitary endeavour, it is also always a collective process and achievement. This collective nature is evident in the book itself and we greatly appreciate the contribution of those interviewed for the book, namely Morten Koch Andersen, Tzanetos Antypas, Bill Bowring, Başak Çali, Moataz El Fegiery, Basil Fernando, Lesley Ann Foster, Siri Frigaard, Charles Garraway, Eric Holt-Giménez, M. C. Iqbal, Med S. K. Kaggwa, Ibrahima Kane, Huma Shakeb Khan, Cephas Lumina, Benyam Dawit Mezmur, Ramanou Nassirou, Önder Özkalipçi, Eibe Riedel, Oswaldo Ruiz-Chiriboga, Soliman M. Santos, Elham Saudi, Mandira Sharma, Clive Stafford Smith and Sohail A. Warraich, as well as Robert Francis Garcia for his contribution. We are also grateful for the valuable research assistance and other contributions by a good number of people, particularly Menna Seged Abraha, Katerina Akestoridi, Laila Alodaat, Julie Bardeche, Madeeha Dani, Georgios Dimitropoulos, Mariam Fazal Faruqi, Sarah Fulton, Andrew Hagiopan, Yusuke Hara, Melanie Horn, Jose Sebastiao Manuel, Laura Imogen Mcleish, Julie Marie Olesen, Guillermo Otalora, Kharunya Paramaguru, Maja Pecana, Eleni Polymenopoulou, Veronica Ranza, Mervat Rishmawi, Virginie Rouas, Fahad Siddiqui, Salma Yusuf and Parisa Zangeneh.

We also thank Marta Walkowiak, Valerie Appleby and Caitlin Lisle at Cambridge University Press for their encouragement and support throughout, and Margaret Humbert for her outstanding editorial work.

Our greatest debt belongs to those whose attitude inspired the book, that is all those who cannot stand injustice and have, by word or by deed, given substance to what a life in dignity, freedom and equal rights means.

1 International Human Rights Law and Notions of Human Rights: Foundations, Achievements and Challenges

CONTENTS

1.1 INTRODUCTION

The term human rights is frequently used as if it were self-explanatory. It is tempting and not uncommon to view 'human rights' as something intrinsically good. Human rights are often labelled (somewhat mockingly) as the new religion, a label which illustrates the elevated status they appear to enjoy. On closer inspection, it becomes evident that the term human rights is used freely and sometimes loosely by members of different disciplines and the public at large, meaning different things – both positive and negative – to different people, depending on the context and the purpose for which it is used. It is therefore important to clarify the meaning(s) of the term by tracing its genealogy and examining its use in various contexts.

This undertaking cannot be confined to charting the development of international human rights law. Equating human rights with rights recognised in international treaties and/or other legal sources may in practice suffice when addressing particular human rights issues. Beyond this, it amounts to taking a purely positivist position that provides little guidance in response to a crucial question. Can a claim that something be recognised as a human right, for example the right to same-sex marriage, be justified, even if it is currently not explicitly recognised in law?

Human rights have an important dual function: they are claims based on particular values or principles and often also legal rights that entail entitlements and freedoms. Philosophical and political conceptions of human rights are broader than international human rights law, which is essentially a normative term referring to rights validated in recognised sources. While the two spheres are closely intertwined, they do not necessarily share a causal or automatic relationship, i.e. that every claim must transform into a legally recognised right. Nor is the relationship always harmonious. A legally recognised right may be defined too narrowly and may therefore exclude certain categories: for example age may not explicitly fall within the purview of the right to non-discrimination, or conversely a recognised right may be wider than thin theories of human rights based on a limited number of core rights.

To take the meaning of human rights for granted, or simply to refer to formulas denoting rights that we have by virtue of being human, would ignore the controversy surrounding their foundations and validity. Theories of human rights abound, including substantive (based on moral values or foundational postulates), formal (constructive, pragmatic, discourse), subaltern (human rights as distinctive practices born out of struggle) and post-modern (empathy for the other) approaches, as well as political theories, such as liberal or socialist notions of human rights. It is in particular the purported universality of human rights, i.e. their applicability to everyone, everywhere and anytime, that has given rise to enduring debates. Those often, somewhat misleadingly, labelled 'cultural relativists' have raised important challenges regarding the supposed origins, validity, scope of application and politics of human rights. The question of political use and/or abuse of the language of human rights reaches beyond the universality debate, but is an integral part of what can be seen as an increased probing of the 'innocence' of human rights. These overlapping debates may be seen as bewildering if not downright counterproductive, potentially undermining support for human rights at a time when much needs to be done to ensure their effective protection. However, downplaying or dismissing the importance of these debates may lead to a failure to answer satisfactorily the question of what we mean when we refer to human rights, which is critical in situations where the very idea is being challenged. It is perhaps inevitable that the notion of human rights is and will remain charged and will be used for differing if not contradictory ends. This does not mean that the notion is entirely open-ended, but it counsels against using it lightly without having considered its multiple dimensions. For human rights advocates, developing an understanding that is critically aware of these aspects is arguably the best way towards being convincing in the recurring public debates about human rights.

1.2   THE DEVELOPMENT OF HUMAN RIGHTS AND INTERNATIONAL HUMAN RIGHTS LAW

The founding document of international human rights law, i.e. the Universal Declaration of Human Rights (UDHR), refers in its preamble and article 1 to claims and freedoms that human beings enjoy by virtue of their humanity: that is, inherent rights. These rights are based on the principles of dignity, equality and liberty, and are underpinned by notions of solidarity. While the notion of human rights is arguably of more recent origin, it is part of a broader development that can be traced back to the earlier stages of human history.

At the core of human rights lie fundamental questions about the nature of human beings and their relationship with each other as members of societies, including 'international society'. In this context human rights address the relationship of individuals to others, in particular to those in a position of power (especially civil and political rights, equality and non-discrimination) and the relationships of groups and their members to others (minority rights, right to self-determination and rights of indigenous peoples); the settlement of disputes and administration of justice (fair trial in modern parlance); rights to participate in the polis (particularly freedom of expression and related rights, including the right to vote); and the material (in the broadest sense) conditions for a life of dignity and freedom (social, economic and cultural rights; the right to development).

This section traces the historical development of human rights and its most prominent manifestation, international human rights law. It examines the antecedents and formation of human rights with a view both to locating them in a broader socio-political history and to identifying their specific nature. This undertaking is important at a time when the validity of human rights, though seemingly triumphant, is being called into question on account of their association with particular historical and political developments and ideas that are associated with Western secular liberal democracies. Reflecting on shared concerns throughout history and identifying strands of thought and practices that have contributed to their development can, in this context, open up perspectives that provide human rights with broad-based legitimacy.

1.2.1   Foundations

International human rights law is a rather late addition to the body of international law whose modern origins are commonly located in the seventeenth and eighteenth centuries.[1] International law governed the relationship

---

[1] See for a thorough account, W. G. Grewe, *The Epochs of International Law* (Walter de Gruyter, 2000), and for a concise summary, S. C. Neff, 'A Short History of International Law', in M. D. Evans (ed.), *International Law*, 5th edn (Oxford University Press, 2018) 3–27.

between states, which were recognised as its sole subjects. States were considered absolutely sovereign, which meant that the treatment of citizens and other individuals on their territories fell within their exclusive prerogative. While certain human rights concerns, such as religious persecution, were at times raised, individual or collective rights as understood today did not form part of the corpus of international law. This explains why international human rights law, when emerging with considerable force following World War II, drew heavily on ethical imperatives, concepts of rights and historical sources, as well as national declarations and constitutions. This was evident in the preparatory work to the UDHR, which was informed by the views of a number of philosophers and intellectuals about the nature and content of human rights and borrowed substantially from national rights declarations.[2]

Ancient and traditional cultures and societies, and the world's major religions, share a deep concern about human nature, ethics and justice. The major religions were faced with the task of constructing an ethical framework for the conduct of their members. This often took the form of commandments and the definition of desirable if not obligatory conduct, adherence to which would bring the rewards promised by each religion. This ranged from the principle of *ahimsa*, non-violence, shared by Hindus, Jains and Buddhists, to the ten commandments of the Old Testament, including 'thou shalt not kill', and the vision of a just society based on respect for the sanctity of life in Islam, complemented by exhortations to limit wealth and distribute material goods fairly.[3] Indian rulers such as Kautilya (350–283 BC) extolled the virtue of the rule of law in the treatise *Arthashastra*, or, as in the case of Asoka (304–232 BC), declared religious tolerance.[4] African societies also developed intricate principles and rules that governed the rights and duties of their members.[5] While notions of individual autonomy and rights were known in some societies, the question of how human beings treat each other and how best to exercise power in a polis was frequently framed as a matter of virtuous conduct and justice in conformity with reason, religious or customary commands. The principal concern was therefore the creation of a harmonious and just society rather than the protection of the rights of individuals. Nevertheless, it is clear that the principles, commandments and practices sketched out above have contributed to the development of modern human rights law.[6]

---

[2] See below at 1.2.6.

[3] See for a good account of 'early ethical contributions to human rights', M. R. Ishay, *The History of Human Rights: From Ancient Times to the Globalization Era* (University of California Press, 2008) 16–61.

[4] Ibid., 29–30.

[5] See M. Mutua, *Human Rights: A Political and Cultural Critique* (University of Pennsylvania Press, 2002) 71–93, and the work of F. M. Deng on the Dinka, a good overview of which can be found in W. Twining, *General Jurisprudence: Understanding Law from a Global Perspective* (Cambridge University Press, 2009) 378–93.

[6] As evident in the UN Educational, Scientific and Cultural Organization (UNESCO) inquiry informing the UDHR. See below at 1.2.6.

1.2.2 The American and French Declarations of Rights

The United States (US) Declaration of Independence (1776) (and later the Bill of Rights (1791)) and the French Declaration of the Rights of Man and of the Citizen (1789) were the outcome of political struggles that drew on natural law and liberal theories of rights.[7] The American Declaration emphasised the right to life, liberty and the pursuit of happiness, while the French Declaration stressed the right to liberty, property, security and resistance to oppression. Both declarations had a considerable influence on international human rights law, particularly the UDHR.[8] However, a critical analysis shows that the declarations foreshadowed a number of problems that have continued to haunt international human rights law and are at the heart of many of today's debates. Their shortcomings are readily apparent: the declarations speak of the rights of 'man'; the rights granted are predominantly civil and political, reflecting and privileging certain class interests; and the documents failed to address a number of practices that violate fundamental rights. It is indeed a (telling) paradox that it was not seen as contradictory that these rights were declared while the American settlers were invading indigenous peoples' land, destroying their cultures and practising slavery. At the same time, France (and other states) pursued a policy of imperialism and colonialism and large groups of individuals in their own societies, such as women, were effectively excluded and barred from the enjoyment of rights.[9]

From their inception, the language of rights found in the declarations faced a virulent backlash and attacks from various schools of thought. Those opposed to the liberal bourgeois ideas reflected in the French Declaration, such as Edmund Burke (1729–1797), criticised the abstract and individualistic nature of rights.[10] Burke defended traditional rights, claiming that these reflected long-standing developments and inhered organically in the community. Rights were complemented by duties and did not allow the overthrow of government. This 'conservative' perspective has proved highly influential

---

[7] See in particular the works of Thomas Hobbes, John Locke, Thomas Paine, Jean-Jacques Rousseau and Montesquieu. On the historical context and particularly the French Declaration, see J. Waldron (ed.), *Nonsense upon Stilts: Bentham, Burke and Marx on the Rights of Man* (Methuen, 1987) 7–28.

[8] See in this context also S. Moyn, *The Last Utopia: Human Rights in History* (The Belknap Press of Harvard University Press, 2010), who argues that the declarations recognised citizens' rights and that today's human rights are radically different, and essentially a recent development, which he locates in the 1970s. Further, P. Alston, 'Book Review: Does the Past Matter? On the Origins of Human Rights' (2013) 126 *Harvard Law Review* 2043, particularly at 2066ff.

[9] See in this context U. Baxi, *The Future of Human Rights*, 3rd edn (Oxford University Press, 2008) 59–95.

[10] See account in Waldron, above note 7, 77–95.

in informing communitarian critiques of the concept of human rights[11] and finds its echoes in contemporary debates on a British Bill of Rights.[12]

The French Declaration was derided as 'nonsense upon stilts' by writers such as Jeremy Bentham (1748–1832), who launched a scathing attack on the notion of natural rights.[13] Bentham argued that rights were only rights if they had been recognised by law, i.e. they must be posited and do not have an independent existence. As the foremost utilitarian thinker, Bentham viewed the primary purpose of rights as maximising aggregate happiness (based on security, subsistence, abundance and equality). The utilitarian attack was characterised by a strong adherence to positivism as a means to escape the metaphysical uncertainty, if not fiction, of natural law. However, legal positivism's faith in a formal law-making process as self-validating bears the inherent risk that the very existence of a law is seen as sufficient justification for its commands irrespective of its substance. The risk posed by extreme positivism was starkly exposed in the twentieth century after the Nazi period and the fall of communist states, such as the German Democratic Republic (GDR), when officials justified violations by referring to existing national laws. Germany's judiciary responded to this challenge by invoking the Radbruch formula. Gustav Radbruch (1878–1949) argued that statutory law should be set aside if it is entirely incompatible with the idea of justice, in particular where the law deliberately denies equality and does not seek to advance the ultimate goal of any law, i.e. to serve justice.[14] Radbruch's formula marked a partial return to natural law which was also propagated by other legal philosophers such as Ernst Bloch (1885–1977), who had become disenchanted with the decoupling of law and justice inherent in positive law.[15]

The Industrial Revolution in Europe was characterised by stark inequalities and the inhuman conditions in which a large number of children and adults had to work and live.[16] Unsurprisingly, the nineteenth-century working

---

[11] See on communitarianism, W. Kymlicka, *Contemporary Political Philosophy*, 2nd edn (Oxford University Press, 2002) 212–21.

[12] L. Maer and A. Horne, 'Background to proposals for a British Bill of Rights and Duties', SN/PC/04559 (3 February 2009), online at http://researchbriefings.parliament.uk/Research Briefing/Summary/SN04559#fullreport. See further C. Gearty, *On Fantasy Island: Britain, Europe, and Human Rights* (Oxford University Press, 2016).

[13] Reproduced, with commentary, in Waldron, above note 7, 34–45.

[14] See on the practice of German courts in respect of crimes committed by officials of the GDR, *Streletz, Kessler and Krenz* v. *Germany* (ECtHR) (2001) para. 22, and the findings of the ECtHR, at para. 87: 'that a State practice such as the GDR's border policing policy, which flagrantly infringes human rights and above all the right to life, the supreme value in the international hierarchy of human rights, cannot be covered by the protection of Article 7 § 1 of the Convention [prohibition of retroactive application of criminal law]'.

[15] See for a discussion of Bloch's ideas, C. Douzinas and A. Gearey, *Critical Jurisprudence: The Political Philosophy of Justice* (Hart, 2005) 99–103.

[16] See e.g., F. Engels, *The Condition of the Working Class in England* (Penguin Classics, 2006 (first published in 1844)).

class and labour movements had mixed views of the conceptions of rights embodied in the American and French declarations. Karl Marx (1818–1883) argued in his work 'On the Jewish Question' that human rights as defined in the declarations, in particular the right to property, were used to secure the interests of the capitalist class.[17] He saw human rights as antithetical to a communist society that would overcome the antagonism between the individual and the state by providing for everyone according to his or her needs. Workers, trade unions, socialist movements and leftist political parties have against this background often been critical of the notion of human rights and the very apparatus of the state and the law meant to protect these rights. Nevertheless, it is clear that these actors have made important contributions to the development of human rights law, particularly in respect of the right to non-discrimination, political rights, economic, social and cultural rights, as well as collective rights.[18]

Notwithstanding these criticisms, the American and French declarations exerted symbolic significance and became important reference points as the language of rights and liberties was increasingly invoked to buttress demands for equality, freedom and self-determination.

1.2.3   The Struggle for Rights in the Nineteenth Century

The nineteenth century witnessed a growing struggle for rights which was often inspired by the language of the declarations. Feminists, for example, advocated a Declaration of the Rights of Women (Olympe de Gouges (1748–1793) in 1790) and non-discrimination (Mary Wollstonecraft, 1759–1797).[19] Although these endeavours were unsuccessful at the time, they laid the foundation for later women's rights movements.[20] Another major movement evolved to call for the abolition of slavery, an ancient practice that had been transformed into a globalised commercial enterprise negating liberty and dignity and inflicting extreme suffering. The abolitionist movement had been active since the late eighteenth century,[21] but the practice of slavery only ended after a series of struggles, such as those by François-Dominique Toussaint-L'Ouverture (1743–1803), who led a successful anti-colonial

---

[17] See discussion in Waldron, above note 7, 122–4. See further P. O'Connell, 'On the Human Rights Question' (2018) 40 *Human Rights Quarterly* 962.

[18] Ishay, above note 3, 118–72.

[19] M. Wollstonecraft, *A Vindication of the Rights of Women* (Penguin Classics, 2004 (first published 1792)). Olympe de Gouges' Declaration of the Rights of Women can be found in M. R. Ishay, *The Human Rights Reader*, 2nd edn (Routledge, 2007) 175–80.

[20] See Chapter 11.

[21] J. R. Oldfield, *Popular Politics and British Anti-slavery: The Mobilisation of Public Opinion against the Slave Trade, 1787–1807* (Frank Cass, 1998).

uprising in Haiti,[22] and the American Civil War.[23] The transnational movement advocating the abolition of the slave trade played a pivotal role in universally outlawing slavery, as reflected in a series of international treaties.[24] These developments set important international precedents for the recognition of dignity, equality and freedom as fundamental principles applying to the whole of humanity. Equally, nationalist movements throughout the nineteenth and the twentieth centuries invoked the principles of the declarations to demand self-determination and independence for colonised countries.[25] However, power relations and international law edifices developed in the nineteenth and early twentieth centuries combined to delay the end of colonialism,[26] a practice that was marked by large-scale rights violations. The legacy of colonialism continues to exert a profound and largely adverse influence on the protection of human rights, particularly in the way power is exercised at the national and international level.

In the realm of international law the American and French declarations, for all their influence on national constitutions, did not translate into a state practice that recognised human rights or which pierced the veil of sovereignty. The nineteenth century witnessed nascent developments in the field of international humanitarian law, which grew out of a desire to limit excesses on the battlefields.[27] However, international humanitarian law was primarily conceived as a system that imposed an obligation of restraint on the warring parties rather than one that conferred any subjecthood on individuals. One seeming exception to the lack of protection of individuals under international law at the time was the diplomatic protection relating to the minimum standard of treatment of 'aliens'.[28] According to this rule, injury to an alien, including what would be considered human rights violations by

---

[22] J. D. Popkin, *You are All Free: The Haitian Revolution and the Abolition of Slavery* (Cambridge University Press, 2010). See for a brief overview, N. Stammers, *Human Rights and Social Movements* (Pluto Press, 2009) 63–7.

[23] D. Waldstreicher, *The Struggle against Slavery: A History in Documents* (Oxford University Press, 2002).

[24] J. S. Martinez, *The Slave Trade and the Origins of International Human Rights Law* (Oxford University Press, 2012), highlights in particular the innovative use of anti-slavery courts to combat the slave trade.

[25] F. Cooper, *Africa since 1940: The Past of the Present* (Cambridge University Press, 2002) 66–84. See also B. Anderson, *Imagined Communities: Reflections on the Origin and Spread of Nationalism*, rev. edn (Verso, 2006), and for radical forms of the anti-colonial struggle, F. Fanon, *The Wretched of the Earth* (Penguin Classics, 2001 (first published in 1961)).

[26] See in particular A. Anghie, *Imperialism, Sovereignty and the Making of International Law* (Cambridge University Press, 2004).

[27] See Chapter 16.

[28] See on diplomatic protection, in particular the work of the International Law Commission (ILC), including the 2006 Draft Articles on Diplomatic Protection, online at http://legal.un.org/ilc/.

today's standards, constituted an injury to the state of which the alien was a national. The state could in turn exercise its right to diplomatic protection on behalf of the individual (as a right of the state, not the individual) and demand appropriate forms of reparation under the rules of state responsibility. This rule became prominent in the nineteenth century when it was often used as a device of imperial powers to protect the economic interests of their nationals, in particular against expropriation. This reflected the inequalities between states and generated considerable opposition.[29] Diverging standpoints came to the fore over the applicable standard of treatment, particularly in the Americas. Some states insisted that it be equality of treatment with nationals, which could result in the lowest common denominator, while others stressed the need for an independent minimum standard of treatment irrespective of national law and practice.[30] The use of diplomatic protection at the time was not based on the recognition of individual rights, but the notion has since undergone considerable changes, assuming a potentially stronger role in the field of international human rights law.[31]

1.2.4   World War I, the League of Nations and Human Rights

World War I marked the culmination of a prolonged power struggle between European states and came at a time of growing calls for independence and the overthrow of old orders such as that of tsarist Russia. Nationalism, imperialism and the availability of industrially produced weapons in combination with a wanton disregard for human life resulted in a disastrous war that shattered the existing order. This was to have a profound influence on the development of international human rights, which was, however, initially not reflected in the international legal order. It strengthened the position of women, who had become more publicly engaged as a result of the war and now demanded equal rights, with the suffragettes in the United Kingdom (UK) calling for women's right to vote;[32] it buttressed calls by socialist movements for the realisation of social and economic rights;[33] and it laid the foundation for the recognition of the right to self-determination and minority rights.

---

[29] Anghie, above note 26, 209.

[30] See e.g., *Harry Roberts (USA)* v. *United Mexican States* (General Claims Commission) (Mexico and United States) (1926), and further E. Borchard, 'The "Minimum Standard" of Treatment of Aliens' (1940) 38 *Michigan Law Review* 445.

[31] See *Ahmadou Sadio Diallo (Republic of Guinea* v. *Democratic Republic of the Congo)*, Preliminary objections (ICJ) (2007) 599, para. 39.

[32] See H. Smith, *The British Women's Suffrage Campaign: 1866–1928*, 2nd edn (Longman, 2009).

[33] Ishay, above note 3, 176–8.

The crisis also gave birth to international institutions, marking a significant shift in the system of international relations and international law. Besides the International Labour Organization (ILO) established in 1919, the most important institution was the League of Nations, set up 'to promote international co-operation and to achieve international peace and security'.[34] It did not have an explicit human rights mandate and the language of its preamble speaks to the traditional sovereignty paradigm of international law: 'maintenance of justice and a scrupulous respect for all treaty obligations in the dealings of organised peoples with one another'. Even so, the League of Nations established a system of minority protection, mainly for Central, Eastern and South-eastern Europe, Turkey and Iraq, which was seen as integral to maintaining peace following the break-up of the Habsburg and Ottoman empires in the region.[35] Treaties under the system, as well as declarations made by states, which were to be supervised by the League Council, provided for the protection of the right to life and liberty, freedom of religion and non-discrimination. They also guaranteed minority rights such as the use of a particular language or education. While the League's minority system was incomplete and inadequately supervised, it established important principles for protection and international human rights monitoring, and provided the basis for the subsequent development of minority rights under international human rights law.

World War I also bolstered demands for self-determination following the rise of nationalist movements and declarations by the then US president, Woodrow Wilson, which resulted in reconfigurations in Eastern Europe.[36] However, in other regions, the colonial powers largely succeeded in containing such demands by delaying transfer of sovereignty through the mandate system established by the League of Nations. Article 22 of the Covenant of the League of Nations set out the general framework of the mandate system and article 23 stipulated minimum standards of treatment of the 'native inhabitants', besides entrusting the League with 'secur[ing] and maintain[ing] fair and humane conditions of labour' and supervising both the implementation of agreements relating to trafficking and drugs, as well as the arms trade. However, instead of paving the way for genuine self-determination and protection of rights, the mandate system introduced the development paradigm into international relations, marking 'the move from exploitative colonialism (imperialism) to

[34] See R. Henig and A. Sharp, *Makers of Modern World Subscription: The League of Nations* (Haus Publishing, 2010).

[35] See L. Thio, *Managing Babel: The International Legal Protection of Minorities in the Twentieth Century* (Martinus Nijhoff, 2005) 27–98; P. Thornberry, *International Law and the Rights of Minorities* (Clarendon Press, 1991) 38–52.

[36] See Chapter 10.2.1.

cooperative colonialism (development)'.[37] In addition, the monitoring exercised by the League was generally seen as weak and ineffective.[38]

1.2.5   World War II, the Holocaust and the Foundations of the International Human Rights System

The measures taken following World War I proved inadequate and failed to build a stable international order. Instead, the global crisis in the 1920s contributed to the rise of extremist political movements and aggressive nationalist states, particularly in Germany, Italy and Japan, and ultimately resulted in World War II. The war was characterised by its brutality and enormous death toll. Its significance for the development of international human rights law is largely due to the parallel Holocaust, the systematic destruction of the Jewish people based on a racist ideology, as well as murderous campaigns targeting Sinti and Roma, homosexuals, persons with disabilities, political opponents and others, planned with the use of modern bureaucracy and executed in an industrial manner by Nazi Germany.[39] The shock to the international system caused by these developments triggered a reordering of the international system. The years 1945–1950 were a truly foundational period for the development of international human rights law and related fields, providing a window in which states were willing to create institutions and a legal framework to address a series of concerns.

The objective of the United Nations (UN), which was established in 1945, was to put in place an effective international organisation built on a system of collective security with strong enforcement powers. Owing to the impetus from states such as the USA, following Franklin Delano Roosevelt's declaration of the four freedoms (freedom of speech and expression, freedom of worship, freedom from want and freedom from fear), and from public figures and groups, the question of human rights had been on the agenda since the very beginning of the UN. The USA, also due to the advocacy and lobbying of civil society organisations, and Latin American countries were influential in efforts to enshrine human rights provisions in the UN Charter.[40] The Charter's preamble proclaims that UN members are determined 'to reaffirm faith in

---

[37] B. Rajagopal, *International Law from Below: Development, Social Movements and Third World Resistance* (Cambridge University Press, 2003) 50–72, quote at 71.

[38] Ibid., 70–1; Anghie, above note 26, 149–56 and, further, S. Pedersen, *The Guardians: the League of Nations and the Crisis of Empire* (Oxford University Press, 2015).

[39] See Z. Bauman, *Modernity and the Holocaust* (Polity Press, 2000). For first-hand accounts of persecution, see P. Levi, *If This Is a Man* (Orion Press, 1959); V. Klemperer, *I Will Bear Witness 1933–1941: A Diary of the Nazi Years* (Modern Library, 1999) and *I Will Bear Witness 1942–1945: A Diary of the Nazi Years* (Modern Library, 2001).

[40] See G. T. Mitoma, 'Civil Society and International Human Rights: The Commission to Study the Organization of Peace and the Origins of the UN Human Rights Regime' (2008) 30

fundamental human rights, in the dignity and worth of the human person, in the equal rights of men and women and of nations large and small'. Article 1(3) lists human rights as one of the purposes of the UN, and articles 55 and 56 make human rights an integral part of the UN's international economic and social cooperation obligations. Human rights are also part of the mandate of the Economic and Social Council (ECOSOC) (articles 62 and 68) and of the international trusteeship system (article 76(c)). As the texts of articles 1(3) and 55 demonstrate, the Charter's drafters perceived human rights protection as imperative to a new international order conducive to peace, thus emphasising its instrumental value in international relations. The creation of the UN Commission on Human Rights pursuant to article 68 also signalled the importance of the UN as an institutional setting for the development of the international human rights regime.

Parallel developments witnessed the UN War Crimes Commission (1943–1948),[41] the Nuremberg and Tokyo war crimes trials (1945–1949 and 1946–1948 respectively), which laid the foundation for international criminal law,[42] and the adoption of the Genocide Convention (Convention on the Prevention and Punishment of the Crime of Genocide) in 1948.[43] The substantial expansion of the scope of application and protection of international humanitarian law through the four Geneva Conventions adopted in 1949, and the recognition of refugee rights in the Convention Relating to the Status of Refugees (the Refugee Convention) in 1951, are further milestones.

1.2.6　The UDHR: Origins, Content and Significance

The work on establishing a universal human rights system began in the early 1940s and culminated in the UDHR in 1948, which was seen as an integral part of the International Bill of Human Rights then envisaged by the UN. The UDHR is the UN's foundational human rights document and the cornerstone for the international human rights system, setting a framework

Human Rights Quarterly 607. See on the Latin American contribution more broadly, P. G. Carozza, 'From Conquest to Constitutions: Retrieving a Latin American Tradition of the Idea of Human Rights' (2003) 30 *Human Rights Quarterly* 281.

[41] See 'Symposium: The United Nations War Crimes Commission and the Origins of International Criminal Justice' (2014) 25 (1–2) *Criminal Law Forum.*

[42] See T. Taylor, *The Anatomy of the Nuremberg Trial: A Personal Memoir* (Alfred A. Knopf, 1992); N. Boister and R. Cryer, *The Tokyo International Military Tribunal: A Reappraisal* (Oxford University Press, 2008); and, on the subsequent Nuremberg trials, K. J. Heller, *The Nuremberg Trials and the Origins of International Criminal Law* (Oxford University Press, 2011).

[43] See R. Lemkin, *Axis Rule in Occupied Europe: Laws of Occupation, Analysis of Government Proposals for Redress* (Carnegie Endowment for International Peace, 1944), 79–95; W. Schabas, *Genocide in International Law*, 2nd edn (Cambridge University Press, 2009). See further Chapter 17.

for the understanding and content of rights that has stood the test of time.[44] States differed on whether to make a Bill of Rights an integral part of the Charter, and once it was decided that it should be separate whether to have a non-binding declaration followed by a legally binding covenant or to agree on such a covenant from the outset. The majority in the UN Commission on Human Rights, which had been established by ECOSOC in 1946 and had eighteen members at the time, opted for a declaration as a first step to agreeing on basic principles and as an educational tool. It was envisaged that the declaration would be followed by a covenant and measures of implementation to form an International Bill of Human Rights. The Commission tasked a committee of eight members from Australia, Chile, China, France, Lebanon, the USSR, the UK and the USA with drafting the UDHR, under the leadership of Eleanor Roosevelt. The process took two years, during which time the drafting committee consulted leading thinkers for their views on human rights. The draft articles were subject to intense scrutiny and sustained debates in the Commission, ECOSOC and the UN General Assembly (UNGA).[45] Most states were in support of a universally shared set of principles. However, several objections were raised to the draft articles at the time.[46] Communist countries in particular criticised the draft for not paying due regard to sovereignty, different stages of economic development and economic, social, cultural and collective rights. South Africa objected to racial equality because of its apartheid system and Saudi Arabia objected to the freedom to change one's religion.[47]

The UNGA adopted the UDHR on 10 December 1948 (that date was later declared International Human Rights Day). Forty-eight of the then fifty-eight member states of the UNGA voted in favour and eight states abstained

---

[44] See on the UDHR, A. Eide, G. Alfredsson, G. Melander, L. Rehof, A. Rosas and T. Swinehart (eds.), *The Universal Declaration of Human Rights: A Commentary* (Oxford University Press, 1992); G. Johnson and J. Symonides, *The Universal Declaration of Human Rights: A History of its Creation and Implementation, 1948–1998* (UNESCO Publishing, 1998); J. Morsink, *The Universal Declaration of Human Rights: Origins, Drafting, and Intent* (University of Pennsylvania Press, 1999); M. A. Glendon, *A World Made Anew: Eleanor Roosevelt and the Universal Declaration of Human Rights* (Random House, 2002); W. Schabas (ed.), *The Universal Declaration of Human Rights: The Travaux Préparatoires*, 3 vols. (Cambridge University Press, 2013).

[45] Documents can be found at UN, The Universal Declaration of Human Rights: An Historical Record of the Drafting Process, online at www.un.org/Depts/dhl/udhr.

[46] See for the broader points of contention, including British concerns over the applicability of rights to its colonies and US concerns that racial inequality in the US would come under international scrutiny, C. N. J. Roberts, *The Contentious History of the International Bill of Human Rights* (Cambridge University Press, 2014), particularly chs. 2–5.

[47] See in particular, UN doc. A/PV. 183, Verbatim Record of the Hundred and Eighty-third Plenary Meeting, Palais de Chaillot, Paris, Friday (10 December 1948), online at http://research.un.org/en/docs/ga/meetings.

(Byelorussia, Czechoslovakia, Poland, Saudi Arabia, the Ukrainian Soviet Socialist Republic, the Union of South Africa, the Union of Soviet Socialist Republics and Yugoslavia), with two members being absent. The individual provisions were also put to a vote. There was a remarkable degree of agreement, with unanimous votes for most rights, the only exceptions being the first recital of the preamble and articles 1, 2(2) (principle of non-distinction), 14 (right to asylum), 19 (freedom of expression), 20 (freedom of assembly and association), 27 (cultural life) and 29 (duties and limitations).[48]

The UDHR endorses the universality of human rights according to which all human beings have the same inherent rights, which should be recognised and observed universally 'in a spirit of brotherhood'. This is reflected in the first recital of the preamble – 'Whereas recognition of the inherent dignity and of the equal and inalienable rights of all members of the human family is the foundation of freedom, justice and peace in the world' – and in article 1 – 'All human beings are born free and equal in dignity and rights.' The UDHR sets out the rights referred to as a 'common standard of achievement for all peoples and all nations'. It formulates these rights in plain language in line with its mission to be an educational tool for the promotion of human rights. Article 2 stipulates the right to non-discrimination, articles 3–20 civil rights and liberties, article 21 political rights, articles 22–7 economic, social and cultural rights, article 28 the right to an international order in which the declaration's rights can be realised, article 29 duties and limitations of rights, and article 30 the principle that the rights granted in the UDHR do not confer a right to destroy the same. With the exception of minority rights and collective rights, the UDHR encompasses most rights later recognised in the main international human rights treaties, though the rights are formulated in a broad rather than a detailed manner (compare, for example, article 10 UDHR with article 14 of the International Covenant on Civil and Political Rights (ICCPR)).

The UDHR's status was subject to some debate during the drafting stage, with some representatives arguing that it constituted an authoritative interpretation of the UN Charter. Most representatives and commentators held the view that it was essentially a non-binding declaration of principles.[49] This reading appears to be in line with the UDHR's purpose of serving as a document that is accessible and of general validity, and acts as a springboard for the development of international human rights law. It also reflects the fact that the UDHR declares rights of universal application without specifying the obligations of duty-holders such as states or providing enforcement mechanisms. While the UDHR as such is not binding, many if not most of its provisions have by now been recognised as customary international law through

[48] Ibid.   [49] See discussion in Morsink, above note 44, 8.

their recognition in other treaties and declarations as well as in national laws and jurisprudence.[50]

The UDHR was hailed as a major achievement at the time and since.[51] However, it has also been subject to scathing criticism for its supposed empty rhetoric[52] and ethnocentrism.[53] The latter is based on the argument that the UN was not representative of all peoples at the time and that the UDHR reflects strong Western influences.[54] It is certainly correct that the UDHR is liberal in spirit with an emphasis on individual rights, owing a lot to continental European and Latin American notions of rights. However, it would be misleading to portray the UDHR as a straightforward 'Western' imposition. The very universality of the declaration is in considerable part a compromise forged in lengthy sessions and debates which included a discussion of ideological and cultural differences. The UDHR reflects some of the concerns raised by women, emphasises economic, social and cultural rights, and recognises duties, in particular, as limitations of rights. It was formulated against the background of decolonisation, with some newly independent states such as India contributing to debates. This is not to deny that the UDHR is also a political document that reflects prevailing power relationships at the time – forming part of broader ideological battles on the eve of the Cold War – but it is equally clear that there was a strong, shared desire to formulate a set of generally valid rights in response to the atrocities of World War II. It is indeed its clarity of vision, language and structure that has proved to be enduring.

For all its apparent shortcomings, such as the lack of recognition of collective rights, the UDHR has provided standards that have enabled actors to debate and develop the nature and content of international human rights and demand their recognition and protection.[55] Notably, a number of newly independent states have endorsed the UDHR, not out of any apparent compulsion but as a symbolic statement of sharing the ideals and principles contained therein. The idea of the universality of human rights may have suffered since then, but it is clear that the UDHR still constitutes its most impressive articulation.

---

[50] See Chapter 2.2.2.1.

[51] See e.g., UN events on marking the sixtieth anniversary of the UDHR, www.un.org/en/events/humanrightsday/udhr60/pdf/IK_HRDay%202008_En_20081126.pdf.

[52] See in particular criticism by Hersch Lauterpacht discussed in Roberts, above note 46, 26–50.

[53] See Moyn, above note 8, particularly at 66–73.

[54] See A. Schwab and P. Pollis, *Toward a Human Rights Framework* (Praeger, 1982) 4, and, in contrast, Å. Samnoy, *Human Rights as International Consensus: The Making of the Universal Declaration of Human Rights, 1945–1948* (Chr. Michelsen Institute, 1993) 105.

[55] M. Mutua, 'Standard Setting in Human Rights: Critique and Prognosis' (2007) 29 *Human Rights Quarterly* 547, at 556, captures this point by saying that 'the UDHR should be seen more as a credible promise than a holy text'.

1.2.7   Cold War and Decolonisation

The Cold War and decolonisation are arguably the two most important factors that shaped the development of international human rights law from the 1950s to the late 1980s.

The divide into political camps – in particular the USA and other 'Western' states versus 'socialist' states and later several newly established states – slowed down the realisation of the International Bill of Human Rights. Differences over the nature of rights and suitable modes of protection resulted in the adoption of two treaties in 1966, the ICCPR and the International Covenant on Economic, Social and Cultural Rights (ICESCR), which constitute the main general treaties for the respective body of rights. The ICCPR sets out key civil and political rights, which states parties undertake to respect and to ensure. These include the right of self-determination, the right to life, the prohibition of slavery and torture, and the rights to liberty and security of person, to a fair trial and to privacy, as well as freedom of movement, religion, expression, assembly and association.[56] The ICESCR equally provides for the right of self-determination, and a number of economic, social and cultural rights, such as the rights to work, to social security, to an adequate standard of living, to health, to education and to take part in cultural life.[57] States parties are obliged to realise these rights progressively. The UN Human Rights Committee and the Committee on Economic, Social and Cultural Rights monitor states parties' compliance with their obligations under the respective Covenant, i.e. the ICCPR and the ICESCR.[58] The Cold War also witnessed the increasing politicisation of human rights, which were mainly used by Western states, foremost among them the USA, to evaluate the conduct of other states critically, to demand that certain action be taken and, in so doing, to demonstrate their own superior legitimacy.[59] One outcome of

---

[56] See Chapter 8 on civil and political rights.
[57] See Chapter 9 on economic, social and cultural rights.
[58] See further Chapter 5.
[59] According to its website, 'The US Department of State submits [human rights] reports on all countries receiving assistance and all United Nations member states to the US Congress in accordance with the Foreign Assistance Act of 1961 and the Trade Act of 1974.' The influential reports can be found at www.state.gov/j/drl/rls/hrrpt. See also R. Müllerson,

the intensified human rights diplomacy was the Final Act of the Conference on Security and Co-operation in Europe in 1975, signed by thirty-five 'capitalist' and 'communist' states, which – while emphasising sovereignty and non-intervention – included provisions for the protection of human rights. The process resulted in the establishment of the Organization for Security and Co-operation in Europe (OSCE) and contributed significantly to greater human rights diplomacy and more weight being accorded to human rights in communist states.[60] However, it did little to change the political economy of human rights, which were still selectively invoked or ignored to serve political ends.[61]

Decolonisation was a complex and uneven struggle and political process. The UN Charter recognised the obligation to 'promote ... [t]he well-being of the inhabitants' (of non-self-governing territories) and to 'ensure, with due respect for the culture of the peoples concerned, their political, economic, social, and educational advancement, their just treatment, their protection against abuses, and to promote self-government'.[62] It also created a trusteeship system towards this end. However, colonising states frequently resisted domestic uprisings and decolonisation efforts through force and violations. Notorious examples are the suppression of the Mau Mau, by the British forces in Kenya,[63] and of the Algerian independence movement by France.[64] Political movements and leaders from emerging and newly independent states were targeted, such as Patrice Lumumba (1925–1961) in what is now the Democratic Republic of the Congo, and Ho Chi Min (1890–1969) in Vietnam; this contributed to precipitating political instability and war. White settler regimes resisted decolonisation in the country formerly known as Rhodesia (1965–1979), now Zimbabwe, and reinforced the system of apartheid in South Africa (1948–1994). These developments provided the impetus to anti-racism initiatives in the UNGA and led to the adoption of

---

Human Rights Diplomacy (Routledge, 1997) 102–17, and on US foreign policy on human rights more broadly, D. P. Forsythe, Human Rights in International Relations, 3rd edn (Cambridge University Press, 2012) 205–21, with further references.

[60] D. J. Galbreath, The Organization for Security and Co-operation in Europe (Routledge, 2007).

[61] Baxi, above note 9, 30–2.

[62] Art. 73 UN Charter.

[63] See D. Anderson, Histories of the Hanged: Britain's Dirty War in Kenya and the End of Empire (Weidenfeld and Nicolson, 2005), and C. Elkins, Imperial Reckoning: The Untold Story of Britain's Gulag in Kenya (Henry Holt, 2005). See on the case brought by four Kenyan survivors of torture against the United Kingdom before the High Court of England and Wales, which resulted in a landmark settlement in June 2013, www.leighday.co.uk/Our-expertise/international-claims/Kenya.

[64] See Fanon, above note 25; M. Evans, Algeria: France's Undeclared War (Oxford University Press, 2012), and further B. Ibhawoh, Human Rights in Africa (Cambridge University Press, 2018).

the International Convention on the Elimination of All Forms of Racial Discrimination (ICERD) in 1965 and the International Convention on the Suppression and Punishment of the Crime of Apartheid (ICSPCA) in 1973.[65]

Newly independent states were often politically vulnerable internally because of their artificial nature, particularly in Africa, and externally because of great power interests and their economic fragility and dependency. 'Third World' states sought to meet this challenge by stressing their political sovereignty and calling for development and a reform of the international economic system. Attempts to institute a New International Economic Order based on greater economic equality and share of resources between states failed in the 1970s.[66] Subsequently, similar political efforts were channelled into calls for the recognition of the right to development.[67] The surrounding debates have brought to the fore different conceptions of rights, in particular concerning the collective nature of human rights.[68] While the legacy of colonialism and the challenges stemming from the decolonisation process still loom large in international law, it is already clear that this process has added important dimensions to the understanding of human rights and the development of international human rights law.

1.2.8   The Growth of International Human Rights Law

A series of struggles, advocacy by the international human rights movement, the increasing importance of human rights in international relations, a determination to tackle (at least some) persistent problems, and a concerted effort to develop a more coherent system have contributed to the rapid growth of standard-setting since the 1970s, in particular at the UN level. This standard-setting consisted of the adoption of a series of treaties, declarations and other instruments that further developed the normative body of international human rights law. These sources further elaborate specific individual rights already recognised in the UDHR and ICCPR, such as the Convention against Torture and Other Cruel, Inhuman or Degrading Treatment or Punishment (CAT) (1984), or govern specific violations not expressly stipulated in the International Bill of Human Rights, such as the International Convention for the Protection of All Persons from Enforced Disappearance (CPED) (2006). The increasing awareness of the need to recognise – and provide better protection for – the rights of members

---

[65] See Baxi, above note 9, 53–5.

[66] Declaration for the Establishment of a New International Economic Order, UNGA resolution 3201 (S-VI) (1 May 1974). See M. Bedjaoui, *Towards a New International Economic Order* (Holmes Meier, 1979).

[67] See in particular, the Declaration on the Right to Development, UNGA resolution 41/128 (4 December 1986).

[68] See Chapters 2.3.2 and 10.2.

of particular groups is reflected in the Convention on the Elimination of All Forms of Discrimination against Women (CEDAW) (1979) and the seminal Convention on the Rights of the Child (CRC) (1989), the treaty with the most states parties in the field of human rights. It became increasingly clear that generic sets of rights such as those contained in the ICCPR do not adequately capture the situation of members of groups who face systematic discrimination and disadvantages on account of their status. This has led to the adoption of treaties such as the International Convention on the Protection of the Rights of All Migrant Workers and Members of Their Families (ICRMW) (1990) and the Convention on the Rights of Persons with Disabilities (CRPD) (2006). After a prolonged struggle, collective group rights have recently been recognised in the UN Declaration on the Rights of Indigenous Peoples (2007), which may over time result in a treaty protecting the rights of indigenous peoples.[69] Human rights conferences[70] and initiatives to address global economic and environmental problems, as well as related emerging concerns such as the role of business in the violation of human rights, have spurred the growth of soft law in the field of human rights.[71]

In a parallel development, a series of treaties and resolutions have been adopted at the regional level, particularly in the European, American and African systems, often as a result of specific historical experiences and advocacy, thereby adding important regional dimensions to the understanding of human rights.[72] The process of standard-setting and institution-building has been complemented by a growth in human rights jurisprudence at the national, regional and international levels, which has contributed to clarifying the normative content of rights and to generating the impetus for the adoption of treaties, such as the CPED (2006).[73]

Traditional international human rights law, with its focus on the state both as protector and (potential) violator, lacks an important dimension, namely individual criminal liability and mechanisms to ensure accountability in order to respond to serious human rights violations. This was seen as an evident weakness of the system that had remained unaddressed since the Nuremberg and Tokyo trials. However, a change in political constellations following the end of the Cold War, the establishment of ad hoc tribunals by the UN Security Council (UNSC) in the 1990s in response to the conflict in the former Yugoslavia and the genocide in Rwanda, strong NGO movements,

---

[69] See Chapter 10.4.
[70] In particular the World Conference on Human Rights, which resulted in the Vienna Declaration and Programme of Action on 25 June 1993. See also M. Nowak (ed.), *World Conference on Human Rights, Vienna, June 1993: The Contributions of NGOs: Reports and Documents* (Manz, 1994).
[71] See Chapters 2.2.4 and 19.3.
[72] See Chapter 6.
[73] See on relevant developments and jurisprudence, Chapter 8.6.

and the leadership of several states resulted in the re-emergence of international criminal justice efforts. This culminated in the establishment of the International Criminal Court (ICC) in 1998 and led to the setting up of several mixed/hybrid courts, such as those in East Timor, Cambodia and Sierra Leone.[74] In an important broadening of the scope of international criminal law, the statutes of international tribunals recognise that war crimes can also be committed in internal armed conflicts.[75] In parallel, several human rights treaty bodies, the International Court of Justice (ICJ) and others have recognised the applicability of human rights in the course of armed conflicts.[76] These developments have resulted in the growing convergence of international human rights law, international humanitarian law and international criminal law, in particular when addressing violations in internal armed conflicts. International human rights law has also become increasingly important in the context of international refugee law, such as in respect of the interpretation of the notion of persecution, immigration detention, and the scope of the prohibition of refoulement.[77] At the national level, meanwhile, the end of conflicts and/or authoritarian systems has triggered complex processes often referred to as transitional justice.[78] These processes are characterised by the agreed upon need to address legacies of violations in times of transition. This includes having to determine what should be done in respect of truth, accountability and justice, how the legal system and institutions should be reformed and how to promote reconciliation, particularly with a view to preventing future violence and violations.[79] The principles and rules

[74] See on international criminal law generally, A. Cassese, *International Criminal Law*, 3rd edn (Oxford University Press, 2012); R. Cryer, H. Friman, D. Robinson and E. Wilmshurst, *Introduction to International Criminal Law and Procedure*, 2nd edn (Cambridge University Press, 2010); I. Bantekas, *International Criminal Law*, 4th edn (Hart, 2010); and for resources on tribunals and hybrid courts, www.monash.edu/law/research/projects/icjp/compilation-project/general/tribunals-hybrid-courts.

[75] See arts. 5–8 ICC Rome Statute 1998, particularly para. (2)(c)–(f).

[76] See Chapters 16.4 and 16.5.

[77] See Chapter 13.3.6, and V. Chetail, 'Are Refugee Rights Human Rights? An Unorthodox Questioning of the Relations between Refugee Law and Human Rights Law' in R. Rubio-Marin (ed.), *Human Rights and Immigration* (Oxford University Press, 2014) 19–72.

[78] The field has generated a vast body of documents and literature. See in particular, UN Secretary General, The Rule of Law and Transitional Justice in Conflict and Post-Conflict Societies, UN doc. S/2004/616 (23 August 2004); R. Teitel, *Transitional Justice* (Oxford University Press, 2000); N. Roht-Arriaza and J. Mariezcurrena (eds.), *Transitional Justice in the Twenty-First Century: Beyond Truth versus Justice* (Cambridge University Press, 2006); K. McEvoy and L. McGregor, *Transitional Justice from Below: Grassroots Activism and the Struggle for Change* (Hart, 2008); and the *International Journal of Transitional Justice*.

[79] See in particular, the mandate of the Special Rapporteur on the promotion of truth, justice, accountability and guarantees of non-repetition, UN doc. A/HRC/RES/18/7 (13 October 2011), and the Special Rapporteur's website at www.ohchr.org/EN/Issues/TruthJustice Reparation/Pages/Index.aspx.

of international human rights and international criminal law form an important if not integral part of such processes, which have in turn influenced and
enriched international human rights law.[80]

1.3   CURRENT CHALLENGES

The proliferation of international human rights standards, the increasing recognition of the indivisible, interdependent and interrelated nature of human
rights and the growing number of institutions tasked with protecting human
rights constitute important progress in the field. International human rights
have developed into an impressive body of law – though with some remaining normative gaps – and an increasingly mature regime characterised by
specific rights, obligations and supervisory mechanisms. However, this very
institutionalisation has raised questions about its efficacy and the risk of
state and elite influence and control.[81] Serious violations persist and a number of developments pose a challenge to the system as to how best to address
them in order to become truly effective and credible.

1.3.1   International/Cross-border Dimension of Violations

The process of globalisation coupled with persisting, if not growing, inequalities and conflicts has undermined national rights protection and heightened
the cross-border, international dimension of violations. This became dramatically visible in the plight of refugees who drowned in the Mediterranean
Sea or were stranded in the Indian Ocean.[82] Austerity measures taken in the
wake of the global financial crisis are another example of global developments adversely impacting rights, often of those who are most disadvantaged already.[83] Environmental crimes, such as the dumping of toxic waste,
the arms trade, exploitation, corruption, displacement and trafficking are
further issues of concern. The prevalence of increased human insecurity and
poverty has brought about a greater awareness of the interconnectedness
of violations and the need to develop effective responses.[84] The latter poses

---

[80] See on how Inter-American human rights bodies have dealt with questions of transitional
justice, Chapters 6.3.2 and 6.3.3.
[81] See e.g., Baxi, above note 9; Stammers, above note 22.
[82] See in particular, UNHCR, The Sea Route to Europe: The Mediterranean Passage in the
Age of Refugees (July 2015); I. Mann, *Humanity at Sea: Maritime Migration and the
Foundations of International Law* (Cambridge University Press, 2016).
[83] See in particular, A. Nolan (ed.), *Economic and Social Rights after the Global Financial
Crisis* (Cambridge University Press, 2014).
[84] See in particular, the reports regularly published by the UN Special Rapporteur on extreme
poverty and human rights, online at www.ohchr.org/EN/Issues/Poverty/Pages/SRExtreme
PovertyIndex.aspx.

a number of legal challenges, such as: (1) qualifying cross-cutting practices or particular acts such as corruption as a violation, and developing an
adequate framework of protection; (2) determining the causality between
certain acts and their consequences, such as neo-liberal policies and poverty; (3) identifying responsibility where a multitude of actors are involved,
including international institutions, multinational corporations (MNCs) or
transnational criminal networks; (4) providing a forum in which victims of
these acts are able to obtain effective access to justice and perpetrators are
held to account.[85]

These features are particularly challenging because they are in marked
contrast to the traditional conception of human rights, which focuses on
the state as a territorial unit. In response, local and international movements and coalitions have increasingly called for new standards and systems
of accountability, such as corporate criminal liability, if not fundamental changes to the international economic system altogether.[86] They have
also led efforts using transnational litigation, particularly to hold MNCs to
account.[87] These emerging areas of international human rights law are in a
state of flux but are likely to grow in importance. The present system cannot
ignore the adverse consequences of power relationships and problems in the
global political and economic order and the often closely related range of
damaging activities if it wants to be taken seriously in its role of protecting
human dignity, equality and well-being.

1.3.2   Responsibility of Multiple Actors

International human rights law is based on the responsibility of states, which
has given human rights a distinctively state-centric prism. This is for good
reason, as it has been mainly states that have committed the most serious
violations in the twentieth century. Claims that the power of states is waning
in times of globalisation may to some degree be correct in terms of the state's
economic decision-making power. However, as a cursory reading of annual

---

[85] See in particular, Chapter 19.3.

[86] Rajagopal, above note 37, 219–22; W. Kaleck and M. Saage-Maß, 'Corporate Accountability
for Human Rights Violations Amounting to International Crimes: the Status Quo and its
Challenges' (2010) 8 *Journal of International Criminal Justice* 699; and contributions in
Nolan, above note 83.

[87] D. Stoichkova, *Towards Corporate Liability in International Criminal Law* (Intersentia,
2010); P. Muchlinski, 'The Provision of Private Law Remedies against Multinational
Enterprises: A Comparative Law Perspective' (2009) 4 *Journal of Comparative Law* 148;
S. Joseph, *Corporations and Transnational Human Rights Litigation* (Hart, 2004). See for
cases raising the liability of corporations for human rights abuses before US courts under
the Alien Torts Claim Act, particularly *Kiobel* v. *Royal Dutch Petroleum Co.* (US) (2013),
http://ccrjustice.org/ourcases/current-cases/kiobel.

human rights reports shows, states retain considerable powers in policy-making and immense powers in the sphere of law-enforcement. The exercise of such powers is often at its most intense where economic and political stakes are particularly high, as in many oil-rich countries and/or where the state's power is challenged, as recent developments in the Middle East demonstrate. However, the increasing role of international institutions in the flow of finances and projects, their involvement in conflict and post-conflict situations, the growing number of de facto states and rebel groups using force, the expanding scope of MNC operations, as well as violence and discrimination committed by other private actors have equally raised the question of their respective responsibility and accountability. The adverse impact of the economic and political crisis triggered by international financial institutions in 2008, and the devastation wrecked by the Islamic State in Iraq and Syria, though very different in nature, demonstrate the centrality of these developments for effective human rights protection. While the responsibility of non-state actors (NSAs) has traditionally been located outside the international human rights framework, there is a discernible trend to bring them into the fold. This includes the violation of the rights of women, which was for a long time downplayed if not altogether ignored as a result of the public–private divide according to which the private sphere was not the domain of state interest. These developments have been complemented by a broadening of the positive obligations assumed by states to protect individuals from threats and harm inflicted by NSAs, which points to a widening of the field of application of international human rights law, albeit one that poses considerable challenges to the system.[88]

1.3.3   Effective Monitoring and Implementation

The growth of the international human rights regime has not been matched by an equally effective enforcement system. Human rights treaty bodies have adopted new procedures, and additional protocols have been agreed upon to enhance protection and compliance. Recent additions of note are the protocols to the ICESCR and CRC, which provide a complaints procedure for the violation of economic, social and cultural rights and children's rights respectively, and the Optional Protocol to CAT, which put in place an international preventive mechanism. However, it is clear that the system essentially relies on the goodwill of states, which may be based on a political calculus according to which it is more beneficial to be seen to respect human rights. In practice, a considerable number of states still fail to adequately implement their human rights obligations due to systemic and

---

[88] See Chapters 2.3.4 and 19.2.

institutional shortcomings and/or deliberate disregard. Non-cooperating states that have succeeded in isolating themselves and seemingly violate human rights with impunity pose an even more fundamental challenge to the system.[89]

The limits of the promotion and protection approach of the international human rights treaty and Charter body system raises the question of resort to other means, including force in the case of serious violations. The so-called right to humanitarian intervention has recently been effectively superseded by the responsibility to protect (R2P) doctrine, which emphasises the primary obligation of states to protect their populations and the subsidiary duty of the 'international community', particularly acting through the UNSC, where the state concerned fails to do so.[90] While this doctrine is often either hailed as major progress or criticised as simply another form of interventionism,[91] the problem remains. Are political bodies such as the UNSC, or, in lieu of them, states and other entities, able and best placed to enforce human rights protection? The political (and grossly unrepresentative) nature of the UNSC seems to suggest the contrary, as selective responses to human rights violations illustrate.[92] States may also invoke humanitarian considerations for what appear to be unilateral foreign policy goals. This is problematic because it is often not clear to what degree such policies are underpinned by a genuine desire to promote human rights or whether they are driven by ulterior motives such as hegemony or human rights imperialism. Even where there is some willingness to act out of genuine concern, situations such as Darfur highlight the complexity of interventions falling short of armed force, which is likely to remain the exception.[93] It is clear that human rights diplomacy is of utmost importance in such circumstances but may equally not escape politicisation. While such extreme situations do not indicate an abysmal failure of the international human rights regime, they painfully illustrate the limitations of a system that ultimately depends on the readiness of states and international institutions to take timely action.

[89] See e.g., P. Goedde, 'Legal Mobilization for Human Rights Protection in North Korea: Furthering Discourse or Discord?' (2010) 32 *Human Rights Quarterly* 530. See further Report of the commission of inquiry on human rights in the Democratic People's Republic of Korea, UN doc. A/HRC/25/63 (7 February 2014).

[90] See 2005 World Summit Outcome, UNGA resolution 60/1 (24 October 2005) paras. 138–9.

[91] C. Gray, *International Law and the Use of Force*, 4th edn (Oxford University Press, 2018) 58–64.

[92] See in particular M. Koskenniemi, 'The Police in the Temple: Order, Justice and the UN: A Dialectical View' (1995) 6 *European Journal of International Law* 325. See for a feminist perspective, G. Heathcote, 'Security Council Resolution 2242 on Women, Peace and Security: Progressive Gains or Dangerous Development' (2018) 32 *Global Society* 374.

[93] See Case Study 3.2.

1.3.4   Human Rights Imperialism and Exceptionalism

The international human rights system is an integral part of international relations and as such is subject to political considerations on the part of its actors.[94] This is a truism and the resulting constraints and opportunities for the promotion and protection of human rights are widely recognised. However, the integrity of the system risks being seriously undermined where human rights language is used, or appears to be used, to further the interests of major powers and/or where states seek to rewrite the rules or to exempt themselves from the system with reference to overriding considerations, in particular national security.[95]

The often ambiguous use of human rights language by major powers to justify interventions and conditionality, and the invocation of human rights to protect the commercial interests of powerful economic actors, has generated considerable unease.[96] Human rights are in this context often seen as instruments through which Western states in particular seek to dictate what policies other states ought to pursue, thereby cementing unequal power relationships (as Western states are frequently not subject to the same level of scrutiny by other states) and at times providing the pretext for economic or military interventions that may serve geo-strategic rather than genuine human rights interests. The roles of the USA, international organisations such as the North Atlantic Treaty Organization (NATO), international financial institutions such as the International Bank for Reconstruction and Development (IBRD or World Bank) and the International Monetary Fund (IMF), and the European Union (EU) are pivotal and highly ambiguous in this context.[97] While at least some of these entities also contribute to the promotion and protection of human rights, the conflation of the pursuit of foreign policy interests with human rights language carries the risk of discrediting the latter.

---

[94] See on human rights in international relations, R. J. Vincent, *Human Rights and International Relations* (Cambridge University Press, 1986); Forsythe, above note 59; and more broadly, J. L. Dunoff and M. A. Pollack (eds.), *Interdisciplinary Perspectives on International Law and International Relations: The State of the Art* (Cambridge University Press, 2013).

[95] See in particular, International Commission of Jurists. Assessing Damage, Urging Action: Report of the Eminent Jurist Panel on Terrorism, Counter-Terrorism and Human Rights (2009); M. Goodhart and A. Mihr (eds.), *Human Rights in the 21st Century: Continuity and Change since 9/11* (Palgrave Macmillan, 2011); reports by the Special Rapporteur on the promotion and protection of human rights and fundamental freedoms while countering terrorism, online at www.ohchr.org/EN/Issues/Terrorism/Pages/SRTerrorismIndex.aspx.

[96] Baxi, above note 9, 294–302, who refers to this as the politics of human rights, in contrast to the politics for human rights.

[97] Ibid., 234–75. See also Chapter 19.4.

Under the Bush administration, the USA in particular sought to reinterpret international human rights norms, such as the definition of torture, and international humanitarian law through the introduction of the term 'unlawful enemy combatants' in order to justify measures it had taken in response to terrorist threats.[98] This has privileged security paradigms that seemingly override human rights considerations, the most extreme being the tightly regulated 'legal black hole' of Guantánamo Bay.[99] These developments have caused considerable damage to the fabric of the international human rights system as they may serve as a blueprint for the justification of measures that are evidently clear violations.[100] The national and international struggle against the US 'War on Terror' policy has been impressive and at least partially successful in upholding and reinforcing international human rights law, but has demonstrated how fragile the system is when one of its supposed champions embarks on a policy that is contrary to its own basic tenets.[101] The coming into power of governments based on populist and nationalist sentiments, including the US administration elected in 2016, constitutes a significant challenge. Formerly liberal states have openly challenged the very idea of the value of multinational institutions, thereby calling into question one of the fundamental tenets of the international human rights system.[102]

QUESTIONS

1. What is the link between social, political and philosophical developments in the eighteenth and nineteenth centuries and the contemporary system of international human rights law?

2. What role has decolonisation played in the development of international human rights law?

3. Has international human rights law shown that it is capable of effectively addressing contemporary challenges?

---

[98] See P. Sands, *Torture Team: Rumsfeld's Memo and the Betrayal of American Values* (Palgrave Macmillan, 2008); K. J. Greenberg and J. L. Dratel (eds.), *The Torture Papers: The Road to Abu Ghraib* (Cambridge University Press, 2005).

[99] See J. Steyn, 'Guantanamo Bay: The Legal Black Hole' (2004) 53 *International & Comparative Law Quarterly* 1. The US detention regime has generated a considerable body of literature and reports by UN Special Rapporteurs since its establishment in 2002.

[100] See on the use of torture in particular, US Senate Select Committee, Committee Study of the Central Intelligence Agency's Detention and Interrogation Programme (2014).

[101] See J. Fitzpatrick, 'Speaking Law to Power: The War Against Terrorism and Human Rights' (2003) 13 *European Journal of International Law* 241, and, more broadly, M. Byers and G. Nolte (eds.), *United States Hegemony and the Foundations of International Law* (Cambridge University Press, 2003).

[102] P. Alston, 'The Populist Challenge to Human Rights' (2017) 9 *Journal of Human Rights Practice* 1.

1.4   THE IDEA OF HUMAN RIGHTS: THEORIES AND CRITIQUES

Human rights face a paradox. At a time when they seem to have attained the status of the dominant discourse, their potential shortcomings are also becoming apparent, leading some authors to raise the spectre of the 'end of human rights'.[103] These are fundamental challenges. Satisfactorily addressing questions about the nature and validity of human rights is increasingly important for their effective protection in a rapidly changing world characterised by persistent and newly emerging patterns of threats, such as the detrimental consequences of climate change, globalisation, particularly rising inequality, large-scale poverty and new technologies.[104] While the universal aspiration of human rights remains one of its main attractions as a cross-cultural, worldwide goal and yardstick, it is clear that in order to be true to its claim it must be accompanied by increasing sensitivity to context and to those excluded from both debates and access to protection and legal remedies. The human rights discourse faces a difficult task in these circumstances; that of engaging with broader notions of justice and avoiding undue reliance on overly legalistic and/or narrow approaches to what are often complex political and societal problems without losing its distinctive focus on rights.

Human rights theories can be categorised into several schools.[105] A useful way of doing so is to group theorists into natural scholars (human rights as given), deliberative scholars (as agreed upon), protest scholars (as fought for) and discourse scholars (as talked about).[106] This section provides a brief account of the moral and liberal theories of human rights which have formulated universal postulates with a considerable influence on the development of human rights law. These theories have equally attracted a number of critiques; these will be examined, together with other notions of human rights, not least with a view to understanding whether and how they can live up to their inherent promise.

---

[103] C. Douzinas, *The End of Human Rights: Critical Legal Thought at the Turn of the Century* (Hart, 2000). See also S. Hopgood, *The Endtimes of Human Rights* (Cornell University Press, 2013) and E. Posner, *The Twilight of Human Rights Law* (Oxford University Press, 2014).

[104] See T. Pogge, *World Poverty and Human Rights: Cosmopolitan Responsibilities and Reforms*, 2nd edn (Polity Press, 2008); T. Murphy (ed.), *New Technologies and Human Rights* (Oxford University Press, 2009).

[105] See for good overviews, J. W. Nickel and D. A. Reidy, 'Philosophy', in D. Moeckli, S. Shah and S. Sivakumaran (eds.), *International Human Rights Law* (Oxford University Press, 2010) 39–63; Twining, above note 5, 173–201; C. R. Beitz, *The Idea of Human Rights* (Oxford University Press, 2009).

[106] M.-B. Dembour, 'What Are Human Rights? Four Schools of Thought' (2010) 32 *Human Rights Quarterly* 1.

1.4.1   Moral and Liberal Human Rights Theories

The UDHR is silent and ostensibly agnostic on the foundation of human rights. Several thinkers consulted during the drafting stage offered their own understanding of the nature of human rights, but the drafters of the UDHR took a pragmatic view, fearing that any disagreement about the underlying philosophy of human rights might jeopardise agreement about the contents of the declaration.[107] However, the UDHR's drafting history and language suggest that moral and liberal theories exerted a strong influence on the development and understanding of human rights following World War II.[108] Moral theories of human rights draw on the language of inherent (natural) rights found in the American and French declarations and restated in the UDHR.[109] Human rights are seen as universally applicable standards that transcend time, location and culture. This position provides a strong metaphysical grounding for the universal nature of human rights.[110] However, ideas based on 'epistemic universality'[111] can be challenged on the ground that they do not have any objective validity. The very 'universality' may be the expression of a subjective viewpoint, if not the outcome of a political project that reflects Western bias, as critics of the UDHR have argued.[112] The postulate of an anterior moral theory that informs the development of human rights law may also fail to reflect the complex political processes that result in the recognition of particular rights.[113] Authors have responded to the objections raised against substantive (moral) accounts by grounding theories of human rights in personal autonomy as agency.[114] However, the list of core rights flowing from this is rather narrow and fails to provide a satisfactory basis for addressing global concerns.[115] Others have located human

---

[107] Morsink, above note 44, 125; M. Ignatieff, 'Human Rights as Politics, Human Rights as Idolatry', *The Tanner Lectures on Human Values* (2000) 327, at 328, online at http://tannerlectures.utah.edu/_documents/a-to-z/i/Ignatieff_01.pdf.

[108] See e.g., L. Henkin, *The Age of Rights* (Columbia University Press, 1990) 6–10.

[109] Moral theories may ground human rights in religious or moral principles, notions of personal agency (Gerwith), autonomy (Griffin) or a plurality of values (Tasioulas). See for a concise overview of moral theories, Twining, above note 5, 202–17.

[110] See J. Morsink, *Inherent Human Rights: Philosophical Roots of the Universal Declaration* (University of Pennsylvania Press, 2009).

[111] Ibid., 50.

[112] Mutua, above note 5, 39–70, particularly at 46–7.

[113] This is the main critique of deliberative or constructivist scholars, see e.g., Ignatieff, above note 107, 337. In an interesting observation, Twining, above note 5, 180–1, notes that human rights law may include rights not provided for in moral theories, thus reversing the oft-assumed causality of anterior moral rights.

[114] J. Griffin, *On Human Rights* (Oxford University Press, 2008).

[115] Twining, above note 5, 122–32. See also Twining's discussion of J. Tasioulas's theory of a 'pluralist conception of human interests' that seeks to meet this challenge.

rights in human capabilities,[116] a notion that provides a useful combination of agency and an instrumental approach to the protection of human rights.

Liberal theories played a significant role in shaping the understanding of human rights, both as a concept and as a feature of political and international relations. Liberalism views the individual as an autonomous subject who may exercise his or her rights as long as they do not conflict with the rights of others.[117] The role of the state is to provide for order, security (and basic welfare) without unjustified interference with the rights of individuals. This view resulted in an emphasis on civil and political rights in the early human rights discourse, dubbed the first generation of rights, which at the national level may act as trumping other considerations.[118] It was based on the divide between the public and private sphere, a conception that has been identified as reflecting and entrenching a male bias in international human rights law.[119]

Rawls, who became well-known for his work on justice as fairness, developed a theory of political liberalism at the global level in his work *The Law of Peoples*.[120] He constructed an international system composed of what he termed well-ordered liberal and hierarchical societies, outlaw states, societies burdened by unfavourable conditions and benevolent absolutisms. Further, he stipulated principles that 'well-ordered societies' would embrace and identified situations in which humanitarian intervention would be justified, namely where a state fails to respect basic human rights. In this world, effectively, human rights serve as benchmark for the acceptability of a state, which is primarily to be judged by 'reasonable liberal peoples'. While constituting an interesting attempt at explaining the role of human rights in international relations, Rawls's theory is widely seen as parochial, outdated and unsuitable to address the challenges facing the global system.[121] Even though attempts to construct grand liberal theories have failed, liberal thinking continues to be influential in the invocation of human rights in international relations and prominent in the text and interpretation of treaties, with human rights being celebrated or criticised as a liberal political project.[122] Some of the

---

[116] A. Sen, *Development as Freedom* (Oxford University Press, 1999); M. Nussbaum, *Women and Human Development: The Capabilities Approach* (Cambridge University Press, 2000).

[117] See in particular, J. Rawls, *Political Liberalism* (Columbia University Press, 1996).

[118] R. Dworkin, 'Rights as Trumps', in Waldron, above note 7, 153–67.

[119] See H. Charlesworth and C. Chinkin, *The Boundaries of International Law: A Feminist Analysis* (Manchester University Press, 2000) 28–32.

[120] J. Rawls, *The Law of Peoples* (Harvard University Press, 2001).

[121] See discussion and reference to critics in Twining, above note 5, 159–62, as well as an account of T. Pogge's attempt to reinterpret Rawls's work, 163–72.

[122] See T. Dunne and M. Hanson, 'Human Rights in International Relations', in M. Goodhart (ed.), *Human Rights: Politics and Practice* (Oxford University Press, 2009) 59–74, with further references.

rhetoric used in the Arab uprisings beginning in 2010 has demonstrated the revolutionary potential of liberal language, couched in universal standards, which critiques both national regimes and ('liberal') foreign states that compromise if not betray human rights for the sake of realpolitik.[123]

1.4.2   Meeting the Challenge: Reconstructing Human Rights

A number of interlinked processes, beginning with the Cold War divide and decolonisation, largely destroyed any seemingly existing consensus and resulted in growing scrutiny and criticism of the unspoken assumptions underpinning human rights. With their increasing use as part of foreign policy, in particular by the USA in the 1970s, human rights became widely seen as a political instrument used selectively to create or maintain hegemony.[124] The perceived individualistic, and for many societies supposedly culturally alien, nature of human rights was viewed as an integral part of the process of globalisation and was increasingly objected to.[125] At the national level, civil liberties movements, student and feminist actors and a number of thinkers engaged in alternative practices and critical discourses that questioned both moral and political (liberal) assumptions and biases, in particular male bias, which were seen as inherent in the prevailing doctrine of rights and the reliance on law to protect human rights.[126] This was complemented by post-modern critiques of reason and foundational theories based on the idea of objective truth.[127] These challenges seemingly subsided in the wake of the liberal triumphalism following the breakup of the Soviet Union and the concomitant revolutions in Eastern Europe. However, unease has since resurfaced and arguably intensified,[128] as human rights came to dominate political discourse and assumed a prominent place in foreign policy. Their elevated status has attracted many followers but has also resulted in closer

---

[123] See M. El-Ghobashy, 'The Praxis of the Egyptian Revolution' (2011) 258 *Middle East Report*, online at www.merip.org/mer/mer258/praxis-egyptian-revolution; R. Khalidi, 'Preliminary Historical Observations on the Arab Revolutions of 2011', *Jadaliyya* (21 March 2011), www.jadaliyya.com/pages/index/970/preliminary-historical-observations-on-the-arab-re. See further below Interview 1.1.

[124] Mutua, above note 5, 39–70.

[125] Ibid. See on the Asian values debate, a brief overview with further references in Twining, above note 5, 198–9.

[126] See for a discussion of the relationship between law and politics, C. Gearty, *Principles of Human Rights Adjudication* (Oxford University Press, 2004) 8–30.

[127] See C. Gearty, *Can Human Rights Survive?* (Cambridge University Press, 2006) 17–21; R. Rorty, 'Human Rights, Rationality and Sentimentality', in S. Shute and S. Hurley (eds.), *On Human Rights* (Basic Books, 1993) 111, 115.

[128] As evident in titles such as *The End of Human Rights* (Douzinas), and *Can Human Rights Survive?* (Gearty). See also Baxi, above note 9, 82–5.

inspection and interrogation of their nature and role in national and international politics. This has opened up the human rights discourse and generated what appears at first sight to be a bewildering number of theories that seek to address some, if not all, of the challenges faced.

One of the main challenges to human rights is that they can hardly be called universal if they only reflect the preferences of a particular culture or group of like-minded states, as critics of the 'Western' nature of human rights have claimed. Indeed, any substantive theory risks being accused of positing an understanding of human rights that does not reflect global diversity. Deliberative or discourse theories, many of which have been influenced by Habermas's communication theory, seek to address this challenge by placing emphasis on open-ended arguments in situations of level playing fields.[129] The advantage of this approach is that its democratic nature is seemingly conducive to reaching an understanding if not consensus that strengthens the acceptability of human rights as defined by the participants. This is of particular importance in cross-cultural situations[130] and the UDHR process itself can at least partly be seen as a successful manifestation of this approach.[131] However, its value is limited where rights discourses are framed by elites,[132] in situations of power asymmetry and/or where there is no willingness to engage in dialogue, be it generally or on specific issues seen as non-negotiable.[133]

The difficulty if not apparent futility of agreeing on a foundational theory of human rights has led some authors to turn to pragmatism, arguing that human rights are inherently political and that they should be promoted through education.[134] In a similar vein, constructivist theories seek to draw on areas of overlapping consensus and/or other principles, such as common interests,[135] with a view to identifying common ground if not convincing others to accept the human rights standards in question. The advantage of these theories is their flexible and realistic stance that is cognisant of the political nature of human rights discourses and practices. However, the

---

[129] Habermas's theory focuses on the use of communicative action to reach shared understandings. See overview of discourse theories by Twining, above note 5, 217–24.

[130] A. A. An Na'im, 'Introduction', in A. A. An Na'im (ed.), *Human Rights in Cross-Cultural Perspectives: A Quest for Consensus* (University of Pennsylvania Press, 1992 (paperback)) 1–15, at 1–8.

[131] See above at 1.2.6.

[132] See W. P. Simmons, *Human Rights Law and the Marginalised Other* (Cambridge University Press, 2014 (paperback)), particularly at 107–59.

[133] See Gearty, above note 127, 40: 'There is nothing that allows us to say "You have got to do this" in the endless deliberation that now seems the best we can hope for.'

[134] Rorty, above note 127.

[135] J. Donnelly, *Universal Human Rights in Theory and Practice*, 3rd edn (Cornell University Press, 2013) 16–17, 57–60.

theories provide limited guidance as to why human rights should be valid and may fail to convince others, especially if they are associated with particular political projects such as the promotion of liberal democracy.

Critical legal scholars and movements have articulated one of the most concerted critiques of contemporary conceptions and practices of human rights. They argue that human rights as a language of political discourse is too narrow and crowds out other equally valid if not preferable modes, such as social justice.[136] Further, it is seen as negating policy choices by framing decision-making as a question of rights to be adjudicated upon[137] rather than being subject to political debate.[138] As such, human rights language may not constitute the discourse of emancipation it promises to be. It may overly focus on endless, often individualistic, identity politics that are increasingly couched in terms of rights instead of addressing underlying structural problems and inequalities or fostering solidarity.[139] There is also a risk that rights which have served as challenges to dominant orders are being harnessed and used to serve class, economic or political interests, a concern that is in line with Marxist criticism of human rights.[140] A case in point is the invocation of property rights that have been used to stifle land reforms.[141]

The multitude of discourses have added an important critical dimension to the understanding of human rights. Even though these critical voices have had limited visible impact on the prevailing growth of international human rights law and the role of human rights in international relations, they are vital in ensuring that human rights do not lose what may be considered their defining features: their interrogation of power and violence; their focus on unnecessary and unacceptable suffering; their potential to imagine and demand a different world based on shared core values; and their capacity to give voice to and empower those who have been excluded from legal

---

[136] See M. Koskenniemi, 'The Effect of Rights on Political Culture', in P. Alston (ed.), *The EU and Human Rights* (Oxford University Press, 1999) 99–116; D. Kennedy, 'The International Human Rights Movement: Part of the Problem' (2002) 15 *Harvard Human Rights Journal* 101; D. Kennedy, 'The International Human Rights Regime: Still Part of the Problem?', in R. Dickinson, E. Katselli, C. Murray and O. Pedersen (eds.), *Examining Critical Perspectives on Human Rights* (Cambridge University Press, 2014) 19–34.

[137] See for a critical legal theory approach on the nature of adjudication, particularly in the American context, D. Kennedy, *A Critique of Adjudication* (Harvard University Press, 1998).

[138] Koskenniemi, above note 136, 99–100. See also Gearty, above note 127, 60–98, on this point.

[139] Ibid., and Douzinas, above note 103.

[140] See Baxi, above note 9, 57–8, 252–3; O'Connell, above note 17.

[141] See Mutua, above note 5, 142–4, in the South African context.

recognition and attendant rights (such as stateless persons, migrants and indigenous peoples) or who are otherwise marginalised.[142]

QUESTIONS

1. Do theories of human rights matter? If so, why?

2. Why is the strong appeal of moral theories of human rights at the same time their biggest weakness?

3. Do the critiques of human rights theories point to a fatal flaw in their conception or are they healthy reminders of the importance of a plurality of political practices?

1.5 UNIVERSAL HUMAN RIGHTS: CONTESTATIONS AND PRACTICES

1.5.1 The Debate

The question of universality is one of the recurring debates at the heart of human rights. Universality is invoked as the cornerstone of human rights by some and derided as the embodiment of ethnocentric, politically biased and narrow conceptions thereof by others. It is one of the paradigms of the international human rights system, as evident in the name of the UDHR and expressed in its self-description as 'common standard of achievement for all peoples and all nations'. The term universality is used to denote the nature and validity of rights that are common to all human beings by virtue of their humanity.[143] This 'abstract universality'[144] is reflected in the use of language in the UDHR, such as 'everyone' and 'all human beings'. However, the notion of universality is subject to multiple understandings (for example, as a natural right or political aspiration, as a ground for validity of rights or scope of their application) and the UDHR itself provides a series of essentialist and instrumentalist justifications of human rights.[145] The moral and political dimension of the notion of universality as a founding principle has provided

---

[142] See in particular, Baxi, above note 9. See also Pogge, above note 104; Douzinas, above note 103; Gearty, above note 127 (arguing for compassion); and feminist theories based on the ethics of care – see C. Gilligan, *In a Different Voice: Psychological Theory and Women's Development* (Harvard University Press, 1982).

[143] Donnelly, above note 135, 10.

[144] Baxi, above note 9, 167–9.   [145] Ibid., 164–5.

a strong impetus for the development of international human rights law. However, it has also been subjected to close scrutiny over the years, resulting in several strands of critique, if not outright rejection.

At the core of debates about universality is the tension between a set of rights that supposedly apply to everyone at all times and the lack of (a shared) understanding and practical application, or limited recognition, of these rights around the world. This tension is closely tied up with the political struggle for decolonisation, self-determination and development policies, which includes attempts to define rights and values deemed appropriate in their particular contexts. It has gained further impetus in the clash between global homogenisation and local and regional identity politics.

Critics of universality argue that cultures and societies have developed different understandings of the nature of human beings and of 'rights', which may include a rejection of the notion that rights provide a suitable means of governing social relationships. The idea of universal rights is deemed illusory because rights are informed by and applied in specific societal and cultural contexts.[146] It is also seen as culturally inappropriate, effectively imposing an alien concept (individual rights with a focus on civil and political rights) that is the outcome of a particular historical development and is specific to particular political systems (liberal democracies) on cultures that have different value systems (religious or communitarian, rather than liberal and individualistic).[147] While some reject the notion of universality altogether, others argue that culture provides the context in which universal notions of rights have to be interpreted and appropriated in order to be meaningful and effective.[148] Indeed, there is ample evidence that this process is already taking place in the regional human rights systems and in respect of certain rights, such as the rights of indigenous peoples.

The universality debate is of particular practical importance where consensus over certain practices is lacking, be it ostensibly on religious grounds, as a justification for corporal punishment, or for 'traditional' or 'cultural'

---

[146] See 'Statement on Human Rights, The Executive Board, American Anthropological Association', in (Oct.–Dec. 1947) new series 49 *American Anthropologist* 539. See in contrast, 'Declaration on Anthropology and Human Rights Committee for Human Rights; American Anthropological Association, Adopted by the AAA membership June 1999', online at http://humanrights.americananthro.org/1999-statement-on-human-rights/ and for a discussion of the role played by these documents in the history of anthropology and human rights, M. Goodale, *Surrendering to Utopia: An Anthropology of Human Rights* (Stanford University Press, 2009) 18–39, which also reprints both documents as appendices.

[147] See for a critical perspective, B. Gregg, *Human Rights as Social Construction* (Cambridge University Press, 2013).

[148] See S. E. Merry, 'Transnational Human Rights and Local Activism: Mapping the Middle' (2006) 108 *American Anthropologist* 38; Rajagopal, above note 37, 210.

reasons such as female genital cutting/mutilation (see below at 1.5.2). Rather than simply insisting on absolute standards in these situations, a number of authors call for a dialogue, both between and within cultures,[149] to arrive at a solution that is acceptable for those concerned. As has been rightly highlighted, genuine dialogue about human rights must engage in addressing the content of the subject of disagreement where 'we' must be able to adequately answer challenges, for example why pornography should be tolerated, before postulating a right as a standard for others.[150] The outcome of such dialogue may be the acceptance of universal standards, possibly subject to the phasing out of traditional practices, for example polygamy,[151] the context-specific interpretation of rights – similar to the concept of margin of appreciation applied by the European Court of Human Rights (ECtHR)[152] – or their rejection, for example where one side rejects the right of the other to discuss certain practices, for example because they are seen as commanded by God. The latter position shows the limits of dialogue where differences cannot be bridged. However, the very act of seeking an open dialogue can be helpful in fostering a human rights culture if it is grounded in a 'cosmopolitan' spirit that takes the arguments of others seriously and brings different points of view to the table. The recognition of the need to be context specific must not necessarily equate with an abandonment of universality, which can still provide a valuable framework of culturally transcendent and genuinely universal aspirations.[153]

The universality debate has important political dimensions for international human rights. The charges of ethnocentrism highlight the bias apparent in the mainstream human rights discourse that has for a long time been dominated by authors with a broadly shared cultural background and value system.[154] This practice has been criticised as neo-colonial and patronising, focusing the West's gaze on 'the other' and generating a narrative of savages ('the perpetrators' who are bad), victims (the poor and faceless masses who are good and in need of protection), and saviours (Western human rights organisations and their counterparts).[155] This criticism highlights the reproduction of simplistic views that are prone to reinforce stereotypes and

---

[149] An Na'im, above note 130; M. Baderin, *International Human Rights and Islamic Law* (Oxford University Press, 2005) 5.

[150] J. Waldron, 'How to Argue for a Universal Claim' (1999) 30 *Columbia Human Rights Law Review* 305.

[151] See art. 5 African Protocol on the Rights of Women on the elimination of harmful practices.

[152] See in this context, Baderin, above note 149, 231–5.

[153] See Baxi, above note 9, 185.

[154] Mutua, above note 5, 39–70.

[155] M. Mutua, 'Savages, Victims and Saviors: the Metaphor of Human Rights' (2001) 4 *Harvard International Law Journal* 201.

prejudices and ignore agency. Such an outcome is clearly antithetical to human rights based on notions of respect for dignity, freedom and equality. The interrogation of authorship and power dynamics underlying the development of human rights law, including in the field of human rights work, is therefore an important corrective and ongoing task that is needed to ensure the continuing legitimacy of human rights and their advocates.

A further charge is that notions of universality can be used for ideological purposes in order to mask the intent behind what is essentially a political project. According to this argument, the tenets of universality are derived from liberal democracy and aimed at its promotion as a political ideology. This narrow focus frequently fails to provide adequate solutions to pressing governance issues, such as social justice and land reform in many African countries, or worse, may protect the interests of certain individuals or classes at the expense of the public good.[156] Some of the opposition to universal human rights is ostensibly directed against the export of the political ideology that they seem to imply. Indeed, the language of universal rights may be appropriated to pursue hegemonic objectives and to promote modes of neo-liberal globalisation serving certain power interests.[157] This is a challenge that human rights defenders invoking universal standards must and can address. While there is a political dimension to universal human rights that may be used to justify power relationships, human rights reach beyond this to protect core human freedoms and to limit the exercise of power. This may include the power of the very entities, be it states or others, invoking the universality of human rights.

The politics of universality is evident within the international human rights system in debates over the recognition of rights, in particular collective ones such as the right to development, the validity of reservations to human rights treaties, for example in relation to Sharia (Islamic law), and the inclusion and interpretation of rights in regional treaties.[158] The universal language of human rights primarily employed by Western actors in international relations has also triggered a number of confrontations and largely defensive reactions. This includes the Asian value debate in the 1990s, where states such as Singapore and Malaysia claimed that Asian communitarian values differed from Western individualistic values reflected in international human rights.[159] This debate was closely related to differences over models of

---

[156] Mutua, above note 5, 142–4.
[157] Baxi, above note 9, 170–5; Anghie, above note 26, 279–91.
[158] See Chapter 6, particularly 6.2.5.
[159] See for nuanced and critical discussions of the points raised, Y. Ghai, 'Asian Perspectives on Human Rights' (1993) 23 *Hong Kong Law Journal* 342; A. Sen, 'Human Rights and Asian Values' (Carnegie Council on Ethics and International Affairs, 1997).

development and may have reflected the political interest of Asian states in fending off the use of human rights discourse to attack their economic policies;[160] while it has largely subsided, different approaches to human rights within Asia are still apparent.[161] Another example is the opposition of states with Muslim majorities to what is seen as the imposition of secular notions that violate religious beliefs, such as liberal interpretations of freedom of expression, which have led to concerted efforts at the Human Rights Council (HRC) to redefine the relationship between these rights.[162] The 'universality v. relativism' schism has also resurfaced in debates surrounding the exercise of international criminal justice in Africa where the ICC and other bodies have been portrayed as pursuing Western notions of retributive justice that are contrary to African modes of reconciliation.[163]

These debates, while seemingly focusing on different conceptions of rights, are at their heart also about *ownership* of human rights discourses and practices. While objections to universality raise valid concerns, it is often questionable how representative and genuine they are. The notion of culture as something immutable is essentialist and its use is prone to presenting one strand within a culture as 'the culture'. This may ignore, if not suppress, other voices and thereby replicate the very mode of discourse that universality is accused of. Cultural specificity may also be invoked to deflect criticism over certain practices that are increasingly seen as incompatible with basic rights, such as discrimination against women, and serve as a variant of arguments used to demand non-interference.[164]

However, it is equally clear that arguments surrounding human rights may open up valuable debates, which reflect the fact that they are developed in a continuous process of contestation and contextual adjustment. It is not necessarily the idea of universal human rights but the power relationships and modes of invoking and seeking to enforce them that appear problematic. Building strong and credible national and regional systems that protect and promote fundamental values and rights while being sensitive to local contexts would appear to be the most important step in changing this equation. Indeed, there is a growing realisation of the need to develop a 'decentered

---

[160] Rajagopal, above note 37, 202–16.

[161] See for the fledgling sub-regional ASEAN system of human rights, Chapter 6.6.

[162] See Chapter 8.7.3.

[163] O. Oko, 'The Challenges of International Criminal Prosecutions in Africa' (2007–2008) 31 *Fordham International Law Journal* 343, and generally, V. O. Nmehielle (ed.), *Africa and the Future of International Criminal Justice* (Eleven International, 2012). See further on international criminal law, Chapter 17.

[164] See for a sophisticated critique of both universalist and relativist approaches from an African gender perspective, J. Oloka-Onyango and S. Tamala, '"The Personal is Political" or Why Women's Rights are Indeed Human Rights: An African Perspective on International Feminism' (1991) 17 *Human Rights Quarterly* 692.

understanding of [human rights as] normative construct'[165] and a 'global perspective'[166] that reflects the plurality of voices. 'Relativist' critiques themselves may at times overstate the Western dominance by ignoring the multitude of authors and movements that have contributed, and continue to contribute, to the development of human rights and human rights law. This is particularly evident in the African context, where regional human rights treaties reflect distinctive approaches to human rights, such as an emphasis on duties and collective rights, and novel approaches in areas such as women's rights and the rights of internally displaced persons.

Ultimately, universality is a global concern that cuts across cultures and 'symbolise[s] *universality of collective human aspiration to make power more accountable, governance progressively more just and states incrementally more ethical*.'[167] If seen as a framework to address myriad local, national and international injustices, universality can serve both as an important yardstick and a means to foster global solidarity.

INTERVIEW 1.1

Human Rights and the Uprisings in the Arab World[1]

(Moataz El Fegiery)

Dr Moataz El Fegiery is Middle East and North Africa (MENA) Protection Coordinator at Front Line Defenders, and Co-Founder and Secretary General of the Egyptian Human Rights Forum. He is the former executive director of the Cairo Institute for Human Rights Studies and a member of its board of directors. El Fegiery is the author of *Islamic Law and Human Rights: The Muslim Brotherhood in Egypt* (Cambridge Scholars Publishing, 2016).

What role has the language of and reference to human rights played in triggering the uprisings in the Arab world?

One reason behind the popular revolt in Arab states has been the lack of respect for human rights. For decades, people in Tunisia, Egypt, Syria, Yemen and Libya have been subjected to repressive regimes with poor

---

[1] See further on developments in the region, A. T. Chase, *Human Rights, Revolution, and Reform in the Muslim World* (Lynne Rienner Publisher, 2012); C. Tripp, *The Power and the People: Paths of Resistance in the Middle East* (Cambridge University Press, 2013).

---

[165] J. Habermas, *Time of Transitions* (Polity Press, 2006) 155.
[166] Twining, above note 5.
[167] Baxi, above note 9, 185 (emphasis in original).

human rights records. The quest for social justice, human dignity and freedom has been manifested in the key slogans chanted by demonstrators in different Arab states. In Egypt, for example, the systematic practice of torture and ill-treatment by the security forces under Mubarak's regime prompted activists and youth movements to revolt on 25 January 2011, which is an official holiday, 'the police day', in order to send a clear message to Mubarak and the Ministry of Interior that the misuse of power by the security forces would no longer be acceptable. In the following days, massive popular demonstrations swept across Egypt demanding drastic political changes. The important role that respect for human rights played in chants, blogs and debates during the uprising can in no small part be attributed to the work of local human rights organisations over the last decade that raised public awareness about the patterns of human rights violations through advocacy and litigation. In Egypt, the rise of private media from 2003 onwards has enabled human rights NGOs to reach a wide popular audience across the country.

Were there any objections to the invocation of universal human rights?

Political and social forces that took to the streets in Arab states were diverse and had different political visions for the future of their countries. These forces agreed on the necessity of political change and of addressing the severe injustice created by the policies of the outgoing regimes. While political forces have not necessarily mentioned international human rights law explicitly, the underlying norms became part of the day-to-day political contestations during the revolutionary and transitional periods.

Positions diverge when it comes to the interpretation of human rights. For instance, Islamist political parties such as the Freedom of Justice party established by the Muslim Brotherhood in Egypt clearly state in their platforms that international human rights should be implemented as long as they are in line with Islamic Sharia. Other non-Islamist parties also oppose some aspects of international human rights law as inappropriate for their society's religion and culture. Human rights issues that tend to give rise to controversy in the context of Arab societies are those related to gender equality, freedom of religion, the rights of religious minorities and some aspects of the rights of children, such as the prohibition of child marriage and female genital mutilation.

For all the diversity of views on human rights, it is important to recognise the increasing role played in the region by human rights defenders who tirelessly struggle to embed international human rights in local cultural traditions. In the transitional period in Egypt, for example, human rights NGOs proposed a road map for constitutional, legal and institutional reform based on international human rights law. However, these NGOs have been marginalised and attacked by the transitional authority in Egypt.

How do you view the role of international human rights in these developments? To what degree have they played a part in the politics of transition?

This differs from one country to another based on the forms of transitional authority and transitional arrangements that are in place. In Egypt the Military Council has managed the transitional period poorly, failing to institute tangible human rights reforms. The situation has led to tensions in the relationship between the transitional authority and the human rights community in Egypt, as the latter has been vocal in denouncing the deteriorating status of human rights and the reluctance of the Military Council to implement much-needed reforms. During the transitional period, human rights defenders in Egypt have been subject to an unprecedented campaign of surveillance and persecution. The Muslim Brotherhood, Salafists and other Islamist parties sat at the head of executive and legislative governing institutions, and they played the dominant role in writing the first post-revolution Egyptian constitution. In their short experience in power, Islamists marginalised secularist and liberal Muslims, women and religious minorities. They failed to show any commitments to human rights, judicial independence and the rule of law and their legal and political actions aggravated religious polarisation and societal divides. The Muslim Brotherhood's rule ended dramatically in July 2013 after President Morsi was deposed by the military following massive popular unrest. Nevertheless, the ouster of Morsi has not saved democracy as wished by many Egyptian liberals who joined the protest against the rule of the Muslim Brotherhood and backed the new transitional plan declared by the military. On the contrary, political and civil rights have faced a severe downturn and the prospect of establishing democratic institutions has become gloomy. The changing structure of political power and the political alliances shift in the post-Muslim Brotherhood period have enabled this dramatic decline of rights to occur. The military and other conservative political forces, including remnants of the Mubarak regime, have been significantly empowered after the ouster of the Muslim Brotherhood. Mounting numbers of Egyptians look at the military and its leaders as the country's saviour amid increasing frustration over democracy and its ability to deliver order. Meanwhile, the liberal revolutionary forces go through an intractable crisis, suffering from deep divisions and harsh repression. The Muslim Brotherhood is currently subjected to a high level of repression. However, Islamists continue to be the most organised political force and the current military regime has tolerated the political activism of Salafists to counter the Muslim Brotherhood. In Tunisia, however, there has been a more inclusive transitional process where civil society and all political forces have taken part in the transitional arrangements, with human rights defenders playing a leading role.

The dramatic 2013 fall of the Muslim Brotherhood in Egypt prompted Islamists in Tunisia to conclude a political agreement with the non-Islamist opposition, a deal widely regarded as having secured the transition process in Tunisia.

What is the future of human rights in the Arab region, including in terms of the development of an effective regional human rights system?

The situation looks gloomy in the region today. The use of military force and political violence has significantly expanded, causing grave human rights and humanitarian consequences and immense challenges for the work of human rights defenders. In Syria, Libya and Yemen, state and non-state actors opted to use violence to settle political scores and gain the upper hand in ongoing power struggles. These developments highlight the fragility or decline of the nation state in many countries in the region, giving way to growing sectarianism and tribal political trajectories. The collapse of the democratic process in Egypt since the removal of the Muslim Brotherhood from power in July 2013 by the military escalated instability in the country and led to waves of bloody confrontations between the state and opponents on a level previously unseen in modern Egyptian history. Moreover, conflicting political agendas of international and regional powers aggravated domestic conflicts and turned these crises into proxy wars.

Jihadist Islamists would find no better environment than this to flourish in the region. Growing numbers of violent Islamist groups have systematically and massively used brutal violence against foreign and domestic targets including innocent civilians to take over power in Syria, Iraq, Libya, Yemen and Egypt. The rise of Jihadism is an outcome of a unique religionised political ideology which long existed in the region. However, one cannot see its recent emergence in isolation from a series of inadequate policies pursued by Western and Middle Eastern states, including the cooperation with these violent groups at certain moments to achieve narrow political gains. Moreover, human rights violations and the absence of the rule of law in most Middle Eastern states are contributing to violent radicalisation and recruitment of desperate youths by terrorist groups.

I do not see a prospect for an efficient regional human rights system in the Arab region within the current political circumstances. The League of Arab States (LAS) adopted the Arab Charter of Human Rights in 1994 and modified it in 2004. In 2014, LAS decided to establish an Arab Court of Human Rights to be based in Bahrain. However, the contribution of these mechanisms is very limited within the current tumultuous situation. These mechanisms are flagrantly subject to governmental control and manipulation and fall short of international human rights standards. Independent NGOs and human rights defenders are excluded from the activities of LAS.

Islamist movements are often seen as antithetical to human rights, particularly international human rights standards. Is this view borne out by your research and experience?

Islamists are not monolithic and their discourses on Islamic law and international human rights are highly contingent upon the political and social contexts in different Muslim states and even at different times. For example, the *al-nahda* (renaissance) movement in Tunisia, particularly according to the writings of its leader Rashid al-Ghanoushi, has sought to develop human-rights-friendly interpretations of Islam. In Egypt, the Muslim Brotherhood has been eager to portray its position as being in conformity with international human rights law. However, the group interprets many international human rights restrictively. For instance, its members and leaders have usually been critical of the conception of gender equality in CEDAW. They argue that international women's rights corrupt Islamic social values and morals. Instead, they advocate the concept of complementary roles between men and women. This means that not all rights enjoyed by men are provided for women. This understanding influences the discriminatory positions that have been developed by the Muslim Brotherhood towards marriage, divorce and the political rights of women. However, Islamists' stances on certain international human rights such as gender equality and equal citizenship will continue to be problematic as long as they seek to establish what they call 'the Islamic State' ruled by Sharia.

1.5.2   Experiences in Combating Female Genital Cutting/Mutilation

Female genital cutting (FGC), which will be referred to as female genital mutilation (FGM),[168] consists of the total or partial removal of the female genitalia, or other harmful procedures to the female genitalia. FGM is practised in twenty-eight African and Middle Eastern countries and immigrant communities and affects over a hundred million girls and women. It is a traditional socio-cultural practice and initiation rite based on beliefs surrounding female sexuality and purity, maintained through significant pressure by family members, communities and peers. The cutting is commonly carried

---

[168] The term itself is contested as FGC is seen as neutral in contrast to FGM. There is a considerable body of literature on the law and practice of FGM. See in particular A. Rahman and N. Toubia, *Female Genital Mutilation: A Guide to Laws and Policies Worldwide* (Zed Books, 2000); F. Banda, *Women, Law and Human Rights: An African Perspective* (Hart, 2005) 207–46; World Health Organization (WHO), *Eliminating Female Genital Mutilation: An Interagency Statement, OHCHR, UNAIDS, UNDP, UNECA, UNESCO, UNFPA, UNHCR, UNICEF, UNIFEM, WHO* (2008).

out by traditional female practitioners. It frequently results in pain, harm and lasting health damage to girls and women. Regional and international human rights treaties, treaty bodies and special procedures have classified FGM as a form of gender-based violence that violates a series of rights of the girl-child and women (freedom from torture and other ill-treatment, right to health, right to non-discrimination).[169] States have a positive obligation to protect these rights and to eliminate harmful practices as set out in particular in article 5(a) CEDAW and article 5(b) of the Protocol to the African Charter on Human and Peoples' Rights (ACHPR) on the Rights of Women in Africa; the latter explicitly refers to the prohibition of all forms of FGM.

Beyond its legal qualification and obligations arising under international human rights law, FGM has become a focal point for intense debates about cultural relativism and feminism. What makes FGM particularly challenging is that it is a deep-rooted practice that is often seemingly endorsed by women themselves. If it is only communities or 'cultures' themselves that can define the validity of rights and practices, FGM may be justified on the grounds of the legitimacy it commands.[170] In contrast, universalists, including Western feminists, have called it a violation that is based on discrimination and coercion.[171] The girls and women supporting this practice, so the argument goes, have internalised the dominant discourse that legitimises FGM. Such reasoning, however, denies any agency, particularly if applied to women over the age of eighteen. It has been called 'imperialist' feminism, and advocacy based on the argument that FGM is violent, despicable and wrong has proved ambivalent if not counterproductive.[172] This constellation has pitted those advocating the application of universal human rights standards against others calling for respect for cultural diversity. It has also led to criticism of feminists who supposedly turn a blind eye to forms of 'voluntary' genital mutilation in the West, such as cosmetic surgery.[173] While the

---

[169] See for a brief overview, WHO, ibid., 8–10. See also Report of the Special Rapporteur on torture and other cruel, inhuman or degrading treatment or punishment, Manfred Nowak, UN doc. A/HRC/7/3 (15 January 2008) paras. 50–5.

[170] See in this context contributions in J. K. Cowan, M.-B. Dembour and R. A. Wilson (eds.), *Culture and Rights: Anthropological Perspectives* (Cambridge University Press, 2001).

[171] F. P. Hosken, *Stop Female Genital Mutilation: Women Speak: Facts and Actions* (Women's International Network News, 1995). See also C. J. Walley, 'Searching for Voices: Feminism, Anthropology, and the Global Debate over Female Genital Operations' (1997) 12 *Cultural Anthropology* 405.

[172] See H. Lewis, 'Between Irua and "Female Genital Mutilation": Feminist Human Rights Discourse and Cultural Divide' (1995) 8 *Harvard Human Rights Journal* 1.

[173] See in this context, 'Cosmetic Surgery, Body Image and Sexuality' (2010) 18 *Reproductive Health Matters*. At least some forms of cosmetic surgery, such as piercing of the female genitals, are increasingly considered to constitute FGM. See NHS, *FGM Health Services: FGM Guidance for Professionals*, undated, www.nhs.uk/NHSEngland/AboutNHSservices/sexual-health-services/Pages/fgm-for-professionals.aspx.

controversy surrounding FGM has been intense, the debate has been healthy in as much as it has stressed the need for a cross-cultural understanding and a sharpening of strategies on how best to respond to harmful practices.

Several states have adopted legislation that outlaws FGM, which has in many instances been complemented by awareness campaigns.[174] The prohibition and criminalisation of FGM as a means of protecting women's rights is an important step, both as a public rejection of the practice and as a deterrent. However, experiences show that these measures alone often have limited effectiveness. In the African context this practical challenge has been addressed at two levels. Women's rights groups have formed networks to develop regional awareness and binding regional standards, such as in the African Protocol on the Rights of Women. Civil society groups have also increasingly pursued a community-based approach, which has enjoyed the support of the UN International Children's (Emergency) Fund (UNICEF), other UN agencies and several governments, such as that of Senegal. This approach is based on the insight that legislative measures and campaigns based on women's rights may not bring about a change in practice unless they are complemented by programmes that directly engage affected communities.

The international NGO Tostan has developed what it calls a community empowerment programme. The programme is run by local Tostan facilitators who take a participatory and 'respectful approach that allows villagers to make their own conclusions about FGC and to lead their own movements for change'.[175] The educational programme uses interactive methods to share information and raise awareness, inter alia, of human rights and the harmful impact of FGM. The programme seeks to facilitate dialogue and claims to be non-judgemental, seeking to enable participants to make informed choices. It also takes a community-based, rather than individualistic, approach to changing social convention. According to independent evaluations, the programme has raised villagers' awareness of human rights, reproductive health and the adverse impact of FGM.[176]

---

[174] See e.g., official responses to the FGM debate in the UK, particularly HM Government's Statement: 'International Day of Zero Tolerance to Female Genital Mutilation' (6 February 2014), www.gov.uk/government/uploads/system/uploads/attachment_data/file/295056/HMG_FGM_Declaration.pdf, and various documents that are part of the 'Collection: Female Genital Mutilation', www.gov.uk/government/collections/female-genital-mutilation.

[175] See the Tostan website, www.tostan.org.

[176] See UNICEF Innocenti Digest, *Changing a Harmful Social Convention: Female Genital Mutilation/Cutting* (UNICEF Innocenti Research Centre, 2005, reprinted 2008) 24; UNICEF, *Long-term Evaluation of the Tostan Programme in Senegal: Kolda, Thies and Fatick Regions* (2008).

Tostan's programmes have achieved notable successes; over 4,500 communities have publicly declared that they have abandoned FGM. Other programmes have initiated alternative rites of passage and sought to provide employment opportunities for cutters to change the cultural and economic factors that sustain the practice.

A UNICEF study on FGM identified several key elements of change, namely non-coercive and non-judgemental approaches with focus on empowerment; awareness on the part of the community of the harm caused by FGM; the decision to abandon FGM as a collective choice; public affirmation; organised diffusion from one community to another; and an environment that enables and supports change.[177] These elements, based on practical experiences, demonstrate that discussions which frame the issue of FGM and women's rights as a clash between universal human rights and culture may miss the point. Instead of a stark dichotomy of abstract principles versus immutable culture, experiences show that FGM is often an embedded practice that those concerned may be willing to change under the right circumstances. In this context the language of human rights becomes part of a broader package of persuasion that will only succeed if translated and related to local practices and concerns. The agency of local actors as well as the sensitivity of the actors involved to socio-cultural factors and the needs of local communities are crucial in this regard. This is critical because failure to create an environment conducive to abandoning FGM will inevitably test if not expose the limits of states' ability to fulfil their positive obligations to protect the rights of those concerned. The debate and practices surrounding FGM demonstrate starkly that it is not sufficient to condemn a certain harmful practice by invoking universal human rights; it needs to be tackled through creative and often painstaking engagement before it can be changed for good.

QUESTIONS

1. Should the notion of universality be replaced with that of plurality?

2. Are the debates surrounding universality mainly concerned with the substance of universal human rights, the process by which they are formulated, or the underlying assumptions evident in the mainstream discourse?

3. What lessons do grassroots initiatives to combat FGM hold for the language and application of universal human rights?

---

[177] UNICEF Innocenti Digest, ibid., 13–14.

FURTHER READING

Anghie, A., *Imperialism, Sovereignty and the Making of International Law* (Cambridge University Press, 2004).

An Na'im, A. A. (ed.), *Human Rights in Cross-Cultural Perspectives: A Quest for Consensus* (University of Pennsylvania Press, 1992 (paperback)).

Arendt, H., *The Origins of Totalitarianism* (Schocken Books, 1951).

Baxi, U., *The Future of Human Rights*, 3rd edn (Oxford University Press, 2008).

Brysk, A., and M. Stohl (eds.), *Expanding Human Rights: 21st Century Norms and Governance* (Edward Elgar, 2017).

Cook, R. J. (ed.), *Human Rights of Women: National and International Perspectives* (University of Pennsylvania Press, 1994).

Dickinson, R., E. Katselli, C. Murray and O. Pedersen (eds.), *Examining Critical Perspectives on Human Rights* (Cambridge University Press, 2014).

Donnelly, J., *Universal Human Rights in Theory and Practice*, 3rd edn (Cornell University Press, 2013).

Douzinas, C., and C. Gearty (eds.), *The Meanings of Rights: The Philosophy and Social Theory of Human Rights* (Cambridge University Press, 2014).

Eide, A., G. Alfredsson, G. Melander, L. Rehof, A. Rosas and T. Swinehart (eds.), *The Universal Declaration of Human Rights: A Commentary* (Oxford University Press, 1992).

Evans, T. (ed.), *Human Rights Fifty Years on: A Reappraisal* (Manchester University Press, 1998).

Ferstman, C. et al. (eds.), *Contemporary Human Rights Challenges: The Universal Declaration of Human Rights and Its Continuing Relevance* (Routledge, 2019).

Freeman, M., *Human Rights: An Interdisciplinary Approach*, 2nd edn (Polity Press, 2011).

Gearty, C., and C. Douzinas (eds.), *The Cambridge Companion to Human Rights Law* (Cambridge University Press, 2012).

Goodale, M., *Surrendering to Utopia: An Anthropology of Human Rights* (Stanford University Press, 2009).

Ishay, M. R., *The History of Human Rights: From Ancient Times to the Globalization Era* (University of California Press, 2008).

Jensen, S. L. B., *The Making of International Human Rights: The 1960s, Decolonization, and the Reconstruction of Global Values* (Cambridge University Press, 2016).

Kinley, D., W. Sadurski and K. Walton (eds.), *Human Rights: Old Problems, New Possibilities* (Edward Elgar, 2013).

Lutz-Bachmann, M., and A. Nascimento (eds.), *Human Rights, Human Dignity, and Cosmopolitan Ideals* (Ashgate, 2014).

Moeckli, D., H. Keller and C. Heri (eds.), *The Human Rights Covenants at 50: Their Past, Present and Future* (Oxford University Press, 2018).

Morsink, J., *Inherent Human Rights: Philosophical Roots of the Universal Declaration* (University of Pennsylvania Press, 2009).

Mutua, M., *Human Rights: A Political and Cultural Critique* (University of Pennsylvania Press, 2002).

Nowak, M., *Human Rights or Global Capitalism: The Limits of Privatization* (University of Pennsylvania Press, 2017).

Pogge, T., *World Poverty and Human Rights: Cosmopolitan Responsibilities and Reforms*, 2nd edn (Polity Press, 2008).

Rajagopal, B., *International Law from Below: Development, Social Movements and Third World Resistance* (Cambridge University Press, 2003).

Simmons, W. P., *Human Rights Law and the Marginalised Other* (Cambridge University Press, 2014 (paperback)).

Twining, W., *General Jurisprudence: Understanding Law from a Global Perspective* (Cambridge University Press, 2009).

Waldron, J., *Nonsense upon Stilts: Bentham, Marx and Burke on the Rights of Man* (Methuen, 1987).

2 International Human Rights Law: The Normative Framework

CONTENTS

2.1   INTRODUCTION

The multiple voices making up the field of international human rights are one of its defining characteristics. Diplomats, officials, politicians, social movements, non-governmental organisations (NGOs), academics from various disciplines, commentators and the public at large contribute to debate and practice. They add to, and often complement, the work of (international) lawyers. The interaction of this multitude of actors has stimulated the development of international human rights law. However, it has also increased the scope for misunderstandings and misrepresentations of the law that may be misleading, if not damaging. International human rights law is a legal system that has its own rules and methods, which, even if contested, frame the consideration of arising questions. For example, claims that the death penalty is unlawful under international law, while welcome from an advocacy perspective, may be seen as turning what ought to be the law (*de lege ferenda*) into a statement about what the law is (*de lege lata*). If such a claim were to be framed as a legal argument, it would have to be developed very carefully with adequate references so as not to risk undermining the (legal) credibility of the person or organisation making it. Such a risk is particularly evident when assertions made – such as that a successor government may not be responsible for the violations committed by the government preceding it (in an NGO report on Iraq) – reveal fundamental misconceptions of international law, in this case the difference between the succession of governments and states.[1]

The need for a sound understanding of the normative legal framework and for conceptual clarity applies particularly to those working in the field of international law. The sociology of international law has been aptly described as one of practice ('commentators' such as legal advisors and judges seeking to determine the law), propaganda (states using legal arguments) and principle (academics reflecting on foundational questions).[2] In other words, the standpoint(s) of the various actors are informed by their positions and how they approach the law. This plurality of actors may give rise to prolonged debates, especially where no judicial (or quasi-judicial) body is called upon to adjudicate the legal questions raised, which broadens the scope for legal indeterminacy. This indeterminacy opens space for the progressive development of international human rights law but may equally create tension, particularly where states disagree with certain interpretations. Conflicts also arise because of the ever-widening reach of adjudication of questions of human rights law, such as its application to the extraterritorial conduct of states. This process may result in what has been referred to as the fragmentation of international law, which raises the spectre that different bodies, such as the International Court of Justice (ICJ), international criminal tribunals and human rights treaty bodies, develop diverging interpretations of the law.[3] In these contexts, an informed discourse is important for the coherence and legitimacy of the system.

International human rights law is part of public international law[4] and shares a number of its features, including sources, obligations (primary rules) and state responsibility (secondary rules).[5] While international human rights law has formed within the broader setting of international law, it has developed distinctive features. Traditional international law was an order based on

---

[1] Succession of governments is generally considered not to affect state responsibility whereas state succession may. See P. Dumberry, *State Succession to International Responsibility* (Martinus Nijhoff, 2007).

[2] M. Mendelson, 'Practice, Propaganda and Principle in International Law (Inaugural Lecture)' (1989) 42 *Current Legal Problems* 1.

[3] See Report of the Study Group of the ILC, Fragmentation of International Law: Difficulties Arising from the Diversification and Expansion of International Law, UN doc. A/CN.4/L.682 (13 April 2006) and UN doc. A/CN.4/L.682/Add.1 (2 May 2006).

[4] See in this context, M. T. Kamminga and M. Scheinin (eds.), *The Impact of Human Rights Law on General International Law* (Oxford University Press, 2009).

[5] See on the responsibility of states particularly art. 33 of the ILC Articles on the Responsibility of States for Internationally Wrongful Acts (ARSIWA) and further below at 2.5.

the sovereign interests of states as its sole subjects. In contrast, international human rights law is characterised by its emphasis on common interests that reflect the fundamental values of the international legal order. This value-based approach is evident in the concept of *jus cogens*, or peremptory norm, and the notion of *erga omnes*, obligations owed to the international community as a whole. The substantive emphasis on common interests is mirrored in the preference for multilateral instruments. The making of treaties and declarations, such as the Convention on the Rights of the Child (CRC) or the United Nations (UN) Declaration on the Rights of Indigenous Peoples (UNDRIP), frequently involves a large number of actors, including international civil society. Human rights treaties agreed upon in these processes create regimes that are meant to benefit individual and collective rights-holders rather than serving reciprocal state interests. They also typically encompass monitoring bodies that have sought to develop the distinctive features of human rights treaties in their practice. The Human Rights Committee (HRCtee), for example, has limited the scope for reservations and declared successor states bound by human rights obligations, these being interpretations that diverge from positions considered to reflect general international law.[6] The supervisory features of human rights treaties have raised the question of whether they are self-contained or special regimes, i.e. systems that exclude recourse to other measures of enforcement, a question that goes to the core of the relationship between international human rights law and general international law.

Undoubtedly, international human rights law can form an important component of a new international order[7] or international constitutionalism. However, unilateralism, selectivity and fragmentation, in addition to challenges of effective implementation, are restraining factors that may slow down, if not undermine, 'constitutional' developments at the international level.[8] This chapter examines these dynamics and discusses the key building blocks of international (human rights) law: its sources;[9] its rights and

---

[6] See HRCtee, General Comment 24: Issues relating to reservations made upon ratification or accession to the Covenant or the Optional Protocols thereto, or in relation to declarations under article 41 of the Covenant, UN doc. CCPR/C/21/Rev.1/Add.6 (4 November 1994) and General Comment 26: Continuity of obligations, UN doc. CCPR/C/21/Rev.1/Add.8/Rev.1 (8 December 1997).

[7] See P. Allott, *Eunomia: New Order for a New World*, 2nd edn (Oxford University Press, 2001).

[8] See for a thorough debate and for an approach based on social constructivism, O. Diggelmann and T. Altwicker, 'Is there Something like a Constitution of International Law: Critical Analysis of the Debate on World Constitutionalism' (2008) 68 *Zeitschrift für ausländisches und öffentliches Recht und Völkerrecht* 623.

[9] General principles as one of the sources referred to in art. 38(1) of the ICJ Statute are not dealt with separately in this chapter. See for a brief discussion of human rights as general principles of law, O. De Schutter, *International Human Rights Law*, 2nd edn (Cambridge University Press, 2014) 66–7.

obligations and the scope of their application; and its implementation as well as state responsibility and enforcement.

2.2   SOURCES

2.2.1   Treaties

Treaties are referred to in article 38 of the ICJ Statute as one of the recognised sources of international law. They are bilateral or multilateral agreements between states[10] governed by the Vienna Convention on the Law of Treaties (VCLT) of 1969, which is widely seen as reflecting customary international law.[11] In the human rights sphere treaties take several names, such as 'covenant', 'convention', 'charter' or 'protocol' (the latter where they relate to another treaty). The name of a treaty reflects the symbolic significance attached to it by its drafters but does not entail separate legal consequences. As an agreement, a treaty requires consent, which can be expressed by way of 'signature, exchange of instruments constituting a treaty, ratification, acceptance, approval or accession, or by any other means if so agreed'.[12] The surest way to find out about the actual status of a treaty, i.e. date of adoption, coming into force, states parties, reservations, etc., is to access the databases available online, in particular the UN Treaty Collection.[13]

2.2.1.1   *Treaty-making*

Multilateral human rights treaties are frequently the outcome of a long and often complex deliberative process involving a number of actors. Nevertheless, once agreed upon, their existence and content are often taken for granted and do indeed have a self-validating quality, not least as a matter of positive law. However, there are several reasons why an understanding of the treaty-making process is important. It can shed light on the various interpretations put forward by states, experts and others, which, in the form of the so-called *travaux préparatoires* (preparatory work), can help in interpreting

---

[10] See on the nature of agreements between states and non-state actors, particularly peace agreements, C. Bell, *On the Law of Peace, Peace Agreements and the Lex Pacificatoria* (Oxford University Press, 2008) 127–43.

[11] See A. Aust, *Modern Treaty Law and Practice*, 3rd edn (Cambridge University Press, 2014) 9–12.

[12] See art. 11 VCLT.

[13] The UN Treaty Collection is accessible at http://treaties.un.org. The status of regional treaties can be found on the websites of the respective organisations, namely the Council of Europe (CoE), Organization of American States (OAS) and African Union (AU).

the treaty.[14] In addition, it can reveal the historical context and the political motives, role and positions of states and others, such as international organisations and civil society. It may also explain why certain states have (not) become parties, and why a treaty has been a success or a failure. The position of states in these processes is also important in evaluating whether a specific norm contained in a treaty has the status of customary international law (see below at 2.2.2).

Multilateral treaties go through a series of stages before adoption and coming into force. There is no fixed process or formula for the making of treaties. The idea, initiative or impetus for a treaty can emerge from different sources, which have included individuals (Raphael Lemkin in respect of the Convention against Genocide);[15] NGOs (Amnesty International (AI) and others, Convention against Torture and Other Cruel, Inhuman or Degrading Treatment or Punishment (CAT));[16] states (Trinidad and Tobago, International Criminal Court (ICC)):[17] intergovernmental organisations (IGOs) (the UN, the International Bill of Human Rights);[18] expert commissions (such as the International Law Commission (ILC));[19] or a combination of these.[20] The power of actors, the ability to participate effectively and the capacity to own both the process and the product have been identified as key factors in these processes.[21]

The process of '[h]uman rights treaty negotiations may involve the UNGA [UN General Assembly], the Committee,[22] the Economic and Social Council, the Human Rights Council and an intergovernmental conference'.[23] Depending on the procedures and practice of the body concerned or the conference convened, civil society representatives will have varying degrees of influence.[24] NGOs may be able to observe and lobby delegates, but also

---

[14] Art. 32 VCLT.

[15] See R. Lemkin, *Axis Rule in Occupied Europe: Laws of Occupation, Analysis of Government, Proposals for Redress* (Carnegie Endowment for International Peace, 1944) 79–98; W. Schabas, *Genocide in International Law: The Crime of Crimes*, 2nd edn (Cambridge University Press, 2009) 17–90.

[16] J. H. Burgers and H. Danelius, *The United Nations Convention against Torture: A Handbook on the Convention against Torture and Other Cruel, Inhuman or Degrading Treatment or Punishment* (Martinus Nijhoff, 1988) 13–29.

[17] See UNGA resolution 44/39 (1989).

[18] See Chapter 1.2.5.

[19] See for the ILC's work, http://legal.un.org/ilc/?.

[20] See for further examples, M. Mutua, 'Standard Setting in Human Rights: Critique and Prognosis' (2007) 29 *Human Rights Quarterly* 547.

[21] Ibid., 557.

[22] See for the work of the UNGA's third committee, www.un.org/en/ga/third.

[23] See A. Boyle and C. Chinkin, *The Making of International Law* (Oxford University Press, 2007) 166–83.

[24] See on a duty to consult NGOs, S. Charnovitz, 'Nongovernmental Organizations and International Law' (2006) 100 *American Journal of International Law* 348, at 368–72.

to make submissions, which may be taken into consideration during the drafting.[25] The ICC Rome Statute is a recent example of the important role played by NGOs in the development of international treaties. At the Rome conference NGOs were well represented, gave public statements, lobbied and succeeded in strengthening several areas of the treaty, such as by the inclusion of gender crimes and victims' rights.[26]

Draft texts often undergo a series of changes, with articles added or omitted and the text being amended, as a result of deliberations that reflect the positions of states and their willingness to compromise. Political stakes, leverage, force of personality and argument, as well as the dynamics of the moment, will often dictate the outcome of treaty negotiations. A major factor is the acceptability of the final draft, which poses a perennial dilemma: to what degree should the text of a document be compromised in order to persuade other states to join? This is a delicate balance that needs to be struck at the drafting stage, which is closely related to the procedure for adopting the text. Consensus may enhance acceptability, but may come at the price of compromising the text. Conversely, where a text is adopted by majority, opposition and subsequent non-ratification may undermine the universality and effectiveness of the treaty concerned. Following adoption, the treaty will be open for signature. Multilateral treaties need to have a sufficient number of states parties to command legitimacy. The number of ratifications needed for a treaty to come into force varies, but most instruments set the bar at twenty ratifications.[27] An initially low number of parties may help in creating momentum by making the treaty a reality, which may attract other states to follow. There is, however, an equal risk that a treaty limps along and carries limited weight if the number remains low.[28] This explains why fundamental treaties setting up institutions with universal scope, such as the ICC Rome Statute, require a larger number of states parties (sixty);[29] the high threshold is justified by the universal ambition and the commitments that states parties have to undertake in order to make such a treaty work.

The number of states parties a treaty attracts depends on several factors: degree of consensus; acceptability; strength of ratification campaigns;

---

[25] For further examples of the role of NGOs in treaty-making, see Boyle and Chinkin, above note 23, 41–97; Mutua, above note 20, 593–604.

[26] See in particular, the work of the Coalition for the ICC, www.iccnow.org. See also M. J. Struett, *The Politics of Constructing the International Criminal Court: NGOs, Discourse and Agency* (Palgrave Macmillan, 2008).

[27] Or other means expressing consent to be bound.

[28] See e.g., the 1986 Convention on the Non-applicability of Statutory Limitations to War Crimes and Crimes against Humanity, which had only attracted fifty-five parties as of 1 August 2015.

[29] Art. 126(1) ICC Rome Statute.

international and institutional support for a treaty; and the record of the body established to monitor the treaty's implementation. Examples of treaties with a high number of states parties are both covenants (International Covenant on Civil and Political Rights (ICCPR) and International Covenant on Economic, Social and Cultural Rights (ICESCR)) and the CRC,[30] which are widely seen as treaties to which a state must be party to show a degree of 'human rights acceptability'. Other treaties have been less successful because they are perceived to carry less weight or are politically more controversial. An example is the International Convention on the Protection of the Rights of All Migrant Workers and Members of Their Families (ICRMW), which has been ratified and acceded to by most migrant-sending states, but has received virtually no endorsement by receiving states, which has undermined the object of the treaty.[31]

As instruments, treaties are the hallmark of positive law, i.e. the law posited and explicitly agreed upon by states in a formal procedure. It is mainly for this reason that they are a prized tool in advocacy efforts aimed at standard-setting and strengthening the legal recognition and implementation of human rights. While important, adoption and ratification of treaties are not ends in themselves. The number of treaties and treaty parties does not automatically translate into better protection, as there frequently remains a considerable gap between the treaty rhetoric and motives for becoming a party thereto, on the one hand, and the reality of implementation on the other.[32]

2.2.1.2   *Reservations*

Unless a treaty provides otherwise, states can enter reservations, defined as 'a unilateral statement, however phrased or named, made by a State, when signing, ratifying, accepting, approving or acceding to a treaty, whereby it purports to exclude or to modify the legal effect of certain provisions of the treaty in their application to that State'.[33] In other words, reservations allow states to limit the scope of their obligations; in practice, states often do.[34]

---

[30] As of 27 March 2019, CPED as the latest treaty to come into force had 59 parties, CAT 165, ICESCR 169, ICCPR 172, CRPD 177, ICERD 179, CEDAW 189 and the CRC 196.

[31] Fifty-four states parties as of 1 April 2019.

[32] See in particular, the much discussed study by O. A. Hathaway, 'Do Human Rights Treaties Make a Difference?' (2002) 118 *Yale Law Journal* 1935.

[33] Art. 2(1)(d) VCLT. See also on reservations, the ILC Guide to Practice on Reservations to Treaties (2011).

[34] The text of reservations can be found on the UN Treaty Collection website, http://treaties.un.org, under 'Status of Treaties' following the chart for signatures and ratifications. See also B. A. Simmons, *Mobilizing for Human Rights: International Law in Domestic Politics* (Cambridge University Press, 2009) 98–103.

Reservations to human rights treaties essentially constitute a compromise that seeks to address the fundamental dilemma between sovereignty and the pursuit of collective goals. A categorical position, i.e. prohibiting states from making reservations, risks having fewer states parties, while placing no limits on entering reservations may defeat the object and purpose of a treaty. Reservations are in this light a pragmatic device that allows states to overcome potential stumbling blocks to becoming a party, namely obligations that are not agreeable. However, this pragmatism comes at the price of fragmentation because the fact that not all states have the same obligations may undermine the integrity of a treaty and frustrate its objectives. Reservations therefore raise a series of questions. What are the acceptable limits to making reservations? What should be the consequence of impermissible reservations? And who should decide on the validity of reservations and their consequences?

Some treaties prohibit the making of reservations, whereas others apply the general rule, whether explicitly stated or not, that reservations must not run counter to the object and purpose of the treaty. This rule was developed by the ICJ and incorporated in the VCLT, replacing the previous purely consent-based system under which states could make reservations that other parties were free to accept or reject.[35]

There is no general rule that says when a reservation runs counter to a treaty's object and purpose. However, the practice of states and treaty bodies provides ample illustration and guidance. To begin with, states parties cannot derogate from *jus cogens* norms and non-derogable rights that are fundamental to a treaty.[36] Reservations in relation to other rights may be incompatible with general principles, such as equality, or may undermine the very rationale of the treaty concerned. An example of this kind is the reservation entered by the government of Kuwait to the Convention on the Elimination of All Forms of Discrimination against Women (CEDAW) according to which it 'reserves its right not to implement the provision contained in article 9, paragraph 2, of the Convention,[37] inasmuch as it runs counter to the Kuwaiti Nationality Act, which stipulates that a child's nationality shall be determined by that of his father'.[38] Beyond this, human rights treaty

---

[35] Art. 19 VCLT. See also *Reservations to the Convention on the Prevention and Punishment of the Crime of Genocide* (ICJ) (1951) 21–7.

[36] HRCtee, General Comment 24, paras. 8–10, in which the HRCtee applies this rule equally to rights having the status of customary international law. See, in contrast, 3.1.5.3 of the ILC Guide to Practice on Reservations to Treaties (2011). See also 4.4.3, ibid., on *jus cogens*.

[37] 'States Parties shall grant women equal rights with men with respect to the nationality of their children.'

[38] See reference to text and objections by other states parties, Finland, the Netherlands, Sweden, online at http://treaties.un.org/Pages/ViewDetails.aspx?src=TREATY&mtdsg_no=IV-8& chapter=4&lang= en#31.

bodies and states have frequently raised concerns about general and vague statements that do not provide a sufficiently clear indication of how they affect a state party's obligations and may effectively nullify them.[39] This applies in particular to declarations that a treaty or a specific article is to be interpreted in conformity with national legislation.[40] For example, Saudi Arabia entered the following reservation to CEDAW: '[i]n case of contradiction between any term of the Convention and the norms of Islamic law, the Kingdom is not under obligation to observe the contradictory terms of the Convention'. Finland objected to the reservation, stating that:

A reservation which consists of a general reference to religious law and national law without specifying its contents ... does not clearly define to other Parties to the Convention the extent to which the reserving State commits itself to the Convention and therefore creates serious doubts as to the commitment of the reserving State to fulfil its obligations under the Convention. Furthermore, reservations are subject to the general principle of treaty interpretation according to which a party may not invoke the provisions of its domestic law as justification for a failure to perform its treaty obligations.[41]

As a matter of general practice, human rights treaty bodies regularly recommend, albeit with mixed results, that states parties withdraw reservations made.[42]

General international law, as developed by the ICJ and codified in the VCLT, principally leaves it to other states parties to object to what they consider impermissible reservations. In principle, the relevant treaty provisions apply between the states parties concerned unless the objecting state expressly states its intention that they should not do so.[43] This approach, which is effectively based on reciprocity, is unsatisfactory when applied to international human rights treaties whose primary objective is to create a regime binding all parties. The HRCtee strongly made this point in its General Comment 24, in which it reserved the right to decide whether a particular reservation was compatible with the ICCPR's object and purpose.[44] It held that a reservation by Trinidad and Tobago, according to which the HRCtee was not competent to consider death penalty cases, was incompatible with

---

[39] See art. 57(1) ECHR: 'Reservations of a general character shall not be permitted under this Article', and HRCtee, General Comment 24, para. 19.

[40] See e.g., Bangladesh's reservation to art. 14 CAT and Spain's response thereto, online at http://treaties.un.org/Pages/ViewDetails.aspx?src=TREATY&mtdsg_no=IV-9&chapter=4&lang= en#14.

[41] See http://treaties.un.org/Pages/ViewDetails.aspx?src=TREATY&mtdsg_no=IV-8&chapter=4&lang=en.

[42] See HRCtee, General Comment 24, para. 20, and, generally, the concluding observations of UN human rights treaty bodies.

[43] Arts. 20(4)(b) and 21 VCLT.   [44] HRCtee, General Comment 24, para. 18.

the ICCPR's object and purpose because it 'singles out a certain group of individuals for lesser procedural protection than that which is enjoyed by the rest of the population'.[45] The European Court of Human Rights (ECtHR) found in *Belilos* v. *Switzerland* that Switzerland's declaration on the right to a fair trial was too general and was incompatible with (the then) article 64 of the European Convention on Human Rights (ECHR).[46] Similarly, a declaration made by Turkey that limited the ECtHR's jurisdiction in relation to Northern Cyprus was held to violate (the then) articles 25 and 46 ECHR.[47]

Importantly, as a result of their findings, the ECtHR and the HRCtee have simply excluded invalid reservations with the effect that a state party is bound by the treaty (provision) in question. This is problematic because treaty bodies assume the right effectively to overrule the lack of state consent. As a result, a state that makes a reservation to a human rights treaty faces the risk of being fully bound even if this outcome runs counter to its intention. From the perspective of an effective multilateral regime, severing reservations is preferable to the exclusion of a state party or the de facto acceptance of an incompatible reservation. However, it carries the risk that a state may choose not to become a party where it expects that its reservation may be invalidated. A state that is already a party may oppose the interpretation and question the right of the treaty body to impose an obligation it has not consented to, which may potentially result in a standoff or even the denunciation of a treaty.[48] The repercussions of the approach taken by human rights treaty bodies became highly visible when France, the United States of America (USA) and the United Kingdom (UK) objected strongly to General Comment 24, accusing the HRCtee of effectively usurping the rights of states parties and acting ultra vires (beyond its competence).[49] The ILC's Guide on Reservations to Treaties, whose adoption followed a series of discussions involving treaty bodies and states, provides for a compromise solution according to which states shall take a treaty body's assessment of the permissibility of a reservation into consideration.[50] Notably, according to the Guide, an impermissible reservation is null and void.[51] A state entering an invalid reservation is bound by the treaty unless it has 'expressed

---

[45] *Kennedy* v. *Trinidad and Tobago* (HRCtee) (1999) para. 6.7.

[46] *Belilos* v. *Switzerland* (ECtHR) (1988) paras. 50–60.

[47] *Loizidou* v. *Turkey* (ECtHR) (1995) paras. 15, 27 and 90–8.

[48] Trinidad and Tobago denounced the Optional Protocol after the HRCtee had ruled in *Kennedy* v. *Trinidad and Tobago* (2002) para. 10, that the reservation entered was invalid.

[49] The observations by the UK, the USA and France on General Comment 24 can be found in Report of the HRCtee, UN doc. A/50/40 (3 October 1995) Annex IV (USA and UK), and UN doc. A/51/40 (13 April 1997) Annex VI (France).

[50] Section 3.2.3 of the ILC Guide to Practice on Reservations to Treaties (2011).

[51] Ibid., section 4.5.1.

a contrary intention' or expresses its intention not to be bound. It has to do so within twelve months where the treaty body concerned declares that it considers a reservation invalid.[52] The ILC's approach therefore combines respect for state consent with a qualified severance provision whose application depends on the state's response to a treaty body's declaration that its reservation is invalid.[53]

2.2.2   Customary International Law

Customary international law, namely 'international custom, as evidence of a general practice accepted as law'[54] – in other words state practice accompanied by *opinio juris*, i.e. belief in the binding nature of a rule – is the other main source of international law.[55] Establishing the recognition and content of a rule under customary international law will often be crucial to determine what, if any, legal obligations a state has. The subject matter of several areas of international human rights law may not (yet) be (fully) governed by a treaty. This applies to most human rights at some stage in their development; current examples are the law governing the rights of indigenous peoples[56] and the law governing internally displaced persons.[57] Alternatively, a treaty may govern a particular area of the law but a state may not be a party. Random examples are the US non-ratification of the CRC and Thailand's non-ratification of the Convention relating to the Status of Refugees (Refugee Convention). In addition, alleged violations may date back a long time, for example, torture during colonial times, and it may not be clear whether the prohibition was already recognised at that point. Customary international law is in these circumstances critical to establishing a state's obligation(s) and responsibility and to monitor compliance with international standards.

---

[52] Ibid., section 4.5.3.

[53] See further A. Pellet, 'The ILC Guide to Practice on Reservations to Treaties: A General Presentation by the Special Rapporteur' (2013) 24 *European Journal of International Law* 1061.

[54] Art. 38(1)(b) ICJ Statute.

[55] See on customary international law generally, H. Thirlway, *The Sources of International Law*, 2nd edn (Oxford University Press, 2019) 60–105; ILA, *Final Report of the Committee, Statement of Principles Applicable to the Formation of General Customary International Law* (London Conference, 2000), available on the Association's website, www.ila-hq.org.

[56] The rights of indigenous peoples have been explicitly recognised in UNGA resolution 61/295 (2007) rather than in discrete human rights treaties, though human rights treaty bodies have provided some recognition and protection in their jurisprudence. See below at 2.2.5 and Chapter 10.4.

[57] With the exception of the Protocol on the Protection and Assistance to Internally Displaced Persons (Great Lakes Pact, 2006) and the 2009 African Union Convention for the Protection and Assistance of Internally Displaced Persons (Kampala Convention).

Customary international law is by its nature rather indeterminate. Beyond some well-established categories, such as the prohibition of torture, there is considerable uncertainty about which rights have customary status. This relative flexibility and openness can become an important tool for advocates to make claims that a rule or a right has attained or is in the process of attaining such status under international law. Where such claims gain traction, they can be highly effective. An example would be the long-standing campaign to outlaw the death penalty, which has contributed to its regional abolition in Europe.[58] On the political plane, states can use multilateral channels to develop and garner support for a rule of customary international law or, conversely, to put forward positions that thwart the recognition of rights viewed as contrary to a state's interest.[59] Attempts aimed at achieving the recognition of the right to development illustrate this struggle. While the UNGA issued a landmark resolution on this right in 1986, its customary law status has remained the subject of controversy.[60]

The process of establishing custom, i.e. determining what constitutes evidence, poses a number of methodological challenges.[61] This is particularly pronounced in the field of human rights, where evidence of custom is often largely based on declaratory sources, such as the Universal Declaration on Human Rights (UDHR), rather than on other forms of state practice.[62] The privileging of statements and values expressed in such instruments is problematic as it may open a gap between aspirations and reality, i.e. 'words are cheap'. A further challenge consists in establishing the evidentiary value of conflicting state practice, torture being a well-known and vexing example. While states regularly vote for declarations affirming the absolute prohibition of torture, with national laws stipulating such prohibition, torture is still practised all too frequently. However, the actual practice is widely

---

[58] See Chapter 8.2.5.

[59] See for a critical perspective, B.S. Chimni, 'Customary International Law: A Third World Perspective' (2018) 112 *American Journal of International Law* 1, and 'Symposium on B.S. Chimni, "Customary International Law: A Third World Perspective"' (2018) 112 *AJIL Unbound* 290.

[60] See S. P. Marks, 'The Human Right to Development: between Rhetoric and Reality' (2004) 17 *Harvard Human Rights Journal* 137; and A. Sengupta, 'On the Theory and Practice of the Right to Development' (2002) 24 *Human Rights Quarterly* 837. See also Chapter 14.3.

[61] For a critical assessment of the ICJ's approach see Boyle and Chinkin, above note 23, 278–85.

[62] See on evidence of state practice in the field of human rights, American Law Institute, *Restatement (Third) of the Foreign Relations Law of the United States*, §701(2). See for a recent example of practical application in a related field, the International Committee of the Red Cross (ICRC) landmark study, J.-M. Henckaerts and L. Doswald-Beck (eds.), *Customary International Humanitarian Law*, vol. I: *Rules* and vol. II: *Practice* (ICRC and Cambridge University Press, 2005), and ICRC Customary International Humanitarian Law Database, www.icrc.org/customary-ihl/eng/docs/home.

considered irrelevant where states do not seek to justify it as lawful. This is effectively what the ICJ held in a well-known passage in *Nicaragua* v. *USA*.[63] The rationale for the position is sound because customary international law concerns the normative status of a rule. The discrepancy between normative requirements and realities on the ground is an unfortunate feature of international human rights law, and upholding and reinforcing the normative status of a rule has been one of the key means of limiting existing discrepancies. However, persistent breaches of a norm may undermine its effectiveness if it is seen as something that states pay lip service to but do not adhere to in actual practice.

A different question arises where the right or rule is already governed by a treaty, namely whether treaties count as state practice. For example, when seeking to specify the USA's obligations in respect of the rights of the child (the USA is not a party to the CRC), is it possible to use CRC-related practice as evidence that its standards are of a customary nature? Treaties are a separate source and by becoming a party states incur rights and obligations according to treaty law. However, it would be paradoxical if the very fact of overwhelming treaty membership were to preclude resort to a treaty as evidence of custom.[64] It is therefore generally accepted that treaties count as state practice. This is particularly important for multilateral – so-called law-making – treaties aimed at codifying or 'crystallising' customary international law, which includes major human rights treaties. While treaty practice carries some weight, its evidentiary value for determining the customary status of a particular article or right needs to be assessed with reference to supporting state practice. The question of treaties as state practice needs to be distinguished from the relationship between treaties and customary international law. Treaties governing the same subject matter will be *lex specialis,* but customary international law may still apply where there is a gap or a conflict on jurisdictional grounds.[65] In addition, subsequent practice of states parties may affect the interpretation of a treaty.[66]

The legal consequence of a rule of customary international law is that a state is bound to respect the right in question. This applies irrespective of whether a state has consented to the rule, unless it has persistently objected to it. The exception of a persistent objector is recognised in order to allow states to opt out of permissive custom (with the exception of peremptory norms having *jus cogens* status, see below at 2.2.6), but plays a limited role

---

[63] *Military and Paramilitary Activities in and against Nicaragua (Nicaragua* v. *United States of America)* (ICJ) (1986) paras. 206–9 (regarding the principle of non-intervention).

[64] See R. R. Baxter, 'Multilateral Treaties as Evidence of Customary International Law' (1965–1966) 41 *British Yearbook of International Law* 275.

[65] *Nicaragua* v. *USA*, paras. 175–9.

[66] See in particular art. 31(3)(b) VCLT.

in the practice of international human rights law.[67] New states are widely considered to be bound by customary international law, although this argument can be contested on the grounds that it violates consent, which some consider to be a basis of any obligation under international law; this may also apply to rules, such as state succession to debts incurred by previous colonial governments attributed to the state, which are incompatible with the economic self-determination of states.[68]

2.2.2.1   The UDHR and Customary International Law

The UDHR is paradigmatic for the role of custom in the field of international human rights law. As a UNGA declaration, it constitutes neither a treaty nor a formal source of international law.[69] However, it is often assumed or claimed that the UDHR has the status of customary international law. Such an assertion needs careful consideration. (1) Did the UDHR constitute state practice? Yes, voting for UNGA declarations is recognised as state practice. (2) Was this practice accompanied by *opinio juris?* This question is more difficult to answer in the affirmative because the UDHR was primarily seen as an agreement on, and declaration of, fundamental principles serving as a first step towards a binding International Bill of Human Rights rather than referring to binding rights and obligations or constituting an authoritative interpretation of the UN Charter (a treaty). (3) Has the UDHR been recognised as binding in state practice since its adoption? Answering this question requires evaluating the weight given to the declaration and its individual provisions at the time and an analysis of their subsequent application in state practice. Relevant evidence comprises, in particular, recognition of UDHR articles in treaties; reference to the UDHR or its articles in declarations, resolutions or similar statements; reference to the UDHR or its articles in the practice of international and regional bodies; and incorporation of the UDHR or its articles in national constitutions and legislation as well as their application by national courts and other bodies.

Note that the list refers both to the declaration and its articles, as a lot of relevant state practice concerns particular UDHR provisions rather than the UDHR as a whole. This is important because some UDHR articles have undoubtedly become customary international law, such as the principle of

---

[67] See ILA, *Final Report*, above note 55, 27–9, and P. Dumberry, 'Incoherent and Ineffective: The Concept of Persistent Objector Revisited' (2010) 59 *International & Comparative Law Quarterly* 779.

[68] See further for a critical analysis, M. Craven, 'The Problem of State Succession and the Identity of States under International Law' (1998) 9 *European Journal of International Law* 142, particularly at 157.

[69] See ILA, *Final Report*, above note 55, Part V, 54–65.

non-discrimination or the prohibition of slavery, while others may not have, such as the right to rest and leisure.[70] Determining the customary status of any given UDHR article requires rigorous scrutiny of available state practice (reference in treaties, declarations, number of national laws or judgments, etc.) and weight attached to it (number of states parties, voting for declarations, prevalence of laws or judgments). This can be a painstaking methodological exercise. However, bypassing its rigours risks undermining the credibility of any assertion made regarding the customary status of a particular right.[71]

2.2.3   Judicial Decisions as Source of Law

Article 38 of the ICJ Statute recognises 'judicial decisions ... as subsidiary means for the determination of rules of law'. This provision states the obvious: jurisprudence can provide valuable evidence of the status and content of norms through their interpretation in a given case. It also makes clear that judicial bodies are not considered to have a law-making function.[72] This theoretical premise must not, however, be overstated as such bodies play an increasingly important role in the development of international law.

A number of international treaty bodies apply and interpret international human rights law, drawing on recognised methods of treaty interpretation, namely that '[a] treaty shall be interpreted in good faith in accordance with the ordinary meaning to be given to the terms of the treaty in their context and in the light of its object and purpose'.[73] By definition, this includes bodies specifically tasked with monitoring a particular human rights treaty and interpreting its provisions. Prominent examples at the international level are the HRCtee and the ECtHR, the Inter-American Court of Human Rights (IACtHR) and the African Commission on Human and Peoples' Rights (ACmHPR) as well as the African Court on Human and Peoples' Rights (ACtHPR) at the regional level.[74] Other international judicial bodies are also increasingly called upon to adjudicate human rights questions. The ICJ, in particular,

---

[70] See e.g., H. Hannum, 'The Status of the Universal Declaration of Human Rights in National and International Law' (1995–1996) 25 *Georgia Journal of International and Comparative Law* 287; and critical discussion in B. Simma and P. Alston, 'The Sources of Human Rights Law: Custom, Jus Cogens and General Principles' (1988–1989) 12 *Australian Yearbook of International Law* 82.

[71] See Simma and Alston, ibid., particularly 83–100.

[72] See Boyle and Chinkin, above note 23, 263–311, on the role of courts in law-making.

[73] Art. 31(1) VCLT. See further arts. 31(2)–(4), 32, 33 VCLT, and for an assessment of the practice of UN treaty bodies in this regard, K. Mechlem, 'Treaty Bodies and the Interpretation of Human Rights' (2009) 42 *Vanderbilt Journal of Transnational Law* 905.

[74] See Chapters 5 and 6.

has made important rulings in a series of contentious cases and advisory opinions that have a direct bearing on international human rights law.[75] Recently established international criminal tribunals also refer to, or apply, human rights law in their jurisprudence, for example when interpreting the elements of crimes or when defining the rights of the defence.[76] Regionally, the European Court of Justice (ECJ) (now Court of Justice of the European Union – CJEU) and African regional community courts have issued land-mark judgments in the field of human rights, such as the ECJ in *Carpenter* and *Kadi*[77] and the Economic Community of West African States (ECOWAS) Community Court of Justice in *Mani* v. *Niger*.[78] In addition, domestic courts are frequently seized with cases in which they have to interpret international human rights law. Courts have become particularly prominent in adjudicating a series of highly charged cases in the context of counter-terrorism measures and human rights, such as the UK House of Lords in *A and Others* v. *Secretary of State*, which effectively ended the system of indefinite detention of foreign nationals suspected of terrorism.[79]

These developments have led to an intensification of the adjudication of international human rights law, largely prompted by victims, human rights lawyers and NGOs, as well as states and others in cases before the ICJ.[80] The increased application, along with the scrutiny and cross-referencing that it entails, has resulted in a more sophisticated understanding and maturing of international human rights law. However, it has also increased the risk of fragmentation, and of diverging interpretations, of rules depending on which body is seized with a particular question.[81] As there is no formal hierarchy

[75] See G. Zyberi, *The Humanitarian Face of the International Court of Justice: Its Contribution to Interpreting and Developing International Human Rights and Humanitarian Law Rules and Principles* (Intersentia, 2008); S. R. S. Bedi, *The Development of Human Rights Law by the Judges of the International Court of Justice* (Hart, 2007).

[76] See multiple contributions in C. Eboe-Osuji (ed.), *Protecting Human Rights: Essays in International Law and Policy in Honour of Navanethem Pillay* (Martinus Nijhoff, 2010).

[77] *Mary Carpenter* v. *Secretary of State for the Home Department* (ECJ) (2002) (right of spouse not to be deported); *Kadi and Al Barakaat International Foundation* v. *Council and Commission* (ECJ) (2008) (legal protection against UN Security Council imposed sanctions transposed into EU law).

[78] *Mme Hadijatou Mani Koraou* v. *The Republic of Niger* (ECOWAS CCJ) (2008) (prohibition of slavery).

[79] *A and Others* v. *Secretary of State for the Home Department* (UK) (2004).

[80] E.g., NGO advocacy has been credited with leading to the UNGA resolution referring the *Nuclear Weapons* case before the ICJ for an advisory opinion. See R. Falk, 'The Nuclear Weapons Advisory Opinion and the New Jurisprudence of Global Civil Society' (1997) 7 *Transnational Law & Contemporary Problems* 333, at 340–2.

[81] See ILC, Fragmentation, above note 3, which discusses several cases, including the difference between the jurisprudence of the International Criminal Tribunal for the former Yugoslavia (ICTY) and ICJ on the question of 'overall control' vs 'effective control'. See

between courts, diverging judgments can lead to uncertainty over the state of the law. However, this risk can also be seen as a sign of healthy pluralism where differences in judicial opinion are not resolved through predetermined hierarchies, but where contextual 'translation' at the national level[82] and acceptance by other actors will determine legitimacy. Observing the increased adjudication and potential fragmentation of international human rights law, one should not lose sight of the fact that the development of this body of law is far from linear or comprehensive in coverage. Much will depend on what type of cases comes before the bodies concerned. This will in turn depend on a range of factors, with the work of human rights lawyers and NGOs being particularly influential in determining the human rights questions that these bodies will address. Given the limited resources of human rights treaty bodies they often rely heavily on pleadings and cases brought by NGOs and other interested groups. Compare, for example, the submissions by complainants and the decision of the ACmHPR in a case against Egypt, in which the Commission found that the imposition of the death penalty following allegations of torture and an unfair trial before the Supreme State Security Emergency Court violated several rights under the African Charter on Human and Peoples' Rights (ACHPR).[83]

2.2.4   Soft Law

What is the status of declarations, resolutions, conference statements and other such documents? These instruments, which are not binding as such, are often referred to as 'soft law'. 'Soft law' is not a formal source of law in its own right. Rather, the term is mainly used to describe non-binding instruments that set standards and/or form part of the law-making process. It may also refer to vague provisions in treaties that do not create discernible obligations.[84] Soft law can therefore be understood as a broad category that captures the increasing plurality and complexity of standard-setting and law-making processes. Though strongly contested at times,[85] the term continues to be used as convenient shorthand.

Application of the Convention on the Prevention and Punishment of the Crime of Genocide (*Bosnia and Herzegovina* v. *Serbia and Montenegro*) (ICJ) (2007) paras. 402–6, rejecting the ICTY's approach as 'unpersuasive'.

[82] See in particular K. Knop, 'Here and There: International Law in Domestic Courts' (1999–2000) 32 *New York University Journal of International Law & Politics* 501.

[83] *Egyptian Initiative for Personal Rights and Interights* v. *Arab Republic of Egypt* (ACmHPR) (2011).

[84] See for a good overview, A. Boyle, 'Soft Law in International Law Making', in M. Evans (ed.), *International Law*, 5th edn (Oxford University Press, 2018) 119–37.

[85] P. Weil, 'Towards Relative Normativity in International Law' (1983) 77 *American Journal of International Law* 413.

Soft law instruments can be part of the formative stages of customary international law or treaty-making. States and international organisations frequently adopt resolutions and other such instruments with a view to developing the law. These instruments constitute international law in an embryonic state, which may in time become recognised through one of the formal sources. The UDHR is the best-known example of its kind, but there are several other instances in which a treaty has been preceded by a series of resolutions or other soft law instruments.

In the field of human rights there is a range of documents used for standard-setting aimed at developing best practices and interpreting binding obligations of states. Examples are the UN standards on detention, such as the Standard Minimum Rules for the Treatment of Prisoners, which have been used in the jurisprudence of human rights treaty bodies to determine acceptable conditions of detention.[86] A further example is the Maastricht Guidelines on economic, social and cultural rights developed by a group of experts that has greatly contributed to the normative recognition and justiciability of these rights.[87] Such documents demonstrate the important role that various actors can play in developing and advancing international standards.

Soft law instruments are also increasingly used by international organisations and states when addressing the role of non-state actors (NSAs). Prominent examples are a number of standard-setting instruments and codes of conduct providing that multinational corporations (MNCs) adhere to international human rights standards in their operations.[88] Politically, these instruments are based on the premise that MNCs should be directly engaged and that it is in their best interests to adhere to standards. However, limited evidence of compliance and the lack of adequate monitoring and enforcement mechanisms have resulted in criticism that the essentially voluntary arrangements are not effective.[89]

2.2.5   UNDRIP: A Soft Law Success Story?

UNDRIP was the outcome of a long process of deliberation, in which the actors achieved a high degree of consensus (143 member states voted in favour and 11 states abstained) on a series of controversial matters, such as

---

[86] See e.g., HRCtee, General Comment 21: Replaces General Comment 9 concerning humane treatment of persons deprived of liberty (art. 10) (1992) para. 5, referring to relevant UN standards, which have been consistently applied in the Committee's jurisprudence, such as in *Akwanga* v. *Cameroon* (2011) para. 7.3. The (revised) UN Standard Minimum Rules for the Treatment of Prisoners (Mandela Rules) were adopted by the UN General Assembly, UN doc. A/RES/70/175, Annex (17 December 2015).

[87] Maastricht Guidelines on Violations of Economic, Social and Cultural Rights 1997, which followed the earlier Limburg Principles on the Implementation of the ICESCR 1987.

[88] See Chapter 19.3.   [89] See ibid.

the individual and collective dimension of indigenous peoples' rights, self-determination and land rights. The four states that voted against the declaration – Australia, Canada, New Zealand and the USA – subsequently endorsed it. This development demonstrates the value that soft law instruments can have in generating a pull factor and enhancing prospects of compliance.[90]

UNDRIP shows that soft law can have distinct practical advantages. Actors may prefer using soft law instruments because the very fact that these instruments are non-binding may facilitate reaching consensus. This gives states flexibility to tailor instruments to their needs without having to adhere to the formal requirements involved in treaty-making and amendment, both at the international and national level. However, doubts continue to be expressed over soft law serving as a convenient means for states to escape binding obligations and create mere appearances.[91] Yet in a system whose enforcement mechanisms are relatively weak and where compliance depends on numerous factors, the binding nature of an instrument may not be decisive. This applies especially where states and international organisations have a sufficiently strong interest in adherence. The success of UNDRIP will in this light need to be judged by the extent to which its promise is realised. In practice, while actors have often focused on developing formally binding standards, i.e. treaties, in the field of international human rights law, strategic considerations may weigh in favour of soft law instruments that promise greater acceptance and may act as a stepping stone for a treaty.

POINTS TO CONSIDER

1. Does UNDRIP demonstrate that giving priority to treaty obligations is misplaced?

2. To what extent can the factors contributing to UNDRIP's success be utilised in other areas of international human rights law? Consider, for example, developments in respect of the rights of internally displaced persons.[92]

---

[90] M. Barelli, 'The Role of Soft Law in the International Legal System: The Case of the United Nations Declaration on the Rights of Indigenous Peoples' (2009) 58 *International & Comparative Law Quarterly* 957. See for a critical perspective on the compromises made in the making of UNDRIP, K. Engle, 'On Fragile Architecture: The UN Declaration on the Rights of Indigenous Peoples in the Context of Human Rights' (2011) 22 *European Journal of International Law* 141.

[91] See for an overview of positivist critiques of soft law, J. d'Aspremont, 'Softness in International Law: A Self-serving Quest for New Legal Materials' (2008) 19 *European Journal of International Law* 1075.

[92] See documents relating to relevant international standards on the website of the UN Special Rapporteur on the human rights of internally displaced persons, www.ohchr.org/EN/Issues/IDPersons/Pages/IDPersonsIndex.aspx.

2.2.6 *Jus Cogens* and *Erga Omnes*

The notions of *jus cogens* and *erga omnes* are at the heart of claims that international law is being transformed from a system based on state consent to a constitutional order based on higher values.[93] *Jus cogens* was initially conceived as a principle governing the invalidity of treaties, i.e. delineating the limits of what states could agree on as a matter of treaty law. This rule is laid down in articles 53 and 64 of the VCLT. Article 53 provides that:

A treaty is void if, at the time of its conclusion, it conflicts with a peremptory norm of general international law. For the purposes of the present Convention, a peremptory norm of general international law is a norm accepted and recognized by the international community of states as a whole as a norm from which no derogation is permitted and which can be modified only by a subsequent norm of general international law having the same character.

An obvious example would be an agreement between two states to torture a person, which would on the face of it be invalid (the example is not as outlandish as it seems given reports about complicity of states in interrogating suspected terrorists).[94] Beyond this narrow scope, *jus cogens* is widely understood to denote a hierarchy of fundamental norms.[95] The resulting, somewhat mythical, status given to *jus cogens* has been mocked and criticised;[96] not surprisingly, the use of the notion opens up the long-standing debate between positive law and natural law, with *jus cogens* seen as a Trojan horse for the revival of the latter.[97]

While the notion of *jus cogens* is often used to elevate certain claims, its source, contents and legal consequences are not fully settled and its practical significance is frequently misunderstood. As a general rule, *jus cogens* norms are formed in the same way as customary international law. Their peremptory status can only be changed if the *opinio juris* that vested the norm with its fundamental nature changes in line with state practice, although this is slightly paradoxical, allowing state practice to change a norm that is deemed

---

[93] A. Orakhelashvili, 'Peremptory Norms as an Aspect of Constitutionalisation in the International Legal System', in S. Muller and M. Frishman (eds.), *The Dynamics of Constitutionalism in the Age of Globalization* (TMC Asser Press, 2009) 153–80. See for a concise overview, D. Shelton, 'International Law and "Relative Normality"', in M. Evans (ed.), *International Law*, 4th edn (Oxford University Press, 2014) 137–65, particularly at 142–52.

[94] See Chapter 18.8.1.

[95] See for a feminist critique of *jus cogens* as prioritising male perspectives, H. Charlesworth and C. Chinkin, 'The Gender of *Jus Cogens*' (1993) 15 *Human Rights Quarterly* 63.

[96] A. D'Amato, 'It's a Bird, it's a Plane, it's *jus cogens*' (1990) 6 *Connecticut Journal of International Law* 1.

[97] See D. Dobois, 'The Authority of Peremptory Norms in International Law: State Consent or Natural Law?' (2009) 78 *Nordic Journal of International Law* 133.

absolute and of superior value.[98] In practice, courts either have been reluctant to use the term *jus cogens* or have often not elaborated on how they have derived a finding that a norm has attained such status.[99]

The starting point in seeking to delineate the corpus of peremptory norms is often the ICJ's famous dictum in the *Barcelona Traction* case, which mentioned genocide, slavery and racial discrimination as obligations *erga omnes* (which may imply their *jus cogens* status, see below).[100] The prohibition of torture has also been referred to as a *jus cogens* norm by courts and human rights treaty bodies.[101] The fact that a right is non-derogable may be indicative, but not all such rights are understood to constitute *jus cogens*.[102] As there is no clear-cut methodology or list of *jus cogens* rights, their acceptance will essentially remain a matter of state practice and judicial interpretation. This opens space for indeterminacy and for the making of broad claims that seek to elevate the status of the norms invoked.[103] A pertinent example that illustrates the possible range of positions is the right to development; while some contest that this has been recognised as a binding right, others have accorded it *jus cogens* status.[104]

Many human rights appear to be natural candidates for *jus cogens* classification and have indeed been referred to, if not recognised, as such.[105] However, claims that a rule has attained *jus cogens* status are at times not only misconceived, they are also often not necessary if the principal aim is to demonstrate that a norm has binding force. This raises the question of the additional legal value of *jus cogens* status beyond its symbolic weight. Other than the invalidity of treaties, judicial decisions and state practice suggest that states have a duty not to recognise (or contribute to the perpetuation of) situations resulting from violations of *jus cogens* norms and to take measures to bring such situations to an end. In its advisory opinion in the *Wall* case, the ICJ found that states had a duty 'not to recognise the illegal situation resulting

---

[98] See critical remarks on this point by D'Amato, above note 96.

[99] See Shelton, above note 93.

[100] *Barcelona Traction, Light and Power Company, Limited* (*Spain* v. *Belgium*) (ICJ) (1970) para. 33.

[101] See Chapter 8.3.

[102] See e.g., art. 11 ICCPR: 'No one shall be imprisoned merely on the ground of inability to fulfil a contractual obligation', which is non-derogable pursuant to art. 4(2) ICCPR.

[103] See U. Linderfalk, 'Normative Conflict and the Fuzziness of the International ius cogens Regime' (2009) 69 *Zeitschrift für ausländisches und öffentliches Recht und Völkerrecht* 961.

[104] See e.g., M. Bedjaoui, 'The Right to Development', in M. Bedjaoui (ed.), *International Law: Achievements and Prospects* (UNESCO and Martinus Nijhoff, 1991) 1177–204, at 1183; S. Chowdhury and P. de Waart, 'Significance of the Right to Development: An Introductory View', in S. Chowdhury, E. Denters and P. de Waart (eds.), *The Right to Development in International Law* (Martinus Nijhoff, 1992) 7–23, at 21. See further Chapter 14.3.

[105] See Shelton, above note 93, 142–52.

from the construction of the wall' arising from the breach of the right to self-determination and fundamental principles of human rights (held to apply *erga omnes*).[106] Further, it has been recognised that international crimes may not be subject to amnesties[107] and that the international community, through the UN, has a responsibility to protect those at risk of such crimes.[108] However, beyond this the legal consequences of *jus cogens* are less clear.[109]

For example, in the case of *Al-Adsani* v. *United Kingdom*, the ECtHR recognised that the prohibition of torture is a *jus cogens* norm, but declined to find that it trumps state immunity where a torture victim brings a suit in a third state.[110] The fact that the judgment was based on the narrowest of margins (nine to eight votes) shows that the notion of *jus cogens* can pose considerable challenges, both of a legal and policy nature, for courts and others seized with interpreting the law, where cases pit fundamental values against deeply entrenched rules of international law based on sovereign equality. The call to focus on the values underlying *jus cogens* as a means of a flexible and contextual interpretation of the law rather than the 'mechanical paradigm of non-derogability' is merited.[111] Yet *jus cogens* is bound to remain a notion that galvanises international lawyers, perhaps for the very reason of its great but elusive, even mystical, promise.[112]

Erga omnes is closely related to but is conceptually different from *jus cogens*. It denotes obligations that a state has towards all other states because of the fundamental nature of a particular norm. The scope of the obligation means that all states, as an exception to general rules of international law, have an interest and standing. As stipulated in article 48(1)(b) of the ILC Articles on Responsibility of States for Internationally Wrongful Acts (ARSIWA), states may 'invoke the responsibility of another state ... if the obligation breached is owed to the international community as a whole'. This shift beyond bilateral and reciprocal forms of responsibility applies in particular in the field of human rights characterised by multilateral, shared concerns.[113] Since the ICJ dictum

---

[106] *Legal Consequences of the Construction of a Wall in the Occupied Palestinian Territory* (ICJ) (2004) para. 159.

[107] *Prosecutor* v. *Furundzjia* (ICTY) (1998) para. 155.

[108] See 2005 World Summit Outcome, UNGA 60/1 (24 October 2005) paras. 138–9. See also S. Zifcak, 'The Responsibility to Protect', in Evans, above note 84, 484–517.

[109] See for an engaging discussion of some of the issues raised, A. Bianchi, 'Human Rights and the Magic of *jus cogens*' (2008) 19 *European Journal of International Law* 491.

[110] *Al-Adsani* v. *United Kingdom* (ECtHR) (2001) 273, para. 61. See also *Jurisdictional Immunities of the State* (*Germany* v. *Italy: Greece intervening*) (ICJ) (2012) paras. 92–7. See also *Jones and Others* v. *United Kingdom* (ECtHR) (2014) paras. 186–215.

[111] Bianchi, above note 109, 505.   [112] Ibid.

[113] See further M. Koskenniemi, 'Solidarity Measures: State Responsibility as a New International Order?' (2001) 72 *British Yearbook of International Law* 337; I. Scobbie, 'The Invocation of Responsibility for the Breach of "Obligations under Peremptory Norms of General International Law"' (2002) 13 *European Journal of International Law* 1201.

in the *Barcelona Traction* case, the notion of *erga omnes* has been recognised in the ARSIWA and referred to in jurisprudence.[114] While it has been suggested that all human rights norms apply *erga omnes*,[115] the scope of the obligation is subject to further development in state practice and through judicial determination. It would seem logical that *jus cogens* norms apply *erga omnes*. However, the opposite is not taken for granted[116] and many doctrinal questions remain concerning the relationship of the two concepts and the scope of *erga omnes*.[117]

In practical terms, states can invoke the responsibility of another state (or states) that is in breach of its *erga omnes* obligation to demand that it ceases the wrongful act, guarantees non-repetition and provides reparation to the injured party or beneficiaries.[118] However, the utility of *erga omnes* is somewhat limited because it does not in and of itself confer jurisdiction that does not otherwise exist, as held by the ICJ when Portugal invoked the principle of self-determination in the *East Timor* case to this effect.[119] Where the court or body concerned has jurisdiction, the *erga omnes* nature of the norm at issue may replace the need for a state, as an admissibility criterion, to demonstrate that one of its interests has been affected. Incidentally, this is already standard procedure for inter-state applications under human rights treaty body complaints procedures, where states are assumed to have an interest in compliance by other states parties with the treaty obligations irrespective of whether their own interests are at stake.[120]

QUESTIONS

1. Is the distinction between binding sources of law and soft law artificial, and is it time to abandon it?

2. Why has the notion of *jus cogens* played such an important role in the context of international human rights law?

---

[114] See e.g., in respect of the right to self-determination, *Legal consequences of the separation of the Chagos Archipelago from Mauritius in 1965* (ICJ) (2019) para. 180. For an overview, C. J. Tams, *Enforcing erga omnes Obligations in International Law* (Cambridge University Press, 2005); J. Crawford, *State Responsibility: The General Part* (Cambridge University Press, 2013) 66–7; ILC Draft Articles on Responsibility of States for Internationally Wrongful Acts with commentaries, 2001, in *Yearbook of the International Law Commission* vol. II, part II (United Nations, 2001) 110–16, 126–7.

[115] See HRCtee, General Comment 31: The nature of the general legal obligation imposed on states parties to the Covenant, UN doc. CCPR/C/21/Rev.1/Add.13 (26 May 2004) para. 2.

[116] T. Meron, 'On a Hierarchy of International Human Rights' (1986) 80 *American Journal of International Law* 1, at 11; M. Byers, 'Conceptualising the Relationship between jus cogens and erga omnes Rules' (1997) 66 *Nordic Journal of International Law* 211, at 237.

[117] See Byers, ibid.   [118] Art. 48 ARSIWA.

[119] *East Timor (Portugal v. Australia)* (ICJ) (1995) para. 29.

[120] See on this point in particular, HRCtee, General Comment 31, para. 2.

2.3   PRINCIPLES, RIGHTS, OBLIGATIONS AND SCOPE OF APPLICATION

2.3.1   Principles

Equality, freedom, dignity and solidarity are principles prominently referred to in article 1 UDHR,[121] and instrumentally linked to 'freedom, justice and peace in the world' in the UDHR's preamble. These principles permeate international human rights law; by informing the recognition and implementation of rights, and their interpretation,[122] they provide important pillars and yardsticks for the international human rights architecture.

1. Equality: As stated by the HRCtee '[n]on-discrimination, together with equality before the law and equal protection of the law without any discrimination, constitute a basic and general principle relating to the protection of human rights'.[123] This entails both a right not to be discriminated against on any of the prohibited grounds and a duty incumbent on states to observe the principle by guaranteeing and implementing rights 'without distinction of any kind'.[124]

2. Freedom: While there is no generic right to freedom, its fundamental role, both as freedom from constraint and freedom to do something, is evident in several rights, such as the right to liberty and security and to freedom of movement. The primacy of the freedom to (or not to) do something also finds expression in the rule that the onus is on the state to justify any interference with recognised rights, such as the right to privacy, and freedoms, such as freedom of religion, expression, assembly and association.[125]

3. Dignity: Respect for the notion of human dignity provides a crucial *raison d'être* for rights if not a right itself, for example as set out in article 3 of the Protocol to the African Charter on Human and Peoples' Rights on the Rights of Women in Africa and article 10(1) ICCPR. The notion of dignity is important both for the recognition of new rights and for measures to protect rights against emerging threats. It is also of increasing relevance in giving substance to rights in adjudication.[126]

---

[121] Note that art. 1 UDHR does not use the term solidarity but stipulates that human beings 'should act towards one another in a spirit of brotherhood'.

[122] See in particular, reference in art. 31(1) VCLT to interpreting treaty 'in light of its object and purpose'.

[123] HRCtee, General Comment 18: Non-discrimination (Thirty-Seventh Session, 1989) para. 1.

[124] See e.g., art. 2(1) ICCPR.

[125] See further Chapter 8.7.3.

[126] See C. McCrudden, 'Human Dignity and Judicial Interpretation of Human Rights', (2008) 19 *European Journal of International Law* 655, and further C. McCrudden (ed.),

4. Solidarity: Solidarity underpins the collective effort of securing rights with a view to achieving a world order characterised by 'freedom, justice and peace'. It also takes the form of specific obligations, such as in article 2(1) ICESCR, 'to take steps, individually and through international assistance and co-operation' to achieve the full realisation of the rights recognised in the Covenant, though the nature of this obligation remains controversial.[127]

Both individually and jointly, these fundamental principles serve as an important reminder that specific rights and corresponding obligations should not be viewed in isolation, but form part of a broader system that rests on agreed upon core values.

2.3.2   The Concept of Rights

A right requires a right-holder. Traditionally, states were considered the only subjects of international law, i.e. as having rights because of their statehood and being able to bring claims against each other. This included the exercise of diplomatic protection where states could raise a claim on behalf of their nationals concerning the violation of minimum standards (many of which would fall within today's human rights guarantees) by a third state.[128] However, importantly, this was seen as the right of a state 'to ensure, in the persons of its subjects, respect for the rules of international law'.[129] While minimum standards for the treatment of aliens and protection for minorities may have provided the nucleus, it was only after 1945 that the individual (in the broadest sense) became recognised as a subject of international law.[130] This means that individuals can hold rights and bring claims, where avenues are available. It also means that individuals are liable for certain breaches of international law, in particular international crimes. The question of whether the individual or the state is, or should be, the true subject of international law, and to what degree the subject status of individuals is dependent on

---

Understanding Human Dignity (Oxford University Press, 2013). See also J. Waldron, *Dignity, Rank and Rights* (Oxford University Press, 2012).

[127] See Chapter 9.3.

[128] *Barcelona Traction* (ICJ) (1970) paras. 78–9. See further I. Brownlie, *Principles of Public International Law* (Oxford University Press, 2008) 57–67; P. Okowa, 'Issues of Admissibility and the Law on International Responsibility', in Evans, above note 84, 450–83, at 454–69.

[129] *Mavrommatis Palestine Concessions* (PCIJ) (1924) 2.

[130] See A. A. Cançado Trindade, *The Access of Individuals to International Justice* (Oxford University Press, 2011) 1–16; R. McCorquodale, 'The Individual and the International Legal System', in Evans, above note 84, 259–85; A. Orakhelashvili, 'The Protection of the Individual in International Law' (2001) 31 *California Western International Law Journal* 241; and Chapter 1.2.

the state, has been widely debated.[131] What matters for practical purposes is that treaties and customary international law recognise individuals as rights-holders, and hence as subjects. Significantly, the recognition of rights is independent of the existence of available remedies, i.e. the fact that an individual may not be able to claim his or her right before any body neither deprives the right of its quality nor the individual of his or her status as a subject.[132]

Rights can be divided into several categories with respect to their: (1) origin and source of validity (natural and positive rights – see Chapter 1); (2) subject or right-holder (individual and group rights); (3) subject matter (civil and political rights; economic, social and cultural rights; collective rights); (4) type (negative or positive rights); and (5) nature (absolute and other, particularly qualified rights).

Most of the rights recognised in international human rights treaties are conceptualised as individual rights. This harks back to the notion that human beings have rights by virtue of their humanity, which was traditionally understood to apply to individuals only. While some of the most prominent human rights in the early twentieth century had a collective dimension (for example, minority rights), these rights were understood to belong to the individual members of minorities, not to any collective entity.[133] Several objections have been raised against the recognition of collective rights, ranging from the position that human rights can by definition only be vested in the individual, to a number of pragmatic concerns. These include questions of delineation: how to identify groups that should qualify as the right-holder; the nature of rights granted, such as the right to development; the exercise of such rights (representation); conflict between group rights and individual rights; and utility, namely whether group rights are necessary and best suited to protect the interests and values in question.[134] Politically, Western states and scholars have often been suspicious of collective rights because they were seen as a vehicle for what were considered political demands by socialist and 'Third World' states, in particular in relation to the right to development.[135] This intransigence over the recognition of collective rights

---

[131] See literature ibid. with further references.

[132] Appeal from a Judgment of the Hungaro/Czechoslovak Mixed Arbitral Tribunal (PCIJ) (1933) 208, 231.

[133] HRCtee, General Comment 23: The rights of minorities (art. 27), UN doc. CCPR/C/21/Rev.1/ Add.5 (8 April 1994) paras. 1 and 3; P. Thornberry, *International Law and the Rights of Minorities* (Clarendon Press, 1991) 113–37.

[134] J. Donnelly, *Universal Human Rights in Theory and Practice*, 2nd edn (Cornell University, 2003) 208–11. See also Chapter 10.2.

[135] See for the political background, B. Rajagopal, *International Law from Below: Development, Social Movements and Third World Resistance* (Cambridge University Press, 2007) 216–22.

has fuelled the debate about the (lack of true) universality of human rights.[136] However, collective rights have now been recognised in treaties, particularly the ACHPR, UN declarations, especially in relation to indigenous peoples, and in the jurisprudence of human rights treaty bodies.[137] While several challenges remain, such as who is entitled to exercise collective rights, how to identify corresponding duty-holders and obligations, such as in respect of the right to development, and how to resolve conflicts between individual and collective rights, the recognition of collective rights has become a fact of international human rights law. Given the collective nature of many human rights violations, it can be expected that collective rights will be of increasing importance in years to come.

Civil and political rights, economic, social and cultural rights as well as collective rights have been referred to as the three generations of rights, reflecting a narrative according to which these rights have been recognised in that order, which may also be taken to indicate a shift in emphasis.[138] The metaphor of generations has served as convenient shorthand, but constitutes a rather crude and at least partly inaccurate way of describing the development of international human rights law. For practical purposes, each of the three categories has some features which distinguish it from the other categories. However, the main traditional distinction, i.e. that economic, social and cultural rights have resource implications and are therefore not justiciable, and that collective rights are not genuine rights, has increasingly been called into question.[139] The move towards a more nuanced and holistic understanding of rights is reflected in the oft-repeated mantra that human rights are 'indivisible, interdependent and interrelated', which also serves the political goal of strengthening all sets of rights.[140]

Rights can be negative, i.e. freedom from something, such as the right not to be enslaved, or positive, i.e. the right to something, such as the right to education. By their nature rights can either be absolute or subject to limitations or qualifications. Absolute rights, such as freedom from slavery, allow for no exceptions and cannot be derogated from. Even in highly exceptional situations, such as states of emergency, states are not permitted to interfere with such rights.[141] However, not all non-derogable rights are absolute rights.

---

[136] See Chapter 1.5.1.
[137] See Chapter 10.
[138] See K. Vasak, 'Le droit international des droits de l'homme' (1974) 140 *Recueil des Cours* 333, at 343–5.
[139] See on justiciability, Chapter 9.6.
[140] See Vienna Declaration and Programme of Action, UN doc. A/Conf.157/23 (12 July 1993) paras. 5 and 18.
[141] See HRCtee, General Comment 29: States of Emergency (art. 4), UN doc. CCPR/C/21/Rev.1/Add.11 (31 August 2001) paras. 7–16. See on states of emergency below at 2.3.5.

For example, the right to life is not absolute, as the use of lethal force may be lawful under international human rights law (and international humanitarian law) in particular circumstances.[142] Several rights, such as the right to liberty and security, can be interfered with, for example by way of detention, where the legal grounds for such interference are adhered to, and may be subject to derogations.[143]

Qualified rights, such as the right to privacy and freedom of expression, may be, and frequently are, restricted on specific grounds relating to the rights of others, national security, public order or public morals.[144] These grounds, which are set out in so-called clawback clauses, must be based on law, be proportionate and not allow states to deprive the rights of their essence.[145] Qualified rights provide states with considerable scope to restrict the exercise of rights and are therefore frequently subject to complex interpretation, which needs to balance the rights of individuals with the rights of others and societal concerns as put forward by the state.[146] While qualified rights can be derogated from, the need and scope for derogation is limited as states may already invoke security considerations when restricting such rights; special circumstances, such as an emergency, may, however, influence the proportionality of measures taken.[147] This distinction between absolute and derogable rights was first developed in the field of civil and political rights. The Committee on Economic, Social and Cultural Rights (CESCR) has now interpreted economic, social and cultural rights to contain a core obligation of 'minimum essential levels of each of the rights'.[148] This was an important step in strengthening the status of these rights because the ICESCR's formula that they were to be realised progressively depending on available resources provided no clearly identifiable minimum standards, while seemingly giving states parties considerable leeway in fulfilling their obligations.[149]

---

[142] See e.g., art. 2(2) ECHR and art. 15(2) ECHR.

[143] See Chapter 8.4.4.

[144] See e.g., art. 8 ECHR and art. 19(3) ICCPR.

[145] See for a concise summary of applicable standards in the ICCPR context, HRCtee, General Comment 34: Freedoms of opinion and expression, UN doc. CCPR/C/GC/34 (12 September 2011) paras. 21–36.

[146] See in particular, Chapter 8.7.

[147] See on the derogability of these rights, HRCtee, General Comment 29, para. 5, and, generally, L. Doswald-Beck, *Human Rights in Times of Conflict and Terrorism* (Oxford University Press, 2011). See further on states of emergency and derogation of rights, below at 2.3.5.

[148] CESCR, General Comment 3: The nature of States parties obligations (art. 2, para. 1) (14 December 1990) para. 10.

[149] Report of the UN High Commissioner for Human Rights (focusing on the progressive realisation of economic, social and cultural rights under international human rights law), UN doc. E/2007/82 (25 June 2007).

2.3.3   The Right to Equality and Non-discrimination

The right to equality and non-discrimination is truly fundamental. The struggle for human rights is in large measure a struggle against the indignities of inequality and subordination, with slavery, apartheid and gender discrimination constituting particularly prominent examples. Equality is not only important in its own right; lack of equality is also at the heart of many violations, as those discriminated against are often less powerful and therefore more vulnerable to multiple abuse. Several general human rights treaties provide that states have to guarantee all rights without discrimination, and include separate provisions setting out the right to equality between men and women and equal protection before the law.[150] The express rationale of some treaties, notably the International Convention on the Elimination of All Forms of Racial Discrimination (ICERD) and CEDAW, is to prohibit discrimination, here on the grounds of race and of sex respectively, and to take measures towards its elimination.

The prohibition of discrimination requires that like cases are treated alike. States must not discriminate on any of the prohibited grounds, and must ensure that individuals are not discriminated against in their private relations.[151] There is a broad range of prohibited grounds, as evident in article 2(1) ICCPR: 'race, colour, sex, language, religion, political or other opinion, national or social origin, property, birth or *other status*' (emphasis added). The prohibition covers both direct and indirect discrimination. The former explicitly distinguishes between two groups, for example, by applying different rules to men and women such as in army recruitment, which used to be a male preserve for combat soldiers, or with regard to persons of certain nationality or race as opposed to others, such as during apartheid. Indirect discrimination can be more difficult to establish, as the comparable groups are on the face of it treated alike but the treatment has a disproportionate impact on one group. An example of this is requiring certain qualifications that only members of one group are likely or able to meet, but not members of the other. Such treatment does not amount to discrimination where it is objectively justified, such as where a certain qualification, for example, a professional bar exam, is required to practise as a lawyer. However, this raises the problem of a state's failure to address existing inequalities, for example,

---

[150] See in particular, arts. 2(1) and 26 ICCPR; art. 2(2) ICESCR; art. 2(1) CRC; art. 1(1) ICRMW; arts. 3–5 CRPD; art. 14 ECHR and Protocol 12 to the ECHR; arts. 1(1) and 24 ACHR as well as arts. 2 and 19 ACHPR.

[151] See HRCtee, General Comment 28, art. 3 (The Equality of Rights between Men and Women), UN doc. HRI/GEN/1/Rev.9 (vol. I) (2008) paras. 4 and 31; and CESCR, General Comment 20, Non-discrimination in economic, social and cultural rights (art. 2, para. 2 of the ICESCR) UN doc. E/C.12/GC/20 (2 July 2009) para. 11.

where members of certain ethnic minorities or women find it particularly difficult to enter the bar in the country concerned. States may therefore have to take affirmative action, also known as positive discrimination, with a view to redressing such inequalities.[152] A prominent, albeit controversial, example of affirmative action concerns quotas for women's political representation.[153] Fredman's transformative approach reconceptualises substantive equality as a four-dimensional concept, consisting of redressing disadvantage; redressing stigma, stereotyping, and humiliation; the participative dimension: social inclusion and political voice; and accommodating difference and structural change.[154]

2.3.4   Obligations

By becoming a party to a treaty, or as a matter of customary international law, a state incurs obligations. The basic binary distinction is between negative and positive obligations. Traditionally, liberties and civil and political rights were conceived as essentially imposing 'negative' duties on the state, i.e. to refrain from interfering with a right, for example 'do not arbitrarily detain a person'. However, it is evident that states must also take certain measures to ensure rights. For example, states should not only abstain from arbitrarily taking life, but must also take measures to protect the life of those within their jurisdiction against apparent risks.[155] This dual obligation is articulated well in article 2(1) ICCPR, according to which each state party 'undertakes to *respect* and to *ensure* to all individuals within its territory and subject to its jurisdiction the rights recognized in the present Covenant' (emphasis added). This encompasses 'legislative, judicial, administrative, educative and other appropriate measures [taken] in order to fulfil [a state's] legal obligations'.[156] The general obligation to protect rights means that a state has to take measures to prevent and repress violations, irrespective of whether they are committed by state or NSAs, and provide adequate remedies in case of breach.[157] This duty is one of means, not result, as it may

---

[152] HRCtee, General Comment 28, para. 3 and CESCR, General Comment 20, para. 9. See also art. 4 CEDAW. See on the difference between affirmative action measures and 'reasonable accommodation' (arts. 2 and 5 CRPD), Committee on the Rights of Persons with Disabilities, General Comment 6 (2018) on equality and non-discrimination, UN doc. CRPD/C/GG/6 (26 April 2018) para. 25(c).

[153] See J. McCann, *Electoral Quotas for Women: An International Overview*, Research Paper Series 2013–2014 (Parliament of Australia, 14 November 2013).

[154] S. Fredman, 'Substantive Equality Revisited' (2016) 14 *International Journal of Constitutional Law* 712.

[155] See Chapter 8.2.6.

[156] HRCtee, General Comment 31, para. 7.   [157] Ibid., para. 8.

be impossible to prevent certain violations.[158] States have to exercise 'due diligence', i.e. take all measures that can reasonably be taken in the circumstances in order to ensure the rights granted. This may consist of a series of measures, for example criminalising certain forms of rape, overhauling ineffective systems of investigations in rape cases and changing judicial interpretations that address obstacles to effective protection.[159] Treaties may also specify measures, such as the enactment of legislation, reviews, provision of training and other similar steps, which states have to take in order to fulfil their obligations.[160] In the field of economic, social and cultural rights, states have a duty to protect, promote and fulfil rights. This entails taking measures so that rights are not infringed by others; it also means being proactive, to the point of implementing direct measures to provide certain goods and services if these are needed to fulfil minimum standards, such as food to prevent starvation.[161]

The broadening of positive obligations in international human rights law is significant and potentially far reaching. It signals that states have duties beyond simple non-interference as conceived in traditional liberal theories, and must actively consider the impact of policies and measures, or lack thereof, on human rights protection. This duty has resulted in a streamlining of human rights, the extent of which is still being developed in the ever-growing jurisprudence of human rights bodies on positive obligations.[162]

2.3.5   Derogation in Times of Emergency

Extraordinary situations such as natural disasters, riots, acts of terrorism or wars confront states with a challenge, if not crisis. Such situations raise the question as to what measures states may take in response, particularly whether extraordinary circumstances justify or even require extraordinary powers. Preserving the state and public order and security in times of crisis, it may be argued, calls for absolute powers.[163] However, this option is

---

[158] As articulated succinctly in the landmark case of *Velásquez Rodríguez* v. *Honduras* (IACtHR) (1988) paras. 172–7.

[159] See e.g., *M. C.* v. *Bulgaria* (ECtHR) (2005) paras. 109–87, and *Vertido* v. *The Philippines* (CtEDAW) (2010) paras. 8.1–8.10.

[160] See e.g., arts. 4(1), 5, 10, 11, 13 and 14 CAT.

[161] See e.g., CESCR, The Right to Adequate Food (art. 11), UN doc. E/C.12/1999/5 (12 May 1999) para. 15.

[162] Positive obligations have been discussed particularly in the context of ECtHR jurisprudence; see A. R. Mowbray, *The Development of Positive Obligations under the European Convention on Human Rights by the European Court of Human Rights* (Hart, 2004); D. Xenos, *The Positive Obligations of the State under the European Convention on Human Rights* (Routledge, 2012).

[163] See in this context particularly the work of Carl Schmitt, discussed extensively in the seminal work of G. Agamben, *State of Exception* (Chicago University Press, 2005).

problematic as it may easily result in authoritarianism and abuse of power. There are numerous examples where states have abused emergency powers, turning what should have been a response to an extraordinary situation into the norm.[164] Several decades of emergency laws in Egypt, Israel and Syria are cases in point.[165] At the other end of the spectrum would be a response that limits states to using powers within the existing rights framework. The fact that qualified rights already permit balancing and the risk of abuse are good arguments in favour of such a position. International human rights law, however, has essentially chosen a compromise solution, providing states with the option of taking special measures. States may derogate from certain rights, but such derogation is subject to limitations and safeguards. This model is followed in key treaties, such as the ICCPR, the ACHR and the ECHR.[166] However, notably, the ACHPR does not allow for any derogation.[167] The international human rights law approach grapples with, and at times barely masks, an in-built tension between political prerogatives and legal constraints, which raises the question of the limits of a formal, legalistic approach to dealing with crisis situations.[168]

Any derogation presupposes the existence of a 'public emergency'. This has been defined as a situation that 'threatens the life of the nation'.[169] The ECtHR, in its first judgment in *Lawless* v. *Ireland*, described it as 'an exceptional situation of crisis or emergency which affects the whole population and constitutes a threat to the organised life of the community of which the State is composed'.[170] The jurisprudence on whether or not such a situation exists has been characterised by considerable deference, particularly in the European context where states have been granted a wide margin of appreciation in the determination of what constitutes an emergency.[171]

A state of emergency does not vest a state with absolute powers and licence to ignore or violate human rights. Several rights are non-derogable, and must therefore be respected fully in times of emergency. Treaties explicitly set out several non-derogable rights, such as the right to life (with the exception of lawful acts of war), the prohibition of torture and other ill-treatment, the prohibition of slavery and non-retroactivity of the law.[172] In addition, human

---

[164] See e.g., F. Ní Aoláin and O. Gross, '*A Skeptical View of Deference to the Executive in Times of Crisis*' (2008) 41 *Israel Law Review* 545; REDRESS, *Extraordinary Measures, Predictable Outcomes: Security Legislation and the Prohibition of Torture* (2012).

[165] See REDRESS, ibid., 25.

[166] Art. 15 ECHR; art. 27 ACHR and art. 4 ICCPR.

[167] *Article 19* v. *Eritrea* (ACmHPR) (2007) para. 87.

[168] See W. E. Scheuerman, '*Human Rights Lawyers* v. *Carl Schmitt*', in E. J. Criddle (ed.), *Human Rights in Emergencies* (Cambridge University Press, 2016) 175–201.

[169] Art. 4 ICCPR.   [170] *Lawless* v. *Ireland* (No.3) (ECtHR) (1961) para. 28.

[171] See further Ní Aoláin and Gross, above note 164.

[172] Art. 15 ECHR, art. 27 ACHR and art. 4 ICCPR.

rights treaty bodies and courts, especially the HRCtee and the IACtHR, have considerably broadened the scope of non-derogable rights. This includes, in particular, essential judicial guarantees, such as the right to habeas corpus, and the right to an effective remedy.[173] It is also recognised that the principle of non-discrimination is largely non-derogable.[174] This jurisprudence substantially limits the scope of rights that may be derogated from.

During emergencies, states frequently target the right to liberty and security, the right to a fair trial and qualified rights, such as freedom of expression, though strictly speaking no derogation is necessary from the latter rights as they are already subject to balancing considerations. Even where a right is derogable, any measures taken are subject to a proportionality test. They must be strictly necessary to counter the threat (not blanket in scope), have a link to the threat, be limited in time and non-discriminatory.[175] Adherence to these requirements is subject to judicial scrutiny. In addition, where states invoke emergencies, for example to justify prolonged detention without judicial supervision, adequate safeguards against abuse must be in place.[176]

States of emergency are also subject to important formal requirements. States need to proclaim a state of emergency, specify the rights derogated from, and notify the human rights treaty bodies concerned.[177] In the absence of such notification, treaty bodies may treat the state as if it has not derogated from the rights concerned, thereby effectively preventing a state from invoking derogation as justification for a breach. Further, a state of emergency must be lifted as soon as there is no longer a threat to the life of the nation, as it is considered a temporary, extraordinary measure.[178]

The legal framework applicable to states of emergency is well developed. However, there are considerable concerns that states invoke emergency rationales, either explicitly or implicitly, by using the language of security and counter-terrorism to undermine human rights. In this manner they

---

[173] See HRCtee, General Comment 29, paras. 6–16; *Habeas Corpus in Emergency Situations (Arts. 27(2), 25(1) and 7(6) American Convention on Human Rights)* (IACtHR) (1987); *Judicial Guarantees in States of Emergency (Arts. 27(2), 25 and 8 American Convention on Human Rights)* (IACtHR) (1987).

[174] Compare the grounds of prohibited discrimination in emergencies in art. 4(1) ICCPR, which are narrower than art. 2(1) ICCPR, and do not include, e.g., national origin. See further HRCtee, General Comment 29, para. 8. See on the prohibition of discrimination on grounds of nationality in the European human rights system, *A and Others* v. *United Kingdom* (ECtHR) (2009).

[175] See HRCtee, General Comment 29, particularly paras. 4, 5 and 8.

[176] Compare *Aksoy* v. *Turkey* (ECtHR) (1996) paras. 67–87 with *Brannigan and McBride* v. *United Kingdom* (ECtHR) (1993) paras. 36–66.

[177] HRCtee, General Comment 29, para. 17, and *Legal Consequences of the Construction of a Wall in the Occupied Palestinian Territory* (ICJ) (2004) para. 127.

[178] HRCtee, General Comment 29, para. 2.

vest authorities with extremely broad powers while limiting protection by restricting, if not altogether excluding, remedies, oversight and accountability.[179] The result is veritable states of exceptionalism antithetical to the rule of law, and, by definition, human rights protection.

2.3.6 Scope of Application

The scope of application of a human rights treaty is confined to a state's jurisdiction. This is understood to be primarily territorial, which means that states have to respect and ensure the rights of all individuals within their territory.[180] In principle, this applies to 'everyone' within the state territory without distinction,[181] with the exception of rights which by their nature belong to members of certain groups, such as citizens' rights and the rights of minorities.[182] Article 16 of the ECHR goes further by providing states considerable latitude to restrict rights by stipulating that '[n]othing in Articles 10, 11 and 14 shall be regarded as preventing the High Contracting Parties from imposing restrictions on the political activity of aliens'.[183] A further qualified exception can be found in article 2(3) of the ICESCR, according to which '[d]eveloping countries, with due regard to human rights and their national economy, may determine to what extent they would guarantee the economic rights recognized in the present Covenant to non-nationals'.

There are a growing number of situations where the conduct of states outside their territory has a bearing on human rights, which raises the question of the extraterritorial application of human rights treaties.[184] These situations include clandestine operations, such as extraordinary renditions, as well as military or other operations, such as targeted killings, custodial torture in an occupied country, cooperation with states violating certain rights or maritime interception of refugees on the high seas. At first sight, international human rights treaties do not apply because these acts take place outside

---

[179] See generally Doswald-Beck, above note 147, and O. Gross and F. Ní Aoláin, *Law in Times of Crisis: Emergency Powers in Theory and Practice* (Cambridge University Press, 2006).

[180] See e.g., art. 2(1) ICCPR, which, somewhat ambiguously, states that '[e]ach State Party to the present Covenant undertakes to respect and to ensure to all individuals *within its territory* and *subject to its jurisdiction* the rights recognized in the present Covenant' (emphasis added).

[181] HRCtee, General Comment 31, para. 10.

[182] See e.g., arts. 25 and 27 ICCPR respectively. See on the status of 'non-citizens' in particular, D. Weissbrodt, *The Human Rights of Non-Citizens* (Oxford University Press, 2008).

[183] See critical analysis by M.-B. Dembour, *When Humans Become Migrants: Study of the European Court of Human Rights with an Inter-American Counterpoint* (Oxford University Press, 2015) 46–51.

[184] See Chapter 7.2.1.4.

the state's territory. However, treaty bodies and courts have widened the scope of application, largely using the test of 'effective control' to determine whether the existing degree of control justifies bringing certain conduct within the jurisdiction of the state concerned.[185] Military engagements abroad and the internationalised nature of anti-terrorism measures, such as the use of drones, are bound to lead to further litigation and challenges, both to delineate the territorial scope of human rights law and to apply human rights standards extraterritorially.[186]

2.4   IMPLEMENTATION

Upon becoming party to a treaty a state commits itself to give effect to a series of obligations in the domestic sphere (and extraterritorially in so far as applicable).[187] Treaties, or customary international law for that matter, are built on the assumption that states will comply with their obligations. Compliance denotes the degree to which a state succeeds in respecting and ensuring human rights. It also refers to a phenomenon of international relations and politics that describes complex processes affecting a state's ability and willingness to meet its obligations under international law. Theories abound in this respect, ranging from the convergence of interests that motivate states to comply, the legitimacy of international law, to the importance of the interplay between international institutions and domestic political processes.[188] While state-centric perspectives emphasise the role of coercion and interests in securing compliance, there is an increasing focus on bottom-up approaches that stress the value and impact of persuasion and the role played by domestic institutions and actors.[189] In practice, both

---

[185] See in particular, M. Milanovic, *Extraterritorial Application of Human Rights Treaties: Law, Principles, and Policy* (Oxford University Press, 2011).

[186] See Case Study 8.1.

[187] See e.g., art. 2(2) ICCPR.

[188] See in particular, H. H. Koh, 'Why do Nations Obey International Law?' (1997) 106 *Yale Law Journal* 2599; R. Goodman and D. Jinks, 'Incomplete Internalization and Compliance with Human Rights Law' (2008) 19 *European Journal of International Law* 725; T. M. Franck, *The Power of Legitimacy Among Nations* (Oxford University Press, 1990); O. C. Okafor, *The African Human Rights System, Activist Forces and International Institutions* (Cambridge University Press, 2007) 12–62 (focusing primarily on the relationship between institutions and domestic forces). See for a review of recent literature, E. Stubbins-Bates, 'Sophisticated Constructivism in Human Rights Compliance Theory' (2014) 25 *European Journal of International Law* 1169.

[189] See ibid., and further, Simmons, above note 34, and the rather US-centric stewardship model proposed by E. Hafner-Burton, *Making Human Rights a Reality* (Princeton University Press, 2013).

international 'pressure' and 'internalisation' play an important role in fostering compliance, though both approaches may fail or even be counterproductive depending on the particular context. Implementation serves as the measure of a state's compliance with its obligations. As a general rule, states have discretion as to how they implement a treaty in their domestic order unless a treaty specifies implementing modalities.[190] An example of the latter is article 4 of the International Convention for the Protection of All Persons from Enforced Disappearance (CPED), according to which '[e]ach State Party shall take the necessary measures to ensure that enforced disappearance constitutes an offence under its criminal law'. Beyond these prescriptions, states may choose how best to give effect to the obligations incurred. Article 26 VCLT provides that states must do so in good faith.

The obligation to give effect to treaty rights binds all branches of the state, requiring the state to take legislative, administrative, judicial and other measures,[191] which includes adopting human-rights-based approaches in policy-making and institutional reforms as appropriate. States must bring their laws into conformity with the requisite treaty standards because they cannot rely on national laws that are at variance with their international obligations,[192] for example legislation providing for judicially sanctioned corporal punishment. This is logical as any other result would effectively nullify obligations meant to serve as general overriding standards.[193] Yet international law does not prescribe a particular mode of incorporation; what matters is that states fulfil their obligations. Modes of incorporation are traditionally distinguished as monism, where international law and domestic law are part of the same legal order and the former takes precedence over the latter, mainly applicable in civil law countries, and dualism, where international law is separate and not directly applicable in the domestic order unless incorporated, a mode mainly followed in common law countries.[194]

The practice of states does not necessarily fall neatly into either category, as national practices often combine both elements and interpret international law in the local context.[195] There is, therefore, a need to establish for each country: (1) the constitutional and statutory law recognition of international human rights treaties and customary international law; (2) the rank of these sources within the national legal order; and (3) the judicial interpretation

---

[190] HRCtee, General Comment 31, paras. 4 and 13.

[191] Ibid., para. 7.

[192] Art. 27 VCLT.

[193] It is also for this reason that reservations to the effect that human rights treaty provisions are to be interpreted in line with national legislation are generally considered invalid. See above at 2.2.1.2.

[194] See for a good overview, E. Denza, 'The Relationship between International and National Law', in Evans, above note 84, 383–411.

[195] See ibid., and Knop, above note 82.

concerning the relationship between the international and the national legal system. International human rights treaty bodies regularly exhort states to adopt specific implementing legislation that would give the treaty concerned a clear status in domestic law.[196] Several constitutions expressly recognise ICCPR and ICESCR rights,[197] and several states have adopted statutory laws implementing supranational, particularly regional, treaties.[198] However, even where international treaties have constitutional status, statutory law is often not in conformity with relevant international standards. This anomaly is particularly prevalent in states that become parties to treaties but do not have the legislative commitment to carry out the requisite reforms, and/or a judiciary empowered and willing to strike down laws incompatible with international standards.[199]

The judiciary plays a particularly important role in the protection of all sets of rights and in ensuring that states and their organs adhere to international obligations. Traditionally, courts are often seen to show a preference for relying primarily on national law in their jurisprudence. However, national courts have developed a growing awareness of their role in applying relevant international standards, though practice differs considerably.[200] Some courts have flatly rejected the binding nature of international treaty standards. For example, the Sri Lankan Supreme Court held in the *Singarasa* case that the ICCPR had no binding force under domestic law and refused a retrial even though the HRCtee had found that Singarasa

---

[196] See in particular general comments/recommendations on the implementation of treaty obligations and concluding observations on states parties' reports by various treaty bodies, which regularly exhort parties to implement the respective treaty in domestic law where they have not done so already.

[197] C. Heyns and F. Viljoen, *The Impact of the United Nations Treaties on the Domestic Level* (Kluwer Law International, 2002) 7–46; C. Harland, 'The Status of the International Covenant on Civil and Political Rights (ICCPR) in the Domestic Law of States Parties: An Initial Global Survey Through UN Human Rights Committee Documents' (2002) 22 *Human Rights Quarterly* 187.

[198] See both Heyns and Viljoen and Harland, ibid. See also e.g., Ireland's European Convention on Human Rights Act, 2003, and Nigeria's African Charter on Human and Peoples' Rights (Ratification and Enforcement) Act 1990, ch. 10.

[199] See e.g., on Sudan's Bill of Rights, L. Oette, 'Law Reform in Times of Peace Processes and Transitional Justice: The Sudanese Dimension', in L. Oette (ed.), *Criminal Law Reform and Transitional Justice: Human Rights Perspectives for Sudan* (Ashgate, 2011) 11–31, at 22–9.

[200] See generally M. Kirby, 'Domestic Courts and International Human Rights Law: The Ongoing Judicial Conversation (The Hondis Lecture 2008)' (2009) 27 *Netherlands Quarterly of Human Rights* 291; N. Jayawickrama, *The Judicial Application of Human Rights Law: National, Regional and International Jurisprudence* (Cambridge University Press, 2002); B. Conforti (ed.), *Enforcing International Human Rights in Domestic Courts* (Kluwer Law International, 1997); A. Nollkaemper, *National Courts and the International Rule of Law* (Oxford University Press, 2011).

had been convicted and sentenced to thirty-five years' imprisonment under anti-terrorism laws in violation of the right to a fair trial.[201] In another case, Sudan's Constitutional Court effectively held that immunity from prosecution granted to officials under national law was compatible with human rights standards without adequately considering international jurisprudence, which holds otherwise.[202]

In contrast to Sri Lanka's Supreme Court, the Spanish Supreme Court awarded an applicant €600,000 compensation for mental damages, holding that the state, pursuant to its interpretation of Spain's constitution, was obliged to implement CEDAW's views.[203] Other courts have upheld international standards even in the face of pressing security concerns, such as the UK House of Lords in several cases, leading to fundamental changes in the UK anti-terrorism scheme;[204] or courts have taken a lead role in progressively interpreting constitutional rights, thus advancing the development of international human rights law. An example is the South African Constitutional Court in the *Grootboom* case, in which a group of persons who had been evicted sought an order from the government to provide them with adequate basic shelter or housing; the Court held that the state must devise and implement a programme 'to provide relief for people who have no access to land, no roof over their heads, and who are living in intolerable conditions or crisis situations', setting a precedent on the right to housing and protection against forced evictions.[205] Ultimately, it is not the reference to international standards but the recognition and protection of rights that courts are able to provide which matters. Examples are Germany's Constitutional Court, Colombia's Constitutional Court and the Indian apex courts, which have significantly enhanced our understanding of rights, and, in the Indian case, the availability of remedies.[206] The jurisprudence of domestic courts constitutes important state practice and can be expected to play an even more important role with the increasing awareness of international standards. However, it is equally clear that decisions in individual cases, including their implementation, will depend on a number of domestic factors

---

[201] *Singarasa* v. *Attorney General* (Sri Lanka) (2006).

[202] *Farouq Mohamed Ibrahim Al Nour* v. *(1) Government of Sudan; (2) Legislative Body (Sudan)* (2008).

[203] *Judgment* No. 1263/2018 (Spain) (2018).

[204] See T. Bingham, *The Rule of Law* (Allen Lane, 2010) 133–59.

[205] See *Government of the Republic of South Africa and Others* v. *Grootboom and Others* (South Africa) (2000); art. 39(1) of the South African Constitution mandates South African courts to consider international law when interpreting the Bill of Rights.

[206] See on India the various contributions in C. Raj Kumar and K. Chockalingam (eds.), *Human Rights, Justice and Constitutional Empowerment* (Oxford University Press, 2007). See also for discussion of relevant jurisprudence, Chapter 9.6.

characterising the delicate relationship between the legislature and the executive on the one hand and the judiciary on the other. The importance of an independent judiciary in this context could not have been better put by the late Lord Bingham in his landmark book on the rule of law: '[t]here are countries in the world where all judicial decisions find favour with the powers that be, but they are probably not places where any of us would wish to live'.[207]

2.4.1   The Role of National Human Rights Institutions

A number of states have established national human rights institutions (NHRIs). According to the Paris Principles, NHRIs should be independent bodies tasked with promoting and protecting human rights, using a range of measures in respect of all spheres of human rights.[208] The high hopes initially placed in NHRIs have given way to a more nuanced assessment.[209] It has become increasingly clear that many NHRIs lack one or more of the key features of independence, powers and/or capacity. In addition, the faith in the ability of NHRIs to provide protection may be misplaced where they act as poor substitutes for courts in a system where the rule of law is weak. Nevertheless, besides providing a measure of protection and justice, some NHRIs have played useful or even leading roles, particularly where they have enhanced awareness of human rights and have been able to identify a country's human rights problems and articulate a domestic human rights vision in equal measure.[210] Such NHRIs can form a critical part of broader civil society efforts to demand respect for human rights, which are often at the heart of enhanced implementation.

---

[207] Bingham, above note 204, 65.

[208] Principles relating to the Status of National Institutions (The Paris Principles), UNGA resolution 48/134 of 20 December 1993. See further G. de Beco and R. Murray, *A Commentary on the Paris Principles on National Human Rights Institutions* (Cambridge University Press, 2014). See on NHRIs, Office of the High Commissioner for Human Rights (OHCHR), *National Human Rights Institutions: History, Principles, Roles and Responsibilities*, Professional Training Series no. 4 (rev. 1) (United Nations, 2010); R. Murray, *The Role of National Human Rights Institutions at the International and Regional Levels: The Experience of Africa* (Hart, 2007).

[209] See International Council on Human Rights Policy, *Assessing the Effectiveness of National Human Rights Institutions* (2005); R. Goodman and T. Pegram (eds.), *Human Rights, State Compliance, and Social Change: Assessing National Human Rights Institutions* (Cambridge University Press, 2011),

[210] See e.g., Afghanistan's Independent Human Rights Commission, www.aihrc.org.af/en, and Kenya's National Commission on Human Rights, www.knchr.org. See for further information on the work of NHRIs and OHCHR, www.ohchr.org/en/countries/nhri/pages/nhrimain.aspx.

INTERVIEW 2.1

Reflections on the Work of Uganda's Human Rights Commission

(Med S. K. Kaggwa)

Med S. K. Kaggwa is a distinguished Ugandan lawyer who is the former Chairperson of Uganda's Human Rights Commission (UHRC)[1] and Commissioner of the African Commission on Human and Peoples' Rights.

What are the mandate and powers of Uganda's Human Rights Commission?

The UHRC is an 'A' status independent NHRI established under article 51(1) of the Constitution of the Republic of Uganda and the UHRC Act of 1997 that is mandated to:

Receive and investigate, at its own initiative or on a complaint made by any person or group of persons against the violation of any human right; to visit places of detention or related facilities with a view to assessing and inspecting conditions of the inmates and make recommendations; to establish a continuing programme of research, education and information to enhance respect of human rights; and to recommend to Parliament effective measures to promote human rights including provision of compensation to victims of violations of human rights, or their families.

It is also mandated to create and sustain within society the awareness of the provisions of this Constitution as the fundamental law; to create awareness about human rights and civic obligations; to monitor the government's compliance with international treaty and convention obligations on human rights; and to perform such other functions as may be provided by law.

Under article 52(2), the UHRC is required to publish periodical reports and submit annual reports to Parliament on the state of human rights and freedoms in the country. Importantly, the UHRC also has a quasi-judicial function as stipulated under article 53(1) of the Ugandan Constitution which empowers it to provide redress to victims of human rights violations through tribunals.

Article 54 of the Constitution guarantees the independence of the UHRC. The UHRC is expected to be independent and should not, in the performance of its duties, be subject to the direction or control of any person or authority. However, article 52(3)(b) of the Constitution permits the Commission to request the assistance of any department, bureau, office, agency or person in the performance of its functions.

---

[1] www.uhrc.ug. The interview was conducted in 2012 while he was still in office.

What would you say has been its most valuable achievement?

The UHRC's establishment, powers and functions comply with the UN Paris Principles and it is accredited with 'A' status by the International Coordinating Committee of National Human Rights Institutions. It has regularly reported on the state of human rights in the country up to this day; fourteen annual reports have been produced and submitted to Parliament with recommendations for improvement. These reports provide some measure of accountability to the public.

In 2009 Parliament discussed findings and recommendations contained in UHRC reports that had been submitted from 1997 to 2007.[2] Recommendations on human rights and freedoms in the country were analysed and recommended for further action by various government institutions. Parliament also approved the creation of a human rights committee to discuss recommendations made by the UHRC and monitor government compliance with human rights among other responsibilities. For instance, the UHRC had always recommended to Parliament the enactment of a law that prevents torture. In 2006 the UHRC together with NGOs under the Coalition Against Torture drafted the Prevention and Prohibition of Torture Bill 2010, which was passed by Parliament on 26 April 2012 and subsequently entered into force as the Prevention and Prohibition of Torture Act 2012.

The UHRC has established nine regional offices. In addition to the regional offices, with support from the UN Development Programme (UNDP) it has established sub-regional offices in the north and north-eastern parts of Uganda to take services closer to the local population that were majorly affected by the Lord's Resistance Army insurgency. These offices are well coordinated by the Directorate of Regional Services. The UHRC has established a Right to Health Unit, Vulnerable Persons Unit and a Human Rights Defenders' Desk under the Directorate of Monitoring and Inspections. The two units and the Human Rights Defenders' Desk are responsible for monitoring the implementation of the right to health, the rights of vulnerable groups and the rights of human rights defenders.

The UHRC has also helped to establish district human rights desks and committees in seventy-six districts of the country in order to ensure protection and promotion of human rights at that level. These have been able to support the UHRC in mediating some cases of human rights violations at the district-level such as Tororo and Kiruhura. However, some of the human rights desks and committees are not functional due to lack of funding.

The UHRC has a good working relationship with security agencies, which never used to be the case in the past. It is allowed to freely inspect places of detention (police cells, prisons and military detention facilities). It also

---

[2] www.parliament.go.ug/new/.

receives prompt responses to investigation inquiries especially from the Uganda People's Defence Forces and prisons. This progress is attributed to the numerous human rights training programmes carried out by the UHRC for security agents.

The institution is considered credible both at national and international level. On several occasions the UHRC has been a point of reference and has been called upon to carry out capacity-building for other NHRIs in the region. UHRC commissioners and staff have been called upon as experts/ resource persons to share experiences and best practices on the establish- ment, powers and functions of an NHRI with NHRIs of Kenya, Sierra Leone, Sudan, Tanzania, Somaliland, Ethiopia, Malawi and Swaziland. As a result of its credibility the UHRC has previously chaired the African Network of National Institutions and Commonwealth Forum for National Human Rights Institutions.

What are the main challenges it faces?

The government takes a long time to honour UHRC tribunal awards or com- pensate victims of human rights violations.[3] The failure to have a single entity coordinating civic education programmes in the country often leads to duplication of results and imbalances in the coverage of interventions. In addition, inadequate financial resources make it difficult for the UHRC to fully implement its broad mandate.

With only nine regional offices in the country, the UHRC still faces a challenge in ensuring that human rights services are accessed by people in geographically distant and hard to reach areas. The limited funding for the institution's activities has been exacerbated by a decline in donor funding. The institution relies significantly on government funding in addition to funding received from its donors.[4] Funds received from donors on the other hand are usually earmarked for particular programmes. Therefore it becomes difficult to ensure that the Commission's mandate is met within the different budget allocations.

What steps have you taken to address these challenges?

The UHRC uses a mobile complaints handling system. In this system, staff in regional offices travel to distant places within their areas of jurisdiction to receive complaints and also to sensitise people to their rights. Through its annual reports on the state of human rights in the country, the UHRC urges the government to put in place a mechanism where the victims of human rights violations are compensated urgently. As already mentioned,

---

[3] UHRC, 14th Annual Report (2011) 14.
[4] UHRC, 13th Annual Report (2010) 134.

with effect from 1 July 2011 the UHRC established sub-regional field offices in the northern and north-eastern parts of Uganda in order to take services closer to the rural population.[5]

What contributions can NHRIs make, and what are their limitations?

NHRIs have a responsibility to monitor government's compliance with international treaties. This often includes analysis of government policies and laws to ensure that they are consistent with human rights principles. By this means, NHRIs can ensure that national laws protect the rights of all categories of people including human rights defenders.

NHRIs are also an appropriate source of information on the human rights situation in the country. Such information can be used to publicise national human rights concerns at the international level in search for an appropriate remedy.

The hope that NHRIs effectively guarantee human rights has not been fulfilled in many countries. What do you see as the main reason for the apparent weakness of some NHRIs, and how do you think it can be overcome at the regional and international level?

Most NHRIs have limited funding to fully implement all the activities they should be carrying out as per their mandates and the Paris Principles. NHRIs have very limited capacity to investigate human rights violations and also monitor the human rights situation in conflict areas. In addition, the procedure for appointing chairpersons and commissioners varies from one NHRI to another. It therefore becomes hard to ensure protection and promotion of human rights at a uniform level in various countries, particularly where the NHRI lacks the necessary independence and does not conform to the UN Paris Principles.

Recommendations: NHRIs ought to lobby their respective governments for an increase in funding to be able to implement their mandates. They could also rely on funding from donors or any other source to support implementation of their mandates as long as they do not compromise the independence of the institution. NHRIs can coordinate efforts to promote dialogue between conflicting parties and mediate through or with networks and coalitions. They could also coordinate efforts to ensure that victims of the conflict, such as those in Northern Uganda, have access to remedies and reparation, which can constitute a challenge in transitional contexts. Finally, NHRIs can work through networks and coalitions at the national, regional and international level for technical and financial support in the protection and promotion of human rights within their areas of jurisdiction.

---

[5] UHRC, 14th Annual Report (2011) 50.

2.5   STATE RESPONSIBILITY AND HUMAN RIGHTS TREATIES AS SELF-CONTAINED REGIMES

The ILC's ARSIWA are regularly referred to by international courts and in state practice and are largely seen as codifying customary international law on the attribution of state responsibility and its consequences.[211] The articles set out general rules and govern the obligations owed by states responsible for a wrongful act, such as a violation of human rights, to other states and the international community as a whole.[212] Their rules of attribution and legal consequences are important in the human rights context, particularly where states invoke human rights violations as being of an *erga omnes* character or as a violation of their rights, and inform the jurisprudence in human rights cases.[213] As far as the practice under human rights treaties is concerned, human rights treaty bodies and courts monitor compliance of states with their obligations through reporting, inquiries and individual and inter-state complaints procedures.[214] Their decisions determine whether a state has breached its treaty obligations and spell out the legal consequences under the treaty, i.e. cessation and the various forms of reparation that such a finding entails. This set-up has raised the question of whether human rights constitute a so-called self-contained or special regime that excludes recourse to other mechanisms and counter-measures,[215] such as sanctions.[216] For example, where a human rights treaty provides for an inter-state complaints procedure, it seems reasonable to suggest that states should have recourse to this procedure as the most spe-cialised available instead of taking other steps, such as countermeasures. The rationale is clear; the system has been set up for a particular purpose and has developed its own procedures and jurisprudence. It is therefore in

---

[211] See for a concise overview, C. Crawford and S. Olleson, 'The Character and Forms of International Responsibility' in Evans, above note 84, 415–49, and for a detailed study, S. Ollesen, *The Impact of the ILC's Articles on Responsibility of States for Internationally Wrongful Acts*, Preliminary Draft (British Institute of International and Comparative Law, 2007).

[212] See art. 33(1) ARSIWA. Art. 33(2) clarifies that this is 'without prejudice to any right, arising from the international responsibility of a State, which may accrue directly to any person or entity other than a State'. See also the virtually identical art. 33(2) of the ILC Draft Articles on the Responsibility of International Organisations (2011).

[213] See ICJ judgment on the *Application of the Convention on the Prevention and Punishment of the Crime of Genocide (Bosnia and Herzegovina v. Serbia and Montenegro)* (2007); and advisory opinion, *Legal Consequences of the Construction of a Wall in the Occupied Palestinian Territory* (2004), discussed further in Ollesen, above note 211.

[214] See in particular, Chapters 5–7.

[215] See arts. 49–55 ARSIWA.

[216] See discussion in ILC, Fragmentation, above note 3, paras. 123–94, with further references.

the interest of functional integrity and efficiency that states use the specialised system.

Following extensive debates within the ILC, and in light of judicial practice, there are no cogent policy reasons or support to make international human rights treaties closed systems and bar states from having recourse to general countermeasures.[217] It is nevertheless reasonable for states parties to use a special regime unless the remedies it provides 'would be manifestly unavailable or ineffective or where it would be otherwise unreasonable to expect recourse to it'.[218] In such circumstances, states may either have recourse to other international bodies, including the ICJ, which has been increasingly seized with questions of international human rights law, or use proportionate countermeasures. However, countermeasures frequently pose both legal and political challenges. The international human rights system is multilateral and embedded in the UN, particularly its specialised bodies, i.e. the Human Rights Council (HRC), and regional political bodies, such as the Council of Europe (CoE), the European Union (EU), the African Union (AU) and the Organization of American States (OAS). Proponents may claim that unilateral sanctions or even the use of force in the form of 'humanitarian intervention' are necessary where these institutional structures are ineffective. However, such unilateral moves are frequently seen as politically motivated and aimed at establishing regional or international hegemonies. This has prompted developments to formulate doctrines, such as the responsibility to protect (R2P), according to which the UN has primary responsibility to take effective action where a state (and, implicitly, institutional systems of protection) fails in its duty to protect those within its territory from serious human rights violations, namely international crimes.[219]

QUESTIONS

1. The role of NHRIs is frequently overrated. Rather than providing an effective means for the promotion and protection of human rights, they have more often than not become a façade that embodies the weakness rather than the strength of a national system. Discuss.

2. The system for the enforcement of international human rights obligations is under-developed and ineffective. Discuss.

---

[217] The HRCtee seems to imply this in its General Comment 31, para. 2.
[218] ILC, Fragmentation, above note 3, para. 152.
[219] 2005 World Summit Outcome, paras. 138–9, and Zifcak, above note 108.

2.6   PRACTICAL APPLICATION: THE ROLE OF LAW REFORM

The mismatch between ratification and effective implementation of treaties is one of the most glaring shortcomings of the international human rights system. It calls into question its basic premise of setting out standards that states parties will seek to adhere to, if not realise immediately. In practice, it is often a combination of factors and complex dynamics, including the interplay between national and international actors, that determine the nature of implementation, if any, as an examination of legislative reforms aptly demonstrates.

Best practice in the area of legislative reform is relatively easy to identify. States should actively seek to incorporate relevant human rights standards in their domestic legislation. This can be done by conducting compatibility studies and identifying those laws or provisions that need to be repealed, amended or adopted in order to bring domestic law into conformity with international standards.[220] Such studies should ideally be undertaken before a state becomes party to a treaty but may for practical purposes follow it. They should be complemented by legislation that recognises the rights concerned and provides for effective protection. Such legislation should, where applicable, form part of broader policies, and be accompanied by institutional reforms and the training of officials to whom it is addressed. The rights reflected in such legislation should also be an integral element of broader human rights education and awareness-raising programmes so that those whose rights are concerned know what their rights are and how best to exercise them. In turn, this requires that the rights are justiciable and that effective remedies are available in case of breach.

Reality frequently fails to live up to these best practices. This applies in particular to the reform of statutory laws. A common refrain is to say that a state lacks political will to bring its laws into conformity with international standards. While this may well be true, as a general statement it often obscures more than it reveals unless it is clear what is meant by 'political will'. This is obvious where a government flatly refuses to undertake specific reforms or, worse, pursues or even adopts legislation that runs counter to its obligations, such as draconian emergency laws following a *coup d'état* or in times of crisis,[221] or laws that impose severe punishment for consensual homosexual acts.[222] However, actual practice is frequently less clear-cut, with

---

[220] Heyns and Viljoen, above note 197, 7–46.

[221] See in particular, information about emergency powers worldwide, available at STEM-State of Emergency Mapping, online at www.emergencymapping.org/.

[222] See Report of the UN High Commissioner for Human Rights, Discriminatory Laws and Practices and Acts of Violence Against Individuals Based on their Sexual Orientation and

reforms failing to materialise because they are caught in a web of multiple political, institutional and practical obstacles. International institutions and/ or domestic civil society for their part may lack the awareness or may not give priority to a particular issue and therefore fail to generate the momentum needed to make the government concerned act. Even where such actors exercise some influence, a government may refrain from passing legislation if the political (or financial) cost is deemed too high. For example, in South Africa, trauma crisis and counselling support, the morning-after pill and legal representation for victims were excluded from legislation governing sexual violence on the grounds of resource constraints.[223]

Resistance to legislative reforms can take numerous forms. Law-enforcement agencies are often strongly opposed to legislation that results in restrictions to their power and/or greater oversight and accountability. For example, in India the armed forces have opposed calls for the repeal of the Armed Forces Special Powers Act in force in Kashmir and the north-east of India, which grants them extraordinary powers in contravention of international human rights standards.[224] Religious groups may decisively influence the debate on reforms, for example in respect of abortion or blasphemy laws affecting reproductive rights and the freedom of expression.[225] Nationalist groups may be opposed to granting rights to minorities, and public sentiment may result in restricting the rights of certain categories of persons, such as migrants and refugees.[226] External political pressure, such as structural adjustment programmes advocated by international agencies, may contribute to a political climate detrimental to reforms protecting basic

---

Gender Identity, UN doc. A/HR/C/19/41 (17 November 2011), which was published against a background of a series of anti-homosexuality bills or laws contemplated or adopted in countries such as Uganda and Nigeria.

[223] See R. Manjoo, G. Kweka and S. O. Ofuani, 'Sexual Violence and the Law: Comparative Legislative Experiences in Selected Southern African Countries', in Oette, above note 199, 269–95, at 287–8.

[224] See AI, *India: Security Forces Cannot Claim Immunity under AFSPA, Must Face Trial for Violations* (7 February 2012), online at www.amnesty.org/au/news/comments/27815/.

[225] See on the criminalisation of abortion, Interim report of the Special Rapporteur on the right of everyone to the enjoyment of the highest attainable standard of physical and mental health, UN doc. A/66/254 (3 August 2011), and on blasphemy laws in Pakistan, UN Special Rapporteur on the independence of judges and lawyers, Ms Gabriela Knaul, Preliminary observations on the official visit to the Islamic Republic of Pakistan, Islamabad (29 May 2012), online at www.ohchr.org/EN/NewsEvents/Pages/DisplayNews.aspx?NewsID=12194&LangID=E.

[226] The treatment of refugees and their 'rightlessness' had already been highlighted by Hannah Arendt in her seminal work, *The Origins of Totalitarianism* (Schocken Books, 1951). See on the political context also M. A. Schain, 'The State Strikes Back: Immigration Policy in Europe' (2009) 20 *European Journal of International Law* 93.

[227] See Report of the Independent Expert on the Effect of Economic Reform Policies and Foreign Debt on the Full Enjoyment of all Human Rights, Bernards Mudho, UN doc.

rights.[227] In addition to these political factors, the institutional set-up may not be conducive. Several states seemingly lack the capacity to draft good implementing legislation. Law reform commissions, where in place, can help in identifying areas for reform and ensuring that technical expertise benefits from consultation.[228] However, even here political priorities or approaches taken may undermine reforms. A telling example concerns attempts to ban polygamy in Uganda, which faltered, also as the result of a consultation with rural communities that found some support for the practice.[229] The outcome of the law-making process itself depends on gaining sufficient political support often also at the federal level, which may compromise reforms. The time within which legislation has to be adopted is another factor that frequently derails or substantially delays reform proposals.[230]

How can international standards be used to bring about legislative reforms where domestic law fails to guarantee and protect rights? This is one of the key strategic questions facing domestic actors. International human rights treaty bodies, UN special procedures mandate-holders or other bodies may have identified laws in need of reform. This may help in raising awareness but does not by itself guarantee that the requisite steps will be taken. Indeed, such recommendations are routinely ignored. Worse, international 'pressure' and reference to international standards may even create a backlash. National actors therefore often have to develop their own strategies and activities to challenge laws incompatible with international standards.

The campaign to change the *Hudood* laws in Pakistan is an instructive example of the multifaceted challenges.[231] The *Hudood* laws were adopted in 1979 by the then military ruler Zia ul-Haq as part of a policy of Islamisation. The law rendered *zina* (extramarital sexual intercourse) subject to harsh, fixed punishments, including flogging and stoning. Significantly, it also turned rape into a form of *zina* to which Islamic laws of evidence applied. This meant that four male eyewitnesses had to testify to the rape; if insufficient evidence was available to sustain an allegation, especially in case of

---

A/HRC/4/10 (3 January 2007) paras. 26–69; M. R. Abouharb and D. Cingranelli, *Human Rights and Structural Adjustment* (Cambridge University Press, 2007).

[228] See e.g., the substantive work undertaken by South Africa's Law Reform Commission, www.justice.gov.za/salrc/.

[229] Uganda's polygamy laws have thereafter been challenged by human rights groups before Uganda's Constitutional Court. See J. Shore, 'Human Rights Group Challenges Uganda's Polygamy Laws', Centre for Human Rights and Humanitarian Law, *The Human Rights Brief* (6 April 2010).

[230] It took twenty-two years and countless lapsed bills to turn the constitutional prohibition of torture in the Philippines into an anti-torture law in 2009.

[231] The following account draws on S. A. Warraich, 'Through the Looking Glass: The Emergence, Confused Application and Demise of Pakistan's *Hudood* Rape Laws', in Oette, above note 199, 243–67.

pregnancy, a woman faced prosecution for *zina*. The law resulted in a moral witch hunt and confused application by specially constituted Sharia councils, which often turned rape victims into suspects. Pakistani women's rights groups found it difficult to campaign against the laws given the repressive political climate and the prevalence of conservative morals supporting the law in rural areas. Religious factions accused these groups of pursuing a Western agenda as a means of discrediting them, especially following criticism from Western countries, such as in cases that upheld the punishment of stoning.

In these circumstances, women's rights activists adopted a two-track approach, which aimed at exposing the discriminatory and harmful impact of the law. They used local meetings, theatre performances and a variety of publications to undermine the laws in the public eye, in particular in rural areas. In parallel, human rights lawyers defended those accused of *zina* before the courts, seeking to demonstrate the flawed and inconsistent application of the law. These measures, accompanied by sustained international criticism, served to erode support for the laws in Pakistan, which were increasingly seen as an ill-conceived embarrassment even by several Islamic scholars. In the wake of this change in public mood, several civil society groups, supported by some political parties, campaigned and lobbied for a repeal of the laws. This campaign faced hostile reactions from religiously motivated parties. However, ten years after Pakistan had ratified the CEDAW in 1996, the efforts resulted in some significant changes, albeit in the form of a compromise package that, while repealing the *zina* law, retained a number of discriminatory pieces of legislation.

The Pakistani experience holds important lessons. It is difficult to repeal laws that find their way on to the statute book even where they are seemingly discredited. This is especially the case where they can claim some legitimacy, which can be religious but may equally derive from security considerations or similar rationales. Opponents of such legislation have to embark on sustained engagement, combining awareness-raising, litigation, advocacy and lobbying in order to bring about at least some limited changes. This engagement also illustrates the nature of the struggle over legislative reforms, which are often about symbolic legitimacy. In times of severe political repression, the legal system can become a site for exposing apparent flaws, which has the advantage that one can refer to texts (and international commitments of states) rather than to (often contested) information about facts. This painstaking work may in time result in a change of attitudes and/or may prepare the ground for genuine reforms once the opportunity arises. A change of government or the end of a conflict constitutes an important opening for legislative reforms. However, by its very nature, law reform is a complicated process whose outcome is a reflection of a number of political factors and legal considerations.

INTERVIEW 2.2
The Campaign to Repeal Pakistan's *Hudood* Laws
(Sohail A. Warraich)

Sohail Warraich is a women's rights activist who actively campaigned for the repeal of the *Hudood* laws, working on behalf of the Shirkat Gah women's resource centre and performing street plays with his theatre group that exposed how the law victimised women.

How did you get involved in the campaign to repeal the Hudood laws?

I had just joined university when I read the news of punishment of flogging pronounced under the *Zina* Ordinance to Safia Bibi, a blind girl, for being pregnant outside of marriage. Her plea was one of rape. The international press also publicised this case and the Women's Action Forum (WAF) strongly protested against it. This case introduced me to the *Zina* Ordinance and its problems. Though Safia was acquitted upon appeal, the injustices of this law continued in case after case. In 1987 Shahida Parveen from Karachi was given a sentence of stoning to death by the trial court. She had remarried after being divorced by her first husband but following her remarriage her former husband claimed that she was still married to him. He claimed that had he divorced her he would have followed the procedure given in law. Shahida and her second husband were tried under the *zina* law and convicted. She was sentenced to stoning to death while her second husband was sentenced to a hundred lashes. This verdict shocked everyone. Amnesty International issued an action alert against Shahida's sentence. That was my first active participation for the repeal of the *Zina* Ordinance. After that, I learnt more about the problems of this law and joined protest meetings and demonstrations organised by WAF and other rights groups. The theatre group I worked for (Ajoka Theatre) performed street plays on the injustices suffered by rape victims under this law. In the early 1990s, I joined the Shirkat Gah women's resource centre, a leading women's rights organisation, which was at the forefront in the campaign for the repeal of *Hudood* ordinances. In 2006, the enactment of the Women's Protection Act, which repealed many provisions of the *Zina* and *Qazaf* Ordinances, was a first major success of the campaign against these laws, but the struggle has to continue until their total repeal.

What was the key to the successful campaign?

A firm, clear position and consistency in demanding repeal of *Hudood* laws over the years was key to the campaign, which was ultimately met with success to the extent that major amendments to these laws were introduced to prevent abuse. Women's rights activists for years demanded repeal of these laws without mincing words. The relevant positions were based on the rights of people rather than shifting stances.

Case after case also provided opportunities to protest against the verdicts and further campaign against these laws. The old argument that any law can be misused was successfully countered from a number of cases demonstrating that the potential for abuse and misuse was from within the law rather than being its mere misapplication. Explaining to people in very simple words with examples from actual cases in which contradictory verdicts had been pronounced proved helpful in removing misperceptions about the widely propagated 'Islamic' nature of these laws. To this end, I wrote handbills in simple Urdu and, together with my colleagues, wrote campaign materials including a small booklet titled *Why Hudood Ordinances Should be Repealed*, in Urdu and English. It was widely distributed at public meetings and also sent to members of Parliament.

What were some memorable moments in the campaign?

In fact for me the memorable moment was the case of Zafran Bibi, who was sentenced to stoning to death by a trial court in March 2002. This case again exposed the absurdity and unjust nature of this law, as happened in some of the previous cases. Zafran was a married pregnant woman and her husband was serving a sentence in a jail. She went to the police station with her father-in-law to register a complaint of rape against another man. She was sent for a medical examination and being found pregnant was held under the offence of *zina*. Before the conclusion of the trial she gave birth to a female child. During trial her statement that she gave birth to a child was taken as her confession of having committed *zina*. She was sentenced under *hadd* (maximum fixed punishment which was stoning to death for a married Muslim man or a woman). This case helped the campaign a lot. It exposed the ambiguities and injustices of this law to everyone. It became a lot easier to talk about repeal of these laws with the help of this case. A momentum built and there were public meetings on the injustices of these laws and demands for repeal were strengthened. In the public meetings and handbills, extracts were used from the verdicts of higher courts including the Federal Shariat Court where the application of the law was criticised and injustices were exposed. In many verdicts of the 1990s, the courts referred extensively to the *zina* law, short of asking for amendments or repeal. The courts' observations and remarks provided first-hand material for the campaign against *Hudood* laws.

Zafran Bibi's case occurred at a very critical and decisive time. It exposed the inherent contradictions, inequalities and extreme potential for misuse in the provisions of *zina* and rape in the *Hudood* law, and the judgment of the Federal Shariat Court demonstrated that the defenders and proponents of *Hudood* laws were left with only very weak arguments. The longest paragraph of the judgment was not on the merits of the case itself but rather on the admonition of organisations and individuals who protested against the verdict of stoning to death.

From the *Zafran* case onwards the campaign gained a different momentum. During month-long debates over the Bill, inside and outside Parliament there were many memorable moments. Some of the debates on TV exposed the hollow defence of these laws by traditional clerics and their anti-women mindset. In most of these debates clerics were invited and some of the TV channels and other factions of the media portrayed the issue as religious alone, on which these clerics were the sole authority. These debates showed that the battle on these laws was an issue of political power, spearheaded by certain conservative forces, rather than a purely legal question. It gave a real opportunity to discover the obstructions and difficulties faced by legislative reform brought in the name of religion and how religion was used as an instrument to prevent reform. Reports about government committees constituted to bargain with leaders of religious political parties and their allied clerics and the bargains being negotiated were hilarious as well as embarrassing. Finally, when the amendments happened, the so-called 'divineness' attached to the *Hudood* laws was dented. Though the result achieved was short of what we desired, in political terms it was a landmark. That will never be forgotten.

What are the lessons for other countries?

The first and foremost is that criminal laws (especially those related to sexual acts and offences) introduced in the name of Islam in some Muslim majority states are a political tool to gain some 'legitimacy' and support for the rulers and also to keep control through harsher punishments. Experience tells us that these laws are enacted in haste, carry inherent inequalities and are aimed at disadvantaged sections of the society. They are divisive in nature and divide society on the basis of sex and religion.

The cover of Islam is used to silence any opposition to these laws. The suggestion from Pakistan's experience is to contest these laws from your own positions of strength. Public support can be gained by taking the problems of law to the public and linking them to their lives. Emblematic cases can be used to agitate against these laws. There is no monolithic Sharia and in each Muslim majority state each sect has its own interpretations. So attempts to fight on arguments from within religion may not be of much help. In certain circumstances that can be a tactic, but not a real long-term strategy. There can be arguments from within the religious discourse against a particular text of laws enforced in a jurisdiction, but that may mean replacing one text with another which on the face of it may seem better than before but may ultimately bring similar problems.

FURTHER READING

Boisson de Chazournes, L., and M. G. Kohen (eds.), *International Law and the Quest for its Implementation: Liber amicorum Vera Gowlland-Debbas* (Brill, 2010).

Boyle, A., and C. Chinkin, *The Making of International Law* (Oxford University Press, 2007).

Crawford, J., *State Responsibility: The General Part* (Cambridge University Press, 2013).

Criddle, E. J. (ed.), *Human Rights in Emergencies* (Cambridge University Press, 2016).

De Beco, G. and R. Murray, *A Commentary on the Paris Principles on National Human Rights Institutions* (Cambridge University Press, 2014).

Fellmeth, A. X., *Paradigms of International Human Rights Law* (Oxford University Press, 2016).

Goodman, R., 'Human Rights Treaties, Invalid Reservations and State Consent' (2002) 96 *American Journal of International Law* 531.

Goodman, R., and D. Jinks, *Socializing States: Promoting Human Rights Through International Law* (Oxford University Press, 2013).

Gross, O., and F. Ní Aoláin, *Law in Times of Crisis: Emergency Powers in Theory and Practice* (Cambridge University Press, 2006).

Heyns, C., and F. Viljoen, *The Impact of the United Nations Treaties on the Domestic Level* (Kluwer Law International, 2002).

Kamminga, M. T., and M. Scheinin (eds.), *The Impact of Human Rights Law on General International Law* (Oxford University Press, 2009).

Lagoutte, S., T. Gammeltoft-Hansen and J. Cerone (eds.), *Tracing the Roles of Soft Law in Human Rights* (Oxford University Press, 2016).

Linos, K., and T. Pegram, 'What Works in Human Rights Institutions' (2017) 111 *American Journal of International Law* 628.

Meron, T., *Human Rights and Humanitarian Norms as Customary Law* (Clarendon Press, 1989).

Mutua, M., 'Standard Setting in Human Rights: Critique and Prognosis' (2007) 29 *Human Rights Quarterly* 547.

Human Rights Standards: Hegemony, Law and Politics (State University of New York Press, 2016).

Nollkaemper, A., *National Courts and the International Rule of Law* (Oxford University Press, 2011).

Orakhelashvili, A., *Peremptory Norms in International Law* (Oxford University Press, 2006).

Simmons, B. A., *Mobilizing for Human Rights: International Law in Domestic Politics* (Cambridge University Press, 2009).

Symposium, 'Assessing the Work of the International Law Commission on State Responsibility' (2002) 13 *European Journal of International Law* 1053.

Symposium, 'The International Law Commission's Guide to Practice on Reservations to Treaties' (2013) 24 *European Journal of International Law* 1055.

Tams, C. J., *Enforcing Obligations Erga Omnes in International Law* (Cambridge University Press, 2005).

Thirlway, H., *The Sources of International Law*, 2nd edn (Oxford University Press, 2019).

Websites

International Law Association: www.ila-hq.org/, particularly Human Rights Law Committee, www.ila-hq.org/en/committees/index.cfm/cid/1027

International Law Commission: www.un.org/law/ilc/

National Human Rights Institutions: www.ohchr.org/EN/Countries/NHRI/Pages/NHRIMain.aspx

UN Treaty Collection: https://treaties.un.org/

3 Human Rights in Practice

CONTENTS

3.1   INTRODUCTION

Human rights are constructed by multiple actors acting within the given political and legal structures, and challenging and changing them in the process. While the political struggle for human rights is universal and potentially engages all human beings, our focus is on key agents, both the 'true authors' of human rights[1] and others who play an influential role. The 'human rights movement' includes individuals and communities fighting for

---

[1] See on the authorship and ownership of human rights, U. Baxi, *The Future of Human Rights*, 3rd edn (Oxford University Press, 2008) 32–58.

their rights, non-governmental organisations (NGOs), the somewhat amorphous 'civil society', social movements and transnational networks that engage in local and global power struggles. More recently, the term 'human rights defenders' has become a widely used category to embrace the range of actors concerned.

The human rights movement is by no means uniform and a series of challenges, both within the movement and in respect of its role as a political actor, have become more pronounced with the increasing power of human rights and its advocates. This development has cast the light on human rights advocates, such as NGOs, and has raised questions both of legitimacy – who are you to make claims in the name of human rights or on behalf of certain people? Are you living up to human rights principles in your own practice? – and effectiveness – are you really making the positive difference in people's lives you claim to make? Responses to these challenges testify to a growing self-awareness and critical assessment of the nature of human rights work, which includes an evaluation of the efficacy of strategies used to promote and protect human rights. Inevitably, human rights advocates are increasingly drawn into the political domain and are faced with the difficult task of marrying principle with pragmatism. This chapter explores the tensions arising in these contexts and assesses the strategies used by human rights actors, namely documentation, human rights reporting, advocacy, awareness-raising, training and education and, where relevant, litigation (which is considered in more detail in Chapters 7 and 15).

3.2   CIVIL SOCIETY

The last decades have witnessed a growing emphasis on civil society, both as a collective group of actors that promote human rights and as a societal structure or forum that enables the exercise of rights.[2] This development has to a considerable degree been due to the waning of political ideologies and traditional parties at the national level and the process of globalisation at the

---

[2] T. Risse, 'The Power of Norms vs. the Norms of Power: Transnational Civil Society and Human Rights', in A. M. Florini (ed.), *The Third Force: The Rise of Transnational Civil Society* (Carnegie Endowment for International Peace, 2000) 177–210; S. Batliwala, 'Grassroots Movements as Transnational Actors: Implications for Global Civil Society' (2002) 13 *Voluntas: International Journal of Voluntary and Non-profit Organizations* 393; J. Keane, *Global Civil Society?* (Cambridge University Press, 2003); B. de Sousa Santos and C. A. Rodriguez-Garavito, *Law and Globalization from Below: Towards a Cosmopolitan Legality* (Cambridge University Press, 2005); M. Edwards (ed.), *The Oxford Handbook of Civil Society* (Oxford University Press, 2011); J. Ehrenberg, *Civil Society: The Critical History of an Idea* (New York University Press, 1999). See on the UN and Civil Society, online at www.un.org/en/civilsociety/index.shtml.

international level.[3] In the process, non-state actors, including NGOs, social movements and transnational networks have grown in size and importance.[4] While the notion of 'civil society' is often invoked, if not celebrated, its meaning remains subject to diverging interpretations and its role contested.

National civil society has been described '[as] the intermediary layer between the public sphere of the state and the private sphere of households and organizations within it that are voluntary and autonomous'.[5] Its international counterpart, 'global' civil society, has been defined as 'the sphere of ideas, values, institutions, organisations, networks, and individuals located between the family, the state and the market and operating beyond the confines of national societies, polities, and economies'.[6] This broad definition makes it clear that civil society cannot be simply equated with NGOs. Nevertheless, it is equally clear that NGOs form an important organised element of civil society. This is evident in definitions such as those of the World Bank, which understands 'the term civil society to refer to the wide array of non-governmental and not-for-profit organizations that have a presence in public life, expressing the interests and values of their members or others, based on ethical, cultural, political, scientific, religious or philanthropic considerations. Civil Society Organizations (CSOs) therefore refer to a wide array of organizations: community groups, NGOs, labor unions, indigenous groups, charitable organizations, faith-based organizations, professional associations, and foundations.'[7]

These definitions suggest that civil society is clearly separate from both the state and the economic sphere.[8] This is seemingly reflected in the stance of civil society actors who decide to keep a marked distance from political parties and processes, focusing instead on using their moral credibility to influence public opinion in order to achieve their objectives. This makes for a clear and important demarcation. However, locating civil society entirely outside the political sphere creates a questionable dichotomy. It favours

---

[3] J. Keane, 'Global Civil Society', in H. Anheier, M. Glasius and M. Kaldor (eds.), *Global Civil Society 2001* (Oxford University Press, 2001) 23–47.

[4] M. E. Keck and K. Sikkink, *Activists beyond Borders: Advocacy Networks in International Politics* (Cornell University Press, 1998).

[5] H. M. Zafarullah and Md. H. M. H. Rahman, 'Human Rights, Civil Society and Nongovernmental Organizations: The Nexus in Bangladesh' (2002) 24 *Human Rights Quarterly* 1011, at 1016–17.

[6] *Global Civil Society Yearbook*, 2001, quoted in M. Glasius, 'Dissecting Global Civil Society: Values, Actors, Organisational Forms' *openDemocracy* (2 November 2010).

[7] The World Bank, *Defining Civil Society*, online at http://web.worldbank.org/WBSITE/ EXTERNAL/TOPICS/CSO/0,contentMDK:20101499~menuPK:244752~pagePK: 220503~piPK:220476~theSitePK:228717,00.html.

[8] See M. Shaw, 'Civil Society', in L. Kurtz (ed.), *Encyclopaedia of Violence, Peace and Conflict* (Academic Press, 1999) 269–78.

models leading to an 'NGOization',[9] and may come at the expense of remoteness from democratic processes and a broader public appeal. Yet in the practice of many countries, particularly in repressive regimes and transitional periods, actors may engage simultaneously in human rights work and political activities that blur the boundaries between the two spheres.[10] Moreover, the interaction between various voluntary groups and political and economic actors is often fluid. NGOs, for example, are frequently funded by states or by regional or international institutions and enter into strategic partnerships with them.[11]

'Civil society' is commonly associated with the idea of people doing something good. While this may often be true, it is important to recognise that civil society is a multifaceted sphere that forms part of political processes. This means that civil society groups may adopt diametrically opposed positions, some of which may be highly questionable from a human rights perspective. The struggle over the right to abortion between proponents, particularly women's rights groups, and opponents, such as the Catholic Church and others, is an illustration of such dynamics in the field of reproductive rights.[12] What makes civil society valuable, therefore, is not that it provides a particular ('human rights friendly') view of the world, but that it allows the political space in which rights, and competing versions thereof, can be advocated and, ideally, exercised.

3.3   SOCIAL MOVEMENTS

Human rights advocacy may be founded on 'self-interest', such as the rights of workers, indigenous peoples or lesbian, gay, bisexual, transgender or intersex persons (LGBTI), or flow from an ethical belief, such as in the case of human rights NGOs or faith-based organisations, forming part of 'the human rights movement'.[13] Such groups and others often come together to

---

[9] B. Rajagopal, *International Law from Below: Development, Social Movements and Third World Resistance* (Cambridge University Press, 2003) 260–1.

[10] See e.g., L. Laakso, 'Opposition Politics in Zimbabwe' (2003) 7 *African Studies Quarterly* 19, and C. Tilly and L. J. Wood, *Social Movements 1768–2012*, 3rd edn (Paradigm Publishers, 2012) 1ff.

[11] J. Keane, *Cosmocracy* (Centre for the Study of Democracy, 2002) 27, online at http:// johnkeane.net/cosmocracy/.

[12] See J. M. Joachim, *Agenda Setting, the UN, and NGOs: Gender Violence and Reproductive Rights* (Georgetown University Press, 2007) 133–62; R. Fleishman, 'The Battle against Reproductive Rights: The Impact of the Catholic Church on Abortion Law in Both International and Domestic Areas' (2000) 14 *Emory International Law Review* 277.

[13] A. Neier, *The International Human Rights Movement: A History* (Princeton University Press, 2012). See also multiple contributions from around the world in 'Commemorative Issue: Human Rights in Motion' (2014) 20 *Sur-International Journal on Human Rights*.

form social movements that are characterised by 'collective challenges ... by people with common purposes and solidarity in sustained interactions with elites, opponents and authorities'.[14] These movements constitute important forms of mobilisation by a cross-section of actors who frequently focus, either directly or indirectly, on human rights issues. The anti-slavery movement, suffragettes advocating women's rights, the struggle for decolonisation, and anti-apartheid and anti-racism campaigns are particularly prominent instances of successful (and often internationalised) campaigns.[15] A key feature of such social movements is the fight against injustice, both at the national and international level. This may target local or single-issue violations, such as the fight against development projects, caste-based discrimination or corruption in India, or global concerns, such as campaigns against the adverse impact of globalisation.[16] However, it is important to recognise that some of the methods of social movements may be used by other forces for different causes, such as campaigns against immigration and migrants, that can be seen as antithetical to human rights. In other words, the form of mobilisation does not inherently determine its content.

Social movements do not necessarily frame their cause in human rights terms. Even where a movement deals with an issue that clearly raises human rights concerns, such as poverty or racism, its members may decide not to use human rights language if they believe that it will not resonate and be effective in mobilising others and influencing opinion and behaviour. In the United States (USA), for example, campaigners are said to have frequently preferred to use the language of civil rights because the term 'human rights' is associated with foreign policy and other countries.[17] Notably, though, movements such as #Blacklivesmatter, which was created in 2012 after the lack of justice for the killing of Trayvon Martin, have explicitly framed their demands using human rights language.[18] In the field of economic, social and cultural rights, social movements may find the language of social justice more potent, such as in the European context with its roots in social democracy and green politics in particular, as well as Christian ideals. How

---

[14] S. Tarrow, *Power in Movement: Social Movements and Contentious Politics*, 3rd edn (Cambridge University Press, 2011) 9. See also Tilly and Wood, above note 10, 1–11, and, further, G. Edwards, *Social Movements and Protests* (Cambridge University Press, 2014).

[15] See Keck and Sikkink, above note 4.

[16] M. Mohanty, P. N. Mukherji with O. Tornquist (eds.), *People's Rights: Social Movements and the State in the Third World* (Sage, 1998).

[17] A. C. Finnegan, A. P. Saltsman and S. K. White, 'Negotiating Politics and Culture: The Utility of Human Rights for Activist Organizing in the United States' (2010) 2 *Journal of Human Rights Practice* 307.

[18] See http://blacklivesmatter.com/ferguson, demanding, inter alia, that the US Government 'recognize the full spectrum of our human rights and its obligations under international law'.

best to frame a campaign that clearly has a human rights dimension can for these reasons constitute a considerable challenge for social movements. This is, however, not merely an instrumental question. Movements may have ambivalent if not deeply hostile attitudes towards the state and institutions, which may affect their views on human rights law and its utility as a means of addressing their grievances. Rather than operating within existing legal frameworks, the very thrust of social movements may be to transform systems that are based on non-recognition, exclusion and ultimately violence.[19]

Social movements have increasingly articulated forms of resistance that address injustices with a view to challenging elite agendas and institutionalised decision-making processes. This development has been hailed as an alternative human rights discourse that redefines civil society and democracy 'based on cultural politics of identity, autonomy and territory',[20] and 'offers a local and indigenous ... way of questioning the violence of the postcolonial development state'.[21] This rejection of the state and the search for autonomous political space is, however, open to criticism in so far as it may undermine broader democratic forces and processes, which may in turn weaken the protection of human rights. None the less, social movements must be credited with having addressed a number of blind spots in the existing system, including too much faith in institutional forms of protection that may effectively maintain the status quo and reinforce exclusion. This has brought about a reconfiguration of the human rights paradigm, particularly an increased recognition of collective rights and the need for systems to be more responsive to the demands and particular circumstances of those who are different from the 'mainstream'.

3.4   NGOs

3.4.1   General Considerations

NGOs have taken on an ever more important role in the national, regional and international promotion and protection of human rights. The precursors of NGOs date back to the nineteenth century with the emergence of organisations such as Anti-Slavery International.[22] NGOs became recognised as international actors in the formative stages of the United Nations (UN), as reflected in article 71 of the UN Charter and in the Economic and Social

---

[19] Rajagopal, above note 9, 262.   [20] Ibid., 236.
[21] Ibid., 254. For an in-depth discussion see also N. Stammers, *Human Rights and Social Movements* (Pluto Press, 2009) 131–213.
[22] See www.antislavery.org/english. M. Kaye, *1807–2007: Over 200 Years of Campaigning Against Slavery* (Anti-Slavery International, 2005), online at www.antislavery.org/includes/documents/cm_docs/2009/1/18072007.pdf.

Council (ECOSOC) resolution 288(X) (1950), which referred to NGOs and gave them consultative status.[23] Today, there are thousands of NGOs working in the field of human rights and related areas, as a glimpse at the – by no means exhaustive – list of NGOs with consultative status at the UN demonstrates.[24]

The ECOSOC eligibility criteria for consultative status in particular provide some useful guidance on the constitutive elements of NGOs. ECOSOC resolution 1996/31[25] considers as an NGO '[a]ny such organization that is not established by a governmental entity or intergovernmental agreement' (organisations set up by governments to appear like NGOs are often, slightly ironically, referred to as GONGOs). In addition to qualitative criteria, such as conformity 'with the spirit, purposes and principles' of the UN Charter and possession of recognised standing within its field, the resolution sets out key organisational elements. NGOs must have established premises, a democratically adopted constitution, as well as democratic and transparent decision-making processes. They should also have authority to speak for their members, a representative structure and appropriate accountability mechanisms.

Other criteria, such as those relating to profit-making, political nature and registration, are potentially problematic. The assumption that NGOs are not-for-profit, which is largely based on the ideal that they undertake valuable (and charitable) work for the public good, is increasingly called into question.[26] NGOs need to generate money to sustain themselves and carry out their activities. As a result, they secure funds from individuals, institutions (trusts, foundations or other such donors) or (inter)governmental bodies. However, such funds may be difficult to obtain for particular types of activities and moreover generate dependency on – often shifting – donor agendas. In addition, in several countries, national laws restrict NGO access to funds.[27] Furthermore, some NGOs may wish to provide employment for their beneficiaries, such as displaced persons, a purpose that is typically not covered by funding. Making a profit that relates to aims, such as the sale of publications,

---

[23] Consultative status enables NGOs to attend meetings (e.g. at the UN HRC), and make written submissions and oral presentations during meetings.

[24] See http://csonet.org/index.php?menu=17.

[25] ECOSOC resolution 1996/31: Consultative Relationship between the United Nations and Non-governmental Organizations.

[26] Judge L. Fernando and A. W. Heston, 'Introduction: NGOs between States, Markets, and Civil Society', in Judge L. Fernando and A. W. Heston (eds.), *The Role of NGOs: Charity and Empowerment*, The Annals of the American Academy of Political and Social Science (Sage, 1997) 8–20, at 11: 'The distinction between for-profit and nonprofit continues to become blurred. In their drive toward financial self-sufficiency, NGOs function as for-profit organizations.'

[27] See e.g., 'NGO laws in Sub-Saharan Africa' (2011) 3 *Global Trends in NGO Law*, and (2010) 1 *Survey of Arab NGO Laws*, online at the International Center for Not-for-Profit Law, www.icnl.org.

or profit intended solely to further the objectives of the organisation, such as rehabilitation for victims of human rights violations, may therefore be seen as compatible with the notion of NGOs outlined above.[28] The European Convention on the Recognition of Legal Personality of International Non-Governmental Organisations appears to recognise as much, given its emphasis on the 'non-profit-making *aim*' (article 1, emphasis added) of NGOs. However, engaging in profit-making activities raises critical issues for NGOs, such as becoming more market oriented, and may encourage abuse, such as using their mandate as a cover for business activities. It will therefore often constitute good practice to limit such activities, if not refrain from them altogether.

NGOs may carry considerable political weight and many of their members may, and often do, share certain political affiliations. However, they should be distinguished from political parties whose ultimate purpose is to participate in the political system and seek to govern. This is recognised in a useful definition that views NGOs as 'independent voluntary association[s] of people acting together on a continuous basis, for some common purpose, other than achieving government office, making money [see above] or illegal activities'.[29]

NGOs are commonly registered as charities or voluntary organisations or similar structures in their home country or, in the case of international NGOs, in the place of their headquarters.[30] However, restrictive national legislation or repression may prevent organisations from registering, or lead to revocation of their registration, in violation of their freedom of association.[31] International resolutions governing consultative status or questions of legal personality require that NGOs are registered and limit the grounds on which such registration may be denied. For example, registration within a member state of the European Convention on the Recognition of Legal Personality of International Non-Governmental Organisations is constitutive of legal personality in all member states.[32] However, registration remains a problem if

---

[28] J. Bennett, S. Gibbs, R. James and P. Ryder, *NGO Funding Strategies: An Introduction for Southern and Eastern NGOs* (INTRAC, 1996) 1.

[29] P. Willets, *What is a Non-Governmental Organisation?* (undated), online at www.staff.city.ac.uk/p.willetts/CS-NTWKS/NGO-ART.HTM.

[30] See e.g., the UK Charities Act 2011.

[31] See for detailed studies in the European context the three annual reports of the Expert Council on NGO Law, *Conditions of Establishment of Non-Governmental Organisations*, OING Conf/ Exp (2009); *The Internal Governance of Non-Governmental Organisations*, OING Conf/Exp (2010); and *Sanctions and Liability in Respect of NGOs*, OING Conf/Exp (2011). See also the successful appeal of the Human Dignity Trust, an NGO that supports gay and lesbian rights, against the initial refusal of the Charity Commission to register it as a charity, *The Human Dignity Trust and the Charity Commission for England and Wales* (UK) (2014).

[32] Art. 2 of the European Convention on the Recognition of Legal Personality of International Non-Governmental Organisations, CoE, European Treaty Series no. 124. See also Guidelines for Participation by Civil Society Organizations in OAS, CP/RES. 759 (1217/99) para. 2.

not a paradox where NGOs are expected to operate formally within a system that may be deeply hostile to their very existence.

3.4.2   Human Rights NGOs

Broadly speaking, human rights organisations include any NGO that commits itself to promoting and/or protecting human rights. The ultimately rights-oriented nature of their mandate distinguishes human rights NGOs from related NGOs, such as those working in the humanitarian, development or environmental field. However, such distinctions can be somewhat artificial, as some of these NGOs may equally engage in human rights activities, either directly or indirectly. An example is the organisation Médecins Sans Frontières, which provides humanitarian services but also documents human rights violations (*témoignage* = bearing witness), an approach that has brought it into conflict with governments when operating in conflict zones, such as Darfur.[33]

Many human rights NGOs initially replicated the separation found in the International Bill of Human Rights between civil and political rights on the one hand and economic, social and cultural rights on the other.[34] Amnesty International (AI), for example, began in the 1960s with a mandate to protect peaceful political prisoners.[35] Following sustained demands for a change in focus that would enable it to respond to the multifaceted nature of human rights violations worldwide, the organisation decided in 2001 to broaden its mandate to include economic, social and cultural rights. This reflects a strong pull towards a broader mandate, as constituencies expect the weight of an organisation to be used to address a range of problems, which may, however, come at the expense of heightened efficacy. At AI this change was characterised by at times heated debates between its members, many of whom were concerned that it would jeopardise what they viewed as the core function of the organisation.[36]

These debates illustrate the difficulties related to mandates, which are at the core of an NGO's identity. The mandate circumscribes what an NGO should be doing and thereby defines its profile. It may be broad or very specific, and may

---

[33] Médecins Sans Frontières, *The Crushing Burden of Rape: Sexual Violence in Darfur* (2005), online at www.doctorswithoutborders.org/sites/usa/files/sudan03.pdf; 'Second Arrest in Sudan; Dutch Coordinator For MSF in Darfur Held This Morning' (31 May 2005), online at www.doctorswithoutborders.org/news-stories/press-release/second-arrest-sudan-dutch-coordinator-msf-darfur-held-morning.

[34] See M. Mutua, 'Standard Setting in Human Rights: Critique and Prognosis' (2007) 29 *Human Rights Quarterly* 547, at 592–3.

[35] See P. Benenson, 'The Forgotten Prisoners' *The Guardian* (28 May 1961), www.theguardian.com/uk/1961/may/28/fromthearchive.theguardian.

[36] S. Hopgood, *Keepers of the Flame: Understanding Amnesty International* (Cornell University Press, 2006) 92–6, 181–8.

cover all types of human rights, a certain category of rights,[37] or specific rights, such as freedom from torture;[38] or certain groups, such as children's rights[39] or minority rights.[40] NGOs may be associated with a particular area of expertise, or even specific projects at times, such as the Association for the Prevention of Torture with the campaign for the adoption of the Optional Protocol to the Convention against Torture (OPCAT).[41] A shift in the nature of violations, political realities or funding opportunities may tempt NGOs to broaden their mandate, either explicitly or de facto. However, such a move frequently creates tensions within (between the 'old guard' and reformers) and may even weaken an NGO where it compromises what are seen as its core strengths.

Human rights NGOs are also sometimes characterised by their organisational set-up, particularly whether or not they function as membership organisations, or described according to their modus operandi, i.e. advocacy, policy-making, capacity-building, legal, etc.[42] This may be useful for a better understanding of the approach taken by the NGO in question; however, what matters for NGOs in practice is that they are able to identify and use the strategies that are most effective to achieve their objectives. In terms of their territorial reach, national NGOs frequently link with external actors and use the international arena to bring about domestic change,[43] while international NGOs for their part often work at the national level to strengthen domestic protection efforts and achieve thematic objectives, such as campaigning for the abolition of the death penalty where it still exists.

3.4.3   Assessing the Role of Human Rights NGOs

NGOs have become major players at various levels. Nationally, they have often been at the forefront of campaigns that resulted in reforms, such as in respect of sexual violence in Southern African countries,[44] and as strategic

[37] See e.g., the Center for Economic and Social Rights, www.cesr.org.
[38] These include organisations such as Amnesty International, Association for the Prevention of Torture (APT), International Federation of ACAT (Action by Christians for the Abolition of Torture; FIACAT), International Rehabilitation Council for Torture Victims (IRCT), REDRESS, and World Organisation Against Torture (OMCT).
[39] See for regional examples, the Africawide Movement for Children, www.africawide movement.org.
[40] See Minority Rights Group International, www.minorityrights.org.
[41] www.apt.ch.
[42] See for a good overview of the nature of NGOs and their activities, International Council on Human Rights Policy (ICHRP), *Human Rights Organisations: Rights and Responsibilities*, Final Draft Report (2009) paras. 12–28.
[43] Keck and Sikkink, above note 4. See also Case Study 3.1 below.
[44] See R. Manjoo, G. Kweka and S. O. Ofuani, 'Sexual Violence and the Law: Comparative Legislative Experiences in Selected South African Countries', in L. Oette (ed.), *Criminal Law Reform and Transitional Justice: Human Rights Perspectives for Sudan* (Ashgate, 2011) 269–95.

litigators, as was the case with the right to food in India.[45] Regionally and internationally, NGOs have been pivotal in using available treaty and charter bodies and in developing standards, such as women's rights coalitions campaigning for the adoption of the African Protocol on the Rights of Women, as well as the coalitions for an anti-landmine treaty and the International Criminal Court (ICC) Rome Statute.[46] Successful collaboration of national and international NGOs and other actors gives credibility to the boomerang theory, according to which national actors utilise supranational fora to exert pressure on governments and bring about change.[47] It also plays a part in the context of the spiral theory, where NGOs form part of the forces that lead states to move from denial to accommodation, and, ideally, compliance.[48]

The increasing power and influence wielded by NGOs has raised a number of questions about their nature and work, as well as their role as political actors, which centre on legitimacy, accountability and effectiveness.[49] Legitimacy refers to the supposed democracy deficit of NGOs. While NGOs themselves draw legitimacy from their cause, others have questioned whether 'self-appointed groups [are] an adequate substitute for mass movements'.[50]

---

[45] In 2001, the People's Union for Civil Liberties launched ground-breaking public interest litigation on behalf of starving people before India's Supreme Court on the right to food. The Supreme Court held that the Indian government had a direct responsibility to prevent starvation. It ordered that the country's food stocks be used without delay to prevent hunger and starvation and that all the food-based schemes across India be fully implemented. See *People's Union for Civil Liberties* v. *Union of India & Ors* (India) (2003).

[46] See Mutua, above note 34, 589–604; F. Banda, *Women, Law and Human Rights: An African Perspective* (Hart, 2005) 66–78; International Campaign to Ban Landmines, www.icbl.org; F. Faulkner, *Moral Entrepreneurs and the Campaign to Ban Landmines* (Rodopi, 2007); and for a critical perspective, K. Anderson, 'The Ottawa Convention Banning Landmines, the Role of International Non-governmental Organizations and the Idea of International Civil Society' (2000) 11 *European Journal of International Law* 91. See also M. Glasius, *The International Criminal Court: A Global Civil Society Achievement* (Routledge, 2006).

[47] See Keck and Sikkink, above note 4.

[48] See T. Risse, S. C. Ropp and K. Sikkink (eds.), *The Power of Human Rights: International Norms and Domestic Change* (Cambridge University Press, 1998); T. Risse, S. C. Ropp and K. Sikkink (eds.), *The Persistent Power of Human Rights: From Commitment to Compliance* (Cambridge University Press, 2013), particularly T. Risse and S. C. Rope, 'Introduction and Overview', 3–25.

[49] P. J. Spiro, 'NGOs and Human Rights: Channels of Power', in S. Joseph and A. McBeth (eds.), *Research Handbook on International Human Rights Law* (Edward Elgar, 2010) 115–38; M. T. Kamminga, 'The Evolving Status of NGOs under International Law: A Threat to the Inter-State System?', in P. Alston (ed.), *Non-State Actors and Human Rights* (Oxford University Press, 2005) 93–112; H. Slim, *By What Authority? The Legitimacy and Accountability of Non-governmental Organisations* (ICHRP, 2002); Mutua, above note 34, 604–19.

[50] R. Pinkney, *NGOs, Africa and the Global Order* (Palgrave Macmillan, 2009), back cover and Introduction, 1–10.

The answer may be 'no', but it must equally be recognised that the growth of NGOs corresponds with the demise of political ideologies and mass movements and is an effect rather than the cause of that demise. Indeed, it is notable that many of those who were active in party politics in a number of countries later became actively engaged in NGOs as an alternative form of politics. NGOs therefore represent a specific form of public engagement. They may be, and often are, a part of social or mass movements. Moreover, an NGO may derive legitimacy from the nature of its engagement and representation, which applies particularly to membership organisations. In the field of human rights NGOs are presumed to act in the broader public interest. This is particularly the case where they seek the protection of rights that have been widely recognised. However, even where an NGO acts as a pressure group for rights not (yet) recognised, its work can be considered as an integral part of a pluralistic society.

A further critique of NGOs concerns their composition and mode of operation. NGOs are often seen as professional elites who interact with other elites and, while claiming to represent marginalised persons or groups, 'are very different from the people they seek to save'.[51] This criticism, which is seemingly directed at certain types of NGOs, draws on notions of voluntarism and grassroots self-organisation where people take action either as a matter of principle or to pursue a common cause. While this type of commitment constitutes an ideal, some interventions such as complex litigation are time-consuming and require considerable professional skills. Nevertheless, the critique highlights the risk that NGOs may become too self-referential and concerned with project cycles and the careers of their members rather than the well-being of those they claim to represent or whose cause they purport to advance.

At the international level, NGOs may develop a self-righteousness that is divorced from the realities on the ground, an accusation that has been repeatedly levelled against major international human rights NGOs.[52] This is seemingly illustrated by the fact that it is often highly educated Western elites who travel and speak on behalf of persons or groups with whom they have little in common or only limited contact.[53] These actors are viewed as carriers of Western bias, or even neo-imperialism, who, even with the best of intentions, advance liberal notions and objectives that may set false

[51] See M. Mutua, *Human Rights: A Political and Cultural Critique* (University of Pennsylvania Press, 2002) 36–7.

[52] See on the role of international NGOs as 'Missionaries or Imperialists?', Pinkney, above note 50, 157–83. See on the problem of 'human rights messengers' from the 'West' (state functionaries, development planners and programmers) and their 'evangelical claim', Baxi, above note 1, 34–6.

[53] D. Kennedy, 'The International Human Rights Movement: Part of the Problem' (2002) 15 *Harvard Human Rights Journal* 101, at 121.

priorities,[54] such as focusing on civil and political rights violations instead of the adverse impact of globalisation. National NGOs collaborating with international NGOs are in this scheme of things frequently elite beneficiaries who are not genuinely representative of the people and may not be interested in addressing deep-seated structural problems.[55] These problems are compounded by the way NGOs are funded where they rely on external donor funding that often comes from Western governments or intergovernmental bodies.[56] This means that funds may be used to advance certain foreign policy goals, create dependency and open the door to corruption.

The issue of corruption leads on to the question of accountability.[57] It is increasingly seen as contradictory and ironic that NGOs frequently call for transparency and accountability, but may seemingly be unable or unwilling to follow such standards themselves.[58] This has become particularly acute given the potential for abuse inherent in the power of NGOs in relation to the framing of critical issues and resources, as well as individuals and groups of persons whom they claim to represent or interact with. Many NGOs have recognised that accountability is imperative to maintaining their credibility, which is their major asset, both in terms of garnering public support for their positions and obtaining funds. Transparency is also critical to counter-attacks by governments and others that may wrongly accuse NGOs of misconduct, often as a pretext for banning national NGOs or expelling/preventing entry of international NGOs or undermining their work more generally. NGOs have therefore taken a number of initiatives to affirm their responsibility and take appropriate action, for example in the form of codes of conduct and the international NGO Accountability Charter,[59] with a view to ensuring respect for human rights in their own work and striving for best practices in relation to governance, effectiveness, independence, truthfulness and transparency vis-à-vis their various constituencies.[60] These are important first steps that signal a shift from NGOs as 'moral' forces to political actors who must not only say that they do good but also demonstrate that this is actually the case.

Effectiveness essentially concerns the question of whether NGOs are doing what they are supposed to be doing, whether they are doing it well and

---

[54] Ibid., 114–16. See also Mutua, above note 51, 39–70.

[55] Banda, above note 46, 289–91; Mutua, above note 34, 593.

[56] See N. Banks, D. Hulme and M. Edwards, 'NGOs, States and Donors Revisited: Still too close for comfort?' (2015) 66 *World Development* 707.

[57] The ICHRP prefers the term responsibility. See ICHRP, above note 42, para. 83.

[58] See for a brief overview, ibid., paras. 79–82. See also J. McGann and M. Johnstone, 'The Power Shift and the NGO Credibility Crisis' (2006) 8 *International Journal of Not-for-Profit Law* 65; M. Marschall, 'Legitimacy and Effectiveness: Civil Society Organizations Role in Good Governance', *Transparency International*, 1 November 2002.

[59] See www.ingoaccountabilitycharter.org.   [60] ICHRP, above note 42, paras. 132–206.

whether they have the intended impact. This is critical for NGOs' legitimacy. In other words, are their claims in respect of any of these points justified? Unlike companies or political parties who (ideally) face the judgement of the market or the electorate respectively, NGOs report back to their donors or their members, where applicable. Beyond this, it is often difficult to tell to what degree an NGO has been effective. Many NGOs undertake evaluations, which can be a useful tool, especially where they are carried out throughout project cycles and with the active participation of beneficiaries.[61] However, while some NGOs may be able to point to successes, such as the adoption of the Rome Statute in the case of the Coalition for the ICC, the long-term nature of their work, for example advocating reforms in repressive regimes, frequently makes it difficult, if not impossible, to identify tangible impacts. These realities call for a nuanced assessment of what constitutes effectiveness, including such broad notions as creating rights awareness, which is ideally based on considerable empirical work where researchers chart the impact of NGOs' human rights work over a substantial period of time.[62]

The criticism levelled against NGOs can act as a healthy mirror to counteract complacency or self-congratulatory attitudes. Questions of legitimacy deficit, limited accountability, concern over effectiveness and unequal power relationships between national and international NGOs are all too real. However, it is important not to lose sight of the fact that a large number of NGOs respond to genuine problems and needs and frequently play a critical role in opening political space. The uprisings in the Arab world in 2010 and 2011, for example, showed that NGOs had forged close links with bloggers, youth movements and other political actors, and were often part and parcel of developments rather than constituting aloof elites.[63] While unequal power relationships between international and national NGOs remain, which often reflect global realities more generally, national and regional NGOs in the Americas, Africa and Asia have taken innovative approaches and made considerable progress in developing their capacity. This is changing the international dynamics towards a more pluralistic approach. Western-based international NGOs are often still dominant because they are close to the centres of power and are frequently better resourced (though they have equally suffered from reduced funding made available in the wake of the global economic crisis and a growing demand for regionalisation if not

---

[61] See e.g., C. Thomas, 'Evaluation at Minority Rights Group' (2009) 1 *Journal of Human Rights Practice* 488.

[62] Ibid.

[63] See Interview 1.1 with Moataz El Fegiery; L. Al-Zubaidi, 'Digital Activism: Arabs Can Do It Themselves: Interview with Sami Ben Gharbia', in (2011) 2 *Perspectives: Political Analysis and Commentary from the Middle East, Special Issue: People's Power: The Arab World in Revolt* 86.

localisation). However, there is an increased realisation that the legitimacy of NGOs demands more substantial equality, which is also reflected in the debates and decisions made by international NGOs.[64] None the less, there remains a risk that international NGOs unduly dictate what is best and how things are done. What is needed, therefore, is a self-reflective practice of how best to join forces based on a spirit of mutual respect and solidarity.

3.5   HUMAN RIGHTS DEFENDERS

'Human rights defenders' is a broad term that is not confined to NGOs with an explicit human rights mandate or 'human rights activists', but includes 'individuals, groups and associations ... contributing to ... the effective elimination of all violations of human rights and fundamental freedoms of peoples and individuals'.[65] The category therefore reflects realities in which anyone can defend human rights irrespective of his/her/their profession, which captures the multiple efforts by individuals and groups around the world.[66] While there is no need for formal recognition, according to the Office of the High Commissioner for Human Rights (OHCHR), human rights defenders have certain responsibilities, and therefore need to accept the universality of human rights, defend human rights and do so peacefully.[67] The notion of human rights defenders derives its importance from the fact that it has been endorsed by the UN and entails a set of rights and obligations, as well as protection mechanisms. NGO advocacy and UN concern resulted in the 1998 UN Declaration on Human Rights Defenders adopted by consensus by the UN General Assembly (UNGA).[68] Significantly, this resolution, which was motivated by the desire to give legitimacy to the work of human rights defenders and to enhance protection, recognises that '[e]veryone has the right, individually and in association with others, to promote and to strive for the protection and realization of human rights and fundamental freedoms at the national and international levels'. It constitutes an important recognition of

---

[64] Hopgood, above note 36, 161–75.

[65] Declaration on the Right and Responsibility of Individuals, Groups and Organs of Society to Promote and Protect Universally Recognized Human Rights and Fundamental Freedoms, UNGA resolution 53/144 (8 March 1999). See also Commentary on the Declaration, July 2011, online at www.ohchr.org/Documents/Issues/Defenders/CommentarytoDeclarationon defendersJuly2011.pdf.

[66] See on the status of a human rights defender, which was contested by the respondent state in that case, *Human Rights Defender et al.* v. *Guatemala* (IACtHR) (2014) paras. 125–32.

[67] OHCHR, *Human Rights Defenders: Protecting the Right to Defend Human Rights*, Fact Sheet No. 29 (2004) 9–10.

[68] Ibid. See also Mutua, above note 34, 564–5.

the valuable work done by human rights defenders and identifies a number of existing rights and corresponding duties of states, which have undoubtedly been formulated with a view to countering practices that states have used to restrict the work of human rights defenders. The declaration's rights are largely based on the freedom of expression, assembly and association, including the right to 'form, join and participate in non-governmental organizations, associations or groups'. The declaration also addresses prerequisites for human rights work, such as the right to receive funds, including from abroad, and to engage in activities such as advocacy, trial observation and complaints, as well as the right to an effective remedy and protection.

The protection of human rights defenders has become a major concern. Defenders have been increasingly subjected to harassment, threats, arbitrary arrest, detention and unfair trials, various forms of ill-treatment and extrajudicial killings. There are numerous examples where those who bear witness to human rights violations and/or seek to counter them have themselves been targeted.[69] This applies in particular to sensitive cases where individuals or organisations collect evidence that may expose corrupt practices, jeopardise business interests (of both government and non-state actors) and contribute to criminal prosecutions. Cases in point are the suspicious death in custody, allegedly as a result of ill-treatment, of the Russian lawyer Sergei Magnitsky who had investigated a major tax fraud implicating several officials; the killing in Sri Lanka of Lasantha Wickrematunge, a well-known investigative journalist whose newspaper had run a series of articles about human rights violations;[70] and the murder of human rights defender Jesús María Valle Jaramillo in Colombia after having 'actively denounced the crimes perpetrated by paramilitary elements, as well as the collaboration and acquiescence between the latter and members of the National Army'.[71] The arbitrary arrests and unfair trials

---

[69] Report of the Special Rapporteur on the situation of human rights defenders, Addendum: Summary of Cases Transmitted to Governments and Replies Received, UN doc. A/HRC/16/44/ Add.1 (28 February 2011); IACHR, Report on the Situation of Human Rights Defenders in the Americas, OEA/Ser.L/V/II.124, doc. 5 rev. 1 (7 March 2006); IACHR, *Second Report on the Situation of Human Rights Defenders in the Americas*, OEA/Ser.L/V/II, doc. 66 (31 December 2011).

[70] See, REDRESS, 'Allegation letter regarding Mr Sergei Magnitsky (Russian Federation)' (21 December 2010), online at www.redress.org/case-docket/ allegation-letter-to-un-special-rapporteurs-on-torture-and-on-the-independence-of-thejudiciary-and-; L. Wickrematunge, 'And Then They Came for Me' *Sunday Leader* (11 January 2009) (editorial published after his killing), at www.thesundayleader.lk/20090111/ editorial-.htm.

[71] *Valle Jaramillo* v. *Colombia* (IACtHR) (2008) para. 73. See also *Human Rights Defender et al.* v. *Guatemala*, paras. 130–2, which concerned the killings of a community activist who had engaged in activities to promote a series of rights and of an activist engaged in the promotion of union rights, the right to truth and women's rights.

resulting in the execution of Ken Saro Wiwa and other Ogoni people who had fought against the ills of oil exploration during Nigeria's dictatorship in the 1990s is another infamous example of an egregious violation.[72] Those who protest on behalf of indigenous peoples, ethnic minorities or other marginalised groups, such as women's rights or LGBTI groups, have also been under attack, as illustrated by the killing of the Ugandan gay rights activist David Kato in 2011.[73] Foreign nationals may equally be targeted and states have resorted to questioning, threats and expulsion of international NGO members, human rights activists and UN staff members whose presence has attracted unwelcome attention to their human rights record.[74] Human rights defenders are also increasingly at risk of reprisals from non-state actors, such as the Islamic State.[75]

The UN has responded to these developments by establishing the position of Special Representative of the UN Secretary-General on Human Rights Defenders in 2000, which was later replaced by the UN Special Rapporteur on the situation of human rights defenders in 2008.[76] The Special Rapporteur has identified a number of developments of concern and exercises an important protective function where human rights defenders are at risk. Dialogue with governments and others is critical to prevent violations but may often not be sufficient, in which case it becomes crucial to react promptly to serious threats. The UN and others have advocated putting in place mechanisms to help in a quick and informal way where human rights defenders face adverse repercussions, such as by granting visa exemptions. These efforts have been complemented by European Union (EU)/Council of Europe (CoE) initiatives to support human rights defenders in the region and beyond.[77] However,

---

[72] See *International Pen and Others* v. *Nigeria* (ACmHPR) (1998).

[73] N. Pillay, UN High Commissioner for Human Rights, 'What David Kato's Death can Teach the World' (1 February 2011), online at www.ohchr.org/en/NewsEvents/Pages/DisplayNews.aspx?NewsID=10750&LangID=E.

[74] See e.g., the measures taken against NGOs in Sudan, Report of the Special Rapporteur on the situation of human rights defenders, Addendum: Summary of Cases Transmitted to Governments and Replies Received, UN doc. A/HRC/13/22/Add.1 (24 February 2010) paras. 2114–18.

[75] See e.g., FrontLineDefenders, 'Iraq-Human rights lawyer Samira Saleh Al-Naimi abducted and killed by ISIS' (26 September 2014), www.frontlinedefenders.org/node/27353.

[76] See www.ohchr.org/EN/Issues/SRHRDefenders/Pages/SRHRDefendersIndex.aspx. See also IACHR, Rapporteurship on Human Rights Defenders, http://oas.org/en/iachr/defenders/default.asp, and ACmHPR, Special Rapporteur on human rights defenders, www.achpr.org/mechanisms/human-rights-defenders.

[77] See EU Delegation to the UN, EU Council Conclusions on the 10th Anniversary of EU Guidelines on Human Rights Defenders (23 June 2014), http://eu-un.europa.eu/articles/en/article_15216_en.htm.

there are limits to the level of protection various official actors can provide in practice and human rights defenders themselves are increasingly using innovative strategies and are taking precautionary measures to minimise the risk.[78] There are now an increasing number of NGOs and networks, such as Protection International,[79] whose principal mandate is to provide protection to human rights defenders.[80]

Beyond the issue of protection, human rights defenders, particularly NGOs, continue to be subjected to a barrage of restrictive practices aimed at controlling their work. In early 2010, several NGOs expressed their concerns at attempts made by several states in the UN Human Rights Council (HRC) to narrow the definition of human rights defenders and 'better' regulate their work so as to avoid the 'political abuse' of NGO status and 'evasion of national laws'.[81] These attempts, which were ultimately unsuccessful, illustrate the atmosphere of distrust and hostility in which many human rights defenders have to operate. While some human rights defenders are reported to have engaged in questionable practices, including corruption, the thrust of the latest debate is clearly directed against the right to challenge state practices recognised in the UN Declaration on Human Rights Defenders, which is still anathema to many governments. None the less, some states have adopted laws for the protection of human rights defenders, and the HRC and the UNGA have responded by reiterating the need for protection, including of women human rights defenders.[82]

---

[78] See E. Nesossi, 'Political Opportunities in Non-democracies: The Case of Chinese *weiquan* lawyers' (2015) 19 *The International Journal of Human Rights* 961; F. Van der Vet and L. Lyytikäinen, 'Violence and Human Rights in Russia: How Human Rights Defenders Develop their Tactics in the Face of Danger, 2005–2013' (2015) 19 *The International Journal of Human Rights* 979.

[79] See www.protectioninternational.org. See also www.frontlinedefenders.org, and for a regional initiative, the East and Horn of Africa Human Rights Defenders Project, www.defenddefenders.org.

[80] See on the issue of protection more broadly, REDRESS, *Ending Threats and Reprisals against Victims of Torture and Related International Crimes: A Call to Action* (2009).

[81] On 23 March 2010, a joint NGO statement expressed alarm at attempts during the negotiations to selectively quote from, rewrite, or restrict the clear provisions of the Declaration on Human Rights Defenders in order to regulate the work of NGOs and restrict protection only to those working on issues that governments had accepted or agreed with. See www.forum-asia.org/2010/100323-HRC13-FA-Joint-Item8-GD-re%20 HRD%20draft%20resolution-FINAL.pdf.

[82] Human Rights Council, *Protecting Human Rights Defenders*, UN doc. A/HRC/22/L.13 (15 March 2013); UN General Assembly, *Protecting Women Human Rights Defenders* (30 January 2014). See also the list of measures that the IACtHR set out for the respondent state to implement an effective policy for the protection of human rights defenders, *Human Rights Defender et al.* v. *Guatemala*, paras. 263–4.

CASE STUDY 3.1
NGOs and Human Rights Protection in Sudan

After its military coup in 1989, the Sudanese regime embarked on a crackdown against civil society activists and political opposition characterised by serious human rights violations, including a wave of bans, arbitrary arrests and detention, unfair trials, torture and extrajudicial killings.[1] Throughout the 1990s any work related to human rights inside Sudan was extremely difficult due to the prevailing repressive atmosphere. Later, in 2001 and 2002, lawyers, doctors and journalists were able to establish two human rights organisations in Sudan, the Khartoum Centre for Human Rights and Environmental Development and the Amal (Hope) Centre for the Rehabilitation of Victims of Torture, which operated closely with a London-based organisation of Sudanese victims in exile. While the Khartoum Centre engaged in legal aid litigation and advocacy, the Amal Centre provided – for the first time in Sudan – regular specialised treatment for victims of violations, including for victims of rape in Darfur after 2004.

The centres quickly gained in reputation, due to a combination of the capacity of their staff and their ability to monitor human rights violations and to reach out to a broad network inside Sudan and internationally. This development, taking place against the backdrop of the conflict in Darfur characterised by massive violations and political changes following the North–South peace agreement in 2005, brought with it a series of opportunities and challenges. There were only few human rights organisations in Sudan with some capacity, which meant that international organisations were keen to work with the centres and donors were eager to fund a broad range of activities. As a result, the Khartoum Centre and the Amal Centre, particularly in Darfur, had to cope with increasing demand that stretched their own capacities.

These developments also left the centres vulnerable to corruption and security interference, with one leading staff member accused of having misused considerable sums of money and of reporting back to the Sudanese security services about internal affairs. The staff and the centres' network came under increasing pressure in the form of repeated arrests, interrogation, raids of meetings and other measures, some of which had been sanctioned by a newly enacted law, the Organisation of Humanitarian and Voluntary Work Act 2006, which allowed the authorities greater control over the growing number of human rights NGOs. This situation deteriorated following the application for an arrest warrant for Sudan's President al-Bashir by the ICC Prosecutor in July 2008. According to a complaint brought before, and upheld by the African Commission on Human and Peoples' Rights (ACmHPR), two human rights defenders associated with the Khartoum Centre were tortured in November 2008 and its then director was threatened with torture.[2] Amid further threats

---

[1] See *Amnesty International and Others* v. *Sudan* (ACmHPR) (1999).
[2] *Monim Elgak, Osman Hummeida and Amir Suliman* v. *Sudan* (ACmHPR) (2014).

the key staff members decided to leave the country and the Centre was closed down by the authorities, who froze its accounts and confiscated the Centre's belongings, including its extensive human rights library, notwithstanding the presence of UNMIS, the UN Mission in Sudan, in Khartoum. Other organisations suffered a similar fate while some NGOs and individuals were able to continue their human rights work in an extremely repressive environment. The story of the Khartoum Centre and the Amal Centre, which played a critical role in documenting and monitoring violations and providing legal and medical support to victims in the period 2001–2009, demonstrates the often fragile position of national NGOs and their members. They must frequently work in situations where there is a need to respond to serious human rights violations and to interact with a range of national, regional and international actors while at the same time building their own capacity, ensuring the effective functioning of the organisation and navigating a repressive political environment. National NGOs may in such situations overreach themselves, and their members or associates may risk losing touch with local realities where they have easy access to money and are fêted internationally; international actors, such as other NGOs and donors, for their part need to be careful not to inadvertently encourage corruption or exposure of national human rights defenders to security threats because their ability to protect individuals or organisations from harm or closure may be limited.

POINTS TO CONSIDER

1. To what extent does the story of the Khartoum Centre and the Amal Centre bear out concerns that have been raised about the relationship between national NGOs and international actors?

2. What violations of the UN Declaration on Human Rights Defenders are evident in the case study?

3. Are developments in Sudan exceptional or do they raise generic concerns that illustrate the need to make the international system pertaining to the work of human rights defenders, particularly NGOs, more effective?

3.6   LEGAL PROFESSIONALS AND HUMAN RIGHTS

The broad definition of human rights defenders rightly suggests that the promotion and protection of human rights is not the domain of any particular type of actor or profession. Nevertheless, it is clear that the legal profession plays an important role, both in the development of standards and their practical application. The dominance of lawyers and the supposedly increasingly legalistic approach to human rights has been lamented but constitutes a reality that is perhaps inevitable, at least as far as the growth of and recourse to international human rights *law* is concerned.

The legal profession comprises lawyers, judges, prosecutors, legal advisors, academics and others who may pursue rather different objectives and approaches in respect of human rights. Indeed, they are often pitted against each other. What unites them is that they typically use the law to argue for or against the recognition, or particular interpretation, of human rights, or responsibility for a breach in a given instance. Unsurprisingly, legal professionals have been both at the forefront of the human rights movement, for example the International Commission of Jurists,[83] and at the heart of repressive regimes that ignore the rule of law and violate human rights. There is a long list of legal officials, attorney generals and judges who have effectively served as handmaidens of regimes. This has included drafting infamous laws that are blatantly discriminatory or providing for broad powers and/or punishments that serve as a recipe for human rights violations.[84] It has also consisted in politically motivated prosecutions, staging of show trials and/or handing down clearly disproportionate punishments. The role of legal professionals was particularly notorious in the Soviet Union under Stalin and in Nazi Germany, with the Prosecutor-General Andrey Vyshinsky and the judge of the Nazi Peoples' Court Roland Freisler representing two particularly infamous prototypes.[85] In a number of countries, judges have failed to uphold human rights, for example by imposing the death penalty after blatantly unfair trials.[86] Legal professionals, such as US legal advisors in the context of the so-called War on Terror, have tried to reinterpret human rights law so as to justify practices that amounted to violations, in this instance of the prohibition of torture.[87] Notably, academics have at times sought to lend a degree of credibility to such endeavours.[88]

---

[83] See www.icj.org.

[84] This observation applies to virtually any regime that enacts such legislation. See for a particularly pertinent example, the role of jurists in Nazi Germany, I. Müller, *Hitler's Justice: The Courts of the Third Reich* (Harvard University Press, 1992); A. E. Steinweis and R. D. Rachlin (eds.), *The Law in Nazi Germany: Ideology, Opportunism, and the Perversion of Justice* (Berghahn Books, 2013). See on resistance by German Jewish lawyers, L. Oette, 'Document and Analyze: The Legacy of Klemperer, Fraenkel, and Neumann for Contemporary Human Rights Engagement' (2017) 39 *Human Rights Quarterly* 832.

[85] Müller ibid.; A. Vaksberg, *Stalin's Prosecutor: The Life of Andrei Vyshinsky* (Grove, Weidenfeld, 1991).

[86] See for an excellent study of how the legal system and the judiciary were employed in Sudan to prop up the then Nimeri regime, which resulted in the execution of the 'Sudanese Muslim reformer', Mahmoud Muhammad Taha, in 1983, A. A. An-Na'im, 'The Islamic Law of Apostasy and its Modern Applicability: A Case Study from Sudan' (1986) 16 *Religion* 197.

[87] See in particular, P. Sands, *Torture Team: Rumsfeld's Memo and the Betrayal of American Values* (Palgrave Macmillan, 2008).

[88] See e.g., J. Addicott, 'No Torture, No Prosecution' *Opinio Juris* (8 May 2009). See also the account of a journalist who, after his position on the acceptability of interrogation methods was challenged, voluntarily underwent waterboarding: C. Hitchens, 'Believe Me, It's Torture' *Vanity Fair* (August 2008).

While law is a contested sphere, i.e. actors have different views on how to interpret rights and obligations depending on their standpoint, the realm of acceptability is arguably left behind where an overwhelming body of opinion strongly rejects the arguments put forward. This is particularly the case where the legal professionals concerned are aware that their arguments legitimise violence for political ends. In noteworthy contrast, many legal professionals have taken a stance to defend human rights. Examples include lawyers who provide legal assistance, often pro bono (free of charge), in politically sensitive cases, legally oriented NGOs using advocacy and legal avenues to bring about broader changes or hold perpetrators of violations accountable, or a combination of actors, for example when pursuing Pinochet in Spain and the United Kingdom (UK).[89] Legal professionals are increasingly using the media or journalistic methods to reach a broad audience when contesting particular practices, such as in respect of violations alleged to have been committed in the war against terrorism and in the course of armed conflicts in Afghanistan and Iraq.[90] Professional bodies, such as bar associations, can also play an important role, though they often work in repressive environments where they either lack independence or find it difficult to engage effectively in human rights work. Nevertheless, some associations, such as in Pakistan, have taken prominent action in defence of the independence of the judiciary, protesting and successfully calling for the reinstatement of Chief Justice Muhammad Chaudhry, who had, in their view, been unfairly dismissed by the then President Musharraf in 2007.[91]

Legal officials are often pivotal to human rights protection, particularly during transitional periods or where a government with a strong commitment to human rights, or at least certain rights, is in power. Their role is particularly important where they stand up to human rights violations. However, as the targeting of magistrates and ombudsmen in countries such as Colombia demonstrates,[92] it is clear that their room for manoeuvre is limited where there is a lack of protection, particularly where high-ranking officials or influential individuals are implicated in human rights violations.

---

[89] See in particular, A. Dorfman, *Exorcising Terror: The Incredible Unending Trial of General Augusto Pinochet* (Seven Stories Press, 2002) 32; N. Roht-Arriaza, *The Pinochet Effect: Transnational Justice in the Age of Human Rights* (University of Pennsylvania Press, 2006) 208.

[90] E.g. Phil Shiner of Public Interest Lawyers, in the *Baha Mousa* case. See also Sands, above note 87.

[91] See Notes, 'The Pakistani Lawyers' Movement and the Popular Currency of Judicial Power' (2010) 123 *Harvard Law Review* 1705; International Bar Association, *The Struggle to Maintain an Independent Judiciary: A Report on the Attempt to Remove the Chief Justice of Pakistan* (2007).

[92] See Report of the Special Rapporteur on the situation of human rights defenders, Mission to Colombia, UN doc. A/HRC/13/22/Add.3 (4 March 2010).

The role of judges in human rights protection has been widely acknowledged. Indeed, judges themselves have repeatedly affirmed their responsibility in this regard.[93] There are numerous examples of judges at the national, regional and international level who have applied and consciously developed the scope of international human rights law, including in politically tense contexts such as counter-terrorism policies in the UK.[94] One of the most remarkable examples of judicial activism in this regard is public interest litigation in South Asia, particularly India, where Indian judges relaxed the rules of standing and interpreted fundamental rights broadly so as to protect human rights more effectively.[95] This has resulted in an impressive body of jurisprudence but limited changes on the ground due to lack of enforcement, which highlights the limits of the law as a tool for social change where judicial and political forces are not in agreement.

A number of academics working in the field of human rights have close links with NGOs and/or litigate human rights cases.[96] Several universities run human rights centres and clinics that often provide valuable research and have carried out important work to support advocacy and litigation efforts.[97] Universities also provide a forum for discourse and nurture new generations of human rights scholars and activists. However, due to repressive environments and resource constraints, it is often universities in Western countries that can provide such opportunities, including for overseas students, thereby reinforcing existing divides. Nevertheless, efforts are being made around the world to establish centres that provide local spaces and respond to regional if not wider concerns, and it will be important to support initiatives that are of lasting value in building a global community of human rights lawyers.[98]

---

[93] See e.g., the Bangalore Principles of Judicial Conduct, 2002, adopted by the Judicial Group on Strengthening Judicial Integrity, at the Round Table Meeting of Chief Justices held at the Peace Palace (The Hague, 25–26 November 2002).

[94] See in this regard, T. Bingham, *The Rule of Law* (Allen Lane, 2010) 133–59.

[95] See S. Deva, 'Public Interest Litigation in India: A Critical Review' (2009) 28 *Civil Justice Quarterly* 19.

[96] See Interview 6.2 with Bill Bowring.

[97] See e.g., the Centre for Human Rights of the Faculty of Law, University of Pretoria, which was established 'as part of domestic efforts against the apartheid system of the time' and has now 'positioned itself in an unmatched network of practising and academic lawyers, national and international civil servants and human rights practitioners across the entire continent, with a specific focus on human rights law in Africa, and international development law in general'. See www.chr.up.ac.za. See for a further example from Iran, M. M. Meghdadi and A. Erfani-Nasab, 'The Role of Legal Clinics of Law Schools in Human Rights Education: Mofid University Legal Clinic Experience' (2011) 15 *Procedia Social and Behavioral Sciences* 3014; on the US experience, D. R. Hurwitz, 'Lawyering for Justice and the Inevitability of International Human Rights Clinics' (2003) 28 *Yale Journal of International Law* 505; and in the UK, L. Welchman, 'The International Human Rights Clinic at SOAS', in A. Alemanno and L. Khadar (eds.), *Reinventing Legal Education: How Clinical Education Is Reforming the Teaching and Practice of Law in Europe* (Cambridge University Press, 2018) 247–71.

[98] See further F. S. Bloch (ed.) *The Global Clinical Movement: Educating Lawyers for Social Justice* (Oxford University Press, 2011).

3.7   HEALTH PROFESSIONALS AND HUMAN RIGHTS

Health professionals occupy a particularly sensitive position in respect of human rights. Their knowledge and skills can be used either to commit or facilitate violations or, alternatively, to document and respond to breaches, mitigate their consequences or, ideally, prevent them. Doctors and health professionals have been implicated in notorious violations, such as experiments and killings during the Holocaust,[99] and have assisted in the execution of the death penalty and torture.[100] It was not least in protest against the conduct of their professional colleagues that health professionals started engaging in efforts aimed at the protection of human rights. This has included providing treatment and rehabilitation to victims of serious violations,[101] and entailed developing tools, such as the Istanbul Protocol and the Minnesota Protocol, to document torture and extrajudicial killings respectively.[102] These are important instruments, as medical reports and forensic findings frequently constitute crucial evidence both in human rights cases and in criminal trials relating to human rights violations. Psychologists and psychiatrists also assess the consequences of violations for victims, families and communities at large,[103] and these can be highly valuable in legal proceedings, such as when determining adequate reparation measures.[104] Significantly, initiatives have not been confined to individuals. Health professionals have established and run important NGOs, such as Physicians for Human Rights,[105]

[99] H. H. Fryhofer, *The Nuremberg Medical Trial: The Holocaust and the Origin of the Nuremberg Medical Code* (Peter Lang, 2004); R. J. Lifton, *The Nazi Doctors: Medical Killing and the Psychology of Genocide* (Basic Books, 2000).

[100] See e.g., British Medical Association, *Medicine Betrayed: The Participation of Doctors in Human Rights Abuses* (Zed Books, 1992); S. Austin, *Report to the Special Committee of the Board of Directors of the American Psychology Association: Independent Review Relating to APA Ethical Guidelines, National Security Interrogations and Torture* (2 July 2015).

[101] See in particular the website of the International Rehabilitation Council for Torture Victims, www.irct.org, and the Dignity Danish Institute against Torture, https://dignityinstitute.org.

[102] 'Manual on the Effective Investigation and Documentation of Torture and Other Cruel, Inhuman or Degrading Treatment or Punishment (Istanbul Protocol)', submitted to the UN High Commissioner for Human Rights (9 August 1999), and Manual on the Effective Prevention and Investigation of Extra-legal, Arbitrary and Summary Executions, UN doc. E/ST/CSDHA/12 (1991), revised version, The Minnesota Protocol on the Investigation of Potentially Unlawful Death (2016).

[103] See e.g., D. Somasundaram, *Scarred Minds: The Psychological Impact of War on Sri Lankan Tamils* (Sage, 1998); S. Priebe et al., 'Experience of Human Rights Violations and Subsequent Mental Disorders: A Study Following the War in the Balkans' (2010) 71 *Social Science Medicine* 2170.

[104] See e.g., *Gutiérrez Soler* v. *Colombia* (IACtHR) (2005) para. 127(5).

[105] See www.physiciansforhumanrights.org.

and professional bodies have committed themselves to human rights standards. The World Medical Association, for example, has issued a number of
resolutions on the role and duties of health professionals in relation to particular situations and violations, including the duty to speak out against
violations.[106]

3.8   HUMAN RIGHTS FIELD OFFICERS

Human rights field operations have become an important component of
many UN, OHCHR, Organization of American States (OAS), African Union
(AU) or Organization for Security and Co-operation in Europe (OSCE) missions or programmes, which are typically mandated by resolutions or agreements with the host country.[107] While this practice is taken for granted today,
it is actually a fairly recent development that began in the early 1990s, with
the first deployment of human rights field workers to El Salvador (1991)
and then to Cambodia, Haiti and former Yugoslavia.[108] The mandate of missions differs depending on the situation, but several core areas of human
rights field work have been identified on the basis of surveys carried out
in 2004 and 2008, namely 'monitoring, reporting, advocacy/intervention,
capacity-building, engaging with humanitarian and development partners,
support to peace processes and transitional justice, in-mission sensitisa-
tion and participation in UN governance of transitional territories'.[109] In the
beginning, human rights field workers operated with limited guidance and
often in an ad hoc fashion. This was soon considered inadequate, if not outright irresponsible, because it could put both people in-country and human
rights field officers themselves at risk. For example, handing out question-
naires to detainees in Rwanda to report about their treatment is said to have
resulted in acts of retaliation against them because no precautions or protective measures had been taken by the human rights field officers at the time.[110]

---

[106] See e.g., Resolution on the Responsibility of Physicians in the Documentation and
Denunciation of Acts of Torture or Cruel or Inhuman or Degrading Treatment (54th
World Medical Association (WMA) General Assembly, September 2003 as amended by the
58th WMA General Assembly, October 2007); Resolution on Health and Human Rights
Abuses in Zimbabwe (58th WMA General Assembly, October 2007); Council Resolution on
Genocide in Darfur (176th WMA Council Session, May 2006); all online at www.wma.net.

[107] See B. G. Ramcharan (ed.), *Human Rights Protection in the Field* (Brill, 2006); M. O'Flaherty
(ed.), *The Human Rights Field Operation: Law, Theory and Practice* (Ashgate, 2007).

[108] See M. O'Flaherty and G. Ulrich, 'The Professional Identity and Development of Human
Rights Field Workers', in M. O'Flaherty and G. Ulrich (eds.), *The Professional Identity of
the Human Rights Field Worker* (Ashgate, 2010) 9–10.

[109] Ibid., 23.

[110] W. G. O'Neill, 'The Guiding Principles for Human Rights Field Officers Working in Conflict
and Post-Conflict Environments: A Commentary', in O'Flaherty and Ulrich, above note
108, 33–48, at 39.

The situation in mission countries is frequently characterised by a series of complex political, legal and practical challenges and the need to provide effective protection against ongoing violations. Operating in such environments requires a range of skills, necessitating increasing professionalism on the part of international and national officers. The Human Rights Law Centre of the University of Nottingham, together with several partners, took the initiative of drawing up two major documents that provide guidance on critical issues, namely the 2008 *Guiding Principles for Human Rights Officers Working in Conflict and Post-Conflict Environments* and the *Statement of Ethical Commitments of Human Rights Professionals*.[111] Both documents set out relevant principles in some detail and have proved useful tools. However, there are still concerns about the limited practical training and guidance that human rights field officers receive prior to deployment.[112] They often have to develop the relevant knowledge and skills on the job and make a number of difficult choices in what is typically a highly politicised and fluctuating environment, both within organisations and in the host country itself. This includes questions on how to respond to violations (effective protection without putting anyone at risk), engaging with authorities (having to rely on cooperation while being critical at the same time), and relating to civil society (which may not be responsive enough or too close – human rights operations may also weaken civil society by recruiting talented personnel). It also concerns ethical questions as to how human rights field officers relate to others, particularly vulnerable persons and victims of violations, and how they conduct themselves in the host country generally.[113] Beyond allegations of misconduct of individual officers forming part of broader concerns about abuses by UN personnel,[114] in-country missions can have other unintended impacts, such as inflating prices, and human rights officers frequently operate in and share a space of power imbalance vis-à-vis the majority of the population.

---

[111] Text can be found in O'Flaherty and Ulrich, above note 108, 419–39.

[112] J. Horowitz, 'OHCHR Pre-deployment Human Rights Training: Adapting to the Evolving Roles, Responsibilities, and Influence of UN Human Rights Officers' (2010) 2 *Journal of Human Rights Practice* 49.

[113] See Principle no. 10: 'Do No Harm', 2008 Guiding Principles.

[114] See UN Secretary-General, A Comprehensive Strategy to Eliminate Future Sexual Exploitation and Abuse in United Nations Peacekeeping Operations, UN doc. A/59/710 (24 March 2005); E. P. Flaherty and S. Hunt, 'Rule without Law: Injustice at the United Nations?' (April 2006) 21 *Geneva Post Quarterly* 21; and C. Ferstman, *Criminalizing Sexual Exploitation and Abuse by Peacekeepers*, United States Institute of Peace, Special Report 335 (September 2013).

INTERVIEW 3.1

Experiences of a UN Human Rights Officer

(Huma Shakeb Khan)

Huma Shakeb Khan worked as a UN human rights officer in Iraq. She joined the mission in 2009 and has served in various places across Iraq, with Erbil, the capital of the autonomous Kurdish region, being her duty station in 2012.

What training and guidance did you receive prior to deployment to Iraq?

I received a four-day security training which was geared towards military questions and was fairly racist in its approach towards Iraq and Iraqis. It was extremely gender insensitive and I have never used a single thing from that training in my three years of work in Iraq. The training was mandatory and the contractor charged large amounts of money from the mission. In truth, it felt more like a scam. The UN's only concern seemed to be about security before deploying their staff. There was a brief session on cultural sensitivity and we were not given any reading material about Iraq, so we were basically left to our own devices in finding out more about the country.

What have been the main human rights problems in Iraq during your time there?

The problems in Iraq and the autonomous Kurdish region differ from each other considerably. In the Kurdish region weak institutions are one of the key problems. Security institutions do not abide by the rule of law, the anti-terror law is misused, and weak democratic institutions allow freedom of expression to be compromised. Violence against women and ill-treatment of migrant workers are further problems, as well as ensuring that the work of oil companies does not result in harm to the local people and environment. One of the main issues is the disputed territories between the autonomous Kurdish region and the federal government of Iraq. These areas have a significant Kurdish population and the demography has changed a lot due to the policies of the former regime that had expelled a large number of Kurds, though many of them returned after 2003. In these areas both Kurdish and Iraqi military arrest people without following proper legal procedure and enforced disappearances are still common. In addition, there are several insurgent groups and attacks on civilians are common.

What is your typical day like working in Erbil?

We live in a compound which has an office and accommodation. I am in the office by 8.30 a.m. In Erbil it is easy to move outside. So on a regular day I have a few meetings outside, and sometimes within the compound either with victims, NGO or UN agencies. I usually work until 6–7 p.m. In the evenings, I either stay in my room after dinner or go out somewhere with colleagues. Previously we could only leave the compound in the presence of security officers but the situation has improved a lot, particularly compared to places like Kirkuk and Baghdad. Some colleagues have lived there for two years and may not have seen a single regular Iraqi shop or market.

How do you monitor the human rights situation, and how effective is this monitoring?

We conduct visits to places of detention, meet with detainees in private, visit government and NGO-run shelters, meet with civil society and follow up cases in court. We also go to the various districts and sub-districts and meet witnesses and victims. In other parts of Iraq one has to rely a lot on local staff, phone calls and civil society to obtain information, which changes the nature of monitoring. The mandate in the Kurdish region focuses more on technical assistance and supporting the government.

It is hard to measure the impact of monitoring. In the Kurdish region it has had some impact as the government is keen to collaborate with international organisations and is receptive, and the UN is generally well liked for the role it played during the Kurdish uprising. In other parts of Iraq the UN is mainly associated with the occupation forces and thus does not really command a lot of respect from local actors. In addition to dealing with the government concerned, there are a lot of internal struggles within the UN system as we are part of a political mission run by the Department of Political Affairs, which can lead to a clash between the political aspects of the mission and human rights, usually ending in favour of the former.

What are the biggest challenges you experienced in fulfilling your tasks?

As a human rights activist I used to struggle a lot with the diplomatic nature of the organisation. It is a constant balancing act, which can be valuable in so far as it means that we gain more attention from the government than activists do. Moreover, working in an extremely insecure environment makes work really challenging. There are also several blind spots, such as the role played by NATO in Iraq, which affected human rights, but that is not within our mandate. The UN's weakness in respect of the occupation of Iraq also makes it difficult to 'preach' to Iraqis. I try to work around this by keeping issues at a very local level, offering assistance in improving and acknowledging the limitations of the organisation.

What lessons can be learned from your experience for individual human rights officers and for field operations more generally?

Human rights work takes place in a particular political and social context, which defines international human rights law. Human rights officers need to be very aware and keen to understand that context and work with local team members and interlocutors to define the issues accordingly. It is important to not come across as being on a civilising mission where the world is divided between 'uncivilised' and 'civilised'. Having examples from different countries to show how things can be done is helpful in this respect. Keeping polite and humble always helps. Drawing upon civil society organisations from within the country always strengthens the work of human rights officers and one should invest in developing meaningful partnerships. Finally, it is important to understand the difference in the work of the UN compared to Human Rights Watch (HRW) or AI. Each one has its own value although they are very different. The UN has to work in close collaboration with the government concerned as per our respective mandates in field missions. Maintaining that constant dialogue and offering assistance is very important for UN human rights officers. In some sense working in the UN's human rights component means being part diplomat, part activist. It is a difficult balance to keep but that is the key to understanding the role of the UN human rights field officer.

QUESTIONS

1. Is civil society a liberal vision that has little relevance where marginalised groups and communities face systemic discrimination and denial of justice?
2. Has the increasing professionalisation of human rights NGOs suffocated the human rights movement?
3. What is the practical utility of using the term human rights defenders?
4. Why is the role of the medical profession so important in the protection of human rights?

3.9   HUMAN RIGHTS STRATEGIES

All human rights defenders essentially share the same goal, i.e. how best to promote and protect human rights. Over time, the various actors, including NGOs, national human rights institutions, regional and international actors (such as field officers and special procedures mandate-holders) have developed an array of strategies to achieve this objective. This section examines the nature, use and effectiveness of several key strategies, namely documentation, fact-finding and human rights reporting; monitoring; advocacy; and awareness-raising and capacity-building (litigation is addressed in Chapter 15).

3.9.1   Documentation and Fact-finding

Documentation refers to any measures taken with a view to establishing an accurate record of an incident or patterns of human rights violations; in other words, to find out the 'truth' of what happened. This practice serves multiple purposes. Documenting violations may be part of monitoring by individuals, NGOs and specifically mandated bodies, including ad hoc commissions of inquiry. The materials and information obtained may be used for awareness-raising, advocacy, for example, reporting violations and calling for action, litigation – as evidence – and to inform political and policy responses, such as the UN Security Council (UNSC) mandating peacekeeping troops or setting up a criminal tribunal. Documentation also serves to establish an alternative record to official versions of events, which are often characterised by various forms of denial;[115] such a record may become particularly important during subsequent transitional periods where there may be greater political will to act on findings.[116]

There is no uniform standard for documenting human rights violations whose main aim is to obtain as much information as possible about the 'what', 'who', 'where', 'when' and 'how' of an incident or patterns of violations, as well as the 'why', i.e. the context and factors that help explain them. Doctors, lawyers and others have produced a number of important manuals on how best to document particular types of violations, such as the Istanbul Protocol on torture, the Minnesota Protocol on extrajudicial killings and the International Protocol on the Documentation and Investigation of Sexual Violence in Conflict, which set out in detail what information to obtain from victims (torture, sexual violence) or witnesses (all) in relation to alleged violations.[117] Systematic documentation of violations, which is often the function of commissions of inquiry or fact-finding missions such as those on Darfur, Gaza, Libya or Syria, primarily consists of interviewing and taking statements of victims and witnesses, reviewing documents (for example, legislation, instructions, custody records, policy papers), on-site observations, collecting material evidence, assessment of available audiovisual materials (for example, photographs or satellite images of locations) and forensic evidence, including medical reports, autopsies and exhumation

---

[115] See in particular, S. Cohen, *States of Denial: Knowing about Atrocities and Suffering* (Polity Press, 2001).

[116] See on the methods used and challenges faced in this regard by various truth commissions, P. Ball, H. F. Spirer and L. Spirer (eds.), *Making the Case: Investigating Large Scale Human Rights Violations Using Information Systems and Data Analysis* (American Association for the Advancement of Science, 2000).

[117] Istanbul Protocol (1999); Minnesota Protocol (2016); International Protocol on the Documentation and Investigation of Sexual Violence in Conflict: Best Practice on the Documentation of Sexual Violence as a Crime or Violation of International Law, 2nd edn (2017).

findings.[118] The documentation of long-term violations of economic, social and cultural rights may require using additional methods, such as compiling statistics to demonstrate the impact of policies and measures on issues such as food, health and education over a period of time.[119]

Documentation increasingly relies on video materials, satellite images and mapping, which have been used in a number of instances to expose the consequences of conflict, such as in Darfur,[120] or the consequences of large-scale violations, for example the environmental impact of oil exploration in Ogoni land adversely affecting economic, social and cultural rights.[121] The availability and prevalence of audio-visual evidence is perhaps the most important development in respect of documentation. Taken by witnesses, victims and often the perpetrators themselves, these images have been widely distributed with considerable impact, particularly in the case of photographs of abuse taken by US wardens in the Iraqi prison of Abu Ghraib.[122] The photos of the body of Khaled Said, who had been beaten to death by police, played an important role in triggering public protests in Egypt in 2010. Photos of detainees tortured to death in Syria are viewed as important evidence in exposing practices and putting together cases against Syrian government officials held to be responsible for the commission of international crimes.[123] Another recent example of footage that exposed serious violations is the graphic evidence broadcast by Channel 4, UK, of international crimes committed in the last phase of the Sri Lankan war in 2009 that was used by the

---

[118] Report of the International Commission of Inquiry on Darfur to the United Nations Secretary-General (25 January 2005) paras. 12–25; Report of the United Nations Fact-finding Mission on the Gaza Conflict, UN doc. A/HRC/12/48 (25 September 2009) paras. 159–64; and Report of the International Commission of Inquiry to Investigate all Alleged Violations of International Human Rights Law in the Libyan Arab Jamahiriya, UN doc. A/ HRC/17/44 (1 June 2011) paras. 1–10. For an overview of the practical issues affecting the Gaza mission's documentation work, see Chapter 4.7.1. See further T. Boutruche, 'Credible Fact-finding and Allegations of International Humanitarian Law Violations: Challenges in Theory and Practice' (2011) 16 *Journal of Conflict and Security Law* 105, and P. Alston and S. Knuckey (eds.), *The Transformation of Human Rights Fact-finding* (Oxford University Press, 2016).

[119] See on statistical indicators, below at 3.9.3.

[120] See AI's 'Eyes on Darfur' project, online at www.eyesondarfur.org. See on the use of geo-mapping as a new tactic, www.newtactics.org/geo-mapping-human-rights/geo-mapping-human-rights.

[121] See UN Environment Programme (UNEP), *Environmental Assessment of Ogoniland* (2011), online at www.unep.org/nigeria, which is not a human rights report, but whose findings are important for an assessment of Nigeria's compliance with its obligations.

[122] See 'Torture Scandal: The Images that Shocked America', *The Guardian* (undated), online at www.guardian.co.uk/gall/0,8542,1211872,00.html.

[123] Human Rights Watch, *If the Dead Could Speak: Mass Deaths and Torture in Syria's Detention Facilities* (2015).

UN Panel of Experts on Accountability for War Crimes in Sri Lanka.[124] NGOs such as Witness[125] systematically use video advocacy to document and highlight a range of violations.[126]

The broadening of documentation through new technologies has resulted in a considerable shift in the ongoing struggle between truth-seeking and denial, making it increasingly difficult to conceal violations. However, several challenges remain. The nature of documentation often depends on what should be documented, as defined, for example, by the mandate of a mission or of an organisation. As a result, breaches of certain rights or violations by perpetrators such as non-state actors may be overlooked or under-represented. The documentation itself may be ad hoc or limited, particularly where there is lack of timely access to crucial information or where capacity and resources are not available, especially to undertake the long-term documentation of patterns of violations. Documenting violations often requires ingenuity and insistence in the face of denial and obfuscation. A commission of inquiry into disappearances in Sri Lanka, for example, was only able to find out the number of detained persons in custody when it compared the custody records (which had a falsified entry) with the records for food allocation (which showed the real number of inmates).[127] Members of fact-finding missions and monitoring bodies have repeatedly reported how they grappled with the authorities to gain access to crucial locations or to individuals that allowed them to obtain a more accurate record.[128] However, even where they gain access and documentation is carried out according to accepted standards, the material often requires an element of interpretation where facts are not unambiguous.[129]

Where documentation is not in line with best practice, vital proof may be lost. For example, it may be impossible to verify the remains of individuals who have been 'disappeared', which may be a particular problem where local populations have access to mass graves. Interviews with victims of human

---

[124] 'Egypt: "We are all Khaled Said"', BBC (17 February 2011), online at www.bbc.co.uk/worldservice/programmes/2011/02/110217_outlook_egypt_protests_khaled_said.shtml; 'Sri Lanka's Killing Fields', Channel 4 (14 June 2011), online at www.channel4.com/programmes/sri-lankas-killing-fields/4od.

[125] See www.witness.org.

[126] S. Gregory, 'Cameras Everywhere: Ubiquitous Video Documentation of Human Rights, New Forms of Video Advocacy, and Considerations of Safety, Security, Dignity and Consent' (2010) 2 *Journal of Human Rights Practice* 191.

[127] See Interview 8.2 with M. C. M. Iqbal.

[128] See e.g., A. Cassese, *Inhuman States, Imprisonment, Detention and Torture Today* (Polity Press, 1996); M. Nowak, 'Fact-Finding on Torture and Ill-Treatment and Conditions of Detention' (2009) 1 *Journal of Human Rights Practice* 101.

[129] P. Alston, 'The Challenges of Responding to Extrajudicial Executions: Interview with Philip Alston' (2010) 2 *Journal of Human Rights Practice* 355, at 356.

rights violations may only be possible once, and crucial information may be lost if it is not elicited at the right time. It is therefore important, for use in criminal proceedings, that they adhere to particular standards of criminal procedure, in case they are rejected as hearsay, especially if the original victim or witness cannot be present at the trial. Beyond their evidentiary value, interviews also raise broader questions of confidentiality and security. Those taking interviews have a particular responsibility towards victims and witnesses to avoid further traumatisation and prevent harm.[130] The reality that the protection of those documenting violations and of witnesses itself is a major concern reinforces the need to adhere to best practices. This concern is particularly acute where states are reluctant to cooperate and actively thwart documentation, putting victims, witnesses and human rights defenders at risk.[131] Human rights defenders therefore increasingly use special databases, such as Martus, 'to document human rights violations systematically and securely'.[132]

INTERVIEW 3.2

Documenting Human Rights Violations in Volatile Environments: The Libyan Experience

(Elham Saudi)

Elham Saudi is Director of Lawyers for Justice in Libya (LFJL), an NGO working closely with a network of Libyan lawyers and human rights defenders to 'defend and promote justice through the promotion of human rights, the rule of law and democracy'.[1]

How did your organisation seek to document violations during the conflict in Libya?

As an organisation started in the diaspora, LFJL had to find innovative and collaborative ways to document violations occurring on the ground.

1. Capacity-building of legal professionals: the need to document violations became apparent very early in the Libyan revolution, as the Gaddafi regime attacked civilians from the first moment. LFJL began its training of lawyers on the ground as early as April 2011, less than two months

[1] www.libyanjustice.org.

---

[130] Istanbul Protocol (1999) paras. 119–59.
[131] See in the context of proceedings of international criminal tribunals, REDRESS, above note 80, 52–5.
[132] See www.martus.org.

from the start of the revolution. At this early stage, only the eastern part of Libya was liberated. We therefore arranged for two young lawyers to come to Egypt where we, with international investigative experts, trained them on the documentation of violations. On their return, they trained the remaining members of the fact-finding committee set up by the legal department of the National Transitional Council (NTC).

We conducted further training by Skype for those in places which had not yet been liberated. In addition to these 'guerrilla' style trainings, we held a workshop in Tunisia in September, after the liberation of Tripoli, for over thirty people from more than ten cities in Libya, which benefited from the expertise of a number of international NGOs. Training lawyers in Libya was challenging during the conflict because of the obvious security concerns and so we had to use measures such as Skype instead of telephone lines and external training. It was difficult to work with people for substantial periods of time in order properly to engage with the detailed process of documenting violations. This was one of the reasons why the events were held outside Libya to ensure enough 'space' and clarity of focus to absorb the information in a setting that is distant from the conflict.

2. Standardisation of documentation: in order to simplify both the training and documentation processes, we decided to produce a pro forma witness statement. In cooperation with various organisations, we produced this document and used it as the basis for all our training. This provided a pro forma that ensured that many of the key questions were asked and was intended to minimise the scope for leading questions or for testimonies based on 'collective' memory and not a recollection of actual facts. The form also encouraged corroborative evidence by cross-referring to such evidence. Finally, the forms ensured that identification data (e.g. name, address, etc.) were retained by LFJL and not shared with international bodies. This was to ensure security: first, by not having documented the identification data in the same place as the testimony so that if Gaddafi forces found the files – remember this was still during the conflict – they could not easily trace the witnesses and, second, to ensure that the details of those providing were not divulged, intentionally or inadvertently, without informed consent at the time of the use of the testimony by any international bodies. The form was used by those lawyers we trained, but also by others trained by them and, most importantly, the official fact-finding committees set up by the NTC and outlined in (3) below.

3. Network of fact-finding committees: following the initial training in Egypt, we discussed the need for documentation on a nation-wide scale with the then still nascent NTC. In cooperation with the NTC's legal department, we developed the concept of fact-finding committees tasked with investigating all alleged violations committed since 15 February 2011 across the country. Each committee would be appointed by the NTC,

thus providing a form of legitimacy for their work and, we hoped, easier access to victims and witnesses. We also hoped that this process would enlist a sense of responsibility and accountability with the NTC itself. LFJL assisted the NTC, at that time the publicly known members consisting mainly of people from the east of Libya, with identifying suitable lawyers and investigators in key cities. The committees did some excellent work, some of which was crucial to both the ICC file and that of the Commission of Inquiry.

4. A link to international advocacy and accountability: during the conflict, LFJL was in the privileged position of having direct access to international bodies both for advocacy and accountability. Key among these were the HRC in Geneva, the Foreign and Commonwealth Office in London, the African Commission in Banjul and the ICC in The Hague. We were able to serve as a link between the networks we had helped establish in Libya and these bodies. For example, we were able to allow all those participating in the Tunisia workshop time with ICC investigators to share their findings, learn on developing their work and be recognised for their crucial role in the ICC process.

What were the main challenges to establishing an accurate record of violations?

There were several. The speed with which events were uncovering meant that those working on the ground had to be creative and resourceful in documenting violations and securing evidence. On our side, it meant we also had to be resourceful about how we ensured that the documentation would stand up to scrutiny and be useful in the future. Further, the small population in Libya means that on a community by community basis people know each other personally. This made it difficult for knowledge not to be presumed by those conducting interviews and also for 'collective' memory not to play a part in the documentation of the violations. Also, the regional nature of some of the subsequent fighting meant that there was a degree of 'selective' documentation taking place. Finally, the sense of victor's justice, which emerged with the powerful militias, means that there is the risk of an unbalanced account of violations emerging. Although reinforced by the NTC in its Law 38 granting an amnesty for acts done in the name of the 17 February Revolution, this sense of skewed justice is not being tolerated by civil society, which is active in demanding accountability for all acts. This gives some hope that with time a more thorough record of what has happened in the Libyan conflict, including in the rape file, will be established.

Did you find any evidence of rape?

Yes, our network of lawyers found evidence in two regions. Through the testimony of medical doctors who had treated women with injuries and symptoms consistent with rape and limited victim testimony, as well as some video footage confiscated from the mobile telephones of some regime soldiers, we were able to establish that rape had occurred. We were not, however, able to get a full picture of the extent to which it happened and may be regarded as systematic. The publicity that the question of rape received almost instantly halted the flow of information on these crimes to us. The shame factor of being named a victim of rape in a conservative culture appeared to be a dissuading factor, with a handful of those from whom we had secured witness testimonies withdrawing their consent to our using those testimonies in any international or local case.

What were the consequences of reports that claims about rape had been unfounded or exaggerated?[2]

The primary consequence of such reports was not dissimilar to the consequence of when the reports of rape received significant attention – disengagement by those affected. The reporting of rape, in whatever guise, resulted in a withdrawal of cooperation by victims and witnesses. The fear of being 'exposed' once more by becoming a public subject meant that some victims with whom we started conversations decided to stop speaking. We saw this with female and male victims of rape.

A further consequence, which I believe is the result of the fear created by the stories of rape – exaggerated or not – is the use of an accusation of rape as a threat to secure confessions for other violations. We have had at least two testimonies by persons detained by militias who were threatened with a charge of rape in this manner. This not only brings into question all confessions of rape but also highlights how far we are as a community from dealing with the true repercussions of this part of the conflict.

How do you view the work done by others, such as the ICC or the Commission of Inquiry, in documenting violations in Libya?

The primary flaw with the work of both the ICC and the Commission of Inquiry was the limited time spent on the ground, building rapport and investing in their counterparts within Libya. They did not take their mandate as active and so did little to help improve the local system, building rapport and seeing their mandate as helping to improve the local system. The perception that they were, to varying degrees, 'in bed with' the transitional authorities was not very helpful either. In my view the ICC lost an opportunity to

---

[2] P. Coburn, 'Amnesty Questions Claim that Gaddafi Ordered Rape as Weapon of War', *Independent* (24 June 2011), online at www.independent.co.uk/news/world/africa/amnestyquestions-claim-that-gaddafi-ordered-rape-as-weapon-of-war-2302037.html.

establish its credentials in Libya. It had the perfect storm of a wide mandate, a population willing to speak and share its information and a legal community willing to assist; yet its tangible involvement stagnated after the issue of the initial arrest warrants and it was often hampered by its own red tape.

What are the lessons from the Libyan experience for documenting violations in similar contexts?

The key lesson is adaptability. In a fast-moving conflict, in a country with a vast landscape, and where culture and custom play a strong role, it was vital not to adapt a 'cut and paste' approach to the documentation of violations. This was most clearly demonstrated in the rape cases. There was a presumption on the part of some of the media and advocacy and investigative authorities that highlighting rape cases would create a 'safe' environment for victims to come forward. This approach is familiar to those in the West and often bears fruit. However, in Libya, a conservative country where 'honour', in its most proscribed definitions, is paramount, the attention that rape cases received served as a deterrent for victims. We often heard the phrase 'I don't want my name to be known like Iman El Obeidi's',[3] when attempting to persuade victims to provide testimonies. 'It is personal', we were told, and 'I would prefer for the world not to be involved.'

[3] Iman Obeidi publicly complained about being raped by Gaddafi forces during the war and her case became instantly known across Libya and worldwide. She later fled the country.

3.9.2   Human Rights Reporting

States, national human rights institutions, regional and international bodies, NGOs, think tanks, journalists and individuals publish reports relating to human rights, which may focus on law, policy and/or practice. Human rights reports, particularly by the UN or UN-appointed bodies and NGOs, can be highly influential. They are one of the most important means of establishing a record of human rights situations, including violations, and often explicitly counter official versions of events. Reports frequently identify the underlying factors, nature and consequences of violations in a wide range of contexts. They are also an integral part of monitoring and their findings can play a critical role in advocacy efforts. Reports contribute to debates about the development of standards, legislative or institutional reforms, changes in policy, for example an end to military cooperation or, in urgent situations, serve as one of the factors resulting in preventive action. Human rights reports are also frequently relied upon in legal proceedings to corroborate allegations concerning specific methods and patterns of violations,[133] which may also help to investigate international crimes and establish individual liability.[134] More generally, human rights reports help to generate awareness, both in a particular context and more broadly, for example by casting the spotlight on un-/under-reported types of violations.[135] However, critical observers have argued that human rights reports 'depoliticise human rights violations by drawing attention away from structural processes of class or ethnic power, and reduce violations to a set of technical problems concerning the functioning of the legal system'[136] and make 'human rights violations ... seem random, accidental or arbitrary', instead of explaining their context of 'planned misery' and 'the logic of particular socio-economic arrangements'.[137] Their problematic narrative and portrayal of actors has also been the subject of scathing criticism.[138]

AI, and later HRW, in particular have developed a widely recognised model for human rights reports to ensure an accurate record of violations and/or analysis of an issue that is informed by an understanding of the given context. Researchers undertake background research about the thematic right or country-specific situation, examine available documentation, consult with a wide range of experts, activists and others on the situation relating to the particular issue, for example migrant workers in Middle Eastern countries,[139]

---

[133] E.g., a 2000 UN Expert Report and 2003 Global Witness report were used in the case against Guus van Kouwenhoven, a Dutch businessman, who was accused of supplying arms to Charles Taylor, the former President of Liberia, in exchange for logging rights. See *Kouwenhoven* case (The Netherlands) (2006) and (2008). See also Global Witness, *The Usual Suspects. Liberia's Weapons and Mercenaries in Cote d'Ivoire and Sierra Leone: Why it's Still Possible, How it Works and How to Break the Trends* (2003), online at www.globalwitness.org/library/usual-suspects; Report of the Panel of Experts appointed pursuant to Security Council Resolution 1306 (2000) in relation to Sierra Leone, UN doc. S/2000/1195 (20 December 2000).

[134] See generally M. Bergsmo and W. H. Wiley, 'Human Rights Professionals and the Criminal Investigation and Prosecution of Core International Crimes', in S. Skåre, I. Burkey and H. Mørk (eds.), *Manual on Human Rights Monitoring: An Introduction for Human Rights Field Officers*, 3rd rev. edn (Norwegian Centre for Human Rights, 2008) 1–30, and further, L. S. Sunga, 'How Can UN Human Rights Special Procedures Sharpen ICC Fact-finding?' (2011) 15 *The International Journal of Human Rights* 187, at 198.

[135] See e.g., ICHRP and Transparency International, *Corruption and Human Rights: Making the Connection* (2009), and Discriminatory Laws and Practices and Acts of Violence against Individuals Based on their Sexual Orientation and Gender Identity, Report of the UN High Commissioner for Human Rights, UN doc. A/HRC/19/41 (17 November 2011).

[136] R. A. Wilson, 'Representing Human Rights Violations: Social Contexts and Subjectivities', in R. A. Wilson (ed.), *Human Rights, Culture and Context: Anthropological Perspectives* (Pluto Press, 1997) 134–60, at 148.

[137] S. Marks, 'Human Rights and Root Causes' (2011) 74 *Modern Law Review* 57, at 75.

[138] M. Mutua, 'Savages, Victims and Saviors: The Metaphor of Human Rights' (2001) 42 *Harvard International Law Journal* 201.

[139] HRW, *Slow Reform: Protection of Migrant Domestic Workers in Asia and the Middle East* (2010); International Federation of Human Rights (FIDH) and Egyptian Organization for Human Rights (EOHR), *Migrant Workers in Saudi Arabia* (2003).

and ideally visit locations and those concerned to collect and verify available information. Any factual allegation and information should be corroborated by another source so as to ensure reliability. The style of writing is as objective as possible, combining factual information and case stories with legal and policy analysis, as well as recommendations. A report is then vetted internally (some NGOs share drafts with governments concerned for their comments) and published.[140]

A report is a tool and should therefore form part of a broader strategy that considers both thematic priorities and its use, including media strategy, advocacy and follow-up. However, it is not always clear what impact particular reports will have (which forms part of the prior strategic assessment) or have had (evaluation), which raises the broader question of effectiveness. In 2005, for example, HRW produced a report on violations committed during the presidency of Alberto Fujimori in Peru.[141] Following the publication of the report, Fujimori was extradited from Chile to Peru, and convicted by the Peruvian Supreme Court on charges of serious human rights violations. HRW argued that its report was crucial in providing evidence for the extradition of Fujimori and in changing the perception that there was no evidence against him.[142] However, the report was not mentioned explicitly in the judgment of the Chilean Supreme Court in which it decided to extradite Fujimori. Moreover, Peruvian and other international actors had also worked to counter perceptions of Fujimori's innocence.[143] These considerations show the difficulty of attributing and assessing impact, an assessment that may also be influenced by an organisation's interest in advancing its reputation. In practice, reports of this nature are frequently one among several factors that contribute to, and influence, complex processes that may eventually result in accountability.

Reports may also have unintended adverse consequences. For example, a human rights report documenting abuses committed by serving officials in Afghanistan[144] was said to have inadvertently contributed to, if not prompted, the latter's decision to approve an amnesty for all combatants involved in the 1992 and 1993 conflict covering crimes perpetrated during that period.[145]

---

[140] Hopgood, above note 36, 74–92.
[141] HRW, *Probable Cause: Evidence Implicating Fujimori* (2005), online at www.hrw.org/en/reports/2005/12/21/probable-cause.
[142] HRW, 'Peruvian Court Convicts Fujimori for Human Rights Violations' (5 May 2009), online at www.hrw.org/en/news/2009/05/05/peruvian-court-convicts-fujimori-human-rights-violations.
[143] L. Mallinder, 'Law, Politics and Fact-finding: Assessing the Impact of Human Rights Reports' (2010) 2 *Journal of Human Rights Practice* 166, at 173.
[144] HRW, *Blood-Stained Hands: Past Atrocities in Kabul and Afghanistan's Legacy of Impunity* (2005), online at www.hrw.org/en/reports/2005/07/06/blood-stained-hands.
[145] Mallinder, above note 143, 174.

This example shows that the impact of reports can be unpredictable and that a nuanced assessment is needed about what type of report and demands may best support effective strategies at a particular point in time. While reports by NGOs and/or official bodies may be effective and lead to identifiable results, their long-term impacts are often less apparent. As pointed out by Manfred Nowak, the former UN Special Rapporteur on torture:

I have not been able to objectively assess, either on the basis of follow-up missions or on other methods of fact-finding, whether my missions and reports had any sustainable impact on the goal of eradicating torture and of improving the general conditions of detention in the countries visited.[146]

This rather sobering assessment shows the need for further empirical research to evaluate impact, which would require studies using social science methods to better understand what role the various types of human rights reports play, particularly in influencing the perceptions and decision-making of relevant actors.

3.9.3   Monitoring

According to an OHCHR training manual, human rights monitoring is:

a broad term describing the active collection, verification and immediate use of information to address human rights problems. Human rights monitoring includes gathering information about incidents, observing events (elections, trials, demonstrations, etc.), visiting sites such as places of detention and refugee camps, discussions with government authorities to obtain information and to pursue remedies and other immediate follow-up ...[147]

Monitoring can be situation-specific, such as during elections, but is often of a long-term nature to observe and analyse a human rights situation at the local, national, regional or international level.

The UN definition demonstrates that monitoring refers to a range of interventions whose main purpose is to identify what problems, if any, exist in a particular context and, in so far as needed and possible, to take action with a view to ensuring respect for human rights. Monitoring may be conducted by state authorities, national human rights institutions, NGOs, UN human rights field officers, regional and international special rapporteurs, the media and others, and combines documentation and observation with remedial action.[148] In recognition of past failures, mechanisms have been put in place to act where monitoring evidences a risk of conflict and violations, including threats and harassment of individuals. This applies in particular to early

---

[146] Nowak, above note 128, 118.
[147] OHCHR, *Training Manual on Human Rights Monitoring* (United Nations, 2001) 9.
[148] See strong emphasis on interviewing and collecting testimonies, ibid.

warning mechanisms in situations that may result in serious violations, such as the UN Office of the Special Advisor on the Prevention of Genocide.[149]

Long-term monitoring focuses on structural factors and developments over time. It principally applies to all sets of rights, particularly in relation to the positive obligations of states. In practice, it has been used especially in respect of economic, social and cultural rights and the right to development. The duty to 'progressively realise' these rights is one of their distinctive features, which implies that a process is set in train towards better fulfilment of the right concerned. The monitoring of relevant rights, such as the right to health or the right to food, poses considerable methodological and practical challenges. Methods and statistics relating to health or food were primarily formulated in the development context, as reflected in sources such as the World Health Organization (WHO) Statistical Information System and the Human Development Index prepared annually by the UN Development Programme (UNDP).[150] UN human rights bodies and others have stressed the need for human rights-based monitoring but have grappled with developing an adequate framework, including how to use data generated by UN agencies, regional institutions and others that has an apparent bearing on human rights but is primarily used for other purposes.[151] In practice, prior mapping and indicators have been widely used to establish whether states have met certain targets (benchmarks) within a given time frame.[152]

Monitoring can consist of an internal or external evaluation. Ideally, external monitoring is based on constructive engagement informed by a series of principles.[153] In practice, however, states are frequently hostile to being monitored. They may reject the presence of international monitors altogether, for example in the case of Sri Lanka,[154] or may obstruct the work of national and international human rights monitors in myriad ways, for example by revoking licences, threatening personnel with expulsion or denying access

[149] See www.un.org/en/preventgenocide/adviser/index.shtml.

[150] See http://hdr.undp.org/en/statistics.

[151] See in this context, OHCHR, *Training Manual*, above note 147, ch. 20.

[152] See on use of indicators and benchmarks in relation to various rights, Report on Indicators for Promoting and Monitoring the Implementation of Human Rights, UN doc. HRI/MC/2008/3 (6 June 2008) para. 7. For an extensive discussion, see Chapter 9.7.

[153] The OHCHR, *Training Manual*, above note 147, 87–94, lists the following: do no harm; respect the mandate; know the standards; exercise good judgement; seek consultation; respect the authorities; credibility; confidentiality; security; understand the country; need for consistency, persistence and patience; accuracy and precision; impartiality; objectivity; sensitivity; integrity; professionalism; and visibility.

[154] This was one of the recommendations made by several states during the universal periodic review that Sri Lanka's previous government had objected to. Report of the Working Group on the Universal Periodic Review Sri Lanka, UN doc. A/HRC/8/46 (5 June 2008) para. 84.

to certain facilities, persons or documentation.[155] Monitors are in this context frequently confronted with the dilemma of how to respond to apparent human rights violations; if they speak out, they may not be able to continue their monitoring function; if they do not raise the issue (or raise the issue behind closed doors with the government but to no avail) their monitoring risks failing to fulfil its basic objective, namely to ensure enhanced protection.

3.9.4   Advocacy

Advocacy, i.e. the act of arguing for something to be done, denotes the various strategies used to strengthen the promotion and protection of human rights, either in respect of a specific case/situation or more broadly. The breadth of this definition means that there are numerous human rights advocates, beyond well-known advocacy organisations or prominent individual human rights activists. This includes popular movements, UN officials requesting respect for particular rights, such as the UN High Commissioner for Human Rights,[156] and may include states and their representatives who seek to influence other states and international organisations to take a certain course of action that results in greater recognition of, or respect for, human rights.[157]

Human rights advocacy can pursue specific short-term goals, for example prompting UNSC action in response to reports about violations in the context of armed conflicts, such as in Syria from 2011 (ongoing as of 2019), or broader, long-term objectives, such as the creation of a strong international human rights system. The latter advocacy entails campaigning for the recognition of particular rights, the setting of standards and the establishment of effective institutions.[158] Several campaigns have had a considerable degree of success to this end. For example, the women's rights movement succeeded in having a number of specific rights recognised, such as reproductive rights in the African Protocol on the Rights of Women, establishing institutions, such as the complaints procedure under the Optional Protocol to the Convention

---

[155] Nowak, above note 128, 105.
[156] 'Pillay Presents Groundbreaking UN Study on Violence, Discrimination against People because of their Sexual Orientation' (7 March 2012), www.ohchr.org/EN/NewsEvents/Pages/DisplayNews.aspx?NewsID=11917&LangID=E. See for the new High Commissioner on Human Rights, Zeid Ra'ad Al Hussein, in post since September 2014, www.ohchr.org/EN/AboutUs/Pages/HighCommissioner.aspx.
[157] See R. Müllerson, *Human Rights Diplomacy* (Routledge, 1997), in particular 118–47; D. P. Forsythe, *Human Rights in International Relations*, 4th edn (Cambridge University Press, 2017) 256–94.
[158] See for a good overview, Mutua, above note 34.

on the Elimination of All Forms of Discrimination against Women (CEDAW), UN special procedures,[159] and seeking accountability for violations, such as those before the ICC.[160] Other examples are ratification campaigns, such as in relation to the Convention on the Rights of the Child (CRC),[161] the ban on landmines[162] and efforts resulting in developing standards, such as on the rights of indigenous peoples[163] and internally displaced persons (IDPs).[164]

These campaigns show how networks of actors have been able to influence and shape the international system. This is a continuous process as new demands emerge, such as for the recognition and effective protection of LGBTI rights, whose proponents often face a considerable struggle to gain acceptance, even by liberal 'gatekeepers'.[165] Similar mechanisms are at play in national systems where (networks of) actors seek to influence policy-making and practices to bring about legislative, judicial or institutional reforms. However, it is often not possible to neatly separate national, regional and international advocacy efforts. On the contrary, networks of national and international actors, particularly NGOs, together with like-minded states, frequently use international fora as arenas of legitimacy to exert pressure on repressive states with a view to bringing about gradual changes from denial to engagement and compliance.[166] In practice, the outcome of such efforts depends largely on the receptiveness of states. When faced with alleged violations, states have developed sophisticated arsenals of denial[167] and have often successfully built alliances in crucial fora that allow them to escape censure and the need for change. The model of transnational networks sketched out above was developed in the 1990s and was based on a world where 'liberal' states wielded considerable influence, including in

---

[159] See UN Working Group on the issue of discrimination against women in law and in practice, www.ohchr.org/EN/Issues/Women/WGWomen/Pages/WGWomenIndex.aspx; UN Special Rapporteur on violence against women, its causes and consequences, www.ohchr.org/EN/ Issues/Women/SRWomen/Pages/SRWomenIndex.aspx.

[160] See on Crimes of Sexual Violence, 'Case Study: The Women's Caucus for Gender Justice in the ICC', online at www.endvawnow.org/en/articles/1193-campaigns-for-institutional-change.html.

[161] For further examples, see U. Oberdörster, 'Why Ratify? Lessons from Treaty Ratification Campaigns' (2008) 61 *Vanderbilt Law Review* 681, at 697.

[162] See above at 3.4.3.

[163] C. Charters, L. Malezer and V. Tauli-Corpuz (eds.), *Indigenous Voices: The UN Declaration on the Rights of Indigenous Peoples* (Hart, 2013).

[164] African Union Convention for the Protection and Assistance of Internally Displaced Persons in Africa (Kampala Convention), 2009.

[165] B. Clifford (ed.), *The International Struggle for New Human Rights* (University of Pennsylvania Press, 2009).

[166] Keck and Sikkink, above note 4.

[167] Cohen, above note 115, and Mutua, above note 34, 602–4.

international fora, such as the UN human rights bodies. However, power relationships have shifted significantly over the last decade, which has changed political dynamics and may make it more difficult to achieve greater human rights protection.

Advocacy consists of several methods that can be used to influence the targeted actors, be they governments, regional or international institutions or non-state actors. Advocates may use public campaigns (reports, letter writing, collecting signatures, demonstrations, media appearances), lobbying (speaking directly with influential persons) and complementary means such as litigation to achieve the desired result, often combining these methods as needed.[168] In the sustained and ultimately successful efforts to change Pakistan's *Hudood* rape laws, actors reached out to local communities and used litigation, street theatre, the media, reporting and lobbying.[169] Developing effective advocacy therefore requires a range of skills, including strategic vision, thematic understanding, political acumen, network building talents and public relations know-how.

One major challenge for those engaging in advocacy is to assess its efficacy. This is important for several reasons. Advocacy is resource and time intensive. Actors therefore need to decide what advocacy efforts are worthwhile; members of organisations or funders, for their part, may request some evidence that the advocacy effort made has achieved its objective or is making progress towards this end. Ultimately, not being able to show that advocacy works, or believing that it does not make a difference, may lead some actors to question its very *raison d'être* and undermine the morale of those engaged in it. Worse, advocacy may even unintentionally do more harm than good.[170] In practice, evaluating the impact of advocacy is fraught with difficulties. 'First, one must establish criteria for success. What degree of change qualifies a network campaign as effective?'[171] Second, if such change has been identified, to what degree can it be attributed to the particular advocacy, given that this is frequently one among several factors and that decision-makers may not acknowledge that changes were made in response? While this impact may often prove difficult to establish, there are evident success stories, particularly where a campaign had a clear goal which was eventually achieved, such as the adoption of a treaty protecting specific rights, for example the Convention on the Rights of Persons with Disabilities (CRPD).[172]

---

[168] See ICHRP, above note 42, para. 22.
[169] See Interview 2.2 with Sohail A. Warraich.
[170] G. Andreopoulos and Z. Arat (eds.), *The Uses and Misuses of Human Rights: A Critical Approach to Advocacy* (Palgrave Macmillan, 2014).
[171] S. D. Burgerman, 'Mobilizing Principles: The Role of Transnational Activists in Promoting Human Rights Principles' (1998) 20 *Human Rights Quarterly* 905, at 912.
[172] M. Sabatello and M. Schulze (eds.), *Human Rights & Disability Advocacy* (University of Pennsylvania Press, 2013).

The outcome of advocacy is particularly difficult to measure where the goals are long-term and where immediate changes are unlikely in the present circumstances, such as advocating legislative and institutional reforms in repressive regimes. However, as the campaigns in apartheid South Africa showed, these efforts created an important alternative discourse that both undermined the legitimacy of the regime(s) at the time and prepared the ground for changes following the end of apartheid.[173] The multiple efforts undertaken to close Guantánamo Bay, including campaigns, NGO and UN reports in addition to litigation, provide a similarly instructive example of long-term impact even though developments following a change in the US administration showed that considerable political and practical difficulties may perpetuate violations and militate against immediate solutions.[174]

3.9.5   Awareness-raising, Capacity-building and Human Rights Education

Awareness-raising refers to the process of engaging – by means of information-sharing, educational activities or other communication – with particular groups or the public at large. Its aim is to foster a better understanding of human rights in general and/or alerting the target group to a specific human rights issue and ways of how best to address it. Ideally, awareness-raising positively influences those targeted and helps in promoting the goal pursued, such as 'to foster respect for the rights and dignity of persons with disabilities' and 'to combat stereotypes, prejudices and harmful practices relating to persons with disabilities'.[175] Raising human rights awareness serves multiple objectives. It is a cornerstone of promotion: rights-holders, authorities, judges and others need to know what human rights are and what they entail in order to assert, implement or adjudicate them. Accordingly, it is recognised that states 'have the primary responsibility to promote and ensure human rights education and training', including adequate human rights training for 'state officials, civil servants, judges, law-enforcement officials and military personnel'.[176] The Universal Declaration of Human Rights (UDHR) goes further, stating in its preamble that 'every individual and every organ of

---

[173] P. J. Schwikkard, 'Reflections on Law Reform Pertaining to Arrested, Detained and Accused Persons in South Africa', in L. Oette (ed.), *Criminal Law Reform and Transitional Justice: Human Rights Perspectives for Sudan* (Ashgate, 2011) 139–53, at 153.

[174] See in this context, AI, *USA – Guantanamo: A Decade of Damage to Human Rights and 10 Anti-Human Rights Messages Guantanamo Still Sends* (2011), and Human Rights First Campaign, Close Guantanamo, www.humanrightsfirst.org/campaigns/close-guantanamo.

[175] See art. 8(1)(a),(b) CRPD.

[176] See art. 7(4), UN Declaration on Human Rights Education and Training, UNGA resolution 66/ 137 (19 December 2011). See also art. 10 of the Convention against Torture (CAT) and art. 23 of the International Convention for the Protection of All Persons from Enforced Disappearance (CPED) for treaty-based obligations to train law-enforcement officials and others in relation to the prohibition of torture and enforced disappearance respectively.

society ... shall strive by teaching and education to promote respect for these rights and freedoms ... to secure their universal and effective recognition and observance'. It therefore sees teaching and education as the building blocks for a human rights culture that spans the national and the international sphere. Raising awareness of human rights also serves an instrumental purpose as part of advocacy campaigns. Imparting knowledge about the nature and importance of human rights, or framing an issue as a question of human rights, is often an essential component of such campaigns. This is particularly the case when mobilising grassroots constituencies or seeking the recognition of new rights.

Awareness-raising is also closely related to capacity-building in the field of human rights, which refers to 'the process by which individuals, organizations, institutions and societies develop abilities to perform functions, solve problems and set and achieve objectives'.[177] For example, marginalised communities, such as the Dalits in India, may frame and articulate their grievances as human rights issues and may be able to use legal and other channels to seek prevention and claim accountability and justice.[178] Such an approach may not necessarily result in enhanced protection or the desired outcome and a shift to internationalised advocacy and the concomitant need to mainstream discourses may depoliticise efforts and limit the impact of such strategies.[179] Nevertheless, it can signify an important step towards empowerment of individuals and groups demanding respect for their rights rather than being beneficiaries who are at the mercy of local authorities and others.[180] Awareness of the international human rights regime can also be critical for national human rights activists and others who want to use available avenues to highlight human rights concerns, request urgent intervention and seek accountability and justice.

Human rights education is an integral component of awareness-raising, which the UN in particular has promoted since the very beginning of its human rights-related work.[181] In the most recent development, the HRC set

---

[177] Note by the UN Secretariat, Definition of Basic Concepts and Terminologies in Governance and Public Administration, UN doc. E/C.16/2006/4 (5 January 2006) para. 33.

[178] P. Kumar Shinde, *Dalits and Human Rights* (Isha Books, 2005); B. Clifford, '"Dalit Rights Are Human Rights": Caste Discrimination, International Activism, and the Construction of a New Human Rights Issue' (2007) 29 *Human Rights Quarterly* 167.

[179] J. Lerche, 'Transnational Advocacy Networks and Affirmative Action for Dalits in India' (2008) 39 *Development and Change* 239.

[180] See also art. 2(2)(c) UN Declaration on Human Rights Education and Training: 'Education for human rights, which includes empowering persons to enjoy and exercise their rights and to respect and uphold the rights of others.'

[181] See preamble and art. 26(2) UDHR; the UN Educational, Scientific and Cultural Organization (UNESCO) recommendation concerning education for international understanding, cooperation and peace and education relating to human rights and fundamental freedoms adopted by the Geneva Conference at its eighteenth session (Paris, 19 November 1974); the UN Decade for Human Rights Education (1995–2004).

up an open-ended working group, which in 2011 led to the adoption of the UN Declaration on Human Rights Education and Training.[182] The Declaration evidences a broad understanding of human rights education and training, which: comprises all educational, training, information, awareness-raising and learning activities aimed at promoting universal respect for and observance of all human rights and fundamental freedoms and thus contributing to, inter alia, the prevention of human rights violations and abuses by providing persons with knowledge, skills and understanding and developing their attitudes and behaviours, to empower them to contribute to the building and promotion of a universal culture of human rights.[183]

It adds that '[h]uman rights education and training is a lifelong process that concerns all ages'.[184] This outlook is reflected in the work of many NGOs and human rights educators who have developed multiple approaches to the teaching of human rights, and have produced a wealth of educational materials.[185]

While the advantages of human rights education are widely recognised, it is equally clear that there are fundamental challenges. The very subject of human rights itself is open to various interpretations and often contested; while this can be positive if taught in a manner that encourages a contextual understanding, respect for tolerance and diversity informed by fundamental rights, it may easily result in skewed visions and distortions. Governments may interpret human rights education in a selective fashion that differs significantly from the UN Declaration and the approaches of NGOs or human rights teachers. This may include taking rather a narrow view of human rights education. For example, Australia's Second/Third Reports to the Committee on the Rights of the Child, when reporting on the aims of education under article 29 CRC,[186] only focused on anti-racism programmes and policies, protecting children from sexual abuse and improving school discipline.[187] In the UK, human rights education has been criticised for neglecting economic, social and cultural rights and collective rights, as well as failing to acknowledge problematic aspects of the UK's own record and the fact that human

---

[182] UNGA resolution 66/137 (16 February 2011).   [183] Ibid., art. 2(1).

[184] Ibid., art. 3(1).

[185] See P. Gerber, 'Human Rights Education: A Slogan in Search of a Definition', in S. Joseph and A. McBeth (eds.), *Research Handbook on International Human Rights Law* (Edward Elgar, 2010) 541–66.

[186] Art. 29(1) CRC provides: 'States Parties agree that the education of the child shall be directed to … (b): The development of respect for human rights and fundamental freedoms, and for the principles enshrined in the Charter of the United Nations.'

[187] Second and Third Periodic Reports of States Parties due in 1998 and 2003: Australia, UN doc. CRC/C/129/Add.4 (29 December 2004) paras. 372–84, discussed by Gerber, above note 185, 550–4. See on an initiative in the Australian state of Victoria, E. Branigan and P. Ramcharan, 'Human Rights Education in Australia: Reflections on the Meaningful Application of Rights and Values in Practice' (2012) 4 *Journal of Human Rights Practice* 233.

rights are born out of social struggles.[188] The purpose of human rights teaching may also be very different, for example either forming part of general, formal education or being a cornerstone of targeted efforts aimed at bringing about broader transformation,[189] which may result in conflicting approaches and widely diverging outcomes depending on the approach taken, which may not produce 'true citizens of the world'.[190]

In legal education, human rights law may form part of constitutional/ public law, regional systems, for example EU law, or public international law. However, the subject is often optional or confined to postgraduate studies. Many law students still leave university without having developed a clear understanding of human rights and human rights law. This is a particularly acute problem in countries where lawyers and activists are faced with human rights violations, or their legacy, but may lack the knowledge and requisite skills that would help them deal with the issues arising in such contexts. The staple response of international actors has been to provide human rights training for officials, judges and lawyers, such as in the case of Iraq following the end of the Saddam Hussein regime. Carefully designed training programmes that meet actual needs, address gaps in knowledge and enhance the skills of participants can be useful measures in such circumstances.[191] However, training has often been used as a poorly designed short-cut measure where external actors with limited understanding of the situation and needs of participants share largely theoretical knowledge. Such training is often attractive for organisers, trainers and funders who can claim successful project implementation; meanwhile, participants enjoy the opportunity to travel and frequently receive handsome per diems. For these reasons, there is a risk that training lacks a sense of focus, i.e. that it is not an integral part and means of a broader, organically developed long-term strategy but becomes an end in its own right. The larger impact of such training beyond evaluation by its participants is often not clear, particularly where officials receive training but the structural conditions facilitating violations remain in

---

[188] B. Bowring, 'Human Rights and Public Education' (2012) 42 *Cambridge Journal of Education* 53.

[189] Gerber, above note 185. See for an analysis of, and case study (India) on, various models of human rights education ('global citizenship', 'coexistence' and 'transformative action'), M. Bajaj, 'Human Rights Education: Ideology, Location, and Approaches' (2011) 33 *Human Rights Quarterly* 481.

[190] See on the potential of such education, U. Baxi, 'Human Rights Education: The Promise of the Third Millennium?' in G. J. Andreopoulos and R. P. Claude (eds.), *Human Rights Education for the Twenty-first Century* (University of Pennsylvania Press, 1997) 142–54.

[191] See www.humanrightseducation.info/ and www.ohchr.org/en/publicationsresources/ pages/trainingeducation.aspx for the main UN websites. See also International Human Rights Network, 'What is effective training?', online at www.ihrnetwork.org/files/7.%20 What%20is %20Effective%20Training.PDF.

place.[192] To be effective, developing and implementing human rights training should therefore be an integral element of a carefully designed strategy that identifies realistic objectives, including follow-up and sustainability.

The focus on training also risks masking deeper structural problems. Legal education in countries marked by years of dictatorship or conflict often declines markedly, resulting in a noticeable gap in knowledge and skills between the older and younger generations. Training is a means to narrow this gap but cannot by itself replace good university education. Support for human rights work, from funders and/or from other universities, adds an important financial and moral dimension that can act as a welcome boost for universities and lecturers who often work in extremely difficult circumstances. Evaluating approaches in this regard should form part of broader reflections on how capacity can be generated from within countries on a sustainable basis.

CASE STUDY 3.2
Responding to Serious Human Rights Violations in Darfur, Sudan – Strategies, Critiques, Impact

The conflict in Darfur, Sudan (2003–) has been characterised by massive human rights violations that have been attributed primarily to the government of Sudan and the Janjaweed (militias), but also to rebel groups.[1] The UN and the AU responded by undertaking a number of fact-finding missions and inquiries, issuing resolutions and, in the case of the UNSC, referring the situation to the Prosecutor of the ICC in 2005.[2] The UN and AU also worked together to provide protection on the ground through the AU/UN Hybrid Mission in Darfur (UNAMID), whose presence the government of Sudan agreed to in 2007.[3] In 2008 the ICC applied for an arrest warrant against Sudan's President al-Bashir

---

[1] See in particular, Report of the International Commission of Inquiry on Darfur, 2005, and J. Flint and A. de Waal, *A New History of a Long War*, 2nd edn (Zed Books, 2008).

[2] UNSC resolution 1593 (2005). See for an overview, L. Oette, 'Peace and Justice, or Neither? The Repercussions of the al-Bashir Case for International Criminal Justice in Africa and Beyond' (2010) 8 *Journal of International Criminal Justice* 345, at 347–50. See for a critical assessment, F. Grünfeld and W. N. Vermeulen in cooperation with J. Krommendijk, *Failure to Prevent Gross Human Rights Violations in Darfur: Warnings to and Responses by International Decision Makers (2003–2005)* (Brill, 2014).

[3] UNSC resolution 1769 (2007).

---

[192] See for an interesting case study on the political question of whether to conduct human rights training in repressive systems, D. Kinley and T. Wilson, 'Engaging a Pariah: Human Rights Training in Burma/Myanmar' (2007) 29 *Human Rights Quarterly* 368.

(which was issued in 2009), which triggered considerable debate and opposition by the Arab League, the AU and others.[4] The AU made a renewed effort to resolve the crisis in 2009 through the AU High-level Panel on Darfur, which was mandated to 'examine the situation in depth and submit recommendations to the Council on how best the issues of accountability and combating impunity, on the one hand, and reconciliation and healing, on the other, could be effectively addressed'.[5]

The situation constituted a major challenge for national and international NGOs and other human rights actors who worked in an environment characterised by constant flashpoints. This included the crisis in Darfur, major milestones in the implementation of the Comprehensive Peace Agreement (2005–2011),[6] such as elections and the referendum concerning the independence of the South, conflicts in other parts of Sudan and 'routine' human rights violations. This often meant that actors seemingly had to follow events rather than being able to pursue coherent strategies. There were also a number of practical challenges. National NGOs simultaneously had to respond to complex factual and political developments, to operate in a repressive environment and to build their capacity. Meanwhile, regional and international actors, particularly the AU and the UN, struggled to fulfil their mandate to monitor and protect human rights due to multiple structural factors, including frequently facing obstruction and adverse reactions ranging from a lack of cooperation to expulsion of their staff members.

The Darfur crisis has been characterised by the creative, and at times controversial, use of human rights strategies. Documenting violations was difficult because of inaccessibility, security concerns and the limited capacity of local actors. However, actors have been able, by employing a range of methods, to obtain valuable information about violations. This included clandestine expert missions to the area, interviews, particularly with refugees in neighbouring Chad, but also with militia leaders and others, leaks, satellite images, videos and photography, as well as medical evidence.[7] Much of this documentation was undertaken by NGOs and concerned individuals, including

---

[4] See Oette, above note 2, 357–64.
[5] Darfur: The Quest for Peace, Justice and Reconciliation, Report of the African Union High-level Panel on Darfur (AUPD), PSC/AHG/2 (CCVII) (29 October 2009).
[6] The Comprehensive Peace Agreement settled the conflict between the Government of Sudan and the southern Sudan People's Liberation Movement/Army.
[7] See the evidence provided by the ICC Prosecutor, reports by major international human rights organisations and the documentary film by A. Sundberg and R. Stern, *The Devil Came on Horseback* (2007). See also A. C. Tsai et al., 'Medical Evidence of Human Rights Violations against Non-Arabic Speaking Civilians in Darfur: A Cross-Sectional Study' (2012) 9 *PLOS Medicine* 1.

international humanitarian NGOs in Darfur and local groups. The UN and the AU undertook fact-finding missions that provided detailed accounts[8] and the ICC carried out its own investigations, although it did not officially visit Darfur. These sources yielded a considerable body of evidence, and some reports, such as those by the UN Commission of Inquiry, have been highly influential, resulting in the ICC referral. The government of Sudan, meanwhile, has persistently downplayed the scale of violations and attributed casualties and incidents to both sides and banditry.[9] While this clearly constitutes a tactic of denial, there are certain issues, such as the scale of rape, which remain contested, largely because of the difficulty of reliably documenting violations.

The Darfur crisis caught the attention of a broad cross-section of actors and resulted in major advocacy campaigns. The highly vocal Save Darfur campaign came under stringent criticism for its allegedly simplistic portrayal of the conflict and exaggeration of the scale of violations.[10] It was accused of having mobilised the public in states such as the USA, while failing to engage politically with Sudan and within Africa. Accordingly, it was considered to be part of the problem of external interference rather than the solution.[11] This criticism highlights potentially problematic aspects of advocacy used to influence policies, such as calling for troops to be deployed to Darfur, which may further aggravate the situation. However, the criticism ignores the plurality of advocacy efforts, including by regional networks such as the Darfur consortium, which pursued more nuanced strategies.[12] In practice, one of the main problems has been the lack of concerted domestic advocacy and mobilisation, not least due to the repressive environment (though considerable efforts have been made to build the capacity of local actors), which shielded Khartoum (the capital of Sudan, often used synonymously with the government) from more serious domestic repercussions.

Human rights violations in Darfur also became the subject of litigation before human rights treaty bodies, such as the ACmHPR in 2009,[13] while

---

[8] Report of the International Commission of Inquiry on Darfur, 2005, and Report of the African Commission on Human and Peoples' Rights' Fact-Finding Mission to the Republic of Sudan in the Darfur Region, 8–18 July 2004, EX.CL/364 (XI) (20 September 2004).

[9] See Interview with President Omar al-Bashir, *BBC* (14 May 2009), online at http://news.bbc.co.uk/1/hi/programmes/hardtalk/8050309.stm.

[10] M. Mamdani, *Saviors and Survivors: Darfur, Politics, and the War on Terror* (Verso, 2009) 48–71. See for a contrasting account, R. Hamilton, *Fighting for Darfur: Public Action and the Struggle to Stop Genocide* (Palgrave Macmillan, 2011).

[11] Mamdani, above note 10, 297.

[12] L. Oette, 'Book Review: Mahmood Mamdani, *Saviors and Survivors, Darfur, Politics and the War on Terror*' (2010) 54 *Journal of African Law* 313.

[13] *Sudan Human Rights Organisation and Centre on Housing Rights and Evictions (COHRE) v. Sudan* (ACmHPR) (2009).

several cases are pending before the ICC.[14] These efforts have contributed to building up a body of evidence concerning human rights violations in Darfur, but have largely failed to make a difference in practice because of the limited enforcement powers of the bodies involved. While the threat of ICC prosecutions is considerable and has resulted in a number of legal and political responses on the part of the government of Sudan, the evidence after more than ten years of conflict illustrates the limits of international human rights law, international humanitarian law and international criminal law in providing protection and justice. Nevertheless, the multiple initiatives comprising documentation, reporting, advocacy, awareness-raising and litigation have resulted in an important record that may yet prove decisive for greater human rights protection and justice, particularly after the popular uprising that began in December 2018 resulted in the downfall of President al-Bashir in April 2019.

[14] See for current status, www.icc-cpi.int/en_menus/icc/situations%20and%20cases/situations/situation%20icc%200205/Pages/situation%20icc-0205.aspx.

POINTS TO CONSIDER

1. What factors explain the innovative approaches to documentation in response to violations in Darfur?
2. Do efforts in respect of Darfur show that advocacy is frequently at risk of being self-serving if not irrelevant altogether?
3. What lessons do developments in Sudan hold for the international human rights movement?

QUESTIONS

1. What makes documentation so fundamental in the promotion and protection of human rights?
2. What methodological and practical difficulties does monitoring pose?
3. Is there any evidence that advocacy enhances human rights promotion and/or protection?
4. Should there be a change in approaches taken towards human rights training?

FURTHER READING

Alston, P., and S. Knuckey (eds.), *The Transformation of Human Rights Fact-Finding* (Oxford University Press, 2016).

Andreassen, B. A., H.-O. Sano and S. McInerney-Lankford (eds.), *Research Methods in Human Rights: A Handbook* (Edward Elgar, 2018).

Baehr, P., *Non-governmental Human Rights Organizations in International Relations* (Palgrave Macmillan, 2009).

Baxi, U., *The Future of Human Rights*, 3rd edn (Oxford University Press, 2008).

Becker, J., *Campaigning for Justice: Human Rights Advocacy in Practice* (Stanford University Press, 2013).

Charnovitz, S., 'Nongovernmental Organizations and International Law' (2006) 100 *American Journal of International Law* 348.

Clifford, B. (ed.), *The International Struggle for New Human Rights* (University of Pennsylvania Press, 2009).

Cotesta, V., *Global Society and Human Rights* (Brill, 2012).

Dupuy, P.-M., and L. Vierucci (eds.), *NGOs in International Law: Efficiency in Flexibility?* (Edward Elgar, 2008).

Goodhart, M. (ed.), *Human Rights: Politics and Practice* (Oxford University Press, 2009).

Hodson, L., *NGOs and the Struggle for Human Rights in Europe* (Hart, 2011).

Keck, M. E., and K. Sikkink, *Activists beyond Borders: Advocacy Networks in International Politics* (Cornell University Press, 1998).

Kennedy, D., *The Dark Side of Virtue: Reassessing International Humanitarianism* (Princeton University Press, 2004).

Landman, T., and E. Carvalho, *Measuring Human Rights* (Routledge, 2010).

Nelson, P. J., and E. Dorsey, *New Rights Advocacy: Changing Strategies of Development and Human Rights NGOs* (Georgetown University Press, 2008).

O'Flaherty, M., and G. Ulrich (eds.), *The Professional Identity of the Human Rights Field Worker* (Ashgate, 2010).

OHCHR, *Training Manual on Human Rights Monitoring* (United Nations, 2001).

Pinkney, R., *NGOs, Africa and the Global Order* (Palgrave Macmillan, 2009).

Rajagopal, B., *International Law from Below: Development, Social Movements and Third World Resistance* (Cambridge University Press, 2007).

Ramcharan, B. G. (ed.), *International Law and Fact-Finding in the Field of Human Rights* (Martinus Nijhoff, 2014).

Risse, T., S. C. Ropp and K. Sikkink (eds.), *The Persistent Power of Human Rights: From Commitment to Compliance* (Cambridge University Press, 2013).

Sikkink, K., *Evidence for Hope: Making Human Rights Work in the 21st Century* (Princeton University Press, 2017).

'Special Issue: Critical Perspectives on the Security and Protection of Human Rights Defenders' (2015) 19 *International Journal of Human Rights*.

Stammers, N., *Human Rights and Social Movements* (Pluto Press, 2009).

Websites

ACmHPR, Special Rapporteur on human rights defenders: www.achpr.org/mechanisms/human-rights-defenders

Inter-American Commission on Human Rights (IACHR), Rapporteurship on Human Rights Defenders: http://oas.org/en/iachr/defenders/default.asp

OHCHR, 'OHCHR in the World: Making Human Rights a Reality on the Ground': www.ohchr.org/EN/Countries/Pages/WorkInField.aspx

OHCHR, Publications and Resources: www.ohchr.org/EN/PublicationsResources/Pages/Publications.aspx

UN Special Rapporteur on the situation of human rights defenders: www.ohchr.org/EN/Issues/SRHRDefenders/Pages/SRHRDefendersIndex.aspx

4 The United Nations Charter System

CONTENTS

4.1   INTRODUCTION

The United Nations (UN) Charter was not designed to address human rights, at least directly, but was instead a mechanism primarily intended to maintain and secure international peace and security. None the less, some scant references to human rights are visible therein, but as will be discussed in this chapter these were not originally meant to confer strict obligations on states or otherwise to establish a global order of rights-holders. Despite these shortcomings the human rights framework of the Charter remains crucially important because in the seventy or so years since its adoption many of the Charter's principal organs and their subsidiary institutions have been instrumental in the promotion and protection of human rights worldwide. Given that the Charter is a living instrument it is only natural that organs originally devoted to human rights have fallen into desuetude and others have surfaced to take their place. Thus, the Charter represents a constantly changing battleground of ideas, institutions, actors and activities within which politics and human rights are at odds. In the midst of this battleground, however, one finds a plethora of actors, both states and non-governmental organisations (NGOs), that seek to close this gap between politics and rights.

Although initially this seemed like a vain uphill struggle on account of the fact that the UN is quintessentially a political organisation, since the end of the Cold War in the early 1990s there has been a shift towards a more visible human rights-centred approach. This is evidenced from the increased depoliticisation of human rights institutions, the adoption of a human rights agenda by the UN Security Council (UNSC) and the mainstreaming of human rights within the Organisation as a whole. Thus, as will become evident in the next section, the UN Charter can no longer be construed in accordance with the political climate and notions of state sovereignty prevailing in 1945. In equal manner, article 2(7) of the Charter, which forbids the Organisation to intervene in the domestic affairs of states, necessarily now excludes human rights violations from its ambit.

A comprehensive discussion of the UN's human rights work and institutions is an infinite task given that every atom of the Organisation is engaged in one way or another in the promotion or protection of rights. As a result, a large part of this chapter is devoted to the examination of the principal human rights institution, the Human Rights Council (HRC), and the various mechanisms operating under its wing. This includes a discussion of the universal periodic review (UPR), the HRC's complaint procedure, as well as its so-called special procedures. The chapter then goes on to analyse the important human rights dimension of the UN General Assembly (UNGA) and the UNSC, since both possess authority to take direct action against violations, in addition to their standard-setting capacity. Institutions that have produced important human rights work, but whose mandate is otherwise peripheral to human rights, such as the International Court of Justice (ICJ), are mentioned in this chapter but are not extensively analysed. Equally, space precludes us from examining specialised agencies such as UN International Children's (Emergency) Fund (UNICEF) and the UN High Commissioner for Refugees (UNHCR).

It should be pointed out that Charter-based institutions are distinguished from treaty organs engaged in human rights work, such as the Human Rights Committee (HRCtee) of the International Covenant on Civil and Political Rights (ICCPR).[1] Although all of these treaty organs reside within the UN they are in fact independent from the Organisation itself, unless treaty members have entered into a collaboration agreement to the contrary with the UN. As a result, treaty organs are not susceptible to the authority of the UNSC, as is the case with Charter-based organs.

---

[1] The Committee on Economic, Social and Cultural Rights (CESCR), on the other hand, is not a treaty organ, but was founded by ECOSOC resolution 1985/17 (28 May 1985). For reasons of coherence its work is explored in the chapters dealing with international treaty systems (Chapter 5) and ESC rights (Chapter 9).

4.2   THE HUMAN RIGHTS DIMENSION OF THE CHARTER

The Charter is rightly viewed as having a *constitutional* force over and above other international treaties and obligations assumed by states because article 103 thereof expressly says so. This necessarily implies that the human rights provisions of the Charter prevail over any conflicting provisions contained in other treaties and are derogable solely in accordance with the Charter. This observation is of practical significance only if the Charter's human rights provisions are couched in the form of concrete obligations for member states. If not, and particularly if the language employed is hortatory, then the risk is that human rights may be marginal to the Charter framework and outside the strict purview of the mandate assigned to its organs and institutions. A literal reading of the Charter demonstrates that human rights were not a priority among delegates to the San Francisco conference that preceded its adoption, and in fact the majority of members were averse to any reference to them. It is well known that even the meagre human rights provisions in the Charter were the result of the determined efforts by human rights lobbyists and Eleanor Roosevelt, wife of the then United States (US) president.

Be this as it may, the *travaux préparatoires* (preparatory work) of the San Francisco conference are of little use in analysing the human dimension of this constitutional instrument, as are its human rights provisions. The preamble and article 1(3) of the Charter prescribe the purposes of the Organisation, which includes among others the reaffirmation of fundamental human rights, equal rights for men and women and self-determination of peoples. This is followed by article 55 which provides that the UN shall 'promote ... universal respect for, and the observance of, human rights and fundamental freedoms for all without distinction as to race, sex, language or religion'. The purposes of article 55 are to be achieved by 'all members pledg[ing] to take joint and separate action in cooperation with the Organisation', in accordance with article 56. If one considers that pledges within the UN are not viewed as binding promises and that the 'promotion' and 'observance' of human rights constitute weak, and rather ineffective, obligations, it is evident that from a strict textual reading the Charter is not a legal basis for the assumption of serious human rights obligations.

Like most contemporary treaties, the UN Charter is a living instrument which by necessity must be construed in accordance with the evolutionary method of interpretation.[2] Evolutionary treaty interpretation is possible, even if not stipulated in the original text, where, in accordance with article 31(1) VCLT, it is supported by good faith, context and the treaty's object and

---

[2] Express acceptance of this method was made, e.g., by the Inter-American Court of Human Rights (IACtHR) in *The Right to Information on Consular Assistance in the Framework of the Guarantees of Due Process of Law* (IACtHR) (1999) para. 193.

purpose. The subsequent human rights practice and shared understanding of UN member states, particularly post-1960, reinforces both context and the Charter's human rights-oriented object and purpose (article 31(3) VCLT).[3]

An illustration is poignant. The cornerstone of the Charter in 1945 and in subsequent years was the containment of armed conflict across international frontiers with a view to averting yet another world war. As a result UN member states were willing to turn a blind eye to authoritarian regimes that committed genocide or blatantly abused fundamental human rights. Thus, human rights on many occasions lost out to the Charter's strict reading of international peace and security as the Organisation's paramount priority. Such an interpretation is no longer viable for several practical reasons. For one thing, it is now universally acknowledged that international peace and security may just as well be threatened by domestic conflicts, either because they tend to spill over into neighbouring nations, or because they cause large migration and refugee flows, or otherwise destabilise entire regions. The disintegration of the former Yugoslavia is a powerful reminder. Moreover, it is now well understood that the absence of rule of law and human rights leads sooner or later to weak, fragile or indeed failed states. The Fund for Peace maintains an annual 'failed/fragile states index' which is premised on twelve indicators, a number of which are pertinent to this discussion: massive refugee or internally displaced person movements, uneven economic development, criminalisation/delegitimisation of the state, widespread violation of human rights, lack of the rule of law, and the security apparatus operating as a state within a state.[4] Finally, the entrenchment of human rights has become so fundamental to the activities and *raison d'être* of the international community that even the very notion of peace and security cannot be divorced or read separately from human rights.[5] As a result, the rather hortatory or weak language of the Charter should not mislead us into thinking that fundamental rights are not an integral part of the UN's principal external aims and priorities. It is necessary therefore to construe the provisions of the Charter in conformity with fundamental human rights.

---

[3] See S. Fish, *Is There a Text in the Class? The Authority of Interpretative Communities* (Harvard University Press, 1980), who coined the theory of interpretative communities and according to which sovereign actors have formed an interpretative community in which they share common understandings about certain notions, including human rights, and interpret these notions in a relatively uniform manner.

[4] See the Fund for Peace, 'Fragile states index 2018', online at http://fundforpeace.org/fsi/2018/04/24/fragile-states-index-2018-annual-report/.

[5] UNGA resolution 65/281 (20 July 2011), preamble, which stresses that 'peace and security, development and human rights are the pillars of the UN system and the foundations for collective security and well-being'. Equally, the UNSC has underlined the perils of HIV/AIDS for regional security and post-conflict reconstruction; UNSC resolution 1983 (7 June 2011).

The dynamic nature of the UN Charter is especially evident in respect of the institutions originally destined to promote and observe human rights. The chief protagonist was one of the five principal organs of the Organisation, namely the Economic and Social Council (ECOSOC). ECOSOC in turn set up the Commission on Human Rights (CommHR), the predecessor to what is now the HRC.[6] As will be discussed in the next section, although the Commission largely failed to take effective measures to protect and enforce human rights[7] it did none the less succeed in pushing forward a standard-setting agenda, followed by the drafting of substantive human rights treaties. The Commission is credited with the Bill of Rights, which consists of the Universal Declaration of Human Rights (UDHR), in addition to the ICCPR and the International Covenant on Economic, Social and Cultural Rights (ICESCR). It was also responsible for the drafting of other important treaties, such as the International Convention on the Elimination of All Forms of Racial Discrimination (ICERD). Yet ECOSOC has remained largely peripheral to the human rights developments stemming from within the Organisation and did not live up to the expectations of the Charter's drafters. On the other hand, the UNGA, and particularly its third (social, humanitarian and cultural affairs) committee, the UNSC and their respective subsidiary organs, have adopted a mix of significant political decisions and legal initiatives in the field of human entitlements. Equally, the ICJ, although by no means designed to address individual complaints or human rights disputes, has on many occasions addressed violations through the prism of state responsibility, while at the same time taking the opportunity to elaborate upon relevant human rights rules.[8]

The slow realisation of rights within the Organisation is explained by the fact that its principal organs are political in nature – save for the ICJ – and this is also true in respect of many of their subsidiary organs. Political, as opposed to independent, appointees are not impartial and owe allegiance to the governments that appointed them. This has inhibited bodies such as ECOSOC and the CommHR from responding even to the most flagrant violations that have come to their attention. During the Cold War, UN institutions largely declined to collaborate with, or make use of, information provided by external stakeholders, particularly human rights NGOs. Although it is

---

[6] At the same time ECOSOC set up another Commission, that on the Status of Women.

[7] In fact, the Commission adopted a statement in 1947 whereby it argued that it had no power to take any action with respect to complaints alleging violations of human rights (CommHR report of first session E/259 (1947) paras. 21–2). For a background analysis, see T. Gonzales, 'The Political Sources of Procedural Debates in the United Nations: Structural Impediments to Implementation of Human Rights' (1981) 13 *New York University Journal of International Law and Politics* 427, at 450.

[8] See R. Higgins, 'Human Rights in the International Court of Justice' (2007) 20 *Leiden Journal of International Law* 745.

true that most European nations generally welcome the participation of civil society, countries with poor human rights records fiercely resisted private intrusions into their domestic affairs. The Organisation has now become responsive to external stakeholders and this is evident, for example, in the mandate of the HRC, its complaints procedures and the UPR, all of which will be analysed shortly. The following sections and subsections will focus on the mandate and work of the OHCHR and the HRC.

4.3 THE OFFICE OF THE HIGH COMMISSIONER FOR HUMAN RIGHTS

The Office of the High Commissioner for Human Rights (OHCHR) was established in 1993 by the UNGA, its purpose being to mainstream[9] and coordinate the Organisation's human rights activities as well as to promote and ensure realisation of rights – particularly by making recommendations to other UN bodies – within the framework of the Charter and the Bill of Rights.[10] The OHCHR is by far the largest human rights entity within the UN, with a staff of 1,300 as of 2019. Unlike the HRC, which addresses human rights issues through an intergovernmental lens and procedures, the OHCHR is independent from states and is a subsidiary organ of UNGA. The OHCHR's work is largely supportive in nature, while at the same time it seeks to coordinate the vast and diverse human rights agendas within the UN. Had it not been for the OHCHR, none of the UN human rights mechanisms, treaty bodies, special procedures, HRC,[11] expert committees, and peacekeeping (as far as the latter's human rights dimension is concerned) would have been possible. The OHCHR is key to operationalising new human rights mechanisms adopted by UN entities. A recent illustration is the International, Impartial and Independence Mechanism (IIIM) for the investigation and prosecution of persons responsible for crimes in Syria since 2011,[12] in respect of which the OHCHR has set out its terms of reference and has an input in the selection of its personnel.

   In furtherance of its capacity-building role, the OHCHR has set up field presences and missions throughout the globe, thereby assisting states to fulfil their human rights obligations, as well as promoting ratification and implementation of human rights treaties. In the pursuit of its mandate, the OHCHR engages, in addition to states, with national human rights institutions (NHRIs), as well as NGOs.

---

[9] Although this task seems to have now been shouldered by the HRC, on the basis of UNGA resolution 65/281 (20 July 2011) Annex, para. 42.

[10] UNGA resolution 48/141 (20 December 1993) para. 4.

[11] Although the OHCHR assists the work of the HRC, it is wholly independent and distinct from the HRC.

[12] UNGA resolution 71/248 (11 January 2017).

The independent (from states) nature of the OHCHR has been enhanced by a succession of influential and outspoken Commissioners. This has led to more vibrant human rights diplomacy and the maintenance of a vocal and public profile. By way of illustration the OHCHR did not hesitate to criticise the USA for its handling of the Guantánamo detainees, demanding that they be entitled to fundamental rights under human rights and humanitarian law.[13]

4.4   THE HRC

The HRC, although among the newest human rights bodies in the UN system, is certainly among the most important. Its establishment was the result of the acute politicisation and lack of credibility of its predecessor,[14] the CommHR and ECOSOC. While it is true that the Commission achieved significant landmarks in both standard-setting and rule-making through the promulgation of declarations and treaties, it also struggled with the political agendas of several of its member states, many of which were anti-human rights oriented. A number of nations were driven to hold seats in the Commission with the sole purpose of obfuscating and preventing condemnation of their human rights records, as well as those of their allies.[15] It is true to say that with the exception of South Africa – which was, however, politically isolated – the Commission never really managed to condemn or seriously investigate the gross human rights abuses committed by any country against its own people. This state of affairs was tolerated because of the lack of an alternative option, particularly during the Cold War, the futility of attempting to amend the relevant part of the UN Charter and also because the liberal democracies in the Commission were satisfied that this body was at the very least contributing to the promulgation of positive human rights law. By the early 2000s it had become apparent that the Commission could no longer fulfil a serious role in the protection and monitoring of human rights worldwide and that it would have to be replaced by a new institution that was not prone to political manipulation and which would, moreover, enjoy the confidence of public and private actors alike.

A number of events prompted the need for the creation of the HRC, besides the over-politicisation and loss of credibility of its predecessor. For one thing, the USA and its European allies had long lost the requisite majority to thwart

---

[13] See CommHR, Situation of Detainees at Guantánamo Bay, UN doc. E/CN.4/2006/120 (15 February 2006).

[14] Report of the High-level Panel of Threats, Challenges and Change, A More Secure World: Our Shared Responsibility, UN doc. A/59/565 (1 December 2004) para. 283.

[15] UN Secretary-General Report, In Larger Freedom: Towards Development, Security and Human Rights for All, UN doc. A/59/2005/Add.3 (26 May 2005) paras. 140–7.

Third World politics within the Commission. Secondly, the monitoring and complaint mechanisms of the Commission had become merely ceremonial and had been replaced in practice by the various UN treaty mechanisms and the work of treaty bodies. Thirdly, much of the work which would otherwise have been the domain of the Commission had been assumed by the Third Committee of the UNGA and to a much lesser degree by the UNSC. Fourthly, the political 'aberration' previously associated with the notion that the UN could collaborate with civil society organisations in the field of human rights had long been replaced by a global climate where such collaboration was welcome at all levels. Lastly, following the end of the Cold War era, which was plagued by the complete inability of the UN to tackle human rights catastrophes such as that of Cambodia, industrialised nations and their populations were now inclined to be vocal against human rights abuses.

By and large, the UN's human rights agenda could certainly have survived without bodies such as the Commission or the HRC, given that all its organs, bodies and entities are already actively engaged with human rights issues. Moreover, human rights are incorporated and streamlined in all UN activities and operations.[16] So why the need for yet another dedicated, yet still political, human rights body? As the global guarantor of peace and security, including human rights, the UN no doubt needs a permanent standing body dedicated solely to advancing, protecting and monitoring human rights, lest the otherwise welcome diffusion and overlap of human rights agendas within the Organisation risk becoming random, uncoordinated and perhaps also conflicting. The ideal permanent body must, moreover, enjoy significant political clout, otherwise it is in jeopardy of being ignored, side-lined or made irrelevant. Such *clout can only be derived from the active participation of sovereign states at the helm, as opposed to a self-standing court, quasi-court or civil society organisations. The latter, as important as they are, can only play a complementary role to that of states in the protection and promotion of rights, particularly with respect to countries that openly and blatantly flout most human entitlements. Finally, apart from condemnatory resolutions by the UNSC and the UNGA, there exists no other mechanism within the UN system where states can discuss their human rights issues in an open and non-confrontational manner with a view to exposing such problems and potentially – although certainly not always – finding solutions. Despite their

---

[16] By way of illustration, all entities within the UN system involved in development projects adopted, in 2003, a Statement on a Common Understanding of a Human Rights-based Approach (HRBA) to Development Cooperation. Therein it is stated that all projects must be guided by the Bill of Rights and that development cooperation 'contributes to the development of the capacities of "duty-bearers" to meet their obligations and of "rights-holders" to claim their rights'. Equally, mainstreaming gender perspectives into all policies and programmes of the UN was formally institutionalised in 1997. See UN doc. E/1997/66 (12 June 1997).

*※ Yeah she got a lot

precedential value, human rights tribunals and treaty mechanisms are only useful for resolving individualised violations and do not allow the international community to address the offending state, with the aid of NGOs, in an elaborate discussion of all its human rights problems. The HRC aspires to assume this unique role.

Unlike the Commission, which was set up by ECOSOC, the HRC was set up by the UNGA and is a subsidiary organ thereof.[17] Its task is to carry on the work of the Commission, as well as assume its responsibilities,[18] and as a result its creation was not meant to sever all ties with the past. Its legal status allows it to bring all matters relating to human rights, whether urgent or long-term, for discussion before the UNGA, which certainly enjoys far more exposure and political power than ECOSOC. The HRC was entrusted with three major responsibilities: (1) a thorough and ongoing review of the human rights record of all UN members, through a mechanism known as UPR; (2) examination and investigation of situations concerning gross and systematic violations of human rights; and (3) optimisation of the UN's institutional capacity to deal with human rights.

The first two will be examined in discrete sections of this chapter, so it is prudent briefly to discuss institutional optimisation at this stage. Since 1945 every entity within the UN has assumed some kind of human rights function and over time this has given rise to unnecessary duplication and overlap. This is not only costly, but risks generating friction and inefficiency. The HRC is responsible for rationalising and coordinating the various human rights mandates and functions, save for the standing work of the UNGA and the UNSC. Moreover, despite the fact that the UN is automatically associated with human rights, it is not self-evident that all its departments and institutions are guided by a specific human rights agenda and policy. By way of example, a strategy of sanctions designed to prevent a regime from amassing nuclear weapons but which causes malnutrition, child mortality and deaths as a result of the lack of health care is clearly devoid of a human rights orientation. Equally, policies that promote rights but which do not take into consideration the particular needs of women and girls are devoid of a gender perspective. It was therefore crucial that the HRC was entrusted with mainstreaming gender and human rights considerations into all UN policies and actions.[19]

If all of these laudable aspirations which the new HRC is poised to fulfil are to be achieved, it needs to be impartial, objective, transparent and results oriented. This is a tall order given the politicised nature of its predecessor and certainly cannot be achieved by mere rhetoric. That is why the UNGA decided on the imposition of certain, seemingly stringent, conditions for the election of

---

[17] UNGA resolution 60/251 (3 April 2006) para. 1.   [18] Ibid., para. 5(g).
[19] Ibid., paras. 3 and 6.

states to the forty-seven members comprising the HRC. Although membership of the Council is open to all UN members, the UNGA 'shall take into account the contribution of candidates to the promotion and protection of human rights and their voluntary pledges and commitments made thereto'.[20] Although this falls rather short of requiring a solid human rights record of potential members, it does represent a significant departure from past practices and no doubt states with poor records may find themselves dissuaded or simply discouraged. Moreover, in extreme cases, the UNGA, by a two-thirds majority of present and voting members, may suspend a particular member engaged in gross and systematic violation of human rights.[21] In practice, because membership to the Council is highly valued from a strategic perspective, states have vied for election and in their pledges to the UNGA made a distinct effort to demonstrate their commitment to human rights both domestically and internationally. Of course, this may be meaningless for countries with a history of repression and abuse,[22] but even so they risk being isolated by other HRC members. Certain groups of states have gone as far as publicly declaring their voting criteria, as was the case with European Union (EU) members which committed themselves not to vote for candidates that were subject to UN sanctions for human rights violations.[23] The USA, although a member of the Council since 2009, initially voted against resolution 60/251 (which effectively created the HRC) because it only required a simple majority for the election of members as opposed to a more stringent two-thirds majority, and also because it did not automatically exclude candidates subject to UN sanctions.[24]

Yet the system is far from perfect and has faced legitimacy concerns from the outset. Membership of the HRC is based on equitable geographical distribution among the various regional groups.[25] Ideally, states will compete for available seats and will thus be elected by their regional peers on the basis of their human rights record. In practice, many regional groupings operate manufactured (or closed) slates, meaning that competition within the group is discouraged because seats are allocated under the table by mutual

---

[20] Ibid., para. 8.   [21] Ibid.

[22] E.g., see Egyptian Pledge, UN doc. A/61/878 (23 April 2007) 5, where the then (autocratic) Mubarak regime pledged, inter alia, to preserve the freedom of the press and of the judiciary and to strengthen civil society and political dialogue! The texts of all 2007 election pledges are available online at www.un.org/ga/61/elect/hrc/.

[23] H. Upton, 'The Human Rights Council: First Impressions and Future Challenges' (2007) 7 *Human Rights Law Review* 29, at 33.

[24] In fact, in April 2008 the Bush administration announced that it would be withholding a portion of its contribution to the 2008 UN regular budget, equivalent to the country's share of the HRC budget. In June of the same year it further announced that the USA would engage with the HRC 'only in matters of deep national interest'. The Obama administration reversed this hostile climate and in 2009 the USA was elected to the HRC, submitting its first UPR in 2010. In June 2018, the USA withdrew from the HRC on account of the Council's supposed political bias.

[25] UNGA resolution 60/251, para. 7.

You go girl!

agreement between group members. Astonishingly, Syria's candidacy for the Council was unopposed within the Asian group in the run-up to the 2011 elections, despite global reports that its security forces had killed more than 800 demonstrators at the time, just before the Syrian conflict erupted in full and sank the country into chaos. Following widespread condemnation, the Asian group finally urged Syria to withdraw its candidacy and nominated Kuwait in its place.[26]

Despite these shortcomings the Council is a far cry from its predecessor where the withdrawal of a candidacy for persistent human rights violations would have seemed laughable. This conclusion is reinforced by the suspension of Libya from the Council by the UNGA on 1 March 2011,[27] only nine months after it was elected on a closed African slate. The practice of closed slates has been the subject of much criticism by the EU, and in the EU Parliament's Priorities for the 24th (2014) session of the HRC, it was emphasised that:

> elections to the [HRC] need to be competitive, and expresses its opposition to the arranging of uncontested elections by regional groups; reiterates the importance of standards for [HRC] membership as regards commitment and performance in the human rights field, and urges the member states to insist on such standards when defining the candidates they will vote for.[28]

These developments certainly indicate an evolving dynamic permeating the operation and membership of this new institution. The UPR mechanism, examined in 4.4.1, justifies a reserved excitement about this dynamic.

4.4.1   The UPR

The UPR is a creature born out of UNGA resolution 60/251.[29] It assumes that an HRC composed as far as possible of countries that promote and implement human rights can serve as a forum for a holistic, honest, yet non-confrontational, discussion of each nation's persistent human rights issues. The UNGA made it clear that this reporting mechanism should not duplicate existing reporting obligations, must avoid becoming burdensome to the UN and its member states and should moreover add value to the promotion of human rights. Before going any further it is important to examine in what way the UPR is different from similar reporting mechanisms within the UN system, particularly the seven treaty-based mechanisms and any Charter-based

---

[26] Human Rights Watch, 'UN: Limited Choice Marks Rights Body Election' (20 May 2011).
[27] UNGA resolution 65/265 (1 March 2011).
[28] EU Parliament resolution of 13 March 2014 on EU priorities for the 25th session of the UN Human Rights Council (2014/2612(RSP)) paras. 2 and 5.
[29] UNGA resolution 60/25, para. 5(e).

periodic reports. Charter-based reporting is no longer available; its last manifestation, a periodic self-reporting mechanism,[30] was formally terminated in 1980 as being obsolete and far too marginal to be of any relevance.[31] The reporting dimension of the treaty bodies, on the other hand, has fared much better and has enhanced the effectiveness of individual communications, general comments, inter-state complaints and on-site inquiries, where available. None the less, despite the extensive comments and recommendations of the various treaty bodies in their responses to national reports, these are necessarily confined to the limited number of rights contained in their respective treaties. Moreover, this process is confined only to those states that have ratified the treaties.

By contrast, under the UPR states are reviewed on the basis of obligations arising from the UN Charter, the UDHR, instruments to which they are parties and any unilaterally assumed voluntary pledges and commitments.[32] These may in fact turn out to be more extensive than most treaty obligations. Even further, although the treaty bodies are not supported by an enforcement mechanism, their comments and recommendations on the parties' periodic reports are not meant to serve as mere points of discussion. On the contrary, because the obligations arising out of human rights treaties are binding, the recommendations of the treaty bodies aim, among other things, to demonstrate where and how compliance is poor or ineffective. In this sense the treaty bodies' periodic reporting mechanisms are not necessarily free from friction and compulsion. Finally, treaty bodies employ for their reporting processes independent experts, whereas the UPR is premised on peer review, which is conducted by the representatives of states elected to the HRC.

The reader may well ponder what makes a country that is not a party to any, or simply a few, treaty-based mechanisms decide to take part in a UPR where the entirety of its human rights record risks being scrutinised before the rest of the world. The simple answer to this question lies in the fact that even the most brutal regime, with the exception perhaps of North Korea, is weary of perpetual political and financial isolation and is cognisant that its human rights record will eventually surface, thanks to the pace of modern media and the speed of information exchange. As a result, even countries with the poorest of human rights records have submitted themselves to the scrutiny of the UPR.

The process is relatively straightforward. To start with, states are under an obligation to submit a national report discussing the state of human rights in their country, which ideally should be prepared on the basis of a broad

---

[30] ECOSOC resolution 624B (XXII) (1 August 1956).
[31] UNGA resolution 35/209 (17 December 1980).
[32] HRC resolution 5/1 (18 June 2007) Annex, para. 1.

consultation with all relevant stakeholders.[33] This national report should not exceed twenty pages, unlike the extensive reports submitted before human rights treaty bodies. No doubt, these national reports will attempt to paint a favourable picture and in many cases deflect attention from serious abuses or hide behind laws that were never meant to be respected or implemented by the authorities. In order for the HRC to assess the national report the UPR provides for the compilation of two distinct sources of information that are made publicly available: (1) information contained in the reports of treaty bodies, special procedures, including observations and comments by the state concerned, and other relevant UN documents which shall not exceed ten pages;[34] (2) a summary of credible information provided by other relevant stakeholders, namely NGOs, which again must not exceed ten pages.[35] In practice, given the vibrancy and organisation of the international human rights NGO movement, the information provided in national reports is quite literally picked apart in the NGO summaries. By way of illustration, in the course of Uzbekistan's 2008 UPR presentation, NGOs consistently emphasised that torture was not only widespread but publicly sanctioned in Uzbekistan and that the country had failed to implement the right to fair trial, having resorted to exaction of forced confessions, denial of defence rights and government appointment of judges.[36] In respect of Myanmar, the contributing NGOs contested the suggestion of the government that the new Constitution was transparent and democratic, noting, inter alia, that article 445 thereof effectively granted a blanket amnesty to government officials for past and future serious crimes.[37]

The national report along with the compiled information is then processed and reviewed by a working group consisting of three rapporteurs, selected by the drawing of lots among the members of the HRC and from different regional groupings (also known as the troika).[38] The review is conducted through an interactive dialogue, which may involve the participation of observer states and other stakeholders.[39] The purpose of this format is to pose meaningful and pressing questions to the reviewed state by any interested party sharing particular human rights concerns, thus also avoiding giving the impression that the troika operates in a quasi-judicial manner. A list of questions or issues may be prepared in advance by observer nations and submitted to the state under review with a view to facilitating its preparation and providing some focus for the interactive dialogue.[40] In practice, this list of issues and questions has become a significant part of the process,

---

[33] HRC resolution 5/1, Annex, para. 15(a).   [34] Ibid., para. 15(b).   [35] Ibid., para. 15(c).
[36] NGO summary on Uzbekistan, UN doc. A/HRC/WG.6/3/UZB/3 (16 September 2008) paras. 8, 9 and 14.
[37] NGO summary on Myanmar, UN doc. A/HRC/WG.6/10//MMR/3 (18 October 2010) paras. 5 and 12.
[38] HRC resolution 5/1, Annex, para. 18(d).   [39] Ibid., para. 18(b) and (c).   [40] Ibid., para. 21.

particularly since many of the issues raised have evoked strong responses on account of their sensitive nature.

In 2009 the Uzbek delegation, for example, reacted forcefully to allegations that it had covered up its military repression of government dissent in Andijan province which resulted in the loss of hundreds of lives, noting that this was a national security issue which it was not willing to discuss further.[41] In other instances, the list of questions against liberal democracies has addressed a variety of non-mainstream human rights issues. In 2011 the USA, for example, was criticised, among other things, for its poverty discrepancy between blacks and whites, for rapes in prison and discrimination against indigenous peoples.[42] No doubt, states are compelled to respond to the questions posed, even if to dismiss them. The interactive dialogue itself, with the presence of observers and stakeholders, is scheduled to last no more than three hours.[43] This is followed by the deliberation of the troika and the adoption of a so-called outcome. Prior to its adoption, the country under review will have a chance to respond to the issues raised.[44] The outcome is equivalent to the report adopted by treaty bodies and consists of a summary of the proceedings, a conclusion and/or recommendations and a list of the voluntary commitments of the state concerned.[45]

Because the UPR is founded on the principle of cooperation, country involvement and non-confrontation, the conclusion/recommendation section of the outcomes does not criticise countries under review. Instead, it offers suggestions for improvement, shares best practices, and offers the possibility of cooperation, technical assistance and capacity-building, among other things.[46] States may accept a recommendation or take note of it. The idea underlying the UPR is to identify problems, discuss them with the state concerned and offer assistance to overcome them. In practice, most countries tend to adopt at least some of the recommendations offered in the course of their UPR.[47] At the same time it has to be acknowledged that the HRC, special procedures and treaty bodies have identified a plethora of instances where states have paid mere lip service even to pledges made by themselves. The HRC may decide if and when any specific follow-up is necessary, and in situations where a state fails to take any remedial action the HRC may address

---

[41] Report of the Working Group on the Uzbek UPR, UN doc. A/HRC/10/83 (11 March 2009) para. 97.

[42] Report of the Working Group on the United States, UPR, UN doc. A/HRC/16/11 (4 January 2011) paras. 76 and 78–9.

[43] HRC resolution 5/1, Annex, para. 22.   [44] Ibid., paras. 28–32.   [45] Ibid., para. 26.

[46] Ibid., para. 27.

[47] Chad, for example, agreed to ratify the Optional Protocol to the Convention against Torture and to establish a national prevention mechanism, something applauded by the Committee against Torture (CtAT). See Concluding Observations on Chad, UN doc. CAT/C/TCD/CO/1 (4 June 2009) para. 36.

as it deems appropriate all instances of persistent non-cooperation.[48] In 2011 the HRC adopted a brief decision on non-cooperation with the UPR, which although addressed to Israel at the time, was held to be of general application. The decision effectively urged all UPR stakeholders to exert pressure on the non-cooperative state to submit to the process.[49] Interestingly, Israel resumed its UPR assessment in 2013, which indicates that even such pressure can be effective.

Overall, the UPR, despite its drawbacks, has managed to make deliberation transparent and open to external actors, particularly NGOs, and has forced governments to respond to questions they would otherwise prefer not to engage with. At the end of the first UPR cycle in 2012, all UN member states had been subjected to review. Of the 21,000 recommendations issued, 74 per cent had been accepted.[50] By mid-2019 the third cycle was halfway completed. Empirical evidence suggests that NGOs have grown in experience from the UPR and in the process have unified their efforts through partnerships and established more effective follow-up monitoring procedures.[51] In some countries, NGOs are either considered illegal or their members are liable to persecution. As a result, NGO submissions for countries like Saudi Arabia are made by entities operating abroad.[52]

4.4.2   The HRC's Complaints Procedure

Given the myriad individual complaint mechanisms available through the UN's treaty bodies and regional human rights tribunals, an additional procedure seems rather superfluous. This is all the more true considering that the so-called 1503 procedure,[53] the predecessor to the HRC's current complaints mechanism, is confidential, time-consuming and oriented towards achieving a friendly settlement with the culprit state, rather than addressing the plight of the victims. As a result, it is not self-evident why the UNGA thought it wise

---

[48] HRC resolution 5/1, paras. 37–8. In practice, special procedures also warn recalcitrant countries about failing to implement both their pledges as well as the most pertinent recommendations addressed to them in their UPR. See Special Rapporteur on North Korea, UN doc. A/HRC/16/58 (21 February 2011) para. 74.

[49] See Report of the HRC on the Work of its Seventh Organizational Meeting, UN doc. A/HRC/OM/7/1 (4 April 2013).

[50] UPR Info, 'Beyond Promises: The Impact of the UPR on the Ground' (2014) 13, online at www.upr-info.org/sites/default/files/general-document/pdf/2014_beyond_promises.pdf.

[51] UPR Info, 'The Butterfly Effect: Spreading Good Practices of UPR Implementation' (2016).

[52] See Summary of Stakeholders' Submission on Saudi Arabia, UN doc. HRC/WG.6/31/SAU/3 (24 August 2018).

[53] It is known as such because it was enunciated in ECOSOC resolution 1503 (XLVIII) (27 May 1970), as amended by ECOSOC resolution 2000/3 (19 June 2000). CommHR resolution 2000/109 (16 April 2000) further reduced the procedural steps for the filing of communications from five to four.

to renew the life cycle of the 1503 procedure.[54] There are some cogent reasons. For one thing, whereas individual complaint mechanisms require the consent of states for the submission of communications by their nationals, the 1503 procedure does not. Moreover, the procedure is triggered only with respect to gross and systematic violations of human rights,[55] not mere individual and isolated infractions. In terms of effectiveness the 1503 procedure was largely discredited because it failed to seriously investigate many of the widespread violations of its era, including the glaring crimes of the Argentine junta in the 1980s and those of the Fujimori regime in Peru. The case of the Rwandan genocide is also illustrative. Although the Commission had ample information a year before the genocide that it was in fact impending, it none the less decided to keep the situation confidential under the 1503 procedure. What is more alarming is that Rwanda at the time held a seat on the Commission.

Other criticisms against the Commission are that it addressed only a limited number of civil and political rights, thus excluding altogether economic, social and cultural rights, and demonstrated a deep political bias which rendered it unable to act against particular governments.[56] Between 1974 and 2005 a total of eighty-four countries were examined, with violations ranging from mass killings and disappearances to forced labour and religious persecution.[57] Although little information has become publicly available, it is known at least that the CommHR adopted condemnatory resolutions only in respect of seven countries, while three were referred directly to the public 1235 procedure (as opposed to the confidential nature of the 1503 mechanism).[58]

The revamped 1503 complaints procedure[59] has remedied many of the defects of its predecessor, and as a result of the proliferation of treaty-based and regional communications mechanisms its role is practically limited to being an early warning system and a complementary political pressure tool.

[54] See para. 3 of UNGA resolution 60/251, wherein the UNGA decided to retain this mechanism.

[55] ECOSOC resolution 1503, para. 1.

[56] P. Alston, 'The Commission on Human Rights', in P. Alston (ed.), *The United Nations and Human Rights: A Critical Appraisal* (Clarendon Press, 1995) 151.

[57] H. Tolley, 'The Concealed Crack in the Citadel: The UN Commission on Human Rights' Response to Confidential Communications' (1984) 6 *Human Rights Quarterly* 420.

[58] ECOSOC resolution 1235 (XLII) (6 June 1967). This followed the 1503 procedure and was originally intended to allow the Commission to consider the situations in South Africa, Rhodesia and Portuguese colonies. However, the Sub-Commission on Human Rights, now disbanded, hijacked the process and allowed NGOs to make oral interventions or circulate statements, which in turn allowed it to recommend to the Commission that it establish a committee of experts to consider situations in Greece and Haiti during 1967. A shocked Commission then adopted the 1503 confidential procedure to avoid further political embarrassment. The rationale of the 1235 procedure has none the less been retained in the revamped procedure under HRC resolution 5/1, Annex, para. 109(d).

[59] Its modalities are elaborated in HRC resolution 5/1, Annex, part IV.

Quite significantly it is expressly applicable to all rights and not only to those considered fundamental, as long as their violation is gross, of course.[60] It is also hailed as victim-oriented on account of the fact that it requires the HRC to reach an outcome within a maximum of two years from the submission of the complaint to the state and also because it provides for the involvement of the complainant.[61] Given that the procedure is directed towards gross, and therefore ongoing, human rights violations it is evident that a two-year process involving deliberations with the culprit state is inadequate for addressing urgent situations. It is also unlikely that the UNSC will be in the dark in relation to gross and widespread human rights violations likely to endanger peace and security, and no doubt other early warning mechanisms, both intergovernmental and private, will be more alert to the first signals of crimes and violations. Much like the use of the ICJ to impose interim measures in the *Bosnian Genocide case*,[62] which although unable to yield any immediate relief for the victims was none the less able to put pressure on Serbia, the revamped 1503 procedure will ultimately serve as a complementary forum for political pressure.

From a procedural point of view it is no different from other complaint mechanisms. In order to be considered admissible an application must not be politically motivated, should adequately describe alleged violations and be submitted by the victim or any person or group with direct and reliable information, even second-hand, as long as the information is not based exclusively on media reports. Moreover, local remedies need to have been exhausted, assuming they are effective, and the case should not have been referred to another human rights procedure.[63] Communications are filtered for the purposes of admissibility, including an assessment of whether the alleged violations are indeed gross and persistent, by a working group on communications that is staffed by members of the HRC's advisory committee.[64] Once considered admissible the complaints filtered are passed to a working group on situations, whose task is to investigate the allegations. This is composed of HRC members serving, however, in their personal capacity.[65] As already noted, the procedure is confidential, albeit the plenary of the HRC is notified of all proceedings.[66] The state under investigation must cooperate and make every effort to provide a response no later than three months after receiving

---

[60] Ibid., para. 85.

[61] Ibid., paras. 85 and 105–8. Minimal is an understatement, given that the complainant has no access to what is being discussed in the relevant proceedings administered by the working groups.

[62] Case Concerning *Application of the Genocide Convention* (*Bosnia v. FRY*), Provisional Measures Order (ICJ) (1993).

[63] HRC resolution 5/1, Annex, para. 87.   [64] Ibid., paras. 91–5.   [65] Ibid., paras. 96–7.

[66] Exceptionally, the HRC may decide to conduct a public meeting in those situations of 'manifest and unequivocal lack of cooperation', in accordance with para. 104, ibid.

the request. Five potential outcomes are available from this process: (1) full discontinuation; (2) retention of the situation under review followed by a request to the state to provide further information; (3) retention under review and appointment of a country rapporteur; (4) discontinuation of the confidential procedure and reverting to a public consideration of the situation; and (5) recommendation of technical assistance, capacity-building or advisory services through the OHCHR to the state under consideration.[67]

A case study is pertinent. Following several allegations of widespread and systematic human rights violations in Eritrea, the HRC proceeded to converse with the Eritrean government in confidence. None the less, the information received, both oral and written, was deemed inadequate and incomplete and hence the HRC decided to discontinue the confidential process and take up public consideration of the matter, including empowering the Special Rapporteur on the human rights situation in Eritrea to investigate allegations contained in the complaints.[68]

4.5   SPECIAL PROCEDURES

It was in 1980 that the then Sub-Commission on the Promotion and Protection of Human Rights recommended to the CommHR the establishment of a Working Group on enforced or involuntary disappearances (WGEID), which were at the time common place among South America's dictatorial regimes.[69] The Working Group was immensely successful because it proved flexible and was able to visit numerous countries for on-site investigations, something which neither the Commission nor the Sub-Commission was able to do.[70] Moreover, the Working Group was able to respond quickly to urgent situations and as a result it became a useful paradigm for human rights reporting and investigation.

The function and nature of special procedures is quite different from that of other Charter-based and human rights treaty bodies. Special procedures are set up to scrutinise and/or investigate specific countries where acute human rights violations are alleged to have taken place, or investigate and report on the trends, developments and implementation of particular rights around the world. The former are known as country-specific mandates, whereas the latter are known as thematic mandates. Thematic mandates may be established in the form of a working group or by means of an independent expert or special rapporteur. Although their establishment has never been driven by particular methodological imperatives, for instructive

you love thematic stuff

---

[67] Ibid., para. 109.   [68] HRC resolution 21/1 (9 October 2012).

[69] CommHR resolution 20 (XXXVI) (29 February 1980).

[70] The Sub-Commission had prior to 1980 set up intersessional and sessional working groups, such as those on slavery (1975) and the administration of justice (1974).

purposes thematic mandates can be distinguished in three ways by reference to their pursuits, namely: (1) those that seek to investigate and analyse the state and implementation of rights clearly established in the Bill of Rights (for example, enforced or involuntary disappearances, torture, freedom of religion or belief, racism and racial discrimination); (2) those highlighting the impact of contemporary situations on the enjoyment of rights (for example, those of people of African descent, the effects of foreign debt and other related international financial obligations of states on the full enjoyment of human rights, mercenaries, countering terrorism, and extreme poverty); and (3) those that investigate the status and viability of new and emerging rights (for example, international solidarity, transnational corporations and their impact on rights, contemporary forms of slavery and migrants).[71]

What distinguishes the UN's special procedures from other Charter-based mechanisms is that all mandate-holders are independent from any government. In fact, although a certain degree of lobbying is necessarily involved, interested candidates are urged to apply independently. In practice, such posts have largely been assumed by academics (although a number have been also held by activists), largely because they are able to combine their academic activities with the exigencies of their mandates. This is by no means a trivial issue because other than their expenses mandate-holders are not entitled to a salary and it is natural, given the time-consuming nature of these posts, that they only attract the wealthy or academics (equipped with human rights expertise) able to work around their professional schedules. Since most thematic mandates demand a team of full-time staff to deal with the increasing load of communications and research, it is evident that mandate-holders from developing nations have little, or no, access to the level of resources and funding of their wealthier counterparts. This in turn has been counterproductive for the work of some mandates and the UNGA recently addressed this critical issue by requesting the OHCHR to make available requisite funding from the UN budget as well as from extra-budgetary sources.[72]

Special procedures are not meant to process individual complaints in the manner practised by Charter-based mechanisms (for example the 1503 procedure) or treaty bodies, which exercise a judicial or quasi-judicial function. Equally, they have no authority to demand that offending states undertake any particular action.[73] Finally, UN member states have no general reporting obligations towards any of the special procedures, and no obligation

---

[71] By September 2015 there were thirty-nine thematic mandates and fourteen country mandates.

[72] UNGA resolution 65/281 (20 July 2011) Annex, paras. 31–4.

[73] Of course, this has not stopped special procedures, in cases of recalcitrant governments, of notifying the UNSC, recommending that it take appropriate action to ensure that the culprit government respect its human rights obligations. See Report of the Special Rapporteur on Belarus, UN doc. E/CN.4/2006/36 (16 January 2006) para. 80.

to respond to particular allegations. None the less, special procedures have played an immensely significant role in shaping human rights policies in areas insufficiently understood by policy-makers,[74] as well as in addressing urgent human rights crises in a manner that other bodies with judicial authority could not. By way of illustration, it has been aptly demonstrated by the Special Rapporteur on the right to food, among other UN bodies, that the right of access to food is affected by domestic agricultural policies, gender discrimination and global market fluctuations, as well as because 'global food systems have been shaped to maximize efficiency gains and produce large volumes of commodities, they have failed to take distributional concerns into account'.[75] Equally, the independent expert on debt and human rights has adduced concrete evidence that government debt affects all fundamental rights.[76]

Moreover, the work of special mandates often leads to very distinct standard-setting tools in areas of law where other forms of regulation or norm-creation are non-existent. We have already referred to the Guiding Principles on Foreign Debt and Human Rights, but one may also single out the *Handbook for Realizing the Human Rights to Water and Sanitation*[77] and the Draft Basic Principles on the right to effective remedies for trafficked persons.[78]

The following sections aim to show how mandate-holders have employed the three tools in their armoury to make their mandates flexible, responsive and relevant. It is precisely because of their flexibility and immediate response to violations that special procedures mandate-holders are a constant nuisance for many countries. More often than not they have been made the object of political attack and have been asked to resign.[79] In one case the Special Rapporteur on the independence of judges and lawyers was convicted and incarcerated by his native Malaysian courts because it was considered that he had defamed certain private firms, which he accused of being involved in corruption. The ICJ emphatically pointed out that things

---

[74] Some special procedures have even proceeded to issue general comments in the same manner as treaty bodies. See the WGEID, 'General Comments on Enforced Disappearance as a Continuous Crime', online at www.ohchr.org/Documents/Issues/Disappearances/GC-EDCC.pdf.

[75] Final Report of the UN Special Rapporteur on the right to food, 'The Transformative Potential of the Right to Food', UN doc. A/HRC/25/57 (24 January 2014) para. 10.

[76] See 'Guiding Principles on Foreign Debt and Human Rights', UN doc A/HRC/20/23 (10 April 2011) Annex.

[77] Available online at www.ohchr.org/EN/Issues/WaterAndSanitation/SRWater/Pages/Handbook.aspx.

[78] Available online at www.ohchr.org/Documents/Issues/Trafficking/Consultation/ConsultationEffectiveRemedy/DraftBasicPrinciples.pdf.

[79] See 'Statement by US Ambassador to the HRC for the Resignation of Special Rapporteur Richard Falk' (7 July 2011), online at http://geneva.usmission.gov/2011/07/07/donahoe-statement/.

said or done in the course of a Special Rapporteur's mandate are immune from prosecution.[80]

INTERVIEW 4.1
With Former UN Independent Expert
(Cephas Lumina)

Cephas Lumina, a Zambian national, was UN Independent Expert on the effects of debt on the enjoyment of human rights from 2008 to 2014. The interview was carried out when he was still in office. He was subsequently appointed to the Committee on the Rights of Children.

How are you able to combine your position as Special Rapporteur with your busy academic and professional schedule? Do you receive any secretarial or other assistance from the UN or other bodies?

It is very difficult to combine academic and professional responsibilities with work as a UN special procedures mandate-holder. A number of colleagues either have low teaching loads or have been granted leave of absence by their institutions in order to devote more time to UN work. Unfortunately, this has not been the case with me and I was constrained to leave my academic position because the workload did not leave me sufficient time for my academic work and my home institution was not very supportive in this regard.

   Although the OHCHR is enjoined to provide administrative assistance, this is quite limited due to budgetary constraints, which means that fewer human and financial resources are available to support the work of the special procedures. I personally receive no support from other sources (I think due to the contentious nature of my mandate), but some of my colleagues get extra funding from some countries which allows them to engage additional support staff or undertake thematic studies. There are also problems flowing from a high staff turnover in the OHCHR, which is attributable to staff career movements and cumbersome UN recruitment procedures. Some of the support staff work on short-term contracts and therefore are forced to seek longer-term, and more secure, job opportunities elsewhere. To illustrate the gravity of the problem, I have had a total of seven OHCHR staff supporting my mandate since I assumed it in May 2008 until early 2012 (some lasting only a couple of months)!

---

[80] *Difference Relating to Immunity from Legal Process of a Special Rapporteur of the Commission on Human Rights* (ICJ) (1999) paras. 39ff.

Do you think that affected individuals and communities are aware of your mandate and that by communicating with you they feel they can make a difference?

No. Many individuals and communities do not seem to be aware of my mandate and in particular the connection between foreign debt and human rights. I do not know the reasons for this but I suspect that generally there is little public awareness of the UN special procedures and how they can assist affected individuals and communities. Personally, I have endeavoured to increase the visibility of my mandate by participating in public events such as conferences and by drawing global attention to the human rights implications of foreign debt through media statements focusing on a range of issues, including climate change and commercial creditor litigation against impoverished countries.

In practice, how receptive have governments and international finance institutions been to your reports and recommendations?

Developing countries have generally been very receptive to my reports and recommendations while developed countries and international financial institutions have not. That said, there are occasions when I have engaged constructively with the World Bank and the African Development Bank, both of which have been involved in the consultations that have been held concerning the Draft Guiding Principles on foreign debt and human rights which I am developing in the context of my mandate. Norway and Australia have also engaged with the mandate and commented positively on aspects of my country mission reports. I have engaged with the [International Monetary Fund] IMF and the Asian Development Bank during missions but their response has generally not been encouraging.

What are your primary sources of information?

I draw my information from a broad range of sources but this depends on the type of report I have to produce. For thematic reports, I rely principally on academic research, official (UN and government) documents and studies by NGOs. For country mission reports, I rely on official documents (including national legislation and policy documents), UN documents, academic research and information from discussions with government officials and other stakeholders (such as development partners and NGOs).

4.5.1   Communications

A good number of special procedures are entitled to receive information concerning human rights violations from governments, NGOs, intergovernmental organisations, victims and witnesses. When credible information is furnished, showing that a violation within the scope of the mandate has occurred or is about to occur, the mandate-holder possesses the discretion to intervene with the government concerned and communicate its findings. The Code of Conduct for special procedures sets out the relevant admissibility criteria,[81] which are the same as those required for the complaints procedure of the HRC, described above (see 4.4.2). Two types of communication are available. The first concerns situations that are ongoing, life-threatening or in respect of which harm is imminent and thus require urgent action. Such communications are known as urgent appeals and their motivation is to inform the state of the situation with a view to making an immediate intervention terminating or preventing the violation. The second type concerns violations that have already occurred and in respect of which the relevant communications are known as letters of allegation. In neither case does the mandate-holder have authority to make the case public or condemn the target government – a case is publicised when the Special Rapporteur submits his/her report to the HRC or the UNGA – but rather urges it to take all appropriate action to investigate and address the allegations. In practice, the press releases issued by mandate-holders can be sharp and rather accusatory,[82] which is a sign of the confidence and respect they enjoy.

In 2017, 534 communications were sent to 117 states and 25 non-state actors and 1,843 individual cases were handled, of which 655 concerned women. A total of 484 replies were received, which translates to a response rate of 68 per cent. Of these, 164 communications were followed up by special procedures mandate-holders.[83]

4.5.2   Country Visits

Country visits are an integral part of the work of the special procedures because they allow mandate-holders to perform on-site investigations in respect of urgent situations and draft accurate and detailed reports. Yet no state is obliged to provide access to Special Rapporteurs, or any other mechanism for that matter, to conduct on-site investigations. Country visits are only possible following a standing invitation or an ad hoc invitation issued by the requesting nation. Standing invitations allow all mandate-holders to visit the country concerned for work related to their mandate without the need to make a formal request. Even so, Special Rapporteurs must notify the authorities in advance of each visit and the institutions or persons they

---

[81] HRC resolution 5/2 (18 June 2007) Annex. Available online at www.ohchr.org/Documents/HRBodies/SP/CodeofConduct_EN.pdf.

[82] See press release by Special Rapporteur on the right to food, 'Madagascar's Hungry Population is Taken Hostage Denounces UN Special Rapporteur' (22 July 2011).

[83] HRC, 'Facts and Figures with Regard to Special Procedures in 2017' UN doc. A/HRC/37/37/Add.1 (13 March 2018) 2.

intend to converse with. In 2017, a total of 86 country visits to 64 countries were made and 118 standing invitations by UN member states had been made.[84] During the 1980s and 1990s, at a time when states zealously guarded their domestic jurisdiction from external scrutiny over their human rights practices and thus refused all country visits, mandate-holders stationed themselves in neighbouring countries that provided them access and interviewed refugees and those in flight. This was particularly true in respect of the Israeli and Chilean country mandates.

Once an invitation is issued, the government should not stifle the mission with administrative or other hurdles, or by imposing conditions. In fact, a coherent body of customary principles seems to have emerged pertinent to fact-finding missions,[85] which are wholly applicable to country visits. This includes full freedom of movement and inquiry, access to all requested facilities, contact with all requested persons and organisations (confidential and unsupervised where relevant), including prisoners and NGOs, and full access to documentary material relevant to the mandate. It is also crucial that the government provide assurance that no person interviewed or in contact with the special rapporteurs will suffer threats, harassment or punishment.[86] In practice, reprisals are common, as will be analysed shortly.

Besides facilitating the investigative work of special procedures, country visits have given rise to an additional dimension that is of great significance. Any visit is always an event much talked about in the media of the visited nation and the public perception is that a UN human rights body would not undertake an official visit unless a serious issue was at stake. This tension obviously trickles down to the country's political institutions, which are keen, in most cases, to appease public sentiment and the nation's image abroad. A visit therefore may act as a pressure point for a number of changes.

4.5.3   Annual Reports

The reporting function of special procedures may seem trivial compared to the dispatch of communications and country visits. None the less, both annual and ad hoc reports are extremely important. Reports provide a unique insight into particular human rights situations for the benefit of public institutions as well as other private stakeholders. Given the independence of

---

[84] Ibid.

[85] See F. Viljoen, 'Fact-finding by UN Human Rights Complaints Bodies: Analysis and Suggested Reforms' (2004) 8 *Max Planck Yearbook of UN Law* 49; see also Declaration on Fact-finding by the UN in the Field of Maintenance of International Peace and Security, UNGA resolution 46/59 (9 December 1991) Annex.

[86] Terms of Reference for Fact-finding Missions by Special Rapporteurs/Representatives of the Commission on Human Rights, UN doc. E/CN.4/1998/45 (20 November 1997) Appendix V.

Special Rapporteurs, their reports are both critical and revealing, and as a result the information contained in them is often attacked by target states. This evidently renders them all the more valuable and in practice they are employed as authoritative secondary sources of law and fact by scholars and UN institutions, as well as by international courts and tribunals. We have already explained that the UPR relies to a great extent on the reports issued by special procedures. Moreover, in situations where the law is yet to crystallise, is unregulated by treaty or lacks concrete state practice, as in the case of transnational corporations, human rights defenders, the right to development, or the impact of sovereign debt on human rights and other matters, the reports of special procedures' mandate holders usually mould and shape legal developments.

CASE STUDY 4.1
Reprisals against Those Collaborating with UN Human Rights Procedures

A little-exposed facet of the work of the various procedures of the HRC concerns the fate of the individuals providing information, making complaints or simply collaborating with the HRC and its institutions. Although, as explained, most of the procedures involve a large degree of confidentiality, it is inevitable that during country visits the identity of those conversing with Special Rapporteurs is made known, as is also the case *mutatis mutandis* when urgent communications are issued in respect of particular violations. Reprisals against such persons take the form of harassment, intimidation, arbitrary arrests, physical aggression, refusal to issue travel documents, death threats and killings. The HRC has identified the seriousness of the problem, which greatly undermines the entirety of its human rights work, and has called for governments to take urgent and remedial action.[1] It should be stressed that reprisals are committed not only by government agents, but also by non-state actors, as the following case aptly illustrates.

On February 2005 Sister Dorothy Stang was shot several times as she walked to attend a meeting in the town of Anapu, in Brazil. The victim was an environmentalist, human rights defender and member of the Pastoral Land Commission, whose aim is to defend the rights of rural land workers and bring about land reform. On October 2004 Sister Dorothy had met the UN Special Rapporteur on the independence of judges and lawyers, during the latter's visit to Belem, Brazil and a week prior to her murder she had met the Brazilian Human Rights Minister to report that four local farmers had received death threats from loggers and landowners. Following immediate communications

[1] HRC resolution 12/2 (12 October 2009).

from several UN special procedures the government of Brazil initiated prosecutions and soon after made several arrests.[2]

In other cases where the culprits were government-sanctioned agents, the authorities generally took no remedial action. While on the one hand the issue highlights the vulnerability of victims, defenders and collaborators, on the other hand it demonstrates that UN procedures are perceived as a powerful tool against violations by those who commit them.

[2] CommHR Report, Cooperation with Representatives of United Nations Human Rights Bodies, UN doc. E/CN.4/2006/30 (6 February 2006) paras. 6ff.

QUESTIONS

1. What are the benefits and disadvantages of independent and government-appointed human rights posts within the UN's machinery?

2. Is there any institution, principal organ or body – other than the UNSC – which presides over and oversees the work of other human rights entities within the UN Charter framework?

3. Is the UN legally bound by international human rights law? Your response should consider whether the UN is bound institutionally (for example in respect of its employees' labour rights), as well as with regard to its external operations.

4. The human rights procedures and mechanisms operated by UN institutions – other than the UNSC – do not carry the element of compulsion which one finds in most international courts and tribunals. How effective do you consider they are and what recommendations would you make to render them more effective?

5. What is the additional value generated by the UPR, given that most states already face extensive reporting obligations on account of their membership to multilateral universal human rights treaties?

4.6 THE UNGA AND HUMAN RIGHTS

The UNGA is a principal organ of the Organisation under article 7 of the UN Charter. It is political in nature but unlike other organs its membership is universal and each state is entitled to a single vote of equal value. With very few exceptions, its resolutions are not binding on member states, but at the very least all its unanimous, or near-unanimous, resolutions are highly persuasive. The UNGA's influence and law-making capacity is also manifest in the fact that states are careful in their statements and endorsements of resolutions adopted therein because of possible estoppel implications (i.e. they cannot renege on statements made before the UNGA because they constitute binding unilateral acts).[87] Moreover, it is strongly argued that unanimous resolutions that are subsequently re-endorsed provide concrete evidence of consistent state practice (whether in the form of *usus* or *opinio juris*) and thus may well crystallise into custom.[88] As a result, the standard-setting work of the UNGA in the field of human rights assumes increased significance.

The UNGA possesses a rather broad power to deal with human rights, given that articles 10 and 11 of the UN Charter authorise it to discuss any questions or matters within the scope of the Charter and make appropriate recommendations to the states concerned, as well as the UNSC. Exceptionally, the UNGA is not competent to deal with an issue that is under examination by the UNSC. The UNGA's vast workload is diffused through six committees and despite the many linkages between their respective thematic mandates, for the purpose of this section the third committee deals directly with human rights. In practice, all committees address human rights in one way or another. Unlike the UNSC, the UNGA has from the outset maintained that human rights are not encompassed under article 2(7) of the UN Charter and are thus susceptible to discussion and investigation. It supported this view on the basis that articles 1, 2 and 55 of the Charter render the enforcement of human rights a matter of international concern. As a result, the UNGA recommended in 1946 the suspension of Spain (under Franco) from UN membership[89] and later rejected the applicability of article 2(7) to the Soviet invasion of Hungary, arguing that this was in violation of article 2(4) and moreover constituted genocide.[90]

From a practical perspective the UNGA's human rights work has three dimensions: (1) promotion of human rights and humanitarian law through standard-setting resolutions (for example, the UDHR), discussion of emerging issues, such as HIV/AIDS and poverty, as well as acting as a forum for the adoption of treaties; (2) condemnation of specific human rights violations and, where competent, taking measures against offending states, culminating in the expulsion from certain UN entities, such as that of Libya from the HRC;[91] and

---

[87] Art. 1 of the ILC's Guiding Principles applicable to Unilateral Declarations of States iterates the customary rule whereby: '[d]eclarations publicly made and manifesting the will to be bound may have the effect of creating legal obligations. When the conditions for this are met, the binding character of such declarations is based on good faith; states concerned may then take them into consideration and rely on them; such states are entitled to require that such obligations be respected.'

[88] G. Sloan, 'General Assembly Resolutions Revisited: (Forty Years Later)' (1987) 58 *British Yearbook of International Law* 39.

[89] UNGA resolution 39(I) (12 December 1946).

[90] UNGA resolution 1132(XI) (10 January 1957); UNGA resolution 1133(XI) (14 September 1957), and especially UNGA resolution 1127(XI) (21 November 1956).

[91] UNGA resolution 65/265 (1 March 2011).

(3) establishment and funding of peacekeeping, peace-enforcement, observer and other missions with a view to dispatching them to troubled areas. The UNGA's authority in setting up peacekeeping missions is crucial because of its exclusive authority under article 17 of the Charter to decide on budgetary issues, with money being the most necessary prerequisite for such missions to materialise.[92] Transitional, or post-conflict, justice and management are now a significant aspect of the UNGA's human rights agenda, although in practice their implementation is undertaken by the HRC and the OHCHR.[93]

4.7   THE UNSC

Although it is not readily obvious, the UNSC has the potential to be the most effective institution in the protection of human rights. This is reinforced by the stipulation in articles 24 and 25 of the Charter, which confer upon it primary responsibility for the maintenance of international peace and security through the adoption of resolutions that are binding on all UN member states. We have already alluded to the fact that the contemporary architecture of international peace and security encompasses human rights and humanitarian law, and given that the UNSC is designed to be a quick-response mechanism to crises and unfolding international situations, its vested authority necessarily renders it an ideal forum for immediate action. This is unlike any other human rights organ or institution within the UN or otherwise, all of which are unable to respond immediately and/or with (armed or other) force if necessary, against offending states or non-state actors. While it is well known that during the Cold War the UNSC was effectively precluded from taking any action with respect to situations of gross human rights violations, since the early 1990s this has no longer been the case. Of course, when reading UNSC resolutions one must not forget that these are primarily intended as political decisions, and as a result significant political considerations underlie them.[94] At the same time, and while the UNSC is not bound to any institutional precedent, it cannot lightly disregard its own resolutions on the same or similar matters.[95] This is true irrespective of the veto power

---

[92] For the biennium 2014–2015 the UNGA authorised a budget for its peacekeeping operations at a cost of $114 million; UNGA resolution 68/248 (16 January 2014).

[93] The UNGA may even leave the initiative to the HRC. E.g., the HRC dispatched an independent commission of inquiry in respect of the 2010 post-electoral violence in Côte d'Ivoire without a prior resolution from the UNGA, relying on the basis of its founding mandate in UNGA resolution 60/251. See HRC resolution 16/25 (25 March 2011).

[94] E. Papastavridis, 'Interpretation of Security Council Resolutions under Chapter VII in the Aftermath of the Iraqi Crisis' (2007) 56 *International & Comparative Law Quarterly* 53.

[95] This of course does not mean that the UNSC must establish the same mechanisms in respect of similar situations, as is the case with criminal tribunals. Logistical, financial and political considerations may certainly preclude their establishment in particular cases.

held by the UNSC's permanent members and it is now common practice for persistent rights violators to be identified.

The human rights work of the UNSC is not susceptible to neat categorisations for the simple reason that on many occasions human rights considerations are only obvious as secondary effects; moreover, the UNSC deals with crises as and when they arise and only rarely maintains an annual agenda of particular issues, as does the UNGA, for example. Thus, the UNSC's human rights 'jurisprudence' may be derived principally from resolutions concerning specific country situations and secondarily from general thematic resolutions. The latter type is employed typically in order to reinforce and bolster existing rules and in a handful of cases also for the purpose of standard-setting. By way of illustration, resolution 1261 and its successors concerned the recruitment and use of children in armed conflict, stressing that this was an international crime and a violation of children's rights.[96] These resolutions effectively quashed any appeal to cultural sensitivities that may have been entertained by various warlords under the guise of tribal custom, thus reinforcing the relevant rules in the Convention on the Rights of the Child (CRC) and paving the way for the Optional Protocol to the CRC on the Involvement of Children in Armed Conflict, adopted a year later.[97] Of equal standard-setting value is resolution 1325 and its successors, which urged states to ensure increased participation of women at all decision-making levels and called on all actors negotiating peace agreements to adopt a gender perspective.[98]

The UNSC's authority as a potent protector of rights is reflected in its practices for determining country situations. For one thing, unlike other organs that meet periodically, the UNSC can, and does, meet at any time. Moreover, it need not receive an official request or communication in order to deliberate on a crisis and in practice it is only a matter of hours – unfortunately not always – from the start of a crisis before a meeting is convened, albeit the Council does not always adopt a resolution straight away. Given that an important facet of any armed conflict, humanitarian disaster or brutal repression is human plight and the violation of rights – the other being the spill-over into neighbouring nations – the UNSC has employed its general powers under chapter VII in various forms. Depending on the cooperation

---

[96] UNSC resolution 1261 (30 August 1999). See also UNSC resolution 1612 (26 July 2005) and UNSC resolution 2175 (29 August 2014), regarding the obligation to respect humanitarian law and civilians in armed conflict; equally, UNSC resolution 2150 (16 April 2014), reaffirming the crime of genocide and the responsibility of states to prosecute.

[97] See Chapter 12.4.3.1.

[98] UNSC resolution 1325 (31 October 2000) paras. 1 and 8; equally, UNSC resolution 2171 (21 August 2014) operative para. 18, which reiterates the 'continuing need to increase success in preventing conflict by increasing the participation of women at all stages of mediation and post-conflict resolution and by increasing the consideration of gender-related issues in all discussions pertinent to conflict prevention'.

of the target state, the escalation of violence and the threat to human safety and well-being, the UNSC may well decide to dispatch an observer mission, a peacekeeping or a peace-enforcement contingent. Whereas the objective of the first of these is to monitor and report on the prevailing situation, the latter two play a substantive role in the protection of civilian populations from the calamities of conflict and may assist in containing the conflict itself. What is more, if these missions are authorised to use armed force (under the UNSC's standard terminology of 'all necessary means' on the basis of article 42 of the Charter) in order to fulfil their mandate, they are no longer idle bystanders to violations but can effectively protect the victims. In the case of Somalia, where armed factions were indiscriminately killing civilians and looting food supplies, thus raising the risk of widespread famine, the UNSC authorised the UN operation in Somalia (UNOSOM) to use all necessary means to establish a secure environment for humanitarian relief operations.[99]

Exceptionally, UNSC resolutions condemning particular acts of repression against civilians are used as a platform by certain nations, with or without opposition by others, as justification for subsequent forceful measures. By way of illustration, although resolution 688 against Iraqi repression of the country's Kurdish population was merely condemnatory,[100] it was none the less relied upon by Western European nations to set up a safe haven and a no-fly zone in northern Iraq. This type of implied authorisation is not widely accepted as legitimate under international law, irrespective of the nature or the objective upon which the relevant action relies; yet it has been routinely invoked by three of the UNSC's permanent members, namely France, the USA and the UK, to the chagrin of Russia and China.[101] Unilateral coercive measures of this nature are unlawful under international law[102] as they are prohibited under the UN Charter, are not considered lawful countermeasures[103] and produce an adverse impact (even if unintended) on the enjoyment of fundamental human rights in the target state.   ✻ LA Nc E

Besides urgent action through the deployment of military contingents, the UNSC has been concerned with post-conflict justice, victims and national reconciliation. Chief among its political objectives has been the eradication of impunity and to this end the UNSC has not hesitated to establish international criminal tribunals for the prosecution of those most responsible for

---

[99] UNSC resolution 794 (3 December 1992) para. 10.
[100] UNSC resolution 688 (5 April 1991) with para. 3 insisting that Iraq allow access to humanitarian organisations to all those in need of assistance.
[101] See C. Gray, 'From Unity to Polarisation: International Law and the Use of Force against Iraq' (2002) 13 *European Journal of International Law* 1, at 8ff.
[102] HRC resolution 24 (24 September 2013), although the matter is not free from academic and political controversy. But see OHCHR, Report on the Impact of Unilateral Coercive Measures on Human Rights, Particularly Socio-Economic Rights of Women and Children in Targeted States, UN doc. A/HRC/27/32 (10 July 2014).
[103] See Arts. 49–50 ILC Articles on State Responsibility.

serious violations of human rights and humanitarian law. The International Criminal Tribunal for the former Yugoslavia (ICTY),[104] the International Criminal Tribunal for Rwanda (ICTR)[105] and the tribunal for Lebanon[106] are paradigmatic of this objective. Despite the UNSC's lesser involvement in the establishment of subsequent tribunals (for example, Sierra Leone, Cambodia and Iraq), it is no less determined to fight impunity.

The endorsement and spread of criminal justice mechanisms necessarily means that the UNSC is not only addressing states as violators of rights, but also non-state actors, something which is alien to inter-state human rights courts and tribunals.[107] Indeed, the UNSC has not only directly condemned non-state actors[108] but has ordered measures involving the use of force or the enforcement of criminal jurisdiction against them. This is true, for example, in respect of Somali pirates.[109]

Yet although it is now unquestionable that the UNSC is a capable and willing defender of rights, there is still considerable debate as to whether the UNSC's choice of enforcement, particularly the use of collective sanctions (as opposed to unilateral sanctions), is compatible with fundamental human rights. The UNSC may well infringe human rights even if its actions aim to address human rights violations. Here are three useful illustrations:

The UNSC imposes an import embargo on the brutal and dictatorial regime of country A, the effect of which is to significantly impede the availability of basic medicines, food and water to its civilian population and as a result a large number of children and vulnerable persons die.

The UNSC imposes targeted sanctions against specific individuals suspected of terrorist-related offences, encompassing asset freezing and arrest. The sanctions are final and binding on member states and the suspects have no recourse to any appeal or review mechanism.

The UNSC orders the use of armed force against country A, which is ruled by a brutal dictator. The UNSC is aware that the regime will strenuously resist its downfall and is fully prepared to sacrifice the lives of many of its people in the process in order to defend itself against a multinational force.

In all of these cases the UNSC has to make difficult decisions that directly affect the fundamental rights of a large number of people, despite other possible benefits, such as democracy-building, rule of law and cessation

---

[104] UNSC resolution 827 (25 May 1993).   [105] UNSC resolution 955 (8 November 1994).

[106] UNSC resolution 1757 (30 May 2007).

[107] It is no accident, therefore, that the UNSC possesses authority under art. 13(b) of the ICC Statute to refer situations to the ICC. A significant number of those indicted are members of non-state groups.

[108] UNSC resolution 814 (26 March 1993) para. 13, calling on Somali factions to desist from breaching humanitarian law and reaffirming their criminal liability for any violations.

[109] UNSC resolution 1950 (23 November 2010) para. 12. See I. Bantekas, *International Criminal Law*, 4th edn (Hart, 2010) 301–2.

of human rights violations. Although it is generally acknowledged that the UNSC's practice in scenario (2) would be disproportionate and lacking legal support,[110] the other two find an equal amount of support and opprobrium. Yet the UNSC should not lightly infringe fundamental rights under the guise of collateral damage and should explore other alternatives before deciding to employ sanctions that are likely to affect the rights of entire populations.[111] The Iraq sanctions regime provides an instructive lesson in this respect, not least because it eventually resulted in major changes to the UNSC's practice towards smarter sanctions.[112] While the comprehensive sanctions imposed against Iraq in the aftermath of the 1990 Gulf War excluded foodstuff and medicine used for humanitarian purposes, it soon became apparent that these limited exceptions were insufficient to provide for the needs of the population. After much wrangling, resolution 986 was adopted in 1995, allowing Iraq to export oil in exchange for foodstuff, medicine and humanitarian goods.[113] The Oil for Food programme thus introduced was referred to as 'a temporary measure to provide for the humanitarian needs of the Iraqi people'.[114] However, the programme's design and implementation undermined its effectiveness, as a result of a combination of factors, particularly the lack of availability of adequate funds for infrastructure, blocking of dual-purpose goods by the Sanctions Committee, as well as corruption and maladministration. The resulting persistent humanitarian crisis led to repeated adjustments of the programme, which, ultimately, failed adequately to offset the adverse impact of sanctions imposed against Iraq at the time.[115] It is for this reason that there is widespread disinclination against all types of broad sanctions because they are deemed incompatible with the enjoyment of human rights.[116]

You! are incompatible w/ failure

---

[110] In *Kadi and Al Barakaat International Foundation* v. *Council of the European Union* (CJEU) (2008) paras. 335–7 and 349, the Court of Justice of the European Union (CJEU) held that the imposition of targeted sanctions (freezing orders in the case at hand) against a suspected terrorist by the EU without any remedy whatsoever in the form of judicial review or a hearing violated the right of effective judicial protection. In similar fashion in *R (on the application of Al-Jedda)* v. *Secretary of State for Defence* (UK) (2007) Lord Bingham argued that UNSC resolutions authorising extensive powers of detention 'must ensure that the detainee's rights under art. 5 [of the ECHR] are not infringed to any greater extent than is inherent in such detention'.

[111] CESCR, General Comment 8, UN doc. E/C.12/1997/8 (12 December 1997) para. 3.

[112] C. C. Joyner, 'United Nations Sanctions after Iraq: Looking Back to See Ahead' (2003) 4 *Chinese Journal of International Law* 329.

[113] UNSC resolution 986 (14 April 1995) para. 8.   [114] Ibid., preamble.

[115] UNSC, Report of the Second Panel Established pursuant to the Note by the President of the Security Council (S/1999/100) of 30 January 1999, concerning the Current Humanitarian Situation in Iraq (30 March 1999) UN doc. S/1999/356 Annex II. H. von Sponeck, *A Different Kind of War: The UN Sanctions Regime in Iraq* (Berghahn Books, 2006).

[116] Sub-Commission on the Promotion and Protection of Human Rights, 'The Adverse Consequences of Economic Sanctions on the Enjoyment of Human Rights', UN doc. E/CN.4/Sub.2/2000/33 (2000) para. 71.

QUESTIONS

1. Is the UN bound by the three instruments encompassed within the Bill of Rights? More generally, is the UN bound by customary human rights law?

2. You are the legal advisor to a small human rights NGO. Through your investigations it transpires that the government of country A is engaged in the enforced disappearance of its political dissidents. The abductees number in the hundreds and their family members are too scared to confront the local authorities or approach any international bodies. Under the circumstances, which institution or organ within the UN would you inform and what would you expect to achieve? Justify your response.

3. What is the function of standard-setting within the UN?

4. Does the practice of the HRC include the 'name and shame' technique?

5. If the UNSC authorises the use of armed force in order to oust a brutal regime it risks setting in motion a war that may cost thousands of lives. Should it instead rely on sanctions or should it support a popular uprising by financial, technological and political assistance? Discuss with reference to the invasion of Iraq in 2003, the Egyptian uprising in 2011 and the Venezuela uprisings of 2018.

6. Following the adoption of resolution 1373 (2001) by the UNSC in the aftermath of 9/11 a number of countries justified the violation of fundamental rights in order to ensure compliance with the terms of the resolution which demanded that states take all necessary measures to prevent and punish terrorist attacks.[117] Should the UNSC's resolutions expressly stipulate conformity with fundamental human rights, or is this already implicitly understood?

4.7.1   Fact-finding in Practice: The UN Mission in the Gaza Conflict

Following the Israeli army's incursion into the Gaza strip in late December 2008 (known as operation Cast Led), a significant number of civilian casualties were reported, in addition to a pattern demonstrating the destruction of Gaza's economic and social infrastructure. The HRC decided to set up a fact-finding mission to:

investigate all violations of international human rights law and international humanitarian law by the occupying power, Israel, against the Palestinian people throughout the occupied Palestinian territory, particularly in the occupied Gaza strip, due to the current aggression, and calls upon Israel not to obstruct the process of investigation and to fully cooperate with the mission.[118]

---

[117] The UN Human Rights Committee, among other treaty bodies, emphasised in its examination of state reports that all measures adopted for the implementation of resolution 1373 should be in full compliance with the International Bill of Human Rights. See UN Concluding Observations on Moldova, UN doc. CCPR/CO/75/MDA (5 August 2002) para. 8.

[118] HRC resolution A/HRC/S-9/L.1 (12 January 2009) para. 14.

The terms of the mandate are important in this case because although it demands that all violations be investigated, thus implying any committed by Palestinians as well, the remainder of the mandate, and the inclusion of words such as [Israeli] aggression, clearly pre-empt the investigation by suggesting that only Israeli military actions be scrutinised. The ambassador of Israel to the country's permanent mission to the UN in Geneva, in a letter to the head of the UN fact-finding mission, Richard Goldstone, refused to extend his country's cooperation to the mission on the following grounds:

This grossly politicised resolution prejudges the issue at hand, determining at the outset that Israel has perpetrated grave violations of human rights and implying that Israel has deliberately targeted civilians and medical facilities and systematically destroyed the cultural heritage of the Palestinian people. It calls for urgent international action directed only against Israel and, as regards the proposed fact-finding mission, makes clear that it regards its mandate as exclusively focused on Israeli violations of human rights and humanitarian law. The fact that several distinguished individuals approached to head the Mission declined reflects the problematic nature of the mission and its mandate.[119]

The four-person mission, composed of three legal experts and a military analyst, received personal attacks during the course of its work and one member, Professor Chinkin, was accused of conflicting interests. In an interview following the completion of the report, Goldstone made the point that:

Obviously nobody enjoys being attacked. A lot of the attacks have been in intemperate terms not so much in the media but in emails and private messages and that's unpleasant but let me immediately say that it hasn't affected our work. We've gone ahead and did what we had undertaken to do and what our mandate required us to do and the fact we were attacked I don't think came as a surprise to any of us. The vehemence of some of it may have surprised me speaking for myself but if one does this sort of work one's going to be attacked. It's not the first time and probably not the last.[120]

WOMEN POWER

Chinkin's alleged bias was based on a letter she signed along with other leading academics, which was published in *The Times*, where she and her colleagues argued against the legality of operation Cast Led. In fact, the letter made no reference to human rights or international humanitarian law (IHL) violations; it simply examined operation Cast Led from a jus ad bellum perspective.

Goldstone rightly dismissed all claims of bias as 'clutching at straws'.[121] The USA complained, among other things, that during the mission's on-site

---

[119] Letter dated 7 April 2009, in Report of the Fact-finding Mission: Human Rights in Palestine and Other Occupied Arab Territories [Fact-Finding Report], UN doc. A/HRC/12/48 (25 September 2009) Annex II, at 436.

[120] Unofficial transcript of the press conference of 29 September 2009.   [121] Ibid.

visits to Gaza there was a visible presence of Hamas security in the vicinity, thus exacerbating the mission's bias. Goldstone retorted that none of the mission's members noticed any inappropriate presence of Hamas police during the investigation of witnesses and that even if they were in the vicinity they could not 'in any way [have] overheard or in any way exercised any direct influence on any of the witnesses we saw'.[122] The narration of these incidents is intended to highlight the political intricacies behind the appointment and mandate of a human rights investigative mission and the variety of pressures on individual members.

Based on these criticisms, and despite the terms of the HRC's resolution, Goldstone wisely expanded the HRC resolution's mandate by deciding to investigate alleged violations by both sides to the conflict. This clearly provided an additional degree of legitimacy to the final report and the overall work of the mission. It is not unusual for fact-finding missions or other UN subsidiary organs to construe their mandates expansively, whether in temporal or substantive terms. Such a construction is generally dictated by the material exigencies of each particular mission, albeit in respect of the Gaza mission it was prescribed by a desire to rectify the perception of bias without impairing in any way its original mandate.

Fact-finding missions are not (generally) meant to ascertain the criminal liability of perpetrators but to provide a clear picture of events to the appointing body. As a result, the missions are free to employ any type of evidence and mechanism of inquiry, although ultimately the quality of the evidentiary material will determine the quality of the report and its recommendations. In the present instance, the Gaza mission placed particular emphasis on the plight of the victims and resorted to some degree of narrative storytelling. The readers will be able to judge for themselves whether this was an appropriate mechanism under the circumstances. The mission had intended to conduct on-site investigations in Gaza and Israel and interview victims and participants on both sides. However, as a result of Israel's refusal to cooperate the mission was not only precluded from visiting Israel and the West Bank but was unable to enter Gaza, save through Egyptian territory. It was thus forced to ascertain the Israeli side of events from material evidence and witness statements in Gaza and affected neighbouring countries. Besides interviews, it employed reports from international organisations, NGOs, medical records, video and satellite images provided by the UN Operational Satellite Applications Program (UNOSAT), forensic analysis of weapons and ammunition remnants collected at incident sites, publicly available material[123] and

---

[122] Ibid.

[123] A number of Israeli soldiers involved in the operation had by that time narrated personal stories to the Israeli press, which in turn made them public.

public hearings in Gaza and Geneva.[124] In numerous cases the mission held that NGO data was more reliable than official government data. By way of illustration, in considering the number of Palestinians who lost their lives during the operation, it relied on NGO reports because the data presented was generally more consistent as compared to official Palestinian and Israeli data.[125]

The storytelling dimension of the report, setting out the historical context of the conflict and the basis of operation Cast Led, was apparent from the use of so-called public hearings. These were broadcast live and their purpose was:

> to enable victims, witnesses and experts from all sides to the conflict to speak directly to as many people as possible in the region as well as in the international community. The mission is of the view that no written word can replace the voice of victims. While not all issues and incidents under investigation by the Mission were addressed during the hearings, the thirty-eight public testimonies covered a wide range of relevant facts as well as legal and military matters. The mission had initially intended to hold hearings in Gaza, Israel and the West Bank. However, denial of access to Israel and the West Bank resulted in the decision to hold hearings of participants from Israel and the West Bank in Geneva ... Participants in the hearings were identified in the course of the mission's investigations, and had either first-hand experience or information or specialized knowledge of the issues under investigation and analysis. In keeping with the objectives of the hearings, the mission gave priority to the participation of victims and people from the affected communities.[126]

This mechanism resembles public confessions free of criminal liability accepted in the course of truth and reconciliation commissions,[127] as well as the rationale for the participation of victims in international criminal proceedings. It is innovative for the purposes of a fact-finding mission whose role is generally to ascertain facts, not to give a voice to the victims. Yet it does not wholly seem out of place given that fact-finding missions have in the past tended to focus excessively on the type and scale of violations, and in doing so dehumanising somewhat the victims of the crimes. It is not far-fetched to claim that the aim of fact-finders has typically been to recount the scale and intensity of violations as opposed to the victims' suffering, with a view to offering political space and legitimacy to their mandators to undertake further action, whether through sanctions or the establishment of criminal tribunals. Offering a personalised voice to the victims, on the other hand, assists in giving a voice to the facts and restoring the victims' faith in the

---

[124] Fact-Finding Report, above note 119, para. 159.   [125] Ibid., para. 30.   [126] Ibid., para. 166.
[127] P. Parker, 'The Politics of Indemnities: Truth Telling and Reconciliation in South Africa' (1996) 17 *Human Rights Law Journal* 1.

relevant process.[128] It is a welcome follow-up to the practice of UN special procedures to narrate in their reports the specific crimes committed by governments and non-state actors against their victims, most of which are spelt out by name.[129] The Israeli opposition to these public hearings is instructive:

> This procedure is unprecedented as part of fact-finding operations. The very point of a fact-finding mission is that a team of experts bring their experience and judgment to bear in assessing the available evidence and drawing responsible conclusions – not that raw evidence, perhaps of questionable authenticity, is directly broadcast into the public arena. Such a trial by public opinion, which of necessity cannot give any weight to confidential or sensitive information, can serve little purpose in ascertaining the truth, and is only likely to prejudice public opinion in advance of any other conclusion.[130]

No doubt, UN investigations and fact-finding are not straightforward exercises. There will always be states with opposing interests that will stifle country visits or prevent its agents and nationals from providing testimony of any kind. Such states and their allies will attack the integrity of the mission, and members will be subject to attacks, not necessarily physical, against their persons. Heads of missions need to be creative and not be afraid to explore new methodologies while fulfilling their mandate. Most importantly, they must ensure that their very mandate is even-handed, objective and fair and if it is not, to employ their discretionary or implied powers to mold it as such. Ultimately, a mission is not legitimised by its hard work, but largely by its fairness and impartiality.

FURTHER READING

Alston, P., 'Reconceiving the UN Human Rights Regime: Challenges Confronting the New UN Human Rights Council' (2006) 7 *Melbourne Journal of International Law* 185.

Alston, P., and J. Crawford (eds.), *The Future of UN Human Rights Treaty Monitoring* (Cambridge University Press, 2000).

Alston, P., and F. Mégret (eds.), *The United Nations and Human Rights: A Critical Appraisal* (Oxford University Press, 2015).

Barber, M., *Blinded by Humanity: Inside the UN's Humanitarian Operations* (IB Tauris, 2016).

Charlesworth, H., and E. Larking (eds.), *Human Rights and the Universal Periodic Review: Rituals and Ritualism* (Cambridge University Press, 2014).

Fassbender, B., *Securing Human Rights? Achievements and Challenges of the UN Security Council* (Oxford University Press 2011).

---

[128] One should not, of course, be oblivious to the risk that listening to victims alone creates a one-sided truth and prevents a clear understanding of the roots of the conflict. In a study encompassing 120 interviews of ordinary people among Bosnia's three ethnic communities, each vehemently denied the crimes committed by his or her own ethnic group, emphasising that they were perpetrated by members of the other groups. J. N. Clark, 'Transitional Justice, Truth and Reconciliation: An Under-explored Relationship' (2011) 11 *International Criminal Law Review* 241, at 256–7.

[129] See e.g., Report by the Special Rapporteur on Torture, Mission to Nepal, UN doc. E/CN.4/2006/6/Add.5 (9 January 2006) 16ff.

[130] Letter dated 2 July 2009, in Fact-Finding Report, above note 119, at 448.

Franck, T. M., and H. S. Fairley, 'Procedural Due Process in Human Rights Fact-finding by International Agencies' (1980) 74 *American Journal of International Law* 308.

Freedman, R., *The United Nations Human Rights Council: A Critique and Early Assessment* (Ashgate, 2013).

Genser, J., and B. S. Ugarte (eds.), *The United Nations Security Council in the Age of Human Rights* (Cambridge University Press, 2016).

Ghanea, N., 'From the UN Commission on Human Rights to UN Human Rights Council: One Step Forwards or Two Steps Sideways?' (2006) 55 *International & Comparative Law Quarterly* 695.

Katayanagi, M., *Human Rights Functions of United Nations Peacekeeping* (Martinus Nijhoff, 2002).

Lauren, P. G., 'First Principles of Racial Equality: History and the Politics of Diplomacy of Human Rights Provisions in the United Nations Charter' (1983) 5 *Human Rights Quarterly* 1.

Mertus, J., *The United Nations and Human Rights: A Guide for a New Era* (Routledge, 2009).

Nolan, A., R. Freedman and T. Murphy (eds.), *The United Nations Special Procedures System* (Brill, 2017).

Ramcharan, B. G., *The United Nations High Commissioner for Human Rights: The Challenges of International Protection* (Martinus Nijhoff, 2002).

The UN Human Rights Council (Routledge, 2011).

Rudolf, B., 'The Thematic Rapporteurs and Working Groups of the United Nations Commission on Human Rights' (2000) 4 *Max Planck Yearbook of United Nations Law* 289.

Schwelb, E., 'The International Court of Justice and the Human Rights Clauses of the Charter' (1972) 66 *American Journal of International Law* 337.

Shelton, D., *The United Nations System for Protecting Human Rights* (Routledge, 2014).

Subedi, S., *The Effectiveness of the UN Human Rights System: Reform and Judicialisation of Human Rights* (Routledge 2017).

Verdirame, G., *The UN and Human Rights: Who Guards the Guardians?* (Cambridge University Press, 2013).

Websites

HRC: www.ohchr.org/EN/HRBodies/HRC/Pages/HRCIndex.aspx

NGO Monitor: www.ngo-monitor.org/article/the_un_human_rights_council_ecosoc_and_ngos_

UN and civil society: www.un.org/en/civilsociety/index.shtml

UN human rights: www.un.org/en/rights

UN human rights documents: http://research.un.org/en/docs/humanrights

Universal Periodic Review: www.ohchr.org/EN/HRBodies/UPR/Pages/UPRMain.spx

UN Watch: www.unwatch.org/en

5 The UN Human Rights Treaty System

CONTENTS

I love gender AND sexual

5.1 INTRODUCTION

United Nations (UN) treaty bodies constitute the main institutional vehicle for the application of international human rights law. Bodies such as the UN Human Rights Committee (HRCtee) are by no means the only international mechanisms that address issues of human rights protection. Indeed, bodies as diverse as the International Labour Organisation (ILO)[1] and the World Bank[2] employ special procedures dealing with human rights questions. International tribunals and courts, particularly the International Court of Justice (ICJ), are increasingly adjudicating cases that have a bearing on

---

[1] www.ilo.org. See for a good overview and nuanced assessment of the ILO's contribution to the promotion of social justice and human rights, particularly labour rights, and its supervisory system, G. Oberleitner, *Global Human Rights Institutions: Between Remedy and Ritual* (Polity Press, 2007, reprinted 2008) 106–12.

[2] See on the World Bank 1993 Inspection Panels, ibid., 129–35; S. Skogly, *Human Rights Obligations of the World Bank and the International Monetary Fund* (Cavendish, 2001) 35–6 and 180–5; and, more generally, M. Darrow, *Between Light and Shadow: The World Bank, the International Monetary Fund and International Human Rights Law* (Hart, 2003).

international human rights law.[3] Yet human rights treaty bodies fulfil a special role in that they are the only entities within the UN system that states have explicitly mandated to monitor compliance with their human rights treaty obligations.

Treaty bodies fulfil a range of functions, from promotional activities to monitoring and adjudicating complaints. These tasks, which are taken for granted today, are the result of states' willingness to vest treaty bodies with the mandate of monitoring compliance. This constituted a remarkable shift away from earlier notions of sovereignty in a system where states were, essentially, the sole authors, interpreters and enforcers of rights and obligations. What accounts for this change and why do states agree to be part of such regimes? This question, which has attracted considerable attention in recent years, poses a particular challenge because it does not seem to conform to the realist views that used to hold considerable sway in international relations, according to which states use institutions as a means to exercise power. Alternative theories emphasise states' interests (enhancing reputation and avoiding sanctions) or point to 'acculturation'.[4] This denotes a process of interaction of various actors which generates a pull to build and join credible human rights mechanisms as part of an international order. Indeed, these mechanisms form part of broader international institution building, particularly at the UN level. The development of UN treaty bodies has witnessed a steady growth after a slow beginning in which it took over twenty years and numerous debates to set up the first two, the Committee on the Elimination of Racial Discrimination (CERD) and the HRCtee.

The proliferation of treaties, treaty bodies and increased ratification does not automatically equate to a coherent and effective international system that is well placed to achieve its objectives, particularly strengthening protection at the international and national level. On the contrary, this development may strain the capacity of the parties and institutions involved and lead to duplication as well as system fatigue. The discussions surrounding states' reporting obligations before UN treaty bodies illustrates these capacity challenges. Treaty bodies have struggled with state compliance, both procedurally (reporting) and substantively (implementing human rights obligations),

DISGUSTING CUNT · *DONT PICKUR NOSE*

---

[3] The ICJ has increasingly addressed human rights questions, both in its contentious and advisory jurisdiction. See S. Sivakumaran, 'The International Court of Justice and Human Rights', in S. Joseph and A. McBeth (eds.), *Research Handbook on International Human Rights Law* (Edward Elgar, 2010) 299–325; B. Simma, 'Mainstreaming Human Rights: The Contribution of the International Court of Justice' (2012) 3 *Journal of International Dispute Settlement* 7.

[4] See for a good overview of the various theories, O. C. Okafor, *The African Human Rights System, Activist Forces and International Institutions* (Cambridge University Press, 2007) 12–62; Oberleitner, above note 1, 6–22.

YASSS QUEEN!

and this continues to be an area of major concern. These factors have contributed to the perceived weakness of UN treaty bodies and triggered a series
of reform proposals. Paradoxically, this process is taking place at the same
time as a growing number of national and international actors seek to use
these very bodies to advance human rights promotion and protection, which
inadvertently deepens existing institutional and systemic challenges.

This development raises serious questions about the ability of these bodies
to respond adequately to human rights concerns. Beyond these operational
difficulties lurk more fundamental issues concerning the very nature of a
system that depends on states and in which treaty bodies 'oscillate between
the desire to supervise and the need to cooperate'.[5] The search for gradual
improvement takes place in an institutional framework whose dynamics
may make it incapable of addressing 'larger issues of power, domination,
and legitimacy'.[6] Mandate constraints, bureaucracy and the still largely
state-centric nature of the process, all contribute to a situation where the
bodies may not respond effectively to serious violations and/or fashion
effective remedies. Nevertheless, their work provides an important forum for
developing international human rights law and engaging with states; this
very engagement allows domestic actors, non-governmental organisations
(NGOs), other states and international institutions to seek changes that may
over time result in an improved human rights situation. However, the task
of strengthening the role of treaty bodies in the protection of human rights
will continue to pose a considerable challenge to a system that is ultimately
based on the 'goodwill' of states, which it constantly has to test in order to
be effective.

5.2   COMMON FEATURES OF INTERNATIONAL HUMAN RIGHTS TREATY BODIES

Debates surrounding the drafting of international human rights treaties
centred not only on the substance of the instruments but also on what, if
any, type of body should be mandated to exercise monitoring functions.
The idea of setting up bodies composed of independent experts to monitor
state conduct in the domestic sphere constituted a departure from the then
prevailing notion of state sovereignty; it was not entirely unprecedented,
though. The Permanent Mandates Commission established under article 22
of the Covenant of the League of Nations had earlier operated a petitions
procedure against the Mandatory that also dealt with human rights-related

[5] B. Rajagopal, *International Law from Below: Development, Social Movements and Third World Resistance* (Cambridge University Press, 2003) 66–7.
[6] Ibid., 67.

matters.[7] Subsequently, proposals made by states in the formative years of the UN human rights system show the breadth of options pondered, ranging from calls for an International Court of Human Rights (Australia)[8] to a rejection of special monitoring bodies on the ground that they would represent an unwarranted interference with state sovereignty (Romania).[9] The model of treaty bodies that eventually emerged inevitably reflects a compromise that has resulted in the dynamics and challenges evident today.

Beginning with the CERD in 1969,[10] followed in 1976 by the most prominent body, the HRCtee,[11] the total number had risen to ten treaty bodies by 2011 (which remained unchanged as of 2019). These include the Committee on the Elimination of Discrimination against Women (CtEDAW) (1982),[12] the Committee against Torture (CtAT) (1987),[13] the Committee on the Rights of the Child (CtRC) (1991),[14] the Committee on Migrant Workers (CMW) (2003),[15] the Committee on the Rights of Persons with Disabilities (CtRPD) (2008),[16] and the Committee on Enforced Disappearances (CED) (2011).[17] In addition, the Subcommittee on Prevention of Torture (SPT) was set up under the Optional Protocol to the Convention against Torture (OPCAT) in 2006.[18] With the exception of the Committee on Economic, Social and Cultural Rights (CESCR), all international human rights treaty bodies are established by states parties and based on the founding treaty that sets out their respective mandate and functions.[19] Their close institutional links, including reporting

---

[7] Ibid., 67–71; A. Anghie, 'Colonialism and the Birth of International Institutions: Sovereignty, Economy, and the Mandate System of the League of Nations' (2002) 34 *New York University Journal of International Law and Politics* 513, at 523–8. See for the complaints procedure relating to the minority rights instruments of the League of Nations, P. Kovács, 'The Protection of Minorities under the Auspices of the League of Nations', in D. Shelton (ed.), *The Oxford Handbook of International Human Rights Law* (Oxford University Press, 2015) 325–41, at 327–32.

[8] A. Devereux, 'Australia and the International Scrutiny of Civil and Political Rights: An Analysis of Australia's Negotiating Policies, 1946–1966' (2003) 22 *Australian Yearbook of International Law* 47, at 54–60.

[9] See for references to debates in the General Assembly in 1952, Y. Tyagi, *The UN Human Rights Committee: Practice and Procedure* (Cambridge University Press, 2011) 58–60.

[10] Arts. 8–16 ICERD: www2.ohchr.org/english/bodies/cerd/index.htm.

[11] Arts. 28–45 ICCPR: www2.ohchr.org/english/bodies/hrc/index.htm.

[12] Arts. 17–22 CEDAW: www2.ohchr.org/english/bodies/cedaw/index.htm.

[13] Arts. 17–24 CAT: www2.ohchr.org/english/bodies/cat/index.htm.

[14] Arts. 43–5 CRC: www2.ohchr.org/english/bodies/crc/index.htm.

[15] Arts. 72–8 ICRMW: www2.ohchr.org/english/bodies/cmw/index.htm.

[16] Arts. 34–9 CRPD: www.ohchr.org/EN/HRBodies/CRPD/Pages/CRPDIndex.aspx.

[17] Arts. 26–36 CPED: www.ohchr.org/EN/HRBodies/CED/Pages/CEDIndex.aspx.

[18] Arts. 5–16 OPCAT: www.ohchr.org/EN/HRBodies/OPCAT/Pages/OPCATIndex.aspx.

[19] ECOSOC resolution 1985/17 (28 May 1985). See on steps taken to correct this anomaly, HRC resolution 4/7 (30 March 2007): Rectification of the legal status of the Committee on Economic, Social and Cultural Rights. For an analysis of the CESCR's work, see also Chapter 9.

to the UN General Assembly (UNGA) and being serviced by the Office of the High Commissioner for Human Rights (OHCHR) and financed out of the UN budget, means that human rights treaty bodies effectively form part of the UN human rights architecture.[20]

Human rights treaty bodies fulfil their monitoring function primarily by means of considering states parties' reports and adjudicating on complaints. In addition, several treaty bodies, such as the CtAT,[21] CtEDAW,[22] CED,[23] CtRPD,[24] CtRC[25] and CESCR[26] are mandated to conduct confidential inquiries upon receipt of reliable information of systematic or serious violations or, in the case of the CERD, through early warning and urgent action procedures.[27] The SPT differs from other bodies; it considers neither states parties' reports nor complaints. Instead, in line with its preventive function it focuses on visits to states parties, providing advice on, and to, national preventive mechanisms and offering cooperation.[28]

It is tempting to measure the strength of a treaty body by reference to its power to adjudicate complaints because this is still frequently seen as the function that really matters, drawing on analogies with national law. Complaints procedures are undoubtedly important, especially those providing individuals with access to international justice.[29] However, these procedures do not automatically result in enhanced respect for rights and implementation of states parties' obligations. What must therefore be considered crucial is the ability of treaty bodies to utilise all means at their disposal to contribute to the development of an international 'culture' in which human rights

[20] See for a brief overview, including facts and figures, N. Pillay, *Strengthening the United Nations Human Rights Treaty Body System*, A report by the United Nations High Commissioner for Human Rights (United Nations, June 2012) 16–19: www2.ohchr.org/english/bodies/HRTD/docs/HCReportTBStrengthening.pdf.

[21] Art. 20 CAT. The Committee had completed ten confidential inquiries by April 2019: Turkey (1994), Egypt (1996 and 2017), Peru (2001), Sri Lanka (2002), Mexico (2003), Federal Republic of Yugoslavia (Serbia and Montenegro) (2004), Brazil (2008), Nepal (2012) and Lebanon (2014). See www.ohchr.org/EN/HRBodies/CAT/Pages/ InquiryProcedure.aspx.

[22] Art. 8 Optional Protocol CEDAW. The Committee had made five inquiries by April 2019 relating to Mexico, Canada, the Philippines, the United Kingdom and Kyrgyzstan. See www.ohchr.org/EN/HRBodies/ CEDAW/Pages/InquiryProcedure.aspx.

[23] Art. 33 CPED. See also art. 34 CPED.

[24] Arts. 6 and 7 Optional Protocol CRPD.

[25] Arts. 13 and 14 Optional Protocol CRC on a Communications Procedure.

[26] Arts. 11 and 12 Optional Protocol ICESCR.

[27] See Guidelines for the Early Warning and Urgent Action Procedures, Annual Report, UN doc. A/62/18, Annexes, ch. III, adopted at the CERD's 71st session in August 2007. See for the practice of using these procedures, www.ohchr.org/EN/HRBodies/CERD/Pages/Early WarningProcedure.aspx.

[28] Art. 11 OPCAT.

[29] See in particular, A. A. Cançado Trindade, *The Access of Individuals to International Justice* (Oxford University Press, 2011), and Chapter 7 on complaints procedures.

Is this book ur new hairat? (us your slaying it!)

are recognised and translated into actual promotion and protection at the national level.

Human rights treaty bodies are composed of between ten and twenty-five members who are elected by states parties and commonly serve for four years and up to eight years if re-elected.[30] The 'ideal' body comprises a group of individuals of high repute, outstanding expertise, dedication and independence[31] who represent various regions of the world. This ideal has been met to varying degrees by the various bodies; the HRCtee, in particular, has been credited for the capacity of its members, which reflects its prominent role and status. However, the lack of equitable geographical representation and gender balance in human rights treaty bodies has been a cause for concern and steps have been taken to address these shortcomings.[32]

The committees work on a part-time basis and meet in regular intervals in Geneva for brief sessions to review states parties' reports and, depending on the body, to consider individual communications, work on general comments or address other matters falling within their mandate. The working methods of the committees are set out in their respective rules of procedure, which detail the role of committee members, decision-making, publicity of meetings and so on.[33] The periodic sessions become an intense focus of committee work and an important forum for interaction with states parties, UN agencies, NGOs and others. However, the geographic location of the committee work, while having logistical advantages, can contribute to a sense of remoteness, especially for actors from the Americas, Asia and Africa. Webcasting of Committee sessions and having more regional meetings are some of the initiatives taken to make committee work more accessible.[34]

---

[30] Art. 8 ICERD; arts. 28–34 ICCPR; art. 17 CEDAW; art. 17 CAT; art. 43 CRC; art. 72 ICRMW; art. 34 CRPD; art. 26 CPED; arts. 5–10 OPCAT.

[31] See on this point in particular, Guidelines on the Independence and Impartiality of Members of the Human Rights Treaty Bodies ('the Addis Ababa guidelines'), UN doc. A/67/222 (2 August 2012) Annex I.

[32] See Promotion of equitable geographical distribution in the membership of the human rights treaty bodies, UNGA resolution 64/173 (18 December 2009), and Composition of the staff of the Office of the United Nations High Commissioner for Human Rights, UNGA resolution 16/10 (26 March 2011); Pillay, above note 20, 74–7; and on gender representation, H. Charlesworth, 'Not Waving but Drowning: Gender Mainstreaming and Human Rights in the United Nations' (2005) 18 *Harvard Human Rights Journal* 1; G. Heathcote, *Feminist Dialogues on International Law: Successes, Tensions, Futures* (Oxford University Press, 2019) 191–4.

[33] The text of the rules of procedures can be found on the websites of the treaty bodies; see www.ohchr.org/EN/HRBodies/Pages/HumanRightsBodies.aspx.

[34] See Inter-Committee Meeting of the human rights treaty bodies, The structure of the dialogue between treaty bodies and States parties, the structure and length of concluding observations, and the mode of interaction of treaty bodies with stakeholders, in particular national human rights institutions and civil society actors, UN doc. HRI/ICM/2011/2 (18 May 2011) para. 66, and Report of the Chairs of the human rights treaty bodies on their twenty-third meeting, Implementation of Human Rights Instruments, UN doc. A/66/175 (22 July 2011) para. 8.

The growing number of states parties' reports and communications, together with the need for enhanced coordination between the various bodies, increasingly strains the capacity of the committees. They are served throughout the year by their respective secretariats through the OHCHR, but there are consistent complaints that the time allocated and the resources available are inadequate to undertake the work effectively without overstretching the personal capacity of those involved.[35] In practice a lot depends on the initiative of individual committee members and the dynamics of the bodies concerned, and their level of engagement and output can differ markedly. The lack of remuneration (expenses only) may underscore the integrity of the committee members, but is prone to limit the additional time such individual experts are able to spend on committee work.

Problems of capacity, coordination and limited visibility in the broader public have contributed to calls for the strengthening, if not the wholesale reform, of the treaty body system.

5.3   REPORTING PROCEDURE

5.3.1   Overview

LMAO

Periodic reporting, the only generally accepted procedural obligation of states, has a special place in the work of human rights treaty bodies.[36] The reporting procedure serves multiple goals. Its overall objective is to ensure that states parties comply with their treaty obligations or, as article 2(2) of the International Covenant on Civil and Political Rights (ICCPR) puts it, 'to give effect to the rights recognised'. It provides an opportunity for states to review their law and practice, to develop a better understanding of the nature of problems identified, including by developing adequate policies, and to evaluate progress made in respect of implementation. The reporting procedure also offers an occasion for civil society and other national and international actors, including UN agencies, to provide input and scrutinise state conduct. Viewed from this perspective, reporting is essentially an enabling process engaging a number of actors, with the committees concerned acting as focal points that guide, help to evaluate and assist states on how best to implement their obligations.[37] This understanding is based on the implicit instrumental assumption that states are more likely to comply if engaged in a 'constructive

---

[35] See Pillay, above note 20, 27–8, 32–4.
[36] See generally OHCHR, *Manual on Human Rights Reporting under Six Major International Human Rights Instruments* (United Nations, 1997); A. Bayefsky (ed.), *The UN Human Rights Treaty System in the 21st century* (Kluwer Law International, 2000).
[37] See e.g., art. 40 ICCPR and OHCHR, *The United Nations Human Rights Treaty System: An Introduction to the Core Human Rights Treaties and the Treaty Bodies*, Fact Sheet no. 30 (2005) 27; P. Alston, 'The Purposes of Reporting', in OHCHR *Manual*, above note 36, 19–24.

dialogue (also called constructive discussion)', which is the approach pursued by the treaty bodies.[38] The process has been described as a form of ritual, which, for all its apparent shortcomings of being a second-order review, provides an important space for engagement and 'moral imagination'.[39]

Reporting procedures were first mooted in 1956[40] and later incorporated as a general obligation of states parties in subsequent treaties.[41] However, treaty bodies grappled with framing this obligation and developing a suitable format for reports. This was largely due to the vague wording of relevant provisions and resistance by some committee members to subjecting states' records to a critical examination, including the adoption of concluding observations. This prompted treaty bodies to adopt a series of general comments to clarify states parties' reporting obligations.[42] Since then, the reporting practice has developed, resulting in the adoption of harmonised guidelines on reporting.[43] Treaty bodies generally follow a similar format. An initial report is to be submitted within one or two years of a state becoming a party, depending on the treaty in question.[44] It is expected to set out the legislative, institutional and administrative framework in relation to the rights concerned and the report effectively serves as a baseline for later reports. The committee concerned considers the report based on information received from a variety of sources, including other UN agencies, national human rights institutions and NGOs. A list of issues, which is put to the state party before the session and allows NGOs and others to submit further information, subsequently forms the basis of discussions with the state delegates.

At the end of this process the committee deliberates and adopts concluding observations that set out positive developments, areas of concern and recommendations.[45] This includes requesting the state party to inform the

---

[38] See Harmonized Guidelines on Reporting under the International Human Rights Treaties, including Guidelines on a Common Core Document and Treaty-specific Documents, UN doc. HRI/MC/2006/3 (10 May 2006) para. 11.

[39] T. Kelly, 'Two Cheers for Ritual: The UN Committee against Torture' (2018) 9 *Humanity* 93. See also M. O'Flaherty, 'The United Nations human rights treaty bodies as diplomatic actors', in M. O'Flaherty et al. (eds.) *Human Rights Diplomacy: Contemporary Perspectives* (Martinus Nijhoff Publishers, 2011) 155–71.

[40] ECOSOC resolution, E/Res/624 B (XXII) (1 August 1956).

[41] See Alston, above note 37, 19–20.

[42] See e.g., HRCtee General Comments 1 and 2 (both 1981) and 30 (2002), online at www.ohchr.org/EN/HRBodies/CCPR/Pages/CCPRIndex.aspx.

[43] See UN doc. HRI/MC/2006/3. See also Consolidated Guidelines for State Reports under the International Covenant on Civil and Political Rights, UN doc. CCPR/C/66/GUI/Rev.2 (26 February 2001).

[44] Art. 9 ICERD; art. 40 ICCPR; art. 18 CEDAW; art. 19 CAT; art. 44 CRC; art. 73 ICRMW; art. 35 CRPD; art. 29 CPED. See for an overview, Pillay, above note 20, 20.

[45] The concluding observations are available on the OHCHR website, www.ohchr.org, both by treaty body (see sessions) and by country (see name of the country). The Universal Human Rights Index, http://uhri.ohchr.org, provides a search function according to treaty body, state and specific rights.

committee concerned of measures taken to implement its recommendations within a certain time period. For example, the HRCtee identifies a number of important recommendations that states should implement within one year and which are supervised by a follow-up rapporteur who draws up follow-up reports.[46] The state party may respond to the concluding observations, an option that is often used by states, primarily to object to some findings or recommendations made.[47] Next, the state party is obliged to submit further (periodic) reports (the period varies under the various rules of procedures, from two years (CERD) to five years (most treaty bodies)).[48] Periodic reports are more targeted in nature. States are expected to report on relevant developments in the reporting period and to set out what measures they have taken to comply with the recommendations made in the preceding concluding observations of the treaty body concerned. Following the initiative of the CtAT in 2007, the HRCtee and the CMW introduced a new optional reporting procedure 'whereby [the HRCtee] would send states parties a list of issues ... and consider their written replies in lieu of a periodic report'.[49] This measure was introduced to make reporting more targeted and efficient, and initial responses by states parties were favourable, resulting in an increase of reports submitted.[50] Upon receipt of the report the reporting cycle continues as set out above.

The increased participation of civil society actors has considerably changed the nature of the reporting procedure. NGOs and others can play an important role in the review of law and practice during the preparation of reports. Ideally, this already constitutes part of a broader domestic dialogue about a state's human rights performance.[51] Indeed, some states involve NGOs, national human rights institutions and others at the drafting stage, but the practice is far from uniform. Where it is based on a genuine dialogue rather than consultation for the sake of it this practice has the potential to result

[46] See e.g., Concluding Observations on Colombia, UN doc. CCPR/C/COL/CO/6 (4 August 2010) para. 27: 'In accordance with rule 71, paragraph 5, of the Committee's rules of procedure, the state party should provide, within one year, relevant information on its implementation of the recommendations made by the Committee in paragraphs 9, 14 and 16' (relating to impunity, extrajudicial killings and forced disappearances).

[47] See e.g., Comments by the Government of the People's Democratic Republic of Algeria, UN doc. CCPR/C/DZA/CO/3/Add.1 (19 November 2007), contesting the accuracy of the Committee's findings and several of the concerns it raised, such as in relation to amnesties, secret detention, enforced disappearances, torture and pre-trial detention in the counter-terrorism context, freedom of expression, assembly and association and the status of women.

[48] Pillay, above note 20, 20.

[49] See HRCtee, Focused Reports Based on Replies to Lists of Issues prior to Reporting (LOIPR): Implementation of the New Optional Reporting Procedure (LOIPR procedure), UN doc. CCPR/C/99/4 (29 September 2010) para. 1.

[50] Pillay, above note 20, 48.   [51] UN doc. HRI/MC/2006/3, para. 10.

in a contextualised report reflecting existing challenges and shortcomings. This stands in contrast to reports that simply restate the law or use selective and often irrelevant information, or otherwise do not present an accurate picture of affairs. The treaty bodies have responded to such shortcomings through the adoption of detailed guidelines and by pursuing dialogue with state delegates, as well as, on occasion, by requesting supplementary reports. However, states frequently appear either unable or unwilling to provide a sufficiently detailed and/or accurate report.[52] The information provided by UN agencies, NGOs and others provides an important counterweight and alternative source of information.[53] Drawing on a rich pool of information enables treaty bodies to identify a list of issues that are relevant in light of the actual practice and to ask probing questions during the constructive dialogue.[54] This includes highlighting specific cases or incidents that have been taken up by treaty bodies to illustrate systemic problems, enhance engagement and make follow-up more targeted.[55]

The increased level of engagement is frequently reflected in the concluding observations of treaty bodies. Concluding observations, that is the 'verdict' of the treaty body, are often the most contentious part of the reporting process. Inevitably, such observations raise issues and include recommendations that are objected to by states. Irrespective of what one considers to be the legal nature of concluding observations – positions range from an 'authoritative pronouncement on whether a state has or has not complied with its obligations'[56] to mere opinions or recommendations[57] – they will have to

---

[52] This may take the form of a clearly inadequate report, such as the one-page initial report submitted by Nepal to the CtAT, UN doc. CAT/C/16/Add.3 (16 December 1993), or rather sophisticated but highly 'selective' reports, such as Uzbekistan's report to the CtAT, UN doc. CAT/C/UZB/3 (28 July 2006).

[53] 'Alternative' or 'shadow' reports can be found on the respective treaty bodies websites under 'The Committee and its Work', 'Sessions'. See A. Clapham, 'The UN Human Rights Reporting Procedures: An NGO Perspective', in J. Crawford and P. Alston (eds.), *The Future of UN Human Rights Treaty Monitoring* (Cambridge University Press, 2000) 175–98, and OHCHR, *Working with the United Nations Human Rights Programme: A Handbook for Civil Society* (United Nations, 2008) ch. IV, at www.ohchr.org/Documents/Publications/NgoHandbook/ngohandbook4.pdf.

[54] However, see the critical account of the frustrating reality of treaty body proceedings, T. Kelly, 'The Cause of Human Rights: Doubts about Torture, Law, and Ethics at the United Nations' (2011) 17 *Journal of the Royal Anthropological Institute* 728.

[55] See e.g., the detailed List of Issues, China, Advanced Unedited Version (2015), and India, UN doc. CEDAW/C/IND/Q/4–5 (28 October 2013).

[56] T. Buergenthal, 'The UN Human Rights Committee' (2001) 5 *Max Planck Yearbook of United Nations Law* 341, at 351.

[57] See e.g., *Jones* v. *Ministry of Interior Al-Mamlaka Al-Arabiya AS Saudiya (the Kingdom of Saudi Arabia)* (UK) (2006), on the CtAT's comments on art. 14 CAT in relation to Canada's state party report; Lord Bingham of Cornhill, para. 23: 'no more than a recommendation'; Lord Hoffmann, para. 57: 'no value'.

be sufficiently specific, practical and persuasive to command the authority needed to enhance the prospect for implementation.[58] This includes the soundness of the legal arguments made, which have at times been the subject of controversy. A prominent example is the United States' (US) disagreement over the interpretation of the law by the HRCtee. The latter's concluding observation had challenged several of the states parties' interpretations of its obligations in the context of counterterrorism operations, including the definition of torture and the applicability of the ICCPR to the Guantánamo Bay detention regime.[59] This was a highly politicised incident that directly challenged the foundations of the extraordinary legal regime that the then US government had sought to erect. More generally, however, it is clear that concluding observations can be highly authoritative and are increasingly referred to in legal arguments made and in jurisprudence on human rights issues, such as by the ICJ in the *Wall* case.[60]

INTERVIEW 5.1

Using Shadow Reports to Promote Gender Equality and Combat Sexual Violence: South Africa

(Lesley Ann Foster)

Gender discrimination, sexual violence and other *de jure* or *de facto* violations of women's rights constitute major problems in South Africa. In 2011 South Africa was due for review before CtEDAW. Several NGOs used the opportunity to submit alternative reports, including an NGO shadow report.[1] CtEDAW issued its concluding observations on the report on 5 April 2011.[2]

---

[1] *South African NGO Shadow Report*, submitted to the CEDAW Committee's 48th Session (17 January–4 February 2011) online, at https://tbinternet.ochr.org/Treaties/CEDAW/ Shared%20Documents/ZAF/INT_CEDAW_NGO_ZAF_48_10363_E.pdf.
[2] UN doc. CEDAW/C/ZAF/CO/4.

---

[58] See C. Heyns and F. Viljoen, *The Impact of the United Nations Human Rights Treaties on the Domestic Level* (Kluwer Law International, 2002) 26–7, and Tyagi, above note 9, 252–9, on the nature of concluding observations.
[59] Comments by the Government of the United States of America on the concluding observations of the Human Rights Committee, UN doc. CCPR/C/USA/CO/3/Rev.1/Add.1 (12 February 2008). See for subsequent developments, HRCtee, Concluding Observations on the Fourth Periodic Report of the United States of America, UN doc. CCPR/C/USA/CO/4 (23 April 2014).
[60] The ICJ referred to the HRCtee's concluding observations on Israel's second period report when discussing the applicability of the ICCPR to the occupied territories in *Legal Consequences of the Construction of the Wall in the Occupied Palestinian Territory* (ICJ) (2004) para. 110.

The following is an interview with Dr Lesley Ann Foster, executive director of the Masimanyane Women's Support Centre,[3] which took the lead in preparing the NGO shadow report.

What did you hope to achieve by submitting the shadow report?

The then UN Special Rapporteur on Violence against Women, Radhika Coomaraswamy, had visited South Africa saying that it had the highest levels of violence against women in the world for a country not at war. This remark, together with the group's own knowledge and experience, provided sufficient motivation for us to focus on this issue. Another thing that counted in the group's favour was that violence against women had been raised high on the political agenda and it had been acknowledged as one of the most critical issues facing the country. We adopted a broad understanding of violence against women. It encompassed many other facets of women's rights, such as education, employment, literacy, health, welfare and similar issues, all with links to violence against women. Our main objective was to see a strengthening of the state's response to violence against women. We had identified various challenges in the implementation of state policies and called for a better legislative framework as well as improved institutional arrangements.

How did you succeed in having so many NGOs join the endeavour? *this stands for N° GAY OP S (Carson)*

We started off with a strong network of partner organisations. Next we purposefully identified the groups we knew should be included. Anyone else could join, so when groups expressed an interest we let them be a part of it. We asked various organisations to conduct the focus group discussions or participate in the field work. This included marginalised groups, including people working on lesbian, gay, bi-sexual and transgender (LGBT) issues, a transgender group and a sex workers group. We did not contact the group of disabled women whom we work with and this was a gap in our recent report. We made sure that everyone was given the opportunity to input into the process. We went into communities and trained women's groups on the principles of the Convention on the Elimination of All Forms of Discrimination against Women (CEDAW) and then invited them to participate in the process. All of this made it possible to draw people into developing the shadow report and participating in different ways in the process.

What was the division of labour between NGOs in preparing the report?

The approach of how to write a report on violence against women generated much discussion. An audit of the available skills was done. The group had medical expertise, legal expertise, media, education, financial and advocacy and lobbying skills. Most of the group had strong links to various networks.

---

[3] Now Masimanyane Women's Rights International, www.masimanyane.org.za.

It was also helpful that they came from different provinces within the country so were able to provide information on violence against women in different geographical, social, cultural and political settings.

How did you ensure the accuracy of information used?

We recorded the focus group discussions using electronic tools (video and recording devices). We also used published research and official state documents. All those involved in the process were briefed on the CEDAW and provided training on research, which helped in selecting and verifying relevant information.

How was the report received and used by the committee?

The final report was distributed to all the participating organisations throughout the country and every government minister and department was sent a copy. This was done after the report was sent to the CEDAW committee members. There were very audible grumblings in government circles about the report and some attempts were made to discredit the information contained in it. A harsh attack by the head of the government delegation was made to one of our representatives whom she knew well. The attack centred on her view that we were out of order in providing alternative information and that we should have been supportive of the government as it was a government of the people for the people. She did not accept our view that we had an important monitoring role to play.

The report was read by the CEDAW committee members. We then had a lunch briefing with the committee prior to our state reporting. They asked for clarifications on issues raised in the report and asked us to elaborate our concerns. They asked us what questions should be put to our state. This was very useful and extremely powerful. Eighteen out of the final twenty-six recommendations made by the CtEDAW focused on aspects of violence against women as highlighted in the NGO shadow report. Perhaps one of the most significant concluding comments was the suggestion that the South African government develop specific equality legislation. All of the concluding comments were sound suggestions which the group welcomed.

Some members of the group travelled back to South Africa with the government delegation. During the trip some discussion took place and the delegation acknowledged that the presence of the NGO delegation was a good thing. The representatives said that the concluding comments gave the delegation bargaining tools for greater political commitment and resource allocation for addressing women's rights in the country. They realised that if the report had been accepted without an honest critique and recommendations it would have led to complacency within government. This was an important shift.

Are you using the concluding observation in domestic advocacy, if so, how and with what impact?

We are currently disseminating the concluding observations. We have a national advocacy strategy in place to take up some of the issues on an ongoing basis. We are exploring further use of the convention, such as by applying the Optional Protocol to the CEDAW. We are also considering requesting an inquiry into some forms of discrimination in the country. The government has taken some action. It used the report to develop a strategy for addressing violence against women in the country, including research on lived realities of women. Extensive legislative reform took place and more than 4,000 laws were reviewed to ensure non-discrimination against women and girls. Equality legislation was developed but has not as yet been passed. Extensive programmes have been established in the country to support women and girls who are victims of gender-based violence. Research has been commissioned by the national government to develop the data systems related to violence against women.

What are the lessons you learned from the process?

Shadow reporting is a vital strategy for getting international attention on the plight of women in your country. We learned that you have to be prepared and you need to understand how the system works. We also learned that the work after the reporting session is as important as the development of the shadow report. One needs to use every opportunity to teach women about discrimination and inequality. Finally, we have learned that the state and women themselves do not have a strong enough understanding of discrimination.

5.3.2   Strengthening the Reporting Procedure

Non-compliance with treaty reporting is one of the notorious, systemic challenges confronting the UN human rights treaty system. Many states have failed to submit any reports or submitted them several years after they were due.[61] The reasons for this are both state-specific and systemic. States may lack the political incentive or have limited capacity, including lack of adequate data, to submit reports in time. The treaty bodies have limited 'enforcement' powers and there is no apparent political cost for late submissions, unlike with the universal periodic review (UPR) which is a much more state-driven political process.[62] One major problem facing the system

---

[61] According to Pillay, above note 20, 21, only 16 per cent of reports 'were submitted in strict accordance with the due dates established in the treaties or by the treaty bodies. As of April 2012, a total of 626 reports – 315 initial reports and 311 periodic reports – were overdue'; see ibid., 23.

[62] See Chapter 4.4.1 for a discussion of the UPR.

is the growing number of reporting obligations that states find increasingly difficult to meet.[63] The treaty bodies and the OHCHR have taken a series of measures to address non-reporting and delays.[64] These include supporting states in building their capacity to prepare and submit reports, encouraging states to submit core documents[65] and offering states the possibility to report on a list of issues rather than submitting a full periodic report.[66] Treaty bodies may 'name and shame' late or non-reporting states, or decide to consider the situation in a state even in the absence of a report on the basis of other information received.[67] In practice, the threat of doing so has often been sufficient to prompt a state to engage and ultimately submit a report.[68] This demonstrates a degree of effectiveness which ironically may generate the reverse problem. The treaty bodies themselves may not have the capacity to consider reports within a reasonable time if reporting were to increase, which would in all likelihood considerably add to the already existing backlog.[69]

This challenge, together with concerns about adequate coordination and lack of impact of treaty bodies, led to a concerted review process in the 2000s.[70] In the course of this process the OHCHR proposed the establishment of a unified standing treaty body. It argued that the creation of such a body would

[63] See Report by the Secretariat, Concept Paper on the High Commissioner's Proposal for a Unified Standing Treaty Body, UN doc. HRI/MC/2006/2 (22 March 2006) para. 16; Pillay, above note 20, 25.

[64] See W. Kälin, 'Examination of State Reports', in H. Keller and G. Ulfstein (eds.), *UN Human Rights Treaty Bodies* (Cambridge University Press, 2012) 16–72, at 32, and Tyagi, above note 9, 188–210, for the HRCtee.

[65] The core document should contain general information about the state, the general framework for the promotion and protection of human rights, information on non-discrimination and equality and effective remedies; see UN doc. HRI/MC/2006/3, paras. 31–59.

[66] See UN doc. CCPR/C/99/4.

[67] E.g., in relation to Gambia, in 2008 the HRCtee considered the situation in the absence of a report in 2002, and 'declared the state party to be in breach of its obligation to cooperate with the Committee in the performance of its functions under Part IV of the Covenant', and, in 2009, 'referred [the matter] to the High Commissioner for Human Rights, Report of the Special Rapporteur for follow-up on concluding observations', UN doc. CCPR/C/95/2/ rev.1 (26 May 2009) 2–3.

[68] See e.g., Concluding Observations of the Human Rights Committee: Rwanda, UN doc. CCPR/ C/RWA/CO/3 (7 May 2009) para. 2.

[69] See UN doc. A/66/344, para. 11: 'As of May 2011, 263 reports were pending consideration under the nine treaty bodies with a reporting procedure.' See 12, Table 2 for an overview of the backlog, and para. 21: 'The observation, made by an independent expert reporting on the same issue to the United Nations in 1997, that the treaty system "can function only because of the large-scale delinquency of states" remains true today (see UN doc. E/ CN.4/1997/74, para. 48).'

[70] Reform efforts date back to the 1980s; see UNGA resolution 43/115 (8 December 1988) para. 15. See for the important role played by the UN Secretary-General, Strengthening of the United Nations: An Agenda for Further Change, UN doc. A/57/387 (9 September 2002) paras. 52–4; In Larger Freedom: Towards Development, Security and Human Rights for All, UN doc. A/59/2005 (21 March 2005) para. 147.

provide ... a framework for a comprehensive, cross-cutting and holistic approach to implementation ... a consistent approach to interpretation of provisions in the treaties ... extend ... the period of the dialogue ... members ... be available on a permanent basis ... be more visible ... [provide a] unified monitoring structure.[71]

In addition, a comprehensive, overall assessment of the implementation of international legal obligations under human rights treaties for countries in one single document ... would be more likely to attract heightened attention from political bodies such as ... [the] Human Rights Council or the Security Council.[72]

In spite of these apparent advantages the proposal did not garner much support. This was due to concerns that it might undermine protection for specific rights and that the attempt to integrate all treaties would be fraught with difficulties. In 2009 the UN High Commissioner for Human Rights initiated a treaty body strengthening process involving a range of relevant stakeholders, with a major focus on measures aimed at harmonising the working methods of treaty bodies, as expressed in the Dublin Statement on the Process of Strengthening of the United Nations Human Rights Treaty Body System.[73] NGOs welcomed this process and submitted a number of proposals to make the system more visible and accessible for NGOs to contribute.[74] The process culminated in a major report by the UN High Commissioner for Human Rights in 2012, which compiled a series of recommendations. These included: establishing a comprehensive reporting calendar ... enhancing independence and impartiality of members and strengthening the election process; establishing a structured and sustained approach to capacity-building for States parties for their reporting duties ... increasing accessibility and visibility of the treaty body system, through webcasting of public meetings and use of other new technologies; a simplified focused reporting procedure ... alignment of other working methods to the maximum extent without contradicting the normative specificities of the treaties; limitation of the length of documentation.[75]

There is a clear understanding of the problems and needs as reflected in the measures suggested. These include availability of greater resources to respond to the increased workload resulting from the expansion of treaty

---

[71] UN doc. HRI/MC/2006/2, paras. 27–35.   [72] Ibid., para. 36.

[73] See www2.ohchr.org/english/bodies/HRTD/docs/DublinStatement.pdf. See for further documents generated as part of the review process, OHCHR, 'The Treaty Body Strengthening Process', online at www.ohchr.org/EN/HRBodies/HRTD/Pages/TBStrengthening.aspx.

[74] Dublin Statement on the Process of Strengthening the United Nations Human Rights Treaty Body System: Response by Non-governmental Organizations, November 2010 (recommendations include holding occasional meetings outside of Geneva, advance notice for NGOs, communications, protection against reprisals for NGOs, enhanced membership of treaty bodies, better coordination), online at www2.ohchr.org/english/bodies/HRTD/docs/FinalDublinStatResponseNGOs.pdf.

[75] Pillay, above note 20, 10–11.

bodies and states parties, improved communications, more targeted reporting and follow-up and better coordination between the treaty bodies.[76] In 2014, the UNGA adopted resolution 68/268, which draws on the High Commissioner's proposals and sets out a series of measures to be put in place whose effectiveness is to be reviewed periodically.[77]

These measures, if implemented, would contribute to enhanced efficiency. However, it is questionable whether they will be sufficient to satisfactorily address the underlying factors, particularly fragmented mandates, limited powers and the low visibility of UN treaty bodies. This raises the more fundamental question of whether the current system is based on structures and processes that can be successfully strengthened or whether it suffers from systemic shortcomings that require a radical rethink and reforms. The risks to the human rights treaty body architecture inherent in such drastic changes have acted as a bulwark that has kept the current system in place. Ongoing concerns, if not frustration, with a system seen as dysfunctional may give renewed impetus to the idea of a unified standing treaty body, or even a World Court of Human Rights,[78] which several observers believe would be the authority needed to give human rights the standing it warrants at UN level.

It would seem tempting to dismiss the reporting procedure as an onerous and futile 'soft' mechanism that generates the illusion of progress but in reality produces a dialogue that allows states and other actors in the system to be seen as doing something while largely maintaining the status quo. However, for all its apparent and supposed weaknesses the reporting procedure has become an integral part of the system that has contributed, at least to some degree, to the promotion and protection of human rights. It has within its confines: (1) produced an impressive source of information and record in respect of states' implementation of their human rights treaty obligations; (2) advanced to varying degrees the interpretation and understanding of rights and obligations under the various treaties; (3) provided a forum and instrument for human rights advocacy; and (4) contributed to some changes in law and practice, although the state record of implementing recommendations is patchy.[79] In addition to strengthening the technical aspects of reporting in order to increase efficiency, the main task for treaty bodies is to enhance implementation. This

---

[76] Ibid.; Measures to Improve Further the Effectiveness, Harmonization and Reform of the Treaty Body System, UN doc. A/66/344 (7 September 2011).

[77] Strengthening and enhancing the effective functioning of the human rights treaty body system, UNGA resolution 68/268 (21 April 2014). See 'Status of the human rights treaty body system', Report of the Secretary-General, UN doc. A/73/309 (6 August 2018).

[78] See J. Kozma, M. Nowak and M. Scheinin, *A World Court of Human Rights: Consolidated Statute and Commentary* (Neuer Wissenschaftlicher Verlag, 2011); T. Buergenthal, 'A Court and Two Consolidated Treaty Bodies', in Bayefsky, above note 36, 299–302.

[79] The most thorough study on implementation is that of Heyns and Viljoen, above note 58. See also, UN doc. HRI/MC/2006/2, paras. 11–14.

includes better visibility and most importantly fostering practices that enable domestic actors, particularly civil society, to use the process as an advocacy tool to improve the human rights situation in the country concerned.

QUESTIONS

1. Is the reporting system fundamentally flawed or simply in the process of becoming an effective means of monitoring of, and engagement on, states' human rights record?

2. What is the evidence that the model of 'constructive dialogue' adopted by the treaty bodies has really been constructive?

3. Would the establishment of a unified standing body proposed by the OHCHR constitute the breakthrough needed to substantially strengthen the reporting procedure or would it weaken the more targeted protection existing human rights treaty bodies are mandated to provide?

4. What are the strategic openings and challenges for NGOs in the reporting process?

5.4   GENERAL COMMENTS/RECOMMENDATIONS

General comments (also referred to as general recommendations by the CtEDAW and the CERD) are written instruments that treaty bodies adopt, with varying frequency, to set out their views as to the rights and obligations under the treaty concerned.[80] These comments are an integral aspect of the treaty body practice and a vital tool for the interpretation of the respective treaties. The practice of adopting general comments was pioneered by the CERD in 1972, based on the power of treaty bodies to make general recommendations in relation to their function of examining states parties' reports.[81] This direct link was particularly evident in the first generation of general comments that specified states parties' reporting obligations. Subsequently, general comments have become instruments that enable treaty bodies to interpret treaty provisions with a view to promoting effective rights protection and the implementation of treaties. They can serve a number of purposes, combining legal analysis with important policy and practice direction functions.[82]

---

[80] The General Comments can be found in UN doc. HRI/GEN/1/Rev.9 (vols. I and II) (27 May 2008), and on the websites of the respective treaty bodies.

[81] See Report on the Working Methods of the Human Rights Treaty Bodies Relating to the State Party Reporting Process, UN doc. HRI/ICM/2010/2 (10 May 2010) para. 120, based on art. 9(2) ICERD.

[82] See the study by H. Keller and L. Grover, 'General Comments of the Human Rights Committee and their Legitimacy', in H. Keller and G. Ulfstein (eds.), *UN Human Rights Treaty Bodies* (Cambridge University Press, 2012) 116–98, at 143.

The adoption of a general comment typically involves a number of stages that are followed with some variation by all treaty bodies. A member or members of a treaty body propose(s) the drafting of a general comment. If this proposal is supported, a member or a group composed of several members is tasked with preparing a draft or drafts for consideration by the committee. The draft is then further revised and formally adopted after a detailed discussion of its contents.[83] In this process the committee consults with a range of actors from within the UN system, such as specialised agencies, and from without, such as NGOs.[84] In practice, general comments are the outcome of particular dynamics within the treaty body. Is there a readiness to use general comments generally or in relation to a particular issue? Who is taking the lead? How well-informed and capable are the drafters? And how successfully does the body overcome any differences to produce an authoritative draft?

The practice of adopting general comments differs markedly between committees. Whereas many bodies adopt one general comment every two years on average, others, notably the CtAT, have only adopted four in over twenty years. The HRCtee had adopted an impressive number of thirty-six general comments by April 2019, and these constitute an important guide to its understanding of the ICCPR.[85] These comments broach the obligation of states parties under the Covenant and the Optional Protocol, reporting obligations, general questions such as reservations and the majority of substantive rights (including revised comments in relation to several important articles). Compared to the initial, rather cursory, general comments of treaty bodies, the more recent ones are greatly substantive. They include at times detailed analysis of the treaty bodies' jurisprudence and relevant international law as well as consideration of topical themes, such as sanctions,[86] non-citizens,[87] refugees,[88] as well as children and HIV/AIDS.[89] General comments have served to clarify the fundamental norms of a treaty, such as

---

[83] See Buergenthal, above note 56, 388; UN doc. HRI/ICM/2010/2, paras. 122–4.

[84] See e.g., the General Discussion on the preparation for a General Comment on Article 9 (Liberty and Security of Person) of the International Covenant on Civil and Political Rights, Palais des Nations, Room XII – 25 October 2012, and the range of documents submitted in the process which resulted in the adoption of the HRCtee's General Comment 35, www.ohchr.org/EN/HRBodies/CCPR/Pages/GConArticle9.aspx.

[85] Available online at www.ohchr.org/EN/HRBodies/CCPR/Pages/CCPRIndex.aspx. See on the role of General Comments in the Committee's practice, Keller and Grover, above note 82, 116–98, and Tyagi, above note 9, 277–307.

[86] CESCR, General Comment 8: The Relationship between Economic Sanctions and Respect for Economic, Social and Cultural Rights, UN doc. E/C.12/1997/8 (12 December 1997).

[87] CERD, General Comment 30: Discrimination against Non-Citizens, UN doc. HRI/GEN/1/Rev.7/Add.1 (4 May 2005).

[88] CEDAW, General Recommendation 32 on the gender-related dimensions of refugee status, asylum, nationality and statelessness of women, UN doc. CEDAW/C/GC/32 (14 November 2014).

[89] CtRC, General Comment 3: HIV/AIDs and the Rights of the Children, UN doc. CRC/GC/2003/3 (17 March 2003).

the application of non-discrimination to violence against women,[90] and the relationship between torture and other forms of cruel, inhuman or degrading treatment or punishment.[91] In an innovative step, in November 2014 the CtRC and the CtEDAW adopted a joint general recommendation/general comment on harmful practices.[92] The CtRC has also adopted two joint general comments, with the CMW, in the context of international migration.[93] General comments can act as key reference points for states parties, such as on the nature of their obligations, and others where they articulate important principles of international law.[94] This function has been particularly valuable for bodies that do not (or did not) have the competence to hear complaints. The CESCR in particular has used its general comments to develop a sophisticated understanding of states parties' obligations necessitated by the controversies surrounding the nature of economic, social and cultural rights and of corresponding obligations,[95] which in turn has been referred to in national jurisprudence.[96]

General comments are not binding or vested with any formal legal status. Instead, they are widely seen as interpretations of the respective treaties by an authoritative body, which may also serve to restate and clarify its jurisprudence.[97] As such, general comments have become influential not only for the practice of treaty bodies but also because they are cited as authoritative in the jurisprudence of other national and international bodies.[98] It is

---

90 CtEDAW, Violence against Women, General Recommendation 12 (1989); General Recommendation 19 (1992) and 35 (2017) on gender-based violence against women, updating General Recommendation 19.

91 CtAT, General Comment 2: Implementation of Article 2 by States Parties, UN doc. CAT/C/GC/2 (24 January 2008).

92 Joint General Recommendation/General Comment 31 of the Committee on the Elimination of Discrimination against Women and General Comment 18 of the Committee on the Rights of the Child on Harmful Practices, UN doc. CEDAW/C/GC/31-CRC/C/GC/18 (14 November 2014).

93 Joint General Comment 3 (2017) of the CMW and 22 (2017) of the CRC on the general principles regarding the human rights of children in the context of international migration, UN doc. CMW/C/GC/3-CRC/C/GC/22 (16 November 2017) and Joint General Comment 4 (2017) of the CMW and 23 (2017) of the CRC on State obligations regarding the human rights of children in the context of international migration in countries of origin, transit, destination and return, UN doc. CMW/C/GC/4-CRC/C/GC/23 (16 November 2017).

94 HRCtee, General Comment 31: The Nature of the General Legal Obligation imposed on States Parties to the Covenant, UN doc. CCPR/C/21/Rev.1/Add.13 (26 May 2004).

95 This practice started with its General Comment 3 on general obligations, which was followed by comments concerning the states parties' obligations in relation to substantive rights.

96 See e.g., *Government of the Republic of South Africa and Others* v. *Grootboom and Others* (South Africa) (2000) paras. 29–31, 45.

97 See Tyagi, above note 9, 301–7, with further references. However, see Keller and Grover, above note 82, 133, who refer to the US and UK position rejecting 'the idea that the Committee is "the" authoritative interpreter of the Covenant'.

98 See e.g., the ICJ in the *Wall* Advisory opinion, para. 136 (reference to General Comment 27); *Ahmadou Sadio Diallo (Republic of Guinea* v. *Democratic Republic of the Congo)* (ICJ) (2010) para. 66 (General Comment 15); para. 77 (General Comment 8).

therefore apt to refer to general comments as 'important instruments in the lawmaking process of the [Human Rights] Committee'[99] and compare them to advisory opinions.[100] Indeed, the ICJ believes that 'it should ascribe great weight to the interpretation adopted by this independent body [the HRCtee] that was established specifically to supervise the application of that treaty'.[101]

The legitimacy of general comments has been attributed to a number of factors, which a recent study based on a series of interviews with committee members identified as determinacy, symbolic validation, coherence, adherence and democratic decision-making.[102] While many general comments have been favourably received, their authority has been challenged in some notable instances. The HRCtee's General Comment 24 is an example that elicited considerable controversy. Several states, namely the United Kingdom (UK), the USA and France, took exception to the HRCtee's position that it, rather than the states parties themselves, has the competence to decide on the validity of reservations, as has been the traditional understanding in international law.[103] The General Comment was the subject of close scrutiny and questions were raised about the Committee's reasoning and limited legal analysis.[104] Such reactions generate moments of tension that can damage the relationship between states and treaty bodies and serve to undermine the latter's authority. However, the committees, being the guardians of the treaty in question, also have a responsibility to strengthen the effectiveness of human rights treaties. Using general comments to break new ground to this effect can be a risky undertaking, but may over time be vindicated if a sufficient number of relevant actors subscribe to the treaty bodies' position, which in turn generates momentum for others to follow.[105]

5.5   COMPLAINTS PROCEDURES AND JURISPRUDENCE OF TREATY BODIES

5.5.1   Overview

Treaty-based complaints procedures (individual and inter-state communications) are an important means to monitor compliance of states parties with their obligations and to develop the law under the respective treaty. Importantly, and exceptionally as compared to other areas of international

---

[99] Buergenthal, above note 56, 387.   [100] Ibid., 386.   [101] *Ahmadou Sadio Diallo*, para. 66.
[102] Keller and Grover, above note 82.
[103] See observations by the USA, the UK and France on General Comment 24, in Report of the HRCtee, UN doc. A/50/40 (3 October 1995), Annex IV (USA and UK), and UN doc. A/51/40 (13 April 1997), Annex VI (France).
[104] See K. Korkelia, 'New Challenges to the Regime of Reservations under the International Covenant on Civil and Political Rights' (2002) 13 *European Journal of International Law* 437, at 446–68; E. A. Baylis, 'General Comment 24: Confronting the Problem of Reservations to Human Rights Treaties' (1999) 17 *Berkeley Journal of International Law* 277.
[105] See further Chapter 2.2.1.2 on reservations.

law, individual complaints procedures provide victims of human rights violations with a remedy at the international level.[106] This is in contrast to related areas, such as international refugee law and international humanitarian law, where no comparable treaty bodies and procedures exist. However, UN human rights treaty bodies are not vested with the automatic competence to consider communications. They can only deal with individual cases where states parties make a declaration to this effect or become parties to an optional protocol.[107] The lack of a compulsory complaints procedure reflected the reluctance of states to expose themselves to any scrutiny other than the reporting procedure. This has slowly changed as many states (with some significant exceptions, see further below) have now recognised the competence of treaty bodies to consider complaints of alleged human rights violations.[108]

Procedures for inter-state cases before the various treaty bodies differ. Communications may be heard by the committee concerned (Convention against Torture (CAT), International Convention on the Protection of the Rights of All Migrant Workers and Members of Their Families (ICRMW) and the International Convention for the Protection of All Persons from Enforced Disappearance (CPED))[109] or dealt with by ad hoc conciliation commissions (International Convention on the Elimination of All Forms of Racial Discrimination (ICERD) and ICCPR[110]). Disputes regarding the interpretation and application of the respective treaty may be settled through negotiation, arbitration, or, ultimately, referral to the ICJ (ICERD, CEDAW, CAT, ICRMW and CPED).[111] The rather elaborate UN treaty system for inter-state complaints has not been used. This may appear odd at first sight because states included the relevant provisions in the first place and a number of states parties have made declarations accepting the complaints procedures concerned. States' reluctance to use formal inter-state procedures before treaty bodies to resolve disputes may be attributed to a preference for political bodies, such as the UN Human Rights Council (HRC), to address human rights concerns and a desire to avoid adverse diplomatic repercussions. However, there have been

---

[106] See further Chapter 7.

[107] Optional protocols become necessary where the primary treaty, as is the case with the ICCPR, does not provide for a complaints procedure. See more recently, the Optional Protocols to the ICESCR and CRC (Complaints Procedures).

[108] See http://treaties.un.org/Pages/Treaties.aspx?id=4&subid=A&lang=en.

[109] Art. 21 CAT; art. 74 ICRMW; art. 32 CPED.

[110] Arts. 11–13 ICERD (automatic/compulsory) and arts. 41–43 ICCPR (upon declaration).

[111] Art. 22 ICERD; art. 29 CEDAW; art. 30 CAT; art. 92 ICRMW; art. 42 CPED. See for an interpretation of art. 22 ICERD (dispute settlement between ICERD states parties and referral to the ICJ), case concerning *Application of the International Convention on the Elimination of All Forms of Racial Discrimination (Georgia v. Russian Federation)* (ICJ) (2011) paras. 115–84; on art. 29 CEDAW, *Armed Activities on the Territory of the Congo (New Application: 2002) (Democratic Republic of the Congo v. Rwanda)* (ICJ) (2006) paras. 87–93; and on art. 30 CAT, *Questions Relating to the Obligation to Prosecute or Extradite (Belgium v. Senegal)* (ICJ) (2012) paras. 42–55.

a growing number of inter-state cases over the breach of human rights obligations before other courts, namely the European Court of Human Rights (ECtHR) and the ICJ.[112] Notably, in several judgments, the ICJ adjudicated cases with reference to the ICCPR, among other applicable sources.[113] This suggests that states prepared to use formal proceedings prefer to resort to courts, where possible. The reason for this may be the prospect of obtaining a binding judgment that carries greater weight than quasi-judicial or other dispute settlement procedures for inter-state cases provided for in the UN human rights treaty system.

By April 2019 eight treaty bodies had the competence to receive individual communications. Individual complaints mechanisms are either provided for in the respective treaty, such as ICERD, CAT, ICRMW (procedure not in force as of April 2019) and CPED,[114] or in an optional protocol, as is the case with the ICCPR and the Convention on the Rights of Persons with Disabilities (CRPD). The Optional Protocols to the CEDAW (1999), the International Covenant on Economic, Social and Cultural Rights (ICESCR) (2008) and the Convention on the Rights of the Child (CRC) (on complaints procedure) (2011) were adopted twenty years, forty-two years and thirty-two years respectively after the adoption of the treaty setting out the substantive rights. This time lag shows that the acceptance of individual complaints procedures is often the outcome of protracted processes. These processes are usually driven by a range of actors comprising civil society organisations, like-minded states parties, UN bodies and individual experts, who frequently encounter considerable obstacles when advocating changes to the system. These include objections based on the supposed lack of justiciability of rights (ICESCR)[115] and the reluctance to vest bodies such as the CtEDAW with the power to consider complaints in what are seen as sensitive areas. The challenges surrounding the recognition of an individual complaints procedure were also evident in recent debates in the HRC concerning an optional protocol to the CRC.[116]

The level of state acceptance of the various treaty bodies' competence to consider communications varies considerably.[117] There is a significant regional imbalance which undermines the universal reach of procedures. The USA, India, China and Middle Eastern states in particular have not accepted the competence of treaty bodies to receive complaints against them. Even

---

[112] See Chapter 6.2.5 on the ECtHR.

[113] See in particular, the *Wall* Advisory Opinion and *Ahmadou Sadio Diallo*.

[114] Art. 14 ICERD; art. 22 CAT; art. 77 ICRMW; art. 31 CPED.   [115] See Chapter 9.6.1.

[116] See Optional Protocol to the CRC on a communications procedure, UN doc. A/HRC/ RES/17/ 18 (14 July 2011), and documents of the Open-ended Working Group on an Optional Protocol to the CRC to provide a communications procedure, online at www.ohchr.org/EN/ HRBodies/HRC/WGCRC/Pages/OPenEndedWorkingGroupIndex.aspx.

[117] The status of ratifications and acceptance of treaty bodies' competence to consider complaints is available online at www.ohchr.org/EN/HRBodies/Pages/HumanRightsBodies.aspx.

where states have recognised such competence, there are sizeable differences in the number of communications that reach the various committees. The HRCtee has dealt with by far the most complaints, followed by the CtAT, CERD, CtEDAW and CtRPD.[118] The respective committee(s) often plays a valuable role for some countries or in some regions while it may be of marginal interest in others. In this context, it is important not to see the number of communications brought against a particular state as a reliable indicator of the seriousness of the human rights situation in a country, though this may constitute one factor influencing whether or not cases are brought. Other factors include awareness, the presence of activist lawyers and NGOs taking up cases, the availability of effective domestic remedies that make recourse to the treaty bodies unnecessary, a preference for regional procedures where available and the degree of belief in the utility of the procedure.[119] Finally, state acceptance of complaints procedures has not automatically translated into compliance with decisions made.[120]

5.5.2   The HRCtee

Of the 172 states parties to the ICCPR, 116 had become parties to the optional protocol as of 1 May 2019. The HRCtee had found 975 violations in a total of 2,474 communications with respect to 89 states as of March 2016.[121] It has developed an impressive body of jurisprudence that has been marked by its response to systemic and/or serious violations in several countries and regions and by the development of its case law on particular rights. The 1970s and 1980s were characterised by a large number of decisions against Uruguay in cases involving torture and enforced disappearances.[122] Colombia and Zaire (now Democratic Republic of the Congo) featured prominently in the 1980s in respect of serious violations committed in the course of conflict and dictatorship.[123] Jamaica in the late 1980s and throughout the 1990s and Trinidad and Tobago in the 1990s and 2000s were the subject of dozens of views, particularly in respect of the death penalty regime in place in both countries. These included findings that the mandatory death penalty was incompatible with the

---

[118] The relevant statistics are provided in the overview for each treaty body following in this chapter, with the exception of CtESCR and CtRC due to their limited caseload to date.

[119] Heyns and Viljoen, above note 58, 28–30.   [120] See Chapter 7.5.

[121] See statistical survey of complaints considered, online at www.ohchr.org/EN/HRBodies/CCPR/Pages/CCPRIndex.aspx.

[122] Beginning with the case of *Massera* v. *Uruguay* (HRCtee) (1979), the first HRCtee decision on the merits that found violations of arts. 7, 9(1–4), 10(1), 14(1–3) and 25. All of the Committee's first twelve views concerned Uruguay, with a total of forty-eight views as of 2018.

[123] See e.g., *Herrera* v. *Colombia* (HRCtee) (1987) paras. 10.1–11 (violation of arts. 6, 7 and 10(1)); *Muteba* v. *Zaire* (HRCtee) (1984) paras. 10.1–12 (violation of arts. 7, 9(3–4), 10(1), 14(3)(b–d) and 19); *Mpandanjila et al.* v. *Zaire* (HRCtee) (1986) paras. 8.1–9 (violation of arts. 9(1), 10(1), 12(1), 14(1), 19 and 25).

right to life, an emphasis on compliance with the right to a fair trial as prerequisite for the imposition of the death penalty and holding that the so-called death row phenomenon may constitute inhuman and degrading treatment.[124]

In the 2000s and 2010s the geographic focus broadened. It has included Australia (particularly in relation to immigration detention);[125] Algeria and Libya (particularly enforced disappearances);[126] Belarus (denial of various rights resulting from political repression);[127] Central Asian states, particularly Tajikistan, Kyrgyzstan and Uzbekistan (mainly torture and imposition of the death penalty following an unfair trial);[128] Russia (multiple violations);[129] and several Asian states, particularly Nepal (multiple violations, particularly conflict-related violations, including enforced disappearance),[130]

---

[124] See *Kennedy* v. *Trinidad and Tobago* (HRCtee) (1999) para. 7.3 (mandatory death penalty); *Price* v. *Jamaica* (HRCtee) (1996), paras. 9.2–9.3 (death penalty following an unfair trial); *Pratt and Morgan* v. *Jamaica* (HRCtee) (1989), para. 15 (commutation as appropriate remedy); *Johnson* v. *Jamaica* (HRCtee) (1998) para. 10.4 (death row).

[125] See in particular, *Griffiths* v. *Australia* (HRCtee) (2014) paras. 7.1–8 (violation of art. 9(1) and (4)); *F. K. A. G. et al.* v. *Australia* (HRCtee) (2013) paras. 9.1–10 (violation of arts. 7 and 9(1) and (4) and art. 9(2) in respect of five authors); *M. M. M. et al.* v. *Australia* (HRCtee) (2013) paras. 10.1–11 (violation of arts. 7 and 9(1) and (4)). See also *Blessington and Elliot* v. *Australia* (HRCtee) (2014) paras. 7.1–8 (imposition of life sentence on juveniles, violation of arts. 7, 10(3) and 24), and *Horvath* v. *Australia* (HRCtee) (2014) paras. 8.1–9 (non-enforcement of judgment providing compensation for police misconduct, violation of art. 2 (3) in connection with arts. 7, 9(1) and (5), 10(1) and 17).

[126] See *Sassene* v. *Algeria* (HRCtee) (2014) paras. 7.1–8, with reference to relevant case-law against Algeria, violation of arts. 6(1), 7, 9, 10(1), 16 and 17 (author, Zaier) and arts. 6(1), 7, 9, 10(1), 16 and 17 (author's husband, victim of enforced disappearance); *Al Rabbasi* v. *Libya* (HRCtee) (2014) paras. 7.1–8 (violation of arts. 6(1), 7, 9, 14(1) and (3)(b) and 16 (victim of enforced disappearance) and art. 7, alone and read in conjunction with art. 2(3) (author, brother of victim of enforced disappearance)).

[127] See *Selyun* v. *Belarus* (HRCtee) (2015) paras. 7.1–7.8 (violation of arts 6, 7, 9(3) and 14(2) and 3(b)(d) and (g)); *Yuzepchuk* v. *Belarus* (HRCtee) (2014) paras. 8.1–9 (violation of arts. 6, 7, 9(3) and 14(1) and (3)(e) and (g)); *Lozenko* v. *Belarus* (HRCtee) (2014) paras. 7.1–8 (violation of arts. 19(2) and 21); *Korneenko and Milinkevich* v. *Belarus* (HRCtee) (2009) paras. 8.1–9 (violation of arts. 19(2), 25 and 26).

[128] See *Ashirov* v. *Kyrgyzstan* (HRCtee) (2017) paras. 7.1–8 (violation of arts. 7 in conjunction with 2(3) and 14(1)); *Iskandarov* v. *Tajikistan* (HRCtee) (2011) paras. 6.1–6.7 (violation of arts. 7, 9(1) and (3), 14(1) and 3(b), (d–e) and (g)); *Akhadov* v. *Kyrgyzstan* (HRCtee) (2011) paras. 7.1–7.8 (violation of arts. 6, 7, 9 and 14(1) and (3)(g)); *Kasimov* v. *Uzbekistan* (HRCtee) (2009) paras. 9.1–9.10 (violation of arts. 7 and 14(3)(b) and (g)).

[129] See *Lantsova* v. *Russia* (HRCtee) (2002) paras. 8.1–8.10 (violation of arts. 6 and 10(1)), and *Khoroshenko* v. *Russia* (HRCtee) (2011) paras. 9.1–9.10 (violation of arts. 6, 7, 9(1–4) and 14(1) and (3)(a–b), (d) and (g)).

[130] *Neupane et al.* v. *Nepal* (HRCtee) (2017) paras. 10.1–10.11 (violation of arts. 6, 7, 9 and 16, in conjunction with art. 2(3); and authors' rights under arts. 7 and 7 read in conjunction with 2(3)); *Chaulagain* v. *Nepal* (HRCtee) (2014) paras. 11.1–12 (violation of arts. 6(1), 7, 9 and 10, all read in conjunction with art. 2(3); as well as the author's rights under art. 7, read in conjunction with art. 2(3)); and *Bhandari* v. *Nepal* (HRCtee) (2014) paras. 8.1–9 (violation of arts. 6(1), 7, 9 and 16, and art. 2(3) in conjunction with arts. 6(1), 7, 9 and 16 with regard to the victim of enforced disappearance as well as arts. 7 and 2(3) read in conjunction with art. 7 (author)). See also, Interview 7.1 with Mandira Sharma.

the Philippines and Sri Lanka (mainly in relation to the death penalty before its abolition in the Philippines, as well as torture, arbitrary arrests and detention and unfair trials).[131] The HRCtee has over the years also heard a number of complaints in relation to particular states for which it constitutes the only available international complaints procedure. This included Spain in respect of the right to an appeal as part of the right to a fair trial, primarily because Spain had until 2009 not been a party to Protocol no. 7 to the European Convention on Human Rights (ECHR), which recognises such a right.[132]

A large number of cases before the HRCtee concern articles 2, 6, 7, 9, 10 and 14, which reflects the prevalence and close nexus of arbitrary detention, torture, other ill-treatment and enforced disappearance, or unfair trials and the death penalty, as well as the lack of effective remedies. The HRCtee has made an important contribution to the international jurisprudence in this respect.[133] It has also adopted a number of influential views in respect of other articles, including on freedom of expression,[134] freedom of religion,[135] non-discrimination[136] and minority rights.[137]

---

[131] See *Wilson* v. *Philippines* (HRCtee) (2003) paras. 7.1–8 (violation of arts. 7, 9(1–3) and 10(1–2)); *Singarasa* v. *Sri Lanka* (HRCtee) (2004) paras. 7.1–7.5 (violation of arts. 14(1), (2) and (3)(c), (f–g), 5, 2(3) and 7); *Rajapakse* v. *Sri Lanka* (HRCtee) (2006) paras. 9.1–10 (violation of arts. 7, 9(1–3), 10 as well as 2(3)). See also *X* v. *Sri Lanka* (HRCtee) (2017) paras. 7.18 (violation of art. 7, read alone and in conjunction with art. 2(3), and of art. 26), which concerned the inadequate investigation of rape complaints by a woman who belonged to the Tamil minority and had been a minor at the time of the rape.

[132] See *Gayoso Martinez* v. *Spain* (HRCtee) (2009) paras. 9.1–10 (violation of art. 14(5)), and *S. S. F. et al.* v. *Spain* (HRCtee) (2014) (no violation).

[133] *Bleier* v. *Uruguay* (HRCtee) (1982) paras. 13.1–14 (violation of arts. 6, 7, 9 and 10(1)); *Sharma* v. *Nepal* (HRCtee) (2008) paras. 7.1–10 (violation of arts. 6, 7, 9, 10 and 2(3)); *Alzery* v. *Sweden* (HRCtee) (2006) paras. 11.1–12 (violation of arts. 7 and 2 and art. 1 of the Optional Protocol). See also HRCtee, General Comment 32: art. 14: Right to Equality before Courts and Tribunals and to a Fair Trial, UN Doc. CCPR/C/GC/32 (23 August 2007) and General Comment 36 (2018) on art. 6 of the International Covenant on Civil and Political Rights, on the right to life, UN doc. CCPR/C/GC/36 (30 October 2018).

[134] See HRCtee, General Comment 34: art. 19: Freedoms of Opinion and Expression, UN doc. CCPR/C/GC/34 (12 September 2011) and, e.g., *Yong-Joo Kang* v. *Republic of Korea* (HRCtee) (2003) paras. 7.1–8 (political opinion) (violation of arts. 10(1 and 3), 18, 19 and 26).

[135] See e.g., on the right to conscientious objection to military service, *Hudaybergenov* v. *Turkmenistan* (HRCtee) (2015) paras. 7.1–8 (violation of arts. 7, 10(1) and 18(1)).

[136] See on art. 26, *Zwaan-de Vries* v. *The Netherlands* (HRCtee) (1987) paras. 10–16, and *Albareda et al.* v. *Uruguay* (HRCtee) (2011) paras. 9.1–10. On discrimination resulting from restrictive abortion laws, see *Mellet* v. *Ireland* (HRCtee) (2016) paras. 7.1–8 (violation of arts. 7, 17 and 27), and largely similar case of *Whelan* v. *Ireland* (HRCtee) (2017) paras. 7.1–8 (same findings). On the prohibition of access to divorce proceedings for same-sex couples married abroad, see *C* v. *Australia* (HRCtee) (2017) paras. 8.1–9 (violation of art. 26), and on the refusal to have the sex changed on the birth certificate of married transgender persons, *G* v. *Australia* (2017) paras. 7.1–8 (violation of arts. 17 and 26).

[137] On art. 27, see *Lovelace* v. *Canada* (HRCtee) (1981) paras. 13.2–19 (violation); *Lubicon Lake Band* v. *Canada* (HRCtee) (1990) paras. 32.1–33 (violation); *Länsman et al.* v. *Finland* (HRCtee) (1994) paras. 9.1–10 (no breach); *Diergaardt et al.* v. *Namibia* (HRCtee) (2000) paras. 10.1–11 (violation of art. 26, not 27); *Mahuika et al.* v. *New Zealand* (HRCtee)

The HRCtee's jurisprudence constitutes an authoritative record of violations in the cases brought before it. While the value of its views as a remedy for individuals has been undermined by limited state compliance,[138] it has vindicated claims, set precedents and served as an advocacy tool for tackling systemic violations.[139] In conjunction with the reporting system its jurisprudence has eroded the acceptability of certain practices. This has contributed to changes in the practice of states parties, such as the suspension or abolition of the death penalty.[140]

The views of the HRCtee have been referred to by other courts, including the ICJ, human rights treaty bodies, other UN bodies, national courts and others.[141] The importance of the ICCPR as part of the International Bill of Human Rights, the nature of issues raised before the Committee and the standing of individual committee members have all contributed to the authority that the HRCtee's jurisprudence generally commands. However, there are several grounds on which the HRCtee's jurisprudence can be, and has been criticised, including by its own members. These include its handling of facts and evidentiary problems – the HRCtee has no fact-finding capacity and relies on written submissions rather than hearings – and the paucity of its reasoning, generally attributed to the limited time and resources available and the search for consensus. Critics also mention taking positions that have far-reaching consequences with limited explanation and reference to the jurisprudence of other bodies.[142]

A(?) Independent young women

5.5.3   Breadwinners, Social Security and Discrimination: *Zwaan-de Vries* v. *The Netherlands*

The author, Mrs F. H. Zwaan-de Vries, was denied benefits under the Dutch Unemployment Benefits Act in 1979/1980, which excluded married women 'who were neither breadwinners nor permanently separated from their husbands', but not married men.[143] The legislation had been based on the view

---

(2000), paras. 9.1–9.9 (no breach); *Mavlonov and Sa'di* v. *Uzbekistan* (HRCtee) (2009) paras. 8.6–9 (violation); *Poma Poma* v. *Peru* (HRCtee) (2009) paras. 7.1–8 (violation); *Georgopoulos et al.* v. *Greece* (HRCtee) (2010) paras. 7.1–8 (violation).

[138] See Chapter 7.5.

[139] See for an assessment of its impact, Heyns and Viljoen, above note 58, 15–19.

[140] Reference to this development is made in *Lumanog and Santos* v. *Philippines* (HRCtee) (2008) para. 8.2.

[141] A. Nollkaemper and R. van Alebeek, *The Legal Status of Decisions by Human Rights Treaty Bodies in National Law*, ACIL Research Paper no. 2011–02 (11 April 2011) 18–19.

[142] See e.g., controversy surrounding the case of *Kennedy* v. *Trinidad and Tobago*, in which the HRCtee denied the validity of Trinidad and Tobago's reservation to the Optional Protocol, including individual, dissenting, opinions of Committee members Nisuke Ando, Prafulachandra N. Bhagwati, Eckart Klein and David Kretzmer, ibid.

[143] *Zwaan-de Vries* v. *The Netherlands*, paras. 10–16.

that 'all married men who had jobs could be regarded as their family's bread-winner'. In 1985, in implementing a European Economic Community Council directive, the Netherlands amended its legislation in order to provide for equal treatment. The author argued that she had been a victim of discrimination (article 26 ICCPR) in relation to social benefits. In response, the state party posed the question of whether the way it had fulfilled its obligations under article 9 (right to social security) in conjunction with articles 2 and 3 ICESCR could become, by way of article 26 ICCPR, the object of an examination by the HRCtee. It further argued that if the Committee were to find article 26 ICCPR applicable, the article would need to be interpreted so as to impose simply an obligation of periodic review to ensure that a state took measures to progressively eliminate discrimination in its national legislation. In addition, the state party claimed that the notion of breadwinner was not discriminatory as the provisions of the Act were 'based on reasonable social and economic considerations which are not discriminatory in origin'.

On the merits, the Committee held that:

article 26 does not merely duplicate the guarantees already provided for in article 2. It derives from the principle of equal protection of the law without discrimination, as contained in article 7 [UDHR], which prohibits discrimination in law or in practice in any field regulated and protected by public authorities. Article 26 is thus concerned with the obligations imposed on States in regard to their legislation and the application thereof ... what is at issue is not whether or not social security should be progressively established in the Netherlands but whether the legislation providing for social security violates the prohibition against discrimination contained in article 26 and the guarantee given therein to all persons regarding equal and effective protection against discrimination. The right to equality before the law and to equal protection of the law without any discrimination does not make all differences of treatment discriminatory. A differentiation based on reasonable and objective criteria does not amount to prohibited discrimination within the meaning of article 26 ... Under [the Act] a married woman, in order to receive ... benefits, had to prove that she was a 'breadwinner' –a condition that did not apply to married men. Thus a differentiation which appears on one level to be one of status is in fact one of sex, placing married women at a disadvantage compared with married men. Such a differentiation is not reasonable ...[144]

The case set an important precedent for the interpretation of article 26 ICCPR, giving it a broad scope of application in relation to any legislation, even where the latter purports to regulate social rights. The finding of discrimination was the inevitable consequence of this interpretation given the outdated terms of the law. It was facilitated by the fact that the Netherlands had already changed the very legislation to provide for equal treatment, which constituted an implicit acknowledgement. The Netherlands reacted

---

[144] Ibid., paras. 12.3–14.

strongly to the decision and even threatened to withdraw from the Optional Protocol to the ICCPR.[145]

While the Netherlands ultimately refrained from denouncing the Optional Protocol, other states such as Jamaica, Guyana and Trinidad and Tobago have done so. It is clear that the HRCtee has to tread a fine balance. The acceptance of its views in a given case, and of the legitimacy of the HRCtee as a quasi-judicial body, depends to a considerable degree on the persuasiveness of its views, which require careful reasoning where they seemingly depart from widely held understandings. *Zwaan-de Vries* v. *The Netherlands* broke important ground in this regard.[146]

5.5.4   The CERD

Fifty-eight of the 179 states parties had made a declaration under article 14 of the ICERD (recognising CERD's competence to hear individual complaints) as of 11 May 2018.[147] The CERD has registered a much lower number of complaints than the HRCtee (62 concerning 15 states parties by May 2018), which shows that its complaints procedure remains underutilised.[148] The majority of communications have concerned a few states parties only (particularly Australia, Denmark, France, Germany, the Netherlands, Norway, Sweden and Slovakia). As a result, its jurisprudence has to date not fully captured the manifold forms of violations and problems arising in the context of racial discrimination, which has limited its overall impact. Nevertheless, the CERD's decisions have highlighted inadequate responses to racial discrimination and racial hatred, such as the lack of effective investigations of racist incidents in Denmark,[149] and of 'reported statements of racial discrimination' in Germany[150] as well as the tolerance of hate speech in Norway.[151] The

---

[145] See C. Tomuschat, *Human Rights: Between Idealism and Realism*, 2nd edn (Oxford University Press, 2008) 51–2.

[146] See further HRCtee, General Comment 28, art. 3 (The Equality of Rights between Men and Women), UN doc. HRI/GEN/1/Rev.9 (vol. I) (2008) para. 31.

[147] Report of the Committee on the Elimination of Racial Discrimination, UN doc. A/73/18 (2018) para. 2.

[148] Ibid., para. 44.

[149] *Ahmad* v. *Denmark* (CERD) (2000) paras. 6.1–8 (violation of art. 6); *Gelle* v. *Denmark* (CERD) (2006) and *Adan* v. *Denmark* (CERD) (2010) both paras. 7.1–8 (both violations of arts. 2(1)(d), 4 and 6); *Dawas and Yousef Shava* v. *Denmark* (CERD) (2012) paras. 7.1–8 (violation of arts. 6 and 2(1)(d)). See also, *L. K.* v. *Netherlands* (CERD) (1993) paras. 6.1–6.8 (lack of diligent investigation into threats of racial violence – violation of arts. 6 and 4).

[150] *TBB – Turkish Union in Berlin/Brandenburg* v. *Germany* (CERD) (2013) paras. 12.1–14 (violation of arts. 2(1)(d), 4 and 6).

[151] *The Jewish Community of Oslo* v. *Norway* (CERD) (2005) paras. 10.1–11 (violation of arts. 4 and 6).

CERD also dealt with cases such as the removal of the word 'Nigger' from a sign put up in an Australian town in 'honour of a well-known sporting and civic personality' (the word 'Nigger' had been the latter's nickname), which reflected that changed perceptions can make the public display of certain words racially offensive.[152] It further found that practices such as mandatory HIV/AIDS and drugs testing for foreign native speaker teachers in Korea constituted a breach of the state party's obligation 'to guarantee equality in respect of the right to work'.[153] Importantly, in two employment-related cases, the CERD stipulated that 'presumed victims of racial discrimination are not required to show that there was discriminatory intent against them'.[154]

Within the given limitations, the CERD's jurisprudence has contributed to the clarification of the notion of racial discrimination, the difference between direct and indirect discrimination and the positive obligations of states in response to (allegations of) racial discrimination, particularly the nature of effective remedies.

5.5.5   Still Facing Discrimination: *Durmic v. Serbia and Montenegro*

In *Koptova v. The Slovak Republic*, the CERD found that two municipal resolutions banning Romany families from entering the towns concerned constituted a violation of article 5(d)(i) of the ICERD (prohibition of discrimination in the enjoyment of civil rights, in particular 'the right to freedom of movement and residence within the border of the State').[155] In *Ms L. R. et al. v. Slovak Republic (Dobsina)*, the cancellation of a low-cost housing project for Romas following a hostile local petition was found to constitute discrimination in relation to housing in violation of article 5(d)(iii). In both cases there was a lack of effective remedy.[156]

In *Durmic v. Serbia and Montenegro*:

in 2000 the Humanitarian Law Center (HLC) carried out a series of 'tests' across Serbia, to establish whether members of the Roma minority were being discriminated against while attempting to access public places. It was prompted to such action by numerous complaints alleging that the Roma were denied access to clubs, discotheques, restaurants, cafes and/or swimming pools, on the basis of their ethnic origin ... two Roma individuals ... and three non-Roma individuals, attempted to gain access to a discotheque in Belgrade. All were neatly dressed, well behaved and were not under the influence of alcohol. Thus, the only apparent difference between them

---

[152] *Hagan v. Australia* (CERD) (2003) paras. 7.1–7.4 (violation of arts. 2(1)(c), 5, 6 and 7).

[153] *L. G. v. Republic of Korea* (CERD) (2015) para. 7.4 (violation of art. 5(e)(i)), also finding, in para. 7.3, a violation of arts. 2(1)(c) and (d), and 6. See also a similar case brought before the HRCtee, *Vandom v. Republic of Korea* (2018).

[154] *Gabaroum v. France* (CERD) (2016) para. 7.2, also *V. S. v. Slovakia* (CERD) (2015) para. 7.4.

[155] *Koptova v. Slovak Republic* (CERD) (2000).

[156] *Ms L. R. et al. v. Slovak Republic* (Dobsina) (CERD) (2005).

was the colour of their skin. There was no notice displayed to the effect that a private party was being held and that they could not enter without showing an invitation. The two individuals of Roma origin were denied entry to the club on the basis that it was a private party and they did not have invitations. When the petitioner asked the security guard how he could obtain an invitation there and then, he was told that it was not possible and that the invitations were not for sale ... The three non-Roma individuals were all allowed to enter, despite having no invitations for the so called private party and making this clear to the security personnel at the time.[157]

A criminal complaint submitted to the Public Prosecutor to investigate a case of racial discrimination did not result in any prosecution and a case brought before the Constitutional Court remained pending for over fifteen months without any response. Following a detailed discussion of challenges to admissibility the CERD found a violation of articles 5(f) and 6 of the ICERD, holding, inter alia, that:

The State party has ... failed to establish whether the petitioner had been refused access to a public place, on grounds of his national or ethnic origin in violation of article 5(f) of the Convention. Owing to the police's failure to carry out any thorough investigation into the matter, the failure of the public prosecutor to reach any conclusion and the failure of the Court of Serbia and Montenegro even to set a date for the consideration of the case some six years after the incident, the petitioner has been denied any opportunity to establish whether his rights under the Convention had been violated.[158]

The decisions cast an important spotlight on racial discrimination against the Roma, demonstrating a pattern in which discriminatory acts are followed by wholly inadequate responses of the authorities and judicial systems, effectively denying legal protection. They added to the growing evidence of the systemic nature of this group-specific discrimination in the region and form an important part of broader efforts to combat discrimination and the 'right-lessness' of the Roma.[159]

5.5.6   The CtAT

The competence of the CtAT to hear individual complaints pursuant to article 22 CAT has been recognised by 68 of the 165 states parties as of May 2018.[160] By 15 August 2015 the CtAT had concluded 539 cases, finding a violation in 107 out of the 272 cases in which it rendered a decision. In total, 697 communications had been received regarding 34 states parties.[161]

---

[157] *Durmic* v. *Serbia and Montenegro* (CERD) (2006) paras. 2.1–2.2.   [158] Ibid., para. 9.5.
[159] See in this regard in particular, the work of the European Roma Rights Centre, www.errc.org.
[160] Report of the CtAT, UN doc. A/73/44 (2018) para. 56.
[161] Statistical survey of individual complaints considered can be found at www.ohchr.org/en/hrbodies/cat/pages/catindex.aspx.

The majority of complaints have concerned alleged violations of article 3 CAT (*refoulement*) brought mainly against Australia, Canada, Denmark, France, the Netherlands, Sweden and Switzerland. The CtAT's jurisprudence on article 3 includes several important decisions, including in the context of extraordinary renditions,[162] Dublin transfers in the European Union context,[163] and in relation to situations where the risk of torture emanates from non-state actors (Somalia).[164] The Committee held that the circumstances of expulsion, here abandoning around '40 migrants some of whom were severely injured, in the border area separating Morocco and Mauritania without adequate equipment and with minimal supplies of food and water, and forc[ing] them to walk some 50 kilometres through an area containing anti-personnel mines' constituted ill-treatment in breach of article 16.[165] The Committee has also specified states parties' obligation to investigate allegations of torture effectively and to provide reparation, including in several cases against Algeria,[166] Burundi,[167] Kazakhstan,[168] Serbia and Montenegro, Spain and Tunisia, which highlighted systemic shortcomings.[169] It considered the issue of acquiescence in respect of a state's failure to protect individuals against violence by non-state actors, namely mob violence against a Roma settlement in Montenegro,[170] and prisoner-on-prisoner violence in Venezuela.[171] It also found that solitary confinement for twenty-one days amounted to ill-treatment.[172] In addition the CtAT has ruled on the scope of universal jurisdiction as part of the ramifications of the *Habré* case, the former Chadian

---

[162] Return to Egypt was considered a violation of art. 3 in *Agiza* v. *Sweden* (CtAT) (2005) paras. 13.1–13.14 (see 5.5.7), but not in *Attia* v. *Sweden* (CtAT) (2003) paras. 12.1–13.

[163] *A. N.* v. *Switzerland* (CtAT) (2018) paras. 8.1–9 (violation of arts. 3, 14 and 16).

[164] *Elmi* v. *Australia* (CtAT) (1999) paras. 6.4–7 (violation of art. 3).

[165] *Barry* v. *Morocco* (CtAT) (2014) para. 7.2 (violation of art. 16).

[166] *Bendib* v. *Algeria* (CtAT) (2013) paras. 6.1–7 (violation of art. 1 in conjunction with 2(1), 12, 13 and 14).

[167] *Ndagijimana* v. *Burundi* (CtAT) (2018) paras. 8.1–9 (violation of art. 1, read alone and in conjunction with art. 2(1) and arts. 12, 13 and 14).

[168] *Evloev* v. *Kazakhstan* (CtAT) (2013) paras. 9.1–10 (violation of art. 1 in conjunction with arts. 2(1), 12, 13, 14 and 15); *Bairamov* v. *Kazakhstan* (CtAT) (2014) paras. 8.1–9 (same violations as in Evloev).

[169] *Nikolic* v. *Serbia and Montenegro* (CtAT) (2005) paras. 6.2–7 (violation of arts. 12 and 13); *Dimitrijevic* v. *Serbia and Montenegro* (CtAT) (2004) paras. 5.3–6 (violations of arts. 2(1), 1, 12, 13 and 14); *Guridi* v. *Spain* (CtAT) (2005) paras. 6.4–7 (violation of arts. 2, 4 and 14); *Bouabdallah Latief* v. *Tunisia* (CtAT) (2003) paras. 10.3–11 (violation of arts. 12 and 13); *Keremedchiev* v. *Bulgaria* (CtAT) (2008) paras. 9.2–10 (violation of arts. 12 and 16); *Hanafi* v. *Algeria* (CtAT) (2011) paras. 9.1–10 (violation of arts. 1, 2(1), 11, 12, 13 and 14); *Sonko* v. *Spain* (CtAT) (2011) paras. 10.1–10.8 (violation of arts. 12 and 16).

[170] *Hajrizi Dzemajl et al.* v. *Yugoslavia* (CtAT) (2002) paras. 9.1–10 (violation of arts. 16, 12 and 13). See also *Osmani* v. *Serbia* (CtAT) (2009) paras. 10.3–11 (violation of arts. 16, 12 and 13).

[171] *Larez* v. *Venezuela* (CtAT) (2015) paras. 6.1–7 (violation of arts. 2(1), 11, 12 and 14, read separately and in conjunction with art. 1, with regard to Mr Guerrero Larez (who disappeared), and under art. 16 with regard to the complainants).

[172] *Vogel* v. *New Zealand* (CtAT) (2017) paras. 7.1–8 (violation of art. 16).

president, accused of being responsible for international crimes, who had fled to Senegal, which has engaged several treaty bodies and courts.[173] These cases show the potential of CtAT to contribute significantly to the jurisprudence on the prohibition of torture, particularly if it engages in more in-depth considerations of the normative questions posed in a given case rather than their cursory treatment that is characteristic of some of its decisions.

5.5.7   Rendered Defenceless: *Agiza* v. *Sweden*

In 1998 Ahmed Hussein Mustafa Kamil Agiza, an Egyptian national, was tried *in absentia*, convicted and sentenced to twenty-five years' imprisonment for belonging to a terrorist group. In 2000 he claimed asylum in Sweden. Following the views of the Swedish security police, the government denied him asylum. According to an investigation by the Parliamentary Ombudsman he was deported to Egypt in 2001 on an aircraft provided by the American Central Intelligence Agency. The complainant alleged that he was tortured by the Egyptian state security officers upon his return. After finding the complaint admissible, on the merits, the CtAT considered in detail whether there was a substantial risk of torture upon the complainant's return, finding that:

> it was known, or should have been known, to the State party's authorities at the time of the complainant's removal that Egypt resorted to consistent and widespread use of torture against detainees, and that the risk of such treatment was particularly high in the case of detainees held for political and security reasons … It follows that the state party's expulsion of the complainant was in breach of article 3 of the Convention. The procurement of diplomatic assurances, which, moreover, provided no mechanism for their enforcement, did not suffice to protect against this manifest risk.[174]

Importantly, in its assessment of the procedural dimension of article 3, the CtAT found that:

> in order to reinforce the protection of the norm in question and understanding the Convention consistently, the prohibition on refoulement contained in article 3 should be interpreted the same way to encompass a remedy for its breach, even though it may not contain on its face such a right to remedy for a breach thereof … The nature of refoulement is such, however, that an allegation of breach of that article relates to a future expulsion or removal; accordingly, the right to an effective remedy contained in article 3 requires, in this context, an opportunity for effective, independent and impartial review of the decision to expel or remove, once that decision is made, when there is a plausible allegation that article 3 issues arise.[175]

On the facts, the CtAT found that the lack of judicial or independent administrative review of the government's decision to expel the complainant

---

[173] *Guengueng* v. *Senegal* (CtAT) (2006) paras. 9.1–12 (violation of arts. 7 and 5(2)). See also Chapter 7.7.

[174] *Agiza* v. *Sweden*, para. 13.4.   [175] Ibid., para. 13.6.

constituted a breach of article 3 CAT and that the state party had also violated its duty under article 22 CAT to cooperate with the Committee.

Agiza v. *Sweden* set an important precedent in the jurisprudence on extraordinary renditions, showing how states' security cooperation undermines the prohibition of *refoulement* and exposes individuals to the risk of torture.[176] It proved to be influential in cases before other human rights treaty bodies, particularly the largely similar *Alzery* case decided by the HRCtee.[177] Most importantly for the interpretation of CAT, the CtAT read a general procedural obligation to provide an effective remedy into article 3 and the Convention as a whole, thereby strengthening legal protection, particularly against future violations.[178]

5.5.8   The CtEDAW

Of 189 states parties, 109 had recognised the competence of the CtEDAW to hear complaints under the Optional Protocol to CEDAW as of 9 March 2018.[179] The CtEDAW assumed its function of considering individual complaints in 2001. It had decided relatively few cases (56) as of 24 January 2019 and these concerned a still limited, but increasing number of states parties, with Austria, Belarus, Brazil, Bulgaria, Canada, Denmark, Finland, Georgia, Hungary, Kazakhstan, Mexico, the Netherlands, Peru, the Philippines, Republic of Moldova, Russia, Slovakia, Spain, Tanzania, Timor-Leste and Turkey found to have violated their obligations under the treaty.[180] The CtEDAW's jurisprudence has primarily addressed positive obligations, particularly the duty to take effective action to provide protection against domestic violence,[181] also in relation to children and child custody,[182] and other sexual violence,[183]

---

[176] See Chapter 17.8.   [177] *Alzery* v. *Sweden*.

[178] See further on article 3, CtAT, General comment 4 (2017) on the implementation of article 3 of the Convention in the context of article 22, UN doc. CAT/C/GC/4 (4 September 2018).

[179] Report of the Committee on the Elimination of Discrimination against Women, UN Doc. A/73/38 (2018) 41, paras. 1–2.

[180] Statistical survey of individual complaints considered can be found at www.ohchr.org/en/hrbodies/cedaw/pages/cedawindex.aspx.

[181] *A. T.* v. *Hungary* (CtEDAW) (2005) paras. 9.1–9.6 (violation of arts. 2(a–b) and (e), 5(a) and 16); *Yildrim* v. *Austria* (CtEDAW) (2007) and *Goekce* v. *Austria* (CtEDAW) (2007) both paras. 12.1–12.2 (violation of arts. 2(a), (c–f), 3 and 1); *V. K.* v. *Bulgaria* (CtEDAW) (2011) paras. 9.1–9.15 (violation of arts. 2(c–f), 1, 5(a) and 16(1)); *Jallow* v. *Bulgaria* (CtEDAW) (2012) paras. 8.1–8.8 (violation of arts. 2(b–f), 5(a) and 16(c–d), (f), read in conjunction with arts. 1 and 3); *González Carreño* v. *Spain* (CtEDAW) (2014) paras. 9.1–10 (violation of arts. 2(a–f), 5(a) and 16(1), read jointly with art. 1).

[182] *J. I.* v. *Finland* (CtEDAW) (2018) paras. 8.1–9 (violation of arts. 2(a), (c), (d), (f), 15(a) and 16(1)(d), (f), read jointly with art. 1 and the Committee's General Recommendation 35); *M. W.* v. *Denmark* (CtEDAW) (2016) paras. 5.1–6 (violation of art. 2, read in conjunction with art. 1 and art. 5(a) and (b), and 16(1(d)); *X and Y* v. *Georgia* (CtEDAW) (2015) paras. 9.1–10 (violation of arts. 2(b)–2(f), in conjunction with arts. 1 and 5(a), as well as the Committee's General Recommendation 19).

[183] *S. V. P.* v. *Bulgaria* (CtEDAW) (2012) paras. 9.1–9.10 (violation of art. 2(a–c), (e–g) read together with arts. 1, 3 and 5(a–b), 12 and 15(1)).

including a case of femicide.[184] The CtEDAW dealt with a case on involuntary sterilisation of a Roma woman, which highlighted the intersection between racial and gender-based discrimination.[185] It has also recognised intersectional discrimination in access to health care as a violation,[186] and in the case of an aboriginal woman who did not have effective legal protection when seeking to regain her property.[187] In an important precedent, the CtEDAW found that the state party's condoning of discriminatory customary inheritance laws violated multiple rights under CEDAW.[188] The CtEDAW has strengthened reproductive rights in a case where a girl who had become pregnant as a result of sexual abuse was denied surgery.[189] In addition, it has addressed the removal of maternity benefits[190] and found violations in cases of stereotyping in employment matters[191] and criminal proceedings.[192] The importance of CEDAW in the custodial context was underscored in a case concerning humiliating treatment of women and conditions in detention facilities.[193] The nature of these cases and the approach taken by the CtEDAW point to the important role that it can play in strengthening the rights of women in international human rights law.[194]

---

[184] *Reyes and Morales* v. *Mexico* (CtEDAW) (2017) paras. 9.1–10 (violation of art. 2(b), (c) and art. 5, read in conjunction with art. 1).

[185] *Szijarto* v. *Hungary* (CtEDAW) (2006) paras. 11.1–11.5 (violation of arts. 10(h), 12 and 16(1)(e)).

[186] *Teixeira* v. *Brazil* (CtEDAW) (2011) paras. 7.1–8 (violation of arts. 12, 2(c), (e) and 1).

[187] *Kell* v. *Canada* (CtEDAW) (2012) paras. 10.1–11 (violation of arts. 2(d), (e), 16(1) and 1).

[188] *E. S. and S. C.* v. *United Republic of Tanzania* (CtEDAW) (2015) paras. 7.1–8 (violation of the rights of the authors) under arts. 2(c), 2(f), 5(a), 13(b), 15(1), 15(2), 16(1)(c) and 16(1)(h)).

[189] *L. C.* v. *Peru* (CtEDAW) (2011) paras. 8.6–9 (violation of arts. 2(c), (f), 3, 5, 12 and 1).

[190] *De Blok* v. *The Netherlands* (CtEDAW) (2014), paras. 8.1–9 (violation of art. 11(2)(b)).

[191] *R. K. B.* v. *Turkey* (CtEDAW) (2012) paras. 8.1–10 (violation of arts. 2(a), (c), 1, 5(a) and 11(1)(a), (d)). See on sexual harassment in the workplace, *Belousova* v. *Kazakhstan* (CtEDAW) (2015) paras. 10.1–11 (violation of art. 2(e), read in conjunction with arts. 1, 5(a) and 11(1)(a), (f)).

[192] *Vertido* v. *The Philippines* (CtEDAW) (2010) below at 5.5.9; *R. P. B.* v. *The Philippines* (CtEDAW) (2014) paras. 8.1–9 (violation of art. 2(c), (d), (f), read in conjunction with art. 1); *X.* v. *Timor Leste* (CtEDAW) (2018) paras. 6.1–7 (violation of arts. 2(a), (c), (d), (f), and 15, read jointly with art. 1 and the Committee's General Recommendations 19, 28, 33 and 35).

[193] *Abramova* v. *Belarus* (CtEDAW) (2011) paras. 7.1–7.8 (violation of arts. 2 and 5(a)).

[194] See also assessment by J. Connors, 'Optional Protocol', in M. A. Freeman, C. Chinkin and B. Rudolf (eds.), *The UN Convention on the Elimination of All Forms of Discrimination against Women: A Commentary* (Oxford University Press, 2013) 617–18: 'The Committee has not had the opportunity to develop a comprehensive jurisprudence, although it has made significant contributions in some areas, in particular violence against women and women's right to reproductive health … [its] views on communications and the results of the single inquiry have been influential in the creation of women's human rights jurisprudence, including in relation to the State's obligation to exercise due diligence to prevent or prosecute human rights violations, which has been relied on by the [ECtHR] and [IACtHR]' (footnotes omitted).

5.5.9   'We Don't Believe You': *Vertido* v. *The Philippines*

Karen Tayag Vertido alleged that she had been raped by the former president of the Davao City Chamber of Commerce and Industry in March 1996. She underwent a medical examination and complained to the police. The case eventually reached a trial court where it remained pending from 1997 to 2005.[195] Two experts testified that the author suffered from post-traumatic stress disorder due to the rape. There were no further witnesses and the accused claimed 'that the sexual intercourse was consensual'. In April 2005 the Regional Court of Davao City acquitted the accused, relying on several criteria established in a previous Supreme Court ruling.

After finding the case admissible the CtEDAW considered:

the author's allegations that gender-based myths and misconceptions about rape and rape victims were relied on by Judge Hofileña-Europa in the Regional Court of Davao City in its decision ... leading to the acquittal of the alleged perpetrator, and will determine whether this amounted to a violation of the rights of the author and a breach of the corresponding state party's obligations to end discrimination in the legal process under articles 2(c), 2(f) and 5(a) of the Convention.[196]

It found that the length of the trial breached the author's right to a remedy in relation to article 2(c) CEDAW, stating: 'while acknowledging that the text of the Convention does not expressly provide for a right to a remedy, [it] considers that such a right is implied in the Convention'.[197] Further, '[t]he Committee finds that one of [the guiding principles applied in the case], in particular, according to which "an accusation for rape can be made with facility", reveals in itself a gender bias ... '.[198] Moreover:

It is clear from the judgment that the assessment of the credibility of the author's version of events was influenced by a number of stereotypes, the author in this situation not having followed what was expected from a rational and 'ideal victim' or what the judge considered to be the rational and ideal response of a woman in a rape situation ... [the author had reacted 'both with resistance at one time and submission at another time', which the judge saw as contradictory]. Further misconceptions are to be found in the decision of the Court, which contains several references to stereotypes about male and female sexuality being more supportive for the credibility of the alleged perpetrator than for the credibility of the victim.[199]

Moreover, '[w]ith regard to the definition of rape, the Committee notes that the lack of consent is not an essential element of the definition of rape in the Philippines Revised Penal Code ... rape constitutes a violation of women's right to personal security and bodily integrity and that its essential element was lack of consent'.[200] The Committee then recommended that the state

---

[195] *Vertido* v. *The Philippines* (CtEDAW) (2010) (violation of art. 2(c),(f), 5(a), 1).
[196] Ibid., para. 8.2.   [197] Ibid., para. 8.3.   [198] Ibid., para. 8.5.   [199] Ibid., paras. 8.5–8.6.
[200] Ibid., para. 8.7.

party pay compensation to the author and undertake far-reaching reforms in its legislation on rape and procedures in rape cases, including:

Appropriate training for judges, lawyers, law enforcement officers and medical personnel in understanding crimes of rape and other sexual offences in a gender-sensitive manner so as to avoid revictimization of women having reported rape cases and to ensure that personal mores and values do not affect decision-making.[201]

The views of the Committee provide an anatomy of how a legal system fails rape victims. Given the prevalence of gender stereotypes worldwide the decision reaffirms the Committee's understanding of rape and clarifies states parties' obligations to treat rape cases in an expeditious and non-discriminatory manner. While not explicitly referring to it, the case can be viewed in light of judgments by other bodies, such as the ECtHR in *M. C. v. Bulgaria* (ECtHR) (2005), in which states failed in their positive obligation to adequately respond to rape allegations. It therefore forms part of a growing jurisprudence that both exposes domestic failings in rape cases and helps in developing best practices.

5.5.10 The CtRPD

Ninety-two of the 177 states parties to the CRPD were, as of 21 September 2018, also parties to its Optional Protocol that recognises the competence to hear complaints brought by or on behalf of victims or groups of victims claiming to be victims.[202] Following the coming into force of the Optional Protocol to the CRPD, the CtRPD had, by September 2018, decided 26 cases that had been brought against Argentina, Australia, Austria, Brazil, Denmark, Germany, Hungary, Italy, Lithuania, Saudi Arabia, Sweden, Tanzania and the UK, finding violations in 16 cases.[203] The cases highlighted a series of shortcomings in the law and practice of states parties that fail to take the rights of persons with disabilities adequately into consideration. Denial of reasonable accommodation, i.e. 'necessary and appropriate modification and adjustment not imposing a disproportionate or undue burden, where needed in a particular case, to ensure to persons with disabilities the enjoyment or exercise on an equal basis with others of all human rights and fundamental freedoms' (article 2 CRPD), was at issue in several cases. In its first case, the CtRPD addressed a conflict of interest, with the state privileging pub-lic interest, that is the city development plan, over the applicant's interests

---

[201] Ibid., para. 8.9(iv).

[202] Report of the Committee on the Rights of Persons with Disabilities on its twentieth session (27 August – 21 September 2018), UN doc. CRPD/C/202/2 (12 December 2018) para. 1.

[203] Ibid., paras. 8–9 on latest jurisprudence, and information available on the UN OHCHR jurisprudence database.

to use the land to build facilities for essential hydrotherapy.[204] The state's failure to address the specific circumstances and needs of the applicant in its planning policy was found to have violated the applicant's rights under the Convention. States parties had also violated their obligation to provide reasonable accommodation in cases concerning access of visually impaired persons to their bank accounts (see further 5.5.11), lack of equal recognition and failure to be properly represented in court,[205] refusal to provide Auslan interpretation to enable participation of deaf people in jury service,[206] and conditions of detention that lacked accessibility to facilities and services.[207] Hungary's fundamental law 'which allows courts to deprive persons with intellectual disability of their right to vote and to be elected', and the deprivation of the six authors who suffered from 'intellectual disability' of their right to vote, was held to violate the right to equal recognition before the law and the right to participate in political and public life.[208] Germany's approach to providing support with a view to integrating persons with disabilities into the labour market was found to be flawed, inter alia resting on a medical model of disability incompatible with the Convention and hampered by administrative complexities.[209] Significantly, the CtRPD held that indefinite detention of persons with cognitive impairments who had been charged with criminal offences constituted discriminatory treatment, and hence amounted to a violation of the right to liberty.[210] In another communication concerning detention, the Committee found that a young man with a prior, slight hearing impairment had been subjected to solitary confinement, abuse and torture, which resulted in loss of hearing in the absence of adequate medical care, and a denial of his right to a fair trial.[211] In a further landmark case, it held that the lack of state action to protect persons with Albinism, here a failure to investigate, may result in re-victimisation amounting to psychological

---

[204] *H. M.* v. *Sweden* (CtRPD) (2012) paras. 8.1–9 (arts. 5(1), 5(3), 19(b), 25 and 26, read alone and in conjunction with arts. 3(b), (d), (e), and 4(1)(d) CRPD).

[205] *Makarova* v. *Lithuania* (CtRPD) (2017) paras. 7.1–8 (violation of arts. 12(3) and 13(1)).

[206] *Beasley* v. *Australia* (CtRPD) (2016) paras. 8.1–9 (violation of arts. 3, 5(1) and 29(b)). See also *J. H.* v. *Australia* (CtRPD) (2018) paras. 7.1–8 (violation of arts. 5(2) and (3), and 21(b), (e)).

[207] *X* v. *Argentina* (CtRPD) (2014) paras. 8.1–9 (arts. 9(1)(a–b), 14(2) and 17 CRPD).

[208] *Bujdosó and five others* v. *Hungary* (CtRPD) (2013) paras. 9.1–10 (art. 29, read alone and in conjunction with art. 12 CRPD). See on access to electronic voting, *Given* v. *Australia* (CtRPD) (2018) paras. 8.1–8.10 (violation of art. 29(a)(i) and (ii), read alone and in conjunction with arts. 5(2), 4(1)(a),(b),(d),(e), (g) and 9(1) and (2)).

[209] *Gröninger et al.* v. *Germany* (CtRPD) (2014) paras. 6.1–7 (art. 27(1)(d–e) and (h), read together with art. 3(a–c) and (e), as well as arts. 4(1)(a–b) and 5(1) CRPD).

[210] *Noble* v. *Australia* (CtRPD) (2016) paras. 8.1–8.10 (violation of arts. 5(1) and (2), 12(2) and (3), 13(1), 14(1)(b) and 15)).

[211] *Al Adam* v. *Saudi Arabia* (CtRPD) (2018) paras. 11.1–12 (violation of art. 13(1) read alone and in conjunction with arts. 4, 15, 16 and 15).

torture and/or ill-treatment.[212] In its early jurisprudence, the CtRPD also had the opportunity to elaborate on key concepts. It held that the 'difference between illness and disability is a difference of degree and not a difference of kind',[213] and that states enjoy a certain margin of appreciation 'when assessing reasonableness and proportionality of accommodation measures'.[214] The CtRPD's focus, in its recommendations, on both individual remedies, and broader, particularly legislative reforms, underscores the potential of the procedure to challenge, and result in changes to, deeply engrained practices detrimental to the rights of persons with disabilities.

5.5.11   Shortchanged: *Nyusti and Takács* v. *Hungary*

Szilvia Nyusti and Péter Takács, the authors of the communication,[215] both have 'severe visual impairments'. They alleged that they were discriminated against because, contrary to their contract with a Hungarian bank (OTP), they were 'unable to use the automatic teller machines (ATMs) without assistance, as the keyboards of the ATMs operated by OTP are not marked with Braille, nor do the ATMs provide audible instructions and voice assistance for banking card operations'. As a result, even though they paid the same fees as sighted clients, they received inferior services. Their bank, which the authors had sued for a breach of Hungary's 2003 Equal Treatment Act, argued that the 'positive discrimination' sought was a government responsibility under the Act. The Hungarian Supreme Court found in favour of the defendants on this point. The respondent state, in the case: effectively takes a position that, under its existing legal framework, the obligation to provide for accessibility of information, communications and other services for persons with visual impairments on an equal basis with others does not apply to private entities, such as OTP ['the bank'], and does not affect contractual relationships.[216]

The CtRPD rejected this argument, recalling that:

States Parties should, in particular, take appropriate measures to develop, promulgate and monitor the implementation of minimum standards and guidelines for the accessibility of facilities and services open or provided to the public (art. 9, para. 2(a), of the Convention), and ensure that private entities that offer facilities and services which are open or provided to the public take into account all aspects of accessibility for persons with disabilities (art. 9, para. 2(b)).[217]

While the CtRPD acknowledged that Hungary had taken measures with a view to enhancing accessibility, it found a violation of article 9(2)(b) CRPD,

---

[212] *X.* v. *Tanzania* (CtRPD) (2017) paras. 8.1–8.7 (violation of art. 17, read in conjunction with art. 4).
[213] *S. C.* v. *Brazil* (CtRPD) (2014) para. 6.3.   [214] *Jungelin* v. *Sweden* (CtRPD) (2014) para. 10.5.
[215] *Nyusti and Takács* v. *Hungary* (CtRPD) (2013).   [216] Ibid., para. 9.3.   [217] Ibid., para. 9.4.

observing 'that none of these measures have ensured the accessibility to the banking card services provided by the ATMs operated by OTP for the authors or other persons in a similar situation'.[218] In its recommendations, among other measures, it requested the state party to:

create a legislative framework with concrete, enforceable and time-bound benchmarks for monitoring and assessing the gradual modification and adjustment by private financial institutions of previously inaccessible banking services provided by them into accessible ones. The State party should also ensure that all newly procured ATMs and other banking services are fully accessible for persons with disabilities.[219]

The case squarely addresses a key aspect of accessibility, effectively forcing the state to make sure that private entities do not directly or indirectly discriminate against persons with disabilities. The authors had taken their legal challenge up to the Hungarian Supreme Court and by obtaining a favourable decision from the CtRPD, exposed a flawed understanding shared by the private company in question, the executive and the judiciary. The CtRPD's decision demonstrates that it is not willing to accept half-hearted measures of implementation and, instead, insists that the state party shows concretely how it complies with its obligations. While the substance of the case concerns what may be considered a comparatively minor disadvantage, its potential repercussions are significant for all states parties to the CRPD.

5.5.12 Achievements and Challenges

The individual complaints procedure before international treaty bodies has contributed to the development of international human rights law. It has also provided some form of remedy for individuals and brought about changes as a result of subsequent implementation.[220] However, several treaty bodies, such as the CERD, the CtAT and the CtEDAW, remain under-utilised. Ironically, this development also shields them to some degree from the opposite problem, namely an increasing caseload that would adversely affect the effectiveness of complaints procedures.

   Several crucial areas remain unaddressed in the current system of complaints procedures. This applies in particular to economic, social and cultural rights, which is changing after the coming into force of the Optional Protocol to the ICESCR in May 2013.[221] The individual complaints procedure for children's rights (in force since April 2014) also constitutes an important contribution to the system, not least because it has the potential to let

---

[218] Ibid., para. 9.6.   [219] Ibid., para. 10(2)(a).   [220] See Chapter 7.5.

[221] The CESCR had adopted views in four cases (three against Spain, one against Ecuador) as of 8 October 2018, with thirteen cases declared inadmissible, according to information available on the OHCHR jurisprudence database. See further discussion in Chapter 9.6.1.

children themselves more clearly articulate their best interests.[222] However, an increase in existing complaints procedures will pose a challenge in its own right, particularly for the coherence and capacity of the system to ensure effective rights protection.

The fourfold increase in recourse to individual complaints procedures since 2000 prompted the OHCHR in 2012 to propose a series of measures, particularly aligning working approaches by means of common practices to strengthen the system of individual complaints procedures, inquiries and country visits.[223] The challenges facing the system run deeper than operational matters. Their function as expert bodies that examine complaints on a part-time basis without having public hearings or undertaking fact-finding, and which issue decisions that often do not attract great visibility and are repeatedly not complied with, limits their effectiveness. This is particularly evident in the lack of implementation. Treaty bodies have sought to address this problem by strengthening follow-up procedures, including by means of follow-up rapporteurs, though with limited success to date.[224] While important, these top-down measures may on their own be insufficient to enhance implementation. As highlighted by observers, making the complaints procedure an effective and meaningful remedy for victims and an advocacy tool will require broader changes to the system, focusing particularly on its relevance in the domestic context.[225]

INTERVIEW 5.2
Working for the CESCR
(Eibe Riedel)

Dr Eibe Riedel is Professor Emeritus, having previously taught public law and international law at several universities in Germany, Britain, Switzerland and Australia. Among a number of other positions held, he has been a member of the CESCR since 1997, where his term expired on 31 December 2012.

How would you describe your experience as a member of the CESCR – rewarding, frustrating, or a bit of both?

A bit of both, but mainly rewarding. And a lot of work.

---

[222] The CtRC had adopted views in four cases (two against Spain, one against Belgium, and one against Denmark) as of 31 January 2019, with a further eight cases declared inadmissible; see further Chapter 12.

[223] Pillay, above note 20, 68–74.

[224] See Open Society Justice Initiative, *From Judgment to Justice, Implementing International and Regional Human Rights Decisions* (Open Society Foundations, 2010) 117–36.

[225] See Chapter 7.5.

The reporting procedure has been much maligned; how do you assess its effectiveness and prospects for its strengthening or more fundamental reforms?

This is a very broad question that cannot be answered easily. With permanent cuts in financial resources for all the treaty bodies, any method of strengthening the system seems flawed. What is needed in the medium term is a proper reform of the entire system towards a unified treaty body monitoring. After initial failure in 2004, this real reform drive has to start soon – with ten treaty bodies making the whole process cumbersome, unwieldy, and at times repetitive and unfocused – both in the state reporting and during the committee questionings. If work started on reforms now, I reckon it would take about ten years to achieve it.

Do general comments sometimes play the role of a Trojan horse for fundamental reinterpretations of treaty provisions or general rules of international law? If so, where are the limits?

Sometimes they may indeed give the appearance of Trojan horses – but the process is really quite transparent. The issue remains how far interpretation can go. Views differ considerably as to how far interpretation (legitimate) and acting like a legislator (illegitimate) can go. My own view is that general comments should only interpret the Committee's approach in dialogues with states parties, explaining the meaning of terms used in the ICESCR. But sometimes, newer developments have to be taken on board, like the issue of the right to water, deduced from articles 11 and 12 ICESCR. By way of example, maybe have a look at the CESCR statement on resource allocation and the standard of reasonableness and proportionality in the Committee's work, adopted a little while ago when the Optional Protocol was discussed[1] to explain how far the Committee can go and what the 'margin of appreciation/discretion' of states parties really entails.

Considering the procedure under the Optional Protocol to the ICESCR, the question of justiciability, and the experience of other UN treaty bodies with individual complaints procedures, what do you see as the main challenges and prospects for the Committee once the Optional Protocol comes into force?

Again a very big question.[2] In a nutshell: the Committee should take great care not to overstep its role once the Optional Protocol is in force [as of May 2013]. It would be wise to choose micro-level issues first and to keep away

---

[1] See www2.ohchr.org/english/bodies/cescr/docs/statements/Obligationtotakesteps-2007.pdf.
[2] See E. Riedel, 'New Bearings to Social Rights: The Communications Procedure under the ICESCR', in U. Fastenrath, R. Geiger, D. Khan, A. Paulus, S. von Schorlemer and C. Vedder (eds.), *From Bilateralism to Community Interest: Essays in Honour of Bruno Simma* (Oxford University Press, 2011) 574–89.

from macro-issues like the extraterritorial application of ICESCR rights, or poverty generally, or environment protection issues on a large scale. This would definitely frighten off many states from ratifying. The fact that a reference to article 1 of both Covenants – which never played a role in the practice of the HRCtee – was kept in the Optional Protocol, despite no treaty body practice on it, will frighten off many countries that have large minorities and self-determination problems. In 2008 about fifty states voiced clear objections to that issue in an individual communications procedure. Those macro-questions should be left to the HRC, the General Assembly, ECOSOC or even to the Security Council. In fact, the CESCR only refers to self-determination occasionally in the state reporting procedure and then usually in conjunction with a particular part III article.

Once the Optional Protocol is in force and in operation [as of May 2013] I expect that interpretation of the broadly and vaguely formulated Covenant provisions will be easier and help to focus discussions, as happened with the Optional Protocol to the ICCPR. To be successful the cases dealt with have to be really convincing individual – or groups of individuals – cases, showing clear violations in order to attract proper worldwide attention. I would warn against over-ambitiousness, at least at the beginning, because that would scare off many potential ratifiers.

What role do NGOs play as users of the system and as critical supporters of the CESCR?

NGOs continue to play a crucial role in the whole procedure(s). But sometimes, they overdo it; for example, by raising budget issues in a very broad manner or by negating discretionary powers of states in making policy choices. When NGOs provide carefully drafted alternative or parallel reports Committee members find them really helpful. Sometimes, though, they are one-issue over-statements, or even alternative government positions, of the opposition that may just have lost a general election. But the information is crucial, anyway, for the Committee to do its work properly. Civil society has been excellent in propagating Henry Shue's triple obligations, as popularised by Asbjoern Eide, 'respect, protect, fulfil', which by now most states know of and accept almost without opposition, even though the Covenant is silent on that issue.

POINTS TO CONSIDER

1. Have UN treaty bodies played a leading role in the development of international human rights law?

2. Is the proliferation of individual complaints procedures the way forward or is it time for a radical rethink? What are the issues that a more effective system should address?

3. How do the practical challenges facing treaty bodies affect their legitimacy?

FURTHER READING

Alen, A., J. Vande Lanotte, E. Verhellen, F. Ang, E. Berghmans, M. Verheyde and B. Adamson (eds.), *A Commentary on the United Nations Convention on the Rights of the Child* (Martinus Nijhoff, 2005).

Baderin, M., and R. McCorquodale, 'The International Covenant on Economic, Social and Cultural Rights: Forty Years of Development', in M. Baderin and R. McCorquodale (eds.), *Economic, Social and Cultural Rights in Action* (Oxford University Press, 2007) 3–24.

Bantekas, I., M. A. Stein and D. Anastasiou (eds.), *The UN Convention on the Rights of Persons with Disabilities* (Oxford University Press, 2018).

Bassiouni, M. C., and W. A. Schabas (eds.), *New Challenges for the UN Human Rights Machinery: What Future for the UN Treaty Body System and the Human Rights Council Procedures?* (Intersentia, 2011).

Cholewinski, R. (ed.), *Migration and Human Rights: The United Nations Convention on Migrant Workers' Rights* (Cambridge University Press, 2009).

Flynn, E., *From Rhetoric to Action: Implementing the UN Convention on the Rights of Persons with Disabilities* (Cambridge University Press, 2013).

Freeman, M., C. Chinkin and B. Rudolf (eds.), *The UN Convention on the Elimination of All Forms of Discrimination against Women* (Oxford University Press, 2013).

Joseph, S., and M. Castan, *The International Covenant on Civil and Political Rights: Cases, Materials, and Commentary*, 3rd edn (Oxford University Press, 2013).

Keller, H., and G. Ulfstein (eds.), *UN Human Rights Treaty Bodies: Law and Legitimacy* (Cambridge University Press, 2012).

Langford, M. (ed.), *Social Rights Jurisprudence: Emerging Trends in International and Comparative Law* (Cambridge University Press, 2008) (various contributions on the role of several committees).

McGoldrick, D., *The Human Rights Committee: Its Role in the Development of the International Covenant on Civil and Political Rights*, 2nd edn (Clarendon Press, 1994).

Murray, R., E. Steinerte, M. Evans and A. Hallo de Wolf, *The Optional Protocol to the UN Convention against Torture* (Oxford University Press, 2011).

Nowak, M., *UN Covenant on Civil and Political Rights: CCPR Commentary*, 2nd edn (Engels, 2005).

Nowak, M., and E. McArthur, *The United Nations Convention against Torture: A Commentary* (Oxford University Press, 2008).

Oberleitner, G. (ed.), *International Human Rights Institutions, Tribunals and Courts* (Springer, 2018).

Odello, M., and F. Seatzu, *The UN Committee on Economic, Social and Cultural Rights: The Law, Process and Practice* (Ashgate, 2013).

Saul, B., D. Kinley and J. Mowbray, *The International Covenant on Economic, Social and Cultural Rights: Commentary, Cases and Materials* (Oxford University Press, 2014).

Schöpp-Schilling, H. B., and C. Flinterman (eds.), *The Circle of Empowerment: Twenty-Five Years of the UN Committee on the Elimination of Discrimination against Women* (The Feminist Press, 2007).

Scovazzi, T., and G. Citroni, *The Struggle against Enforced Disappearance and the 2007 United Nations Convention* (Martinus Nijhoff, 2007).

Sohn, L. B., and T. Buergenthal, *International Protection of Human Rights* (Bobbs-Merrill, 1973).

Thornberry, P., *The International Convention on the Elimination of all Forms of Racial Discrimination: A Commentary* (Oxford University Press, 2016).

Tobin, J. (ed.), *The UN Convention on the Rights of the Child: A Commentary* (Oxford University Press, 2019).

Wolfrum, R., 'The Committee on the Elimination of Racial Discrimination', (1999) 3 *Max Planck Yearbook of United Nations Law* 489.

Websites

OHCHR: www.ohchr.org (providing links to all
human rights treaty and charter bodies, i.e. HRC
and Special Procedures, country-specific documents; text of international treaties and status of
ratification)

UN: www.un.org (main UN organs)

Universal Human Rights Index Database:
www.ohchr.org/EN/HRBodies/Pages/
UniversalHumanRightsIndexDatabase.aspx (provides
easy access to country-specific human rights information emanating from international human rights
mechanisms in the United Nations system: the
treaty bodies, the special procedures and the UPR)

6 Regional Human Rights Treaty Systems

CONTENTS

6.1 INTRODUCTION

Initial concerns that regional human rights systems may undermine the universality of rights have largely given way to a more positive appreciation of their role.[1] Regional human rights systems provide a crucial layer of protection. They are closely connected with regional political developments and integration which potentially gives them more traction than the United

---

[1] See Vienna Declaration and Programme of Action, UN doc. A/CONF.157/23 (12 July 1993) para. 37.

Nations (UN) system. Moreover, increasing references to their jurisprudence and practice evince how they contribute to, and enrich, international human rights law.

An examination of regional human rights systems suggests the following typical process. States agree on the need for closer regional cooperation if not integration. Human rights are accepted as one element of, and a yardstick for, the regional political order. A foundational human rights instrument is adopted. Further, a human rights body with a mandate to promote human rights and monitor states parties' compliance with their treaty obligations is (eventually) set up. Over time, responding to demands and with a view to strengthening the effectiveness and credibility of the system, substantive rights are broadened and the role of victims (and others, particularly non-governmental organisations (NGOs)) in raising the issue of, or complaining about, human rights violations is enhanced. As the system matures this momentum eventually results in the establishment of a judicial body. Parallel efforts to foster regional political integration reinforce the importance of human rights at all levels as a marker of the system's ability to provide a stable order based on the rule of law and the protection of fundamental rights.

The European, Inter-American and African human rights systems share a number of these idealised features, which indicates that there is a pull to develop a stronger normative framework and monitoring mechanisms. However, a look at their development demonstrates that these goals are not always shared across a region (see, for example, the ambiguous role of the United States of America (USA) in the Inter-American system). Regional political support for human rights systems can vary considerably, which may in turn affect the latter's effectiveness. Moreover, a focus on institutional features where the availability of a judicial body is often equated with a strong system may obscure what is one of the latter's fundamental tasks, namely contributing to the development of a regional human rights culture and enhanced domestic protection. Lawyers, NGOs, human rights defenders, the media, like-minded politicians and states all play a crucial role in this context in using, defending and developing regional instruments to transform them into living systems that make a positive impact, particularly at the national level.

Regional human rights systems, being simultaneously creatures and 'masters' of states, and frequently forming part of broader political dynamics, face a number of common challenges. These include: (1) the adequacy of the legal and institutional framework; (2) the capacity of bodies to fulfil their mandate effectively; (3) their responsiveness to human rights violations, particularly systemic and massive violations; (4) their effectiveness in ensuring compliance; and (5) their ability to contribute to regional acceptance of and respect for human rights. The effectiveness of a system depends to a large degree on its legitimacy, that is the authority it commands, which in turn requires that a sufficient number of states are supportive. The persuasiveness of responses by the relevant bodies, both in relation to individual cases and systemic problems, their awareness of political realities and their ability to fashion a human rights culture that reflects regional features and offers space for national actors are critical factors in this regard.

Assessments of the record of regional human rights systems vary considerably. They range from being a driving force for the advancement of human rights to being essentially conservative and ineffective because of their limited ability to respond to gross and systematic violations, deference to states and the lack of strong enforcement powers.[2] In practice, normative and institutional developments testify to the continuing relevance of regional human rights systems, as is evident in the growing recourse to them. Indeed, one of the major challenges for regional human rights bodies is that they are at risk of becoming a victim of their own success; it is in particular the capacity problems encountered that raise serious questions about their effectiveness. It is against this background that this chapter examines the historical development, legal framework, institutional set-up and practice, as well as the impact and challenges facing the major regional human rights system today. It also examines the prospects for their development in various parts of Asia, which to date have no, or only extremely weak, systems in place.

6.2   THE EUROPEAN HUMAN RIGHTS SYSTEM

6.2.1   Overview

The European Convention on Human Rights (ECHR) and the European Court of Human Rights (ECtHR)[3] are the cornerstones of the larger European human rights architecture that has been developed largely under the aegis of the Council of Europe (CoE).[4] Forming part of regional responses to World War II, the CoE was established in 1949 in a process driven by France, Italy, the United Kingdom (UK), Ireland and the Benelux and Scandinavian countries.[5]

---

[2] See O. C. Okafor, *The African Human Rights System, Activist Forces and International Institutions* (Cambridge University Press, 2007) 67–90, for a critical review and analysis of positions, particularly in the African context.

[3] See www.echr.coe.int.

[4] See www.coe.int.

[5] See in particular, E. Bates, *The Evolution of the European Convention on Human Rights: From its Inception to the Creation of a Permanent Court of Human Rights* (Oxford University Press, 2010). See on the CoE, J. Petaux, *Democracy and Human Rights for Europe: The Council of Europe's Contribution* (CoE, 2009); R. Kicker (ed.), *Pioneer and Guarantor for Human Rights* (CoE, 2010).

It constitutes the main European intergovernmental political body, with the Committee of Ministers (CoM) and the Parliamentary Assembly as its main organs. The CoE's aim 'to achieve a greater unity between its members for the purpose of safeguarding and realising the ideals and principles which are their common heritage and facilitating their economic and social progress' is to be pursued 'by agreements and common action ... in the maintenance and further realisation of human rights and fundamental freedoms'.[6] Crucially, CoE membership is made conditional upon acceptance of the rule of law and human rights.[7] This was part of an essentially political project of liberal Western European states to create a stable political order, which was also developed as a contrasting model to communist countries at the time.[8] Today, the CoE is the primary body in the field of human rights, both in terms of standard-setting and monitoring. It has developed into an impressive system with forty-seven member states, having witnessed a substantial expansion following the disintegration of the Soviet Union, and now includes states in Eastern Europe, the Caucasus, Turkey, Ukraine and Russia, with Belarus and Kazakhstan being the only non-member states in the region.

A number of human rights treaties were developed within the CoE setting and adopted by its CoM. The ECHR, which was adopted in 1950 and entered into force in 1953, largely focused on civil and political rights and was influenced by the Universal Declaration of Human Rights (UDHR), which is referred to in its preamble. Significantly, in the light of recurring opposition to the ECHR and the ECtHR in the UK, it was a conservative British lawyer, Sir David Maxwell Fyfe, who played a leading role in the drafting.[9]

The almost exclusive focus on civil and political rights in the ECHR reflects its political outlook, and bias, at the time. Partly responding to this lacuna, the CoE adopted the European Social Charter on 18 October 1961, with the European Committee of Social Rights (ECSR) becoming its main supervisory body. The Charter's aim was to secure 'the enjoyment of social rights ... without discrimination' (preamble), with a strong focus on the right to work. However, this aim was compromised by its selective approach which allows states to opt for a certain number of articles that they agree to be bound by.[10] The adoption and acceptance of the Charter therefore came at the expense of a unified normative framework. This fact,

---

[6] Art. 1 Statute of the Council of Europe 1949.

[7] Art. 3, ibid.

[8] See Bates, above note 5, 5–8.

[9] See A. Donald, J. Gordon and P. Leach, *The UK and the European Court of Human Rights*, UK Equality and Human Rights Commission Research Report 83 (Metropolitan University, Human Rights and Social Justice Research Institute, 2011) 8–9.

[10] Art. 20(1) European Social Charter, 1961, and part III, art. A(1) of the European Social Charter (Revised), 1996. See Chapter 9.6.2.

together with limited visibility, undermined its potential to strengthen economic, social and cultural rights, which still play a secondary role in the European system.[11] Other treaties followed, particularly the European Convention for the Prevention of Torture (1987), which developed into an important preventive mechanism supervised by the European Committee for the Prevention of Torture and Inhuman or Degrading Treatment or Punishment (CPT).[12] The European Charter for Regional and Minorities Languages (1992) and the Framework Convention for the Protection of National Minorities (1995), whose implementation is monitored by the CoM, represent further important instruments. In the wake of the dramatic political changes on the continent in the late 1980s and the early 1990s, the Framework Convention recognises the importance of the rights of minorities and provides a framework for their regional protection.[13] Beyond the CoE, the European Union (EU) (see below at 6.2.8) and the Organization for Security and Co-operation in Europe (OSCE) have played important roles in addressing questions of human rights protection in Europe within their respective mandates.[14]

6.2.2   The ECHR

The ECHR recognises key political and civil rights, including: (1) rights of an absolute nature, i.e. the prohibition of torture, slavery and forced labour and the prohibition of retroactive punishment which cannot be derogated from in times of emergency (article 15); (2) non-derogable rights that are subject to limited exceptions, namely the right to life (articles 2 and 15(2)); (3) rights that may be derogated from within limits, such as the right to liberty and security (article 5), and the right to a fair trial (article 6); and (4) qualified rights, that is the right to respect for private and family

---

[11] See further D. Harris and J. D. Arcy, *The European Social Charter: The Protection of Economic and Social Rights in Europe*, 2nd edn (Transnational Publishers, 2001); G. de Búrca, B. de Witte and L. Ogertschnig (eds.), *Social Rights in Europe* (Oxford University Press, 2005), particularly part II. See for a critical account, T. Novitz, 'Remedies for Violations of Social Rights within the Council of Europe: The Significant Absence of a Court', in C. Kilpatrick, T. Novitz and P. Skidmore (eds.), *The Future of Remedies in Europe* (Hart, 2000) 231–52, at 232–5.

[12] See www.cpt.coe.int. See for reflections combined with a practical account of its work, A. Cassese, *Inhuman States: Imprisonment, Detention and Torture in Europe Today* (Polity Press, 1996).

[13] M. Weller (ed.), *The Rights of Minorities: A Commentary on the European Framework Convention for the Protection of National Minorities* (Oxford University Press, 2005); A. Verstichel, A. Alen, B. de Witte and P. Lemmens (eds.), *The Framework Convention for the Protection of National Minorities: A Useful Pan-European Instrument?* (Intersentia, 2008).

[14] See www.osce.org. See for the nature of its work, OSCE, *Annual Report 2011*; D. J. Gaelbreath, *The Organisation for Security and Cooperation in Europe* (Routledge, 2007).

life, freedom to manifest one's religion or beliefs,[15] freedom of expression as well as freedom of peaceful assembly and association guaranteed in articles 8–11 respectively. The Convention obliges all states parties (called High Contracting Parties) to secure these rights within their jurisdictions (article 1). This entails both negative (for example to refrain from torture) and positive obligations, as stipulated, for example, in article 2(1) on the right to life ('protected by law'), and, more broadly, as inherent in the right to a fair trial in article 6. Significantly, the ECHR requires states to provide an effective remedy in case of breach of any of the Convention rights (article 13).

However, there were several notable omissions in the scope of rights initially recognised in the ECHR, which necessitated the adoption of a number of subsequent protocols. The first of these (1952) recognised – in a rather curious mixture – the right to property, the right to education and the right to free elections. Further protocols mainly concerned criminal justice matters and the scope of the right to a fair trial, including the prohibition of imprisonment for debt, the right of appeal in criminal matters, compensation for wrongful conviction and the right not to be punished twice, thereby closing some of the existing gaps compared to other treaties, such as the International Covenant on Civil and Political Rights (ICCPR).[16] Freedom of movement, the prohibition of expulsion of nationals, the prohibition of collective expulsion of aliens, and procedural safeguards relating to the expulsion of aliens, were also recognised.[17] Significantly, the CoE also took steps to abolish the death penalty, which was implicitly recognised in article 2(1) ECHR. Protocol no. 6 (1983) abolished the death penalty save in time of war, and Protocol no. 13 (2002) brought the process to a conclusion with the complete abolition of the death penalty. A further notable addition is Protocol no. 12, which recognises the general prohibition of discrimination, thereby going beyond article 14 ECHR, which only applies to non-discrimination in relation to the rights granted in the Convention.[18] While the adoption of these protocols has largely addressed the normative gaps evident in the ECHR it has contributed to a fragmentation of the system; as treaties, the protocols are subject to separate ratification, which has been uneven in practice and has resulted in different levels of protection.[19]

---

[15] Note that art. 9(1) ECHR does not allow interference with the internal aspect of the freedom to hold thoughts and beliefs.

[16] See arts. 1 of Protocol no. 4, and arts. 2, 3 and 4 of Protocol no. 7.

[17] See arts. 2, 3 and 4 of Protocol no. 4, and art. 1 of Protocol no. 7.

[18] See for a concise account of the ECtHR's jurisprudence on Art. 14 ECHR, O. de Schutter, *International Human Rights Law*, 2nd edn (Cambridge University Press, 2014) 642–5.

[19] See http://conventions.coe.int/Treaty/Commun/ListeTraites.asp?MA=3&CM=7&CL=ENG for a link to the status of ratification for each protocol.

6.2.3   Key Institutions

The ECHR supervisory mechanism is effectively a complaints procedure, providing for both individual and inter-state complaints. The original system consisted of: (1) a European Commission of Human Rights, which was created in 1954 and was competent to receive individual complaints and to bring them before the court where states had recognised its competence to do so; (2) the ECtHR, which became operational in 1959 and could hear inter-state cases and individual complaints brought before it by the Commission provided the state concerned had accepted its jurisdiction; and (3) the CoM responsible for the enforcement of judgments. In this model, the Commission effectively acted as a quasi-judicial filter for cases to be brought before the ECtHR, which was to act in a judicial capacity.[20] The Commission played a leading role in the development of the system and issued some landmark decisions, notably its report on the *Greek* case in 1969 in response to a series of violations committed by the then Greek dictatorship (1967–1974).[21] However, a growing caseload that had resulted from a greater awareness and a significant increase in member states following political changes in Eastern and South-eastern Europe prompted a fundamental reform of the system in the 1990s. Protocol no. 11 (1998) abolished the Commission and created a court with two chambers. In what was a revolutionary step for international human rights treaty bodies whose competences are often curtailed by states jealously guarding their sovereignty, the Protocol provided mandatory direct individual access to the Court. The CoM retained its role of supervising the execution of judgments in what is the present two-tier system.

6.2.4   The ECtHR: Structure and Functions

The ECtHR has forty-seven judges (one per member state), who are elected by the CoE's Parliamentary Assembly 'from a list of three candidates nominated by the High Contracting Party'[22] and sit in their personal capacity.[23] Following the changes made in Protocol no. 14, the Court sits in 'single-judge formations' (admissibility), committees of three judges and a Chamber of seven judges deciding on admissibility and merits, as well as a Grand Chamber (GC) of seventeen judges.[24] The GC is strictly speaking not an appeal body. Rather, its main function is to develop and ensure the consistency of the Court's

[20] See arts. 20–37 of the 1950 ECHR.
[21] The *Greek case, Denmark* v. *Greece*; *Norway* v. *Greece*; *Sweden* v. *Greece*; *Netherlands* v. *Greece* (ECmHR) (1969). See on the role of the European Commission, e.g., D. Harris, M. O'Boyle and C. Warbrick, *Law of the European Convention on Human Rights* (Oxford University Press, 1995) 571–603.
[22] Art. 22 ECHR.   [23] Art. 21 ECHR.   [24] Art. 26 ECHR.

jurisprudence in the interpretation or application of the ECHR, including its protocols.[25] The GC may decide to hear a case where a Chamber relinquishes jurisdiction or where a party requests referral following a Chamber judgment.[26]

Individual complaints form the bulk of the ECtHR's work. By the end of 2018 it had issued more than 21,000 judgments, the bulk of which followed the adoption of Protocol no. 11 (1999).[27] In contrast, there have only been twenty-six inter-state cases, most of which, unsurprisingly, have been of a high-profile nature.[28] The Court has by January 2019 issued five judgments in inter-state cases.[29] It can also issue advisory opinions but has used this power on only three occasions because of the narrow remit provided for in article 47 ECHR.[30] This is bound to change following the entry into force of Protocol no. 16, which provides that the highest national courts designated by the contracting parties 'may request the Court to give advisory opinions on questions of principle relating to the interpretation or application of the rights and freedoms defined in the Convention or the protocols thereto'.[31]

6.2.5   Jurisprudence of the ECtHR

6.2.5.1   *Development of the ECtHR's Jurisprudence*

A brief review of the ECtHR's history shows that it adjudicated few cases in its early years – issuing seven judgments on the merits in its first decade – beginning with *Lawless* v. *Ireland* in 1960.[32] Initially, the majority of judgments, many of which have come to be seen as landmark cases, concerned the right to liberty and security, the right to a fair trial and the right to freedom of expression, as well as in two cases the prohibition of

---

[25] Art. 30 ECHR.   [26] Art. 31 ECHR.   [27] ECtHR, *Overview 1959–2018* (2019) 2–4.

[28] See overview at www.echr.coe.int/Documents/InterStates_applications_ENG.pdf.

[29] *Ireland* v. *United Kingdom* (ECtHR) (1978), (2018) (Revision); *Cyprus* v. *Turkey* (IV) (ECtHR) (2001); *Cyprus* v. *Turkey* (IV) (ECtHR) (2014) (Just Satisfaction); *Denmark* v. *Turkey* (ECtHR) (2000); and *Georgia* v. *Russia* (I) (ECtHR) (2014).

[30] Decision on the *Competence of the Court to give an advisory opinion* (ECtHR) (2004); Advisory opinion on *Certain legal questions concerning the lists of candidates submitted with a view to the election of judges to the European Court of Human Rights* (ECtHR) (2008); Advisory opinion on *Certain legal questions concerning the lists of candidates submitted with a view to the election of judges to the European Court of Human Rights* (No. 2) (ECtHR) (2010).

[31] Art. 1(1) of Protocol no. 16, CETS 214 Human Rights (Protocol no. 16) (2 October 2013). The Court adopted its first advisory opinion under Protocol no. 16 in April 2019, which concerned the recognition in domestic law of a legal parent–child relationship between a child born through a gestational surrogacy arrangement abroad and the intended mother.

[32] *Lawless* v. *Ireland* (No. 1) (ECtHR) (1960).

torture and other ill-treatment (*Ireland* v. *the United Kingdom* and *Tyrer* v. *United Kingdom*).[33] It was only in the early 1990s (205 judgments in total by 1990) that the number of decisions and judgments began to grow steadily, with the Court handing down over a hundred annually since 1996, a figure that has risen to over a thousand annually since 2005. The 1990s brought about a significant shift that led the Court increasingly to consider both systemic and serious, large-scale violations in different contexts. Largely as a result of NGO-driven litigation the Court was seized with a number of cases concerning serious violations in the northeast of Turkey.[34] It was also faced with a series of deep-seated structural problems in post-communist countries that had become parties to the ECHR, particularly Romania, Bulgaria and Poland, in relation to ill-treatment, the administration of justice and property rights.[35] In addition, Ukraine's and Russia's acceptance of the Court's jurisdiction in 1997 and 1998 respectively resulted in a steady rise of cases against them, many of which have been characterised by serious violations.[36] In recent years, the Court has also ruled on several high-profile cases concerning the conduct of armed forces and counter-terrorism measures, including outside the territory of ECHR contracting parties.[37] These developments were complemented by a large number of repeat cases concerning systemic violations, particularly in respect of the length of proceedings in Italy[38] and the regulation of property rights in Poland.[39] The significant increase in the number and nature of cases culminated in unprecedented challenges to the system, which will be considered in more detail at 6.2.7.

The ECtHR has made a major and influential contribution to the development of international human rights law. This applies in particular to its

---

[33] *Ireland* v. *the United Kingdom* (ECtHR) (1978); *Tyrer* v. *United Kingdom* (ECtHR) (1978). See further M. R. Madsen, 'The Protracted Institutionalization of the Strasbourg Court: From Legal Diplomacy to Integrationist Jurisprudence', in J. Christofferson and M. R. Madsen (eds.), *The European Court of Human Rights between Law and Politics* (Oxford University Press, 2013) 43–60.

[34] By 2018 there had been a total of 3,532 judgments in cases against Turkey, which is the highest number of judgments for any contracting state. See ECtHR, *Statistics 1959–2018*, 3.

[35] Ibid., 6–7.

[36] Both states accounted for 17 per cent of the total number of judgments by 2018. See ibid.

[37] See *Jaloud* v. *The Netherlands* (ECtHR) (2014); *Al-Jedda* v. *United Kingdom* (ECtHR) (2011); *Al-Skeini and Others* v. *United Kingdom* (ECtHR) (2011); *Al-Saadoon and Mufdhi* v. *United Kingdom* (ECtHR) (2010); *Saadi* v. *Italy* (ECtHR) (2009); *Othman* (Abu Qatada) v. *United Kingdom* (ECtHR) (2012); *Babar Ahmad and Others* v. *United Kingdom* (ECtHR) (2012); *Al Nashiri* v. *Romania* (ECtHR) (2018); *Abu Zubaydah* v. *Lithuania* (ECtHR) (2018).

[38] In 1,194 out of 2,396 judgments against Italy. See ECtHR, *Statistics 1959–2018*, 8. See in particular *Bottazzi* v. *Italy* (ECtHR) (1999) and *Scordino* v. *Italy* (ECtHR) (2007).

[39] See in particular *Broniowski* v. *Poland* (ECtHR) (2005) and (2006).

jurisprudence on the right to life, especially in respect of positive obligations,[40] the prohibition of torture and other ill-treatment,[41] including sexual violence,[42] the prohibition of slavery and forced labour,[43] the right to liberty and security,[44] and the right to a fair trial,[45] including the right of access to justice.[46] It also comprises leading judgments that gave a broad reading to aspects of the right to privacy,[47] including in relation to environmental concerns[48] and an extensive (and in parts controversial) jurisprudence on qualified rights such as freedom of expression[49] and freedom of assembly and association, including in relation to trade unions.[50] It has broadened the

[40] See *Tagayeva and Others* v. *Russia* (ECtHR) (2017); *Lambert and Others* v. *France* (ECtHR) (2015); *Centre for Legal Resources on behalf of Valentin Câmpeanu* v. *Romania* (ECtHR) (2014); *Anguelova* v. *Bulgaria* (ECtHR) (2002); *Osman* v. *United Kingdom* (ECtHR) (1998); *Öneryildiz* v. *Turkey* (ECtHR) (2005); *Kelly and Others* v. *United Kingdom* (ECtHR) (2001).

[41] *Bouyid* v. *Belgium* (ECtHR) (2015); *Cestaro* v. *Italy* (ECtHR) (2015); *Vinter and Others* v. *United Kingdom* (ECtHR) (2013); *El-Masri* v. *The Former Yugoslav Republic of Macedonia* (ECtHR) (2012); *Aksoy* v. *Turkey* (ECtHR) (1996); *Selmouni* v. *France* (ECtHR) (2000); and *Soering* v. *United Kingdom* (ECtHR) (1989); *Chahal* v. *United Kingdom* (ECtHR) (1996); *M. S. S.* v. *Belgium* and *Greece* (ECtHR) (2011); *Hirsi Jamaa* v. *Italy* (ECtHR) (2012); *Saadi* v. *Italy*, in relation to non-refoulement.

[42] *O' Keeffe* v. *Ireland* (ECtHR) (2014); *Aydin* v. *Turkey* (ECtHR) (1997); *M. C.* v. *Bulgaria* (ECtHR) (2005); *Opuz* v. *Turkey* (ECtHR) (2010); *V. C.* v. *Slovakia* (ECtHR) (2011); and *M. and C.* v. *Romania* (ECtHR) (2011).

[43] *Rantsev* v. *Cyprus and Russia* (ECtHR) (2010) (trafficking).

[44] *Butkevich* v. *Russia* (ECtHR) (2018) (arrest, detention and trial of journalist covering protests, also violation of arts. 6 and 10); *Identoba and others* v. *Georgia* (ECtHR) (2015); *Stanev* v. *Bulgaria* (ECtHR) (2012).

[45] *Engels and Others* v. *Netherlands* (ECtHR) (1976); *König* v. *Federal Republic of Germany* (ECtHR) (1978); *Burdov* v. *Russia* (ECtHR) (2002).

[46] *Golder* v. *United Kingdom* (ECtHR) (1975); *Zubac* v. *Croatia* (ECtHR) (2018).

[47] See e.g., *Big Brother Watch and Others* v. *United Kingdom* (ECtHR) (2018). The right to respect for private and family life, home and correspondence in art. 8 has spawned a rich jurisprudence that has been particularly important in such diverse areas as personal identity, data protection, reproductive rights, family life, housing, correspondence, stop and search, and immigration. See for a selection of key cases, A. Mowbray, *Cases and Materials on the European Convention on Human Rights*, 3rd edn (Oxford University Press, 2012) 488–597.

[48] See *López Ostra* v. *Spain* (ECtHR) (1994); *Guerra and Others* v. *Italy* (ECtHR) (1998); *Hatton and Others* v. *United Kingdom* (ECtHR) (2003); *Dubetska and Others* v. *Ukraine* (ECtHR) (2011); *Deés* v. *Hungary* (ECtHR) (2010).

[49] *Magyar Jeti Zrt* v. *Hungary* (ECtHR) (2018); *Magyar Helsinki Bizottság* v. *Hungary* (ECtHR) (2016). See further Chapter 8.7.

[50] See *Young, James and Webster* v. *United Kingdom* (ECtHR) (1981); *Sørensen and Rasmussen* v. *Denmark* (ECtHR) (2006); *The National Union of Rail, Maritime and Transport Workers* v. *United Kingdom* (ECtHR) (2014); and *Sindicatul 'Păstorul Cel Bun'* v. *Romania* (ECtHR) (2013).

scope of the right to property[51] and affirmed the right to vote, particularly for prisoners.[52] In its more recent jurisprudence the Court – though not always entirely consistently – has strengthened the rights of minorities[53] and individuals facing discrimination, including on the basis of sexual orientation and gender identity.[54]

6.2.5.2   *The ECtHR's Interpretation of the ECHR*

The ECtHR has developed a number of important doctrines in its interpretation of the ECHR. As a general principle, it has sought to interpret the Convention authoritatively and in the most effective fashion while at the same time respecting the principle of subsidiarity (according to this principle, which is grounded in sovereignty, it is foremost states themselves that are responsible for guaranteeing the rights granted).[55] When faced with how to construe terms such as 'law' or 'civil rights' in articles 5 and 6 ECHR respectively, the Court gave them an 'autonomous meaning' under the Convention.[56] This was an important step in establishing its authority vis-à-vis national systems and developing a coherent understanding of the Convention. The Court has stressed that the Convention is part of a constitutional order, which, in combination with considerations of effectiveness, underpins the purposive interpretation of its provisions.[57] It views the Convention as a living instrument whose provisions need to be 'interpreted in light of present-day conditions',[58] which may also include changing its own interpretation of the ECHR over time.[59] On several occasions it has refused to recognise and accommodate 'traditional' views when considering the compatibility of laws or practices with the Convention, including, for example, discrimination against children born outside marriage[60] and the criminalisation of homosexual

---

[51] See *Öneryildiz* v. *Turkey* and *Broniowski* v. *Poland*.

[52] See *Hirst* v. *United Kingdom* (ECtHR) (2006).

[53] See *D. H. and Others* v. *The Czech Republic* (ECtHR) (2008) and *Oršuš and Others* v. *Croatia* (ECtHR) (2011).

[54] See *Goodwin* v. *United Kingdom* (ECtHR) (2002); *Y. Y.* v. *Turkey* (ECtHR) (2015). See further P. Johnson, *Homosexuality and the European Court of Human Rights* (Routledge, 2013).

[55] See further G. Letsas, *A Theory of Interpretation of the European Convention on Human Rights* (Oxford University Press, 2007).

[56] See e.g., *König* v. *Federal Republic of Germany*, paras. 88–9.

[57] See *Loizidou* v. *Turkey* (ECtHR) (1995) para. 75.

[58] *Tyrer* v. *United Kingdom* (ECtHR) (1978) para. 31.

[59] *Selmouni* v. *France*, para. 101.

[60] *Marckx* v. *Belgium* (ECtHR) (1979) and *Vermeire* v. *Belgium* (ECtHR) (1993) (violation of arts. 8 and 14).

conduct.[61] However, it has been less willing to overturn practices such as in respect of the right to privacy where it has identified a lack of European consensus.[62]

The ECtHR has relied heavily on the principle of proportionality, stating that 'inherent in the whole of the ECHR is a search for a fair balance between the demands of the general interest of the community and the requirements of the protection of the individual's fundamental rights'.[63] This principle has been particularly important when considering whether states could justifiably restrict the exercise of qualified rights. The margin of appreciation developed in this context is perhaps the most prominent of the ECtHR's doctrines.[64] First articulated in *Handyside* v. *UK* (1976), the Court has used it as a device that gives states some discretion in applying Convention guarantees, particularly when determining what measures are necessary to restrict rights on grounds such as public morals, which involve certain value judgements.[65] The Court has also given states some flexibility in determining whether a factual situation exists that threatens the life of the nation (application of article 15)[66] and in respect of positive obligations.[67] The margin of appreciation is based on the principle of subsidiarity, which is now set to be enshrined in the ECHR's preamble once Protocol no. 15 enters into force.[68] It is a pragmatic device for the Court to defer to states' assessment where it considers it inappropriate to make an assessment itself. The discretion inherent in this margin is not unlimited as the Court has repeatedly stressed that its application 'goes hand in hand with European supervision'.[69] In addition, the scope of the margin differs considerably. States have been given a fairly broad

---

[61] *Dudgeon* v. *United Kingdom* (ECtHR) (1982) (violation of art. 8).

[62] See for a critical assessment of the Court's approach in this regard, M.-B. Dembour, *Who Believes in Human Rights? Reflections on the European Convention* (Cambridge University Press, 2006), particularly at 197–201, 206–10 and 238–41.

[63] *Soering* v. *United Kingdom*, para. 89.

[64] See in particular Y. Arai-Takahashi, *The Margin of Appreciation Doctrine and the Principle of Proportionality in the Jurisprudence of the ECHR* (Intersentia, 2002); Letsas, above note 55, 80–98.

[65] *Handyside* v. *United Kingdom* (ECtHR) (1976) paras. 48–50.

[66] *Demir and Others* v. *Turkey* (ECtHR) (1998) para. 43; *A and Others* v. *United Kingdom* (ECtHR) (2009) paras. 173–4.

[67] *M. C.* v. *Bulgaria*, paras. 154–5.

[68] Art. 1 of Protocol no. 15 (2013) provides that '[a]t the end of the preamble to the Convention, a new recital shall be added, which shall read as follows: "Affirming that the High Contracting Parties, in accordance with the principle of subsidiarity, have the primary responsibility to secure the rights and freedoms defined in this Convention and the Protocols thereto, and that in doing so they enjoy a margin of appreciation, subject to the supervisory jurisdiction of the European Court of Human Rights established by this Convention"'.

[69] *Handyside* v. *United Kingdom*, para. 49.

margin where there is a lack of European consensus, where they make value judgements and where conflicting rights or interests need to be balanced, for example restricting freedom of expression on grounds of public morals and the protection of rights of others.[70] However, in areas where interference may encroach on the core of a right, such as political freedom of expression, the Court has been much less generous in trusting the assessment of states. This is evident in a series of Austrian cases where journalists faced prosecutions and fines for 'defamation' of politicians.[71]

On the whole, the ECtHR has been mindful of diverging national approaches and largely respectful of the jurisprudence of national courts, as it is clear that in order to maintain its legitimacy it must strike a delicate balance between its supervisory role and respect for states' systems.[72] Observers and actors from different political backgrounds have repeatedly criticised (or commended) the ECtHR both for its broad interpretation of the ECHR and for being too deferential when key national interests or sensitivities are at stake.

6.2.5.3   Responses to the ECtHR's Jurisprudence

The ECtHR has been the subject of at times scathing criticism for its supposed deference to contracting states.[73] A detailed review of its jurisprudence showed how the Court has, with few exceptions, privileged states' responses over the rights of migrants.[74] Further, in a number of cases the Court has seemingly accepted state reliance on moral values or local sentiments at the expense of a robust affirmation of rights, especially in the field of artistic work.[75] This comes perilously close to accepting majoritarian views, an approach that runs counter to the very essence of liberal models of defending individual rights. This applies in particular to those who claim a right to be

---

[70] *Müller and Others* v. *Switzerland* (ECtHR) (1988) paras. 32 and 36; *Mouvement Raëlien Suisse* v. *Switzerland* (ECtHR) (2012) paras. 59–66; *Wingrove* v. *United Kingdom* (ECtHR) (1997) paras. 58, 61 and 64.

[71] See e.g., *Lingens* v. *Austria* (ECtHR) (1986) paras. 39–47.

[72] See on the Court's legitimacy in particular, the research output of the project on the 'Legitimacy and Authority of Supranational Human Rights Courts', online at http:// ecthrproject.wordpress.com.

[73] Dissenting opinion of Judge Spielmann in *Müller* v. *Switzerland*; Dembour, above note 62, 162–6.

[74] M.-B. Dembour, *When Humans become Migrants: Study of the European Court of Human Rights with an Inter-American Counterpoint* (Oxford University Press, 2015).

[75] See e.g., *Müller and Others* v. *Switzerland*, paras. 32, 36 and 43. In contrast, see *Klein* v. *Slovakia* (ECtHR) (2006) paras. 45–55.

different. In *Refah Partisi and Others* v. *Turkey* and *Leyla Şahin* v. *Turkey*, the Court gave preference to the protection of Turkey's secular state when pitted against freedom of religion, freedom of association and women's rights.[76] *Lautsi* v. *Italy*, where the GC reversed a Chamber judgment on freedom of religion following a public outcry in Italy over the ban of crucifixes in the classroom, is another case in point.[77]

Such cases raise broader questions of the political stance taken by the ECtHR, which has been accused of being too accommodating and 'conservative'.[78] However, the jurisprudence of the Court is rather mixed in this regard. In several instances it has given a broad interpretation to rights, for example by identifying positive obligations to provide protection against environmental pollution pursuant to articles 2 and 8.[79] It has also issued a number of judgments against states that were highly politically charged. These include *McCann* v. *UK*, where the Court held that the killing of three IRA operatives by British security forces violated their right to life because of failings in the planning of the operation; *Hirst* v. *UK*, concerning prisoners' right to vote; and several cases relating to serious violations in the conflicts in Turkey and Russia discussed in Interview 6.2.

Conversely, some of the ECtHR's jurisprudence may be viewed as reassuring states that it will not rule against them in highly sensitive cases of national interest. *Banković* v. *Belgium*, *Lautsi* v. *Italy*, *Refah Partisi* v. *Turkey* and *Gäfgen* v. *Germany* are examples pointing to such practice.[80] Several rulings made in 2014, such as *Hassan* v. *UK* (preventive detention in Iraq), *Ibrahim and Others* v. *UK* (restriction of access to a lawyer) and *Hutchinson* v. *UK* (life imprisonment), seemed to give credibility to perceptions that the Court does not want to antagonise its fraught relationship with the British government further.[81] While this approach is prudent in so far as the Court is

---

[76] *Refah Partisi (The Welfare Party) and Others* v. *Turkey* (ECtHR) (2002) paras. 49–136; *Leyla Şahin* v. *Turkey* (ECtHR) (2005) paras. 30–123 and 163–6. See Chapters 8.7.2 and 8.7.4 for further discussion, including of *S. A. S.* v. *France* (ECtHR) (2014).

[77] *Lautsi and Others* v. *Italy* (ECtHR) (2011). See for a prompt, critical response, L. Zucca, 'A Comment on Lautsi', *EJIL Talk* (19 March 2011), online at www.ejiltalk.org/a-comment-on-lautsi; and further, D. McGoldrick, 'Religion in the European Public Square and in the European Public Life – Crucifixes in the Classroom?' (2011) 11 *Human Rights Law Review* 451.

[78] See S. Meckled-García and B. Çali, 'Lost in Translation: The Human Rights Ideal and International Human Rights Law', in S. Meckled-García and B. Çali (eds.), *The Legalization of Human Rights: Multidisciplinary Perspectives on Human Rights and Human Rights Law* (Routledge, 2006) 10–29.

[79] See e.g., *Öneryildiz* v. *Turkey*; *Hatton* v. *United Kingdom*.

[80] *Banković and Others* v. *Belgium and Others* (ECtHR) (2001) (discussed briefly in Chapter 7.2.1.4); *Lautsi* v. *Italy*; *Refah Partisi* v. *Turkey*; *Gäfgen* v. *Germany* (ECtHR) (2010) (discussed in Chapter 8.3.4).

[81] *Hassan* v. *United Kingdom* (ECtHR) (2014); *Ibrahim and Others* v. *United Kingdom* (ECtHR) (2016); *Hutchinson* v. *United Kingdom* (ECtHR) (2015). See critical analysis, with particular

more likely to enjoy the acceptance of states if it respects certain 'red lines', it potentially undermines itself as a guardian of rights, especially in difficult circumstances. This is particularly the case where the Court's reasoning is seen as too cursory (or categorical) and lacking in critical engagement with fundamental underlying questions.[82] The strong dissenting opinions in cases such as *Lautsi* v. *Italy*, *Gäfgen* v. *Germany* and *Leyla Şahin* v. *Turkey* provide glimpses of the dissatisfaction that such reasoning is bound to cause, both within and outside the Court.[83] The Court's reasoning has also been criticised in other cases, such as in *Behrami and Behrami* v. *France* and *Saramati* v. *France, Germany and Norway*, a case concerning the responsibility of national troops acting in Kosovo under UN authorisation.[84] In *Kononov* v. *Latvia*, the GC appeared to realise that the Chamber's application of international law had been highly questionable when it reached a judgment diametrically opposed to that of the Chamber. It held that article 7 ECHR (prohibition of retrospective application) did not prevent Latvia from prosecuting Mr Kononov for war crimes committed in 1994 even though applicable domestic law at the time did not recognise war crimes.[85]

6.2.6   Impact

The ECHR and ECtHR have had a profound impact on the development of international and national human rights law. The ECHR is, somewhat ironically, one of the colonial legacies that left its imprint in national systems of human rights protection,[86] and the ECtHR's jurisprudence has been referred to by national, regional and international courts and bodies. The system is at the heart of the regional human rights culture in Europe, with the ECHR as the main reference point for human rights that underpins the CoE's work. As interpreted by the ECtHR and national courts, the ECHR has also become increasingly influential for the EU. Respect for human rights is one

reference to the ECtHR's jurisprudence in the *Othman (Abu Qatada)* v. *UK* and *Austin and Others* v. *UK* (ECtHR) (2012) cases, H. Fenwick, 'An Appeasement Approach by the European Court of Human Rights?' (5 April 2012), online at https://ukconstitutionallaw. org/2012/04/05/helen-fenwick-an-appeasement-approach-in-the-european-court-of-human-rights/.

[82] See in this regard, critique by Judge Loucaides, 'Reflections of a Former European Court of Human Rights Judge on his Experiences as a Judge' (26 July 2010), online at www.errc.org/cikk.php?page=8&cikk=3613. See further regular, and annual ('Best and Worst ECtHR judgments') reviews of ECtHR judgments on the blog, www.strasbourgobservers.com.

[83] See dissenting opinions by Judge Malinverni joined by Judge Kalaydjieva in *Lautsi* v. *Italy*; joint partly dissenting opinion of Judges Rozakis, Tulkens, Jebens, Ziemele, Bianku and Power in *Gäfgen* v. *Germany*; and of Judge Tulkens in *Leyla Şahin* v. *Turkey*.

[84] See on *Behrami and Behrami* v. *France* and *Saramati* v. *France, Germany and Norway* (ECtHR) (2007), Chapter 7.2.1.2.

[85] *Kononov* v. *Latvia* (ECtHR) (2010).

[86] K. Vasak, 'The European Convention of Human Rights Beyond the Frontiers of Europe' (1963) 12 *International & Comparative Law Quarterly* 1206.

of the accession criteria for EU membership, and it has been used as a yardstick for countries such as Bulgaria, Romania and Turkey.[87] The Charter for Fundamental Rights, now incorporated in the Lisbon Treaty, draws on the ECHR.[88] Plans for the EU to become a party to the ECHR further underscore the Convention's status as the central European human rights instrument with the ECtHR as the final arbiter.

At the national level the ECHR has been directly incorporated in its member states[89] and consistently applied, or referred to, by national courts.[90] The ECtHR's jurisprudence has affected a number of rights and compelled states to undertake a series of legislative and institutional changes. These include granting particular rights, such as equal rights for children born out of wedlock in Belgium,[91] and strengthening the rights of mentally disabled persons in Russia.[92] They also comprise reforms in the administration of justice, particularly providing adequate remedies, such as in several post-communist countries,[93] or in policing practices, such as in the UK.[94] The potential application of the ECHR to acts committed abroad, particularly where forces are engaging in operations extraterritorially, such as the UK's forces in Iraq,[95] significantly extends its reach and has profound consequences for member states engaged in armed conflict beyond their borders. Systemic shortcomings, such as chronic delays in legal proceedings in Italy, or deep-seated discrimination, such as is faced by migrants across the continent or the Roma in several Eastern European countries, have been particularly taxing, often generating a large number of cases without resulting in the changes needed to ensure effective protection. Even though it has repeatedly emphasised states' positive duty to investigate violations, the ECtHR has found it difficult to break cultures of impunity, particularly in the Turkish and Russian context, as Interviews 6.1 and 6.2 demonstrate.

---

[87] According to the Copenhagen membership criteria, a 'candidate country must have achieved stability of institutions guaranteeing democracy, the rule of law, human rights and respect for and protection of minorities'.

[88] See 6.2.8.

[89] See R. Blackburn and J. Polakiewicz (eds.), *The European Convention on Human Rights and its Member States, 1950–2000* (Oxford University Press, 2001).

[90] See M. Andenas and E. Bjorge, *National Implementation of ECHR Rights: Kant's Categorical Imperative and the Convention*, University of Oslo Faculty of Law Legal Studies Research Paper Series (2011) no. 2011–15.

[91] *Marckx* v. *Belgium* and *Vermeire* v. *Belgium*.

[92] *Shtukaturov* v. *Russia* (ECtHR) (2008). See also Mental Disability Advocacy Centre, 'Russia: Strategic Litigation Leads to Law Reform', online at http://mdac.info/node/708.

[93] See in particular *Broniowski* v. *Poland*; *Kudla* v. *Poland* (ECtHR) (2000); and *Burdov* v. *Russia* (No. 2) (ECtHR) (2009).

[94] See A. Donald et al., *Evaluating the Impact of Selected Cases under the Human Rights Act on Public Services Provision* (Equality and Human Rights Commission, 2009) 28–39.

[95] See *Al-Jedda* v. *United Kingdom*; *Al-Skeini and Others* v. *United Kingdom*.

INTERVIEW 6.1

The Nature and Impact of Litigation Concerning Turkey

(Başak Çali)

Turkey – a party to the ECHR since 1954, having accepted the right of individual petition in 1987 – has experienced military dictatorships and conflict in the Kurdish-populated south-east of the country. Its reliance on a secular nation state built on a strong military led to systemic problems that were frequently characterised by serious human rights violations. In the 1990s Turkish lawyers, academics and NGOs such as the Essex European Court of Human Rights Litigation Project,[1] the Human Rights Association, Diyarbakir[2] and the Kurdish Human Rights Project[3] identified litigation before the ECtHR as one of the strategies to seek justice and bring about systemic changes. The goal of this endeavour was to establish a public record of violations and to compel Turkey to hold perpetrators accountable, provide reparation and undertake substantial reforms. The litigation resulted in a large number of cases that provided an anatomy of violations, especially in the south-east of the country, and shortcomings in the Turkish legal system. Turkey had a strong incentive to comply because of its wish to accede to the EU. It has paid considerable amounts of compensation and carried out a series of legislative reforms, such as removing immunity for officials or abolishing the death penalty at the time of the *Öcalan* case.[4] However, the ECtHR's overall impact has been limited by the fact that Turkey has been less willing to investigate and prosecute serious human rights violations, and impunity remains a problem.

Dr Başak Çali is a legal academic and practitioner. She is Professor of International Law at the Hertie School of Governance and Founding Director for the Center of Global Public Law at Koç University Law School and has litigated cases before the ECtHR. She recently completed a major study on the legitimacy and authority of supranational human rights courts and has examined the impact of cases brought before the ECtHR from South-east Turkey between 1996 and 2006 on the acknowledgement of state violence in Turkey.[5]

---

[1] See the Essex Human Rights Centre, www.essex.ac.uk/hrc/.

[2] See http://en.ihd.org.tr.

[3] See www.khrp.org.

[4] *Öcalan* v. *Turkey* (ECtHR) (2005).

[5] B. Çali, 'The Logics of Supranational Human Rights Litigation, Official Acknowledgement and Human Rights Reform: The Southeast Turkey Cases before the European Court of Human Rights, 1996–2006' (2010) 35 *Law and Social Inquiry* 311.

You write that '[s]upranational human rights courts are institutional sites that provide specialized vocabulary, structure, and opportunities for participation in addressing state violence and the process of acknowledgement'. What is the ECtHR's record in relation to Turkey in this regard?

The South-east Turkey cases discuss exactly that. While the cases themselves offer this crucial vocabulary and enabled victims of human rights violations to access justice, the judgments are not the final say on acknowledgement of state violence, in particular in the context of counter-terrorism operations. That is, human rights judgments can act as tools of acknowledgement only if state authorities are willing to accept them as such. In Turkey we have seen resistance to that.

NGOs and others have pursued a number of cases and the ECtHR has established a considerable record of violations. However, you still suggest that litigation failed to act as a catalyst for domestic acknowledgement. What are the factors that explain the failed 'transmission' of these cases?

In my study I argue that such factors are mostly discursive and political (some also call them ideological or ideational). In other words Turkey is not a country that faces shortcomings in its material or institutional capacity to implement human rights judgments. I argue that Turkish ruling elites have not seen the counter-terrorism operations from a human rights perspective and have, therefore, regarded judgments against themselves as taking sides, i.e. supporting the terrorists against the Turkish state. This has been a major obstacle for recognising the human rights violations for what they are.

You take issue with a reading that views Europe's (ECtHR, CoE and EU) reform efforts vis-à-vis Turkey as exemplary in bringing about major domestic changes. What approach other than the 'technical-bureaucratic' one you criticised could the European bodies have taken in engaging with Turkey in what are surely long-term processes?

One of the ECtHR's weaknesses has been its lack of attention to truth and acknowledgement in its approach to remedies. On the one hand this is understandable. The ECHR as well as a large proportion of the Court's case law has not been about adjudicating gross and systemic human rights violations. The CoM also has not taken a bold stance. For example, it has never asked Turkey to publicly apologise to the victims or institute other processes of public acknowledgement or healing. It has limited itself to asking for statistics of prosecutions of security forces involved in human rights violations. In contrast, such apologies are an everyday practice in the Inter-American Human Rights System. This leaves the EU – an institution pretty much free to make demands from Turkey under its Copenhagen accession criterion of human rights. However, the EU has side-lined truth and acknowledgement in favour of an approach demanding that Turkey grant more rights to its Kurdish citizens. This has meant that – albeit for different reasons – no international pressure was there to help push the acknowledgement of violations other than the voices of the judgments themselves. The approach I advocate is clear: international organisations should have insisted on public acknowledgement of state violence.

What are the broader lessons that can be learned from the impact of ECtHR litigation in Turkey?

The ECtHR litigation in Turkey has addressed very diverse issues, ranging from state-sponsored violence to freedom of expression, from property rights to administration of justice and arbitrary detention. The impact of such litigation has also varied depending on the issue – this is not surprising and is to be expected in other countries, too. The South-east Turkey cases are special in one sense, as official bodies challenged the very basis of these judgments, the evidence provided by the witnesses and the authenticity of victims. While Turkey has paid monetary compensation and carried out a number of legislative reforms, the prosecution rates of state officials have remained low and the violations have never been officially acknowledged. It is, of course, not reasonable to expect too much from the ECtHR judgments. I think that full implementation is generally more puzzling than no implementation when we analyse judgments from supranational human rights courts with no final authority over states. Lessons we learn from the South-east Turkey litigation are that: (1) each issue in each country brings with it a complex constellation of factors that explain why human rights judgments are implemented, contested or ignored, and these should be addressed even when litigating a case; (2) different remedies face different levels of resistance in terms of implementation. The remedies that require a change in mindset are those that are hardest to implement.

In Russia, developments show some parallels. Domestic NGOs, such as the Nizhny Novgorod Regional Committee against Torture[6] and Memorial,[7] as well as external actors, such as the European Human Rights Advocacy Centre,[8] seized on the opportunity offered and brought a number of applications before the ECtHR. These cases concerned both systemic problems of law enforcement and the administration of justice, as well as serious violations committed in the conflict in Chechnya.[9] Russia introduced some

---

[6] See www.pytkam.net.
[7] See www.memo.ru/eng.
[8] See http://ehrac.org.uk.
[9] See for a good overview, http://ehrac.org.uk/about-our-work/human-rights-litigation/.

changes as a result, but systemic challenges regarding the rule of law remain. This includes in particular impunity for serious human rights violations committed in counter-terrorism operations and in the conflict in Chechnya. An important feature of developments in Russia is the readiness of numerous individuals and lawyers in Russia independently to take cases to Strasbourg. While this has resulted in a large number of inadmissibility decisions, it has given Russian cases before the ECtHR a pluralistic complexion. It also means that the ECHR and recourse to the ECtHR are increasingly seen as an integral extension of Russia's legal system and that domestic actors are much more aware of the ECHR's role and value, both as an additional remedy and as a means to advocate change.

INTERVIEW 6.2

The Nature and Impact of Litigation Concerning Turkey and Russia
(Bill Bowring)

Bill Bowring is a Professor at Birkbeck College and a Barrister at Field Court Chambers, Gray's Inn, who has litigated over a hundred cases against Armenia, Azerbaijan, Estonia, Georgia, Latvia, Russia and Turkey before the ECtHR. He has published widely on international law, human rights and Soviet and Russian law.[1]

How would you describe the nature of cases that you brought against Turkey and Russia before the ECtHR?

First, with the Kurdish Human Rights Project, I litigated a number of cases against Turkey in the 1990s. Significant cases in which applicants I represented won concerned the positive duty of the state to protect freedom of expression,[2] death in custody by torture,[3] and disappearance of an applicant's two sons at the hands of the army.[4]

In 2003 I founded the European Human Rights Advocacy Centre (EHRAC), in partnership with the Memorial Human Rights Centre in Moscow and the Bar Human Rights Committee, with a €1 million grant from the European

---

[1] See in particular, B. Bowring, *The Degradation of the International Legal Order? The Rehabilitation of Law, and the Possibility of Politics* (Routledge, 2008); B. Bowring, *Law, Rights and Ideology in Russia: Landmarks in the Destiny of a Great Power* (Routledge, 2013).

[2] *Özgür Gündem* v. *Turkey* (ECtHR) (2000).

[3] *Aktaş* v. *Turkey* (ECtHR) (2003).

[4] *Ipek* v. *Turkey* (ECtHR) (2004).

Commission. We litigated the first six Chechen cases against Russia.[5] We also brought the first environmental case against Russia – *Fadeyeva* v. *Russia*[6] – as well as many Chechen, environmental, discrimination and other cases since then. I am now representing the applicant in *Carter* v. *Russia* (murder of Aleksandr Litvinenko).

The Turkish judgments are important in the Russian context as they are constantly referred to in the pleading and judgments, especially in the Chechen cases which still continue.

What has been the main goal of bringing cases before the ECtHR?

We take a case to complain about specific violations suffered by specific victims. The objective, in our cases, which often take at least five to six years until judgment, is to vindicate the individual applicants' complaints. Therefore, the main goal is to win a judgment against the state in question. Cases vary. In most cases what the applicants want is certainly not money but affirmation by the highest judicial organ in Europe of the truth of what has happened to them and their relatives. However, in the many disappearance cases against Turkey and Russia, what the applicants really want from enforcement is a thorough and effective investigation into the disappearance of their children and close relatives and the identification and prosecution of those responsible. The enforcement procedures of the CoE are so far less than effective.

What would you say are the main achievements of litigation in relation to Russia before the ECtHR?

Russia has in every case paid the just satisfaction ordered by the Court, providing some measure of justice for individual victims. As a result of *Kalashnikov* v. *Russia*[7] and eighty more cases up to *Ananyev* v. *Russia*[8] there have been real reforms in the penitentiary system. Russia is now subject to pilot judgments in *Ananyev* v. *Russia* (conditions in pre-trial detention), in addition to *Burdov* v. *Russia No. 2* (non-enforcement of judgments),[9] and has responded constructively. The Chechen cases have given the applicants and the whole Chechen people unassailable accounts of what happened from 1999 onwards. Russian law textbooks and commentaries are now full of Strasbourg judgments, which shows that the

---

[5] *Khashiyev* v. *Russia*; *Akayeva* v. *Russia*; *Isayeva* v. *Russia*; *Yusupova* v. *Russia*; *Bazayeva* v. *Russia*; *Isayeva and Others* v. *Russia* (ECtHR) (all 2005).

[6] *Fadeyeva* v. *Russia* (ECtHR) (2005).

[7] *Kalashnikov* v. *Russia* (ECtHR) (2003).

[8] *Ananyev and Others* v. *Russia* (ECtHR) (2012).

[9] *Burdov* v. *Russia* (No. 2) (ECtHR) (2009).

ECHR and the ECtHR jurisprudence have become an integral part of the Russian legal system.

What are the challenges for the ECtHR to fulfil its role effectively in relation to countries such as Russia?

The main challenge is for states to implement the Convention properly in their domestic systems as they have bound themselves to do. In every CoE member state this is a long and complex process. Russia has in fact done not at all badly in complying with the twenty-nine obligations it undertook in 1996 on joining the CoE. The UK is presently the only member state defying the Court (*Hirst* v. *UK*).[10]

The European system also has its own limitations, particularly: (1) the ECHR, like the 1789 *Déclaration des droits de l'Homme et du Citoyen*, for the most part protects only civil and political rights and is effectively an eighteenth-century document, somewhat antiquated compared to the ICCPR, American Convention on Human Rights (ACHR) and the African Charter on Human and Peoples' Rights (ACHPR); (2) the Court is often excessively deferential to states; (3) despite reforms, cases take from six to twelve years after exhaustion of domestic remedies; (4) enforcement is very slow, opaque and weak.

You mentioned the UK. What are your views on the government's plans to replace the Human Rights Act with a British Bill of Rights? How do you expect this to be perceived in countries such as Russia?

In my view British hostility to the ECHR and to the judgments of the Strasbourg Court can be traced back to British condemnation of the French *Déclaration*, and our antipathy since 1789 to lists of enforceable rights. Although Britain ratified the ECHR in 1951, we did not allow individuals to complain to the Court until 1966, and only (partially) incorporated the ECHR into UK law in 1998 in the Human Rights Act, which came into force in 2000, but preserves parliamentary supremacy by ensuring that UK courts cannot overrule acts of Parliament on human rights grounds. Until 2000, it was not possible to argue the ECHR before the UK's courts. Both Turkey and Russia incorporated the ECHR into their domestic law when they ratified, in Russia's case in 1998, and from that moment complainants could argue the ECHR and its case law in the Russian courts. If the UK was to repeal the Human Rights Act that would not only be a step backwards for the UK but would set a very bad example to all forty-seven states in the ECHR system, Russia in particular.

---

[10] *Hirst* v. *United Kingdom* (ECtHR) (2006).

POINTS TO CONSIDER

1. How effective has litigation been in securing individual justice and addressing systemic human rights problems in Turkey and Russia?

2. What are the lessons from the Turkish and Russian experience for human rights lawyers dealing with countries confronted with systematic and systemic violations?

6.2.7   The Struggle for Efficiency, Effectiveness and Institutional Reforms

The ECtHR is facing two critical challenges: how to cope with its caseload and how to enhance implementation of its judgments. The problems caused by forever rising numbers of applications, particularly increasing delay in the resolution of cases and the need for more resources, have been apparent since the 1990s. Protocol no. 11, which effectively abolished the European Commission of Human Rights, was meant to streamline procedures. However, a growing number of member states and the greater awareness and willingness of those within their jurisdictions to resort to the Court has since resulted in an exponential rise in applications. In 2011 there was a monthly deficit of over a thousand in respect of 'cases allocated and cases disposed of', which resulted in a 9 per cent increase of pending applications, totalling 151,600 by the end of the year.[96] This situation was seen as unsustainable. The Court and CoE have pursued two parallel responses to this crisis, in the form of pilot judgments and by means of procedural and structural reforms.

The pilot-judgment procedure was developed in response to systemic problems resulting in a series of applications that essentially address the same issue and clog the system. Instead of dealing with each application individually the ECtHR started using a new procedure in the case of *Broniowski* v. *Poland*, which concerned over 80,000 claims for compensation relating to expropriation of property.[97] The purpose of the procedure is to settle a large number of pending cases and prevent repeat applications by inducing the state effectively to resolve systemic problems. The procedure may be initiated by the Court 'on its own motion or at the request of one or both parties'.[98] If, in its pilot judgment, the Court identifies a systemic problem giving rise to violations it adjourns all pending cases and grants states a limited period of time to address the matter, including by providing effective national remedies, or face the prospect of a series of adverse judgments. In its practice,

---

[96] See ECtHR, *Analysis of Statistics 2011* (2012) 4–6.
[97] *Broniowski* v. *Poland*.
[98] Rule 61(2) Rules of Court.

the ECtHR has issued several high-profile pilot judgments that concerned a range of systemic issues, such as excessive length of domestic proceedings, non-enforcement of domestic judgments, or prison conditions.[99]

The pilot-judgment procedure constitutes an innovative approach that has had some success, particularly where domestic bodies, such as constitutional courts, have been supportive and states have had an interest in resolving the underlying issues.[100] It therefore holds some promise for the ECtHR having a 'constitutional' impact and contributing to the strengthening of domestic procedures and remedies. However, a series of practical questions remain concerning selection, application and impact of the procedure on individual claimants.[101]

A number of individuals, states and bodies within the CoE framework have been working to identify what other steps can be taken to increase the effectiveness of the system. One major outcome was Protocol no. 14, which was opened for signature in 2004 and came into force in 2010 after substantial delays caused by Russia's initial non-ratification.[102] The Protocol introduces a number of changes aimed at streamlining procedures.[103] Significantly, a single judge can rule on the admissibility of applications (instead of three judges previously). Cases can be dismissed where they are manifestly inadmissible or 'where the applicant has not suffered a significant disadvantage'.[104] The latter formula is problematic because it curtails the right to individual access for violations.[105] It is therefore subject to certain safeguards[106] and the Court's dealing with cases on this ground merits close

---

[99] P. Leach, H. Hardman, S. Stephenson and B. Blitz, *Responding to Systemic Human Rights Violations: An Analysis of 'Pilot Judgments' of the European Court of Human Rights and their Impact at National Level* (Intersentia, 2010) 15–23, and ECtHR, *Factsheet-Pilot Judgments* (January 2019), online at www.echr.coe.int/Documents/FS_Pilot_judgments_ENG.pdf, which refers to cases concerning violations of the right to the protection of property, prolonged non-enforcement of court decisions and lack of domestic remedy, excessive length of proceedings and lack of domestic remedy, exclusion of convicted prisoners from voting, inhuman and/or degrading conditions of detention, and failure to regularise residence status of persons unlawfully removed from the register of permanent residents.

[100] Leach et al., ibid., 177–8.

[101] Ibid., particularly 171–85.

[102] This delay necessitated the adoption of Protocol no. 14bis in 2009.

[103] See P. Lemmens and W. Vandenhole (eds.), *Protocol no. 14 and the Reform of the European Court of Human Rights* (Intersentia, 2005).

[104] Art. 35(3)(b) ECHR.

[105] See X. B. Ruedin, 'De minimis non curat the European Court of Human Rights: The Introduction of a New Admissibility Criterion Article 12 of Protocol No. 14' (2008) 1 *European Human Rights Law Review* 80.

[106] Art. 35(3)(b) ECHR provides, in particular, that 'no case may be rejected on this ground which has not been duly considered by a domestic tribunal'. However, this safeguard is to be removed upon entry into force of Protocol no. 15 (2013); see art. 5 of that protocol.

scrutiny.[107] Conversely, a committee of three judges can rule on the admissibility and merits where 'the underlying question in the case ... is already the subject of well-established case-law of the Court'.[108] Protocol no. 14 also seeks to facilitate friendly settlements and strengthens the role of the Court in the enforcement of judgments upon referral by the CoM.[109] Once in force, Protocol no. 15 (2013) will introduce a further significant procedural change, reducing the time limit within which cases have to be brought to the Court from six months to four months.[110]

The measures set out in Protocol no. 14 appear to have made the ECtHR more efficient. In 2014, a total of '56,200 applications were allocated to a judicial formation, an overall decrease of 15% compared with 2013 (65,800) ... It is the first time since 2003 that the allocated number of cases has decreased.'[111] However, there is general consensus that more needs to be done to resolve the challenges facing the system.[112] Enhancing domestic implementation through legislative and institutional reforms as well as judicial protection is key, because it would make recourse to the Court unnecessary.[113] It is clear that domestic actors, including NGOs, the media, parliamentarians, courts and others, such as national human rights institutions,[114] play a vital role in bringing about the requisite changes in what is an ongoing, long-term task.

Is the only solution to the current problems facing the ECtHR for it effectively to become a constitutional court of Europe? In response to this question, it has been suggested that the Court should focus only on fundamental questions, which would shift the emphasis towards national implementation.[115] The pilot-judgment procedure and the admissibility requirements in

---

[107] See e.g., *Shefer* v. *Russia* (ECtHR) (2012); and further, N. Vogiatzis, 'The Admissibility Criterion under Article 35(3)(b) ECHR: A "significant disadvantage" to Human Rights Protection' (2016) 65 *International & Comparative Law Quarterly* 185.

[108] Art. 28(1)(b) ECHR.

[109] Arts. 39 and 46(3) and (4) ECHR.

[110] See art. 4 of Protocol no. 15.

[111] ECtHR, *Analysis of Statistics 2014* (January 2015) 4; 43,000 allocations is the comparable figure for 2018, ECtHR, *The European Court of Human Rights: Facts & Figures 2018* (2019).

[112] See Report of the Group of Wise Persons to the Committee of Ministers, CM(2006)203 (2006), and website for updates, online at www.echr.coe.int/ECHR/EN/Header/The+Court/ Reform+of+the+Court/Conferences.

[113] See Brighton Declaration, adopted by the High Level Conference on the Future of the European Court of Human Rights in April 2012, online at www.echr.coe.int/Documents/ 2012_Brighton_FinalDeclaration_ENG.pdf.

[114] Such as, e.g., the Joint Committee on Human Rights in the UK, www.parliament.uk/ business/committees/committees-a-z/joint-select/human-rights-committee/human-rights-judgments.

[115] See S. Greer, 'What's Wrong with the European Convention on Human Rights?' (2008) 30 *Human Rights Quarterly* 680, and J. Christofferson, 'Individual and Constitutional

Protocol no. 14 ('no significant disadvantage') already point to a more constitutional role for the Court. Further, article 1 of Protocol no. 16 envisages that the highest national courts 'may request the Court to give advisory opinions on questions of principle relating to the interpretation or application of the rights and freedoms defined in the Convention or the protocols thereto'. The suggested shift would have a positive impact on the Court's resources and would allow it to further develop its jurisprudence on fundamental questions of wider importance. However, it has triggered serious concerns that it would undermine the individual relief that is by many seen as being at the heart of the system.[116] There is indeed a risk that individual complaints may be curtailed and that the Court may become selective in responding to European human rights problems. The debate surrounding the nature of the Court demonstrates current fault lines; it also shows that there are no easy solutions to the problems facing it. As developments over the last two decades show, the system cannot escape continuous adjustments. How to effectively function and move beyond crisis management is vital for an institution which, despite all its achievements to date, faces recurring political challenges and is at risk of frustrating those whose rights it is meant to protect.

6.2.8   The EU

The precursor to the EU, the European Community (EC), was meant to be an organisation aimed at European integration principally through the movement of goods, persons, services and capital. Hence, it was not concerned with human rights per se. However, it is clear that the EU, an international organisation based on a 'unique economic and social partnership between 28 countries',[117] has a special role in the promotion and protection of human rights in Europe and beyond in the course of its external human rights policy.[118] While early, ambitious attempts to include human rights protection in

Justice: Can the Power Balance of Adjudication be Reversed?', in J. Christofferson and M. R. Madsen (eds.), *The European Court of Human Rights between Law and Politics* (Oxford University Press, 2013) 181–203. The move towards a more constitutional role is to some extent reflected in paras. 30–4 of the 2012 Brighton Declaration. However, para. 31 of the Declaration equally stresses that '[t]he right of individual application remains a cornerstone of the Convention system'.

[116] See for the position taken by many NGOs, 'Joint Statement for the High Level Conference on the Future of the European Court of Human Rights', Izmir, Turkey (26–27 April 2011), online at www.amnesty.eu/content/assets/Doc2011/Joint_statement_future_of_ECHR_ior610082011en.pdf.

[117] See http://europa.eu/about-eu/basic-information/index_en.htm, as of May 2019 when the question of the United Kingdom's withdrawal from the EU was pending.

[118] See P. Alston (ed.), *The EU and Human Rights* (Oxford University Press, 1999); D. Ehlers (ed.), *European Fundamental Rights and Freedoms* (De Gruyter, 2007).

the system failed, the European Court of Justice (ECJ; later renamed Court of Justice of the European Union (CJEU)) subsequently developed a notable jurisprudence on human rights through its interpretation of Community law.[119] However, it was not until the 1992 Maastricht Treaty (Treaty on European Union) that human rights were formally recognised in EU law. At present, article 6(3) of the Treaty on European Union, as revised by the Lisbon Treaty,[120] stipulates that '[f]undamental rights, as guaranteed by the European Convention for the Protection of Human Rights and Fundamental Freedoms and as they result from the constitutional traditions common to the Member States, shall constitute general principles of the Union's law'.[121] The Charter of Fundamental Rights of the European Union of 2000, which became binding as an integral part of the Lisbon Treaty,[122] presently con-stitutes the EU's major human rights instrument. It encompasses a range of civil, political, economic, social and cultural rights that are contained in its six chapters (dignity, freedoms, equality, solidarity, citizens' rights and justice).[123] However, EU policies and practices in respect of human rights have been contradictory. In contrast to its leading role in areas such as developing anti-discrimination instruments, the EU's policies and conduct in other fields have been the subject of considerable criticism. This applies particularly in respect of asylum and immigration,[124] the EU's limited pro-gress in effectively protecting rights of minorities, such as the Roma,[125] its handling of the debt crisis,[126] and inconsistencies in its external human rights engagement.[127]

The relationship between the EU and the ECtHR constitutes a critical and complex question for human rights protection in Europe. The role of the EU vis-à-vis its member states, particularly its ability to mandate action that may result in a breach of states' obligations under the ECHR, inevitably raised the question whether the EU itself should be bound by European human rights

---

[119] See A. T. Williams, *Human Rights and the European Court of Justice: Past and Present Tendencies*, Warwick Research Papers (2011) no. 2011/06.

[120] Treaty of Lisbon amending the Treaty on European Union and the Treaty Establishing the European Community, EN 17 December 2007 OJ C306/1.

[121] Consolidated Version of the Treaty on European Union, 26 October 2012 OJ C326.

[122] Art. 6(1) Treaty on European Union.

[123] See W. B. T. Mock (ed.), *Human Rights in Europe, Commentary on the Charter of Fundamental Rights of the European Union* (Carolina Academic Press, 2010); S. Peers et al. (eds.), *The EU Charter of Fundamental Rights: A Commentary* (Hart, 2014).

[124] See E. Guild and P. Minderhoud (eds.), *The First Decade of EU Migration and Asylum Law* (Brill, 2011).

[125] G. de Búrca, 'The Road not Taken: The European Union as a Global Human Rights Actor' (2011) 105 *American Journal of International Law* 649.

[126] See Chapter 14.6.

[127] See in the context of migration policies, L. Oette and M. A. Babiker, 'Migration Control à la Khartoum: EU External Engagement and Human Rights Protection in the Horn of Africa' (2017) 36 *Refugee Survey Quarterly* 64.

law. National courts, such as the German Constitutional Court,[128] as well as the ECtHR, have shown considerable reluctance to find that the EU may provide lesser protection than that granted in national constitutions or the ECHR respectively.[129] This unresolved situation was considered unsatisfactory and contributed to the drafting of the Charter of Fundamental Rights. The Charter, which, among other rights, also essentially contains ECHR rights, is binding on the EU and on member states 'only when they are implementing [European] Union law'.[130] The Lisbon Treaty also resolved another fundamental question, namely providing that the EU 'shall accede' to the ECHR[131] and thus become subject to the jurisdiction of the ECtHR (interestingly, the EU had already become a party to the Convention on the Rights of Persons with Disabilities (CRPD), which allows supranational organisations to do so).[132] Discussions about the modalities of becoming a party resulted in a draft accession agreement between the EU and CoE in 2013. However, the planned accession has been called into question following an opinion by the CJEU in 2014, in which it held that the accession agreement had on several grounds failed to account for the autonomy and specificity of EU law, including judicial review by the CJEU.[133] It therefore found that the agreement was not compatible with EU law.[134] The judgment has delayed, though not necessarily entirely derailed, accession. Should the accession proceed, it is clear that such a step would have significant ramifications. It places the ECtHR firmly at the apex of the European human rights architecture. The Court can be expected to be seized with cases that may have potentially far-reaching repercussions for EU policies. Such a development would pose a challenge regarding the scope of review, namely whether the EU would still benefit from a presumption of compliance.[135] At the same time, the broadened scope of the CJEU's jurisdiction, which is now mandated to apply the Fundamental Charter, has raised the possibility of divergence arising from the parallel jurisdiction of both courts (as well as the ECSR).[136] Judging by

---

[128] See decisions known as *Solange I* (Germany) (1974) and *Solange II* (Germany) (1986).

[129] See in particular *Bosphorus* v. *Ireland* (ECtHR) (2006) paras. 150–8.

[130] Art. 51(1) of the Charter.

[131] Art. 6(2).

[132] Art. 42 CRPD.

[133] *Request for an Opinion pursuant to Article 218 (11) TFEU* (CJEU) (2014).

[134] See for a prompt, critical reply, S. Peers, 'The CJEU and the EU's accession to the ECHR: A Clear and Present Danger to Human Rights Protection' (18 December 2014), online at http://eulawanalysis.blogspot.it/2014/12/the-cjeu-and-eus-accession-to-echr.html.

[135] As applied in *Bosphorus* v. *Ireland*, para. 156. The presumption is rebuttable if the 'protection of Convention rights was manifestly deficient'.

[136] Importantly, art. 52(3) of the Charter provides that '[i]n so far as this Charter contains rights which correspond to rights guaranteed by the Convention for the Protection of Human Rights and Fundamental Freedoms, the meaning and scope of those rights shall be the same as those laid down by the said Convention. This provision shall not prevent Union law providing more extensive protection'.

the ECJ's and CJEU's jurisprudence to date, it is reasonable to expect that it will take a pragmatic line that seeks to reflect the ECtHR's jurisprudence as much as possible.[137] Nevertheless, the scope for legal uncertainty inherent in these developments cannot be denied.

QUESTIONS

1. For all its supposed progressiveness, the ECtHR has been rather conservative in its overall approach and has frequently refrained from demanding fundamental changes that appeared merited with a view to securing stronger rights protection. Would this statement constitute a fair assessment of the Court's record to date?

2. Should the ECtHR become more akin to a constitutional court and only hear cases of fundamental importance?

3. Are the Fundamental Rights Charter in the Lisbon Treaty and EU accession to the ECHR the final steps towards a coherent European human rights system?

6.3   THE INTER-AMERICAN HUMAN RIGHTS SYSTEM

6.3.1   Overview

The origins of the Inter-American system date back to regional efforts in the nineteenth century to strengthen cooperation based on mutual respect and non-intervention, which resulted in the establishment of the Pan American Union in 1889–1890.[138] Following World War II, in a process aimed at establishing a peaceful, democratic and liberal regional order, the Organization of American States (OAS) was established in 1948 by virtue of the OAS Charter, with twenty-one member states at the time (thirty-five as of December 2018). One of its first steps was the adoption of the American Declaration on the Rights and Duties of Man, 1948, which predated the UDHR. The American Declaration has a strong emphasis on civil and political rights. Notably, it also acknowledges a number of economic, social and cultural rights and a list of duties, drawing inspiration, among other sources, from

---

[137] See e.g., *Schmidberger* v. *Republik Österreich* (CJEU) (2003) paras. 71–3.

[138] See generally D. Harris and S. Livingstone (eds.), *The Inter-American System of Human Rights* (Clarendon Press, 1998); J. M. Pasqualucci, *The Practice and Procedure of the Inter-American Court of Human Rights*, 2nd edn (Cambridge University Press, 2013); R. K. Goldman, 'History and Action: The Inter-American Human Rights System and the Role of the Inter-American Commission on Human Rights' (2009) 31 *Human Rights Quarterly* 856.

the four freedoms formulated by Roosevelt in 1943.[139] The OAS Charter and the American Declaration constituted the initial normative framework for human rights protection. However, in the first decade it was not complemented by any institutional mechanisms and it took until 1959 to set up the Inter-American Commission on Human Rights (IACHR). The difficulty in reaching agreement on and developing effective procedures was evident, as it was only in 1965 that the Commission was given the power to examine individual complaints based on a violation of the OAS Charter and/or the American Declaration.[140]

In a parallel process, the ACHR was adopted in 1969 after a ten-year drafting period. The Convention focuses mainly on civil and political rights. Notably, it recognises the right to a juridical personality, the right to a name and the right to a nationality,[141] reflecting regional concerns over deprivations of these rights. The Convention also stipulates rights of the child, democratic rights (the right to participate in government) and the progressive development of economic, social and cultural rights.[142] This range of rights gives the Convention a fairly broad scope, which comes, however, at the expense of specific guarantees in relation to the rights of the child and economic, social and cultural rights.[143]

The resulting gap was in part rectified through the adoption of an additional protocol on economic, social and cultural rights in 1988.[144] Further treaties were adopted as part of responses to certain types of serious violations experienced in the region. This comprises the Inter-American Convention to Prevent and Punish Torture in 1985, the Inter-American Convention on Forced Disappearance of Persons in 1994 and the Inter-American Convention on the Prevention, Punishment and Eradication of Violence against Women, 1994, which added important normative layers of protection and international precedents in their respective fields of application.

The adoption of the ACHR and the establishment of the Inter-American Court of Human Rights (IACtHR) in 1979 resulted in a two-track system of human rights protection:

1. The majority of states in the region, twenty-three at present, have become parties to the ACHR, twenty of which have accepted the jurisdiction of the IACtHR.[145] Individual petitions are first brought before the IACHR.

---

[139] Chapter 1.2.5.
[140] Goldman, above note 138, 868.
[141] Arts. 3, 18 and 20 ACHR.
[142] Arts. 19, 23 and 26 ACHR.
[143] See on the political dynamics resulting in the weak status of economic, social and cultural rights, Goldman, above note 138, 860–3, 879, 885.
[144] The other such protocol adopted is the Additional Protocol to the American Convention on Human Rights to Abolish the Death Penalty (1990).
[145] Art. 62 ACHR.

The Commission is empowered to consider cases brought by 'any person or group of persons, or any non-governmental entity legally recognized in one or more member states',[146] and may submit a case to the IACtHR where it finds a violation and a friendly settlement cannot be reached.[147]

2. Cases against other states (that have either not become a party to the ACHR or which do not recognise the jurisdiction of the IACtHR) can only be considered by the IACHR. Where the state concerned, such as the USA or Canada,[148] is not a party to the ACHR, the Commission applies the OAS Charter and the American Declaration.[149]

6.3.2   The IACHR

The IACHR, which is composed of seven independent members elected by the OAS General Assembly and based in Washington DC, has a broad promotional and protective mandate.[150] This includes:

- awareness-raising, including by means of thematic reports. Several of these reports have been highly influential in identifying and addressing human rights problems in specific situations and in the region at large;[151]
- observation of the human rights situation in member states, including by way of conducting country visits. The Commission had conducted ninety-eight visits by the end of 2018.[152] It has published over fifty country

---

[146] Art. 44 ACHR.   [147] Art. 51 ACHR.

[148] The USA and Canada have not become parties by virtue of a combination of concerns, particularly regarding the impact of the ACHR on federal law-making and competences, and on individual rights, such as the right to life on abortion policies. See *Enhancing Canada's role in the OAS: Canadian Adherence to the American Convention on Human Rights: Report of the Standing Senate Committee on Human Rights* (Senate of Canada, 2003); C. Cerna, 'The United States and the American Convention on Human Rights: Prospects and Problems of Ratification', in D. Forsythe (ed.), *The United States and Human Rights: Looking Inward and Outward* (University of Nebraska Press, 2000) 94–109.

[149] According to art. 23 of its Rules of Procedure of 2009, petitions can be brought before the IACHR concerning violations of the OAS Charter, the American Declaration, as well as (against parties to) the ACHR and other listed treaties, namely the Additional Protocol to the ACHR in the Area of Economic, Social and Cultural Rights: 'Protocol of San Salvador', the Protocol to the ACHR to Abolish the Death Penalty, the Inter-American Convention to Prevent and Punish Torture, the Inter-American Convention on Forced Disappearance of Persons, and/or the Inter-American Convention on the Prevention, Punishment and Eradication of Violence Against Women: 'Convention of Belém do Pará'.

[150] See art. 106 OAS Charter and art. 41 ACHR. Information about the work of the IACHR is available on its website at www.cidh.oas.org.

[151] See e.g., Report on Terrorism and Human Rights, OEA/Ser. L/V/II.116 doc. 5 rev. 1 corr. (22 October 2002), and Report on Citizen Security and Human Rights, OEA/Ser. L/V/II doc. 57 (31 December 2009).

[152] See www.oas.org/en/iachr/activities/countries_all.asp for updated status on in loco visits.

reports, which often provide a detailed account of human rights problems encountered, thereby producing an important record of the human rights situation in the continent;[153]

- making recommendations to OAS member states regarding the regional protection of human rights. The Commission has issued several resolutions, including on transnational challenges such as the human rights of migrants and on specific situations, such as granting precautionary measures in respect of detainees in Guantánamo Bay;[154]
- considering petitions by individuals and NGOs. The Commission's caseload has grown steadily and it received 2,957 petitions in 2014, with the majority relating to Mexico, Colombia, Nicaragua, Peru, Brazil, Argentina and Ecuador;[155] and
- submitting cases to the IACtHR. The Commission has referred an average of around twelve cases per year to the Court since 2003 (with an average of fewer than five cases previously), with eighteen cases referred to the Court in 2018.[156]

The IACHR has also created a system of rapporteurships, which monitor and promote respect for specific thematic rights.[157]

The IACHR has been credited for its role in responding to serious human rights violations in the 1970s and 1980s. Notwithstanding the adoption of the ACHR in 1969, the Inter-American system was confronted with serious human rights violations and apparent non-compliance by military dictatorships such as those in Argentina, Chile, Paraguay and Uruguay. Steps taken by the Commission in response, such as an on-site visit to Argentina in 1979 and subsequent exposure of human rights violations, have been viewed as an important factor in reducing violations and undermining the legitimacy of the then regime.[158] Similarly, the Commission played a critical

---

[153] The country reports are available on the IACHR's website. See e.g., Honduras: Human Rights and the Coup d'Etat, OEA/Ser. L/V/II doc. 55 (30 December 2009).

[154] See resolution 3/08, Human Rights of Migrants, International Standards and the Return Directive of the EU, and resolution 2/11, Regarding the Situation of the Detainees at Guantánamo Bay, United States, MC 259–02, and Guantánamo Bay Precautionary Measures (2002).

[155] Statistical data are included in the IACHR's annual report 2018, 58.

[156] Ibid., 75.

[157] Freedom of expression, rights of women, rights of migrants, rights of the child, rights of human rights defenders, rights of indigenous peoples, rights of persons deprived of liberty, rights of persons of African descent and against racial discrimination, and rights of LGBTI persons. See www.oas.org/en/iachr/mandate/rapporteurships.asp.

[158] Report on the Situation of Human Rights in Argentina, OEA/Ser. L/V/II.49, doc. 19 corr. 1 (11 April 1980). See also Goldman, above note 138, 873; S. Canton, 'The Inter-American Commission on Human Rights: 50 Years of Advances and the New Challenges' (Summer 2009) Americas Quarterly, online at www.americasquarterly.org/Inter-American-Commission-Human-Rights.

part in responding to conflict, repression and impunity in countries such as Colombia, Guatemala and Peru in the 1980s and 1990s.[159] The Commission has equally developed a strong focus on assistance in transitional processes, such as in Colombia.[160] It has also paid special attention to the promotion and protection of rights in respect of specific groups, such as the rights of women and indigenous peoples, or in particular contexts, such as counter-terrorism.[161] Over the years the Commission has contributed to the development of American human rights law through its thematic reports and petitions. Several cases before it concerned critical issues, such as the protection of unborn life in the *Baby Boy* case,[162] and the death penalty.[163] Considering the breadth of its mandate it comes as no surprise that the Commission, like other bodies of its kind, suffers from limited resources and a lack of capacity that threaten to undermine the efficiency and effectiveness of its work.[164]

6.3.3   The IACtHR

The IACtHR was established in 1979. It is composed of seven judges elected by the states parties to the ACHR at the OAS General Assembly[165] and is based in Costa Rica. The IACtHR has contentious jurisdiction over cases in relation to alleged violations of the ACHR and any other protocols to which a state is a party.[166] It can also issue advisory opinions regarding

---

[159] Goldman, above note 138, 875–8; V. Abramovich, 'From Massive Violations to Structural Patterns: New Approaches and Classic Tensions in the Inter-American Human Rights System' (2009) 11 *SUR-International Journal of Human Rights* 7, at 23.

[160] See in this regard, Statement by the Inter-American Commission on Human Rights on the Application and Scope of the Justice and Peace Law in Colombia, OEA/Ser. L/V/II.125, doc. 15 (1 August 2006); Violence and Discrimination against Women in the Armed Conflict in Colombia, OEA/Ser. L/V/II doc. 67 (18 October 2006); Principal Guidelines for a Comprehensive Reparation Policy, OEA/Ser. L/V/II.131, doc. 1 (19 February 2008); Truth, Justice and Reparation: Fourth Report on Human Rights Situation in Colombia, OEA/Ser. L/V/II, doc. 49/13 (31 December 2013).

[161] See for the IACHR's reports, www.cidh.oas.org/publi.eng.htm.

[162] '*Baby Boy' Abortion* case (IACHR) (1981). See further Chapter 11.2.3.

[163] See *Felix Rocha Diaz* v. *The United States* (IACHR) (2015); *Peter Cash* v. *The Bahamas* (IACHR) (2014); *Edgar Tamayo Arias* v. *The United States* (IACHR) (2014).

[164] See Report of the Special Working Group to Reflect on the Workings of the Inter-American Commission on Human Rights with a view to Strengthening the Inter-American Human Rights System for consideration by the Permanent Council, OEA/Ser. G, GT/SIDH-13/11 rev. 2 (13 December 2011) 7–16.

[165] Arts. 52–4 ACHR.

[166] Arts. 62 and 19(6) Additional Protocol on Economic, Social and Cultural Rights. See generally on the scope of the IACtHR's jurisdiction (with a particular focus on the Convention of Belém do Pará), *González et al.* ('*Cotton Field*') v. *Mexico* (IACtHR) (2009) paras. 31–81.

the interpretation of the ACHR or other OAS treaties.[167] The exercise of its contentious jurisdiction is circumscribed by two important factors: (1) the state(s) concerned has/have to recognise the IACtHR's competence to hear contentious cases;[168] (2) only the IACHR or states parties can submit cases.[169] This means that the IACHR acts as gatekeeper in the individual complaints procedure. Unlike the ECHR system, individuals cannot bring cases directly before the IACtHR. Initially, applicants did not have any independent role in proceedings. This was problematic where their views diverged from that of the Commission, which was increasingly seen as an anomaly that over time prompted the IACtHR to develop changes in its practice.[170] Under the 2001 and 2009 Rules of Procedures the victims and their representatives have been given a prominent role and effectively function as parties following the referral of a case; they 'may submit their brief containing pleadings, motions and evidence autonomously and shall continue to act autonomously throughout the proceedings',[171] which signals a decisive shift towards the recognition of victims as parties. In addition, the role of Inter-American defender has been established to represent victims who do not have the benefit of legal assistance.[172]

By the end of March 2019, the IACtHR's Series C on contentious cases had reached 374, many of which had been initiated by national and regional NGOs, such as the Centre for Justice and International Law (CEJIL).[173] The inter-state procedure, in contrast, has effectively remained dormant, with not a single judgment on the merits.[174] In the 1980s and 1990s the IACtHR was seized with a limited number of cases of serious violations, including massacres, enforced disappearances, torture and lack of judicial protection, as well as unfair trials.[175] In the 2000s the IACtHR adjudicated a

---

[167] Art. 64 ACHR.   [168] Art. 62 ACHR.   [169] Art. 61 ACHR.

[170] See *Five Pensioners* v. *Peru* (IACtHR) (2003) paras. 152–7; L. Burgorgue-Larsen and A. Ubeda de Torres, *The Inter-American Court of Human Rights: Case Law and Commentary* (Oxford University Press, 2011) 40–7.

[171] Art. 25(1) Rules of Procedure (2009), online at www.corteidh.or.cr/sitios/reglamento/nov_2009_ing.pdf.

[172] Art. 37 Rules of Procedure (2009).

[173] See www.cejil.org. See more generally on strategic litigation in the Inter-American system, Abramovich, above note 159, 14–16.

[174] One case was declared inadmissible by the Inter-American Commission for failure to exhaust domestic remedies. See *Nicaragua* v. *Costa Rica* (IACHR) (2007). See on another inter-state case, *Franklin Guillermo Aisalla Molina, Ecuador* v. *Colombia* (IACHR) (2010).

[175] The IACtHR issued judgments on the merits in a total of twenty-two cases between 1987 and 2000, including its first, *Velásquez Rodríguez* v. *Honduras* (IACtHR) (1988) (enforced disappearance); *Aloeboetoe* v. *Suriname* (IACtHR) (1991) (attack by soldiers on community); '*Street Children*' *Villagrán Morales et al.* v. *Guatemala* (IACtHR) (1999) (abduction, torture and murder of minors).

series of cases characterised by large-scale and systematic violations, many of which had been committed in the course of armed conflict and counter-insurgency (such as in Colombia, Guatemala and Peru), and had taken place in a climate of impunity.[176] The IACtHR was also increasingly called upon to rule on inadequate responses to violations in countries such as Bolivia, Brazil and Mexico, reflecting the influence of transitional justice processes.[177] In addition, it focused on collective rights, notably in respect of the rights of indigenous peoples, which have served as international precedents.[178] The IACtHR's jurisprudence on children's rights has also been noteworthy for its focus on strengthening the protection of children and their rights.[179] It has also developed a far-reaching jurisprudence on migrant rights, including on the right to nationality,[180] consular assistance,[181] non-discrimination,[182] immigration detention,[183] expulsion[184] and extradition.[185] Moreover, the IACtHR issued landmark rulings in cases of sexual violence, such as *Castro-Castro Prison* v. *Peru*, where its interpretation of rape and

---

[176] See in particular, the 'massacre' cases, *Mapiripán Massacre* v. *Colombia* (IACtHR) (2005); *Pueblo Bello Massacre* v. *Colombia* (IACtHR) (2006); *Ituango Massacres* v. *Colombia* (IACtHR) (2006); *La Rochela Massacre* v. *Colombia* (IACtHR) (2007); *Plan de Sánchez Massacre* v. *Guatemala* (IACtHR) (2004); *Las Dos Erres Massacre* v. *Guatemala* (IACtHR) (2009); *Miguel Castro Castro-Prison* v. *Peru* (IACtHR) (2006).

[177] *Gomes Lund et al.* v. *Brazil* (IACtHR) (2010); *Ticona Estrada et al.* v. *Bolivia* (IACtHR)(2008); *Radilla Pacheco* v. *Mexico* (IACtHR) (2009). See also Abramovich, above note 159, 8.

[178] See *Yakye Axa Indigenous Community* v. *Paraguay* (IACtHR) (2005); *Sawhoyamaxa Indigenous Community* v. *Paraguay* (IACtHR) (2006); *Saramaka People* v. *Suriname* (IACtHR) (2007); *Xákmok Kásek Indigenous Community* v. *Paraguay* (IACtHR) (2010); *Kuna Indigenous People of Madungandí and the Emberá Indigenous People of Bayano* v. *Panama* (IACtHR) (2014); and *Afrodescendant Communities displaced from the Cacarica River Basin (Operation Genesis)* v. *Colombia* (IACtHR) (2013). See also Abramovich, above note 159, 20–2.

[179] See in particular the *Street Children* case and advisory opinion *Juridical Condition and Human Rights of the Child* (IACtHR) (2002), and, for more recent cases, *Mendoza et al.* v. *Argentina* (IACtHR) (2013) and *Gonzales Lluy et al.* v. *Ecuador* (IACtHR) (2015) (HIV infection resulting from blood transfusion). See for an analysis of the IACtHR's jurisprudence, M. Feria Tinta, *The Landmark Rulings of the Inter American Court of Human Rights on the Rights of the Child: Protecting the Most Vulnerable at the Edge* (Martinus Nijhoff, 2008).

[180] *The Girls Yean and Bosico* v. *Dominican* Republic (IACtHR) (2005).

[181] *The Right to Information on Consular Assistance in the Framework of the Guarantee of the Process of Law* (IACtHR) (1999) and *Juridical Conditions and Rights of the Undocumented Migrants* (IACtHR) (2003).

[182] *Juridical Conditions and Rights of the Undocumented Migrants.*

[183] *Vélez Loor* v. *Panama* (IACtHR) (2010).

[184] *Expelled Dominicans and Haitians* v. *Dominican Republic* (IACtHR) (2014); *Pacheco Tineo family* v. *Bolivia* (IACtHR) (2013).

[185] *Wong Ho Wing* v. *Peru* (IACtHR) (2015).

forced nakedness have proved influential, and the *Cotton Field* case on due diligence obligations in respect of gender-based violence.[186] It has also recognised the rights of LGBTI persons in several recent cases,[187] and in an advisory opinion.[188] In 2017, the IACtHR for the first time found a violation of article 26 (economic, social and cultural rights) in a case concerning the dismissal of a former trade union leader and president of an employee organisation.[189] Overall, the IACtHR's recent jurisprudence has been viewed as signalling a shift in focus 'to structural violence by police on marginal communities, collapsed prison systems and deeply problematic judiciaries'.[190] This jurisprudence in contentious cases has been complemented by a series of important advisory opinions, such as on the derogability of judicial protection during states of emergency,[191] the environment and human rights,[192] as well as the rights of undocumented migrants and the institution of asylum.[193]

Faced with patterns of systematic violations the IACtHR has been cognisant of their political context and dimension, particularly marginalisation, discrimination, institutional rule of law weaknesses and impunity.[194] It has articulated a number of principles and fashioned approaches that have broken new ground in the international understanding of human rights. One prominent example is its jurisprudence on forced disappearances. The IACtHR found that this practice entails multiple (and ongoing) violations, recognised family members as victims in their own right and

---

[186] *Castro-Castro Prison* v. *Peru*, paras. 304–13; *González et al. ('Cotton Field')* v. *Mexico*, paras. 222–411; *Veliz Franco et al.* v. *Guatemala* (IACtHR) (2014); *Espinoza Gonzáles* v. *Peru* (IACtHR) (2014); *Velásquez Paiz* v. *Guatemala* (IACtHR) (2015). See on rape also *Favela Nova Brasilia* v. *Brazil* (IACtHR) (2017) and *Women Victims of Sexual Torture in Atenco* v. *Mexico* (IACtHR) (2018).

[187] *Atala Riffo and Daughters* v. *Chile* (IACtHR) (2012); *Flor Freire* v. *Ecuador* (IACtHR) (2016); *Duque* v. *Colombia* (IACtHR) (2016).

[188] *Gender identity, and equality and non-discrimination with regard to same-sex couples* (IACtHR) (2017).

[189] *Lagos del Campo* v. *Peru* (IACtHR) (2017). See on art. 26 also *Cuscul Piraval et al.* v. *Guatemala* (IACtHR) (2018).

[190] P. Engstrom and A. Hurrell, 'Why the Human Rights Regime in the Americas Matters', in M. Serrano and V. Popovski (eds.), *Human Rights Regimes in the Americas* (United Nations University Press, 2010) 29–55, at 42.

[191] *Habeas Corpus in Emergency Situations* (IACtHR) (1987); *Judicial Guarantees in States of Emergency* (IACtHR) (1987).

[192] *The Environment and Human Rights* (IACtHR) (2017).

[193] *Juridical Conditions and Rights of the Undocumented Migrants*; and *Rights and guarantees of children in the context of migration and/or in need of international protection* (IACtHR) (2014); *The Institution of Asylum* (IACtHR) (2018).

[194] See on the point of structural inequality in particular, Abramovich, above note 159.

identified positive obligations of the state to investigate alleged violations where the perpetrators cannot be identified.[195] It has also been at the forefront of the development of the right to truth, which includes access to state-held information.[196] This comes within the context of its strong emphasis on states' duty to combat impunity, holding in particular that amnesties are incompatible with the duty to investigate and offer effective access to justice for violations such as the right to life and freedom from torture.[197]

The IACtHR's approach is characterised by its *pro-homine* stance[198] and sensitivity towards the human rights problems facing the region. It has developed a practice of hearing detailed evidence, which makes its judgments important records of violations in their own right. The IACtHR's interpretation of the ACHR demonstrates a strong focus on effectiveness, particularly effective remedies. Its jurisprudence on reparation in particular is considered to constitute a major contribution to human rights law.[199] However, the IACtHR has at times been criticised for articulating positions that may find limited support in international human rights law, such as locating the question of labour protection of undocumented migrant workers as a question of non-discrimination having attained the status of *jus cogens*[200] and for introducing notions, such as the *proyecto de vida* (life plan) as a component of reparation,[201] without applying them consistently in its jurisprudence.

---

[195] See in particular the landmark case of *Velásquez Rodríguez* v. *Honduras*, as well as *Goiburú* v. *Paraguay* (IACtHR) (2006), and *La Cantuta* v. *Peru* (IACtHR) (2006).

[196] See *Bámaca Velásquez* v. *Guatemala* (IACtHR) (2000) paras. 197–202; *La Cantuta* v. *Peru*, para. 128; *Gomes Lund* v. *Brazil*, paras. 138–9, 151, 173, 200, 201, 211, 217, 219, 240, 297.

[197] See in particular, *Barrios Altos* v. *Peru* (IACtHR) (2001) paras. 41–4, and *Gomes Lund* v. *Brazil*, paras. 149–80.

[198] According to this principle, the IACtHR interprets the ACHR in a way that 'awards the greatest degree of protection to the human beings under its guardianship'; see further Pasqualucci, above note 138, 12–14.

[199] See Chapter 15.10.

[200] See *Juridical Condition and Rights of the Undocumented Migrants*, para. 101. See critical comments on this approach, J. Cavallaro and S. E. Brewer, 'Reevaluating Regional Human Rights Litigation in the Twenty-First Century: The Case of the Inter-American Court' (2008) 102 *American Journal of International Law* 768, at 822–4. See in defence of this approach, Dembour, above note 74, 309–11.

[201] T. M. Antkowiak, 'Remedial Approaches to Human Rights Violations: The Inter-American Court of Human Rights and Beyond' (2008) 46 *Columbia Journal of Transnational Law* 351, at 371, fn. 101. See also Chapter 15.10.8.

6.3.4   Impact

The IACHR and IACtHR have played an important role in responding to systematic and widespread violations in the region. This includes their emphasis on victims' rights, access to justice and accountability, which has contributed to a significant shift in the regional human rights culture. At the domestic level, states have taken a number of legislative and institutional measures to bring their systems into conformity with the ACHR, either in response to specific judgments or independently, even though compliance has been uneven.[202] This forms part of the growing normative influence of the Inter-American system and its impact on political and judicial actors in the region.[203] However, several problems remain. At the sub-regional level, the non-ratification of the ACHR by the USA and Canada, in combination with the lack of recognition of the IACtHR's jurisdiction by several Central American states, has given the system a decidedly Latin American orientation. This signals embedded fault lines that still hinder the development of a truly American system. At the national level, marginalisation and impunity remain deeply engrained and the Inter-American system has struggled to make an impact on underlying structural political and economic factors that foster violations.[204]

The Inter-American system also faces familiar institutional challenges.[205] While the caseload of the IACHR and the IACtHR – the latter because of the limited number of referrals – is still light in comparison to that of the ECtHR, a growing awareness and willingness to resort to these regional mechanisms is putting an increasing strain on the system.[206] The inadequate resources made available have already forced the IACtHR to reduce the number of hearings, which undermines one of its important functions as a public forum to expose human rights violations.[207] These developments may in time result in further reforms, considering experiences in the European system, and provide victims with direct access to the IACtHR.

---

[202] See F. Basch, L. Filippini, A. Laya, M. Nino, F. Rossi and B. Schreiber, 'The Effectiveness of the Inter-American System of Human Rights Protection: A Quantitative Approach to its Functioning and Compliance With its Decisions' (June 2010) 12 *SUR-International Journal of Human Rights* 9, and Open Society Justice Initiative (OSJI), *From Judgment to Justice, Implementing International and Regional Human Rights Decisions* (Open Society Foundations, 2010) 63–92. See also Chapter 7.5.

[203] See for detailed studies, Cavallaro and Brewer, above note 200, and Engstrom and Hurrell, above note 190.

[204] See in particular Abramovich, above note 159.

[205] See IACHR, Position Document on the Process of Strengthening of the Inter-American System for the Protection of Human Rights, OEA/Ser. L/V/II, doc. 68 (8 April 2012).

[206] Ibid.

[207] Cavallaro and Brewer, above note 200, 797–808. See for the budget, IACtHR, Annual Report 2014 (2015) 77–81.

INTERVIEW 6.3

An Intimate Experience of the IACtHR as Litigant and Senior Staff Attorney

(Oswaldo Ruiz-Chiriboga)

Dr Oswaldo Ruiz-Chiriboga is Assistant Professor, Department of Legal Studies at the Central European University. He worked as a lawyer for CEJIL before serving for six years as Senior Staff Attorney at the IACtHR.[1]

What has been your experience as a litigant before the Inter-American human rights system?

My first exposure came from November 2001 to October 2002 when I coordinated the work of the students of the Human Rights Clinic at the Pontifical Catholic University of Ecuador. We represented victims in several cases before the IACHR and in one case before the IACtHR (*Tibi* v. *Ecuador*).[2] From 2003 to 2005, I worked for CEJIL, which is a major NGO that engages with the Inter-American system at several levels. In my work on the Legal Defence Programme, I led cases on human rights from Honduras and Nicaragua before the Commission and Court. This included researching the case background and precedents, drafting and editing briefs, attending hearings, developing legal arguments, communicating with client NGOs and victims and negotiating with state agents, among other functions. Since I was the only Ecuadorian at CEJIL I also worked closely with its Washington DC office on all the Ecuadorian cases. In addition, as part of my work on the training and dissemination programme, and the Campaign to Strengthen the Inter-American System, I travelled around Central America conducting meetings, seminars and courses with NGOs, public servants, victims of human rights violations and indigenous peoples, among others.

You later on became Senior Staff Attorney at the Court. What did this role entail and how has it changed your views of the Court?

I served in the Court from February 2005 until September 2010. As Senior Staff Attorney I coordinated one of the then six working groups of the

---

[1] Oswaldo Ruiz-Chiriboga maintains a blog on the Inter-American system (in Spanish) at http://corteidhblog.blogspot.co.uk. He is one of the editors of *The Inter-American Court of Human Rights: Theory and Practice, Present and Future*; see below at Further Reading.

[2] *Tibi* v. *Ecuador* (IACtHR) (2004).

Court's permanent Registry (nowadays there are seven groups). Under the general supervision of the Court's Registrar I was in charge of 20 per cent of the cases pending before the Court, exercising executive and operational authority over the unit. This consisted of judicial support, coordination and supervision of the work of interns and junior attorneys. The work entailed a range of tasks. In particular, I drafted legal documents and opinions and provided the necessary legal direction on substantive and procedural issues. This included complex or novel questions on a wide range of international law and human rights issues, including violent conflicts and democratic transitions. My most important task was to assist the Court's judges in drafting the Court's decisions, judgments and advisory opinions.

Serving as a staff attorney was a wonderful experience. It showed me how the Court is able to deal with all its duties and functions even though it does not have sufficient financial and human resources. As is well known, the Court's budget is not enough to cover all its needs, which has forced it to look for external funding. The lack of resources has many implications, the most important being the work overload of all the attorneys. We had to deal with all the contentious cases, advisory opinions and provisional measures. Moreover, since the Court is also in charge of monitoring the compliance of its judgments we had to analyse all the compliance reports submitted by the states and the observations sent by the Commission and the victims' representatives. In short, a case is not over when the Court delivers its judgment. It is only closed when the state has complied with the judgment and this can take years. This fact increases the workload of the Court because it has to deal with pending but also already decided cases. Finally, another consequence of the inadequate funding of the Court is the poor quality of the translations of its decisions.

What impact has the Inter-American Commission and the Court's jurisprudence had in your country?

In *Chaparro Álvarez and Lapo Íñiguez* v. *Ecuador*,[3] the Court ordered the state to modify its Constitution and its national law, because: (1) the habeas corpus remedy was decided by majors and not by judges; and (2) the national law posed arbitrary burdens on persons accused of drug-dealing (the individual had to pay a fee for the administration of his/her seized goods, even if he or she was acquitted). Ecuador complied with

---

[3] *Chaparro Álvarez and Lapo Íñiguez* v. *Ecuador* (IACtHR) (2007).

these orders. However, it is hard to say that the Court's judgment played a significant role in the relevant constitutional amendment, because during that time the country was already in the process of adopting a new Constitution and local stakeholders had a considerable voice. In general terms, I think that one of the major impacts of the Court's judgments in Ecuador and the region is its doctrine of 'Conventionality Control', i.e. the duty of national judges to interpret and apply domestic law in accordance with the Convention.

Overall, what do you see as the strengths and weaknesses of the Inter-American system?

Some of the main points of concern are the insufficient budget for both the Commission and Court; delays in the procedure before the Commission; and lack of transparency in the process of appointing and electing judges and commissioners that may affect the impartiality of the Court and the Commission. OAS states have raised several points of concern regarding the work of the Commission, pointing out weaknesses in the procedure of precautionary measures, friendly settlements, preparation of annual reports and the work of the rapporteurships, though I am not sure how justified they are, except in respect of the system of rapporteurships. In addition, the Court has at times not been clear in its interpretation of the Convention and other regional treaties, for instance in *Acevedo Buendía et al. v. Peru*[4] it declared it has contentious jurisdiction over article 26 ACHR (economic, social and cultural rights), but in doing so it ignored the Protocol of San Salvador. On other occasions the Court has imported decisions of other tribunals, particularly the ECtHR, without considering that such decisions were based on the European regional consensus, which may not be similarly present in the Americas.

As to its strengths, the Court is very open to interpreting the Convention in such a way that groups traditionally excluded, for instance indigenous peoples, could find international protection for their cultural particularities. It is also the leading tribunal on reparation issues. In addition, the Court has modified its Rules of Procedure to expedite the process before it, to facilitate the participation of victims, to allow the participation of new actors (the Inter-American Defender, for instance) and to minimise the expenses of victims (for example the Fund for Victims).

---

[4] *Acevedo Buendía et al. ('Discharged and Retired Employees of the Comptroller') v. Peru* (IACtHR) (2009).

In light of this, what do you see as the main challenges facing the Inter-American system today?

The main challenges include achieving universality of the Inter-American system by encouraging ratification of its treaties by all the OAS member states; ensuring full compliance with the recommendations and decisions made; improving procedures and ensuring strict observance of the regulatory frameworks in the individual petitions system; increasing efficiency and expediency in the processing of petitions and cases and moving towards greater transparency in the management of the system, particularly the Commission.

QUESTIONS

1. What are the defining characteristics of the Inter-American system?
2. Is it possible to speak of a truly American human rights system?
3. Have the Inter-American bodies successfully responded to human rights problems prevailing in the continent?
4. What role did the Inter-American system play in the context of national transitions from dictatorships, such as those in Argentina and Peru?

6.4   THE AFRICAN HUMAN RIGHTS SYSTEM

6.4.1   Overview

Human rights formed part of the broader agenda of the Pan African Congresses in the anti-colonial struggle prior to independence.[208] However, the Organisation of African Unity (OAU) established in 1963 largely omitted any mention of human rights, emphasising decolonisation, state sovereignty and development instead. It was only in the late 1960s that proposals for an African human rights instrument began to be put forward that ultimately

---

[208] See on the development of the African human rights system, K. O. Kufuor, *The African Human Rights System: Origin and Evolution* (Palgrave Macmillan, 2010); F. Ouguergouz, *The African Charter on Human and Peoples' Rights: A Comprehensive Agenda for Human Rights* (Martinus Nijhoff, 2003) 19–48; F. Viljoen, *International Human Rights Law in Africa*, 2nd edn (Oxford University Press, 2012) 151–69; M. Killander, 'African Human Rights Law in Theory and Practice', in S. Joseph and A. McBeth (eds.), *Research Handbook on International Human Rights Law* (Edward Elgar, 2010) 388–413.

resulted in the adoption of the ACHPR in 1981 and the establishment of the African Commission on Human and Peoples' Rights (ACmHPR). The ACHPR is remarkable as it covers a wide spectrum of civil and political rights, though not always drafted with sufficient precision, such as the right to a fair trial,[209] as well as economic, social and cultural rights. It is the only major human rights treaty that recognises a set of collective rights, including the right to development, the right to peace and security and the right to a satisfactory environment.[210] The ACHPR also lists a number of individual duties 'towards his [and her] family and society, the state and other legally recognized communities and the international community'.[211] The emphasis on duties, together with the recognition of collective rights, has been viewed as a genuine African feature of the treaty.[212] Yet the impact is limited because there are no procedures to enforce these duties and hold individuals liable for a breach; in practice, the relevant provisions (articles 27–9) serve to qualify rights, that is they provide the grounds on which states may restrict the exercise of rights such as freedom of expression.[213]

After a hesitant beginning, the African human rights system has gained considerable momentum since the 1990s. Political changes and democratisation processes in several states, institutional reforms at the regional level and increasing NGO engagement have contributed to a stronger focus on human rights and several instruments were adopted that addressed various apparent lacunae in the regional system of protection. These include the African Charter on the Rights and Welfare of the Child (1990), the Protocol on the Rights of Women in Africa (2003), the African Charter on Democracy, Elections and Governance (2007),[214] and the African Union (AU) Convention for the Protection and Assistance of Internally Displaced Persons in Africa (Kampala Convention) 2009.[215]

---

[209] Compare art. 7 ACHPR to art. 6 ECHR; art. 8 ACHR and art. 14 ICCPR. The shortcoming has been largely rectified by means of the Principles and Guidelines on the Right to a Fair Trial and Legal Assistance in Africa, doc./OS(XXX)247 (2001).

[210] See arts. 19–24 ACHPR.

[211] Art. 27 ACHPR.

[212] See in particular M. Mutua, *Human Rights: A Political and Cultural Critique* (University of Pennsylvania Press, 2002) 82–92.

[213] See *Tanganyika Law Society and The Legal and Human Rights Centre* v. *Tanzania* (ACtHPR) (2013) paras. 106–9, and, for a discussion of the ACmHPR's jurisprudence in this regard, K. Olaniyan, 'Civil and Political Rights in the African Charter: Articles 8–14', in M. Evans and R. Murray (eds.), *The African Charter on Human and Peoples' Rights: The System in Practice 1986–2006*, 2nd edn (Cambridge University Press, 2008) 213–43, at 220–3.

[214] See on this Charter, including its status as a human rights instrument, 'The African Charter on Democracy, Elections and Governance at 10' (2019) 63 Supplement S1 *Journal of African Law*.

[215] For current status, see OAU/AU treaties, conventions, protocols and charters, online at http://au.int/en/treaties.

Important institutional developments include in particular the establishment of the AU in 2002 (including all African states).[216] In notable contrast to its predecessor, one of the AU's objectives as set out in its Constitutive Act of 2000 is to 'promote and protect human and peoples' rights in accordance with the [ACHPR] and other relevant human rights instruments'.[217] The Act explicitly mentions '[r]espect for democratic principles, human rights, the rule of law and good governance; humanity' as one of the AU's principles.[218] As an exception to the principle of non-interference the Act also recognises 'the right of the Union to intervene in a member State pursuant to a decision of the Assembly in respect of grave circumstances, namely: war crimes, genocide and crimes against humanity'.[219] Significantly, the AU established a number of bodies and procedures with a bearing on human rights and has generally assumed a more proactive role in this field, albeit with a rather mixed record to date.[220] In addition, a protocol to establish an African Court on Human and Peoples' Rights (ACtHPR) (to become part of the African Court of Justice and Human Rights) was adopted in 1998 to provide stronger judicial human rights protection in the region.[221]

Sub-regional developments complement the African human rights architecture. States in the crisis-ridden Great Lakes region have agreed on the Great Lakes Pact, an impressive instrument that seeks to strengthen human rights, accountability and justice in the area.[222] However, its impact has been limited due to the lack of adequate institutional mechanisms.[223] Human rights have also become an important component of sub-regional economic integration. Significantly, the courts of regional economic communities, particularly the East African Community (EAC), the Economic Community of West African States (ECOWAS) and the Southern African Development Community (SADC), prior to its effective suspension in 2010, have increasingly interpreted their jurisdiction as enabling them to adjudicate human

---

[216] See http://au.int/en/about/nutshell; and on the AU's historical development, R. Murray, *Human Rights in Africa: From the OAU to the African Union* (Cambridge University Press, 2004) 1–48; Viljoen, above note 208, 151–69.

[217] Art. 3(h) Constitutive Act of the AU.

[218] Art. 4(m) Constitutive Act of the AU.

[219] Art. 4(h) Constitutive Act of the AU.

[220] See for a good overview, Viljoen, above note 208, 169–212.

[221] Protocol to the ACHPR on the Establishment of an ACtHPR (adopted 10 June 1998, in force since 25 January 2004) (1998 Protocol).

[222] See for further information and the text of the Pact the website of the International Conference on the Great Lakes Region, online at www.icglr.org/index.php/en.

[223] See for an in-depth assessment, D. Clancy, 'Lessons from a State of Flux: The International Justice Laboratory of the Great Lakes Pact', in L. Oette (ed.), *Criminal Law Reform and Transitional Justice: Human Rights Perspectives for Sudan* (Ashgate, 2011) 197–226.

rights cases.[224] Some of these developments have met with resistance or non-compliance, and the proliferation of mechanisms does not necessarily equate with increased effectiveness. Nevertheless, they testify to the growing regional efforts to address human rights at the normative and institutional level. The recognition of the close link between respect for human rights, a stable and democratic order and economic development must count as an important factor behind these changes, which have received added impetus thanks to creative litigation by NGOs and the largely human rights-friendly jurisprudence of the courts.

6.4.2   The ACmHPR

The ACmHPR is based in the Gambia and composed of eleven members who are elected by the AU Assembly of Heads of State and Government and serve in their personal capacity.[225] It has a broad mandate to promote and protect human rights as laid down in article 45 ACHPR. Its promotional mandate includes the consideration of states parties' reports, the study of human rights issues and country-specific situations, including by means of fact-finding missions, and a system of special rapporteurs and working groups.[226] The Commission's protection mandate comprises the consideration of individual and inter-state complaints, a competence that it derived from articles 55 and 56 ACHPR.[227] The Commission meets biannually for its general sessions to fulfil its mandate and may convene special (extraordinary) sessions where called for.[228]

In what was effectively its first decade, the ACmHPR adopted a number of important decisions in the 1990s. These concerned a series of cases, mainly brought by NGOs making use of the broad standing provided for in the Charter, which predominantly addressed mass violations (including violations of the right to life, prohibition of torture, right to liberty, right

---

[224] See in particular, L. N. Murungi and J. Gallinetti, 'The Role of Sub-Regional Courts in the African Human Rights System' (2010) 7 *SUR-International Journal of Human Rights* 119. For latest developments, see the websites of the respective courts, www.eacj.org; www.courtecowas.org; www.sadc.int/about-sadc.

[225] Art. 13 ACHPR. See on the ACmHPR more generally, arts. 30–44 ACHPR, and its website, www.achpr.org.

[226] See Viljoen, above note 208, 289–390.

[227] See on the ACmHPR's 'protective, promotional and interpretive' mandate and the 'different procedures and activities by which the ACmHPR carries out this mandate and which generate findings', R. Murray and D. Long, *The Implementation of the Findings of the African Commission on Human and Peoples' Rights* (Cambridge University Press, 2015) 44–68.

[228] The session reports are available on the ACmHPR's website, www.achpr.org.

to a fair trial and mass expulsions).[229] However, the Commission's decisions were largely confined to short findings of violations, lacked broader visibility and were frequently not complied with. The execution of Ken Saro Wiwa by Nigeria's dictatorship, in blatant disregard of an interim measure by the Commission calling for the suspension of the punishment, is one of the most glaring examples in this respect.[230] Following a series of important cases against Nigeria in the 1990s,[231] the Commission developed its jurisprudence throughout the 2000s. The violations and countries concerned have become more varied, with several high-profile cases against Guinea, Zimbabwe, Eritrea, Angola, Côte d'Ivoire, Sudan and Cameroon.[232] Its first inter-state decision, *Democratic Republic of Congo* v. *Burundi, Rwanda and Uganda*, which concerned the responsibility of the defendant states for a series of violations committed in the course of the conflict in the Democratic

---

[229] See in particular, *Krishna Achuthan (on behalf of Aleke Banda), Amnesty International (on behalf of Orton and Vera Chirwa), Amnesty International (on behalf of Orton and Vera Chirwa)* v. *Malawi* (ACmHPR) (1994); *Organisation mondiale contre la torture, Association Internationale des juristes démocrates, Commission internationale des juristes, Union interafricaine des droits de l'Homme* v. *Rwanda* (ACmHPR) (1996); *Free Legal Assistance Group, Lawyers' Committee for Human Rights, Union Interafricaine des Droits de l'Homme, Les Témoins de Jehovah* v. *Democratic Republic of Congo* (ACmHPR) (1996); *Union interafricaine des droits de l'Homme, Fédération internationale des ligues des droits de l'Homme, RADDHO, Organisation nationale des droits de l'Homme au Sénégal and Association malienne des droits de l'Homme* v. *Angola* (ACmHPR) (1997); *Amnesty International and Others* v. *Sudan* (ACmHPR) (1999); and in the early 2000s, *Malawi African Association, Amnesty International, Ms Sarr Diop, Union interafricaine des droits de l'Homme and RADDHO, Collectif des veuves et ayants-Droit, Association mauritanienne des droits de l'Homme* v. *Mauritania* (ACmHPR) (2000); and *Movement burkinabé des droits de l'Homme et des peuples* v. *Burkina Faso* (ACmHPR) (2001).

[230] *International Pen and Others* v. *Nigeria* (ACmHPR) (1998) para. 115: 'This is a blot on the legal system of Nigeria that will not be easy to erase. To have carried out the execution in the face of pleas to the contrary by the Commission and world opinion is something that we pray will never happen again. That it is a violation of the Charter is an understatement.'

[231] By May 2019, Nigeria was the state with the highest number of cases in the African system. See www.achpr.org/communications and http://caselaw.ihrda.org. See for an account of the impact of the African system on Nigeria, Okafor, above note 2, 91–154.

[232] See *Institute for Human Rights and Development in Africa (on behalf of Sierra Leonean refugees in Guinea)* v. *Guinea* (ACmHPR) (2004); *Zimbabwe Human Rights NGO Forum* v. *Zimbabwe* (ACmHPR) (2006); *Article 19* v. *Eritrea* (ACmHPR) (2007); *Institute for Human Rights and Development in Africa (on behalf of Esmaila Connateh & 13 others)* v. *Angola* (ACmHPR) (2008); *Mouvement ivoirien des droits humains (MIDH)* v. *Côte d'Ivoire* (ACmHPR) (2008); *Sudan Human Rights Organisation & Centre on Housing Rights and Evictions (COHRE)* v. *Sudan* (ACmHPR) (2009); *Association of Victims of Post Electoral Violence & Interights* v. *Cameroon* (ACmHPR) (2009). See also Statistics on the Implementation of the African Charter on Human and Peoples' Rights, 30 years later (ACmHPR, 2011).

Republic of Congo, is remarkable for its parallel application of international human rights law and international humanitarian law by virtue of articles 60 and 61 ACHPR.[233] *Social and Economic Rights Action Center (SERAC) and Center for Economic and Social Rights (CESR)* v. *Nigeria*, which concerned multiple violations committed in the context of oil extraction in Ogoniland, is a leading case, setting a major precedent for its broad application of economic, social and cultural rights.[234] It contains important considerations on collective rights, a jurisprudence that was later complemented in cases of indigenous peoples[235] and groups targeted in the course of armed conflict, such as in Darfur, Sudan.[236] The Commission has in its recent jurisprudence also increasingly emphasised the positive obligations of states to secure rights, such as to take measures to protect individuals from post-election violence in Cameroon.[237] It also issued several rulings that exposed systemic shortcomings in national law and practice, finding respondent states' responsible for a failure to hold accountable perpetrators of serious violence such as torture,[238] including sexual violence,[239] and provide justice to victims.[240]

The ACmHPR's interpretation of the ACHPR has by and large not been underscored by clearly articulated doctrines.[241] Instead, it has been rather pragmatic, drawing freely on a range of sources to support its reasoning.[242] It has emphasised the lack of derogability of rights and has interpreted

---

[233] *Democratic Republic of Congo* v. *Burundi, Rwanda, Uganda* (ACmHPR) (2003). See on the Commission's position on the application of international humanitarian law in cases before it, *Thomas Kwoyelo* v. *Uganda* (ACmHPR) (2018) paras. 149–55.

[234] *Social and Economic Rights Action Center (SERAC) and Center for Economic and Social Rights (CESR)* v. *Nigeria (Ogoniland* case) (ACmHPR) (2001).

[235] *Centre for Minority Rights Development (Kenya) and Minority Rights Group (on behalf of Endorois Welfare Council)* v. *Kenya (Endorois* case) (ACmHPR) (2009).

[236] *Sudan Human Rights Organisation and Centre on Housing Rights and Evictions (COHRE)* v. *Sudan.*

[237] See *Association of Victims of Post Electoral Violence & Interights* v. *Cameroon*, paras. 83–112; *Zimbabwe Human Rights NGO Forum* v. *Zimbabwe*, paras. 142–64.

[238] See on art. 5 of the Charter particularly *Gabriel Shumba* v. *Zimbabwe* (ACmHPR) (2012) paras. 142–66.

[239] *Egyptian Initiative for Personal Rights and Interights* v. *Egypt* (ACmHPR) (2011).

[240] *Abdel Hadi, Ali Radi & Others* v. *Republic of Sudan* (ACmHPR) (2013); *Monim Elgak, Osman Hummeida and Amir Suliman (represented by FIDH and OMCT)* v. *Sudan* (ACmHPR) (2014). See on the compatibility of blanket amnesties with states parties' obligations, obiter dictum in *Kwoyelo* v. *Uganda*, paras. 283ff.

[241] However, see for the ACmHPR's jurisprudence on aspects of admissibility, particularly exhaustion of domestic remedies, F. Viljoen, 'Communications under the African Charter: Procedure and Admissibility', in Evans and Murray, above note 213, 76–138.

[242] According to art. 60 ACHPR, '[t]he Commission shall draw inspiration from international law on human and peoples' rights'.

clawback clauses ('according to the law', 'before the law') broadly to include international law standards, thereby preventing states from narrowing the scope of applicability of rights.[243] The Commission has endorsed the principles of subsidiarity and the margin of appreciation in a recent case but has otherwise not applied these doctrines in its jurisprudence.[244]

The ACmHPR's approach, while seemingly progressive in some instances, appears at times to lack coherence and consistency. It has construed obligations broadly, holding that due diligence is an obligation of results not means.[245] It has also read rights into the ACHPR, such as the right to housing and food in *Social and Economic Rights Action Center (SERAC) and Center for Economic and Social Rights (CESR) v. Nigeria*,[246] which can be viewed either as progressive interpretation or a dangerously loose construction of the treaty that was not necessary to achieve the desired level of protection.[247] Conversely, it has adopted a rather narrow interpretation of state responsibility and obligations where a more purposive one could have been expected to advance the effective protection of human rights, such as in its interpretation of Zimbabwe's fulfilment of its positive obligations in relation to serious violations attributed to the ruling party ZANU-PF.[248] Its fashioning of remedies for violations had been rather general, notably not specifying amounts of compensation,[249] although some, particularly more recent, decisions have identified a series of specific remedies.[250] The jurisprudence of the Commission therefore provides a rather mixed picture characterised by an element of unpredictability that leaves considerable scope for further development.

---

[243] See in particular, *Media Rights Agenda and Constitutional Rights Project v. Nigeria*, paras. 65–70.

[244] *Garreth Anver Prince v. South Africa* (ACmHPR) (2004) paras. 50–4.

[245] *Association of Victims of Post Electoral Violence and Interights v. Cameroon*, para. 111.

[246] The Commission also found a violation of the right to adequate housing, on a combined reading of arts. 14, 16 and 18 of the Charter in *Mbiankeu Geneviève v. Cameroon* (ACmHPR) (2015) paras. 120–4.

[247] See for critical comments on this point, Viljoen, above note 208, 327–8.

[248] *Zimbabwe Human Rights NGO Forum v. Zimbabwe*, paras. 135–87.

[249] With the earlier exception of *Egyptian Initiative for Personal Rights & Interights v. Egypt*, para. 275, where it endorsed the request of the complainants for EP 57,000 (around €6,600) for each of the victims. See now also *Geneviève v. Cameroon*, para. 153; *Hossam Ezzat & Rania Enayet (represented by Egyptian Initiative for Personal Rights & Interights) v. Egypt* (ACmHPR) (2016) para. 185(e).

[250] See in particular *Social and Economic Rights Action Center (SERAC) and Center for Economic and Social Rights (CESR) v. Nigeria*; *Sudan Human Rights Organisation and Centre on Housing Rights and Evictions (COHRE) v. Sudan*; and *Endorois* case. See on this point also OSJI, above note 202, 100–4, and, further, REDRESS, *Reaching for Justice. The Right to Reparation in the African Human Rights System* (2013).

CASE STUDY 6.1
Modise v. *Botswana* and the Question of Nationality Rights

John K. Modise v. *Botswana* is a landmark case on the right to a nationality.[1] Modise, who was born in South Africa but grew up in Botswana, was deported to South Africa because of his political activities. With neither Botswana nor South Africa recognising his citizenship status Modise ended up spending seven years in a South African homeland, and after being deported from there, had to spend five weeks in no-man's land before being admitted back to Botswana on humanitarian grounds. The case revolved around Botswana's refusal to grant Modise nationality, which was found to violate his right to equal protection of the law and to the recognition of his legal status. His deportation and subjection to a miserable state of uncertainty was also held to violate the prohibition of torture and inhuman treatment, the right to family life, freedom of movement, the right to property and the right to participate freely in the government of his country. The case highlighted a number of the many problems surrounding nationality which have beset the continent, and led to the first case decided by the African Committee of Experts on the Rights and Welfare of the Child[2] and initiatives to draft a separate instrument on citizenship rights.[3]

[1] *John K. Modise* v. *Botswana* (ACmHPR) (2000). See on statelessness also *The Nubian Community in Kenya* v. *Kenya* (ACmHPR) (2015).
[2] *IHRDA and Open Society Justice Initiative (OSJI) (on behalf of children of Nubian descent in Kenya)* v. *Kenya* (ACtERWC) (2011). See on the revocation of Sudanese nationality in the wake of South Sudan's secession/independence, *African Centre for Justice and Peace Studies (ACJPS) and People's Legal Aid Centre (PLACE)* v. *Sudan* (ACtERWC) (2018).
[3] See Recommendations of the Civil Society Meeting on African Union mechanisms and the Protection of Refugee, IDP and Citizenship Rights (2009) para. 18, online at www.refugee-rights.org/Publications/PR/2009/CRAI.communique.102209.pdf.

POINT TO CONSIDER

1. **Why is the *Modise* case so emblematic of the challenges facing human rights protection in the African context?**

6.4.3   Impact

The ACmHPR's sessions have become an important forum for the deliberation of human rights in Africa. In its jurisprudence it has begun to develop the contours of a regional human rights culture. Further cross-fertilisation can be expected with sub-regional courts and the ACtHPR, which is examined at 6.4.4 and 6.4.5. However, the Commission's impact has been hampered by a chronic lack of resources, which has undermined the visibility, efficiency and quality of its work and has resulted in ever-increasing delays.[251] One response to this situation has been the Commission's increasingly restrictive rulings on admissibility, which has introduced an element of uncertainty and has limited effective access to the main African human rights body.[252] In addition, pressure exerted by states through the AU appears to have adversely influenced decision-making, such as in relation to the situation in Zimbabwe.[253] Attempts by the AU in 2018 to constrain the Commission's independence are a further indication of the backlash it has faced in recent times.[254] The Commission's impact has also been undermined by insufficient state compliance.[255] This is due to the weak enforcement mechanisms, including by the AU and ACtHPR, and the limited incorporation and application of the ACHPR, which suggests inadequate domestic awareness and follow-up.[256] Yet the situation varies considerably between countries such as Nigeria, where the ACHPR was made part of national law and has been applied by the judiciary,[257] and others, where there has been less visible impact, such as in Sudan. However, owing to the increasing mobilisation of regional and domestic human rights lawyers and NGOs, greater bottom-up impetus can be expected to enhance the role of the ACHPR at the domestic level and across the continent.[258] This will also lead to increased pressure on the system to respond more urgently to a series of regional human rights challenges, including women's rights, rights of lesbian, gay, bisexual, transgender and intersex (LGBTI) persons, HIV/AIDS, marginalisation and entrenched poverty, which have to date been insufficiently addressed in the Commission's jurisprudence.

---

[251] See concerns set out in Joint Letter of Litigants to the Working Group on Communications of the African Commission on Human and Peoples' Rights (4 December 2011), online at www.cihrs.org/?p=353&lang=en.

[252] See the growing number of cases declared inadmissible, particularly for being submitted out of time (see further Chapter 7.2.3.1) and closed for 'lack of diligent prosecution', www.achpr.org/communications.

[253] Viljoen, above note 208, 188–9.

[254] See in particular AU, EX.CL/Dec. 1015 (XXVIII) (28–29 June 2018).

[255] See F. Viljoen and L. Louw, 'State Compliance with the Recommendations of the African Commission on Human and Peoples' Rights, 1994–2004' (2007) 101 *American Journal of International Law* 1; OSJI, above note 202, 93–115.

[256] See in particular, the detailed consideration of the role of various actors by Murray and Long, above note 227, 69–188.

[257] Okafor, above note 2, 148–54.

[258] Ibid., in particular 300–1.

6.4.4   The ACtHPR

The desire to create a judicial body that addresses some of the ACmHPR's weaknesses was the driving force behind NGO advocacy and regional diplomacy to set up a regional human rights court.[259] This movement resulted in the 1998 Protocol which set up the ACtHPR and came into force in 2004. The ACtHPR took up its work in 2006 with its seat in Tanzania. However, a controversial decision made in 2004 to merge the African Court of Justice (ACJ)[260] and the ACtHPR complicated matters during the interim period.[261] In 2008 the AU adopted a protocol to merge the two courts (which replaces the 1998 and 2003 Protocols for each of the respective courts) with a view to the creation of the African Court of Justice and Human Rights one year after the deposit of the fifteenth ratification.[262] The merged court is envisaged to consist of a general affairs and a human rights section. The present ACtHPR, and future merged court, has advisory and contentious jurisdiction, can make provisional orders, issue binding judgments and has an explicit mandate to award reparation and refer binding judgments to the AU Assembly for enforcement.[263] In short, the Court has the potential to substantially strengthen protection and visibility of human rights in Africa.

The protocols establish a two-tier system. Individuals or NGOs can bring cases directly before the Court only following prior acceptance of the Court's competence by member states; otherwise they have to rely on the ACmHPR for doing so.[264] The fact that only nine states had recognised the competence of the Court to receive individual and NGO communications directly as of March 2019 demonstrates the initial reluctance of states to broaden access in a way that would put the Court in a position to fulfil what is arguably its core function.

Only seven states have ratified the merger protocol as of February 2019. The decision in June 2014 to adopt a further protocol on amendments to the

---

[259] See www.africancourtcoalition.org.

[260] The ACJ was set up by a protocol in 2003 (which came into force in 2009).

[261] See for an account of these developments, I. Kane and A. C. Motala, 'The Creation of a New African Court of Justice and Human Rights', in Evans and Murray, above note 213, 406–40.

[262] See Protocol on the Statute of the African Court of Justice and Human Rights (adopted on 1 July 2008) (2008 Protocol).

[263] Arts. 27–31, 1998 Protocol; arts. 35, 45, 46, 2008 Protocol. The provisions applying to the human rights section are broadly similar to the ones contained in the 1998 Protocol, with the exception of the enforcement procedure which envisages an enhanced role for the AU Assembly in the execution of judgments.

[264] Art. 34(6), 1998 Protocol; art. 30(f), 2008 Protocol. Art. 34(6) of the 1998 Protocol was unsuccessfully challenged in *Femi Falana* v. *The African Union* (ACtHPR) (2012) (Dissenting Opinion – Sophia Akuffo, Bernard Ngoepe and Elsie Thompson).

protocol on the statute of the African Court of Justice and Human Rights, vesting it with criminal jurisdiction, has added a new layer of complexity.[265] None the less, the new merged court will in all likelihood be established at some point in the near future. In the meantime, the ACtHPR will be tasked with developing its case law. Its first case was a non-starter and declared inadmissible because it had been brought by an individual against Senegal, a state that had not recognised the ACtHPR's competence to receive such complaints.[266] Since then, it has been seized with a growing number of cases, many of which, particularly in its early period, have been declared inadmissible. In its jurisprudence, the Court has addressed shortcomings in Tanzania's criminal justice system raised in a series of similar cases,[267] the killing of a journalist in Burkina Faso and lack of adequate investigation,[268] criminal sanctions for defamation,[269] the minimum age of marriage[270] and the minimisation of genocide law in Rwanda.[271] In a noteworthy development, the Court held that the African Charter on Democracy, Elections and Governance constitutes a human rights instrument,[272] which gives an indication of the potential scope of its jurisdiction.[273] In 2015, it also issued its first judgment on reparation.[274] In a significant development the ACtHPR adopted provisional measures against Libya in the early stages of the conflict in 2011 to 'immediately refrain from any action that would result in loss of life or violation of physical integrity of persons' following an application by the ACmHPR.[275] While there were no indications that Libya complied with

---

[265] Protocol on Amendments to the Protocol on the Statute of the African Court of Justice and Human Rights (27 June 2014).

[266] *Michelot Yogogombaye* v. *The Republic of Senegal* (ACtHPR) (2009).

[267] See e.g., *Mohamed Abubakari* v. *Tanzania* (ACtHPR) (2016). These cases, which typically concerned thirty years' imprisonment for armed robbery, are noteworthy for finding several violations of the right to a fair trial, including lack of legal aid provision.

[268] *Nobert Zongo and Others* v. *Burkina Faso* (ACtHPR) (2014).

[269] *Lohé Issa Konaté* v. *Burkina Faso* (ACtHPR) (2014).

[270] *APDF & IHRDA* v. *Mali* (ACtHPR) (2018), finding multiple violations of the Maputo Protocol, the African Charter on the Rights and Welfare of the Child, and the Convention on the Elimination of All Forms of Discrimination against Women.

[271] *Ingabire Victoire Umuhoza* v. *Rwanda* (ACtHPR) (2017). See also reference to the Court's 2016 ruling on Rwanda's withdrawal of its declaration made under art. 34(6) of the Protocol (individual petition), which was, unsuccessfully, aimed at suspending pending cases against Rwanda.

[272] *Actions pour la protection des Droits de l'Homme* (APDH) v. *Côte d'Ivoire* (ACtHPR) (2016).

[273] According to art. 2(1) of the 1998 Protocol, the Court's jurisdiction 'shall extend to all cases and disputes sumitted to it concerning the interpretation and application of the Charter, this Protocol and *any other relevant Human Rights instrument* ratified by the State concerned' (emphasis added).

[274] *Nobert Zongo and Others* v. *Burkina Faso* (ACtHPR) (2015).

[275] In the matter of *African Commission on Human and Peoples' Rights* v. *Great Socialist People's Libyan Arab Jamahiriya* (ACtHPR) (2011).

the order, the decision provided a glimpse of the types of interventions the ACtHPR can make. It was also the first time that the Commission referred a matter to the ACtHPR. Subsequently, the Court ruled on two significant cases brought before it by the Commission, one concerning the secret detention of Saïf Al Islam Kadhafi and lack of respect for his right to a fair trial,[276] and the other on the rights of the Ogiek peoples in Kenya.[277]

6.4.5   African Regional Economic Courts

A review of judicial developments in Africa would be incomplete without a brief reference to its regional economic courts.[278] These courts are principally mandated to adjudicate matters falling within the scope of the treaties governing regional economic unions. Upon application by individuals and NGOs, several regional economic courts have interpreted their broad jurisdiction to include the competence to hear human rights cases. The ECOWAS Community Court of Justice, which has an explicit human rights mandate,[279] issued a landmark judgment in which it found that Niger had violated the prohibition of slavery and ordered a series of remedial measures.[280] In another case it found that Gambia, the respondent state, was responsible for prolonged arbitrary detention in breach of the right to liberty and security and the right to a fair trial. It ordered the respondent state to pay US $100,000 compensation, which was in noteworthy contrast to the ACmHPR's then general practice of not specifying amounts of compensation.[281] In another case against Gambia, the Court found that the country's legislation on sedition, criminal libel, defamation and false news publication violated freedom of speech and expression, and that the respondent state had arbitrarily detained and tortured several of the applicants who were journalists.[282] The East African Court of Justice, in a case concerning violations of

---

[276] *African Commission on Human and Peoples' Rights* v. *Libya* (ACtHPR) (2016).

[277] *African Commission on Human and Peoples' Rights* v. *Kenya* (ACtHPR) (2017).

[278] S. T. Ebobrah, 'Litigating Human Rights before Sub-regional Courts in Africa: Prospects and Challenges' (2009) 17 *African Journal of International and Comparative Law* 79; Murungi and Gallinetti, above note 224.

[279] See arts. 9(4) and 10(d) of the ECOWAS Supplementary Protocol A/SP.1/01/05 amending the Protocol (A/P1/7/91) relating to the ECOWAS Community Court of Justice (19 January 2005).

[280] *Mme Hadijatou Mani Koraou* v. *The Republic of Niger* (ECOWAS CCJ) (2008). See H. Duffy, '*Hadijatou Mani Koraou* v. *Niger*: Slavery Unveiled by the ECOWAS Court' (2009) 9 *Human Rights Law Review* 151.

[281] See *Manneh* v. *Gambia* (ECOWAS CCJ) (2008). In a subsequent case against Gambia, the Court awarded US $200,000 compensation for unlawful arrest, detention and torture: *Musa Saidykhan* v. *The Gambia* (ECOWAS CCJ) (2010).

[282] *Federation of African Journalists and Others* v. *Gambia* (ECOWAS CCJ) (2018).

fair trial rights in Uganda, considered itself competent to consider human rights matters notwithstanding article 27(2) of the EAC Treaty, according to which such jurisdiction is subject to a separate protocol.[283] It acknowledged that it is precluded from adjudicating 'on disputes concerning human rights violations *per se*' (emphasis in original), but stressed that it 'will not abdicate from exercising its jurisdiction of interpretation [of the EAC treaty] under Article 27 (1) merely because the reference includes allegation of human rights violation'.[284]

The growing number of judgments by regional economic courts is evidence of the creative use made by individuals and NGOs of existing opportunities to litigate human rights cases. It also demonstrates the willingness of African regional courts to exercise their jurisdiction effectively to address human rights concerns, which is often seen as integral to the legitimacy of economic and political unions. However, the practice raises difficult questions, particularly whether regional economic courts have jurisdiction to adjudicate human rights cases, and if so, what law to apply. The proliferation of courts with jurisdiction over human rights carries the risk of fragmentation or inconsistencies, and of forum shopping (there is no need to exhaust domestic remedies), thus potentially sidelining the ACmHPR.[285] It is also politically controversial as states have objected to the regional economic courts' exercise of jurisdiction over human rights matters. This applies particularly to a highly politically charged case against Zimbabwe where the SADC tribunal ruled in 2008 that the expropriation of the land of the applicant (a white farmer) had been discriminatory and that the respondent state should pay fair compensation.[286] The government of Zimbabwe refused to comply with the order, claiming that it was not binding. The High Court of Zimbabwe ruled that the judgment could not be enforced and SADC itself, apparently yielding to pressure from Zimbabwe, effectively suspended the tribunal[287] and, in 2012, decided to negotiate a new protocol that would confine the tribunal's mandate to the interpretation of the SADC treaty and protocols in

---

[283] *Katabazi and 21 Others* v. *Secretary General of the East African Community and Another* (East African Court of Justice) (2007).

[284] Ibid., 16.

[285] See for an assessment, Murungi and Gallinetti, above note 224, 130–1.

[286] *Mike Campbell (PVT) and Others* v. *Republic of Zimbabwe* (SADC Tribunal) (2008). See also *Luke Munyandu Tembani* v. *Republic of Zimbabwe* (SADC Tribunal) (2009).

[287] See P. N. Ndlovu, '*Campbell* v. *Republic of Zimbabwe*: A Moment of Truth for the SADC Tribunal' (2011) 1 *SADC Law Journal* 63; D. Matyszak, *The Dissolution of the SADC Tribunal* (19 August 2011), online at www.researchandadvocacyunit.org. The decision to suspend the Tribunal was unsuccessfully challenged before the ACmHPR in *Luke Munyandu Tembani and Benjamin John Freeth (represented by Norman Tjombe)* v. *Angola and Thirteen Others* (2013), and the ACtHPR in *Request for an Advisory Opinion by Pan African Lawyers' Union and the Southern Africa Litigation Centre* (2013).

inter-state disputes.[288] This is a salutary lesson on how judicial activism can backfire, with the SADC developments seemingly constituting a victory for state sovereignty. However, in a region where activist forces are becoming increasingly vocal and effective in creating political space for contestation, satisfactorily addressing human rights concerns is a challenge that regional institutions cannot ignore lest they compromise their legitimacy. This task, as well as the one of building a coherent system based on the consistent application of the Charter combined with effective remedies, constitutes the main challenge facing the African human rights system.

INTERVIEW 6.4

Making the System Work

(Ibrahima Kane)

Ibrahima Kane, AU Advocacy Director, Open Society Foundations, has been working to promote and protect human rights in Africa for over three decades, engaging at the grassroots level as well as in strategic litigation and helping to strengthen regional human rights systems. In the course of his work, he has become one of the major civil society voices on human rights in Africa.

The African human rights system has repeatedly been described as weak and ineffectual. What is your response to such assessments?

If a human rights system is evaluated through the number of cases examined by the different bodies that compose the system and implemented by states parties against which they are filed, we can definitely talk about a weak system because in almost thirty years of existence, fewer than 700 cases were handled by three human rights bodies, i.e. the African Commission on Human and Peoples' Rights (African Commission) (more than 600 cases), the African Committee of Experts on the Rights and Welfare of the Child (African Committee) (9 cases) and the African Court on Human and Peoples' Rights (African Court) (59 cases). According to a recent survey by the African Commission, only 25 per cent of its decisions/recommendations have been implemented so far.

However, the work of the system is not limited to the case law. For example, in implementing their promotional mandate, the African Commission and the African Committee have immensely contributed to the contextualisation of the key provisions of the respective treaties, either in adopting additional protocols, such as the Protocol on the rights of women, the draft Protocol on the specific aspects of the right to a nationality and the

---

[288] SADC, Final Communiqué of the 32nd Summit of SADC Heads of State and Government (Maputo, 18 August 2012) para. 24.

eradication of statelessness in Africa, or in interpreting the content of rights and liberties enshrined in their treaties. The number of initiatives taken by the bodies (creation of special mechanisms, adoption of Guidelines and Principles and general comments, missions of inquiry, promotional visits and conferences, etc.) has shown their ability to be creative and to respond to the real needs of Africans. In addition, at the sub-regional level like in West Africa, new bodies were created to better promote human rights. The ECOWAS Community Court of Justice is a court of first instance and victims of human rights do not even need to exhaust legal remedies. More importantly, the Court can organise its hearings in the country where the violations are alleged to have occurred. I must also confess that the African system is very young and, as someone once said, being young is good because it helps to correct the wrongs. So it is wise to suggest that the system is still under construction.

You have engaged closely with the African Commission and other human rights bodies in the region. How has this worked in practice and how effective have you been in your work?

The African human rights system provides a 'world' of possibilities provided that one puts a lot of effort into communicating with the key actors and shows a willingness to help in improving the different mechanisms. Supporting the activities of the African Commission or the African Court is not easy given that for years the AU did not provide them with enough financial and human resources. In addition, the rules of these bodies are sometimes so complex and time-consuming that many organisations prefer to do their own work instead of helping the bodies to perform their respective mandates.

During the last twenty years, I managed to create between the organisations I have worked for and the various bodies enough confidence that allowed me to be proactive in dealing with human rights issues on the continent. We helped in drafting a large number of Guidelines and Principles, in organising seminars and conferences and in finalising the work on key draft protocols. Working with members of the African Commission or judges of the African Court has been a fantastic opportunity to discuss some critical issues regarding the effectiveness and the perceptions that the rest of the stakeholders have of the system. For example, our persistent criticism of the composition of the African Commission, with a large number of Ambassadors and senior states officials, led to the creation of a working group, whose mandate was to revise the Commission's Rules of Procedure. The members of the African Commission showed increasing confidence to work with us, which I believe was mainly related to the fact that we acted with professionalism, openness and made sure that the financial and technical resources were available.

There have been several important developments in the region, particularly an increasing number of normative texts, institutions and judicial bodies adjudicating human rights cases. What are the promises and challenges that this development entails for the African human rights system?

Despite all the efforts undertaken to improve its effectiveness, the African human rights system still faces a number of challenges:

1. The lack of financial and technical resources: the annual budget provided by the AU only covers 30 to 40 per cent of the needs of the system. Almost all the human rights treaty bodies are understaffed and the majority of their current staff is junior.
2. The various bodies hardly talk to each other and this is quite worrying given the fact that some of them have a structural relationship, such as the African Commission and the African Court.
3. Access to the mechanisms is still a problem. Banjul (African Commission) and Arusha (African Court) are still very far from many African capitals and communication systems in the Gambia and Tanzania are not very efficient.
4. There are a lot of gaps in the current legal framework for the protection of rights on the continent and states are very slow in adopting and ratifying new treaties.
5. African civil society organisations are still weak and their input and influence on the system is still limited.
6. Implementation of the decisions and recommendations of the bodies is still a problem.

Yet what makes me confident in the system is the progress made by many states in putting human rights at the heart of their daily actions. 2016 has been declared the year of human rights in Africa by the AU, and this is a clear indication to African states that there is no future on the continent if human dignity and life are not fully respected. In addition, ordinary sessions of the African Commission are now well attended by states parties and the number of inter-states cases is increasing (two in one year). The AU has also taken the lead in the fact-finding missions when massacres occurred on the continent (South Sudan, Central African Republic, etc.). We can, without any doubt, say that human rights seem to have a brighter future on the continent. At the same time, I believe that only our continued efforts, as human rights activists, will help the system to deliver its promises.

What are the lessons that the African system may hold for the development of regional human rights systems elsewhere?

Three main lessons can so far be learnt from the 30 years of experience of the African human rights system:

1. The vagueness of a regional human rights normative framework should always be seen as a strength of the system.
2. It is difficult to protect rights in a context of general poverty, lack of good governance and weak institutions, be it at the regional or national level.
3. The realisation of human rights on a continent is always a transnational process which requires a lot of collaboration between the different stakeholders.

If we look at new systems such as in the Association of Southeast Asian Nations (ASEAN) context it is important to support the work of the institutional actors and, from a civil society perspective, to take an approach that is both strategic and constructive.

Another important lesson is the need for more dialogue based on objective criticism. African activists and NGOs have had more influence than big Western NGOs in this respect; using the flexibility inherent in the system has been more useful than teaching it lessons. Having said that, it is critical that regional institutions learn from other systems; the African system has certainly benefited from the European and the Inter-American systems in this regard.

What areas do you see as current or emerging frontiers for human rights protection in Africa?

There are several pressing issues: first and foremost, our continent is still struggling to find the best means to respond to the massacres that it is experiencing at a large scale. Citizenship and nationality are also a major concern. Well over 60 per cent of children born in Africa do not have a birth certificate, which has greatly contributed to discrimination based on nationality and statelessness. Discrimination more generally, including on the grounds of sex and sexual orientation, is still a key problem across the continent. Other issues concern freedom of movement in Africa and the rights of victims of terrorism, which has become a major scourge. Another challenge is how to advance economic, social and cultural rights, which is extremely difficult given the realities on the ground. However, initiatives such as the Charter for the Public Service in Africa (2001) are a first step to put the framework in place that is needed to implement these rights more effectively. We should not forget that human rights are rights for the normal citizen when he/she can use the law to effectively 'force' the state to comply with its treaty obligations and to change his/her own daily life. I don't think that we Africans even have a choice concerning our human rights system. It is the only one we have and we have to ensure that it serves the people of our continent who, for more than four centuries, are still struggling to protect their rights and dignity.

1. Has the ACmHPR developed a jurisprudence that adequately responds to, and reflects, the multiple human rights challenges in the continent?

2. Does the fact that states need to recognise the standing of individuals and NGOs before the African Court inspire confidence that it will be able to become an effective judicial body?

3. Can the regional economic courts act as catalysts for a stronger African human rights system or is their human rights jurisprudence a passing phenomenon?

4. Is the African human rights system at risk of fragmentation?

6.5   THE ARAB HUMAN RIGHTS SYSTEM

The founding of the League of Arab States (the Arab League) dates back to 1945 and its inter-governmental human rights body, the Permanent Arab Committee on Human Rights, was established in 1968. Yet normative and institutional developments have lagged behind its regional counterparts.[289] The Arab Charter on Human Rights of 2004 entered into force in 2008 (15 states parties as of 30 January 2019) after its controversial 1994 predecessor had failed to attract a sufficient number of ratifications. The Charter sets out an Arab approach to human rights that situates the latter in the particular political, including post-colonial, and cultural context while proclaiming adherence to universality.[290] It contains both progressive elements, as it comprises all sets of rights, including the rights of minorities and the right to development, and problematic provisions. The latter include the controversial reference to Zionism, the right to equality between men and women within the framework of Sharia, the imposition of the death penalty on minors if provided in national law, the lack of prohibition of cruel, inhuman or degrading punishment, the confinement of certain economic, social and cultural rights to citizens, and overly broad limitations on freedom of thought and religion.[291] Its article 43 stipulates that '[n]othing in this Charter

---

[289] See M. Rishmawi, 'The League of Arab States and Human Rights', in S. Sheeran and N. Rodley (eds.), *Routledge Handbook of International Human Rights Law* (Routledge, 2016) 483–504; K. D. Magliveras, 'The Protection of Human Rights and Fundamental Freedoms in the League of Arab States and in the Arab-Islamic World: An Overview (2018) 1 *Diritti umani e diritto internazionale* 105.

[290] See in particular its preamble and art. 1.

[291] M. Rishmawi, 'The Arab Charter and the League of Arab States: An Update' (2010) 10 *Human Rights Law Review* 169.

may be construed or interpreted as impairing the rights and freedoms protected by the domestic laws of the States parties or those set forth in the international and regional human rights instruments which the States parties have adopted or ratified, including the rights of women, the rights of the child and the rights of persons belonging to minorities'. This 'saving clause' raises the obvious challenge of how the Charter's provisions can be reconciled with states parties obligations set out in these instruments. The Charter established the Arab Committee on Human Rights, composed of seven members, as its treaty body. Initially, its composition and operation has prompted criticism on account of the limited independence of its members, and the lack of gender balance.[292] Significantly, its mandate is restricted; it cannot receive individual complaints, as it is confined to reviewing states parties' reports.[293] The review process has involved civil society but has been viewed as rather generic and ineffective.[294] In 2014, the Arab League adopted the Statute of the Arab Court of Human Rights. The process and outcome raised concerns about the lack of civil society consultation, the controversial choice of Bahrain as the designated seat of the Court and inadequate guarantees ensuring its independence. In addition, the Court's mandate is viewed as overly state-centric, only providing for inter-state complaints and complaints by accredited NGOs.[295] This set-up does not augur well for the development of the system, but close observers and civil society participants have nonetheless emphasised the need to build on the emerging Committee practice and engage with the system.[296] The magnitude of human rights challenges in the region, both structural and acute, is enormous. Further reforms are called for to address the chasm between the aspirations and demands articulated in popular protest and civil society movements, and the normative and institutional shortcomings within the Arab League setting.

6.6   TOWARDS AN ASIAN HUMAN RIGHTS SYSTEM?

Asia has not witnessed the impetus that led to the establishment of a human rights system as an important part of a regional or sub-regional political body. However, the call by the 1993 Vienna Conference on Human Rights

---

[292] M. Rishmawi, *The League of Arab States Human Rights Standards and Mechanisms, Towards Further Civil Society Engagement: A Manual for Practitioners* (Open Society Foundation, 2015) 41.

[293] Art. 41 of the Arab Charter on Human Rights.

[294] GIZ and German Institute for Human Rights, *The Arab Human Rights System: Annex to the ABC of Human Rights for Development Cooperation* (GIZ, 2017) 4.

[295] See for a detailed analysis, International Commission of Jurists, *The Arab Court of Human Rights: A Flawed Statute for an Ineffective Court* (2015).

[296] Rishmawi, above note 292.

to establish 'regional and sub-regional arrangements for the promotion and protection of human rights' was taken up by ASEAN, which, fourteen years later, adopted the ASEAN Charter in 2007. The Charter envisages the establishment of an ASEAN human rights body, which was inaugurated as the ASEAN Intergovernmental Commission on Human Rights (AICHR) on 23 October 2009.[297] The AICHR is mandated to promote and protect human rights and fundamental rights. This is to be done primarily through awareness-raising, capacity-building, provision of advisory services and technical assistance, the development of common approaches and positions on human rights matters, as well as the preparation of studies on thematic issues. It has also been tasked with elaborating an ASEAN Declaration on Human Rights, which it adopted on 19 November 2012.[298] The AICHR is composed of ten members, meets biannually, and adopts a model of decision-making 'based on consultation and consensus'. Its promotional mandate and consultative functions reflect ASEAN member states' reluctance to establish a body with quasi-judicial, let alone judicial, functions.

The AICHR model does not follow the typology of human rights bodies in other regions and its apparent weakness has raised concerns about its ability to develop a regional human rights culture and contribute to the effective protection of rights.[299] However, the evolutionary process envisaged does provide a point of reference for engagement and contestation for civil society actors and others to advocate stronger human rights protection. Judging by the experiences of other institutions, the AICHR may be receptive to calls for a progressive interpretation and a broadening of its mandate. Indeed, this would provide it with an opportunity to gain and maintain credibility as a human rights body. While the work of the AICHR progressed slowly, its very establishment constitutes an important development that is bound to hold critical lessons for regional human rights protection in Asia.

---

[297] Cha-Am Hua Hin Declaration on the Inauguration of the ASEAN Intergovernmental Commission on Human Rights (23 October 2009), online at www.asean.org/storage/images/archive/15thsummit/Declaration-AICHR.pdf. See H. D. Phan, 'The evolution towards an ASEAN human rights body' (2008) 9 *Asian Pacific Journal on Human Rights and the Law* 1; J. Munro, 'The Relationship between the Origins and Regime Design of the ASEAN Intergovernmental Commission on Human Rights' (2011) 15 *International Journal of Human Rights* 1185.

[298] The text of the declaration is available online at www.asean.org/news/asean-statement-communiques/item/asean-human-rights-declaration. See further N. Doyle, 'The ASEAN Human Rights Declaration and the Implications of Recent Southeast Asian Initiatives in Human Rights Institution-Building and Standard-Setting' (2014) 63 *International & Comparative Law Quarterly* 67; G. J. Naldi and K. Magliveras, 'The ASEAN Human Rights Declaration' (2014) 3 *International Human Rights Law Review* 183.

[299] D. A. Desierto, 'Universalizing Core Human Rights in the "New" ASEAN: A Reassessment of Culture and Development Justifications against the Global Rejection of Impunity' (2009) 1 *Göttingen Journal of International Law* 77.

6.7   COMPARISON OF REGIONAL SYSTEMS

The review of regional human rights systems yielded important findings for each of the systems, but also for other regions where systems are weak and/ or deficient, such as in respect of ASEAN to date and the Arab League, or non-existent, such as in South Asia.[300] The situation in these regions may change following political developments, particularly in the Middle East, which would in turn pose anew the question of what constitutes an effective regional human rights system. The general case for such a system has been widely recognised. Indeed, regional systems can make a significant contribution to 'regional universality', bridging international standards and domestic implementation and developing a distinctive regional human rights culture.

Experience to date suggests that the desire for greater regional political unity is a critical factor and can serve to generate the impetus for the establishment of regional human rights systems. In their initial phase, such systems tend to reflect considerable compromises between the member states' intention to create a credible system and their intention to retain control over the institutions mandated to monitor its effective application and implementation. Regional human rights bodies frequently seek to use and expand their powers, not least to attain a degree of legitimacy. This has resulted in frictions, and member states may undermine the effectiveness of bodies by not providing adequate resources.[301] Nevertheless, most systems have largely succeeded in developing stronger institutional human rights cultures over time, although their political and popular acceptance can be precarious. The strength of systems and their impact depends to a large degree on their embeddedness in the overall political culture and their contribution to the resolution of conflict and political transitions. The growth of regional networks of actors that claim and thereby reinforce respect for the principles and goals for which the system had been set up is another important element. These interrelated factors and the degree to which they contribute to domestic implementation processes, including by empowering local actors, are critical for the effectiveness of regional human rights systems.

As a general rule, it is important that the type of human rights system chosen is suitable in the particular circumstances. For example, there may be some merit in creating bodies with a strong promotional mandate first rather

---

[300] S. Dhaliwal, *Human Rights Mechanism in South Asia* (Routledge, 2017).

[301] See further M. R. Madsen, P. Cebulak and M. Wiebusch, 'Backlash against international courts: explaining the forms and patterns of resistance to international courts' (2018) 14 *International Journal of Law in Context, Special Issue 2: Resistance to International Courts* 197.

than focusing predominantly or exclusively on judicial bodies. However, it is equally clear that complaints procedures that provide access for individuals (and NGOs) play a pivotal role. They compel states to respond to specific allegations and to demonstrate their respect for human rights through taking concrete measures, in contrast to other procedures largely based on a rather broad constructive dialogue. Against this background it is the public in the region, particularly individuals, NGOs and the media, that plays a crucial role in articulating legitimate expectations that reflect local and regional priorities based on experiences of suffering and notions of justice.

QUESTIONS

1. Is there a natural progression from bodies with a largely promotional mandate to fully fledged judicial bodies in the development of regional human rights systems?

2. Are there common lessons that can be gleaned from the existing regional systems for other regional bodies contemplating the setting up of a new human rights system?

FURTHER READING

General

Buckley, C. M., A. Donald and P. Leach (eds.), *Towards Convergence in International Human Rights Law: Approaches of Regional and International Systems* (Brill Nijhoff, 2017).

Cerna, C. M. (ed.), *Regional Human Rights Systems* (Ashgate, 2014).

Shelton, D., and P. Wright-Carroza, *Regional Protection of Human Rights*, 2nd edn (Oxford University Press, 2013).

European Human Rights System

Bates, E., *The Evolution of the European Convention on Human Rights: From its Inception to the Creation of a Permanent Court of Human Rights* (Oxford University Press, 2010).

Christofferson, J., and M. R. Madsen (eds.), *The European Court of Human Rights between Law and Politics* (Oxford University Press, 2013).

Grabenwarter, C., *European Convention on Human Rights: Commentary* (Beck, 2014).

Greer, S., *The European Convention on Human Rights: Achievements, Problems and Prospects* (Cambridge University Press, 2006).

Harris, D. J., M. O'Boyle, C. Warbrick, E. Bates and C. Buckley, *Law of the European Convention on Human Rights*, 4th edn (Oxford University Press, 2018).

Hodson, L., *NGOs and the Struggle for Human Rights in Europe* (Hart, 2011).

Mowbray, A., *Cases and Materials on the European Convention on Human Rights*, 3rd edn (Oxford University Press, 2012).

Peers, S., T. Hervey, J. Kemmer and A. Ward (eds.), *The EU Charter of Fundamental Rights: A Commentary* (Hart, 2014).

Rainey, B., E. Wicks and C. Ovey, *Jacobs, White & Ovey: The European Convention on Human Rights*, 7th edn (Oxford University Press, 2017).

Schabas, W. A., *The European Convention on Human Rights: A Commentary* (Oxford University Press, 2015).

Seatzu, F., and A. Ubeda de Torres, *The Law and Practice of the European Social Committee* (Routledge, 2015).

Van Aaken, A., and I. Motoc (eds.), *The European Convention on Human Rights and General International Law* (Oxford University Press, 2018).

Websites

ECSR: ww.coe.int/t/dghl/monitoring/socialcharter/ ECSR/ECSRdefault_en.asp.

CoE: www.coe.int

ECtHR: www.echr.coe.int

EU: http://europa.eu

Inter-American Human Rights System

Antkowiak, T. M., and A. Gonza, *The American Convention on Human Rights: Essential Rights* (Oxford University Press, 2017).

Burgorgue-Larsen, L., and A. Ubeda de Torres, *The Inter-American Court of Human Rights: Case Law and Commentary* (Oxford University Press, 2011).

Engstrom, P. (ed.), *The Inter-American Human Rights System: Impact Beyond Compliance* (Palgrave Macmillan, 2018).

Haeck, Y., O. Ruiz-Chiriboga and C. Burbano-Herrera (eds.), *The Inter-American Court of Human Rights: Theory and Practice, Presence and Future* (Intersentia, 2015).

Harris, D., and S. Livingstone (eds.), *The Inter-American System of Human Rights* (Clarendon Press, 1998).

Medina Quiroga, C., *The American Convention on Human Rights: Crucial Rights and their Theory and Practice* (Intersentia, 2014).

Pasqualucci, J. M., *The Practice and Procedure of the Inter-American Court of Human Rights*, 2nd edn (Cambridge University Press, 2013).

Serrano, M., and V. Popovski (eds.), *Human Rights Regimes in the Americas* (United Nations University Press, 2010).

Websites

IACHR: www.oas.org/en/iachr

IACtHR: www.corteidh.or.cr

OAS: www.oas.org

African Human Rights System

Evans, M., and R. Murray (eds.), *The African Charter on Human and Peoples' Rights: The System in Practice 1986–2006*, 2nd edn (Cambridge University Press, 2008).

Kufuor, K. O., *The African Human Rights System: Origin and Evolution* (Palgrave Macmillan, 2010).

Murray, R., *The African Charter on Human and Peoples' Rights: A Commentary* (Oxford University Press, 2019).

Okafor, O. C., *The African Human Rights System, Activist Forces and International Institutions* (Cambridge University Press, 2007).

Sloth-Nielsen, J. (ed.), *Children's Rights in Africa: A Legal Perspective* (Routledge, 2016).

Ssenyonjo, M. (ed.), *The African Regional Human Rights System: 30 years after the African Charter on Human and Peoples' Rights* (Martinus Nijhoff, 2012).

Viljoen, V., *International Human Rights Law in Africa*, 2nd edn (Oxford University Press, 2012).

Websites

ACmHPR: www.achpr.org

ACtHPR: www.african-court.org

African Committee of Experts on the Rights and Welfare of the Child: www.acerwc.org

See on the jurisprudence of all three of the above also African Human Rights Case Law Analyser: http://caselaw.ihrda.org

AU: www.au.int

Community Court of Justice – ECOWAS: www.courtecowas.org

East African Court of Justice: www.eacj.org

SADC Tribunal: www.sadc.int/about-sadc/ sadc-institutions/tribun/

Arab League Human Rights System

Rishmawi, M., 'The League of Arab States and Human Rights', in Gibney, M., and A. Mihr (eds.), *The SAGE Handbook of Human Rights* (Sage, 2014) 615–35.

Websites

Arab Human Rights Committee: www.lasportal.org/
ar/humanrights/Committee/Pages/default.aspx
(Arabic)

ASEAN Human Rights System

Duxbury, A., and H.-L. Tan, *Can ASEAN Take
Human Rights Seriously?* (Cambridge University
Press, 2019).
Nasu, H., and B. Saul (eds.), *Human Rights in the
Asia-Pacific Region: Towards Institution Building*
(Routledge, 2011).

Saul, B., and C. Renshaw, *Human Rights in Asia
and the Pacific: Critical Concepts in Asian
Studies Volumes I–IV* (Routledge, 2014).
Tan, H.-L., *The ASEAN Intergovernmental
Commission on Human Rights: Institutionalising
Human Rights in South East Asia* (Cambridge
University Press, 2011).

Websites

ASEAN Intergovernmental Commission on Human
Rights: www.aichr.org

7 Individual Complaints Procedures

CONTENTS

7.1 INTRODUCTION

Complaints procedures offer a unique opportunity for individuals and groups to have claims of human rights violations considered and their rights vindicated in a judicial or quasi-judicial procedure. For non-governmental organisations (NGOs) and human rights lawyers, complaints procedures are an important avenue to pursue strategic objectives, in addition to supporting victims in individual cases. States, on the other hand, may find themselves having to defend allegations of specific or systemic violations. Ideally, complaints procedures act as a mirror that provides an opportunity for states to bring their practices into conformity with the respective treaty. In practice, however, states often view unfavourable decisions as unwarranted criticism, which may create difficulties at the implementation stage. The treaty bodies themselves are in theory neutral arbiters that apply the treaty provisions and rules of procedures. However, inevitably, their position as bodies created by states, and relying on states' cooperation on the one hand and seeking the effective protection of human rights on the other, raises a host of challenges in actual practice.

This chapter is written generically from the perspective of litigants (which will mainly be referred to as applicants throughout the chapter), examining the common stages of admissibility, merits, decision, remedies and implementation that are characteristic of complaints procedures before treaty bodies (the term is used in this chapter to refer to both United Nations (UN) treaty bodies and regional human rights commissions and courts). Questions considered include in particular:

1. Jurisdiction: who can bring a case against whom in relation to what types of violation alleged to have been committed, when and where?
2. Exhaustion of domestic remedies: what are the reasons for requiring a litigant to take legal steps (pursue remedies) first in the state where the alleged violation occurred? Is it always clear what steps need to be taken? Are there any exceptions? Who carries the burden of proof?
3. Others: are there any time limits for submitting applications? Can a case be brought before more than one treaty body? Does it need to be written in a particular language, etc.? As for the merits, what does it take to prove a complaint?
4. And finally, what is the nature of the decisions treaty bodies can make and the types of remedies awarded?

For the post-decision phase, the chapter examines the challenge of implementation. In particular, what steps can treaty bodies and litigants take, and have they taken, to enhance the prospect of a state complying with a decision? In addition, we briefly consider specific procedures which play an important role in practice, though they are only relevant where resorted to, or agreed upon, by the parties. These include interim (provisional) measures and friendly settlements. Questions to be considered include: when can interim measures be used, are they binding, how effective are they in practice? What are the conditions for friendly settlements, and are they necessarily a good outcome if this is what parties agree on?

The stages and features of regional and international complaints procedures are broadly similar and the following is a generic overview rather than a detailed examination of all available procedures; where applicable, notable differences or different approaches taken by the respective treaty bodies are indicated. Inter-state complaints share most features of individual complaints procedures and are not dealt with separately given their limited relevance to date.[1]

7.2   ADMISSIBILITY

Admissibility refers to the procedural requirements that need to be fulfilled for a judicial or quasi-judicial body to consider the substance of a case, i.e. its merits, though bodies may rule on admissibility and merits simultaneously. The admissibility criteria are laid down in the applicable treaty – including optional protocols where the main treaty does not envisage a complaints procedure – that sets out the mandate and functions of the treaty body concerned.[2] These criteria determine who may bring a case against which state about what kind of violation. They also reflect, through the requirement to exhaust domestic remedies, the principle that supranational bodies are not meant to replace domestic courts. Rather, their role is to monitor whether states have complied with their obligation to respect and protect rights 'within their jurisdiction'.

In practice, many if not most cases fail at the admissibility hurdle, particularly on the grounds of a failure to exhaust domestic remedies. An inadmissibility decision does not necessarily preclude an applicant from lodging another case concerning the same matter if circumstances have changed, particularly where domestic remedies have been exhausted subsequently.[3] However, given the length of proceedings before supranational bodies, applicants whose case is declared inadmissible may face added evidentiary challenges domestically and may have missed time limits to pursue domestic remedies. Equally important, an applicant may lose the belief that the supranational bodies will remedy the alleged violation. Inadmissibility decisions by supranational bodies can therefore effectively spell the end of any efforts to remedy violations even where the underlying claim of a violation

---

[1] Inter-state complaints have primarily featured in the European system. See S. C. Prebensen, 'Inter-State Complaints under Treaty Provisions: The Experience under the European Convention on Human Rights', in G. Alfredsson, J. Grimheden and B. Ramchjaran (eds.), *International Human Rights Monitoring Mechanisms: Essays in Honour of Jakob Th. Möller*, 2nd rev. edn (Martinus Nijhoff, 2009) 439–64.

[2] Art. 14 ICERD; art. 22 CAT; art. 77 ICRMW; art. 31 CPED; Optional Protocols to ICCPR, CEDAW, CRPD, ICESCR, CRC (Communication Procedure); arts. 34 and 35 ECHR; arts. 44–7 ACHR; arts. 55 and 56 ACHPR.

[3] See e.g., *Rules of Procedure of the HRCtee*, UN doc. CCPR/C/3/Rev. 10 (11 January 2012) rule 98(2): 'If the Committee has declared a communication inadmissible under article 5, paragraph 2, of the Optional Protocol, this decision may be reviewed at a later date by the Committee upon a written request by or on behalf of the individual concerned containing information to the effect that the reasons for inadmissibility referred to in article 5, paragraph 2, no longer apply.'

is justified. Applicants and anyone advising individuals or groups who contemplate bringing a case before a supranational body must therefore be careful to ensure that the admissibility requirements have been fulfilled so that a case will be heard on its merits.

7.2.1   Jurisdiction

7.2.1.1   *Rationae Personae:* Who can Bring a Complaint?

As a general rule, anyone claiming to be a victim of a violation can submit an application, which is, depending on the treaty in question, also referred to as a communication or complaint. The rationale behind this rule is that those who claim that their rights have been violated have an interest and are entitled to a remedy. A person claiming to be a victim of a violation of the International Covenant on Civil and Political Rights (ICCPR) or the European Convention on Human Rights (ECHR), for example, must show that he or she is directly affected, i.e. that the acts or omissions in question must have a direct bearing on his or her right(s).[4] This notion can be broad as it has been interpreted, for example, to provide standing for a member of the Roma community in relation to offensive remarks made against his community even though he had not been personally targeted.[5] In contrast, an NGO acting on behalf of victims, without having itself suffered any violation of its rights, was not recognised to have standing under the ECHR.[6] The same notion of victim applies to a group of persons whose members have suffered violations or a group that suffered a violation of its collective right(s) (where the complaints procedure in question provides standing for such claims). The position of legal persons differs; whereas the Optional Protocol to the ICCPR only allows individuals to claim violations,[7] the European Court of Human Rights (ECtHR) grants standing to legal persons where their rights

---

[4] See for the notion of victim in the HRCtee's jurisprudence, *Aumeeruddy-Cziffra et al.* v. *Mauritius* (HRCtee) (1981) para. 9.1; *B. d. B. et al.* v. *Netherlands* (HRCtee) (1989) para. 6.6; and the ECtHR, *Klass and Others* v. *Germany* (ECtHR) (1978) para. 33 and *Amuur* v. *France* (ECtHR) (1996) para. 36. The African and the Inter-American systems distinguish between petitioner and victim. See in this regard the distinction made between 'original claimants' and 'parties to the case' (victims or alleged victims) in art. 2 of the IACtHR's Rules of Procedure (2009).

[5] *Aksu* v. *Turkey* (ECtHR) (2012) paras. 50–4.

[6] *Stichting Mothers of Srebenica and Others* v. *The Netherlands* (ECtHR) (2013) paras. 114–17 (the directly affected victims were found to have standing).

[7] See art. 1 of the Optional Protocol to the ICCPR. The HRCtee does not recognise standing of persons or groups alleging a violation of the right to self-determination; see *Diergaardt et al.* v. *Namibia* (HRCtee) (2000) para. 10.3, and *Lubicon Lake Band* v. *Canada* (HRCtee) (1990) para. 13.3. *Länsman III* v. *Finland* (HRCtee) (2005) para. 6.1. See also Y. Tyagi, *The UN Human Rights Committee: Practice and Procedure* (Cambridge University Press, 2011) 401, with further references.

have been affected, such as a newspaper outlet in relation to freedom of expression.[8]

The criterion of being 'directly affected' is problematic where an actual violation has not yet taken place. For example, it would be unreasonable to wait for a violation of the right to privacy to materialise and face criminal sanctions for homosexual conduct. It may also be unclear whether a violation is already taking place or about to occur, such as where a person is subjected to telephone tapping in violation of his or her right to privacy without knowing it. Treaty bodies and courts have therefore recognised that applications can be brought in these circumstances but only if a violation is reasonably foreseeable or imminent.[9]

Applicants before the Human Rights Committee (HRCtee) or the ECtHR may authorise someone else, including NGOs, to act on their behalf.[10] In exceptional circumstances, 'when it appears that the individual in question is unable to submit the communication personally', such as in the case of enforced disappearance, 'a communication submitted on behalf of an alleged victim may, however, be accepted if submitted by next of kin close to the case'.[11] As a general rule, applicants must show a 'sufficient link' (HRCtee)[12] or a personal and specific link to the direct victim, such as family members of someone who died as a result of an alleged violation (ECtHR).[13] In an exceptional case, the ECtHR granted standing to an NGO as de facto representative of 'a highly vulnerable person with no next-of-kin, Mr Câmpeanu, a young Roma man with severe mental disabilities who was infected with HIV, who spent his entire life in the care of the state authorities and who

---

[8] E.g., *The Sunday Times* v. *UK* (ECtHR) (1980). See in the African system, *Zimbabwe Lawyers for Human Rights and Associated Newspapers of Zimbabwe* v. *Zimbabwe* (ACmHPR) (2009), particularly para. 178. Legal persons cannot claim to be victims in the Inter-American system. However, the IACtHR recognised that individuals, such as shareholders, may in specific circumstances be able to vindicate their rights 'even when they are encompassed in a legal figure or fiction created by the same system of law'; *Cantos* v. *Argentina* (IACtHR) (2001) para. 29. See further the Court's advisory opinion, *Entitlement of legal entities to hold rights under the Inter-American Human Rights System* (IACtHR) (2016).

[9] *Norris* v. *Ireland* (ECtHR) (1988) paras. 28–34, and *Toonen* v. *Australia* (HRCtee) (1994) para. 5.1 (homosexuality); *Klass and Others* v. *Germany*, para. 34 (telephone tapping). See for the Inter-American system, *International Responsibility for the Promulgation and Enforcement of Laws in Violation of the Convention* (Arts. 1 and 2 of the American Convention on Human Rights) (IACtHR) (1994) paras. 40–50, and *Suárez Rosero* v. *Ecuador* (IACtHR) (1997) para. 98.

[10] Rule 36 of the ECtHR's 2011 Rules of Court. See also *P. K. and Others* v. *Spain* (CtAT) (2008) para. 8.3, which the CtAT found inadmissible on account of the acting NGO's failure to obtain authorisation from the migrant they were claiming to represent.

[11] Rule 96(b) of the HRCtee's 2012 Rules of Procedure.

[12] See *Massera et al.* v. *Uruguay* (HRCtee) (1979) para. 5.

[13] See *Yaşa* v. *Turkey* (ECtHR) (1999) paras. 61–6.

died in hospital, allegedly as a result of neglect'.[14] Next of kin may also have standing as victims of a violation in their own right, such as the right not to be subjected to inhuman treatment where a (close) relative has been forcibly disappeared.[15]

States are often reluctant to give standing to individuals, groups or organisations, other than the direct victims, out of concern that this would open the 'floodgates' for public interest litigation. The question of how broadly or narrowly standing is defined is therefore a measure of the control states seek to retain over those permitted to use procedures. In contrast to the Optional Protocol to the ICCPR and the ECHR, article 44 of the American Convention on Human Rights (ACHR) and article 55 of the African Charter on Human and Peoples' Rights (ACHPR) considerably broaden standing for cases brought before the Inter-American Commission of Human Rights (IACHR) and the African Commission on Human and Peoples' Rights (ACmHPR) respectively.[16] The African Commission has emphasised the rationale for this relaxation in cases where the victims themselves may be unable to bring cases: '[it] has adopted an *actio popularis* approach where the author of a communication need not know or have any relationship with the victim. This is to enable poor victims of human rights violations on the continent to receive assistance from NGOs and individuals far removed from their locality'.[17] The broad standing also enables NGOs to bring strategic cases in response to mass violations or systemic breaches.[18] It therefore facilitates access to international justice and opens avenues for public interest litigation.[19]

---

[14] *Centre for Legal Resources on behalf of Valentin Câmpeanu* v. *Romania* (ECtHR) (2014) para. 104. In contrast, see *Bulgarian Helsinki Committee* v. *Bulgaria* (ECtHR) (2016) paras. 50–61.

[15] *Kurt* v. *Turkey* (ECtHR) (1999) para. 134; *Sharma* v. *Nepal* (HRCtee) (2008) para. 7.9. See in the context of the Inter-American system, *Ituango Massacres* v. *Colombia* (IACtHR) (2006) Separate Concurring Opinion of Judge S. García Ramírez, paras. 10–12.

[16] Notably, the broad standing has been retained for the ACtHPR. See art. 5(3) of the 1998 Protocol to the ACHPR and art. 30 of the 2008 Protocol on the Statute of the African Court of Justice and Human Rights.

[17] *Article 19* v. *Eritrea* (ACmHPR) (2007) para. 65.

[18] See in particular, *Centre for Minority Rights Development (Kenya) and Minority Rights Group (on behalf of Endorois Welfare Council)* v. *Kenya* (ACmHPR) (2009); *Interights, Institute for Human Rights and Development in Africa, and Association mauritanienne des droits de l'Homme* v. *Mauritania* (ACmHPR) (2004); *Social and Economic Rights Action Center (SERAC) and Center for Economic and Social Rights (CESR)* v. *Nigeria* (ACmHPR) (2001). See for an *actio popularis* in an individual case, *Spilg and Mack & Ditshwanelo (on behalf of Lehlohonolo Bernard Kobedi)* v. *Botswana* (ACmHPR) (2013) paras. 76–82.

[19] See more broadly on the 'exercise of the right of access to international justice', A. A. Cançado Trindade, *The Access of Individuals to International Justice* (Oxford University Press, 2011) 17–49.

7.2.1.2   *Against Whom can a Complaint be Brought?*

Applicants can only bring cases against a state that is party to the treaty concerned and has recognised the competence of the treaty body to consider complaints (unless they have denounced such competence, for example Trinidad and Tobago).[20] This is automatically the case before the IACHR and ACmHPR, which have compulsory jurisdiction relating to the relevant Organization of American States (OAS) instruments and the ACHPR respectively,[21] as well as before the ECtHR following changes in 1998 (Protocol no. 11) that revolutionised the European system. Other treaty bodies and courts only consider applications where the state concerned has explicitly accepted their jurisdiction. The African Court on Human and Peoples' Rights (ACtHPR), for example, found the first case brought before it inadmissible because the respondent state had not recognised its competence to hear cases lodged by individuals.[22]

Applicants cannot bring cases against non-state actors (NSAs) because individuals, armed rebel groups, businesses or others falling within this category are not recognised as parties to human rights treaties. The same applies in principle to international organisations[23] though this may change should the European Union (EU) become a party to the ECHR.[24] Yet the involvement of international organisations raises complex questions of attribution. Can a state be held responsible for acts or omissions in contexts where it acted as part of multinational forces and/or purported to act pursuant to binding resolutions by international organisations?[25] The jurisprudence of human rights treaty bodies is not settled in this regard. In the *Behrami* case, the applicants argued that the French KFOR (international forces in Kosovo) troops' failure to clear cluster bombs dropped by the North Atlantic Treaty Organization (NATO), which resulted in the killing of one boy and serious

---

[20] The treaty body will also not have jurisdiction for acts occurring after a state party has effectively denounced the treaty in question. See e.g., Trinidad and Tobago's declarations in relation to the ICCPR Optional Protocol and the ACHR with effect from 26 August 1998 and 29 May 1999 respectively.

[21] See Chapters 6.3.2 and 6.4.2.

[22] *Michelot Yogogombaye* v. *The Republic of Senegal* (ACtHPR) (2009).

[23] See *Luke Munyandu Tembani and Benjamin John Freeth (represented by Norman Tjombe)* v. *Angola and Thirteen Others* (ACmHPR) (2013) paras. 15 and 80; as well as the decisions by the ACtHPR which concerned regional organisations but were not decided on *rationae persona* grounds, *Femi Falana* v. *African Union* (ACtHPR) (2012) and *Efoua Mbozo'o Samuel* v. *the Pan African Parliament* (ACtHPR) (2011).

[24] See Chapter 6.2.8. Note, however, that the EU became party to the CRPD in 2010 pursuant to art. 42 (though not its Optional Protocol to date).

[25] See further Chapter 19.4 for a more extensive discussion.

injuries to another, constituted a violation of the right to life. The ECtHR refused to entertain the application *rationae personae* on the grounds that the acts in question were attributable to the international organisation, here the UN Mission in Kosovo (UNMIK) acting pursuant to UN Security Council (UNSC) authorisation. In *Saramati*, the detention authorised by a Norwegian and later a French KFOR commander in a station located in a sector led by Germany – which the applicant alleged to constitute a violation of articles 5, 6 and 13 ECHR – was equally found not to be attributable to the states concerned because the UNSC retained 'ultimate authority and control'.[26] The decision was heavily criticised, particularly for its interpretation of the rules of attribution and its policy implications of depriving the ECHR of any application.[27]

In contrast, in the later case of *Al-Jedda*, the ECtHR rejected the argument that the United Kingdom (UK) was not responsible for the internment of civilians in Iraq because it was carried out pursuant to UNSC resolutions, holding that the 'Security Council had neither effective control nor ultimate authority and control over the acts and omissions of troops within the multinational force'.[28] This case demonstrates the centrality of the criterion of 'ultimate authority and control' used by the ECtHR to attribute responsibility. Subsequently, in *Nada v. Switzerland*, the ECtHR held that the contracting state's decision to impose an entry ban was based on the national implementation of UNSC resolutions, and therefore fell within Switzerland's jurisdiction.[29] In addition, the ECtHR has made clear that the collective veil will not always be available where states transfer part of their sovereignty to an international organisation, namely the EU, and the international organisation does not provide for equivalent protection,[30] particularly where 'the protection of Convention rights was manifestly deficient'.[31]

---

[26] *Behrami* v. *France* and *Saramati* v. *France, Germany and Norway* (ECtHR) (2007) paras. 121–52, particularly at 144–52.

[27] M. Milanovic and T. Papic, 'As Bad as it Gets: The European Court of Human Rights' Behrami and Saramati Decision and International Law' (2009) 58 *International & Comparative Law Quarterly* 267.

[28] *Al-Jedda* v. *United Kingdom* (ECtHR) (2011) para. 84. See also *Jaloud* v. *The Netherlands* (ECtHR) (2014) paras. 140–51 on the responsibility of the respondent state acting pursuant to a UN resolution and under the command of a foreign state (here the USA and the UK).

[29] *Nada* v. *Switzerland* (ECtHR) (2012) paras. 117–23. See also *Al-Dulimi and Montana Management Inc.* v. *Switzerland* (ECtHR) (2016) paras. 93–6.

[30] See in particular, *Bosphorus Hava Yollari Turizm Ve Ticaret Anonim Sirketi* v. *Ireland* (ECtHR) (2006) paras. 143–56.

[31] Ibid., para. 156.

CASE STUDY 7.1
Protection against the Implementation of UNSC Sanctions: *Sayadi and Vinck* v. *Belgium*

The UNSC has increasingly imposed sanctions against individuals believed to be involved in terrorism. These individuals are placed on lists and may face serious restrictions, including the freezing of all their financial assets. In *Sayadi and Vinck* v. *Belgium*, the authors had been placed on such a list as a result of information provided by the Belgian authorities. They brought a case against Belgium before the HRCtee, alleging a series of violations. Belgium argued that the case was inadmissible because the implementation of UNSC resolutions was a matter for the European Community, which had transposed them into regulations, and that the authors were precluded 'from disputing United Nations rules concerning the fight against terrorism before the Committee'.[1] The HRCtee held that:

While [it] could not consider alleged violations of other instruments such as the Charter of the United Nations, or allegations that challenged United Nations rules concerning the fight against terrorism, the Committee was competent to admit a communication alleging that a State party had violated rights set forth in the Covenant, regardless of the source of the obligations implemented by the State party.[2]

In a nuanced decision, it then found that Belgium was responsible for the violations resulting from placing the individuals on the sanctions list even though Belgium was later unable to have the names removed from it.[3] Some of the Committee members dissented, arguing that the communication was unsubstantiated because article 103 UN Charter[4] takes priority over competing obligations under the Covenant.[5] This decision is an important piece in a series of cases that revolved around the question as to what extent human rights treaty bodies may review UNSC resolutions and European implementing regulations and provide adequate human rights protection.[6]

---

[1] *Sayadi and Vinck* v. *Belgium* (HRCtee) (2008) para. 4.11.
[2] Ibid., para. 7.2.
[3] Ibid., paras. 10.1–11.
[4] Art. 103 UN Charter: 'In the event of a conflict between the obligations of the Members of the United Nations under the present Charter and their obligations under any other international agreement, their obligations under the present Charter shall prevail.'
[5] See dissenting opinions of Ms Ruth Wedgwood and Mr Ivan Shearer.
[6] See *Bosphorus* v. *Ireland* (ECtHR) (2006); *Kadi* v. *Commission* (CJEU) (2010) and another sanctions case pending before the Grand Chamber in August 2015: *Al-Dulimi and Montana Management Inc.* v. *Switzerland* (ECtHR) (2013).

7.2.1.3   *Rationae Materiae:* What Rights?

An applicant must allege the violation of a right that falls within the scope of the relevant treaty and binds the state party concerned, which also excludes rights in respect of which a valid reservation has been entered.[32] An applicant cannot, for example, claim a violation of the right to property before the HRCtee or the right to self-determination before the ECtHR because the respective treaties do not guarantee these rights as such. Nor can an applicant claim a violation of rules of international humanitarian law per se because human rights treaties do not confer jurisdiction to rule on such violations.[33] Instead, an applicant would need to demonstrate that the alleged violation, such as the bombing of a village, falls within the scope of the treaty concerned, such as constituting a violation of the right to life, as in the case of *Isayeva* v. *Russia*.[34] Beyond these rather clear-cut cases, applications may give rise to difficult legal questions, for example whether tax proceedings concern 'civil rights and obligations' and therefore fall within the scope of article 6 ECHR.[35]

7.2.1.4   *Jurisdiction in Respect of Extraterritorial Conduct*

Applications are increasingly brought in relation to violations alleged to have taken place outside a state's territory. Such applications may be simply considered inadmissible *rationae loci* for lack of territorial link. However, these cases frequently raise complex questions of jurisdiction that are closely

---

[32] *Kozlova and Smirnova* v. *Latvia* (ECtHR) (2001). See Chapter 2.2.1.2 on reservations.

[33] However, see case of *Bámaca Velásquez* v. *Guatemala* (IACtHR) (2000) paras. 208–9: the court 'can observe that certain acts or omissions that violate human rights, pursuant to the treaties that they do have competence to apply, also violate other international instruments for the protection of the individual, such as the 1949 Geneva Conventions and, in particular, common Article 3'. See also *Democratic Republic of Congo* v. *Burundi, Rwanda, Uganda* (ACmHPR) (2003), where the ACmHPR made extensive reference to international humanitarian law pursuant to art. 60 ACHPR. See also Chapter 16.5.

[34] See e.g., *Isayeva and Others* v. *Russia* (ECtHR) (2005) paras. 162–201.

[35] *Ferrazzini* v. *Italy* (ECtHR) (2002) paras. 14–31.

related to the material applicability of a treaty. A state's obligation to respect human rights under the respective treaties is in principle confined to its territorial jurisdiction. For example, article 2(1) ICCPR stipulates that a state party 'undertakes to respect and to ensure to all individuals within its territory and subject to its jurisdiction the rights recognized in the present Covenant'. This is in line with the general rule of international law according to which jurisdiction refers primarily to state territory, including air space as well as aircraft and vessels that are registered in the state or fly its flag.[36] In most cases the act or omission complained of will have taken place on the territory of a state and the jurisdiction of the treaty body will be apparent. This includes cases that have a link to other countries, such as sending someone to a country where he or she is at risk of torture, because the state action in question, for example deportation, takes place on its territory.[37]

Jurisprudence is less clear on the circumstances under which treaties apply to conduct abroad (extraterritorial application) beyond the recognised exceptions of 'acts of diplomatic and consular agents ... present on foreign territory'[38] and 'the exercise of extra-territorial jurisdiction by a Contracting State when, through the consent, invitation or acquiescence of the Government of that territory, it exercises all or some of the public powers normally to be exercised by that Government'.[39] A look at the potential scope of cases shows the importance of this issue. Does the kidnapping or arrest of a person by agents of a state party in a third country bring the case within the purview of the treaty concerned?[40] Does the killing of a person at an army checkpoint, for example by Dutch troops in Iraq,[41] or the detention of a person in a war conducted abroad, such as by UK troops in Iraq and Afghanistan,[42] and subsequent transfer to the local authority, fall within the jurisdiction of the Netherlands or the UK respectively? Does the interception or rescue of migrants on the high seas and taking them on board of a vessel fall within the jurisdiction of the state carrying out such acts?[43] What about the conduct of Turkey in Northern Cyprus, that of the USA in Guantánamo Bay and of Israel in the occupied

---

[36] See on jurisdiction, J. Crawford, *Brownlie's Principles of Public International Law*, 8th edn (Oxford University Press, 2012) 456–86; C. Stalker, 'Jurisdiction', in M. Evans, *International Law*, 5th edn (Oxford University Press, 2018) 289–315.

[37] As explicitly recognised in art. 3 CAT and the jurisprudence of international treaty bodies. See Chapter 8.3.6.

[38] *Al-Skeini and Others* v. *United Kingdom* (ECtHR) (2011) para. 134.

[39] Ibid., para. 135.

[40] *Burgos* v. *Uruguay* (HRCtee) (1981) paras. 12.1–12.3.

[41] *Jaloud* v. *The Netherlands*.

[42] *Al-Skeini and* Others v. *United Kingdom*; *Al-Saadoon and Mufdhi* v. *United Kingdom* (ECtHR) (2010); *R (on the application of Evans)* v. *Secretary of State for Defence* (UK) (2011); *Hassan* v. *United Kingdom* (ECtHR) (2014).

[43] *Hirsi Jamaa* v. *Italy* (ECtHR) (2012) paras. 76–82; *P. K. and Others* v. *Spain*, para. 8.2.

territories?[44] And what about the use of firepower in a combat situation in a third country[45] or the bombing of a television station in a non-member state?[46] Human rights treaty bodies, and national courts, have largely used the criterion of 'effective control' to establish whether such acts fall within a state's jurisdiction.[47] Determining whether a state exercises 'effective control' is a question of fact that depends on physical control over a person or military presence and other factors evidencing the state's 'control over an area outside its territory'.[48] However, the application of this criterion has been far from consistent and has caused a considerable deal of controversy and legal uncertainty.[49]

Extending the application of treaties to conduct abroad may from a teleological perspective strengthen the effective protection of human rights. However, it frequently encounters considerable resistance on the part of states that oppose such interpretation.[50] The European experience is instructive in this regard because it has generated most of the existing case law. In one of its most controversial cases, concerning the NATO bombing of a television station in Belgrade, *Banković and Others* v. *Belgium and Sixteen Other Contracting States*, the ECtHR found the ECHR inapplicable, holding that there was no effective control of the territory and its inhabitants.[51] In a potentially far-reaching paragraph, it stressed that the protection of the Convention was meant to guarantee a public European order and did not extend 'beyond the legal space (*espace juridique*) of the Contracting States'.[52] Equally, the UK House of Lords had adopted a narrow reading, finding that UK troops operating in Iraq exercised 'effective control' where

---

[44] *Loizidou* v. *Turkey* (ECtHR) (1995); Concluding observations of the HRCtee on the USA, UN doc. CCPR/C/USA/CO/3/2006 (15 September 2006) para. 10; and Israel, UN doc. CCPR/C/ISR/CO/3/2010 (3 September 2010) para. 5.

[45] Compare *Issa and Others* v. *Turkey* (ECtHR) (2005) paras. 65–81, with *Al-Skeini* v. *United Kingdom*, paras. 149–50 (during occupation) and *Jaloud* v. *The Netherlands* (control over an area) paras. 140–53.

[46] *Banković and Others* v. *Belgium and Others* (ECtHR) (2001).

[47] *Jaloud* v. *Netherlands*, para. 139, provides an overview of the ECtHR's jurisprudence. See also *Mohammad Abdullah Saleh Al-Asad* v. *The Republic of Djibouti* (ACmHPR) (2014) para. 134, and HRCtee, General Comment 31, Nature of the General Legal Obligation Imposed on States Parties to the Covenant, UN doc. CCPR/C/21/Rev.1/Add.13 (26 May 2004) para. 10: 'This means that a State party must respect and ensure the rights laid down in the Covenant to anyone within the power or effective control of that State Party, even if not situated within the territory of the State Party.'

[48] HRCtee, General Comment 31, ibid., and *Al-Skeini* v. *United Kingdom*, para. 139.

[49] See further Chapter 16.6.1.

[50] Such as the UK in *Al-Skeini* v. *United Kingdom*, Turkey in *Loizidou* v. *Turkey*, and the USA in relation to extraterritorial counter-terrorism operations, UN doc. CCPR/C/USA/CO/3/2006, para. 10 and *Djamel Ameziane* v. *United States* (IACHR) (2012).

[51] *Banković and Others* v. *Belgium and Others*, paras. 54–82.

[52] Ibid., para. 80. See for a detailed discussion of the *Banković* case, M. Milanovic, 'From Compromise to Principle: Clarifying the Concept of State Jurisdiction in Human Rights Treaties' (2008) 8 *Human Rights Law Review* 411.

an individual was in custody but not in a combat situation,[53] a distinction that seems rather artificial, particularly where the troops concerned are in control of an area.

7.2.1.5   The Long Reach of the ECHR: *Al-Skeini* v. *UK*

The *Al-Skeini* v. *UK* judgment substantially clarified the ECtHR's jurisprudence. The case concerned the killing of six civilians at the hands of UK troops, both in custody and on the streets of Basra, Iraq, and the UK's failure to comply with its procedural duty under article 2 ECHR to investigate the killings effectively. The outcome of the case hinged on the question of jurisdiction. Once the ECtHR found that the UK's 'authority and responsibility for the maintenance of security in South East Iraq' provided the jurisdictional link under article 1 ECHR,[54] a finding of a violation of article 2 ECHR became almost inevitable due to the apparent lack of independence of investigations.[55] The judgment effectively abandoned the Court's reservation that the ECHR does not apply extraterritorially (see *Banković*). However, it retains a case-by-case approach that focuses on the element of direct control over a person and/or effective control over an area to establish a jurisdictional link. In a persuasive concurring opinion Judge Bonello criticised the Court for having missed an opportunity to develop a more coherent approach to the question of extraterritorial application based on functional considerations according to which 'a State has jurisdiction for the purposes of Article 1 whenever the observance or the breach of any of these functions [negative and positive obligations in respect of human rights] is within its authority and control'.[56]

One important follow-up question is what rights should apply; for example whether occupying forces, such as in Iraq, should ensure the rights under the ECHR, which has given rise to debates about the risk of 'human rights imperialism' by applying regional standards beyond the

---

[53] *Al-Skeini & Ors* v. *Secretary of State for Defence* (UK) (2007) summarised in *Al-Skeini* v. *United Kingdom*, paras. 83–8.

[54] Ibid., para. 149.

[55] Ibid., paras. 151–77. See also on the procedural limb of art. 2, *Jaloud* v. *The Netherlands*, paras. 157–228.

[56] See the Concurring Opinion of Judge Bonello, *Al-Skeini* v. *United Kingdom*, para. 11. See also HRCtee, General Comment 36 on article 6 of the International Covenant on Civil and Political Rights, on the right to life (2018) para. 22: '[States] must also take appropriate legislative and other measures to ensure that all activities taking place in whole or part within their territory and in other places subject to their jurisdiction, but having a direct and reasonably foreseeable impact on the right to life of individuals outside their territory ... are consistent with article 6 ...'

territory of member states.[57] While there are still grey areas in this respect, a state effectively exercising public authority extraterritorially should be responsible for ensuring the rights it is able to protect, particularly in relation to its own conduct.[58] Given the multiple instances in which states act abroad it can be expected that the jurisdictional question will continue to vex human rights treaty bodies, although a teleological approach focusing on effective protection appears best suited to these situations, not least so as to avoid a situation described by Judge Bonello of states acting as 'gentlemen at home, hoodlums elsewhere'.[59]

POINTS TO CONSIDER

1. Do you agree with Judge Bonello's functional approach, or would this be 'tantamount to arguing that anyone adversely affected by an act imputable to a Contracting State, wherever in the world that act may have been committed or its consequences felt, is thereby brought within the jurisdiction of that State for the purpose of Article 1 of the Convention'?[60]

2. The UK argued (see Judge Bonello's concurring opinion) that exporting the ECHR to Iraq would amount to 'human rights imperialism'. Discuss.

In an interesting reverse scenario, Moldova argued in 2004 in the *Ilaşcu* case that it did not exercise jurisdiction over Transdniestra, a breakaway region that had effectively been under Russian control since 1991. The ECtHR rejected this argument, finding that a state retains jurisdiction over its territory 'even where the exercise of the State's authority is limited in part of its territory'.[61] This was an important ruling because it strengthened the protection of persons, such as Ilaşcu, who find themselves in the power of a de facto authority. The ECtHR tempered the legal consequences, though, by finding that the limited control did affect the nature of Moldova's positive obligation to prevent and remedy violations.[62]

---

[57] R. Wilde, 'Compliance with Human Rights Norms Extraterritorially: 'human rights imperialism?', in B. de Chazournes and M. G. Kohen (eds.), *Human Rights and the Quest for its Implementation* (Brill, 2010) 319–48.

[58] Concurring Opinion of Judge Bonello in *Al-Skeini* v. *United Kingdom*, para. 32, and further R. Wilde, 'Triggering State Obligations Extraterritorially: The Spatial Test in Certain Human Rights Treaties' (2007) 40 *Israel Law Review* 503, and Milanovic, above note 52, at 424.

[59] Concurring Opinion of Judge Bonello in *Al-Skeini* v. *United Kingdom*, para. 18. See Chapter 9.7 on the extraterritorial application of economic, social and cultural rights.

[60] *Banković and Others* v. *Belgium and Others*, para. 75.

[61] *Ilaşcu and Others* v. *Moldova and Russia* (ECtHR) (2005) paras. 300–31, at 313; also *Assanidze* v. *Georgia* (ECtHR) (2004) paras. 132–50. The approach taken in *Ilaşcu* was upheld in *Mozer* v. *Moldova and Russia* (ECtHR) (2016) paras. 96–100.

[62] *Ilaşcu and Others* v. *Moldova and Russia*, paras. 332–5.

7.2.1.6   *Rationae Temporis:* When?

Applicants can only bring a case that falls within the period for which a
state has recognised the competence of a treaty body to consider applications against it, for example following the entry into force of the Optional
Protocol to the ICCPR for the state concerned. This is based on the general
rule of non-retroactivity of obligations (because of a lack of state consent for
the preceding period).[63] However, applicants may exceptionally bring cases
in circumstances that qualify this general rule. The most important situations are ongoing violations, such as enforced disappearances,[64] or violations
of property rights,[65] which commenced before the state concerned became
bound by the complaints procedure but continued to generate effects thereafter.[66] The consideration of other violations, such as the inordinate length
of proceedings, is in principle confined to the period after a state is subject
to the complaints procedure. However, treaty bodies have qualified this principle and have considered relevant factors prior to that date.[67] In the case of
trials, for example, the HRCtee has held that the upholding of convictions by
higher courts allows it to consider proceedings as a whole where a judgment
constitutes an affirmation of the original violation, which it was precluded
from considering because of non-retroactivity.[68] Importantly, a state may
also be held responsible for its failure to comply with its positive obligation
to investigate violations even where they occurred prior to it being bound.
The HRCtee initially held that the duty to investigate was not an independent
obligation that could be detached from the violation of a substantive ICCPR

---

[63] See *Janowiec and Others* v. *Russia* (ECtHR) (2013) para. 128; and further *Blečić* v. *Croatia*
(ECtHR) (2006) paras. 51–93 (court termination of tenancy before entry into force); *E. J.
and C. M. Drake* v. *New Zealand* (HRCtee) (1997) para. 8.2 (1951 peace treaty with Japan
that was alleged not to provide adequate compensation for New Zealand nationals and
residents); *R. A. V. N. et al.* v. *Argentina* (HRCtee) (1990) para. 5.2 (amnesty laws).

[64] See *Varnava and Others* v. *Turkey* (ECtHR) (2009) for an overview of jurisprudence of
international bodies, at paras. 93–106, and of the ECtHR, at paras. 130–50. See also *J. E.
Zitha and P. J. L. Zitha* v. *Mozambique* (ACmHPR) (2011) paras. 73–94.

[65] See e.g., *Loizidou* v. *Turkey* (ECtHR) (1997) paras. 48–64, and *Hutten-Czapska* v. *Poland*
(ECtHR) (2007) paras. 152–3.

[66] But a state may limit jurisdiction to acts that had begun after a certain date; see e.g.,
Serrano Cruz Sisters v. *El Salvador* (IACtHR) (2004) paras. 57–79.

[67] See for an overview of ECtHR jurisprudence, *Šilih* v. *Slovenia* (ECtHR) (2009) paras. 140–7
and *Janowiec and Others* v. *Russia*, paras. 136–51.

[68] Here conviction under Sri Lanka's Prevention of Terrorism Act based on evidence
allegedly extracted under torture, see *Singarasa* v. *Sri Lanka* (HRCtee) (2004) para. 6.3. The
CESCR held that 'judicial or administrative decisions of the national authorities are also
considered as part of the "facts" ... when they are the result of proceedings that are directly
related to the initial events, acts or omissions that gave rise to the violation and provided
that they allow redress to be obtained for the alleged violation, in accordance with the law
applicable at the time.' *Calero* v. *Ecuador* (CESCR) (2018) para. 9.5.

right. However, it later found that it has jurisdiction where proceedings had already been pending at the time the ICCPR and the Optional Protocol came into force for the state party.[69] The ECtHR, in holding that the procedural obligation to investigate alleged violations under articles 2 and 3 ECHR had developed into a separate and autonomous duty, found that procedural acts or omissions might constitute an interference that brings a case within the Court's jurisdiction.[70] However, it qualified this general rule by requiring a 'genuine connection' between the substantive violation and the procedural steps, 'a significant proportion [of which] will have been or ought to have been carried out after the critical date [entry into force]'.[71] This connection could 'in certain circumstances ... also be based on the need to ensure that the guarantees and the underlying values of the Convention are protected in a real and effective manner'.[72] A case concerning the termination, in 2004, of investigations by Russian authorities into the war crimes committed in Katyn, Poland, during World War II, whereby some procedural steps had been taken in the early 1990s, illustrated the difficulties of determining such a link in cases dating back a long time. After setting out relevant principles, the Court concluded 'that there were no elements capable of providing a bridge from the distant past into the recent post-ratification period [after 1998] and that the special circumstances justifying a connection between the death and the ratification [such as newly discovered evidence] have not been shown to exist'.[73] Nevertheless, the jurisprudence shows that applicants may under certain circumstances be able to bring cases alleging a violation of the duty to investigate even where they are barred from raising the violation giving rise to such duty, as in the case of extrajudicial killings.

7.2.2   Exhaustion of Domestic Remedies

The requirement to exhaust domestic remedies frequently constitutes one of the most formidable challenges for applicants. The exhaustion rule recognises that victims have a right of access to justice and that states have the

---

[69] Compare *R. A. V. N. et al.* v. *Argentina*, para. 5.3, with *Mariama Sankara et al.* v. *Burkina Faso* (HRCtee) (2006) para. 6.3.

[70] See *Janowiec and Others* v. *Russia*, para. 132. For the IACtHR, see also *Serrano Cruz Sisters* v. *El Salvador*, paras. 77–96, particularly at para. 77 ('independent facts' even though court barred from examining actual violations alleged because of limitation pursuant to El Salvador's declaration); *Moiwana Community* v. *Suriname* (2005) paras. 37–44.

[71] *Šilih* v. *Slovenia*, paras. 159–67, particularly para. 163. See further *Janowiec and Others* v. *Russia*, paras. 145–8 and *Mocanu and Others* v. *Romania* (ECtHR) (2014) paras. 205–11.

[72] *Šilih* v. *Slovenia*, para. 163 and *Janowiec and Others* v. *Russia*, paras. 149–51.

[73] *Janowiec and Others* v. *Russia* (ECtHR) (2012) para. 140, upheld by the Grand Chamber in 2013, para. 160.

primary duty, and should be given the opportunity, to remedy violations at the domestic level. The rule reflects the subsidiarity of supranational human rights treaty bodies, which are not meant to replace national courts or act as appeal courts.[74] From a pragmatic perspective the rule also prevents a supranational body from being seized with a large number of cases (although the floodgate argument has not stopped an enormous volume of applications reaching the ECtHR). The jurisprudence on the exhaustion of domestic remedies varies considerably between treaty bodies and even in the practice of individual bodies over time. This is unsurprising given the difficulty of determining whether domestic remedies are available and effective. This determination also has a political dimension because it implies a verdict on the capacity of the domestic legal system in question to respond adequately to an alleged violation.

7.2.2.1   What Remedies Must be Exhausted?

An applicant needs to exhaust remedies that are available and effective. A remedy is considered available if it is accessible in theory and practice[75] and can be 'pursued without impediment'.[76] It is effective where it offers a prospect of success, that is redress for the violation complained about.[77] In principle, applicants must pursue all available remedies, including appeals to the highest courts and fundamental rights petitions.[78] However, there are several recognised exceptions. There is no need to exhaust purely discretionary procedures such as pardons because they are not based on the determination of rights.[79] In cases of serious violations, such as alleged violations of the right to life or the prohibition of torture, purely administrative or disciplinary proceedings are not considered sufficient or effective.[80] In these instances remedies must be of a judicial nature; they must also be capable of establishing

---

[74] E.g., *Selmouni v. France* (ECtHR) (2000) para. 74; *Kudla v. Poland* (ECtHR) (2000) para. 152; *Velásquez Rodríguez v. Honduras* (IACtHR) (1988) para. 61; *Dawda Jawara v. The Gambia*, (ACmHPR) (2000) para. 31; *T. K. v. France* (HRCtee) (1989) para. 8.3. See on the application of the principle in public international law, P. Okowa, 'Issues of Admissibility and the Law on State Responsibility', in M. Evans, above note 36, 477–508, at 500–5.

[75] *Akdivar and Others v. Turkey* (ECtHR) (1997) para. 66.

[76] *Dawda Jawara v. The Gambia*, para. 32.

[77] Ibid., *Sejdovic v. Italy* (ECtHR) (2006) para. 46; *Godínez Cruz v. Honduras* (IACtHR) (1990) paras. 67–9; *Patino v. Panama* (HRCtee) (1994) para. 5.2.

[78] *A. H. v. Sweden* (CtAT) (2006).

[79] *Singarasa v. Sri Lanka*, para. 6.4; *Prince v. Jamaica* (HRCtee) (1992) para. 5.1; *Constitutional Rights Project v. Nigeria* (ACmHPR) (1995) para. 10.

[80] See in particular, HRCtee decisions in *Vicente et al. v. Colombia* (HRCtee) (1997) para. 5.2; *Coronel et al. v. Colombia* (HRCtee) (2002) para. 6.2.

the facts and the criminal responsibility of those responsible. This means, for example, that a respondent state cannot refer to the possibility of pursuing a case before a national human rights commission that lacks binding powers where an applicant shows that effective judicial remedies are not available.[81] This jurisprudence demonstrates the link between the nature of violations and the types of remedies that are considered effective in the circumstances.

Remedies need not be exhausted if they are futile, for example where there is already settled case law by the highest courts on the point raised.[82] Equally, there is no need to exhaust unduly prolonged remedies, which are by their very nature considered ineffective as recognised in several treaties and the jurisprudence of treaty bodies.[83] There are no hard and fast rules on when a remedy is unduly prolonged – treaty bodies generally consider the conduct of the parties and the complexity of the case to determine whether the length of time is reasonable.[84] Applicants are, for example, able to rely on this rule where investigations into alleged violations have been pending for years without any evidence of progress or where judicial proceedings have dragged on for several years, particularly where remedies have been turned into 'delaying instruments'.[85]

Other exceptions to the general rule of exhaustion are based on structural policy considerations. The ACmHPR, in particular, has repeatedly held that it would be impracticable to require applicants to exhaust domestic remedies in cases of serious or massive violations where – even though the violations must have been known to the state – it failed to take adequate action.[86] The ECtHR also held for some time that applicants need not exhaust domestic remedies in the south-east of Turkey 'where an administrative practice consisting of a repetition of acts incompatible with the Convention and official tolerance by the State authorities has been shown to exist, and is of such a nature as to make proceedings futile or ineffective'[87] – a practice that

---

[81] *Ilesanmi* v. *Nigeria* (ACmHPR) (2005) para. 42. Conversely, it is not sufficient for an applicant to submit a case before a national human rights institution without also seeking recourse to courts, see *Alfred B. Cudjoe* v. *Ghana* (ACmHPR) (1999) para. 13; *Brough* v. *Australia* (HRCtee) (2006) para. 8.7.

[82] *Länsman et al.* v. *Finland* (HRCtee) (1994) para. 6.2; *Pressos Compania Naviera S. A. and Others* v. *Belgium* (ECtHR) (1996) para. 27.

[83] Art. 5(2)(b) Optional Protocol to the ICCPR; art. 56(5) ACHPR; art. 46(1)(c) ACHR.

[84] See e.g., *Zongo and others* v. *Burkina Faso* (ACtHPR) (2014) paras. 72–106; *Todorov* v. *Bulgaria* (ECtHR) (2005) para. 45. See for a detailed review of the HRCtee's jurisprudence on this point, Tyagi, above note 7, 487–92.

[85] *Las Dos Erres Massacre* v. *Guatemala* (IACtHR) (2009) paras. 119 and 121; *Rajapakse* v. *Sri Lanka* (HRCtee) (2006) para. 9.4.

[86] See e.g., *Sudan Human Rights Organisation and Centre on Housing Rights and Evictions (COHRE)* v. *Sudan* (ACmHPR) (2009) para. 102.

[87] *Akdivar* v. *Turkey*, para. 67. See also on 'administrative practice', *Georgia* v. *Russia* (I) (ECtHR) (2014) paras. 122–59.

resulted in a large number of cases before the Court. Such jurisprudence makes it easier for applicants to pursue cases, but may result in difficulties at the enforcement stage if a state opposes the interpretation of the treaty body concerned.

Applicants need not exhaust domestic remedies that are not accessible. This rule has been applied where someone cannot return to a country to pursue a case out of fear for his or her life, particularly following a violation.[88] It also applies where someone has been subjected to threats preventing him or her from accessing legal remedies, either personally or through lawyers. This includes situations where a 'general fear in the legal community to represent [a person] prevents a complainant ... from invoking domestic remedies', as found by the Inter-American Court of Human Rights (IACtHR) in its advisory opinion on *Exceptions to the Exhaustion of Domestic Remedies*.[89]

The IACtHR held that a lack of means to afford legal assistance does not absolve a person from having to exhaust domestic remedies unless 'it can be shown that an indigent needs legal counsel to effectively protect a right which the Convention guarantees and his indigency prevents him from obtaining such counsel'.[90] This finding entails that states have to offer legal aid where needed to secure effective access to remedies. Other courts, such as the ECtHR, have been reluctant to consider lack of resources as a ground on which applicants can forgo the requirement to exhaust domestic remedies.[91] Applicants relying on this argument therefore run a considerable risk of their case being declared inadmissible.

In terms of procedure, applicants bear the initial burden of proof to show that they have exhausted domestic remedies or that effective remedies are not available. Where the applicant makes out a prima facie case to this effect the state must demonstrate that effective remedies were available, i.e.

[88] *Monim Elgak, Osman Hummeida and Amir Suliman (represented by FIDH and OMCT) v. Sudan* (ACmHPR) (2014) paras. 48–55; *Mbiankeu Geneviéve v. Cameroon* (ACmHPR) (2015) paras. 75–6. In contrast, see *Givemore Chari (represented by Gabriel Shumba) v. Republic of Zimbabwe* (ACmHPR) (2012) paras. 60–70 (need to exhaust domestic remedies). See on the contradictory aspects of the ACHPR's jurisprudence in this regard, F. Viljoen, 'Communication under the African Charter: Procedure and Admissibility', in M. Evans and R. Murray (eds.), *The African Charter on Human and Peoples' Rights: The System in Practice 1986–2006*, 2nd edn (Cambridge University Press, 2008) 76–138, at 121–3.

[89] *Exceptions to the Exhaustion of Domestic Remedies (Arts. 46(1), 46(2)(a) and 46(2)(b) of the American Convention on Human Rights)* (IACtHR) (1990) para. 32.

[90] Ibid., para. 31; *Hilaire, Constantine and Benjamin et al. v. Trinidad and Tobago* (IACtHR) (2002) para. 152(b). See also *Purohit and Moore v. The Gambia* (ACmHPR) (2003) paras. 36–8; *Henry v. Jamaica* (HRCtee) (1991) para. 7.3: 'it is not the author's indigence which absolves him from pursuing constitutional remedies, but the State party's unwillingness or inability to provide legal aid for this purpose'.

[91] *Van Oosterwijck v. Belgium* (ECtHR) (1981) para. 38.

'sufficiently certain in theory and practice', but have not been exhausted.[92] If the state succeeds in doing so the applicant has to exhaust any remaining remedies.[93] Arguments to this effect are frequently at the heart of admissibility decisions and constitute one of the major hurdles that applicants need to overcome.

7.2.2.2   'An Affront to Common Sense and Logic': *Dawda Jawara* v. *The Gambia*

Dawda Jawara, the complainant, was 'the former Head of State of the Republic of The Gambia. He allege[d] that after the Military coup of July 1994, that overthrew his government there has been "blatant abuse of power by ... the military junta". The military government is alleged to have initiated a reign of terror, intimidation and arbitrary detention.' The respondent state party claimed that the complainant had not exhausted domestic remedies, arguing that 'he should have sent his complaint to the police who would in turn have investigated the allegations and prosecuted the offenders "in a court of law"'. The African Commission held that 'in a situation where the jurisdiction of the courts have [sic] been ousted by decrees whose validity cannot be challenged or questioned, as is the position with the case under consideration, local remedies are deemed not only to be unavailable but also non-existent'.[94] Moreover, '[t]he complainant in this case had been overthrown by the military, he was tried in absentia, former Ministers and Members of Parliament of his government have been detained and there was terror and fear for lives in the country. It would be an affront to common sense and logic to require the complainant to return to his country to exhaust local remedies'.[95]

Consequently, the African Commission found the case admissible and in so doing established an important precedent for the understanding of what constitutes an effective remedy.

QUESTION

1. **A human rights defender who has credible evidence that he has been tortured because of his work and who left the country concerned out of fear for his safety considers that he would face further risk of torture if he were to return to pursue the case. Would he still need to pursue domestic remedies, possibly through a lawyer?**

---

[92] *Dalia* v. *France* (ECtHR) (2001) para. 38.
[93] *S. H. B.* v. *Canada* (HRCtee) (1987) para. 7.2; *Epözdemir* v. *Turkey* (ECtHR) (2002) (mere doubt not sufficient).
[94] *Dawda Jawara* v. *The Gambia*, para. 34.   [95] Ibid., para. 36.

7.2.3　Other Procedural Requirements

7.2.3.1　Time Limits

There is no uniform practice concerning the time within which an application has to be submitted. Before both the ECtHR and the IACHR applications need to be brought within six months after the final decision or six months from the time either of the act constituting the alleged violations or after it becomes clear that no effective remedies are available.[96] As held in *Varnava v. Turkey*, the 'object of the six-month time-limit under Article 35 §1 is to promote legal certainty'.[97] The rule can pose significant challenges for applicants who have to make sure that they submit applications in time. These include situations where an applicant mistakenly pursues remedies that may be considered ineffective, and, in so doing, fails to adhere to the six-month limit.[98] The only UN treaties that include an express time limit (of one year) are the recently adopted Optional Protocols to the International Covenant on Economic, Social and Cultural Rights (ICESCR) and Convention on the Rights of the Child (CRC).[99] Other complaints procedures may reject applications that are submitted after an unduly long time on the ground that they constitute an abuse of the right. The HRCtee has clarified its understanding of what constitutes an abuse of right by stipulating a general, comparatively generous, five-year period from the exhaustion of domestic remedies or three years after the 'conclusion of another procedure of international investigation or settlement'.[100] The ACHPR provides that applications should be submitted 'within a reasonable time from the time domestic remedies are exhausted'.[101] The ACmHPR has for a long time applied this rule generously, but has since the late 2000s begun to declare cases inadmissible for having been submitted out of time where it considers that the applicant(s) did not convincingly show why the application could not have been made earlier.[102]

---

[96] See e.g., *Bayram and Yildrim v. Turkey* (ECtHR) (2002). See on ineffective investigations and the applicant's duty of diligence, *Mocanu and Others v. Romania*, paras. 258–83. The period will be reduced to four months in respect of cases to be brought before the ECtHR upon the coming into force of Protocol no. 15.

[97] *Varnava and Others v. Turkey* (ECtHR) (2009) para. 156.

[98] See for an overview of relevant jurisprudence, P. Leach, *Taking a Case to the European Court of Human Rights* (Oxford University Press, 2011) 4.101; D. J. Harris et al., *Law of the European Convention on Human Rights*, 3rd edn (Oxford University Press, 2014) 61–7.

[99] Art. 3(2)(a) Optional Protocol to the ICESCR and art. 7(h) Optional Protocol to the CRC on a communications procedure.

[100] Rule 96(c) of the HRCtee's Rules of Procedure.

[101] Art. 56(6) ACHPR.

[102] See e.g., *Michael Majuru v. Zimbabwe* (ACmHPR) (2008) para. 110 (twenty-two months considered too long in the circumstances); *Article 19 and Others v. Zimbabwe* (ACmHPR) (2010) (two years); *Darfur Relief and Documentation Centre v. Sudan* (ACmHPR) (2009) paras. 78–9 (twenty-nine months).

This jurisprudence, which is far from consistent, shows that an indeterminate limit, such as 'within a reasonable time', introduces an element of uncertainty and possibly of arbitrariness.[103]

7.2.3.2   *Duplication*

Complaints procedures provide that applications are inadmissible if the same matter is being examined (Optional Protocol to the ICCPR; ACHR; International Convention for the Protection of All Persons from Enforced Disappearance (CPED)) or has been examined (ACHPR) by the same body or 'another procedure of international investigation or settlement' (both grounds under the Convention against Torture and Other Cruel, Inhuman or Degrading Treatment or Punishment (CAT); International Convention on the Protection of the Rights of All Migrant Workers and Members of Their Families (ICRMW); Optional Protocols to the Convention on the Elimination of All Forms of Discrimination against Women (CEDAW), ICESCR, Convention on the Rights of Persons with Disabilities (CRPD), and CRC, and the ECHR where it has already been examined by the Court or submitted to another procedure). The rationale behind this rule is to prevent forum shopping, to contribute to the settlement of disputes and to reduce the scope for diverging decisions. The requirement is less restrictive for applicants than it may appear at first sight because it effectively requires that the application is identical in relation to the facts, the parties concerned and the allegations raised in another case, and does not rely on new information.[104] Moreover, it only applies where the other body examines the complaint, which the CESCR found not to be the case for an ECtHR inadmissibility decision 'worded in general terms and [which] does not provide specific reasons for its finding'.[105] Further, it is confined to other binding complaints procedures. Procedures that cannot consider complaints, determine responsibility and afford remedies, such as the UN special procedures (with the possible exception of the Working Group on Arbitrary Detention),[106] confidential UN Charter body proceedings, such as the Human Rights Council's (HRC) complaints procedures, or preventive bodies, such

---

[103] See also critical comments by F. Viljoen, *International Human Rights Law in Africa*, 2nd edn (Oxford University Press, 2012) 319–20.

[104] See e.g., *Fanali* v. *Italy* (ECtHR) (1983) para. 7.2; *Smirnova and Smirnova* v. *Russia* (ECtHR) (2002); *Varnava and Others* v. *Turkey*, para. 118.

[105] *Sierra et al.* v. *Spain* (CESCR) (2016) para. 6.5.

[106] See *Niyonzima* v. *Burundi* (CtAT) (2015) para. 7.1 (reporting of case to Working Group on Arbitrary Detention did not render case inadmissible because mandate of that body concerns arbitrary deprivation of liberty, not torture).

as the European Committee for the Prevention of Torture and Inhuman or Degrading Treatment or Punishment (CPT), fall outside of its scope.[107] These factors considerably limit the importance of this admissibility criterion in practice.

7.2.3.3   Well-foundedness

Applicants must demonstrate that their case is not manifestly ill-founded or unsubstantiated (HRCtee), a notion that allows treaty bodies to dismiss claims that are deemed without merit.[108] This requirement involves a preliminary examination of the substance of the case. Applications have been found to be manifestly ill-founded where they effectively asked the treaty body to act as court of appeal, where there is no apparent violation or where the allegations are not sufficiently substantiated.[109] Effectively, this means that an applicant has to make out a prima facie case and adduce at least some evidence that supports any claims made. Protocol no. 14 to the ECHR has added a related, and controversial, criterion of 'no significant disadvantage', which means that the Court may declare applications inadmissible even where they may be well-founded but are not considered sufficiently serious to merit its attention.[110]

7.2.3.4   Abuse of Rights

'Abuse of rights' is a general and flexible device in the hands of treaty bodies to dismiss applications that are designed to cause annoyance, use offensive language or are otherwise considered inappropriate.[111] The criterion of offensive language can be problematic where the body concerned applies value judgements to applications of victims who may have a strong sense of injustice and thereby deprive them of the opportunity to hear a case on the merits.[112] In practice, the criterion of abuse of rights does not play a major role, but it is still one that applicants need to be mindful of.

---

[107] See for a review of relevant jurisprudence Tyagi, above note 7, 466–71, and *Nikolai, Ljubov and Oleg Mikolenko* v. *Estonia* (ECtHR) (2006).

[108] See e.g., art. 3(2)(e) Optional Protocol to the ICESCR; art. 35(3)(a) ECHR; art. 47(b), (c) ACHR.

[109] See e.g., *Hussain and Singh* v. *Guyana* (HRCtee) (2005) para. 5.4. See also *Mohammed Abdullah Saleh Al Asad* v. *The Republic of Djibouti* (ACmHPR) (2014) paras. 136–77 (rendition case, inadmissible).

[110] Art. 53(3)(b) ECHR. See for its application, e.g., *Shefer* v. *Russia* (ECtHR) (2012).

[111] See in particular, art. 3 Optional Protocol to the ICCPR; art. 35(3)(a) ECHR; art. 56 ACHPR.

[112] Art. 56(3) ACHPR. See critical comments by Viljoen, above note 103, 314–15.

7.2.3.5   *Anonymity*

Most complaints procedures require that applications are not lodged anonymously.[113] The reason for this is that the treaty body needs to know who it is dealing with; it also enables the respondent state to better respond to the facts. However, the requirement can be problematic where an applicant fears that the disclosure may put him or her at risk of reprisals. This is a genuine risk in many cases, as the relevant jurisprudence and UN reports demonstrate. For example, in *Aksoy*, the first torture case against Turkey, the applicant was killed before the ECtHR could hear the case on the merits.[114] Bodies therefore accept exceptions, such as the use of pseudonyms, as long as it is clear who is behind the application.[115] In practice, applicants may find it difficult to hide their identity, particularly given the factual evidence they need to provide to substantiate their claims.

7.3   MERITS

Once a case has been found admissible (and sometimes simultaneously) a human rights treaty body considers the merits to determine whether the rights of the applicant(s) have been violated, in other words whether the allegations made are well-founded and reveal a breach of the state party's obligations. This determination is not confined to the violations claimed by the applicant; rather, treaty bodies can determine on their own motion what violations the proven facts disclose.[116] The evidentiary rules in proceedings before human

---

[113] Art. 3 Optional Protocol to the ICCPR; art. 35(2)(a) ECHR; art. 46(d) ACHR; art. 56(1) ACHPR.

[114] *Aksoy* v. *Turkey* (ECtHR) (1996) para. 22.

[115] *Shamayev and Others* v. *Georgia and Russia* (ECtHR) (2005) para. 275. Note the specific protection provided for in art. 4(1) Optional Protocol to the CRC (Communication Procedure), according to which '[t]he identity of any individual or group of individuals concerned shall not be revealed publicly without their express consent'.

[116] See in particular, F. Viljoen, 'Fact-finding by UN Human Rights Complaints Bodies: Analysis and Suggested Reforms' (2004) 8 *Max Planck Yearbook of United Nations Law* 49. See for an example of a case where the complainants did not invoke any particular provision of the CAT, but the CtAT found that the case raised an issue under art. 3 and possibly art. 16 of the Convention, *Njamba and Balikosa* v. *Sweden* (HRCtee) (2010) para. 1.1. However, see *Chaulagain* v. *Nepal* (HRCtee) (2014) Partly dissenting opinion of Committee members Víctor Manuel Rodríguez-Rescia and Fabián Salvioli, paras. 3 and 4: 'The problem frequently faced by the Committee is more structural in nature and has to do with the incomprehensible – and, we believe, misguided – practice of refraining from applying the principle of *iura novit curia* in the consideration of communications. The Committee should analyse the cases it has before it based on the established facts and, on that basis, should determine which Covenant rights have been violated, regardless of whether this coincides with what has been claimed by the authors of the communication.'

rights treaty bodies, particularly quasi-judicial bodies, are characterised by less rigidity than those before national courts. As a general rule, the applicant carries the burden of proof in the sense that he or she has to make out a prima facie case.[117] This means having to adduce sufficient evidence to disclose a violation of his, her or their rights by the respondent state party, otherwise the application is (partly or fully) unfounded. In practice, this burden is eased in a series of circumstances. Where a state party does not respond to an application or fails to contest the allegations, the facts are considered proven where the applicant makes out a prima facie case.[118] In addition, the burden of proof is effectively reversed where the state party's lack of cooperation prevents the establishment of the facts, such as where it withholds crucial documents.[119] This rule also applies where it can be shown that a person was taken into custody in good health but sustains injuries or even dies while in detention without the state giving a satisfactory explanation.[120] The rationale behind this exception is that the circumstances lie exclusively in the sphere of the state and it is frequently virtually impossible for applicants to prove state responsibility. Moreover, where the facts disclose state interference with a qualified right, such as the right to privacy, the state party needs to show that such interference was necessary and proportionate.[121]

The standard of proof, that is the level of proof required for a treaty body to uphold a complaint, differs between treaty bodies and is not clearly defined. Most bodies appear to apply a standard akin to that known from civil proceedings, namely preponderance of probabilities (more likely than not).[122] The ECtHR has applied a higher standard of proof 'beyond reasonable doubt', which it has defined as 'the coexistence of sufficiently strong, clear and concordant inferences or of similar unrebutted presumptions of fact'.[123] While it has been emphasised that this standard is not identical to that applied in national criminal proceedings, it seems to be inappropriately high for human rights cases and its application has been repeatedly criticised.[124]

---

[117] See in particular, J. Kokott, *The Burden of Proof in Comparative and International Human Rights* (Kluwer Law International, 1998).

[118] See e.g., *Bailey* v. *Jamaica* (HRCtee) (1993) paras. 9.2–11.1.

[119] *Akkum and Others* v. *Turkey* (ECtHR) (2006) para. 211. See for an early example of the HRCtee's jurisprudence, *Bleier* v. *Uruguay* (HRCtee) (1982) para. 13.3.

[120] *Tomasi* v. *France* (ECtHR) (1993) para. 108; *Selmouni* v. *France*, para. 87; *Kurt and Others* v. *Turkey* (ECtHR) (2007) para. 124. See also *Velásquez Rodríguez* v. *Honduras*, paras. 135–8.

[121] See e.g., *Van der Velden* v. *the Netherlands* (ECtHR) (2006); *Coster* v. *United Kingdom* (ECtHR) (2001); *Leander* v. *Sweden* (ECtHR) (1987).

[122] See for a brief overview, R. Murray, 'Evidence and Fact Finding by the African Commission', in Evans and Murray, above note 88, 139–70, at 159–62.

[123] *Salman* v. *Turkey* (ECtHR) (2000) para. 100.

[124] Partly Dissenting Opinion of Judge Bonello, *Veznedaroğlu* v. *Turkey* (ECtHR) (2001), particularly para. 12.

Evidence is freely admissible and courts have shown flexibility in its assessment, often stressing that this is required by the nature of human rights cases.[125] Proceedings before UN treaty bodies are in writing only, relying mainly on affidavits and documentary evidence.[126] In contradistinction, the IACtHR has developed an elaborate practice of hearing witnesses and expert testimony in oral proceedings. This is important for applicants because it enables them to put a comprehensive account of alleged violations on the record and before the Court for consideration.[127] The regional human rights courts and bodies can also undertake fact-finding missions to establish the evidence.[128] However, practice is rather ad hoc and hampered by the lack of power to compel witnesses.

Applicants in human rights proceedings are well-advised to draw on as many credible sources of evidence as possible to substantiate any allegations made. Types of evidence may include victim and witness statements (affidavits), official documents (including judgments, documentation by national human rights institutions, custody records and policy papers) and expert testimony (particularly medical reports).[129] Reports by both national and international organisations and human rights bodies frequently play an important role in recording cases and establishing patterns of violations that can be relied on to enhance the credibility of claims made.[130] Courts may also consider audio-visual materials (satellite images, photographs and videos) as evidence.[131]

---

[125] *Ireland* v. *the United Kingdom* (ECtHR) (1978) para. 209; *Velásquez Rodríguez* v. *Honduras*, paras. 122–38.

[126] See e.g., art. 5(1) Optional Protocol to the ICCPR and rule 100(1) of the HRCtee's Rules of Procedure.

[127] J. Cavallaro and S. E. Brewer, 'Reevaluating Regional Human Rights Litigation in the Twenty-First Century: The Case of the Inter-American Court' (2008) 102 *American Journal of International Law* 768. See for a recent example, *García Lucero et al.* v. *Chile* (IACtHR) (2013).

[128] See Cavallaro and Brewer, ibid., 780, 793–6, 803–8, 814–16; P. Leach, C. Paraskeva and G. Uzelac, *International Human Rights and Fact-Finding: An Analysis of the Fact-finding Missions Conducted by the European Commission and Court of Human Rights* (Human Rights and Social Justice Research Institute, Metropolitan University, 2009); Murray, above note 122, 146–8.

[129] See A. Kjaerum, 'Combating Torture with Medical Evidence: The Use of Medical Evidence and Expert Opinions in International and Regional Human Rights Tribunals' (2010) 20 *TORTURE* 119, particularly on the distinction between documentary medical evidence and expert opinion.

[130] *Sudan Human Rights Organisation and Centre on Housing Rights and Evictions (COHRE)* v. *Sudan*, paras. 151–3; *Baboeram et al.* v. *Suriname* (HRCtee) (1985) para. 12.2.

[131] See the Center for Research Libraries, *Human Rights Electronic Evidence Study: Final Report* (The Center for Research Libraries, 2012), particularly 146–8. See also for an example of a video admitted as evidence in front of the IACtHR, *Gangaram Panday* v. *Suriname* (IACtHR) (1994) paras. 2(e), 8 and 52–6. According to the OHCHR, 'Procedure

Human rights courts may admit third parties to submit *amici* on particular points of law as 'friends of the court' where this is considered to be in the 'interests of the proper administration of justice'.[132] Although interveners are supposedly neutral, *amicus curiae* submissions can provide an excellent opportunity for NGOs to advocate a particular interpretation of rights and broaden the scope of analysis and thereby possibly advance jurisprudence in the field of human rights.[133] In practice, *amici* have played an important role in providing information and setting out questions of law that have been referred to by parties and formed part of the deliberations of the respective court.[134]

7.4   DECISIONS BY HUMAN RIGHTS TREATY BODIES

A glimpse at the decisions of human rights treaty bodies shows that decision-making is by majority, which sets out its reasoning in the decision.[135] Separate concurring opinions (to elaborate on a point of law or principle) and dissenting opinions (to set out the grounds on which the judge(s)/member(s) disagree with the majority) are an integral and instructive part of many decisions. Such opinions can provide an invaluable insight into the different positions within a treaty body; they are frequently relied upon by those who criticise particular reasoning and/or decisions and may be so persuasive as to lead to changes in jurisprudence.

The types of decision differ between treaty bodies and courts. Proceedings before UN treaty bodies and regional human rights commissions are

for complaints by individuals under the human rights treaties', 'it has not been the practice to receive oral submissions from the parties or audio or audio-visual evidence (such as audio cassettes or videotapes)'. See www.ohchr.org/EN/HRBodies/TBPetitions/Pages/IndividualCommunications.aspx.

[132] See e.g., art. 36(2) ECHR and rule 44(3)(a) ECtHR Rules of Procedure.

[133] M. Schachter, 'The Utility of Pro Bono Representation of US-Based Amicus Curiae in Non-US and Multi-National Courts as a Means of Advancing the Public Interest' (2004) 28 *Fordham International Law Journal* 88; A. Wilkowska-Landowska, '"Friends of the Court": The Role of Human Rights Non-governmental Organisations in the Litigation Proceedings' (2006) (2) *Human Rights Law Commentary*, online, at www.nottingham.ac.uk/hrlc/publications/humanrightslawcommentary.aspx.

[134] See e.g., the joint NGO *amicus* in the case of *Al-Saadoon and Mufdhi* v. *the United Kingdom* (Application no. 61498/08), *Written Comments by the Bar Human Rights Committee of England and Wales, British Irish Rights Watch, the European Human Rights Advocacy Centre, Human Rights Watch, the International Commission of Jurists, the International Federation for Human Rights, Justice, Liberty and Redress* (9 April 2009), online at www.liberty-human-rights.org.uk/sites/default/files/al-saadoon-and-mufdhi-v-uk-european-court-of-human-rights-2010.pdf.

[135] However, see Tyagi, above note 7, 552–6, on the HRCtee's practice to rely on consensus as much as possible.

quasi-judicial and such bodies adopt decisions. There is a continuing debate about the legal nature of these decisions, which some bodies refer to as 'views' or 'opinions'. Some observers, and frequently states parties or domestic courts, such as the Sri Lankan Supreme Court, claim that they are purely recommendatory.[136] The formal arguments put forward in support of this position are not very convincing. While there is general agreement that they are not binding as such, decisions of treaty bodies are recognised as 'authoritative interpretations' of the respective treaties that determine to what extent, if any, a state has failed to comply with its obligations.[137] As a consequence, states parties are required to take the necessary measures to remedy any violations found and bring their conduct into conformity with their obligation to give effect to treaties, such as required under article 2 ICCPR.[138]

In practice, there are considerable differences concerning the types of remedy identified by treaty bodies and awarded by courts. Remedies in the decisions of treaty bodies (other than courts) are often of a general and standardised nature. Treaty bodies tend to refrain from specifying amounts of compensation, stipulating that the state party should provide adequate compensation or reparation in line with national or international standards.[139] They also frequently request states parties to take measures against the perpetrators of violations, particularly to undertake investigations and ensure the prevention of 'similar violations in the future'. Yet practice has been far from consistent and UN treaty bodies have not developed an elaborate jurisprudence on reparation. In the regional systems, the IACHR has tended to be more specific and elaborate than the ACmHPR in respect of the reparations recommended. However, the African Commission has recently issued decisions that demonstrate greater emphasis on the nature of remedies.[140]

Human rights courts issue binding judgments on the merits that the parties undertake to comply with.[141] These judgments are final. The only exceptions are ECtHR Chamber judgments that may be brought before

---

[136] *Singarasa* v. *Attorney General* (Sri Lanka) (2006). In contrast, see Judgment No. 1263/2018 (Spain) (2018), in which the Spanish Supreme Court enforced the CtEDAW decision in the case of *González Carreño* v. *Spain* (CtEDAW) (2014) by awarding the applicant €600,000 compensation.

[137] HRCtee, General Comment 33: The Obligations of States Parties under the Optional Protocol to the International Covenant on Civil and Political Rights, UN doc. CCPR/C/GC/33/CRP.3 (25 August 2008) para. 13.

[138] Ibid., particularly paras. 14–15.   [139] See Chapter 15.10.7.   [140] Ibid.

[141] Arts. 44 and 46(1) ECHR; arts. 67 and 68 ACHR; arts. 28(2) and 30 of the 1998 Protocol to the ACHPR and art. 46 of the 2008 Protocol on the Statute of the African Court of Justice and Human Rights.

the Grand Chamber where they raise fundamental matters and the Grand Chamber accepts a request made.[142] The ECtHR has repeatedly stated that its judgments are declaratory. It has largely confined itself to stating that a judgment constitutes satisfaction but, especially in cases of violations of articles 2, 3 and 5 ECHR, where requested by the applicant, the ECtHR awards specific amounts of compensation for pecuniary and non-pecuniary harm.[143] This practice is based on the Court's interpretation of its competence to award 'just satisfaction', according to which it is primarily for the respondent state to take the measures necessary to comply with its obligations, under the supervision of the Committee of Ministers (CoM). The ECtHR's approach has been repeatedly criticised for its 'conservative' nature, but the Court has in some recent judgments ordered states to take specific measures, such as retrial or release, which may indicate a willingness to develop its own reparation regime.[144] However, these cases are still exceptional and the ECtHR's jurisprudence on reparation remains under-developed. The IACtHR's jurisprudence, based on article 63 ACHR, provides a stark contrast, standing out for its deliberately progressive, detailed and victim-oriented approach towards awarding reparation that both reflects the nature of harm and seeks to bring about systemic changes to ensure compliance.[145] The ACtHPR has not had the opportunity to develop its jurisprudence on reparation.[146] Notably, the Court has the mandate to award appropriate remedies, a power that many hope it will use with a view to strengthening the effectiveness of the African human rights system.[147]

---

[142] Art. 43 ECHR.   [143] See Chapter 15.10.7.

[144] See P. Leach, 'Beyond the Bug River: A New Dawn for Redress before the European Court of Human Rights?' (2005) 2 *European Human Rights Law Review* 148, referring to cases such as *Ilaşcu and Others* v. *Moldova and Russia*, and *Assanidze* v. *Georgia*. However, the Court has largely failed to use opportunities to widen the scope of reparation awarded. See in particular, arguments put forward in *Varnava and Others* v. *Turkey*, Intervention Submission by the Redress Trust (2 October 2008), which were ignored by the Court; see *Varnava and Others* v. *Turkey*, paras. 215–25. The Court has, though, become more prescriptive in some recent cases, such as in respect of systemic problems, here impunity for enforced disappearances, see *Aslakhanova and Others* v. *Russia* (ECtHR) (2012) paras. 222–39.

[145] See for a recent example of the breadth and detailed nature of reparation measures awarded, *Cabrera García and Montiel Flores* v. *Mexico* (IACtHR) (2010) paras. 208–61.

[146] However, note the first ruling of the Court on reparation in *Nobert Zongo and Others* v. *Burkina Faso* (ACtHPR) (2015).

[147] Art. 27 of the 1998 Protocol to the ACHPR and art. 45 of the 2008 Protocol on the Statute of the African Court of Justice and Human Rights.

7.5   IMPLEMENTATION OF DECISIONS AND JUDGMENTS

Implementation represents one of the main challenges for litigants because non-compliance[148] is a systemic problem in the international human rights system. The fact that most human rights treaties provide for no or only rudimentary enforcement procedures suggests that their significance was not well-appreciated at a time when the primary focus was on standard-setting. The assumption that states parties that voluntarily subject themselves to a complaints procedure could be expected to comply with any decisions made has proven highly questionable. Indeed, implementation has become one of the Achilles heels of complaints procedures given the prevalence of partial or complete non-compliance. This is due to a range of factors, particularly the lack of adequate legal and institutional frameworks that would facilitate implementation.[149] Conversely, commitment to human rights, the use of rulings to advance domestic human rights agendas and domestic preferences leading to the honouring of long-standing obligations, however 'begrudgingly', have been identified as key factors for compliance.[150] The available data show that compliance with the decisions of UN treaty bodies is inconsistent;[151] the same applies to decisions by the ACmHPR.[152] Most states comply with orders issued by the IACtHR or the ECtHR to pay compensation.[153] In both systems, states have also undertaken a series of general measures, particularly legislative reforms, to give effect to judgments.[154] However,

---

[148] R. Murray and D. Long, *The Implementation of the Findings of the African Commission on Human and Peoples' Rights* (Cambridge University Press, 2015) 41, usefully distinguish between 'measuring compliance (as the desired result) ... and monitoring implementation (as one process by which compliance may be achieved)'.

[149] See Tyagi, above note 7, 579–80, for the HRCtee and, more broadly, Open Society Justice Initiative, *From Rights to Remedies: Structures and Strategies for Implementing International Human Rights Decisions* (2013), which emphasises the role of key institutions, namely executive-level mechanisms, parliaments, the judiciary and national human rights institutions.

[150] C. Hillebrecht, *Domestic Politics and International Human Rights Tribunals: The Problem of Compliance* (Cambridge University Press, 2013), particularly 19–40.

[151] Several states have a persistent record of partial or complete non-compliance. See e.g., the 2014 *Annual Report of the HRCtee*, UN doc. A/69/40 (vol. I) paras. 258–65. However, in several cases, compensation was paid and some legislative reforms and changes were made, see Tyagi, above note 7, 626–9, for a brief overview.

[152] F. Viljoen and L. Louw, 'State Compliance with the Recommendations of the African Commission on Human and Peoples' Rights, 1994–2004' (2007) 101 *American Journal of International Law* 1.

[153] Hillebrecht, above note 150, 13 and 51.

[154] Peru abolished its amnesty laws following the case of Barrios Altos and several European states changed their legislation, particularly with a view to complying with pilot judgments. See further Chapters 6.2.6 and 6.3.4.

respondent states have largely failed to undertake investigations and hold the perpetrators accountable where ordered or obliged to do so;[155] this is a serious challenge as impunity constitutes one of the main factors that perpetuate a climate that facilitates human rights violations.[156]

The UN treaty bodies have responded to unsatisfactory implementation by taking various measures, such as setting timelines for reporting back on steps taken, the appointment of special rapporteurs for follow-up on views, and the inclusion of references to the lack of implementation in concluding observations on states parties' reports.[157] However, these measures ultimately rely on persuasion or naming and shaming because there are no effective sanctions. This means that they have been of limited use where needed most, that is when dealing with recalcitrant states. The development of more effective enforcement procedures remains a major challenge for the credibility of the UN human rights treaty system and has been one of the arguments for a unified human rights body or even a world court on human rights.

In the regional systems, the IACHR operates a system in which it may request parties for information, hold hearings and issue reports on the state of compliance.[158] The ACmHPR has committed itself to establishing follow-up mechanisms, but limited progress has been made beyond reporting on the status of implementation.[159] Successful cases of implementation have been attributed to the efforts of litigants and other bodies rather than the Commission's follow-up activities.[160]

'Enforcement' procedures differ in the Inter-American and European system (the system before the ACtHPR is not considered further because of lack of sufficient practice at the time of writing). The IACtHR strengthened the system when it found that it had implied powers to follow up on judgments.[161] It has changed its rules of procedure and developed a practice of convening regular meetings with the parties involved, which appears to be conducive to enhanced compliance.[162] However, this practice requires intense engagement and may by itself prove insufficient to overcome entrenched

---

[155] Hillebrecht, above note 150, 51.

[156] Open Society Justice Initiative (OSJI), *From Judgment to Justice, Implementing International and Regional Human Rights Decisions* (2010) 33–92.

[157] See Tyagi, above note 7, 584–6, for an overview of the action that the HRCtee can take.

[158] Art. 48(1) of the 2009 Rules of Procedure.

[159] Resolution on the Importance of the Recommendations of the African Commission on Human and Peoples' Rights and rule 112 of the 2010 Rules of Procedure. See further Murray and Long, above note 148, 119–39.

[160] OSJI, above note 156, 104–8.

[161] *Baena Ricardo* v. *Panama* (IACtHR) (2003).

[162] Art. 69 of the IACtHR's 2010 Rules of Procedure. The Court also regularly issues orders on compliance with judgments, available on its website at www.corteidh.or.cr.

systemic problems hindering implementation. The European system is unique in so far as a political body, the Council of Europe's (CoE) CoM, is tasked with supervising the execution of judgments. This includes individual and general measures and the CoM regularly monitors steps taken by the respondent states.[163] However, it has had limited success in challenging systemic non-compliance, such as by Russia and Turkey in relation to conflict-related violations.[164] In practice, NGOs increasingly provide information about the status of implementation to enable the CoM to exercise its mandate more effectively,[165] but limited political will and institutional resistance still remain major obstacles. Protocol no. 14 responded to criticisms concerning the division of tasks between the ECtHR and the CoM by giving the Court a greater role in the execution of judgments.[166]

It is clear that any institutional supranational 'enforcement' procedures have inherent limitations. There is no authority in international law with binding enforcement powers comparable to national systems; the ultimate sanction for non-compliance may be sanctions by, or exclusion from, the political body in question, but these steps require a considerable degree of political support.[167] From a functional perspective, the threat of exclusion may work as an effective threat for a state that wants to be part of a system, but fails where this is not the case and it is most needed. Human rights treaty bodies and courts therefore have to rely largely on their legitimacy, which includes persuasiveness of decisions made and a collective interest in making the system work, including by means of compliance.[168]

---

[163] Art. 46(2) ECHR; Reports on the execution of judgments can be found online at www.coe.int/t/cm/humanrights_en.asp.

[164] See Interviews 6.1 and 6.2. See also interim resolution CM/ResDH(2011)292: Execution of the judgments of the European Court of Human Rights in 154 cases against the Russian Federation concerning actions of the security forces in the Chechen Republic of the Russian Federation.

[165] See e.g., 'Communication from a group of the NGOs in the Mikheyev group of cases against the Russian Federation: Information made available under Rule 9.2 of the Rules of the Committee of Ministers for the supervision of the execution of judgments and of the terms of friendly settlements', DH-DD(2010)385E /1 September 2010.

[166] See art. 46(5) ECHR.

[167] See Protocol no. 14 to the Convention for the Protection of Human Rights and Fundamental Freedoms, amending the control system of the Convention, Explanatory report (CETS no. 194) Agreement of Madrid (12.5.2009) para. 100: 'None the less, it appeared necessary to give the Committee of Ministers, as the competent organ for supervising execution of the Court's judgments, a wider range of means of pressure to secure execution of judgments. Currently the ultimate measure available to the Committee of Ministers is recourse to Article 8 of the Council of Europe's Statute (suspension of voting rights in the Committee of Ministers, or even expulsion from the Organisation).'

[168] See B. Çali, A. Koch and N. Bruch, 'The Legitimacy of Human Rights Courts: A Grounded Interpretivist Analysis of the European Court of Human Rights' (2013) 35 *Human Rights Quarterly* 955.

Participants and observers increasingly recognise the importance of complementing a top-down institutional perspective with bottom-up approaches to enhance compliance.[169] This turns the focus firmly on the domestic sphere and the ability of domestic actors and institutions to have decisions made implemented. Human rights treaty bodies have affirmed that states are expected to comply with their decisions.[170] Accordingly, it should be sufficient to simply request payment of adequate compensation (which is often subject to negotiations), as well as asking the state to take the additional measures needed to provide the remedies granted or recommended. In practice, states repeatedly fail to do so. The strength of the position of an applicant then depends on whether domestic law recognises the binding force of decisions by human rights treaty bodies – which is often the case for human rights courts, but not UN treaty bodies[171] – so that they are enforceable. In the absence of such legislation, domestic courts have repeatedly declined to give effect to decisions by UN treaty bodies. One glaring example is the decision of Sri Lanka's Supreme Court in the *Singarasa* case. The HRCtee had found that Singarasa's conviction and sentence to thirty-five years' imprisonment under the Prevention of Terrorism Act had been in violation of his right to a fair trial under article 14 ICCPR. When lawyers sought a retrial in Sri Lanka in line with the Committee's views, Sri Lanka's Supreme Court found that there was no obligation on the Sri Lankan government under domestic law to enforce the views.[172]

The legal status of decisions by treaty bodies and the availability of national implementation mechanisms are important. However, it is clear that implementation also depends on other factors, such as the degree of legitimacy of the body concerned and the extent to which the domestic legal community contributes to it. The strength and support of civil society, including NGOs and the media, to advocate implementation is often equally critical. This applies particularly where implementation is part of domestic political processes, such as reforms during transitional periods, or takes place within a broader political context, for example where it is used as a yardstick for membership in a regional organisation, such as in respect of EU accession.

---

[169] See O. C. Okafor, *The African Human Rights System, Activist Forces and International Institutions* (Cambridge University Press, 2007) 12–62; Hillebrecht, above note 150.

[170] HRCtee, General Comment 33, paras. 14–15.

[171] ILA, *Final Report on the Impact of Findings of the United Nations Human Rights Treaty Bodies* (Berlin Conference, 2004).

[172] *Singarasa* v. *Sri Lanka*.

CASE STUDY 7.2
Restoring Ancestral Lands to Indigenous Peoples – *Mayagna (Sumo) Awas Tingni Community* v. *Nicaragua*

In 2001 the IACtHR found that Nicaragua, through its failure to demarcate the communal lands of the Awas Tingni Community and other measures, had breached the applicants' right to judicial protection (article 25 ACHR) and the private right to property (article 21 ACHR) in relation to articles 1(1) and 2 ACHR.[1] It held that the 'State must adopt the legislative, administrative, and any other measures required to create an effective mechanism for delimitation, demarcation, and titling of the property of indigenous communities, in accordance with their customary law, values, customs and mores ... [which was to be carried out] within a maximum term of 15 months, with full participation by the Community and taking into account its customary law, values, customs and mores'.

The Court also decided that '[t]he State must invest, as reparation for the immaterial damages, in the course of 12 months, the total sum of US$50,000 ... in works or services of collective interest for the benefit of the Awas Tingni Community, by common agreement with the Community and under the supervision of the Inter-American Commission'. The approach taken by the Court reflects what may be called a participatory approach when awarding reparation for a breach of the collective rights of indigenous peoples. While Nicaragua enacted legislation in 2003 to give effect to the judgment, it took until 2008 when a change in government finally resulted in over 70,000 hectares of land being given to the community. This is an important example of compliance through legislative reforms and other measures, which has been attributed to the role played by President Ortega, a factor that demonstrates the importance of political support in implementing judgments.[2]

[1] *Mayagna (Sumo) Awas Tingni Community* v. *Nicaragua* (IACtHR) (2001).
[2] See further Open Society Justice Initiative (OSJI), *From Judgment to Justice, Implementing International and Regional Human Rights Decisions* (2010) 72–4.

POINTS TO CONSIDER

1. What is innovative about the IACtHR's approach in respect of reparation for the violation of collective rights?

2. Can 'political will' be said to be *the* factor when it comes to the implementation of decisions and judgments?

7.6   ADDITIONAL PROCEDURAL OPTIONS

7.6.1   Interim Measures

Applicants can request interim measures (also referred to as provisional measures) at any stage of proceedings before the final decision, and often do so at the very beginning of the procedure. These measures are important where an applicant is at risk of an imminent violation of his or her rights; their main purpose is to prevent a deterioration of a situation that adversely affects rights and leads to harm that cannot be made undone. Treaty bodies have either explicit or implied powers to order (request) interim measures, either upon application or *ex officio* (on their own motion).[173] Interim measures may be ordered where the treaty body has jurisdiction and there is prima facie evidence of a serious risk that action taken or threatened by a state, including a failure to act, may result in irreparable harm to the rights of a party. Interim measures have been ordered primarily to stay the imminent deportation, expulsion or extradition or other transfer of detainees that may result in a violation of rights[174] and to suspend the execution of the death penalty.[175] Treaty bodies have also ordered such measures to protect the health of detainees[176] and to protect complainants, including groups such as communities[177] and employees,[178] from threats.[179] The decision to order interim measures in the form of a stay of deportation or stay of execution is provisional. Its main objective is to preserve rights; interim measures should therefore not be prejudicial and impact on the determination of merits, not least because the decision to order such measures is not based on a full consideration of the available evidence.

---

[173] Art. 63(2) ACHR; rule 39 ECtHR 2009 Rules of Court; rule 98 of the ACmHPR's 2010 Rules of Procedure; E. Rieter, *Preventing Irreparable Harm: Provisional Measures in International Human Rights Adjudication* (Intersentia, 2010); C. B. H. Herrera, *Provisional Measures in the Case Law of the Inter-American Court of Human Rights* (Intersentia, 2010). See also Order of the IACtHR (2009) *Provisional Measures regarding Venezuela, Matter of Liliana Ortega et al.*, paras. 3–4, even independent of any pending case.

[174] *Cruz Varas and Others* v. *Sweden* (ECtHR) (1991); *Weiss* v. *Austria* (HRCtee) (2003) para. 8.3. See on the 'rise and fall of rule 39 [interim measures] requests' before the ECtHR, M.-B. Dembour, *When Humans become Migrants: Study of the European Court of Human Rights with an Inter-American Counterpoint* (Oxford University Press, 2015) 434–6.

[175] *Öcalan* v. *Turkey* (ECtHR) (2005); *International Pen and Others* v. *Nigeria* (ACmHPR) (1998); *Pratt and Morgan* v. *Jamaica* (HRCtee) (1989); Tyagi, above note 7, 516, fn. 619: over two hundred requests; *LaGrand* case (*Germany* v. *United States*) (ICJ) (2001).

[176] *Altesor* v. *Uruguay* (HRCtee) (1982) para. 4.

[177] Order of the IACtHR (2007) *Provisional Measures regarding Nicaragua Case of the Mayagna (Sumo) Awas Tingni Community.*

[178] Order of the IACtHR (2004) *Matter of Miguel Agustín Pro Juárez Human Rights Center et al. regarding Mexico.*

[179] *Fernando* v. *Sri Lanka* (HRCtee) (2005) para. 5.5.

Most treaty bodies have recognised that interim measures have binding force. This interpretation is not as obvious as it seems. Indeed, the question of the binding nature of interim measures had been problematic because of the lack of explicit provisions to that effect. In the earlier judgment of *Cruz Varas* v. *Sweden*, the ECtHR held that the binding force of interim measures, which were only envisaged in the rules of procedures of the Court, cannot be derived from the right to an individual petition.[180] This jurisprudence was reversed[181] in light of several leading judgments, such as by the IACtHR in the *Constitutional Court* case and the International Court of Justice (ICJ) in the *LaGrand* case, which held that interim measures are binding.[182] Indeed, it would run counter to a purposive interpretation of human rights treaties to deny the binding power of interim measures. This would effectively leave it within states parties' discretion whether or not to comply and undermine the very protection of the treaty rights in question that interim measures seek to preserve.[183]

In practice, one of the main challenges for applicants is to act in time so that the treaty body concerned can order interim measures before irreparable harm has occurred. However, even where interim measures have been ordered, states have repeatedly failed to comply. The executions of Ken Saro Wiwa in Nigeria, of Joey Ramiah in Trinidad and Tobago and of the LaGrand brothers in the USA are cases in point.[184] In another example, UK troops handed over two applicants to Iraqi authorities in breach of an interim order not to do so because they were at risk of facing the death penalty.[185] Acting contrary to interim measures would normally constitute a violation of the respective treaty, such as the right to bring individual petitions before the ECtHR or the Optional Protocol to the ICCPR.[186] Yet these legal consequences, and the affirmation of the binding force of interim measures, do not appear to constitute sufficient safeguards in all cases. This is highly problematic, particularly where it results in a violation of substantive rights and is damaging for the human rights treaty system as it undermines the authority of treaty bodies. Given the limited capacity of treaty bodies to impose sanctions

---

[180] *Cruz Varas and Others* v. *Sweden*, para. 99.

[181] *Mamatkulov and Askarov* v. *Turkey* (ECtHR) (2005) paras. 103–29.

[182] Order of the IACtHR, *Provisional Measures regarding the Case of the Constitutional Court* v. *Peru* (2000) para. 14 (operative part), and *LaGrand*, paras. 100–9.

[183] *LaGrand*, paras. 102–3.

[184] *International Pen and Others* v. *Nigeria*; *Hilaire, Constantine and Benjamin et al.* v. *Trinidad and Tobago*, paras. 196–200; *LaGrand* respectively.

[185] *Al-Saadoon and Mufdhi* v. *United Kingdom* (ECtHR) (2009) paras. 162–6.

[186] See ECtHR in *Mamatkulov and Askarov* v. *Turkey*, paras. 99–129; ignoring an interim order constituted a breach of the right to individual petition (art. 34); *Ruzmetov* v. *Uzbekistan* (HRCtee) (2006) para. 5.3, finding a breach of the Optional Protocol.

for non-compliance, finding the means that deter states from violating interim measures will continue to be a major challenge for the effectiveness of complaints procedures.

7.6.2   Friendly Settlements

Friendly settlements are a means at the disposal of the parties, i.e. the applicant(s) and respondent state(s), to settle a case amicably, which is explicitly provided for in the procedures for the European, Inter-American and African courts, as well as in the Optional Protocols to the ICESCR and CRC.[187] A settlement can typically be reached at all stages of proceedings before the decision on the merits, is confidential in nature and concludes the case where a respective treaty body is satisfied that it is compatible with respect for human rights.[188] In the European system, this takes the form of a decision that sets out the facts and the solution reached, after which the case is struck off the list.[189]

Friendly settlements have been agreed upon in a number of cases. Respondent states have paid compensation (normally *ex gratia*), have issued apologies and have agreed to undertake legislative changes, including in the course of pilot-judgment procedures.[190] These settlements play an important role in the system of complaints procedures. Indeed, they have many advantages. They save time, reduce the caseload of treaty bodies and allow the parties to negotiate terms that are agreeable and that states may be more likely to comply with. It is for these reasons that treaty bodies encourage friendly settlements. For states, avoiding an adverse judgment and a public finding of state responsibility provides an additional incentive. Litigants, on the other hand, may feel pressurised to accept an offer and often face a dilemma over whether to agree to friendly settlements; doing so deprives them of the opportunity to obtain a finding on the merits that may include a public vindication by holding the state responsible for the violations alleged. The dilemma can be particularly acute where the case is of strategic importance and NGOs and others have a strong interest in it being pursued further, although ultimately it is for the applicant(s) to decide. In addition, a case may involve a large number of victims who may be divided over whether to agree to a friendly settlement.

---

[187] Art. 39 ECHR; art. 49 ACHR; art. 9 Protocol to the ACHPR; art. 7 Optional Protocol to the ICESCR; art. 9 Optional Protocol to the CRC Communication Procedure.

[188] See H. Keller, M. Forowicz and L. Engi, *Friendly Settlements Before the European Court of Human Rights* (Oxford University Press, 2010); IACHR, *Impact of the Friendly Settlement Procedure*, OEA/Ser.L/V/II. doc. 45/13 (18 December 2013).

[189] See e.g., art. 39 ECHR.

[190] *Broniowski* v. *Poland* (ECtHR) (2006).

QUESTIONS

1. A UNSC resolution authorises the use of force against Somali pirates. A European state deploys an armed contingent to the region, which kills several pirates in the course of its operations. Their relatives claim that the pirates were captured, ill-treated and executed. A lawyer who has been approached by the relatives lodges a case before the ECtHR following the exhaustion of domestic remedies, alleging a violation of articles 2 and 3 ECHR. What objections is the state likely to raise concerning admissibility, considering in particular the location of the alleged violation and the international context in which the operation had taken place?

2. A woman brings a case before the HRCtee, alleging that her husband has been abducted by state agents. She has eyewitness accounts to show that he was taken into custody by members of the armed forces. Would this be sufficient to make out a prima facie case and obtain a decision on the merits that her husband has been the victim of an enforced disappearance and the violation of several rights that this may entail?

3. In the same case, consider that the alleged abduction had taken place in 2005. The applicant had complained several times to local authorities but no action had been taken. The state ratified the ICCPR and its Optional Protocol with effect from 2010. Can the applicant bring a case before the HRCtee alleging a substantive violation, such as that the enforced disappearance amounts to torture, or a procedural violation, i.e. failing to investigate her complaint, or both?

4. Is the need to exhaust domestic remedies still the rule given the many exceptions recognised by treaty bodies?

5. Do supranational individual complaints procedures constitute effective remedies for victims of human rights violations?

6. Under what circumstances should applicants consider requesting interim measures?

7. Why are friendly settlements a double-edged sword for applicants?

INTERVIEW 7.1
Nepal before the Human Rights Committee
(Mandira Sharma)

The Advocacy Forum is the first Nepalese NGO that started using the individual complaints procedure before the HRCtee (Nepal acceded to the Optional Protocol to the ICCPR in 1991). It has brought a series of cases that address the legacy of serious human rights violations and the culture of impunity in Nepal. The following is an interview with Mandira Sharma, Advocacy Forum's founding director who served as its director until May 2010. She was instrumental in developing their litigation strategy.

How many cases have you brought in relation to what violations, and what has been the outcome?

We have brought eight cases on behalf of sixteen victims to date. Those eight cases concern torture, extrajudicial executions, and enforced disappearance and sexual violence. Seven cases have already been decided. In all these seven cases the committee has found violations of multiple articles of the ICCPR as we have argued. Following the decisions the government has provided interim relief in the form of monetary compensation to victims. We are continuously working to secure implementation of other recommendations. This process has helped to raise the awareness of the government officials on this subject, encouraged victims and enhanced the knowledge of civil society organisations, lawyers and human rights activists about the practical use of UN mechanisms such as the HRCtee.

How do victims of alleged violations contact you and how do you select cases (including type of violations)?

We have been working with the victims for the last twenty years. Initially, we ourselves used to go to the villages, as many victims did not know us or how to contact us. Now we have offices and officers in many districts and we are known to the victims, so they come to us. As we have been providing legal aid to the victims and their families, we are following up those cases carefully. While we exhaust local remedies and victims would not get justice, we explain to them and their family the possibility of going to the HRCtee. If victims want us to help them with this, we start working on the case. Even if we are asked to do so we might not be able to help every victim to go to the Committee, and as a result we select emblematic cases. So, we explain to victims how the jurisprudence established in other cases can be helpful for them locally.

What are your case-specific and strategic considerations in your litigation; in other words, what are your main goals?

The goal is to establish jurisprudence and to have the HRCtee's views on issues which are difficult to address before local courts. For example, we took a case of enforced disappearance to the Committee as the Nepalese government refused to investigate, stating that this would be done by the forthcoming truth and reconciliation commission and the commission of inquiry on enforced disappearance. We wanted the Committee to hold that the government had an obligation to undertake a criminal investigation in the case and that the commission of inquiry was not suitable for this purpose. So, the Committee's view on this is helping us to shape our discourse on this issue. Similarly, we have filed a case of sexual violence where the victim's request to initiate an investigation was denied because of statutes of limitation in Nepalese law – thirty-five days – to file a complaint in cases of rape. In the cases of torture we wanted to establish how the Torture Compensation Act does not fulfil the obligation under the CAT and call for an appropriate legal framework that makes criminal prosecutions possible in torture-related cases.

How difficult is it to substantiate cases, some of which date back to the mid-1990s?

So far we have taken cases where we ourselves have been involved in their investigation, documentation, as well as legal interventions. We have chosen cases where we are confident that the available evidence is sound and sufficient. What is advantageous about taking cases to the HRCtee is that it does not determine individual criminal guilt and that the threshold of evidence is not that high, like beyond reasonable doubt. The Office of the High Commissioner for Human Rights (OHCHR) also had field operations in Nepal so their documentation now has helped us to substantiate information that we have collected. We also consult with the National Human Rights Commission and use the information collected by other organisations as contemporaneous evidence to strengthen the case.

What challenges have you faced in relation to the admissibility of cases?

We are in a peculiar situation in Nepal. One of the difficulties that we face is that Nepal has maintained that all the crimes committed in the past will be dealt with by the Truth and Reconciliation Commission and the Commission of Inquiries on Disappearance. These two mechanisms were set up in 2015 with mandates of two years, but failed to deliver their mandates even after four years of their existence. Currently, the Government is preparing to have commissioners for these commissions again. The government's arguments are based on the lofty plans it has developed, including the National Human Rights Commission. So, while it can at times be difficult to overcome admissibility hurdles, we have been able to demonstrate convincingly how these plans and institutions have not been able to provide effective remedies for victims of violations. Furthermore, some serious violations such as enforced disappearances and torture were not even defined as crimes under national legislation until very recently (the Criminal Code that came into force in August 2018 criminalises both torture and enforced disappearances). So, the authorities do not initiate criminal investigation in these cases. So, we can easily claim that the remedy is not being available and that there is nothing to exhaust at the local level.

How successful have you been in implementing decisions?

The record has been mixed. We have been successful in obtaining interim relief in the form of compensation for victims. We have also been successful in obtaining some legal reform, such as the new criminal code criminalising torture and enforced disappearance. It also addresses the issue of statutory limitation for rape to some extent. The decisions also had a broader impact, raising awareness of government officials about the government's obligations under the ICCPR. Civil society and the legal community are also increasingly taking an interest in the subject. For example, in addition to Advocacy Forum, there are other organisations that now also help victims to access the Committee. The Media has also developed an interest in these cases. Now, every time there is a case filed before the committee or a decision coming out from the committee, the media also takes an interest in reporting the case. We have also realised that many victims would like to take up their case as they have found this a way of gaining recognition of the harm that they suffered and often continue to suffer. However, the authorities have largely failed to undertake investigations in line with the HRCtee's views, an issue on which we continue to work.

How can the HRCtee's impact in Nepal be maximised and what are the main challenges in this regard?

Using the HRCtee's views in emblematic cases to expand the jurisprudence at local level is critical with a view to facilitating implementation of human rights standards as we cannot take each and every case to the Committee. We are collaborating with other organisations to launch the campaign demanding implementation of the Committee's views. We are also publishing the cases (see http://realrightsnow.org/en/). In addition to this the Committee's jurisprudence plays an important role for wider policy reform initiatives, and trainings and awareness-raising. However, the main challenge that we face is that perpetrators still enjoy de facto immunity. Even the decisions of the Nepalese Supreme Court have been ignored. The weak rule of law is therefore at the heart of human rights violations and the lack of accountability and justice. One way of addressing this is to create a link between the implementation of the Committee's views and the universal periodic review (UPR) and international support to Nepal. Once we are able to make this link, the state would be under pressure to observe the HRCtee's views to bring about change at the local level. Another way would also be having a robust follow-up process of the HRCtee itself.

7.7   THE *HISSÈNE HABRÉ* CASE: THE INTERPLAY BETWEEN DOMESTIC, REGIONAL AND INTERNATIONAL PROCEEDINGS

Attempts to bring Hissène Habré to trial have given rise to a remarkable history of legal proceedings that have occupied national, regional and sub-regional courts, the Committee against Torture (CtAT) and the ICJ. The case also resulted in initiatives at the African Union (AU) level to establish a mixed court. Situated at the interface of international criminal law and the human rights obligation to extradite or prosecute, the case is an extraordinary example of the quest for justice before a multitude of judicial, quasi-judicial and political bodies. This endeavour has been well-documented, largely thanks to the efforts of several protagonists, including Souleymane Guengueng of the Association of Victims of Crimes and Political Repression, and Reed Brody, Human Rights Watch (HRW), who also feature in the film *The Dictator Hunter*.[191]

Hissène Habré came to power in Chad in 1982. He is alleged to have been responsible for serious human rights violations, including large-scale torture and extrajudicial killings amounting to international crimes. After being forced from power in 1990, Habré eventually fled to Senegal where he has stayed since. After several years Chadian victims and human rights defenders, particularly the Association of Victims, together with HRW, began using various avenues to bring Habré to trial. First attempts in Senegal failed because the Dakar Court of Appeal in 2000, in a judgment upheld by the Court of Cassation in 2001, ruled that the Senegalese criminal procedure code did not provide for universal jurisdiction[192] over crimes against humanity committed in third countries. In parallel, 'a Belgian national of Chadian origin and Chadian nationals'[193] and others lodged complaints against Habré in Belgium in 2000 and 2001 using Belgian universal jurisdiction laws. Meanwhile, Souleymane Guengueng and others submitted a communication against Senegal before the CtAT. In May 2006 the Committee found that the lack of implementing legislation establishing jurisdiction over acts of torture in Senegal violated article 5(2) CAT.[194] Equally, the failure to prosecute Habré (in the absence of an extradition) was considered a violation of article 7 CAT. Senegal finally changed its legislation in 2007, making international crimes subject to universal jurisdiction. A further constitutional reform of

---

[191] See for a good overview, R. Brody, 'Bringing a Dictator to Justice: The Case of Hissène Habré' (2015) 3 *Journal of International Criminal Justice* 209.

[192] See on universal jurisdiction, Chapter 17.5.

[193] ICJ, 'Belgium Institutes Proceedings against Senegal and Requests the Court to Indicate Provisional Measures', Press Release, no. 2009/13 (19 February 2009).

[194] *Guengueng v. Senegal* (CtAT) (2006).

2008 ensured that proceedings for international crimes would not fall foul of the principle of non-retroactivity. However, Senegal still did not prosecute Habré, invoking financial and logistical challenges.

Meanwhile, in a legal counter-attack, Habré challenged these legislative amendments before the Economic Community of West African States (ECOWAS) Community Court, arguing among other points that they violated the principle of non-retroactivity (prosecuting someone for an offence that was not on the statute books at the time when it was committed). The ECOWAS court, in its far-from-convincing judgment of 18 November 2010, found that the retroactive nature of the law may violate international law.[195] It also considered the exception that this rule did not apply to international crimes, and fashioned a 'compromise' solution, stating that Habré should be tried before an ad hoc court. Another challenge against Senegal's legislation, which similarly argued that it violated the principle of non-retroactivity and ran counter to the search for an African solution, constituted the first case before the ACtHPR.[196] The application was given short shrift and declared inadmissible because Senegal had not accepted the Court's jurisdiction.

Meanwhile, Belgian authorities had investigated the complaints lodged in 2000/2001, and in September 2005 issued an international arrest warrant against Habré for genocide, crimes against humanity, war crimes, torture and other violations. An extradition request made by Belgium was turned down by the *Chambre d'accusation* of the Dakar Court of Appeal. By now, the *Habré* case had become a dilemma for Senegal, which asked the AU to find an African solution. In January 2006 the AU established a committee of eminent African jurists which proposed that a mixed tribunal should be set up to try Habré in Africa. In July 2006, the AU 'mandate[d] the Chairperson of the [African] Union, in consultation with the Chairperson of the Commission, to provide Senegal with the necessary assistance for the effective conduct of the trial'.[197] However, efforts to bring Habré to trial in Africa stalled because of continuing discussions over who should finance it. Belgium, for its part, significantly increased the pressure on Senegal and the AU. In February 2009 it instituted proceedings against Senegal before the ICJ, arguing that 'Senegal's failure to prosecute Mr H. Habré, if he is not extradited to Belgium to answer for the acts of torture that are alleged against him, violates the Convention against Torture'.[198] The ICJ, in a judgment dated 20 July 2012 whose admissibility was based on article 30 CAT, found that Senegal had breached its

---

[195] *Hissène Habré* v. *Republic of Senegal* (ECOWAS CCJ) (2010).

[196] *Yogogombaye* v. *Senegal* (ACtHPR) (2009).

[197] Decision on the Hissène Habré Case and the African Union, doc. Assembly/AU/3 (VII) (2 July 2006).

[198] ICJ, above note 193.

obligations under article 6(2) CAT 'by failing to make immediately a preliminary inquiry into the facts relating to the crimes allegedly committed by Mr Hissène Habré' and under article 7(1) CAT 'by failing to submit the case of Mr Hissène Habré to its competent authorities for the purpose of prosecution'. Consequently, it found that the Republic of Senegal 'must, without further delay, submit the case of Mr Hissène Habré to its competent authorities for the purpose of prosecution, if it does not extradite him'.[199]

The account of multiple proceedings shows that various actors have used legal avenues at the national, regional and international level. Victims and NGOs brought cases (criminal prosecutions in Senegal, CtAT case) which complemented their ongoing advocacy campaigns to have Habré prosecuted. Chad tried Habré *in absentia* (and sentenced him to death for international crimes),[200] lifted his immunity and invited Belgian and Senegalese judges to investigate the case.[201] Habré himself, and those acting in his support, used the ECOWAS court and the ACtHPR to challenge Senegal's legislation. Belgium, meanwhile, has emerged as the major state player. It has used proceedings before the ICJ, ostensibly for Senegal to extradite or prosecute Habré; indirectly, it also put pressure on the AU and others involved to expedite initiatives to try Habré.

The *Habré* case represents a momentous struggle to hold a former head of state accountable that is being fought out at the legal and political level. The struggle achieved a major breakthrough in late 2012 with the creation of the Extraordinary African Chambers within the Senegalese Courts.[202] Habré was indicted for war crimes, crimes against humanity and torture in July 2013. His trial before the Extraordinary African Chambers, in which over a thousand victims had applied as civil parties, commenced in July 2015, and he was found guilty of the crime of torture, crimes against humanity and war crimes, and sentenced to life imprisonment on 30 May 2016.[203] A subsequent appeal was dismissed on 27 April 2017, although he was acquitted for the crime against humanity of rape.[204] The Court also awarded reparation to

---

[199] *Questions relating to the Obligation to Prosecute or Extradite* (*Belgium* v. *Senegal*) (ICJ) (2012) para. 122.

[200] S. Czajkowski, 'Chad Court Sentences Ex-dictator Habre to Death in absentia', *Jurist* (16 August 2008).

[201] See Brody, above note 191, also on 'the ripple effect in Chad'.

[202] The Statute of the Chambers is available at www.hrw.org/news/2013/09/02/statute-extraordinary-african-chambers. See further S. Williams, 'The Extraordinary African Chambers in the Senegalese Courts: An African Solution to an African Problem?' (2013) 11 *Journal of International Criminal Justice* 1139.

[203] *Ministère Public* v. *Hissein Habré* (EAC) (2016). See for the website of the Extraordinary African Chambers (in French), www.chambresafricaines.org/index.php/l-affaire-habre.html.

[204] *Le Procureur Général* v. *Hissein Habré* (EAC) (2017).

thousands of civil party victims of several violations, ranging from 20 million Central African Francs (FCFA) (rape and sexual violence), to 15 million FCFA (arbitrary detention, torture, prisoners of war) and 10 million FCFA (indirect victims).[205] Meanwhile, on 25 March 2015, the N'Djamena Criminal Court convicted twenty former security officials who had served under the Habré regime for torture, and imposed sentences ranging from five years' imprisonment to lifelong hard labour. It also ruled that Chad and the convicted persons had to pay the equivalent of US $125 million to over 7,000 victims.[206] The case history illustrates the difficulty of implementation in the face of political resistance, and legal and financial obstacles. It also demonstrates how the persistence of key protagonists has kept up the imperative for accountability, clarified Senegal's obligations, prompted the AU into action and influenced Chad's response. These efforts have resulted in an outcome that sets an important precedent in the region, strengthens international human rights and provides a measure of justice for the victims of the Habré regime.

POINT TO CONSIDER

1. Over fifteen years of pursuing legal avenues before national, regional and international bodies and courts resulting in the trial of Habré demonstrate the importance of persistence rather than the limits of complaints procedures to ensure justice. Discuss.

FURTHER READING

Burgorgue-Larsen, L., and A. Ubeda de Torres, *The Inter-American Court of Human Rights: Case Law and Commentary* (Oxford University Press, 2011).

Duffy, H., *Strategic Human Rights Litigation: Understanding and Maximising Impact* (Hart, 2018).

Evans, M., and R. Murray (eds.), *The African Charter on Human and Peoples' Rights: The System in Practice 1986–2006*, 2nd edn (Cambridge University Press, 2008).

Gerards, J. (ed.), *Implementation of the European Convention on Human Rights and of the Judgments of the ECtHR in National Case-law: A Comparative Analysis* (Intersentia, 2014).

Hillebrecht, C., *Domestic Politics and International Human Rights Tribunals: The Problem of Compliance* (Cambridge University Press, 2013).

Joseph, S., and M. Castan, *The International Covenant on Civil and Political Rights: Cases, Materials and Commentary*, 3rd edn (Oxford University Press, 2013).

Keller, H., M. Forowicz and L. Engi, *Friendly Settlements before the European Court of Human Rights: Theory and Practice* (Oxford University Press, 2010).

---

[205] See list of victims, ibid., Annex.

[206] HRW, 'Chad: Habré-era Agents Convicted of Torture: 20 Convicted, $125 Million in Reparations to Victim Ordered' (25 March 2015).

Leach, P., *Taking a Case to the European Court of Human Rights*, 4th edn (Oxford University Press, 2017).

Murray, R., and D. Long, *The Implementation of the Findings of the African Commission on Human and Peoples' Rights* (Cambridge University Press, 2015).

Open Society Justice Initiative, *From Judgment to Justice, Implementing International and Regional Human Rights Decisions* (2010).

Open Society Justice Initiative, *From Rights to Remedies: Structures and Strategies for Implementing International Human Rights Decisions* (2013).

Pasqualucci, J. M., *The Practice and Procedure of the Inter-American Court of Human Rights*, 2nd edn (Cambridge University Press, 2013).

Rieter, E., *Preventing Irreparable Harm: Provisional Measures in International Human Rights Adjudication* (Intersentia, 2010).

Websites

ACmHPR: www.achpr.org

ACtHPR: www.african-court.org

ECtHR: www.echr.coe.int

IACHR: www.oas.org/en/iachr

IACtHR: www.corteidh.or.cr

ICJ: www.icj-cij.org

OHCHR: www.ohchr.org (providing links to all human rights treaty bodies)

Compilations and Databases Providing Access to Documents and Judgments

American Society of International Law, Electronic Resource Guide: www.asil.org/resource/humrts1.htm

Bayefsky: UN Human Rights Treaty System: www.bayefsky.com

Commonwealth and International Human Rights Law Database: commonwealth-and-international-law-database/index.html

OMCT Handbook Series, Second Edition ('OMCT's Handbook Series consists of four volumes, each one providing a detailed guide to the practice, procedures, and jurisprudence of the regional and international mechanisms that are competent to examine individual complaints concerning the violation of the absolute prohibition of torture and ill-treatment'): www.omct.org/monitoring-protection-mechanisms/reports-and-publications/2014/11/d22956

Project Diana Online Human Rights Archive: http://avalon.law.yale.edu/subject_menus/diana.asp

University of Minnesota Human Rights Library: www1.umn.edu/humanrts

World Courts: www.worldcourts.com

8 Civil and Political Rights

CONTENTS

8.1 INTRODUCTION

Civil and political rights emerged out of fundamental rights conceptions protecting life, integrity, liberty and opinion of a person against an overbearing state. The twentieth century demonstrated that these rights were at risk in multiple contexts, ranging from genocidal campaigns, dictatorships and arbitrary law-enforcement to armed conflict and a breakdown of law and order. Rights such as the right to life and freedom from ill-treatment may also be at risk from other sources, namely non-state actors in the domestic and other spheres, which have taken on a growing importance in the wake of states' withdrawal from public functions. While international human rights standards have been developed to provide adequate protection in these circumstances, their implementation requires certain structures without which it is unlikely that core civil and political rights can be effectively protected. The rule of law, the administration of justice and democratic institutions are key components in this regard. While international human rights law does not mandate that a particular political system be in place, it is difficult to see how rights can be effectively protected without having at least a minimum of checks and balances.

Equally, however, a democratic system as such is not a panacea for rights protection. Indeed, there are deep-seated structural factors that can, and have, undermined the effective protection of rights in all systems. Social exclusion, inequality and discrimination in particular are prone to significantly increase vulnerability, as evident in the higher likelihood of persons from certain ethnic or class or national backgrounds being subject to arbitrary arrest, detention, ill-treatment and other violations.[1] As a yardstick of power relations in a society, social exclusion, inequality and discrimination are also closely related to lack of access to justice, which both reflects and compounds vulnerabilities and impunity. The absence of effective remedies and accountability of those responsible has been identified as a central factor contributing to the perpetuation of violations.[2] The resulting impunity constitutes both a cause and a manifestation of a malfunctioning system that fails to protect. Against this background this chapter identifies the normative content of the right to life, the prohibition of torture and other cruel, inhuman or degrading treatment or punishment (other ill-treatment), the right to liberty and security, the right to a fair trial and qualified rights, particularly freedom of expression, and examines the challenge of ensuring their effective protection. It also considers the issue of enforced disappearance, one of the most serious violations that has spawned a rich jurisprudence but has only recently become the explicit object of an international treaty.

8.2   THE RIGHT TO LIFE

8.2.1   Practice

Life is at risk both through a state's use of force and its failure to provide adequate protection from threats to life.[3] The use of lethal force comprises the deliberate killing of individuals or groups, including targeted extrajudicial

---

[1] See e.g., Interim Report of the Special Rapporteur of the Commission on Human Rights on the question of torture and other cruel, inhuman or degrading treatment or punishment, UN doc. A/55/290 (11 August 2000) paras. 34–7; and Report of the Special Rapporteur on extreme poverty and human rights, UN doc. A/72/502 (4 October 2017). See for a more in-depth discussion, Chapter 13.3.4.

[2] See Principle 1 of the Updated Set of Principles for the Protection and Promotion of Human Rights through Action to Combat Impunity, UN doc. E/CN.4/2005/102/Add.1 (8 February 2005).

[3] See for a good overview, *UN Special Rapporteur on Extrajudicial Executions Handbook*, which is part of the Project on Extrajudicial Executions of the Centre for Human Rights and Global Justice, New York University School of Law, online at www.extrajudicialexecutions.org.

executions,[4] torturing to death in custody, enforced disappearances (where they result in murder), (unlawful) killings in armed conflicts, massacres or even genocides. Members of marginalised groups and opposition movements, as well as journalists, have been particularly vulnerable to extrajudicial killings. In addition, while there is a growing trend towards the abolition of judicially sanctioned killing, i.e. capital punishment, according to Amnesty International records, fifty-three countries imposed 2,591 death sentences in 2017, and twenty-three countries carried out 993 executions by means of beheading, hanging, lethal injection and shooting.[5]

Lethal force may also be used without the direct intention to kill but in the knowledge that this may be the outcome, for example the use of live ammunition to quell a protest.[6] The state may also accidentally cause the death of persons through its agents, for example soldiers mistakenly shooting a passer-by during an exercise, or through potentially lethal operations, such as accidents at state-run nuclear power stations.

Individuals and groups face numerous threats to their life from sources other than the state. This is often most pronounced during armed conflict where rebel groups may be responsible for more killings than governmental forces.[7] The multiple executions by the group Islamic State in Iraq and Syria are a particularly egregious example of such violations.[8] Life is also threatened during peace-time, both in relation to acts of violence, such as deadly domestic violence[9] and sexual violence,[10] as well as health hazards

---

[4] See in particular, Report of the Special Rapporteur on extrajudicial, summary or arbitrary executions, Addendum: Study on Targeted Killings, UN doc. A/HRC/14/24/Add.6 (28 March 2010) and C. Finkelstein, J. D. Ohlin and A. Altman (eds.), *Targeted Killings: Law and Morality in an Asymmetrical World* (Oxford University Press, 2012).

[5] Amnesty International, *Death Sentences and Executions 2017* (2018) 5–7. Note that the figures do not include China where 'data on the use of the death penalty remained classified as a state secret', ibid., at 6.

[6] See on the protection of the right to life in the context of policing assemblies, Report of the Special Rapporteur on extrajudicial, summary or arbitrary executions, UN doc. A/HRC/17/28 (23 May 2011) paras. 12–133.

[7] See e.g., Report of the Special Rapporteur on extrajudicial, summary or arbitrary executions, Addendum Follow-up to country recommendations: Afghanistan, UN doc. A/HRC/17/28/Add.6 (27 May 2011) paras. 17–33.

[8] See in particular, documents of the 22nd special session of the Human Rights Council on the human rights situation in Iraq in light of abuses committed by the Islamic State in Iraq and the Levant and associated groups, 1 September 2014.

[9] See in particular, *Opuz* v. *Turkey* (ECtHR) (2010); Committee on the Elimination of Discrimination against Women (CtEDAW) jurisprudence. It is estimated that 'approximately 5,000 women are murdered each year by family members in honour-related violence'. See Report of the Special Rapporteur on violence against women, its causes and consequences, UN doc. A/66/215 (1 August 2011) para. 32.

[10] See in particular, *González et al. ('Cotton Field') v. Mexico* (IACtHR) (2009).

emanating from private actors, such as the operation of dangerous plants.[11] As discussed in more detail in 8.2.7, the state has a duty to protect life in these circumstances.

8.2.2   Sources

The right to life is recognised in all major international and regional human rights instruments.[12] Its mention as the first substantive right in most of these treaties reflects its fundamental importance. The recognition in treaty law is complemented by international standards, such as the Principles on the Effective Prevention and Investigation of Extra-legal, Arbitrary and Summary Executions[13] and the Basic Principles on the Use of Force and Firearms by Law Enforcement Officials.[14] The right not to be arbitrarily deprived of one's life is considered to have attained the status of customary international law[15] and to be non-derogable.[16] The taking of life may also constitute an international crime, namely genocide (particularly killing members of a group), crimes against humanity (murder, extermination, persecution and other inhumane acts committed as part of a widespread or systematic attack directed against any civilian population) or a war crime (particularly wilful killing or murder).[17]

8.2.3   The Prohibition of Arbitrary Deprivation of Life

Even though the right to life has repeatedly been referred to as a 'fundamental right',[18] it is not absolute in so far as international treaties such as the International Covenant on Civil and Political Rights (ICCPR), American

---

[11] See e.g., *Öneryildiz* v. *Turkey* (ECtHR) (2005).

[12] See art. 3 UDHR; art. 6 ICCPR; art. 6(1) CRC; art. 9 International Convention on the Protection of the Rights of All Migrant Workers and Members of Their Families (ICRMW); art. 10 Convention on the Rights of Persons with Disabilities (CRPD), and at the regional level art. 2 ECHR; art. 4 ACHR and art. 4 ACHPR.

[13] Recommended by UN ECOSOC resolution 1989/65 (24 May 1989).

[14] Adopted by the Eighth UN Congress on the Prevention of Crime and the Treatment of Offenders, Havana, Cuba (27 August to 7 September 1990).

[15] Restatement (Third) of the Foreign Relations Law of the United States, §702; Rule 89 of the ICRC Customary International Humanitarian Law Database (ICRC-CIHL Database), online at www.icrc.org/customary-ihl/eng/docs/home.

[16] HRCtee, General Comment 36 on article 6 of the International Covenant on Civil and Political Rights, on the right to life (30 October 2018) para. 2, and General Comment 24: Issues relating to reservations made upon ratification or accession to the Covenant or the Optional Protocols thereto, or in relation to declarations under art. 41 of the Covenant, UN doc. CCPR/C/21/Rev.1/Add.6 (4 November 1994) para. 10. See also art. 15(2) ECHR: 'No derogation from Article 2, except in respect of deaths resulting from lawful acts of war … '

[17] See arts. 6–8 of the ICC Rome Statute respectively.

[18] See e.g., *Baldéon García* v. *Peru* (IACtHR) (2006) para. 82; *McCann and Others* v. *United Kingdom* (ECtHR) (1996) para. 147.

Convention on Human Rights (ACHR) and African Charter on Human and Peoples' Rights (ACHPR) permit the use of force resulting in the deprivation of life that is not 'arbitrary'. Under article 2(2) of the European Convention on Human Rights (ECHR), the use of such force may be justified (1) 'in defence of any person from unlawful violence'; (2) 'in order to effect a lawful arrest or to prevent the escape of a person lawfully detained';[19] and (3) 'in action lawfully taken for the purpose of quelling a riot or insurrection'.[20] Killings that are lawful under international humanitarian law are recognised as a further exception.[21]

As a general rule the use of force must be regulated by law and must be exceptional.[22] Where its use may be justifiable it must be absolutely necessary and strictly proportionate to the legitimate aim sought.[23] This means that there are no less serious alternatives available to achieve the aim, for example using baton rounds instead of live ammunition to disperse a crowd. It requires that the means used, i.e. lethal force, is not out of proportion to the aim pursued, for example shooting to arrest an unarmed man who has committed a petty theft. Determining proportionality in the particular circumstances can pose considerable difficulties, as international jurisprudence demonstrates.

8.2.4   *McCann* v. *United Kingdom*: Absolute Necessity in the European Court of Human Rights's Jurisprudence

McCann v. *United Kingdom* is a leading case in which the European Court of Human Rights (ECtHR) interpreted the circumstances under which the use of lethal force 'in defence of any person from unlawful violence' under article 2(2)(a) ECHR is absolutely necessary. In that case the applicants alleged that the killing of their relatives by British soldiers in Gibraltar as part of a 'shoot-to-kill' policy constituted a violation of the right to life. The Court agreed that the soldiers honestly believed for good reason that the three known Irish Republican Army (IRA) operatives were about to launch an attack, which

---

[19]   *Nachova and Others* v. *Bulgaria* (ECtHR) (2006) para. 95.

[20]   *Guleç* v. *Turkey* (ECtHR) (1999) para. 71.

[21]   See Chapters 16.3 and 16.4.

[22]   See *Nachova and Others* v. *Bulgaria*, para. 96; *Case of Cruz Sánchez and Others* v. *Peru* (IACtHR) (2015) paras. 257–66. See also arts. 1 and 11 of the Basic Principles on the Use of Force and Firearms by Law Enforcement Officials (August/September 1990), and art. 3 of the Code of Conduct for Law Enforcement Officials, UNGA resolution 34/169 (17 December 1979).

[23]   See *McCann and Others* v. *United Kingdom*, para. 149, and on the limited application of the principle in cases of deliberate, state-sanctioned killings, *Pueblo Bello Massacre* v. *Colombia* (IACtHR) (2006) para. 133.

in principle justified the use of force in the particular circumstances even where the belief turned out to be wrong. However, in a significant expansion of the scope of a state's obligation, the Court broadened its consideration of proportionality to include the planning and conduct of the operation. It found that the planning did not take the requisite precautionary measures and that consequently the use of force had not been absolutely necessary.[24] Several dissenting judges in *McCann* v. *United Kingdom* expressed their concern about reasoning that is based on the benefit of hindsight in respect of operational questions. While the Court needs to be careful not to lightly substitute its own views for that of the state in this regard, the test developed by the ECtHR in *McCann* has an important legal policy dimension. It takes a holistic view of what is 'absolutely necessary' and compels law-enforcement officials to plan and control actions in such a way that the use of force is minimised or truly becomes a measure of last resort. Such an approach takes into consideration that operations are the result of a series of decisions for which the state remains responsible. This is appropriate, as responsibility should be seen in the overall context and not be artificially limited to focusing solely on the actual belief of the law-enforcement official(s) using force at the end of a chain of events, which may be genuine, but mistaken because of earlier erroneous judgments.

QUESTIONS

1. What is the importance of the *McCann* v. *United Kingdom* ruling from a legal policy perspective aimed at ensuring that the right to life is effectively protected in all circumstances?

2. In 2005 Charles de Menezes, a Brazilian living in London where he worked as an electrician, was mistakenly identified as a terrorist who it was believed was about to attack the London underground. After a series of operational errors de Menezes was allowed to board a train where police officers killed him with multiple shots at point-blank range without warning, in line with the police policy at the time. The ECtHR's Grand Chamber ruled on the procedural aspects of the case, particularly the decision not to prosecute any individual in relation to de Menezes's death (finding no violation as the parties had settled the substantive aspect of the case through payment of compensation).[25] What is the significance of the case for states' operations in counter-terrorism cases?

---

[24] *McCann and Others* v. *United Kingdom*, paras. 202–14.
[25] See *Armani da Silva* v. *United Kingdom* (ECtHR) (2016).
[26] Art. 6(2) ICCPR; art. 2(1) ECHR; art. 4(2) ACHR.

CASE STUDY 8.1
The Killing of Bin Laden and the Right to Life

On 2 May 2011 Osama Bin Laden, the then head of Al-Qaeda, was killed in a raid conducted by a United States (US) military unit in Abbottabad, Pakistan, apparently without the prior express consent or knowledge of the Pakistani authorities.[1] Accounts of the circumstances of the killing have been conflicting. In particular, it is not clear whether Bin Laden tried to defend himself when confronted by US forces.[2] The killing of Bin Laden raised a series of complex questions concerning its lawfulness under international law, including international humanitarian law and international human rights law,[3] which forms part of the broader debate about 'targeted killings'.[4] US government officials asserted that international humanitarian law applied and that the killing was lawful because Bin Laden had been a legitimate target and had not given himself up.[5] This position would be correct if the 'conflict' between the USA and Al-Qaeda at the time could be characterised as a situation of armed conflict. This is questionable and contested, not least because it is difficult to determine whether asymmetrical warfare of this kind reaches the requisite threshold and whether a situation of armed conflict continues to apply even if there has been no resort to force or violence for quite some time.[6] If the circumstances qualify as an armed conflict at the time, the lawfulness of the killing would depend on the rules of international humanitarian law, particularly the question of whether Bin Laden was a legitimate target and, if so, whether he had surrendered at the time of his killing (which would have rendered his killing unlawful).[7]

---

[1] See A. S. Deeks, 'Pakistan's Sovereignty and the Killing of Osama Bin Laden' (5 May 2011) 15 *American Society of International Law Insights.*

[2] See for an immediate request for a clarification of the facts to assess the lawfulness of the use of lethal force, Osama bin Laden: statement by the UN Special Rapporteurs on summary executions and on human rights and counter-terrorism (6 May 2011). See for an official US account, 'Press Briefing by Press Secretary Jay Carney' (5 March 2011), online at www.whitehouse.gov/the-press-office/2011/05/03/press-briefing-press-secretary-jay-carney-532011.

[3] See B. Van Schaack, *The Killing of Osama Bin Laden & Anwar Al-Aulaqi: Uncharted Legal Territory,* Santa Clara University Legal Studies Research Paper no. 02–12 (2012) 7–10; A. P. V. Rogers and D. McGoldrick, 'Assassination and Targeted Killing: The Killing of Osama Bin Laden' (2011) 60 *International & Comparative Law Quarterly* 778.

[4] See Chapter 18.6.2.

[5] See for an overview, Van Schaack, above note 3, 7–10.

[6] Ibid., 24–31.

[7] See Chapter 16.2.1 on 'combatant' status and the concept of 'taking a direct part in hostilities'.

POINTS TO CONSIDER

1. What questions would need to be considered when examining the compatibility of the killing with international human rights law, in relation to both where it was done and how it was carried out?
2. What grounds may justify the use of lethal force?
3. Would a shoot-to-kill policy be lawful?[8]

[8] See also Chapter 16.6.2.

8.2.5   The Death Penalty under International Law

The ICCPR, the ECHR and the ACHR explicitly acknowledge the death penalty as an exception to the right to life,[26] and the death penalty has been interpreted as not constituting an 'arbitrary' deprivation of life under the ACHPR.[27] However, the language of article 6(6) ICCPR already acknowledges the desirability of the abolition of the death penalty.[28] This objective has found expression at the international level in the Second Optional Protocol to the ICCPR, aiming at the abolition of the death penalty, which had eighty-seven parties as of 27 March 2019. At the regional level, developments are most advanced in the Americas and Europe,[29] as reflected in the Protocol to the ACHR to Abolish the Death Penalty and Protocols no. 6 and no. 13 to the ECHR. The latter two protocols successively and effectively abolished the death penalty in the European system.[30] The African Commission on Human and Peoples' Rights (ACmHPR) called for a moratorium on the death penalty, and the majority of African states have either abolished capital punishment or observe a moratorium.[31] Despite this trend the death penalty as such is arguably not yet unlawful under present

[27] *Interights et al. (on behalf of Mariette Sonjaleen Bosch) v. Botswana* (ACmHPR) (2003) para. 43.
[28] See further P. Hodgkinson and W. A. Schabas (eds.), *Capital Punishment: Strategies for Abolition* (Cambridge University Press, 2004); R. Hood and C. Hoyle, *The Death Penalty: A Worldwide Perspective*, 5th edn (Oxford University Press, 2015).
[29] A. Sarat and J. Martschukat (eds.), *Is the Death Penalty Dying? European and American Perspectives* (Cambridge University Press, 2011).
[30] See *Öcalan v. Turkey* (ECtHR) (2005) paras. 150–75, and *Al-Saadoon and Mufdhi v. United Kingdom* (ECtHR) (2009) paras. 115–22, where it considered (para. 120) 'that Article 2 has been amended so as to prohibit the death penalty in all circumstances. Against this background, the Court does not consider that the wording of the second sentence of Article 2 §1 continues to act as a bar to its interpreting the words "inhuman or degrading treatment or punishment" in Article 3 as including the death penalty.'
[31] See ACmHPR, General Comment 3 on the African Charter on Human and Peoples' Rights: The Right to Life (Article 4) (2015) paras. 22–3 and *Groupe de Travail sur les Dossiers*

international human rights law. Where it is still imposed and applied, however, the death penalty is subject to a series of conditions, particularly procedural safeguards that must be complied with strictly for it to be lawful. It may only be imposed for the most serious crimes[32] and must not be mandatory because a court has to be able to consider mitigating or special circumstances when imposing it as a punishment.[33] Certain categories of persons should be exempt from the death penalty, namely children who were under eighteen years of age at the time when the crime was committed[34] and mentally ill persons.[35] A person may only be sentenced to death following a fair trial (which in death penalty cases will invariably be subject to particularly close scrutiny),[36] including the right to an appeal.[37] The imposition of the death penalty must also not be discriminatory.[38] Where foreign nationals face the death penalty they need to be granted consular assistance.[39] These conditions, which reflect the serious, irreversible nature of the death penalty, raise the threshold in terms of crimes, categories of persons and nature of trials, which, taken together, considerably limit the scope for the punishment to be lawfully imposed.

The death penalty has a close relationship with the prohibition of torture and other cruel, inhuman or degrading treatment or punishment. Its imposition following an unfair trial has been considered inhuman treatment.[40] Separately, the conditions of waiting for one's execution (death row phenomenon) may in certain circumstances amount to inhuman treatment.[41]

Judiciaires Stratégiques v. *Democratic Republic of Congo* (ACmHPR) (2013) paras. 68–9, where the Commission stressed the abolitionist trend.

[32] See HRCtee, General Comment 36, paras. 35–6; *Restrictions to the Death Penalty (Arts. 4(2) and 4 (4) American Convention on Human Rights)* (IACtHR) (1993); *Hilaire, Constantine and Benjamin et al.* v. *Trinidad and Tobago* (IACtHR) (2002) para. 102.

[33] *Hilaire, Constantine and Benjamin et al.* v. *Trinidad and Tobago*, paras. 98–109; *Weerawansa* v. *Sri Lanka* (HRCtee) (2009) para. 7.2.

[34] Art. 37(a) CRC and art. 6(5) ICCPR.

[35] *Sahadath* v. *Trinidad and Tobago* (HRCtee) (2002) para. 7.2.

[36] See e.g., *Khoroshenko* v. *Russian Federation* (HRCtee) (2011) para. 9.11; *Öcalan* v. *Turkey*, para. 166; *International Pen and Others* v. *Nigeria* (ACmHPR) (1998) para. 103.

[37] See art. 4(6) ACHR; HRCtee General Comment 36, para. 41; *Khalilov* v. *Tajikistan* (HRCtee) (2005) paras. 7.5–7.6.

[38] HRCtee General Comment 36, para. 44.

[39] *The Right to Information on Consular Assistance in the Framework of the Guarantees of the Due Process of Law* (IACtHR) (1999) para. 137; *LaGrand* case (*Germany* v. *United States*) (ICJ) (2001) para. 77.

[40] *Öcalan* v. *Turkey*, paras. 167–75; *Al-Saadoon and Mufdhi* v. *United Kingdom*, paras. 120–2; *Mwamba* v. *Zambia* (HRCtee) (2010) para. 6.8.

[41] *Soering* v. *United Kingdom* (ECtHR) (1989) paras. 92–111; *Hilaire, Constantine and Benjamin et al.* v. *Trinidad and Tobago*, paras. 168–9. But see *Ashby* v. *Trinidad and Tobago* (HRCtee) (2002) para. 10.6, according to which 'detention on death row for a specific period does not violate, as such, article 7 of the Covenant in the absence of further compelling circumstances'.

Further, the method of execution itself may constitute cruel punishment.[42] In addition, the failure to inform relatives of the execution and the burial place has also been found to violate the prohibition of ill-treatment.[43]

It is cogent to argue that the death penalty itself is inherently and invariably inhuman.[44] If followed, this reasoning would make the death penalty unlawful under international law by shifting the focus from the right to life to the prohibition of inhuman treatment or punishment, if not torture. This is problematic in so far as it would run counter to the death penalty constituting an explicit exception to the right to life. However, it may be justifiable as a subsequent interpretation of the treaty by its parties, such as in the ECHR context, with the effect that the exception to the right to life becomes obsolete.[45] An argument can also be made a fortiori that if corporal punishment is unlawful (see below at 8.3.5) then this must apply even more so to the death penalty.[46] The Human Rights Committee (HRCtee), in its revised general comment on the right to life referred to a number of factors (subsequent agreements and practice) as suggesting 'that considerable progress may have been made towards establishing an agreement among the States parties to consider the death penalty as a cruel, inhuman or degrading form of punishment'.[47] Current debates show that the death penalty is increasingly seen as an anomaly in the international human rights system.

8.2.6   Positive Obligations to Protect the Right to Life

Several treaties expressly stipulate that the right to life shall be protected by law.[48] This obligation has been interpreted as requiring states to: (1) regulate the protection of life and prohibit the arbitrary deprivation of life;[49] (2) take measures to protect an individual or persons at risk; (3) minimise the

---

[42] *Ng* v. *Canada* (HRCtee) (1993) paras. 16.2–16.4 (gas asphyxiation). See on lethal injection, a subject of increasing concern following several botched executions, *Felix Rocha Diaz* v. *The United States* (IACHR) (2015).

[43] See e.g., *Schedko* v. *Belarus* (HRCtee) (2003) para. 10.2; *Spilg and Mack & Dithwanelo (on behalf of Lehlohonolo Bernard Kobedi)* v. *Botswana* (ACmHPR) (2013) paras. 174–7.

[44] Report of the Special Rapporteur on torture and other cruel, inhuman or degrading treatment or punishment, UN doc. A/HRC/10/44 (14 January 2009) paras. 29–48.

[45] *Al-Saadoon and Mufdhi* v. *United Kingdom*, para. 120.

[46] This point was raised by the Special Rapporteur on torture, above note 44, para. 38.

[47] HRCtee, General Comment 36, para. 51.

[48] Art. 6(1) ICCPR; art. 6 CRC; art. 9 ICRMW; art. 19 CRPD; art. 2(1) ECHR; art. 4(1) ACHR.

[49] See on the beginning of life, left open in the *Baby Boy* case (IACHR) (1981) paras. 18–31; *Artavia Murillo et al. ('In Vitro Fertilization')* v. *Costa Rica* (IACtHR) (2012) paras. 185–264 (embryo not a person); *Vo* v. *France* (ECtHR) (2004) paras. 74–95, and conversely, on the end of life (right to die), rejected in *Pretty* v. *UK* (ECtHR) (2002) para. 39. See also *Lambert and Others* v. *France* (ECtHR) (2015) 136–82, judicial authorisation of withdrawal of artificial nutrition and hydration no violation of art. 2 ECHR.

risk of potentially lethal hazards;[50] (4) criminalise, investigate, prosecute and punish unjustified killings; and (5) provide effective remedies in case of breach.

8.2.6.1   Providing Protection against Threats to Life

Irrespective of the source of the risk to life, be it state or non-state actors, it is recognised that states have a 'primary duty ... to put in place a legislative and administrative framework designed to provide effective deterrence against threats to the right to life'.[51] This includes subjecting unjustified killings to proportionate criminal and disciplinary sanctions as appropriate.[52] States must also ensure that pertinent laws, such as abortion laws, do not result in a situation that effectively puts persons at risk; here, women forced to undergo life-threatening illegal abortions.[53]

In the leading ECtHR case of *Osman* v. *United Kingdom*,[54] Mr Osman was killed by his son's teacher who had developed an obsession with his son. The school received a series of complaints about the teacher's conduct, graffiti of a sexual nature appeared around the school and a brick was thrown through the window of Mr Osman's property. Later, the teacher was seen near Mr Osman's house, but though the police were informed they did not take any measures at the time. The teacher 'on being arrested ... stated: "why didn't you stop me before I did it, I gave you all the warning signs?"' The Court found that:

it must be established to its satisfaction that the authorities knew or ought to have known at the time of the existence of a real and immediate risk to the life of an identified individual or individuals from the criminal acts of a third party and that they failed to take measures within the scope of their powers which, judged reasonably, might have been expected to avoid that risk.[55]

---

[50] See e.g., *Öneryildiz* v. *Turkey*, para. 90; *Albekov and Others* v. *Russia* (ECtHR) (2008) para. 88.

[51] *Öneryildiz* v. *Turkey*, para. 89. See also *Pueblo Bello Massacre* v. *Colombia*, para. 120; *Camargo* v. *Colombia* (HRCtee) (1982) paras. 13.1–13.3.

[52] See e.g., *Mapiripán Massacre* v. *Colombia* (IACtHR) (2005) para. 232. The ECtHR held that in certain cases, namely where the killing was not intentional, civil sanctions may be sufficient; see *Vo* v. *France*, para. 90, and *Calvelli and Ciglio* v. *Italy* (ECtHR) (2002) paras. 51–7. This reasoning was subject to strong criticism in the Partly Dissenting Opinion of Judge Rozakis joined by Judges Bonello and Strážnická.

[53] See HRCtee, Concluding Observations: Venezuela, UN doc. CCPR/CO/71/VEN (26 April 2001) para. 19; HRCtee, General Comment 36, para. 8.

[54] *Osman* v. *United Kingdom* (ECtHR) (1998) paras. 115–22. See for a discussion of the positive obligation in the jurisprudence of the ECtHR and the IACtHR, Concurring Opinion of Judge Diego García-Sayán in Relation to the Judgment of the IACtHR in *González et al.* ('Cotton Field') v. *Mexico*, paras. 3–15. For its application in the counter-terrorism context, here the hostake-taking in Beslan, see *Tagayeva and Others* v. *Russia* (ECtHR) (2017) paras. 481–93.

[55] *Osman* v. *United Kingdom*, para. 116.

On the facts, it held that 'the applicants have failed to point to any decisive stage in the sequence of the events leading up to the tragic shooting when it could be said that the police knew or ought to have known that the lives of the Osman family were at real and immediate risk from Paget-Lewis [the teacher]'.[56] The *Osman* test has served as a foundation for subsequent cases and has been used to guide policing in the United Kingdom (UK).[57] While the ECtHR's approach is pragmatic and seemingly offers the authorities considerable leeway,[58] it comes at the expense of more precise guidance.

POINTS TO CONSIDER

1. Are the standards developed in *Osman* sufficient to ensure that the authorities prioritise the protection of the right to life?

2. What is the significance of these standards in the context of domestic violence?[59]

The nature of the authorities' duty to protect life depends on the circumstances. A heightened duty applies particularly where there is a known risk, for example a series of attacks on human rights defenders and/or journalists. Where a person at risk complains about being followed and targeted, the authorities need to investigate promptly, prosecute the perpetrators where appropriate and offer special protection.[60] This is also the case where it is clear that persons belonging to a certain group that is vulnerable have previously been targeted, such as young, marginalised women who had been victims of a spate of murders in Mexico.[61] A heightened duty to exercise due diligence is also recognised in the custodial context where the state needs to

---

[56] Ibid., para. 121.

[57] A. Donald et al., *Evaluating the Impact of Selected Cases under the Human Rights Act on Public Services Provision* (Equality and Human Rights Commission, 2009) 28–39.

[58] *Osman* v. *United Kingdom*, para. 116: 'bearing in mind the difficulties involved in policing modern societies, the unpredictability of human conduct and the operational choices which must be made in terms of priorities and resources, such an obligation must be interpreted in a way which does not impose an impossible or disproportionate burden on the authorities'.

[59] See further Chapter 11.2.3.

[60] *Gongadze* v. *Ukraine* (ECtHR) (2005) paras. 164–71 and 175–180; *Luna López* v. *Honduras* (IACtHR) (2013) paras. 124–5; *Zimbabwe Human Rights NGO Forum* v. *Zimbabwe* (ACmHPR) (2006) para. 160. Where there is evidence linking the police to prior threats and the authorities subsequently fail to respond to complaints, the state may be held directly responsible for a violation (of art. 6 ICCPR). See *Pathmini Peiris* v. *Sri Lanka* (HRCtee) (2011) para. 7.2.

[61] *González et al. ('Cotton Field')* v. *Mexico*, paras. 249–402.

protect the life of those under its physical control.[62] This obligation entails putting in place custodial safeguards against violence by officials and providing adequate medical assistance.[63] The state also needs to protect prisoners against self-harm and violence from other prisoners.[64] Such violence may engage the responsibility of the state both under the right to life and the prohibition of ill-treatment.[65] The general principle has broad application. It requires the authorities to consider the vulnerability of certain prisoners to violence at the hands of others – including because of the nature of the crime they have committed – and the risk that some, particularly violent or mentally ill, prisoners may pose to others and to take adequate precautionary measures. A tragic example is the case of *Edwards* v. *UK* where the authorities ignored these risks and a young detainee was killed by his violent cell mate who had a history of mental illness.[66]

8.2.6.2   *Duty to Investigate, Prosecute and Punish and to Provide Redress*

The violation of the right to life is both facilitated and compounded by impunity. Responses to allegations of such a violation have frequently been characterised by inaction, delays, lack of victim and witness protection, the taking of inadequate measures particularly of a forensic nature and limited if non-existent independence of the investigating authorities.[67] Legal barriers such as amnesty or immunity laws or unduly short statutes of limitation, which bar prosecutions, or making cases against suspected (army) perpetrators subject to the jurisdiction of military courts, have also constituted major obstacles.[68]

The Inter-American Court of Human Rights (IACtHR) has developed a particularly rich jurisprudence in which it has taken a contextual approach to identify the factors contributing to impunity and its impact on victims and

---

[62] *Salman* v. *Turkey* (ECtHR) (2000) para. 99; *Anguelova* v. *Bulgaria* (ECtHR) (2002) para. 110; HRCtee, General Comment 36, para. 25.

[63] As stipulated in the UN standards on the treatment of detainees, see below note 163, and developed in jurisprudence. See on the rights of mentally ill persons in mental health institutions, *Ximenes Lopes* v. *Brazil* (IACtHR) (2006) paras. 101–11 and 120–50.

[64] European Committee for the Prevention of Torture and Inhuman or Degrading Treatment or Punishment, CPT Standards, CPT/Inf/E (2002) 1 – Rev. 2010, 21, para. 27; *Larez* v. *Venezuela* (CtAT) (2015) para. 6.7.

[65] See *Paula and Audrey Edwards* v. *United Kingdom* (ECtHR) (2002) para. 57.

[66] Ibid.

[67] See in this regard Independent Study on Best Practices, including Recommendations, to assist States in strengthening their domestic capacity to combat all aspects of impunity, by Professor D. Orentlicher, UN doc. E/CN4/2004/88 (27 February 2004).

[68] See on the compatibility of such barriers with states' human rights obligations, *Barrios Altos* v. *Peru* (IACtHR) (2001) para. 41; *Marguš* v. *Croatia* (ECtHR) (2014) paras. 99–141; *Mocanu and Otheres* v. *Romania* (ECtHR) (2014) paras. 326–48; HRCtee, General Comment 36, para. 27.

society at large.[69] In the seminal case of *Velásquez Rodríguez* it held that states have a duty to investigate alleged violations of the right to life, irrespective of the identity of the perpetrators.[70] This is important because a state may still be held responsible for a procedural failure even where its responsibility for the substantive violation cannot be established. The obligation requires that – where the seriousness of the violation warrants it – criminal laws are in place and that state authorities undertake an investigation, either following a complaint or *ex officio* (on their own motion) upon receiving credible information about a violation of the right to life, which needs to be prompt, impartial and effective.[71] Effectiveness requires the authorities to take all necessary investigative steps capable of establishing the facts and the identity of the perpetrators.[72] Where investigations produce sufficient evidence the authorities must prosecute the perpetrator(s) and, if convicted, subject them to adequate punishments.[73] In addition, victims of violations, particularly relatives, need to be informed of the outcome of investigations and must have access to effective remedies.[74]

8.2.7   A Right to Survival?

Traditionally, the right to life has been understood as a civil right that protects against extrajudicial killings and other unjustified use of life-threatening or lethal force.[75] Recognising a duty of the state to provide the basics necessary for survival would potentially transform the right, or elements of it, into an economic, social and cultural right. A nexus between the right to life and 'survival and development' is explicitly made in article 6 of the Convention

---

[69] See in particular, *La Cantuta* v. *Peru* (IACtHR) (2006) paras. 110, 115, 157, 160, 222, 226, 227, 239, including Separate Opinion of Judge S. García Ramírez.

[70] *Velásquez Rodríguez* v. *Honduras* (IACtHR) (1988) paras. 172–7.

[71] See e.g., *Mapiripán Massacre* v. *Colombia*, para. 219; *Hugh Jordan* v. *United Kingdom* (ECtHR) (2001) paras. 105–8.

[72] *Nachova and Others* v. *Bulgaria*, para. 113; *Cepeda Manuel Vargas* v. *Colombia* (IACtHR) (2010) paras. 116–22, at para. 118: 'In complex cases, the obligation to investigate includes the duty to direct the efforts of the apparatus of the State to clarify the structures that allowed these violations, the reasons for them, the causes, the beneficiaries and the consequences, and not merely to discover, prosecute and, if applicable, punish the direct perpetrators.'

[73] *Öneryildiz* v. *Turkey*, paras. 91–118; *Mapiripán Massacre* v. *Colombia*, paras. 296–9; *Pathmini Peiris* v. *Sri Lanka*, para. 7.4.

[74] *Hugh Jordan* v. *United Kingdom*, para. 109; *González et al.* (*'Cotton Field'*) v. *Mexico*, para. 424 (lack of information about investigations one of the factors constituting degrading treatment of relatives).

[75] See *African Commission on Human and Peoples' Rights* v. *Kenya* (AfCtHPR) (2017) para. 154: 'The Court considers that it is necessary to make a distinction between the classical meaning of the right to life and the right to decent existence of a group. Article 4 of the Charter relates to the physical rather than the existential understanding of the right to life.'

on the Rights of the Child (CRC).[76] Beyond this, there is limited jurisprudence evidencing a broader understanding. The HRCtee has emphasised that it 'would *be desirable* for State parties to take all possible measures to reduce infant mortality and increase life expectancy, especially in adopting measures to eliminate malnutrition and epidemics'.[77] The right to life and the rights of the child under the ACHR have been interpreted by the IACtHR to include a right to a dignified existence.[78] The failure to 'curb' the forced begging of *talibés* children (aged 4–12) living in abject conditions was held, by the African Committee of Experts on the Rights and Welfare of the Child, to constitute a violation of the child's right to survival and development under article 5 of the African Charter on the Rights and Welfare of the Child.[79] Beyond the violation of children's right to life, the dismal living conditions of displaced persons following a massacre were referred to as contributory reasons by the IACtHR in the context of finding a violation of the right to life.[80] The complainants' argument that environmental degradation, pollution and the destruction of land and farms of the Ogoni in Nigeria had resulted in a violation of the right to life was endorsed by the ACmHPR in the *Ogoniland* case.[81] The ECtHR, in *Cyprus* v. *Turkey*, left open whether article 2 ECHR entails a minimum level of general health care.[82] In *Mehmet Şentürk and Bekir Şentürk* v. *Turkey*, the Court found that denial of emergency treatment on account of inability to pay constituted a violation of the right to life.[83] While the ECtHR's case law indicates a measure of reluctance to extend the scope of the right to life, it is equally clear that states must be considered to have an obligation to take steps that can reasonably be expected to ensure the survival of individuals falling within their jurisdiction, both in relation to general conditions of life and environmental degradation.[84]

---

[76] Art. 6(2) CRC: 'States Parties shall ensure to the maximum extent possible the survival and development of the child.' See M. Nowak, *A Commentary on the United Nations Convention on the Rights of the Child, Article 6: The Right to Life, Survival and Development* (Martinus Nijhoff, 2005).

[77] HRCtee, General Comment 6: The right to life (30 April 1982) para. 5 (emphasis added). See also HRCtee, Concluding observations: Democratic People's Republic of Korea, UN doc. CCPR/CO/72/PRK (27 August 2001) para. 12.

[78] '*Street Children*' *Villagrán Morales et al.* v. *Guatemala* (IACtHR) (1999) paras. 144 and 191. See further at Chapter 9.3 and Chapter 12.4.3.

[79] *The Centre for Human Rights (University of Pretoria) and La Rencontre Africaine Pour la Defense des Droits de l'Homme (Senegal)* v. *Government of Senegal* (ACtERWC) (2014) paras. 40–5.

[80] *Mapiripán Massacre* v. *Colombia*, para. 186.

[81] *Social and Economic Rights Action Center (SERAC) and Center for Economic and Social Rights (CESR)* v. *Nigeria (Ogoniland case)* (ACmHPR) (2001) para. 67.

[82] *Cyprus* v. *Turkey* (ECtHR) (2002) paras. 216–22, in particular at 219.

[83] *Mehmet Şentürk and Bekir Şentürk* v. *Turkey* (ECtHR) (2013) paras. 79–97.

[84] See HRCtee, General Comment 36, paras. 26 and 62; ACmHPR, General Comment 3, para. 43.

The jurisprudence of national courts, notably India's apex courts, point the way to a broader and more comprehensive understanding of the right to life as governing all aspects of life.[85]

QUESTIONS

1. What is problematic about the proposition that the death penalty itself constitutes a violation of the prohibition of torture and other ill-treatment, considering the current status of the right to life under international law?

2. Have treaty bodies interpreted the duty to protect life in such a way that it is sufficiently clear what measures states need to take to counter existing threats?

8.3   THE RIGHT TO BE FREE FROM TORTURE AND OTHER ILL-TREATMENT

8.3.1   Practice

The practice of torture persists in many countries despite its absolute prohibition under international law.[86] Authoritarian and dictatorial states have a history of deliberately using torture as a means to control and repress the population and destroy their 'enemies'.[87] Torture is also a weapon of war used to instil terror and gather intelligence in order to weaken the enemy. Democratic and other countries alike have resorted to torture for counter-insurgency purposes, often facilitated by emergency laws.[88] The response to the 9/11 attacks in the USA was characterised by resort to torture and other ill-treatment,[89] the practice of extraordinary rendition – transferring someone outside the protection of the law to a country for interrogation

---

[85] See Chapter 9.12.

[86] See in particular, reports by the UN Special Rapporteur on torture, www.ohchr.org/EN/Issues/Torture/SRTorture/Pages/SRTortureIndex.aspx; and REDRESS, *Justice for Torture Worldwide: Law, Practice and Agendas for Change* (2013). See also N. Rodley and M. Pollard, *The Treatment of Prisoners under International Law*, 3rd edn (Oxford University Press, 2009).

[87] See K. Millet, *The Politics of Cruelty: An Essay on the Literature of Political Imprisonment* (Norton, 1995); M. Feitlowitz, *A Lexicon of Terror: Argentina and the Legacies of Torture*, revised and updated version (Oxford University Press, 2011).

[88] D. Rejali, *Torture and Democracy* (Princeton University Press, 2007). In the colonial context, see M. Lazreg, *Torture and the Twilight of Empire: From Algiers to Baghdad* (Princeton University Press, 2007).

[89] See in particular, US Senate Select Committee on Intelligence, *Committee Study of the Central Intelligence Agency's Detention and Interrogation Programme* (2014).

where he or she is at risk of, or will be subject to, torture[90] – and allegations of complicity in the torture of terrorist suspects.[91] Torture also frequently constitutes part of routine law-enforcement.[92] This practice is often tolerated if not encouraged in order to 'combat crime' but is simultaneously self-serving as a tool of power for corrupt and brutal law-enforcement officials.[93] Non-state actors have also used torture methods, although it is often difficult to establish the nature and extent of practices in these contexts.[94] Gender-based violence, particularly sexual violence, is widespread and has been recognised as a form of torture.[95]

There is a large arsenal of torture methods, i.e. any treatment capable of inflicting severe physical or mental pain or suffering. Where there is effective monitoring and a risk of accountability, methods of torture tend to be of a nature that does not leave physical traces, whereas torture is often crude and extremely brutal in countries where the law-enforcement, security and armed forces act with little or no restraint.[96] The multiple consequences of torture, particularly post-traumatic stress disorder, have been well documented over the years.[97] The impact of torture is not confined to the individual subjected to it; it also often has a detrimental effect on the families who bear the brunt of the suffering of the survivor/victim. Beyond this, torture can paralyse communities and instil fear in entire societies, which is often part and parcel of its perverse rationale.[98]

---

[90] See e.g., *Al Nashiri* v. *Poland* (ECtHR) (2014) paras. 511–19; also *Al Nashiri* v. *Romania* (ECtHR) (2018); *Abu Zubaydah* v. *Lithuania* (ECtHR) (2018).

[91] See Joint Study on Global Practices in Relation to Secret Detention in the Context of Countering Terrorism, UN doc. A/HRC/13/42 (19 February 2010), particularly paras. 132–58. See Chapter 18.8.

[92] See e.g., *Mikheyev* v. *Russia* (ECtHR) (2006).

[93] S. Jensen and M. K. Andersen (eds.), *Corruption and Torture: Violent Exchange and the policing of the urban poor* (Aalborg Universitetsforlag, 2017).

[94] REDRESS, *Not only the State: Torture by Non-State Actors, Towards Enhanced Protection, Accountability and Effective Remedies* (2006). See also Chapter 19.5.1.

[95] See Report of the Special Rapporteur on torture and other cruel, inhuman or degrading treatment or punishment, UN doc. A/HRC/7/3 (15 January 2008) paras. 44–58 and REDRESS, *Justice for Torture*, above note 86, 14–18.

[96] Rejali, above note 88.

[97] See Manual on the Effective Investigation and Documentation of Torture and Other Cruel, Inhuman or Degrading Treatment or Punishment (Istanbul Protocol), submitted to the UN High Commissioner for Human Rights (9 August 1999). See also IRCT, Torture Journal: Journal on Rehabilitation of Torture Victims and Prevention of Torture, www.irct.org/torture-journal.

[98] For a detailed case study, see A. Doney, 'The Psychological After-Effects of Torture: A Survey of Sri Lankan Ex-Detainees', in D. Somasundaram, *Scarred Minds: The Psychological Impact of War on Sri Lankan Tamils* (Sage, 1998) 256–87.

8.3.2 Sources

The prohibition of torture and other ill-treatment is enshrined in a series of international and regional instruments.[99] The most detailed treaty is the Convention against Torture and Other Cruel, Inhuman or Degrading Treatment or Punishment (CAT) and at the regional level, the Inter-American Convention to Prevent and Punish Torture. There are also separate treaties focusing on the prevention of torture, namely the European Convention for the Prevention of Torture and Inhuman or Degrading Treatment or Punishment and the Optional Protocol to CAT (OPCAT).

Torture and other ill-treatment are prohibited under international humanitarian law.[100] Moreover, torture is considered an international crime subject to universal jurisdiction and constitutes an element of genocide, war crimes and crimes against humanity.[101]

8.3.3 The Absolute Prohibition of Torture

The prohibition of torture is absolute and non-derogable,[102] having attained the status of *jus cogens*.[103] This absolute prohibition is the outcome of long political struggles and the recognition that torture is so egregious that it cannot be justified under any circumstances. Nevertheless, there are recurring demands to permit exceptions which have become particularly prominent in the 'torture debate' largely, but not exclusively, triggered by the 'War on Terror'.[104] The debate has revolved around the 'ticking bomb scenario': should it be lawful to torture an individual if this would possibly result in the lives of (a large number of) people being saved?

While the state has a duty to protect the life and security of anyone within its jurisdiction there are good reasons why torture should not be an acceptable way of doing so. From a rule of law perspective, torture is incompatible

---

[99] Art. 5 UDHR; arts. 7 and 10 ICCPR; art. 37 CRC; art. 10 ICRMW; art. 15 CRPD; art. 3 ECHR; art. 5 ACHR and art. 5 ACHPR.

[100] See ICRC-CIHL Database, rule 90.

[101] See in particular, arts. 5–8 CAT, arts. 6(b) (genocide), 7(1)(f) (crimes against humanity), 8(2)(a)(ii) and 8(2)(c)(i) (war crimes) ICC Rome Statute.

[102] Arts. 1 and 2(2) CAT; arts. 4(2) and 7 ICCPR; arts. 3 and 15(2) ECHR; arts. 5 and 27(2) ACHR; and art. 5 ACHPR.

[103] See e.g., *Prosecutor v. Furundzija* (ICTY) (1998) paras. 153–7; CtAT, General Comment 2: Implementation of article 2 by States parties, UN doc. CAT/C/GC/2 (24 January 2008) para. 1; *Questions relating to the Obligation to Prosecute or Extradite* (*Belgium* v. *Senegal*) (ICJ) (2012) para. 99.

[104] See in particular, Y. Ginbar, *Moral, Practical and Legal Aspects of the Ticking Bomb Justification for Torture* (Oxford University Press, 2008); J. Waldron, *Torture, Terror and Trade-Offs: Philosophy for the White House* (Oxford University Press, 2010); D. Luban, *Torture, Power, and Law* (Cambridge University Press, 2014).

with the presumption of innocence and due process; information extracted under torture must therefore not be used in judicial proceedings.[105] As an interrogation method it is apparent that information extracted under torture is frequently not reliable, a point emphatically underscored by the US Senate Select Committee Study of the Central Intelligence Agency's Detention and Interrogation Programme.[106] Crucially, allowing torture in specific circumstances risks turning the exceptional into the rule. Indeed, the Israeli experience where interrogators routinely relied on the ticking bomb exception appears to support this slippery slope argument.[107] Vesting judges with the power to issue 'torture warrants' in ticking bomb situations, as has been suggested,[108] and thereby judicially sanction 'state violence', appears both unrealistic and highly inappropriate. Ultimately, the torture debate concerns the limits of the exercise of state power and the core of human dignity. Even if there are utilitarian grounds, international human rights law is based on the premise that a person should not be turned into a mere object and that the state should not be allowed to negate if not destroy someone's personality. Indeed, the absolute nature of the prohibition of torture has been defended on the ground that it constitutes an archetype of national legal systems and international law on the relationship between law and violence, meaning 'a particular provision in a system of norms which has a significance going beyond its immediate normative content, a significance stemming from the fact that it sums up or makes vivid to us the point, purpose, principle, or policy of a whole area of law'.[109]

8.3.4   The Case of *Gäfgen* and the German Torture Debate

The German case of *Gäfgen* illustrates the difficult legal and moral questions raised by the absolute prohibition of torture. Magnus Gäfgen, a young law student, kidnapped and murdered an eleven-year-old boy, Jacob Metzler, in order to extort money from the family to lead a lavish lifestyle. The police apprehended him following the hand-over of the ransom. Thinking that Jacob was still alive, the head of the Frankfurt police and one of his officers threatened Gäfgen that he would be subjected to severe pain if he did not reveal the boy's whereabouts. Gäfgen – terrified by the threat – admitted

---

[105] See in particular, art. 15 CAT.

[106] US Committee, above note 89.

[107] See *Public Committee Against Torture* v. *The State of Israel* (Israel) (1999). See on the necessity defence also *Tbeish* v. *Attorney General* (Israel) (2018). See further Public Committee against Torture-Israel, *Israel-Briefing to the Human Rights Committee: For the Committee's Review of the Fourth Periodic Report on Israel* (September 2014) paras. 2–6.

[108] A. Dershowitz, 'Is There a Torturous Road to Justice?' *Los Angeles Times* (8 November 2001).

[109] Waldron, above note 104, 228.

that he had already killed Jacob and led the police to the place where he had hidden the child's body. Gäfgen was later tried, convicted and sentenced to life imprisonment for murder.

The case triggered a major debate in Germany, both within the legal profession and the broader public, with many supporting the acts of the police director because he had acted to save a child's life.[110] The German courts affirmed the absolute prohibition of torture but did not rule that Gäfgen's conviction had been unlawful. Gäfgen then took his case to the ECtHR. Eventually, the Grand Chamber held that: (1) the threat of torture fell within article 3 (constituting inhuman treatment but not torture); (2) the punishment of the police director and the police officer (they received a suspended fine, the lowest possible punishment) had not satisfied the procedural requirement to adequately punish violations of article 3; and (3) the substantial delay of ruling on Gäfgen's compensation claim (more than three years at the time) had breached his right to an effective remedy for torture.[111] However, the Grand Chamber found no violation in relation to the most controversial aspect of the case, namely the admission of evidence, particularly the discovery of Jacob Metzler's body, obtained as a result of the threat of torture (which it considered under article 6).[112] The majority of the Grand Chamber agreed with Germany's argument that the evidence had not been material because Gäfgen had confessed voluntarily at the end of the trial. Gäfgen's lawyer had rejected this argument, saying that Gäfgen had been left with no genuine choice, knowing that he would have been convicted on the basis of the available evidence irrespective of the confession. This position found support in a scathing dissenting opinion that criticised the Court's artificial construct of a 'break in the causal chain' on account of Gäfgen's confession and emphasised that the absolute nature of the prohibition requires that all evidence obtained in breach should be excluded.[113] Such a finding, however, would have necessitated a retrial. It is clear that the majority must have been keenly aware that this would have prompted an outcry in Germany, which may have been a factor influencing its judgment, although this remains

---

[110] See further on the academic debate, S. Greer, 'Is the Prohibition against Torture, Cruel, Inhuman and Degrading Treatment Really "Absolute" in International Human Rights Law?' (2015) 15 *Human Rights Law Review* 101; N. Mavronicola, 'Is the Prohibition Against Torture and Cruel, Inhuman and Degrading Treatment Absolute in International Human Rights Law? A Reply to Steven Greer' (2017) 17 *Human Rights Law Review* 479.

[111] *Gäfgen* v. *Germany* (ECtHR) (2010) paras. 75–132.

[112] Ibid., paras. 133–88. The court's jurisprudence on the compatibility of the use of evidence extracted or derived contrary to art. 3 ECHR with the right to a fair trial under art. 6 ECHR is problematic in so far as it appears to distinguish between torture, in which case such use renders a trial inherently unfair, and other ill-treatment where its assessment depends on the circumstances.

[113] *Gäfgen* v. *Germany*, Joint Partly Dissenting Opinion of Judges Rozakis, Tulkens, Jebens, Ziemele, Bianku and Power.

a matter of conjecture. Ultimately, the judgment shows that affirming the absolute prohibition of torture is often only the first step, with the crucial question being what legal consequences should flow from its absolute nature in a given case.

POINTS TO CONSIDER

1. Does the judgment of the ECtHR Grand Chamber do justice to the facts?
2. What is the legal significance of the *Gäfgen* case?

8.3.5 The Definition of Torture and Other Forms of Ill-treatment and Punishment

The prohibition under international law encompasses both torture and other forms of ill-treatment. While there is a noticeable trend not to differentiate sharply between the two,[114] certain obligations, such as the duty to establish universal jurisdiction and to extradite or prosecute a person alleged to have committed torture, are not explicitly recognised for other forms of ill-treatment. Further, torture still carries a special stigma. In addition, the nature of the remedies may be influenced by a finding of torture, including the amount of compensation awarded. A clear understanding of the legal meaning of torture can therefore be of considerable importance in a given case.

The definition in article 1 CAT is widely seen as the most authoritative and has been referred to by most international and regional human rights treaty bodies in their jurisprudence. Broken down into its constitutive elements the definition sets out the following elements of torture:[115]

- Infliction of severe mental or physical pain or suffering: an act of torture can be objectively severe, i.e. applying electroshocks or rape, or may be severe because of the circumstances, including the duration, impact and personal characteristics, i.e. subjective elements, such as 'sex, age and state of health'.[116] Importantly, the definition comprises not only physical pain but also mental pain or suffering, such as mock executions which the laws of many countries still do not recognise as torture.

---

[114] CtAT, General Comment 2. However, see also M. Nowak, 'What Practices Constitute Torture? US and UN Standards' (2008) 28 *Human Rights Quarterly* 809.

[115] See for a thorough discussion and attempt at redefining torture, S. Dewulf, *The Signature of Evil: (Re)Defining Torture in International Law* (Intersentia, 2011).

[116] *Ireland* v. *United Kingdom* (ECtHR) (1978) para. 162; *Selmouni* v. *France* (ECtHR) (2000) paras. 100–5; *Loayza Tamayo* v. *Peru* (IACtHR) (1997) para. 57; *Hajrizi Dzemajl et al.* v. *Yugoslavia* (CtAT) (2002) paras. 8.6 and 9.2.

- Intent: the intentional infliction is one of the factors distinguishing torture from other forms of ill-treatment. For example, poor conditions of detention as such do not amount to torture unless they are used, either solely or in combination, to deliberately inflict severe pain or suffering for a particular purpose.
- Purpose: the purpose element makes it clear that torture is a means to an end in the context of abuse of power. The 'classical' purpose is to extract information or a confession, but article 1 CAT is broader in scope. It also includes several other purposes, and 'for reasons based on discrimination of any kind', which can be particularly important in cases of sexual violence. The list of purposes is illustrative rather than exhaustive, i.e. 'such purposes as', and it is difficult to envisage circumstances where an official inflicts severe pain or suffering, even for ostensibly purely selfish purposes, where no link could be made to any of the purposes mentioned.[117]
- Official involvement: the formula used in article 1 CAT 'inflicted by or at the instigation of or with the consent or acquiescence of a public official or other person acting in an official capacity' serves to attribute responsibility. The CAT definition therefore excludes 'torture' by non-state actors, such as rebel groups (unless they exercise state-like functions).[118] However, an act such as domestic violence, prisoner-on-prisoner violence or a pogrom by a mob, committed by private individual(s) may come within the ambit of torture if the officials concerned acquiesce, such as by encouraging the commission or continuation of relevant acts, including through inaction.[119] In these situations, the lack of due diligence to prevent and respond to relevant acts constitutes the crucial nexus that potentially broadens the scope of torture to a wider range of actors.[120] Beyond the confines of article 1 CAT, there is an increasing debate as to whether the public official requirement is intrinsic to the notion of torture, which is of immense relevance for the scope of acts and actors that may fall within the definition.[121] Notably, torture as an element of war crimes or a crime against humanity does not require the involvement of a public official.[122]

[117] See Dewulf, above note 115, particularly 338–55. Note that the crime against humanity of torture under art. 7(2)(d) of the ICC Rome Statute does not require the purpose element, requiring instead that the act is inflicted on someone in custody or under the effective control of the perpetrator.

[118] See in particular, *Elmi* v. *Australia* (CtAT) (1999) para. 6.5.

[119] *Opuz* v. *Turkey*, paras. 158–76; *Wilson* v. *Philippines* (HRCtee) (2003) para. 7.3; *Hajrizi Dzemajl* v. *Yugoslavia*, para. 9.2.

[120] CtAT, General Comment 2, para. 18. See further REDRESS, *Redress for Rape: Using International Jurisprudence on Rape as a Form of Torture or Other Ill-Treatment* (2013).

[121] See Separate Opinion of Judge Cecilia Medina Quiroga in *González et al.* ('Cotton Field') v. *Mexico*, paras. 7 and 16; Dewulf, above note 115, 363–99.

[122] See for a concise overview, Dewulf, above note 115, 376–81.

The definition of torture contained in article 2 of the Inter-American Convention to Prevent and Punish Torture is similar to that in article 1 CAT, but is broader in that it does not require 'severe' pain or suffering, and refers to 'any purpose', and to 'methods upon a person intended to obliterate the personality of the victim or to diminish his physical or mental capacities, even if they do not cause physical pain or mental anguish'.[123]

Article 3 ECHR is structured differently, simply prohibiting torture, inhuman or degrading treatment or punishment. The ECtHR has developed a rich, though at times controversial, jurisprudence on the definition of torture in which it distinguishes between forms of ill-treatment (which must reach the required threshold of a 'minimum level of severity'[124]) and torture (deliberate inhuman treatment causing very serious and cruel suffering).[125] The Court has therefore applied a seemingly high threshold for an act to be considered torture. It seemed to acknowledge as much when it stated in *Selmouni* v. *France* that it considers that certain acts which were classified in the past as 'inhuman and degrading treatment' as opposed to 'torture' could be classified differently in future. It takes the view that the increasingly high standard being required in the area of the protection of human rights and fundamental liberties correspondingly and inevitably requires greater firmness in assessing breaches of the fundamental values of democratic societies.[126]

This was widely seen as a barely veiled reference to its earlier, heavily criticised finding in *Ireland* v. *UK* that the five techniques (wall standing, hooding, subjection to noise, sleep deprivation and deprivation of food and drink) constituted inhuman treatment, but did not amount to torture.[127] In a noteworthy development, Ireland requested the ECtHR to revise its judgment in that case, based on 'thousands of recently released documents and taking account of the legal advice received'.[128] The Court dismissed the request in 2018.[129]

The difference between article 1 CAT and the definition developed by the ECtHR has given rise to a debate between those who view purpose as the central element in distinguishing between torture and other ill-treatment – with a high entry threshold for ill-treatment – and those who consider severity

---

[123] See on its application in the Court's jurisprudence, *Espinoza Gonzáles* v. *Peru* (IACtHR) (2014) para. 143.

[124] See *Bouyid* v. *Belgium* (ECtHR) (2015) paras. 87–91 and, 110–13.

[125] See e.g., *Jalloh* v. *Germany* (ECtHR) (2007) paras. 67–8; *Selmouni* v. *France*, para. 96; *Cestaro* v. *Italy* (ECtHR) (2015) paras. 171–90 (in French).

[126] *Selmouni* v. *France*, para. 121.

[127] *Ireland* v. *United Kingdom*, para. 167; *Selmouni* v. *France*, para. 101.

[128] Statement by Minister Flanagan on the 'Hooded Men' case, Department of Foreign Affairs and Trade, Ireland, Press Office (2 December 2014).

[129] *Ireland* v. *United Kingdom* (ECtHR) (2018). See M. Boyle, 'Revising the verdict in Ireland v. UK: time for a reality check?' *EJIL Talk* (6 April 2018).

as a more suitable device to recognise the scale of different forms of ill-treatment.[130] This debate, though highly relevant for a clear understanding of the nature of torture, has had limited resonance in the jurisprudence of treaty bodies; even the ECtHR seems to invoke both article 1 CAT and its own definition, which may be seen as part of an attempt to show that a certain act constitutes torture under all possible definitions.[131]

A further element of torture introduced by the then Special Rapporteur on torture Manfred Nowak is that of 'powerlessness'.[132] While this notion has potentially negative connotations for victims, the element of powerlessness can play a useful role in respect of the degree of factual control and in capturing the crucial (and terrifying) power imbalance inherent in torture situations. It can therefore be important when distinguishing between custodial ill-treatment and other situations, such as the use of excessive force during demonstrations.

Beyond the rather flexible formula developed by the ECtHR, other forms of inhuman, cruel or degrading treatment not amounting to torture are not defined in international law. By its nature ill-treatment is a broad category with a wide field of application, as evidenced by the often casuistic jurisprudence.[133] Examples include inhuman conditions of detention, denial of medical care, destruction of homes and excessive use of force.[134] Notably, rendering individuals, such as asylum seekers, destitute may also constitute ill-treatment, such as held by the ECtHR in *M. S. S.* v. *Belgium and Greece*.[135] Treatment has been defined as degrading if it arouses 'feelings of fear, anguish and inferiority capable of humiliating and debasing the victim',[136] such as unnecessary strip searches[137] or confinement of a prisoner in a metal cage in a courtroom.[138]

---

[130] See M. Evans, 'Getting to Grips with Torture' (2002) 51 *International & Comparative Law Quarterly* 365.

[131] See e.g., *Jalloh* v. *Germany*, para. 48. See on the African Commission's interpretation of article 5 of the African Charter on Human and Peoples' Rights, *Gabriel Shumba* v. *Zimbabwe* (ACmHPR) (2012) paras. 143–4.

[132] See Special Rapporteur on torture, above note 95, paras. 28–30, 45, 52, 57.

[133] See the excellent chapter on this category in Waldron, above note 104, 276–319.

[134] See e.g., *Ananyev and Others* v. *Russia* (ECtHR) (2012) (pilot judgment on inhuman and degrading conditions in pre-trial detention); *Todorov* v. *Ukraine* (ECtHR) (2012) paras. 51–5 (denial of adequate medical care); *Dulaş* v. *Turkey* (ECtHR) (2001) paras. 49–56 (destruction of homes); *Güler and Öngel* v. *Turkey* (ECtHR) (2011) paras. 23–31 (excessive use of force during protests); *Abdullah Yasa and Others* v. *Turkey* (ECtHR) (2013) paras. 34–51 (tear gas).

[135] *M. S. S.* v. *Belgium and Greece* (ECtHR) (2011). See for an analysis of the Court's jurisprudence, M.-B. Dembour, *When Humans become Migrants: Study of the European Court of Human Rights with an Inter-American Counterpoint* (Oxford University Press, 2015) 402–41.

[136] *Ireland* v. *United Kingdom*, para. 167.

[137] See e.g., *Wieser* v. *Austria* (ECtHR) (2007) paras. 39–41.

[138] *Svinarenko and Slyadnev* v. *Russia* (ECtHR) (2014) paras. 113–39.

The category of cruel, inhuman or degrading punishment has been applied in particular to corporal punishments. Treaty bodies have been uniform in their jurisprudence, according to which officially sanctioned corporal punishment is a degrading attack on a 'person's dignity and physical integrity',[139] for example in cases of birching on the Isle of Man (UK), the use of a tamarind switch in Jamaica, the cat-o'-nine-tails in Trinidad and Tobago or flogging in Sudan.[140]

The second sentence of article 1(1) CAT excludes from the definition of torture 'pain or suffering arising only from, inherent in or incidental to lawful sanctions'. This provision may be read as justifying any sanctions prescribed under national law, including corporal punishments. However, such an interpretation would give states unfettered discretion to define the scope of application of article 1, even to the point of passing laws that stipulate punishments clearly falling within the definition of torture. It is for this reason that most observers consider that 'lawful' refers to both national and international law, a reading that effectively makes the provision redundant. If the sanction constitutes torture according to the second sentence of article 1(1) CAT it can no longer be a valid exception; if it does not constitute torture there is no need for an exception.[141] None the less, several states retain judicial corporal punishment, which raises the question of whether there can be regional or religiously based exceptions. However, the absolute nature of the prohibition of torture under customary international law leaves no room for any contravening practice.[142] The issue of cruel, inhuman or degrading punishment has also been considered in the context of certain detention regimes. These include being kept in isolation, being locked up in a small room for twenty-three hours a day[143] and life imprisonment without the possibility of release,[144] the nature and consequences of which may reach

---

[139] *Tyrer* v. *the United Kingdom* (ECtHR) (1978) para. 33.

[140] Ibid., paras. 28–35; *Osbourne* v. *Jamaica* (HRCtee) (2000) para. 9.1; *Caesar* v. *Trinidad and Tobago* (IACtHR) (2005) paras. 56–89 (in which the Court found the punishment to amount to torture); *Curtis Francis Doebbler* v. *Sudan* (ACmHPR) (2003) paras. 29–44.

[141] M. Nowak, 'Challenges to the Absolute Nature of the Prohibition of Torture and Ill-treatment' (2005) 23 *Netherlands Quarterly of Human Rights* 674.

[142] See REDRESS and SHRM, *No More Cracking of the Whip: Time to End Corporal Punishment in Sudan* (2012) 28–31. See also Committee on the Rights of the Child (CtRC), The right of the child to protection from corporal punishment and other cruel or degrading forms of punishment (arts. 19, 28 para. 2; 37, inter alia), UN doc. CRC/C/GC/8 (2 March 2007).

[143] *G.B.* v. *Bulgaria* (ECtHR) (2004) paras. 82–8.

[144] See *Kafkaris* v. *Cyprus* (ECtHR) (2009) paras. 95–108; *Vinter and Others* v. *the United Kingdom* (ECtHR) (2012) paras. 87–96; also *Babar Ahmad and Others* v. *United Kingdom* (ECtHR) (2012) paras. 205–44. However, see *Hutchinson* v. *the United Kingdom* (ECtHR) (2015) paras. 18–26, where the ECtHR deferred to the national courts' response to *Vinter and Others* v. *the United Kingdom*.

beyond what detainees can be expected to suffer in the course of lawful deprivation of their liberty.[145]

8.3.6   Obligations

Under the prohibition, states have a negative obligation to refrain from engaging in any torture or other ill-treatment and a positive obligation to prevent, investigate, prosecute and punish, and redress such acts. As is clear from article 2 CAT, the overarching duty and primary objective of the prohibition is to prevent acts of torture through 'effective legislative, administrative, judicial or other measures'. The effective implementation of the prohibition requires state actors to take a series of measures in law and practice that are designed to significantly reduce the risk of torture.[146] These include incorporating the prohibition of torture in national law,[147] stipulating that statements extracted under torture are inadmissible[148] and providing custodial safeguards. Safeguards such as prompt access to a lawyer of one's choice, the right to inform family members of the arrest, the right to challenge the lawfulness of detention before a judge, keeping custodial records and regular health checks are all meant to minimise the risk of torture, particularly during the initial phase of detention.[149] Visiting mechanisms, particularly in the form of regular independent external monitoring, can serve as an important deterrent and as a form of engagement that may result in gradual changes leading towards enhanced compliance. Such mechanisms are in place at the national, regional and international level.[150] According to international treaties and best practices, visiting mechanisms should be independent, composed of a group of mixed professionals with the required

---

[145] See Interim report of the Special Rapporteur of the Human Rights Council on torture and other cruel, inhuman or degrading treatment or punishment, UN doc. A/66/268 (5 August 2011) (on solitary confinement and isolation).

[146] General Recommendations of the Special Rapporteur on the question of torture, UN doc. E/CN4/2003/68 (17 December 2002) para. 26. See on the effectiveness of preventive measures, R. Carver and L. Handley, *Does Torture Prevention Work?* (Liverpool University Press, 2016).

[147] L. Oette, 'Implementing the Prohibition of Torture: The Contribution and Limits of National Legislation and Jurisprudence' (2012) 16 *The International Journal of Human Rights* 717. See on making torture a crime under national law, art. 4 CAT and *Cestaro* v. *Italy*, para. 209.

[148] Art. 15 CAT, see Report of the Special Rapporteur on torture and other cruel, inhuman or degrading treatment or punishment, UN doc. A/61/259 (14 August 2006) paras. 44–62; *Singarasa* v. *Sri Lanka* (HRCtee) (2004) paras. 7.1–7.5.

[149] CtAT, General Comment 2, para. 13.

[150] In particular the CPT in Europe, the Subcommittee on Prevention of Torture (SPT) under the OPCAT, and the ICRC. See also Association for the Prevention of Torture, www.apt.ch.

expertise and adequately resourced.[151] The mechanisms need to have unrestricted access to all detention facilities at short notice and the opportunity to interview detainees in private. Some states have responded positively to recommendations by visiting bodies such as the European Committee for the Prevention of Torture and Inhuman or Degrading Treatment or Punishment (CPT) in Europe and there are considerable hopes that the preventive mechanisms under OPCAT will have an equally positive impact worldwide. Finally, states must not expose individuals to the risk of torture or other ill-treatment in other countries, a principle known as *non-refoulement* explicitly stipulated in article 3 CAT (torture) and generally recognised in international jurisprudence.[152]

Impunity is a major factor perpetuating torture and the approach underpinning the CAT is that of combating crime. Accordingly, states must make torture a crime in their national laws and must extradite or prosecute anyone present on their territory suspected of having committed an act of torture, which requires states to establish universal jurisdiction over acts of torture.[153] Individuals alleging torture must have an effective right to complain and states have a corresponding duty to investigate allegations of torture promptly, impartially and effectively.[154] Where sufficient evidence is found, perpetrators of torture must be subject to adequate punishments.[155] Anyone suspected of torture should not benefit from immunities, amnesties or pardons, and torture should not be subject to statutes of limitation.[156] Accountability is also an important element of the right of torture victims to an effective remedy and reparation, which is recognised as a separate right in article 14 CAT and in the jurisprudence of human rights treaty bodies and courts as being inherent in the relevant treaties.[157]

---

[151] Second Annual Report on the Subcommittee on Prevention of Torture and Other Cruel, Inhuman or Degrading Treatment or Punishment, UN doc. CAT/C/42/2 (7 April 2009) paras. 33–42.

[152] See CAT, General Comment 4 on the implementation of article 3 of the Convention in the context of article 22, UN doc. CAT/C/GC/4 (4 September 2018), and further Chapters 5.5.7 and 18.8.

[153] Arts. 4–8 CAT. See on its role in the *Habré* case, Chapter 7.7.

[154] See in particular arts. 12 and 13 CAT. Note that art. 12 stipulates an *ex officio* obligation, i.e. upon receiving credible information that acts of torture may have been committed, the authorities need to commence an investigation even in the absence of a complaint.

[155] *Gäfgen* v. *Germany*, paras. 121–5; *Zontul* v. *Greece* (ECtHR) (2012) paras. 95–109.

[156] See e.g., *Guridi* v. *Spain* (CtAT) (2005) para. 6.7; *Barrios Altos* v. *Peru*, paras. 41–4; *Mocanu and Others* v. *Romania* (ECtHR) (2014) para. 326; HRCtee, General Comment 31, para. 18.

[157] See CAT, General Comment 3: Implementation of article 14 by States parties, UN doc. CAT/C/GC/3 (19 November 2012), particularly paras. 16–17, 41–2. See further Chapters 15.9 and 15.10.

INTERVIEW 8.1

The Role of Medical Documentation in Combating Torture: Istanbul Protocol

(Dr Önder Özkalipçi)

The Istanbul Protocol was developed in the 1990s by a coalition of human rights organisations, doctors and lawyers and has since become an important, internationally recognised manual and guide on how to document and investigate torture cases. The following is an interview with Dr Önder Özkalipçi, one of the three project coordinators at the time, who has also conducted a series of trainings on the Istanbul Protocol around the world.

Why 'Istanbul Protocol'?

The idea of calling the guidelines 'Istanbul Protocol' emerged during the first meeting of the authors and contributing organisations in 1996 – the name reflects the fact that the main meetings were held in the Forensic Medicine Department of the Medical Faculty, Istanbul University.

What explains the prominent role played by Turkish activists and organisations in drafting the Istanbul Protocol?

First of all, the Istanbul Protocol is a joint product of seventy-five experts from forty different organisations. A number of non-governmental organisations (NGOs), such as Physicians for Human Rights-USA and Action for Torture Survivors-Geneva, and individuals made important contributions, which was facilitated by three coordinators (Vincent Iacopino, Caroline Schlar and myself). At the time, torture was an important public health problem in Turkey (unfortunately it still is today). Several key organisations, namely Human Rights Foundation of Turkey, Turkish Medical Association and Forensic Physicians Society of Turkey, teamed up to respond to this challenge. Our thinking was that if we could succeed in making a strong contribution to an international document that could be accepted by the UN, then this might help our struggle against torture and ill-treatment in our own country. The Istanbul Protocol is clearly the outcome of international collaboration and an international document, but it is equally true that the Turkish experience and expertise was an important element that inspired and invigorated the work of colleagues from other countries.

What are the main challenges relating to the documentation and investigation of torture?

Besides attempts to justify torture that are at times evident in public opinion, impunity is the biggest challenge in practice. By definition, the crime of torture is committed by state officials or 'at the instigation of or with the consent or acquiescence of state officials or other persons acting in official capacities'. This means that perpetrators already operate within a state network that allows them to cover the traces of their crime and rely on 'friends' within the system. One of the key tools of protecting perpetrators is to delay investigations. Investigations last so long that the case is dismissed because of the expiry of time limits for prosecutions, the perpetrator may become an important state official or retires or dies because of old age, or the evidence is lost.

Given these challenges the independence of the experts taking part in the investigation is critical. In several countries, forensic doctors work under the authority of the Ministry of Justice or Ministry of Interior. How can you prevent doctors from being subject to pressure by high state officials if they are working in the same ministry as the alleged perpetrator(s)? In practice, this has been a real problem for medical experts when preparing medical reports documenting torture. Threats are another major concern. There is always the risk of threats to the victim, his or her family, lawyers and the experts playing a role in the investigation, such as medical experts and even prosecutors and judges. Sadly, one of our colleagues, Dr Germán Antonio Ramírez Herrera, who took part in trainings on the Istanbul Protocol and submitted a detailed report that included several medico-legal reports on serious human rights violations, was assassinated in Ecuador in 2010. We know of several other cases of threats to forensic experts and there is still a long way to go worldwide. Lack of standards and knowledge of how best to investigate allegations of torture is another issue. In many cases the 'doctors' help the perpetrators, deliberately or inadvertently, because of the poor quality of their medical reports. Where a doctor concludes 'no evidence', a prosecutor or judge finds it easier not to prosecute or convict the perpetrator(s).

How does the Istanbul Protocol assist in addressing these challenges?

Essentially, the Istanbul Protocol highlights the responsibility of states to investigate allegations of torture promptly and effectively and provides the tools on how to do this in practice. States must work towards improving the quality of investigations. Training medical doctors how to document and prepare a report on the physical and psychological findings of torture and making judges and prosecutors aware of the value of high quality medico-legal reports remains a priority task.

Has the Istanbul Protocol been used in practice, and has it made a difference?

Yes, there are dozens of examples of decisions from national or international courts that cite the Istanbul Protocol when ruling on allegations of torture. High quality medical reports prepared in line with the Protocol's standards are challenging the forensic systems of countries. After years of training and engagement countries such as Georgia, Serbia, Turkey, Mexico and Egypt have begun introducing positive changes such as using medical report templates consistent with relevant standards and making significant investments to forensic medicine. The Committee against Torture (CtAT) has also started recommending training on the Istanbul Protocol in its concluding observations on states parties' reports. If states implement these trainings effectively there is some hope that the prevalence of torture decreases, although we all know that the global picture of torture is not very satisfactory today.

What is the broader significance of the Istanbul Protocol in the struggle against torture?

The Istanbul Protocol is an important tool for legal and health professionals who should work together to combat torture more effectively – such cooperation has considerable potential to bring about changes. Ultimately, a manual or protocol cannot protect individuals from torture if there is no rule of law. However, guidelines that represent best practices agreed upon by professionals worldwide can contribute to societies based on the rule of law where, we would hope, torture is the exception and – should it happen – its perpetrators will be punished.

The Istanbul Protocol is being updated in 2018 and 2019 in a process coordinated by four UN bodies and four NGOs. What has prompted this update, and what do you expect it to achieve?

The last twenty years have seen plenty of changes in both the legal and medical fields. There is a need to reflect these changes and update the Istanbul Protocol. For example, references to the UN Commission on Human Rights, which was replaced by the Human Rights Council in 2006, are out of date. The important OPCAT monitoring system, including the Subcommittee on Prevention of Torture, only started working several years after the Istanbul Protocol was submitted in 1999. Many changes of this kind are needed in a manual aimed at providing guidance on the investigation of torture allegations.

The group that drafted the Istanbul Protocol (seventy-five experts from forty organisations from fifteen countries) 'owned' the Protocol and led and supported the efforts for its global recognition and implementation. Now there are more than twice as many organisations and professional experts involved. This will strengthen the network of those having a keen interest in making the documentation and investigation of torture more effective. As a result, I expect us to be stronger in facing the challenge of implementing the IP globally.

8.4   THE RIGHT TO LIBERTY AND SECURITY OF PERSON

8.4.1   Practice

The modern system of imprisonment grants states considerable power to deprive persons of their liberty and control their freedom.[158] This power inevitably gives rise to concerns that are particularly pronounced in respect of special detention regimes, including prison camps, preventive detention (based on the alleged threat of a person or the need to protect public safety irrespective of any suspicion of having committed a crime), immigration detention, detention under emergency laws (curtailing detainee's rights) and secret detention (lack of acknowledgement), such as in the 'War on Terror'.[159] Many of these detention regimes are characterised by their lack of due process and safeguards, which has often facilitated other violations, notably torture and enforced disappearance, and resulted in the denial of fair trials that require effective defence from the outset.[160] In addition, detention regimes tend to be far from 'neutral'. Individuals who belong to marginalised communities or groups are more likely to be targeted by the authorities, such as members of ethnic or other minorities, foreign nationals, Afro-Americans in the USA or Muslims in the UK following the terrorist attacks, and are therefore particularly vulnerable to the state's power to arrest and detain.[161] Arrest and detention can entail devastating and potentially irreversible consequences such as stigmatisation, loss of employment, the breakdown of a relationship, psychological damage and illnesses contracted in prison. This makes it imperative that the public's interest in punishment and/or safety is counterbalanced by adequate due process guarantees against arbitrariness applying to all forms of detention, including confinement in psychiatric hospitals.

---

[158] See M. Foucault, *Discipline and Punish: The Birth of the Prison* (Penguin, 1991).

[159] Reports of the Working Group on Arbitrary Detention, UN doc. A/HRC/7/4 (10 January 2008) paras. 59–68; and A/HRC/13/30 (18 January 2010) paras. 72–80; Joint Study, above note 91, paras. 57–86.

[160] Ibid.

[161] See in particular, reports of the UN Working Group on Arbitrary Detention, online at www.ohchr.org/EN/Issues/Detention/Pages/WGADIndex.aspx.

8.4.2   Sources

The right to liberty and security is recognised in several international and regional instruments,[162] which are complemented by UN 'soft law' standards that can be, and have been used to specify states' obligations.[163] International humanitarian law includes numerous provisions on arrest and detention, particularly regarding the internment of prisoners of war.[164] Systematic or widespread 'imprisonment or other severe deprivation of physical liberty in violation of fundamental rules of international law' constitutes a crime against humanity[165] and unlawful confinement (as a grave breach) a war crime.[166] The prohibition of arbitrary arrest and detention is considered to constitute customary international law.[167] Moreover, certain aspects of the right to liberty and security, such as the right to habeas corpus, are viewed as non-derogable and permissible derogations are subject to a strict proportionality test.[168]

8.4.3   Scope of the Right to Liberty and Security

The right prohibits arbitrary deprivation of liberty and guarantees security.[169] The term liberty refers to 'physical liberty' as opposed to 'mere restriction of freedom of movement'.[170] Deprivation of liberty differs from restriction

---

[162] Art. 9 UDHR; art. 9 ICCPR; art. 37(b) CRC; art. 14 CRPD; art. 16 ICRMW; art. 17 CPED; art. 5 ECHR; art. 7 ACHR; art. 6 ACHPR.

[163] UN Standard Minimum Rules for the Treatment of Prisoners (Mandela Rules), UN doc. A/RES/70/175 (17 December 2015) Annex; UN Body of Principles for the Protection of All Persons under Any Form of Detention or Imprisonment, adopted by General Assembly resolution 43/173 (9 December 1988).

[164] See for a concise overview, ICRC-CIHL, Database rule 99.

[165] Art. 7(1)(e) ICC Rome Statute.   [166] Art. 8(2)(a)(vii) ICC Rome Statute.

[167] HRCtee, General Comment 24: Issues relating to reservations made upon ratification or accession to the Covenant or the Optional Protocols thereto, or in relation to declarations under article 41 of the Covenant, UN doc. CCPR/C/21/Rev.1/Add.6 (4 November 1994) para. 8. According to §702(e) of the US Restatement (Third) on Foreign Relations, 'prolonged arbitrary detention' violates customary international law.

[168] HRCtee, General Comment 29: States of Emergency (article 4) UN doc. CCPR/C/21/Rev.1/Add.11 (31 August 2001) para. 4. See also *Habeas Corpus in Emergency Situations (Arts. 27(2), 25(1) and 7(6) American Convention on Human Rights)* (IACtHR) (1987) paras. 11–13; *Judicial Guarantees in States of Emergency (Arts. 27(2), 25 and 8 American Convention on Human Rights)* (IACtHR) (1987) paras. 20–30 and 36–40.

[169] See HRCtee, General Comment 35: Article 9 (Liberty and Security of Person), UN doc. CCPR/C/GC/35 (16 December 2014). The ECtHR and IACtHR have largely focused on the right to liberty. See for the IACtHR's understanding of the concept, *Chaparro-Álvarez and Lapo-Íñiguez v. Ecuador* (IACtHR) (2007) paras. 52–3.

[170] *Guzzardi* v. *Italy* (ECtHR) (1980) para. 92 (confinement akin to open prison constituting deprivation of liberty); *Austin and Others* v. *the United Kingdom* (ECtHR) (2012) paras. 52–69 (kettling no deprivation of liberty; however, see joint dissenting opinion on this point by Judges Tulkens, Spielmann and Garlicki); *Adil Soltan Oglu Gahramanov* v. *Azerbaijan* (ECtHR) (2013) paras. 34–47 (stopped at airport, no violation).

upon liberty – which may constitute an interference with the right to freedom of movement – in terms of its degree or intensity rather than its nature or substance.[171] It has an objective and subjective element, i.e. confinement to a certain limited place for a not negligible length of time without valid consent.[172] The subjective element is particularly important in cases of psychiatric confinement, in which it acts as a safeguard where the individual concerned is not in a position to express his or her consent.[173]

8.4.4   Justification of Arrest and Detention

International human rights law prohibits the 'arbitrary' deprivation of liberty. Importantly, it is not sufficient that arrest or detention are permitted by national law; this would give states carte blanche to allow deprivation on the flimsiest of grounds, as is indeed often the case, particularly under emergency laws.[174] As stated by the HRCtee in the defining case of *Mukong* v. *Cameroon*, 'arbitrariness' is 'not to be equated with "against the law" but must be interpreted more broadly to include elements of inappropriateness, injustice, lack of predictability and due process of law ... remand in custody pursuant to lawful arrest must not only be lawful but reasonable in the circumstances'.[175]

As a general rule, a state must comply with the (substantive) law that may justify deprivation of liberty and the (procedural) law stipulating arrest and detention procedures, which themselves must be reasonable, foreseeable and proportionate.[176] The authorities must demonstrate the existence of grounds that justify arrest, such as reasonable suspicion of a crime having been committed, or continued detention, for example to prevent flight, interference with evidence or the recurrence of crime.[177] Notably, some grounds, such as imprisonment for debt or disability, are explicitly prohibited under international human rights law as a justification for arrest or detention.[178] The ECHR differs from other treaties as it sets out a list of exhaustive grounds on which the deprivation of liberty is permitted.[179] These include the arrest and

---

[171] *Guzzardi* v. *Italy*, para. 93.
[172] *Storck* v. *Germany* (ECtHR) (2005) paras. 74–8.
[173] Ibid.
[174] *Amnesty International and Others* v. *Sudan* (ACmHPR) (1999) para. 59.
[175] *Mukong* v. *Cameroon* (HRCtee) (1994) para. 9.8.
[176] See *Tibi* v. *Ecuador* (IACtHR) (2004) para. 98; *Gusinskiy* v. *Russia* (ECtHR) (2005) paras. 52–5, 62–9; *Steel* v. *United Kingdom* (ECtHR) (1998) para. 54.
[177] *A.* v. *Australia* (HRCtee) (1997) para. 9.4.
[178] Art. 11 ICCPR; art. 1 of Protocol no. 4 to the ECHR; art. 14(1)(b) CRPD.
[179] However, see *Hassan* v. *United Kingdom* (ECtHR) (2014) paras. 96–107, a case of preventive detention during armed conflict not explicitly covered by any of the grounds set out in art. 5 ECHR, where the Court held that it would, where requested

detention of persons suspected of having committed criminal offences,[180] of persons of 'unsound mind, alcoholics or drug addicts or vagrants'[181] and in the immigration and deportation/extradition context.[182]

International human rights treaties stipulate a number of procedural safeguards against arbitrary arrest and detention.[183] As a first step, anyone arrested must be promptly informed of the reasons for his or her arrest.[184] This is meant to enable the arrested or detained person to effectively exercise his or her rights, with a view to challenging the lawfulness of the deprivation of liberty and defending any criminal charges where applicable.[185] Judicial control constitutes the most important safeguard against arbitrary deprivation of liberty. In criminal cases states have to ensure that any suspect is brought promptly before a judge or judicial authority,[186] that is normally within the first forty-eight hours.[187] This rule recognises that anyone facing criminal charges is particularly vulnerable and that there is a heightened interest in ensuring

---

by the respondent state, interpret and apply art. 5 'in the light of relevant provisions of international humanitarian law' even without a formal derogation. See also partly dissenting opinion of Judge Spano joined by Judges Nicolaou, Bianku and Kalaydjieva.

[180] See e.g., *Lawless* v. *Ireland* (No. 3) (ECtHR) (1961); *Fox, Campbell and Hartley* v. *UK* (ECtHR) (1990) para. 32.

[181] See e.g., *Winterwerp* v. *Netherlands* (ECtHR) (1979) paras. 38–42 ('unsound mind'); *Enhorn* v. *Sweden* (ECtHR) (2005) paras. 40–56 (HIV); *De Wilde, Ooms and Versyp* v. *Belgium* (ECtHR) (1971) paras. 66–70 ('vagrants'); *Witold Litwa* v. *Poland* (ECtHR) (2000) paras. 72–80 ('alcoholic'). W. A. Schabas, *The European Convention on Human Rights: A Commentary* (Oxford University Press, 2017) 220, refers to this wording of art. 5(1)(e) ECHR as 'somewhat embarrassingly archaic'.

[182] In *Saadi* v. *United Kingdom* (ECtHR) (2008) paras. 61–80, the Court found that a state may detain a person under the first limb of art. 5(1)(f) ECHR 'to prevent his effecting an unauthorised entry' as long as the state had not authorised the entry. In *Suso Musa* v. *Malta* (ECtHR) (2013) paras. 94–107, the Court found a violation of both limbs of art. 5(1)(f) ECHR, on account of conditions and length of detention to prevent unauthorised entry and the lack of realistic prospect of the applicant's deportation under the second limb of art. 5(1)(f) ECtHR. See for critical discussion of the ECtHR's jurisprudence, and a more favourable account of the IACtHR's judgment in *Vélez Loor* v. *Panama* (IACtHR) (2010), Dembour, above note 135, 359–401.

[183] HRCtee, General Comment 35, paras. 24–48 and Working Group on Arbitrary Detention, United Nations Basic Principles and Guidelines on Remedies and Procedures on the Right of Anyone Deprived of Their Liberty to Bring Proceedings Before a Court, UN doc. A/HRC/30/37 (6 July 2015).

[184] Art. 9(2) ICCPR; art. 5(2) ECHR; art. 7(4) ACHR and principle M.2(a) of the Principles and Guidelines on the Right to a Fair Trial and Legal Assistance in Africa, 2001.

[185] *Juan Humberto Sánchez* v. *Honduras* (IACtHR) (2003) para. 82; *Fox, Campbell and Hartley* v. *UK*, para. 40.

[186] A public prosecutor is not a 'judicial authority', see *Kulomin* v. *Hungary* (HRCtee) (1996) para. 11.3 and *Tibi* v. *Ecuador*, para. 117.

[187] See *Berezhnoy* v. *Russia* (HRCtee) (2016) para. 9.2, referring to the forty-eight hours' limit and 'especially strict standards of promptness' of twenty-four hours in case of juveniles. In *Brogan and Others* v. *United Kingdom* (ECtHR) (1988) para. 62, the Court found that

judicial control of executive action at the earliest opportunity.[188] States have repeatedly sought to extend the period between arrest and appearance before a judicial authority, particularly in emergency situations. However, human rights treaty bodies have allowed limited extensions only where they are shown to be necessary and where adequate safeguards are in place, knowing well that detainees are most at risk of torture and other ill-treatment in the initial days of detention.[189] A detainee on remand also has a right to be tried within a reasonable time (taking into consideration the complexity of the case and conduct of the parties) or to be released pending trial.[190] This right flows from the presumption of innocence and continued detention can only be justified on specific, narrow grounds, such as to prevent escape. It reaches its absolute limit where the time spent on remand exceeds the maximum length of imprisonment a detainee would face in the case of conviction.[191]

Beyond the specific rules applying to criminal cases anyone deprived of his or her liberty has the right to challenge the lawfulness of detention, which entails the (non-derogable) right to have his or her case speedily heard by a court, also referred to as habeas corpus.[192] This right provides an important safeguard, particularly against 'institutionalised' deprivation of liberty, such as in psychiatric hospitals, or excessive detention regimes, such as in the immigration context.[193] Habeas corpus proceedings must examine the factual and legal grounds for detention. This has proved difficult where authorities have relied on confidential information on national security grounds. Importantly, an applicant must be able 'effectively to challenge the allegations' and the state concerned must provide procedures, so that the right of the defence can be exercised.[194]

Custodial safeguards, in addition to preventing unlawful arrest and detention, are meant to minimise the risk of torture and other ill-treatment and

'even the shortest of the four periods of detention, namely the four days and six hours spent in police custody ... falls outside the strict constraints as to time permitted by the first part of Article 5 para. 3 (art. 5–3): See also *Borisenko* v. *Hungary* (HRCtee) (2002) para. 7.4 (three days too long).

[188] *Tibi* v. *Ecuador*, para. 114; principle M.3(b) of the 2001 African Fair Trial Principles.

[189] Contrast *Brannigan and McBride* v. *United Kingdom* (ECtHR) (1993) paras. 32 and 56, with *Aksoy* v. *Turkey* (ECtHR) (1996) para. 78. See also *Castillo Petruzzi et al.* v. *Peru* (IACtHR) (1999) paras. 109–12. The ACHPR does not provide for derogability as reaffirmed in principle R. 2(a) of the 2001 African Fair Trial Principles.

[190] *Wemhoff* v. *Federal Republic of Germany* (ECtHR) (1968) paras. 4–17; *Suárez-Rosero* v. *Ecuador* (IACtHR) (1997) paras. 38–66; principle M.1(e) of the 2001 African Fair Trial Principles; HRCtee, General Comment 35, paras. 36–8.

[191] See for an in-depth discussion, *W.* v. *Switzerland* (ECtHR) (1994) para. 43, and Dissenting Opinion of Judge Pettiti.

[192] Art. 9(4) ICCPR; art. 5(4) ECHR; art. 7(6) ACHR; principle M.5 of the 2001 African Fair Trial Principles.

[193] *Shtukaturov* v. *Russia* (ECtHR) (2008) paras. 121–35 ('applicant with mental disorder'); *Vélez Loor* v. *Panama*, paras. 119–39.

[194] *A and Others* v. *United Kingdom* (ECtHR) (2009) paras. 217–24.

guarantee the rights of the defence. Incommunicado detention, i.e. holding someone without access to the outside world, is the very antithesis of these safeguards. It violates the right to liberty and also constitutes a form of ill-treatment, if not torture, in its own right.[195] The right of access to a lawyer of one's choice is another crucial safeguard that applies from the earliest stage of proceedings.[196] However, it may exceptionally be restricted for compelling reasons, provided that such restriction does 'not unduly prejudice the rights of the accused under Article 6'.[197] As the judgment in *Ibrahim and Others* v. *United Kingdom*, which primarily concerned 'safety interviews' of terrorism suspects, illustrates, such an approach may be problematic where it provides authorities with considerable leeway at the initial interrogation phase as long as any adverse consequences, 'taken cumulatively' are mitigated by 'counter-balancing safeguards'.[198]

For foreign nationals, access to a consular official – referred to in article 36(1) Vienna Convention on Consular Relations – has been recognised as a human right, which is particularly important given the vulnerable position of foreign nationals.[199] In practice, its effectiveness depends on the ability and willingness of consular officials to take action to protect the rights of their nationals. In addition to due process rights during arrest and detention, international human rights law also recognises a right to compensation for 'arbitrary' arrest and/or detention.[200] This right serves as vindication for the violation suffered and, ideally, acts as a deterrent for the state.

8.4.5   Administrative Detention: Law and Power in the Pursuit of Policy

Preventive detention, also referred to as administrative detention, is ostensibly aimed at preventing a danger to the public. It is not explicitly prohibited in international human rights law[201] but is considered problematic because

---

[195] See at 8.3.5.

[196] *Öcalan* v. *Turkey*, paras. 131–7; *Bulacio* v. *Argentina* (IACtHR) (2003) paras. 130 and 132.

[197] *Salduz* v. *Turkey* (ECtHR) (2009) para. 55.

[198] *Ibrahim and Others* v. *The United Kingdom* (ECtHR) (2014), particularly paras. 213 and 224, and judgment of the Grand Chamber in the case (2016) paras. 255–311. See also *Beuze* v. *Belgium* (ECtHR) (2018) paras. 114–50, and criticism of the approach taken in the Joint Concurring Opinion of Judges Yudkivska, Vučinić, Turković and Hüseynov in *Beuze* v. *Belgium*.

[199] *LaGrand* case, para. 77. See also *Avena and other Mexican nationals* (*Mexico* v. *United States of America*) (ICJ) (2004) 12, paras. 58–106; *The Right to Information on Consular Assistance in the Framework of the Guarantees of the Due Process of Law; Chaparro Álvarez and Lapo Íñiguez* v. *Ecuador* (IACtHR) (2007) para. 164; principle M. 2(e) of the 2001 African Fair Trial Principles.

[200] Arts. 9(5) ICCPR; art. 5(5) ECHR, principle M. 1(h) of the 2001 African Fair Trial Principles.

[201] Art. 5 ECHR is an exception as it does not list preventive detention as one of the grounds of legitimate arrest and detention (other than in the immigration context, see art. 5(1)(f) ECHR). See *Lawless* v. *Ireland* (no. 3) paras. 10–15. However, the ECtHR effectively permitted the short-term preventive detention of football fans pursuant to an order as being in compliance with art. 5(1)(b) in *Ostendorf* v. *Germany* (ECtHR) (2013) paras. 65–105.

it essentially constitutes detention without trial. This form of detention is therefore subject to strict requirements; it must be defined by law, necessary (to achieve the legitimate object pursued) and subject to continuous judicial review.[202]

In practice, preventive detention has been an integral part of states' arsenal to control and stifle opposition. It has been revived in the context of counter-terrorism operations, including in the detention regimes of Guantánamo Bay (USA) and Belmarsh prison in the UK, which have raised serious concerns about their compatibility with the right to liberty and security.[203] Indeed, it has been argued that prolonged detention without trial constitutes a form of ill-treatment in its own right.[204]

The Israeli administrative detention regime illustrates the risks inherent in this form of detention. Thousands of Palestinians from the occupied territories have been held in administrative detention by Israeli authorities over the years, particularly during the various uprisings.[205] Several pieces of military laws provide Israeli authorities with wide-ranging powers, namely the Emergency Powers (Detention) Law 1979, the Order Regarding Security Provisions (Consolidated Version) (no. 1651) 2009, and the Incarceration of Unlawful Combatants Law 2002.[206] Under the latter law,[207] the military may detain an individual suspected of having participated in 'hostile acts against the State of Israel' or being a member of a force perpetrating such acts for up to fourteen days without judicial review. It may also restrict access to a lawyer for up to seven days on security grounds. Detention may be renewed for up to six months at a time under judicial supervision as long as the person concerned is considered to constitute a risk to public security. Besides this Act, which is used to detain persons from the Gaza strip, administrative detention in the West Bank is governed by the Order

---

[202] HRCtee, General Comment 35, para. 15. See for a good analysis of the risk of preventive detention and the approach of the IACtHR, Concurring Opinion of Judge Sergio García Ramírez to the Judgment in the case of *Bayarri* v. *Argentina* (IACtHR) (2008).

[203] Situation of detainees at Guantánamo Bay Report of the Chairperson of the Working Group on Arbitrary Detention, Ms L. Zerrougui et al., UN doc. E/CN.4/2006/120 (15 February 2006) paras. 17–29; and *A and Others* v. *United Kingdom*, paras. 162–72.

[204] This argument was rejected by the ECtHR in *A and Others* v. *United Kingdom*, paras. 126–36, on the ground that the detainees were not without prospects of release because effective remedies were available. However, see *F. K. A. G.* v. *Australia* (HRCtee) (2013) and *M. M. M.* v. *Australia* (HRCtee) (2013) para. 9.8 and para. 10.7 respectively, where the HRCtee found a violation in cases of indefinite detention.

[205] Recent B'Tselem statistics show that as of March 2015, Israeli prison services held 412 residents of the occupied territories in administrative detention. See online at www.btselem.org/administrative_detention/statistics.

[206] See Hamoked and B'Tselem, *Without Trial: Administrative Detention of Palestinians by Israel* (2009) 4.

[207] Law no. 5762/2002.

Regarding Security Provisions, Military Order 1651.[208] This Order author-ises the Israeli Defence Forces to detain a person for an initial ninety-six hours without judicial supervision. Detention may be ordered for up to six months, where the commander 'has reasonable cause to believe that reasons of regional security or public security require that a certain person be held in detention', a period which may be extended for a further six months. The terms 'regional security or public security' are not defined. Combined with the fact that the regular judicial review takes place in routine proce-dures, which may be based on classified information and conducted in the absence of the detainee, detainees are effectively hardly able to challenge the legality of detention.

Israel has justified this practice with reference to 'the provisions of inter-national humanitarian law'.[209] However, even under international human-itarian law, such detention should be exceptional.[210] Moreover, the regime has been criticised for its lack of due process, its use as an alternative to criminal proceedings, its frequent and extensive application,[211] including for the detention of political opponents and Palestinians more generally, and its incompatibility with international standards.[212] The example demonstrates the difficulty of ensuring that adequate safeguards are in place in a sys-tem designed to maximise executive control based on security paradigms. Inherently, such detention regimes render detainees vulnerable to other vio-lations, particularly torture. Given the legacy of abuse of systems of preven-tive detention worldwide, there are good reasons to minimise if not prohibit it altogether.

---

[208] See Order Regarding Security Provisions [Consolidated Version] (Judea and Samaria) (no. 1651) 5770–2009, arts. 271–94.

[209] See with reference to discussion of the jurisprudence of Israeli courts, T. Stahlberg and H. Lahmann, 'A Paradigm of Prevention: Humpty Dumpty, the War on Terror and the Power of Preventive Detention in the United States, Israel and Europe' (2011) 59 *American Journal of Comparative Law* 1051, at 1066–73. The HRCtee has expressed its regrets over the position of Israel that the Covenant does not apply to individuals within its jurisdiction but outside its territory, and was 'concerned at the position of the State party that international human rights law does not apply when international humanitarian law is applicable'. See HRCtee, Concluding Observations: Israel, UN doc. CCPR/C/ISR/CO/4 (21 November 2014) para. 5.

[210] See ICRC-CIHL, Database, rule 99.

[211] See CtAT, Concluding observations on the fifth report of Israel, UN doc. CAT/C/ISR/CO/5 (3 June 2016) para. 22, where the Committee reiterates its concerns regarding detention under the law 5762-2002, and expressed grave concerns that 'there were 700 persons, including 12 minors, in administrative detention'.

[212] See concerns expressed in Report of the Special Rapporteur on the promotion and protection of human rights and fundamental freedoms while countering terrorism – Mission to Israel, including visit to Occupied Palestinian Territory, UN doc. A/HRC/6/17/Add.4 (16 November 2007) paras. 22–9; HRCtee, Concluding observations, above note 209, para. 10.

Immigration detention has become another focal point for concerns over administrative detention.[213] As part of broader deterrence policies, states have increasingly resorted to detaining asylum seekers and other migrants, following arrival, during refugee status determination or awaiting deportation or removal. Places of detention are often called 'reception centres' or 'removal centres', and states have argued that individuals held in these centres are not deprived of their liberty. However, most of these places are detention centres, and many are prison-like. This signals the increasing securitisation (immigrants as threat) and criminalisation (criminalising unauthorised entry, overstaying and similar conduct) of asylum seekers and migrants.[214] Notably, Guantánamo Bay was first used for immigration detention purposes, setting the template for a practice aimed at minimising if not altogether removing legal constraints.[215] These developments are highly problematic because most individuals so detained have never committed any crime (other than falling foul of immigration rules, with the exception of those awaiting deportation following criminal conviction). Yet they are frequently subject to mandatory, and at times indefinite, administrative detention with limited judicial safeguards. Ultimately, such detainees become hostages of a system in which political imperatives override the rule of law.

Several bodies, such as the Office of the UN High Commissioner for Refugees (UNHCR) and the IACtHR, have emphasised that immigration detention must be truly exceptional and subject to effective legal safeguards.[216] However, the ECtHR has given states some latitude to detain refugees and migrants,[217] as have several European Union (EU) legal instruments.[218] The practice of Australia, the UK and the US to routinely if not mandatorily detain asylum seekers has

---

[213] See in particular, A. Nethery and S. J. Silverman (eds.), *Immigration Detention: The Migration of a Policy and its Human Impact* (Routledge, 2015); D. Wilsher, *Immigration Detention: Law, History, Politics* (Cambridge University Press, 2012); G. Cornelisse, *Immigration Detention and Human Rights: Rethinking Territorial Sovereignty* (Martinus Nijhoff, 2012); and www.globaldetentionproject.org.

[214] This process has been referred to as crimmigration; see J. Stumpf, 'The Crimmigration Crisis: Immigrants, Crime, and Sovereign Power' (2006) 56 *American University Law Review* 367.

[215] A. Daystari, *United States Migrant Interdiction and the Detention of Refugees in Guantánamo Bay* (Cambridge University Press, 2015).

[216] UNHCR, *Detention Guidelines: Guidelines on the Applicable Criteria and Standards Relating to the Detention of Asylum Seekers and Alternatives to Detention* (2012); *Vélez Loor* v. *Panama*, paras. 91–101. See also Committee on Migrant Workers (CMW), General Comment 2 on the rights of migrant workers in an irregular situation and members of their families, UN doc. CMW/C/GC/2 (28 August 2013) paras. 23–35.

[217] See above note 182.

[218] See art. 26 of the Asylum Procedures Directive (2013/32/EU); arts. 8–11 of the recast Receptions Conditions Directive (2013/33/EU); art. 28 of the recast Dublin regulation (EU/604/2013) concerning the detention of asylum seekers; arts. 15–18 of the Returns Directive (2008/115/EC).

been the subject of increasing concern, criticism and adverse rulings.[219] Such detention is frequently arbitrary and in violation of legal safeguards, such as effective judicial review. It has a highly detrimental impact on detainees who are often left in a state of limbo for years, such as where it is uncertain whether they can be deported.[220] The adverse mental health consequences of such detention on persons who are often already traumatised and on vulnerable persons such as children have been well documented.[221] These consequences, conditions of detention and the treatment of detainees, often at the hands of privatised service providers in charge of operating centres, may and do in several instances amount to inhuman or degrading treatment if not torture.[222] High rates of self-harm and recurring riots are a clear indication not only of the human toll of this practice but also of legal and institutional regimes that are arbitrary and fail to provide protection, either by virtue of policy design, indifference, or both.

QUESTIONS

1. Is preventive detention a suitable response to security threats; what alternatives exist under international law?

2. What is the difference between the prohibition of 'arbitrary' arrest and detention in the ICCPR and the system provided for in the ECHR?

3. Why is the adherence to the various obligations arising from the right to liberty and security so central for the protection of multiple rights?

8.5   THE RIGHT TO A FAIR TRIAL

8.5.1   Practice

The administration of justice is at the heart of human rights protection and the rule of law. It denotes a system based on the fundamental tenets of an independent judiciary, effective access to justice and equality of

---

[219] See e.g., *F. K. A. G.* v. *Australia*; *M. M. M.* v. *Australia*; *Detention Action* v. *Secretary of State for the Home Department (Equality Human Rights Commission intervening)* (UK) (2014) para. 221 (on adverse impact of fast-track detention on refugee status determination); IACHR, *Report on Immigration in the United States: Detention and Due Process*, OEA/Ser.L/V/II, doc. 78/10 (30 December 2010).

[220] See for an excellent study, which provides first-hand perspectives of individuals in UK immigration detention, M. Bosworth, *Inside Immigration Detention* (Oxford University Press, 2014).

[221] T. Storm and M. Engberg, 'The Impact of Immigration Detention on the Mental Health of Torture Survivors Is Poorly Documented – A Systematic Review' (November 2013) 60 *Danish Medical Journal* 1, which reviews fifteen studies on the impact of detention on mental health.

[222] See e.g., *M. S. S.* v. *Belgium and Greece*, paras. 223–34; *F. K. A. G.* v. *Australia* and *M. M. M.* v. *Australia*, para. 9.8 and para. 10.7 respectively; CtAT: Concluding Observations USA, UN doc. CAT/C/USA/CO/3–5 (19 December 2014) para. 19.

arms. Conversely, its absence has facilitated and contributed to perpetuating myriad violations. Authoritarian and dictatorial states have frequently used criminal trials as an extension of state power, applied by a pliant judiciary in proceedings stripped of due process. This is particularly apparent in proceedings that subject civilians, often members of the opposition, to the jurisdiction of special or military courts.[223] The systemic failure to ensure the independence of the judiciary and due process is still a common feature in many countries.[224] Beyond deliberate maladministration, many systems face major structural problems that may result in a denial of justice, ranging from lack of basic infrastructure and personnel, corruption and delays to inadequate guarantees of defence rights, to name just some recurring problems. The lack of access to justice in particular is a fundamental problem. Systemic inequalities frequently impact adversely on the ability of members of particular groups, such as foreign nationals, minorities, women and the poorer strata of society more generally, to access justice, creating a vicious circle that enhances their vulnerability to other human rights violations.[225]

8.5.2   Sources

The right to a fair trial is recognised in a series of international and regional instruments.[226] The ICCPR and ECHR provide that the right applies in proceedings relating to criminal charges and civil rights and obligations, with article 8 ACHR going further by rendering it applicable to all proceedings. Notwithstanding some variations, the core of the right to a fair trial is guaranteed in all of these instruments. This treaty-based recognition is

---

[223] See in particular, F. Andreu-Guzmán, *Military Jurisdiction and International Law: Military Courts and Gross Human Rights Violations* (International Commission of Jurists, 2004).

[224] See regular reports of the Special Rapporteur on the independence of judges and lawyers, Summary of information, including individual cases, transmitted to Governments and replies received, e.g., UN doc. A/HRC/17/30/Add.1 (19 May 2011).

[225] See Report of the Special Rapporteur on extreme poverty and human rights, UN doc. A/67/278 (9 August 2012); Access to Justice in the promotion and protection of the rights of indigenous peoples: restorative justice, indigenous juridical systems and access to justice for indigenous women, children and youth, and persons with disability: Study by the Expert Mechanism on the Rights of Indigenous Peoples, UN doc. A/HRC/27/65 (7 August 2014); and for a country-specific example, Office of the High Commissioner for Human Rights (OHCHR) Nepal, *Opening the Door to Equality: Access to Justice for Dalits in Nepal* (2011).

[226] Art. 10 Universal Declaration of Human Rights (UDHR); art. 14 ICCPR; art. 40(2)(iii) CRC; art. 18 ICRMW; art. 11(3) CPED; art. 6 ECHR; arts. 8 and 25 ACHR; art. 7 ACHPR. See also art. 13 CRPD.

complemented by a number of international and regional standards.[227] The right to a fair trial also forms part of international humanitarian law[228] and its violation may constitute a war crime.[229] These sources are testimony to the importance of the right to a fair trial, whose essential components are widely seen to represent customary international law.[230]

Essential judicial guarantees are not subject to derogations. Where permitted, derogations to the right to a fair trial during times of emergency must be strictly necessary.[231] As emphasised by the HRCtee, '[t]he guarantees of fair trial may never be made subject to measures of derogation that would circumvent the protection of non-derogable rights',[232] particularly in relation to article 6 ICCPR (trials resulting in the death penalty) and article 7 ICCPR (evidence extracted under torture admitted at trial).

8.5.3   Main Features of the Right to a Fair Trial

8.5.3.1   *General Principles*

The independence and impartiality of the judiciary is an absolute guarantee and a crucial component of the right to a fair trial, referring both to the position of judges (appointment; security of tenure; safeguards against interferences and appearance of independence)[233] and the institutional independence of the judiciary from the executive and legislature.[234] Tribunals must also be impartial, that is free from undue bias (fair and seen to be fair).[235] A judicial system has to be accessible to all whose rights are affected so that it can fulfil its elementary function, i.e. the dispensation of justice. The right of access to justice has been recognised as an integral part of the right to a fair trial

---

[227] See in particular, Basic Principles on the Independence of the Judiciary, adopted by the Seventh UN Congress on the Prevention of Crime and the Treatment of Offenders (UNCPCTO) (Milan, 26 August to 6 September 1985), and endorsed by UNGA resolutions 40/32 (29 November 1985) and 40/146 (13 December 1985); Basic Principles on the Role of Lawyers and Guidelines on the Role of Prosecutors, both adopted by the Eighth UNCPCTO (Havana, 27 August to 7 September 1990); 2001 African Fair Trial Principles.

[228] See ICRC-CIHL, Database, rule 100.

[229] See art. 8(2)(a)(vi) and (c)(iv) ICC Rome Statute.

[230] See references in ICRC-CIHL Database, rule 100.

[231] See in particular, *Judicial Guarantees in States of Emergency (Arts. 27(2), 25 and 8 American Convention on Human Rights)*.

[232] HRCtee, General Comment 32: Article 14: Right to equality before courts and tribunals and to a fair trial, UN doc. CCPR/C/GC/32 (23 August 2007) para. 6.

[233] S. Trechsel, *Human Rights in Criminal Proceedings* (Oxford University Press, 2005) 53–61, with further references.

[234] See HRCtee, General Comment 32, para. 19, and Report of the Special Rapporteur on the independence of judges and lawyers, UN doc. A/HRC/11/41 (24 March 2009) paras. 14–84, 95–104.

[235] Trechsel, above note 233, 61–79.

by the HRCtee and in the Inter-American system through the combination of articles 8 and 25 ACHR.[236] The ECtHR has read it into the right to a fair trial in the seminal case of *Golder* v. *UK*.[237] Golder, a prisoner, was refused permission by the UK Home Secretary to consult a lawyer in order to bring a libel case against a prison officer. The majority of the Court found that the right to a fair trial applied to both court proceedings and the opportunity to bring a case, which has become an integral part of the Court's subsequent jurisprudence on article 6 ECHR. However, it is important to recall that a state is not required to create a substantive right where none exists.[238] Where such a right is in principle available, restrictions must have a legitimate aim and be proportionate.[239]

'Fairness' is the hallmark of justice. This central component of proceedings is reflected in the right to equality before courts and tribunals, a far-reaching right that imposes a positive obligation on states to provide equal access to courts and procedural rights in their legal systems. Equality of arms is a fundamental principle according to which the parties to proceedings must have equal procedural rights (unless distinctions can be objectively justified) and be able to present their case – in principle in a public hearing – without being at a substantive disadvantage vis-à-vis the other party or parties.[240] It differs from non-discrimination, which concerns the administration of justice rather than the adversarial relationship of the parties.[241] However, discrimination may also violate equality of arms, for example where an indigent foreign national is not provided with legal aid or language assistance to argue his or her case.[242]

8.5.3.2   *Criminal Proceedings*

Criminal proceedings are of a particularly sensitive nature because of what is at stake for the parties, particularly the defendant. Several principles and specific rights apply to criminal proceedings only. Their main purpose is to

---

[236] HRCtee, General Comment 32, paras. 9–11; Judicial Guarantees in States of Emergency; A. A. Cançado Trindade, *The Access of Individuals to International Justice* (Oxford University Press, 2011) 63–75; 2001 African Fair Trial Principles C(b)(i) and K; F. Francioni (ed.), *Access to Justice as a Human Right* (Oxford University Press, 2007); Report of the Special Rapporteur on the independence of judges and lawyers, UN doc. A/HRC/8/4 (13 May 2008) paras. 15–54.

[237] *Golder* v. *United Kingdom* (ECtHR) (1975).

[238] *Al-Adsani* v. *United Kingdom* (ECtHR) (2001) paras. 46–7.

[239] See e.g., L. Doswald-Beck, *Human Rights in Times of Conflict and Terrorism* (Oxford University Press, 2011) 319–30.

[240] HRCtee, General Comment 32, para. 13.

[241] See on the relationship between the principle of equality and the prohibition of discrimination, Trechsel, above note 233, 94–5.

[242] HRCtee, General Comment 32, para. 13.

ensure equality of arms and protect defendants against the potential abuse of state power in the administration of criminal justice. The principle of legality governing criminal proceedings includes in particular the prohibition of retroactive substantive laws that flows from the maxim *nullem crimen sine lege* (no criminal responsibility for conduct that does not constitute a crime) and *nulla poena sine lege* (no punishment without law).[243] It is based on the notion that individuals should know what conduct is liable to what punishment at any given time so as to have the choice of acting in compliance with the law or face punishment.[244] Importantly, the principle does not apply to crimes recognised in international law, thus enabling national systems to disregard objections to the retroactive prosecution of international crimes,[245] such as in the case of *Kononov* v. *Latvia*.[246] The presumption of innocence is another important principle which is reflected in rules on the right to remain silent and the burden of proof being on the state. It is meant to protect against unjust convictions and safeguard the reputation of persons accused of having committed crimes.[247] The principle of *ne bis in idem* or double jeopardy (no one should be prosecuted twice for the same crime) protects the individual from repeated prosecutions, thereby compelling the authorities to prepare their case carefully, and promotes legal certainty.[248]

The right of the defence in criminal proceedings comprises both equality of arms and a set of specific rights for the defendant.[249] These include the right of the defendant to be present at trial,[250] to be defended by a lawyer of his or her choice[251] and to free legal aid 'when the interests of justice so require'.[252] The rights of the defence can conflict with other principles of the administration of justice, such as protecting the anonymity of witnesses. This

---

[243] See in this regard also arts. 22 and 23 of the ICC Rome Statute.

[244] See art. 15 ICCPR; art. 7 ECHR; art. 9 ACHR; art. 7(2) ACHPR.

[245] Art. 15(2) ICCPR. See in this respect particularly *Streletz, Kessler and Krenz* v. *Germany* (ECtHR) (2001). See for discussion of these and further cases, Doswald-Beck, above note 239, 300–17.

[246] *Kononov* v. *Latvia* (ECtHR) (2010). See Chapter 6.2.5.3. See also *Maktouf and Damjanovic* v. *Bosnia and Herzegovina* (ECtHR) (2013) paras. 65–76 (potentially more severe punishments for war crimes constituted violation of art. 7 ECHR).

[247] HRCtee, General Comment 32, para. 30. See in particular *John Murray* v. *United Kingdom* (ECtHR) (1996) para. 54, where the ECtHR held that the right to remain silent was not violated where an accused was found at the scene of a crime and, at his later trial, a court drew inferences from his lack of explanation and refusal to provide evidence.

[248] HRCtee, General Comment 32, paras. 54–7.

[249] See art. 14(3) ICCPR; art. 6(3) ECHR; art. 8(2) ACHR; art. 67 ICC Rome Statute. See General Comment 32, paras. 31–41. See for victim's right and fair trial, Trechsel, above note 233, 36–41.

[250] Art. 14(3)(d) ICCPR.

[251] Ibid.; art. 6(3)(c) ECHR; art. 8(2)(d) ACHR; art. 7(1)(c) ACHPR.

[252] Art. 14(3)(d) ICCPR; art. 6(3)(c) ECHR; art. 8(2)(e) ACHR.

presents a challenge, as a successful prosecution often depends on evidence given by informants, persons at risk of reprisals and vulnerable witnesses such as children or victims of sexual violence. Where the defence is not able to cross-examine a witness at trial the judicial authorities must adopt procedures that 'sufficiently counterbalance ... the handicaps under which the defence labour[s]', such as arrangements made to question witnesses in special hearings where the defence counsel is present.[253] Finally, states have to provide for compensation in cases of miscarriages of justice, which serves as an important right of those who have been wronged and as deterrent against the abuse of the criminal justice system.[254]

CASE STUDY 8.2
The Problem with Military and Special Courts

Military justice is governed by principles of military discipline and expeditiousness. It is generally accepted that military personnel may be subject to the jurisdiction of military courts in relation to service-related offences. However, there have been recurring concerns over subjecting civilians to the jurisdiction of military courts, primarily because the presence of members of the forces on the bench does not guarantee independence.[1] Politically, military courts, also known as courts-martial, have been repeatedly (ab)used to try rebels and political opposition members without the benefit of a fair trial (and conversely of shielding military personnel from full accountability for human rights violations).[2] One such example is *Akwanga* v. *Cameroon*, where Mr Akwanga, a political opponent, had been targeted, tortured and unjustly sentenced to twenty years' imprisonment by a military court.[3] In a highly critical individual opinion in that case, the HRCtee member Fabián Omar Salvioli reiterated his position that the Committee's line of reasoning, which still permits military courts to have jurisdiction over civilians in exceptional cases, is out of step with the development of international human rights law. Salvioli argues that the Committee fails to make the clear distinction between military and civilian trials needed in light of the negative experiences throughout history. In his opinion,

---

[1] F. Andreu-Guzmán, *Military Jurisdiction and International Law: Military Courts and Gross Human Rights Violations* (International Commission of Jurists, 2004).
[2] See Opinion of Fabián Omar Salvioli in *Akwanga* v. *Cameroon* (HRCtee) (2011) para. 7.
[3] Ibid., para. 2.6.

---

[253] *Doorson* v. *the Netherlands* (ECtHR) (1996) para. 72; *Van Mechelen and Others* v. *the Netherlands* (ECtHR) (1997) para. 54.
[254] Art. 9(5) ICCPR; art. 3 Protocol no. 7 to ECHR; art. 10 ACHR. See also HRCtee, General Comment 32, paras. 52–3.

only the absolute prohibition of civilians being tried by military courts would be compatible with the right to a fair trial guaranteed in article 14 ICCPR.[4]

The practice of security courts in Egypt illustrates how the use of emergency legislation and extraordinary measures becomes routine and facilitates a range of violations.[5] Three men were sentenced to death by the Supreme State Emergency Security Court in November 2006 for their alleged participation in a series of attacks on Egyptian tourist resorts in 2004 and 2005. The men were subjected to torture while in detention and were only given access to legal presentation at the trial stage. The Court convicted them, relying on confessions extracted under torture; the verdict was subject to ratification by the President and could not be appealed. The ACmHPR found Egypt to be in breach of the prohibition of torture, the right to a fair trial and the independence of the judiciary (articles 5, 7 (1)(a) and (d), and 26 ACHPR), emphasising in particular that '[t]ribunals that do not use the duly established procedures of the legal process shall not be created to displace the jurisdiction belonging to the ordinary courts or judicial tribunals'.[6]

[4] Ibid., Individual Opinion of Committee Member Mr Fabián Omar Salvioli.
[5] *Egyptian Initiative for Personal Rights and Interights* v. *Arab Republic of Egypt* (ACmHPR) (2011).
[6] Ibid., para. 204.

POINT TO CONSIDER

1. **Is jurisprudence too accommodating when considering that proceedings seemingly antithetical to the right to a fair trial, such as the trial of civilians before military courts, may be justifiable in certain circumstances?**

8.6   ENFORCED DISAPPEARANCE AS MULTIPLE HUMAN RIGHTS VIOLATION

Enforced disappearance is a method that has been used by states to establish complete control over a person by rendering him or her invisible. It has often been used systematically, mostly through covert plain-clothes operations, as a means to facilitate the torture and/or killing of its targets. By its nature it constitutes a form of state terror, aimed at spreading uncertainty and fear of an all-powerful state.[255] The practice greatly enhances the vulnerability

[255] See e.g., *Goiburú et al.* v. *Paraguay* (IACtHR) (2006) para. 65, which refers to a decision by the National Court of Spain that characterised 'Operation Condor' as 'a sort of "international terror mechanism"'.

of anyone subjected to it and frequently has profound psychological – and, depending on the circumstances, physical – consequences. It also leads to anxiety and uncertainty for relatives and friends of the disappeared who may therefore be victims of ill-treatment in their own right.[256]

The practice of enforced disappearances was a modus of state terror and murder used by regimes such as Nazi Germany, and later became a particularly notorious practice of Latin American dictatorships to combat (and kill) opponents, including members of ethnic communities.[257] In Argentina, for example, many victims were drugged and then thrown naked from an aircraft or helicopter into the sea, where they would drown. The UN Working Group on Enforced or Involuntary Disappearances had, by May 2018, 'transmitted a total of 57,149 cases' of enforced disappearances since 1980.[258] This number, while indicating the prevalence of the practice, does not reflect its true extent. By its very nature it is difficult to verify how many persons have been forcibly disappeared, and estimates of the number of persons disappeared in some countries alone, such as Iraq, are significantly higher than the overall number of complaints received by the Working Group.[259] The practice has, over the last thirty years, not been confined to a few countries or a particular region, as the UN Working Group has received more than one hundred complaints each in respect of over twenty countries.[260] Iraq (16,566) and Sri Lanka (12,549) stand out as having the highest number of cases.[261]

Legal developments relating to enforced disappearance owe a lot to the concerted efforts by relatives of the disappeared, lawyers and human rights defenders, particularly in Latin America, who have persistently raised the issue.[262] This has spawned multiple responses both at the domestic level,

---

[256] M. Blaauw and V. Lähteenmäki, '"Denial and silence" or "acknowledgement and disclosure"' (2002) 84 *International Review of the Red Cross* 767.

[257] See in particular, the findings of truth commissions, e.g., in Argentina, Bolivia, Chile, Guatemala and Uruguay.

[258] Report of the Working Group on Enforced or Involuntary Disappearances, UN doc. A/HRC/39/46 (30 July 2018) para. 5 and Annex II.

[259] The UN Working Group on Enforced or Involuntary Disappearances reported that there were 16,419 outstanding cases in Iraq as of May 2018 (Working Group, ibid., Annex II). Other estimates put the number of disappeared between 250,000 and 1 million (International Commission on Missing Persons, *Iraq*, online at www.icmp.int/where-we-work/middle-east-and-north-africa/iraq/).

[260] UN Working Group on Enforced or Involuntary Disappearances, Annex II. Over a hundred cases were transmitted between 1980 and 2018 to the Governments of Algeria, Argentina, Chile, China, Colombia, Democratic People's Republic of Korea, Egypt, El Salvador, Ethiopia, Guatemala, Honduras, India, Indonesia, Iran, Iraq, Lebanon, Mexico, Morocco, Nepal, Nicaragua, Pakistan, Peru, Philippines, Russian Federation, Sri Lanka, Sudan, Syrian Arab Republic, Timor-Leste, Turkey and Yemen.

[261] Ibid., Annex II.

[262] P. Rice, 'Survivors and the Origin of the Convention for the Protection of All Persons from Enforced Disappearance', in A. S. Moore and E. Swanson (eds.), *Witnessing Torture: Perspectives of Torture Survivors and Human Rights Workers* (Palgrave Macmillan, 2018) 157.

particularly following political transitions, and at the regional human rights level. The Inter-American Commission on Human Rights (IACHR) and the IACtHR were seized with a number of cases, with the Court's judgment in *Velásquez Rodríguez* setting a leading precedent. The Court noted that 'the forced disappearance of human beings is a multiple and continuous violation of many rights under the Convention that the States Parties are obliged to respect and guarantee',[263] which entails a positive obligation to prevent, and effectively respond to allegations of such violations.[264]

In 1994 the Inter-American Convention on Forced Disappearance of Persons was adopted. At the international level, concerns over the practice resulted in the 1992 Declaration on the Protection of All Persons from Enforced Disappearance,[265] but were not at the time translated into any binding international treaty. Rather, it was left to human rights treaty bodies and regional courts to grapple with a number of complex legal questions raised by the multiple violations characteristic of enforced disappearance. It was generally accepted that enforced disappearance constitutes a violation of the right to liberty and security of the person (where the link to the state could be made), which is the thrust of the legal definition of enforced disappearance (see below).[266] It was also recognised that victims have a right to a remedy and states a corresponding duty to investigate, prosecute and punish the perpetrators.[267] However, it was less clear what other rights enforced disappearances violated in a given case. Do they constitute torture or other ill-treatment in their own right (i.e. even in the absence of evidence that the disappeared person was ill-treated)?[268] Where a person remains disappeared,

---

[263] *Velásquez Rodríguez* v. *Honduras*, para. 155. On enforced disappearance as a continuous crime, see also Working Group on Enforced or Involuntary Disappearances, General Comment on Enforced Disappearance as a Continuous Crime, UN doc. A/HRC/16/48 (26 January 2011) 10–12; General Comment on the Right to the Truth in Relation to Enforced Disappearances, ibid., 12–17.

[264] *Velásquez Rodríguez* v. *Honduras*, paras. 166, 176–7; *Juan Humberto Sánchez* v. *Honduras* (IACtHR) (2003) para. 184; *Quinteros* v. *Uruguay* (HRCtee) (1983) para. 15; *Kurt* v. *Turkey* (ECtHR) (1999) para. 124.

[265] UNGA resolution 47/133 (18 December 1992).

[266] *Velásquez Rodríguez* v. *Honduras*, paras. 155, 187; *Bleier Lewenhoff* v. *Uruguay* (HRCtee) (1982) para. 14; *Kurt* v. *Turkey*, paras. 123–4; *Mouvement Burkinabé des Droits de l'Homme et des Peuples* v. *Burkina Faso* (ACmHPR) (2001) para. 44.

[267] *Bautista* v. *Colombia* (HRCtee) (1995) para. 8.6; *Aboussedra* v. *Libyan Arab Jamahiriya* (HRCtee) (2010) para. 9; *Aouabdia* v. *Algeria* (HRCtee) (2011) para. 9; *Varnava and Others* v. *Turkey* (ECtHR) (2009) para. 149; *Mouvement Burkinabé des Droits de l'Homme et des Peuples* v. *Burkina Faso*, para. 42; *Goiburú et al.* v. *Paraguay*, para. 84.

[268] *Kurt* v. *Turkey*, para. 116 (needed specific evidence); *Çakici* v. *Turkey* (ECtHR) (1999) para. 92 (testimony given by witness who shared a room with the victim was sufficient to prove torture); *El Masri* v. *The Former Yugoslav Republic of Macedonia* (ECtHR) (2012) para. 202 (forcible incommunicado detention); *Aslakhanova and Others* v. *Russia* (ECtHR) (2012) para. 142 (mere fact of being held incommunicado in unacknowledged detention, witnessing the ill-treatment of his father and neighbours, would have caused Mr Shidayev

what are the factors that allow a finding of a violation of the right to life?[269] Under what circumstances do enforced disappearances constitute a violation of the rights of others, particularly the right of family members not to be subjected to inhuman treatment?[270] What are the rights of victims in relation to the right to truth (which was largely developed in the context of enforced disappearances)?[271] Treaty bodies and courts have developed their own, and at times diverging, jurisprudence, with the IACtHR taking a broader and the ECtHR a more restrictive approach to recognising violations of rights other than the right to liberty and security. In addition, the enforced disappearance of persons has been explicitly recognised as a crime against humanity.[272]

The adoption of the International Convention for the Protection of All Persons from Enforced Disappearance (CPED) in 2006 was seen as an important addition to the international legal framework and a step towards enhanced protection. Article 2 CPED reflects what is now commonly considered to constitute 'enforced disappearance', namely:

considerable anguish and distress); *Velásquez Rodríguez* v. *Honduras*, para. 187 (mere subjection of an individual to prolonged isolation and deprivation of communication is in itself cruel and inhuman treatment); *Goiburú et al.* v. *Paraguay*, para. 157; *Aouabdia* v. *Algeria*, paras. 7.4–7.5 (incommunicado detention amounted to a violation of art. 7 ICCPR); *Article 19* v. *Eritrea* (ACmHPR) (2007) para. 102; *Amnesty International and Others* v. *Sudan*, para. 54 (incommunicado detention amounted to a violation of art. 5 ACHPR).

[269] *Bámaca Velásquez* v. *Guatemala* (IACtHR) (2000) paras. 130, 173 (presumption of execution after passage of eight years without any news given the state practice of forced disappearances and extrajudicial killings); *Mojica* v. *Dominican Republic* (HRCtee) (1994) para. 5.6 (since state party did not deny that Rafael Mojica had disappeared and that his disappearance had been caused by state agents, the right to life had not been effectively protected); *Aslakhanova and Others* v. *Russia*, para. 101: '[h]aving regard to the numerous previous cases concerning disappearances in Chechnya and Ingushetia which have come before it, the Court has found that in the particular context of the conflict, when a person was detained by unidentified State agents without any subsequent acknowledgment of the detention, this could be regarded as life-threatening'.

[270] *Varnava and Others* v. *Turkey* (ECtHR) (2009) para. 200 (depends on circumstances, particularly nature of the 'failure by the authorities to respond to the quest for information by the relatives'); *Valle Jaramillo et al.* v. *Colombia*, para. 119 (presumption that close family members suffered). See also *Amnesty International and Others* v. *Sudan*, para. 54; *Sharma* v. *Nepal* (HRCtee) (2008) para. 7.9; *Aouabdia* v. *Algeria*, para. 7.6 (finding that the suffering caused to the relative by the enforced disappearance constituted a violation of art. 5 ACHPR (Sudan) and art. 7 ICCPR (Nepal and Algeria) respectively).

[271] *Bámaca-Velásquez* v. *Guatemala*, para. 201; *Anzualdo Castro* v. *Peru* (IACtHR) (2009) para. 113; Working Group, General Comment on the Right to the Truth in Relation to Enforced Disappearances, above note 251, 12–17; *Al Nashiri* v. *Poland*, para. 495; *Aslakhanova and Others* v. *Russia*, para. 215 and para. 223, where the ECtHR referred to the duty to 'account for the circumstances of the death and the location of the grave' (with reference to *Varnava and Others* v. *Turkey*) which it derives from art. 3 ECHR. See further *El Masri* v. *The Former Yugoslav Republic of Macedonia*, Joint Concurring Opinion of Judges Tulkens, Spielmann, Sicilianos and Keller.

[272] Art. 7(1)(i) ICC Rome Statute; see also art. 5 CPED.

the arrest, detention, abduction or any other form of deprivation of liberty by agents of the State or by persons or groups of persons acting with the authorization, support or acquiescence of the State, followed by a refusal to acknowledge the deprivation of liberty or by concealment of the fate or whereabouts of the disappeared person, which place such a person outside the protection of the law.

The Convention is modelled in large part after CAT, requiring states to make enforced disappearance a crime subject to universal jurisdiction that they are duty-bound to investigate, prosecute and punish as well as provide reparation for.[273] Unsurprisingly, another strong emphasis is on effective safeguards, which are stipulated in some detail and the non-observance of which should be subject to sanctions.[274] Notably, the Convention reflects the jurisprudence of treaty bodies and regional courts according to which relatives who suffered harm are to be considered victims and have the right to truth and reparation.[275] Nevertheless, questions such as whether enforced disappearance constitutes a violation of the prohibition of torture and the right to life would still need to be considered separately. The Convention entered into force on 23 December 2010, having mainly been ratified or acceded to by Latin American and European states, but also some African states and, significantly, Iraq. It is still premature to assess the Convention's impact, but the existence of a UN treaty regime on enforced disappearance constitutes an important development.

INTERVIEW 8.2

Inquiries into Enforced Disappearances in Sri Lanka

(M. C. M. Iqbal)

Sri Lanka is one of the countries with the highest number of recorded disappearances in the world, committed both in campaigns against uprisings in the south of the country (1971 and 1987–1990) and in the context of the conflict in the north-east of the country (which lasted, with some interruptions, from 1983 to 2009). In 1995, the then President Chandrika Bandaranayke established three zonal commissions to inquire into disappearances since 1988, and another all-island commission was appointed in 1998. The commissions received around 30,000 complaints (including multiple complaints). In addition to those, approximately 16,000 complaints which did not come within the mandates of these commissions had been received and were eventually passed on to the National Human Rights Commission of Sri Lanka for further

---

[273] Arts. 3 (duty to investigate), 6 (duty to prosecute), 7 (duty to punish) and 24 (right to reparation) CPED.

[274] Arts. 17 and 18 (safeguards), and 22 (sanctions) CPED.   [275] Art. 24 CPED.

action. The commissions were able to meticulously document the practice of enforced disappearances and recommended prosecution of the perpetrators and reparation for the victims. However, more than a decade later, with the exception of a few isolated prosecutions and limited amounts of compensation paid to victims, these recommendations have not been implemented. The following is an interview with M. C. M. Iqbal, former Secretary of two zonal Commissions of Inquiry and Secretary of the Committee of Inquiry into Disappearances of the Human Rights Commission of Sri Lanka, who has published several articles on the subject.[1]

What were some of the most striking findings of the Commissions of Inquiry about the nature and extent of violations?

Many innocent young men who happened to be either children of those who were not supporters of the government of the time, or young men who had been actively involved in criticising the government, had been taken away on suspicion that they were insurgents and had disappeared. A graphical analysis of the dates and places revealed that the peaks of disappearances had been a few days before and after the presidential and parliamentary elections that took place in 1989 and the 1990s, which is indicative of their political nature.

There was evidence that most persons abducted, arrested or detained had been tortured in places specially maintained for this purpose in order to extract information before they were caused to be disappeared. At a particular period, bodies or parts of the bodies of persons who had been killed had been allowed to remain on roadsides and culverts for long periods, purportedly to instil fear among the people who were against the then government. There had been evidence that interested persons had provided the police and security forces with lists with names of persons who had been taken away after calling for them by name at the houses of the respective persons. In some instances this had resulted in persons who had the same name as the person they had been looking for being taken away and disappearing.

You have interviewed victims and studied thousands of files. Can you describe a case that has left a particularly lasting impression?

A young man who had been a victim of an abduction and had been released after rehabilitation spoke about a torture chamber that existed then at the St Sylvester's College, Kandy. He said that he was detained in this chamber and was tortured. From time to time detainees were taken away in the night, supposedly to be transferred to other detention centres. He was among those taken away on a particular date to be transferred to another centre. A few of them were taken with their hands tied in a truck through a dark stretch of

---

[1] See in particular at http://groundviews.org.

road with two other vehicles following. From time to time, one by one, a military officer would push a detainee down from the moving vehicle and ask him to run. While he was running someone from the second vehicle would shoot down the detainee. He said an officer from the third vehicle would stop near the fallen detainee, pour petrol on his face and set fire to it. When it was his turn to be pushed down, someone from the third vehicle shouted, 'enough for the day, petrol is over'. Thereafter he was taken back to the camp where the other detainees who heard what happened nicknamed him the *chance karaya* (the lucky one). Sometime later he was sent along with a few others for rehabilitation and released after a few years.

By its very nature enforced disappearances are secretive and tend not to be recorded. How were the commissions able to verify that persons had disappeared?

The commissions used a range of steps such as checking lists of detainees obtained from all detention centres, employment records, corroborative evidence, such as a copy of a complaint to the International Committee of the Red Cross (ICRC), police or other persons in authority and observing the demeanour of complainants. It also interviewed witnesses, including those who had been released in some way or had escaped. The commissions also had to be creative, in particular by looking for supplementary evidence of being in police custody subsequent to removal or abduction. For example, there were discrepancies between the information books (IB) in the police stations, which did not mention persons taken in to be disappeared, and the diet registers for food provided, which did. Similarly, in some cases there were no official records of the officer-in-charge or any other police officer having travelled to the area from which the disappearance had taken place. The commission then found that the driver of the vehicle used by the police had entries in his running chart, which demonstrated he had travelled to that particular place with other police officers on the relevant dates.

The Commissions made a number of specific recommendations which have by and large not been implemented. Why did successive governments not act on the recommendations?

The interim reports of the commissions identified several perpetrators. The then president issued a directive to the army commander and the Inspector General of Police asking them to take prompt action against the perpetrators identified and report within one month of the steps that had been taken. This directive was the headline in some of the newspapers of the day. A couple of days later another headline appeared in the newspapers stating that no such order had been issued. Discrete inquiries revealed that the then Deputy Minister of Defence who was in the midst of a military operation against the

Liberation Tigers of Tamil Eelam (LTTE) had asked the President whether she wanted him to fight the terrorists now or instead start a fight against the security forces and the police based on the findings of the commissions. That was the end of that directive.

The cases in which perpetrators had been identified were handed over by the President to the Missing Persons Unit of the Attorney-General's Department for them to initiate prosecutions. The Attorney-General's Department needed further evidence to be recorded by the Criminal Investigation Department (CID). That was because the inquiries by the commissions were confined only to the point where 'credible material indicative of the perpetrator' is elicited. It was not for the commissions to look for 'evidence beyond reasonable doubt'. But the Attorney-General needed that evidence to initiate legal action. The CID's Disappearances Investigation Unit dealt with these cases. The brotherly feeling among the members of the Disappearances Investigation Unit who were themselves police officers led to these cases being handled at a snail's pace, if at all, and often with half a mind. Consequently, most of the cases, which had been filed very much later, eventually failed, partly because of the way in which the Unit and the Missing Persons Unit handled these cases and partly because by the time the cases came for trial it was almost twenty years after the incident and many material witnesses were no more or not with their memory in a good state.

Have you faced any repercussions for speaking out publicly on the need to act on the recommendations?

Yes. I had to face consequences for speaking out about them at different levels. I was a lecturer on human rights at the Institute of Human Rights in Sri Lanka where many police and military officers were following a course to obtain their diploma in human rights which was a must then, for their promotions. One of the topics I had to lecture on was the manner in which disappearances of persons took place in Sri Lanka and how the rights of individuals had been violated in the process. At discussion stages many of the students from the police and the security forces had argued with me on the human rights issues concerned. Subsequently, a petition had been sent to the Institute asking them not to allow me to lecture as my lectures were derogatory about the conduct of the security forces and the police in the past. The Institute ignored this petition and I was asked to continue to lecture for several years, much to the chagrin of my students from the forces.

The organisations of parents and guardians of the disappeared used to invite me for their annual meetings. Some of its members continued to ask me from time to time why no action was being taken against the perpetrators whom they had identified and referred to while giving evidence. I had to appease them by reassuring them that action would be taken in due course. As a follow-up to this, wherever possible I had been putting pressure on the authorities through my writings and other disclosures, reminding the authorities of the need to deal with the perpetrators identified by the commissions. Perhaps it was some of them who repeatedly threatened me over the telephone that if I did not stop working for the international organisation for which I was working while I was in Sri Lanka during 2007, that I would be killed. I left the country thereafter.

What are the consequences of the failure to act for the victims and society at large?

The commissions on disappearances conducted their inquiries and investigations in all earnest, and the people in general and the complainants in particular were anxiously waiting to see identified perpetrators punished and abducted or disappeared persons to be found. The failure of successive governments to diligently implement most of the recommendations of the commissions led to the people losing faith in such institutions and the perpetrators becoming emboldened. Eventually it was found the successive governments continued to use abductions and disappearances of persons as a convenient method of dealing with dissent or with those who became a thorn in their sides. One could say without hesitation that the non-implementation of the recommendations of the commission on specific provisions in the terms of reference of these commissions, viz. to deal with perpetrators according to the law, to consider the measures recommended to prevent such incidents in the future, and to make appropriate changes to the existing laws which facilitated abductions and disappearances, eventually led to the proliferation of impunity and the breakdown of law and order in the country.

QUESTIONS

1. Has the adoption of CPED closed an important normative gap in international human rights law?
2. What is the broader relevance for international human rights law of the rights and duties identified in the jurisprudence on enforced disappearance?
3. What lessons does the experience of Sri Lanka's Commissions of Inquiry hold for the effective protection of rights?

8.7   QUALIFIED RIGHTS, WITH A PARTICULAR FOCUS ON FREEDOM OF EXPRESSION

8.7.1   Practice

The exercise of freedom of expression, assembly and association serves as a critical measure of a pluralistic and tolerant society and as a key to participatory rights in its political life. Taken together with the freedom of thought, conscience and religion as well as the right to privacy, i.e. rights that largely protect the space of an individual against unwarranted interference, they constitute core civil and political rights. However, with the exception of the internal dimension of freedom of thought, conscience and religion, these rights are not absolute. The degree to which, and the grounds upon which, they may be restricted, are therefore frequently the subject of intense debates. There can be marked 'cultural' differences, particularly in respect of freedom of expression. Some countries favour an almost unlimited liberty, such as the USA, whereas others ban speech seen as offensive or glorifying totalitarian regimes, such as Nazi Germany, or as unacceptable attacks on religion. The curtailment of these rights is often the hallmark of repression and the defining feature of totalitarian regimes and authoritarian states. However, even some nominally democratic states have a poor record of protecting these fundamental freedoms. Political and community activists, human rights defenders and journalists are particularly vulnerable to intimidation, harassment, ill-treatment and murder. Dozens of journalists and media workers are killed every year; in many cases the authorities are either seemingly implicated or palpably fail to protect those at risk. The murder of Anna Politkovskaya in Russia[276] and of Lasantha Wickrematunge, who wrote an editorial predicting his murder shortly before he was shot dead in Sri Lanka,[277] are two particularly chilling examples of attacks on investigative journalists that form part of broader attempts to hide the truth, stifle dissent and silence critical voices. The importance of critical voices became strikingly clear during the uprisings in the Arab world, where the exposure, debate and sharing of information by bloggers and others provided the impetus for the exercise of freedom of expression and assembly in the form of mass demonstrations across the region.[278]

8.7.2   Sources

Freedom of expression, assembly and association are recognised in the ICCPR and all regional human rights treaties, as well as in International Labour Organization (ILO) treaties in the case of freedom of association.[279] Freedom

---

[276] See 'In praise of … Anna Politkovskaya' *The Guardian* (9 October 2006), online at www.theguardian.com/commentisfree/2006/oct/09/russia.media.

[277] L. Wickrematunge, 'I hope my murder will be seen not as a defeat of freedom but an inspiration' *The Guardian* (13 January 2009), online at www.theguardian.com/commentisfree/2009/jan/13/wickrematunga-final-editorial-final-editorial.

[278] See Al Jazeera, 'Blogging on the Nile: We Look at the Role of Social Media in Egypt and at the Bloggers who Sowed the Seeds of a Multi-media Uprising', online at www.aljazeera.com/programmes/witness/2011/02/20112181938841767.html.

[279] Arts. 19, 21, 22 ICCPR; arts. 10 and 11 ECHR; arts. 13, 15, 16 ACHR; arts. 9–11 ACHPR; ILO Conventions 87 (1948) (Freedom of Association and Protection of the Right to Organise) and 98 (1949) (Right to Organise and Collective Bargaining).

of expression has a broad scope of application encompassing political and artistic expression, the media as well as commercial advertising.[280] It also includes the right of access to information, which is particularly important in relation to personal data and information. Whereas the ECtHR had primarily interpreted article 10 ECHR to protect against state interference in receiving information, with recent jurisprudence signalling a change to this approach,[281] the IACtHR has interpreted it more broadly as a right of substantive access to information.[282]

The main differences between the relevant treaty provisions are the grounds on which the rights can be restricted. These grounds include protecting the rights or reputation of others, national security, public order, or public health or morals. Article 10 ECHR goes further by recognising 'preventing the disclosure of information received in confidence' and 'maintaining the authority and impartiality of the judiciary' as legitimate grounds. These grounds appear to give states considerable leeway, particularly in relation to such vague notions as national security or public morals. However, as is clear from the jurisprudence of human rights treaty bodies, restricting freedom of expression on any of these grounds can only be justified if it is prescribed by law, necessary and proportionate in the circumstances and providing it does not impair the essence of the right.[283] Courts such as the ECtHR have provided states with a margin of appreciation to assess the proportionality of restrictions, particularly in the sphere of public morals, on the ground that they are in a better position to judge what is in the public interest.[284] While acknowledging local and national differences such a margin carries the risk of privileging majoritarian or state-centric interpretations of rights. It is also for this reason that other bodies, such as the HRCtee, recently affirmed that they do not assess the scope of freedom of expression 'by reference to a "margin of appreciation"'.[285]

While freedom of expression, assembly and association are not explicitly non-derogable, the HRCtee suggested that the grounds provided to restrict these freedoms already vest states with sufficient powers during

---

[280] HRCtee, General Comment 34: Article 19: Freedoms of opinion and expression, UN doc. CCPR/C/GC/34 (12 September 2011) paras. 11–12.

[281] *Magyar Helsinki Bizottság* v. *Hungary* (ECtHR) (2016) paras. 117–80.

[282] *Claude Reyes et al.* v. *Chile* (IACtHR) (2006) paras. 61–103. See further IACHR, *The Inter-American Legal Framework Regarding the Right to Access to Information*, 2nd edn, OEA/Ser.L/V/II. CIDH/RELE/INF.9/12 (7 March 2011). See also Report of the Special Rapporteur on the promotion and protection of the right to freedom of opinion and expression, UN doc. A/68/362 (4 September 2013).

[283] HRCtee, General Comment 34, paras. 21–36; Doswald-Beck, above note 239, 414–43.

[284] See Chapter 6.2.5.

[285] HRCtee, General Comment 34, para. 36. However, see *Hertzberg et al.* v. *Finland* (HRCtee) (1982), where the Committee appears to grant national authorities a 'margin of discretion'.

emergencies.[286] This means that emergency situations can be considered when assessing the proportionality of measures to restrict rights, such as the freedom of assembly on national security grounds, but may not have to be invoked to derogate from the right.[287]

8.7.3   Freedom of Religion vs Freedom of Expression

Salman Rushdie's *Satanic Verses* and the *Jyllands-Posten* Danish cartoons of Prophet Mohammed are two instances in which the exercise of freedom of expression met with protests and violent responses on the ground that they were insulting to religion. On 7 January 2015, twelve persons were killed in an attack on the French satirical magazine *Charlie Hebdo*, among them five cartoonists, with the assailants reportedly shouting 'we have avenged the prophet' when leaving the scene of the crime.[288] While such incidents have been particularly pronounced in relation to issues portrayed as fundamental to Islam, the potential for tensions is by no means confined to this faith. Indeed, it raises fundamental questions about the relationship between freedom of expression and freedom of religion, including the protection of individuals and minorities against discrimination and attacks on religion. Attempts made by the Organization of the Islamic Conference in the then Commission on Human Rights and later in the Human Rights Council (HRC) to prohibit the 'defamation of religions'[289] have met with considerable resistance because they are seen as overly restricting freedom of expression.[290] There is also an apparent risk of political manipulation and of making freedom of expression contingent on the sentiments of the majority.

In the ICCPR, freedom of expression is subject to restrictions under article 19(3) and the limitations provided for in article 20, which prohibits propaganda for war and advocacy of national, racial or religious hatred. However, such hatred is only prohibited where it 'constitutes incitement to discrimination, hostility or violence'. Most commentators agree that the broad nature of these terms give rise to a degree of legal uncertainty and that there is a need to

---

[286] HRCtee, General Comment 29, paras. 5–6.

[287] See in the Inter-American system, *Zambrano Vélez* v. *Ecuador* (IACtHR) (2007) paras. 51–2.

[288] P. Vale, 'Paris Gunman Shouts "We Have Avenged The Prophet Mohammed" in Newly-Released Video Footage', *Huffington Post* (13 January 2015).

[289] Compare for a recent shift in emphasis, 'Combating defamation of religions', UN doc. A/HRC/RES/13/16 (15 April 2010); 'Combating intolerance, negative stereotyping and stigmatization of, and discrimination, incitement to violence, and violence against persons based on religion or belief', UN doc. A/HRC/RES/16/18 (12 April 2011).

[290] S. Parmar, 'The Challenge of "Defamation of Religions" to Freedom of Expression and the International Human Rights' (2009) 3 *European Human Rights Law Review* 353.

demonstrate both 'hatred' and its causal link to the prohibited incitement.[291] Article 20 ICCPR is intended to counter vicious propaganda targeting vulnerable individuals and communities rather than protecting belief systems as such, as is evident from its high threshold. Article 18 ICCPR (freedom of religion) for its part arguably provides protection against attacks on religion only in so far as they interfere with the freedom to hold a belief and exercise one's religion.[292] Prohibiting 'defamation of religion' would therefore need to be justifiable under the grounds stipulated in article 19(3) ICCPR, namely respect for the rights or reputation of others; protection of national security or of public order (*ordre public*), or of public health or morals. As is clear from jurisprudence, this requires a careful assessment of the circumstances, i.e. whether it would be proportionate to restrict freedom of expression, even if it was considered 'offensive'.[293] The question of religious hatred has also been discussed in the context of article 4 of the International Convention on the Elimination of All Forms of Racial Discrimination (ICERD), which prohibits racial discrimination, with the Committee on the Elimination of Racial Discrimination (CERD) holding that 'discrimination based exclusively on religious grounds was not intended to fall within the purview of the Convention'.[294]

The exercise of the individual right to manifest one's religion or express one's opinion is seen as a normal state of affairs unless it infringes on the rights of other persons or clearly runs counter to legitimate public concerns. As qualified rights have by their nature to be interpreted with reference to the particular context, the balancing of rights is bound to result in differences of opinion on where the appropriate line should be drawn and who should decide in this respect. Observers have called for a duty of self-restraint and a need to use freedoms responsibly.[295] While this sounds eminently reasonable, different actors will have different understandings and perceptions of what acceptable limits are, and a duty of self-restraint may be seen as stifling freedom of expression. Ultimately, authorities, courts and human rights treaty bodies need to make the difficult decision of where the limits of tolerance are, while being mindful that the liberty underlying this very tolerance forms the essence of the right.

---

[291] See Expert seminar on the links between articles 19 and 20 of the ICCPR: *Freedom of expression and advocacy of religious hatred that constitutes incitement to discrimination, hostility or violence* (Geneva: United Nations, 2–3 October 2008), online at www.ohchr.org/Documents/Issues/Expression/ICCPR/Seminar2008/CompilationConferenceRoomPapers.pdf.

[292] See on the scope of the right, HRCtee, General Comment 22: The right to freedom of thought, conscience and religion (article 18), UN doc. CCPR/C/21/Rev.1/Add.4 (30 July 1993).

[293] HRCtee, General Comment 34, para. 11.   [294] See *P. S. N. v. Denmark* (CERD) (2007) para. 6.3.

[295] V. Muntarbhorn, '"Religion" and "Expression" in the Human Rights Framework: Walking the Middle Path', Conference Paper no. 7, 2008 Expert seminar, above note 291.

8.7.4   To Wear or Not to Wear: Freedom of Conscience and Religion, the Rights of Women and the Veil

The veil has become a highly symbolic feature which has triggered intense debates about freedom of religion and women's rights. While women are in some countries virtually given no choice but to cover their heads and faces, others, such as France, have banned the wearing of full-face veils in public, or, in the case of Turkey, prohibited wearing the veil in public buildings.[296] Unsurprisingly, these laws and regulations have been challenged before courts and human rights treaty bodies have grappled with the issues raised. In *Hudoyberganova v. Uzbekistan*, the HRCtee found that regulations banning the wearing of religious symbols at a public university violated the applicant's right to freedom of thought, conscience and religion.[297] While this constituted a recognition of the right to wear a veil in principle, which is also echoed in its General Comment 22,[298] the Committee equally recognised that this freedom was subject to restrictions. In the particular case, since the state party provided no justification, the Committee found a violation.[299] The ECtHR, in contrast, held in *Şahin v. Turkey* that a ban on the wearing of headscarves at Turkish universities did not violate article 9 ECHR. It found that the grounds provided by Turkey to justify the ban, namely protecting the secular order of the state and the rights of others, were legitimate and proportionate in the circumstances. This judgment has been the subject of considerable criticism, particularly from a feminist perspective.[300] The Court did not consider the right to privacy under article 8, which, according to its own jurisprudence, provides for a considerable sphere of 'personal autonomy'.[301] Doing so would have enabled the court to better appreciate the agency of Leyla Şahin – the woman affected by the ban – that is to what extent her choice was personal and should be respected and take priority. Instead, the Court accepted Turkey's views that the veil, being an expression of Islamic fundamentalism, negated gender equality.[302]

Granting a state a wide margin of appreciation in this field raises concerns as it affects a series of rights, including the right to education. More

---

[296] See Z. Ashraf, 'Contested Meaning of the Veil and Political Ideologies of Iranian Regimes' (2007) 3 *Journal of Middle East Women's Studies* 75; W. G. Leane, 'Rights of Ethnic Minorities in Liberal Democracies: Has France Gone Too Far in Banning Muslim Women from Wearing the Burka?' (2011) 33 *Human Rights Quarterly* 1032; Z. A. Saktanber and G. Çorbacioglum, 'Veiling and Headscarf-Skepticism in Turkey' (2008) 15 *Social Politics: International Studies in Gender, State and Society* 514.

[297] *Hudoyberganova v. Uzbekistan* (HRCtee) (2004) para. 6.2.

[298] HRCtee, General Comment 22, para. 4.   [299] *Hudoyberganova v. Uzbekistan*, para. 6.2.

[300] *Leyla Şahin v. Turkey* (ECtHR) (2005); J. Marshall, 'Conditions for Freedom? European Human Rights Law and the Islamic Headscarf Debate' (2008) 30 *Human Rights Quarterly* 631.

[301] M.-B. Dembour, *Who Believes in Human Rights? Reflections on the European Convention* (Cambridge University Press, 2006) 213.

[302] *Şahin, Leyla v. Turkey*, paras. 104–23. Supportive, and calling for a contextual approach, is K. Bennoune, 'Secularism and Human Rights: A Contextual Analysis of Headscarves,

generally, the case raised broader questions about the limits of tolerance, particularly the degree to which a state may enforce its vision of society. The Court, by yielding to Turkey's version of secularism, ultimately endorsed a system based on uniform notions that may pay scant regard to the rights of the individual. Irrespective of the outcome, the ECtHR's handling of the case therefore constituted a missed opportunity to engage in more depth with this fundamental question. The Court's response to France's ban of wearing a full veil in public has equally been characterised by far-reaching deference. In a broad reading of what constitutes a legitimate aim under articles 8 and 9 ECHR, the Court found in *S.A.S.* v. *France* that 'under certain conditions the "respect for the minimum requirements of life in society" ... – or of "living together"– [the grounds invoked by France] can be linked to the legitimate aim of the "protection of the rights and freedoms of others"'.[303] While the Court was aware of a number of concerns that had been raised about the disproportionate nature of the blanket ban, it none the less considered it proportionate, 'having regard in particular to the breadth of the margin of appreciation'.[304] Judges Nussberger and Jäderblom, in their joint partly dissenting opinion, questioned the notion of 'living together' as providing a legitimate aim, set out a different approach to pluralism, tolerance and broadmindedness and criticised the majority for considering the ban proportionate, including its failure to adequately take into account the adverse impact on the women concerned.[305] The HRCtee, in two decisions of December 2018, explicitly rejected reliance on 'the concept of living together', which it considered 'very vague and abstract', finding that '[t]he right to interact with any individual in public and the right not to be disturbed by other people wearing the full-face veil are not protected by the Covenant and therefore cannot provide the basis for permissible restrictions within the meaning of article 18(3)' [freedom of religion].[306]

QUESTIONS

1. Do you agree with the legal reasoning and policy considerations evident in the ECtHR's judgment in *Şahin* v. *Turkey* and *S. A. S.* v. *France*?

2. What approach may it have chosen to strike a different balance between the competing versions?

Religious Expression and Women's Equality Under International Law' (2006–2007) 45 *Columbia Journal of Transnational Law* 367.

[303] *S.A.S.* v. *France* (ECtHR) (2014) para. 121.   [304] Ibid., para. 157.

[305] Ibid., Joint Partly Dissenting Opinions of Judges Nussberger and Jäderblom.

[306] *Yaker* v. *France* (HRCtee) (2018) para. 8.10, similarly *Hebbadi* v. *France* (HRCtee) (2018) para. 7.10. The Committee also found that the criminal ban 'constitutes a form of intersectional discrimination based on gender and religion', violating art. 26 of the Covenant: *Yaker* v. *France*, para. 8.17; *Hebbadi* v. *France*, para. 7.17.

3. **Do the grounds permitting restrictions of the freedom of expression provide states with too much latitude, especially considering the fundamental importance of the right for the promotion and protection of human rights more generally?**

4. **Has the tension between freedom of expression and freedom of religion been satisfactorily resolved in jurisprudence and UN practice?**

FURTHER READING

Bielefeldt, H., N. Ghanea and M. Wiener, *Freedom of Religion or Belief: An International Law Commentary* (Oxford University Press, 2016).

Carver, R., and L. Handley, *Does Torture Prevention Work?* (Liverpool University Press, 2016).

Casey-Maslen, S., and S. Connolly, *Police Use of Force under International Law* (Cambridge University Press, 2017).

Doswald-Beck, L., *Human Rights in Times of Conflict and Terrorism* (Oxford University Press, 2011).

Franck, T. M., 'The Emerging Right to Democratic Governance', (1992) 86 *American Journal of International Law* 46.

Joseph, S., and M. Castan, *The International Covenant on Civil and Political Rights: Cases, Materials, and Commentary*, 3rd edn (Oxford University Press, 2013).

Macken, C., *Counter-Terrorism and the Detention of Suspected Terrorists: Preventive Detention and International Human Rights Law* (Routledge, 2011).

McGoldrick, D., *Human Rights and Religion: The Islamic Headscarf Debate in Europe* (Hart, 2006).

McGonagle, T., and Y. Donders (eds.), *The United Nations and Freedom of Expression and Information: Critical Perspectives* (Cambridge University Press, 2015).

Murray, R., E. Steinarte, M. Evans and A. Hallo de Wolf, *The Optional Protocol to the UN Convention against Torture* (Oxford University Press, 2011).

Nowak, M., *UN Covenant on Civil and Political Rights: CCPR Commentary*, 2nd edn (Engels, 2005).

Torture: An Expert's Confrontation with an Everyday Evil (University of Pennsylvania Press, 2018).

Nowak, M., and E. McArthur, *The United Nations Convention against Torture: A Commentary* (Oxford University Press, 2008).

Office of the High Commissioner for Human Rights in Cooperation with the International Bar Association, *Human Rights in the Administration of Justice: A Manual on Human Rights for Judges, Prosecutors and Lawyers*, Professional Training Series no. 9 (United Nations, 2003).

Parry, Sir E. J. (ed.), 'Special Issue: Torture and the Quest for Justice' (2012) 16 *The International Journal of Human Rights*.

Rodley, N., and M. Pollard, *The Treatment of Prisoners under International Law*, 3rd edn (Oxford University Press, 2009).

Schabas, W. A., *The Abolition of the Death Penalty in International Law*, 3rd edn (Cambridge University Press, 2002).

Šimonović, I. (ed.), *Death Penalty and the Victims* (OHCHR, 2016).

Tomuschat, C., E. Lagrange and S. Oeter (eds.), *Right to Life* (Martinus Nijhoff, 2010).

Trechsel, S., *Human Rights in Criminal Proceedings* (Oxford University Press, 2005).

Vermeulen, M. L., *Determining State Responsibility under the International Convention for the Protection of All Persons from Enforced Disappearance* (Intersentia, 2012).

Websites

UN special procedures

Special Rapporteur on extrajudicial, summary or arbitrary executions: www.ohchr.org/EN/Issues/Executions/Pages/SRExecutionsIndex.aspx

Special Rapporteur on freedom of religion or belief: www.ohchr.org/EN/Issues/FreedomReligion/Pages/FreedomReligionIndex.aspx

Special Rapporteur on the promotion and protection of the right to freedom of opinion and expression: www.ohchr.org/EN/Issues/FreedomOpinion/Pages/OpinionIndex.aspx

Special Rapporteur on the rights to freedom of peaceful assembly and of association: www.ohchr.org/EN/Issues/AssemblyAssociation/Pages/SRFreedomAssemblyAssociationIndex.aspx

Special Rapporteur on torture and other cruel, inhuman or degrading treatment or punishment: www.ohchr.org/EN/Issues/Torture/SRTorture/Pages/SRTortureIndex.aspx

Working Group on Arbitrary Detention: www.ohchr.org/EN/Issues/Detention/Pages/WGADIndex.aspx

Working Group on Enforced or Involuntary Disappearances: www.ohchr.org/EN/Issues/Disappearances/Pages/DisappearancesIndex.aspx

Selected NGOs

Amnesty International: www.amnesty.org

Article 19: www.article19.org

Association for the Prevention of Torture: www.apt.ch

Centre for Civil and Political Rights: www.ccpr-centre.org

Dignity, Danish Institute against Torture (see in particular its extensive documentation centre and library on torture): www.dignityinstitute.org

FIDH – International Federation for Human Rights: www.fidh.org/International-Federation-for-Human-Rights

Human Rights Watch: www.hrw.org

Index on Censorship: www.indexoncensorship.org

International Coalition against Enforced Disappearance: www.icaed.org/home

International Commission of Jurists: www.icj.org

International Rehabilitation Council for Torture Victims (IRCT): www.irct.org

Penal Reform International: www.penalreform.org

REDRESS: www.redress.org

World Organisation against Torture (OMCT): www.omct.org

9 Economic, Social and Cultural Rights

CONTENTS

9.1 INTRODUCTION

Economic, social and cultural (ESC) rights include a number of entitlements, such as the right to work and the enjoyment of just and favourable conditions of work; the right to form and join trade unions; the right to social security; the protection of the family, mothers and children; the right to an adequate standard of living, which includes adequate food, clothing and housing and continuous improvement of living conditions; the right to the highest attainable standard of mental health; the right to education; and the right to participate in cultural life and enjoy the benefits of scientific progress. All these are protected under the International Covenant on Economic, Social and Cultural Rights (ICESCR).

Several differences are traditionally cited to distinguish the disparate legal nature of ESC rights from civil and political rights. Whereas states are obliged to implement the latter immediately, most ESC rights are subject to progressive realisation under the terms of the ICESCR. Moreover, because civil and political rights are considered negative obligations and thus generally only require entrenchment in the legal order of states, they are justiciable and enforceable before the courts. On the other hand, several states suggest that ESC rights are not justiciable, not only because they are not immediately realisable but also because their implementation requires funds and resources which parties to the ICESCR may not possess. Thus, resource scarcity is a significant impediment to the fulfilment of ESC rights, as well as a justification for those states that are unwilling to invest money in social welfare services, especially towards the vulnerable, marginalised and the indigent. These issues will be explored in detail in this chapter.

It will also be demonstrated that ESC rights are by no means the poor relative of civil and political rights. In fact, many of the latter are meaningless without ESC rights. By way of illustration, the right to life is to some degree dependent on adequate food and water, decent housing and health care. Equally, a decent education is a good platform for an informed exercise of the freedom of expression. It will be shown that ESC rights are not vague obligations but to a large degree are now susceptible to qualitative and quantitative measurement. One of the sections in this chapter analyses in detail the advancement of indicators and benchmarks that have been developed since the mid-1990s in order to set out realistic targets for states with a view to assessing their performance.

The final sections of the chapter concentrate on four distinct ESC rights: the right to education, the right to health and the rights to food and water. These should be read together with the right to development, where it is explained that most developmental objectives generally overlap with ESC rights. There, it will be demonstrated that several ESC rights that are not perceived as justiciable in certain nations were brought before the courts as necessary extensions of other justiciable civil and political rights (indirect justiciability).

9.2   BRIEF HISTORICAL CONTEXT OF ESC RIGHTS

ESC rights are clearly recognised in articles 22–7 of the Universal Declaration of Human Rights (UDHR) as well as article 55(a) and (b) of the United Nations (UN) Charter, and were later elaborated in more detail in the ICESCR. Yet even to this day scholars argue about the intention of the drafters of the ICESCR, which were at the time divided into two political camps, socialist or Soviet-bloc nations on the one hand and Western liberal states on the other. For the socialist bloc the provision of a comprehensive and free social welfare system encompassing all ESC rights was a natural extension of its political ideology and state organisation. Most liberal democracies conditioned ESC rights, such as that of work and adequate living standards, on the forces of free-market economics, which rested on private initiative, non-state interference and the promotion of entrepreneurship. The idea was that a well-functioning market economy would generate enough jobs and wealth for all members of society to enjoy high quality ESC benefits. Even so, some liberal democracies, but certainly not all, put in place a social safety net for those unable to take advantage of the bounties of the free-market system.

As a result, most liberal states objected to the assimilation of ESC rights with civil and political rights, at least in terms of their implementation.[1] The USSR at the time argued that ESC rights should be immediately enforceable and justiciable, which was vehemently opposed by the United States of America (USA), its Western allies and most developing nations. Thus, the USA and its allies pressed the Commission on Human Rights to remove ESC rights from the text of the impending covenant that it was in the process of drafting. When the matter came to the General Assembly it swiftly overturned the Commission's decision[2] and subsequently the Commission prepared a single draft covenant containing seventy-three articles governing both ESC and civil and political rights. It was at this point that the heated debates between the two political camps intensified, leading to a compromise solution whereby ESC rights were to be incorporated in a covenant that was distinct from civil and political rights.[3] Scholars such as Whelan and Donnelly attribute this Western persistence to technical questions of legal implementation (namely objections to justiciability and immediate implementation), rather than substantive ideological concerns.[4] The truth lies somewhere in the middle. Whereas it is true that ESC rights were not central to certain liberal states[5] – a prime example being the lack of welfare for the

---

[1] A. Kirkup and T. Evans, 'The Myth of Western Opposition to Economic, Social and Cultural Rights? A Reply to Whelan and Donnelly' (2009) 31 *Human Rights Quarterly* 221, at 228–9.

[2] UNGA resolution 421(V) (4 December 1950).

[3] UNGA resolution 543(VI) (5 February 1952), noting however that ESC and civil and political rights are interconnected and interdependent.

[4] D. J. Whelan and J. Donnelly, 'The West, Economic and Social Rights and the Global Human Rights Regime: Setting the Record Straight' (2007) 29 *Human Rights Quarterly* 908.

[5] S. L. Kang, 'The Unsettled Relationship of Economic and Social Rights in the West: A Response to Whelan and Donnelly' (2009) 31 *Human Rights Quarterly* 1006, at 1007–8. Other liberal democracies, such as Germany, have elevated universal social welfare to a

multitude of victims of the Great Depression in the USA[6] – they none the less accepted and protected most ESC rights in their legal systems; yet their conception of fulfilment was fundamentally different from that of the USSR. Standing out among its other liberal counterparts, particularly the set of countries that now form the European Union (EU), the USA has been nothing less than vociferous in proclaiming that ESC rights are not rights at all but goals which states aspire to achieve. By way of illustration, in response to a 2007 questionnaire on the domestic implementation of the right to water from the Office of the High Commissioner for Human Rights (OHCHR), the US position paper bluntly conceded that its government 'does not share the view that a right to water [broadly understood] exists under international human rights law'.[7] Such a position expressed by the world's superpower certainly hampers efforts to give prominence to ESC rights worldwide, but has not halted the tide of laws, constitutional amendments and judicial pronouncements in many parts of the globe to bring about the justiciability of ESC rights. In fact, some courts are prepared to accept that the existence of a serious risk of harm ('owing to a well-founded fear of being persecuted') associated with refugee determination, encompasses not merely violations of fundamental civil and political rights, but also socio-economic rights, such as access to food and medical treatment.[8]

As will be explained in following sections, the perceived legal differences between civil and political and ESC rights were ultimately reflected in their respective monitoring in the two covenants. Whereas the implementation of civil and political rights is monitored by the Human Rights Committee (HRCtee), whose mandate is derived from the International Covenant on Civil and Political Rights (ICCPR) itself, the drafters of the ICESCR decided against

---

constitutional principle. Article 20(1) of Germany's Basic Law (the *Grundgesetz*) establishes the so-called *Sozialstaatsklausel*, or social state principle, which obliges the government to provide the minimum core ESC rights so that people can live with dignity. The Federal Constitutional Court (the *Bundesverfassungsgericht*) has interpreted this minimum core to include essential foodstuff, housing, clothing and health care (BVerfGE 82, 60 (80), 1990). This has given rise, among other things, to a constitutional entitlement to a minimum of benefits, as decided by the Federal Administrative Court (BVerwGE 1, 159 (1954)).

[6] It should be noted, however, that in direct response to the Great Depression the Roosevelt administration implemented a set of economic programmes between 1933 and 1936 whose aim included, among others, the provision of relief to the poor and the unemployed.

[7] 'Views of the USA on human rights and access to water, submitted to OHCHR' (June 2007) para. 4. It did, however, go on to say that water rights are an important part of water governance in the USA and a complex array of entitlements exist primarily at the state level.

[8] *Chen Shi Hai* v. *Minister for Immigration and Multicultural Affairs* (Australia) (2000); *Chen* v. *Holder* (US) (2010) at 334, which iterated that persecution may also be in the form of economic deprivation. For a discussion of socio-economic rights of refugees, see Chapter 13.3.6.

a monitoring mechanism and objected to the possibility of an optional pro-tocol giving rise to individual complaints. When the ICESCR came into force in 1976, the UN Economic and Social Council (ECOSOC) set up working groups composed of government experts to assist with the review of country reports. Their operation was generally considered unsatisfactory, leading one group in 1985 to propose transforming the existing system into a committee of independent experts. This suggestion was endorsed by ECOSOC, which went ahead and set up the Committee on Economic, Social and Cultural Rights (CESCR).[9] Although it was only provided with the power to review the parties' periodic reports and offer non-binding recommendations, it has gone ahead and issued general comments, in the mould of the HRCtee, and in more recent years these comments have slowly begun to use the language of 'violations' attributable to actions and omissions of states parties.[10]

9.3   PROGRESSIVE REALISATION AND THE NATURE OF STATE OBLIGATIONS

The nature of obligations addressed to states in their implementation of ESC rights is predicated on article 2(1) of the ICESCR, which reads as follows:

Each state party to the present Covenant *undertakes to take steps*, individually and through international assistance and co-operation, especially economic and technical, to the *maximum of its available resources*, with a view to achieving *progressively* the full realisation of the rights recognised in the present Covenant by all appropriate means, including particularly the adoption of legislative measures (emphasis added).[11]

This language is in stark contrast to the obligations contained in article 2(1) of the ICCPR, which stipulates that each party undertakes to 'respect and ensure to all individuals ... the rights recognised in the present Covenant', as well as article 2(3), according to which parties undertake to 'ensure that any person whose rights or freedoms ... are violated shall have an effective remedy'. Therefore, it would seem that the rights in the ICESCR are framed as goals that are to be achieved progressively, contingent on the maximum use of a nation's available resources. In addition, whereas the ICCPR directly addresses its intended rights-holders (i.e. 'everyone shall have the right'),

---

[9] ECOSOC resolution 1985/17 (28 May 1985).

[10] See e.g., CESCR Concluding Observations on Israel, UN doc. E/C12/1/Add. 27 (4 December 1998) para. 11, in respect of Israel's alleged discriminatory practices between Jewish and Palestinian property rights.

[11] This definition is essentially reproduced with minor variations in art. 26 of the ACHR, as well as art. 1 of the 1988 Additional Protocol to the American Convention on Human Rights in the Area of Economic, Social and Cultural Rights (San Salvador Protocol).

the ICESCR does so through the medium of the state (i.e. 'state parties to the present Covenant recognise the right of everyone'). As a result, it has been questioned whether an obligation that is not immediately enforceable, not overtly justiciable and which is contingent on available resources can ever give rise to an entitlement at all.

It is beyond doubt that ESC rights are binding on states. This is true not only in respect of those obligations that are subject to immediate implementation, but in respect of all rights.[12] This is so because every right in the ICESCR entails obligations of conduct and obligations of result. These may be broken down to three further levels of obligation, namely to respect, protect and fulfil. The obligation to respect requires states to refrain from interfering directly or indirectly with the enjoyment of the right, such as by denying or impeding access or enforcing discriminatory practices. The obligation to protect requires states to take measures that prevent third parties from interfering with the right. In relation to the right to health, for example, this includes the adoption of legislation or other measures ensuring equal access to health care and health-related services provided by third parties; ensuring that the privatisation of the health sector does not constitute a threat to the availability, accessibility, acceptability and quality of health facilities, goods and services;[13] and controlling the marketing of medical equipment and medicines by third parties. Finally, the obligation to fulfil requires the adoption of appropriate legislative, administrative, budgetary, judicial, promotional and other measures.[14]

As far as the duty to fulfil is concerned, the CESCR has iterated that it involves an obligation to facilitate and a duty to provide. Facilitation requires the creation of appropriate conditions that lead to the enjoyment of the right in question, such as the establishment of a national health policy in respect of the right to health. The duty to provide requires states to provide the commodity that is the essence of a particular right (for example, water, food and health services) 'whenever an individual or group is unable, for reasons beyond their control' to enjoy the right by the means at their disposal.[15] This

---

[12] ESC rights that have been recognised by the CESCR as being of immediate application include arts. 3, 7(a)(i), 8, 10(3), 13(2)(a), (3) and (4) and 15(3) ICESCR. CESCR General Comment 3: nature of ICESCR obligations, UN doc. E/1991/23 (14 December 1990) paras. 5 and 7; CESCR General Comment 9: domestic application of ICESCR, UN doc. E/C12/1998/24 (3 December 1998) para. 10.

[13] See CESCR General Comment 24 on state obligations under ICESCR in the context of business activities', UN doc. E/C.12/GC/24 (10 August 2017), particularly paras. 21–2.

[14] CESCR General Comment 14: right to health, UN doc. E/C12/2004 (11 August 2000) paras. 33–6.

[15] CESCR General Comment 12: right to food, UN doc. E/C12/1999/5 (12 May 1999) para. 15; CESCR General Comment 14, para. 37; CESCR General Comment 15: right to water, UN doc. E/C12/2002/11 (20 January 2003) para. 25.

is no doubt a controversial point of view because it is said to ignore the fundamental premise of the ICESCR, i.e. progressive realisation. None the less, the CESCR's view is in full conformity with the accepted position that water and food, among other things, should not be treated as commodities but as means necessary for survival and welfare.

In respect of those ESC rights that require the state to provide a resource (for example water) or a service (for example health care) the CESCR has formulated a set of criteria against which the obligation to fulfil should be assessed. The first concerns availability of the resource in question. Water, for example, must be sufficient and continuous for consumption, sanitation, cooking and other purposes. The second is quality, meaning that it should be safe. The third is accessibility, without discrimination, which consists of physical, economic and information accessibility.[16]

The concept of progressive realisation of the rights guaranteed in the Covenant derives from the reality that most, if not all, states are unable to provide the entire range of ESC rights, at least with immediate effect, because of resource constraints. Unlike civil and political rights, which are generally viewed as requiring negative obligations of non-interference (for example right to life, freedom of expression, freedom of assembly) and are thus (erroneously) seen as devoid of implementation costs,[17] ESC rights are positive in nature and are not susceptible to implementation without dispensing significant resources. As a result, states have been unwilling to assume the onerous obligations associated with ESC rights if not accompanied by the condition that their realisation would be progressive, as opposed to immediate. No doubt this saving clause has been abused and has served as a basis for justifying inaction, principally through claims of state indigence.[18] In most cases there is usually an underlying culture of corruption, clan favouritism and weak public institutions.

In *Bermúdez Urrego* v. *Transmilenio* the petitioner argued that the public transport system of Bogota provided no accessibility to wheelchair users. In discussing possible remedies for the violation of the petitioner's freedom of movement, the Colombian Constitutional Court held that freedom

---

[16] CESCR General Comment 15, ibid., para. 12.

[17] This is not, however, true. States are under an obligation to take positive measures to protect civil and political rights. For example, there exists an obligation to protect the right to life and other personal freedoms by maintaining an effective police force or by averting deadly terrorist attacks. See Chapter 18.4.

[18] See S. Leckie, 'Another Step towards Indivisibility: Identifying the Key Features of Violations of Economic, Social and Cultural Rights' (1998) 20 *Human Rights Quarterly* 81, at 94. In *Cuscul Pivaral and Others* v. *Guatemala* (IACtHR) (2018), the inaction of the government in offering effective and accessible retroviral drugs to HIV sufferers was found to have violated the obligation to progressively implement the right to health.

of movement in this context was a progressive right, subject to two important observations. First, a right is not considered progressive simply because it entails a positive action on behalf of the state. The protection of some rights may, in some circumstances, be so urgent as to warrant an immediate response. Secondly, that a right is to be ensured progressively does not mean that it cannot be enforced. The Court emphasised that 'taking rights seriously equally demands taking their progressive nature seriously'. It held that: (1) the progressive definition of the level of enjoyment of a right cannot continuously exclude certain groups of the population (such as persons with disabilities); (2) the state must gradually make advances as to the fulfilment of the right; and (3) the state may define the level of fulfilment that it is prepared to ensure, albeit rationally, and this must be made public by legislation and the right itself must be made justiciable.[19]

In a case involving failure to provide necessary school furniture and undertake school audits, the South African High Court (Eastern Cape) emphasised that this constituted a 'serious impediment for children attempting to access the right to basic education'. This right, provided in section 29(1)(a) of the South African Constitution, was found to be an unqualified right that is immediately realisable without being subject to progressive realisation. The Court noted that the right to basic education is quintessentially 'an empowerment right'.[20]

Article 2(1) of the ICESCR envisages progressive realisation of rights through the 'taking of steps' 'by all appropriate means'. The Committee has rightly commented that:

While the full realisation of the relevant rights may be achieved progressively, steps towards that goal must be taken within a reasonably short time after the Covenant's entry into force for the States concerned. Such steps should be deliberate, concrete and targeted as clearly as possible towards meeting the obligations recognised in the Covenant.

The fact that realisation over time, or in other words progressively, is foreseen under the Covenant should not be misinterpreted as depriving the obligation of all meaningful content. It is on the one hand a necessary flexibility device, reflecting the realities of the real world and the difficulties involved for any country in ensuring full realisation of ESC rights. On the other hand, the phrase must be read in the light of the overall objective, indeed the raison d'être, of the Covenant which is to establish clear obligations for States parties in respect of the full realisation of the rights in question. It thus imposes an obligation to move as expeditiously as possible towards that goal.[21]

---

[19] *Bermúdez Urrego* v. *Transmilenio* (Colombia) (2002).

[20] *Madzodzo and Others* v. *Minister of Basic Education* (South Africa) (2014); see also *Governing Body of Juma Musjid Primary School and Others* v. *Essay NO and Others* (South Africa) (2011).

[21] CESCR, General Comment 3, paras. 2 and 9, emphasis added.

That states are under an obligation to implement ESC rights, even if these have not been rendered justiciable, follows from their indivisibility from civil and political rights. People are living organisms, composed of myriad functions that are inseparable from the whole. In this sense, the right to life is not meaningful only when the state refrains from killing or protects individuals from crime, as this is simply one of the many dimensions of life. Others include access to food and water for immediate survival. When bare survival has been achieved, living a decent life that amounts to well-being[22] (which includes adequate access to housing, health care, education and other things) is important because without well-being political rights seem luxurious and theoretical pursuits to those who cannot afford to provide the bare essentials for their families. It is for this reason that most, if not all, ESC rights have been rendered justiciable by domestic and international judicial bodies as necessary correlations of civil and political freedoms and entitlements. In subsequent chapters this indirect justiciability will be demonstrated in respect of the right to development[23] and the right to sustainable development.[24]

The IACtHR is among those international tribunals that have provided a broad interpretation to civil and political rights so as to encompass by extension ESC rights. In the *Street Children* case, state agents of Guatemala were found to have practised abhorrent systematic violence against abandoned street children, including executions and torture. The Court employed articles 4 (right to life) and 19 (rights of the child) of the American Convention on Human Rights (ACHR) in order to construct the right to a dignified existence, which it stipulated should be guaranteed by the state. It found that in the case at hand Guatemala had deprived street children of the minimum conditions for a dignified life and prevented them from the full and harmonious development of their personalities.[25]

---

[22] Well-being is a central notion in the pursuit of the right to development, which is explained in Chapter 14.2.

[23] See Chapter 14.3.1.

[24] See Chapter 14.3.2.

[25] 'Street Children' *Villagrán Morales et al.* v. *Guatemala* (IACtHR) (1999) paras. 144, 191; in its Advisory opinion on *Juridical Condition and Human Rights of the Child* (IACtHR) (2002) para. 84, it was held that a dignified life for children separated from their families encompassed the right to education and the right to health. See J. L. Cavallaro and E. Schaffer, 'Less as More: Rethinking Supranational Litigation of Economic and Social Rights in the Americas' (2004) 56 *Hastings Law Journal* 217, at 272, who argue in favour of an expansive construction of the right to life and property in order to encompass a large number of ESC rights.

9.4 RESOURCE IMPLICATIONS: THE OBLIGATION TO UTILISE 'MAXIMUM AVAILABLE RESOURCES'

Article 2(1) of the ICESCR, as do other instruments related to the fulfilment of economic and social rights,[26] stresses that states are obliged to realise ESC rights by making the maximum use of their available resources. No doubt, although the resources of one nation will vary, and sometimes staggeringly so, from those of another, the assessment of a nation's available resources and its maximum utilisation of these resources towards implementing a particular right may be measured by reference to objective criteria. First of all, it is crucial to define and ascertain what falls within a state's available resources. The question is by no means simple, since one could argue that human capital, intellectual property rights, uncollected taxes and government loans constitute public resources, although not yet realisable/tangible monetary assets. Economists generally contend that a country's available resources should not be measured only by the ratio of governmental expenditure to gross domestic product (GDP), which represents the market value of a country's products and services in any one year. Available resources should also include development assistance, borrowing and running a deficit, as well as the monetary space made possible by central banks by, for example, currency devaluations, fluctuation of interest rates and others. This is referred to as the fiscal space diamond.[27]

Budgeting for human rights gives rise to an altogether different proposition. National budgets serve four distinct functions, namely: (1) control, by holding agencies accountable in respect of revenues and expenditures; (2) fiscal, for its contribution to economic stability and growth; (3) political, by prioritising activities and allocating resources; and (4) planning, by setting out goals and outcomes. A human rights-based approach to national budgeting necessitates that budgets are transparent, accountable, participatory, sustainable, flexible and capable of stimulating human development (according

---

[26] Art. 4 CRC; art. 4(2) CRPD. See also CtRC, General Comment 5: general measures of implementation, UN doc. CRC/GC/2003/5 (27 November 2003) paras. 6–8 and 51. The CtRC has criticised most countries for their failure in this regard. See Concluding Observations on Slovenia, UN doc. C/CRC/15/Add.230 (26 February 2004) para. 15, which called for the development of a 'systematic and detailed allocation of resources in order to provide a clear picture of trends in budget allocations and [which] ensures that resources are made available ... to the maximum extent of available resources in order to meet the needs of all children and correct poverty-related disparities'.

[27] See UN Development Programme (UNDP), 'The Fiscal Space Challenge and Financing for MDG Achievement', online at http://content.undp.org/go/cms-service/stream/asset/jsessionid=axMCGVWNrEb4?asset_id=2223965, at 7.

to the UN's Human Development Index (HDI)). It is important when looking at a budget to understand how much was spent, on what and whether it enhanced the end-users' standard of living. A budget that respects human rights and development must demonstrate a high degree of: (1) adequacy, essentially that a state has made the maximum use of its available resource; (2) priority, whereby allocation has been made on the basis of a rights assessment; (3) equity, in the sense that allocating policies are not discriminatory. Even so, one must be careful to read budgets in a way that reflects their real allocation of resources. For example, disaggregated (i.e. broken down in as many discreet categories as possible) data reveal whether the most vulnerable have benefited as much as other groups. The same is true with respect to various forms of taxation. As will be shown elsewhere, flat taxation schemes are generally discriminatory against financially weaker classes as opposed to progressive taxation. In addition, per capita allocation (i.e. money spent per person), as opposed to average allocation helps identify inequalities in social spending patterns.

The maximum utilisation of a state's resources, in particular, raises a number of compelling arguments. For example, would a country's failure to allocate funds to implement basic ESC rights be justified on the ground that it is obliged to service its foreign debt which accounts for 90 per cent of its annual resources? The European Court of Human Rights (ECtHR)[28] and the European Committee on Social Rights (ECSR) have both adamantly held that states cannot under any circumstances justify violations of entrenched rights on account of subsequent loan or fiscal obligations assumed by treaty or contract, irrespective of the conditions imposed by their lenders in such agreements.[29] The CESCR has pointed out the minimum requirements for the implementation of ESC rights, irrespective of a country's financial situation. These consist of the so-called minimum core obligations, which will be discussed in the next section, consisting of the minimum essential levels pertinent to each right.[30] Resource constraints can only under very exceptional circumstances be claimed as a justification to deny implementation of minimum core obligations.[31] Moreover:

even in times of severe resource constraints whether caused by a process of adjustment, of economic recession, or by other factors the vulnerable members of society can and indeed must be protected by the adoption of relatively low-cost targeted programmes.[32]

---

[28] *Capital Bank AD* v. *Bulgaria* (ECtHR) (2005) para. 90.
[29] *Federation of Employed Pensioners of Greece (IKA-ETAM)* v. *Greece* (ECSR) (2012) paras. 66–81; *Pensioners' Union of the Agricultural Bank of Greece (ATE)* v. *Greece* (ECSR) (2012) 48.
[30] CESCR, General Comment 3, para. 10.   [31] Ibid.
[32] CESCR, General Comment 3, para. 12.

No doubt, states have often claimed that although they are utilising the maximum of their resources these are none the less insufficient.[33] In most cases, however, they do not make the best use of their resources and this is something that is often pointed out by judicial institutions and intergovernmental entities.[34]

One poignant example concerns the distributive failures of so-called regressive tax regimes. These generally rely on the assumption that the rich will invest money in the economy if their personal and property taxes are reduced, taking into account that they already pay corporate tax and provide mass employment. As a result, regressive regimes balance their shortfall by imposing higher taxes on goods and services, which are, however, consumed by low- and middle-income households. Thus, they generate inequitable outcomes and fail to distribute wealth across the population because the poor end up paying more of their income on taxes than the rich.[35] Countries adhering to regressive regimes are clearly not making the maximum use of their resources and should consider reverting to progressive taxation where the wealthy are taxed according to their real income. But such a system cannot work if the global financial system allows the wealthy to emigrate to a handful of tax havens. In many cases, however, states simply fail in their task to use maximum available resources on account of limited administrative capacity, excessive bureaucracy[36] or, as in the case of Paraguay, through their inability simply to collect taxes. There are several indexes by which to measure economic inequality, which itself may explain structural problems with a state's economy, e.g. tax policies that effectively discriminate against the poor and low-income classes. An index/coefficient regularly employed by CESCR is the Gini index, which measures economic inequality in a given

---

[33] See R. Robertson, 'Measuring State Compliance with the Obligation to Devote the Maximum Available Resources to Realising Economic, Social and Cultural Rights' (1994) 16 *Human Rights Quarterly* 693.

[34] In the *Settlement Agreement between AJIC and the City of Buenos Aires* (Argentina) (2011), decided by the Superior Tribunal of Justice, the local government had under-utilised its financial resources by 32 per cent in respect of financing early childhood education. Ultimately, the parties reached a settlement, following findings of violations by lower courts regarding the right to education. The settlement contained an agreement whereby a permanent auditor was appointed to monitor the progress of relevant works, as well as a bimonthly work group to monitor implementation of the agreement, comprised of representatives from both camps.

[35] The German Federal Constitutional Court has held that the state's power of direct taxation – as opposed to indirect taxation – cannot be used to deprive people of the means for their 'existential minimum' (BVerfGE 82, 60(85), BVerfGE 87, 153(69)).

[36] CESCR Concluding Observations on Romania, UN doc. E/C.12/ROU/CO/3–5 (9 December 2014) para. 7.

population. The Gini index ranges from 0 (or 0 per cent) to 1 (or 100 per cent), with 0 representing perfect equality and 1 representing perfect inequality. In its assessment of the South African report, the country's Gini coefficient of 0.63 was found by the CESCR to be one of the worst globally. The CESCR partly explained this on the basis of South Africa's tax policies which do not allow the mobilization of the resources required to reduce such inequalities, these not being sufficiently progressive. In addition, it found that value added tax, as well as other taxes on household items, to have had a serious impact on low-income households, for which there had been no human rights impact assessments.[37]

There is some debate about whether the assessment of resource availability and its appropriate utilisation should be a justiciable matter, in addition to encompassing unavoidable political considerations. The CESCR, although admitting that determinations of this nature are not ordinarily justiciable, has gone on to say that courts are already involved in a considerable range of matters encompassing resource implications and possess the authority to do so 'within the limits of the appropriate exercise of their functions of judicial review'.[38] None the less, there exists a significant thread of jurisprudence in constitutional democracies whereby domestic courts have questioned the authority of the state to divert resources for the implementation of particular ESC rights, subsequently ordering their redirection or suggesting the need for reforms.[39] By way of illustration, the South African Constitutional Court in the *Treatment Action Campaign* case decided, among other issues, that the non-public availability of a drug that was found to prevent the transmission of HIV from mothers to babies was unreasonable and breached the right of poor mothers and their newborns to effective health care.[40]

Similarly, the Argentine Supreme Court has issued orders in a long list of cases to public authorities and hospitals demanding that they provide

---

[37] CESCR, Concluding Observations on the Report of South Africa, UN doc. E/C.12/ZAF/CO/1 (29 November 2018) para. 21.

[38] CESCR, General Comment 9, paras. 10 and 14.

[39] In *Campaign for Fiscal Equity* v. *State of New York* (US) (2003), the New York Court of Appeals suggested that New York state reform its school finance system so that it could provide a sound basic education to all of its districts. Upon the state's failure to implement any reforms, the court ordered that US $5.6 billion be allocated to annual school-operating expenses and another US $9.2 billion for a five-year capital projects programme. The state's appeal against the order was rejected: *Campaign for Fiscal Equity* v. *State of New York* (US) (2006). This led the New York governor in early 2007 to adopt the State Education Budget and Reform Act which envisaged significant state-wide increases in education aid.

[40] *South African Minister of Health* v. *Treatment Action Campaign* (South Africa) (2002).

HIV and other life-saving medication and treatment to the indigent.[41] The Mexican Supreme Court has ruled that refusal by the authorities on the basis of fiscal constraints to construct a new, or re-model existing, respiratory facilities for HIV sufferers (respiratory infections and diseases are the most common cause of death for HIV sufferers) violated the right to the highest attainable standard of health. The government was obliged, and was in fact ordered, to make the necessary budget allocations in accordance with its duty to use the maximum of its available resources.[42] In the same fashion the Colombian Constitutional Court has issued *amparo* and *tutela* injunctions, which are intended to protect people from unlawful and arbitrary governmental acts through urgent judicial review.[43] The right of amparo is stipulated in article 25(1) of the ACHR. In the *Rivera* case the Constitutional Court ordered a lower court to determine whether the petitioner was in a situation of 'absolute indigence' for the purpose of providing him with free medical treatment. The test for indigence was found to be premised on: (1) absolute incapacity to sustain oneself by one's own means; (2) the existence of a vital need which, if left unsatisfied, would seriously injure human dignity; and (3) the material absence of family support. If all three conditions were found to have been satisfied the lower court could order the state to contribute to that person's sustenance.[44]

As a result, it is wrong to suggest that courts are ill-placed, or that they do not possess the authority, to question and annul budgetary decisions that affect the implementation of ESC rights. In fact, an important function of judicial review is to prevent the implementation of government acts that carry a financial impact on rights.

---

[41] *Campodónico de Beviacqua, Ana Carina* v. *Ministerio de Salud y Banco Drogas Neoplásicas* (Argentina) (2000). A year earlier, the Venezuelan Supreme Court in *Cruz Bermúdez and Others* v. *Ministerio de Sanidad y Asistencia Social* (Venezuela) (1999), ordered the distribution of HIV drugs to 170 indigent sufferers.

[42] *Case Special Unit 13 (Pabellón 13)* (Mexico) (2014).

[43] In *Restrepo and López* v. *Salud Colmena* (Colombia) (2001) two HIV sufferers were denied testing since they were not included in the mandatory state-financed health plan. Neither could afford to pay for the tests. On the basis of the right to life the Constitutional Court held that diagnostic tests were essential to protect the right to health of HIV patients as well as to monitor the progress and effectiveness of HIV treatments. Thus, it ordered the private hospital (Salud Colmena) to carry out these tests free of charge, further authorising it to charge this additional cost to a government fund.

[44] *Rivera* case (Colombia) (1992). This is in conformity with case T-426/1992 (Colombia) (1992) which reproduces the German doctrine of 'minimum level of existence' (*Existenzminimum*).

CASE STUDY 9.1
United States Budget Allocated to Primary and Secondary Education

In 2004 the USA ranked eighth in its commitment to public education spending. In 2003–4 it spent US $472.3 billion, which represented almost 6 per cent of the country's GDP. This appears to demonstrate a significant commitment to government-funded education; numbers are deceptive, however. The level of public funding for education is dependent on local property taxes, not on a system of wealth redistribution that promotes equal quality of education for all children irrespective of income. As a result, wealthier neighbourhoods generate more money for public schools than low-income and deprived neighbourhoods. It is estimated that affluent public schools spend US $15,000 for each student, whereas poorer schools can only afford an amount close to US $4,000. It is evident that school districts with the largest percentage of minority students receive the least amount of general education revenues.[1] Under the terms of the ICESCR the USA would have failed to utilise its maximum available resources to fulfil the right to education because of the discrimination inherent in the current system of public education funding.

[1] Center for Women's Global Leadership, 'Maximum Available Resources and Human Rights: Analytical Report' (2011) 7.

9.5   MINIMUM CORE OBLIGATIONS

In one of its first general comments the CESCR made it clear that, at the very least, states are under an obligation to ensure the satisfaction of the minimum essential levels of each ESC right. It has referred to these as minimum core obligations.[45] For example, in cases of severe food shortages or serious epidemics threatening the very existence of a population, or a group thereof, the state is obliged to provide essential foodstuffs and vaccine or other health care. Although minimum core obligations are not derogable,[46] in extreme cases where 'every effort has been made to use all the resources [at the disposal of a state] in an effort to satisfy, as a matter of priority, minimum core obligations' the state in question is not considered at fault.[47]

[45] CESCR, General Comment 3, para. 10.   [46] CESCR, General Comment 14, para. 18.
[47] CESCR, General Comment 3, para. 10.

It has been suggested that minimum core obligations anticipate three accomplishments: (1) provision of a specific direction in the implementation of ESC rights by disassembling the inherent relativism of their otherwise 'progressive realisation'; (2) advancement of a baseline level of protection irrespective of socio-economic policies and disparate levels of available resources; and (3) signalling an acceptable global redistributive debate.[48] At the same time, however, what remains unanswered is whether the minimalist approach associated with minimum core obligations presupposes differentiated standards between developed and developing countries. Some critics have further argued that the continued insistence on the performance of developing states, in respect of assessing minimum core obligations has steered focus away from low- and middle-income classes in the developed world.[49] To respond to the question of whether differentiated standards are justified – which necessarily poses a relativist dimension – one must first assess the values pertinent to human existence recognised under general international law. The majority of the globe's population still lives in abject poverty, suffering unnecessary deaths from diseases, infections and malnourishment. The UN's HDI has consistently emphasised that human development and well-being should be measured on the basis of longevity, knowledge and decent living standards.[50] Under this light, a needs-based core minimum set of obligations premised on the preservation of bare survival would not meet the HDI threshold and is in any event antithetical to the notion that the right to life is not exhausted by biological survival alone but is instead multidimensional. As a result, several scholars have rejected the needs-based approach, arguing in favour of value-based core minimum obligations by putting emphasis on what it means to be human, encompassing within their methodology the notions of dignity, equality and freedom.[51]

This line of thinking seems to conform more closely to the CESCR's approach, given that its formulation of core minimum obligations in respect of rights such as water require much more than the formulation of needs-based policies by states parties.[52] The Committee is not alone in

[48] K. Y. Young, 'The Minimum Core of Economic and Social Rights: A Concept in Search of Content' (2008) 33 *Yale Journal of Intenational Law* 113, 121–2.

[49] M. Craven, *The International Covenant on Economic, Social and Cultural Rights: A Perspective on its Development* (Oxford University Press, 1995) 143–4.

[50] UNDP, *Human Development Report* (Oxford University Press, 1990) 11. For a fuller discussion, see Chapter 14.2.

[51] See Young, above note 48, 128–38.   [52] CESCR, General Comment 15, para. 37.

its value-based conception of the minimum core. In fact, the German Constitutional Court has long developed the doctrine of 'minimum level of existence' (*Existenzminimum*), whereby the state is constitutionally obliged to establish a social welfare system that enables people to live with dignity.[53] Equally, in the USA the courts have employed their power of judicial review in order to suggest budgetary reforms that overturn existing economic and social policies, as is the case with the discrepancy in quality of public secondary education offered to under-privileged classes.[54] The courts were not merely content that children attended school, but emphasised that the level of secondary education should be such as to prepare students for higher education and render them capable of competing in the employment market.[55] This by no means suggests a bare minimum.

The implementation of minimum core obligations does not always require the infusion of tangible resources but may simply demand a change of policies. By way of illustration, food and employment security in poor nations could be significantly boosted by the protection of small-scale farming, access to subsidies or micro-financing and insistence on local consumption with a view to minimising cost. In this manner valuable foodstuffs would not be exported cheaply out of countries reliant on them for their well-being and farmers could continue to grow their produce without fear of being outpriced or taken over by large collectives.[56]

Despite the fact that core minimum obligations must be construed as value-based rather than needs-based, in emergency situations it is not expected that the state should implement the higher thresholds of ESC rights. In the *Grootboom* case, which concerned the eviction of homeless people from their informal settlements, the South African Constitutional Court held that even though the government was working towards a housing policy to provide adequate, low-cost housing for the poor, it was under a legal duty to accommodate as a matter of priority the 'absolutely homeless'.[57]

---

[53] BVerfGE 1, 97 (104); BVerfGE 45, 187 (229).

[54] *Campaign for Fiscal Equity* v. *State of New York* (2003).

[55] The House of Lords in *R* v. *East Sussex Council ex parte Tandy* (UK) (1998) adopted a similar stance in a case where a disabled child unable to physically attend school had its home tuition hours reduced from five to three by its local council on financial grounds. The Lords argued that although the Council was entitled to choose how to best spend its resources, it was none the less obliged to offer all children a 'suitable education', as per section 298 of the Education Act 1993.

[56] See Chapter 20.3.1, dealing with globalisation.

[57] *Government of South Africa and Others* v. *Grootboom and Others* (South Africa) (2000).

9.6   JUSTICIABILITY OF ESC RIGHTS

The concept of justiciability concerns whether a particular claim is susceptible to judicial scrutiny on the basis of mandatory procedural rules.[58] For some time, especially during the deliberations on the drafting of the ICESCR, it was contended that ESC rights did not possess a justiciable character. In order to justify this line of thinking it was argued that these were not in fact rights entailing legal entitlements but rather policy directives, or that their progressive realisation rendered them unsusceptible to judicial determination.[59] It was further argued that the courts could not possibly have a say on how governments determined their fiscal priorities. In the *Nigerian Education* case, for example, the government claimed that education was not a legal entitlement for its citizens and that as a result of widespread corruption it lacked the funds necessary to cover the shortfall to its educational budget, effectively denying large numbers of children the right to education. The ECOWAS court confirmed that the right to primary education was both justiciable and binding on Nigeria irrespective of the resources available to it.[60]

These types of anti-justiciability claims led a number of countries to avoid adopting legislation that would have made ESC claims justiciable before local courts. The Swiss Federal Supreme Court, for example, determined that the rights enshrined in the ICESCR were not justiciable because they did not manifest the characteristics of directly applicable norms.[61] Such arguments focusing on the alleged absence of direct applicability tend to bypass the fact that the rights in question are in one way or another enshrined in national constitutions. Even so, through a process of strategic litigation initiated mainly by human rights NGOs, local courts have been urged to entertain claims based on the violation of ESC rights, whether directly or by reference to civil and political rights. The Indian Supreme Court, for example,

---

[58] See M. J. Dennis and D. P. Stewart, 'Justiciability of Economic, Social and Cultural Rights: Should There be an International Complaints Mechanism to Adjudicate the Rights to Food, Water, Housing and Health?' (2004) 98 *American Journal of International Law* 462, at 474–5, who take a narrow view, arguing that a claim should be considered justiciable only where its adjudication contributes to a practical result that is susceptible to implementation. For a comprehensive analysis of many of the cases cited in this section, see International Commission of Jurists, 'Courts and the Legal Enforcement of Economic, Social and Cultural Rights: Comparative Experiences of Justiciability' (2008).

[59] This argument was rejected by the Colombian Constitutional Court, especially in situations where the government has not taken the requisite steps to fulfil the right in question: *Bermúdez Urrego* v. *Transmilenio*.

[60] *Social and Economic Rights Action Center (SERAC)* v. *Federal Republic of Nigeria and Universal Basic Education Commission* (ECOWAS) (2010).

[61] *T* v. *Neuchâtel County Compensation Bank and Administrative Court* (Switzerland) (1995).

subsumed the right to a healthy environment, adequate housing and other matters under the right to life. At a time when India lacked a constitutional provision guaranteeing the right to a healthy environment the country's Supreme Court relied on article 21 of the Constitution contending that the right to life guaranteed therein encompassed the enjoyment of a healthy environment, including clean air and uncontaminated potable water.[62] In *MC Mehta* v. *Union of India*, which concerned the discharge of untreated effluents from a tannery into the River Ganges, the Supreme Court ordered the tannery's closure despite the inevitable job losses, emphasising that human health and a balanced natural environment were of greater importance.[63] This line of construction by which the right to life has been found to encompass the right to a healthy environment has been followed by other constitutional courts.[64]

The IACtHR and the IACHR have adopted a similar methodology in respect of ESC rights that are not written into the American Convention. In *Bosico* v. *Dominican Republic*, for example, two Haitian children born in the Dominican Republic were denied birth certificates and nationality by the authorities of that country and as a result were not allowed to attend school and were deprived of a juridical personality. The Court found a violation of article 3 (right to juridical personality), article 19 (children's rights) and article 20 (right to nationality), among others, in order to affirm the obligation of states to provide without discrimination an education that is free and which fosters children's intellectual development.[65]

In countries where ESC rights have found their way into national constitutions[66] the courts have developed a significant string of caselaw confirming their justiciable character. It should be pointed out that the courts are not necessarily the best forum for implementing ESC rights, as this is a task best suited to the executive power of central and regional governments by means of action plans and practical measures, such as the supply of pharmaceutical

---

[62] *Charan Lal Sahu* v. *Union of India* (India) (1990); but especially *Subhash Kumar* v. *State of Bihar* (India) (1991).

[63] *MC Mehta* v. *Union of India (Ganges water pollution* case) (India) (1998).

[64] *Farooque* v. *Bangladesh* (Bangladesh) (1997); *Shehla Zia* v. *WAPDA* (Pakistan) (1994), adopted by the Pakistan Supreme Court; *Presidente de la sociedad MARLENE SA* v. *Municipalidad de Tibás* (Costa Rica) (1994); *Antonio Mauricio Monroy Cespédes case* (Colombia) (1993).

[65] *Girls Yean and Bosico* v. *Dominican Republic* (IACtHR) (2005) para. 185. See M. F. Tinta, 'Justiciability of Economic, Social and Cultural Rights in the Inter-American System of Protection of Human Rights: Beyond Traditional Paradigms and Notions' (2007) 29 *Human Rights Quarterly* 431, at 445–51. See also M. B. Dembour, *When Humans Become Migrants: Study of the European Court of Human Rights with an Inter-American Counterpoint* (Oxford University Press, 2015) 313–51.

[66] For example, Colombian Constitution 1991, ch. II, arts. 42–77.

drugs and housing. None the less, a free and independent judiciary plays an important role in clarifying the exact content of obligations, monitoring their implementation against possible discrimination, and determining the validity of omissions to fulfil based on reasonableness and proportionality; sometimes this role is further enhanced by its ability to demand specific action.[67] In an Indian case, a destitute woman died on a busy Delhi street four days after giving birth, having no access to food or medical aid. Because of the publicity of the incident, the Delhi High Court entertained the case through its own motion. It went on to order the local authority to set up five homeless shelters exclusively for destitute, homeless and lactating women and to ensure the operability of a system for such women to be taken to the shelters if they could not go themselves and for the services to be publicised.[68]

Reasonableness, defined as an action that is appropriate under the circumstances and proportionality (which is a test for discerning balance between two opposing propositions), whether directly or indirectly, have been invoked by a number of courts in order to assess the propriety of governmental restrictions upon ESC rights. They have been further incorporated in article 8(4) of the 2008 Optional Protocol to the ICESCR.[69] The South African Supreme Court has been instrumental in this regard, particularly through its much celebrated *Grootboom* judgment, but similar decisions have been reached elsewhere. In the *Multiple Sclerosis* case, the Argentine Supreme Court was called upon to decide the validity of a regulation issued by the Ministry of Health which excluded multiple sclerosis treatment from the country's mandatory minimum health insurance plan. This regulation affected patients already under the plan, with the Court deeming it unreasonable and contrary to the right to health.[70]

A poignant facet of ESC rights concerns the obligation to refrain from deliberately imposing retrogressive measures, such as would reverse any achievements made in the realisation of a particular right.[71] Retrogressive measures essentially deny existing rights-holders their legitimate entitlements and many states during the post-2008 global financial crisis justified

---

[67] In fact, the CESCR routinely criticises countries that fail to make ICESCR rights justiciable and which further place limitations on the exercise of socio-economic rights. See CESCR, Concluding Observations on Vietnam, UN doc. E/C.12/VNM/CO/2–4 (15 December 2014) paras. 7–9.

[68] *Court on its own Motion* v. *Union of India* (India) (2011).

[69] This stipulates that in the examination of individual communications for violations of ESC rights, the CESCR shall 'consider the reasonableness of the steps taken by the state party ... bearing in mind that the state party may adopt a range of possible policy measures for the implementation of the rights set forth in the Covenant'.

[70] *Asociación de Esclerosis Múltiple de Salta* v. *Ministerio de Salud-Estado Nacional (Multiple Sclerosis case)* (Argentina) (2003).

[71] CESCR, General Comment 3, para. 9. However, this is best framed as a qualified obligation.

cuts to pensions, education and health by reference to spiralling public debt.[72] The odious set of measures imposed by Greece's bilateral and multilateral lenders, for example, between 2010 and 2014 on education, health and pensions, among others, adversely affected the living conditions of the infirm, the elderly and low-income households. Retrogressive measures have been successfully challenged before national courts, particularly in the areas of pensions, health care and education.[73]

Finally, it should be remembered that because justiciability does not only encompass claims against public authorities, the actions and omissions of private actors may also be challenged before the courts. Although non-state actors are not charged with specific ESC obligations under the ICESCR or general international law, to the extent that they effectively discharge economic and social rights in substitution for the state they have been viewed by some courts as legitimate duty-holders and have thus accepted the justiciability of claims brought against them. In *Etcheverry* v. *Omint* the applicant, who was an HIV sufferer, was provided membership to a private health plan by his employer. When he later became redundant he sought to continue his membership through private funds but the insurance company refused. The Argentine Supreme Court held that private health providers were under a duty to protect the right to health of their customers and that their special relationship was not simply of a contractual nature.[74] International bodies dealing with ESC rights claims but with no jurisdiction against non-state actors, such as the ECSR, will typically find that the state concerned has violated its obligations under the European Social Charter by failing to take action against recalcitrant private actors.[75] This alternative is also open to national courts through the function of judicial review.

The following sections discuss the two available international quasi-judicial mechanisms that deal with individual and collective complaints associated with violations of ESC rights; the Optional Protocol to the ICESCR and

---

[72] The Greek Supreme Administrative Court (*Symvoulio Epikrateias*), at the height of the financial crisis, upheld the constitutional nature of the measures (essentially) imposed upon the Greek government by its creditors on the rationale that otherwise the country would become insolvent! See *Symvoulio Epikrateias* judgment no. 668/2012 (Greece) (2012). Effectively therefore, the Court's assessment of constitutionality and human rights is predicated solely on sovereign insolvency and finances.

[73] The Latvian Constitutional Court in the *Pensions* case (Latvia) (2009) and the Romanian Constitutional Court, judgment no. 872 (2010) held that pension cuts implemented on the basis of loan agreements with the IMF were unconstitutional.

[74] *Etcheverry* v. *Omint Sociedad Anónima y Servicios* (Argentina) (2001).

[75] The CESCR in its General Comment 19 (right to social security), UN doc. E/C12/GC/19 (4 February 2008) para. 65, noted that a state violates its duty to provide social security where it fails to adequately regulate the activities of private companies that deny this entitlement to rights-holders.

the European Social Charter. In addition to these, the San Salvador Protocol on Economic Social and Cultural Rights establishes a weak periodic reporting mechanism, as well as an outlet for individual communications, but only in respect of two specific rights (article 19(6)): the right to form and participate in trade unions under article 8(a) and the right to education in accordance with article 13. Finally, the African Charter on Human and Peoples' Rights (ACHPR) incorporates several ESC rights and does not distinguish their justiciable character from that of other rights.

9.6.1   Individual Communications and the ICESCR Optional Protocol

On account of the unique legal nature of ESC rights (i.e. their progressive realisation, resource constraints and others), it was inconceivable to the majority of states during the drafting of the Covenant that a body equivalent to the UN HRCtee could receive individual communications. This was further reinforced by those who doubted whether the rights in the Covenant were justiciable in the first place before the parties' domestic courts. With the issue of non-justiciability having long been disposed of, the idea of a complaints procedure began to be discussed within the UN in 1991 and in 2001 the Commission on Human Rights appointed an independent expert on the Question of an Optional Protocol to the ICESCR.[76] The baton was later passed to a working group[77] and following a series of high-level discussions the text of the Protocol was adopted by the UN General Assembly in late 2008.[78] This was by no means a smooth ride and despite the strong consensus from many quarters there was also significant dissent, with some commentators claiming that empowering a committee with powers over the implementation of ESC rights risks establishing a judicially controlled command economy through a counter-democratic process.[79]

The Protocol envisages three particular types of communication: individual or group complaints, inter-state communications and an inquiry procedure. The idea behind all three (all of which are common to the global human rights treaties) is for the target state to reach a settlement with the complainant or consider reforming those laws and institutions that are found to infringe a particular right. Although the CESCR's recommendations are not meant to be binding as such, they are highly authoritative and states are

---

[76] CommHR resolution 2001/30 (20 April 2001).

[77] CommHR resolution 2003/18 (22 April 2003).

[78] For a background to events and discussions leading to its adoption, see C. de Albuquerque, 'Chronicle of an Announced Birth: The Coming into Life of the Optional Protocol to the International Covenant on Economic, Social and Cultural Rights: The Missing Piece of the International Bill of Human Rights' (2010) 32 *Human Rights Quarterly* 144.

[79] Dennis and Stewart, above note 58, 466.

expected to comply. Under article 2, communications may be received by, or on behalf of, individuals or groups of individuals, implying that the procedure is open to minority groups, indigenous persons, trade unions and even NGOs. Significantly, and in line with the jurisprudence of other international bodies, the violation need not have taken place on the territory of the state party but may occur in any place where the party exercises effective control. A communication may not be admissible if it does not reveal that the author has suffered a clear disadvantage; even so, the Committee may still consider the communication if it raises a serious issue of general importance.[80] Following the admissibility stage the Committee will examine the communication and simultaneously transmit it to the target state for further statements and explanations.[81] Upon examination the Committee transmits its views, along with its recommendations, to the parties. The target state must give due consideration to the views and recommendations of the Committee and come back within six months with a response on any subsequent action taken.[82]

Given the sparse use made of inter-state complaints before other human rights mechanisms, it would be unlikely that this one would constitute a shining exception. Finally, the inquiry procedure is triggered by the receipt of reliable information indicating grave or systematic violations of ESC rights, upon which the CESCR will invite the target state to cooperate in the examination of available information and submit its observations. This procedure is equally confidential and upon reaching its findings the CESCR will transmit its views to the state concerned, which has six months to respond.[83]

9.6.2   The ECSR

Within the context of the Council of Europe (CoE) a relatively vibrant and successful mechanism came into existence following the adoption of the European Social Charter in 1961. Unlike the ICESCR, which addresses a broad range of economic and social rights, the Charter largely protects labour and workplace-related rights, albeit it also encompasses the right to protection of health and to social security,[84] among others. The Charter is monitored by the European Committee of Social Rights (ECSR), which is composed of independent experts. Member states are under an obligation to submit a report every two years discussing the measures they have taken to protect and fulfil the rights stipulated in the Charter, which the Committee duly evaluates. The other

---

[80] Art. 4, Optional Protocol to the ICESCR.   [81] Art. 6, ibid.
[82] Art. 9(1) and (2), ibid.
[83] Art. 11, ibid.
[84] Arts. 11 and 12, European Social Charter.

function of the Committee is to receive collective complaints alleging unsatisfactory application of the Charter. Such complaints can only be submitted by international organisations of employers and trade unions, NGOs listed under the CoE and representative national organisations of employers and trade unions within the jurisdiction of the targeted state party.[85] Individual communications are not available under the Charter.[86] The Committee's jurisprudence to date has made particular impact in the field of social security and has cemented the obligation of states to protect ESC rights irrespective of financial commitments to private or intergovernmental lenders.[87]

QUESTIONS

1. Some liberal democracies take the view that persons who do not contribute to the economy by working and paying taxes should not be entitled to public goods such as health care, water and housing. Discuss by reference to the role of the state.

2. By setting out minimum core obligations the citizens of developed nations risk being disadvantaged because the focus of minimum core obligations is on what poor nations can or should provide for their people. Discuss.

3. Country A has limited resources and is poor. In designing its national educational plan it reckons that if it were to educate more scientists, particularly doctors, nutritionists, agricultural experts and others it could ultimately offer a better life to all its people. In doing so the government is forced to cut educational funding from all remote villages. It justifies this decision by claiming that 95 per cent of rural children ultimately end up as farmers and that therefore providing them with six years of education is a waste of money that could be better spent on training much needed scientists. In any event, this will help rural populations because they will have access to much improved health care, housing, water and crop management. Is this exclusion justified under human rights law, including the right to sustainable development?

4. It is not the place of the courts to decide on budget allocation because this involves executive considerations. Discuss whether the courts' ordinary judicial review powers cover, or should cover, budgetary matters that affect the enjoyment of civil and political and ESC rights. Would the denial of elections be a plausible justification to a claim that a government does not have enough money to hold them? Why should a similar argument refusing to uphold fundamental ESC rights be any different?

---

[85] Art. 1, 1995 Additional Protocol to the European Social Charter.
[86] See generally G. de Búrca and B. de Witte, *Social Rights in Europe* (Oxford University Press, 2005).
[87] See Chapter 19.4.2.

5. **The new mantra in the post-2008 financial crisis era is that governments should reduce their deficits by drastically curbing public spending. This entails loss of work for many, the charging of end-user fees for services that would otherwise be free, such as health care, and the reduction of social welfare services to the vulnerable. Is economic recovery and growth under these terms compatible with fundamental ESC rights? If not, design a brief policy that conforms to social justice, respects ESC rights and yet is financially viable.**

9.7   EXTRATERRITORIALITY OF ESC RIGHTS

The extraterritorial nature of human rights obligations has been discussed in other chapters, especially as regards belligerent occupation.[88] Unlike the ICCPR (article 2(1)), the ICESCR does not limit the application of rights to persons within a state's territory. This does not, however, mean that the rights in question automatically assume an extraterritorial character. This was certainly not the intention of its drafters. Even so, the obligation of states to respect, protect and fulfil ESC rights extraterritorially stems from general international law and particularly the law on state responsibility.[89] Paragraph 9 of the 2011 Maastricht Principles on Extraterritorial Obligations of States in the Area of ESC Rights, states that such an obligation arises in:

situations over which [a state] exercises authority or effective control, whether or not such control is exercised in accordance with international law;

situations over which State acts or omissions bring about foreseeable effects on the enjoyment of economic, social and cultural rights, whether within or outside its territory;

situations in which the State, acting separately or jointly, whether through its executive, legislative or judicial branches, is in a position to exercise decisive influence or to take measures to realise ESC rights extraterritorially, in accordance with international law.

The Maastricht Principles iterate nothing more than general international law. In a globalised world, powerful states are able to exert a significant amount of financial, fiscal, trade or other similar control over their weaker counterparts. Such control does not amount to belligerent occupation, even

---

[88]   See Chapter 16.6.

[89]   In *Georgia* v. *Russian Federation* (ICJ) (2008) para. 109, a question posed to the Court was whether the CERD, which like the ICESCR does not contain a jurisdictional provision, applies extraterritorially. Despite the absence of such a provision, the ICJ held that the CERD generally applies 'to the actions of a state party when it acts beyond its borders'.

though they may produce similar or even more detrimental effects to the population in question.[90] Hence, it is unlikely that international law does not consider that states effectively controlling the fate of ESC rights in third nations have no obligation to reverse the effects of their actions. Such a gap in the law would render ESC rights meaningless in the era of globalisation.

Scholars and practitioners generally acknowledge three general extraterritorial dimensions arising from the ICESCR and general international law. These are: (1) multilateral sanctions established by the UN Security Council; (2) military occupation; and (3) international assistance and cooperation.[91] Others add the positive 'duty' to address the question of global poverty.[92] Künnemann further proposed a typology of 'internal, external and international obligations of states towards victims'.[93] Although international assistance and cooperation seems the more likely contender because it is specifically demanded in article 2(1) of the ICESCR,[94] it is in fact framed in unilateral terms or as a non-binding promise, rather than a binding obligation.[95] The reality is that states whose internal ESC obligations are impacted by the actions of states (and their agents), which in most cases will involve direct interference in domestic affairs, are entitled to seek cessation and other remedies, as well as apply countermeasures in accordance with general international law.

9.8   INDICATORS AND BENCHMARKS FOR MEASURING COMPLIANCE

One of the shortcomings associated with the monitoring of states' obligations to respect, protect and fulfil human rights is the lack of verifiable quantitative criteria through which to measure with some degree of accuracy success and failure. This shortcoming is even more visible in the field of ESC rights,

---

[90] See e.g., Chapter 14.6, which deals with indebted states and the financial control exerted over them by their lenders.

[91] See F. Coomans, 'The Extraterritorial Scope of the International Covenant on Economic, Social and Cultural Rights in the Work of the United Nations Committee on Economic, Social and Cultural Rights' (2011) 11 *Human Rights Law Review* 1.

[92] M. Salomon, 'Is There a Duty to Address World Poverty?' Robert Schuman Centre for Advanced Studies Policy Paper 3 (2012).

[93] R. Künnemann, 'Extraterritorial Application of the International Covenant on Economic, Social and Cultural Rights', in F. Coomans and M. T. Kamminga (eds.), *Extraterritorial Application of Human Rights Treaties* (Intersentia, 2004) 201–31.

[94] See CESCR, General Comment 3, The Nature of State Parties' Obligations (1990) para. 14, where it was held that: 'international cooperation for development and thus for the realization of economic, social and cultural rights is an obligation of all states' which is 'particularly incumbent upon those states which are in a position to assist others in this regard'.

[95] On international assistance, see Chapter 14.4.

which encompasses mostly positive obligations required to realise the various entitlements. The idea of introducing practical indicators as a tool for measuring the implementation of rights has been discussed since the early 1990s,[96] but it was not until the recommendations of Paul Hunt, a UN Special Rapporteur, that the move to indicators started to become more methodical, informed and streamlined. Human rights indicators consist of specific information relevant to a state in respect of an event, activity or outcome related to human rights norms and standards used to assess and monitor the promotion and protection of rights.[97] In large part this information is of a quantitative character in the form of numbers and percentages. Examples include the percentage of persons covered by social security, access to health care, education enrolment rates and the number of women with a fixed income.

The formulation of indicators is subject to several considerations. First, indicators must be anchored in the normative content of particular rights, as opposed to simply reflecting the socio-economic or developmental content of the right. By way of illustration, health indicators compiled by the World Health Organization (WHO) serve largely different objectives from indicators assessing implementation of the right to health. The latter are not intended to determine the general levels of health in a particular nation, but rather to assess to what degree adequate health care is available, accessible and known to the population.[98] As a result, human rights indicators require ascertaining the various attributes of rights, which are generally found in the definitions of international treaties and their elaboration by their respective treaty bodies. The attributes of the right to food, for example, are found in article 11 of the ICESCR and General Comment 12 of the CESCR on the right to adequate food. They consist of nutrition, food safety, consumer protection and food availability.[99] These, in turn, are derived from the CESCR's recognition that economic and social rights must be available, accessible (physically and economically, non-discriminatory and people must be well-informed) and of a decent quality.[100]

The second consideration is to avoid divorcing cross-cutting human rights norms in the choice of indicators, as would be the case if one were to distinguish non-discrimination, equality, participation, indivisibility and empowerment instead of considering them as elements of a single unit.[101]

---

[96] See e.g., the Vienna Declaration and Program of Action, world conference on human rights, UN doc. A/CONF 157/24 (1993) para. 98.

[97] Report on Indicators for Monitoring Compliance with International Human Rights Instruments, UN doc. HRI/MC/2006/7 (11 May 2006) para. 7.

[98] P. Hunt, 'The Right of Everyone to Enjoy the Highest Attainable Standard of Physical and Mental Health', UN doc. A/58/427 (10 October 2003) para. 10.

[99] Report on Indicators, above note 97, para. 15.

[100] See e.g., CESCR General Comment 15, para. 12, referring to the right to water.

[101] Report on Indicators, above note 97, para. 13.

Without these, all other rights are rendered meaningless. In fact, the OHCHR conceded that many of the assessments made by development agencies with regard to North Africa and Arab regions prior to the uprisings of 2011 failed to take adequate account of the increasing inequality and social injustice prevailing there.[102]

It is now well settled that human rights indicators are structured along the lines of a tripartite configuration: they are structural, process and outcome based.[103] Structural indicators reflect the ratification/implementation of legal instruments and the establishment of institutional mechanisms, such as justiciability and access to justice more generally and the enactment of relevant laws. Process-based indicators reflect the degree to which laws are transformed into concrete policies, as is the case with national health and educational plans, universal immunisation programmes, public interventions and other matters. Outcome-based indicators reflect attainments in the realisation of human rights. Outcome indicators may, however, be misleading because they concern results which could well have arisen for other reasons. For example, an increase in life expectancy need not necessarily be the result of universal immunisation, but also of better nutrition, access to clean water, improved health awareness, education and other factors. Thus, process indicators are in a sense more important for the enjoyment of a right than outcome indicators. It is also essential for all indicators to be disaggregated, that is to account specifically for disadvantaged and marginalised groups, women, children, minorities and to distinguish between low-, middle- and high-income groups in order to better assess disparities in the enjoyment of particular rights between various segments of the population.[104]

As has already been explained, indicators serve to confer objective attributes upon the various human rights. Once these have been clearly set out their realisation must be measured against individualised benchmarks. These benchmarks will vary from country to country on the basis of available resources and technical capacity and will serve to commit each country to the particular performance standard agreed. By way of illustration, if an outcome indicator for the right to adequate housing demands that affordable and decent accommodation be made available to 80 per cent of low-income households, an appropriate and realistic benchmark for developing country X may be an increase of ten percentile points every year over a period of ten years. On the other hand, industrialised country Y, 75 per cent of whose low-income population enjoys subsidised, cheap or public accommodation, may adopt a

---

[102] ECOSOC, Report of the OHCHR, UN doc. E/2011/90 (26 April 2011) para. 10. The World
        Bank's country brief on Tunisia is specifically mentioned.
[103] Report on Indicators, above note 97, paras. 16–19.
[104] Ibid., para. 31. CtEDAW General Recommendation 9 (1989) emphasises the need for
        disaggregated data in order to understand the precise situation of women.

benchmark of covering its 5 per cent shortfall within the space of a year. It is crucial to point out that benchmarks are set out in consultation with target states on the basis of their capabilities and certainly never unilaterally by international monitoring bodies or quasi-judicial entities. This process is typically referred to as scoping. This process of consultation is also envisaged in respect of indicators, for the sole reason that because they are not expressly written into treaties, states parties may end up refusing to be bound by them. There are of course a limited number of situations where indicators are only contextually and not universally specific, as is the case with particular diseases and epidemics.[105] It is important to emphasise that the data by which the satisfaction of the benchmarks are to be assessed can be sought from government sources, intergovernmental organisations and NGOs.[106]

In practice, there is no standard set of indicators applicable to each ESC right, apart from the few indicators stipulated in the ICESCR.[107] As a result, the CESCR does not measure obligations on the basis of predefined lists of criteria, as is otherwise the case with the indicators and benchmarks elaborated in the context of the Sustainable Development Goals, which have been accepted by all participants to the process.[108] In fact, in a number of its general comments, the CESCR has called on parties to consider obtaining guidance on appropriate indicators from specialist bodies such as the WHO, the Food and Agriculture Organization (FAO), the International Labour Organization (ILO) and others.[109] As a result, although the indicators originally developed by these organisations were not geared towards the realisation of human rights, they have subsequently gone on to initiate workshops in order to formulate indicators premised on a human rights approach. The CESCR, as well as other treaty bodies, now requires a specific format for state reporting purposes, obliging states to make wide use of disaggregated indicators.[110]

It is clear that in order for indicators to be meaningful, the collection of appropriate data must be made compulsory. Such an obligation, in the context of a human rights treaty, expressly exists only in article 31 CRPD. However, given that the reporting requirements of states necessitate the

[105] ECOSOC Report 2011, above note 102, para. 14.

[106] Ibid., para. 17.

[107] Art. 12 ICESCR mentions reductions to stillbirth rates and infant mortality in relation to the right to health, whereas art. 10(f) CEDAW refers to reduction of female student dropout rates in respect of the right to education.

[108] See Chapter 14.5.

[109] CESCR, General Comment 15, para. 53.

[110] See Compilation of Guidelines on the Form and Content of Reports to be Submitted by States Parties to the International Human Rights Treaties, UN doc. HRI/GEN/2/Rev.6 (3 June 2009) at 26ff.

collection and compilation of data in order for treaty bodies to assess their compliance, requests for further and more comprehensive data collection schemes are now commonplace.[111] Although there exists no single and comprehensive methodology by which to collect human rights-related data, the CRPD Committee's 2016 Reporting Guidelines[112] provide that states should report on:

226 Steps taken to develop data collection tools in accordance with the human rights-based approach to disability and focusing on the disabling barriers experienced by persons with disabilities.

227 Steps taken to incorporate human rights-based indicators in data collection and analysis respecting, among others, human rights and fundamental freedoms, ethics, legal safeguards, data protection, confidentiality and privacy.

228 Steps taken to ensure the full and meaningful participation of representative organizations of persons with disabilities in the full process (design/planning, implementation, analysis and dissemination) of data collection and research, through among others, capacity building of those organisations.

229 Steps taken to establish coordinated systems between all entities collecting data on persons with disabilities which ensures reliability and diminishes discrepancies.

230 Steps taken to further disaggregate data, by age, sex and other relevant factors, in order to identify and address the barriers faced by persons with disabilities in exercising their rights, for the purpose of formulating and implementing policies to give effect to the Convention.[113]

Interestingly, the CRPD Committee does not read the state obligation in article 31 as a matter solely engaging national statistical agencies, but as a collective, coordinated and continuous effort encompassing also non-state actors.[114]

---

[111] See e.g., CERD, 'General Recommendation no. 24 (Information on the demographic composition of the population)'; CEDAW, 'General Recommendation no. 9 (Statistical data concerning the situation of women)'; CRC Ctee, 'General Comment No. 5 (General measures of implementation of the Convention on the Rights of the Child' (all contained in UN doc. HRI/GEN/1/Rev.9 (27 May 2008); CEDAW/CRC, Joint General Recommendation/General Comment No. 31 of the Committee on the Elimination of Discrimination against Women and No. 18 of the CRC Ctee, UN doc. CEDAW/C/GC/31-CRC/C/GC/18 (14 November 2014).

[112] 'Guidelines on periodic reporting to the Committee on the Rights of Persons with Disabilities, including under the simplified reporting procedures, adopted by the Committee at its 16th Session' (15 August – 2 September 2016), available at www.ohchr.org/EN/HRBodies/CRPD/Pages/CRPDIndex.aspx.

[113] Ibid., paras. 226–31.

[114] See M. Pedersen, 'Article 31: Statistics and Data Collection', in I. Bantekas, M. A. Stein and D. Anastasiou (eds.), *The UN Convention on the Rights of Persons with Disabilities: A Commentary* (Oxford University Press, 2019) 924, 930.

CASE STUDY 9.2
Indicators on the Right to Food[1]

List of illustrative indicators on the right to adequate food (UDHR, art. 25) (* MDG-related indicators)

	Nutrition	Food Safety and Consumer Protection	Food Availability	Food Accessibility
Structural	• International human rights treaties, relevant to the right to adequate food ratified by the state • Date of entry into force and coverage of the right to adequate food in the Constitution or other forms of superior law • Date of entry into force and coverage of domestic laws for implementing the right to adequate food • Number of registered and/or active NGOs (per 100,000 persons) involved in the promotion and protection of the right to adequate food • Time frame and coverage of national policy on nutrition and nutrition adequacy norms	• Time frame and coverage of national policy on food safety and consumer protection • Number of registered and/or active civil society organisations working in the area of food safety and consumer protection	• Time frame and coverage of national policy on agricultural production and food availability • Time frame and coverage of national policy on drought, crop failure and disaster management	
	• Proportion of received complaints on the right to adequate food investigated and adjudicated by the national human rights institution, human rights ombudsperson or other mechanisms and the proportion of these responded to effectively by the government • Net official development assistance (ODA) for food security received or provided as a proportion of public expenditure on food security or Gross National Income			
Process	• Proportion of targeted population that was brought above the minimum level of dietary energy consumption* in the reporting period • Proportion of targeted population covered under public nutrition supplement programmes • Coverage of targeted population under public programmes on nutrition education and awareness • Proportion of targeted population that was extended access to an improved drinking water source* in the reporting period	• Disposal rate or average time to adjudicate a case registered in a consumer court • Share of public social sector budget spent on food safety and consumer protection advocacy, education, research and implementation of law and regulations relevant to the right • Proportion of food-producing and -distributing establishments inspected for food quality standards and frequency of inspections • Proportion of cases adjudicated under food safety and consumer protection law in the reporting period	• Proportion of female-headed households or targeted population with legal title to agricultural land • Arable irrigated land per person • Proportion of farmers availing extension services • Share of public budget spent on strengthening domestic agricultural production (e.g. agriculture-extension, irrigation, credit, marketing) • Proportion of per capita availability of major food items sourced through domestic production, import and food aid • Cereal import dependency ratio in the reporting period	• Share of household consumption of major food items for targeted population group met through publicly assisted programmes • Unemployment rate or average wage rate of targeted segments of labour force • Proportion of targeted population that was brought above the poverty line in the reporting period • Work participation rates, by sex and target groups • Estimated access of women and girls to adequate food within household • Coverage of programmes to secure access to productive resources for target groups
Outcome	• Prevalence of underweight and stunted children under five years of age* • Proportion of adults with body-mass index (BMI) < 18.5	• Number of recorded deaths and incidence of food poisoning related to adulterated food	• Per capita availability of major food items of local consumption	• Proportion of population below minimum level of dietary energy consumption* / proportion of under-nourished population • Average household expenditure on food for the bottom three deciles of population or targeted population
	• Death rates, including infant and under-five mortality rates, associated with and prevalence of malnutrition (including under/overnutrition and inadequate intake of nutrients)			
	All indicators should be disaggregated by prohibited grounds of discrimination, as applicable and reflected in metasheets			

[1] Report on Indicators for Monitoring Compliance with International Human Rights Instruments, UN doc. HRI/MC/2006/7 (11 May 2006) 24.

9.9   THE RIGHT TO HEALTH

Just like other ESC rights, health is a necessary condition for the achievement of all other civil and political as well as economic and social freedoms and entitlements. Yet although all nations aspire to have healthy populations that are productive, they are at the same time wary of investing a large part of their GDP in health-related expenditures because of the spiralling costs of health care. As a result, a number of countries have turned to private health provision in order to redistribute public wealth in other areas of concern. The obvious problem in such cases is that those who cannot afford private health care will suffer ill health or even lose their lives.

Article 12(1) of the ICESCR provides a 'right of everyone to the highest attainable standard of physical and mental health'.[115] It is evident that the Covenant does not articulate a right to be healthy, which cannot be guaranteed even by the best possible medical attention.[116] Rather, it recognises the right to enjoy high standards of health, which represents a proposition that is largely dependent on a series of positive obligations. These obligations are of a twofold nature: on the one hand they require the provision of adequate health care services, while on the other they oblige the authorities to satisfy the underlying determinants of health, including basic shelter, food, water, sanitation, safe working environment, freedom from pollution, disease prevention and others.[117] This definition of the right to health with its two corresponding components is broader than the definition of 'health' in the preamble to the Constitution of the WHO, which defines health as a 'state of complete physical, mental and social well-being and not merely the absence of disease or infirmity'.[118] Although health and well-being can never adequately be subject to quantitative computation, health indicators can paint a relatively clear picture about the availability and accessibility of health care. Article 12(2) of the ICESCR and article 24(2) of the CRC demand at the very least: (1) the reduction of stillbirth rates and infant mortality and healthy development of the child; (2) improvement of environmental and industrial hygiene; (3) prevention, treatment and control of epidemic, endemic and other diseases; (4) provision of necessary medical assistance and health care to all children; (5) the combating of child disease and malnutrition; and (6) ensuring appropriate pre-natal and post-natal health care for mothers.

---

[115] Similarly worded provisions are found also in art. 5 ICERD; art. 12 CEDAW; art. 24 CRC; art. 10 San Salvador Protocol; art. 16 ACHPR; art. 11 European Social Charter.

[116] CESCR, General Comment 14, paras. 8–9.

[117] Ibid., para. 11.

[118] Ibid., para. 4. The difference here is justified by the fact that the WHO definition focuses on structural factors (system), whereas the right to health is centred on individual health.

Neither the Covenant nor the CESCR requires that health care and its socio-economic necessities be provided free of charge. The CESCR does, however, emphasise that health care must be available, affordable and offered without discrimination.[119] Affordability should not be construed narrowly. For example, persons who can purchase medicines and treatment by paying 20 per cent of their monthly salary cannot be said to afford their medicines in the same way as others forced to sell their house. Affordability, therefore, must be assessed by reference to a person's material capacity to live a dignified life. This has certainly been the position of the South African and Argentine Constitutional and Supreme Courts respectively in their dealings with HIV/AIDS sufferers who could not afford access to essential drugs. Although, as already explained, the South African Constitutional Court chooses to justify government restrictions only if they are reasonable, in the *Treatment Action Campaign* case it could find no reasonable basis for withholding a drug which prevented the transmission of HIV by mothers to their newborn.[120] Its Argentine counterpart has not demanded reasonableness in its ruling favouring unimpeded access to life-saving medicines, although this is probably implicit in its judgments. Rather, its primary consideration was the direct constitutional stipulation and the internationally recognised rights to life and health.[121]

A significant dimension in the interpretation of the right to health is that of gender. Women are routinely given no voice as regards their sexual reproductive rights and little attention is paid to their particular health risks, especially pre-natal care, child mortality and the effects of domestic violence.[122] It is imperative, therefore, that states be obliged to integrate a gender perspective in their national health plans.[123] In 1991 the Philippines delegated responsibility for 'people's health and safety' to local governments. The city of Manila issued executive order EO 003 whereby it adopted an affirmative prolife stance, thus denying affordable access to contraception, sexual health

---

[119] Ibid., para. 12.

[120] *South African Minister of Health* v. *Treatment Action Campaign.* This case seems to contradict *Soobramoney* v. *Minister of Health, KwaZulu-Natal* (South Africa) (1998), where the Court ruled that the authorities were right in prioritising the distribution of scarce medical resources and as a result refused dialysis treatment to an elderly patient who later died. Even so, *Soobramoney* should not be read as a denial of affordable health care. This result is further fortified by public health exceptions to intellectual property rights. See Chapter 20.4.

[121] *Asociación Benghalensis and Others* v. *Ministerio de Salud y Acción Social* (Argentina) (2000).

[122] In *Government of Namibia* v. *LM and Others* (Namibia) (2014), the Namibian Supreme Court accepted that HIV-infected women had been forcibly sterilised without their consent, an occurrence that is widespread in Africa.

[123] CESCR, General Comment 14, paras. 20–1.

information and related services. This situation culminated in unsafe abortions, maternal deaths, diseases (including HIV/AIDS), exposure of vulnerable women in abusive relationships and other calamities. The Committee on the Elimination of Discrimination against Women (CtEDAW) found this situation to constitute a systematic violation of access to affordable health care and family planning and emphasised that such delegation of powers does not extinguish the primary human rights obligations of the federal state.[124]

Perhaps more than any other ESC right, the realisation of both strands of the right to health in developing countries is dependent significantly on international cooperation. What is striking in the modern world is that technological advances in medicine and drugs do not translate into an enhancement of the living standards of the billions of poor. This has given rise to a conflict between the right to health on the one hand and the right of pharmaceutical companies to protect their patented drugs from being manufactured and sold at smaller cost by generic producers. This tension is explained more fully in Chapter 20. It suffices therefore here simply to iterate the trend whereby developing nations are now able to produce generic (cheap) drugs in order to protect their indigent populations from the spread of easily treatable diseases and infections. Courts in countries where poverty is rife, but with industries able to produce cheap generic drugs, routinely develop legal arguments in order to deny the original patent-holder of exclusive rights. The Indian High Court, for example, has denied the existence of so-called patent linkage, which would have otherwise prevented the licensing of generic drugs by non-patent holders.[125]

INTERVIEW 9.1

Greek NGO Implements the Right to Health for the Socially Excluded
(Tzanetos Antypas)

Tzanetos Antypas was Director of Praksis, a Greek NGO active in the creation, application and implementation of programmes related to the provision of humanitarian and medical services, particularly to socially excluded groups.[1] The timing of the interview is significant, because it took place in 2011, at a time when Greece's sovereign creditors had not yet imposed the full range of austerity measures.

---

[1] Translation from Greek was carried out by the authors. The organisation's website is online at www.praksis.gr/.

---

[124] CtEDAW, Inquiry concerning the Philippines, UN doc. CEDAW/C/OP.8/PHL/1 (22 April 2015).
[125] *Bayer Corp and Another* v. *Union of India and Others* (India) (2010). The court went on to add that patent protection was now often viewed as 'the ugly face of globalization, seemingly a hazard to public health and travesty of social justice'.

According to your analyses, how many people in Greece, both immigrants and Greeks, lack access to public health care services and why?

On the basis of our data, it is evident that the situation is different for the two population groups. As far as third country nationals are concerned, their legal status determines their access to public health care. Even so, it is possible to estimate that one third of third country nationals living in Athens and visiting our clinic have problems accessing public health care services. For people without proper documentation, in particular [i.e. illegal entrants], things are quite hard indeed. They do not have access to any public health care service, save for emergencies, which are treated with some cost to the patient and are available only during the duration of the emergency itself.

As regards Greek nationals served by our services we observed a rather acute increase in the number of patients visiting our clinics, at a rate of 15 per cent, which accounts mainly for pharmaceutical and medical treatment.

How does your organisation substitute the absence of the state?

Through the provision of entry-level medical services via our clinics in Athens and Thessaloniki, which have been working since 1996 and 1997 respectively, Praksis is able to serve indigent segments of the population that face hurdles in accessing public health care facilities. Such populations include the Greek indigent, homeless, uninsured persons, financial immigrants, asylum seekers, refugees and any other socially excluded and vulnerable group such as addicts, Roma, trafficking victims, those released from prison, street children, as well as any person with poor access to health care, psycho-social or legal support.

What are the principal medical and social needs of the increasing poor population?

Principal needs mainly consist of pharmaceutical drugs for chronic illnesses (given that these increase the cost of living in the long run), as well as the treatment of illnesses caused by poor living conditions. Moreover, dental treatment is in high demand by a large segment of the people treated in our clinics because it is a service that is costly and is not offered free of charge by the national health system, whether for Greeks or third country nationals living in Greece.

What measures would you recommend for the application of the right to health in respect of all those living in Greece, taking into consideration the country's financial situation?

Support and reinforcement of [private not-for-profit] organisations and groups that are active in the provision of health care services to vulnerable populations, since such groups and organisations are able to cover the needs of said populations with far lower cost in comparison to public entities;

support and reinforcement of private initiative in the provision of pharmaceutical products. In other words, there needs to be support for the production of drugs by Greek pharmaceutical companies since this would decrease the cost of health care generally in public hospitals, as well as the cost to patients;

decentralisation of the health system through the support of regional health care institutions (for example support for community medical centres) since these will end up receiving the bulk of referrals and incidents that demand entry-level treatment at lower cost in comparison to a centralized institution with similar referrals and incidents;

promulgation of a law detailing relevant procedures for the legalisation of newly arrived third party nationals. The legalisation of their residence in Greece will culminate in the payment of national insurance premiums which ultimately will lead to increased earnings for the national health system.

9.10   THE RIGHT TO WATER

Water is a limited natural resource that is essential for the preservation of life, in addition to its utility in cooking food, sanitation and sewerage, personal hygiene and religious rites, among others. In 2011 it was estimated that nearly one billion people lacked access to an improved source of drinking water and 2.6 billion did not have access to improved sanitation.[126] This is a far cry from the targets set by the MDGs and the failure is largely the result of inadequate funding, but also poor water management and absence of a clear vision.

Before examining the particular contours of the right to water it is necessary to emphasise that it is a resource that is freely given (unlike, for example, agriculture, which requires cultivation of seeds). Thus, if it is to be treated as a good, or commodity, the value of water should reflect only the investment necessary to clean, purify and transport it to households. Even so, given that it constitutes an ingredient of life, by denying it to those who cannot afford to pay its additional investment cost, one is necessarily depriving the poor of their right to life. This tension is particularly reflected in those countries that possess limited water resources and those that have privatised their water distribution systems. It is also useful to point out that domestic water consumption accounts for less than 10 per cent of total use,

---

[126] SR Report on the Human Right to Safe Drinking Water and Sanitation, UN doc. A/66/255 (3 August 2011) paras. 9–12.

the rest being consumed by irrigation in agriculture and industry. This does not mean that agriculture should cease, but certain sectors that consume high levels of water, such as cotton, should not be given priority over food crops and domestic use, especially where water is scarce.

The right to water has been affirmed by the CESCR by reference to the right to an adequate standard of living in article 11(1) of the ICESCR. While this provision does not specifically mention water, its list of essentials (i.e. food, clothing and housing) is merely indicative through the word 'including'.[127] Given that the right to the highest attainable standard of health requires water for drinking and sanitation,[128] it is equally implicit in this right also. It is also implicit in the right to life, among others, as already stated.[129] In its General Comment 15, dedicated especially to the right to water, the CESCR elaborated the particular qualities of this entitlement. The right contemplates a degree of adequacy which, according to the CESCR, should not be measured merely according to volumetric quantities.[130] In practice, however, most institutions follow the WHO Guidelines on Domestic Water Quantity, Service Level and Health, which sets fifty litres per person daily as the minimum for basic hygienic and consumption requirements.[131]

The South African Supreme Court in *Mazibuko and Others* v. *City of Johannesburg* adopted a different approach. One of the issues in the case concerned the installation of a pre-paid meter in an impoverished Soweto neighbourhood that allocated twenty-five litres per person daily (ten kilolitres monthly per household being free of charge), well below the WHO's Guidelines. In keeping with earlier jurisprudence, the Court refused to determine a minimum core, adding that the City was not under a constitutional obligation to provide any particular amount of free water; rather, it was under a duty to take reasonable measures progressively to realise the achievement of the right. The Court found the policy to be reasonable because it charged excessive use, avoided waste and catered to everyone's needs, including the provision of free water for the indigent.[132]

---

[127] UNGA resolution 64/292 (28 July 2010) explicitly recognised the right to water as a distinct entitlement.

[128] For the importance of sanitation as a fundamental component of the right to water, see CESCR, General Comment 15, para. 29.

[129] It is also directly recognised as a distinct right in a long list of international instruments, including art. 14(2)(h) CEDAW, art. 24(2) CRC, art. 28(2)(a) CRPD and in numerous provisions of international humanitarian law.

[130] CESCR, General Comment 15, para. 11.

[131] Online at www.who.int/water_sanitation_health/diseases/WSH03.02.pdf.

[132] *Mazibuko and Others* v. *City of Johannesburg* (South Africa) (2009) paras. 77ff., per O'Regan J.

Water must be of a specified quality, in the sense that it must be safe for consumption and thus free from micro-organisms, chemicals and other substances.[133] It should moreover be accessible to individual users, both physically and economically.[134] It is not always feasible to bring water into houses in shanty towns or dwellings in remote villages because of the lack of infrastructure. None the less, it is accepted that water should be within reasonable walking distance, otherwise physical accessibility is essentially denied. The CESCR emphasises that water must be 'affordable for all', not necessarily free for all. This is subject to several reservations. First, there exists a 'special obligation' to provide water and sanitation to those who cannot afford them, including marginalised and vulnerable groups.[135] Secondly, the concept of affordability means that water charges may be set in such a way that higher- and middle-income people subsidise those on lower incomes, with a view to the latter enjoying water free of charge or at very little cost.[136] This is the case, for example, with the Chilean Law 18,788, where the subsidisation of water is assessed on the income of households.[137] States can additionally minimise water prices by the adaptation of low-cost techniques and technologies.[138] Finally, the price of water should not be susceptible to commodity-like fluctuations or the interventions of private water providers[139] and thus must be treated as a public good.

The obligation to provide water of a decent quality and quantity to all people is meaningless if states are not under compulsion to protect the environment where potable water is found. More so, states are responsible for preserving and augmenting their water resources so that they can be available for future generations.[140]

---

[133] CESCR, General Comment 15, para. 12(b). Guaranteed also in arts. 23 and 42 of the Ecuador Constitution. The Indian Supreme Court in *Subhash Kumar* v. *State of Bihar and Others* (India) (1991), held that the right to life guaranteed under art. 21 of the Constitution encompasses the enjoyment of pollution-free water.

[134] General Comment 15, para. 12(c).

[135] Ibid., para. 15.

[136] In fact, the Special Rapporteur on water and sanitation in her 2011 Report, para. 19, stresses that 'obtaining water at no cost may actually harm low-income households by depriving service providers of the revenue needed to expand and maintain the service and risks being unsustainable'.

[137] Centre on Housing Rights and Evictions (COHRE), *Legal Resources for the Right to Water and Sanitation* (2008) 77.

[138] General Comment 15, para. 27.

[139] Ibid., para. 24.   [140] Ibid., para. 28.

CASE STUDY 9.3
The Deprivation of Water Rights as Cruel and Inhuman Treatment

In *Mosetlhanyane and Others* v. *Attorney-General (Kalahari Bushmen case)*,[1] the Botswana Court of Appeal was confronted with a claim by a group of Kalahari bushmen who had occupancy rights over an arid land but who were not permitted by the government to extract underground water. In fact, a mining company had originally dug a deep hole in the area, which once abandoned was fitted with a pump and had since been used by the indigenous group for extracting underground water, this being their only source of water. The government recognised, albeit reluctantly, that although the indigenous group possessed occupancy rights,[2] all underground streams were public property and were not subject to unilateral use, even by the land's super-adjacent occupants. In court it was shown that the lack of water had caused a number of maladies to the bushmen. The Court cited with approval General Comment 15 of the CESCR and held that it was irrational for one to possess occupancy rights but not water rights, especially if no other water is available, in which case the person was effectively denied his right of occupancy. As a result, the bushmen were granted water rights in a quantity that was necessary for their needs.

The Court went on to invoke article 7(1) of the Constitution, which protects all persons from inhuman or degrading treatment. It held that the deprivation of water to a population lawfully occupying land which was arid amounted to such treatment and ordered the authorities to restore the applicant's pump.

[1] *Mosetlhanyane and Others* v. *Attorney-General (Kalahari Bushmen case)* (Botswana) (2011).
[2] The group's occupancy rights were recognised a few years prior in *Sesana and Others* v. *Attorney-General* (Botswana) (2006).

9.11   THE RIGHT TO EDUCATION

Education and its availability raise two practical issues. First, while the provision of quality education is expensive, no meaningful development can be achieved without it. The lack of education is a particular characteristic of those living in extreme or moderate poverty. The US Supreme Court in its landmark case of *Brown* v. *Board of Education* noted that 'it is doubtful that any child may reasonably be expected to succeed in life if he is denied the opportunity of an education'.[141] Secondly, without a quality education most

[141] *Brown* v. *Board of Education of Topeka* (US) (1954) at 493.

civil and political rights are meaningless. Freedom of expression, assembly, democratic governance and others can only be realised if the rights-holders are capable of understanding and pursuing their rights in the first place. Since the drafting of article 13 of the ICESCR on the right to education, a number of controversies have arisen. Chief among these is the spiralling cost of public education, particularly in an era of financial constraint, which has caused many nations to partially privatise elements of their educational system or otherwise introduce direct and indirect user fees. Other controversies include discrimination in the quality of education provided to vulnerable groups, which leads to their social exclusion.

Besides the ICESCR, the right to education is enshrined, among others, in article 17(1) of the ACHPR, articles 3 and 13 of the San Salvador Protocol, article 2 of Protocol I to the European Convention on Human Rights (ECHR), article 11(3) of the 1999 African Charter on the Rights and Welfare of the Child, article 5(e)(v) of the International Convention on the Elimination of All Forms of Racial Discrimination (ICERD), article 28 of the CRC and article 8(1) of the Declaration on the Right to Development. Moreover, the preamble to the UNESCO Constitution elevates education to a sacred duty because it leads to the achievement of dignity, understanding of peoples, development and the exchange of ideas and knowledge. All of these instruments to a large degree converge as to the projected aims and objectives of education, which also determine its quality. Thus, education must be directed towards the full development of the human personality, human dignity, enable persons to effectively participate in a free society and promote understanding between all groups and nations. In more recent years, two further elements have been recognised by the CESCR as inherent to this process: gender equality and respect for the environment.[142]

Education is distinguished on the basis of three layers, each corresponding to a more advanced level of study, namely primary, secondary and tertiary (or university) education. In between these there are several sub-categories, particularly basic, technical or vocational education. Article 13(2)(a) of the ICESCR expressly stipulates that primary education should be universal, without discrimination, and provided free of charge irrespective of a country's financial situation.[143] This is an immediate, not a progressive duty,

---

[142] CESCR, General Comment 13, UN doc. E/C12/1999/10 (8 December 1999) para. 5.

[143] In *SERAC* v. *Federal Republic of Nigeria and Universal Basic Education Commission*, the Nigerian government argued that because of corruption, funds destined for the realisation of basic and primary education were no longer available. As a result, it was unable to fulfil its pertinent obligations. The ECOWAS Court held that the right to primary education is universal and not subject to any resource limitations and ordered Nigeria to rectify the situation.

despite the fact that public resources in the form of teachers' salaries, school buildings and books are required.[144] Yet even if governments secure all the necessities for free education, a number of marginalised children may still be excluded through indirect costs.[145] For example, physical inaccessibility will naturally hinder children living in remote areas from travelling to school several miles away. The same is true of schools demanding specific uniforms and books, the cost of which burdens those families who cannot afford them. The CESCR noted in respect of Paraguay, for example, that because many rural schools do not have adequate, separate toilet facilities for each sex, this has a deterrent effect on school attendance among girls and teenagers.[146] Finally, the universality of primary education means that states must take appropriate measures to compel all children to attend primary school, despite the misgivings of their parents, whether because children are considered breadwinners or because of gender discrimination, in addition to cultural practices and beliefs. Although the CESCR has explained that primary education must 'take into account the culture, needs and opportunities of the community',[147] this should not be used as a guise for social exclusion. Consider a situation where the children of a marginalised ethnic minority within country X are given free education only through their minority language, but not in the dominant language. Although this might seem to satisfy the cultural needs of the minority, it perpetuates the social exclusion of the group's new generation and its continued marginalisation.[148] This is why it is imperative that minority members receive a broad education equal to that of the majority,[149] unless the difference in treatment is based on objective and reasonable justification.[150]

---

[144] See *Madzodzo and Others* v. *Minister of Basic Education.*

[145] Although the ICESCR does not impose an obligation on parties to provide day-care and preschool access, the Brazilian Federal Supreme Court has inferred such an obligation from the country's constitutional mandate regarding the right to education: case *RE 436996/SP* (Brazil) (2005).

[146] CESCR Concluding Observations on Paraguay, UN doc. E/C.12/PRY/CO/4 (20 March 2015) para. 30.

[147] Ibid., at para. 31, regarding the failure of Paraguay to promote the preservation and use of indigenous languages; CESCR, General Comment 13, para. 9. Culturally sensitive education was endorsed as far back as 1935 by the Permanent Court of International Justice (PCIJ) in the case concerning *Minority Schools in Albania* (PCIJ) (1935) at 3, 17.

[148] The HRCtee in its concluding observations on Georgia pointed out that the lack of Georgian language skills 'could lead to marginalization and under-representation of minorities in different public and private spheres'; UN doc. CCPR/C/GEO/CO/3 (15 November 2007) para. 17.

[149] Art. 4(4), 1992 UN Declaration on Minority Rights.

[150] In *D. H. and Others* v. *Czech Republic* (ECtHR) (2008) para. 196, the ECtHR held that where a difference in treatment is based on race or ethnicity, 'the notion of objective and reasonable justification must be interpreted as strictly as possible'.

As far as secondary and university education are concerned, article 13 of the ICESCR makes some practical distinctions. Unlike primary education, which must be compulsory and universal, secondary education is to be made generally available and accessible to all, but its fee component is subject to progressive, as opposed to immediate, realisation. University education must equally be made accessible to all, but unlike the other two layers there does not exist a general right to higher education. Rather, accessibility is assessed by capacity alone, which is measured by a degree of competition between candidates. Although states are under an obligation to progressively abolish fees in public universities in accordance with article 13(2)(c) of the ICESCR, this should not be given a restrictive interpretation. In countries like the UK, which have introduced significant higher education fees, prospective students are not required to pay upfront and are eligible for low-interest, subsidised loans that also cover their accommodation and maintenance. These loans are repayable only when students start earning an average salary. The fees in this case, although clearly retrogressive, link education with a guarantee of employability and should not be viewed as an absolute denial of higher education rights.

9.12   THE RIGHT TO FOOD

Despite human advances in sciences, close to one billion people currently suffer from under-nourishment.[151] This number is staggering if one considers that under-nourishment exists when caloric intake is below the minimum dietary energy requirements (MDER) and is essentially a synonym for hunger. This situation is unjustifiable because the global food crisis is not the result of food shortage; rather, it is the result of poor availability and accessibility on account of socio-economic factors. Food crises, also described as famines, began to receive media attention in the late 1970s and were originally viewed from a humanitarian perspective. Essentially, the international community undertook an anti-hunger role through the provision of relief shipments to the destitute. However, from the mid-1990s onwards it became evident that a combination of sharp population increases, climatic change, commodification of agricultural produce, uneven trade liberalisation in the agricultural sector and poor crop management and sustainability had led to soaring food prices beyond the reach of the poor. The problem could no longer be handled through anti-hunger policies, but instead required a holistic approach to the question of food accessibility and availability.

---

[151] FAO, *The State of Food Insecurity in the World* (2010) 8.

This holistic approach is encapsulated in the right to food, which is articulated in article 11 of the ICESCR.[152] There are two strands to this entitlement. In its generic form the right to food is derived from the right to an adequate standard of living, whereby food must be available 'in a quantity and quality sufficient to satisfy the dietary needs of [all] individuals, free from adverse substances and acceptable within a given culture', while at the same time its availability must be sustainable and should not interfere with the enjoyment of other human rights.[153] Thus, food need not necessarily be dispensed by the state for free, but the state is under a concrete obligation to take all means at its disposal to make food affordable and available to all with a view to securing a dignified life.[154] States are certainly able to increase food production by, among other things, subsidising small-scale farming, as well as decreasing the cost of food through the elimination of taxes and tariffs on basic foods. In addition, as already discussed, they can impose a tax on the wealthy to offset the residual cost of food production in favour of the poor. Equally, apart from its positive obligations, the state should refrain from action that removes existing access to food, particularly mass displacement, introduction of toxic substances into the food chain and others of a similar nature.[155] In the *Ogoniland* case, for example, the Nigerian government had allowed foreign oil companies to take over the land occupied by the Ogoni, thus leading to widespread land and water contamination and expulsion through terror tactics. All of this resulted, as the ACHPR pointed out, in the violation of the Ogoni's right to food.[156] Strategic litigation concerned with the right to food in the developing world challenges the soundness of food and agricultural concessions to foreign investors in situations where local communities rely on those resources for their survival.[157]

The other component of the right to food is the right to be free from hunger, articulated in paragraph 2 of article 11 of the ICESCR. Although this

---

[152] The right to food is also protected in art. 25 UDHR; arts. 12 and 14 CEDAW; arts. 25 and 27 CRC; and arts. 12, 15, 17 of the San Salvador Protocol, albeit the right to food is not directly justiciable in the Protocol. The right to food was also explicitly recognised in principle 3 of the 2009 FAO Declaration of the World Summit on Food Security, FAO doc. WSFP 2009/2 (16–18 November 2009). See FAO, 'The Right to Food and Access to Justice: Examples at the National, Regional and International Levels' (2009).

[153] CESCR, General Comment 12, paras. 6–8.

[154] Special Rapporteur on the right to food, Report on the Right to Food, UN doc. E/CN4/2001/ 53 (7 February 2001) para. 14.

[155] Special Rapporteur on the right to food, Report on the Right to Food, UN doc. E/CN4/2006/ 44 (16 March 2006) para. 22.

[156] *SERAC and Center for Economic and Social Rights* v. *Nigeria* (ACmHPR) (2001) paras. 65–6.

[157] See e.g., *Jagannath* v. *Union of India and Others* (India) (1997), where the Indian Supreme Court upheld the traditional fishing rights of a coastal community whose access to food (fish) was curtailed by the issuance of limited fishing licences to private investors.

provision largely describes the measures required of states unilaterally and collectively, the right to be free from hunger has been viewed by the CESCR as a minimum core obligation as follows:

Every state is obliged to ensure for everyone under its jurisdiction access to the minimum essential food which is sufficient, nutritionally adequate and safe, to ensure their freedom from hunger.[158]

The right to be free from hunger best addresses the plight and food needs of peoples and populations. First, it requires states to plan ahead by, for example, improving methods of production or introducing appropriate food conservation on the basis of scientific knowledge.[159] Its second dimension entails the urgent distribution of food to those who are destitute and in circumstances where food is inaccessible. Such situations are typical not only in the aftermath of an earthquake, tsunami or other natural disaster, but also where people have been displaced or are habitually excluded from enjoying food. This latter category is usually forgotten by governments on account of their low socio-economic status – coupled with a complete lack of basic education – which means that whatever their personal circumstances they possess little, or no, voting power.

The *Rajasthan Hunger* case[160] is instructive of this particular dimension. As an introduction to the case it should be pointed out that India and China account for 40 per cent of the world's undernourished population.[161] In terms of actual numbers, 200 million Indians fall within this category and it is not surprising that in their majority they comprise Dalits ('untouchables'), women, poor tribal communities, children and other vulnerable populations living on the fringes of society. It is estimated that up to 2 million children die every year in India as a direct or indirect result of under-nourishment.[162] By 2001 a growing number of hunger-related deaths were unfolding in Rajasthan, despite the existence of sufficient food supplies in nearby government storage. In fact, the food was left to rot and was reportedly in the process of being eaten by rodents. The underlying government indifference and poor management was found by the Indian Supreme Court to violate the constitutionally recognised right to life (article 21) as read against the directive principle on nutrition contained in article 47 of the Constitution. The government not only refused to implement the Indian Famine Code, which

---

[158] CESCR, General Comment 12, para. 14.

[159] Art. 11(2)(a) ICESCR.

[160] *People's Union for Civil Liberties* v. *Union of India and Others* (India) (2003). See also *Kishen Pattnayak and Another* v. *State of Orissa* (India) (1989), where the right to food as a corollary to the right to life was first expounded.

[161] FAO, *The State of Food Insecurity in the World*, above note 151, at 10.

[162] Special Rapporteur, Report on the Right to Food, above note 155, para. 7.

permitted the release of grain stocks in situations of famine, but further argued that it did not have sufficient resources as a result of the crisis. The Court naturally dismissed all these arguments and went on to issue several directives to the authorities demanding that they identify beneficiaries and make food accessible to them.[163]

A similar result was reached by the Colombian Constitutional Court in the *Abel Antonio Jaramillo* case.[164] There, thousands of internally displaced persons were left without any assistance by the Colombian authorities, including food. The Court held that the exposure of these people to conditions of food deprivation, among others, was a violation of their right to food, the minimum requirements of which the state was under an obligation to provide to all in need. It went on to request the authorities to formulate an adequate plan to assist the victims. In similar fashion, the Supreme Court of Nepal in a judgment issued in April 2011 examined the plight of several districts facing acute food shortages with an estimated under-nourished population of 300,000. While reaffirming the constitutional right to food, it held that the state must take every available measure to protect its citizens from food scarcity caused by natural disaster.[165]

The right to food should be examined by reference to two important international efforts to boost global food supplies and prevent hunger. These consist of the 1996 Rome Declaration on World Food Security, reviewed thereafter through a series of World Food Summits (WFS) organised by the FAO and the UN's SDGs. Some countries have criticised the absence of any mention of the root causes of global food insecurity from FAO summits and declarations, particularly the impact of agricultural subsidies on poor farmers, the conversion of grains and cereals into fuel, the consequences of financial speculation on food prices and the imposition of conditionalities on developing nations. Indeed, developed nations are disinclined to discuss such issues in the context of food security alone and prefer to incorporate them in the agenda of the World Trade Organization (WTO).

A significant achievement of the 2002 WFS was the subsequent endorsement in 2004 of a set of Voluntary Guidelines on the Progressive Realisation of the Right to Adequate Food in the Context of National Food Security. The importance of the guidelines lies in the fact that they were endorsed by all WFS not only as a matter of policy but also as pledged targets. Increasingly, they are also relied on by governments and the courts. The aforementioned Nepalese Supreme Court judgment seems to have been influenced by several sections of the guidelines.

---

[163] See FAO, *The State of Food Insecurity in the World*, above note 151, at 26, 56–7.
[164] *Abel Antonio Jaramillo and Others* v. *La Red de Solidaridad Social and Others* (Colombia) (2004) at 25.
[165] Reported by www.fao.org/righttofood/news-and-events/news-detail/en/c/124029/.

QUESTIONS

1. If a state has inadequate water resources, is it justified in rationing water to its people even slightly below the minimum threshold stipulated by the WHO?

2. Free-market economists argue that states should not intervene in the running and operation of markets because this does not allow them to reach their full potential, which in turn would create numerous benefits for societies. Critically discuss, with reference to the global surge in food prices which exposes three-quarters of the world's population to acute food deprivation although there is enough food for everyone.

3. There is an inherent tension between the values protected under intellectual property law (i.e. the property rights of the inventor) and the right of the sick and suffering to life-saving medicines in accordance with the right to health. Discuss.

4. Why is it important that benchmarks be agreed to by the target state and adapted to its particular circumstances?

5. When dealing with private actors that dispense in substance those ESC rights guaranteed by the state (for example, water and sewerage, private social security and health care) are the remedies available under human rights law more effective for the victims? It may be argued that if victims were assimilated to consumers clearly enjoying the pertinent ESC rights they could turn against the providers of services on the basis of both contract and tort. In this manner they could enforce their rights directly against the 'violators'. Discuss.

9.13   CULTURAL RIGHTS

All rights encompass a cultural dimension and it is within this that all rights must be implemented. It should be noted, however, that practices perpetuating inequality and which are antithetical to universal notions of rights have no place in human rights discourse, even if branded as cultural. The existence of cultural rights as such presupposes both a 'culture' or 'cultures' and the notion of 'cultural identity'. When we talk about the mores and norms associated with a grouping of individuals (society or social system) what we are really investigating is the culture of the group. Culture, in its anthropological sense, consists of a set of shared meanings communicated by language or other forms (e.g. symbols) between group members.[166] The role

---

[166] But see also the definition of 'culture' in art 2(a) of the Fribourg Declaration on Cultural Rights.

of the anthropologist is to first 'discover' these shared meanings and then translate them into (same, similar, approximate or other) concepts which the observer clearly understands. In its more narrow sense, it comprises cultural (group) identity as a way of life and intangible heritage. 'Cultural identity' may be understood as 'the sum of all cultural references through which a person, alone or in community with others, defines or constitutes oneself, communicates or wishes to be recognized in one's dignity.[167] Its meaning and scope has been the subject of debate. It is perhaps for this reason that a right to a cultural identity, although 'extensively discussed' at least since the early 1980s at UNESCO level,[168] has never been explicitly guaranteed in international human rights instruments. Intangible heritage, on the other hand, has been held to include the arts, native languages, literature, food, cult, religious traditions, traditional medicines, textile arts and others of similar nature.

The scope of 'cultural rights' has initially orbited around the right 'to take part in cultural life', guaranteed in article 15(1)(a) ICESCR.[169] The meaning of 'cultural life' has evolved over time. In the 1950s, shortly after the UN specialized agency on the protection of education, science and culture (UNESCO) was created, international efforts to protect 'culture' have been confined to the protection of education and the preservation of cultural assets. Debates on cultural identity have been scarce, and even when present, focused primarily on 'race'.[170] It is only in the late 1990s that the need to protect identities in the sense of 'being different' became more visible within the international human rights discourse, encompassing other potential grounds for discrimination such as religion, disability, gender or sexuality. Regional human rights bodies have contributed to the empowerment of cultural identities, dotting them – to some extent – with justiciability. Symonides argued in 1999 that the scope of cultural rights depends on the very meaning that one offers to the term culture: culture may be perceived as 'creative artistic and scientific activities' as well as, in a broader sense, 'the sum of human activities, the totality of values, knowledge and practice'.[171] Yet, under international law, only five human rights are expressly labelled as 'cultural': the right to education; the right to participate in cultural life; the right to enjoy

---

[167] Art 2(b) Fribourg Declaration, ibid.

[168] See Y. Donders, 'A Right to Cultural Identity in UNESCO', in F. Francioni and M. Scheinin (eds.), *Cultural Human Rights* (Brill, 2008) 317, 331.

[169] For a fuller elaboration, see art. 5 of the Fribourg Declaration.

[170] E.g. Declaration on Race and Racial Prejudice, Paris, 27 November 1978, art 1(2): 'All individuals and groups have the right to be different, to consider themselves as different and to be regarded as such', reiterated in the UNESCO Declaration of Principles of Tolerance (1995).

[171] J. Symonides, 'Cultural Rights, A Neglected Category of Rights', in J. Symonides (ed.), *Human Rights: Concepts and Standards* (UNESCO, 1998) 560.

the benefits of scientific progress and its applications; the right to benefit from the protection of the moral and material interests resulting from any scientific, literary or artistic production of which the person is the author, and the freedom of scientific research and creative activity'.[172]

The IACHR has developed a pioneering jurisprudence in relation to indigenous cultural rights,[173] as has the IACtHR,[174] while the 2016 American Declaration on Indigenous Rights has been a unique instrument affirming 'the right of indigenous persons to their own cultural identity and cultural heritage'.[175] The ECtHR has underlined the importance of minority cultural identities for the preservation of cultural diversity – and this, despite the a priori exclusion of cultural rights from its mandate. By way of example, in relation to several joint cases related to Roma evictions by the British authorities the Court underlined the importance of cultural diversity and pluralism within society by stating that the preservation of cultural diversity 'is of value to the whole community'.[176] More recently, in relation to the rights of the Polish minority of Upper Silesia, the grand Chamber of the Court hailed cultural diversity and minority consciousness, by stating that 'pluralism is also built on the genuine recognition of, and respect for, diversity and the dynamics of cultural traditions, ethnic and cultural identities, religious beliefs, artistic, literary and socio-economic ideas and concepts' and that 'the harmonious interaction of persons and groups with varied identities is essential for achieving social cohesion'.[177] 'Cultural identities' in the UNESCO Convention on the Protection of Cultural Diversity (2005) play a central role, especially in connection to the preservation of cultural diversity and an entitlement to receive quality education.[178]

---

[172] See 'Right to take part in cultural life' (article 15(1)(a) of the Covenant), Background paper submitted to the CESCR, UN doc. E/C.12/40/9 (9 May 2008) and generally, S. Borelli and F. Lenzerini (eds.), *Cultural Heritage, Cultural Rights, Cultural Diversity* (Brill, 2012); E. Stamatopoulou, *Cultural Rights in International Law* (Martinus Nijhoff, 2007).

[173] By way of example, see *Case of Plan de Sánchez Massacre* v. *Guatemala* (2004) (IACtHR) para. 49; *The Mayagna (Sumo) Awas Tingni Community* v. *Nicaragua* (2001) (IACtHR) para. 135; *Case of Saramaka People* v. *Suriname* (2007) (IACtHR) para. 121; *Comunidad Moiwana* v. *Suriname* (2016) (IACtHR) para. 86.

[174] See *ACHPR* v. *Kenya* (2017), in which it was held that the expulsion of the Ogiek indigenous community from its ancestral land violated its right to culture, as well as its cultural development.

[175] American Declaration on the Rights of Indigenous Peoples (2016) art. 13(1).

[176] *Chapman* v. *UK* [GC] (2001) (ECtHR) para. 93. Cf. the case of *D. H. and Others* v. *The Czech Republic* [GC] (2008) (ECtHR) (concerning compulsory education for Roma in minority schools leading to segregation) and *Muñoz Díaz* v. *Spain* (2008) (ECtHR) (in relation to the recognition of a marriage in Spain celebrated under the Roma traditions).

[177] *Gorzelik and Others* v. *Poland* [GC] (2005) (ECtHR) para. 92.

[178] Arts. 1 and 5.

This said, several developments in international human rights law have resulted in the 'enlargement' of cultural rights. The 'right to participate in cultural life', in particular, has been gradually interpreted so broadly as to include a right of 'access to and enjoyment of cultural heritage'. This is precisely the case with article 15 paragraph 1(a) ICESCR as a starting point that guarantees the right to participate in cultural life. This development coincides with the adoption of General Comment 21 by the CESCR[179] in which it acknowledged a right of access to cultural heritage in article 15 ICESCR.[180] Such recognition is significant given that the protection of cultural heritage was already encompassed in the process of periodic review in relation to article 15 ICESCR – especially the 'promotion of awareness and enjoyment of the cultural heritage of national ethnic groups and minorities and of indigenous peoples'.[181]

But why are cultural rights important? Clearly, they empower human rights discourse. The cultural dimension of human rights law enhances their indivisibility and interdependence. This includes the understanding that challenges for human rights are substantially different in various parts of the world. Freedom of expression and censorship are paradigmatic of the variety of cultural issues raised by an appreciation of culture. For instance, what is the meaning of freedom of expression, or of the arts, in those states that fully control the media or those that systematically impose restrictions? What is the impact on rights when poverty impedes knowledge, or when the absence of libraries, cinemas, or museums hinders cultural exchange and the diffusion of artworks? Equally, what is the impact on rights in states that systematically impose restrictions on the arts and literature, or worse, when dissident (or simply non-conformist) artists impose self-censorship or are forced into exile?

---

[179] CESCR, 'General Comment No. 21, Right of everyone to take part in cultural life (art. 15, para. 1(a), of the International Covenant on Economic, Social and Cultural Rights)', UN doc. E/C.12/GC/21 (21 December 2009).

[180] Ibid., para. 15(b), in which the CESCR flagged that the right to participate in cultural life contains three key components, namely: participation in, access to, and contribution to cultural life. As the Committee points out, 'access to culture' encompasses 'the right of everyone ... to know and understand his or her own culture and that of others through education and information, and to receive quality education and training with due regard for cultural identity', and further, a right 'to benefit from the cultural heritage and the creation of other individuals and communities'. See also the relevant report of the independent expert in the field of cultural rights, Mrs Farida Shaheed, UN doc. A/HRC/17/38 (21 March 2011).

[181] A. Yupsanis, 'The Meaning of "Culture" in Article 15(1)(a) of the ICESCR – Positive Aspects of CESCR's General Comment No. 21 for the safeguarding of minority cultures' (2012) 55 *German YBIL* 345, 359 and fn. 76.

Cultural rights further empower individuals and groups, particularly disadvantaged groups, as right holders of cultural rights – even in respect of primarily individual rights (such as the right to the arts). This freedom of the arts includes the right of the public to access the arts; access to culture for all, or a culture of one's choice; consultation and participation in cultural activities.

Finally, it should not be forgotten that the promotion of cultural diversity and access to culture contributes to understanding cultural and religious diversity, which in turn can lead to the elimination of 'cultural conflicts' that have appeared as 'global controversies'. In fact, due to its social and symbolic functions, as well as its increased capacity to communicate ideas, visual art and other forms of figurative representation constitute extremely fertile ground for the expansion of cultural conflicts. By way of illustration, controversies involving religious beliefs have been pivoting around objects of either artistic or sacred significance: the Christian crucifixes in the case of the Italian public schools, minarets in the case of Switzerland, headscarves in France and the denigrated copies of the Qur'an in Germany have all served as symbols in debates over cultural and religious identities. Access to culture may ultimately serve to emphasise our common heritage rather than differences. Moreover, empowering cultural rights as a whole could potentially offer a more sustainable solution to the debate over freedom of expression and religious sensibilities and contribute to 'cultural peace'.[182]

FURTHER READING

Agbakwa, S., 'Reclaiming Humanity: Economic, Social and Cultural Rights as the Cornerstone of African Human Rights' (2000) 5 *Yale Human Rights and Development Law Journal* 177.

Alston, P., 'US Ratification of the Covenant on Economic, Social and Cultural Rights: The Need for an Entirely New Strategy' (1990) 84 *American Journal of International Law* 365.

Alston, P., and G. Quinn, 'The Nature and Scope of States Parties' Obligations under the International Covenant on Economic, Social and Cultural Rights' (1987) 9 *Human Rights Quarterly* 156.

Baderin, M. A., and R. McCorquodale (eds.), *Economic, Social and Cultural Rights in Action* (Oxford University Press, 2007).

Betten, L., 'The Implementation of Social and Economic Rights by the ILO' (1998) 6 *Netherlands Quarterly of Human Rights* 29.

Bilchitz, D., *Poverty and Fundamental Rights: The Justification and Enforcement of Socio-Economic Rights* (Oxford University Press, 2007).

Cepeda-Espinoza, M. J., 'Transcript: Social and Economic Rights and the Colombian Constitutional Court' (2010–2011) 89 *Texas Law Review* 1699.

Chenwi, L., 'Putting Flesh on the Skeleton: South African Judicial Enforcement of the Right to Adequate Housing of those Subject to Evictions' (2008) 8 *Human Rights Law Review* 105.

Coomans, F. (ed.), *Justiciability of Economic and Social Rights: Experiences from Domestic Systems* (Intersentia, 2006).

Courtis, C., 'The Right to Food as a Justiciable Right: Challenges and Strategies' (2007) 11 *Max Planck Yearbook of UN Law* 317.

---

[182] See E. Polymenopoulou, 'Does One Swallow Make a Spring? Artistic and Literary Freedom at the European Court of Human Rights' (2016) 16 *Human Rights Law Review* 511.

Davies, D. M., 'Socio-economic Rights: Do they Deliver the Goods?' (2008) 6 *International Journal of Constitutional Law* 687.

De Schutter, O., and E. Decaux (eds.), *Commentaire article par article du Pacte international relatif aux droits économiques, sociaux et culturels* (Pedone, 2017).

De Schutter, O. et al. (eds.), *Routledge Handbook of Food as a Commons* (Routledge, 2018).

Filmer-Wilson, E., 'Human Rights-based Approach to Development: The Right to Water' (2005) 23 *Netherlands Quarterly of Human Rights* 213.

Fukuda-Parr, S., T. Lawson-Remer and S. Randolph, *Fulfilling Social and Economic Rights* (Oxford University Press, 2015).

Gauri, V., and D. M. Brinks (eds.), *Courting Social Justice: Judicial Enforcement of Social and Economic Rights in the Developing World* (Cambridge University Press, 2008).

Langford, M., W. Vanderhole and M. Scheinin (eds.), *Global Justice, State Duties: The Extraterritorial Scope of Economic, Social and Cultural Rights in International Law* (Cambridge University Press, 2014).

Leijten, I., *Socio-Economic Rights and the European Court of Human Rights* (Cambridge University Press, 2018).

Minkler, L. (ed.), *The State of Economic and Social Human Rights: A Global Overview* (Cambridge University Press, 2013).

Nolan, A. (ed.), *Economic and Social Rights after the Global Financial Crisis* (Cambridge University Press, 2014).

O'Keefe, R., 'The Right to Take Part in Cultural Life under Article 15 of the ICESCR' (1998) 47 *International & Comparative Law Quarterly* 904.

Polymenopoulou, E., 'Cultural Rights in the Case-law of the International Court of Justice' (2014) 27 *Leiden Journal of International Law* 447.

Riedel, E., G. Giacca, and C. Golay, *Economic, Social and Cultural Rights in International Law: Contemporary Issues and Challenges* (Oxford University Press, 2014).

Saul, B., D. Kinley and J. Mowbray, *The International Covenant on Economic, Social and Cultural Rights: Commentary, Cases and Materials* (Oxford University Press, 2014).

Ssenyonjo, M., *Economic, Social and Cultural Rights in International Law* (Hart, 2016).

Young, K. G., and A. Sen (eds.), *The Future of Economic and Social Rights* (Cambridge University Press, 2019).

Websites

Centre for Economic and Social Rights: www.cesr.org/

CESCR: www.ohchr.org/en/hrbodies/cescr/pages/cescrindex.aspx

ESCR-Net: www.escr-net.org/

Social and Economic Rights Action Center (Nigeria): www.serac.org/

UN Educational, Scientific and Cultural Organization (UNESCO), Culture: http://en.unesco.org/themes/protecting-our-heritage-and-fostering-creativity

UN Special Rapporteur on the right to food: www.ohchr.org/EN/Issues/Food/Pages/FoodIndex.aspx

UN Special Rapporteur on the right to health: www.ohchr.org/EN/Issues/Health/Pages/SRRightHealthIndex.aspx

Hungry Cities: hungrycities.net

10 Group Rights: Self-determination, Minorities and Indigenous Peoples

CONTENTS

10.1 INTRODUCTION

Rights pertaining to groups, as opposed to individual members thereof, are also known as collective rights or solidarity rights. However, not every conceivable group possesses such rights by the mere fact that it is organised as a collective (for example, political parties, activists, persons with disabilities and others are not endowed with collective rights). Rather, collective rights are limited to particular groupings and are typically conferred by treaty, soft law or customary international law. They are premised on the rationale that certain entitlements are meaningless outside the group and that their justiciable character is dependent on the group's continued existence and coherence. Thus, the notion of statehood is redundant without a stable population that wishes to form a nation, and it is exactly in this populace, through its duly appointed representatives, that the state finds expression. As a result, the powers of the state are vested in its people and it is natural that they be endowed with entitlements that cannot be conferred on discrete individuals. By way of illustration, although the right to elect and be elected is meaningful in its personal dimension, the choice to form, secede or unite with another state cannot be exercised individually. Instead, such decisions are best taken by the affected collective acting as a single corpus in accordance with predefined rules. General international law informs a large part of the discussion on group rights, albeit, as will become evident, human rights considerations have increasingly been viewed as central to the rights of peoples.

This chapter will analyse the right of self-determination in respect of its external and internal dimension, the rights of minorities and the rights of indigenous peoples. Self-determination is the point of reference for any discussion of indigenous and minority rights, although it is far broader than both of these. Minority rights in turn are not considered collective entitlements in relevant international human rights instruments. None the less, as the reader will come to appreciate, they are not altogether devoid of a collective character. Indigenous rights are largely based on soft law and some of their fundamental premises (for example, land rights) are hotly disputed by interested states. Yet it is indisputable that the international community recognises that the vulnerable status of indigenous peoples necessitates a distinctive approach based on the adoption of measures that allow the preservation of their culture and traditions, while on the other hand helping them to develop, whether technologically, financially, educationally or otherwise. Group rights are controversial primarily because they give rise to questions of 'us' and 'others' in addition to challenging traditional notions of state sovereignty.

10.2   THE NATURE OF COLLECTIVE RIGHTS

The existence of collective rights is not self-evident. International law is rather hesitant to grant particular rights to groups as such, not because it refuses to acknowledge their distinct identity, but because states are wary of the effects of collective entitlements. There is also the argument in favour of the individualisation of rights in order to offer protection and remedies to the immediate victim. For example, the killing by police forces of a protestor may be perceived as a violation of the victim's right to life, as well as an attack on the protestors as a whole. Whereas human rights law would view the attack against the protestors as a violation of their freedom of expression or the right of peaceful assembly, it could not possibly render all protestors victims of the unlawful killing as this would, at the very least, hamper the family of the deceased in seeking its rightful redress. Moreover, although not impossible, it is difficult to collectivise freedom of expression and assembly in those cases where the participants do not share more or less the same ideas, beliefs and characteristics. Even so, there is no guarantee that all participants will wish to subsume their individual entitlements into a more impersonal group entitlement. This was certainly the underlying rationale in the construction of the International Bill of Human Rights, which was criticised by developing nations for its perceived Western bias in favour of the individual to the detriment of the person's community. The critique is that although the idea of individually justiciable rights is attractive because it is not dependent on the actions or omissions of other actors (for example, clan leaders), in fact the separation (or distinction) of the individual from the group reduces the power and protection offered by the group. This Western bias, it is further argued, is evident from the fact that the International Bill of Human Rights wholly disregarded the centrality of interdependence inherent in community life in the developing world. It is no wonder, therefore, that the African Charter on Human and Peoples' Rights (ACHPR) has, in addition to self-determination, included a significant list of solidarity or collective rights. These include the right to continued existence (article 20), the right to development (article 22), the right to peace and security (article 23) and the right to a generally satisfactory environment (article 24).

The debate on collective rights is far from over in international human rights discourse. Three broad types of collective entitlements may be distinguished: those stemming from the right to self-determination, those required for the protection of non-majority group members and others predicated on the collectivisation of certain individual rights. Collective rights based on self-determination presuppose the existence of a group with common characteristics centred around actual or potential forms of statehood, underpinned by the concept of *peoples*. The protection of peoples is achieved through rights, as well as through international criminal justice mechanisms. The crime of genocide, for example, constitutes an indirect way of protecting the right to life of the target group's members. Their human rights dimension is justified by the fact that the benefits from the relevant entitlement produce no conflicts between individual members of the group. For example, the right to development and the right of peoples over their natural resources concern values that produce benefits for all and which are not susceptible to individual ownership to the exclusion of others.

On the other hand, groups that do not qualify as *peoples* (i.e. non-majority groups) cannot obviously rely on entitlements stemming from the right to self-determination. Although the welfare interests of such groups, including minorities and indigenous peoples, cannot possibly conflict or harm the welfare of the majority, until recently there was strong opposition to the granting of collective entitlements. It was feared that such entitlements would ultimately lead to claims of self-determination by the non-majority group. In reality, the collective entitlements of such groups are guaranteed either by the granting of individual rights – as is the case with article 27 of the International Covenant on Civil and Political Rights (ICCPR) – or through policy initiatives that do not possess collective normativity. LBGTI persons, for example, can rely on non-discrimination where their rights have been affected as a result of their sexual orientation. LGBTI persons do not, however, possess distinct justiciable group rights. The non-majority groups discussed in this paragraph enjoy different levels of protection under human rights law, with indigenous peoples generally deemed to possess a group entitlement, despite the absence of hard law.

The collectivisation of individual rights towards achieving the welfare of peoples is a challenging notion. It is not clear whether the right to peace, the right to a healthy environment or the right to be free from corruption should, from a policy, strategic litigation or other enforcement perspective, be framed in collective terms. By way of illustration, the Indian Supreme Court has done an excellent job of protecting the right to a healthy environment (and implicitly the environment itself) through public interest litigation based on the right to life and the right to information, without having to construct a collective entitlement.[1] From a practical perspective, the successful outcome of an individual suit produces environmental effects for the entire community as a result of its trickle-down effect. Although the collective rights analysed in this chapter have served their purpose well, a collective rights-based approach may not always constitute the optimum option for the pursuit of community objectives. Collectivised individual rights may therefore be viewed as policy objectives realised through individual rights mechanisms, rather than as collective entitlements. This observation, however, is not meant in any way to decrease the immense utility of collective rights.

In whatever manner collective rights are perceived and put into practice, care should be taken that they are not implemented in a way that prejudices the individual rights of group members. Thus, the constitutional recognition of indigenous customary law should not be employed by chief elders to impose discriminatory and derogatory treatment on vulnerable members. These members should have access to adequate relief outside the framework of customary law if they so wish. Equally, the promotion of individual rights should not be used to effectively diminish communal values or erode particular groups. This is particularly true in cases where certain privileges are afforded only to members of the majority, thus forcing non-majority groups to 'assimilate'.

10.2.1 External Self-determination

Article 1(2) of the United Nations (UN) Charter mentions self-determination as one of its purposes, in particular as a principle whose respect ensures friendly relations between nations. The employment of self-determination in article 1 of the ICCPR and the International Covenant on Economic, Social and Cultural Rights (ICESCR) is of a different nature. It is not referred to

---

[1] See Chapter 9.6.

merely as a principle, or a means to achieve specific targets (i.e. friendly relations); it is framed as a right of peoples. This bifurcation of the concept into two distinct instruments reflects its historical evolution in the course of the twentieth century.[2] In the aftermath of World War I, President Wilson of the United States of America (USA) included it (as point 6) in his famous 'Fourteen Points'. The idea was that since the war in Europe had to a large degree been caused by the unjust displacement of national minorities outside the borders of their homeland, which in turn led to abuses, lack of representation and ultimately revolt, it was only natural that an attempt should be made to avoid a future repetition of such injustices. Wilson, without apparently a clear understanding of the ramifications, espoused the view that any territorial settlements following the war should be 'in the interest and for the benefit' of the populations concerned.[3] Wilson had intimated therefore that the carving up of Europe should be guided not by the territorial claims of the victors but by the self-government interests of the civilian populations.[4] That this was an unrehearsed idea is evident from the fact that its implementation necessarily required a plethora of secessions and the creation of mini-states with an uncertain future. It is quintessentially for this reason that Wilsonian self-determination was soon downplayed and remained a mere principle of international relations until the end of World War II.

Its elevation to the status of a right came about when the discussion on decolonisation commenced in the General Assembly of the UN (UNGA) in the early 1960s. There, it was agreed that peoples under colonial rule and alien domination were entitled to self-rule and a determination of their own political status.[5] Naturally, these two dimensions of the entitlement cannot be exercised by some members of a group to the exclusion of others and so the right as a whole is of a collective nature and can only be exercised and enforced as such. As a result, it requires broad consensus among the

---

[2] It should be emphasised, however, that the drafters of the UN Charter did not disregard the human rights dimension of self-determination. For example, art. 80(1) thereto considers that the trusteeship system established under its predecessor, the League of Nations, continues to produce rights for peoples. See *Legal Consequences for States of the Continued Presence of South Africa in Namibia (South-West Africa* case) (ICJ) (1971) paras. 58ff.

[3] A. Cassese, *Self-Determination of Peoples: A Legal Reappraisal* (Cambridge University Press, 1995) 19–23.

[4] The position on overseas colonies was, none the less, abundantly clear. A mechanism of mandates was set up which subjected peoples residing therein and 'not yet able to stand by themselves under the strenuous conditions of the modern world' to a process designed to improve their well-being and development. This process was held to constitute a 'sacred trust of civilisation' according to art. 22 of the League of Nations Covenant. See *International Status of South-West Africa* (ICJ) (1950) at 132, which noted that the other corollary to this process was the prohibition of annexation.

[5] UNGA resolution 1514(XV) (1960) Declaration on the granting of independence to colonial countries and peoples.

constituent peoples. Of course, self-determination lends itself also to individual entitlements, such as the right to elect and be elected,[6] the right to peaceful assembly and others. However, it is the collective entitlement that is paramount in the Charter and the two Covenants and it is this which is the subject of controversy and limitations by international law. To understand why this is so, it is pertinent at this stage to distinguish between the external and internal dimensions of self-determination. The external dimension dismisses any kind of colonial or racist rule and alien domination and endows victim populations with a right to dispose of such oppressive rulers.[7] It thus prohibits all types of external interference and intervention with the governance of a territory and of its peoples.[8] The internal dimension, on the other hand, refers to the right of peoples to freely determine their own political status and pursue their economic, social and cultural development.[9] It also encompasses the right to freely dispose of natural wealth and resources.[10] The internal dimension therefore informs the political organisation of the state based on the wishes of its people.

The external dimension is plagued by a paradox. Peoples are allowed, on the one hand, to rid themselves of an oppressive regime, yet they are prevented as far as possible from disrupting the territorial integrity of the state. In between the two ends of the paradox it is accepted that oppressed peoples are entitled to secede (and even to employ force) in their collective pursuit of self-government. Moreover, it is also accepted that non-oppressed peoples may demand to secede from the parent state by means of a constitutionally validated plebiscite or by other agreement, as was the case with the break-up of the Soviet Union, the independence of Montenegro from Yugoslavia and the secession of South Sudan from Sudan. The paradox is expressly stipulated in the Friendly Relations Declaration which allows peoples in their pursuit of self-determination to 'establish a sovereign and independent state, [a] free association or integration with an independent state or the emergence into any other political status',[11] as well as to seek and receive support thereof. None the less, it emphasises that none of these entitlements:

---

[6] This individual dimension has been recognised by the CERD in its General Comment 21 (23 August 1996) para. 4.

[7] Art. 1(3) ICCPR; art. 1(4) Protocol Additional to the 1949 Geneva Conventions and Relating to the Protection of Victims of International Armed Conflicts (1977 Protocol I).

[8] UNGA resolution 2625(XXV) (24 October 1970) Declaration on principles of international law concerning friendly relations and co-operation among states in accordance with the Charter of the UN (Friendly Relations Declaration) principles 1 and 3; HRCtee, General Comment 12 (13 March 1984) para. 6.

[9] Art. 1(1) ICCPR.   [10] Art. 1(2) ICCPR.

[11] These three possibilities of statehood were conceded as early as 1960 through UNGA resolution 1541(XV) (15 December 1960), entitled 'Principles which should guide members to determine whether or not an obligation exists to transmit the information called for under art. 73 UN Charter'.

shall be construed as authorizing or encouraging any action which would dismember or impair, totally or in part, the territorial integrity or political unity of sovereign and independent states conducting themselves in compliance with the principle of equal rights and self-determination of peoples as described above and thus possessed of a government representing the whole people belonging to the territory without distinction as to race, creed or color.[12]

This clearly suggests that although the territorial integrity of states is a paramount principle of international relations, it may give way in those cases where peoples are under oppressive rule that stifles their right to representative government.

Even so, secession is not encouraged as a means of resisting an oppressive regime because it is perceived as leading to instability and hence is only sparingly 'authorised' by the international community in practice.[13] One has to look at the process of decolonisation itself, which involved the least possible amount of territorial dissolution, even at the expense of national and tribal homogeneity. Colonial powers (and later the newly independent African nations) invoked the principle of *uti possidetis* in order for the new entities to inherit pre-colonial boundaries and thus avoid the ignition of territorial conflicts.[14] From the point of view of human rights, however, this artificial drawing of boundaries created a plethora of ethnic and tribal enclaves that were cut off from the public life of the state and which inhibited the development of national consciousness, ultimately igniting tribalism. Moreover, the proponents of *uti possidetis* paid little regard to the demands of peoples, minorities and the ancestral rights of indigenous peoples. Not surprisingly, most post-colonial governments represented only tribal majorities or particular elites. As a result of the oppression that naturally followed, numerous ethnic groups in Africa waged wars of secession under the banner of self-determination, but the newly installed governments consistently argued that self-determination was only applicable against colonialism. Since colonialism had been removed, they contended that self-determination had become moot. This argument was no doubt wrongly conceived. If self-determination was destined to expire in the aftermath of decolonisation, this would have

---

[12] Friendly Relations Declaration, above note 8, principle 5.

[13] The Badinter arbitration committee which was appointed to deal with the legal ramifications of the break-up of the former Yugoslavia noted that Serbians living in Croatia did not enjoy the right to secede or join the territory of what was then the Federal Republic of Yugoslavia (now Serbia). Opinion no. 2 emphasised that 'whatever the circumstances, the right to self-determination must not involve changes to existing frontiers at the time of independence, except where the States concerned otherwise agree'. Reproduced in A. Pellet, 'The Opinions of the Badinter Arbitration Committee: A Second Breath for the Self-determination of Peoples' (1992) 3 *European Journal of International Law* 178, at 183.

[14] See M. Shaw, 'The Heritage of States: The Principle of *Uti Possidetis* Today' (1996) 67 *British Yearbook of International Law* 75.

been expressly stated in both the UN Charter and common article 1 of the Covenants, or would have been deleted therefrom. On the contrary, self-determination is a continuing right, the protection and promotion of which is addressed to all states at all times.

For the purposes of external self-determination it should be pointed out that the beneficiaries of the right, designated under the term 'peoples', encompass majority groups or entire populations of states. In this sense, peoples may be identified by reference to race, ethnicity, language or religion, or typically by a combination thereof. Any other grouping that does not comprise a majority of the population (i.e. minorities or indigenous groups) does not enjoy the external dimension of the right to self-determination, only its internal dimension. Simply put, minorities and sub-national groups do not possess an entitlement (under the banner of self-determination) to secede.[15] As a result, in the absence of a constitutional plebiscite, or acute oppression, and then only exceptionally, sub-national groups do not enjoy the right to external self-determination, even if they constitute a numerical majority in a particular geographical location.

10.2.2   Exceptionalism in the External Dimension of Self-determination

We have alluded to the fact that although peoples may validly seek to violently secede from the parent state when under oppression, in practice this is effectuated only when the international community provides its blessing. This finds expression in the language and rhetoric of exceptionalism. The term denotes that even though a particular situation is treated by extraordinary standards that are not in conformity with the ordinary dictates of the law, there is no departure from the law. In the situation at hand, exceptionalism seeks to insulate and safeguard against any instance of unilateral secession, while at the same time providing a viable outlet to situations where the continuity of a state is no longer feasible or desirable. Exceptionalism is thus closer to the 'freely expressed will of peoples' dimension of self-determination than any other political or legal paradigm in history, despite its arbitrary character and absence of all sense of legal certainty. Three distinct sub-paradigms are identified in this book on the basis of exceptional state practice: (1) unilateral secession of peoples from a failed state; (2) consensual secession by means of a plebiscite or agreement; and (3) plebiscite or agreement imposed externally in order to end long-standing conflicts or oppressive rule.

---

[15] *Frontier Dispute* case (*Burkina Faso* v. *Mali*) (ICJ) (1986) at 567; *Report on the Situation of Human Rights of a Segment of the Nicaraguan Population of Miskito Origin* (IACHR) (1984), OEA/Ser.L/V/II.62, doc. 10, Rev. 3 (29 November 1983) at 78–9; see also statement of the USA in the Report of the Working Group established in accordance with UN CommHR resolution 1995/32 (1999), UN doc. E/CN.4/2000/84 (1999) para. 49.

Consensual secession is a theoretical possibility in the constitutional arrangements of federal states,[16] even though not always expressly mentioned, but is naturally discouraged in practice. Representatives of the French-speaking Québecois of Canada pursued their secessionist claim by a referendum which they ultimately lost by a slim majority. This spurred the government of Canada to request its Supreme Court to offer an opinion as to whether the secession of Quebec would in any event be considered lawful under both Canadian and international law. The Court held that although the Constitution did not sanction unilateral secession, Canada would have no basis for denying it to the Québecois in the event of a positive referendum. The position under international law was found not to favour disintegration as long as the state in question represented the whole of the people or peoples resident within its territory, 'on a basis of equality and without discrimination, and respected the principles of self-determination in its own internal arrangements'.[17]

The third paradigm is not readily susceptible to generalisations or predictions. It is premised on the notion that certain parts of the international community are willing to concede that under exceptional circumstances the persistent oppression of a people justifies secession instigated and manoeuvred by the international community if in this manner the oppression ceases and peace is restored.[18] No doubt, this is subject to the obvious disclaimer that the state in question does not enjoy sufficient kudos internationally and is largely stigmatised as a 'pariah'. The exceptional element here is that this paradigm has been applied to *peoples* (in the manner discussed above) as well as numerical minorities. Two poignant cases are cited in support of this concession: Kosovo and South Sudan. After many years of conflict between the predominantly Arab Muslim Northern Sudan against the largely Christian and Animist South, an agreement was brokered in 2005 with the intervention of external actors whereby the peoples of the South would decide their political status.[19] As a result, a referendum took place in January

---

[16] Art. 39(1) of the Ethiopian Constitution states that: 'every nation, nationality or people in Ethiopia shall have the unrestricted right to self-determination up to secession'. This is subject to a defined number of constitutional conditions, particularly a demand by a two-thirds majority of the nation's legislature and a successful referendum. Paragraph 5 defines the terms 'nation', 'nationality' and 'people' as a 'community having the following characteristics: people having a common culture reflecting considerable uniformity or similarity of custom, a common language, belief in a common bond and identity, and a common consciousness the majority of whom live within a common territory'.

[17] *Reference re Secession of Quebec* (Canada) (1998) para. 130.

[18] This was also the implicit position of the ACmHPR in *Katangese Peoples' Congress* v. *Zaire* (ACmHPR) (1995) para. 6.

[19] First came a comprehensive peace agreement which was composed of a number of protocols on power-sharing, wealth-sharing, conflict resolution and boundary delimitation, followed by an interim national constitution. One of these protocols, signed in Machakos, stipulated in art. 2(5) that: '[a]t the end of the six year interim period there shall be an internationally monitored referendum, organized jointly by the GoS [Government of Sudan] and SPLM/A [the Southern entity], for the people of South Sudan

2011 by which the South Sudanese chose to secede from Sudan proper with an overwhelming majority of 98 per cent.

Whereas the South Sudanese clearly constitute a people for the purposes of article 1(1) of the ICCPR, Kosovo Albanians do not, being a minority among ethnic Serbians; albeit both may equally be viewed as majorities in their respective regions. Much like the South Sudanese, the largely ethnic Albanian population of Kosovo was the object of oppression by the post-communist government of the Federal Republic of Yugoslavia. Following a mass exodus of refugees and internally displaced persons in 1999 the territory of Kosovo came under international administration and control, pending a final solution on its future political status. In 2009 Kosovo declared its unilateral secession from Serbia while still under international administration. Although its status is still not entirely clear, a number of countries objected to the legitimacy of its declared statehood and made their position known to the International Court of Justice (ICJ), which by 2009 had been asked to determine whether the unilateral declaration was consonant with international law. Although the ICJ's advisory opinion lacks real legal value, given its mere iteration that the declaration itself is legitimate[20] – without, however, examining whether self-determination under the circumstances justifies secession – the position of intervening states demonstrates an impasse. The USA and the majority of European Union (EU) member states, with the exception of Spain, Romania, Greece and Cyprus, have espoused the view that the Kosovars are entitled to secede because they qualify as *peoples*, have expressed their will as such, in addition to their victimisation during their oppression. Yet all states emphasised that this was an exceptional case that was not meant to set a precedent! Moreover, all Latin American nations,[21] as well as China,[22] Russia,[23] Belarus, Vietnam and others have argued that unilateral secession is void under international law because it violates the principle of territorial integrity and in any event is not available to minorities.

10.2.3   A Test for Sovereignty in the Era of Fiscal 'Occupation'

A test of sovereignty must be pragmatic, based on objective criteria, and linked to self-determination. Given that the 'effective' absence of sovereignty mirrors the impact of belligerent occupation, this will be employed

to confirm the unity of Sudan by voting to adopt the system of government established under the peace agreement, or to vote for secession'.

[20]   *Accordance with International Law of the Unilateral Declaration of Independence in respect of Kosovo* (ICJ) (2010) paras. 78–121.

[21]   See Written statement of Argentina, online at www.icj-cij.org/docket/files/141/15666.pdf.

[22]   Written statement of China, online at www.icj-cij.org/docket/index.php?p1=3&p2=1&k=21 &case=141&code=kos&p3=1.

[23]   Written Statement of Russia, online at www.icj-cij.org/docket/index.php?p1=3&p2=1&k= 21&case=141&code=kos&p3=1.

to test the effective exercise of sovereignty in the modern era. It should be reminded that an occupation exists where territory is *effectively* occupied, irrespective of whether this is admitted or disguised by legal or other means by the occupier.[24] A country is sovereign where it is *effectively empowered*, without pressure or coercion, to make all policy decisions required to run the state machinery and satisfy the fundamental needs of all its people (at the very least), both individual and collective. Where a state's effective power to implement these two items is in any way curtailed or diminished by the actions of third parties (states or international organisations), that state is no longer sovereign. Because states can generally ward off even the predatory acts of private actors, the latter cannot on their own diminish a state's sovereignty, unless they pursue their claims through another state.

A state's policy and decision-making power is effectively curtailed where: (1) it has been substituted in these functions by a third state or an organ appointed by that third state or a group of states; (2) it is prevented from taking a particular action, such as unilateral default or designing its own debt restructuring mechanism; (3) where it is forced to violate fundamental domestic laws, including its constitution or the clear outcome of a referendum; or (4) where external pressure is exerted against its government and institutions with the aim of creating volatility and uncertainty concerning its finances so that it succumbs to such pressure and the demands behind it.[25] Clearly, in all of these circumstances, the fact that a state formally consents to the action stripping it of its effective policy and decision-making power is illegitimate and also illegal.[26] If sovereignty is the *sine qua non* condition for statehood and thus for the existence of the community of nations, it is inconceivable that states may validly sign away their sovereignty in the manner just described. It is like saying that a person may validly contract to sell his healthy heart because freedom of contract overrides any other considerations. In the same manner, governments (as agents of their people) cannot contract out of the rights enjoyed by their people.

The conclusion to be drawn is that where a state is not sovereign, it is either failed or under effective occupation. A failed state may be sovereign (in the sense of empowerment) but suffer from weak institutions. A state not truly sovereign as a result of the actions of third states, while retaining its statehood, should be deemed as being under a *sui generis* occupation by these third states or the institutions controlled by them (such as international financial institutions). This reality deserves to be more widely recognised

---

[24] See specifically *Loizidou* v. *Turkey* (ECtHR) (1997) and *Al-Skeini and Others* v. *UK* (ECtHR) (2011).

[25] See I. Bantekas, 'Sovereign Debt and Self-Determination', in I. Bantekas and C. Lumina (eds.), *Sovereign Debt and Human Rights* (Oxford University Press, 2018) 267.

[26] UNGA Res 63/319 (29 September 2015) art. 1.

and regulated by a fusion between the law of military occupation[27] and the law of state responsibility, as well as by a revised and much more human rights-compliant international law on the responsibility of international organisations.[28]

The vast majority of states require financing to meet infrastructural and other public needs. Quite clearly, a state is unable to formulate or execute policy or indeed make internal or foreign-related political decisions without sufficient capital and access to financial resources. To make things even more complicated, a state's access to (hard currency) capital is determined by (mostly unwritten) market rules, such as the value of its sovereign bonds in the international markets or its overall creditworthiness. Both of these (bond value and creditworthiness) are chiefly predicated on perceptions and conduct exercised by private actors, such as investors, lenders and credit rating agencies.[29] If a country wants to raise its financial profile in order to attract investment or increase its external trade, it may have to enter into agreements that are ultimately injurious to the welfare of its people, or even to its economy and development as a whole. The WTO agreements, several multilateral and bilateral investment treaties (BITs), and even debt relief schemes have been effectively forced upon developing states and in most cases, although they have increased inward investment or exports, have caused deterioration in the living standards of their people.[30]

---

[27] See E. Benvenisti, *The International Law of Occupation* (Oxford University Press, 2013) for a general understanding of the rights and duties of the occupying power. But see also A. Evans-Pritchard, 'Greece Is Being Treated like a Hostile Occupied State' *The Telegraph* (13 July 2015).

[28] It is clear that if states are able to attribute otherwise personal actions to intergovernmental organizations (IGOs) to escape their human rights obligations, then in equal manner the states affected by the measures adopted by such IGOs can claim that they were required by treaty to adhere to them. In both cases there is an artificial absence of obligations and a corresponding absence of liability. Such a result is untenable and lacks legal foundation and has rightly been condemned by international and domestic courts, despite claims to the contrary by collaborating states. This type of liability is recognised in art. 61 of the ILC Articles on the Responsibility of International Organisations, which reads:

A State member of an international organization incurs international responsibility if, by taking advantage of the fact that the organization has competence in relation to the subject-matter of one of the State's international obligations, it circumvents that obligation by causing the organization to commit an act that, if committed by the state, would have constituted a breach of the obligation.

[29] See A. Darbellay-Susso, *Regulating Credit Rating Agencies* (Edward Elgar, 2013). See also UNGA resolution 62/186 (31 January 2008) para. 22, on the role of credit rating agencies and the need for transparency.

[30] See generally A. Nicolaides and C. M. van der Bank, 'Globalisation, NEPAD, Fundamental Human Rights, South African and Continental Development' (2013) 1 *International Journal of Development and Economic Sustainability* 54.

In equal measure, the economies of developing states are simply drops in the vast oceans of volatility of international markets. They may eke a living when their staple agricultural produce achieves a decent price, but risk financial doom when prices drop (for whatever reason) the next year. The same is true in respect of the volatility of international currency exchange rates. Given, additionally, the sensitivity of international markets and their exogenous shocks, even a negative statement by a person of authority against the economy of another state may bring the latter into disrepute to some degree, and as its integrity is undermined, so too will be its capacity to borrow at low interest or sell its sovereign bonds. As a result of all these phenomena or circumstances, it is clear that states may be prevented from pursuing the economic and political will of their people because of their dire economic status.

The constraints on fiscal self-determination is nowhere more evident than in the machineries for debt relief. The Paris Club and the IMF impose several conditionalities on applicant states in this respect. It suffices to state here that conditionalities imposed under the Paris Club and the IMF's Highly Indebted Poor Countries Initiative (HIPC) have been classified as structural or quantitative.[31] Structural conditionalities require the applicant state to undertake political, legislative and institutional reforms, whereas their quantitative counterparts demand the achievement of macroeconomic targets, such as the reduction of fiscal deficits and the accumulation of international reserves. It is a fiction that debtor states *consent* to the conditionalities agreed with the IMF or the Paris Club. The international finance architecture is structured in such a way that developing states or states in distress are unable to make alternative choices. By way of illustration, over-indebted states are naturally excluded from private financial markets, or if they are not, the interest available to them is so high that it ultimately makes borrowing impossible. At the same time, their currency would have been devalued to such an extent that it is internationally undesirable, and in all probability they will suffer from a trade deficit or imbalance. States distressed in this manner, in addition to being unable to meet their domestic fiscal needs, will be pressured by their creditors to repay their external debts. Ultimately, in the absence of liquidity and constant pressure, indebted states are forced to submit to their creditors' demands in the form of conditionalities. Even though these are negotiated between debtors and creditors, there is little to no transparency involved and in practice the negotiating power of the debtor is significantly diminished, if not outright extinguished.[32]

---

[31] N. Villaroman, 'The Loss of Sovereignty: How International Debt Relief Mechanisms Undermine Economic Self-Determination' (2009) 2 *Journal of Politics and Law* 3, 6.

[32] See Chapter 14.6.

It is clear from this discussion that states are effectively disposed of their sovereign decision-making power as well as their ability to make fiscal or other social policy, both of which constitute the essence of self-determination. The international finance architecture does not allow indebted states to opt out or to effectively declare and pursue unilateral insolvency, or indeed design their own debt and fiscal restructuring.

CASE STUDY 10.1
Participatory Budgeting in Porto Alegre, Brazil

Participatory budgeting (PB) is a mechanism through which the governed have direct access to the decision-making fora that determine where and how public finances are spent, as well as the range of taxes to be collected. There is no single model of PB and potentially it could involve participation in all fiscal and budgetary matters. Its roots lie in a social experiment implemented in the wealthy southern region of Porto Alegre in Brazil and its municipality therein in 1989 as a result of the election of the Workers' Party, whose campaign agenda was premised on democratic participation and 'the inversion of spending priorities'.[1] The implementation of PB has only occurred at the local government level and has since been adopted by over 250 municipalities in Brazil and exported to over twenty countries around the world. It is not a process that can be achieved overnight with the mere promulgation of local laws in the expectation that local citizenry will demonstrate a keen and spontaneous desire to participate in the design of a public budget. In fact, it is a slow process whereby the active engagement of participants must be sought from the neighbourhood level. Moreover, it is essential that the responsibilities of local governments and participants, as well as their respective roles, be clearly delineated from the outset. These procedures must involve a significant input from the participants and not be solely dictated or designed by the authorities. When the rules of the game are put in place the participants and the authorities may discuss allocation of available resources.

PB typically involves the spending of discretionary resources, which in the case of poor municipalities could amount from zero to 15 per cent of the budget. The percentage that is allocated to discretionary purposes and which is thereafter susceptible to PB has traditionally been earmarked by participants either to serve public works or in order to address general spending policies.

[1] See B. Wampler, *Participatory Budgeting in Brazil: Contestation, Cooperation and Accountability* (Pennsylvania University Press, 2007).

The participants are derived from all walks of life and possess diverse reasons for wanting to take part in this exercise; non-governmental organisations (NGOs) do so because of a desire to materialise their programmatic goals; private business in order to support local commerce; and random individuals because of a dream of social justice, among others. In terms of actual participation, depending on how the rules of the game have been designed, voting is cast by means of neighbourhood representation, or simply by universal balloting.[2]

PB may be viewed as an ideal microcosmic manifestation of self-determination in a very particular sector of public affairs. Can it constitute a blueprint for broader public access in other affairs of government, or would such participation make government unnecessarily cumbersome and bureaucratic? What is the ideal level of direct public engagement in the decision-making processes of governance?

[2] A. Shah, *Participatory Budgeting: Public Sector Governance and Accountability* (World Bank Publications, 2007). It is worth noting that art. 5(1) of Lome Convention IV (1990) 29 ILM 783, stipulated that man is the 'main protagonist and beneficiary of development, which entails respect for the promotion of human rights ... The role and potential of initiatives taken by individuals and groups shall also be recognised and fostered in order to achieve in practice real participation of the population in the development process.' This is a direct reference to participatory democracy and makes a link between the process of development and public participation in fiscal affairs.

QUESTIONS

1. UN Security Council resolution 713 (25 September 1991) imposed an arms embargo on the entire territory of the former Yugoslavia in order to prevent the warring parties from arming themselves and protracting the conflict. As a result, however, Bosnia and Herzegovina was unable to exercise its inherent right to self-defence, which resulted in genocide against its people. Is the survival of a people an integral part of the external dimension of self-determination? If so, may it be invoked by itself and other states as justification for defying a Security Council resolution of this nature?

2. The UNGA and a specially appointed rapporteur have adopted the position that the employment of mercenaries prevents and distorts the freedom of peoples to determine their political status, thereby impairing their right to self-determination. Do you agree with this argument? Should a people whose authoritarian government employs mercenaries and flagrantly violates human rights be allowed also to employ mercenaries in order to pursue its self-determination claims?

3. What are the positive and negative outcomes of a policy that provides a secessionist entitlement to all minorities and indigenous peoples?

4. Many countries in the developing world subject their exploration and extraction
   contracts with foreign mining companies to the law of contract, rather than
   public/constitutional law. As a result, they claim that the terms of the agreement
   are confidential and not susceptible to parliamentary and public scrutiny, lest
   they breach their contractual obligations. Discuss with reference to the right of
   peoples over their natural resources.

10.3   MINORITIES AS A SUBJECT OF HUMAN RIGHTS

There is no normative definition of the term 'minority' under treaty or soft
law. None the less, there is a broad consensus that it encompasses objective
and subjective elements. The objective dimension suggests the existence of a
group that constitutes a non-dominant minority of the entire population of
a country, even if its numbers are otherwise substantial. In practical terms,
a minority group amounts to at least less than half of the entire population. Moreover, members of the group must share some characteristics, such
as race, religion, language, ethnicity or nationality. The subjective element
is less visible, but is the cohesive substance that defines and sustains the
group's identity as such: that is, the members' sense of belonging, which is
reflected in cultural characteristics, ultimately giving rise to group solidarity.[33] This solidarity ensures the continuing existence of the group, given that
even a racial minority may in time become assimilated with the dominant
racial group and implicitly renounce, or become oblivious to, its particular
identity.[34] It is accepted that the existence of a minority is not dependent on
the concentration of its members in specific regions; thus, they may just as
well be dispersed throughout the territory of a nation.[35] A divided Human
Rights Committee (HRCtee) has expressed the view, however, that the protection afforded under international law encompasses only minorities within
a state, not otherwise majority group members living in minority regions.
In the case at hand, the Committee rejected the linguistic minority status
of anglophone Canadians (otherwise an overall Canadian majority) living

---

[33] F. Capotorti, Study on the rights of persons belonging to ethnic, religious and linguistic
minorities, UN doc. E/CN.4/Sub.2/384/Add 1–7 (1991) para. 568.

[34] In its concluding observations on Denmark, the HRCtee stated that the country's Supreme
Court erred in failing to recognise the Thule tribe of Greenland as a separate group capable
of vindicating its traditional rights, despite the tribe's perception to the contrary. It urged
Denmark to consider applying the principle of self-identification in the determination of
group membership: UN doc. CCPR/C/DNK/CO/5 (16 December 2008) para. 13.

[35] HRCtee, Concluding Observations on the Fourth Periodic Report of Germany, UN doc.
A/52/40, Supp. 40 (1997) para. 183.

among francophone Québecois (a minority group in Canada) in the predominantly francophone region of Quebec, Canada.[36] The objective identification of minorities necessarily means that their status as such is not inhibited by their members' lack of citizenship[37] or immigrant status. Moreover, the very fact that a country has adopted full equality laws for all persons within its jurisdiction does not extinguish the objective existence of minorities and the pertinent rights of their members.[38]

Once the essential characteristics of the minority group are established one must then ascertain who can claim membership and on what grounds, if any, such membership may be revoked. It will be demonstrated in the following sections that membership is a matter of personal self-identification, albeit subject to certain limitations,[39] lest any person could claim this status and genuine group members could equally be expelled arbitrarily. For reasons which will be explored below the entitlement that arises from the international law of minorities is of an individual nature, as opposed to a group right. This individual right, as modelled in article 27 of the ICCPR, has been reproduced, with minor modifications, in all subsequent instruments and its nature is therefore undisputed. Yet the proper construction of this right is meaningless outside the framework of the group itself and as a result it is a legal fiction to divorce the individual from the group. It should be stressed that for reasons of cogency and stability only a closed number of minorities are recognised in international law (i.e. ethnic, religious, linguistic, national). This therefore excludes other non-dominant groups whose members share a common characteristic, such as lesbian, gay, bisexual, transgender and intersex (LGBTI), communists, members of a particular gender and others. Such persons are protected under equality laws and in many cases their vulnerability may require the adoption of positive discrimination measures by the state.[40]

---

[36] *Ballantyne, Davidson and McIntyre* v. *Canada* (HRCtee) (1993) para. 11.2.

[37] HRCtee, Concluding Observations on the Report of Norway, UN doc. A/49/90 (1996) para. 94; Commentary to the UN Declaration on the Rights of Persons belonging to National, or Ethnic, Religious and Linguistic Minorities (Declaration Commentary), UN doc. E/CN.4/Sub.2/AC.5/2005/2 (4 April 2005) para. 10.

[38] The HRCtee chastised Gabon for denying the existence of minorities on its territory: UN doc. CCPR/70/CO/GAB (10 November 2000) para. 17.

[39] The leading case is *Lovelace* v. *Canada* (HRCtee) (1981) para. 14; see also case concerning the *Minority Schools in Albania* (PCIJ) (1935), where the PCIJ stated that the existence of a minority was not subject to a legal, but a factual determination; art. 3(1) of the 1994 Framework Convention for the Protection of National Minorities, ETS no. 157; art. 32(6) of the 1990 Conference on Security and Cooperation in Europe (CSCE) Copenhagen Document on the Human Dimension (1990) 29 ILM 1305.

[40] None the less, the HRCtee in its Concluding observations on Namibia, referred to 'sexual minorities' in order to denote the absence of anti-discrimination laws applicable to LGBTI: UN doc. CCPR/CO/81/NAM (August 2004) para. 22. A similar comment was made with

The current international legal framework on minority protection is based on non-discrimination and equality with members of the majority, while at the same time safeguarding and promoting through positive action the minority's distinct right to culture. The many minority rights instruments, both soft and hard law, essentially express the same principles and thus much of the analysis will be premised on the jurisprudence emanating from article 27 of the ICCPR and the 1992 UN Declaration on Minority Rights.[41]

10.3.1 The Historical and Political Context: Should Minorities be Treated Differently from Majorities?

Not much thought is put into the idea that a distinct regime on minorities must be adopted in domestic laws in order for the particular needs of minorities to be distinguished from those of the local majorities. This argument seems rational on the face of it because it suggests the obvious: that a vulnerable group whose cultural and other existence is threatened by the assimilating vigour of a majority should be protected from the threat of forced assimilation, especially where the possibility of seceding is not on the table. Yet this assumption runs counter to certain theoretical human rights foundations. Chief among these is that the ideal liberal model of rights, and state organisation, should be grounded on the promotion of diverse multicultural societies.[42] The driving force behind diversity is that it enriches experiences, beliefs, ideas, cultures, technological advancement and provides a better understanding of the world.[43] Moreover, multiculturalism has the potential of contributing to the diffusion of ethnic and other differences between people and is therefore a catalyst for peace and conflict prevention.[44] At the other

reference to Poland's inability to avoid discrimination against its sexual minorities: UN doc. CCPR/C/ 82/POL (2 December 2004) para. 18. LGBTI literature, however, is generally disinclined to attach the (legal) label of minority to LGBTI communities and their attendant rights. See Chapter 11.3.2.

[41] UNGA resolution 47/135 (18 December 1992), Declaration on the Rights of Persons Belonging to National or Ethnic, Religious and Linguistic Minorities.

[42] See e.g., art. 151(1) of the Consolidated Treaty Establishing the European Communities, OJ C325/33 (24 December 2002), which requires the Community to strengthen the various cultures of its member states while respecting their national and regional diversity; 2001 UNESCO Universal Declaration on Cultural Diversity, UNESCO doc. 31C/Res25, Annex I; *Timishev* v. *Russia* (ECtHR) (2007) paras. 56 and 58; *Oršuš and Others* v. *Croatia* (ECtHR) (2011) paras. 147–8.

[43] H. Steiner, 'Ideals and Counter-ideals in the Struggle over Autonomy Regimes for Minorities' (1991) 66 *Notre Dame Law Review* 1539, at 1547.

[44] Report of the UN independent expert on minority issues, Effective Protection of the Minorities Declaration, UN doc. A/65/287 (12 August 2010) paras. 32–8. The expert pointed to an academic study demonstrating that the risk of conflict increases if socio-economic inequalities are combined with inequality of access to political decision-making, stressing moreover that inequality in cultural status adds a further risk factor.

extreme lies the state-centric notion that national cohesion and political stability are antithetical to any imperative in favour of ethnic diversity.

If policy-makers were to adopt the principle of multiculturalism in their effort to construct a legal regime for minorities they would be forced to reject the solution of autonomy because in most cases it is inherently divisive. Autonomy, or self-rule, would moreover signal intolerance and convey the message that nothing positive can be derived from diversity. Equally, a regime of autonomy does not guarantee the absence of discrimination by the minority against dissenting members and other minorities. In essence, therefore, one would be propagating a model based on purity of some sort, whether ethnic, racial, national, linguistic or other. This model perpetuates mistrust and endangers fracture and the likelihood of conflict. But are there effective alternatives to assimilation and division for minorities and should multiculturalism serve as the guiding principle? Contemporary practice clearly disfavours assimilation[45] because it is involuntary and carries all the hallmarks of quasi-genocide where it is pursued in a forceful manner. At the same time there is an aversion to the forceful imposition of multiculturalism as a general rule of international law on the ground that it may well be opposed by the peoples of a particular nation. As a result, two broad models have emerged depending on whether the minority is perceived in its collective or from the perspective of its members:

1. autonomy, power-sharing, or other levels of self-government in order to address historic wrongs, bring about federal devolution of power or others; and
2. minority rights for each member of the group, not with a view to discrimination, but in order to preserve the group's distinct culture and solidarity among its members.

Although autonomy and self-government regimes are less frequent, they are none the less entrenched in numerous constitutions[46] and have recently been imposed by the international community on post-conflict nations, as was the case with the former Yugoslavia. These regimes are tantamount to a collective minority right because the entitlement is not addressed to individual members but to the group as such. This is, however, as far as the international community wants to recognise collective entitlements – comparable to the self-determination of peoples – in respect of minorities. Irrespective

---

[45] Assimilation of minorities and indigenous peoples should be distinguished from assimilation policies in respect of migrants, which is generally viewed as a legitimate objective of the state. See the USA's universal periodic review (UPR) Report, UN doc. A/HRC/WG.6/9/USA/1 (23 August 2010) para. 91.

[46] Art. 2 of the Spanish Constitution 'recognises and guarantees the right to autonomy of the nationalities and regions which make it up and the solidarity among all of them'.

of, and in conjunction with, autonomy regimes, human rights law provides individual rights to minority members. This is aptly demonstrated in article 27 of the ICCPR which reads as follows:

In those states in which ethnic, religious or linguistic minorities exist, persons belonging to such minorities shall not be denied the right, in community with the other members of their group, to enjoy their own culture, to profess and practice their own religion, or to use their own language.

Although this clearly refers to an individual entitlement, it cannot exist in isolation from the group ('in community with other members of the group') and as the HRCtee has observed, the rights under article 27 'depend in turn on the ability of the minority group to maintain its culture, language or religion'.[47] This observation is nowhere more apparent than in the case of land traditionally inhabited by minorities, as well as indigenous peoples. Such lands containing among other things ancestral burial grounds, traditional hunting and religious connotations may manifest a group's culture.[48] From an anthropological perspective this type of culture represents a group's way of life through the communication of shared values.[49] As a result, where the group's culture is under attack the focus on the purely individual entitlement is problematic and perhaps unworkable. This is exemplified by the HRCtee's approach in the *Lubicon Lake Band* case. There, the complainant argued that the provincial government of Alberta had expropriated land belonging to the Lubicon Lake indigenous group so that private companies could mine it under a concession agreement for oil and gas. The Committee merged the relevant issues under article 27, holding that the protected culture of a group encompasses its economic[50] and social activities. Thus, if its primary source of income were to be lost on account of an oil and gas concession then the life and culture of the group would be threatened.[51]

The individualistic focus of article 27 of the ICCPR reflects a rather contemporary approach. Indeed, the post-World War I peace treaties established population exchanges along ethnic lines with a view to setting up homogeneous states. Where this was not achievable the minorities in question were subjected to a regime of protection that was premised around a collective right. This was certainly considered exceptional and the expectation was that this measure would be of temporary effect as a result of the minorities' gradual assimilation. By the time the Universal Declaration of Human Rights (UDHR) was under discussion, countries with significant minorities rejected a

---

[47] HRCtee, General Comment 23, para. 6.2.   [48] Ibid., para. 7.

[49] See R. O'Keefe, 'The Right to Take Part in Cultural Life under Article 15 of the ICESCR' (1998) 47 *International & Comparative Law Quarterly* 904.

[50] *Paadar family* v. *Finland* (HRCtee) (2014) para. 7, which concerned the compulsory slaughter of reindeer of a Saami community.

[51] *Lubicon Lake Band* v. *Canada* (HRCtee) (1990) paras. 32–3.

draft provision that would have provided a collective entitlement to minorities on the ground that it would encourage dissension.[52] This is the rationale for the individualistic model introduced by article 27 of the ICCPR.

More importantly, the entitlement enshrined in article 27 constitutes a *sui generis* right to a community identity and is not the by-product of other pertinent rights in the ICCPR. Despite the language in article 27 denoting a negative obligation on the part of the state –'shall not be denied the right' – the HRCtee has expressly emphasised the positive obligation of states, noting that:

Positive measures of protection are, therefore, required not only against the acts of the state party itself, whether through its legislative, judicial or administrative authorities, but also against the acts of other persons within the state party.[53]

The adoption of positive measures, in addition to ensuring the application of non-discrimination, was recognised as early as 1935 by the Permanent Court of International Justice (PCIJ) in its advisory opinion on *Minority Schools in Albania*. The Court held that Albania was under an obligation to 'ensure for the minority element suitable means for the preservation of their racial peculiarities, their traditions and their national characteristics', which entailed facilitation of the right to establish and control 'charitable, religious and social institutions, schools and other educational establishments, [including] the right to use their own language and to exercise their religion freely therein'.[54]

10.3.2 Membership Rights

It has already been stressed that the existence of a minority is a matter of fact and not the subject of a legal or administrative determination. This leaves open two important questions. (1) Can anybody validly claim membership to a minority group? (2) Are minorities at liberty to definitively self-designate every element of their status? The first question should in general terms be answered in the negative. A person may claim membership of a minority group, with special privileges and protection thereof, only if he or she possesses the objective criteria attributable to the group and has partaken in its distinct culture since birth. This excludes persons who have acquired the distinct feature of the group, where possible, after birth but have no direct cultural link with the group. By way of illustration, a German fluent in the Basque language may be validly excluded from the special status offered to the Basque minority in Spain. This exclusion may come from both the group

[52] J. P. Humphrey, 'The United Nations Sub-commission on the Prevention of Discrimination and Protection of Minorities' (1968) 62 *American Journal of International Law* 870.
[53] HRCtee, General Comment 23, para. 6.1.   [54] *Minority Schools in Albania*, at 17.

itself, as well as the state. Neither the group nor the state, however, possesses the authority to deny outright membership to persons born within the group but who for various reasons have left the communal space of the group. A person does not lose his or her lawful minority identity by reason of a conscious departure from the group for whatever reason. Rather, such departure may only affect the ability of the person to enjoy certain rights offered only to members living within the group's communal space during that person's absence.

In the *Lovelace* case, which concerned the right of indigenous women to rejoin their tribe, the applicant was a female member of the indigenous Canadian Tobique band who was born in the band's reservation. As a result of her marriage to a non-Indian she ceased to enjoy membership in accordance with article 12(1)(b) of Canada's Indian Act. Following her divorce the applicant was prevented from returning to her parents in the reserve and argued that she was effectively denied the cultural benefits of living within the community, the right to a home and the right to her minority identity. In this tug-of-war between the wishes of the group and individual self-identification the HRCtee naturally favoured the latter. It held that:

Persons who are born and brought up on a reserve, who have kept ties with their community and wish to maintain these ties must *normally* be considered as belonging to that minority within the meaning of the Covenant. (emphasis added)[55]

The Committee's use of the word 'normally' suggests that situations may arise where the severance of a former member from the communal space of the group may be justified, especially where this is 'reasonable or necessary to preserve the identity of the tribe'.[56] Thus, persons whose ancestors fled the group may reasonably be excluded where their large numbers and modern lifestyle would endanger the continued enjoyment of the group's traditional existence. The group's protected existence need not only concern the preservation of its traditional lifestyle, but also its financial well-being.

The HRCtee has long maintained a distinction between the prohibition of denying group membership where objective criteria are met, and the lawful withdrawal of membership rights to those who live outside the group's communal space. In the *Kitok* case the complainant was a native Saami of Sweden whose family had herded reindeer for over one hundred years and had inherited breeding rights in the Sorkaitum village. However, under Swedish law a person loses his breeding rights if engaged in any other profession for a period of three years. The HRCtee accepted the rationale of the Swedish government in introducing this legislation, its purpose being to improve the living conditions of those Saami for whom reindeer husbandry

---

[55] *Lovelace* v. *Canada*, para. 14.   [56] Ibid., para. 17.

constituted their primary income.[57] Effectively, if all Saami were allowed to occasionally engage in reindeer husbandry they would be denying those making a living from it of their future existence, bearing in mind that this activity was an 'essential element in the culture of the ethnic community'.[58] This was therefore a reasonable curtailment of the particular entitlement for the continued viability and welfare of the community as a whole.[59] The Committee emphasised, however, that such a measure did not and could not have the effect of stripping an ethnic Saami of his or her identity.[60]

Let us now discuss the other question posed at the beginning of this section. Is it open to a minority to designate its status in accordance with the wishes of the majority of its members? By way of illustration, the Treaty of Lausanne described the community living in the north-eastern region of Greece, Thrace, as a Muslim minority. The majority of this community has long desired to be designated as an ethnic Turkish minority, something which Greece had strenuously resisted, not only because of the Lausanne Treaty, but also on account of the fact that this community encompassed a considerable number of Pomaks and other Muslims who did not view themselves as Turks. Given the objective identification of minorities under international law it is artificial to deny the existence of a Turkish minority to those members of the Muslim community who identify themselves as such.[61]

It would be impractical to list all the range of protective measures that are affordable to minority members under human rights law as these will vary from situation to situation. The rationale of this body of law, however, is predicated on the axiom that forced assimilation is unacceptable. Minority protection itself is grounded on four pillars: protection of the existence, non-exclusion, non-discrimination and non-assimilation of minorities.[62] The necessary corollary to these requirements is the obligation to respect cultural pluralism through positive action that promotes the distinctive cultural traits of the group internally (for example, by establishing minority-language schools) as well as more broadly within the country.[63] The extent to which a minority culture is accepted, respected and celebrated by the majority is dependent on conscious affirmative action and not hortatory

---

[57] *Kitok* v. *Sweden* (HRCtee) (1988) para. 4.2.   [58] Ibid., para. 9.2.   [59] Ibid., para. 9.8.

[60] Ibid., para. 9.7.

[61] In *Narrain et al.* v. *Mauritius* (HRCtee) (2012), the Mauritian Constitution envisaged four groups for electoral purposes, namely, Hindu, Muslim, Sino-Mauritian and general population for those whose 'way of life' distinguished them from the other three groups. Even though the applicants claimed that they did not feel as falling within any of the four groups, the HRCtee did not grant them an unlimited right of self-identification. Rather, it held that the state could impose mandatory classification (for the purposes of the elections at least), but no updated figures of community affiliation existed and hence the maintenance of the current system was arbitrary (para. 15.5).

[62] Declaration Commentary, above note 37, paras. 21–4.   [63] Ibid., para. 28.

legislative drafting. The non-exclusion of linguistic minorities, for example, may be achieved by recognising their language among the official languages of the state, or by requiring public authorities to employ it when dealing with minority members. Switzerland has granted official status to all four languages spoken by various groups on its territory.[64] Section 6(1) of the South African Constitution of 1996 has gone even further, granting official status to eleven languages and in addition promoting the languages commonly used by ethnic minorities in the country.[65] Of course, the officialisation of all minority languages is an expensive venture which stretches the resources of the state and is not viable everywhere. As a result, article 3(2) of the 1992 Spanish Constitution makes minority languages official only at the regional level.

Even so, given that minority members are generally among the most vulnerable populations of all nations,[66] there is a danger that an incessant preservation of the group's distinct culture among group members may ultimately isolate the members from any sort of advancement. By way of example, if a state places minority children in separate classes because they lack command of the dominant language, something common in European nations with Roma populations, but fails to apply this policy to all children with similar language deficiencies, it is discriminating against the group.[67] Offending states typically contend that Roma children with poor language skills are unable to attend ordinary classes and that they are privileged to be taught in their own language until they catch up. Where educational policies prevent minority children from commanding the dominant language and the country's culture alongside majority children, there is a heightened risk of grooming an estranged generation with limited skills and qualifications, thus leading it to poverty and social exclusion.[68] This is why it is imperative that minority members receive a broad education equal to that of the majority,[69] unless the difference in treatment is based on objective

---

[64] Art. 4 of the Federal Constitution of the Swiss Confederation.

[65] Constitution of South Africa 1996, s. 6(5)(b). See K. Henrard, 'Language Rights and Minorities in South Africa' (2001) 3 *International Journal on Multicultural Societies* 78.

[66] There have of course existed some notable exceptions, such as the minority racist regime of South Africa and the minority Sunni leadership in Iraq during the reign of Saddam Hussein.

[67] *Oršuš and Others* v. *Croatia*, paras. 158–62. On other cases involving the educational segregation of Romani children, see *D. H. and Others* v. *Czech Republic* (ECtHR) (2008); *Sampanis and Others* v. *Greece* (ECtHR) (2008); *Lavida and Others* v. *Greece* (ECtHR) (2013).

[68] The HRCtee in its Concluding Observations on Georgia pointed out that the lack of Georgian language skills 'could lead to marginalization and under-representation of minorities in different public and private spheres': UN doc. CCPR/C/GEO/CO/3 (15 November 2007) para. 17.

[69] Art. 4(4), UN Minorities Declaration.

and reasonable justification.[70] Preservation of a minority's culture and life-style does not mean that the state should allow group members to subsist on the fringes of society. Culture is not a synonym for backwardness or under-development. Thus, states are under an obligation to educate minority children, even if their parents are of a contrary view. Equally, the European Committee of Social Rights (ECSR) has repeatedly noted in respect of the Roma and Traveller communities that their particular situation must be taken into account by states. As a result they should not be allowed to live in substandard conditions without access to health or sanitary services simply because they are nomadic peoples.[71]

In equal measure, the law applicable to minority members (chiefly arising under a treaty intended to confer on them particular rights) should not be construed as something that one may not freely depart from, if it is in their very best interests to do so. In *Molla Sali* v. *Greece*, the applicant, a member of Greece's Muslim minority of Western Thrace, had concluded a will before a civil notary just before the death of her husband. The will excluded the deceased's two sisters, who claimed that recourse to a civil notary was contrary to the personal (Islamic) law of minority members under the 1923 Treaty of Lausanne. The ECtHR emphasised that denying members of a religious community to exit the minority's legal constrains and resort to regular law has a discriminatory impact and further violates the right to self-identification. The Court relied on international law to make the point that the protection offered by minority law did not have the effect of subjecting group members to a particular cultural or legal regime without their consent.[72]

Finally, although some reference has been made to autonomy and self-rule, it should be emphasised that one of the key elements in the international human rights regime for minorities is the quest for their right to effective participation in decision-making at the regional level in matters that affect them.[73] The UN Minorities Commentary provides some indication of how this may be implemented in practice:

[70] In *D. H. and Others* v. *Czech Republic*, para. 196, the ECtHR held that where a difference in treatment was based on race or ethnicity, the notion of objective and reasonable justification must be interpreted as strictly as possible.

[71] *Interights* v. *Greece* (ECSR) (2009); equally by the same Committee, *Centre on Housing Rights and Evictions (COHRE)* v. *Italy* (ECSR) (2010).

[72] *Molla Sali* v. *Greece* (ECtHR) (2018) paras. 154–7.

[73] Art. 2(2), UN Minorities Declaration; CERD, Concluding Observations on Estonia, UN doc. CERD/C/EST/CO/8–9 (23 September 2010) para. 14; the HRCtee deplored the low representation of minorities at local level in Croatia, UN doc. CCPR/C/HRV/CO/2 (4 November 2009) para. 18. According to the ECtHR in *Mathieu-Mohin and Clerfayt* v. *Belgium* (ECtHR) (1987), this right is not violated where a linguistic minority is obliged to elect parliamentary representatives that belong to the linguistic majority in the region, as long, of course, as this does not impair the situation of the minority or lead to arbitrariness.

Where minorities are concentrated territorially, single-member districts may provide sufficient minority representation. Proportional representation systems, where a political party's share in the national vote is reflected in its share of the legislative seats, may assist in the representation of minorities. Some forms of preference voting, where voters rank candidates in order of choice, may also facilitate minority representation and promote inter-communal cooperation.

Much like the rationale inherent in avoiding 'over-protection' that leads to the group's isolation from the wider community, it is also wise to avoid establishing segregated institutions and public mechanisms. In the spirit of multiculturalism the Declaration warns that:

> Public institutions should not be based on ethnic or religious criteria. Governments at local, regional and national levels should recognise the role of multiple identities in contributing to open communities and in establishing useful distinctions between public institutional structures and cultural identities.[74]

This segregation may be an inevitable reality during transitional periods in post-conflict situations so as to deter the various groups from engaging in hostile acts, but it cannot remain a perpetual policy. The Dayton Peace Agreement that ended the Bosnian civil war envisaged a constitutional provision whereby membership of the House of Peoples and the Presidency was reserved solely to those who identified themselves as belonging to one of the three 'constituent people' (i.e. Bosniac, Serbs and Croats). This was certainly a welcome arrangement at the time in order to ensure peace, but fifteen years later it was found by the European Court of Human Rights (ECtHR) to be discriminatory on racial and ethnic grounds against non-constituent peoples, such as local Roma and Jews.[75]

CASE STUDY 10.2
The Malay *Bumiputra* Policy

Following the independence of Malaysia from the British in 1957 the successor government was of the opinion that indigenous Malays were financially disadvantaged in comparison to other ethnic groups, particularly the country's Chinese community. The ethnic Chinese minority had acquired some affluence as a result of commercial entrepreneurship, whereas the Malay majority lacked universal education, access to government and in rural areas people were considered 'backward'. As a result, it was decided that a degree of positive

---

[74] Declaration Commentary, above note 37, paras. 45 and 47.
[75] *Sejdić and Finci v. Bosnia and Herzegovina* (ECtHR) (2009) paras. 45–50.

discrimination was required in order to bring the level of the indigenous majority to par with the Chinese minority. This principle was enshrined in article 153(1) of the Malaysian Constitution as an express exception to the general rule in article 8(2) which prohibits discrimination of citizens on any ground, as follows: It shall be the responsibility of the [Head of state] to safeguard the special position of the Malays and natives of any of the states of Sabah and Sarawak and the legitimate interests of other communities in accordance with the provisions of this Article.

Those defined as ethnic Malays (or Bumiputras) were subsequently granted privileges over and above other minority members under the pretext that by doing so inter-ethnic tensions would be diminished. This amounted to outright discrimination in all fields of public and private life. By way of illustration, companies must have a minimum *Bumiputra* equity ownership if they are to be listed on the Malaysian stock exchange. Equally, minorities are discriminated against in employment opportunities in the public sector, subsidies for housing and in most other fields. Of course, the effect of these policies has culminated in discrimination against all minority groups and many ethnic Chinese have been forced to leave the country.

Do you consider this policy to be sound from the point of view of advancing a relatively poor and under-developed ethnic group? Is this justified from an affirmative action perspective, especially given that positive discrimination is directed against members of a minority?

QUESTIONS

1. The determination of whether an ethnic minority should possess some degree of autonomy or self-rule should be made not only by members of the minority, but also by the people of the majority. Discuss.

2. Multiculturalism requires tolerance, the preservation and promotion of which is an obligation incumbent on states according to the ECtHR.[76] In a post-conflict nation where ethnic rivalry continues to ignite fierce hostilities, what type of minority regime would you recommend? How would you implement multiculturalism, if at all?

3. Are minority rights tantamount to equality rights?

4. The HRCtee has held that the right of minority members to profess and practise their religion does not impose an obligation on states to fund private religious

---

[76] *Serif* v. *Greece* (ECtHR) (1999) para. 53.

schools.[77] Is this consistent with the principle of equality, particularly where the state funds religious majority schools?

5. A sizeable group of German nationals claim to be an ethnic Prussian minority. There is no longer a Prussian state, its lands having been incorporated into what are today Germany, Poland and Russia. Can the group be considered an ethnic minority for the purposes of the ICCPR and the UN Minorities Declaration?

6. The Roma traditional lifestyle involves constant movement within the territory of states and settlement for short periods in empty land plots. Can states restrict this movement, taking into account that this is the cornerstone of the Roma's cultural identity?[78]

10.4   INDIGENOUS PEOPLES: IS THERE A NEED FOR ADDITIONAL PROTECTION?

Indigenous peoples are the original inhabitants of a territory before it was conquered or colonised and who continue to live there. From the point of view of human rights, it is important to ponder on the following issues: (1) the criteria for indigenous identity and whether any particular protection is warranted in countries primarily inhabited by indigenous peoples; (2) whether the term 'peoples' implies a right of self-determination; (3) whether there is a need for special human rights rules in addition to those that apply to all persons under general international law; and (4) whether indigenous rights are collective rights.

Indigenous claims before treaty bodies have been largely predicated on the law pertinent to minority rights, as is the case with the HRCtee. The majority of the cases examined in the previous section by the HRCtee under article 27 of the ICCPR concerned indigenous groups. It should not surprise us that the term 'indigenous' is not defined in a comprehensive multilateral treaty with universal force; this is also the case with other equally important legal concepts, such as terrorism. The absence of a binding legal definition of 'indigeneity' is probably welcome because it is not susceptible to immutable understandings, particularly given that law is generally averse to concepts such as 'spiritual' or 'culture', which play a large part in the social and anthropological construction of indigenous peoples.[79] None the less, there is significant consensus as to the

---

[77] *Waldman* v. *Canada* (HRCtee) (1999) para. 10.6, noting, however, that if a state chooses to fund the schools of one religious group it is discriminatory not to fund the schools of other religious communities; see also the *Belgian Linguistic case (No. 2)* (ECtHR) (1968), where the ECtHR held that the right to education does not provide a guarantee to the children or the parents of linguistic minorities that their overall education will be provided in their mother tongue.

[78] See *Coster* v. *UK* (ECtHR) (2001).

[79] Para. 9 of the UNESCO Heritage Committee 2012 Operational Guidelines refers to 'world heritage' (mixed cultural and natural heritage) as follows: 'Cultural landscapes often reflect

essential characteristics of indigenousness. A very sketchy definition is articulated in article 1(1) of International Labour Organization (ILO) Convention 169 on Indigenous and Tribal Peoples. However, the most authoritative definition was that offered by UN Special Rapporteur Martínez Cobo:

Indigenous communities, peoples and nations are those which, having a historical continuity with pre-invasion and pre-colonial societies that developed on their territories, consider themselves distinct from other sectors of the societies now prevailing in those territories, or parts of them. They form at present non-dominant sectors of society and are determined to preserve, develop and transmit to future generations their ancestral territories, and their ethnic identities, as the basis of their continued existence as peoples, in accordance with their own cultural patterns, social institutions and legal systems.[80]

Certain features are indispensable, particularly historical continuity, occupation of ancestral lands and attachment thereto, as well as distinctiveness in culture and social institutions, from the dominant groups. By way of illustration, most indigenous peoples enjoy a spiritual attachment to their land,[81] something alien to industrialised nations, as is the case with Australian aboriginals. Much like minorities, the determination of indigenous status is based on self-identification and the same principles apply *mutatis mutandis*.[82] Although genetics may be useful in some clear-cut cases they have little utility for those of mixed race. In such cases it is generally agreed that cultural circumstances play a more significant role for the construction of an indigenous identity.[83] The Inter-American Court has stated that '[t]he identification of [an indigenous community or people], from its name to its membership, is a social and historical fact that is part of its autonomy'.[84]

While it is relatively easy to identify indigenous groups in recently colonised territories, such as North and South America and Australia, it is not so in Africa or Asia where the local populations are by and large indigenous in the literal sense and dominant. It is for this reason that post-colonial governments in both Africa and Asia have refused to accept the existence of indigenous

---

specific techniques of sustainable land-use, considering the characteristics and limits of the natural environment they are established in, *and a specific spiritual relation to nature*' (emphasis added).

[80] UN doc. E/CN.4/Sub.2/1986/7/Add.4 (1986) para. 379.

[81] See the relevant discussion in *South Fork Band and Others* v. *United States* (US) (2009).

[82] See art. 1 ILO Convention 169; arts. 9 and 33(1) UNDRIP, UNGA resolution 61/295 (13 September 2007); CERD General Recommendation VIII (22 August 1990); CERD, Concluding Observations on Indonesia, UN doc. CERD/C/IDN/CO/3 (15 August 2007) para. 15, demanding that Indonesia 'respect the way in which indigenous peoples perceive and define themselves'; para. 4(a) World Bank OP 4.10, 'indigenous peoples' (as revised in 2013).

[83] *Gibbs* v. *Capewell* (Australia) (1995), per Drummond J, at 584.

[84] *Xákmok Kásek Indigenous Community* v. *Paraguay* (IACtHR) (2010) para. 37.

peoples therein as a distinct category warranting special protection.[85] The African Commission on Human and Peoples' Rights (ACmHPR) has rejected this argument, claiming that in Africa 'the term indigenous population does not mean first inhabitants in reference to aboriginality as opposed to non-African communities or those having come from elsewhere'.[86] Thus, it is legally possible for some African populations to be classified as indigenous on the basis of:

occupation and use of a specific territory; the voluntary perpetuation of cultural distinctiveness; self-identification as a distinct collectivity, as well as recognition by other groups; an experience of subjugation, marginalisation, dispossession, exclusion or discrimination.[87]

In equal measure, peoples not considered indigenous in the literal sense, but on the basis that they 'make up a *tribal* community whose social, cultural and economic characteristics are different from other sections of the national community, particularly because of their special relationship with their ancestral territories, and because they regulate themselves, at least partially, by their own norms, customs, and/or traditions'.[88] As a result, they are protected in the same manner as indigenous peoples. Just like minorities (but more so in the case of indigenous peoples), the fact that some members of an indigenous community choose to live outside the community's territory and on the basis of a non-traditional lifestyle does not affect the distinctiveness of the group, nor its communal use and enjoyment of its property. In the *Kaliña and Lokono Peoples* v. *Suriname*, the respondent state had argued that the indigenous applicants did not constitute a homogeneous group and hence did not enjoy the juridical status of an indigenous group. The Inter-American Court did not agree that all members of the group, past and present, must act uniformly in order to enjoy indigenous status.[89]

The principal concern of many states with the ongoing indigenous legal discourse concerns the self-determination of indigenous groups. This preoccupation is reflected in the shift of terminology in the 1957[90] and 1989 ILO Conventions, from 'populations' in the former to 'peoples' in the latter. This shift in language, however, did not go as far as providing an express

---

[85] See B. Kingsbury, 'Indigenous Peoples in International Law: A Constructivist Approach to the Asian Controversy' (1998) 92 *American Journal of International Law* 414, at 415, who juxtaposes a constructivist perspective to the positivist definition of indigenousness. He understands this as 'embodying a continuous process in which claims and practices in specific cases are abstracted in the wider institutions of international society, then made specific again at the moment of application in the political, legal and social processes of particular cases and societies'.

[86] *UN Declaration on Rights of Indigenous Peoples* (ACmHPR) (2007) para. 13.

[87] *Centre for Minority Rights Development (Kenya) and Minority Rights Group International on behalf of Endorois Welfare Council* v. *Kenya (Endorois case)* (ACmHPR) (2009) para. 150.

[88] *Saramaka People* v. *Suriname* (IACtHR) (2007) para. 84.

[89] *Kaliña and Lokono Peoples* v. *Suriname* (IACHR) (2013) para. 80.

[90] ILO Convention 107 Concerning the Protection and Integration of Indigenous and Other Tribal and Semi-Tribal Populations in Independent Countries.

reference to self-determination. Yet much like the international law pertinent to minorities, it is undisputed that indigenous peoples enjoy *mutatis mutandis* the same level of internal self-determination.[91] One could also claim that where an indigenous group constitutes a clear numerical majority it is also entitled to the external dimension of self-determination in the sense described earlier in this chapter.[92]

The depth of international human rights law should ordinarily render claims for a specialist international indigenous law redundant. To some degree this is true, yet certain demands posited by indigenous peoples are not obviously covered by existing instruments and mechanisms. One such demand concerns indigenous claims to ancestral lands, the application of customary/native laws and dispute mechanisms, the right to spiritual property and spiritual connection to land, the right to have agreements signed with colonisers validated and others. These claims, and many others, are reproduced as collective entitlements in the two ILO Conventions and the UN Declaration on the Rights of Indigenous Peoples (UNDRIP) and are reflective of the particular circumstances and struggles of indigenous peoples. Many of these are not, however, confirmed by the practice of states. For example, the validity of colonial treaties with natives has largely been refuted,[93] as has been the claim to exclusive indigenous land ownership. Equally, indigenous peoples have not reaped the rewards of their traditional knowledge in the pharmaceutical qualities of plants or the intellectual property of their artistic work.[94] Increasingly, indigenous knowledge and its contribution to biodiversity is recognised in international instruments, such as the 1992 Rio Declaration of Environment and Development[95] and the 1992 Convention on Biological Diversity. Article 8(j) of the latter calls on states parties to:

Respect, preserve and maintain knowledge, innovations and practices of indigenous and local communities embodying traditional lifestyles relevant for the conservation

---

[91] See arts. 3–5 UNDRIP.

[92] One should, however, reflect on Engle's critical remark that one of the landmark contributions of UNDRIP has been its denial of external self-determination in favour of autonomy and collective rights (over and above other individual rights). See K. Engle, 'On Fragile Architecture: The UN Declaration on the Rights of Indigenous Peoples in the Context of Human Rights' (2011) 22 *European Journal of International Law* 141.

[93] *Lone Wolf* v. *Hitchcock* (US) (1903); *USA–UK Cayuga Indians* (Arbitral Award) (1926); *Netherlands* v. *USA* (*Island of Palmas* case) (Arbitral Award) (1928) at 858.

[94] Intellectual property (IP) laws and treaties predominantly favour the patent-holder, which is seldom ever the indigenous community. IP-related international instruments protecting indigenous traditional knowledge and art are either framed in soft law, such as the 1989 UNESCO Recommendation on the safeguarding of traditional culture and folklore, or are otherwise weak conventions (as compared to commercially focused IP treaties), such as the 2003 UNESCO Convention on the Safeguarding of Intangible Cultural Heritage and the 2005 UNESCO Convention on the Protection and Promotion of the Diversity of Cultural Expressions; see Chapter 20.4.

[95] Principle 22.

and sustainable use of biological diversity and promote their wider application with the approval and involvement of the holders of such knowledge, innovations and practices and encourage the equitable sharing of the benefits arising from the utilisation of such knowledge, innovations and practices.

Besides the gradual erosion of their cultural heritage and the loss of their ancestral lands, indigenous communities have moreover been the target of much more repugnant violations. It is now well recorded that in many instances indigenous peoples have been unable to defend themselves against forced assimilation, physical genocide through official sterilisation policies as exemplified by Australia's policies against its aboriginal population[96] and statistical ethnocide.[97] The underlying root of such attacks against indigenous peoples is usually 'racism and structural exclusion', as was the case with the genocide of Mayan populations by Guatemala from the 1970s until the mid-1990s.[98]

Besides the possible individual entitlements, what distinguishes indigenous claims from minority claims is that the former are quintessentially collective rights.[99] This is what makes indigenous land rights special and justifies why indigenous peoples enjoy the right to a collective juridical personality, in the absence of which the deeper meaning of their traditional way of life is meaningless.[100]

10.4.1   Indigenous Rights over Traditional Lands

Unlike capitalist societies, whose members have been schooled to view land as a commodity, the indigenous relationship to land may be described as naturalistic, religious, social and spiritual in nature, among other

[96] The Australian case against its aboriginal population is well documented and was in fact legalised through the adoption of the 1918 Aboriginals Ordinance. The Australian policy of enforced assimilation and Aboriginal child removal was initially legalised by the 1918 Aboriginals Ordinance and was subsequently defended on legalistic grounds by the Australian High Court in *Kruger* v. *The Commonwealth* (Australia) (1997). See also *Mestanza Chavez* v. *Peru* (IACHR) (2003), where the Peruvian authorities were found to have harassed an illiterate indigenous Peruvian woman by telling her that giving birth to five children was a criminal offence and that she would have to be sterilised. See 'Mass Sterilisation Scandal Shocks Peru', *BBC News* (24 July 2004), which reported 200,000 enforced sterilisations of indigenous Indians by the Fujimori regime.

[97] P. Thornberry, *Indigenous Peoples and Human Rights* (Manchester University Press, 2013) 16–17, who cites examples of under-counting in order to deliberately marginalise particular indigenous groups.

[98] *Residents of the Village of Chichupac and Neighboring Communities* v. *Guatemala* (IACHR) (2014) para. 322.

[99] *Kichwa Indigenous Peoples of Sarayaku* v. *Ecuador* (IACtHR) (2012) para. 231.

[100] *Kaliña and Lokono Peoples* v. *Suriname*, paras. 86–7; *Kuna Indigenous People of Madungandi and Embera Indigenous People of Bayano* v. *Panama* (IACtHR) (2012) paras. 192–3.

things.[101] The following subsections will deal with this important issue for indigenous peoples, that is, their legal relationship with land they have traditionally occupied. The aim is to demonstrate the claims themselves, as well as the legislative variations adopted by states with significant indigenous populations within the overall framework of international law and human rights advancements.

10.4.2   Indigenous Land Rights in Contemporary International Law

Indigenous rights of occupancy or communal ownership are typically reflected in domestic constitutions and land statutes. In the *Mayagna* case before the Inter-American Court of Human Rights (IACtHR) the government of Nicaragua had granted a timber concession to a private company in respect of land occupied by an indigenous group which never sought occupancy titles. The Nicaraguan government argued that because the law required registration and titling they possessed no valid native title. None the less, evidence furnished showed that the group had occupied the land for at least three hundred years and moreover the right of 'communal ownership of lands' was guaranteed under articles 5, 89 and 180 of the Nicaraguan Constitution. The Court and the Commission agreed that Nicaragua could not expect indigenous groups to undertake all the legal formalities associated with titling and that it had an obligation to demarcate their land, particularly since it had recognised the indigenous nature of the Mayagna. It thus affirmed their right to property under article 21 of the American Convention on Human Rights (ACHR) as follows:

1. The Mayagna Community has communal property rights to land and natural resources based on traditional patterns of use and occupation of ancestral territory. These rights 'exist even without state actions which specify them'. Traditional land tenure is linked to a historical continuity, but not necessarily to a single place and to a single social conformation throughout the centuries. The overall

---

[101] HRCtee, Indigenous Peoples and their Relationship to Land, UN doc. E/CN.4/ Sub.2/2001/21 (11 June 2001) 7–9. See also *Mayagna (Sumo) Awas Tingni Community* v. *Nicaragua* (IACtHR) (2001) para. 149, which held: 'Among indigenous peoples there is a communitarian tradition regarding a communal form of collective property of the land, in the sense that ownership of the land is not centred on an individual but rather on the group and its community. Indigenous groups, by the fact of their very existence, have the right to live freely in their own territory; the close ties of indigenous people with the land must be recognized and understood as the fundamental basis of their cultures, their spiritual life, their integrity, and their economic survival. For indigenous communities, relations to the land are not merely a matter of possession and production but a material and spiritual element which they must fully enjoy, even to preserve their cultural legacy and transmit it to future generations.'

territory of the community is possessed collectively, and the individuals and families enjoy subsidiary rights of use and occupation.

2. Traditional patterns of use and occupation of territory by the indigenous communities of the Atlantic coast of Nicaragua generate customary law property systems; they are property rights created by indigenous customary law norms and practices which must be protected, and they qualify as property rights protected by article 21 of the Convention. Non-recognition of the equality of property rights based on indigenous tradition is contrary to the principle of non-discrimination set forth in article 1(1) of the Convention.

3. The Constitution of Nicaragua and the Autonomy Statute of the Regions of the Atlantic Coast of Nicaragua recognise property rights whose origin is found in the customary law system of land tenure which has traditionally existed in the indigenous communities of the Atlantic Coast. Furthermore, the rights of the community are protected by the American Convention and by provisions set forth in other international conventions to which Nicaragua is a party.

4. There is an international customary law norm which affirms the rights of indigenous peoples to their traditional lands.[102]

This IACtHR jurisprudence suggests that indigenous peoples may possess an inherent right under international law to communal ownership – subject to non-discriminatory restrictions that serve public social interests – other than through official conferral by the apparatus of the state. The essence of this observation is that native title is deemed to exist irrespective of official recognition. Such recognition serves merely to demarcate indigenous land and guarantee all the rights over it against third parties. Communal indigenous rights:

encompass a broader and different concept [of territorial rights] that relates to the collective right to survival as an organized people, with control over their habitat as a necessary condition for reproduction of their culture, for their own development and to carry out their life aspirations. Property [or communal ownership] of the land ensures that the members of the indigenous communities preserve their cultural heritage.[103]

This line of thinking supports the exceptional nature of indigenous land ownership, as opposed to other forms of ownership. What this means is that although the state cannot discriminate between indigenous and other ownership, in cases of expropriation for example, it should adopt measures that take into consideration the particular relationship of indigenous peoples with their land. The IACtHR succinctly noted that:

---

[102] *Mayagna (Sumo) Awas Tingni Community* v. *Nicaragua*, para. 140.
[103] *Yakye Axa Indigenous Community* v. *Paraguay* (IACtHR) (2005) para. 146.

This does not mean that every time there is a conflict between the territorial interests of private individuals or of the state and those of the members of the indigenous communities, the latter must prevail over the former. When states are unable, for concrete and justified reasons, to adopt measures to return the traditional territory and communal resources to indigenous populations, the compensation granted must be guided primarily by the meaning of the land for them.[104]

This right to communal ownership is made explicit in article 26 of the 2007 UNDRIP, which provides as follows:

1. Indigenous peoples have the right to the lands, territories and resources which they have traditionally owned, occupied or otherwise used or acquired.
2. Indigenous peoples have the right to own, use, develop and control the lands, territories and resources that they possess by reason of traditional ownership or other traditional occupation or use, as well as those which they have otherwise acquired.
3. States shall give recognition and protection to these lands, territories and resources. Such recognition shall be conducted with due respect to the customs, traditions and land tenure systems of the indigenous peoples concerned.

Article 26 of UNDRIP seems to be more representative of state practice than article 14(1) of ILO Convention 169. The latter obliges member states to recognise the rights of ownership and possession of indigenous peoples over lands which they traditionally occupy. UNDRIP on the other hand subsumes all rights over land to 'traditional ownership or traditional occupation'.

10.4.3   Indigenous Ownership as a Right to Property

A study of the World Bank documented the precise spectrum of land rights afforded to indigenous groups in thirty-three client countries.[105] With respect to Asia, in China, Thailand and Vietnam all land is owned fully by the state.[106] In the Philippines, in accordance with article 7 of the Indigenous Peoples Rights Act 1977, indigenous groups are entitled to claim ownership over ancestral lands as well as all natural resources. In Malaysia, some native title is recognised, but in most cases indigenous peoples do not possess title and

---

[104] Ibid., para. 149.
[105] See International Bank for Reconstruction and Development (IBRD) Operations Evaluation Department, 'Implementation of Operational Directive 4.20 on Indigenous Peoples: An Independent Desk Review', (2001) at 5–38, online at https://uobdu.files.wordpress.com/2011/05/world-bank-od-4-20.pdf.
[106] China reserves special treatment for ethnic minorities and has set up autonomous regions, but these laws should not be viewed as also protecting indigenous peoples, despite some overlap.

are considered 'tenants-at-will'.[107] Similarly, in Indonesia all land belongs to the state but indigenous people enjoy some limited customary (i.e. local custom) land tenure as long as there is no conflict with ordinary property law. In Cambodia, indigenous groups enjoy communal ownership rights over their lands, which is tantamount to private ownership.[108]

In South America the situation is slightly more clear and coherent. In Argentina, although community ownership of ancestral lands is recognised, it is generally hampered by bureaucratic procedural hurdles and is unavailable to indigenous peoples who have relocated to urban areas. Communal ownership rights are equally recognised in Chile, Colombia, Peru, Ecuador, Bolivia and Venezuela. In Brazil, indigenous persons retain exclusive possession and use, albeit ownership is vested in the state. In Central America the situation is more or less equally consistent. With the exception of Mexico and El Salvador, which do not recognise communal rights of ownership, Honduras, Nicaragua, Panama and Guatemala extend such rights to their indigenous peoples, subject to minor limitations. Russia, the world's largest country, does not recognise land ownership for its indigenous populations.[109]

In India and Pakistan communal ownership is possible but subject to the dictates of regional bodies and the decisions of customary councils of elders, among others. In developed nations we have already seen that land ownership is not generally afforded to indigenous peoples. In Canada, indigenous lands are held in the name of the Crown and only a right to occupy and possess is granted to indigenous persons. The Saami people in Sweden equally only enjoy usufruct rights, whereas in the USA First Nation lands are held in trust by the federal government, in which case the First Nations enjoy either beneficial interests or some limited communal ownership. Exceptionally, New Zealand recognises communal freehold in respect of the Maori. Finally,

---

[107] That indigenous land rights are tantamount to normal property rights under art. 13 of the Constitution has been duly recognised by the Malaysian High Court in *Adong bin Kuwau and 51 Others* v. *The Government of Jahore* (Malaysia) (1997), confirmed by the Malaysian Court of Appeal in *Adong bin Kuwau and 51 Others* v. *The Government of Jahore* (Malaysia) (1998).

[108] Cambodian Land Law 2001, arts. 25–7. The Cambodian government in April 2009 proceeded to adopt legislation through which the titling of customary title could be officially concretised. See UN Economic and Social Council (ECOSOC) Permanent Forum on Indigenous Issues, Information Received from Cambodia, UN doc. E/C.19/2010/12/ Add.5 (16 February 2010). It should, however, be noted that the Cambodian government frequently flouts its indigenous laws by granting concessions on protected lands to foreign investors.

[109] See A. Shapovalov, 'Straightening out the Backward Legal Regulation of Backward Peoples' Claim to Land in the Russian North: The Concept of Indigenous Neomodernism' (2005) 17 *Georgia International Environmental Law Review* 435, where the author argues that Russia adheres to the *terra nullius* doctrine.

in sub-Saharan Africa the situation is somewhat confusing because post-colonial governments have recognised traditional customary tenure rights, albeit these are vested in all persons without distinction between indigenous and non-indigenous.

In a landmark decision the ACmHPR in the *Endorois* case was faced with the eviction of the Endorois people in Kenya from their ancestral lands in order to construct a game reserve and tourist facilities. The contested land was home to a lake which the Endorois believed was formed by God after sinking the ground as punishment against their ancestors, thus forming Lake Bogoria. All their kinsmen were buried adjacent to the lake and all their traditional ceremonies were inextricably linked to it. The Commission confirmed the Endorois' spiritual connection to the land[110] and hence found a violation of article 8 of the ACHPR relating to freedom of religion.[111] The Commission accepted that indigenous rights over traditional lands constituted 'property' and that the rights thereto were 'property rights'.[112] It went on to explain the content of these rights by reference to UNDRIP, as follows:

The jurisprudence under international law bestows the right of ownership rather than mere access. The African Commission notes that if international law were to grant access only, indigenous peoples would remain vulnerable to further violations/dispossession by the state or third parties. Ownership ensures that indigenous peoples can engage with the state and third parties as active stakeholders rather than as passive beneficiaries.[113]

In the view of the African Commission, the following conclusions could be drawn: (a) traditional possession of land by indigenous people has the equivalent effect as that of a state-granted full property title; (b) traditional possession entitles indigenous people to demand official recognition and registration of property title; (c) the members of indigenous peoples who have unwillingly left their traditional lands, or lost possession thereof, maintain property rights thereto, even though they lack legal title, unless the lands have been lawfully transferred to third parties in good faith; and (d) the members of indigenous peoples who have unwillingly lost possession of their lands, when those lands have been lawfully transferred to innocent third parties, are entitled to restitution thereof or to obtain other lands of equal extension and quality.[114]

The Commission is emphatically stating that indigenous peoples possess full property rights over their ancestral lands irrespective of whether the state has registered or titled such land or whether the group has satisfied any formal property requirements.[115] The fact that they constitute property rights

---

[110] *Endorois* case, paras. 156 and 166.   [111] Ibid., para. 173.   [112] Ibid., para. 187.
[113] Ibid., para. 204.   [114] Ibid., para. 209.

distinguishes them from mere access rights or privileges that can be withdrawn or sold to third parties at any time by the government. This is a development that is certainly far more progressive than the legislation applicable in many industrialised nations. The property rights of indigenous peoples involve a particular positive obligation on states. Hence, if an indigenous group enjoys the land for its hunting and fishing needs the state must preserve and sustain the relevant ecosystem. Equally, if a group believes in its spiritual attachment to a lake this must not be exploited in such a way as to deplete or pollute its waters. This is consistent with the jurisprudence of the IACtHR which has held that indigenous groups are owed special measures of protection in order to guarantee the full exercise of their rights.[116]

QUESTIONS

1. The application of native customary law in many instances, especially in Africa, is nothing more than an attempt to deny indigenous peoples universal human rights. Examples include the practice of female genital mutilation, gender-based discrimination and the permissibility of rudimentary dispute resolution mechanisms for which there is no guarantee against arbitrariness. Discuss.

2. The 'treaties' entered into between the early conquerors and indigenous peoples were concluded in territories lacking a legal system and therefore the indigenous subjects were not necessarily endowed with legal personality. Do you consider that the law of contract in your country may render this agreement legally binding? If so, can the relevant private international law treaties be utilised to enforce indigenous 'treaties'?

3. Indigenous and minority women are susceptible to discrimination in two respects: for their minority or indigenous status as such, in addition to their gender. This intersectional discrimination does not always affect male members of the group, as is the case with the practice of rape in the context of ethnic cleansing. Do you consider that in such cases a single, unified, violation should be identified, rather than two distinct ones?

4. The original inhabitants of a particular territory are fully integrated within the dominant group so that they no longer possess any distinct cultural patterns or social institutions. Can they still, none the less, claim entitlements from indigenous rights?

---

[115] Canadian courts distinguish between title and rights and hold that a right may exist independently of a title. See *R* v. *Van der Peet* (Canada) (1996) and *R* v. *Adams* (Canada) (1996), confirmed in *Delgamuukw* v. *British Columbia* (Canada) (1997) para. 138.

[116] *Mayagna (Sumo) Awas Tingni Community*, paras. 148–9 and 151; case of the *Sawhoyamaxa Indigenous Community* v. *Paraguay* (IACtHR) (2006) paras. 118 and 131, and *Yakye Axa Indigenous Community*, paras. 124, 131, 135–7, 154.

10.4.4 Special Considerations in the Design of Indigenous Peoples' Development Plans within the World Bank

Since 1991 the World Bank has required borrowers to mitigate any adverse effects from their intended project on indigenous populations. To this end it has devised a layered process that is designed not only to protect indigenous peoples but also to enhance their developmental advancement. This is important because in theory the Bank is in an ideal position to implement indigenous rights since both the investor and the local government are dependent upon its approval of the loan.

The Bank's Operational Policy (OP) 4.10 on indigenous peoples requires the borrower to engage in a process of 'free, prior, and informed consultation' with the affected indigenous group, which must yield 'broad community support' for the project in order for it to be financed.[117] This is subject to a five-prong process, which consists of the following:

1. screening by the Bank to identify whether indigenous peoples are present in, or have collective attachment to, the project area;[118]
2. a social assessment by the borrower;[119]
3. a process of free, prior, and informed consultation with the affected indigenous peoples' communities at each stage of the project, and particularly during project preparation, to fully identify their views and ascertain their broad community support for the project;[120]
4. the preparation of an indigenous peoples plan (IPP) or an indigenous peoples planning framework (IPPF);[121] and
5. disclosure of the draft IPP or draft IPPF.[122]

In the screening process the Bank seeks to determine the existence of indigenous people in the project area and their attachment to it. To this end it consults qualified social scientists, particularly anthropologists with expertise in the project area. In addition, the Bank also consults the indigenous group and the borrower. Where it determines the existence of indigenous peoples it is then incumbent on the borrower to undertake a social assessment study in order to evaluate the project's effects. Where potentially negative effects are detected the social impact assessment (SIA) must propose alternative measures. The SIA assesses in advance the social consequences that are likely to follow from the project, including probable impacts from environmental manipulation.[123] Although the SIA is not an exact science, it may determine the impact on variables such as community structures and institutions,

---

[117] Para. 1, Operational Policy (OP) 4.10 (as revised in April 2013).   [118] Ibid., paras. 6 and 8.
[119] Ibid., paras. 6 and 9.   [120] Ibid., paras. 6 and 10–11.   [121] Ibid., paras. 6 and 12–13.
[122] Ibid., paras. 6 and 15.
[123] See generally H. A. Becker and F. Vanclay, *The International Handbook of Social Impact Assessment: Conceptual and Methodological Advances* (Edward Elgar, 2006).

changes in social behaviour, local norms, customs and activities, changes in social control mechanisms, creation of employment opportunities and others. It is not untypical of borrowers in general – and governments for that matter – to manipulate the SIA as a political rather than as a planning tool. This may be done in order to justify a particular policy rather than as a tool to mitigate the effects of the policy on the affected population.

The Bank's only guarantee against manipulation is the consensus of the affected people, which itself is subject to manipulation, as will be demonstrated in the following section. Further, the borrower may well demonstrate an increase in income in respect of the group's households, which he may then interpret as a determinant in the rise of livelihood. In many cases this increase is artificial since it is the result of lump sum compensations paid to affected persons whose effects are of a limited duration. As a result, Ashley and Hussein emphasise that poverty reduction is not necessarily reflected in a sudden increase of income, but should be approached from a study of food security, vulnerability, social inferiority, access to productive means and an understanding of the objectives of each household (i.e. in the sense of what is important to them – education for their children, land security, etc.).[124]

Following the drafting of the social assessment plan the borrower must next engage in direct consultation with the indigenous peoples on the basis of three principles: (1) an appropriate gender and inter-generationally inclusive framework encompassing broad civil society representation; (2) employment of appropriate consultation methods to the cultural and social values of the affected people, with special attention to the concerns of women, youth and children and their access to development opportunities; and (3) providing full access and disclosure to the relevant reports and information. Before the Bank can go ahead and approve the loan the borrower must demonstrate that the project has received broad community support on the basis of free, prior and informed consent (FPIC).[125] It is natural, however, at this stage for the affected group and civil society organisations to barter with the borrower for further concessions, knowing full well that their agreement is necessary for the continuation of the project. This is certainly welcome, because it ensures that indigenous concerns are voiced and heard throughout

---

[124] C. Ashley and K. Hussein, *Developing Methodologies for Livelihood Impact Assessment: Experience of the African Wildlife Foundation in East Africa* (Overseas Development Institute Working Paper 129, 2000) 14.

[125] This is not a mere condition imposed by the Bank. Rather, it has been endorsed as a customary principle by human rights treaty bodies in relation to the taking of indigenous lands, whatever their form of land tenure. See *Poma Poma* v. *Peru* (HRCtee) (2009) para. 7.6; Committee on Economic, Social and Cultural Rights (CESCR), Concluding Observations on Colombia, UN doc. E/C.12/Add.1/74 (30 November 2001) para. 33; *Dann, Mary and Carrie* (IACHR) (2002) para. 131.

the process and that indigenous social and cultural demands are met, even if the local government is opposed to them. Any special agreement must be communicated by the borrower to the Bank.[126]

On the basis of the social assessment and in consultation with the affected communities, the borrower prepares an IPP that sets out appropriate measures ensuring that the affected group will receive culturally appropriate social and economic benefits and that any adverse effects are avoided, mitigated or compensated.[127] The role of civil society in the consultation process is critical, because indigenous peoples' access to information and their level of education may lend itself to manipulation by the borrower. By way of illustration, in the absence of civil society the borrower may paint an idyllic picture of the project without emphasising any of its social and environmental evils. Equally, the borrower may attempt to negotiate only with persons of influence and thus ignore the community's broader aspirations.

What has not always been abundantly clear in the Bank's policies on indigenous peoples is whether its focus should be directed at preserving the group's cultural and social status quo, or whether it should also be open to the possibility that the group may wish to radically alter this traditional status. Paragraph 7 of Operational Directive 4.20 of 1991, which has now been replaced by OP 4.10, raised this issue as a dilemma for Bank management as follows:

How to approach indigenous peoples affected by development projects is a controversial issue. Debate is often phrased as a choice between two opposed positions. One pole is to insulate indigenous populations whose cultural and economic practices make it difficult for them to deal with powerful outside groups. The advantages of this approach are the special protections that are provided and the preservation of cultural distinctiveness; the costs are the benefits forgone from development programmes. The other pole argues that indigenous people must be acculturated to dominant society values and economic activities so that they can participate in national development. Here the benefits can include improved social and economic opportunities, but the cost is often the gradual loss of cultural differences.

Paragraph 1 of OP 4.10 addresses this issue by requiring that all Bank-financed projects impart culturally appropriate social and economic benefits. The Policy goes even further by stressing that the Bank may, *at a country's request*, support development policies that help to strengthen local laws in favour of indigenous groups, set up poverty-reduction programmes and projects owned by indigenous peoples, as well as address gender and intergenerational issues,[128] among others.

In practice, this process is expensive and cumbersome for borrowers and to a certain degree intrusive for the target states. Moreover, vulnerable and

---

[126] OP 4.10, para. 11(e).   [127] Ibid., para. 1.   [128] OP 4.20, para. 22.

marginalised indigenous groups are typically exploited for their labour and lands by local elites, including timber and natural resources corporations, non-indigenous farmers and corrupt local government officials. Thus, there are many actors who are averse, if not outright hostile, to the enhancement of the status of indigenous peoples, in terms of legal, social as well as financial status. Hence, the Bank should not simply strive to accept an IPP because it has received broad consensus from the indigenous group in the project area. Rather, it must make every effort to eliminate any possible hostility against the group following the completion of the project and avoid the temptation of temporary financial benefits. The following section provides a case study of a World Bank project that failed to satisfy these demands because both the borrower and the Bank simply focused on the letter of the operational policy and not its spirit.

10.4.5 The Chad–Cameroon Pipeline and the Baka/Bakola: What to Look for in Social Impact Assessments

In the late 1990s the World Bank Group proceeded to provide US$115 million towards financing the Chad–Cameroon pipeline project, which was meant to transport Chadian oil to the Cameroonian coast. Although the Bank's participation represented only 3 per cent of the entire amount it provided appropriate political and financial guarantees. The construction of the Cameroon portion of the pipeline was to traverse the country's Atlantic forest zone, part of which is inhabited by the Baka/Bakola indigenous peoples. These groups are also known as pygmies, but the term carries a pejorative connotation and the Bakola themselves do not accept it, despite the fact that it appears heavily in the literature. They maintain a traditional lifestyle that is distinct not only from that of the general population of Cameroon but also from neighbouring tribal and semi-tribal peoples. Unlike other groups they are principally engaged in hunting, trapping and fishing and only recently began to cultivate as an alternative; yet farming is only of secondary financial importance to them, not only because of their cultural identity but also because they are not land owners.

The traverse of the pipeline through traditional Baka/Bakola lands gave rise to two interrelated issues. The first concerned the social impact of the project on this community whereas the second involved the potential realignment of inter-ethnic relations with neighbouring groups and the state itself. The IPP foresaw that the project would bring progress to the area and proposed both individual and collective compensation which consisted in the construction of huts, the provision of tools and compensation for destroyed crops and farmland. There was also provision for a limited supply of electricity, access to health care and education. There is ample evidence that the borrowers did not adequately consult with all the Bakola and moreover failed to compensate all those affected in the project area.

The project was bound to disrupt the Baka/Bakola traditional lifestyle, given that the pipeline was destined to pass through forestland used for their principal activities of hunting and crop-gathering. This eventuality would necessarily result in their adjustment within more confined forest space or lead them towards agriculture as their exclusive livelihood. Both alternatives involved some social adaptation whose consequences the borrowers and the Bank failed to address. The most serious problem was that of land ownership. Under Cameroonian law customary title to land has been available since 1974 as long as the land is occupied or exploited. Land is deemed occupied where the user has constructed buildings and dwellings, whereas exploitation is demonstrated in cases of farming and grazing. The guiding principle in order for customary title to be granted is therefore 'man's clear control of the land and evident development'.[129] Given the Bakola's hunting and crop-gathering livelihood they can never expect to possess any customary law rights under the existing law. They fare no better in Cameroon's forests. The law there distinguishes between non-permanent forest domains, which may be converted for agricultural use, and permanent forest domains that are reserved for conservation. Forest laws have imposed severe restrictions on Bakola hunting and crop-gathering rights because forest products are limited only to personal use. Moreover, because the Bakola do not technically 'occupy' or 'exploit' converted forest land they have never been able to claim any pertinent rights. This has driven the Baka/Bakola to poverty because they traditionally barter with wild game and forest crops, this being their primary source of income. Moreover, it has forced them to become subservient to other groups which have acquired land ownership. Equally, although Cameroonian law envisages annual proceeds from a logging tax that are to be distributed to local village communities, in practice the Baka/Bakola are excluded by rival groups because they are not recognised as having resident status.[130]

As a result of the legal impediments restricting their primary (hunting and crop-gathering) and secondary financial activities (agriculture and farming), the Bakola have become subservient to neighbouring groups, namely certain Bantu tribes.[131] This situation has been exacerbated by the fact that the Bantu are farmers and therefore have come to own land. This stark inequality

---

[129] Art. 15(1) of Order no. 74-1 (6 July 1974) 'Laying down the land tenure system'.

[130] Centre for Environment and Development, Réseau Recherches Actions Concertées Pygmées (RACOPY) and Forest Peoples Programme (FPP), 'The Situation of Indigenous Peoples in Cameroon: A Supplementary Report Submitted to CERD', UN doc. CERD/C/CMR/19 (27 January 2010) paras. 13 and 47ff.

[131] See G. Ngima Mawoung, 'The Relationship between the Bakola and the Bantu Peoples of the Coastal Regions of Cameroon and their Perception of Commercial Forest Exploitation' (2001) 26 *African Study Monographs* 209.

between the two groups has not been addressed by Cameroon, despite the obvious vulnerability of the Bakola, and has led many of them to be considered Bantu serfs. This inequality has curtailed the Bakola's access to markets to sell or barter their forest products, which has in turn forced them to barter with the Bantu who naturally exploit them. Neither the borrowers nor the Bank thought it wise to alter their subservient and serf (economic and social) status, despite the fact that they desired to escape this cycle of exploitation through the acquisition of land, educating their children and improving their standard of living, while retaining much of their traditional lifestyle. Without delaying the project the Bank should, in similar circumstances, oblige the host state to accept legislative changes alleviating the subservient condition of vulnerable people. In the instant case, this could have been achieved by granting the Bakola land rights and rendering them recipients of the logging tax.

This case study is emblematic of the Bank's perception (not necessarily in bad faith) that the socio-economic status of indigenous peoples must remain untouched. Thus, SIA studies fail to identify the discrimination directed against them by the state and other social groups. In this manner, their cycle of poverty and under-development will be perpetuated.

FURTHER READING

Anaya, S. J., *Indigenous Peoples in International Law* (Oxford University Press, 2004).

Barelli, M., 'The Role of Soft Law in the International Legal System: The Case of the United Nations Declaration on the Rights of Indigenous Peoples' (2009) 58 *International and Comparative Law Quarterly* 957.

Caruso, U., and R. Hofmann, *The United Nations Declaration on Minorities* (Martinus Nijhoff, 2015).

Castellino, J., and E. Dominguez-Redondo, *Minority Rights in Asia: A Comparative Legal Analysis* (Oxford University Press, 2006).

Crawford, J. (ed.), *The Rights of Peoples* (Oxford University Press, 1992).

Doyle, C. M., *Indigenous Peoples, Title to Territory, Rights and Resources: The Transformative Role of Free Prior and Informed Consent* (Routledge, 2014).

French, D. (ed.), *Statehood and Self-Determination* (Cambridge University Press, 2015).

Genna, G. M., and T. Hiroi, *Regional Integration and Democratic Conditionality: How Democracy*

Clauses Help Democratic Consolidation and Deepening (Routledge, 2016).

Gilbert, J., *Nomadic Peoples and Human Rights* (Routledge, 2014).

Indigenous Peoples' Land Rights under International Law: From Victors to Actors (Martinus Nijhoff, 2012).

Keane, D., *Caste-based Discrimination in International Human Rights Law* (Ashgate, 2007).

Kymlicka, W., *Multicultural Odysseys: Navigating the New International Politics of Diversity* (Oxford University Press, 2009).

Lerner, N., *Group Rights and Discrimination in International Law* (Martinus Nijhoff, 2003).

May, S., T. Modood and J. Squires (eds.), *Ethnicity, Nationalism and Minority Rights* (Cambridge University Press, 2014).

McHugh, P., *The Maori Magna Carta: New Zealand Law and the Treaty of Waitangi* (Oxford University Press, 1991).

Newman, D., *Community and Collective Rights: A Theoretical Framework for Rights held by Groups* (Hart, 2011).

Ndahinda, F. M., *Indigenousness in Africa: A Contested Legal Framework for Empowerment of Marginalised Communities* (TMC Asser, 2011).

Pentassuglia, G., *Minority Groups and Judicial Discourse in International Law: A Comparative Perspective* (Martinus Nijhoff, 2009).

Pulitano, E. (ed.), *Indigenous Rights in the Era of the UN Declaration* (Cambridge University Press, 2014).

Raco, R., *State-Led Privatisation and the Demise of the Democratic State* (Routledge, 2016).

Ratner, S., 'Drawing a Better Line: *Uti Possidetis* and the Borders of New States' (1996) 90 *American Journal of International Law* 590.

Reisman, W. M., 'Protecting Indigenous Rights in International Adjudication' (1995) 89 *American Journal of International Law* 352.

Spiliopoulou-Akermark, A., *Justifications of Minority Protection in International Law* (Martinus Nijhoff, 1996).

Tesón, F. R. (ed), *The Theory of Self-Determination* (Cambridge University Press, 2016).

Thornberry, P., *Indigenous Peoples and Human Rights* (Manchester University Press, 2013).

Van Genugten, W., 'Protection of Indigenous Peoples on the African Continent: Concepts, Position Seeking and the Interaction of Legal Systems' (2010) 104 *American Journal of International Law* 29.

Xanthaki, A., *Indigenous Rights and United Nations Standards: Self-Determination, Culture and Lands* (Cambridge University Press, 2010).

Websites

Council of Europe, National Minorities: www.coe.int/en/web/minorities/home

Eurominority.eu: www.eurominority.eu/version/eng/index.asp

European Centre for Minority Issues: www.ecmi.de/

Forest Peoples Programme: www.forestpeoples.org/

International Work Group for Indigenous Affairs: www.iwgia.org/

Minority Rights Group International: www.minorityrights.org/

UN Forum on Indigenous Issues: http://undesadspd.org/indigenouspeoples.aspx

Unrepresented Nations and Peoples Organisation: http://unpo.org/

World Bank and Indigenous Peoples: www.world-bank.org/en/topic/indigenouspeoples

The Human Rights of Women

CONTENTS

11.1   INTRODUCTION

The disadvantages, discrimination and subordination suffered by women globally have been well documented in a variety of contexts.[1] Yet the issue of women's human rights has, until relatively recently, been neglected in international law. The instruments composing the International Bill of Human Rights contain general non-discrimination clauses which include the prohibition of discrimination on the basis of sex or gender, whereby the rights within these instruments are held to be applicable to everyone, regardless of, inter alia, sex.[2] As this chapter will discuss, these generic non-discrimination clauses have, in a number of ways, proved inadequate to

---

Chapter written by the late Dr Rupa Reddy, a former teaching fellow at the School of Law, SOAS, University of London. She had worked with a number of international human rights organisations, including on women's rights projects in the UK and elsewhere, and completed a major study on 'Approaches to Honour-Related Violence in the English Legal System'.

[1] See H. Charlesworth and C. Chinkin, *The Boundaries of International Law: A Feminist Analysis* (Manchester University Press, 2000) ch.1, especially 4–14.

[2] See e.g., art. 2 UDHR; art. 2(1) ICCR and art. 2(2) ICESCR.

capture the specific nature of violations suffered by women and to provide adequate protection. Women's human rights are an overarching phenomenon touching on all aspects of the international human rights framework. The importance of addressing human rights issues as they *specifically* pertain to women and others suffering disadvantage or oppression within gender-based power structures has now been widely recognised.[3]

Informed, determined and vociferous campaigns by national and international women's rights movements and coalitions have brought to light, and attempted to redress, a number of inadequacies within the international human rights system. In particular, they have questioned a number of the assumptions underlying the existing framework of protection, particularly a narrow focus on non-discrimination at the expense of broader concerns reflecting the experiences of women, such as gender-based violence. The culmination of the 1976–1985 United Nations (UN) Decade for Women with the 1995 Beijing Fourth World Conference was instrumental in bringing key issues to the fore, and was followed by the Beijing Declaration and Platform for Action ten years later.[4] The Platform discussed and made recommendations on a wide range of issues, including poverty, education, health, violence against women, armed conflict, political rights and the rights of the girl-child, which showed the breadth of concerns relating to women's rights.[5]

At the heart of this discussion remains the core question: why do the human rights of women still remain so contested and controversial? Conceptual and sociological approaches to cultural and social hierarchies, as well as the practicalities of how far to 'mainstream' women's human rights into existing human rights mechanisms, rather than creating separate regimes specifically aimed at protecting women, have been at the centre of these

[3] For useful introductory background perspectives to these debates, see Chinkin and Charlesworth, above note 1. Also N. Burrows, 'International Law and Human Rights: the Case of Women's Rights', in T. Campbell et al. (eds.), *Human Rights: From Rhetoric To Reality* (Blackwells, 1986) 80–98; and R. Cook, 'Women's International Human Rights Law: the Way Forward' (1993) 15 *Human Rights Quarterly* 230. The 2014 UN OHCHR report 'Women's Rights are Human Rights' also provides a useful introductory overview of the current frameworks in place within the UN system, available at www.ohchr.org/Documents/Events/WHRD/WomenRightsAreHR.pdf.

[4] The conference recommended the adoption of the Beijing Declaration and Platform for Action by UNGA. The full text of the document can be found at www.un.org/womenwatch/daw/beijing/platform/. See also R. Cook, 'Effectiveness of the Beijing Conference: Advancing International Law Regarding Women' (1997) 91 *American Society of International Law Proceedings* 310.

[5] The progress and developments made since the original Platform are outlined in the UN Women Annual Report 2014–2015, online at http://annualreport.unwomen.org/en/2015; and also by the Office of the High Commissioner for Human Rights in the document 'Beijing+20', online at www.ohchr.org/Documents/Issues/Women/WRGS/Beijing20Review.pdf.

[6] See H. Charlesworth, 'Not Waving but Drowning: Gender Mainstreaming and Human Rights within the United Nations' (2005) 18 *Harvard Human Rights Journal* 1, which provides a key contribution to these debates.

debates.[6] The 'generational' hierarchy created by certain approaches within the system, whereby so-called first-generation civil and political rights are deemed to take priority over other rights, also forms an important part of the debates.[7] Furthermore, many violations against women are committed in the private, rather than the public realm. However, international human rights law has traditionally focused on the public, 'male' sphere. An examination of the effects of this 'public/private divide' is therefore also critical for the practical protection of women's human rights. A more recent debate has revolved around the conceptual distinction between sex and gender, and the ways in which this distinction may affect the practical application of the human rights of women. This chapter revisits these debates, and examines how they have affected the development of women's rights in international human rights law.[8] It uses the example of prosecution of 'honour crimes' in the United Kingdom (UK) to highlight the utility, as well as the limitations, of international human rights law, when seeking effective protection of women's rights at the domestic level.

11.2   NORMATIVE FRAMEWORK

11.2.1   Key Violations of Women's Human Rights: The Convention on the Elimination of All Forms of Discrimination against Women

The major approach to the protection of women's human rights, from the UN Charter onwards, has been that of non-discrimination and equality. According to the Human Rights Committee (HRCtee), discrimination, which is prohibited in articles 3 and 26 of the International Covenant on Civil and Political Rights (ICCPR):

should be understood to imply any distinction, exclusion, restriction or preference which is based on any ground such as race, colour, *sex*, language, religion, political or other opinion, national or social origin, property, birth or other status, and which has the purpose or effect of nullifying or impairing the recognition, enjoyment or exercise by all persons, on an equal footing, of all rights and freedoms. (emphasis added)[9]

---

[7] See C. Bunch, 'Women's Rights as Human Rights: Toward a Re-Vision of Human Rights' (1990) 12 *Human Rights Quarterly* 486; and Charlesworth and Chinkin, above note 1, 206–7.

[8] Related issues of women's rights including international refugee law, international humanitarian law and international criminal law will not be examined in this chapter.

[9] HRCtee, General Comment 18: Non-discrimination (Compilation of General Comments and General Recommendations Adopted by Human Rights Treaty Bodies), UN doc. HRI/GEN/1/ Rev.1 (1994) 26. Article 6 also refers to the definitions of non-discrimination set out in the International Convention on the Elimination of all forms of Racial Discrimination (ICERD) and CEDAW.

The prohibition forbids both direct discrimination, for example legislation stipulating that women are entitled to less inheritance than men; and indirect discrimination. The latter denotes measures that are ostensibly neutral, such as that all applicants for a particular employment position need to be of a certain height; but which in practice may have a detrimental impact on one of the prohibited grounds, for example, by excluding a proportionately higher number of women from gaining access. Such indirect discrimination is only justifiable where the difference in treatment is reasonable, such as where the particular work can only be satisfactorily carried out by persons of a certain height.

Earlier approaches within international human rights law to the violation of women's rights were 'protective', such as the 1948 International Labour Organization (ILO) Convention Concerning Night Work of Women Employed in Industry.[10] An interim 'corrective' approach followed, which attempted to protect the rights of women, but without direct comparison to the situation of men, for example in relation to the trafficking of women. At present, the overarching approach to the protection of women's human rights is one of non-discrimination, as embodied in the Convention on the Elimination of All Forms of Discrimination against Women (CEDAW).

CEDAW, or the Women's Convention, is the first major international treaty on the protection of women's rights.[11] CEDAW marks out inequality and discrimination against women as a particular and serious form of human rights violation meriting a specific instrument. The underlying reasoning is in many senses sound, since the specificity of abuses directed towards certain vulnerable groups such as women can be most effectively addressed through particular forms of protection and remedies. However, this very specificity can also potentially result in certain important rights being inadvertently overlooked, dismissed, denigrated or marginalised, a risk that necessitates a closer assessment of CEDAW's effectiveness in protecting women's human rights.

Article 1 of CEDAW states that:

For the purposes of the present Convention, the term 'discrimination against women' shall mean any distinction, exclusion or restriction made on the basis of sex which has the effect or purpose of impairing or nullifying the recognition, enjoyment or exercise by women, irrespective of their marital status, on a basis of equality of men and women, of human rights and fundamental freedoms in the political, economic, social, cultural, civil or any other field.

---

[10] 81 UNTS 285. See also N. Hevener, 'An Analysis of Gender-based Treaty Law: Contemporary Developments in Historical Perspective' (1986) 8 *Human Rights Quarterly* 70.

[11] See A. Hellum and H. Sinding Aasen, *Women's Human Rights: CEDAW in International, Regional and National Law* (Cambridge University Press, 2013) for a comprehensive overview of the global impact, implementation and development of the norms within CEDAW, including through examination of national case studies.

The treaty elaborates on this approach in articles 2 and 3, which oblige states to promulgate policy measures to condemn discrimination against women through legislative and other means, and to take appropriate measures to guarantee the equality of women with men in all fields. The Committee on the Elimination of Discrimination against Women (CtEDAW) has clarified that discrimination under the definition of article 1 does not need to be intentional to fall within the remit of the treaty.[12] CEDAW also goes beyond traditional liberal conceptions of direct non-discrimination by setting out 'temporary special measures' ('affirmative action') to accelerate de facto equality between men and women. According to article 4(1), such measures are not to be considered as discrimination under the Convention, and should be discontinued 'when the objectives of equality of opportunity and treatment have been achieved'. One example of this approach could be to set quotas for the number of women given seats in schools or universities, in order to increase access for women to educational opportunities.[13]

Besides a general prohibition of discrimination, CEDAW includes the right to non-discrimination against women in the fields of education,[14] health care,[15] and employment,[16] including in relation to marriage and maternity rights in the employment context.[17] The treaty builds further on issues relating to maternity, marriage and family relations in article 16, which sets out women's rights to freely enter into marriage and to exercise equal rights and responsibilities in relation to their children.[18] CEDAW also emphasises the rights of women to equality in the administration of property and their legal capacity to administer contracts.[19] In addition, it refers to a number of other specific protections; namely, the right not to be trafficked or exploited in prostitution;[20] political and elective rights and representation in political bodies and international organisations;[21] and the right of women to attain or change nationality, including in relation to their children, regardless of their marital status.[22] As well as recognising the need for specific protections, CEDAW goes beyond the hierarchical generational paradigm established within the broader human rights treaties, by referring to the need for states to eliminate discrimination against women in any other areas of economic, social and cultural rights,[23] and by addressing the particular needs of women in rural contexts.[24]

---

[12] See CtEDAW General Recommendation 28 (2010) on the core obligations of states parties under article 2 of CEDAW, UN doc. CEDAW/C/GC/28 (16 December 2010) especially para. 5.

[13] See CtEDAW General Recommendation 25 (2004) on article 4(1) of CEDAW, on Temporary Special Measures (30th session, 2004) especially paras. 24, 31, 32, 37.

[14] Art. 10 CEDAW.   [15] Art. 12 CEDAW.   [16] Art. 11(1) CEDAW.

[17] Art. 11(2) CEDAW.   [18] Art. 16 CEDAW.   [19] Art. 15 CEDAW.

[20] Art. 6 CEDAW.   [21] Arts. 7 and 8 CEDAW.   [22] Art. 9 CEDAW.

[23] Art. 13 CEDAW.   [24] Art. 14 CEDAW.

11.2.2   Critiques of CEDAW

The advent of a treaty specifically aimed at protecting the rights of women is to be welcomed. Yet a number of criticisms have been made in relation to CEDAW's content and the scope of its provisions. For example, CEDAW's provisions on economic, social and cultural rights do not specifically refer to a number of important rights that have a particularly detrimental effect on the lives of women. An example of this is the right to adequate access to food.[25] As well as acting as primary gatherers and distributers of food, where food is scarce women often deny themselves food, feeding other family members before themselves.[26] As a result, because of this role, women as individuals may not have adequate access to food for themselves; yet this disadvantage may not be captured by more generic non-discrimination provisions, since the latter do not tackle underlying structural causes by imposing more far-reaching positive obligations on states.

The Protocol to the African Charter on Human and Peoples' Rights (ACHPR) on the Rights of Women in Africa is more progressive and provides a marked contrast. Its article 15 sets out the right to food security, stating that:

States Parties shall ensure that women have the right to nutritious and adequate food. In this regard, they shall take appropriate measures to:

(a) provide women with access to clean drinking water, sources of domestic fuel, land, and the means of producing nutritious food;

(b) establish adequate systems of supply and storage to ensure food security.

This provision recognises that the right to adequate as well as safe and nutritious food is only achievable through practical measures which impose positive obligations on states, including in relation to access to other resources such as clean water, fuel and a source of land upon which to subsist. A further criticism concerning CEDAW's conceptual and practical application relates in particular to article 5(a), which requires states parties to take all appropriate measures:

To modify the social and cultural patterns of conduct of men and women, with a view to achieving the elimination of prejudices and customary and all other practices which are based on the idea of the inferiority or the superiority of either of the sexes or on stereotyped roles for men and women.

A number of states have argued that article 5 and other provisions set out in CEDAW, such as article 16, constitute an infringement of their local and

---

[25] Although see CtEDAW, General Recommendation 24 (20th session, 1999) para. 7, which raises the issue of nutrition as an aspect of the right to health, especially in relation to rural women.

[26] See e.g., the case studies examined in C. Chinkin and S. Wright, 'The Hunger Trap: Women, Food and Self-Determination' (1993) 14 *Michigan Journal of International Law* 262.

personal laws. This has resulted in one of the most problematic aspects of CEDAW's application; namely, reservations.[27] CEDAW is one of the most ratified yet most reserved of the six core UN treaties, adding further to questions as to its efficacy.

A number of states have entered general reservations stating that they do not consider themselves bound by provisions of the treaty which would require them to change or amend their state constitutions. Within the context of article 5, reservations have particularly related to marriage, children, divorce and inheritance. More specifically, several states have entered reservations to the effect that CEDAW is not binding in so far as it conflicts with, or is contrary to Islamic Sharia law within their domestic legal systems. Their main contention in doing so seems to be that article 5 effectively impedes their rights to determine and enforce religious and personal law norms around family law. For example, Malaysia declared that:

Malaysia's accession is subject to the understanding that the provisions of the Convention do not conflict with the provisions of the Islamic Sharia' law and the Federal Constitution of Malaysia. With regards thereto, further, the Government of Malaysia does not consider itself bound by the provisions of articles 2(f), 5(a), 7(b), 9 and 16 of the aforesaid Convention.[28]

The reservation entered by Niger is even more specifically related to article 5(a), stating that it 'expresses reservations with regard to the modification of social and cultural patterns of conduct of men and women'. It goes on to specify that this is the case due to the fact that provisions including article 5 'cannot be applied immediately, as they are contrary to existing customs and practices which, by their nature, can be modified only with the passage of time and the evolution of society and cannot, therefore, be abolished by an act of authority'.[29]

However, these reservations have been objected to by several other states parties, on the basis that they conflict with the treaty's object and purpose.[30] The CtEDAW has repeatedly expressed concern as to the number of reservations, in particular in relation to issues related to culture or religion.[31] The

---

[27] See Chapter 2.2.1.2 for a more detailed discussion of the issue of reservations to treaties.

[28] See www.un.org/womenwatch/daw/cedaw/reservations-country.htm.

[29] Ibid.

[30] As according to art. 19 of the Vienna Convention on the Law of Treaties. Examples of states which entered objections in relation to art. 5 reservations by Malaysia include Finland, the Netherlands, Norway and France; and in relation to Niger, by Norway, Denmark and Finland. See www.un.org/womenwatch/daw/cedaw/reservations-country.htm for full details of reservations, and consequent objections to this and other articles of the treaty.

[31] Including CtEDAW General Recommendations 4 (6th session, 1987); 20 (11th session, 1992); and particularly General Recommendation 21 (13th session, 1994) on *equality in marriage and family relations*, paras. 41–5.

controversies over these provisions and the practice of entering reservations in relation to them raise questions about CEDAW's efficacy. In particular, this debate highlights the limited commitment of states to the implementation of the treaty where certain provisions are seen to conflict with alleged local norms around gender roles and equality.[32]

A further criticism of CEDAW has been that its monitoring and enforcement mechanisms are weak. While this is a generic problem of the international human rights system, it has been particularly pronounced in respect of CEDAW due to the absence of a complaints procedure prior to 2000. The adoption of an Optional Protocol to CEDAW has given the Committee a more prominent role. One of its advantages is the fact that not only individual victims themselves, but also groups of victims and non-governmental organisations (NGOs) and others acting on behalf of both of the latter, are able to bring communications before the Committee.[33] However, take-up of the procedure has remained limited, and the implementation of decisions constitutes a major challenge in practice.[34]

11.2.3   CEDAW, Violence against Women and Reproductive Rights

One of CEDAW's major flaws is that it contains no explicit provision in relation to violence against women.[35] This is a conspicuous omission for a treaty which in other regards has made a concerted effort to address comprehensively a number of key areas of violations of women's human rights. Unsurprisingly, the lack of insertion of a specific clause on violence against women has produced sustained criticism, which the Committee attempted to address in the form of CtEDAW General Recommendation 19, which states that:

The definition of discrimination includes gender-based violence, that is, violence that is directed against a woman because she is a woman or that affects women disproportionately. It includes acts that inflict physical, mental or sexual harm or suffering, threats of such acts, coercion and other deprivations of liberty. Gender-based violence may breach specific provisions of the Convention, regardless of whether those provisions expressly mention violence.[36]

---

[32] See B. Clark, 'The Vienna Convention Reservations Regime and the Convention on Discrimination Against Women' (1991) 85 *American Journal of International Law* 281.

[33] See C. Mackinnon, *Are Women Human? And Other International Dialogues* (Harvard University Press, 2007) ch. 6, at 65, for a brief but largely positive commentary on the aims and processes of the CEDAW Optional Protocol.

[34] See Chapter 5.5.8 on CtEDAW complaints procedures. See also A. Edwards, *Violence against Women under International Human Rights Law* (Cambridge University Press, 2011) ch. 3.

[35] Ibid.

[36] CtEDAW General Recommendation 19 (11th session, 1992). See now General Recommendation 35 on gender-based violation against women, updating General

Following this the UN General Assembly (UNGA) also took up the issue of violence against women, adopting the 1994 Declaration on the Elimination of Violence Against Women (DEVAW).[37] Article 1 of DEVAW sets out the definition of violence against women as any act of gender-based violence that results in, or is likely to result in, physical, sexual or psychological harm or suffering to women, including threats of such acts, coercion or arbitrary deprivation of liberty, whether occurring in public or in private life.

The Special Rapporteur on violence against women, its causes and consequences (established in 1994) has also been instrumental in developing the understanding of violence against women and bringing relevant issues to the attention of a range of stakeholders. This has consisted of numerous country- and issue-based reports, such as on the intersections between culture and violence against women,[38] and the due diligence standard as a tool for the elimination of violence against women.[39] Both the Human Rights Council (HRC) and the UNGA have adopted further resolutions on the elimination of violence against women.[40] However, the Special Rapporteur has continued to highlight the problem of the 'normative gap' in the international human rights framework with regards to violence against women, whereby:

The lack of a legally binding instrument on violence against women precludes the articulation of the issue as a human rights violation in and of itself, comprehensively addressing all forms of violence against women and clearly stating the obligations of States to act with due diligence to eliminate violence against women.[41]

In the regional context the Inter-American Convention on the Prevention, Punishment and Eradication of Violence Against Women[42] covers several

---

Recommendation 19 (14 July 2017), which broadens the Committee's understanding of gender-based violence against women.

[37] UNGA resolution 48/104 (20 December 1993).

[38] Report of the Special Rapporteur on violence against women, its causes and consequences, 'Intersections between Culture and Violence against Women', UN doc. A/HRC/4/34 (17 January 2007).

[39] Report of the Special Rapporteur on violence against women, its causes and consequences, 'Integration of the Human Rights of Women and the Gender Perspective: Violence Against Women – The Due Diligence Standard', UN doc. E/CN.4/2006/61 (20 January 2006).

[40] UN Human Rights Council resolution on accelerating efforts to eliminate all forms of violence against women: preventing and responding to rape and other forms of sexual violence, UN doc. A/HRC/Res/23/25 (13 June 2013); and UNGA resolution on the intensification of efforts to eliminate all forms of violence against women and girls, UN doc. A/Res/69/147 (18 December 2014).

[41] Report of the Special Rapporteur on violence against women, its Causes and Consequences, UN doc. A/HRC/26/38 (28 May 2014) para. 68. See also a later addendum to this report (A/HRC/29/27/Add.4), which further expands on the problematic nature of this 'normative gap' in addressing violence against women in international law.

[42] Inter-American Convention on the Prevention, Punishment and Eradication of Violence against Women 'Convention of Belém do Pará' (9 June 1994).

crucial aspects, including a definition which encompasses gender-based violence in both the public and private spheres. Further notable features are provisions relating to a range of civil and political, and economic, social and cultural rights; specific reference to the role of cultural norms in violence against women; and the need for states to employ due diligence standards in relation to violence against women. The definition of violence against women within the Protocol to the ACHPR on the Rights of Women in Africa is potentially even more progressive, given its additional reference to economic harm and situations of armed conflict and war:

'Violence against women' means all acts perpetrated against women which cause or could cause them physical, sexual, psychological, and economic harm, including the threat to take such acts; or to undertake the imposition of arbitrary restrictions on or deprivation of fundamental freedoms in private or public life in peace time and during situations of armed conflicts or of war.[43]

More recently, the Council of Europe Convention on Preventing and Combating Violence against Women and Domestic Violence (Istanbul Convention)[44] recognises the 'structural nature of violence against women as gender-based violence', and specifically highlights domestic violence throughout the text. This Convention, as in the other regional contexts, therefore also takes a wider view of violence against women as occurring in both the public and private spheres, including where perpetrated by non-state actors.[45] The treaty also encompasses a wide range of types of violence,[46] including psychological violence, forced marriage and female genital mutilation (FGM); it further makes clear that states parties must undertake legislative reform where necessary to ensure that justifications for crimes of violence against women, such as 'honour', are unacceptable.[47]

Notwithstanding these normative developments, responses to a number of serious and systemic acts of violence against women continue to be inadequate and unsatisfactory, in both national and international contexts. This chapter does not purport to outline the vast range of physical, emotional and other forms of violence against women which occur daily worldwide.[48] Instead, it will highlight two particular sets of issues of relevance within the international human rights context which intersect with a number of other

---

[43]   11 July 2003 (entry into force November 2005), art. 1(j).

[44]   Convention on Preventing and Combating Violence against Women and Domestic Violence, CETS no. 210 (2011) (entry into force August 2014).

[45]   Ibid., art. 5(2).

[46]   Ibid., ch. V.

[47]   Ibid., art. 42(1).

[48]   See K. Askin and D. Koenig (eds.), *Women and International Human Rights Law* (Transnational Publishing, 1999) vol. I, s. 3.

violations. These are the right to life and the prohibition on torture, which are frequently at issue where violence against women results in serious harm, if not loss of life. As well as the omission of a provision on violence against women, CEDAW does not contain explicit provisions on the right to life or the prohibition of torture. For this reason, much of the jurisprudence in relation to these violations of women's human rights, particularly in the public sphere, has to date emerged from other UN and regional treaty bodies.[49]

With respect to the right to life,[50] until relatively recently the international human rights regime focused on state or public sphere violations, such as the death penalty, state killings and forced disappearances or deaths in custody, to which men have been deemed more susceptible than women.[51] Feminist scholars have argued that while women also suffer these violations of their right to life in the public sphere, a large number of violations of women's right to life also occur in the private or domestic sphere, and have not been adequately addressed by authorities in the majority of domestic legal systems.[52] For example, in England and Wales it is estimated that two women are killed each week as a result of domestic violence inflicted by partners and ex-partners.[53]

Women's right to life can raise complex questions regarding the links and overlaps between the public and private nature of violations. One such example is the ongoing and highly charged debate around abortion within the various regional systems.[54] In the European context there is no absolute prohibition on abortion, and the European Court of Human Rights (ECtHR) has applied the concept of the 'margin of appreciation'[55] in order to allow individual states some degree of control over the time limit within which an abortion can legally be carried out. Abortion laws across European states are characterised by a degree of dissonance in this regard. Under the 1967 UK Abortion Act, abortion is legal until the twenty-fourth week of pregnancy, after which period it is only legally permissible in exceptional cases,

---

[49] E.g., from the HRCtee, CAT and ECtHR, as discussed further below in this section.

[50] See Edwards, above note 34, ch. 6, for an overview of international human rights law on the right to life and violence against women.

[51] Ibid., 263–4.

[52] Ibid., 278–9.

[53] According to statistics collated by the national UK domestic violence organisation Women's Aid, online at www.womensaid.org.uk/information-support/what-is-domestic-abuse/how-common-is-domestic-abuse/.

[54] See also M. K. Eriksson, 'Abortion and Reproductive Health', in Askin and Koenig, above note 48, vol. III, s. 3, on the wider historical context of campaigns around reproductive rights for women.

[55] See Chapter 6.2.5.2, and in particular the discussion on the basis and application of the 'margin of appreciation' within European human rights law.

such as those involving substantial risk to the life of the mother or foe-
tal abnormality. This is a comparatively high time limit in comparison to
other European countries, for example France, Norway or Sweden, where
the time limit is twelve weeks. At the other end of the spectrum, until 2018,
under Irish law, in effect abortion used to be technically illegal, except in
extremely exceptional (and arbitrary) circumstances.[56] In the 2010 case of
A, B and C, a pregnant Irish cancer sufferer sought information about the
risk to her life should she continue the pregnancy. She was not provided
with this information and was thus unable to make an informed decision
as to whether to carry on with the pregnancy, at the potential risk to her
own life. The ECtHR found that the lack of 'any implementing legislative or
regulatory regime providing an accessible and effective procedure' enabling
a woman to establish whether she could obtain a lawful abortion in Ireland
constituted a breach of the protection of her right to privacy.[57] Subsequent
to the case a new Irish law[58] stated that the ending of an unborn life would
be a lawful medical procedure where 'there is a real and substantial risk of
loss of the woman's life from a physical illness';[59] and, moreover, where the
risk 'can only be averted by carrying out the medical procedure' in question.[60] The latter procedure must be 'immediately necessary in order to save
the life of the woman'.[61] This includes situations where 'a real and substantial risk of loss of the woman's life by way of suicide' could only be averted
by the abortion.[62] In May 2018, Ireland voted by a two-thirds majority that
the amendment of the Constitution, which had effectively enshrined highly
restrictive abortion laws, be repealed, leading to a reform of Irish legislation
on abortion.[63]

---

[56] E.g., in circumstances such as those within the key 1992 *X* case where a fourteen-year-old
rape victim who had been prevented from obtaining an abortion within or outside Ireland
was at high risk of committing suicide. See *The Attorney General Plaintiff* v. *X. and Other
Defendants* (Ireland) (1992). The issue of the right to abortion prompted a rare CtEDAW
inquiry: Inquiry concerning the United Kingdom of Great Britain and Northern Ireland
under article 8 of the Optional Protocol to the Convention on the Elimination of All Forms
of Discrimination against Women, UN doc. CEDAW/C/OP.8/GBR/1 (6 March 2018).

[57] *A, B and C* v. *Ireland* (ECtHR) (2010) paras. 267–8. This decision contributed to the
ongoing debate over the need to hold a referendum on public opinion on abortion laws in
Ireland; see C. Ryan, 'Irish Poised to Revisit Abortion Laws', *New York Times* (21 February
2012), www.nytimes.com/2012/02/22/world/europe/22iht-letter22.html?pagewanted=all.
See also *Mellet* v. *Ireland* (HRCtee) (2016), in which the Committee found that the lack
of access to abortion of a fatally injured foetus constitutes a violation of arts. 7 and 17
ICCPR.

[58] Protection of Life During Pregnancy Act 2013, no. 5.

[59] Ibid., s. 7(1)(a)(i).   [60] Ibid., s. 7(2)(a)(ii).

[61] Ibid., s. 8(1)(b).   [62] Ibid., s. 9(1)(a)(i).

[63] A. Reidy, 'Ireland Votes Overwhelmingly to Repeal Abortion Ban: "Yes" Vote Ends 35 Years
of Shame and Secrecy for Irish Women and Girls' (Human Rights Watch, 26 May 2018).

Since the ruling in *Vo* v. *France*,[64] in which the Court declined to recognise the unequivocal right to life of a foetus over that of its mother, European jurisprudence on the question of abortion has been left relatively open, and the position on the relationship between the right to life and privacy of the mother and that of the unborn foetus remains subject to the 'margin of appreciation'. In the African context, the Protocol to the ACHPR on Women's Rights also largely concerns itself with the issue of the right to abortion in therapeutic circumstances. According to its article 14(2)(a), states parties should take all appropriate measures to:

protect the reproductive rights of women by authorising medical abortion in cases of sexual assault, rape, incest, and where the continued pregnancy endangers the mental and physical health of the mother or the life of the mother or the foetus.

The African system thus also appears to leave open the decision on balancing the right to life of the woman with that of the unborn foetus to the discretion of individual states, according to the respective status of the woman and the foetus.[65] The difficulty in deciding where this balance lies, as in other regions, revolves around the time at which the right to life is interpreted as starting, and thus where the responsibility of the state begins. While some states, such as Zimbabwe, allow abortion on very limited medical grounds, others such as South Africa allow the right to seek a legal abortion at up to twelve weeks.[66]

More recently in the inter-American context, there has been a religious led backlash against the use of abortion in a number of countries. Nicaragua, for example, has instituted a total ban on abortion under any circumstances, including those involving rape and incest, and a policy of prosecuting medical professionals and others who are found to be facilitating abortions, irrespective of the circumstances.[67] In Nicaragua, a political rapprochement between the incoming Sandinista leader and the country's Catholic Church leaders led to the erosion of the reproductive rights of women, many of whom had fought and campaigned for the Sandinistas to become the leaders of the country.[68] In the regional context, the very wording of article 4 of the American Convention on Human Rights (ACHR), whereby the right to life is protected 'in general, from the moment of conception' may seem to lend support for such policies on abortion. However, jurisprudence in this region on abortion, such as the decision of the Inter-American Commission

---

[64] *Vo* v. *France* (ECtHR) (2004).
[65] See Edwards, above note 34, 288–9.
[66] See F. Banda, *Women, Law and Human Rights: An African Perspective* (Hart, 2005) 184–6.
[67] See Amnesty International, *The Total Ban on Abortion in Nicaragua: Women's Lives and Health Endangered, Medical Profesionals Criminalised*, AMR 43/001/2009 (27 July 2009).
[68] As noted in ibid.

on Human Rights (IACHR) in the *Baby Boy* case,[69] demonstrates the ambiguity of the wording of article 4. In that case, an abortion performed by a doctor in the interim period between the legislation and the activation of laws rendering abortion legal in the USA, was not deemed to constitute a violation of the right to life. The abortion was performed on a foetus over the age of six months at the request of the pregnant woman and her mother. The doctor was brought to trial and later acquitted of manslaughter by the US Supreme Court; however, the case was brought before the IACHR by a number of Catholic religious activists who argued that the acquittal constituted a violation of the right to life. The Commission's approach in this case was in fact based on the interpretation of the wording of article 4. Thus while 'in general' the right to life starts from conception, in certain circumstances, such as the potential harm to the woman, her right to life should be weighed against the right to life of the foetus. The case illustrates that, as in other regional systems, decisions relating to the interpretation and enforcement of the right to life in relation to controversial issues such as abortion are to a large degree left to the discretion of individual states. In many cases these choices may be based around alleged cultural or religious norms, as, for example, in Ireland and Nicaragua discussed above.

The issue of the interpretation of article 4 arose in a related context in Costa Rica, which banned all forms of in-vitro fertilisation (IVF) treatment in 2000. The Inter-American Court of Human Rights (IACtHR), in a case brought by a number of couples who had been denied treatment examined, inter alia, whether the manner in which the treatment was carried out constituted a violation of the right to life. The Costa Rican Constitutional Court had concluded that the high risk of the loss or destruction of embryos entailed within current IVF techniques jeopardised human life, and thus violated article 4.

However, in re-examining the basis for the ban, the IACtHR discussed not only the meaning of the term 'in general' in the protection given under article 4(1), as in the *Baby Boy* case discussed above; but also what, in the circumstances of IVF treatment, constituted the definition of 'conception', from which moment the embryo could be protected by article 4(1). The IACtHR concluded that the term 'conception' must be understood as occurring only once implantation has occurred in the woman's womb, and that before this event article 4 could not be applied.[70]

The prohibition of torture within the context of state institutions applies in principle to anyone, regardless of gender. The UN and regional treaty bodies have made it clear that rape by state actors can in certain circumstances

---

[69] '*Baby Boy*' abortion case (IACHR) (1981).

[70] *Artavia Murillo et al.* ('*In Vitro Fertilisation*') v. *Costa Rica* (IACtHR) (2012), in particular paras. 181–9.

constitute torture. However, jurisprudence acknowledging and affirming this principle has only emerged relatively recently, and there remains much controversy as to the conceptual and practical utility of attempts to harness existing norms and frameworks around torture in cases of rape.[71] On the one hand, it could be argued that constituting rape as a form of torture, a peremptory norm of international law, places the strongest of obligations on states to prevent such crimes and bring perpetrators to justice.[72] On the other hand, it has been argued that it is highly problematic to fail to acknowledge violence against women, including rape, as serious violations in and of themselves, and instead attempt to fit women's experiences into existing, masculinised understandings of harm.[73] In the leading European case of *Aydin* v. *Turkey*,[74] a seventeen-year-old woman suffered rape and various other forms of abuse while being held in custody. The ECtHR found that the treatment she suffered at the hands of the authorities, particularly the rape, constituted torture in violation of article 3 of the European Convention on Human Rights (ECHR). This approach has also been followed in other regional jurisdictions, including the inter-American system. In *Raquel Marti de Meja* v. *Peru*,[75] the IACHR found that the rape and intimidation of the complainant by a member of the security forces constituted a violation of article 5 ACHR. Additionally, in the *Miguel Castro-Castro Prison* v. *Peru* case,[76] the IACtHR found that female detainees who were forced to remain naked under the constant guard of armed male guards had been subjected to a form of sexual violence constituting a violation of article 5(2) ACHR.

Yet the majority of cases of violence against women, including rape, domestic violence and other forms of abuse, are committed within the private sphere by non-state actors, which means that such cases are seemingly not covered by the Convention against Torture and Other Cruel, Inhuman or Degrading Treatment or Punishment (CAT) and other instruments which were designed to address abuses within the public domain. However, the cases discussed below demonstrate that public authorities do have a duty to protect women from violence by non-state actors, including by means of repressing and adequately responding to violations against women, including domestic violence or rape. Where they fail to protect individuals despite knowing that

---

[71] For a comprehensive examination of current conceptual debates and jurisprudence on the issue of whether rape could, or indeed should, constitute torture in international and regional human rights law, see REDRESS, *Redress for Rape: Using International Jurisprudence on Rape as a Form of Torture or Ill-Treatment* (October 2013).

[72] Ibid., 18–19.

[73] See Edwards, above note 34, 339.

[74] *Aydin* v. *Turkey* (ECtHR) (1997).

[75] *Raquel Marti de Meja* v. *Peru* (IACHR) (1996).

[76] *Miguel Castro-Castro Prison* v. *Peru* (IACtHR) (2006).

there is a risk of torture, they may be deemed to have become acquiescent, which potentially brings these acts within the fold of the CAT definition.[77] This may, for example, include cases where the police do not take action following a well-founded complaint by a woman that she is at risk of an attack, and the risk later materialises.

As a practical consequence of the 'public/private divide', according to which abuses by non-state actors fall outside the remit of international human rights law, in the past states have only rarely been held responsible for violations committed by private actors. More recently, the notion of 'positive obligation' has been developed to address this gap in protection, by imposing a series of specific duties on states to effectively address violations in the private sphere. The Honduran case of *Velásquez Rodríguez*[78] was key in establishing this principle of 'due diligence', whereby the state can be held accountable for human rights violations committed by non-state actors if it does not take adequate steps to ensure that such crimes are adequately investigated, prosecuted and punished. This principle has found broad application in the jurisprudence of international and regional treaty bodies, including in relation to violence against women.[79]

In *A.T.* v. *Hungary*[80] the victim claimed that the state party had failed in its duty to provide her with effective protection from serious physical and mental domestic violence from her former partner over the course of four years. She was unable to prevent him from gaining access to her residence because national legislation did not provide for restraining or protection orders, and the domestic courts did not pay sufficient attention to domestic violence. This situation was exacerbated by a lack of alternatives in the form of adequate state provision for shelters or refuges for domestic violence victims, in this case particularly so because the victim could not gain access to a shelter equipped to accommodate not only herself, but also her two children, one of whom was disabled. The CtEDAW found that the state had breached its obligations under article 2(a), (b) and (e) of CEDAW, in that it had failed to protect the complainant by adopting appropriate legislative and other measures to ensure non-discrimination. By linking this general failure of due diligence obligations with article 16 (family relations) and article 5 (cultural

---

[77] See Report of the Special Rapporteur on torture and other cruel, inhuman or degrading treatment or punishment, UN doc. A/HRC/7/3 (15 January 2008), especially paras. 45–9 on intimate partner violence.

[78] *Velásquez Rodríguez* v. *Honduras* (IACtHR) (1988).

[79] See e.g., Report of the Special Rapporteur on violence against women, its causes and consequences, UN doc. A/HRC/23/9 (14 May 2013) para. 11; CtEDAW General Recommendation 28, paras. 13 and 37(b).

[80] *A. T.* v. *Hungary* (CtEDAW) (2005).

or traditional stereotypes perpetuating the inferiority of women in relation to men), the Committee effectively found that this form of violence against women was a violation of the treaty under due diligence principles. In this respect, the Committee specifically referred to its General Recommendation 19 (now 35) on violence against women, which emphasises:

the Convention calls on States parties to take all appropriate measures to eliminate discrimination against women by any person, organization or enterprise. Under general international law and specific human rights covenants, States may also be responsible for private acts if they fail to act with due diligence to prevent violations of rights or to investigate and punish acts of violence, and for providing compensation.[81]

In *M. C. v. Bulgaria*[82] a fourteen-year-old girl alleged that she had been raped by two men. She claimed that the outcome of the criminal investigation into her assault, which found that the prosecution should not proceed due to a lack of finding of force or physical resistance, constituted a lack of effective protection against rape by the Bulgarian state. The ECtHR criticised the state both for its failure to investigate, punish and prosecute rape, and to enact effective criminal legislation in the prosecution of rape, including through its emphasis on the use of force rather than consent in defining the crime of rape. Consequently, it found that the state had failed in its due diligence obligations under articles 3 and 8 ECHR.[83] Similarly, in a case brought under the CEDAW Optional Protocol, the Committee found a failure on the part of the state to uphold its obligations, reiterating:

there should be no assumption in law or in practice that a woman gives her consent because she has not physically resisted the unwanted sexual conduct, regardless of whether the perpetrator threatened to use or used physical violence.[84]

In the more recent ECtHR case of *Opuz v. Turkey*,[85] the applicant and her mother had suffered sustained and prolonged physical and mental domestic violence at the hands of the applicant's husband. This included severe injuries caused by the applicant's husband running them both over in his car, death threats towards them both and numerous stabbing attacks. The violence culminated in the murder of the applicant's mother. The Court stated that the escalating crimes committed by the applicant's husband:

---

[81] CEDAW General Recommendation 19, para. 9.
[82] *M. C. v. Bulgaria* (ECtHR) (2005).
[83] See ibid., especially paras. 148–87, on violations of arts. 3 and 8 within the case in relation to the due diligence obligations of the state.
[84] *R. B. P. v. Philippines* (CtEDAW) (2014) para. 8.10, upholding its previous decision in *Vertido v. The Philippines* (CtEDAW) (2010) para. 8.5.
[85] *Opuz v. Turkey* (ECtHR) (2010).

were sufficiently serious to warrant preventive measures and there was a continuing threat to the health and safety of the victims. When examining the history of the relationship, it was obvious that the perpetrator had a record of domestic violence and there was therefore a significant risk of further violence.[86]

The Court found that despite this, the state had failed to effectively protect the applicant and prevent further harm to herself or her family, largely through its unwillingness to pursue effective criminal proceedings against the applicant's husband. Notably, the ECtHR refuted the government's argument that state interference in the domestic violence perpetrated would have amounted to a breach of article 8 of the Convention (the right to privacy and family life), because it was a 'private matter'. This stance was deemed incompatible with the positive obligation of the state to secure the victim's rights. The Court stated further that despite realising the serious and escalating nature of the violence perpetrated upon the applicant and her mother:

> it cannot be said that the local authorities displayed the required diligence to prevent the recurrence of violent attacks against the applicant, since the applicant's husband perpetrated them without hindrance and with impunity to the detriment of the rights recognised by the Convention.[87]

As a result, the Court found that the state had failed in its positive obligations and had committed a violation of article 3 ECHR. It also found a violation of the right to life of both the applicant and her mother under article 2.

Cases such as *Opuz* illustrate the interlinked nature of types of violence against women, including the link between the right to life and the prohibition of torture. Emerging jurisprudence demonstrates that international and regional human rights regimes have begun to recognise the importance of tackling the fundamental violation of the human rights of women within the private sphere. In the case of *González et al. ('Cotton Field') v. Mexico*,[88] the Court confirmed that the failure of the state to adopt a 'general policy' to address the widespread and egregious violence against women in the Ciudad Juárez region of Mexico, including rapes, murders and disappearances, amounted to a breach of the due diligence principle. Similarly, a 2015 CtEDAW inquiry instituted under article 8 of the CEDAW Optional Protocol found that there had been grave and systematic violations of a number of articles under the convention on the part of Canada due to the latter's failure to exercise due diligence in the investigation of a high number of cases of

---

[86] Ibid., para. 134.   [87] Ibid., para. 169.

[88] Case of *González et al. ('Cotton Field') v. Mexico* (IACtHR) (2009), in particular paras. 253–61. See also paras. 5–9 of the Latin American Model Protocol for the investigation of gender-related killings of women (femicide/feminicide), OHCHR and UN Women (2014), online at www.un.org/en/women/endviolence/pdf/LatinAmericanProtocolForInvestigation OfFemicide.pdf.

missing and murdered aboriginal women and girls.[89] These developments could thus be seen as an important step forward in terms of mainstreaming violations of women's rights into broader human rights frameworks.

However, as highlighted by the Special Rapporteur on violence against women, due diligence will need to be developed further in order to serve as an effective tool in combating gender-based violence:

> If we confine ourselves to the current conception of due diligence as an element of State responsibility, then obstacles relative to the capacity of the State will be determinative. If, on the other hand, we continue dare to push the boundaries of due diligence in demanding the full compliance of States with international law, including the obligation to address the root causes of violence against women and to hold non-State actors accountable for their acts, then we will move towards a conception of human rights compatible with our aspirations for a just world free of violence.[90]

QUESTIONS

1. Has the development of a specific system to protect the human rights of women, for example in the form of CEDAW, been beneficial or detrimental to the advancement of women's human rights overall?

2. Should women's human rights be mainstreamed into the overarching system of international protection of human rights?

3. What has been the impact of the 'due diligence' principle in relation to the protection of the human rights of women? How effective is this principle in the protection of women's rights within the private sphere and domestic regimes?

11.3   CONCEPTUAL DEVELOPMENT

11.3.1   The Development of Feminist Legal Theory and Women's Human Rights

The conceptual development of rights for women has a long pedigree.[91] However, the majority of discussion has been focused around authors writing within and about Western legal systems and contexts. This has been

---

[89] The articles found to have been violated included arts. 1, 2, 3 and 5 in conjunction with 14 and 15 CEDAW. See Report of the inquiry concerning Canada under article 8 of the optional protocol to CEDAW, UN doc. CEDAW/C/OP.8/CAN/1 (6 March 2015), especially paras. 210–15. See also 'Missing and Murdered Indigenous Women in British Columbia, Canada', Inter-American Commission on Human Rights, OEA/Ser.L/V/II (21 December 2014) for a more detailed overview of these issues.

[90] Report of the Special Rapporteur, above note 39, para. 102.

[91] See A. Fraser, 'Becoming Human: The Origins and Development of Women's Human Rights' (1999) 21 *Human Rights Quarterly* 853, for a historical overview of the history of campaigning around rights for women.

increasingly criticised, and has provided the impetus for a number of major discussions within feminist theory that reflect upon and influence concepts and practice within the current international human rights regime. Debates on the existence and nature of women's human rights predate the emergence of the international human rights system, and had, for example, already been raised by authors including Mary Wollstonecraft[92] in the eighteenth century. Early women's rights activists were also key players in the anti-slavery movement.[93] The adaptation and application of existing liberal human rights theories towards specific rights for women led to an early emphasis on gaining rights for women within the public sphere, as exemplified by feminist campaigning for the women's suffrage movement in the nineteenth and early twentieth centuries. Likewise, the emphasis during the establishment of the early international human rights regime on 'first generation' civil and political rights may also have influenced this initial focus on violations of women's human rights in the public domain.[94]

Rights frameworks based around theories of liberalism focus on concepts of individual rights to non-discrimination and equality.[95] This approach argues that women should be treated on the same footing as men in terms of their participation in public life and their treatment by public institutions, and should not be discriminated against on the basis of their sex. Liberalism rests upon the premise that certain concepts such as equal rights and opportunity, rationality and individual choice are the basis of participation in society and public life. The theory posits that all persons are free and equal, including in relation to areas such as the right to vote, equality before the law, education, employment, as well as property rights and freedom of contract. Despite this, a number of signatory states to treaties whose provisions espouse liberal values, such as the civil and political rights contained within the ICCPR, continue to deny these rights to women. For example, while the right to vote was to a great extent addressed by activist and suffragist movements in the twentieth century, a number of states, such as Saudi Arabia, have remained reluctant to ensure the right to vote for women.[96]

---

[92] See M. Wollstonecraft, *A Vindication of the Rights of Woman* (1792).

[93] See Fraser, above note 91.

[94] See Charlesworth and Chinkin, above note 1, 14–18, and Edwards, above note 34, 39–43 for discussion of the history of feminist activism in relation to international law from the early twentieth century to the present.

[95] See Chapter 1.4.1 for discussion of liberal human rights theories.

[96] Although it should be noted that denial of this right has become increasingly untenable, with the majority of states now according female citizens the right to vote. Saudi Arabia itself only granted its female citizens the right to vote and stand for public office during local elections held in December 2015. See I. Black, 'Saudi Arabia elects up to 17 female councillors in historic election' *The Guardian* (13 December 2015), online at www.theguardian.com/world/2015/dec/13/saudi-arabia-elects-up-to-17-female-councillors-in-historic-election.

11.3.2 Critiques of Liberal and Non-discrimination Approaches to Women's Human Rights

A liberal approach seems practical, since without representation within the public sphere, women lack a means by which to effect changes to laws and systems of government in ways which empower them and allow them to enforce these rights. Liberal feminist theorists and activists seek to gain 'insider' status to influence existing institutions in ways which uphold equality between the sexes, and to openly and legitimately attempt to promote policies and laws based on principles of non-discrimination. In this approach, the problem is not law in or of itself, but 'bad' or wrongly applied law.[97] Feminists such as Eleanor Roosevelt and the members of the Commission on the Status of Women advocated the formal equality approach during their participation in the drafting of early international human rights instruments such as the Universal Declaration of Human Rights (UDHR). However, later feminists, particularly in the second half of the twentieth century, began to criticise the focus on civil and political rights and the precepts of non-discrimination underlying them.[98]

One of the most important critiques of liberal feminism revolves around its failure sufficiently to recognise and respond to problems caused by the so-called 'public/private divide'. The state-centric and individualistic nature of liberal approaches to rights places the focus of reform on the public sphere rather than the private sphere of individuals' lives, which should not be interfered with unless necessary. Feminists have long argued that women's prolonged exclusion from the public sphere means that in practice a number of serious violations of their rights take place in the private sphere, such as in the family or in marriage, which are not adequately reflected in the traditional liberal paradigm of international human rights law.[99]

A second major critique of the liberal feminist approach is its acceptance, and consequent inability to adequately question, the assumption of gender neutrality or objectivity underlying systems of law; in this case, the international human rights law regime. Liberal feminism views gender inequality as an error within the system of law requiring rectification, rather than reflecting an in-built system of domination and hierarchy. Critics argue that underlying the outwardly neutral concept of non-discrimination is a white, male-centric, privileged 'norm' which does not encompass the experience or particular vulnerabilities of women, ethnic minorities and others who do not (and cannot) conform to this standard. International human rights laws and

---

[97] See Charlesworth and Chinkin, above note 1, 40.

[98] Including the debate on 'generations' of rights, as discussed above in relation to the lesser importance attached to economic, social and cultural rights.

[99] See Charlesworth and Chinkin, above note 1, 56–9, and Edwards, above note 34, 64–71.

norms, while notionally positing that human rights are equally applicable to all, in practice enforce standards which reinforce existing power hierarchies around gender, race and other potential types of vulnerability.[100] An example is the use of masculine language and vocabulary in international human rights instruments, such as the use of the masculine pronoun in the majority of the general human rights instruments, which is seen as perpetuating the male-centredness of human rights norms, and excludes female perspectives and experiences.[101]

Building on these critiques, two major schools of feminist thought took differing approaches in order to contest assumptions of the alleged neutrality of liberal legal theory. Cultural or relational feminism builds on critiques of liberal paradigms of equality, positing that the factors that make women different from men should be celebrated and valued. It is an approach most famously argued by psychologist Carol Gilligan, who asserted that women reason in a 'different' voice based more on an ethic of care, responsibility and connection than the abstract, masculine ethic of justice propagated by the legal system and society at large.[102] She argued that this adversarial and hierarchical 'male' approach has been privileged within law, and that as a result the 'different' voice of female reasoning has been subjugated and marginalised within conceptual and practical legal frameworks. This argument has also been applied in relation to international law, for example concerning the adversarial and abstract approach of the language used within international human rights treaties.[103]

Radical feminism has deconstructed and critiqued both liberal and cultural feminist approaches. Catherine Mackinnon in particular has argued that 'under the sameness standard, women are measured according to our correspondence with man' but 'under the difference standard, we are measured according to our lack of correspondence with him'. In either case 'masculinity, or maleness is the referent for both'[104] and a male norm poses as gender neutrality. Thus in this approach, it is only women's difference from men, rather than men's difference from women, that matters. In this way differences between men and women, for example such as those relating to pregnancy, can be left unacknowledged by 'male-centric' legal norms, as reflected in the length of time it took to recognise reproductive rights. Mackinnon further criticises arguments which attempt to acknowledge women's difference positively, on the basis that such arguments make certain attributes seem

---

[100] See Edwards, above note 34, 51–64, for more detailed discussion and examples of this argument in relation to international law.

[101] See Charlesworth and Chinkin, above note 1, 231–2, and Edwards, above note 34, 61–4.

[102] C. Gilligan, *In a Different Voice* (Harvard University Press, 1982).

[103] See Edwards, above note 34, 62–3.

[104] C. Mackinnon, *Feminism Unmodified: Discourses on Life and Law* (Harvard University Press, 1987) 34.

inherently female, rather than being attributed to women by a male system of domination for its own purposes.[105] Radical feminism therefore critiques existing male-dominated hierarchies of power from an external standpoint. Instead it advocates an approach based on how the distribution of power results in gender inequality and constructs the status of women in society; the 'dominance approach'.[106] Using this approach, once the domination of women by men is acknowledged and dealt with, it may finally be possible for the conditions of equality to exist in which women truly can see what or who women are, without the constant comparison to an unattainable male standard.

11.3.3 Critiques of 'Western' Feminist Approaches to Women's Human Rights

Mackinnon's approach has left her open to a number of criticisms from other feminists. Post-modern feminists argue that it places too much emphasis on the law as a decisive and overarching mechanism in relation to the violation of women's rights, rather than on the intersection of law with other cultural or socio-political factors.[107] This critique is especially relevant in relation to the debates on cultural relativism discussed below, particularly the effective implementation of 'universal' human rights norms within local contexts using domestic legal systems.[108] In this respect, Mackinnon's 'dominance approach' has been accused of leaving little scope for resistance or strategies for change, including by actors and organisations working to protect women's human rights within the local context. This approach could therefore be seen as at odds with the long-standing and ongoing struggles of women's human rights activism. It also fails to provide an adequate account of certain violations of women's human rights, such as FGM. In Mackinnon's account, little room remains for female agency in the perpetration of FGM, since she subscribes to a theory of so-called 'false consciousness', whereby women have been passively indoctrinated into the system of male dominance. However, accounts of FGM show that women do not necessarily uniformly subscribe to male accounts of their well-being, and undertake actions such as FGM for wider social and cultural reasons.[109]

---

[105] Ibid., 39.   [106] Ibid., 40.

[107] See C. Smart, *Feminism and the Power of Law* (Routledge, 1990).

[108] See S. E. Merry, *Human Rights and Gender Violence: Translating International Law into Local Justice* (University of Chicago Press, 2009), who argues that human rights law is often only fully accepted where it is implemented in conjunction with other types of local systems and norms.

[109] See also Chapter 1.5.2 for further discussion of the issue of FGM.

A major criticism of Mackinnon's work is that she 'essentialises' the voice of women by not sufficiently taking into account the diversity of their experiences, including in relation to issues of cultural, racial or other forms of diversity.[110] For example, Harris argues that Mackinnon only discusses the issue of race in a way which views the experience of oppression of black women as the same as that of white women, only 'more so'. However, Harris argues that the difference in discrimination is not necessarily only *quantitatively* different from that experienced by white women, but *qualitatively* so, different in its very nature, as well as in its severity.[111] One way to address this critique is through the conceptual tool of 'intersectional discrimination'. Crenshaw has analysed a number of scenarios involving violence against women of colour within the United States of America (USA), and argued that where, for example, race and gender discrimination intersect, black women are found to be marginalised within both feminist and anti-racist agendas, and the discrimination they suffer is either compounded or ignored.[112] More recently, she and other feminist scholars have attempted to further analyse the complexity of intersectional discrimination within the context of international human rights frameworks by using a 'traffic intersection metaphor', whereby differing forms of disempowerment are 'thoroughfares', creating intersections where multiple forms of discrimination and identity overlap and meet, resulting in compound or qualitatively different violations of women's human rights.

The latter analysis was set out in the 2001 UN Office of the High Commissioner for Human Rights (OHCHR) Report on the Gender Dimensions of Racial Discrimination, produced following an Expert Group Meeting in 2000.[113] The report details a number of practical examples of intersectional discrimination within the context of human rights violations. One example given is that of violence against women in situations of armed conflict, where women from specific ethnic or racial groups have been targeted with rape, enforced pregnancy and other forms of sexual violence as a means of 'dishonouring' or ethnically cleansing the group in question. The report argues that the intersection of gender and race in this type of violence illustrates the distinct and compound nature of intersectional discrimination, and that the

---

[110] See Charlesworth and Chinkin, above note 1, 52–6, and Edwards, above note 34, 71–86, for further discussion of debates around essentialism. For a post-colonial, feminist critique, see R. Kapur, *Erotic Justice: Law and the New Politics of Postcolonialism* (Glass House Books, 2005).

[111] A. Harris, 'Race and Essentialism in Feminist Legal Theory' (1989–1990) 42 *Stanford Law Review* 581, at 595–6.

[112] See K. Crenshaw, 'Mapping the Margins: Intersectionality, Identity Politics and Violence Against Women of Colour' (1991) 43 *Stanford Law Review* 1241.

[113] UN OHCHR, Gender and racial discrimination: Report of the Expert Group Meeting, Zagreb, Croatia (21–24 November 2000).

response of national and international human rights regimes must take this into account if they are to effectively protect the human rights of women.

These debates could be taken as reflective of more far-reaching criticisms of 'Western' feminist approaches to international human rights. These 'essentialist' approaches are perceived to have ignored the impact of intersecting forms of discrimination with gender discrimination, as well as the impact of wider historical and global contexts such as colonialism. Following from this is the ongoing conflict between culturally relativist and universal conceptions of human rights norms.[114] Related to these discourses surrounding the power relations inherent around the formulation and application of human rights norms, non-Western feminists have criticised the lack of understanding and perceptions of cultural superiority within much Western feminist human rights discourse.[115] Yet criticism of rights discourse has also come from Western human rights activists who do not wish to be seen as imposing culturally relativist neo-imperialistic human rights norms on other states, as well as from grassroots human rights and women's rights activists. Indeed, local women's rights activists may find rights discourse helpful in their attempts to practically implement human rights strategies. It therefore also needs to be recognised that the language of rights feels 'new and empowering'[116] to many victims of human rights violations, and that it is neither practical, nor necessarily ethical, for others to attempt to remove this discourse from current debates around existing human rights frameworks, or to hinder it.

Criticism of Western feminists riding roughshod over local experiences are closely related to debates about 'culture', which have been used frequently on both sides, either to denigrate or to justify certain practices.[117] Such viewpoints add to the perception of culture as fixed and immutable, rather than selected according to context by powerful members of a group in order to preserve existing power structures such as gender hierarchies.[118] They also overlook the possibility of resistance or contestation within groups as to the nature of 'culture', and that cultural practices or customs can adapt (as in the case of FGM), disappear (as in the case of Chinese foot binding), be revived

---

[114] See Chapter 1.5; Charlesworth and Chinkin, above note 1, 222–9, on women's human rights and cultural relativism.

[115] See Charlesworth and Chinkin, above note 1, 46–8; J. Oloka-Oyango and S. Tamale, '"The Personal is Political", or why Women's Rights are Indeed Human Rights: An African Perspective' (1995) 17 *Human Rights Quarterly* 691, for further discussion of essentialism, the impact of colonialism on feminist discourses, and the need for Third World scholars to add their own contributions to existing feminist theories.

[116] P. Williams, *The Alchemy of Race and Rights* (Harvard University Press, 1991).

[117] See Banda, above note 66, 250–9, for a discussion on African perspectives and debates around what constitutes 'culture', particularly within the human rights industry.

[118] See Report of the Special Rapporteur on violence against women, above note 38.

(as in the case of veiling in European Muslim communities) or be imported (as in the case of the Shia practice of *mut'a*, short-term marriages used to justify the abduction of young girls by fighters in Sunni Algeria during the 1990s).[119] These examples illustrate the ways in which cultural practices or traditions are fluid, and can be exploited according to context in order to perpetuate gender-based human rights violations. Conversely, the fluidity of 'culture' opens up the possibility for feminists of challenging violations of women's human rights.

The debate on culture and cultural relativism has been fundamental in relation to women's rights; as has been succinctly pointed out, 'no social group has suffered greater violation of its human rights in the name of culture than women'.[120] Yet there has been a tendency in Western feminist discourse to 'orientalise' concepts around culture, and allegedly cultural forms of violence against women such as FGM. Thus 'culture' is only seen to be a relevant factor in violence against women in non-Western contexts, despite the existence of high rates of sexual and domestic violence in Western states, as well as other harmful practices such as cosmetic surgery or media portrayals of women as sexual objects.[121] A number of 'Western' feminists have argued that it is hypocritical, patronising and futile to attempt to dictate to local activists the methods by which they could or should prevent such violations. They argue that it is necessary to take a grassroots approach to such issues, so that local actors, including feminist activists, are supported and facilitated (but not dictated to or controlled) by more powerful Western feminist activists.[122] Again, ongoing conflicts around approaches to FGM provide a useful example of the necessity for feminists from a range of contexts to work together to protect the rights of female victims, but in a manner which

---

[119] See J. Bauer and A. Helie, *Documenting Women's Rights Violations by Non-State Actors: Activist Strategies from Muslim Communities* (Montreal: International Centre for Human Rights and Democratic Development and WLUML, 2006) 67–8; and L. Volpp, 'Feminism Versus Multiculturalism' (2001) 1 *Columbia Law Review* 1192, for useful discussions around the uses and abuses of the term 'culture' in relation to the practices relating to women.

[120] A. Rao, 'The Politics of Gender and Culture in International Human Rights Discourse', in J. Peters and A. Wolper (eds.), *Women's Rights, Human Rights: International Perspectives* (Routledge, 1995) 169.

[121] See Report of the Special Rapporteur on violence against women, above note 38, 18–19; and also R. Howard, 'Health Costs of Social Degradation and Female Self-mutilation in North America', in K. E. Mahoney and P. Mahoney (eds.), *Human Rights in the Twenty-first Century: A Global Challenge* (Martinus Nijhoff, 1993).

[122] See also e.g., R. Coomooraswamy, 'To Bellow like a Cow: Women, Ethnicity and the Discourse of Rights', in R. Cook (ed.), *Human Rights of Women, National and International Perspectives* (University of Pennsylvania Press, 1994), on strategies to effectively implement women's human rights within culturally diverse settings.

is not perceived as Western feminist neo-imperialism.[123] As Case Study 11.1 on 'honour crimes' demonstrates, these debates around culture and gender are relevant in domestic arenas, such as the multicultural context of the UK, as well as international ones.

11.3.4   Sex, Gender and Sexuality

A final conceptual issue surrounds the use of the terminology of sex or gender. Most international human rights treaties discuss discrimination on the basis of sex rather than gender, although the terms sex, gender and woman are often used interchangeably in the discourse.[124] This may reflect the liberal focus of the debate during the period in which these instruments were drafted and adopted, and assumes that there is a common standard of equality which can be reached between men and women. Use of the term 'sex' is problematic due to the assumption of male neutrality in legal norms and standards, and its focus on the biological physical attributes of 'male' and 'female'. This may be viewed as essentialist in nature, and may also be interpreted in ways which do not adequately encompass all those in need of protection, for example trans-gendered persons.[125]

By contrast, more recent discussions have attempted to re-examine non-discrimination norms, in relation to conceptualisations around gender, as a broader social construct. A key example of a national instrument reflecting this is the 1996 South African Constitution, which specifically refers to non-discrimination on the basis of sex or gender, and sexual orientation.[126] A further example is that of violence against women. UN standard-setting documents on violence against women specifically refer to issues of gender-based violence as a form of discrimination under article 1 of CEDAW. This approach links and builds on traditional notions of equality and non-discrimination in terms of newer debates around gender, and gender-based violence, as opposed solely to the traditional approach of non-discrimination.

While the UN definitions both refer specifically to women, they also allow for a wider definition of gender which could be extended to vulnerable males, even though the majority of, or a disproportionate number of victims,

---

[123] On the particular issue of FGM, see I. Gunning, 'Arrogant Perception, World Traveling and Multicultural Feminism: The Case of Female Genital Surgeries' (1991–1992) 23 *Columbia Human Rights Law Review* 189. See also Chapter 1.5.2.

[124] See Edwards, above note 34, 13–19, for further discussion of the debates around the terminology of sex and gender.

[125] Although see the recent report by the UN OHCHR, Discriminatory Laws and Practices and Acts of Violence against Individuals Based on their Sexual Orientation and Gender Identity, UN doc. A/HRC/19/41 (17 November 2011).

[126] See art. 9(3) Constitution of the Republic of South Africa no. 108 of 1996.

are indeed still female. This approach takes into account social constructions of masculinity and femininity and allows for examination of broader issues of sexuality, including protection of rights in relation to freedom of sexual orientation, which are still highly under-developed in international human rights law.[127] The terminology around gender-based violence, as opposed to that of violence against women or sex discrimination, highlights the relevance of multiple power hierarchies which can victimise both men and women in a variety of contexts.

QUESTIONS

1. What is the relevance of feminist legal theory in relation to the human rights of women today? How can we use these theories in the current context?

2. How is 'culture' relevant to the human rights of women? How does 'cultural relativism' impact on women's human rights?

3. What is the difference between the terms 'sex' and 'gender' in terms of women's human rights?

4. X is a young man who became the victim of various forms of domestic violence, including physical and emotional abuse, once his family realised he was gay. His family told him that if he 'agrees' to a marriage to be arranged for him, all his previous actions will be forgotten, and he will no longer be subject to further abuse. Despite his attempts to alert the authorities to the abuse he is suffering, they have taken no steps to attempt to help him escape the situation without harm. Does X have a case to make before the CtEDAW?

11.4   WOMEN'S HUMAN RIGHTS AND DOMESTIC CONTEXTS: 'HONOUR CRIMES' IN THE ENGLISH LEGAL SYSTEM

The approach of the English legal system to cases of honour-related violence provides an example of how the issues discussed above operate in practice. Within the UK, honour-related violence has, to date, mostly been reported within ethnic minority communities. For this reason, there has been much debate as to the 'cultural' nature of such violence, and thus the extent to which it should be treated as culturally different, in practice and strategy, to other forms of gender-based violence such as domestic violence. The following discussion and Case Study 11.1 illustrate these issues in relation to the international human rights regime.

---

[127] S. Fried and I. Landberg-Lewis, 'Sexual Rights: From Concept to Strategy', in K. Askin and D. Koenig (eds.), *Women's Human Rights Reference Guide* (Transnational Press, 2000) 91–122.

11.4.1   Definitions and Concepts of 'Honour'

A key working definition of the term 'crimes of honour', which provides a useful bridge between concepts of 'honour' and the forms of violence through which 'honour' is enforced, understands it as encompassing:

a variety of manifestations of violence against women, including 'honour killings', assault, confinement or imprisonment, and interference with choice in marriage, where the publicly articulated 'justification' is attributed to a social order claimed to require the preservation of a concept of 'honour' vested in male (family and/ or conjugal) control over women and specifically women's sexual conduct: actual, suspected or potential.[128]

Anthropologists, feminists and other scholars argue that concepts of 'honour' are highly dependent on the twin concepts of male honour and female shame. In this conceptualisation, women are seen as the property of their male relatives, often due to reasons relating to the guarding of patriarchal control over male children, and the passing down of both the family name and inheritance. This objectification renders women disposable once they are perceived to have committed a transgression, since they are deemed to lack worth if they are no longer 'honourable'.

Honour-related violence can cover a wide spectrum of acts to control women's behaviour, ranging from emotional threats to physical violence. Three key forms of violence are especially notable, due both to their inter-linked nature and their severity. These are so-called 'honour killing', forced marriage and rape. For example, refusal to enter a forced marriage, along with other attempts at sexual or other forms of autonomy on the part of women may result in 'honour killing'. Rape may be used as a form of coercion into forced marriage, and women forced into marriage may also suffer marital rape as a consequence.

Honour-related violence can therefore be seen as a form of violence against women. 'Honour' adheres differentially and unequally to men and women; women are undoubtedly the primary victims of 'crimes of honour'[129] at the hands of largely male perpetrators, and those who transgress 'honour' codes suffer harsher consequences than their male counterparts. Even where men are the victims of an 'honour killing', this usually occurs because the victim is alleged to have ruined a woman's reputation by reneging on a promise of marriage, or through an actual or suspected relationship with her.[130] Accordingly, international and European declarations have

---

[128] See the introduction to their edited collection in L. Welchman and S. Hossain, *'Honour': Crimes, Paradigms and Violence Against Women* (Zed Books, 2005) 4.

[129] P. Sen, '"Honour" Crimes of Value and Meaning', in Welchman and Hossain, ibid., 48.

[130] See H. Siddiqui, 'There is No "Honour" in Domestic Violence, only Shame! Women's Struggles against Honour Crimes in the UK', ibid., 264; A. Gill, 'Reconfiguring "Honour"-

specifically located 'honour crimes' within the sphere of gender violence.[131] How is gender-based violence to be understood, particularly if men can also be victims of 'honour crimes'? Gender has been conceptualised as referring to the differential values historically attributed to masculinity and femininity, resulting in a 'patriarchal power legacy which manifests itself through relations of domination and subordination'.[132] The wording of CtEDAW's General Recommendation 19 provides important clues for an understanding of gender-based violence, which it defines as:

violence that is directed against a woman because she is a woman or that affects women disproportionately. It includes acts that inflict physical, mental or sexual harm or suffering, threats of such acts, coercion and other deprivations of liberty. (emphasis added)[133]

The definition does not necessitate that gender-based violence is always solely directed against women, but that this is disproportionately or primarily the case in most circumstances. This analysis also takes into account broader issues of gender and sexuality. For example, gay men and women may suffer honour-related violence if their sexual orientation becomes known and is deemed to bring shame or dishonour to their family or community.[134]

11.4.2 Practical Legal Approaches to 'Honour Crimes': Culture, Gender and Mainstreaming

This section provides a country-specific examination of approaches to honour-related violence within the English legal system, using case examples and interviews with various actors involved with formulating and implementing relevant legal policy and practice.[135] At present within the English legal system, for the most part, cases of honour-related violence are viewed through the lens of domestic violence, and therefore in practice are 'mainstreamed' into overarching frameworks addressing gender-based violence. The Association of Chief Police Officers, which is the national police

---

based Violence as a Form of Gender-Based Violence', in Idriss and Abbas, above note 3, 219.

[131] See the 1993 United Nations Declaration on the Elimination of Violence Against Women, UNGA resolution 48/104; and Council of Europe, So-called 'Honour Crimes', Parliamentary Assembly, resolution 1327 (4 April 2003).

[132] Y. Erturk, 'Considering the Role of Men in Gender Agenda Setting: Conceptual and Policy Issues' (2004) 78 *Feminist Review* 3.

[133] General Recommendation 19, para. 6. See also General Recommendation 35, paras. 1–2.

[134] K. Anderson, 'Violence Against Women: State Responsibilities in International Human Rights Law to Address Harmful Masculinities' (2008) 26 *Netherlands Quarterly of Human Rights* 173, at 178.

[135] This data emerges from the author's unpublished thesis research, 'Approaches to Honour-related Violence in the English Legal System'.

body in England and Wales responsible for formulating policies to be implemented by all of the police forces under its remit, defines honour-related violence as 'a crime or incident, which has or may have been committed to protect or defend the honour of the family and/or community'.[136] However, it simultaneously also specifically includes honour-related violence within the category of domestic abuse. The current cross-governmental definition of domestic violence is:

Any incident of threatening behaviour, violence or abuse (psychological, physical, sexual, financial or emotional) between adults, aged 18 and over, who are or have been intimate partners or family members, regardless of gender and sexuality (family members are defined as mother, father, son, daughter, brother, sister and grandparents, whether directly related, in-laws or step-family).[137]

A number of elements of this definition of domestic violence, in particular the inclusion of a range of behaviours and perpetrators, and the specific reference to both male and female perpetrators and victims, overlap with elements found within cases of honour-related violence. However, the definition is silent on certain other, additional factors, which have been present in some cases. These include the presence of multiple perpetrators, often in conjunction with the premeditation or pre-planning of crimes, and the involvement of an even wider range of family or community members. An example of the latter which has been reported in the UK are so-called 'bounty hunters' in some communities, who are enlisted to track down and at times harm potential victims who have attempted to escape honour-related violence.[138]

Key police officers and prosecutors[139] have endorsed the approach of, in the majority of cases, mainstreaming honour-related violence into current domestic violence strategies. Both police and Crown Prosecution Service interviewees acknowledged that cases of honour-related violence may often overlap or coexist with domestic violence, while simultaneously retaining certain unique elements. So-called 'cultural' factors were often in practice relevant in relation to tactical policing and prosecution tactics. These include frontline officer awareness and training, victim risk and safety plans, and investigation and evidence gathering, for example through the use of 'organised crime' investigative techniques such as covert listening devices, which are not usually employed in domestic homicide cases. The Association of Chief Police Officers interviewee stated that honour-related violence:

---

[136] *Honour-Based Violence Strategy*, Association of Chief Police Officers, 30 September 2008.
[137] National Policing Improvement Agency and Association of Chief Police Officers, *Guidance on Investigating Domestic Abuse* (2008).
[138] E.g., see Siddiqui, above note 130, 70.
[139] Including Commander Steve Allen, the 2006–2009 Association of Chief Police Officers lead on honour-based violence; and Nazir Afzal, former Crown Prosecution Service lead prosecutor on honour-based violence.

does need an additional set of knowledge, awareness, and some of the tactical responses are different as well, in terms of who you share information with, in terms of the safety plans around victims ... So it's about a victim focus, it's about assessing, recognising and managing risk, it's about safety planning, it's about the quality of evidence gathering ... [but] it's also about holding perpetrators to account ... because it's got these other [aspects], you can't just say well we've got a domestic abuse response, therefore that'll do.[140]

Such strategies could be seen as the implementation of an 'intersectional discrimination' approach in order to address crimes of honour-related violence as effectively as possible, whereby the intersection of gender with race or culture is recognised in the investigation and prosecution of such crimes. NGOs working with victims of honour-related violence have also identified the need for an intersectional approach, for example in relation to the need to provide targeted and specific refuge provision for ethnic minority victims of gender-based violence, including honour-related violence.

The interviewees acknowledged potential problems arising from the stigmatisation and stereotyping of certain communities, within the multicultural context of the UK, if certain elements, such as the involvement of wider family or community members within cases of honour-related violence are seen as 'cultural'. This parallels certain aspects of the debates in international human rights law, in relation to the 'orientalisation' of certain types of women's rights violations as associated with or only practised by certain communities or cultures.

11.4.3   Non-state Actors and Due Diligence: A Human Rights Response?

Within the international human rights framework, actors have emphasised the patriarchal nature of honour-related violence rather than its cultural aspects. For example, the Special Rapporteur on violence against women, its causes and consequences examined 'honour killings' and forced marriage within the context of her report on cultural practices in the family that are violent towards women. However, she took care to emphasise that overarching ideologies of masculinity, and the need to regulate female sexuality are key to the perpetuation of such violence.[141] CtEDAW's General Recommendation 19 refers to forced marriage as a type of 'traditional attitude', yet at the same time firmly places it within the realm of gender-based violence.[142] One outcome of this international recognition of honour-related

---

[140] Association of Chief Police Officers TS1, 2008, 4 (author's transcript).

[141] R. Coomaraswamy, Report of the Special Rapporteur on violence against women, its causes and consequences, 'Cultural Practices in the Family that are Violent towards Women', UN doc. E/CN.4/2002/83 (31 January 2002).

[142] See now General Recommendation 35, para. 14, fn. 18, para. 31(b).

violence as a form of gender-based violence is several UNGA resolutions specifically aimed at the elimination of 'crimes of honour' against women.[143]

Ensuring that violence against women is mainstreamed within a broader framework of both domestic and international human rights is an ongoing and pressing concern of feminist theory and activism. The principles and rights embodied within the European human rights system,[144] which have come into force in the UK legal system through the Human Rights Act,[145] can in this context be employed to protect victims of gender violence. As well as breaching broader principles of non-discrimination (article 14), 'honour crimes' such as 'honour killing' and forced marriage could invoke a number of other articles of the Human Rights Act and the ECHR, including articles 2, 3, 5, 8 and 12 ECHR.

A major question which remains to be addressed in relation to the use of human rights law in cases of honour-related violence is the fact that this violence is being carried out by non-state actors. To what extent, then, in the context of the English legal system, can these crimes be addressed by human rights norms? The triggering of these protections in the international human rights regime revolves around whether or not the state authorities have exercised due diligence in preventing, investigating and punishing crimes of honour-related violence.[146] In the UK context of honour-related violence, the due diligence principle translates into the debate around the extent to which state authorities have failed in their duties to an individual, by not adequately protecting or preventing a violation of their rights by a private actor.

In this scenario, if honour-related violence is seen as primarily culturally motivated, the triggering of these obligations could revolve around the arguments raised by activists and others that public authorities have differentiated between their treatment of violence against women within minority and majority communities due to concerns about multicultural politics. Thus the question of differentiation, and consequently due diligence, becomes once more focused on the issue of culture, with all the attendant problems discussed in this chapter. This approach therefore raises some tentative, but potentially controversial questions. One is whether violence against women

---

[143] Working Towards the Elimination of Crimes Against Women Committed in the Name of Honour, UNGA resolution 57/179 (18 December 2002) and Working Towards the Elimination of Crimes Against Women and Girls Committed in the Name of Honour, UNGA resolution 59/165 (20 December 2004). For more detailed analysis of 'honour crimes' as gender violence within the international human rights framework, see J. Connors, 'United Nations Approaches to "Crimes of Honour"', in Welchman and Hossain, above note 128.

[144] Specifically the ECHR.

[145] The Human Rights Act 1998 entered into force on 2 October 2000.

[146] See S. Farrior, 'The Due Diligence Standard and Violence Against Women' (2004) 14 *Interights Bulletin* 157; also Connors, above note 143, at 25.

in ethnic minority communities is now being over-emphasised in a way which may have negative consequences for overall strategies combating violence against *all women* within the UK. This could be avoided if agencies responsible for preventing and punishing such abuses placed greater emphasis on treating honour-related violence as part of a wider problem of gender-based violence. There is growing support among activists and scholars for the enforcement of due diligence obligations in relation to domestic violence in general (rather than specifically honour-related violence). The basis for this is the argument that the high rates of domestic abuse of all types in the UK mean that state mechanisms have failed in their obligations adequately to respond to and prevent such human rights violations by non-state actors.[147]

The discourse of human rights is undoubtedly of great symbolic and practical importance in the international strategy against gender-based violence. However, within multicultural societies such as the UK, the question is whether this discourse is of specific assistance within the context of attempts to protect potential victims of 'honour crimes'.[148] Therefore a number of questions remain as to the practical utility and implementation of human rights mechanisms within specific domestic legal systems. These are raised by Case Study 11.1.

CASE STUDY 11.1
Banaz Mahmod

Banaz Mahmod was a twenty-year-old Kurdish woman who left an abusive marriage which her family had forced her into. She was brutally raped and murdered after her family discovered that she was involved in a relationship with a young man, which they deemed would bring 'dishonour' to the family and community. Later investigations revealed that the murder was planned, premeditated and carried out by a range of private individuals, including her father, uncle and other male members of her family and wider community. Her mother was also complicit, possibly through fear for her own safety. There were a number of failures on the part of the UK police in this case, which led

---

[147] For more detailed arguments as to why and how positive or horizontal obligations come into effect in relation to domestic violence in the UK, including case law, see S. Choudhry and J. Herring, 'Righting Domestic Violence' (2006) 201 *International Journal of Law, Policy and the Family* 95.

[148] See Charlesworth and Chinkin, above note 1, 211.

to an investigation by the Independent Police Complaints Commission. These included a number of occasions where Banaz reported to police front desk staff that she was in fear of her life from her family because of issues of honour. On each occasion her claims were disregarded because the police officers in question did not believe that they constituted a legitimate threat, due at least in part to their lack of understanding of issues around 'honour', and the possibility of accompanying violence. On another occasion Banaz called the emergency services after breaking a window and escaping from the family residence because she feared her father was about to kill her. The attending female police officer took her to the hospital, yet dismissed her account as 'an attention-seeking ploy or a private family matter', and even considered charging her with criminal damage.[1] The Independent Police Complaints Commission found that the police response to Banaz's plight was 'at best mixed' and that she had been 'let down' by the police in London and the West Midlands in relation to 'delays in investigations, poor supervision, a lack of understanding and insensitivity'.[2] It has been argued by activists and others that the police failures in this case demonstrated an ongoing problem of poor implementation of policy, where the police are still 'merely talking the talk' rather than translating policy into practical strategies to protect victims.[3]

[1] See Gill, above note 1.
[2] See 'IPCC concludes investigation into MPs and West Midlands Police dealings with Banaz Mahmod', Independent Police Complaints Commission (2 April 2008).
[3] See A. Gill, '"Honor Killings" and the Quest for Justice in Black and Minority Ethnic Communities in the United Kingdom' (2009) 20 *Criminal Justice Policy Review* 475. See also J. Payton, 'Collective Crimes, Collective Victims: A Case Study of the Murder of Banaz Mahmod', in Idriss and Abbas above note 3, for discussion of this case, including the police response.

POINTS TO CONSIDER

1. What forms of honour-related violence are present in this scenario, and what role does culture play? To what extent is it useful to view 'honour crimes' either as culture- or gender-based?

2. Should such violence be 'mainstreamed' into existing or overarching domestic frameworks around gender-based violence? If so, why, and to what extent?

3. Did the domestic legal system in this case adequately address the violations caused by non-state actors? Is the 'due diligence' principle worth pursuing in this and other cases of honour-related violence?

FURTHER READING

Adami, R., *Women and the Universal Declaration of Human Rights* (Routledge, 2018).

Askin, K., and D. Koenig, (eds.), *Women and International Human Rights Law*, 3 vols. (Transnational Publishers, 1999).

Banda, F., *Women, Law and Human Rights: An African Perspective* (Hart, 2005).

Charlesworth, H., 'Not Waving but Drowning: Gender Mainstreaming and Human Rights within the United Nations' (2005) 18 *Harvard Human Rights Journal* 1.

Charlesworth, H., and C. Chinkin, *The Boundaries of International Law: A Feminist Analysis* (Manchester University Press, 2000).

Chinkin, C., and S. Wright, 'The Hunger Trap: Women, Food and Self-Determination' (1993) 14 *Michigan Journal of International Law* 262.

Coomaraswamy, R., 'To Bellow like a Cow: Women, Ethnicity and the Discourse of Rights', in R. Cook (ed.), *Human Rights of Women, National and International Perspectives* (University of Pennsylvania Press, 1994).

Crenshaw, K., 'Mapping the Margins: Intersectionality, Identity Politics and Violence Against Women of Colour' (1991) 3 *Stanford Law Review* 1241.

Edwards, A., *Violence Against Women in International Human Rights Law* (Cambridge University Press, 2011).

Fraser, A., 'Becoming Human: The Origins and Development of Women's Human Rights' (1999) 21 *Human Rights Quarterly* 853.

Freeman, M., C. Chinkin and B. Rudolf (eds.), *The UN Convention on the Elimination of All Forms of Discrimination against Women* (Oxford University Press, 2012).

Gunning, I., 'Arrogant Perception, World Traveling and Multicultural Feminism: The Case of Female Genital Surgeries' (1991–1992) 23 *Columbia Human Rights Law Review* 189.

Heathcote, G., *Feminist Dialogues on International Law: Successes, Tensions, Futures* (Oxford University Press, 2019).

Hellum, A., and H. Sinding Aasen, *Women's Human Rights: CEDAW in International, Regional and National Law* (Cambridge University Press, 2013).

Mackinnon, C., *Feminism Unmodified: Discourses on Life and Law* (Harvard University Press, 1987).

Are Women Human? And Other International Dialogues (Harvard University Press, 2007).

Manjoo, R., and J. Jones (eds.), *The Legal Protection of Women from Violence: Normative Gaps in International Law* (Routledge, 2018).

Merry, S. E., *Human Rights and Gender Violence: Translating International Law into Local Justice* (University of Chicago Press, 2009).

Oloka-Oyango, J., and S. Tamale, '"The Personal is Political", or Why Women's Rights are Indeed Human Rights: An African Perspective' (1995) 17 *Human Rights Quarterly* 691.

Sosa, L., *Intersectionality in the Human Rights Legal Framework on Violence against Women: At the Centre or the Margins?* (Cambridge University Press, 2017).

Special Rapporteur on violence against women, its causes and consequences, 'Integration of the Human Rights of Women and the Gender Perspective: Violence Against Women – The Due Diligence Standard as a Tool for the Elimination of Violence Against Women', Y. Eturk, UN doc. E/CN.4/2006/61 (20 January 2006).

'The Intersections between Culture and Gender', Y. Eturk, UN doc. A/HRC/4/34 (17 January 2007).

Welchman, L., and S. Hossain, *'Honour': Crimes, Paradigms and Violence Against Women* (Zed Books, 2005).

Williams, P., *The Alchemy of Race and Rights* (Harvard University Press, 1991).

12 Children's Rights

CONTENTS

12.1 INTRODUCTION

The presumption is that a specialised legal regime for children is warranted because of their inherent vulnerabilities. The vulnerability of children is rather different from that of other vulnerable groups, such as women, indigenous peoples, disabled persons, lesbian, gay, bisexual, transsexual and intersex (LGBTI) persons, in that at different stages of their development they are mostly dependent on others for their survival and cannot (or are not allowed to) partake in social or political life in the same way as adults. Unlike all other vulnerable persons, the well-being of children is entrusted to their parents and guardians, and hence many of the issues facing children have traditionally been perceived through the lens of family relationships and family law, as opposed to human rights law.

The Convention on the Rights of the Child (CRC) and its subsequent protocols has somewhat changed this state of affairs by introducing several principles which transform children from objects to real subjects of the law.[1] Moreover, these instruments highlight the reality that children can and do constitute a 'commodity' for organised crime groups and warlords, whether for sexual gratification, illegal adoptions or as child soldiers. Unless states take active and concerted measures to prevent and punish the perpetrators (and end-users) of such offences, the exploitation of children will remain a profitable enterprise. Without investment in the lives of children through the use of maximum available resources, states will remain weak and children disempowered.

This chapter examines the emergence of a specialised human rights regime for children, as well as the guiding principles found in the CRC. It then goes on to illustrate how poverty and other factors exacerbate the vulnerabilities of children.

12.2   CHILDHOOD: A NON-STATIC CONCEPT

It is perhaps inconceivable today that a child would be fully integrated in the life of adults, bearing in the process the same rights and obligations. Yet until the Renaissance, in Europe childhood was no different from adulthood. Children engaged in exactly the same activities as adults and from a very early age they learned their parents' trade through apprenticeships. In this setting, children were not viewed as weaker or inferior compared to adults, and it was considered natural that they would partake in equal measure in the sustenance and survival needs of the family, tribe or clan. Childhood, as a way of treating and behaving towards children as distinct from adults, emerged with the Renaissance and the Reformation movement, whereby children were viewed as weak and in need of discipline.[2] That era, therefore, developed the notion of childhood in the form of a social construct. From the Renaissance right up to the 1970s, parents (or guardians) were recognised as

---

[1] Besides references to children's rights in general human rights treaties (regional and global), specialised instruments other than the CRC and its protocols also exist. These may be crudely classified as public international law and private international law instruments. The former include: the UN Declaration on the Rights of the Child (UNGA resolution 1386 (XIV) (1959)), the 1973 ILO Minimum Age [for employment] Convention, the 1990 African Charter on the Rights and Welfare of the Child and the 1996 European Convention on the Exercise of Children's Rights. Private international law instruments include: the 1965 Hague Convention on Jurisdiction and Applicable Law relating to Adoptions, the 1996 Hague Convention on Jurisdiction, Applicable Law, Recognition, Enforcement and Co-operation in respect of Parental Responsibility and Measures for the Protection of Children and the 1980 Hague Convention on the Civil Aspects of International Child Abduction.

[2] M. Freeman, *The Rights and Wrongs of Children* (Pinter, 1983) 8–10; P. Aries, *Centuries of Childhood* (Knopf, 1962).

the sole agents of the child. This meant that children had no rights as such and no independent *locus standi* that was distinct from that of their parents or guardians.[3]

The CRC and other instruments before it exemplify a tension between two competing ideas, namely the child liberationist model and the child protectionist or nurturance model. The former advocates absolute autonomy, in the sense that children must be allowed to possess power to decide all issues affecting them, this being the only means to fully realise children's rights.[4] The protectionist school, on the other hand, assumes that children's physical and mental capabilities have been proven by the physical sciences to be different from those of adults, which in turn renders them dependent and vulnerable and therefore in need of specialised protection.[5] None of the two schools in their pure form is without problems. By way of illustration, while children's autonomy is attractive, if taken to extremes it allows sexual freedom at a very young age, as well as unlimited recruitment in armed conflicts. Equally, while the pitfalls stemming from absolute autonomy are remedied by the protectionist theory, its application also risks giving no voice whatsoever to children and imposing on them lifestyles which are antithetical to their needs and desires, but which are otherwise compatible with the interests and desires of their parents and guardians. As will be demonstrated in subsequent sections, the CRC reconciles both schools and incorporates elements of both.

With this in mind, a child is defined under article 1 of the CRC as 'every human being below the age of 18 years, unless under the law applicable to the child, majority is attained earlier'.[6] The 'age of majority' refers to the possession of control over one's person, decisions and actions, and coincides in time with the termination of legal authority exercised by the child's parents or guardians.[7] The age of majority is not the same as the age of sexual consent, the age at which one is allowed to consume alcohol or the age one is allowed to vote. These may well differ from the age of majority.

---

[3] In a landmark judgment, the US Supreme Court in *Re Gault* (US) (1967) emphasised that children accused of crimes enjoy the same constitutional guarantees as adults, including the opportunity to confront and cross-examine witnesses.

[4] J. Holt and R. Farson, *Escape from Childhood* (Dutton, 1974).

[5] Freeman, above note 2, at 23.

[6] In Iran, e.g., the age of majority for boys is 15 and 9 for girls. See www.youthpolicy.org/factsheets/country/iran/. It is not a far leap for art. 1041 of the Iranian Civil Code to allow marriage before the age of puberty, thus essentially rendering young girls sexual slaves.

[7] Although an unborn child may in some circumstances be regarded as a 'child', in most jurisdictions the term 'child' refers to a child after it has been born. See *R v. Newham London Borough Council, ex parte Dada* (UK) (1996).

12.3   THE NEED FOR A SPECIALISED PROTECTION REGIME

One of the cardinal principles of human rights is that they apply to all persons irrespective of age, gender, religion or any other particular status. Hence, they equally apply to children. In reality, however, vulnerable persons and groups are unable to exercise their rights in the same way as their more empowered counterparts. By way of illustration, the illiterate and ultra-poor are not only often unaware of their rights but have little access to justice mechanisms. As a result, if they have no recourse to legal aid, no serious political effort towards universal education and if local laws do not allow for representation by civil society, it is evident that their entitlements under international human rights law are meaningless.

Children do not typically possess the means for their own well-being and as such are dependent on their parents or guardians. Even so, the rights afforded to children under general human rights law are not subsumed wholly in the person of the parent. If this were so, the person of the child would be legally inseparable from that of the parent and hence the parent's treatment of the child would not be a matter for human rights law, but the law of property, or some other legal discipline. This may seem absurd if measured against contemporary standards, but it was not long ago that the caning and beating of children by their parents were considered lawful 'disciplinary' methods of parenting.[8] Under the current position, which is reflected in the CRC, children possess an independent (from their parents) legal personality, which encompasses general and specialised human rights entitlements, and, in addition, parents (or other guardians) bear several obligations for their protection, development and well-being. The duties and rights of parents are further supplemented by the state, which has a positive obligation of ensuring that all those involved in the child's upbringing, including the parents, discharge their duties in accordance with the 'best interests' of the child.

The enforcement of children's rights and the two strands upon which such enforcement rests (i.e. independent legal personality counterbalanced with the rights and duties of parents/guardians) suggests that other related areas of law must necessarily be adapted accordingly. For example, under the law of contract a child's legal personality cannot be equated to full legal capacity to enter into complex contracts. The consent of the parent/guardian will always be required in such cases. More importantly, in the greater field of family law seemingly unrelated relationships, such as marital ones (for

---

[8] See *Tyrer* v. *UK* (ECtHR) (1978), which found that such punishment was tantamount to institutionalised violence contrary to art. 3 ECHR (inhuman or degrading treatment or punishment).

example divorce), have a direct bearing on the child.[9] Equally, the legal consequences of adoption or surrogacy juxtapose the positive obligation of the state to ensure the child's best interests, while on the other hand to satisfy that its citizens do not violate the law and engage in conduct that is contrary to public morals.[10] In cases where a child is born from a surrogate mother who under prior and lawful agreement gives up the child to the biological father (and his partner/spouse), the father's country of nationality may not recognise a legal relationship between the biological father and the child. As a result, the child is not considered adopted or the offspring of the father and as a result is not granted the father's nationality if conceived and born abroad, even if the country of birth recognises paternal rights under the surrogacy. The European Court of Human Rights (ECtHR) has held in such cases that overly restrictive surrogacy laws that offend the parent–child relationship do not fall within member states' margin of appreciation and that failure to grant nationality to the child undermines its identity within the society of its parents.[11]

Given the importance of the family unit, since the family is entrusted under law with the function of acting as the primary carer of the child,[12] the family's rights and duties are so intertwined with those of the child that in some cases they are inseparable. The modern concept of 'family' is far more diverse as compared to the traditional model.[13] In its broadest

[9] It should be pointed out here that in civil law systems family law is one of the five components of substantive civil law, the others being property law, contracts, general principles and inheritance law. As a result, very few family lawyers (including judges) possess any expertise in relevant areas, such as developmental psychology, which are crucial in understanding the status and sensitivities of children in law and society.

[10] The ECtHR has been asked numerous times to deal with Islamic *kafala* adoptions, which is a voluntary undertaking, usually by well-off members of the extended family, to provide for the welfare and education of the child. In *Chbihi Loudoudi* v. *Belgium* (ECtHR) (2014), the ECtHR held that the non-recognition of *kafala* by Belgian authorities was in the best interests of the child. In the case at hand, the ECtHR agreed with the Belgian authorities that the maintenance of the single parent–child relationship in Morocco and Belgium with its biological parents served the child's interests much better than an adoption by non-biological parents in Belgium. That inter-state adoptions must only proceed if they are in the interests of the child is confirmed by the 1993 Hague Convention on the Protection of Children and Cooperation in respect of Intercountry Adoption. In *Y. B. and N. S.* v. *Belgium* (CtRC) (2018), the CtRC held that the denial of a humanitarian visa to a five-year-old child taken in under *kafala* fostering arrangements by a Belgian-Moroccan couple violated arts. 3 (child's best interests), 10 (family reunification) and 12 (right to be heard) of the CRC.

[11] *Mennesson and Others* v. *France* and *Labassee* v. *France* (ECtHR) (2014).

[12] Art. 5 CRC includes not only the parents (i.e. family), but also, where applicable, members of the extended family 'or community, as provided for by local custom'. Art. 18(1) and (2) African Charter on Human and Peoples' Rights (ACHPR) notes that 'the family shall be the natural unit and basis of society' and that the state has a duty to assist it.

[13] See F. Banda and J. Ekelaar, 'International Conceptions of the Family' (2017) 66 *International & Comparative Law Quarterly* 833.

sense it is composed of two independent yet interconnected relationships, namely the spouses *inter se* and spouses' children, whereas in its narrowest sense it may consist of single-parent families, non-marital families, families without children, two-adult families without children, etc. The family is protected by two overarching freedoms; privacy and the rights of children. The relationship between the parents and the children is not absolute, but as already noted, it is constrained by the principle of equality and non-discrimination. However, both are subsidiary to the operation of the children's 'best interests' principle, which is paramount in any determination of matters pertinent to children, such as parental care and custody.[14] The reason for this hierarchy between two seemingly equal human rights norms is their tendency for conflict. If one is to assess the best interests of a child in the course of a custody dispute between two parents, one must 'discriminate' in favour of the parent who provides the best possible assurances (for example, safety, stability, loving environment, education prospects, etc.) to the child's well-being. This discrimination is considered necessary because the objective in question is the well-being of the child, which cannot always be served if equality between the parents is taken as the starting point.[15]

12.4   FUNDAMENTAL PRINCIPLES

The CRC recognises four key guiding principles which permeate the understanding and construction of all pertinent rights. Some of these have long been recognised as general principles, but others are new for many states. These principles are meant to be applied contextually (based on the particular circumstances of each case), but also as peremptory principles of construction/interpretation. As a result, they may be applied substantively (for example to interpret the child's right to leisure), as well as in respect of procedural law.[16] These principles are: (1) the best interests of the child (article 3 CRC); (2) respect for the views of the child (article 12 CRC); (3) the right

---

[14] *Maumousseau and Washington* v. *France* (ECtHR) (2007) para. 62; *Gnahoré* v. *France* (ECtHR) (2000) para. 59.

[15] The ECtHR has claimed in unequivocal terms that the award of custody to one parent following divorce or separation constitutes an interference, albeit a legitimate one, to the right to family life of the other under art. 8 ECHR. This interference is justified by the best interests principle enshrined in art. 3 CRC. See *Hoffmann* v. *Austria* (ECtHR) (1993) para. 29. The 'best interests' principle exists also, among others, in art. 24(2) of the EU Charter on Fundamental Rights and arts. 5(b) and 16(1)(d) of the Convention on the Elimination of All Forms of Discrimination against Women (CEDAW).

[16] See CtRC, General Comment 14 (2013) on the rights of the child to have his or her best interests taken as a primary consideration, UN doc. CRC/C/GC/14 (29 May 2013) para. 6.

to life, survival and development (article 6 CRC); and (4) non-discrimination (article 2 CRC).[17]

12.4.1   The Child's Best Interests

The foundational principle underlying any decision, judgment or action (legislative, administrative or other) concerning children is that it must be in the best interests of the child.[18] The application of the 'best interests' principle under article 3(2) CRC must take into account 'the rights and duties [of the child's] parents, guardians or other individuals legally responsible'. A child's best interests must be assessed on an individual basis by the courts and administrative authorities, and hence pertinent decisions must be reasoned as to their effects and outcomes on the particular child.[19] The application of this principle in the field of legislative drafting requires that laws reflect the needs of children in a disaggregated fashion.[20] For example, there should be different types of protection for children who are refugees, members of indigenous communities, marginalised groups (such as Roma), socially excluded, disabled children, abandoned children and others.[21]

Keeping accurate and disaggregated statistical data is therefore important. This is a general obligation on states parties under article 31 CRPD. In the context of article 7 CRPD, which concerns disabled chidren, it serves several practical dimensions.[22] For example, it may show whether a state has reduced the number of disabled children in long-term institutions and whether in turn it has succeeded in placing high numbers in foster care or reintegrated them with their families. Moreover, disaggregated data allows policy-makers to fully appreciate the situation of and discrimination faced

---

[17] See G. Van Bueren, *The International Law on the Rights of the Child* (Martinus Nijhoff, 1995) 15, who refers to general principles and develops a functional framework referred to as the 'four Ps', namely participation, protection, prevention (of harm) and provision (of assistance).

[18] According to art. 3(1) CRC, 'the best interests of the child shall be a primary consideration'. Art. 2 Optional Protocol to the CRC (Communications Procedure) setting out the general principles guiding the functions of the Committee stipulates that the CtRC 'shall be guided by the principle of the best interests of the child'. Under art. 3(2) of the Optional Protocol, the CtRC 'may decline to examine any communication that it considers not to be in the child's best interests'.

[19] See *Y. B. and N. S.* v. *Belgium*, para. 8.3.

[20] CtRC, General Comment 14, above note 16, paras. 10–12.

[21] See e.g., CtRC, General Comment 11 (2009), indigenous children and their rights under the convention, UN doc. CRC/C/GC/11 (12 February 2009) para. 5, which notes that indigenous children face discrimination in several fields, particularly access to health care and education.

[22] See also CtRC, 'General Comment No 9: The Rights of Children with Disabilities', UN doc. CRC/C/GC/9 (27 February 2007) para. 19.

by children with disabilities, particularly indigenous children with disabilities, so as to formulate targeted programmes with a view to tackling the exclusion they face.[23] In some cases, states manipulate data through definitional alterations. Azerbaijan was found by the Committee on the Rights of the Child (CtRC) to have the fifth highest child mortality rate in Europe, but its definition of a 'live birth' was not consistent with the internationally recognised WHO definition.[24] The Committee on the Rights of Persons with Disabilities (CtRPD) deplored the absence of data on disabled children's births so as to be able to correlate these to Azerbaijan's high infant mortality rate and 'particularly how this state of affairs was affecting the birth registration of boys and girls with disabilities'.[25]

A child's best interest must even supersede any related violation of domestic law. In *Paradiso and Campanelli* v. *Italy*, it transpired that the applicants had been untruthful about a surrogacy in Russia because none had a biological relationship with the child. Given that the nine-month-old child was not the product of a lawful surrogacy it was placed in foster care. The ECtHR held that despite the fact that the applicants had breached Italian and international law regarding inter-country adoption, the removal of a child from its family setting (its provisional foster family) was an extreme measure and could be justified only in the eventuality of immediate danger.[26]

According to the ECtHR, the best interests of the child comprise two limbs: maintaining family ties (except where the family has proved particularly unfit) and ensuring the child's development within a sound environment, such as would not harm its health and development.[27]

A particular dimension of the best interests principle is its direct application to entities and institutions other than the courts or the state. Private entities and institutions are not immune from the application of this principle in their dealings with children. Although such an obligation is not conferred on private entities, states parties to the CRC, ICCPR and CRPD are obliged to incorporate such obligation in their domestic laws on the basis of which private entities are obliged to apply the welfare principle. This conclusion is amply reflected in the CtRC's General Comment 9, where it was stated that:

---

[23] CtRPD, 'Concluding Obsevations on the Initial Report of Canada', UN doc. CRPD/C/CAN/CO/1 (8 May 2017) para. 18(a).

[24] CtRC, 'Concluding Observations on the Combined Third to Fifth Periodic Reports of Azerbaijan', UN doc. CRC/C/AZE/CO/3–4 (12 March 2012) para. 34.

[25] CtRPD, 'Concluding Observations on the Initial Report of Azerbaijan', UN doc. CRPD/C/AZE/CO/1 (12 May 2014) paras. 18–19.

[26] *Paradiso and Campanelli* v. *Italy* (ECtHR) (2015).

[27] See *Neulinger and Shuruk* v. *Switzerland* (ECtHR) (2012) para. 136; see generally M. Freeman, *Commentary on the UN Convention on the Rights of the Child: Article 3* (Brill, 2007).

The best interests of the child is of particular relevance in institutions and other facilities that provide services for children with disabilities as they are expected to conform to standards and regulations and should have the safety, protection and care of children as their primary consideration, and this consideration should outweigh any other and under all circumstances, for example, when allocating budgets.[28]

It should, however, be pointed out that even the 'best interests' principle should be construed in such a manner as actually leading to the best interests of a child in particular circumstances. In the case of disabled children, because of the outright rejection of the medical model of disability in the CRPD, the recognition of full legal capacity through, where necessary, supported decision-making is deemed to be in the child's best interests. No doubt, there might well be circumstances where the determination of a disabled child's will and preference is impractical or difficult to ascertain. In such cases, the CtRPD is of the view that the 'best interpretation of will and preferences' must replace 'best interests' determinations.[29] This means that as long as the substitute is not appointed against the person's will, and as long as he or she adopts decisions affecting the disabled child on the basis of its 'best interpretation of will and preferences' rather than a 'best interests' standard, such assistance would not constitute a substituted decision but a supported or facilitated decision.[30] The same view has been expressed by the CtRC as follows: Where the child wishes to express his or her views and where this right is fulfilled through a representative, the latter's obligation is to communicate accurately the views of the child. In situations where the child's views are in conflict with those of his or her representative, a procedure should be established to allow the child to approach an authority to establish a separate representation for the child (e.g. a guardian ad litem), if necessary.[31]

---

[28] CtRC, General Comment 9, above note 22, para. 30; equally CtRC, General Comment 14, above note 16, para. 26. The CRC Committee has identified in what manner the business community is expected to deal with children's rights, including the rights of disabled children. CtRC, General Comment 16 on State Obligations regarding the Impact of the Business Sector on Children's Rights, UN doc. CRC/C/GC/16 (17 April 2013).

[29] CtRPD, 'General Comment No 1: Equal Recognition before the Law', UN doc. CRPD/C/GC/1 (19 May 2014) para. 21; see *RP and Others* v. *UK* (ECHR) (2012) para. 75, which concerned the appointment of an Official Solicitor to represent a mother with learning disabilities in a child care proceeding and where a prematurely born child suffered from serious impairments. The ECtHR referred to arts. 5, 12, 13 and 23 CRPD, but not art. 7 and held that it was on the basis of the best interests of the disabled child that the Official Solicitor should determine what form of guardianship was appropriate.

[30] See I. Bantekas, M. A. Stein and D. Anastasiou (eds.), *The UN Convention on the Rights of Persons with Disabilities: A Commentary* (Oxford University Press, 2018) 363–7.

[31] CRC Ctee, General Comment 14, above note 16, para. 90, on the rights of the child to have his or her best interests taken as a primary consideration.

12.4.2 The Child's Right to be Heard

The right of the child to express its views and be heard is predicated on scientific findings according to which children are able to form views, even before developing their ability to express themselves.[32] As a result, it is natural, but certainly radical (as a legal entitlement) for children not only to have legal standing in matters that affect them, but also substantially to affect pertinent legal relationships through their personal views.[33] Under article 12 CRC children are thus entitled, but not obliged, to express their views in legal or administrative proceedings (for example, custody or adoption) and by implication states are obliged to give due weight to these views.[34] Although the view of a child is enhanced by its age and level of maturity, given the contextual character of this entitlement, the level of a child's maturity is a matter of assessment and can never be presumed;[35] otherwise national authorities would render it defunct in practice.[36] Children's levels of understanding are not uniformly linked to their biological age.[37] The CtRC has chastised states with a mandatory legislation stating an age at which a child is considered capable of expressing its views, emphasising that since age and maturity differ from one child to another, the existence of maturity must be assessed on a case-by-case basis irrespective of age.[38]

The right of a disabled child to always be heard as a substantive and procedural right is distinct from the authority of the entity, judicial or otherwise, before which the child is making a claim, to make a judicial or other determination. The court or other entity deciding a matter affecting a disabled child is not bound by the expressed views of the child. But it cannot ignore its views where its age and maturity are such that not taking these into consideration would not be in the best interests of the disabled child. This is true, for example, in custody or adoption proceedings. Most states pay lip service to the right of children to be heard. While allowing a child to be heard, they provide no guarantees that the courts or administrative authorities will

---

[32] CtRC, General Comment 12 on the right of the child to be heard, UN doc. CRC/C/GC/12 (1 July 2009) para. 21.

[33] Ibid., paras. 32–3.

[34] Ibid., paras. 44–5. The CtRC is also guided by this principle. Pursuant to art. 2 OP CRC (Communication Procedure) '[i]t shall also have regard for the rights and views of the child, the views of the child being given due weight in accordance with the age and maturity of the child'.

[35] General Comment 12 ibid., para. 20.

[36] In *Y. B. and N. S.* v. *Belgium*, para. 8.6, the Committee rejected the respondent state's argument that the five-year-old applicant 'was not capable of forming her own views' and emphasised, in para. 8.7, that '[t]he fact that the child is very young or in a vulnerable situation ... does not deprive him or her of the right to express his or her views, nor reduces the weight given to the child's views in determining his or her best interests'.

[37] CtRC, General Comment 12, above note 32, para. 29.   [38] Ibid., paras. 21 and 52.

actually consider the child's views. By way of illustration, there may be a failure to engage in a true dialogue with the child over several days or sessions of court proceedings; there may be an absence of *in camera* proceedings to ensure the sensitivity of the process; a disabled child may not be given the technological or communicative means to converse with the judge; the maturity of the child may be difficult for the judge to assess because of a child's disability or demeanour. There are of course many more impediments. It is, therefore, imperative that a secure link be established between the right to have a child's views heard and the proper contextualisation and application of such use. This could be achieved, for example, by requiring reasoned decisions with specific mention as to how the child's views were considered and 'respected'[39] and why, if at all, they were rejected. Equally, the decision should explain how the maturity of the child was assessed and the methodology used. This requires a sound and coherent methodological framework that is predicated on scientific criteria and not a random assessment by untrained civil servants or judges. Domestic laws should render decisions not reasoned in the manner explained above as appealable. It comes as no surprise, therefore, that the CtRPD has chastised most states parties for failing to consult, or to adopt appropriate policies and procedures by which disabled children can be consulted in matters that affect them.[40] This is clearly a systemic issue that requires concrete legislative action so that the stakeholders are aware how and when they are expected to participate in the relevant processes.

The CtRC has made a significant distinction between the individual right to be heard, as analysed above, and the collective right of particular groups (of children) to be heard. The latter is not a collective right, in the sense of self-determination, but a *sui generis* entitlement that pertains to groups of children sharing common interests (for example, marginalised, school-children, indigenous). This group right (which is sometimes referred to as a participation right) arises in situations where a policy or action directly affects a group of children. By way of illustration, the removal of a teacher by the school's headmaster, the demolition of a playground, and the introduction of an educational programme for indigenous children are all issues in which the affected children should be allowed to express their views. This is not mere rhetoric but an obligation on all states parties to the CRC.[41]

---

[39] CRPD Ctee, 'Concluding Obsevations on the Initial Report of Cyprus', UN doc. CRPD/C/CYP/CO/1 (8 May 2017) para. 22.

[40] CRPD Ctee, 'Concluding Observations on the Initial Report of Luxembourg', UN doc. CRPD/C/LUX/CO/1 (10 October 2017) para. 17(b); CRPD Ctee, 'Concluding Observations on the Initial Report of Montenegro', UN doc. CRPD/C/MNE/CO/1 (22 September 2017) para. 15(a); CRPD Ctee, 'Concluding Observations on the Initial Report of the UAE', UN doc. CRPD/C/ARE/CO/1 (3 October 2016) para. 16(b).

[41] CtRC, General Comment 12, above note 32, paras. 72–3 and 127ff.

12.4.3   Right to Life, Survival and Development

Unlike adulthood, childhood is a period of continuous growth from birth to infancy, through the preschool age to adolescence. The CtRC has emphasised that:

each phase is significant as important developmental changes occur in terms of physical, psychological, emotional and social development, expectations and norms. The stages of the child's development are cumulative and each stage has an impact on subsequent phases, influencing the children's health, potential, risks and opportunities.[42]

The meaning of 'survival' and its link to the right to life are not apparent in article 6 CRC. However, if one considers that child mortality is highest for neonatal and adolescents it becomes evident that the survival of infants, at the very least, is inextricably linked to the health of their mother. If the authorities do not afford mothers the right to the highest standard of health, the chances of survival for the child will be minimised.[43] In an Indian case, a destitute woman died on a busy Delhi street four days after giving birth, having no access to food or medical aid. Because of the publicity of the incident, the Delhi High Court entertained it on its own motion. It went on to order the local authority to set up five homeless shelters exclusively for destitute, homeless and lactating women, and to ensure that a system is in place for such women to be taken to the shelters if they cannot go themselves, and that its services are publicised.[44] Such judgments essentially call on states to use the maximum extent of their available resources (article 4 CRC). We have commented elsewhere that even poorer states have enough resources to satisfy fundamental socio-economic rights[45] and that there is no excuse for allowing the most vulnerable members of society to perish. Child survival is therefore a concept that is broader and more specialised as regards 'well-being' in the context of the right to development.

The development of children is perceived holistically rather than piecemeal. States are obliged to invest in children, not simply as a matter of obligation under the CRC, but because their human capital is their most valuable asset. As the United Nations (UN) Development Programme's (UNDP) Human Development Report has emphasised, 'investments in early childhood education, a focus on employment opportunities for youth and support for older people enhance life capabilities'.[46] The United Nations Children's Fund (UNICEF) applies a particular methodology for measuring children's

---

[42] CtRC, General Comment 15 on the right of the child to the enjoyment of the highest attainable standard of health, UN doc. CRC/C/GC/15 (17 April 2013) para. 20.

[43] Ibid., para. 18.   [44] *Court on its own Motion* v. *Union of India* (India) (2011).

[45] See Chapter 9.4.   [46] UNDP, *Human Development Report* (2014) 3.

well-being through indicators. These are known as Multiple Indicator Cluster Surveys (MICS) and it is on the basis of MICS that UNICEF assesses funding and recommends measures.[47]

It is now clear that children's vulnerabilities are exploited by organised crime and predatory behaviour (as is the case with paedophile rings), whose existence was either ignored or conveniently silenced in the past, many times regarded as a taboo topic. This is no longer the case. For one thing, the 2002 Optional Protocol to the CRC on the sale of children, child prostitution and child pornography renders such conduct an extraditable international offence (article 5). Children are the victims of such offences and the Protocol makes it clear that irrespective of taboos and local laws their consent should not render them complicit or provide impunity to the perpetrators. As a result, child victims must be cared for at all phases of investigation/prosecution by the authorities and not be exposed to undue risk or harm (article 8). Articles 1 and 3 of the Protocol oblige states to prohibit and punish (even extraterritorially) the sale of children, child prostitution and pornography, including also related conduct, such as sale or transfer of organs for profit, forced labour and illegal adoptions. The next subsection explores the particular status of child soldiers.

12.4.3.1 Child Soldiers

The UN Security Council (UNSC) had since 30 August 1996 condemned the recruitment, deployment and training of children for combat beginning with resolution 1071 in connection with the civil conflict in Liberia. It was only in 1999 that the UNSC not only took up the matter annually on its agenda but condemned all forms of recruitment and deployment of children in armed conflict as a war crime.[48] Article 4(3)(c) of Additional Protocol II (1977) to the 1949 Geneva Conventions states that '[c]hildren who have not attained the age of fifteen years shall neither be recruited in the armed forces or groups nor allowed to take part in hostilities'. A similar provision was also inserted in article 77(2) of Additional Protocol I (1977) and article 38(3) CRC. By the time of the adoption of the International Criminal Court (ICC) Statute in 1998, the Sierra Leone Special Court (SLSC) decided that such conduct was clearly a war crime under customary international law, chiefly because of the near-universal ratification of the CRC and national laws criminalising

---

[47] See http://mics.unicef.org/.

[48] UNSC resolution 1261 (30 August 1999); subsequently, the UNSC has adopted similar resolutions, namely 1314 (11 August 2000), 1379 (20 November 2001), 1460 (30 January 2003), 1539 (22 April 2004), 1612 (26 July 2005), 1882 (4 August 2009) and 1998 (12 July 2011).

child recruitment.[49] By 1998 there was no doubt that child recruitment and related practices were indeed universally recognised war crimes. Article 8(2) (b)(xxvi) of the ICC Statute and article 4 of the SLSC Statute are identical in this respect. This new crime of child recruitment is defined as follows:

> Conscripting or enlisting children under the age of 15 years into armed forces or groups using them to participate actively in hostilities.

The SLSC went a step further, arguing that by the time the 2000 CRC Optional Protocol on the Involvement of Children in Armed Conflict was adopted, the discussion of criminalisation of children below the age of fifteen had been settled and the matter had shifted to raising the standard to include all children below the age of eighteen.[50] There is no contention, of course, that the recruitment of persons above the age of fifteen constitutes an international offence under customary law, since a significant number of countries enlist persons who are at least seventeen, although admittedly they are only exceptionally deployed to combat zones.[51]

The term 'recruitment' should be understood as having the same meaning with the terms 'conscription' and 'enlistment'. Voluntary enlistment is as much a crime as forced enlistment.[52] The SLSC Appeals Chamber in the *CDF* case demonstrated how warlords exploited the vulnerabilities of children by organising initiation rituals where the boys were told 'that they would be made powerful for fighting and were given a potion to rub on their bodies as protection ... before going [into] war'.[53] In the majority of cases, especially in conflicts in Africa, children are enlisted forcefully through abductions.[54]

---

[49] *SLSC Prosecutor* v. *Norman* (SLSC) (2004) paras. 34 and 53; see the 2007 Paris principles and guidelines on children associated with armed forces or armed groups (Paris Principles) and Paris commitments to protect children from unlawful recruitment or use by armed forces or armed groups (Paris Commitments), one of whose objectives is to combat the unlawful recruitment or use of children in armed conflicts; see online at www.icrc.org/eng/resources/documents/misc/paris-principles-commitments-300107.htm.

[50] *SLSC Prosecutor* v. *Norman*, para. 34; under art. 3(a) of the 1999 International Labour Organization (ILO) Worst Forms of Child Labour Convention 182, a 'child' is any person below eighteen years and the worst forms of child labour include forced or compulsory recruitment for use in armed conflict; equally, art. 22(2) of the 1999 African Charter on the Rights and Welfare of the Child.

[51] See generally M. Happold, *Child Soldiers in International Law* (Manchester University Press, 2005); see also art. 77(2) Protocol I (1977), which states that: 'In recruiting among those persons who have attained the age of fifteen years but who have not attained the age of eighteen years the parties to the conflict shall endeavour to give priority to those who are oldest.'

[52] *SLSC Prosecutor* v. *Fofana and Kondewa* ('*CDF*') (SLSC) (2007) paras. 191–2; *ICC Prosecutor* v. *Lubanga* (ICC) (2008) para. 47.

[53] *CDF* Appeals judgment (SLSC) (2008) para. 128.

[54] UNSC resolution 2225 (18 June 2015).

The prosecution of children for war crimes and crimes against humanity has presented a 'difficult moral dilemma' for a number of reasons. In the context of the SLSC, although children were feared for their brutality, the UN Secretary-General noted that they had been subjected to a process of psychological and physical abuse and duress that had transformed them from victims into perpetrators.[55] In a balancing act catering on the one hand for the concerns of humanitarian organisations responsible for rehabilitation programmes, who objected to any kind of judicial accountability for children below eighteen years of age, and on the other adhering to popular demand in favour of punishment for juvenile offenders, the Secretary-General decided in favour of prosecuting juveniles above fifteen years of age, but instructed the prosecutor in such cases to 'ensure that the child rehabilitation program is not placed at risk and that, where appropriate, resort should be had to alternative truth and reconciliation mechanisms, to the extent of their availability'.[56] Despite the aforementioned considerations, parties to armed conflicts continue with impunity to enlist children in armed conflicts and in many cases schools are specifically attacked.[57] UNSC resolution 1379 (2001) called upon the UN Secretary-General to list parties that recruit and use children in the annual report on children and armed conflict. The items on the list have subsequently been expanded, now comprising also killing and maiming and sexual violence in conflict[58] and attacks against schools and hospitals.[59] UNSC resolution 1612 established the monitoring and reporting mechanism (MRM) on grave violations against children in armed conflict.[60] The purpose of the MRM is to provide for the systematic gathering of accurate, timely and objective information on grave violations committed against children in armed conflict.

The current trend suggests that given the alarming number of child soldiers forced into armed conflicts, the prosecution of the recruiters should not be the sole focus of the international community. Rather, justice mechanisms should ensure that former child soldiers can be effectively rehabilitated. To this end, article 26 of the ICC Statute limits jurisdiction to persons who were eighteen years of age at the time they committed a crime, thus excluding child soldiers. Moreover, the ICC Prosecutor's Policy on Children, launched in November 2016, was meant, among others, to reinforce her Office's child-sensitive approach in line with the CRC, thus placing the child's welfare

---

[55] Report of the Secretary-General on the establishment of a Special Court for Sierra Leone, UN doc. S/2000/915 (4 October 2000) para. 22. See also, REDRESS, *Victims, Perpetrators or Heroes? Child Soldiers before the International Criminal Court* (2006), online at www.redress.org/downloads/publications/childsoldiers.pdf.

[56] Art. 15(5) SLSC Statute.   [57] UNSC resolution 2143 (7 March 2014).

[58] UNSC resolution 1882 (4 August 2009).   [59] UNSC resolution 1998 (12 July 2011).

[60] UNSC resolution 1612 (26 July 2005).

over and above any prosecutorial imperatives.[61] The ICC's reparations regime may be collective or individual in nature. In its first reparations order in the *Lubanga* case, the ICC rejected the former child soldiers' pleas for individual reparations and went on to instruct its Trust Fund for Victims to set out a viable programme of collective rehabilitation in lieu of compensation.[62]

12.4.4   Non-discrimination

Given the vulnerable status of the child, it is evident that any discrimination against persons who are responsible directly or indirectly for a child's well-being and development constitutes discrimination against the child itself. As a result, a refusal to accommodate nomadic peoples entails a denial of access to education in respect of their children. In equal measure, the exclusion of (undocumented) migrant women from the health care system of the host state, when offered to all other women, constitutes direct discrimination against the migrant child or unborn child. Article 2 CRC is clear in that no ('or status') discrimination is permitted, even if the status of the child violates the law. For example, undocumented or unregistered children possess exactly the same rights (in the same quality and quantity) as registered children in the country at hand ('within their jurisdiction').

For a long time, the particular public policy considerations of states precluded them from achieving the best possible balance between non-discrimination and the child's best interests. For example, the non-mainstream religious adherence of a parent,[63] or his or her sexual preferences, was used as justification for the removal of custody or even communication rights. The ECtHR and the CtRC have dismissed such discriminatory practices because an assessment of the discriminated parent in question may well reveal that he or she is in fact far better suited than the other to exercise custody.[64] In *Salgueiro da Silva Mouta* v. *Portugal*, the ECtHR found a violation of articles 8 and 14 of the European Convention on Human Rights (ECHR) as a result of the Portuguese courts' decision not to award parental responsibility to a father because he had 'come out' as a homosexual and was living in a relationship with another man. Citing *Hoffmann*, the Court stated that: 'a distinction based

---

[61] Available at www.icc-cpi.int/iccdocs/otp/20161115_OTP_ICC_Policy-on-Children_ENG .PDF.

[62] See *ICC Prosecutor* v. *Lubanga*, Order for Reparations (3 March 2015), as corrected by the Additional Order 'Decision Setting the Size of the Reparations Award for which Lubanga is Liable' (21 December 2017).

[63] In *Hoffmann* v. *Austria*, the ECtHR found a violation of art. 8 ECHR (right to family life) taken in conjunction with art. 14 ECHR (non-discrimination) as a result of the Austrian courts' refusal to award custody to a mother because of her religious beliefs (she was a Jehovah's Witness).

[64] *Salgueiro da Silva Mouta* v. *Portugal* (ECtHR) (1999).

on considerations regarding the applicant's sexual orientation [was] a distinction which is not acceptable under the Convention'.[65]

It would appear that the same result applies in relation to decisions motivated by a parent's sex. Article 14 specifically refers to sex as an impermissible ground of discrimination in the enjoyment of Convention rights.[66] The ECtHR has held that the application of national legislation giving custody to the mother to the exclusion of a role for the father (or requiring the mother's consent to the father playing such a role) in cases where the child of the relationship was born out of wedlock violated articles 8 and 14.[67] As long as the father was involved in the care of the child prior to the break-up of the parents' relationship, there existed a family life protected under article 8, which both parents were entitled to enjoy. No automatic presumption could be made that only the mother was the appropriate caregiver.

It is clear, therefore, that there is no such thing as 'well-intended' discrimination because the likelihood of harming the child's best interests becomes subservient to personal prejudices. Such an outcome is unacceptable under the CRC and other regional human rights treaties. When one parent or guardian is chosen over another following an assessment of the child's best interests this does not amount to discrimination against the other parent or guardian. Case Study 12.1 demonstrates how such discrimination operates in practice, most times 'well-intended', but ultimately flawed.

CASE STUDY 12.1
Discrimination against Fathers in Custody Proceedings: The Critical Role of Neuroscience

As a result of the endemic parental discrimination against women in the global South, where their status remains alarmingly low,[1] the phenomenon of parental discrimination against men before the courts of most industrialised nations has gone generally unnoticed. In most cases, rather than making

---

[1] CtRC, Concluding Observations on Egypt, UN doc. CRC/C/EGY/CO/3–4 (15 July 2011) para. 52(f), noting that states must guarantee equality in divorce and child-rearing responsibilities.

---

[65] Ibid., para. 35.
[66] The same has been pronounced (although somewhat implicitly) by the Court of Justice of the European Union (CJEU) in *Maistrellis* v. *Minister of Justice, Transparency and Human Rights* (CJEU) (2015). It was held that a law refusing parental leave to a father, in circumstances where the mother was not working or seeking paid work, amounted to impermissible sex discrimination and unequal treatment.
[67] See *Zaunegger* v. *Germany* (ECtHR) (2009); *Sporer* v. *Austria* (ECtHR) (2011).

individualised evaluations, the courts confer custody to mothers, even if there were strong indications that the father in question was in fact much better-placed to ensure the child's best interests. Some courts offer no justification for this position, others rely on the traditional family model whereby fathers are presumed breadwinners and mothers full-time carers (which is no longer the case with more and more women in full-time employment)[2] and yet other courts posit the view that mothers enjoy a bio-social advantage over fathers. The presumption that fathers are generally uninterested in greater involvement after separation has been proven wrong through empirical studies.[3] The chief victim arising from such institutionalised discrimination is the child's best interests. In such a socio-legal context there is little incentive for some mothers to change their parenting even if it has raised concerns in the particular circumstances, and in many cases the eventuality of such custody judgments gives rise to financial bargains, where fathers are forced to pay for more visitation time. Ultimately, such judgments entrench and reinforce the stereotypical view of women as only being capable of breeding and raising children.[4]

For a very long time the dominant theory in the dawn of child psychology was that infants and young children possess an inborn attachment to their mother. The connection between mother and child is self-evident, but the 'inborn attachment' was also fed by symbolism inherited from religion and implicit kinship conceptions under the guise of biology. As a result, the social (or cultural) dimensions of kinship have largely dominated popular perceptions of the family, as well as the bonds and relationships between its members. The 'biological bond' perceptions, more specifically, were further reinforced by the allocation of family roles, whereby the mother was the sole carer of her children. To a very large degree, in a male-dominated world of past times, fathers must have implicitly viewed this arrangement as rather convenient. A complicating factor upon the advent of modern psychology was the fact that unlike clinical studies with adults, infants and young children could not express themselves in a way that would produce meaningful outcomes and hence empirical studies on children, let alone infants, was limited to observation. Advances in neuroscience played a significant role in this respect because they allowed scientists to track the development of a brain over time.

---

[2] ILO/World Bank statistics show that between 50 and 60 per cent of women in the industrialised world are economically active. See http://data.worldbank.org/indicator/SL.TLF.CACT.FE.ZS.

[3] P. Parkinson, *Family Law and the Indissolubility of Parenthood* (Cambridge University Press, 2011) 70–7.

[4] In fact, arts. 371–9 of the French Civil Code, and in particular art. 373(2)(11), as amended by Law 2010/769 and Law 2013/404, have aimed to dispel the stereotype that being a woman is equated to being a housewife. To this effect, a Law on Effective Equality of the Sexes has been adopted (Law 2014/873).

The aforementioned perceptions-turned bio-psychological theories could not, however, account for the multitude of discrepancies, namely the healthy mental lives of many children not raised by their mothers (for example, orphans) and vice versa. This missing link was provided by Bowlby's *attachment* theory and the subsequent understanding by social and natural scientists of the diffuse role of each parent on the psychological development of children.[5] These theories, which are now dominant, dismissed the suggestion of one parent's superior role over the other, demonstrating instead that infants develop their sense of safety and stability by attaching themselves to the person or persons who respond promptly and consistently to their cries, smiles and other signals in a process called attachment. Attachment is thus not restricted to the child's biological parent(s), but may also develop with a nanny or adopted parents.[6] Whatever the case, psychologists argue that the infant's secure attachment to its parents provides it with better chances of developing into a happy and well-adjusted adolescent and later adult.[7] It has aptly been demonstrated that infants form the same quality of attachment to fathers as they do to mothers.[8]

Without in any way minimising the role of mothers and motherhood, the father's role in a child's development has been proven crucial not only as regards infants but also later in life.[9] More importantly, mothers and fathers perform different but complementary functions in the healthy development of their children. Several empirical studies have demonstrated the beneficial effects of devoted and caring fathers on infants. It has been shown, for example, that primary school children score higher on tests of empathy if they had secure attachments to their fathers during infancy. These children displayed humane behaviour towards their peers and actually took concrete steps to make them feel better.[10] Equally, infants with involved and caring fathers have

---

[5] See the pioneering work of J. Bowlby, *Attachment*, rev. edn (Pimlico, 1997).

[6] Neuroscience has for some time maintained that affection and love are key factors for the development of an infant's brain, particularly the development of social and emotional brain systems. See S. Gerhardt, *Why Love Matters: How Affection Shapes a Baby's Brain* (Routledge, 2004). Once again, J. Bowlby, *A Secure Base* (Routledge, 2005) constitutes the groundwork for subsequent advances in neuroscience.

[7] M. De Wolff and M. van IJzendoorn, 'Sensitivity and Attachment: A Meta-Analysis on Parental Antecedents of Infant Attachment' (1997) 68 *Child Development* 571.

[8] M. E. Lamb and C. Lewis, 'The Development and Significance of Father–Child Relationships in Two-Parent Families', in M. E. Lamb (ed.), *The Role of the Father in Child Development*, 5th edn (John Wiley and Sons, 2010) 94–153.

[9] In a recent study by A. Sarkadi, R. Kristiansson, F. Oberklaid and S. Bremburg, 'Fathers' Involvement and Children's Developmental Outcomes: A Systematic Review of Longitudinal Studies' (2008) 97 *Acta Paediatrica* 153, it was shown that father engagement reduces the frequency of behavioural problems in boys and psychological problems in young women, further enhancing cognitive development, while at the same time decreasing delinquency and economic disadvantage in low-income families.

[10] H. B. Biller, *Fathers and Families: Paternal Factors in Child Development* (Auburn, 1993).

been shown to score higher in terms of thinking and solving skills,[11] as well as in forming loving relationships with their other brothers and sisters.[12]

The objective of this brief foray into the field of developmental psychology and neuroscience was certainly not aimed at discrediting mothers or suggesting that fathers make better parents. In fact, empirical studies demonstrate the existence of many 'bad' fathers who do not assume positive roles. Rather, the purpose of this case study is to emphasise the need for family courts to dismiss outdated stereotypes about the biological or other superiority of one parent over the other given the undoubted scientific developments. On the whole, the courts must accept in their determination of custody that what is of primary importance is the quality of parenting and the attachments formed by the child to one or the other parent. It is only in this manner that they can form a better view of the child's best interests.

[11] J. K. Nugent, 'Cultural and Psychological Influences on the Father's Role in Infant Development' (1991) 53 *Journal of Marriage and the Family* 475.
[12] B. Volling and J. Belsky, 'The Contribution of Mother–Child and Father–Child Relationships to the Quality of Sibling Interaction: A Longitudinal Study' (1992) 63 *Child Development* 1209.

INTERVIEW 12.1
The State of Children's Rights
(Benyam Dawit Mezmur)

Professor Benyam Dawit Mezmur is a member and former Chairperson (2015–2017) of the CtRC and of the African Committee of Experts on the Rights and Welfare of the Child. In this interview, he takes stock of developments in the field of children's rights, discusses challenges at the international and regional, particularly African level, assesses the impact of litigation, and looks ahead at future prospects. He also reflects on how his work on the subject has influenced his views on international human rights law.

What do you consider to be the main challenges for the protection of the rights of children?

The Convention is the most widely ratified human rights instrument with 196 states parties. The popularity of the CRC, as manifested in its near universal ratification, suggests a high level of normative consensus among the various nations on the idea and content of children's rights as human rights. But the move from near universal ratification to near universal implementation remains an unfinished business.

The different types of challenges that state parties face in the implementation of the Convention are often dependent on a number of factors. These factors include human and financial resources; social stability; how early the Convention has been ratified by a state and internalised; the presence and effectiveness of comprehensive laws on children's rights; the extent to which harmful practices are embedded in society; geographical location, including topography (for instance, sparsely populated state parties, small island states, effects of exposure to climate change, etc); and at times, the type of government arrangement, such as federal or unitary, especially in relation to coordination.

Too many states continue to keep a significant number of children in a 'yes but no' scenario – let me explain and anchor it with examples. A commendably large number of ratifications, yes, but also reservations, some of which go against the object and purpose of the Convention; we mostly seem to agree that article 2 obliges 'States Parties ... ensure the rights ... in the ... Convention to each child within their jurisdiction without discrimination of any kind', but many continue to treat, for instance, girls, children with disabilities, children born outside of wedlock, migrant, asylum-seeking and refugee children, stateless children, children deprived of their family environments, children from indigenous/minority groups, less favourably; taking the views of the child into consideration is an obligation, but we only want to do this in a few exceptions such as custody and adoption; we reckon that birth registration is critical and a right from the start, but relatively expensive and cumbersome registration processes could be okay; definitely all state parties are bound by article 6 on the right to life, survival and development, but, in the year 2016, few still continue to apply the death penalty for offences committed by persons while below the age of eighteen; we mostly agree that child marriage is negative, but more than 150 countries allow exceptions, some of which are too broad; laws and practices that are more akin to 'well said, than well done', rules with unnecessary exceptions, and policies and initiatives that are focused more on quantity than quality (while often short in human and financial resources) seem to permeate and undermine the realization of children's rights.

In part because many states are still struggling to address the already existing and settled issues, the response of many states on emerging issues is often lacking. These emerging issues are sometimes created as a result of the advancement of technology, including the internet. Others emanate because of world events, such as climate change, health hazards (such as Ebola and Zika), instability and armed conflict (such as the so-called Islamic State and its effect on children's rights), the migration crisis, privatisation and increased globalisation, as well as economic crisis which sometimes leads to austerity measures.

The worst dimension of all of this is the price tag to be paid – often a violated childhood!! The best way forward to address these and other similar shortcomings is to use the Convention and its optional protocols as a standard against which laws, policies and other measures are assessed against. In summary, the answer to the vital question that UNICEF posed in a publication in 2014 in the context of the 25th anniversary of the Convention 'does a child born today have better prospects in life than one who was born in 1989?' is 'yes, but not every child'! The same conclusion remains valid as the world prepares to celebrate the 30th anniversary of the Convention.

Which issues pertaining to the rights of children are particularly pronounced, or even unique, in the African context?

Multiple factors are at play here. However, if I were asked to name only five thematic issues that are particularly pronounced, I would probably single out discrimination, child poverty, harmful practices, negative effects of climate change, and conflict. In respect to the latter, for example, the six grave breaches – recruitment and use of children; killing and maiming of children; sexual violence against children; attacks on schools and hospitals; abduction of children; and denial of humanitarian access – the last as a weapon of war is a continuing challenge. In this respect violations by non-state armed groups, including recruitment and use, continue to be a serious problem.

The African continent's child demography is unique, as there is no other continent in the world where children are more central to a continent's future than in Africa. After all, children reportedly account for 47 per cent of its population. A 2017 report by UNICEF – *Generation 2030: Africa 2.0* – has underscored that the population projection of the continent by 2050 suggests that the continent will account for 42 per cent of all global births and almost 40 per cent of all children under eighteen. As a result, with a view to achieving the best out of the demographic dividend, and creating an Africa fit for children, investing in education and health systems remains the leitmotif.

Do you expect an increase in the litigation of the rights of children at the national, regional and international level? If so, what impact do you expect it to have?

In some ways I think an increase at all three levels seems inevitable. There are a number of reasons why I believe so.

Increasingly, globally, access to justice for children is on the rise. More and more national human rights institutions, legal aid clinics, civil society organisations, and more importantly states etc. are facilitating access to justice for children. Also, through human rights education, improved access to information, and other positive developments, children are being empowered more to know their rights, and to challenge their violations.

At the international level, with the coming into force of the Optional Protocol on a communications procedure already five years ago in April 2014, the CRC Committee is having more sense of the various legal issues that are raised in the context of domestic law in state parties to the Optional Protocol. The nature of the case law is slowly but surely diversifying from migration and age determination issues to custody, care, family reunification, alternative custody arrangements including *Kafalah*, abduction, right to vote in state elections, children's rights in the context of the war on terror etc. The same can be said of the jurisprudence coming from the African Committee of Experts on the Rights and Welfare of the Child jurisprudence on issues such as the right to acquire a nationality, using children in the form of begging, contemporary forms of slavery, child soldiers.

I believe that the impact of litigation will probably be mixed, and I hope (I even dare to say 'expect') that it will mostly be positive for children's rights. In some contexts, where there is political and social will to follow through on litigation, outcomes that are positive for pushing the boundaries for children's rights, and the impact will help to strengthen legislative and other appropriate measures, including institutional measures. The possibility to see some positive understanding and cross-fertilisation of jurisprudence, as well as bridging of gaps with other areas of human rights such as disability rights, women's rights, etc. through the litigation of the rights of the child at the national, regional and international level is possible. Whether some of the main role players on children's rights, such as UNICEF and OHCHR, will deepen their roles on child rights litigation will be an interesting development to monitor. However, one cannot be oblivious to the fact that there is the possibility, on some occasions, where setbacks or backlashes will be experienced.

What do you see as gaps in the international law and practice on the rights of children? How should/could these gaps be best addressed?

The added currency that international law in general, and international human rights law in particular, brings to the creation of a world that is fit for everyone is under a lot of pressure. Multilateralism too is being undermined. As a result, the current environment in some quarters that emphasise nationalism, unilateralism, etc. at the cost of the human rights regime should be a cause for concern to all of us.

While the obligations states have under the relevant international and regional child rights instruments is to undertake 'legislative, administrative, and other measures', thirty years into the life of the Convention, significant progress has been made on the legislative part, but not on the 'administrative and other measures' aspect. These include on budgeting, coordination, the role of national human rights institutions, awareness raising, training, monitoring and evaluation of programmes and initiatives.

In 2017, Philip Alston, Special Rapporteur on extreme poverty and human rights penned some thoughts on how 'human rights is under siege', and reading his piece I could not help but notice that his observations are very pertinent to what is happening to child rights in many quarters – the child rights movement too needs to address the populist threat to democracy; the role of civil society (reprisals and the notion of 'you only open your mouth when you go to the dentist'); inequality and exclusion (NGOs working only for minorities, asylum seekers, 'terrorists' and not for the majority); the undermining of international law (reservations, war on terror, trade) and the fragility of international institutions (including OHCHR, UNICEF, ICC, GA, Security Council, etc.). I too believe that the 'honeymoon' phase of children's rights has run its sell-by date, and crucially the movement needs introspection and openness in order to adapt. Making children themselves a central part of this introspection and openness is critical.

How has working on the rights of children shaped your view of the nature and role of the law, particularly international human rights law?

It has shaped my views, and in limited ways even my personality and approach to many things. The capacity of the law for social engineering is absolutely critical. After all the international and regional child rights instruments are legal instruments. But I would also not be original to state that law is often not sufficient. In some parts of the world, the role of formal law is limited because of the existence of deeply embedded non-formal laws and practices, and engaging with these informal structures could be the difference between success and failure. Also, those of us (especially lawyers) working on child rights have to try to get out of our comfort zones and engage better with those working on development, humanitarian action, etc.

When I was chair of the two treaty bodies, I used to tell states that 'as a Committee, we appreciate the distinction between an "active Committee" and "an activist Committee", as well as recognize that it is not by default but by design that the Convention mentions "states" more than 120 times'. As much as we do not have a better organising framework than the human rights discourse for creating a world fit for children, a continued engagement with states should be seen as a 'choiceless choice'.

12.5   CHILDREN'S RIGHT TO BE FREE FROM POVERTY

Child poverty is a deep-rooted problem on an enormous scale. According to UNICEF '[i]n low- and middle-income countries 39 percent of children still struggle to survive in "extreme poverty" – defined internationally as living on less than $1.25 a day [now $1.90] – including some 569 million children aged 18 and under'.[68] However, child poverty is not confined to these countries. In a study of child well-being in thirty-five 'industrialised countries', UNICEF 'found that approximately 30 million children – one child out of every eight across the [Organisation for Economic Cooperation and Development] OECD – are growing up poor'.[69] Poverty is both an objective condition and a subjective experience of what it means being poor. Importantly, it is 'not solely an economic issue, but rather a multidimensional phenomenon that encompasses a lack of both income and the basic capabilities to live in dignity'.[70] What the various definitions of poverty adopted by human rights treaty bodies and others have in common is a level of deprivation that fails to meet basic needs and access to essential services. Drawing on Sen's theory,[71] some definitions, such as that used by the Committee on Economic, Social and Cultural Rights (CESCR), also emphasise the 'sustained or chronic deprivation of the resources, *capabilities*, *choices*, security and power necessary for the enjoyment of an adequate standard of living and other ... rights'.[72] Extreme poverty is understood as 'the combination of income poverty, human development poverty and social exclusion',[73] the debilitating effects of which have become a matter of priority concern for the UN Human Rights Council (HRC).[74]

Poverty affects a series of rights. For children, poverty frequently equates to a negative mirror image of the rights they should enjoy. Poverty makes it more difficult for a child to survive physically,[75] enjoy physical and mental well-being,[76] have adequate means,[77] grow up in a nurturing environment in which he or she can develop his or her personality,[78] acquire knowledge

---

[68] UNICEF *Issue Brief, Child Poverty in the 2015 Agenda* (June 2015) 5.

[69] Ibid. Statistical tables, 'with particular reference to children's well-being' can be found in UNICEF, *The State of the World's Children 2014 In Numbers, Every Child Counts: Revealing Disparities, Advancing Children's Rights* (2014).

[70] Office of the High Commissioner for Human Rights (OHCHR), *Guiding Principles on Extreme Poverty and Human Rights*, undated, 2, online at www.ohchr.org/Documents/ Publications/OHCHR_ExtremePovertyandHumanRights_EN.pdf. The Guiding Principles were adopted in HRC resolution 21/11, A/HRC/21/L.20 (21 September 2012).

[71] A. Sen, *Development as Freedom* (Oxford University Press, 1999).

[72] CESCR, Substantive Issues Arising in the Implementation of the International Covenant on Economic, Social and Cultural Rights: Poverty and the International Covenant on Economic, Social and Cultural Rights, Statement adopted by the Committee on Economic, Social and Cultural Rights on 4 May 2001, UN doc. E/C.12/2001/10 (10 May 2001) para. 8. (emphasis added).

[73] Report of the independent expert on the question of human rights and extreme poverty, Arjun Sengupta, UN doc. E/CN.4/2005/49 (11 February 2005) para. 22.

[74] See in particular the UN Guiding Principles on Extreme Poverty and Human Rights (2012), and the work of the Special Rapporteur on extreme poverty and human rights.

[75] Art. 6 CRC.   [76] Art. 24 CRC.

[77] Arts. 26 (social security) and 27 (standard of living) CRC.   [78] Preamble to the CRC.

and skills (education),[79] enjoy 'rest, leisure, play, recreational activities, cultural life and the arts',[80] and 'achieve their full potential or participate as full and equal members of society'.[81] Instead, poverty frequently hampers children's education, and exposes them to 'exploitation, neglect and abuse',[82] including child labour, crime, trafficking, and domestic or institutional ill-treatment.[83] Several studies demonstrate that poverty, both in terms of income and other types of deprivations, affects children particularly badly, often leading to a downward spiral of missed opportunities, if not misery.[84] Poverty frequently intersects with, and is more pronounced due to, class (for example, working-class children); caste (for example, Dalits); race (for example, poverty among African-Americans in the United States (US)); ethnicity and group status (for example, Roma children, indigenous peoples);[85] nationality and status (for example, migrant children, particularly if unaccompanied) and gender (for example, child marriage).

It is clear that poverty always represents a challenge for, if not a failure of society, including the international community as a whole to protect those who are considered to be most vulnerable.[86] This failure often becomes systemic where poverty is passed on from one generation to another, beginning from the very moment a woman from a poor background is pregnant, which may already negatively affect the life chances of her embryo and future child. The impact of poverty on the core of human dignity and well-being has prompted arguments stipulating a right to be free from poverty.[87]

---

[79] Arts. 28 and 29 CRC.   [80] Art. 31 CRC.

[81] 'Children living in poverty experience deprivation of the material, spiritual, and emotional resources needed to survive, develop and thrive, leaving them unable to enjoy their rights, achieve their full potential or participate as full and equal members of society.' UNICEF, *The State of the World's Children: Childhood under Threat* (2005) 18.

[82] See principle 34 of the UN Guiding Principles on Extreme Poverty and Human Rights.

[83] See on the obligations of states parties to protect children from various forms of exploitation, neglect and abuse, particularly arts. 3(2), 19, 32–6 CRC.

[84] See UNICEF, *Global Study on Child Poverty and Disparities*, undated, online at https://sites.google.com/site/whatithechildpovertystudy/.

[85] Report of the Special Rapporteur on extreme poverty and human rights Magdalena Sepúlveda Carmona: Mission to Mongolia (3–7 December 2012) UN doc. A/HRC/23/36/Add.2 (30 May 2013), and Mission to Paraguay (11–16 December 2011) UN doc. A/HRC/20/25/Add.2 (3 April 2012).

[86] See in particular, preamble of the CRC '[r]ecognizing the importance of international cooperation for improving the living conditions of children in every country, in particular in the developing countries' and art. 2(1) International Covenant on Economic, Social and Cultural Rights (ICESCR); and further T. Pogge, *World Poverty and Human Rights: Cosmopolitan Responsibilities and Reform*, 2nd edn (Polity Press, 2008); M. E. Salomon, *Global Responsibility for Human Rights: World Poverty and the Development of International Law* (Oxford University Press, 2008).

[87] See further C. Chinkin, 'The United Nations Decade for the Elimination of Poverty: What Role for International Law?' (2001) 54 *Current Legal Problems* 553; T. Pogge (ed.), *Freedom From Poverty as a Human Right: Who Owes What to the Very Poor?* (Oxford University Press, 2007).

Such a right has not been explicitly recognised. However, it is clear that the rights guaranteed in several treaties, including the CRC, such as the right to an adequate standard of living, impose an obligation on states to combat poverty, including the underlying discrimination fostering and perpetuating poverty and concomitant rights violations. Equally, several international bodies, especially the UN, have made the eradication of poverty, particularly child poverty, a policy priority.[88]

Effectively combating child poverty requires states to take a series of measures. Ideally, these include a coherent policy, adopting legislation that tackles the causes of child poverty and setting up bodies tasked with protecting children's rights. However, challenges abound. Policies are often designed without adequate participation, implemented without the required level of data and impact assessment, and characterised by fragmentation and lack of coordination.[89] What has become apparent is the need for a concerted effort to address root causes, including structural factors, such as urban–rural divides,[90] and issues such as the lack of registration negatively impacting on access to social security and services,[91] in order for a child poverty reduction strategy to work. While such policies can be, and are often, framed as development-oriented, it is important that they are rights-based so that the best interests of children and the policy impact on their rights is being factored in and assessed throughout. One tool towards this end is budgeting for child rights, also in implementing states' duty progressively to realise the economic, social and cultural rights of children.

A South African study identified three key programmes that the (then) government had pursued 'to reduc[e] child poverty and deliver socio-economic rights',[92] namely a child support grant programme, delivery of free health care to pregnant women and children nought to six, and a primary school nutrition programme. The study developed a sophisticated methodology to inform and monitor budgeting for children's rights to implement the right to education and the right to social security. This included, in particular, allocation of resources and budget priorities, identifying the need to spend more and better on a child's rights, the availability of resources for increased

---

[88] See also OHCHR, Principles and Guidelines for a Human Rights Approach to Poverty Reduction Strategies (2006) and target 1.2 of the Sustainable Development Goals.

[89] See e.g., Report of the Special Rapporteur: Mission to Mongolia, above note 85, para. 18.

[90] Ibid., para. 33.

[91] This issue has been raised by the Special Rapporteur on extreme poverty and human rights following country missions to Timor Leste, Zambia and Bangladesh; see online at www.ohchr.org/EN/Issues/Poverty/Pages/CountryVisits.aspx. See on the right to be registered, particularly art. 7 CRC.

[92] Institute for Democracy in South Africa, *Budgeting for Child Socio-economic Rights, Government's Obligations and the Child's Right to Social Security and Education*, The Popular Version (2002) 4.

spending on a child's rights, and prioritising basic services on the poorest of the poor. It also comprised additional steps such as reducing inequality, including between regions, increasing efficiency and removing obstacles. The study provides a good example of how a contextual analysis of a particular right in light of a state's obligation can help in informing targeted and more effective policy-making and implementation. As a result of advocacy work, the South African government increased the budget allocation for children.[93] In several other countries, particularly in Asia and Africa, budget analysis has also been used to improve resource allocation for children's rights, albeit often focusing on particular rights such as education rather than the entire gamut of rights and the eradication of poverty.[94]

Effective access to justice is a right of children, and an important means of ensuring the protection and realisation of their rights, particularly where policies of implementation are absent or inadequate.[95] However, in practice, the problems experienced by people living in poverty in accessing justice are often particularly pronounced for children due to a combination of factors, including absence of registration, lack of standing and marginalisation.[96] None the less, national courts, such as in India and South Africa, have set important precedents that recognise children's rights and corresponding state duties whose implementation is critical in reducing poverty, such as the right to food, housing and health.[97] Regional and international human rights courts and treaty bodies have also made important rulings in relation to a child's right to be free from poverty in the context of adjudicating specific rights, such as the right to life/freedom from ill-treatment (Guatemala);[98] protection against ill-treatment (forced begging) (Senegal);[99] education (Czech Republic);[100] nationality (Kenya);[101] child marriage (Mali);[102] and the rights

---

[93] Save the Children and Haq: Centre for Children's Rights, *Budget for Children's Analysis: A Beginner's Guide* (2010), online at http://resourcecentre.savethechildren.se/sites/default/files/documents/3134.pdf.

[94] Ibid.

[95] See in particular, Report of the United Nations High Commissioner for Human Rights, Access to Justice for Children, UN doc. A/HRC/25/35 (16 December 2013).

[96] See reports by the Special Rapporteur, above note 85, and, more generally, Report of the Special Rapporteur on extreme poverty and human rights, UN doc. A/67/278 (9 August 2012).

[97] See e.g., *People's Union for Civil Liberties* v. *Union of India and Others* (India) (2003) and *Government of the Republic of South Africa and Others* v. *Grootboom and Others* (South Africa) (2000).

[98] *'Street Children' (Villagrán Morales et al.)* v. *Guatemala* (IACtHR) (1999).

[99] *The Centre for Human Rights (University of Pretoria) and La Rencontre Africaine Pour la Défense des Droits de l'Homme (Senegal)* v. *Government of Senegal* (ACtERWC) (2014).

[100] *D. H. and Others* v. *Czech Republic* (ECtHR) (2008).

[101] *IHRDA and Open Society Justice Initiative (OSJI) (on behalf of children of Nubian descent in Kenya)* v. *Kenya* (ACtERWC) (2011).

[102] *APDF & IHRDA* v. *Mali* (ACtHPR) (2018).

of migrant children (IACtHR advisory opinion).[103] The coming into force of the Third Optional Protocol on a Communications Procedure in April 2014 provided for the first time for a child rights-specific international individual complaints procedure. It allowed children who live in poverty to bring cases claiming a violation of their rights under the CRC, where the state concerned had become a party to the Optional Protocol.

CASE STUDY 12.2
Anti-child Poverty Legislation in the United Kingdom and Austerity Measures

Child poverty has been a long-standing problem in the United Kingdom (UK).[1] Contemporary forms of poverty include low income and access to basic services and facilities, resulting in a series of deprivations. These include not eating three meals a day, exclusion, such as not being able to attend school trips, and adverse health consequences, such as obesity due to poor diet and lack of exercise. It is often questioned whether relative low income, defined as less than 50 per cent of the national median disposable household income, constitutes poverty, especially when compared to 'real' poverty.[2] However, this approach, which essentially takes absolute poverty as a yardstick, has been largely rejected because it fails to appreciate the nature and impact of contemporary forms of poverty.[3] A recent study by the UNICEF Innocenti Research Institute on child poverty argues for a combination of relative low income and measuring deprivation directly, including its depth and duration.[4]

The UK ratified the CRC in 1991. The CtRC regularly raised concerns about child poverty in the UK in its respective concluding observations in 1995, 2002 and 2008.[5] However, in 2008, it also noted the UK policy commitment

---

[1] See e.g., resources available from website of the civil society organisation, Child Poverty Action Group, www.cpag.org.uk/.

[2] See discussion in UNICEF Innocenti Research Centre, *Measuring Child Poverty: New League Tables of Child Poverty in the World's Rich Countries*, Innocenti Report Card 10 (2012) 8 and 23.

[3] Ibid., 10ff.   [4] Ibid., 15–19.

[5] CRC, Concluding Observations: United Kingdom of Great Britain and Northern Ireland, UN doc. CRC/C/15/Add.34 (15 February 1995) para. 15; UN doc. CRC/C/15/Add.188 (9 October 2002) paras. 10 and 45; UN doc. CRC/C/GBR/CO/4 (20 October 2008) paras. 18, 44 and particularly 64.

---

[103] *Rights and Guarantees of Children in the Context of Migration and/or in Need of International Protection* (IACtHR) (2014).

made in 1999 to eradicate child poverty by 2020, which resulted in significant improvements (a one-third reduction in child poverty).[6] The UK's Child Poverty Act 2010 put this policy on a statutory footing, setting out targets to be met by the government to this end, relating to various forms of low income (less than 60–70 per cent of 'median equivalised net household income for the financial year'[7]) and persistent poverty. Under the Act, the Secretary of State is to develop a strategy, taking into consideration:

(a) the promotion and facilitation of the employment of parents or of the development of the skills of parents,

(b) the provision of financial support for children and parents,

(c) the provision of information, advice and assistance to parents and the promotion of parenting skills,

(d) physical and mental health, education, childcare and social services, and

(e) housing, the built or natural environment and the promotion of social inclusion.[8]

Further, when considering measures to be taken, the Secretary of State:

(a) must consider which groups of children in the United Kingdom appear to be disproportionately affected by socio-economic disadvantage, and

(b) must consider the likely impact of each measure on children within each of those groups.[9]

The strategy is to be developed in consultation with local authorities, regional ministries, children and organisations representing children, parents and organisations representing parents, as well as other persons.[10]

The Child Poverty Act is remarkable, transposing what has traditionally been considered a matter of policy-making into legislation that is subject to judicial review.[11] It makes a concerted effort to commit government at all levels to policy implementation, including by providing indicators, setting up bodies such as the Child Poverty Commission, and providing for systems of monitoring. However, the Act has some highly problematic features, particularly its section 16,[12] which mandates economic conditions to be taken into consideration and thereby calls into question the state's duty to use the maximum available resources. This may, in the absence of committing the government to take

---

[6] See UN doc. CRC/C/GBR/CO/4, above note 5, para. 64.

[7] S. 3(2) of the Child Poverty Act of 2010.   [8] S. 9(5) ibid.   [9] S. 9(6) ibid.

[10] S. 10(4) ibid.

[11] E. Palmer, 'The Child Poverty Act 2010: Holding Government to Account For Promises in a Recessionary Climate' (2010) 3 *European Human Rights Law Review* 303, at 313–14.

[12] Matters that must be taken into account when developing a strategy are, pursuant to art. 16(2)(a): 'economic circumstances and in particular the likely impact of any measure on the economy; (b) fiscal circumstances and in particular the likely impact of any measure on taxation, public spending and public borrowing'.

particular measures, open the door to regressive measures that compromise the rights of children, which are framed in terms of needs rather than human rights. In turn, this is prone to undermine the scope for legal protection given the limits of judicial review in questions of resource allocation.[13]

In its May 2014 state report to the CtRC, the UK stressed its commitment to eradicate poverty.[14] It referred to its 2014–2017 strategy, built on:

- raising the incomes of poor children's families by helping them get into work and by making work pay;
- supporting the living standards of low-income families; and
- raising the educational outcomes of poor children.[15]

However, doubts have been raised concerning the efficacy of this approach as children have suffered disproportionately from austerity measures taken by the UK government in response to the economic crisis. The Social Mobility and Child Poverty Commission noted in 2014 that while relative child poverty was at its lowest level, 'absolute child poverty increased by 300,000 between 2010–11 and 2012–13'.[16] It further expressed its concern that:

The impact of welfare cuts and entrenched low pay will bite between now and 2020. Poverty is set to rise, not fall. We share the view of those experts who predict that 2020 will mark not the eradication of child poverty but the end of the first decade in recent history in which absolute child poverty increased. A decade of rising absolute poverty is unprecedented since records began in the 1960s. The clear risk is that the year 2020 will mark not just a failure to meet the government's legal obligation to have ended child poverty but could mark a permanent decoupling of earnings growth and economic growth at the bottom end of the labour market.[17]

These warnings were borne out by the serious concerns expressed by the CtRC in 2016 that, '[t]he rate of child poverty remains high, disproportionately affects children with disabilities, children living in a family or household with a person or persons with a disability, households with many children and children belonging to ethnic minority groups, and affects children in Wales and Northern Ireland the most'.[18] The UK government, instead of taking measures to address the problem of rising child poverty, had introduced legislation, namely '[t]he Welfare Reform and Work Act (2016), which amends the Child

---

[13] See further Palmer, above note 11, at 45, 314–15.

[14] The Fifth Periodic Report to the UN Committee on the Rights of the Child, United Kingdom (May 2014) 38, para. 34.

[15] Ibid.

[16] Social Mobility and Child Poverty Commission, *State of the Nation 2014: Social Mobility and Child Poverty in Great Britain* (October 2014) Foreword and Executive Summary.

[17] Ibid., Foreword.

[18] Concluding observations on the fifth periodic report of the United Kingdom of Great Britain and Northern Ireland, UN doc. CRC/C/GBR/CO/5 (12 July 2016) para. 70(a).

Poverty Act (2010), [which] repealed the statutory target on the eradication of child poverty by 2020 and the statutory obligation[s] ... to produce child poverty strategies'.[19] Professor Philip Alston, the UN Special Rapporteur on extreme poverty and human rights, was scathing in his assessment at the end of his visit to the United Kingdom in late 2018: 'For almost one in every two children to be poor in twenty-first-century Britain is not just a disgrace, but a social calamity and an economic disaster, all rolled into one.'[20]

In times of austerity policies and economic uncertainty coupled with growing unequality, child poverty reduction is at risk of becoming the subject of narrow debates about the definition of poverty and the merits and results of specific measures. Unsurprisingly, the rights of children and the UK's international law obligations in this regard do not figure prominently in such debates. It is therefore often journalists and advocacy groups that draw attention to the realities of child poverty and the experiences of children themselves.[21] Ultimately, as the relative success of measures taken in the first decade of the 2000s demonstrates, in order to effectively reduce child poverty, a concerted policy effort is needed to tackle systemic disadvantages at multiple levels.[22]

[19] Ibid., para. 70(b).

[20] Statement on Visit to the United Kingdom, by Professor Philip Alston, United Nations Special Rapporteur on extreme poverty and human rights (London, 16 November 2018) 1.

[21] See G. Main and J. Bradshaw, *Child Poverty and Social Exclusion, Final Report of 2012 PSE Study* (November 2014) online at www.poverty.ac.uk/sites/default/files/attachments/PSE-Child-poverty-and-exclusion-final-report-2014.pdf.

[22] See contributions in L. Judge (ed.), *Ending Child Poverty by 2020: Progress Made and Lessons Learned* (Child Poverty Action Group, 2012).

QUESTIONS

1. What are the key grounds and justifications for the existence of additional or specialised rights and obligations for the protection of children?

2. Parents have a right to define and shape several of the characteristics of a child under the CRC. To what extent is the child entitled to demand that its own views take precedence over the wishes of its parents?

3. The immune systems of infants and the newborn are susceptible to airborne diseases as a result of climate change or air pollution. If this is true, then what steps should member states to the CRC take to ensure children's survival and their right to life? Is your response affected by the fact that while a country is a party to the CRC it, and other countries, are not parties to the major environmental protection treaties?

4. State A does not allow the members of poor indigenous communities to migrate to the cities in search of a better life. Educational provision in the community's rural environment is exceptionally poor, but is offered by the state. City dwellers in state A are, however, allowed to migrate from one city to another. The state argues that although such policy constitutes discrimination against adult indigenous persons it is not discriminatory against children (and particularly as regards their right to education) because education is offered to both city children and rural (indigenous) children. Discuss.

FURTHER READING

Archard, D., *Children: Rights and Childhood* (Routledge, 2014).

Bhabha, J., *Child Migration and Human Rights in a Global Age* (Princeton University Press, 2014).

Brems, E., E. Desmet and W. Vandehole (eds.), *Children's Rights Law in the Global Human Rights Landscape: Isolation, Inspiration, Integration?* (Routledge, 2017).

Buck, T., *International Child Law* (Routledge, 2014).

Butler, C. W., *Child Rights: The Movement, International Law and Opposition* (Purdue University Press, 2012).

Fortin, J., *Children's Rights and the Developing Law* (Cambridge University Press, 2009).

Freeman, M., *The Future of Children's Rights* (Brill, 2014).

Freeman, M. (ed.), *Children's Rights: New Issues, New Themes, New Perspectives* (Brill Nijhoff, 2018).

Gal, T., and B. Duramy, *International Perspectives and Empirical Findings on Child Participation: From Social Exclusion to Child-Inclusive Policies* (Oxford University Press, 2015).

Grover, S. C., *Children Defending their Human Rights under the CRC Communications Procedure* (Springer, 2014).

Hanson, K., and O. Nieuwenhuys (eds.), *Reconceptualising Children's Rights in International Development* (Cambridge University Press, 2012).

Liefaard, T., and J. E. Doek (eds.), *Litigating the Rights of the Child: The UN Convention on the Rights of the Child in Domestic and International Jurisprudence* (Springer, 2014).

Liefaard, T., and J. Sloth-Nielsen (eds.), *The United Nations Convention on the Rights of the Child: Taking Stock after 25 Years and Looking Ahead* (Brill Nijhoff, 2017).

Mahmoudi, S., P. Leviner, A. Kaldal and K. Lainpelto, *Child-Friendly Justice: A Quarter of a Century of the UN Convention on the Rights of the Child* (Brill, 2015).

Nolan, A., *Children's Socio-economic Rights, Democracy and the Courts* (Hart, 2011).

Parkes, A., *Children and International Human Rights Law: The Right of the Child to be Heard* (Routledge, 2015).

Stoecklin, D., and J-M. Bonvin (eds.), *Children's Rights and the Capability Approach: Challenges and Prospects* (Springer, 2014).

Welch, S., and P. Jones, *Rethinking Children's Rights* (Bloomsbury, 2010).

Websites

Child Soldiers International: www.child-soldiers.org/

CtRC: www.ohchr.org/EN/HRBodies/CRC/Pages/CRCIndex.aspx

European Union rights of the child: http://ec.europa.eu/justice/fundamental-rights/rights-child/index_en.htm

UNICEF: www.unicef.org/

13 The Recognition and Protection of the Human Rights of Vulnerable Groups and Persons

CONTENTS

13.1   INTRODUCTION

The liberal, universal notion of human rights is centred on the abstract person, i.e. 'everyone'. This approach, evident in the Universal Declaration of Human Rights (UDHR), has been increasingly complemented by a focus on particular features or identities of persons and groups, as a result of campaigns and changed mindsets. That focus emerged largely as a result of the heightened awareness of the exposure to discrimination and various forms of violence that these persons or groups face, and the factors that hinder the exercise of individual or collective rights. It has resulted in a more contextual understanding of human rights violations, and the use of an array of terms, particularly discrimination, vulnerability and sometimes marginalisation when referring to the situation of individuals and groups. The greater contextualisation has informed legal and institutional developments, and enabled various actors to tailor states' obligations, particularly in respect of preventive, protective and justice measures relating to (members of) the group concerned. However, the approach taken has been far from coherent in its application in various contexts. This includes the very meaning of the concept of vulnerability, and the legal consequences flowing from it. The approach also faces criticism for producing discourses based on victimisation and attendant interventions. It is viewed as liable to perpetuating stereotypes and failing to bring about the greater transformation needed to effectively tackle the structural causes and conceptions that produce vulnerability in the first place. Further, a focus on group-based vulnerability is prone to reinforce perceptions of a 'normal' person versus categories of vulnerable persons, rather than focusing on vulnerability as a common human condition.[1]

This chapter explores the concept of vulnerability, its recognition and use in international human rights law, and the broader debate on the (potential) advantages and downsides of focusing on vulnerable identities to strengthen protection. Following this overview, it examines core categories of vulnerability that are either already reflected in international human rights law, largely in the form of anti-discrimination instruments, or constitute a priority area in recent debates and legal developments. This includes 'race', gender and sexual orientation, persons with disabilities, persons living in extreme poverty, age (the rights of children are addressed in a discreet chapter), as well as refugees, migrants and internally displaced persons (IDPs). For each of these categories, the chapter examines core notions, highlights specific concerns, charts relevant legal developments and analyses both advances made and remaining challenges.

13.2   VULNERABILITY AND INTERNATIONAL HUMAN RIGHTS LAW

Discrimination is a well-developed legal concept recognised in the International Bill of Human Rights and numerous other instruments.[2] It constitutes a violation of a state's international human rights obligations and frequently acts as gateway to multiple other violations, with the international crime of genocide as its most extreme manifestation. Discrimination might therefore be taken to indicate that a person or certain groups are at a heightened risk of other violations. However, the 'relationship between discrimination and vulnerability' is not clearly conceptualised in the practice of human rights treaty bodies.[3] Vulnerability may therefore stem from, but is not necessarily identical to, discrimination. As a concept, vulnerability is used differently in various disciplines. It denotes the possibility of being

---

[1] See on this notion of vulnerability in particular, Bryan S. Turner, *Vulnerability and Human Rights* (Pennsylvania State University Press, 2006) 25–44.

[2] See Chapter 2.3.3.

[3] A. R. Chapman and B. Carbonetti, 'Human Rights Protections for Vulnerable and Disadvantaged Groups: The Contributions of the UN Committee on Economic, Social and Cultural Rights' (2011) 33 *Human Rights Quarterly* 682, at 693.

exposed to harm and the impact any such harm will have on those affected; policies, such as in the field of disaster management, are aimed at reducing the attendant risks.[4] In the human rights context, the use and interpretation of the notion of vulnerability is far from uniform. Human rights law is based on generic human vulnerability in the sense that it seeks to protect core human values such as life, physical and mental integrity, freedom, equality and dignity. In principle, every person is vulnerable. However, a series of factors, not least the level of resources a person commands, makes vulnerability particular in terms of affecting the likelihood that someone will suffer a violation.[5] Human rights bodies have either acknowledged generic vulnerability while stressing the particular vulnerability of certain groups,[6] or adopted a position whereby certain groups are considered vulnerable by definition or on account of a set of factors.[7] Vulnerability is situation-specific, and has been usefully described as a concept that is 'relational, particular, and harm-based'.[8]

The notion of vulnerability has become increasingly important in human rights discourse and practice. For human rights treaty bodies, vulnerability serves as a contextual device to identify adequate measures of protection and prevention. It may also be a factor requiring specific forms of reparation and enhanced accountability of those who violated the rights of persons considered to be vulnerable. In the interpretation of human rights treaties, bodies and courts have utilised vulnerability to specify positive obligations, to determine whether or not certain conduct falls within the scope of ill-treatment, to assess proportionality and to consider whether treatment is discriminatory.[9]

Vulnerability underpins several human rights instruments. The vulnerability of a child, for example, 'by reason of his [her] physical and mental immaturity', is implied in the preamble of the Convention on the Rights of the Child.[10] It is also part of the definition of trafficking, one element being the 'abuse of a position of vulnerability', whereby vulnerability is understood to

---

[4] B. Wiesner, 'Vulnerability as a Concept, Metric, Model and Tool', *Oxford Research Encylopedias: Natural Hazard Science* (August 2016).

[5] M. A. Fineman, 'The Vulnerable Subject: Anchoring Equality in the Human Condition' (2008) 20 *Yale Journal of Law & Feminism* 1.

[6] L. Peroni and A. Timmer, 'Vulnerable Groups: The Promise of an Emerging Concept in European Human Rights Convention Law' (2013) 11 *International Journal of Constitutional Law* 1056.

[7] See for CESCR, Chapman and Carbonetti, above note 3; and for a broader overview, I. Nifosi-Sutton, *The Protection of Vulnerable Groups under International Human Rights Law* (Routledge, 2017).

[8] Peroni and Timmer, above note 6, 1063ff.

[9] Ibid., 1076ff. for the ECtHR.

[10] See also Convention on the Rights of the Child, General Comment 7: Implementing child rights in early childhood, UN doc. CRC/C/GC/7/Rev.1 (20 September 2006) para. 36.

refer to a situation where victims lack alternatives and adequate protection.[11] Asylum seekers have been considered particularly vulnerable in European Union (EU) law,[12] and by courts, due to their insecure legal status, dependency and, in case of particular categories of asylum seekers, because of the lack of procedural guarantees and special reception needs.[13]

Beyond such explicit recognition, international human rights instruments and bodies have largely adopted a group approach whereby certain groups, and members belonging to it, are considered to be inherently vulnerable. This practice has at times been characterised by limited conceptual development, whereby factors such as disadvantaged positions compared to other groups, and marginalisation are used as indicators denoting vulnerability.[14] The European Court of Human Rights (ECtHR), when referring to vulnerable groups, has relied on stigmatisation and historical prejudice that has had 'lasting consequences resulting in ... social exclusion'.[15] It has developed its jurisprudence in relation to ethnic groups, such as the Roma, persons with mental disabilities, persons living with HIV and asylum seekers.[16] Importantly, this approach conceptualises vulnerability not as an immutable trait but as socially constructed.[17] The Inter-American Court of Human Rights (IACtHR) has equally applied the notion of vulnerability in its jurisprudence, such as in an influential advisory opinion on the rights of migrant children.[18] It has considered vulnerability in the context of 'historical structural discrimination based on economic position',[19] groups that are discriminated against, such as persons with HIV/AIDS,[20] or persons with 'specific needs

[11] Art. 3(a) of the Protocol to Prevent, Suppress and Punish Trafficking in Persons Especially Women and Children, supplementing the United Nations Convention against Transnational Organized Crime (2000).

[12] See in particular art. 21 of the Recast Reception Conditions Directive: 'Member States shall take into account the specific situation of vulnerable persons such as minors, unaccompanied minors, disabled people, elderly people, pregnant women, single parents with minor children, victims of human trafficking, persons with serious illnesses, persons with mental disorders and persons who have been subjected to torture, rape or other serious forms of psychological, physical or sexual violence, such as victims of female genital mutilation, in the national law implementing this Directive.'

[13] *MSS* v. *Belgium and Greece* (ECtHR) (2011) paras. 232, 233, 251.

[14] Chapman and Carbonetti, above note 3.

[15] *Novruk and others* v. *Russia* (ECtHR) (2016) para. 100.

[16] Peroni and Timmer, above note 6, 1064. Critical, M. Bossuyt, 'Categorical Rights and Vulnerable Groups: Moving Away from the Universal Human Being' (2016) 4 *George Washington International Law Review* 717, particularly at 726ff.

[17] O. M. Arnardóttir, 'Vulnerability under Article 14 of the European Convention on Human Rights: Innovation or Business as Usual?' (2017) 3 *Oslo Law Review* 150.

[18] Advisory Opinion OC-21/14, *Rights and Guarantees of Children in the Context of Migration and/or in Need of International Protection* (IACtHR) (2014) paras. 59, 71, 91, 170, 176.

[19] *Case of the Hacienda Brazil Verde Workers* v. *Brazil* (IACtHR) (2016) para. 343.

[20] *Gonzales Lluy et al.* v. *Ecuador* (IACtHR) (2015) para. 290. See *also Jorge Odir Miranda Cortez et al.* v. *El Salvador* (IACtHR) (2009) paras. 70 and 74.

of protection ... either because of his [her] personal condition or the specific condition he [she] is in'.[21] These developments evidence greater awareness and the potential of tailoring the interpretation of states' obligations, and devising both preventive and remedial measures in a more contextual fashion. However, the group approach risks being an overly generic one where groups are simply listed as inherently vulnerable. The group approach may also be under-inclusive where the primary focus is on certain groups only, with some groups, such as persons living in poverty, not consistently included in the canon of vulnerable groups. The notion of vulnerability therefore needs to have a consistently applied, clear doctrinal foundation and be based on generic factors, such as prejudices or social exclusion that can be linked to an enhanced risk to violations, which are interpreted in the light of the context at hand. Designating groups such as women, persons with disabilities or indigenous peoples as vulnerable carries potential downsides, even where it reflects histories and realities of prejudice, exclusion and suffering. It may result in treating groups in an essentialist, stigmatising, victimising and paternalistic fashion.[22] Instead of viewing vulnerability as a label, it has been rightly suggested to treat it as a 'layered concept' that takes into consideration 'broader societal, political and institutional circumstances'.[23] It is therefore important that vulnerability is utilised in a way that respects dignity and agency and facilitates equality. Discourses centred on the need for enhanced protection must against this background not undermine mobilisation for more far-reaching changes and transformations aimed at tackling the causes creating and perpetuating vulnerability.

13.3   VULNERABLE GROUPS AND PERSONS

13.3.1   Race

According to the Durban declaration adopted at the 2001 World Conference against Racism, 'racism, racial discrimination, xenophobia and related intolerance, where they amount to racism and racial discrimination, constitute serious violations of and obstacles to the full enjoyment of all human rights'.[24] The pernicious effect of racism and racial discrimination is widely acknowledged; its causes, manifestations and consequences, including its role in politics and society, have been the subject of rich scholarly literature

---

[21] *Case of Ximenes Lopes* v. *Brazil* (IACtHR) (2006) para. 104.

[22] See R. Kapur, *Erotic Justice: Law and the New Politics of Postcolonialism* (Glass House Press, 2005) 95ff.

[23] Peroni and Timmer, above note 6, 1070–3.

[24] World Conference against Racism, Racial Discrimination, Xenophobia and Related Intolerance, Declaration, 2001.

and debate in multiple disciplines.[25] Yet racism, understood as a world view and acts based on the superiority of certain 'races' over other 'races', faces a paradox. The notion of race, which emerged in discourses in the eighteenth and nineteenth centuries, lacks a scientific basis.[26] The fact that it is socially constructed does, however, not mean that it is less real.[27] On the contrary, notions of race have played a defining role in shaping societal and international relations over the last two centuries. In the context of colonialism, it merged with discourses of 'civilised' countries that bring about civilisation and development, and served to justify myriad forms of colonial oppression.[28] Stratification based on racial views of colonial powers has left an indelible mark in many countries, with apartheid South Africa standing out as a system of institutionalised racism. Notions of racial superiority were also instrumental in justifying slavery and the transcontinental slave trade.[29] The business of slavery and the slave trade was not only extremely brutal in its operation; it has also had lasting influences on the status, living conditions and treatment of persons of African descent in many countries, particularly throughout the Americas. The twentieth century was characterised by the persistence and legacies of these practices, and new forms of racism, which culminated in several genocides, particularly the Holocaust of the Jews and other groups at the hands of Nazi Germany and its collaborators. Notwithstanding sustained efforts to combat racism and racial discrimination, it persists and has witnessed a resurgence in the wake of political and economic instability, and large-scale migration. Lately, it has therefore been particularly pronounced in respect of the treatment of refugees and migrants.[30]

[25] K. Reilly, S. Kaufman and A. Bodino (eds.), *Racism: A Global Reader* (M. E. Sharpe, 2003); L. Back and J. Solomos (eds.), *Theories of Race and Racism: A Reader*, 2nd edn (Routledge, 2009); R. Delgado, *Critical Race Theory: An Introduction* (New York University Press, 2017).

[26] See preamble of the International Convention on the Elimination of All Forms of Racial Discrimination (1965): 'Convinced that any doctrine of superiority based on racial differentiation is scientifically false, morally condemnable, socially unjust and dangerous, and that there is no justification for racial discrimination, in theory or in practice, anywhere.'

[27] See on race as a 'discursive construct', S. Hall, *The Fateful Triangle: Race, Ethnicity, Nation* (Harvard University Press, 2017).

[28] A. Anghie, 'Finding the Peripheries: Sovereignty and Colonialism in Nineteenth-Century International Law' (1999) 40 *Harvard International Law Journal* 1.

[29] See Chapter 1.2.3.

[30] Report of the Special Rapporteur on contemporary forms of racism, racial discrimination, xenophobia and related intolerance, UN doc. A/HRC/38/52 (25 April 2018); M. Bosworth, A. Parmar and Y. Vázquez (eds.), *Race, Criminal Justice, and Migration Control: Enforcing the Boundaries of Belonging* (Oxford University Press, 2018).

Racism and racial discrimination is largely a structurally conditioned practice.[31] An individual experience where, for example, a person is denied employment on account of her colour is against this background not an unfortunate exception, although it may often be portrayed as such, but a manifestation of broader patterns. The Committee on the Elimination of Racial Discrimination (CERD) illustrates this in its General Recommendation 34, finding that:

Racism and structural discrimination against people of African descent, rooted in the infamous regime of slavery, are evident in the situations of inequality affecting them and reflected, inter alia, in the following domains: their grouping, together with indigenous peoples, among the poorest of the poor; their low rate of participation and representation in political and institutional decision-making processes; additional difficulties they face in access to and completion and quality of education, which results in the transmission of poverty from generation to generation; inequality in access to the labour market; limited social recognition and valuation of their ethnic and cultural diversity; and a disproportionate presence in prison populations.[32]

Race or ethnicity is a factor that frequently exposes individuals to a greater risk of violations compared to members of the 'dominant' population. This concerns violations at the hands of both state agents, such as enhanced stop and search, ill-treatment, unfair trials and disproportionate punishments in criminal justice systems,[33] and private actors, where the state fails to provide adequate protection, such as in the field of employment. As widely recognised, vulnerability to violations is amplified, and violations may take specific forms, where race or ethnicity intersects with other factors, such as gender, nationality or socio-economic status.[34] Such violations have in exceptional cases also been based on express legislation and/or policies such as in Nazi Germany or apartheid South Africa. Often, however, they constitute political, social and cultural practices that are deeply embedded and structure relationships in the country concerned.

The combat against racism, which is subsumed under all forms of racial discrimination, has played a pivotal role in the development of international

---

[31] General Recommendation 34 adopted by the Committee, Racial discrimination against people of African descent, UN doc. CERD/C/GC/34 (3 October 2011) para. 5.

[32] Ibid., para. 6.

[33] General Recommendation 31 on the prevention of racial discrimination in the administration and functioning of the criminal justice system, CERD, Sixty-fifth session (2005).

[34] On intersectionality, see General Recommendation 25 on gender-related dimensions of racial discrimination, CERD, Fifty-sixth session (2000), and on the nexus between gender, poverty and race, Report of the Special Rapporteur on violence against women, its causes and consequences, Rashida Manjoo, UN doc. A/HRC/17/26 (2 May 2011) para. 75.

human rights law. It has been characterised by national and international campaigns aimed at, and (largely) resulting in, the suppression of the slave trade, the abolition of slavery, and ending colonialism and apartheid.[35] These developments were supported by a number of international treaties, such as the Slavery Convention of 1926. The United Nations (UN) General Assembly, in the wake of decolonisation, adopted the International Convention on the Elimination of All Forms of Racial Discrimination on 21 December 1965 (ICERD), which followed the UN Declaration on the Elimination of All Forms of Racial Discrimination of 20 November 1963. According to ICERD:

the term 'racial discrimination' shall mean any distinction, exclusion, restriction or preference based on race, colour, descent, or national or ethnic origin which has the purpose or effect of nullifying or impairing the recognition, enjoyment or exercise, on an equal footing, of human rights and fundamental freedoms in the political, economic, social, cultural, or any other field of public life.

The CERD has at times interpreted the notion broadly, including with reference to gender and religion, both of which are not explicitly mentioned in ICERD.[36] This is in line with its approach that the Convention is a living instrument.[37] It has also elaborated on the specific obligations of states parties in its general recommendations, such as on the scope of racist hate speech and its relationship with freedom of expression,[38] and in its jurisprudence.[39] According to one of its former members, '[t]he distinctive rights culture developed by the Committee over the course of time has inspired many, and made an enormous contribution to the solidification of principle that brands racial discrimination an unacceptable State practice'.[40] The issue of racial discrimination has also featured in the practice of other UN treaty bodies and, albeit to a more limited extent, in the jurisprudence of regional human rights courts.[41] The UN Human Rights Council's special procedure system has two mandates directly concerned with racial discrimination, namely the Working Group of Experts on People of African Descent and the Special Rapporteur on contemporary forms of racism, racial discrimination, xenophobia and related intolerance. A glance at the breadth of issues falling within the

---

[35] See Chapter 1.2.3; B. Ibhawoh, *Human Rights in Africa* (Cambridge University Press, 2018) 55ff.

[36] See P. Thornberry, *The International Convention on the Elimination of All Forms of Racial Discrimination: A Commentary* (Oxford University Press, 2016) 126–8, 137–9.

[37] D. Keane and A. Waughray, *Fifty Years of the International Convention on the Elimination of All Forms of Racial Discrimination: A Living Instrument* (Manchester University Press, 2017).

[38] General Recommendation 35, Combating racist hate speech, UN doc. CERD/C/GC/35 (26 September 2013).

[39] See Chapter 5.5.4.   [40] Thornberry, above note 36, 501.

[41] See S. Fredman (ed.), *Discrimination and Human Rights: The Case of Racism* (Oxford University Press, 2001).

latter mandate and dealt with in various reports highlights the challenges that racial discrimination poses, particularly in times of rising populism and xenophobia.[42] At the regional level, this framework is mirrored by instruments such as the Inter-American Convention against Racism, Racial Discrimination and Related Forms of Intolerance (2013), the Inter-American Commission on Human Rights Rapporteurship on the Rights of Persons of African Descent and against Racial Discrimination, the Council of Europe's European Commission against Racism and Intolerance, and race equality instruments of regional economic institutions, such as the EU, particularly in respect of labour law.

International human rights law provides an important counterweight against persistent and new forms of racial discrimination. It does not, however, escape the political challenges of how to deal with ethnic diversity and tensions resulting thereof. This concerns particularly the debate surrounding multiculturalism, integration and assimilation, and migration and immigration more broadly.[43] In this context, international human rights law becomes embroiled in political debates, and may even, inadvertently, reinforce marginalisation where it emphasises the need for special protection.[44] A clear contextual focus and in-depth engagement with structural factors are in such an environment pivotal to overcoming racial discrimination, and securing the rights of those who are at risk thereof, or have experienced it.

13.3.2   Gender, Gender Identity and Sexual Orientation

Gender discrimination and gender-based violence have become a core focus of many legal and institutional responses in the field of international human rights law. This focus is the result of sustained engagement and advocacy of women's (rights) movements. They had to identify, highlight and denounce both the various realities (that were not necessarily acknowledged as violations) faced by women and the male-centric biases in the system of international human rights protection. Notwithstanding the undoubted advancements in the recognition and protection of women's rights, women continue to be exposed to multiple, gender-specific violations. Gender, particularly where understood as a socially constructed concept characterised by notions of male superiority and underpinned by inequalities, stereotyping and social exclusion, constitutes a major structural factor that serves to

---

[42] See further www.ohchr.org/EN/Issues/Racism/SRRacism/Pages/IndexSRRacism.aspx.

[43] See e.g., W. Kymlicka, *Multicultural Citizenship: A Liberal Theory of Minority Rights* (Oxford University Press, 2000), and, for a critical perspective on recent developments, C. Dauvergne, *The New Politics of Immigration and the End of Settler Communities* (Cambridge University Press, 2016).

[44] See for critical views on identity and rights, and identity politics, W. Brown, *States of Injury: Power and Freedom in Late Modernity* (Princeton University Press, 1995) 96ff., and A. Haider, *Mistaken Identity: Race and Class in the Age of Trump* (Verso, 2018).

facilitate, justify and tolerate inequalities and abuses in all spheres of lives. It is therefore recognised that women are particularly vulnerable to violations where gendered notions are prevalent, and are specifically exposed to multiple discrimination, and abuses, where other risk factors, such as race, indigeneity or poverty, are present. The international human rights system has responded to these developments by broadening the notion of discrimination, focusing on gender-based violence and developing a series of instruments, bodies and mechanisms designed to promote and protect women's rights.[45]

The foregrounding of gender as a social construct and gender-based violations as an area of international concern has opened the space for advocacy, and calls to recognise, and better protect, the rights of lesbian, gay, bisexual, transgender and intersex (LGBTI) persons. These persons face multiple discrimination on the grounds of their sexual orientation or gender identity, including discriminatory laws criminalising consensual adult sexual relationships, as well as discrimination in employment, health care, education, in the family and other areas.[46] Individuals have also been exposed to various forms of homophobic or transphobic violence, both by non-state actors and state agents, the latter particularly in the form of torture and other ill-treatment.[47]

While this reality is undeniable, a number of states object to recognising sexual orientation and gender identity as a prohibited ground of discrimination.[48] Other than in some recent regional treaties, there is no explicit reference to these grounds.[49] However, most human rights treaty bodies have interpreted the ground of 'other status' or 'other condition' as prohibiting discrimination based on sexual orientation or gender identity, and consequently found several discriminatory practices to be in violation of states' obligations under the respective human rights treaties.[50] This interpretation can be justified with reference to their immutable or fundamental nature. However, such

---

[45] See Chapter 11.

[46] Report of the United Nations High Commissioner for Human Rights, Discriminatory laws and practices and acts of violence against individuals based on their sexual orientation and gender identity, UN doc. A/HRC/19/41 (17 November 2011).

[47] Report of the Office of the United Nations High Commissioner, Discrimination and violence against individuals based on their sexual orientation and gender identity, UN doc. A/HRC/29/23 (4 May 2015), particularly paras. 20ff.

[48] See e.g., states voting against HRC resolution 27/32: *Human Rights, Sexual Orientation and Gender Identity*, UN doc. A/HRC/RES/27/32 (2 October 2014), adopted by a recorded vote of twenty-five to fourteen, with seven abstentions.

[49] See art. 21 of the Charter of Fundamental Rights of the European Union and art. 4(3) of the Council of Europe Convention on preventing and combating violence against women and domestic violence (2011). In November 2013, the IACHR established a Rapporteurship on the rights of lesbian, gay, bisexual, trans and intersex persons (LGBTI); see further www.oas.org/en/iachr/lgtbi.

[50] See overview in Report of the UN High Commissioner for Human Rights, above note 47, paras. 8–19 and *Atala Riffo and Daughters* v. *Chile* (IACtHR) (2012) paras. 83–93.

an interpretation may be contested by those who view same-sex sexual orientation or choice in matters of gender identity as morally wrong (therefore not deserving protection) or otherwise oppose it. While this question undoubtedly has an important doctrinal dimension, it has become highly politicised and is often portrayed as an attempt to impose 'alien', 'Western' 'lifestyles'. It has generated debates and created tensions within and across countries, and within the broader human rights community and LGBTI persons themselves. Donor interventions promoting rights based on sexual orientation and gender identity have been criticised for being counterproductive in particular settings.[51] LGBTI persons themselves, also as part of broader queer discourses, have objected to being typecast as victims or being confined to what may be viewed as limited, liberal legal spaces of rights protection.[52] Since lack of recognition and denial of agency are often at the heart of violations faced, these voices pose a challenge to develop adequate international human rights law responses. At the normative level, the Yogyakarta Principles on the application of international human rights law in relation to sexual orientation and gender identity (2006), though non-binding, have served as important reference point for the rights of LGBTI persons. These rights reach beyond non-discrimination. As the additional Yogyakarta Principles (YP+10) show, the instrument also responds to concerns such as attacks on LGBTI persons, lack of state protection and recognition, and criminalisation, among other issues.[53] It has been referred to by human rights bodies, such as the IACtHR and the ECtHR. In their jurisprudence, they have increasingly addressed questions and cases surrounding the recognition and protection of LGBTI rights, such as on the right to privacy, the state's positive obligations, and equality and non-discrimination.[54] In a significant development giving LGBTI rights a focal point at the UN, the Human Rights Council created the mandate of an Independent Expert on sexual orientation and gender identity in 2016.[55]

---

[51] See for an interesting case study, M. Wahman and A. C. Drury, 'Leverage, Diplomacy, and African Lesbian, Gay, Bisexual, Transgendered and Intersex Rights – Malawi and Zambia Compared' (2017) 17 *Journal of Human Rights* 622; 'Statement on British "Aid Cut" Threats to African Countries that Violate LBGTI Rights', signed by 'the undersigned African social justice activists' in *Pambazuka News* (27 October 2011).

[52] See for a thoughtful account of debates, V. Hamzic, *Sexual and Gender Diversity in the Muslim World: History, Law and Vernacular Knowledge* (I.B. Tauris, 2016).

[53] http://yogyakartaprinciples.org.

[54] See in particular Advisory Opinion No. 24, *Gender identity, and equality and non-discrimination with regard to same-sex couples. State obligations in relation to change of name, gender identity, and rights deriving from a relationship between same-sex couples (interpretation and scope of Articles 1(3), 3, 7, 11(2), 13, 17, 18 and 24, in relation to Article 1, of the American Convention on Human Rights* (IACtHR) (2017); D. McGoldrick, 'The Development and Status of Sexual Orientation Discrimination under International Human Rights Law' (2016) 16 *Human Rights Law Review* 613.

[55] Protection against violence and discrimination based on sexual orientation and gender identity, UN doc. A/HRC/RES/32/2 (15 July 2016).

CASE STUDY 13.1
A Family Life before National and Regional Courts

The judgment in *Atala Riffo and Daughters* v. *Chile* is a landmark ruling
in the Inter-American human rights system. In March 2002, Ms Atala took
care and custody of her three daughters after having separated from her
husband, Mr Lopez. In 'November 2002, Ms. Emma de Ramón, the partner of
Ms Atala, began living in the same house with Ms Atala, her three daughters
and her eldest son [from Ms Atala's first marriage]'.[1] In January 2003, Mr
Lopez instituted custody proceedings for their three daughters, objecting to
Ms Atala living with her lesbian partner. After protracted legal proceedings,
Chile's Supreme Court awarded custody of the three girls to Mr Lopez. It held,
inter alia, that 'potential confusion over sexual roles that could be caused in
them by the absence from the home of a male father and his replacement by
another person of the female gender poses a risk to the integral development
of the children from which they must be protected'.[2] Following a review of the
practice of regional and international human rights bodies, the IACtHR found
that sexual orientation falls under 'another social condition' in article 1(1) of
the American Convention on Human Rights (ACHR). It held that 'no domestic
regulation, decision, or practice, whether by state authorities or individuals,
may diminish or restrict, in any way whatsoever, the rights of a person based on
his or her sexual orientation'.[3] After examining arguments put forward by the
respondent state and in national proceedings, the Court found that the 'child's
best interest' invoked 'cannot be used to justify discrimination against the
parents based on their sexual orientation'.[4] This applies in particular in case of
'a determination based on unfounded and stereotyped assumptions about the
parent's capacity and suitability to ensure and promote the child's well-being
and development'.[5] Rejecting arguments put forward regarding alleged social
discrimination of the girls, alleged confusion of sexual roles, alleged privilege
of interests and the right to a 'normal and traditional' family, the Court found
a violation of Ms Atala's right to equality under article 24 ACHR, in conjunction
with article 1(1) ACHR.[6] The case illustrates both the importance of the right
to equality and the many challenging questions its application can raise in the
context of family relationships.

---

[1] *Atala Riffo and Daughters* v. *Chile*, para. 30.   [2] Ibid., para. 56.   [3] Ibid., para. 91.
[4] Ibid., para. 110.   [5] Ibid., para. 111.
[6] Ibid., para. 146. The Court also found several other violations, including the right to
privacy.

13.3.3   Persons with Disabilities

It may be surprising to learn that about a billion persons in the world are disabled. This means that one in five persons has some form of disability; yet disabled persons are often invisible and societies share fixed perceptions about the role and capabilities of disabled persons, without really knowing much about their capabilities or their aspirations. Before ascribing rights to disabled persons, the starting point for this discussion should be the common understanding of non-disabled persons regarding the very concept of 'disability'.[56] From a legal point of view, article 1(2) of the UN Convention on the Rights of Persons with Disabilities (CRPD), defines persons with disabilities as including:

> those who have long-term physical, mental, intellectual or sensory impairments which in interaction with various barriers may hinder their full and effective participation in society on an equal basis with others.

This definition is in stark contrast to the traditional understanding of disability through the existence of an impairment, whether physical, sensory, intellectual or mental. Such a perception of disability is clearly predicated on a medical observation, with its emphasis on impairment. This medical approach to disability was dominant until recently and is still espoused in several countries, despite the advent of the CRPD in 2006, which dismisses it altogether.

The medical model of disability focuses exclusively on 'within-individual' (biological, physical and psychological) factors that constitute an impairment.[57] However, a thorough understanding of disability involves a systemic understanding at both individual and social level, which goes beyond the sub-individual level. Reducing disability experience to impairment (loss or diminution of anatomical structure or physiological function or function of the mental-nervous system) leaves aside the experience of disabled people such as their engagement in social activities, the social roles they play and the social relationships they form, as well as the social struggle for

---

[56] See for a more elaborate discussion of the various disability models, D. Anastasiou and I. Bantekas, 'Models of Disability and Human Rights: Beyond Binaries', in M. Langford and M. A. Stein (eds.), *Disability Social Rights* (Oxford University Press, 2019).

[57] M. Oliver, *Understanding Disability: From Theory to Practice* (Macmillan 1996); M. Oliver, *The Politics of Disablement* (Macmillan 1990); see also D. Anastasiou and J. M. Kauffman 'A Social Constructionist Approach to Disability: Implications for Special Education' (2011) 77 *Exceptional Children* 367; D. Anastasiou and J. M. Kauffman, 'The Social Model of Disability: Dichotomy between Impairment and Disability' (2013) 38 *Journal of Medicine and Philosophy* 441; T. Shakespeare, *Disability Rights and Wrongs* (Routledge 2006); M. A. Stein, 'Disability Human Rights' (2007) 95 *California Law Review* 75.

transforming disability services in a disability-friendly social world.[58] This represents a more general view than social constructionism. In the medical model, individuals are viewed as a body part or function, and this can lead to objectification. The objectification of a condition prevents one from seeing the whole person in its environment, and significant parts of personhood, developmental history, experiences and expectations are ignored. This can devalue persons with disabilities and may also involve paternalism. Furthermore, applying a medical perspective to any undesirable phenomenon can lead to a broader undue medicalisation.[59]

A great many problems that people with disabilities, especially those with body-related disabilities (including physical and sensory disabilities), encounter are generated by the built environment, social attitudes and prejudices rather than by their physical limitations.[60] The concern with this paternalistic and medical-centric approach was central in the early mobilisation of the disability movement, as expressed in the following passage from the Policy Statement of the Union of the Physically Impaired Against Segregation (UPIAS, 1974/1976):

Both inside and outside institutions, the traditional way of dealing with disabled people has been for doctors and other professionals to decide what is best for us. It is of course a fact that we sometimes require skilled medical help to treat our physical impairments – operations, drugs and nursing care. We may also need therapists to help restore or maintain physical function, and to advise us on aids to independence and mobility. But the imposition of medical authority, and of a medical definition of our problems of living in society, have to be resisted strongly. First and foremost we are people, not 'patients,' 'cases,' 'spastics,' the 'deaf,' 'the blind,' 'wheelchairs,' or 'the sick.' Our Union rejects entirely any idea of medical or other experts having the right to tell us how we should live, or withholding information from us, or [making] decisions behind our backs.[61]

The inability of the medical model of disability to reflect and encapsulate the disability phenomenon in all its manifestations and contours may be practically illustrated. A person restricted to a wheelchair because of a physical impairment to his or her legs cannot even undertake menial tasks in an urban environment that offers no, or little, wheelchair accessibility. However, if the urban environment were to adapt to wheelchair users through the design of accessible buildings, vehicles and other infrastructure, as well as

---

[58] P. Townsend, 'Elderly People with Disabilities', in A. Walker and P. Townsend (eds.), *Disability in Britain* (Martin Robertson, 1981) 91–118.

[59] Ibid.

[60] Shakespeare, above note 57; J. Morris, *Pride Against Prejudice: A Personal Politics of Disability Paperback* (The Women's Press 1991) 11.

[61] UPIAS Policy Statement adopted 3 December 1974 and amended 9 August 1976, online at http://disability-studies.leeds.ac.uk/files/library/UPIAS-UPIAS.pdf.

the development of IT accessibility, the physical impairment becomes far less important. Imagine now a non-disabled person living in a world of tall buildings with no lifts or stairs (only ropes to climb), or books and journals available only in Braille. This would be a very difficult world even for the fittest and life would be a constant struggle.

Disability organisations and advocates, therefore, have long campaigned for a move away from perceiving disability through the lens of impairment (the medical model) to a model whereby physical, virtual and other environments diminish, wholly or partly, the disadvantages of impairment and in turn enable disabled persons to an equality of opportunities with their non-disabled counterparts. Despite several other milestones, it was the adoption of the CRPD that both highlighted and signalled the death of the medical model.

The CRPD rests on several pillars, some of which are unique to human rights treaty-making. The first is the universal introduction of a social or human rights model of disability, in which the focus is on the creation of enabling environments. Secondly, disability rights in the CRPD are not new rights, but existing rights as adapted and adjusted to creating enabling environments. Thirdly, and in order to realise the first and second pillars, it is imperative that disabled persons enjoy unlimited accessibility. Accessibility, both physical and virtual in public and private spaces is enshrined in article 9 CRPD and is integral to de facto equality and the pursuit of independent living, among other things. In fact, with a view to streamlining accessibility into all walks of life, article 4(1)(f) CRPD obliges states to construct, design and adapt all objects, services, materials and buildings on the basis of a universal design. Article 2 CRPD defines universal design as: 'the design of products, environments, programmes and services to be usable by all people, to the greatest extent possible, without the need for adaptation or specialised design. "Universal design" shall not exclude assistive devices for particular groups of persons with disabilities where this is needed.' Fourthly, it is not only imperative that disabled persons are not discriminated against as compared to non-disabled persons, but that they enjoy de facto equality against non-disabled persons, as well as equality of opportunity. Given the absence of generally enabling environments, de facto equality requires that states take all appropriate measures to ensure the availability of reasonable accommodation. The latter notion is defined in article 2 CRPD as any:

necessary and appropriate modification and adjustments not imposing a disproportionate or undue burden, where needed in a particular case, to ensure to persons with disabilities the enjoyment or exercise on an equal basis with others of all human rights and fundamental freedoms.

Discriminatory action that is oblivious to reasonable accommodation may be highlighted in the plight of persons with HIV or similar virus-based infectious diseases. Their condition per se does not justify being dismissed or otherwise cast aside in the workplace, where it is found that they can still perform their ordinary functions or perform other tasks through reasonable accommodation.[62] Several domestic[63] and international tribunals[64] have held that where an HIV/AIDS-infected person is able to continue working, any interference with his or her employment, particularly where the ground for dismissal or other action against the person relates exclusively to his or her medical condition, is discriminatory and thus prohibited. Fifth, the CRPD demands respect for the dignity of disabled persons, as well as individual autonomy to decide all matters concerning their person and life choices. This also includes full and effective participation and inclusion in society (article 3 CRPD), as well as the right to independent living (article 19 CRPD). This is crucial, because under the medical model intellectually and mentally impaired persons were not considered as being able to decide on matters pertaining to their person, nor live or reside outside an institutional setting. Institutionalisation and absence of legal capacity have been two of the most persistent obstacles to the full realisation of disability rights. In the view of the UN Committee on the Rights of Persons with Disabilities, article 12 CRPD dismisses the application of limited or reduced capacity and introduces what it terms 'universal legal capacity', which states are not permitted to limit on grounds of disability or mental incapacity.[65] The implication is that all forms of substitute decision-making are unlawful under the CRPD. This is a radical proposition and has given rise to heated debates, but without failure the CRPD Committee, in its review of state reports, has condemned overt and disguised practices that fetter the freedom of disabled persons to decide on matters of personal concern, or practices that effectively strip persons with disabilities of individual freedoms (such as the right to found a family or the right to vote).[66] Sixth, far from attracting pity and despair, given appropriate enabling environments, persons with disabilities can and do flourish in all

---

[62] See ILO Recommendation concerning HIV and AIDS and the World of Work, 2010 (No. 200); see also Parliamentary Assembly of the Council of Europe (PACE) Recommendation 1116 (1989) on AIDS and human rights.

[63] *Hoffman* v. *South African Airways* (South Africa) (2000); *M* v. *R* (Switzerland) (2000); *Canada (Attorney General)* v. *Thwaites* (Canada) (1994); *X* v. *Commonwealth* (Australia) (1999).

[64] *IB* v. *Greece* (ECtHR) (2013).

[65] CRPD Committee, General Comment 1 (2014) Article 12: Equal recognition before the law, UN doc. CRPD/C/GC/1 (19 May 2014); A. Dhanda, 'Universal Legal Capacity as a Universal Human Right', in M. Dudley, D. Silove and F. Gale (eds.), *Mental Health and Human Rights: Vision, Praxis, and Courage* (Oxford University Press, 2012); E. Flynn and A. Arstein-Kerslake, 'Legislating Personhood: Realising the Right to Support in Exercising Legal Capacity' (2014) 10 *International Journal of Law in Context* 81.

[66] See L. Series, 'Article 12', in I. Bantekas, A. M. Stein and D. Anastasiou (eds.), *The UN Convention on the Rights of Persons with Disabilities* (Oxford University Press, 2018) 339.

ways of life and hence it is important that all the stigma associated with disability be eliminated, whether by celebrating the contribution and diversity of disabled persons or by educating society as a whole (article 8 CRPD). The awareness-raising obligation contained in the CRPD is innovative and a unique feature of the CRPD.

13.3.4   Persons Living in Extreme Poverty

Poverty is a condition and lived experience that has multiple economic, social and political causes, dimensions and consequences. While the experience and consequences of poverty vary considerably, it is closely associated with low levels of educational attainment, poor health, precarious work and living conditions, stigmatisation and marginalisation. For this reason, the issue of poverty has predominantly been considered through the economic, social and cultural rights prism. In contrast, the violation of civil and political rights of persons living in poverty, such as in the administration of justice (over-criminalisation, lack of legal representation, ill-treatment, inadequate access to justice), or exposure to myriad forms of violence, has been largely neglected.[67] This is an important gap, as violence and lack of respect for the rule of law create, reinforce and perpetuate poverty.[68] Persons living in poverty frequently suffer disadvantages in the criminal justice system due to a combination of factors, particularly lack of social standing, awareness and/ or trust in justice systems, influence and means, which may be particularly pronounced where it intersects with other factors, such as race, or where such persons live in insecure environments, such as street children.[69]

Notwithstanding its apparent human rights dimension, international human rights law has struggled to adequately respond to poverty. It was initially largely framed as an economic problem, to be dealt with by means of development interventions aimed at poverty eradication. However, international actors did not pursue a consistent policy as structural adjustment programmes often aggravated existing conditions.[70] It also became apparent that a purely economic approach is ill-suited to adequately capture poverty. Influenced by Amartya Sen's work, poverty was increasingly framed as a

---

[67] *Report of the Special Rapporteur on extreme poverty and human rights,* UN doc. A/72/502 (4 October 2017).

[68] G. Haugen and V. Boutros, *The Locust Effect: Why the End of Poverty Requires the End of Violence* (Oxford University Press, 2015).

[69] See on access to justice, Report of the Special Rapporteur on extreme poverty and human rights, UN doc. A/67/278 (9 August 2012), and CRC, General Comment 21 (2017) on children in street situations, UN doc. CRC/C/GC/21 (21 June 2017).

[70] See M. Nowak, *Human Rights or Global Capitalism: The Limits of Privatisation* (University of Pennsylvania Press, 2017); M. R. Abouharb and D. Cingranelli, *Human Rights and Structural Adjustment* (Cambridge University Press, 2007).

question of individual capabilities.[71] This enriched the understanding of poverty though generating divergent views as to the meaning of poverty. The definition put forward by the Committee on Economic, Social and Cultural Rights combines various approaches, viewing poverty as 'a human condition characterized by the sustained or chronic deprivation of the resources, capabilities, choices, security and power necessary for the enjoyment of an adequate standard of living and other civil, cultural, economic, political and social rights'.[72] In the international human rights law context, there has been a particular emphasis on extreme poverty. This has been defined as '"the combination of income poverty, human development poverty and social exclusion" (A/HRC/7/15, para. 13), where a prolonged lack of basic security affects several aspects of peoples' lives simultaneously, severely compromising their chances of exercising or regaining their rights in the foreseeable future (see E/CN.4/Sub.2/1996/13)'.[73]

Is there a right to be free from poverty in international human rights law, and, if so, who are the duty-holders?[74] This question, and debate, also has an important international component where states are considered duty-bound to alleviate poverty in other countries, or worldwide.[75]

International treaties have not explicitly recognised a right to be free from poverty. Human rights treaty bodies have considered the impact of poverty on human rights, although without developing a coherent approach in the absence of an explicit framework. This includes limited jurisprudence on discrimination on the grounds of socio-economic status.[76] However, the nexus between poverty and human rights has been explicitly acknowledged. The mandate of the Special Rapporteur on extreme poverty and human rights, established in 1998, represents the UN's focal point on the subject;

---

[71] A. Sen, *Development as Freedom* (Oxford University Press, 2001).

[72] Substantive Issues Arising in the Implementation of the International Covenant on Economic, Social and Cultural Rights: Poverty and the International Covenant on Economic, Social and Cultural Rights: Statement adopted by the Committee on 4 May 2011, UN doc. E/C.12/2001/10 (10 May 2001) para. 8.

[73] UN Guiding Principles on Extreme Poverty and Human Rights (2011) 2. See for an extensive discussion of the notion of poverty, Inter American Commission on Human Rights (IACHR), Report on Poverty and Human Rights in the Americas, OEA/SER.L/V/II.164, doc. 147 (7 September 2017) 21ff.

[74] For a useful overview, see Centre for Economic and Social Rights, *Poverty and Human Rights: Is Poverty a Violation of Human Rights?* (2009).

[75] See above note 73, para. 91, and further, T. Pogge, *World Poverty and Human Rights: Cosmopolitan Responsibilities and Reforms*, 2nd edn (Polity, 2008).

[76] However, see UNCESCR, General Comment 20: Non-discrimination in Economic, Social and Cultural Rights (art. 2, para. 2, of the International Covenant on Economic, Social and Cultural Rights), UN doc. E/C.12/GC/20 (2 July 2009) paras. 27 and 35. See further UN doc. E/C.12/2001/10, above note 72.

the mandate-holders have issued a series of thematic and country-specific reports that have highlighted a range of issues and concerns.[77] The Special Rapporteur also led the process resulting in the adoption of the Guiding Principles on Extreme Poverty and Human Rights by the UN Human Rights Council in 2012. The Principles take the position that:

> Poverty is an urgent human rights concern in itself. It is both a cause and a consequence of human rights violations and an enabling condition for other violations. Not only is extreme poverty characterized by multiple reinforcing violations of civil, political, economic, social and cultural rights, but persons living in poverty generally experience regular denials of their dignity and equality.[78]

The Principles are also noteworthy for drawing on rights-based approaches to development, stressing agency, autonomy, participation and empowerment, transparency and accountability, as well as national strategies and policies, before listing the obligations of states in respect of specific rights. The Guidelines further stipulate a duty of states 'to provide international assistance and cooperation commensurate with their capacities, resources and influence'.[79]

These are important normative advances. Further, progress has been made in meeting the sustainable development goal of poverty eradication.[80] Notwithstanding these developments, poverty remains a challenging structural cause of multiple human rights violations that has in many contexts become even more pronounced as a result of globalisation, conflicts, rising inequality, austerity measures and targeting of persons living in poverty.[81] Human rights-based approaches and legal strategies play an important role in combating poverty and securing the rights of persons living in such condition.[82] Ultimately, though, they will have to be complemented by conducive national and international political and economic systems and institutions to bring about the broader transformation needed.

---

[77] See Commission on Human Rights resolution 1998/25: Human rights and extreme poverty, and for the website of the mandate, whose current mandate-holder is Professor Philip Alston, www.ohchr.org/EN/Issues/Poverty/Pages/SRExtremePovertyIndex.aspx.

[78] Guiding Principles, above note 73, 2.

[79] Ibid., para. 91.

[80] The road to dignity by 2030: ending poverty, transforming all lives and protecting the planet, Synthesis report of the Secretary-General on the post-2015 sustainable development goals, UN doc. A/69/700 (4 December 2014); and further, https://sustainabledevelopment.un.org/topics/povertyeradication and www.worldpoverty.io.

[81] See statements and reports of the UN Special Rapporteur on Extreme Poverty and Human Rights on the Post-2015 Development Agenda, www.ohchr.org/EN/Issues/Poverty/Pages/Post2015Development.aspx.

[82] See for example, recommendations made by the IACHR in its report on poverty and human rights in the Americas, above note 73, 173ff.

INTERVIEW 13.1

Into the Heart of Everyday Violence and Human Rights Violations: Conducting Research on, and with, Marginalised and Vulnerable Persons

(Morten Koch Andersen)

Morten Koch Andersen, Centre for Global Criminology, Department of Anthropology, University of Copenhagen, formerly Dignity, has led and engaged in a series of interdisciplinary research projects on the nexus between violence, human rights and corruption, with a special focus on the administration of justice, legal reform and institutional practices.[1]

How would you describe your research approach?

The research approach is based on partnerships with rights-based organisations in the countries where we work. A key feature in the partnership is trust which over time is built upon common interest for social change, frequent professional and social interactions and deep engagement with people to understand society and politics. For example, in my work in Bangladesh, where I have worked with activists, victims, legal professionals and journalists for more than a decade, we have established a sincere understanding of each other's positions and roles in the global fight for rights and justice. Such relations underpin the analytical work and contribute to the conceptual development and writing of articles.[2]

What are the main challenges of carrying out empirical research with slum dwellers and/or other persons living in poverty?

The main challenge is access. In other words, to find people who are willing to talk about their life and dramatic life events, such as violence or threats of violence. This is especially difficult in situations where the conflict situation is ongoing or remains unsolved without any form of arbitration or settlement; where conflicting parties live in close proximity to each other and/ or are in an unequal power relationship; and where one party has authority to decide or influence decision-making in the area regarding the conflict e.g. landlord, police officer, criminal etc. Most people do not seek outside assistance out of fear they will (again) attract the attention of the perpetrator(s) and because they have little trust that it will bring about some form of redress or settlement. Many victims and others at risk attempt to stay hidden and do not want to attract attention caused by the intervention of human rights activists/organisations.

---

[1] See in particular S. Jensen and M. K. Andersen (eds.), *Corruption and Torture: Violent Exchanges and Everyday Life For the Urban Poor* (Aalborg Universitetsforlag, 2017).

[2] M. K. Andersen, 'Filtering Information: Human Rights Documentation in Bangladesh', *Journal of Human Rights Practice* (advanced online publication, 25 April 2019).

Do you consider the concepts of marginalised and/or vulnerable persons, and a heightened focus on marginalisation and vulnerability in international human rights law, useful approaches to enhance the protection of the rights of persons concerned?

In the field of human rights, what we know – that is, what is knowable and intelligible is – produced by experts based on notions of victimhood and suffering that are created and re-created according to specific standards of documentation and evidence. This includes and often takes as a point of departure treaties on the rights of women, children, persons with disabilities, and declarations on rights of indigenous peoples, rights of persons living in extreme poverty etc. Each of these fields is monitored by organisations and activists with associated mandates, expertise and work capacity. The aim of their work is to make a difference in the world, to help victims and families and change society. However, resources and opportunities are always in demand, and not sufficient to the tasks they have taken upon themselves. This means they have to prioritise their scarce resources and mainly privilege those events that involve and use established notions of victimhood. Often this includes vulnerability, intent and injury combined with urgency of action, which together constitute a case with potential. For example, women and child victims more easily attract public attention because of the (perceived) arbitrariness of victimisation and deeper levels of vulnerability, based on globalised notions of innocence and defencelessness. As such, they fit the category of a blameless, 'proper' victim, which is an illustrative and powerful figure in campaigning. As a result, the very regular – almost mundane or standard – inspections and violence, often beatings, of young men or known criminals in connection with police inquiries into alleged criminal activities rarely attract any attention. Such cases are simply not useful to advocate for political and institutional changes. This also negatively affects other persons living or working in the margins of legality, such as drug addicts, sex workers or slum residents.

What role does human rights law play in addressing the situation of marginalised and/or vulnerable persons?

Language and categories are of course important, especially when we talk about the legal frameworks developed to protect people from harm. However, from the perspective of the victims, international or national laws have often done very little to protect them in their daily dealings with different forms of authorities. This is a global phenomenon. Laws and legal systems are only as good as the political system in which they are situated and meant to operate. If we don't implement laws in practice, that is in the daily administration of justice in the interactions between police and citizens (and non-nationals), then human rights laws become a hollow reference point for the few that have time, interest and resources to care about them. Protection should not be seen as only coming into play reactively after the violation has happened and when a person has chosen to step forward with his or her grievances and injuries seeking redress and compensation. It should be regarded as a preventive safeguard against violations. In other words, we don't necessarily need more laws or standards, what we need is their implementation into rule-of-law practices.

Has your research influenced your views on international human rights law?

Well. Yes and no. The research has confirmed the challenges of human rights, and of those working within the human rights field. Implementation into practice is the main overarching problem and has been so for years, if not since human rights came about as an ideal and global system. On the one hand, it has taught us to be even more attentive to the political spheres of society, the wheeling and dealing of power politics and its implications for policy and practice, and change of policy and practice. On the other, it has shown us that we need to continue to support the activists who work on the ground to change the conditions of the poor and marginal, and that laws are not enough – political openness and leadership combined with institutional capacity and willingness are necessary components for substantial reform and improvement. Without the activists, no one would provide information and knowledge about the effects of unequal rule on ordinary people, and no one would fight for those who cannot fight for themselves, or provide support for those who are committed to fight for rights, equality and justice.

QUESTIONS

1. What is the importance of interdisciplinary, empirical research for the development of international human rights law, and forms of protection?
2. Why is research with persons who are in a vulnerable situation particularly challenging? Consider the role of the researcher, and the position and interests of the persons who are the research subjects.

13.3.5   Old Age

Age creates vulnerabilities at both extremes, namely the young (children) and the old. Unlike the situation of children, where the related vulnerability emanates from the imbalance in power and awareness in relation to adults, the plight of old age is similar to the issues encountered with persons with disabilities. It is not surprising, therefore, that the principles enunciated in the CRPD are commonly applied to explain both the status and attendant rights of old persons, *mutatis mutandis*. In this sense, old age does not in and by itself prevent a person from enjoying the full gamut of rights available to everyone; rather, existing social and physical environments and attitudes, among others, prevent older persons from exercising those rights to their fullest possible degree.[83]

Old age is a challenging phenomenon for states and the international community. A huge amount of investment in human capital and financial resources goes into health care, medical research, nutrition and healthier living, all with the aim of extending the quality and duration of life. While these are fantastic human achievements, they imbalance the demographic ratio between the old (generally, persons over sixty) and the young, chiefly because birth rates are slower as compared to the ageing population, which in turn strains public finances. By way of illustration, the pensionable age limit has increased manifold over the last forty years, while the total amount paid out to pensions has generally decreased in order to finance the unexpected longevity of existing pensioners. Some statistics are useful in order to understand the relevant concerns. Average life expectancy at birth will be thirty years higher in 2050 as compared to 1950. In Europe and North America, between 1998 and 2025, the proportion of persons classified as older will have increased from 20 to 28 per cent and 16 to 26 per cent respectively. Globally, 'the proportion of persons aged sixty years and older will have doubled between 2000 and 2050, from 10 to 21 per cent, whereas the proportion of children is projected to drop by a third, from 30 to 21 per cent'.[84]

While these figures are important in order for states to adapt their demographic agendas, rethink their immigration, pensions and other policies, they cannot in any way entail that the rights of older persons should be subsidiary to financial or demographic considerations. Human rights are enjoyed by 'everyone' to the same degree, irrespective of old age, as enunciated in article 25(1) UDHR and general international human rights law. A terminally ill old person has the same right to health care (with its associated cost) as a child.[85] There is nothing in international or domestic law, or indeed in our value systems, suggesting that the value of life and its attendant dignity should be measured by its projected longevity. As a result, all socio-economic and civil and political rights apply to all persons irrespective of old age. But what type

---

[83] See D. Rodríguez-Pinzón and C. Martin, 'The International Human Rights Status of Elderly Persons' (2003) 18 *American University International Law Review* 915.

[84] Madrid International Plan of Action, Second World Assembly on Ageing (2002) paras. 2 and 3.

[85] See to this effect, CESCR, The Economic, Social and Cultural Rights of Older Persons: General Comment 6, UN doc. E/C.12/1995/16/Rev.1 (12 August 1995) paras. 10–11, in its interpretation of art. 12 ICESCR on the right to health; such tenets of equality have been applied to pensions, by the UN HRCtee in *Brooks* v. *Netherlands* (1987) para. 12.4.

of equality and non-discrimination is required in the context of old persons? equality of opportunity, of consistent outcomes or rather transformative equality?[86] The latter best corresponds to the particular exigencies of older persons. Fredman has posited the four strands of transformative equality as follows: (1) overcoming the cycle of disadvantage, (2) promoting respect for dignity and worth, (3) accommodating difference through structural change, and (4) promoting social and political inclusion and participation.[87] This type of transformative/structural equality is consistent with the CRPD approach,[88] as well as the limited number of international instruments addressing the rights of the elderly (otherwise known as elder rights).

Besides old age discrimination,[89] or welfare in the workplace,[90] the focus of this section is on the set of internationally recognised transformative rights that should be made affordable to older persons, not as new rights but as transformative manifestations of existing rights, justified by reason of their particular vulnerability. The key instruments are the Madrid Political Declaration and International Plan of Action on Ageing; the UN Principles for Older Persons[91] and the Inter-American Convention on Protecting the Human Rights of Older Persons (2015). The principles emanating from these instruments are as follows:

- Independence: Older persons should have the opportunity to work or to have access to other income-generating opportunities, as well as to appropriate educational and training programmes. Moreover, they should be able to live in environments that are safe and adaptable to personal preferences and changing capacities, as well as to reside at home for as long as possible.
- Participation: Older persons should remain integrated in society, participate actively in the formulation and implementation of policies that directly affect their well-being, and share their knowledge and skills with younger generations. This includes the opportunity to seek and develop opportunities for service to the community and to serve as volunteers in positions appropriate to their interests and capabilities.
- Care: Older persons should benefit from family and community care and protection in accordance with each society's system of cultural values.

---

[86] J. Clifford, 'Equality', in D. Shelton (ed.), *The Oxford Handbook of International Human Rights Law* (Oxford University Press, 2013) 420–45.

[87] S. Fredman, *Discrimination Law*, 2nd edn (Clarendon Press, 2011) 25.

[88] See J. L. Corsi, 'Article 5' in Bantekas, Stein and Anastasiou, above note 66, 140–1.

[89] This is a field in which the CJEU has produced a significant body of case. In *Mangold* v. *Helm* (CJEU) (2005), it was held that the prohibition against age discrimination was a principle in both international and EU law.

[90] The ILO is particularly active in this regard. See ILO Convention 128: Invalidity, Old Age and Survivors' Benefits (1967); ILO Recommendation 162: Older Worker (1980).

[91] UNGA resolution 46/91 (16 December 1991).

This includes access to health care to help them to maintain or regain the optimum level of physical, mental and emotional well-being and to prevent or delay the onset of illness. Older persons should be able to enjoy human rights and fundamental freedoms when residing in any shelter, care or treatment facility, including full respect for their dignity, beliefs, needs and privacy and for the right to make decisions about their care and the quality of their lives.

- Self-fulfilment: Older persons should be able to pursue opportunities for the full development of their potential, including access to the educational, cultural, spiritual and recreational resources of society.
- Dignity: Older persons should be able to live in dignity and security and be free of exploitation and physical or mental abuse. Moreover, they must be treated fairly regardless of age, gender, racial or ethnic background, disability or other status, and be valued independently of their economic contribution.

Although these principles are self-evident, the vulnerabilities of older persons routinely allow them to fall prey to exploitation, as well as physical or mental abuse.[92]

13.3.6   Refugees and Migrants

13.3.6.1   The Protection of Persons in Flight or Movement

The following two subsections will explore two distinct, yet very much inter-related phenomena, forced and unforced migration. While during the nineteenth and early twentieth centuries there were few restrictions on the freedom of aliens to settle in countries other than their own, particularly in the new world and territories under colonial rule, in the aftermath of World War I this was no longer the case.[93] Whereas migration was now very much limited and controlled by receiving states according to their own labour needs, the uprooting caused by World War II solidified the need for special protection to persons forced to abandon their own country on account of persecution.[94] Persons subject to such persecution are classified as refugees

---

[92] See WHO, *'Ageing and Life Course: Elder Abuse'* (WHO, 2009); A. Ash, *Safeguarding Older People from Abuse: Critical Context to Policy and Practice* (Policy Press, 2004).

[93] See on the colonial and post-colonial dimension of migration, E. T. Achiume, 'Reimagining International Law for Global Migration: Migration as Decolonization' (2017) 11 *AJIL Unbound* 142.

[94] Prior to the landmark 1951 Refugee Convention, the League of Nations adopted two other instruments to deal with stateless persons and refugees leading up to World War II, namely the 1933 Convention relating to the international status of refugees, 159 LNTS 3663 and the 1938 Convention concerning the status of refugees coming from Germany, 192 LNTS 4461.

under the 1951 Convention relating to the status of refugees (Refugee Convention),[95] whereas (other) migrants are here referred to as those who traverse international frontiers while lacking the element of persecution. Migrants may further be classified as regular, in which case they satisfy the entry requirements of the receiving state, and irregular, on the basis that their entry is illegal because they are not refugees and they do not have the receiving country's consent for entry.[96]

In between refugees and migrants one finds further sub-categories. Persons who are not persecuted as such, but whose flight is necessitated by a natural (e.g. tsunami or earthquake) or man-made disaster (war), may either traverse to a different part of their own country or to another country. Where flight is the result of a man-made or a natural disaster and the person does not cross an international border for fear of persecution, he or she is characterised as an internally displaced person (IDP). Conversely, the status of a person fleeing abroad from the effects of any of the aforementioned disasters is inconsistent.[97] Everyone, particularly civilians, caught in a war zone is susceptible to the risks associated with armed conflict, but such risks in and by themselves do not amount to persecution. As a general rule, therefore, war victims are subject to the protection established by international humanitarian law (IHL), which includes the obligations of the warring parties to respect civilians and distinguish at all times between civilian and non-civilian objectives.[98] In *Adan* v. *Secretary of State for the Home Department*, the House of Lords refused to grant asylum to a Somali fleeing his country's civil war, considering that the civil war did not give rise to a well-founded fear of persecution, even if the war was fought on religious or racial grounds.[99] Such persons may be granted

---

[95] While the 1951 Refugee Convention is the universal instrument for the classification of refugee status and rights thereof, other exceptional and people-specific classifications do exist. The UN Relief and Works Agency for Palestine (UNRWA), for example, in the first Interim Report of its Director, UN doc.A/1451/Rev.1, Supp. 19 (1951) para. 15, took the position that: 'For working purposes, the Agency has decided that a refugee is a needy person, who, as a result of the war in Palestine, has lost his home and his means of livelihood. A large measure of flexibility in the interpretation of the above definition is accorded to chief district officers to meet the many border-line cases which inevitably arise.'

[96] Although states are under no obligation to accept irregular migrants, exceptionally, art. 5 of Directive 2008/115/EC (16 December 2008) on common standards and procedures for returning illegally staying third-country nationals [Returns Directive] stipulates that in deciding to return irregular migrants member states must consider the child's best interests, family life, the applicant's health and the principle of *non-refoulement*.

[97] Exceptionally, in accordance with art. I(2) of the 1969 OAU [now AU] Convention concerning the specific aspects of refugee problems in Africa, the definition of a refugee encompasses, in addition to the 1951 Refugee Convention 'events seriously disturbing public order'.

[98] See Chapter 16.2.1.

[99] *Adan* v. *Secretary of State for the Home Dept* (UK) (1991) para. 311.

exceptional refuge (but not refugee status) on humanitarian grounds.[100] Several courts have taken the view that if the violence in a conflict zone is persecutory in nature and individualised then any person subject to it may validly be entitled to (subsidiary) protection.[101] The UN High Commissioner for Refugees endorsed and elaborated on this position in the guidelines on international protection adopted in 2016.[102]

Another category of persons falling outside the legal definition of refugee are those rendered stateless, whether by choice or compulsion, as long as the flight was not the result of persecution; otherwise, a stateless person may also be a refugee.[103] While international law has always allowed states to control the entry of aliens into their territory as well as the authority to confer nationality, the legal effects of the latter authority against other states are regulated by international law.[104] As a result, it is impermissible for states to strip persons of their sole nationality (thus rendering them stateless),[105] as is also the case with persons residing in a state over several generations or the entirety of their life who are denied the nationality of their country of residence and who possess no other nationality. The Bidoon people in Kuwait, for example, have lived there since time immemorial and constitute 10 per cent of the country's population, but have not been given Kuwaiti

---

[100] Article 15(c) EU Directive 2004/83/EC (29 April 2004) on minimum standards for the qualification and status of third-country nationals or stateless persons as refugees or as persons who otherwise need international protection and the content of the protection granted [Qualifications Directive]. See the CJEU decision in *Meki Elgafaji and Noor Elgafaji* v. *Staatssecretaris van Justitie* (CJEU) (2009), which held that the existence of a serious individual threat may be established where the degree of indiscriminate violence in an armed conflict reaches such a high level that substantial grounds are shown for believing that a civilian, returned to the relevant country would, solely on account of his presence on the territory of that country or region, face a real risk of being subject to that threat.

[101] See *Minister for Immigration and Multicultural Affairs* v. *Abdi* (Australia) (1999) paras. 37, 39; *QD and AH (Iraq)* v. *Secretary of State for Home Dept with the UNHCR intervening* (UK) (2009), where the Court of Appeal held that for the purposes of art. 15(c) EU Qualifications Directive one would have to show that incidents of indiscriminate violence 'were happening on a wide scale and in such a way as to be of sufficient severity to pose a real risk of serious harm ... to civilians generally'. In general terms, art. 15(b) and (c) of the EU Qualifications Directive covers non-targeted harm.

[102] UNHCR, Guidelines on International Protection No. 12: Claims for refugee status related to situations of armed conflict and violence under Article 1A(2) of the 1951 Convention and/ or 1967 Protocol relating to the Status of Refugees and the regional refugee definitions (2 December 2016) HCR/GIP/16/12.

[103] See M. Foster and H. Lambert, *International Refugee Law and the Protection of Stateless Persons* (Oxford University Press, 2019).

[104] *Liechtenstein* v. *Guatemala (Nottebohm case)* (ICJ) (1955).

[105] See 1954 Convention relating to the status of stateless persons, which concerns the rights of such persons in their country of residence and the 1961 Convention on the reduction of statelessness, art. 8 of which prohibits rendering a person stateless.

nationality.[106] Given that no country is obliged to provide asylum to a state-less person who does not meet the relevant criteria,[107] concerned persons would effectively be under the protection of no country and hence would be forced to enter the territory of other nations illegally (in addition to the financial and other burdens imposed on receiving states). With all the various sub-regimes of migration (e.g. refugees, migrants, smuggled or trafficked persons) it is easy to lose sight of the most fundamental of rules, namely that all aliens at international borders are entitled to the enjoyment of fundamental human rights.[108] As a corollary to refugee and migration phenomena it is impermissible for states as a matter of international law to refuse entry to their nationals.[109] This rule is particularly important in situations where refugees or other persons in flight wish to return following the cessation of the conditions that caused them to flee.[110] Technically speaking, the application of this rule to situations where a new state comes into existence whereby certain people were never its nationals, as is the case with Palestinians outside of Israel, is problematic and would need to be resolved through general international law.[111]

13.3.6.2 *The Protection of Refugees in International Law*

The starting point for any discussion on the protection of refugees is the Refugee Convention, which has been ratified by the vast majority of states. Although its ambit was in theory limited to pre-1951 and European refugees, few states in fact chose such a restrictive application and in any event the 1967 Protocol relating to the status of refugees effectively removed the geographic and temporal limits of the Refugee Convention to all persons. According to article 1A(2) of the Refugee Convention, the term refugee shall apply to any person who:

owing to a well-founded fear of being persecuted for reasons of race, religion, nationality, membership of a particular social group, or political opinion, is outside

---

[106] See https://minorityrights.org/minorities/bidoon/.

[107] In fact, the general rule under international law is enshrined in arts. 3 and 4 of the ILC's Draft Articles on Expulsion of Aliens (2014), according to which states are entitled to expel aliens provided such expulsion is in pursuance of a lawful decision and in conformity with international law.

[108] See Principles and Guidelines on human rights at international borders, UN doc. A/69/CRP.1 (23 July 2014).

[109] Art. 12(4) ICCPR.

[110] See E. Rosand, 'The Right to Return Under International Law Following Mass Dislocation: The Bosnia Precedent?' (1998) 19 *Michigan Journal of International Law* 1091.

[111] For an Israeli perspective, see R. Lapidoth, 'The Right of Return in International Law, with Special Reference to the Palestinian Refugees' (1986) 16 *Israel Yearbook of Human Rights* 103.

the country of his nationality and is unable, or owing to such fear, is unwilling to avail himself of the protection of that country; or who, not having a nationality and being outside the country of his former habitual residence as a result of such events, is unable or, owing to such fear, is unwilling to return to it.

This is a loaded definition which national courts have interpreted in different and often progressive ways in order to encompass more categories of persons.[112] It remains fundamental to this day in construing asylum claims. Despite the fact that a person meeting the criteria of article 1A(2) is automatically a refugee, because there does not exist a monitoring body or international enforcement mechanism, the ultimate granting of asylum lies at the 'discretion' of the state where an asylum application is made. This means that national case law on refugee determination is of the utmost importance and in practice progressive case law does find its way into transnational judicial dialogue, which in turn informs pertinent national policies.[113] It should be stated from the outset that it is now generally recognised that refugee rights (including the rights of migrants) are human rights and not simply a *sui generis* body of law that is divorced from the general framework of international human rights. The significance of this observation lies in the fact that states cannot claim that international refugee law was meant to reinforce national security law.[114]

Clearly, the claimant must be outside the country of his or her nationality when making a claim, although the definition also covers those who are already abroad but who are unable to return because of the risk of a particular form of persecution (known as *sur place* refugees);[115] some countries have accepted that asylum claims might be made at their embassies. As a result, refugee status is acquired once the person fleeing persecution leaves his or her country, albeit the protection owed to refugees under the

---

[112] By way of illustration, it has been held that 'different cultural norms and social imperatives may give rise to different sources of persecution ... The concept is not a static one.' *A* v. *Minister for Immigration and Ethnic Affairs* (Australia) (1997) at 293–4. See for a detailed discussion of the interpretation of art. 1, J. C. Hathaway and M. Foster, *The Law of Refugee Status*, 2nd edn (Cambridge University Press, 2014).

[113] Evidence of the impact of such transnational judicial dialogue may be found in H. Lambert, J. McAdam and M. Fullerton (eds.), *The Global Reach of European Refugee Law* (Cambridge University Press, 2013).

[114] See V. Chetail, 'Are Refugee Rights Human Rights? An Unorthodox Questioning of the Relations between Refugee Law and Human Rights Law', in R. Rubio-Marin (ed.), *Human Rights and Immigration* (Oxford University Press, 2014) 20.

[115] See A. Zimmermann and C. Mahler, 'Article 1 A, para. 2', in A. Zimmermann (ed.), *Commentary on the 1951 Convention relating to the Status of Refugees and its 1967 Protocol* (Oxford University Press, 2013) 324ff. In *Khakdar* v. *Russia* (HRCtee) (2014) paras. 11.4 and 13, it was accepted that an Afghan pro-Russian who had lived in Afghanistan for over twenty years would be at risk of death and torture by Taliban insurgents if returned to Afghanistan.

Convention is not granted until such time as the person comes within the de facto jurisdiction of another state. It is obvious that in the majority of cases the refugee's entry into the territory of another state will be unlawful, but no penalties for unlawful entry may be imposed on persons meeting the refugee criteria. In order to bypass their obligation to accept and process a refugee at their border (and ultimately refuse asylum) several states, many acting in common, as is the case with the EU, interdict vessels carrying refugees and migrants on the high seas, or at their common borders, and return them to the continent (or country) of their origin. The UK has even refused to participate or support salvage operations in the Mediterranean under the assumption that this would entice asylum seekers. The absence of a unified EU policy, uneven burden-sharing and disregard for human dignity, among others, was responsible for the loss of life of more than 400 asylum seekers off Italian waters in April 2015.[116] Australia, on the other hand, had pursued a policy of interdicting such persons on the high seas and sending them to island states reliant on its financial aid in the Pacific (Nauru and Papua New Guinea) for processing.[117] Such practices are legally untenable in light of the principle that a state's jurisdiction extends to territory (including vessels)[118] over which it exercises effective control.[119] Moreover, abandoning a refugee on the high seas in fact amounts to *refoulement*. In those cases where refugees unlawfully interned are later 'integrated' with the local population, as is the case with Australia, evidence suggests that they receive minimal support and ultimately become destitute and subject to exploitation.[120]

The claimant must next demonstrate the existence of a serious risk of harm ('owing to a well-founded fear of being persecuted'). The case law of major refugee destination countries demonstrates that the appropriate test for apprehending the seriousness of the risk is an objective, rather than a subjective, one. The risk need not have already occurred (if it has, it is certainly

---

[116] As a result, the EU Joint Foreign and Home Affairs Council announced a ten-point plan to address the aftermath of the disaster on 20 April 2015. Available at: http://europa.eu/rapid/press-release_IP-15-4813_en.htm

[117] See Australian Refugee Council, 'Report on Australia's Man-Made Crisis on Nauru' (3 September 2018), www.refugeecouncil.org.au/nauru-report/2/, which recounts how the remainder of the people are now 'broken'.

[118] *Hirsi Jamaa and others* v. *Italy* (ECtHR) (2012), where an Italian military vessel rescued a vessel sailing towards Italian waters containing African migrants and proceeded to hand them over to Libya. The ECtHR held that Italy was aware of the treatment afforded by the Libyan authorities at the time and hence that its *refoulement* of the immigrants contravened fundamental rights. In any event, the Italian military vessel was tantamount to Italian territory for the purposes of jurisdiction.

[119] See e.g., *Al-Skeini and Others* v. *UK* (ECtHR) (2011).

[120] See 'With Empty Hands: How the Australian Government is Forcing People Seeking Asylum Into Destitution' (18 June 2018), www.refugeecouncil.org.au/with-empty-hands-destitution/.

proof of an impending risk); rather, the fear must be predicated on a forward-looking appraisal whereby there is a reasonable likelihood that it may materialise ('being persecuted' as opposed to 'having been persecuted').[121] In practice, the courts solicit the assistance of country experts who furnish pertinent data, the aim of which is to provide evidence of 'sustained or systemic violations of basic human rights demonstrative of a failure of state protection'.[122] Some courts are prepared to accept that serious harm encompasses not merely violations of fundamental civil and political rights, but also socio-economic rights, such as access to food and medical treatment.[123]

The risk of serious harm must be accompanied by an absence or failure of state protection. Unlike the exhaustion of local remedies rule, there is no requirement that the applicant has even sought protection from his or her country of nationality. The origin of the risk is equally irrelevant. In a world of many failed states it is natural that organised crime and paramilitary groups operate in parallel or well above the organs of the state. As a result, the failure of the state to engage its positive obligation to suppress threats against its people arising from non-governmental entities amounts to a failure to protect under article 1A(2) of the Refugee Convention. Such failure must be assessed objectively, that is, in accordance with the meaning of the term 'unable or unwilling' as this is understood under general international law.[124]

What has generated significant controversy is the nexus between the claimant and his or her status. Essentially, the risk of serious harm must be linked to the person's race, religion, nationality, membership of a particular social group or political opinion, irrespective of whether the person actually enjoys the particular status, so long as he or she is perceived to enjoy that status (even wrongly). Whereas being persecuted on the basis of one's race, religion and nationality is largely self-explanatory, membership of a social group and holding a particular opinion are not. In respect of the latter, it is not necessary that the person has actually acted on his or her opinion or belief,[125] but there is some divergence as to the scope of what constitutes a political opinion. On the one extreme, it is understood as encompassing an

---

[121] *R* v. *Secretary of State for the Home Dept, ex parte Sivakumaran* (UK) (1998); *Immigration and Naturalization Service* v. *Cardoza-Fonseca* (US) (1987).

[122] *Canada (Attorney-General)* v. *Ward* (Canada) (1993) 689; *HJ (Iran) and HT (Cameroon)* v. *Secretary of State for the Home Dept* (UK) (2010). See on acts of persecution in particular art. 9 of the EU Qualification Directive 2011/95/EU.

[123] *Chen Shi Hai* v. *Minister for Immigration and Multicultural Affairs* (Australia) (2000); *Chen* v. *Holder* (US) (2010) at 334, which iterated that persecution may also be in the form of economic deprivation.

[124] *Re Minister for Immigration and Multicultural Affairs, ex parte Miah* (Australia) (2001).

[125] UNHCR, 'Handbook and Guidelines on Procedures and Criteria for Determining Refugee Status' (2011, revised) 79ff.

opinion 'on any matter in which the machinery of state, government and policy may be engaged',[126] whereas on the other it does not cover all issues with a political dimension as this would necessarily extend to all aspects of society.[127]

The non-static nature of the notion of social groups has evolved since 1951 in accordance with our ever-growing understanding of culture, social roles and gender,[128] and on the basis that the protected social groups enjoy 'immutable' or 'unchangeable' characteristics. In fact, the 2002 UNHCR Guidelines on 'Membership of a Particular Social Group' make it clear that:

> the term membership of a particular social group should be read in an evolutionary manner, open to the diverse and changing nature of groups in various societies and evolving international human rights norms.[129]

Although an elaborate examination of all social groups is beyond the scope of this brief section, two groups stand out, namely women and LGBTI persons. As to women, the 2002 UNHCR Guidelines on Gender-related Persecution stipulate that:

> While female and male applicants may be subjected to the same forms of harm, they may also face forms of persecution specific to their sex. International human rights law and international criminal law clearly identify certain acts as violations of these laws, such as sexual violence, and support their characterization as serious abuses, amounting to persecution. ... There is no doubt that rape and other forms of gender- related violence, such as dowry-related violence, female genital mutilation, domestic violence and trafficking are acts which inflict severe pain and suffering – both mental and physical – and which have been used as forms of persecution, whether perpetrated by state or private actors.[130]

As a result, women may be subjected to one or more forms of persecution (rape, female genital mutilation) by their state, tribe or other non-state actors solely on the basis of their gender (but in practice through membership of a women's subgroup). The House of Lords has accepted that a woman raped and ill-treated in Iran, as well as another woman from Sierra Leone facing female genital mutilation there satisfied the existence of a well-founded fear

---

[126] *Canada* v. *Ward* (Canada) (1993) at 693, 746.

[127] By way of illustration, the US Supreme Court has held that resisting recruitment by guerillas did not amount to a political opinion: *Immigration and Naturalization Service* v. *Elias Zacarias* (US) (1992); on the contrary, espousing neutrality during a civil war was found to constitute a political opinion in *Bolanos-Hernandez* v. *Immigration and Naturalization Service* (US) (1984).

[128] See Chapter 11 on gender and women's rights.

[129] UN doc. HCR/GIP/02/02 (7 May 2002) para. 3.

[130] UNHCR, Guidelines on Gender-related Persecution (2002), UN doc. HCR/GIP/02/01 (7 May 2002) para. 9; see also art. 9(2)(a) and (f), EU Qualification Directive.

of persecution as a result of their membership in the social group in the countries under consideration.[131]

In jurisdictions accepting that a person may have a well-founded fear of persecution on account of his or her sexual orientation it is assumed that such orientation is immutable.[132] It is emphasised in judgments and commentaries that in assessing membership of any of the aforementioned groups, membership should not be predicated on the duty to conceal one's identity ('social visibility test').[133] Rather, courts and administrative bodies do not refer to a social group comprising all lesbians or gay men, but rather restrict sexual orientation to a particular country or region, such as 'homosexual men in Bangladesh'.[134]

Having examined which persons qualify as refugees, let us now proceed to the rights affordable to such persons under the Refugee Convention. Unlike other human rights treaties where rights are affordable to all addressees immediately (subject to particular manifestations of progressive realization), the Refugee Convention recognises a system predicated on 'levels of attachment' whereby refugees are progressively entitled to a growing number of entitlements as their relationship with the asylum state deepens.[135] At the most fundamental level a refugee may not be expelled or returned (*refoulé*) to a country where his or her life or freedom would be threatened.[136] This *non-refoulement* principle constitutes the cornerstone of the Convention. Although this principle does not establish a duty to receive (i.e. grant asylum) refugees, in practice it 'amounts to a de facto duty to admit the refugee, since admission is normally the only means of avoiding the alternative, impermissible

---

[131] *Fornah and K v. Secretary of State for the Home Dept* (UK) (2006); see also *Islam v. Secretary of State for the Home Department* and *R v. IAT, ex parte Shah* (UK) (1999); CEDAW Committee Recommendation 32, on the gender-related dimensions of refugee status, asylum, nationality and statelessness of women (14 November 2014); see also E. Arbel, C. Dauvergne and J. Millbank (eds.), *Gender in Refugee Law: From the Margins to the Centre* (Routledge, 2014).

[132] *Canada v. Ward* (Canada) (1993); art. 10(1)(d) EU Qualifications Directive; *MI v. Sweden* (HRCtee) (2013) para. 7.5, where the Swedish authorities refused asylum to a Bangladeshi lesbian woman by focusing on inconsistencies in her account, despite the fact that she was obviously lesbian, was forced to marry and was likely to be prosecuted in her native country.

[133] See *HJ (Iran) and HT (Cameroon) v. Secretary of State for the Home Department*, where the UK Supreme Court sets out the approach to take when considering asylum claims on the grounds of sexual orientation in terms of how to consider whether an individual's fear was well-founded through an examination of their behaviour on return and the consequences of such behaviour.

[134] Zimmermann, above note 115, 426–7.

[135] J. C. Hathaway, 'Refugees and Asylum', in B. Opeskin, R. Perruchoud and J. Redpath-Cross (eds.), *Foundations of International Migration Law* (Cambridge University Press, 2012) 191.

[136] Article 33 Refugee Convention; equally, art. 78 TFEU.

consequence of exposure to risk'.[137] Higher levels of attachment materialise once the refugee is physically present on the territory of the asylum state and later, when he or she is lawfully present or lawfully staying there. At these higher levels the refugee is entitled to a broad range of socio-economic rights with immediate effect, such as the right to movable and immovable property (article 13), the right of association (article 15), access to justice (article 16), the right to work and employment (articles 17–19). As will be demonstrated in the next section, asylum seekers (who do not qualify as refugees) enjoy rights under general international human rights law.[138]

A key policy concern with significant impact on both the fate of asylum applications and the treatment of applicants is that of burden, or responsibility sharing. Despite the intense media spotlight in the West regarding massive refugee flows to Europe, the actual number of refugees in Europe is minimal. Of the 25.4 million refugees registered by UNHCR in mid-2018, 3.5 million were hosted by Turkey, 1 million by Lebanon and Iran and an additional 1.4 million by Uganda and Pakistan.[139] During the same time the European continent hosted 2.6 million refugees,[140] which accounts for approximately 9.7 per cent of the global refugee population. While it is true that states in the global north accept a significant number of refugee applications themselves and agree to grant asylum to some refugees, in many nations in the southern hemisphere the numbers of refugees render the burden ratio staggering. The situation is further compounded by countries such as China, which ignore their obligations under the Refugee Convention and routinely return vulnerable refugees, such as those from North Korea, being fully aware of the risk of execution.[141]

The effects of uneven responsibility sharing on the refugees' fundamental rights are nowhere more evident than in Europe. This has led to several initiatives. At the UN level it is worth mentioning two UN Global Compacts: the first on Migration[142] and another on Refugees,[143] which seek to improve migration governance and cooperation respectively, with regard

---

[137] Hathaway, above note 135, 193.

[138] In *Federaal agentschap voor de opvang van asielzoekers* v. *Saciri and Others* (CJEU) (2014) para. 46, it was held that if a member state chooses to provide material reception to asylum seekers in the form of a financial allowance rather than direct public services, the allowance must be enough to ensure a dignified standard of living; see also art. 13, ILC Draft Articles on the Expulsion of Aliens (2014).

[139] See www.unhcr.org/figures-at-a-glance.html.

[140] UNHCR, *Global Trends: Forced Displacement in 2017* (UNHCR 2017) 13.

[141] See R. Aldrich, 'An Examination of China's Treatment of North Korean Asylum Seekers' (2011) 7 *North Korean Review* 36, who states that China views fleeing North Koreans as 'economic migrants'!

[142] See https://refugeesmigrants.un.org/migration-compact.

[143] See www.unhcr.org/towards-a-global-compact-on-refugees.html.

to refugees.[144] The EU operates its own internal system under the so-called Dublin Regulations (currently Regulation III), whereby an asylum seeker, subject to certain exceptions, must be sent to the EU state of first arrival by the EU state to which he has subsequently moved on in order to lodge an asylum application.[145] Given that asylum seekers in Europe arrive at its external frontiers on foot or by boat it is evident that the Dublin system disproportionately disadvantages countries such as Greece, Spain and Italy. In 'meeting' their obligation, in turn, these countries routinely and systematically violate the rights of detained migrants and refugees, principally as regards the length and quality of detention conditions and access to justice.[146] In *MSS* v. *Greece and Belgium* the ECtHR emphasised that the transfer of an Afghan asylum seeker to Greece by Belgium, in accordance with the then Dublin II regulation, exposed him to risks associated with deficient Greek asylum procedures and appalling detention conditions. As a result, Belgium, along with Greece, was held liable for a breach of articles 3 and 13 of the ECHR.[147] As a result of such violations, article 3(2) of Dublin III regulation now states that:

Where it is impossible to transfer an applicant to the member state primarily designated as responsible because there are substantial grounds for believing that there are systemic flaws in the asylum procedure and in the reception conditions for applicants in that member state, resulting in a risk of inhuman or degrading treatment within the meaning of Article 4 of the Charter of Fundamental Rights of the European Union, the determining member state shall continue to examine the criteria set out in Chapter III in order to establish whether another Member State can be designated as responsible. Where the transfer cannot be made ... the determining member state shall become the member state responsible.[148]

---

[144] For a background, see www.kaldorcentre.unsw.edu.au/publication/2018-global-compacts-refugees-and-migration.

[145] Article 10, EU Regulation 343/2003 (18 February 2003) establishing the criteria and mechanisms for determining the member state responsible for examining an asylum application lodged in one of the member states by a third-country national. Article 3(2) of Regulation 604/2013 [Dublin III] iterates this rule subject to the exception listed.

[146] *F. H.* v. *Greece* (ECtHR) (2014); in *KRS* v. *UK* (ECtHR) (2009), the ECtHR noted that a transfer to Greece under the terms of the Dublin II Regulation presumes that Greece shall respect the person's rights under the ECHR.

[147] *MSS* v. *Greece and Belgium* (ECtHR) (2011).

[148] See *Tarakhel* v. *Switzerland* (ECtHR) (2014), where it was confirmed that although an Afghan family's first landing in Italy should ordinarily have meant that under the Dublin regime the Swiss authorities (where the family subsequently moved on) should send them to Italy, the poor conditions in Italy (and the risk that the family may be split) necessitated that Switzerland assess their applications. See also T. Gammeltoft-Hansen, *Access to Asylum* (Cambridge University Press, 2013) chs. 4–5, who argues that states increasingly outsource migration control to third countries to evade their obligations. At the time of writing, negotiations were ongoing (but pretty much at a standstill) for a new Dublin Agreement.

13.3.6.3   The Protection of Migrants

On the basis of their immigration policies, two extreme state practices may be identified: those recognising permanent settlement, which in turn grant migrants the full gamut of political and socio-economic rights, and those that reject the idea of permanent settlement.[149] The aim of pluralism sought in the first extreme is considered a threat to national unity in the latter and even where immigrants are allowed to settle their integration seldom leads to full inclusion. Portes suggests that opponents of migration fear the profound cultural and structural transformations that migration may cause. 'The fears expressed by opponents of immigration commonly portray a ... movement rising out of the poorer nations of three continents and over-whelming the social systems and the culture of the developed world'.[150] He states that migration has been analysed as a cause of change from a cultural perspective (emphasising its potential for value/normative transformation), as well as from a structural one (highlighting its demographic and economic significance). He also points out that the depth of the processes of change attributed to migration vary from effects that 'simply scratch the surface of society, affecting some economic organizations, role expectations, or norms', to effects that 'may go deep into the culture, transforming the value system, or into the social structure, transforming the distribution of power'.[151]

Before examining the legal dimension of migration it is worth look-ing at some basic data that assist in elucidating this phenomenon. From a demographic perspective, migration is one among three processes that change populations, the others being fertility and mortality. It is univer-sally acknowledged that the balance of births over deaths (known as net natural increase), not net migration, is the major contributor to population growth.[152] Between 1960 and 2010 the global South suffered a net migra-tion loss of 92 million people, which is equivalent to 2 per cent of its 3.85 billion growth within this period. During the same period, the 92 million net migration gain in the global North was equivalent to 28 per cent of its 324.5 million population increase.[153] Whereas in the North the net natural increase is slower as compared to net immigration, the opposite is true in the South, although there is limited data concerning immigrant flows in poorer nations.

[149] S. Castles, H. de Haas and J. M. Miller, *The Age of Migration: International Population Movements in the Modern World* (Palgrave Macmillan, 2013) 14–15.

[150] A. Portes, 'Migration and Social Change: Some Conceptual Reflections' (2010) 36 *Journal of Ethnic and Migration Studies* 15–37, at 154–5.

[151] Ibid., at 1544; D. Mihail and A. Christou (eds.), *Intra-European Youth Mobility and Migration in an Era of Financial Crisis* (Stamoulis, 2015) 24–5.

[152] R. Bedford, 'Contemporary Patterns of International Migration', in Opeskin et al., above note 135, 17.

[153] Ibid.

Table 13.1 UNDP, *Human Development Report* (2013), at 185.

	Stock of emigrants[154]	Stock of immigrants	Net migration rate[155]
	[0% of population]		[per 1,000 people]
	2010	2010	2005–2010
Arab states	5.4	8.0	3.3
East Asia & Pacific	1.1	0.3	−0.5
Europe & Central Asia	10.3	6.5	−0.1
Latin America/Caribbean	5.3	1.1	−1.8
South Asia	1.6	0.8	−1.1
Sub-Saharan Africa	2.5	2.1	−0.5
LDCs	3.3	1.4	−1.4
WORLD	2.9	3.1	0.0

Demographers and immigration experts agree that the various patterns of migration (i.e. temporary, permanent, transiting, mobility, etc.), as well as the means by which this is achieved (particularly irregular migration), make it almost impossible to indicate the extent to which a particular population has been impacted by immigration. The closest we can come is through an assessment of the number of people in a state who were born in another state (so-called immigrant stocks). Table 13.1 provides a snapshot of immigrant movements across the globe, demonstrating that they constitute a small fraction of the overall population sizes.

With these considerations in mind and given the processes of globalisation, as explained in this chapter, oppressive migration policies are incongruous with increased labour demands and the insignificant demographics involved. For the remainder of this section we shall focus on the control of irregular migration and its human rights dimension.

State sovereignty entails the freedom to regulate entry into each nation. With the exception of their refugee obligations and other bilateral and multilateral agreements concerning foreign workers,[156] tourists and other classes of migrants (in the broad sense),[157] states may freely deny entry or

---

[154] Ratio of the stock of emigrants from a country to the population (not to the sum of population and emigrants), expressed as a percentage of the country's population. The definition of emigrant varies across countries, but generally refers to residents who left the country with the intention to remain abroad for more than a year.

[155] Ratio of the difference between the number of in-migrants and out-migrants from a country during a specified period to the average population during the period, expressed per 1,000 people.

[156] The 1990 International Convention on the Protection of the Rights of all Migrant Workers and Members of their Families aims to afford fundamental human rights to both documented and undocumented (or irregular) migrant workers and their families. It has not, however, been ratified by migrant-receiving states.

[157] For example, the 1994 General Agreement on Trade in Services, as well as the freedom of movement and establishment in the context of the EU treaties.

expel any undocumented (irregular) migrants, subject of course to *non-refoulement* considerations. As a result and in accordance with article 79 TFEU, the EU has adopted an elaborate common policy for tackling irregular migration. In this regard, it has established rules on control and surveillance,[158] a mechanism for collecting, processing and exchanging of visa data,[159] and FRONTEX, an agency for border surveillance that has a key role in supporting border control authorities.[160] The UN Special Rapporteur on the Human Rights of Migrants has emphasised that the hostility towards irregular migration is expressed through the externalization of migration control policies and criminalization of labour migration.[161] A typical example of the latter is Streamline Operation, which imposes federal prosecution and imprisonment against all unlawful border-crossers along the USA–Mexico boundary, irrespective of their criminal record or the purpose of their crossing.[162] As a result, this policy has placed a significant strain on local prosecutors and law-enforcement agencies and has distracted them from focusing on drug-trafficking, human trafficking and other real crimes.[163] Australia's Pacific Solution policy, briefly examined in the previous section, falls within this paradigm.

Some human rights exceptions to the state sovereignty paradigm exist, given that the rights enshrined in the UDHR and the two covenants cover 'all persons', including migrants. A distinction should be made between the admission of irregular migrants (which is optional) and the obligation to treat such persons in accordance with fundamental human rights, whether already (illegally) on the territory of the state or at its borders.[164] We have already seen that although states are not obliged to offer temporary shelter

---

[158] Regulation (EC) No. 562/2006 of 15 March 2006 establishing a Community Code on the rules governing the movement of persons across borders (Schengen Borders Code).

[159] Regulation (EC) No. 767/2008 of 9 July 2008 concerning the Visa Information System (VIS) and the exchange of data between member states on short-stay visas (VIS Regulation) and Council Decision 2004/512/EC of 8 June 2004 establishing the Visa Information System (VIS).

[160] Council Regulation (EC) 2007/2004 of 26 October 2004 and Regulation (EC) No. 863/2007 of 11 July 2007.

[161] UN Special Rapporteur Report, UN doc. A/HRC/7/12 (25 February 2008) paras. 13–59.

[162] See M. Valverde, 'What you Need to Know about the Trump Administration's Zero Tolerance Immigration Policy', available at: www.politifact.com/truth-o-meter/article/2018/jun/06/what-you-need-know-about-trump-administrations-zer/.

[163] In fact, because of the bulk of prosecutions, hearings are often conducted en masse with as many as eighty accused pleading guilty simultaneously. This clear deprivation of due process rights has been stricken down by federal courts. See *USA* v. *Roblero-Solis* (US) (2009).

[164] Indefinite detention that is not justified, as would otherwise be the case with 'an individualized likelihood of absconding, danger of crimes against others, or risk of acts against national security' is unlawful. See *FKAG et al* v. *Australia* (HRCtee) (2013) para. 9.3.

to persons who do not satisfy the refugee criteria, they usually do so exceptionally in the event of a humanitarian crisis. The detention criteria already examined in respect of refugees apply *mutatis mutandis* to irregular migrants within the territory of the receiving state.[165] The only difference is that the state may return or expel such persons, but this has to be achieved through a humane process that does not, moreover, expose such persons to inhuman or degrading treatment in the country of origin.[166] In the EU, irregular migrants are granted the choice of voluntary departure, which includes a period that takes into account 'the specific circumstances of the individual case, such as the length of stay, the existence of children attending school and the existence of other family and social links'.[167] Where the migrant does not voluntarily depart, and has exhausted appropriate remedies,[168] he or she may be forcibly removed.[169] Needless to say, there are serious concerns regarding current practices of detention and forced removals.

A rather acute dimension of irregular migration concerns trafficking of persons. For the sake of convenience (and relevance with this section) two broad categories are identified, namely persons trafficked without their consent (e.g. for prostitution) and those who consent to be smuggled, commonly for the purpose of finding a better life in another country. In both cases the smuggler/trafficker can only operate through the processes of organised crime, something which was identified by the international community which adopted two significant protocols in 2000; one relating to the smuggling of migrants[170] and another concerned with trafficking of persons.[171] Both protocols are linked to the 2000 UN Convention against Transnational Organized Crime, which views transnational trafficking and smuggling as organised crime activities. Despite their illegal entry into the territory of a country other than their own, both protocols clearly stipulate that neither the smuggled migrants nor the trafficked persons will incur criminal liability.[172] In fact, besides the extension of fundamental human rights guarantees to both categories,[173] both trafficked[174] and smuggled[175] persons are classified as victims[176] and are entitled to protection against violence from their

---

[165] See arts. 16–18 EU Returns Directive.   [166] Articles 9 and 10, ibid.
[167] Article 7(2), ibid.   [168] Article 13, ibid.   [169] Article 8, ibid.
[170] Protocol against the Smuggling of Migrants by Land, Sea and Air (2001) 40 ILM 335.
[171] Protocol to Prevent, Suppress and Punish Trafficking in Persons, Especially Women and Children (2001) 40 ILM 335.
[172] Article 5 Smuggling Protocol.
[173] Article 8(5) [measures to relieve imminent danger] and art. 9(1)(a) [ensure safety and humane treatment] of the Smuggling Protocol.
[174] Article 2(b) Trafficking Protocol.   [175] Article 16(1)–(4) Smuggling Protocol.
[176] It should be noted that victimhood is only expressly applied to trafficked persons under art. 2(b) of the Trafficking Protocol. However, the deprivations in their country of origin ultimately render those who consent to be smuggled just as vulnerable as victims of trafficking.

traffickers, as well as other appropriate measures to protect their rights to life, freedom from torture and inhuman and degrading treatment. As regards victims of trafficking, in particular, articles 6 to 8 of the Trafficking Protocol require states to recognize their victimhood and offer them all possible physical and legal protection. Although the emphasis is on voluntary repatriation, the Protocol makes the grant of a stay of a limited duration on humanitarian grounds. The Protocol is specifically envisaged as being in harmony with all other human rights instruments, and hence if the criteria of asylum are manifest, the victim may be regarded as a refugee. The same principle is iterated in articles 12–14 of the 2005 Council of Europe Convention on Action against Trafficking in Human Beings. In fact, article 14(1) stipulates that states shall issue a renewable residence permit to victims where: (a) the competent authority considers that their stay is necessary owing to their personal situation, or (b) their stay is necessary for the purpose of their cooperation with the competent authorities in investigation or criminal proceedings.

QUESTIONS

1. Is vulnerability a clearly understood and meaningful concept in international human rights law? What explains its prominence, and what, if any, are the potential drawbacks of focusing on vulnerability?
2. Poverty constitutes one of the major conceptual and practical challenges for international human rights law. Discuss.
3. One of the fundamental premises of the UN Disabilities Convention was that it did not create any rights that did not already exist. Do you agree with this statement or has the Convention actually introduced new rights?
4. A new immigration law in country A sets out objective criteria, namely professional qualifications and income, as criteria for the granting of entry and stay in the country. Opponents of the law argue that it discriminates on the basis of race and class. Would you agree? Would further evidence be needed to sustain the argument, and if so, what kind of evidence would be particularly persuasive? If the law is found to be discriminatory on the grounds of race and/or class, would it be incompatible with international human rights law, or are there exceptions in the field of immigration law?

FURTHER READING

Bagenstos, S. R., *Law and the Contradictions of the Disability Rights Movement* (Yale University Press, 2009).

Bantekas, I., M. A. Stein and D. Anastasiou (eds.), *The UN Convention on the Rights of Persons with*

Disabilities: A Commentary (Oxford University Press, 2018).

Chetail, V. and Bauloz, C. (eds.), *Research Handbook on International Law and Migration* (Edward Elgar, 2014).

Chong, D. P. L., *Freedom from Poverty: NGOs and Human Rights Praxis* (University of Pennsylvania Press, 2010).

Dauvergne, C., *Making People Illegal: What Globalization Means for Migration and Law* (Cambridge University Press, 2008).

Hathaway, J. C., *The Rights of Refugees under International Law* (Cambridge University Press, 2005).

Fineman, M. A., *Vulnerability: Reflections on a New Ethical Foundation for Law and Politics* (Princeton University Press, 2013).

Gallagher, A. T., *The International Law of Human Trafficking* (Cambridge University Press, 2010).

Gallagher, A. T., and F. David, *The International Law of Migrant Smuggling* (Cambridge University Press, 2014).

Goodwin-Gill, G. and J. McAdam, *The Refugee in International Law*, 3rd edn (Oxford University Press, 2007).

International Commission of Jurists, *Sexual Orientation and Gender Identity in Human Rights Law* (2010).

Johnson, P., *Homosexuality and the European Court of Human Rights* (Routledge, 2013).

Keane, D., and A. Waughray, *Fifty Years of the International Convention on the Elimination of All Forms of Racial Discrimination: A Living Instrument* (Manchester University Press, 2017).

Kotiswaran, P. (ed.), *Revisiting the Law and Governance of Trafficking, Forced Labor and Modern Slavery* (Cambridge University Press, 2017).

Martin, C., and D. Rodríguez-Pinzón, *Human Rights of Older People: Universal and Regional Legal Perspectives* (Springer, 2015).

Maru, M. T., *The Kampala Convention and its Contributions to International Law* (Eleven Publishing, 2014).

Nifosi-Sutton, I., *The Protection of Vulnerable Groups under International Human Rights Law* (Routledge, 2017).

Pogge, T. (ed.), *Freedom from Poverty as a Human Right: Who Owes What to the Very Poor* (UNESCO, Oxford University Press, 2007).

Sargeant, M. (ed.), *Age Discrimination and Diversity: Multiple Discrimination from an Age Perspective* (Cambridge University Press, 2011).

Thornberry, P., *The International Convention on the Elimination of All Forms of Racial Discrimination* (Oxford University Press, 2016).

Turner, B. S., *Vulnerability and Human Rights* (Pennsylvania State University Press, 2006).

Weissbrodt, D., and M. Rumsey (eds.), *Vulnerable and Marginalised Groups and Human Rights* (Edward Elgar, 2011).

Websites

Committee on the Elimination of Racial Discrimination: www.ohchr.org/en/hrbodies/cerd/pages/cerdindex.aspx

UN Special Rapporteur on contemporary forms of racism, racial discrimination, xenophobia and related intolerance: www.ohchr.org/EN/Issues/Racism/SRRacism/Pages/IndexSRRacism.aspx

UN Working Group of Experts on People of African Descent: ohchr.org/EN/Issues/Racism/WGAfricanDescent/Pages/WGEPADIndex.aspx

UN Independent Expert on protection against violence and discrimination based on sexual orientation and gender identity: www.ohchr.org/EN/Issues/SexualOrientationGender/Pages/Index.aspx

UN Special Rapporteur on violence against women, its causes and consequences: www.ohchr.org/EN/Issues/Women/SRWomen/Pages/SRWomenIndex.aspx

UN Working Group on the issue of discrimination against women in law and practice: www.ohchr.org/EN/Issues/Women/WGWomen/Pages/WGWomenIndex.aspx

UN Special Rapporteur on Extreme Poverty and Human Rights: www.ohchr.org/EN/Issues/Poverty/Pages/SRExtremePovertyIndex.aspx

OHCHR, Human rights dimension of poverty: www.ohchr.org/EN/Issues/Poverty/DimensionOfPoverty/Pages/Index.aspx

UN Special Rapporteur on the rights of persons with disabilities: www.ohchr.org/EN/Issues/Disability/SRDisabilities/Pages/SRDisabilitiesIndex.aspx

UN Special Rapporteur on the human rights of migrants: https://ohchr.org/EN/Issues/Migration/SRMigrants/Pages/SRMigrantsIndex.aspx

UN Special Rapporteur on the human rights of internally displaced persons: www.ohchr.org/EN/Issues/IDPersons/Pages/IDPersonsIndex.aspx

United Nations High Commissioner for Refugees: www.unhcr.org

United Nations Office on Drugs and Crime, UNODC on trafficking in persons and smuggling of migrants: www.unodc.org/unodc/human-trafficking/

International Labour Organization, Forced labour, modern slavery and human trafficking: www.ilo.org/global/topics/forced-labour/lang--en/index.htm

14 The Right to Development and Sustainable Development

CONTENTS

14.1 INTRODUCTION

Like self-determination and indigenous rights, the right to development (RTD) is a collective entitlement. Yet unlike its other counterparts, it was misunderstood for a long time. Its very existence was erroneously associated solely with foreign aid and charity and was not viewed through the lens of the programmatic positive and negative obligations of ailing states. As will become evident through the course of this chapter, development in its human rights context is primarily a value that translates into individual and communal well-being. This well-being may be linked to industrial or other financial development, although the correlation between the two is neither self-evident nor necessary. If this right to well-being is to make a difference in the lives of people, whether in poor or rich nations, it must be susceptible to quantifiable measurement through which one is able to assess its progress and realisation. In the last decade experts have developed a list of detailed indicators which allow us to assess well-being more accurately. At the same time, wealthy nations have abandoned ad hoc unilateral efforts to assist their poorer neighbours to escape perpetual cycles of poverty by entering into institutionalised multilateral commitments to contribute part of their annual earnings to developmental goals. These goals are also vigorously pursued by multilateral development banks, such as the World Bank and the African Development Bank.

First, we explore the human dimension of development as opposed to the development and financial growth of nations generally. We go on to explore the concept of sustainable development within which RTD exists and then examine the underlying premises of the Millennium Development Goals (MDGs) and their transformation into the Sustainable Development Goals (SDGs). Central in this process is the justiciability of development claims. Finally, the chapter investigates the impact of sovereign debt on development and human rights.

14.2   FROM HUMAN DEVELOPMENT TO SUSTAINABLE DEVELOPMENT

Development is typically associated with the overall wealth of states and is often linked to indicators such as 'growth', 'per capita income' and 'balance of payments', among others. The particular indicators of this type of development are intended to measure the overall wealth of states, not the well-being of their citizens. By way of illustration, whereas a country's gross domestic product (GDP), which represents the market value of its products and services, may be high, the standard of living of its people can still remain relatively low. This is because GDP is not a measure of personal income, nor does it take into account the disparity in the distribution of wealth or the enjoyment of essential services and goods such as health care, education, water and food. The measurement of human well-being is a relatively new phenomenon in the economics and human rights literature. In 1990 the United Nations (UN) Development Programme (UNDP) published its first *Human Development Report* with the aim of demonstrating how economic growth translates into human development. From the outset the report took the approach that:

People are the real wealth of a nation. The basic objective of development is to create an enabling environment for people to enjoy long, healthy and creative lives. This may appear to be a simple truth. But it is often forgotten in the immediate concern with the accumulation of commodities and financial wealth.[1]

[1] UNDP, *Human Development Report* (Oxford University Press, 1990) 9.

Human development is thus defined as enlarging people's choices, chief among these being the ability to lead a long and healthy life, be educated and to enjoy a decent standard of living. The report noted that although income helps formulate human choices, it is merely a *means* and not an *end*. It distinguished between two sides of human development: 'the formation of human capabilities, such as improved health or knowledge ... and the use that people make of their capabilities, for work or leisure'.[2] It identified three key indicators that may be used to measure human development, namely longevity, knowledge and decent living standards.[3] These three indicators are known as the Human Development Index (HDI) and offer markedly different results from the numbers reflecting the GDPs of nations. Of course, democratic governance, a solid income, the enjoyment of human rights and similar factors are also relevant to the processes of human development.

It should be made clear that the distinction between means and ends is key to the human development approach and differentiates the latter from the wealth-based approach to development. Sen and Anand explain that the two approaches to development, namely wealth maximisation and human development, differ in two respects: (1) their ultimate objectives and (2) the effectiveness of distinct instruments. With regard to ultimate objectives, the human development approach affords intrinsic value to the quality of the life people can lead (end) and only instrumental relevance to other elements such as income and wealth that are important only to reach the goal of human well-being (means). In particular, in recognising the importance of economic growth as a means for human development, they argue that the contingent nature of its effectiveness as means (how it is used to promote human development) should be considered. This is also true of its non-uniqueness as a form of means, although others are important too, such as social organisation.[4]

---

[2] Ibid., 10. A. Sen, 'Capability and Well-Being', in M. Nussbaum and A. Sen (eds.), *The Quality of Life* (Oxford University Press, 1993) 30–53, who distinguishes between capabilities and well-being. Sen's capabilities approach demonstrates that well-being differs from welfare in that the latter concerns prosperity in terms of material needs. He measures the developmental progress of states by reference to the capabilities of their citizens (capabilities approach) and distinguishes between positive and negative freedoms. Sen, whose influence was significant in the formulation of the HDI, has argued that only bottom-up development is sustainable, whereas development driven exclusively by governments is unsustainable because of the violation of rights and the lack of empowerment involved in the process. A. Sen, 'Equality of What?' Tanner Lecture on Human Values, Stanford University (22 May 1979) 198, 218. See also A. Sen, *Development as Freedom* (Oxford University Press, 2001).

[3] UNDP, *Human Development Report*, above note 1, 11.

[4] S. Anand and A. Sen, *Sustainable Human Development: Concepts and Priorities* (UNDP Office of Development Studies, 1996).

The 2010 *Human Development Report* underlined the absence of a significant correlation between economic growth and improvements in health and education in the contemporary era.[5] This is attributed to the fact that existing technological improvements and societal structures allow even poor countries to realise significant gains. This means that it is now cheaper to achieve good health, reduce unnecessary mortality, gain access to knowledge and enjoy decent living standards. Yet overall income remains significant because it expands people's freedoms and access to food, shelter, clothing and meaningful employment, which in turn helps them spend more time with their loved ones.[6]

In practice, certain international institutions and many states pay lip service to human development and clearly pursue development agendas that are inspired by the pursuit of financial growth alone. They adhere to the view that financial growth necessarily generates social benefits and is capable of producing adequate social safety nets.[7] The proponents of these views thus see poverty as entailing an absence of material goods, ownership of productive assets and financial opportunities, such as employment; as a result, they fail to consider the lack of empowerment and inclusion.[8] By way of example, the World Bank's Heavily Indebted Poor Countries (HIPC) initiative, which will be explored more fully below, was designed to provide low-interest concessional loans to heavily indebted nations in order to develop their infrastructures and capabilities, as well as allow them to augment their social spending. Although the Bank argues that the HIPC and other similar

---

[5] By way of illustration, although Jamaica is one of the world's highest indebted nations, with a financial growth that is among the weakest globally, its poverty levels have been reduced significantly (14.3 per cent in 2006) and some of its critical social indicators have improved dramatically (e.g. access to basic amenities and life expectancy). This was the result of major social initiatives in the spheres of health, housing and education, despite their numerous shortcomings. See C. Watson-Williams, *Realising Rights through Social Guarantees: The Case of Jamaica*, Final Report Submitted to the World Bank (June 2008) 5–8.

[6] UNDP, *Human Development Report: The Real Wealth of Nations* (Palgrave, 2010) 6.

[7] The term generally refers to policies designed to protect persons who for whatever reason fall below the poverty line and are thus unable to help themselves.

[8] The contemporary view rejects money-centric definitions of poverty. Instead, it emphasises the link between development and freedom, in which case poverty is 'understood as the deprivation of basic capabilities rather than merely as lack of income on its own': UN doc. A/HRC/SF/2008/2 (6 August 2008) para. 12. The CESCR has defined poverty as 'a human condition characterised by the sustained or chronic deprivation of the resources, capabilities, choices, security and power necessary for the enjoyment of an adequate standard of living and other civil, cultural, economic, political and social rights': CESCR statement, UN doc. E/C.12/2001/10 (2001) para. 8. A non money-centric definition is also offered by the EU's European Consensus on Development, para. 11, OJ C46/1 (2006), which notes among other things that poverty 'includes all the areas in which people of either gender are deprived and perceived as incapacitated in different societies and local contexts'.

initiatives have to a large degree achieved their developmental goals,[9] the UN Independent Expert on the Effects of Foreign Debt on the Enjoyment of Human Rights challenges this claim. For one thing, under the HIPC the Bank offers preferential loans only to those countries whose debts are considered unsustainable. Its assessment of debt sustainability, however, is based on the capacity of a country to service its debts, thus excluding from this category countries that pay their debts but in the process are left with no money to realise any economic, social and cultural (ESC) rights.[10] On this basis the Bank has sidelined from the HIPC a number of heavily indebted and poor middle-income countries.[11] These policies are wholly antithetical to the conclusions in the 2014 *Human Development Report*, which noted that the 'universal provision of basic social services can raise social competences and reduce structural vulnerability'. It goes on to show that even poor countries can offer social protection or universal basic services. It uses as examples South Africa's Child Support Grant, which cost 0.7 per cent of GDP in 2008–2009 and reduced the child poverty rate from 43 per cent to 34 per cent. The same is true of Brazil's Bolsa Família programme, which cost 0.3 per cent of GDP in 2008–2009 and accounted for 20–25 per cent of the reduction in inequality.[12]

What these examples show is that the economic aspect of development is not synonymous with growth or financial development more broadly. The latter is just an element of the former, which is associated with improvements in social and political welfare. Therefore, while it could be argued that there is a reciprocal relationship between economic development and human development, the same cannot be said about growth and human development. Quite the opposite: undifferentiated growth does not foster human development and even has negative implications for the natural environment too, given that it is a constituent element of the world system within which human development is pursued. To be sure, the international community has endorsed this observation since growth's detrimental impact on development and the environment was discussed in a series of UN summits and conferences, seeking to address the multifaceted nature of the human dimension of development. At the 1972 Conference on the Human Environment, states declared: 'man has the fundamental right to freedom, equality and adequate

---

[9] C. A. Primo-Braga and D. Dömeland (eds.), *Debt Relief and Beyond: Lessons Learned and Challenges Ahead* (World Bank, 2009).

[10] Report on Effects of Foreign Debt and other Related International Financial Obligations of States on the Full Enjoyment of All Human Rights, particularly Economic, Social and Cultural Rights, UN doc. A/64/289 (12 August 2009).

[11] HRC, Report of the High-level Task Force on the Implementation of the Right to Development on its Sixth Session, UN doc. A/HRC/15/WG.2/TF/2 (24 February 2010) para. 53.

[12] UNDP, *Human Development Report* (UNDP, 2014) 5.

conditions of life in an environment of a quality that permits a life of dignity and wellbeing'.[13] In this statement countries acknowledge that the environment gives people physical sustenance and affords them the opportunity to progress at the social, economic and scientific level, setting the foundations for a direct link between development and environmental sustainability. Development as a collective process of change should aim at 'sustainable living',[14] namely the improvement of the quality of human life while living within the carrying capacity of supporting ecosystems.

The new quest was explicated a decade later by the World Commission on Environment and Development (WCED or Brundtland Commission).[15] The Brundtland report addressed development within the broader context of uneven economic growth and the unbalanced distribution of its benefits and costs among rich and poor countries, as well as inappropriate technology that puts the resource base at risk. It also highlighted the lack of informed decision-making that merges environment, economics and human needs in development planning. The Brundtland report[16] stated that the major objective of development is the satisfaction of everyone's human needs and aspirations for an improved quality of life in perpetuity. Conditions of poverty and inequity are associated with ecological and other crises that hinder the realisation of this objective; hence there is a need for a comprehensive development path that deals with these issues in a comprehensive and integrated manner. The Commission introduced in the development discourse the concept of sustainable development, defined as 'development that meets the needs of the present without compromising the ability of the future generations to meet their own needs'.

Significantly, the Commission reinstated the centrality of human beings in the development process and by making clear that everyone should have their needs met, whether in the present or the future, it sets explicitly universalism as the ethical value that should guide development. Furthermore, there is a direct appeal to social justice because the claim for fulfilment of each generation's needs implies, in essence, a claim of fair and just relations between individuals and the institutions. This is also true in respect of economic and social arrangements that affect generations' ability to meet those needs. Such fairness is founded on the axiom that humans are fundamentally equal and is manifested in the fair distribution of income and wealth, as well as in society's

---

[13] UN Conference on the Human Environment, *Stockholm Declaration on the Human Environment*, UN doc. A/CONF.48/14/Rev.1 (16 June 1972) Principle 1.

[14] IUCN, UNEP, WWF, *Caring for the Earth: A Strategy for Sustainable Living* (Routledge, 2013); UNGA resolution 37/7 (28 October 1982) 'World Charter for Nature'.

[15] UNGA resolution A/38/161 (19 December 1983) 'Process of Preparation of the Environmental Perspective to the Year 2000 and Beyond'.

[16] World Commission on Environment and Development (WCED), *Our Common Future* (Oxford University Press, 1987).

organisational set-up that gives individuals the same opportunity to partici-pate in democratic processes and decision-making.[17] The combination of the two leads to an understanding of human needs *lato sensu* that includes the freedom to achieve dignity and respect of the person through active involve-ment in society's organisational system in addition to the enjoyment of mate-rial goods. Therefore, the objective of sustainable development is current and future societies where people have the opportunity to lead meaningful lives, defined by the achievement of adequate standards of living and the empow-erment to actively choose and decide upon the full range of factors that deter-mine the quality of their lives. That said, the Commission pointed towards a wider spectrum of well-being, therefore embracing the concept of human development as one that informs the content of sustainable development. By extension, the responsibility to guarantee this outcome for present and future generations does not merely reflect the just allocation and utilisation of spe-cific resources in terms of total stock of natural, physical and human capital. It should instead be construed as a general duty to afford generations the entitlement of access to the same opportunity to fulfil their legitimate aspira-tions for a better life in dignity.[18] This involves sharing a generalised capacity to create well-being based upon distributional equity that applies to individ-uals within the same generation (intragenerational equity) and between those in the future (intergenerational equity). On account of this freedom-based understanding of sustainable development, the concept can be defined as 'development that prompts the capabilities of present people without compro-mising the capabilities of future generations'.[19]

To the extent thus that sustainable development represents a shared claim of all to the capability to lead worthwhile lives, it could be argued that the purpose of development is to create the enabling environment in which all people can expand their capabilities, and opportunities can be enlarged for both present and future generations.[20] This is a broader interpretation of the approach taken in the first UN *Human Development Report* (mentioned

---

[17] This is a reflection of Rawls's two principles of justice, namely: (a) equal liberty and (b) difference and fair equality of opportunity. See J. Rawls, *A Theory of Justice* (Harvard University Press, 1999) 266.

[18] This has been defined as *sustainability* by Anand and Sen, above note 4, at 19–21, 27–8. When considered solely as an obligation to maintain resources, a further distinction is made between weak and strong sustainability; see A. Chandani, 'Distributive Justice and Sustainability as a Viable Foundation for the Future Climate Regime' (2007) 2 *Carbon Climate Law Review* 152, 160. However, it is more appropriate to define it from a normative perspective as an exemplification of the commitments to equity inherent in the morals of social justice and universalism which are the normative foundation of the concept of sustainable development.

[19] A. Sen, 'The Ends and Means of Sustainability' (2013) 14 *Journal of Human Development and Capabilities* 6, 11.

[20] UNDP, *Human Development Report 1994* (Oxford University Press, 1994) 13.

above), which identified the elements of human well-being. Due to the parameter of sustainability that requires equal attention to be paid to the lives of people between periods of time, the objective of development can be depicted in the pursuit of sustainable human well-being.[21] Just as human development professes development outcomes beyond the economic outputs of growth, so too sustainable human development purports to a wider net of results in the economic, social and environmental field, since sustainable human well-being is contingent upon the elimination of constraints in all three systems. Indeed, since the introduction of the Brundtland definition of sustainable development, it has been embedded in the international development discourse that sustainable development aims at eradicating poverty, protecting natural resources and changing unsustainable production and consumption patterns. Hence it is a multidimensional undertaking aiming to achieve a higher quality of life for all people that encompasses economic, social and environmental components that are interdependent and mutually reinforcing.[22] The so-called three pillars of sustainable development are hierarchically equal and it is assumed that the realisation of their constituent elements simultaneously and to the same degree, brings about a holistic human-centred approach to development. Sustainable human well-being, it therefore follows, stems from the balanced integration of its aforementioned three dimensions that should be premised upon the principles of dignity, equity, justice, participation and good governance and conform to states' obligations under the UN Charter and human rights treaties.[23] However, this balancing cannot mean same-degree satisfaction because the three pillars are not qualitatively equal due to the incompatibility of their determinative characteristics and their divergent functioning (e.g. material well-being

---

[21] A. B. Zampetti, 'Entrenching Sustainable Human Development in the Design of the Global Agenda after 2015' (2015) 43 *Denver Journal of International Law and Policy* 277, 298.

[22] There is no one single definition of sustainable development. For a sample variety of formulations see: UNGA resolution 51/240 (15 October 1997) 'UN Agenda for Development', at 1; World Summit on Sustainable Development, (26 August–4 September 2002), Johannesburg Declaration on Sustainable Development, UN doc. A/CONF.199/20 (4 September 2002): 'poverty eradication, changing unsustainable patterns of production and consumption and protecting and managing the natural resource base of economic and social development are overarching objectives of, and essential requirements for, sustainable development.' ILA New Delhi Declaration of Principles of International Law Relating to Sustainable Development (2 April 2002), reproduced in (2002) 2 *Politics, Law & Economics* 211, 212: 'The objective of sustainable development involves a comprehensive and integrated approach to economic, social and political processes, which aims at the sustainable use of natural resources of the Earth and the protection of the environment on which nature and human life as well as social and economic development depend and which seeks to realize the right of all human beings to an adequate living standard on the basis of their active, free and meaningful participation in development and in the fair distribution of benefits resulting therefrom, with due regard to the needs and interests of future generations.'

[23] UNGA resolution 66/288 (11 September 2012) 'The Future we Want'.

versus protection of ecosystems). Hence, while all three are necessary for sustainable development, sustainable human well-being requires that a choice is made regarding the degree of satisfaction of each tenet. The question to ask is what determines how this choice is made, particularly since policy choices in the context of development are not detached from moral and political arguments regarding the relationship between the three components of development. This may give rise to different conceptions of sustainable development which is rendered a blanket term and legitimises policies that may adhere to its tripartite framework but do not foster (sustainable) human well-being. This has been a reason why sustainable development is considered a contested and 'vague' concept. The three-pillar model does not address the point, so it is of little avail to look for an answer to the question in it.[24]

Quite clearly, there is a deep disparity between sustainable human and financial development. This tension is exemplified in the instruments analysed in the following section. If development is to be pursued and assessed on the basis of sustainable human well-being it is imperative that it be predicated on human rights norms and considerations, rather than policies from which human rights are absent. This is not mere rhetoric, for it requires policy-makers at all levels to address multidimensional poverty by reference to human rights indicators.[25] A report of the Office of the High Commissioner

[24] M. Lehtonen, 'The Environmental-Social Interface of Sustainable Development: Capabilities, Social Capital, Institutions' (2009) 49 *Ecological Economics* 199, 201; S. Connelly, 'Mapping Sustainable Development as a Contested Concept' (2007) 12 *Local Environment* 259. Recourse to the normative foundation of sustainable development (i.e. universality, human dignity, equity and justice) offers clarification for its foundational principles that are uncontested in the international human rights and development discourse. They can serve as the objective criteria by which to determine the degree of satisfaction of sustainable development components, as well as providing necessary clarity. Consequently, it could be said that the balancing of the pillars is achieved through their prioritisation on the basis of normative standards.

[25] By way of illustration, all entities involved within the UN system in development projects adopted in 2003 a statement on their common understanding of a human rights-based approach (HRBA) to development cooperation. There, it is stated that all projects must be guided by the International Bill of Human Rights and that development cooperation 'contributes to the development of the capacities of "duty-bearers" to meet their obligations and of "rights-holders" to claim their rights'. The HRBA principles are non-discrimination, empowerment, transparency, participation and accountability. See H.-O. Sano, 'Does Human Rights-Based Development Make a Difference?', in M. E. Salomon, A. Tostensen and W. Vandenhole (eds.), *Casting the Net Wider: Human Rights, Development and New Duty-Bearers* (Intersentia 2007) 63–79. The author argues that an HRBA to development has implications for actors and benefits for target groups. Its significance is evaluated on the basis of four dimensions: (1) the link it creates between local and global human rights actions, (2) its impact on national advocacy practices, (3) the clarity it brings to the notion of accountability of state and non-state actors which is defined on the basis of rights, and (4) the stronger protection it affords to the rights of the poor and most marginalised groups. In particular with respect to development,

for Human Rights (OHCHR) provides the following case study to illustrate the point:

A 23-year-old woman arrives at a village clinic ... complaining of pain and discharge stemming from an IUD [intra-uterine device] insertion. She tells the physician that she has already had four unwanted girl children; that her husband is a drunkard who routinely rapes her; and that she is struggling desperately just to keep her daughters and herself alive, but feels that if she could have a son he would be able to support her in later years. What is the health issue here? The treatment of an infection? The ability to freely choose a contraceptive method? The effect of societal son preferences on the woman's childbearing decisions? Or is it, most broadly, that she virtually has no control over her sexual, emotional, or physical well-being because of laws and practices that deny her basic human rights and dignity?[26]

If this case were viewed exclusively from a female health policy perspective, the answers to the points raised would tend to focus on biological processes, yet these hardly constitute the root causes of the problems faced by this woman. A human rights approach, on the other hand, would concentrate on the evident gender inequalities sustained by local laws, customs and cultural practices and would try to address them as root causes of the particular health issue.[27]

14.3   THE RIGHT TO DEVELOPMENT

Despite the fact that international discourse now evolves around 'sustainable development', no right to sustainable development has been acknowledged, because the legal nature of sustainable development is an unsettled matter as explained in the section on justiciability. However, the analysis on the RTD remains relevant since it is recognised as one of the substantive principles of sustainable development. As the UN Working Group on the RTD has stated, the RTD further embraces the different concepts of development of all development sectors, namely sustainable development and human development, as well as indivisibility, interdependence and universality.[28]

---

development is defined as a right and not charity or stemming from donors' self-interests or moral duty to the poor; accountability at the domestic and international level is founded on a common set of rules and norms; while the mutually reinforcing character between development and human rights goals is established, strengthening efforts to achieve both (e.g. framing development claims in human rights language embeds the latter into domestic laws and legal mechanisms through which the repercussions of development initiatives on human well-being can be challenged).

[26] OHCHR, *Claiming the Millennium Development Goals: A Human Rights Approach* (UN, 2008) 11.

[27] Ibid.

[28] UN Commission on Human Rights, 'Report of the Working Group on the Right to Development on its Fifth Session', UN doc. E/CN.4/1996/24 (20 November 1995) para. 76.

Development, at least in the sense conceived in the 1986 Declaration on the RTD,[29] and as arises from other instruments declarations (as outlined in other parts of this chapter) in the context of sustainable development, is unrelated to the financial progress of nations. Moreover, because the entitlement arising from the Declaration is hard to conceptualise, developed countries wrongly perceived this to entail a perpetual obligation to finance their weaker counterparts. A substantial amount of academic writing in the 1980s and 1990s certainly contributed to this confusion by propagating that self-determination (and consequently RTD) obliged industrialised nations to compensate developing states for their loss of earnings during colonisation. This process, it was further argued, allowed developing states to set their own market prices for their commodities and obliged wealthy nations to assist their poorer counterparts financially.[30] Such ideas naturally culminated in the downplaying of the right by wealthy nations, despite the fact that they continued to provide financial assistance, making it clear, however, that such assistance was merely a unilateral undertaking that did not encompass an obligation, or indeed give rise to a legitimate expectation. Although RTD has been subsequently clarified significantly and disengaged from foreign aid, industrialised nations have maintained this position and have persistently rejected proposals for a binding instrument.[31]

A closer reading of the Declaration reveals three fundamental building blocks which help demonstrate that the entitlement is hardly an arbitrary construction, but the natural outcome of the enforcement of the International Bill of Human Rights. These are: 'the constant *well-being*' of all people (article 2(3)), the inextricable nexus between well-being and civil, political and ESC rights (articles 1(1) and 2(2)), and the responsibility of states internally and externally to promote such well-being through the pursuit of all human

Hence, in the context of sustainable development, the RTD should be fulfilled 'equitably' in order to meet developmental and environmental needs of present and future generations. The current Special Rapporteur on the RTD stated that the RTD is a guiding standard when measuring progress in the implementation of the policy framework for sustainable development. See 'Report of the Special Rapporteur on the Right to Development: Note by the Secretariat', UN doc. A/HRC/36/49 (2 August 2017).

[29] UNGA resolution 41/128 (1986).

[30] See M. Bedjaoui, 'The Right to Development', in M. Bedjaoui (ed.), *International Law: Achievements and Prospects* (Martinus Nijhoff, 1991) 1177, at 1182ff. Others, however, took a more pragmatic view, arguing that self-determination only provides a right to pursue development, not a right to live in development. J. Donnelly, 'In Search of the Unicorn: The Jurisprudence and Politics of the Right to Development' (1985) 15 *California Western International Law Journal* 473, at 482ff. (he rejects the existence of a right to development and that it imposes a right to assistance: 'The innate responsibility to help one's fellow man establishes at most a moral obligation to act to promote development, not a right to development', 491).

[31] HRC, Report of the Working Group on the Right to Development on its Eleventh Session, UN doc. A/HRC/15/23 (10 June 2010) paras. 7–12.

rights (articles 4–8). A structured and comprehensive definition that included all three of these elements was articulated, not without dissent, in 2010 by the UN Special Rapporteur on the RTD, which will serve as a working definition for the purposes of this chapter:

> The right to development is the right of peoples and individuals to the constant improvement of their well-being and to a national and global enabling environment conducive to just, equitable, participatory and human-centred development respectful of all human rights.[32]

This conception of development through the lens of well-being and the enjoyment of human rights is not necessarily dependent on aid or other forms of donor assistance, although these would certainly enhance it. Development in this sense may be achieved even with scarce resources if they are allocated equitably, justly and with a view to alleviating human suffering. The vast majority of developing nations are, however, unable to do so because they are poorly managed, highly indebted and structural inequalities (such as poverty) have become so entrenched that they no longer seem out of place or problematic. The link between well-being and human rights in the definition of the RTD is crucial both for its legal nature[33] and for its implementation and justiciability. In respect of its legal nature, although the RTD presupposes the enjoyment of the full gamut of rights encompassed in the International Bill of Human Rights, it is not a mere compilation or synthesis of these rights.[34] Instead, it is an autonomous composite right that is enjoyed both collectively and individually and which is distinguished from the discrete rights that comprise it by the fact that it obliges the duty-bearers to establish an enabling environment for the realisation of individual and collective well-being.

The scheme of entitlements and responsibilities has not been unproblematic. Confusion stems particularly from a misinterpretation of the right's collective aspect that has led to the misunderstanding that the RTD is a

---

[32] HRC, Report of the High-level Task Force on the Implementation of the Right to Development on its Sixth Session, UN doc. A/HRC/15/WG.2/TF/2/Add.2 (8 March 2010) (Right to Development Criteria and Sub-criteria) Annex.

[33] The right's legal nature was settled after the consensus achieved in the Vienna Declaration and Programme of Action that reaffirmed the RTD as a universal and inalienable right and an integral part of fundamental human rights: UN World Conference on Human Rights, 48th Session, *Vienna Declaration and Programme of Action*, UN doc A.CONF.157/23 (1993). Until then, the foundational basis of the RTD and its legitimacy were questioned mainly due to the inclination of Western states to give economic, social and cultural rights inferior status compared to civil and political rights, and even more so to the third generation of rights (solidarity rights such as the RTD, healthy environment, etc.) See M. Assefa Tadeg, 'Reflections on the Right to Development: Challenges and Prospects' (2010) 10 *African Human Rights Law Journal* 325, at 333.

[34] S. Marks, 'The Human Right to Development: Between Rhetoric and Reality' (2004) 17 *Harvard Human Rights Journal* 137, at 149.

right of states (in particular developing states) too.[35] This misunderstanding is based on a surface reading of article 2(3) of the Declaration on the RTD which stipulates that 'states have the right to formulate national development policies'. However, a more careful read of this paragraph provides the necessary clarity: states' right to development policies aims at improving the well-being of *populations* and all *individuals*; it is the latter who are the recipients of these policies. If the provision is also read in conjunction with paragraphs 1 and 2 and article 1, there is no doubt that the Declaration on the RTD consciously casts the human person as the subject of development by affirming the RTD as an inalienable human right. Hence human beings are the intended beneficiaries whether they exercise the right individually or as collective entities such as groups or peoples, in the sense of a nation that seeks to pursue its economic, social and cultural development. On this basis, one can distinguish further between an internal dimension of the RTD that pertains to the exercise of the right by individuals and peoples vis-à-vis their state and an external dimension that asserts the exercise of the right on the international stage, which is claimed by the state on behalf of its peoples. It is in this latter sense that article 2(3) should be interpreted, namely as an invocation of the RTD against the international community which through structural impediments constrains developing states in their effort to realise their peoples' rights. States are the entity through which collective rights such as the RTD are exercised, but this does not render states right-holders. To defend the opposite contradicts also the spirit of human rights law, whose subjects are individuals/people and affords rights to them only while states bear the primary responsibility to realise those rights.

Consistent with this assumption, the binary relation between the holders of the RTD and states is that the latter undertake the obligation to fulfil the right; thus they are duty-bearers of the RTD. In the context of the RTD this duty is not placed solely in the framework of the traditional thinking in human rights law that states' duties are owed primarily to the people within their territory. States are also duty-bearers within the international public order on the premise of international cooperation that draws largely on the interdependence of states as a result of the global economy and governance. In this respect, their international obligations include a positive duty to create the circumstances whereby the prerogative of equality of opportunity for development is enjoyed by all nations. It also gives rise to a negative dimension that inhibits other states from determining their own development policies pursuant to their domestic obligation to uphold human rights and the RTD for the improvement of their peoples' well-being. It becomes apparent, then, that the realisation of the RTD is inextricably linked to the cooperative

---

[35] R. Sarkar, *International Development Law* (Oxford University Press, 2009) 199–253, at 231–2, 252.

role of states, and by and large to that of developed countries, in creating an environment conducive to the realisation of the RTD.[36] In light of this, the states' right under article 2(3) becomes even clearer: it is 'the right to develop human rights-based development policies in the interests of their people made possible through international cooperation'.[37] Notwithstanding states' primary responsibility to realise the RTD, the net of duty-bearers is cast wider against the background of a globalised political economy which has resulted in the proliferation of regulatory regimes that diminish the role of sovereign nation states and lend powers to intergovernmental organisations, transnational corporations, multilateral and bilateral donors. Due to their influence in shaping the economic order and the impact of their policies, interventions or agreements on the enjoyment of ESC rights, and the actions of such actors, cannot be excluded from an inquiry on their responsibility to protect, respect and fulfil human rights, including the RTD. Although the nature of their responsibilities and accountability is a more complex matter (e.g. unlike states, international organisations are not parties to human rights treaties), there is increasing support for the proposition that the current circumstances of international cooperation give rise to the human rights obligations of actors other than states.[38]

An illustration should assist in clarifying this distinction between the individual and collective dimensions of the RTD. The right to free and universal education simply obliges states to offer this entitlement to their young people without discrimination. Education, in the context of the RTD, requires not only that children attend school but that a process has been put in place through which education is linked to knowledge, technology, investment in agriculture, industry and other fields of productivity and employment, all of which will lead to job opportunities, as well as social and financial development.[39]

It becomes apparent that the realisation of individual socio-economic rights in the context of the RTD becomes contingent upon wider social

---

[36] Art 2(3)–(6) Declaration on the RTD.

[37] M. E. Salomon, *Global Responsibility for Human Rights: World Poverty and the Development of International Law* (Oxford University Press, 2007) 114–21.

[38] M. E. Salomon, 'Human Rights, Development and New Duty-Bearers' in Salomon et al., above note 25; Sarkar, above note 35, 221–3; on the impact of business activities on the enjoyment of ESCR, see indicatively CESCR, General Comment 23 (2016) 'on the right to just and favourable conditions of work', UN doc. E/C.12/GC/23 (27 April 2016) paras. 74 and 75; CESCR, General Comment 19 (2007) 'on the right to social security', UN doc. E/C.12/GC/19 (4 February 2008) paras. 45, 46, 71; on state obligations under the CESCR in the context of business activities, CESCR, General Comment 24 (2017); on state obligations under the ICESCR in the context of business activities, UN doc. E/C.12/GC/24 (10 August 2017).

[39] For an analysis of the objectives encompassed in education, and the right thereto, see Chapter 9.11.

arrangements that by implication expand the range of entitlements for the right-holders and the corresponding obligations for the duty-bearers of the RTD. Indeed, the added value of the RTD lies in the fact that it is a right to a particular process of development, meaning that individuals/peoples hold a claim not only to a substantive right that seeks to be fulfilled as the objective of a development policy, e.g. the right to education, but also to the series of actions leading up to the right's fulfilment. These are also essential to achieving development objectives in accordance with the definition of the RTD; namely, that they are centered on justice, equity, participation and human rights standards. Notably, bringing human rights into the process of development, and not only as an end of development policies, adds an important qualitative dimension to the realisation of human well-being. Thus, enlarging individuals' choices and enhancing their freedoms in line with the concept of human development is accomplished through the simultaneous realisation of human rights. By implication, not only are the actions of private and public entities shaped into the obligations and responsibilities of human rights duty-bearers for the purposes of bringing about a specific development outcome as an entitlement, but the integration of human rights in the process of development becomes a legal obligation too. Therefore, the right to development demands a critical approach to the overall development process, from the design of a specific policy to the allocation of resources to the framework of cooperation between competent actors with human rights considerations attached to all these aspects.[40]

It follows that the centrality of human rights is all the more poignant in the implementation of the RTD, whereby three forms are recognised. The first concerns states acting collectively in global and regional partnerships; the second encompasses states acting individually as they adopt and implement policies that affect persons not strictly within their jurisdiction; and the third mode relates to policies and programmes at the national level affecting persons within a state's jurisdiction.[41] Evidently, the implementation of the RTD is not dependent on the actions of external actors in the form of aid or other assistance, but necessarily involves the active engagement of the target state. Before we go on to examine justiciability, queries may well arise regarding how one is able to measure and assess the quantitative and qualitative dimensions of well-being. For years the UN made strenuous efforts to identify a methodology for assessing well-being without at the same time alienating industrialised nations. Although such a methodology has not yet

[40] See A. Sengupta, 'On the Theory and Practice of the Right to Development' (2002) 24 *Human Rights Quarterly* 837, 848–52; S. P. Marks, 'The Human Rights Framework for Development: Seven Approaches', in B. Mushumi, A. Negi and A. Sengupta (eds.), *Reflections on the Right to Development* (Sage, 2005) 23–60.

[41] Arts. 2–4 of the Declaration; see Right to Development Criteria and Sub-criteria, above note 32, paras. 16–17.

been endorsed universally through a binding instrument,[42] there is broad consensus that in common with the work of other human rights treaty bodies, it is possible to distil core attributes of the right and identify indicators in three dimensions – structural, process and outcome[43] – with well-being recognised as the core norm.[44] Three attributes are structured around this, namely comprehensive and human-centred development policy, participatory human rights processes and social justice. Although the three indicators are relevant to all three attributes of the core norm, structure more properly informs the level of commitment; process relates to rules and principles (human rights, participation, accountability and transparency); whereas outcome concerns distributional outcomes, particularly fair distribution of the benefits and burdens of development.[45] Structure, process and outcomes are roughly represented as criteria, sub-criteria and indicators in the roadmap compiled by the UN Working Group on the RTD, which seeks to address and assess how this right may be implemented at the national and international level. An exposition of attribute 3[46] (social justice in development – see Table 14.1) will help explain how structure, process and outcomes are designed to operate.

As is the case with all three attributes, their criteria, sub-criteria and indicators not only use human rights language, but are wholly entrenched within it, thus rendering human rights the yardstick by which development policies and initiatives are to be assessed.[47] As a result, any development policy, no matter how lofty or financially sound, that is in conflict with one or more human rights is incompatible with the RTD. Some cases are clear-cut, others not so. For example, aggregated results on social exclusion initiatives may

---

[42] The second reading of the criteria and sub-criteria with the purpose of refining them was finalised at the seventeenth session of the Working Group on the RTD. See 'Report of the Working Group on the RTD on its seventeenth session', UN doc. A/HRC/33/45 (20 July 2016). The discussion was continued at the eighteenth session when the WG stated that they should be completed by the nineteenth session, in 2018. See 'Report of the Working Group on the RTD on its eighteenth session', UN doc. A/HRC/36/35 (31 May 2017); however, this did not materialise.

[43] See Report on Indicators for Promoting and Monitoring the Implementation of Human Rights, UN doc. HRI/MC/2008/3 (6 June 2008) paras. 17–26. The use of indicators and benchmarks is also discussed in relation to ESC rights in Chapter 9.8.

[44] A more elaborate analysis of indicators and benchmarks is attempted in Chapter 9.8.

[45] Right to Development Criteria and Sub-criteria, above note 32, para. 18.

[46] Ibid., annex, paras. 14–15.

[47] Note the emphasis shifting to assessment as opposed to measurement of development progress, although quantification based on objective criteria is still necessary for policy design. But this shift reveals the importance given to quality alongside quantity in development strategies in that the latter should realise not only humans' economic but social and cultural entitlements as well. W. Mansell and J. Scott, 'Why Bother about a Right to Development?' (1994) 21 *Journal of Law & Society* 171, at 187.

Table 14.1 Attribute 3: Social Justice in Development

Criteria	Sub-criteria	Indicators
3(a) To provide for fair access to and sharing of the benefits of development	3(a)(i) Equality of opportunity in education, health, housing, employment and income	Income inequality; disaggregated outcome data by population groups, for example, male–female, rural–urban, ethnic/racial and socio-economic status
	3(a)(ii) Equality of access to resources and public goods	Public expenditures benefiting poor households
	3(a)(iii) Reducing marginalisation of least developed and vulnerable countries	Global gaps in income and human well-being, mitigating differential bargaining power and adjustment costs of trade liberalisation
3(b) To provide for fair sharing of the burdens of development	3(a)(iv) Ease of immigration for education, work and revenue transfers	Flow of skilled and unskilled migrants from poor to rich countries; flow of remittances
	3(b)(i) Equitably sharing environmental burdens of development	Availability of climate change funds for developing countries; multilateral agreements to reduce negative environmental impacts; distribution of contributions to climate change
	3(b)(ii) Just compensation for negative impacts of development investments and policies	Hazardous industries, dams, natural resource concessions
	3(b)(iii) Establishing safety nets to provide for the needs of vulnerable populations in times of natural, financial or other crisis	Domestic emergency response funds; international humanitarian and reconstruction aid; countercyclical official financial flows
3(c) To eradicate social injustices through economic and social reforms	3(c)(i) Policies aimed at decent work which provide for work that is productive and delivers a fair income, security in the work place and social protection for families	Growth rate per GDP of person employed, employment to population ratio, proportion of people living on less than a dollar a day
	3(c)(ii) Elimination of sexual exploitation and human trafficking	Ratification of the protocol to prevent, suppress and punish trafficking in persons, especially women and children
	3(c)(iii) Elimination of child labour	Extent of child labour; ratification of the convention on the worst forms of child labour
	3(c)(iv) Eliminating slum housing conditions	Proportion of urban population living in slums; access to improved sanitation; and secure tenure
	3(c)(v) Land reform	Access to land; secure land rights; and remedies against land grabs

fail to recognise the plight of particular groups that are routinely excluded, such as indigenous peoples, persons with disabilities and minorities. A need therefore arises for disaggregated policies. Equally, although the indicators may be appropriate for most circumstances, they may require realignment and adjustment in circumstances that are otherwise similar, especially if a disaggregated approach is maintained. By way of illustration, the urban poor of South Africa and the Indian rural poor face distinct health, employment and security issues arising from HIV/AIDS.

The extraterritorial application of RTD should be emphasised in relation to its negative dimension,[48] which is very seldom discussed. In a globalised and interconnected world the actions (including statements) by one state may produce harm (even unintended) for another state. For example, a statement to the effect that state X may be in default of its debt arrears, or that it is not investment-friendly, may have negative outcomes in its trade and investment relations and decrease its credit rating, thus forcing it to borrow with higher interest rates. These acts constitute interference in the domestic affairs of other states, but they also inhibit the RTD. States must therefore refrain from such actions.

14.3.1   Making the RTD Justiciable

It is because of this rights-based foundation of RTD that it has the potential of becoming justiciable before national courts and international human rights bodies.[49] Individuals and groups may challenge a development policy, programme or legislative act on the basis that it infringes other justiciable rights.[50] This indirect *locus standi* is subject to several limitations. In

---

[48] States' extraterritorial obligations (ETOs) conform to the trilogy of respect, protect, fulfil, and this negative dimension corresponds to first of these, according to which states should refrain from interfering directly or indirectly with the enjoyment of rights by persons outside their territories. See CESCR General Comment 24, above note 38, para. 29. De Schutter distinguishes between states' ETOs and global obligations in the framework of the RTD. Both stem from states' obligation to create an enabling international environment for the realisation of the RTD. But he explains that ETOs derive from states' *unilateral* actions/omissions that have an impact on persons or situations outside their territory or jurisdiction and points to the fact that the UNGA Declaration on the RTD is relatively vague on this issue. Yet ETOs can be inferred from art. 4(1) of the Declaration, which imposes on states the duty to adopt international development policies also individually. On the other hand, global obligations derive from states' role as actors in international relations and their duty to cooperate. He concludes on the existence of a hierarchy between states' obligations – national, extraterritorial, global – in the Declaration, all of which are linked to each other in the form of subsidiarity. O. De Schutter, 'The International Dimensions of the Right to Development: A Fresh Start towards Improving Accountability', HRC Working Group on the RTD 19th Session, UN doc. A/HRC/WG.2/19/CRP.1 (22 January 2018) paras. 19ff.

[49] On the justiciability of economic and social rights, see Chapter 9.6.

[50] Of course, it should be remembered that the RTD is directly affirmed also in other instruments. This includes improvement of human well-being in the UN Charter, art. 25 UDHR, arts. 13–15 CEDAW, arts. 3, 24, 27 CRC and art. 28 CRPD; with regard to 'participation', see art. 25 ICCPR, arts. 7 and 14 CEDAW, arts. 12 and 15 CRC, arts. 26, 43–4 Convention of Migrant Workers and Members of their Families, arts. 9, 21, 29, 30 CRPD, arts. 2, 5, 7, 22–23 ILO Indigenous and Tribal Peoples Convention (No. 169) and others. See also art. 22 African Charter on Human and Peoples' Rights, art. 19 of the Protocol to the African Charter on Human and Peoples' Rights on the Rights of Women in Africa; para. 37 of the ASEAN Human Rights Declaration (2012).

practice, actions are generally sustained only if brought by the people of the country implementing development programmes within its jurisdiction. In short, challenges are not typically directed against failure to achieve well-being, but only in respect of violations of civil, political and ESC rights.[51] Yet the reader will ascertain in the examples offered that although reference to the RTD is seldom made by the litigants and the courts,[52] the language and effects of such actions are tantamount to the RTD.

In the late 1990s Chile and South Africa pushed forward legislation aimed at curtailing social security benefits to a large part of their population. Chile did so by privatising its social security system, and South Africa by excluding all those benefiting from non-contributory schemes. In both cases the most vulnerable, such as the poor, the unemployed, part-time workers and women, were effectively denied access to health services, food stamps, microfinancing, pension entitlements and numerous other benefits. The Committee on Economic, Social and Cultural Rights (CESCR) recommended that all workers were entitled to social security benefits, which Chile was obliged to provide, especially to those unable to pay private contributions.[53] In equal measure, the South African Constitutional Court ruled that all the country's citizens were entitled to social security, emphasising that societal welfare indeed depends on the provision of such benefits to the least fortunate.[54]

---

[51] The CESCR has stressed the complementarity between the ICESCR and the Declaration on the RTD, which is manifested in the correspondence between the two instruments, to the extent that monitoring the implementation of the rights enshrined in the Covenant, the Committee contributes also 'to the full realisation of the relevant elements of the RTD'. CESCR, 'Statement on the importance and relevance of the right to development, adopted on the occasion of the twenty-fifth anniversary of the Declaration on the Right to Development', UN doc. E/C.12/2011/2 (12 July 2011) paras. 1 and 7.

[52] Exceptionally, direct reference has been made by the ACHPR in the *Endorois* case (2009), where Kenya was found to have violated the RTD of the Endorois people by failing to ensure their right to participate in the consultations prior to the final decision that lead to the re-zoning of their land. Furthermore, the government failed to compensate them adequately for the dispossession of their land, which resulted in the loss of the community's livelihood (nor did it provide other land for grazing); thus the benefits of development were not distributed equally; similarly, *African Commission on Human and Peoples' Rights* v. *Kenya (in the case of the Ogiek Community of the Mau Forest)*, Judgment (2017) paras. 207–11 (states' duty, individually or collectively, to ensure the exercise of the RTD).

[53] CESCR, Report on Thirty-second and Thirty-third sessions, UN doc. E/C.12/2004/9 (2005) paras. 546 and 569. The Committee noted that women are particularly affected, especially 'housewives' and about 40 per cent of working women who do not contribute to the social security scheme and are consequently not entitled to old-age benefits. It was stressed that working women are left with a much lower average pension than men as their retirement age is five years earlier than that of men.

[54] *Khosa and Others* v. *Minister of Social Development* (South Africa) (2004).

In India and Bangladesh the concept of livelihood has received much prominence from the countries' supreme courts.[55] It was invoked in cases concerning the forceful eviction of slum dwellers or those living in informal settlements. It was held that the right to livelihood derived from the right to life, dignity of person and equal protection, all of which oblige the state to ensure that all people enjoy the basic necessities of life. The evictions amounted to a denial of the slum dwellers' right to livelihood, given that adequate housing is indispensable in order to enjoy the right to life.[56] The Bangladeshi Supreme Court emphasised that a massive eviction from an informal settlement should have been accompanied by a resettlement plan that took into consideration the ability of those evicted to secure alternative accommodation.

Finally, the obligation of a state to secure the well-being of its population encompassed within the RTD is nowhere more evident than in cases involving food shortages and primary health care. In the late 1990s an outbreak of haemorrhagic fever swept Argentina, the government of which failed to produce and distribute the Candid 1 vaccine or otherwise tackle the spread of the fever, which placed 3.5 million people at risk of contracting it. Irrespective of the reasons behind this failure, which included severe budgetary constraints and a national health system that excluded the non-insured, the Argentine Federal Court of Appeals emphasised that one of the pre-eminent objectives of the Constitution was to secure the well-being of the people on the basis of social justice.[57] This is no doubt an implicit reference to the RTD.

These cases demonstrate that the debate regarding the lack of normative character of the RTD and its justiciability is without merit, at least in respect of the internal obligation of states to provide for the well-being of their people. It is inconceivable that states may argue that they would rather not spend their resources to improve the lives of their people, as though quality of life, or life itself, was unimportant compared to other political pursuits, such as defence, structural adjustment, debt servicing and other financial considerations. RTD may be invoked indirectly where a particular right is infringed in a manner that has a bearing on the well-being of vulnerable groups or entire populations.

---

[55] Article 41 of the Indian Constitution expressly envisages the right to livelihood as an expansion of the right to life in the form of a directive principle of state policy.

[56] *Ain o Salish Kendra (ASK)* v. *Government of Bangladesh (Slum-Dwellers case)* (Bangladesh) (1999); *Olga Tellis* v. *Bombay Municipality Corporation* (India) (1985).

[57] *Viceconti* v. *Ministry of Health and Social Welfare* (Argentina) (1998); a similar result was reached by the Ecuadorian Constitutional Tribunal in a case concerning the withdrawal of appropriate retroviral treatment from HIV sufferers: *Mendoza and Others* v. *Minister of Public Health and the Director of the National AIDS/HIV Program* (Ecuador) (2004).

14.3.2   Justiciability of Sustainable Development

The fact that there is no uniformity in the way sustainable development has been articulated[58] does not suffice to deny the consistency in the proclamation of the concept as an objective of state conduct. The latter has been endorsed as such by the international community and states adopt 'constantly and generally' national development strategies and implement international development projects aiming at sustainable development. Hence sustainable development as an objective constitutes a principle of customary law, albeit very general and abstract.[59] The continuous invocation of sustainable development in declarations and treaties demonstrates that it enjoys universal acceptance and that the international community commits strongly to its realisation,[60] but this is not enough to uphold the view that states accept the concept as law *ipso facto*.[61] For instance, intergenerational equity has become part of international law as a principle that underlines environmental treaties. Even so, there is no clear-cut position as to the justiciability and enforceability of future generations' rights. Future generations have only occasionally been granted *locus standi*,[62] and even then one may argue that intergenerational equity does not actually generate rights but only imposes an enforceable duty on states to account for the interests of future generations in the framework of the exercise of existing rights under international law. Hence intergenerational equity's contribution can at most serve as guidance in balancing the interests between generations in

[58] The ILA proposed seven principles relating to sustainable development. 'ILA New Delhi Declaration of Principles of International Law Relating to Sustainable Development' (2002) 2 *Politics, Law & Economics* 211. See also M.-C. Cordonier Segger and A. Khalfan, *Sustainable Development Law* (Oxford University Press, 2005) 95ff., who analyse the emergence and application of these seven principles and comment generally that it 'is doubtful whether the international principles relating to sustainable development are sufficiently substantive at this time to be capable of establishing the basis for an international cause for action'.

[59] See V. Barral, 'Sustainable Development in International Law: Nature and Operation of an Evolutive Legal Norm' (2012) 23 *European Journal of International Law* 377, at 388.

[60] P. Sands, 'International Law in the Field of Sustainable Development' (1994) 65 *British Yearbook of International Law* 303.

[61] See V. Lowe, 'Sustainable Development and Unsustainable Arguments', in A. Boyle and D. Freestone (eds.), *International Law and Sustainable Development* (Oxford University Press, 1999) 24.

[62] *Minors Oposa* v. *Secretary of the Department of Environment and Natural Resources* (1994) (Philippines). Intergenerational equity was recognised in *BGP Properties Pty Lmited* v. *Lake Macquarie City Council* (2004) (Australia). The court analysed the requirements for the implementation of 'ecologically sustainable development', referring, inter alia, to the polluter-pays principle and the principle of intergenerational equity. It examined the precautionary principle, including its development, forms of interpretation and its application in case law.

development processes and outcomes.[63] The same problems arise with respect to intra-generational equity, which has been employed in international law as a result of interpretation of the Rio Declaration's provisions. As such, the principle does not seem to be a self-standing norm and can be applied in adjudication indirectly through the implementation of other principles of sustainable development, such as the principle of common but differentiated responsibilities. Sustainable development lacks a norm-creating character,[64] at least for creating a primary customary rule of conduct. This is consistent with judgments in which sustainable development has not been invoked as a principle of customary law but as one that facilitates the reconciliation of conflicting norms relating to the environment and socio-economic development. In the landmark *Gabcikovo–Nagymaros* case the ICJ stated that:

mankind has, for economic and other reasons, constantly interfered with nature ... Owing to the scientific insights and to a growing awareness to the risks for mankind – for present and future generations – of pursuit of such interventions at an unconsidered and unabated pace, new norms and standards have been developed, set forth in a great number of instruments during the last two decades. Such new norms have to be taken into consideration, and such new standards given proper weight, not only when states contemplate new activities but also when continuing with activities begun in the past. This need to reconcile economic development with protection of the environment is aptly expressed in the concept of sustainable development. For the purposes of the present case, this means that the parties together should look afresh at the effects on the environment of the operation of the Gabcikovo power plant ...[65]

The normative role of sustainable development in balancing competing interests that derive from rules in international economic law, human rights and environmental law has been repeated in WTO arbitral awards. By way of illustration, in the *Shrimp-Turtle* case, sustainable development was characterised again as a concept emphasising the integration of economic and social development and environmental protection.[66] Similarly, the Permanent Court of Arbitration referred to sustainable development in the *Iron Rhine* case[67] between Belgium and the Netherlands, stating that the dictum in the *Gabcikovo–Nagymaros* applies equally in the current case. However, in the framework of reconciliation of environmental law and international

---

[63] Boyle and Freestone, above note 61, 'Introduction', at 14.

[64] Lowe, above note 61, at 37.

[65] *Gabcikovo–Nagymaros case* (ICJ) (1997) para. 140.

[66] *United States-Import prohibition of certain Shrimp and Shrimp Products* (1999) (WTO DSB) para. 129.

[67] *Iron Rhine Arbitration (Belgium v. Netherlands) Award* (PCA) (24 May 2005) paras. 59 and 222, in which it was stated that the integration of environmental protection in development processes is a principle of general international law, citing para. 140 of the ICJ's judgment in *Gabcikovo–Nagymaros*.

development law, the tribunal conferred a duty to prevent, or at least mitigate, the harm caused by development to the environment and elevated it to a principle of general international law.

The analysis suggests that sustainable development has been primarily considered as a normative goal against which the practice of states in development will be measured and evaluated. It does not regulate states' conduct directly by way of imposing constrains. This notwithstanding, its codification in international instruments and the extent to which it has been negotiated by state and non-state actors suggest that its influence in international law goes beyond its procedural relevance. In several instruments it has been articulated as the international community's commitment to *promote*,[68] *achieve*[69] and *contribute to*[70] sustainable development. This implies that states and other stakeholders should take positive steps, including the adoption of specific measures and balanced decision-making in policies, towards sustainable development, which in turn qualifies as an objective for the international community. This is particularly evident in several trade treaties. To be sure, sustainable development constitutes a specific objective for the World Trade Organization since the conclusion of the 1994 Agreement Establishing the WTO, but also for individual countries entering into regional agreements that clearly recognise the promotion of sustainable development as an objective.[71] Additionally, the ICJ has referred to sustainable development as an objective in the *Pulp Mills* case, which was brought before the Court after Argentina filed an application against Uruguay concerning alleged breaches by the latter of obligations incumbent upon it under the Statute of the River Uruguay, a treaty signed by the two states on 26 February 1975 (Statute) for the purpose of establishing the joint machinery necessary for the optimum

[68] UN Convention on Biological Diversity, art. 8(e): 'Promote environmentally sound and sustainable development'; UN Framework Convention on Climate Change, art. 3(4) 'parties have the right to promote sustainable development' and in the preamble 'recognising that all countries ... need access to resources to achieve sustainable development' and Kyoto Protocol to the UN Framework Convention on Climate Change, art. 2(1): 'Each Party included in Annex I, in achieving its quantified emission limitation and reduction commitments under Article 3, in order to promote sustainable development, shall ... '

[69] Johannesburg Plan of Implementation (JPOI) para. 3: 'to achieve the wide shared goals of sustainable development'; Agenda 2030, para. 2: 'We are committed to achieving sustainable development in its three dimensions'; Partnership agreement 2000/483/EC between the members of the African, Caribbean and Pacific Group of States of the one part, and the European Community and its Member States of the other part (2000) in the preamble.

[70] 1994 International Convention to Combat Desertification in Countries experiencing Serious Drought and/or Desertification, Particularly in Africa, art. 2(1), 'with a view to contributing to sustainable development'.

[71] Trade treaties that in the preamble recognise the promotion of sustainable development as an objective. See e.g., (a) 1992 North American Free Trade Agreements (Canada–USA–Mexico) and (b) Free Trade Agreement between Canada and Costa Rica (2002).

and rational utilisation of that part of the river which constitutes their joint boundary. In examining the alleged breach of the applicable article of the Statute, the Court stated that 'reconciling the varied interests of riparian States in a transboundary context and especially in the use of a shared natural resource [is] consistent with the objective of sustainable development'.[72]

CASE STUDY 14.1
Justiciability of Sustainable Development Claims

The relationship between economic interests and their impact on the environment and the rights of local communities has been resolved through the application of human rights provisions in conjunction with the Principles set out in the Stockholm and Rio Declarations in *Bulankulama and others* v. *The Secretary, Ministry of Industrial Development and others* before the Supreme Court of Sri Lanka.[1] The respondents entered into a draft agreement with a leading US mining company for the exploration of phosphate deposits in Eppawela, an agriculturally developed area of great historical importance and archaeological value. The Court emphasised that the protection and improvement of the environment was a constitutional and statutory duty whereby competent national authorities should implement policies aiming at the conservation of the country's natural resources for the benefit of current and future generations, and developers should undertake environmental impact assessments to ensure that development options are sound and sustainable. Interestingly, the Court reiterated that human beings are at the centre of development and they are entitled to a healthy and productive life in harmony with nature (Principle 1 Rio Declaration). States have the right to exploit their own resources, but they must do so pursuant to the environmental and development needs. Hence environmental protection constitutes an integral part of the development process and cannot be ignored (Principle 4 Rio Declaration and 21 Stockholm Declaration). It went on to say that the current case should be decided upon these principles despite their non-binding nature as soft law, and explicitly referred to the components of sustainable development which authorities should pay

---

[1] *Bulankulama and Others* v. *Secretary, Ministry of Industrial Development and Others (Eppawela Case)* (Sri Lanka Supreme Court) (2000).

---

[72] *Pulp Mills on the River Uruguay (Argentina* v. *Uruguay)* (ICJ) (2006) para. 177. In his dissenting opinion Judge Trindade argued that sustainable development should have been applied in the case on the basis of its status as a general principle of international law (by virtue of the evolution of international environmental law through the enunciation of general legal principles), see paras. 132ff.

due regard to. Intergenerational equity should be regarded as axiomatic in the decision-making process for matters concerning the natural environment, which should be also complemented by transparency, fairness and citizen participation. Besides, the precautionary principle and the 'polluter pays' principle are fundamental to the prevention of environmental degradation and for reversing the damages to the region's environment and the non-renewable cultural heritage. The Court placed thus human development in the context of the earth's finite resources and based its reasoning on related principles to the concept of sustainable development.

14.4   GLOBAL PARTNERSHIPS FOR THE FINANCING OF DEVELOPMENT

In a previous section it was explained that two of the ways by which the RTD is implemented concern externally derived aid, whether unilaterally or collectively. Indeed, articles 2(1), 11(1) and 12(1) of the International Covenant on Economic, Social and Cultural Rights (ICESCR) suggest that states should cooperate for the realisation of human rights at the global level. None the less, the *travaux préparatoires* of the Covenant do not support the contention that foreign assistance, whether material or otherwise, was ever couched in terms of an obligation.[73] This position is consistent with the international practice in the field of donor conferences and pledges. One would have naturally thought that states going into donor conferences would be sincere about the funds they were publicly claiming to contribute and that their financial pledges would carry the same legal weight as

---

[73] P. Alston and G. Quinn, 'The Nature and Scope of Parties' Obligations under the International Covenant on Economic, Social and Cultural Rights' (1987) 9 *Human Rights Quarterly* 156, at 186. As a result, this author is not convinced that the right to international solidarity exerts an obligation on states to undertake joint action in response to poverty and other global crises. See, however, the Report of the UN Independent Expert on Human Rights and International Solidarity, UN doc. A/HRC/12/27 (22 July 2009). See M. E. Salomon, *Global Responsibility for Human Rights,* above note 37, 64ff., who argues that whether an obligation of assistance or cooperation (in broader terms) for the realisation of human rights and development exists should be considered as answered on the grounds of evidence in hard and soft international law. Specifically, arts. 55 and 56 UN Charter establish binding obligations on the international community to cooperate on economic and social matters; likewise arts. 22 and 23 ICESCR reaffirm the obligation in relation to the Covenant's rights. Interestingly, the CESCR has elaborated on the nature of this obligation in the context of specific rights (e.g. right to food, health) in its respective General Comments and more generally in General Comment 3 'on the nature of states parties' obligations under the Covenant', UN doc. E/1991/23 (14 December 1990), in which it stressed that 'international cooperation for development and thus for the realisation of ESCR is an obligation of all states'.

promises and other intentional unilateral acts under international law.[74] Yet not only do states routinely renege on funding promises delivered at donor conferences,[75] but more disturbingly their pledges are not considered binding until such time as the pledged funds are delivered to the recipient, in which case there is no right to a refund.[76] This practice exists because states are free to make up the rules in respect of donor conferences[77] and also because it was feared that if binding instruments were employed to collect voluntary contributions many states would be dissuaded from the process altogether. It is only recently that the UN has sought to streamline the process by requiring a degree of formality with regard to pledges.[78] Equally, the World Bank has introduced so-called instruments of commitment to certain human rights and environmental initiatives, which constitute binding agreements requiring parliamentary ratification.[79] These developments have only helped to decrease some empty pledges, but they have in no way reversed the negative situation.

By the end of the 1990s it became evident that the gap between the poor and the very poor had widened so much that even the slightest fluctuation in global food prices could produce waves of famine across the globe.[80] Human development could no longer be left to the devices of poor nations or the odd donor conference set up in the aftermath of a humanitarian disaster. As a result, the Millennium Declaration was adopted by the UN General Assembly (UNGA) in 2000 in the form of a political pledge by the world's leaders, with the aim that it would soon be followed by concrete financial commitments under well-identified targets.[81] The Declaration was meant as a testament of solidarity against global poverty and suffering, and/or respect for human

---

[74] See art. 1 of the ILC Guiding Principles applicable to unilateral declarations of states capable of creating legal obligations.

[75] Although the USA, for example, at the 2002 Monterey Conference pledged, along with other developed nations, to offer 0.7 per cent of its annual GDP, by 2008 it had offered only a fraction of that, a mere 0.18 per cent.

[76] J. E. Archibald, 'Pledges of Voluntary Contributions to the United Nations by Member States: Establishing and Enforcing Legal Obligations' (2004) 36 *George Washington International Law Review* 317, at 317–18 and 329. The UN does not invoke art. 19 of the UN Charter in respect of unpaid voluntary contributions.

[77] R. Sabel, *Procedure at International Conferences* (Cambridge University Press, 1997) 21ff.

[78] UN Secretary-General's Bulletin on establishment and management of trust funds, UN doc. ST/SGB/188 (1 March 1982) para. 29.

[79] See Instrument for the Revised Global Environmental Facility (GEF) of March 2008, Annex C.

[80] By 2014 more than 2.2 billion people are living either near or in multidimensional poverty. This means that more than 15 per cent of the world's population remains vulnerable to multidimensional poverty. At the same time, nearly 80 per cent of the global population lacks comprehensive social protection. About 12 per cent (842 million) suffer from chronic hunger: UNDP, *Human Development Report* (2014), above note 12, at 3.

[81] UNGA resolution 55/2 (18 September 2000).

rights. The centrality of human rights and the RTD in the Declaration's aims is stark. Paragraphs 11 and 24, for example, state that:

We will spare no effort to free our fellow men, women and children from the abject and dehumanising conditions of extreme poverty, to which more than a billion of them are currently subjected. We are committed to making the right to development a reality for everyone and to freeing the entire human race from want.

We will spare no effort to promote democracy and strengthen the rule of law, as well as respect for all internationally recognised human rights and fundamental freedoms, including the right to development.

Following the Millennium Summit the UN Secretary-General finalised the text of the eight agreed MDGs. These are: (1) eradication of extreme poverty and hunger; (2) achievement of universal primary education; (3) promotion of gender equality and empowerment of women; (4) reduction of child mortality; (5) improvement of maternal health; (6) combating HIV/AIDS, malaria and other diseases; (7) ensuring environmental sustainability; and (8) establishment of a global partnership for development. Industrialised states pledged to contribute 0.7 per cent of their GDP[82] to meet these targets, and in addition undertook to support exports from least developed nations, and offer debt relief by cancelling all official bilateral debts, in return for demonstrable commitments to poverty reduction, and providing generous development assistance.[83]

The MDGs, much like the criteria and sub-criteria formulated to assess progress with the RTD, are set against targets whose progress is in turn monitored by a set of indicators. For example, target 1 C of goal 1 (i.e. eradication of extreme poverty and hunger) consists of halving, between 1990 and 2015, the proportion of people who suffer from hunger. This is assessed against the prevalence of underweight children under five years of age and the proportion of populations below the minimum level of dietary energy consumption. The achievement of the first seven substantive goals is predicated to a large degree on goal 8, which seeks to develop a global partnership for development through the delivery of official development assistance (ODA), debt relief, tariff and quota-free access and making available essential drugs and new technologies. Thus, ODA, which consists essentially of direct financial assistance, is complementary to other initiatives and requires that the target state is obliged to work towards implementing the targets and indicators of the MDGs. Paragraph 39 of the 2002 Monterrey Consensus[84] makes it clear

---

[82] See para. 42 of the Monterrey Consensus of the International Conference on Financing for Development, UN doc. A/CONF.198/11 (2002).

[83] See Millennium Declaration, paras. 15–18; MDGs, goal 8, targets A–D.

[84] Monterrey Consensus, above note 82. The Monterey Consensus is a political declaration of the highest calibre aimed at mobilising development assistance and international trade as an engine for development and eliminating external debt. It was followed up in 2008 by the Doha Declaration on Financing for Development.

that ODA is reserved for countries with the least capacity of attracting foreign direct investment and its purpose is to help achieve:

adequate levels of domestic resource mobilisation over an appropriate time horizon, while human capital, productive and export capacities are enhanced. ODA can be critical for improving the environment for private sector activity and can thus pave the way for robust growth. ODA is also a crucial instrument for supporting education, health, public infrastructure development, agriculture and rural development and to enhance food security.

Yet as lofty and important as the MDGs are, they risk denigrating the very values they seek to exalt and protect. First and foremost the rights language entrenched in the Millennium Declaration was not iterated in the MDGs for fear that somehow the goals might be transformed into justiciable entitlements. One might naturally think that although unfortunate, lack of justiciability was a small price to pay for securing the much-needed aid to the world's poor; after all, the goals and their indicators are strikingly similar to the rights found in the International Bill of Human Rights.[85] Sadly, this is not the case.[86]

True, there are many similarities between the goals and ESC rights. However, whereas these rights, as proclaimed in the ICESCR, are meant to apply against all persons without any discrimination, thus reaching the poorest of the poor, the MDGs on many occasions only require states to halve certain poverty indicators. Given the absence of an obligation to disaggregate results in the MDGs, it is tempting for target states to focus on the

---

[85] See P. Alston, 'Ships Passing in the Night: The Current State of the Human Rights and Development Debate Seen Through the Lens of the Millennium Development Goals' (2005) 27 *Human Rights Quarterly* 755, 759, 762 for a human rights critique on the MDGs. For further criticism, see UN System Task Team on the Post-2015 UN Development Agenda, 'Review of the Contributions of the MDG Agenda to foster development: Lessons for the Post-2015 UN development Agenda', Discussion Note (12 March 2012) https://sustainabledevelopment.un.org/content/documents/843taskteam.pdf.

[86] In a 2006 report the OECD estimated that approximately 58 per cent of bilateral aid was tied. Tied aid refers to aid granted under condition that the recipient purchase goods and services from the donor. See OECD, '2005 Development Cooperation Report: Efforts and Policies of the Members of the Development Assistance Committee' (2006) *OECD Journal on Development* 31. By 2010 tied aid had fallen to less than 20 per cent. There is no consensus on the ethical or legal perspectives of this practice under international law, although states are generally keen to hide so-called 'aid for trade', as was the case in the early 1990s when the UK financed the construction of the Pergau dam in Malaysia, which in turn proceeded to buy £1 billion worth of British arms. In *R* v. *Secretary of State for Foreign Affairs ex parte World Development Movement* (UK) (1995), the High Court ruled that the project was not of any economic or humanitarian benefit to the Malaysian people. It should also be noted that the drafters of the Paris Declaration on Aid Effectiveness have pledged to minimise it, and the Development Assistance Committee (DAC) of the OECD issued a (revised) Recommendation on Untying ODA to LDCs and HIPCs, DCD/DAC (2014) 37 Final (12 August 2014), by which it recommends the lifting of all tied aid.

relatively well-off among the poor and make no special provision for vulnerable groups.[87] As a result, the universality element of the relevant right is lost. Moreover, some goals are clearly inconsistent with human rights. By way of illustration, goal 2 calls for universal primary education, ignoring the requirement of free and quality education as enshrined in article 13 of ICESCR. More worrying is the technocratic trend set in the MDGs, with an emphasis on the mobilisation of financial resources over and above the transformation of power relations that play a large part in the creation of poverty and under-development.[88] The MDGs therefore ignore the fundamental role of civil and political rights in the achievement of ESC rights.[89] Hence, multilateral donors seem to entertain the illusion that countries which marginalise their minorities and indigenous populations,[90] which provide employment to their women but provide them with menial jobs, or who allow corrupt leaders to be perpetually re-elected because other candidates do not possess the financial or other means to run for office, can eventually lead their peoples to a high standard of well-being.

Yet data from the last Millennium Development Report does not support this illusion.[91] While significant achievements on many of the MDGs are reported – for instance, the number of people living in extreme poverty has fallen beyond the 50 per cent target of MDG1; 91 per cent of the population in developing countries enrol in primary school (MDG2);[92] infection and deaths from infectious diseases such as malaria have fallen by a rate of 37 and 58 per cent respectively, and the number of people receiving therapy for HIV has

---

[87] OHCHR, above note 26, 4. S. Fukuda-Parr, 'Reducing Inequality – The Missing MDG: A Content Review of PRSPs and Bilateral Donor Policy Statements' (2010) 41 *IDS Bulletin* 26.

[88] Ibid., OHCHR. The Goals' technocratic trend is due to the influence of results-based management (RBM) in the making of their making. RBM is a managerial strategy for development programmes and implementation that lays emphasis on performance by setting and measuring specific outcomes. Notwithstanding the value that lies in such a strategy, its prevalence in design of the MDGs narrowed down the agenda to quantifiable targets and indicators that did not capture the quantitative elements of human development and the scope of objectives in the Millennium Declaration. Ultimately, given the focus on producing results, the MDGs became a minimalist agenda that reflected a narrow understanding of the goals and gave rise to non-inclusive and structurally non-reformist development policies. D. Hulme, 'Lessons from the Making of the Millennium Development Goals: Human Development meets Results-based Management in an Unfair World' (2010) 41 *Institute of Development Studies Bulletin* 15.

[89] HRC, Consolidation of Findings of the High-level Task Force on the Implementation of the Right to Development, UN doc. A/HRC/15/WG.2/TF/2/Add.1 (25 March 2010) paras. 65–6.

[90] The *Human Development Report* (2014), above note 12, at 3, makes the point that although indigenous peoples make up 5 per cent of global population, they account for some 15 per cent of the world's poor.

[91] UN Secretariat, The Millennium Development Goals Report 2015, www.un.org/millenniumgoals/2015_MDG_Report/pdf/MDG%202015%20rev%20(July%201).pdf (UN MDGs Report 2015).

[92] Ibid., at 4.

increased to 13.6 million compared to 800,000 in 2003 (MDG6)[93] – progress has been uneven across regions and countries. Indicatively, the poverty reduction rate in Sub-Saharan Africa was only 28 per cent,[94] while the number of undernourished people has increased by 44 million since 1990, the reason being the region's rapid population growth;[95] access to maternal health care services is still unequal, especially between rural and urban areas, with Central Africa demonstrating the largest gap at 52 percentage points;[96] finally, gender equality remains amongst the most pertinent issues, being evidenced among other things in the disadvantageous position of women in the labour market and public offices.[97] Of course, to reject the MDGs' contribution to the eradication of poverty would be unjustified, but their unconditional success cannot be considered a fact. Instead, it can be inferred that the ambition to 'free all men, women and children from the abject and dehumanising conditions of extreme poverty' enshrined in the Millennium Declaration requires more coherence not only regarding the substantive content of development policies that should view the systemic causes of the challenges to development through a human-rights lens, but also with respect to the tools used to effectuate them. Correspondingly, since development financing is the main instrument, it is therefore imperative that any financing framework possesses the following characteristics: be rights-sensitive and considered against human rights standards and indicators (e.g. removal of tied aid); avoid overly technocratic goals that provide good statistical reading and instead focus on transforming the lives of peoples by prioritising human rights in policy choices and resource allocation; aim to empower all people and disrupt unequal power relations that thwart development for the masses; and make MDG rights justiciable, not necessarily against the donors but in respect of the institutions and mechanisms set up by target states.[98]

---

[93] Ibid., at 6.   [94] Ibid., at 15.   [95] Ibid., at 21.   [96] Ibid., at 40.   [97] Ibid., at 31.

[98] Since the launch of the MDGs, the question of aid effectiveness has become critical for donor states. As a result, in 2005 the Paris Declaration on Aid Effectiveness was adopted with the aim of disbursing and managing ODA more effectively. The Declaration is not binding and established a framework for bilateral partnerships between donors and creditors and individual aid-recipient countries. Aid effectiveness is linked to five mutually reinforcing principles: (1) recipient countries exercise efficient ownership over their development strategies; (2) support is based on recipient countries' strategies and institutions (alignment); (3) harmonisation and transparency of donors' actions; (4) improvement in decision-making and management; (5) mutual accountability of donors and recipients. The Paris Declaration was rigidly technocratic and is only incidentally concerned with development outcomes and hence avoids references to human rights, unlike its follow-up instrument, the 2008 Accra Agenda for Action. Moreover, the OECD DAC published its Action-Oriented Policy Paper on Human Rights and Development in 2007, where it identified ten principles whereby human rights play an inextricable part in donor effectiveness and harmonisation. However, in Evaluating Development Cooperation:

14.5   FROM THE MDGS TO THE SDGS

The described quest for comprehensiveness in the design and implementation of development policies became the centrepiece of the SDGs that were adopted in the framework of Agenda 2030 for Sustainable Development. Considering economic, social and environmental issues as components and overarching objectives of development and combining them with a broader spectrum of topics such as prosperity, the planet, peace, security and justice, the SDGs present an action plan that is more transformative in scope and responds to existing and new development challenges for developing and developed states in the current century. The new set of global goals consists of: no poverty (SDG1), zero hunger (SDG2), good health and well-being (SDG3), quality education (SDG4), gender equality (SDG5), clean water and sanitation (SDG6), affordable and clean energy (SDG7), decent work and economic growth (SDG8), industry innovation and infrastructure (SDG9), reduced inequalities (SDG10), sustainable cities and communities (SDG11), responsible consumption and production (SDG12), climate action (SDG13), life below water (SDG14), life on land (SDG15), peace, justice and strong institutions (SDG16) and partnerships for the goals (SDG17).

Much like the MDGs, the goals are set against targets and indicators focused on measurable outcomes, yet their holistic approach to development is evident at a glance. To illustrate this point, it suffices to consider the wording of the goals. To name a few, SDG1 is concerned with the eradication of poverty in its multidimensional nature and the exclusion of individuals from the economic and other means (such as services) necessary for human well-being wherever it occurs. This makes the goal relevant not only to poor countries but also to developed regions where poverty in relative terms is also recorded; targets on education, to refer back to our earlier example, are not limited to universal primary education, but include secondary, tertiary and lifelong learning (SDG4). The SDGs constitute thus a broader framework of development goals that aspire to become relevant to all individuals, not solely by completing the MDGs' unfinished business, but by expanding the mandate of the systemic framework for development to include the interplay between poverty, inequalities, environmental degradation and institutional impediments to development, namely lack of the rule of law in domestic orders, transparency and accountability of public and private entities and weak regulations to tackle corruption and organised crime.[99]

Summary of Key Norms and Standards (2010) 13–14, the DAC explains its five principles for evaluating development assistance (i.e. relevance, effectiveness, efficiency, impact and sustainability) without any reference to human rights indicators.

[99] The SDGs reflect in their content the outcomes of previous UN summits and conferences. See Agenda 2030, para. 11.

Indeed, alongside the interdependence and indivisibility of the goals, states declared that the agenda is applicable to everyone on the basis of full respect for human dignity and the principles of equity, equality and non-discrimination as expressed in the UN Charter, the UDHR and other human rights treaties and declarations, such as the Millennium Declaration. In fact, in the third preambular paragraph of Agenda 2030 it is stated that the SDGs seek to realise the human rights of all. Within this framework the RTD holds a prominent status and its importance for the realisation of the goals is explicitly recognised.[100] In light of this, human rights seem to have been embedded in the new financing for development framework as well, set at the third international conference on Financing for Development in Addis Ababa. Respect for all human rights underlines states' commitments under the Addis Ababa Action Agenda (AAAA),[101] which pledges to provide a social protection floor for everyone[102] and lays emphasis on develop-ment actors' accountability in relation to their financing promises that are subject to review for the first time.[103] Besides the equitable distribution of resources so that all persons have their most basic needs met, human rights are a key objective for the AAAA,[104] which in this regard aims to establish an international development financing system that is just, cooperative, transparent and premised on human rights standards.[105] Most importantly, the AAAA constitutes an integral part of Agenda 2030,[106] meaning that the human rights principles applicable to the realisation of the socioeconomic

---

[100] Agenda 2030, paras. 10 and 35.

[101] UNGA resolution 69/313 (27 July 2015).

[102] Ibid., para 12.

[103] Ibid., paras. 130–4.

[104] That human rights considerations should permeate development finance programmes was raised by the OHCHR during the third international conference on Financing for Development and the negotiations of the AAAA, its outcome document. It was emphasised that the objective of financing development should be the equitable distribution of resources so that all persons have their most basic needs met and human rights are made a reality for all; see OHCHR, Key Messages on Financing for Development and Human Rights, www.ohchr.org/Documents/Issues/Development/KeyMessageHRFinancingDevelopment.pdf.

[105] Civil society denies that this holds true. On the same note, civil society expressed scepticism about the new financing framework to achieve Agenda 2030 for sustainable development, stating that although the AAAA promulgates the realignment of financial flows with public goals, the agenda does not tackle the structural injustices in the current economic system, and that development finance is not people-centred. See Global Policy Watch, 'Third FfD Failing to Finance Development – Civil Society Response to the Addis Ababa Action Agenda on Financing for Development' (16 July 2015) (blog).

[106] Agenda 2030, paras. 40 and 62.

and environmental SDGs apply to the means-of-implementation targets too, not least since the latter are of equal importance with the rest of the goals.[107]

Notwithstanding the direct bearing on human rights in the making of the goals, the SDG agenda has been criticised for failing to conform to both human rights and the normative standards of the concept of sustainable development. The cornerstone of the critique is found in the predominant role of economic growth as the means to eradicate poverty, and in the favouritism towards mainstream development that reinvigorates the poor-rich divide. SDG8 not only requires that per capita economic growth is sustained but sets a specific threshold of 7 per cent of GDP per year, albeit for developing countries mainly. It also advocates for expanded access to financial services for the accumulation of assets, and an increase in investments with a view to stimulating the economy. While growth cannot be deemed devoid of value for the eradication of poverty, at least in its material sense, there is considerable evidence demonstrating that even though the average annual growth rate of real GDP per capita worldwide is increasing year on year, moderate poverty (less than $2.50 per day) still exists, income disparities are widening while all the more wealth is concentrated on a small portion of the world's population.[108] Obviously, aggregate economic growth does not have the anticipated impact.[109] To be sure, a restructuring of the world's wealth-extracting mechanism is necessary, meaning that the rules on trade, taxation and debt should be changed. Yet the SDGs do not take the bold step to address these issues adequately. The language of the respective goals is vague and no concrete measures to tackle them are mentioned.[110] What this signals, then, is a risk that the transformative nature of the SDGs is compromised.

---

[107] Ibid., para. 61.

[108] The World Bank Group, 'Statistical Appendix in Global Economic Prospects: Broad-based Up-turn but for How Long?' (January 2018) 233, www.worldbank.org/en/publication/global-economic-prospects#data; C. Lakner and C. Sanchez, 'The 2017 Global Poverty Update from the WB' (Let's Talk Development) (16 October 2017), http://blogs.worldbank.org/developmenttalk/2017-global-poverty-update-world-bank.

[109] J. Y. Kim, 'Ending Poverty Requires More than Growth', WBG Press Release No. 2014/434/DEC (10 April 2014) https://ourworldindata.org/extreme-poverty#the-future-of-extreme-poverty.

[110] T. Pogge and M. Sengupta, 'The Sustainable Development Goals as Drafted: Nice Idea, Poor Execution' (2015) 24 *Washington International Law Journal* 571, 575 and fn. 14, 15. For another critical review see I. T. Winkler and C. Williams, 'The Sustainable Development Goals and Human Rights: A Critical Early Review' (2017) 21 *The International Journal of Human Rights* 1023.

INTERVIEW 14.1

Microfinance Non-governmental Organisation (NGO)

(Ramanou Nassirou)

Ramanou Nassirou is the general manager of WAGES (Women and Associations for Gains both Economic and Social), a Togolese microfinance institution that began as a CARE international project in 1994 and has grown since to become the second largest microfinancing institution (MFI) in Togo. As of May 2012, it had a portfolio of 13.6 billion FCFA (the Togo currency) (US$27,200,000) in active loans, 8 billion FCFA (US$16,000,000) in savings deposits, and 168,000 clients, the majority (59 per cent) of whom are women (US $1 = 500 FCFA).

How do you reach and identify your clients? In your assessment do you take into consideration the criteria for poverty set out in the Millennium Development Goals or do you employ your own?

Client outreach is achieved in several ways. As our primary service is providing loans to low-income entrepreneurs and small and medium-sized enterprises (SMEs), our loan officers are in the field for 80 per cent of their working hours. In the field means visiting local markets, small offices, boutiques, roadside stalls, hair salons, workshops, as well as farms and, in essence, any place where business can and does take place. Due to their regular presence among our targeted audience, our public profile, reputation and products are advertised on a daily basis. We furthermore advertise in the local print and radio media and rely heavily on word-of-mouth references from our existing clients.

As for specifically identifying our clients, we use the definition of poverty as established by the MDGs to produce a poverty assessment tool (PAT). Though we serve the low end of the socio-economic ladder, our institution also addresses the financial needs of those outside of this zone, specifically SMEs. Our ability to be a sustainable institution depends on using profits earned from larger loans to subsidise the smaller, and higher-risk loans, as the latter have far lower rates of return. The profit margin of larger loans furthermore allows us to innovate and target marginal groups with special products at lower rates of interest.

Indeed, we have specific loan and savings products tailored to reflect the variety of our clients' business interests and financial situations, most notably in terms of varying interest rates, all of which are calculated on a declining basis. For particularly vulnerable agricultural clients, we lend at an annualised rate of 9 per cent, for all other agricultural loans, 12 per cent, while the remainder of our products are fixed at a standard 18 per cent. For clients at the low end of the socio-economic scale, we have a 'tontine' savings account, which requires a daily deposit over a three-month period before we can establish terms for a loan.

What kind of technical training do you provide to your clients?

We offer a range of specific training opportunities to our clients that serve twin purposes: on the one hand training directly increases the ability of our clients to organise their finances and run their businesses. On the other hand, the training indirectly helps our clients to manage their loans and meet their repayment schedules. We, in other words, have a vested social and self-interest in ensuring that our clients have a minimum understanding of financial and business affairs.

With this in mind our two most common training sessions relate to managing a savings account and managing a loan. Clients are taught how to read and interpret their savings and loan booklets in which all cash transactions are recorded. They are furthermore taught how to foresee financial commitments and plan accordingly; for many, financial planning is done on a day-to-day basis, but long-term planning is harder to do since their income streams can vary tremendously over the course of a year. As for our clients, we help them to build up a certain amount of capital of their own as well as extend them some ourselves.

More specific to agriculturalists and farmers, we provide training on how to transform raw products (such as drying fish for conservation, preserving jams, and so forth) into finished goods and produce them on a saleable scale. We also provide for farmers' training in improved agricultural practices to increase output, in such areas as soil conservation, enrichment, fertilisation, irrigation and complementary crop selection relative to seasons and market demand.

There is also marketing training: this can be as little as having the seller be more friendly, dress better or may be as much as entirely rearranging their stall to better display their products or even relocating. Finally, we also provide functional literacy training, and training sessions to increase awareness of HIV/AIDS and malaria. In overview, the goal of our total training curriculum is to have more knowledgeable, competent and healthy clients, ultimately better able to work, provide for themselves and their families and achieve personal financial security.

Is there any evidence that microloans have helped to empower women or that they have assisted the very poor to raise their standard of living?

In following up with our clients after training sessions and, notably, through their loan life cycles, we have been able to establish that there is a sustained improvement of their socio-economic status.

With our female clients, we have been able to ascertain that they generally achieve greater decision-making ability within their own homes. The empowerment stems from their increased economic independence and the manner in which they utilise their increased cash flow. Instead of relying on their spouses or other family members, they are able to pay for their own expenses and needs, be it for rent, food, health care, school fees, etc. The point is that they now have their own disposable income to do with as they wish. As more active participants in the economic life of their community, they as well have a greater degree of mobility and are better able to participate within the greater community.

14.6   SOVEREIGN DEBT AND THE ENJOYMENT OF FUNDAMENTAL RIGHTS

14.6.1   Accumulation of Sovereign Debt and its Human Rights Dimension

In 1991 Peru was forced to service its foreign debt by doubling its monthly repayment to US$150 million. During that time Latin America was hit by a cholera epidemic, but most poor Peruvians were unable to purchase the necessary drugs because the government had increased the prices of all basic sanitary products in order to raise revenues for its repayment programme. In 2000 the government of Tanzania spent on debt repayment nine times more than it did on the provision of health. It may seem rational that a country must pay its debts, but at the time 1.6 million Tanzanians lived with AIDS and were denied access to essential medicines.[111] In both cases there is a clear conflict between the pressures incumbent on a country to service its foreign (public) debt and its ability to provide basic social services to its people. Thus, debt repayment may in certain situations constitute an impediment to the enjoyment of, at least, the most basic ESC rights, and in many cases also civil and political rights. The issue is not, however, straightforward. For one thing, on what grounds can a country legitimately repudiate or suspend the repayment of a contractually incurred debt? Secondly, given that the ability of states to borrow money allows them to fulfil their human rights obligations by paying for necessary social services, infrastructure and education without burdening their taxpayers (debt as a policy tool) – especially in poor countries – what is the ideal formula at which a debt can be considered sustainable?

Sovereign nations raise revenues through both domestic and international mechanisms. The former include the collection of taxes, customs duties, privatisations and others. At the international level, states borrow from private

---

[111]   C. Barry, 'Sovereign Debt, Human Rights and Policy Conditionality' (2011) 19 *Journal of Political Philosophy* 282, at 286.

banks and international financial institutions (IFIs), but they also issue sovereign bonds and other so-called debt securities. When bonds mature (at a time set out in the body of the bond) states pay the bondholders their initial capital as well as any accrued interest. The capital (or principal) lent and the interest accrued from direct lending and sovereign bond purchases account for a large part of a country's foreign public debt (the other being currency and deposits).[112] Any other lending from local banks or bonds purchased by one's nationals is considered domestic public debt. Sovereign debt is, moreover, distinguished threefold, namely: (1) governmental debt; (2) local authority debt; and (3) public corporation debt. The first two are generally consolidated, whereas unless otherwise specified,[113] the debts of public corporations do not burden the central government. Public debt, whether of foreign or domestic origin, should be distinguished from debt that is private, namely debt incurred by private entities in a state and which is owed to private or public financial institutions or others. Although this observation seems self-evident, it became a focal point in respect of the Greek debt crisis, which is described in Case Study 14.2. It should be emphasised that a state's credit rating determines its access to private lending markets (and the availability of its bonds thereto), as well as the interest rates by which it can borrow. States with poor credit ratings either borrow with high interest rates from private lenders (and correspondingly accumulate more debt in less time than other states) or are excluded from private markets altogether (out of fear of non-repayment). In the latter case, they may resort to emergency funding from IFIs, such as the IMF, but this is a temporary measure with the aim of short-term liquidity and balance-of-payments restoration until such time as the state in question restores its creditworthiness in the private lending markets.

The starting point for this discussion rests on the thesis that the contractual nature of debt obliges the debtor country to honour its undertaking. The more debt accumulated by a state under strict conditions of servicing, the less it is able to cater to the socio-economic needs of its people. The proposition, therefore, that debt is always payable is in stark conflict with the positive obligation of states to fulfil fundamental human rights if by servicing their debt they fail their people. In fact, human rights treaty bodies have made it clear that states cannot invoke their financial obligations to IFIs

---

[112] See art. 1(4), EU Commission regulation 220/2014 (7 March 2014), amending Council regulation 479/2009 as regards references to the European system of national and regional accounts in the EU.

[113] Under Uzbek law, for example, outstanding liabilities of state unitary enterprises are borne by the state. See I. Bantekas, 'The Legal Nature of State Unitary Enterprises in Uzbek Corporate Law' (2013) 27 *Australian Journal of Corporate Law* 346.

(and by implication private lenders) in order to avoid satisfying their human rights obligations.[114] Moreover, the 2014 *Human Development Report* emphasises that 'access to certain basic elements of a dignified life ought to be de-linked from people's ability to pay'.[115] Given, moreover, that states borrow for no other reason than for the benefit of their people, the economic self-determination of sovereign debt is of critical importance; debt contracted by the state but which is used (in the knowledge of the lender) for other private benefit cannot burden the people of that state. This naturally brings into question several principles of general international law. For one thing, despite some contention, no state is 'required to execute pecuniary obligations if this jeopardises the functioning of its public services, disorganises its administration' or has a detrimental effect on fundamental rights.[116] Recent awards by investment tribunals have confirmed this. In the *LG & E* case, an International Centre for the Settlement of Investment Disputes (ICSID) tribunal held that Argentina's crippling financial situation justified an invocation of a state of necessity. This was evident from an unemployment rate of 25 per cent, the fact that half of the country's population lived below the poverty line, the health care system had effectively collapsed and per capita spending on social services had decreased by 74 per cent.[117] Indeed, the near collapse of a domestic economy, in addition to:

the social hardships bringing down more than half of the population below the poverty line; the immediate threats to the health of young children, the sick and the most vulnerable members of the population ... that all this taken together [qualifies] as a situation where the maintenance of public order and the promotion of essential security interest of Argentina as a state and as a country was vitally at stake.[118]

This is not merely an entitlement, but an obligation on the part of states and, as such, human rights obligations supersede conflicting pecuniary obligations. Such a conclusion is consistent with fiscal sovereignty (itself an emanation of economic self-determination) and the tools by which this is exercised.[119] Chief among these is the doctrine of executive necessity, which

---

[114] *Federation of Employed Pensioners of Greece (IKA-ETAM)* v. *Greece* (ECSR) (2012) paras. 66–81; *Pensioners' Union of the Agricultural Bank of Greece (ATE)* v. *Greece* (ECSR) (2012) 48; *Capital Bank AD* v. *Bulgaria* (ECtHR) (2005) para. 90.

[115] UNDP, *Human Development Report* (2014), above note 12, 5.

[116] *Société Commerciale de Belgique (SOCOBEL)* v. *Greece* (PCIJ) (1939). This statement which is attributed to the respondent's counsel was accepted in full by counsel for Belgium.

[117] *LG & E* v. *Argentina* (ICSID) (2006) para. 234.

[118] *Continental Casualty Co.* v. *Argentina* (ICSID) (2008) para. 180.

[119] In *Achmea BV* v. *Slovak Republic* (PCA) (2014) para. 251, the tribunal held that it was not empowered to interfere in the democratic processes of a state, as is the case with its design of a public health care policy. It went on to emphasise that the design and implementation of such a policy 'is for the state alone to assess and the state must balance the different and sometimes competing interests, such as its duty to ensure appropriate

posits the idea that contracts and promises made by government are unenforceable in the public interest if they fetter the future competence and powers of the executive.[120] As a result, it is artificial and wholly illegitimate to construe loan agreements and debts outside the framework of international human rights.[121]

The second exception to general international law is that a succeeding government is not obliged to succeed to pecuniary obligations incurred by its predecessor when these provide no benefit to the people and are otherwise illegal.[122] The principle that governments succeed to all the obligations inherited by their predecessors was not meant to cover odious, illegitimate or illegal debt or to serve as a pretext for the violation of human rights.[123]

As a result of these considerations, states saddled with an odious, illegal or unsustainable debt continue to owe human rights obligations to their people. These obligations supersede other obligations under pertinent debt instruments.[124] States are entitled to employ a variety of mechanisms in order to abide by their human rights obligations. These include unilateral repudiation of debt arising from debt instruments, repudiation of awards in direct conflict with fundamental constitutional guarantees,[125] repudiation of unconscionable concession agreements[126] and finally unilateral insolvency. Although there is significant practice, particularly in the late nineteenth and early twentieth centuries, of states becoming unilaterally insolvent,[127]

---

healthcare to its population and its duty to honour its international investment protection commitments'.

[120] *Watson's Bay and South Shore Ferry Co. Ltd* v. *Whitfield* (Australia) (1919) at 277; *Redericktiebolaget Amphitrite* v. *King* (UK) (1921) at 503.

[121] See CESCR, General Comment 2, para. 9, which emphasised that 'international measures to deal with the debt crisis should take full account of the need to protect economic, social and cultural rights'.

[122] T. H. Cheng, 'Renegotiating the Odious Debt Doctrine' (2007) 70 *Law and Contemporary Problems* 7.

[123] Among the many sources, Bedjaoui, who was the International Law Commission's (ILC) rapporteur on the Vienna Convention on the Succession of States in respect of state property, archives and debts, and hence his opinion is decisive, noted that a debt is considered odious if the debtor state contracted it 'with an aim and for a purpose not in conformity with international law'. M. Bedjaoui, Ninth Report on succession of states in respect of matters other than treaties, UN doc. A/CN.4/301 (1977), reprinted in (1977) *Yearbook ILC*, at 70.

[124] Article 103 of the UN Charter may serve as additional justification for this argument, under the assumption that human rights are central to the aims of the Charter and the parties' obligations.

[125] *BCB Holdings Ltd and Belize Bank Ltd* v. *Attorney-General of Belize* (CCJ) (2013). This is described more fully in Case Study 19.1.

[126] See Chapter 19.3.2.

[127] M. Waibel, *Sovereign Defaults before International Courts and Tribunals* (Cambridge University Press, 2011) 3–19.

this being recognised by investment tribunals as a reality,[128] there is fierce resistance against its eventuality. The benefit of preventing even a heavily indebted state from becoming insolvent is that it will be able to generate funds in perpetuity despite its indebtedness. States can generate funds from the following sources: customs; taxes; expropriation of assets belonging to their nationals, as is the case with imminent domain or extraordinary measures such as confiscation of deposits in banks; sale of state assets; acceptance of odious and neo-colonial concession contracts, particularly as regards strategic infrastructure, monopolies and natural resources; and privatisations among others. However, if states enjoy the right to unilateral insolvency when unable to service their debt without violating fundamental human rights then any default on their debt does not amount to an internationally unlawful act and as such does not incur liability towards their creditors.

14.6.2 Odious, Illegal and Illegitimate Debt

Before we explain the meaning of these concepts, it should be noted that with few exceptions there is an absence of case law and practice. This is not surprising given that creditor states are wary of 'allowing' borrower nations to invoke these concepts as justification for non-payment of sovereign debt, for fear that they may crystallise into custom.[129] As a result, when borrower nations are at the brink of unilateral debt repudiation, their creditors step in to facilitate so-called debt restructuring.[130] This may entail a mixture of partial debt relief/cancellation (usually through informal mechanisms, such as the Paris Club);[131] extended repayment options; further concessional funding; haircut to private debt; as well as a range of conditionalities the aim of which is to sustain the remainder of the debt and ensure prompt repayment of interest and capital. The chief aims of debt restructuring are to avoid at all cost unilateral actions by the borrower, as well as to ensure that the repayment of the debt is not in doubt. However, such negotiated settlements, typically forced upon borrowers lacking short-term liquidity, do not in any way

---

[128] In *Postova Banka AS and Istrokapital SE* v. *Greece* (ICSID) (2015) para. 324, it was held that: 'sovereign debt is an instrument of government monetary and economic policy and its impact at the local and international levels makes it an important tool for the handling of social and economic policies of a state. It cannot, thus, be equated to private indebtedness or corporate debt.'

[129] See e.g., the discussion on the post-Saddam Hussein Iraqi debt, in R. Howse, 'The Concept of Odious Debt in Public International Law', UNCTAD Discussion Paper 185 (2007) at 15–16; 2009 Report on Effects of Foreign Debt, above note 10, paras. 8–9; but see principle 1 of UNGA resolution 69/139 (29 September 2015), Basic Principles on Sovereign Debt Restructuring.

[130] See R. M. Lastra and L. Buchheit (eds.), *Sovereign Debt Management* (Oxford University Press, 2014).

[131] See www.clubdeparis.org/en/.

diminish the right of states to repudiate odious and illegal debt. Indeed, such repudiation is justified by peremptory considerations of justice and equity, but is also founded on sovereignty and self-determination.[132]

The preliminary report of the Greek Truth Committee on Public Debt, whose mandate was to investigate the origins and causes of the public debt of Greece, defined illegitimate debt as:

Debt that the borrower cannot be required to repay because the loan, security or guarantee, or the terms and conditions attached to that loan, security or guarantee infringed the law (both national and international) or public policy, or because such terms and conditions were grossly unfair, unreasonable, unconscionable or otherwise objectionable, or because the conditions attached to the loan, security or guarantee included policy prescriptions that violate national laws or human rights standards, or because the loan, security or guarantee was not used for the benefit of the population or the debt was converted from private (commercial) to public debt under pressure to bailout creditors.[133]

In perhaps the most influential contemporary study on odious debt, commissioned by the UN Conference on Trade and Development (UNCTAD) and authored by Robert Howse, several case studies of illegitimate, odious and illegal debt are set out. Prominent among these is the *Tinoco* arbitration, where a successor Costa Rican government argued that the debts incurred by its predecessor, the dictator Tinoco and his entourage, could not be attributed to the state because none of the loans were in the public interest and the money was used for purely private ends. Chief Justice Taft, who sat as sole arbitrator, agreed with this position, particularly since the Royal Bank of Canada, which paid several cheques to Tinoco, was aware of the dictator's unpopularity in the country and the fact that the money was employed for illegitimate ends.[134] In the case of the Greek debt, analysed in Case Study 13.2, most of the post-2010 bail-out loans were found to be illegitimate because less than 8 per cent was earmarked for public expenditures, the remainder being used to repay existing debt, while the initial debt (for which the loans were granted) was private debt that had forcefully and artificially been converted into public debt.

The Greek Truth Committee further defined odious debt as debt:

which the lender knew or ought to have known, was incurred in violation of democratic principles (including consent, participation, transparency and accountability) and used against the best interests of the population of the borrower state, or is

---

[132] Howse, above note 129, 1.

[133] Truth Committee on Public Debt, Preliminary Report (June 2015), online at www.hellenicparliament.gr/UserFiles/8158407a-fc31-4ff2-a8d3-433701dbe6d4/Report_EN_final.pdf, at 10; see also 2009 Report on Effects of Foreign Debt, above note 10, paras. 8–22.

[134] *Tinoco arbitration (Great Britain v. Costa Rica)* (arbitration tribunal) (1923) at 176.

unconscionable and whose effect is to deny people their fundamental civil, political or economic, social and cultural rights.[135]

If self-determination is to be meaningful, debt which has a detrimental impact on the livelihood, dignity and well-being of a population must be open to debate and approval in accordance with constitutional and international human rights guarantees. Limitation of liability and confidentiality clauses, immunity waivers (for the borrower), conditionalities that infringe fundamental rights or the imposition of measures that stifle democratic debate render the debt instrument invalid and the debt odious. Indeed, in the majority of cases the lenders impose such conditions upon the borrower and hence they possess full knowledge of the odious nature of the agreement. In a recent UNCTAD report entitled 'Sovereign Debt Workouts: Going Forward (Roadmap and Guide)', it was emphasised that debt restructuring currently lacks legitimacy, impartiality, good faith, transparency and sustainability.[136]

The Greek Truth Committee defined illegal debt as:

debt in respect of which proper legal procedures (including those relating to authority to sign loans or approval of loans, securities or guarantees by the representative branch or branches of government of the borrower state) were not followed, or which involved clear misconduct by the lender (including bribery, coercion and undue influence), as well as debt contracted in violation of domestic and international law or which had conditions attached thereto that contravened the law or public policy.[137]

The rule whereby states may not invoke their domestic law as justification for violating their obligations under international law[138] is inapplicable in situations where the lender intended to violate or bypass fundamental provisions of domestic law, particularly of a constitutional nature, through a debt instrument entered into with the borrower. This is because such an agreement violates the principle of legality, fails to satisfy good faith and breaches third parties' legitimate expectations. Surely, the superior character of an agreement under international law was not meant to be used in order to blatantly bypass and violate fundamental constitutional provisions, breach human rights and put third parties' legitimate expectations into doubt.

Given that powerful creditor states are able to interfere in borrower states' constitutional processes and enter into statements or other actions that knowingly culminate in harming the economy of the borrower and the livelihood

---

[135] Truth Committee, Preliminary Report, above note 133, at 10.
[136] UNCTAD, Sovereign Debt Workouts: Going Forward: Roadmap and Guidelines (April 2015), online at http://unctad.org/en/PublicationsLibrary/gdsddf2015misc1_en.pdf, at 4.
[137] Truth Committee, Preliminary Report, above note 133, at 10.
[138] Article 32, ILC Articles on State Responsibility.

of its population (unilateral coercive measures), reference to 'force' in article 52 of the Vienna Convention on the Law of Treaties (VCLT) may be construed as including forms of economic coercion.[139] This type of economic coercion qualifies, among others, as unlawful intervention in one's domestic affairs which, although it does not invalidate consent, may none the less offer a basis for denouncing a loan agreement under article 56(1)(b) VCLT.

14.6.3   Unsustainable Debt

Clearly, what is called for is the introduction of binding responsible banking rules in the field of sovereign loans, and hence the statement in the Monterrey Consensus that debtors and creditors possess a 'shared responsibility' for unsustainable debt is an acknowledgement of the obvious.[140] In domestic law if a bank grants a loan to a minor without his or her parents' consent, it could not retrieve any capital or interest from the parents. Equally, if the same bank were to lend money to a person who possessed no assets or other collateral it would risk losing its capital in case of non-payment by the debtor. As a result, domestic banking is generally a cautious business, but this is not so in respect of sovereign lending because of the special treatment afforded to financial institutions by states. Practice from the post-2008 financial crisis suggests that states are eager to re-capitalise even the most irresponsible banks with taxpayers' money, to the detriment of social spending. In late 2018, the UN Independent Expert on Debt and Human Rights launched his Guiding Principles on Human Rights Impact Assessments of Economic Reforms, which set out the human rights principles and standards that apply to states, international financial institutions and creditors when designing, formulating or proposing economic reforms.[141] It should be pointed out that even where sovereign debt is legitimate, it may none the less be unsustainable. A debt is generally unsustainable where:

> it cannot be serviced without seriously impairing the ability or capacity of the government of the borrower state to fulfil its basic human rights obligations, such as

---

[139] The Final Act of the VCLT includes a declaration, initially tabled by the Netherlands (in reaction to a request by developing countries that consent to a treaty under economic pressure be considered as 'coercion'), stating that: 'The UN Conference on the Law of Treaties ... condemns the threat or use of pressure in any form, military, political, or economic, by any State, in order to coerce another state to perform any act relating to the conclusion of a treaty in violation of the principles of sovereign equality of states and freedom of consent'; Draft Declaration on the Prohibition of the Threat or Use of Economic or Political Coercion in Concluding a Treaty, adopted by the Conference without a formal vote. Draft Report of the Committee of the Whole on Its Work at the First Session of the Conference, UN doc. A/Conf.39/C.1/L.370/Rev.1/Vol.II (1969) at 251–2.

[140] Monterrey Consensus, above note 82, para. 47.

[141] UN doc. A/HRC/40/57 (19 December 2018).

those relating to healthcare, education, water and sanitation and adequate housing, or to invest in public infrastructure and programmes necessary for economic and social development, or without harmful consequences for the population of the borrower state (including a deterioration of the borrower state).[142]

The glaring absence of any human rights considerations is evident in the assessment of debt sustainability. When poor countries apply for debt relief, concessional funding and regular lending, the creditors will have to make an assessment of the applicant's debt sustainability. In practice, debt sustainability is narrowly defined by the ability of a country to pay its debts on the basis of its export earnings alone. By way of illustration, if the projected export earnings of country X are US $100 million in a given year, and the annual repayments on interest and capital on its intended loan amount to US $95 million, its debt will be considered sustainable and it will be eligible for funding. This narrow method of assessment, however, fails to consider the country's expenditures for health, education, housing, infrastructure and other social projects as though they are irrelevant;[143] it only caters for the interests of the lenders. Hence, in the above scenario, the debtor country would be forced to meet its annual social expenditures with US $5 million, although the creditors are aware that the real costs may amount to at least US $20 million. It is no wonder that campaigners are urging multilateral creditors to redefine debt sustainability as the level of debt that allows a country to achieve its MDGs/SDGs targets. The Independent Expert on the Effects of Foreign Debt has suggested that:

Any concept of debt sustainability should include an assessment of what minimum expenditure is required to enable a government to meet its obligations to its citizens, including the provision of basic social services such as health and education. In particular, human rights should be used as a basis for assessing debt sustainability and for the cancellation of all unsustainable debt. Such an approach would consider all indebted countries irrespective of their income and assess the level of debt they could carry without undermining their human rights obligations.[144]

Sovereign debt not only hampers the global financial architecture, it is probably the most serious impediment for the full realisation of all rights and is a major underlying reason for mass phenomena such as irregular migration.

---

[142] Truth Committee, Preliminary Report, above note 133, at 10.

[143] The Paris Club proclaims its commitment to debt relief programmes for poorer nations through two general avenues: (1) longer repayment period (the maximum repayment period is now twenty-three years (including six years of grace) for commercial loans, and forty years (including sixteen years of grace) for ODA loans); (2) debt cancellation, where for the poorest and most indebted countries the level of debt cancellation may reach 67 per cent. Despite these significant initiatives, the Paris Club's instruments and terms make no reference to the HDI, the MDGs or human rights in their assessment of debt sustainability.

[144] 2009 Report on Effects of Foreign Debt, above note 10, para. 55.

A multilateral (as opposed to discrete unilateral) approach would require regional (or highly indebted countries as a grouping) or global efforts to arrive at a treaty based on five key pillars: (1) that debt be payable only when sustainable, calculated strictly on the basis of universally agreed human rights indicators;[145] (2) that debt is transparent and covered by a collective right to truth regarding its causes and origins;[146] (3) that all parties involved in the accumulation of debt, namely lender states and international organisations, bear responsibility, where due; (4) that banking practices worldwide are regulated in such a way that ensures responsibility and a ceiling on interest (it is unacceptable that most global debt is interest-generated (dwarfing the initial capital lent), or predicated on unconscionable practices in which banks invest little (and sometimes no) money but reap huge benefits to the detriment of entire populations); and (5) that foreign investment law and the law applicable to IFIs, such as the World Bank Group and the European Central Bank (ECB), cease to be fragmented from general international law, and particularly fundamental human rights and international environmental law.[147]

CASE STUDY 14.2
The Parliamentary Committee on the Truth about the Greek Debt: The Artificiality of Greek Debt and its Odious Nature

In April 2015 the president of the Parliament of the newly elected government of Greece set up a Truth Committee on Public Debt. This was composed of Greek and foreign experts, economists, lawyers and others, as well as members of grassroots organisations. One of the authors of this book, Ilias Bantekas, was a member of the Committee. All members offered their services pro bono. The object of the Committee was to investigate how Greek foreign debt had accumulated from 1980 to 2014, but especially from 2009 to late 2014, which coincides with the financial crisis.

In June 2008 Greek public debt was about 252 billion euros, which amounted to a debt-to-GDP ratio of 112 per cent, which is certainly sustainable, especially for a developed economy in the eurozone. If this is coupled with a decent

---

[145] See Chapter 9.7.

[146] The only international instrument that obliges and at the same time entitles states to audit their debt is art. 7(9) of EC Regulation 472/2013 on the strengthening of economic and budgetary surveillance of member states in the euro area experiencing or threatened with serious difficulties with respect to their financial stability. National debt commissions, such as those of Greece, Ecuador, Argentina and Brazil, have found this right to stem from their constitutions.

[147] See A. Kulick, *Global Public Interest in International Investment Law* (Cambridge University Press, 2012); see also Chapter 19.3.2.

credit rating, particularly where a state pays its monthly debt arrears on time and is considered creditworthy, the interest charged for its borrowing will remain comparatively low. When such creditworthiness exists and a country maintains a small deficit that is counterbalanced by a manageable debt-to-GDP ratio (i.e. the total amount of public debt as juxtaposed to the GDP), the total amount of a country's overall debt does not lead to a debt crisis. Hence, if a country has an overall debt of only 1 billion euros but produces no revenue while incurring annual public expenses of 100 million euros, its debt-to-GDP ratio will sky-rocket, it will lose its creditworthiness and as a result be forced out of the private lending markets and subsequently the value of its sovereign bonds will be reduced to junk.

Before the circulation of the preliminary report of the Greek Parliament's Truth Committee on Public Debt in June 2015, it was globally assumed that Greece's debt was the result of lavish public expenditures and living 'beyond one's means'. The Committee dispelled this myth and demonstrated how the debt had really been accumulated. It was found that Greece's public debt had remained more or less the same from 1993 to 2009. In fact, two-thirds of the debt's rise was attributable to interest payments alone (simple and compound). Public expenditures during this period were lower in Greece than in the rest of the eurozone, with the exception of defence expenditures. However, what was less noticeable was that between 2000 and 2009 there was a sharp rise in private/consumer debt. This private debt-to-GDP ratio reached its peak at 129 per cent in 2009. Hence, Greek and European private banks found themselves exposed to almost 100 billion euros worth of private debt. Quite clearly, this was not a debt incurred by the state, for which it was not liable.

As the Committee pointed out in its preliminary report, in their effort to avoid the bankruptcy of those private banks which managed to accumulate a private debt of 100 billion euros through irresponsible lending (the majority shares of which had been bought mainly by French and German banks), the governments of France, Germany and Greece conspired to falsify the Greek budget of 2009 so that the country's deficit could appear far larger than it really was. Why? Because in this manner Greece could be forced out of international lending markets and thus incur fiscal supervision by the IMF and the ECB. Their ultimate purpose was to buy some time so that the banks' private debt could be nationalised by Greece, thus transforming it into a public debt. Hence, a private debt was transformed into a public one because the banks could not have forced the Greek state to pay it as it was not incurred by the Greek state. Upon transformation into a 'state' debt, not only were the private banks effectively recapitalised with European Union (EU) taxpayers' money, but the cost of the recapitalisation could subsequently be demanded further from Greece and its people. At what cost? The imposition of the most austere conditionalities ever witnessed and an economic occupation of the country. Did they work?

The austerity measures imposed upon the Greek people not only failed to increase productivity and investment, but even though Greece has succeeded in consecutive surplus budgets, its GDP shrank by 25 per cent and unemployment rose to more than 30 per cent. By late 2014, Greece's debt-to-GDP ratio had risen to 190 per cent. Of the funds granted to Greece under the so-called 'bail-out' programme between 2010 and 2014, less than 8 per cent was earmarked by the creditors for public expenditures, the rest being directed to debt repayment. Yet Greece was made to pay significant fees for this service (legal, financial and other), in addition to the accumulation of interest at exorbitant rates.

The Committee emphasised that all private debt transformed into public debt, along with its attendant interest, was either odious or illegal. Moreover, no loans provided by multilateral and bilateral creditors from 2010 until early 2015 raised an obligation for repayment because they provided no benefit to the Greek state and its people (with 92 per cent going directly for debt repayment), and in fact, despite these loans and the surplus in the country's budget, Greece's public debt continued to grow. As a result, Greece had not in any way become unjustifiably richer from these loans. On the contrary, the measures imposed against the Greek people were wholly antithetical to fundamental human rights as these stem from customary international law, multilateral treaties and the Greek Constitution. Consequently, these 'loans' were held to be odious, illegal or illegitimate. The recommendation of the Committee was that Greece was not only entitled but obliged to unilaterally repudiate such illegal, odious and illegitimate debts on account of its international human rights obligations and economic self-determination.

QUESTIONS

1. Given that the pursuit of well-being knows no borders, the RTD is incumbent also on the governments of even the richest nations.[148] Discuss.

2. So-called 'vulture funds' are made up of private creditors who buy the foreign debt of indebted poor nations at a discounted price, slightly prior to the debt relief initiatives these countries now enjoy. These vulture funds make a profit recovering the full value of the debt, accrued interest, as well as late payment penalties. Given that they invested money into a legitimate subrogated claim, is it just to strip them of the rights granted to them under the debt instrument which they purchased? Discuss in relation to the Debt Relief (Developing Countries) Act, adopted by the United Kingdom (UK) in 2010.

[148] See Save the Children, State of the World's Mothers 2011 (May 2011), which ranks the UK relatively low in children's well-being on account of its poor record of pre-primary enrolment (81 per cent as opposed to 100 per cent in most other European nations), which represents a significant assistance to the poor.

3. What are the obstacles preventing the World Bank from adopting a human rights-based approach (HRBA) to development lending?

4. A fictitious scenario. The donor community declares itself willing to give ten times more aid under condition that it is granted solely under charitable terms, rather than on the basis of the RTD or the MDGs. The money is great and so much can be done with it. Charity is after all benevolent and at par with the RTD. Discuss.

5. The legal basis of the odious/illegitimate debt doctrine seems to be inconsistent with customary international law regarding the succession of governments – which generally posits that succeeding governments are liable for the debts incurred by their predecessors. Discuss.

FURTHER READING

Alston, P., and M. Robinson (eds.), *Human Rights and Development: Towards Mutual Reinforcement* (Oxford University Press, 2005).

Bantekas, I., and Lumina C. (eds.), *Sovereign Debt and Human Rights* (Oxford University Press, 2018).

Blanco, E., and J. Razzaque, 'Ecosystem Services and Human Wellbeing in a Globalised World: Assessing the Role of Law' (2009) 31 *Human Rights Quarterly* 692.

Broberg, M., and Sano, H.-O., 'Strengths and Weaknesses in a Human Rights-based Approach to International Development: An Analysis of a Rights-based Approach to Development Assistance Based on Practical Experiences' (2018) 22 *The International Journal of Human Rights* 664.

Bunn, I. D., 'The Right to Development: Implications for International Economic Law' (2000) 15 *American University International Law Review* 1425.

Fitzmaurice, M., and J. Marshall, 'The Human Right to a Clean Environment: Phantom or Reality? The European Court of Human Rights and English Courts Perspective on Balancing Rights in Environmental Matters' (2007) 76 *Netherlands Journal of International Law* 103.

Fukuda-Parr, S., 'Millennium Development Goal 8: Indicators for International Human Rights Obligations?' (2006) 28 *Human Rights Quarterly* 966.

Ibhawoh, B., 'The Right to Development: The Politics and Polemics of Power and Resistance' (2011) 33 *Human Rights Quarterly* 76.

La Chimia, A., and S. Arrowsmith, 'Addressing Tied Aid: Towards a More Development-oriented WTO' (2009) 12 *Journal of International Economic Law* 707.

Langford, M., A. Summer and A. E. Yamin (eds.), *The Millennium Development Goals and Human Rights: Past, Present and Future* (Cambridge University Press, 2015).

Lienau, O., *Rethinking Sovereign Debt: Politics, Reputation and Legitimacy in Modern Finance* (Harvard University Press, 2014).

Manji, A., 'Eliminating Poverty? Financial Inclusion, Access to Land and Gender Equality in International Development' (2010) 73 *Modern Law Review* 985.

Marks, S. P., *Implementing the Right to Development: The Role of International Law* (Friedrich-Ebert-Stiftung, 2008).

Marks, S. P., and B. A. Andreassen (eds.), *Development as a Human Right: Legal, Political and Economic Dimensions*, new edn (Intersentia, 2010).

Mazur, R. E., 'Realization or Deprivation of the Right to Development under Globalization? Debt, Structural Adjustment and Poverty Reduction Programs' (2004) 60 *GeoJournal* 61.

McInerney-Lankford, S., and H. O. Sano, *Human Rights Indicators in Development: An Introduction* (World Bank Publications, 2010).

Meier, B. M., 'Advancing Health Rights in a Globalized World: Responding to Globalization through a Collective Human Right to Public Health' (2007) 35 *Journal of Law, Medicine and Ethics* 545.

Mitlin, D., and S. Hickey, *Rights-Based Approaches to Development: Exploring the Potential and Pitfalls* (Kumarian Press, 2009).

Paulus, C. G., 'Odious Debts v. Debt Trap: A Realistic Help'? (2005) 31 *Brooklyn Journal of International Law* 83.

Schefer, K. N. (ed.), *Poverty and the International Economic Legal System: Duties to the World's Poor* (Cambridge University Press, 2013).

Sengupta, A., 'On the Theory and Practice of the Right to Development' (2002) 24 *Human Rights Quarterly* 837.

Udombana, N. J., 'The Third World and the Right to Development: Agenda for a New Millennium' (2000) 22 *Human Rights Quarterly* 753.

Websites

African Forum and Network on Debt and Development (AFRODAD): www.afrodad.org/index.php/en/

Committee for the Abolition of Third World Debt: http://cadtm.org/

European Network on Debt and Repayment: www.eurodad.org/

OECD Development Assistance Committee: www.oecd.org/dac/

Sustainable Development Goals: https://sustainabledevelopment.un.org/?menu=1300

UK Department for International Development: www.gov.uk/government/organisations/department-for-international-development

UN Financing for Development: www.un.org/esa/ffd/index.html

UN Right to Development: www.ohchr.org/EN/Issues/Development/Pages/DevelopmentIndex.aspx

15 Victims' Rights and Reparation

CONTENTS

15.1   INTRODUCTION

International human rights law has for a long time focused primarily on standard-setting and the establishment of institutions tasked with promoting human rights and monitoring states' compliance with their obligations. Limited attention was paid to victims as rights-holders and to the availability of effective remedies for the vindication of rights. Yet slowly, conceptual shifts and practices, beginning at the national level, have changed prevailing perceptions of victims as largely passive beneficiaries, resulting in growing calls for victims to play a more active role, particularly in the criminal justice process. The exclusion of victims and their lack of opportunity to participate effectively in proceedings that affect their rights were increasingly seen as an anomaly, raising the fundamental question of whose interests a justice system is supposed to serve.[1] This is reflected in the work of scholars and practitioners in the field of victimology and renewed interest in restorative justice.[2]

This change in thinking gained international currency initially with the 1984 United Nations General Assembly (UNGA) Declaration of Basic Principles of Justice for Victims of Crime and Abuse of Power (Victims' Declaration),[3] and more than twenty years later culminated in the Basic Principles and Guidelines on the Right to a Remedy and Reparation for Victims of Gross Violations of International Human Rights Law and Serious Violations of International Humanitarian Law (Basic Principles).[4] The impetus for victims' rights owes a lot to the increasing availability of regional and international complaints procedures. The growing recourse to these procedures has enabled, if not compelled, regional and international human rights treaty bodies to develop their jurisprudence and, to varying degrees, to strengthen victims' rights in the process. More recently, the establishment of international(ised) criminal tribunals, in particular the International Criminal Court (ICC), has led to a keener appreciation of victims' rights, including the right to protection and the right to participation.[5] These developments are complemented by numerous attempts to take legal action in third countries, in particular on the grounds of universal jurisdiction, which assert and highlight the need for victims' rights in transnational proceedings. Taken together, these multiple efforts are testimony to how victims, supported by their representatives and advocacy organisations, have claimed their space in international human rights law and continue doing so in the face of a series of remaining obstacles to the vindication of their rights.

This emphasis on a victim-centred approach has not remained unchallenged. Critical observers argue that victims' politics lead to a 'privatisation'

[1] J. Doak, *Victims' Rights, Human Rights and Criminal Justice, Reconceiving the Role of Third Parties* (Hart, 2008) 7–11. See further J. C. Ochoa, *The Rights of Victims in Criminal Justice Proceedings for Serious Human Rights Violations* (Martinus Nijhoff, 2013).

[2] See e.g., the work done by the World Society of Victimology, www.worldsociety ofvictimology.org; G. Johnstone, *Restorative Justice: Ideas, Values and Debates* (Willan, 2002); and in the context of international crimes, R. Letschert et al. (eds.), *Victimological Approaches to International Crimes: Africa* (Intersentia, 2011).

[3] UNGA resolution 40/34 (29 November 1985).

[4] UNGA resolution 60/147 (16 December 2006). See for developments at the regional level in particular, Directive 2012/29/EU of the European Parliament and of the Council of 25 October 2012 establishing minimum standards on the rights, support and protection of victims of crime, and replacing Council Framework Decision 2001/220/JHA.

[5] See REDRESS, *The Participation of Victims in International Criminal Proceedings* (2012) and *Ending Threats and Reprisals against Victims of Torture and Related International Crimes: A Call to Action* (2009).

and individualisation of public concerns, feeding a growing 'victims' industry that serves to undermine the agency of individuals and groups to assert their rights as political actors.[6] These are valid concerns. However, it is important not to overlook the vital role that effective rights and remedies play for victims, considering in particular the realities of what it means to suffer serious human rights violations and grave injustices. These violations frequently have devastating consequences for the direct victim(s) and others. Torture, for example, often results in lifelong physical and psychological impairment, being aimed at the destruction of the personality of its victims. Family members experience anxiety while their relative is in custody and often suffer from diminished income following the release or even death of the victim. They also have to bear the brunt of caring for and dealing with victim's attempts to cope with the aftermath of torture, which may be volatile and ultimately 'unsuccessful', without any acknowledgement of their own suffering in the process. Communities, for their part, may be in a state of fear as to who will be next, stifling the freedom of expression and action of their members.

Victims' rights, whether they take the form of a procedural right of access to justice or participation, or a substantive right to reparation, fulfil a number of important functions. Ideally, they allow victims to assert their rights, redress power imbalances manifest in violations, provide a measure of justice and furnish the victim(s) with the means to cope and rebuild their lives. They may also lead to a public acknowledgement of wrongdoing that recognises unlawful suffering, demonstrates society's respect for, and solidarity with, the victim(s), and affirms the rule of law. In addition, victims' rights play an important role in contributing to prevention through deterrence (punishment and/or payment of damages or other forms of reparation) and systemic changes to counter violations, such as legislative and institutional reforms.

Notwithstanding the advancement of victims' rights and the strength of what may be called the victims' rights movement, a series of open questions and challenges remain. Do the rights granted in various treaties and declarations translate into a right to reparation under international law, and, if so, does this apply in relation to all or only some particularly serious human rights violations? Who are the rights-holders and what are their entitlements? Recent developments also raise questions of coherence and effectiveness in light of the proliferation of victims' rights in various bodies of international law, such as international human rights law, international humanitarian law and international criminal law, and of the different approaches taken by various adjudicative bodies. Finally, and crucially, has the growing international recognition of these rights been matched by their effective implementation and enforcement?

---

[6] See on 'victims' politics' below at 15.11.

15.2   THE DEVELOPMENT OF THE RIGHT TO REPARATION

Reparation is a deep-rooted and vital component of any legal order that is central to the notion of justice. It is traditionally based on the understanding that measures need to be taken to restore the order that has been disturbed by the violation. Where this is not (fully) feasible, the wrongdoer(s) must undo the wrong as much as possible to remedy the breach, a principle articulated by the Permanent Court of International Justice (PCIJ) in the *Chorzów Factory* case:

The essential principle contained in the actual notion of an illegal act – a principle which seems to be established by international practice and in particular by the decisions of arbitral tribunals – is that reparation must, as far as possible, wipe out all the consequences of the illegal act and re-establish the situation which would, in all probability, have existed if that act had not been committed.[7]

The notion that a remedy is a corollary to a right is inherent in legal systems around the world.[8] Accordingly, the victim of a breach has an individual right – which can be of a collective nature in the case of a violation of group rights – to claim reparation for the harm suffered as a result. In traditional, state-centred international law, under the rules of state responsibility, reparation was primarily conceived as a secondary obligation owed by states to other states, not individuals, for a breach of a primary obligation. Even under the established rules of injury to aliens, according to which a state had to remedy a breach of an alien's rights (for example foreign investors), reparation was owed to the state of nationality, not the individual(s) whose rights had been violated.[9] This situation changed significantly after World War II with the recognition of a right to a remedy and reparation in various instruments, as well as reparation agreements, schemes and awards at the inter-state level for violations of human rights and humanitarian law. These parallel and to some degree mutually reinforcing developments have been instrumental in advancing the right to reparation. The latter has also been given fresh impetus by debates and measures taken in the context of political transitions. These are situations following the end of a dictatorship or a conflict that are frequently characterised by a large number of victims of gross violations committed over a period of time, typically by multiple perpetrators often involving both state and non-state actors (NSAs). Reparation fulfils a crucial role in these transitional processes. Besides vindicating rights, reparation can signal societal recognition that individuals or communities suffered

---

[7] Case concerning the *Factory at Chorzów* (PCIJ) (1928) 47.

[8] M. C. Bassiouni, 'International Recognition of Victims' Rights' (2006) 2 *Human Rights Law Review* 203, at 206–8; D. Shelton, *Remedies in International Human Rights Law*, 2nd edn (Oxford University Press, 2005) 22–30.

[9] See Shelton, ibid., 58–83.

wrongs, serve to restore civic trust and express solidarity with the victims.[10] Several states have provided at least some reparation in these situations, which contributes to state practice bolstering the right to reparation.[11]

15.3 THE RIGHT TO REPARATION IN INTERNATIONAL HUMAN RIGHTS LAW

15.3.1 Treaties and UN Declarations

The right to an effective remedy for human rights violations was first recognised in article 8 of the Universal Declaration of Human Rights (UDHR): 'Everyone has the right to an effective remedy by the competent national tribunals for acts violating the fundamental rights granted him by the constitution or by law.' In a similar vein, article 2(3) of the International Covenant on Civil and Political Rights (ICCPR) stipulates that 'any person whose rights ... are violated shall have an effective remedy'. The International Covenant on Economic, Social and Cultural Rights (ICESCR) has no comparable provision owing to reservations concerning the justiciability of the rights it protects.[12] Article 6 of the International Convention on the Elimination of All Forms of Racial Discrimination (ICERD) combines states parties' obligation to assure effective remedies against racial discrimination with 'the right to seek from such tribunals just and adequate reparation'. At the regional level, article 13 of the European Convention on Human Rights (ECHR) stipulates that '[e]veryone ... shall have an effective remedy', whereas article 25 of the American Convention on Human Rights (ACHR) provides for a right to judicial protection and recourse that the states parties need to guarantee in their domestic legal order. The African Charter on Human and Peoples' Rights (ACHPR) does not stipulate an explicit right to a remedy. However,

---

[10] P. de Greiff, 'Justice and Reparations', in P. de Greiff (ed.), *The Handbook of Reparations* (Oxford University Press, 2006) 451–77.

[11] See case studies in de Greiff, ibid.; C. Ferstman, M. Goetz and A. Stephens (eds.), *Reparations for Victims of Genocide, War Crimes and Crimes against Humanity: Systems in Place and Systems in the Making* (Martinus Nijhoff, 2009), part VI. However, see Report of the Special Rapporteur on the promotion of truth, justice, reparation and guarantees of non-recurrence, Pablo de Greiff, UN doc. A/69/518 (14 October 2014) para. 6: 'Despite significant progress at the normative level in establishing the rights of victims to reparations and some important experiences at the level of practice, most victims of gross violations of human rights and serious violations of international humanitarian law still do not receive any reparation. Normative progress and even solid practice in some cases should not obscure the implementation gap, which can rightly be said to be of scandalous proportions.'

[12] See on the role of remedies, Committee on Economic, Social and Cultural Rights (CESCR), General Comment 9: The domestic application of the Covenant, UN doc. E/C.12/1998/24 (3 December 1998), and further Chapter 9.6.

the African Commission on Human and Peoples' Rights (ACmHPR) has read such a right into article 7(1)(a) ACHPR, according to which individuals have the right to appeal against acts violating their fundamental rights.[13] The right to an effective remedy is considered non-derogable.[14] In addition, several treaties provide for a right to compensation for specific violations, such as unlawful arrest or detention,[15] miscarriage of justice,[16] and the right to reparation for torture[17] and enforced disappearance, which includes an explicit right to truth.[18] Other human rights treaties also recognise the right to reparation, or elements thereof.[19]

Some authors have questioned whether an individual right to reparation has been recognised in international human rights law, arguing that relevant treaties primarily address procedural duties rather than stipulate substantive rights, and that any such right can only be exercised within existing proceedings before regional or international bodies.[20] However, there is a considerable body of regional and international jurisprudence in which treaty bodies and other courts have effectively interpreted the duty to grant an effective remedy as entailing that a state has to provide substantive reparation in the case of a breach of individual (or collective) rights. In addition, notwithstanding the discretionary powers of human rights treaty bodies, regional courts in particular have developed a consistent practice of awarding compensation particularly for serious violations and, especially in the case of the Inter-American Court of Human Rights (IACtHR), other forms of reparation. The jurisprudence of the Human Rights Chamber of Bosnia and Herzegovina, a hybrid human rights court composed of national and international staff mandated to apply ECHR law, which was in operation from 1996 to 2003, is also noteworthy for its innovative and wide-ranging approach to ordering reparation measures.[21] The Human Rights Committee (HRCtee) has made it clear that '[w]ithout reparation

---

[13] Art. 1 of the Resolution on the Right to Recourse and Fair Trial, adopted at the 11th Ordinary Session of the ACHPR in Tunis, Tunisia, in 1992.

[14] HRCtee, General Comment 29, States of Emergency (article 4); UN doc. CCPR/C/21/Rev.1/Add.11 (31 August 2001) para. 14; *Judicial Guarantees in States of Emergency (Arts. 27(2), 25 and 8 American Convention on Human Rights)* (IACtHR) (1987) paras. 23 and 41.

[15] Art. 9(5) ICCPR; art. 5(5) ECHR.

[16] Art. 14(6) ICCPR; art. 3 Protocol no. 7 to the ECHR.

[17] Art. 14 CAT. See for an important elaboration of its contents, CtAT, General Comment 3: Implementation of article 14 by States parties, UN doc. CAT/C/GC/3 (13 December 2012).

[18] Art. 24 CPED.

[19] See in particular, art. 39 Convention on the Rights of the Child (CRC), as well as art. 21 ACHPR (right of peoples to freely dispose of their wealth and natural resources) and art. 21 ACHR (right to property).

[20] C. Tomuschat, *Human Rights: Between Idealism and Realism*, 3rd edn (Oxford University Press, 2014) 399–419.

[21] See M. Nowak, 'Reparation by the Human Rights Chamber for Bosnia and Herzegovina', in K. De Feyter et al. (eds.), *Out of the Ashes: Reparations for Gross Violations of Human Rights* (Intersentia, 2006) 245–88.

to individuals whose Covenant rights have been violated, the obligation to provide an effective remedy, which is central to the efficacy of article 2, paragraph 3, is not discharged'.[22] Regional human rights treaty bodies and courts have developed the nature, scope and content of the right to an effective remedy and reparation in their jurisprudence, and the IACtHR in particular has repeatedly affirmed that a right to reparation flows from the Convention.[23] In an important ruling, the International Court of Justice (ICJ) affirmed the right to reparation for violations of human rights in its *Israeli Wall* advisory opinion.[24]

The UNGA has recognised the right to reparation in two landmark declarations, namely the Victims' Declaration and the Basic Principles. The latter is the culmination of sustained efforts by core states, such as Chile, the two then Special Rapporteurs, Professor Theo van Boven and Professor Cherif Bassiouni, and several non-governmental organisations (NGOs) to adopt an authoritative instrument that spells out and elaborates on international standards.[25] As an UNGA declaration, the Basic Principles are not binding as such. Indeed, the text stresses their declaratory nature. This apparently cautious approach notwithstanding, the Basic Principles are suffused with the language of rights and their detailed exposition of relevant standards must be seen as an important piece of state practice that strengthens the right to reparation. The Basic Principles already exert a pull-factor that influences perceptions of reparation, treaty-making and jurisprudence. This is particularly evident in the increasing use of the language of the Basic Principles in other instruments and jurisprudence, and reference to the forms of reparation stipulated therein. This is, for example, the case in article 24 of the International Convention for the Protection of All Persons from Enforced Disappearance (CPED) and the HRCtee's General Comment 31. It is also apparent in the practice of human rights courts and treaty bodies, such as in the judgment of the African Court of Human and Peoples' Rights (ACtHPR) in *Zongo and Others* v. *Burkina Faso*,[26] the decision of the Committee against Torture (CtAT) in *Guridi* v. *Spain*[27] and in the ICC context.[28]

---

[22] HRCtee, General Comment 31: Nature of the general legal obligation imposed on states parties to the Covenant, UN doc. CCPR/C/21/Rev.1/Add.13 (26 May 2004) para. 16.

[23] See for a recent example, *Ibsen Cárdenas and Ibsen Peña* v. *Bolivia* (IACtHR) (2010), particularly para. 226 and part IX: Reparations.

[24] *Legal Consequences of the Construction of a Wall in the Occupied Palestinian Territory* (ICJ) (2004) paras. 152–3.

[25] T. van Boven, 'Victims' Rights to a Remedy and Reparation: The New United Nations Principles and Guidelines', in Ferstman et al., above note 11, 19–40; Bassiouni, above note 8, 247–76; D. Shelton, 'The United Nations Principles and Guidelines on Reparations: Context and Contents', in De Feyter et al., above note 21, 11–33.

[26] *Nobert Zongo and Others* v. *Burkina Faso* (ACtHPR) (2015) para. 47.

[27] *Guridi* v. *Spain* (CtAT) (2005) para. 6.8.

[28] See art. 75 ICC Rome Statute. See also *ICC Prosecutor* v. *Thomas Lubanga Dyilo* (*Decision on victims' participation*) (ICC) (2008) para. 92, and critical comments in Separate and Dissenting Opinion of Judge René Blattman, ibid., 49–50, paras. 4–5.

The exercise of the right to reparation will in practice depend on the availability of legal avenues. However, this procedural challenge cannot obscure its recognition as an individual right in international human rights law, which is in principle not contingent on the existence of procedures for its enforcement.[29] This conclusion is supported by emerging practices at the inter-state and national level,[30] and applies in particular to gross violations of human rights as reflected in jurisprudence and the Basic Principles.[31]

15.3.2   Practice at the Inter-state Level

At the inter-state level, reparation for the most serious violations has its origins in war reparations.[32] German reparations to Israel and the victims of the Holocaust must count as the most important example of inter-state reparations, both in terms of the seriousness of the violations and their scale. Until the 1990s such inter-state reparations had largely been dealt with bilaterally, with the understanding that individuals had no right to claim reparation for violations covered in these agreements. However, litigation in the United States (US) in Holocaust-related cases, and in Switzerland in relation to German war crimes during World War II, have strengthened the position of individuals and resulted in the setting up of reparation programmes for the benefit of victims, such as in respect of slave and forced labour.[33] This development is also evident in the setting up of compensation commissions and reparation programmes in cases of mass violations other than the Holocaust,

[29]   See G. Echeverría, 'Do Victims of Torture and Other Serious Human Rights Violations have an Independent and Enforceable Right to Reparation?' (2012) 16 *The International Journal of Human Rights* 698; Report of Special Rapporteur, above note 11, paras. 14–18.

[30]   Also H. Rombouts, P. Sardaro and S. Vandeginste, 'The Right to Reparation for Victims of Gross and Systematic Violations of Human Rights', in De Feyter, above note 21, 345–503, at 365–70. See, however, the more cautious assessment in van Boven, above note 25, 27: 'It should be recognised, however, that as transpired from the German position referred to above, there appears not to be general consensus as to the existence of a customary international law governing individual reparation claims.'

[31]   As pointed out by Bassiouni, above note 8, 251, 'the terms "gross violations of international human rights law" ... should be understood to qualify situations with a view to establishing a set of facts that may figure as a basis for claims adjudication, rather than to imply a separate legal regime'. See also for a discussion of the significance of the reference to gross violations, van Boven, above note 25, 32–4, who highlights art. 26 of the Basic Principles: 'it is understood that the present Principles and Guidelines are without prejudice to the right to a remedy and reparation for all violations of international human rights law and international humanitarian law.'

[32]   Note the difference in terminology: whereas reparation is frequently used to denote the various forms of reparation, the word reparations has traditionally been used in the context of payments and other measures to compensate for/repair war-related damages.

[33]   Foundation Remembrance, Responsibility and Future, www.stiftung-evz.de. See R. Bank, 'The New Programs for Payments to Victims of National Socialist Injustice' (2001) 44 *German Yearbook of International Law* 307. See also the case study on Holocaust and World War II reparations below at 15.12.

such as the UN Compensation Commission (Iraq–Kuwait) and the Eritrea and Ethiopia Claims Commission (in relation to the 1998 war). Operating at an inter-state level through the UN or on the basis of bilateral agreements, these commissions provide that the states (parties) may bring claims on their own behalf or on behalf of their nationals.[34]

Reparation for violations of human rights and humanitarian law has also been awarded in a growing number of inter-state cases. These include *Cyprus v. Turkey* and *Georgia v. Russia* (I) before the European Court of Human Rights (ECtHR), the *Democratic Republic of Congo (DRC) v. Burundi, Rwanda and Uganda* before the ACmHPR, as well as *DRC v. Uganda* and *Republic of Guinea v. DRC* (*Ahmadou Sadio Diallo* case) before the ICJ.[35] In these cases, reparation was due to the state successfully claiming a violation of individual rights and/or of the obligations of the adversarial party. Significantly, the rulings by the ACmHPR in *DRC v. Burundi, Rwanda and Uganda* and the ECtHR in *Cyprus v. Turkey* and *Georgia v. Russia (I)* specified that the victims of violations of human rights and humanitarian law should be the ultimate beneficiaries of any reparation made. The emerging jurisprudence is an important development. It may indicate a greater willingness of states to claim human rights violations (even though such claims may be politically motivated) and provide victims with an additional avenue. The 2012 ICJ judgment awarding compensation in the *Diallo* case sets an important precedent, albeit a series of open questions remain regarding the rights of victims in the course of such proceedings and at the enforcement stage.

15.3.3   State Practice at the National and Transnational Level

Although state practice is far from uniform, most states recognise some form of constitutional or statutory right to reparation in cases amounting to violations of human rights. Individuals, and groups of victims, have been

---

[34] The UN Compensation Commission, which operated from 1991 to 2007, received 'more than 2.6 million claims seeking a total of approximately US$368 billion', submitted by governments on behalf of nationals, corporations or themselves, and by UN agencies on behalf of other individuals. See www.uncc.ch, and L. A. Taylor, 'The United Nations Compensation Commission', in Ferstman et al., above note 11, 197–214. The Eritrea-Ethiopia Claims Commission was based on a bilateral agreement signed in Algiers on 12 December 2000, pursuant to which the parties may bring claims on their own behalf and on behalf of their nationals (natural and juridical persons) before the Permanent Court of Arbitration against the government of (or entities controlled and owned by) the other party. See www.pca-cpa.org/showpage.asp?pag_id=1151. See further H. M. Holtzmann and E. Kristjánsdóttir (eds.), *International Mass Claims Processes: Legal and Practical Processes* (Oxford University Press, 2007).

[35] *Cyprus v. Turkey* (ECtHR) (2014); *Georgia v. Russia* (I) (ECtHR) (2019); Case concerning *Armed Activities on the Territory of the Congo (Democratic Republic of the Congo v. Uganda)* (ICJ) (2005); and *Ahmadou Sadio Diallo, Republic of Guinea v. Democratic Republic of Congo (Compensation owed by the Democratic Republic of the Congo to the*

awarded compensation and other forms of reparation in various jurisdictions, for example in landmark cases such as *Nilabati Behera* v. *State of Orissa* in India for a violation of the right to life (death in custody).[36] In a more recent development a number of states have set up reparation schemes for violations of human rights (and humanitarian law) following the end of conflict or dictatorship.[37] An increasing number of suits brought by individuals in third countries, besides contributing to state practice, have raised the question of the jurisdictional reach of the right to reparation, namely whether it requires states to establish jurisdiction in such cases. The US Alien Torts Claim Act of 1789, though evidently not adopted for that purpose at the time, has become the most prominent legal basis for bringing human rights claims for wrongful acts committed in third countries.[38] This is ironic given that the USA entered a reservation to the effect that it understands article 14 of the Convention against Torture and Other Cruel, Inhuman or Degrading Treatment or Punishment (CAT) to 'provide a private right of action for damages only for acts of torture committed in territory under the jurisdiction of that State Party'. It is open to question, in the absence of explicit treaty provisions, whether states have an obligation to establish jurisdiction that enables victims of violations to bring claims for wrongful acts committed in third countries. Several states and commentators have opposed such an interpretation of article 14 CAT on the ground that the obligations of states parties are confined to their jurisdiction unless otherwise indicated.[39] Yet the text of article 14 CAT could equally be read to apply to all torture victims and a teleological (purposive) interpretation of the Convention to this effect would be in line with its objective of combating torture worldwide. The CtAT considered in its General Comment 3 'that the application of article 14 is not

---

Republic of Guinea) (ICJ) (2012). See also C. McCarthy, 'Reparation for Gross Violations of Human Rights Law and International Humanitarian Law at the International Court of Justice', in Ferstman et al., above note 11, 283–311.

[36] *Nilabati Behera alias Lalita Behera* v. *State of Orissa and Others* (India) (1993).

[37] See for detailed case studies of reparation schemes in Argentina, Brazil, Chile and South Africa, de Greiff, above note 10, and in Colombia, East Timor, Guatemala and Sierra Leone, C. Evans, *The Right to Reparation in International Law for Victims of Armed Conflict* (Cambridge University Press, 2012). See for an analysis of reparation programmes and selected problems, Report of the Special Rapporteur, above note 11.

[38] M. Swan, 'International Human Rights Tort Claims and the Experience of United States Courts: An Introduction to the US Case Law, Key Statutes and Doctrines', in C. Scott (ed.), *Torture as Tort: Comparative Perspectives on the Development of Transnational Tort Litigation* (Hart, 2001) 65–107. However, see the ruling in the case of *Kiobel* v. *Royal Dutch Petroleum* (US) (2013), which emphasises the presumption of extraterritoriality, thereby seemingly limiting the applicability of the Alien Torts Claim Act. See Chapter 19.3.1.

[39] See B. Fassbender, 'Can Victims Sue State Officials for Torture? Reflections on *Rasul* v. *Myers* from the Perspective of International Law' (2008) 6 *Journal of International Criminal Justice* 347. See for recent jurisprudence, *Naït-Liman* v. *Switzerland* (ECtHR) (2018) paras. 45–220.

limited to victims who were harmed in the territory of the State party or by or against nationals of the State party ... article 14 requires States parties to ensure that all victims of torture and ill-treatment are able to access remedy and obtain redress'.[40] However, even where states provide for such jurisdiction, claimants frequently face state immunity as an often insurmountable barrier to holding states accountable.[41]

15.4   THE RIGHT TO REPARATION IN INTERNATIONAL HUMANITARIAN LAW

The right to reparation has a less clear standing in international humanitarian law. Article 3 of the Hague Convention (IV) of 1907 stipulates that belligerents are 'liable to pay compensation' for violations of its provisions. Article 91 of the 1977 Additional Protocol I to the 1949 Geneva Conventions similarly provides that '[a] Party to the conflict which violates the provisions of the Conventions or of this Protocol shall, if the case demands, be liable to pay compensation'. However, there are no provisions in humanitarian law treaties that explicitly stipulate a corresponding individual right. Nor is there any treaty body tasked with hearing complaints and recommending or awarding reparation. This turns the focus sharply to international customary law. Those sceptical of the existence of a right to reparation under international humanitarian law point to the limited jurisprudence.[42] The lack of explicit recognition in other sources is also mentioned.[43] Proponents of such a right argue that international humanitarian law recognises the duty to provide reparation.[44] This has been upheld in the jurisprudence of several courts, in particular in the Netherlands, Greece and Italy.[45] The ICJ in the *Israeli Wall*

---

[40] See CtAT, General Comment 3, para. 22.

[41] See e.g., *Jones and Others* v. *United Kingdom* (ECtHR) (2014). See also the ICJ ruling on enforcement of claims against states in *Jurisdictional immunities of the state* (*Germany* v. *Italy: Greece intervening*), (ICJ) (2012).

[42] See e.g., *Distomo Massacre* case (Germany) (2003) with reference to violations committed during World War II.

[43] According to Tomuschat, above note 20, 411–15, an individual right to reparation has not been recognised in international humanitarian law.

[44] See R. Bank and E. Schwager, 'Is there a Substantive Right to Compensation for Individual Victims of Armed Conflict against a State under International Law?' (2006) 49 *German Yearbook of International Law* 367; L. Zegveld, 'Remedies for Victims of Violations of International Humanitarian Law' (2003) 851 *International Review of the Red Cross* 497; R. Hofmann, 'Draft Declaration of International Law Principles on Compensation for Victims of War (Substantive Issues)', in International Law Association, *Compensation for Victims of War* (Rio de Janeiro Conference, 2008) 2–20. See also Report of the International Commission of Inquiry on Darfur to the United Nations Secretary-General pursuant to Security Council resolution 1564 of 18 September 2004 (UN, 25 January 2005) paras. 593–8. International Committee of the Red Cross (ICRC), CIHL Database, rule 150.

[45] See Hofmann, ibid., 9–11.

advisory opinion and in *DRC* v. *Uganda* equally ruled that states have to provide reparation – 'to natural or legal persons' (*Wall* case) – for violations of international humanitarian law.[46] The fact that ad hoc claims commissions, such as the UN Compensation Commission (Iraq) and the Eritrea and Ethiopia Claims Commission, are set up for the benefit of individual victims is referred to as further evidence of the recognition of the right by the Co-Rapporteur of the International Law Association's (ILA) draft declaration of international law principles on compensation for victims of war.[47] The inclusion of the right to reparation for (serious) violations of international humanitarian law in the Basic Principles and the growing convergence of international human rights law and international humanitarian law in international jurisprudence constitute an important development. However, actual practice is still limited and some states continue to resist recognising an individual right to reparation for violations of international humanitarian law.

15.5   THE RIGHT TO REPARATION IN INTERNATIONAL CRIMINAL LAW

International criminal law has traditionally been concerned with the proscription, prosecution and punishment of crimes of international concern. Victims' rights were largely ignored until the adoption of the ICC Rome Statute. The sole provision of the International Criminal Tribunal for the former Yugoslavia (ICTY) and International Criminal Tribunal for Rwanda (ICTR) on reparation, rule 106(c) of their respective Rules of Procedure and Evidence, provides that for the purpose of a claim made in national proceedings, to which the victims were referred, 'the judgment of the Tribunal shall be final and binding as to the criminal responsibility of the convicted person for such injury'. It very soon became clear that this rule was inadequate. Voices calling for the tribunals to play a greater role in awarding reparation were, in hindsight, prescient but premature.[48] It was only concerted efforts of international NGO coalitions and a greater willingness to acknowledge victims and their rights in proceedings that paved the way for the current ICC regime, which is a milestone as it anchors the right to reparation firmly in international criminal law.

---

[46] *Legal Consequences of the Construction of a Wall*, 136, paras. 149–53; *DRC* v. *Uganda*, para. 259.

[47] Hofmann, above note 44, 11–12.

[48] See suggestions to this effect by Judge Jorda, the then President of the ICTY and Judge Pillay, the then President of the ICTR, in UN doc. S/2000/1063 (3 November 2000) and Letter of 14 December 2000 of the UN Secretary-General, addressed to the President of the Security Council, UN doc. S/2000/1198 (15 December 2000) respectively.

The ICC's reparation regime differs from that of international human rights law in some important respects.[49] In contrast to violations of human rights, reparation is not owed by the state but the individual liable for the commission of international crimes falling within the ICC's jurisdiction. The Court may, pursuant to article 75(2) of the Rome Statute, 'make an order directly against a convicted person specifying appropriate reparation' or 'order that the award for reparations be made through the Trust Fund' for the victims of crime set up under article 79. The Trust Fund, which relies on voluntary contributions and fines collected, is an important structure within the Court's system. It can provide both financial assistance to victims of crimes and reparation in respect of a specific case as set out in article 75. The reparation regime is still at its relatively early stages.[50] The Court had the opportunity to address several important questions in its first ruling on reparation in the *Lubanga* case and the subsequent appeal. The Appeals Chamber stressed the need to distinguish between general principles governing reparations under article 75(1) and the reparations order in a specific case.[51] It emphasised the importance of holding the offender(s) to account and found 'that the legal framework clearly establishes that an order for reparations has to be issued in *all* circumstances against the convicted person. When appropriate, such an order for reparations can – *in addition* – be made through the Trust Fund.'[52] In contrast to the Trial Chamber, the Appeals Chamber held that 'indigence is not an obstacle to the imposition of liability for reparations on the convicted person'.[53] In the circumstances, it rejected challenges to the effect that the Trial Chamber should have awarded individual reparations, in addition to collective reparations.[54] This issue also featured prominently in the *Katanga* case[55] and can be expected to be a recurring challenge given the large number of victims typically eligible in cases before the ICC. In addition, it held that the Trial Chamber must identify victims and 'clearly *define* the harms that result from the crimes for which the person was convicted'.[56] In the

---

[49] See C. Ferstman, 'The Reparation Regime of the International Criminal Court: Practical Considerations' (2002) 15 *Leiden Journal of International Law* 667.

[50] See C. Ferstman and M. Goetz, 'Reparations before the International Criminal Court: the Early Jurisprudence on Victim Participation and its Impact on Future Reparation Proceedings', in Ferstman et al., above note 11, 313–50, and REDRESS, *Justice for Victims: The ICC's Reparation Mandate* (2012).

[51] *The Prosecutor* v. *Lubanga Dyilo (Judgment on the appeals against the 'Decision establishing the principles and procedures to be applied to reparations' of 7 August 2012)* (ICC) (2015) paras. 54–6. See also REDRESS, *Q & A – Conclusion of the appeals in the Lubanga case* (2015).

[52] *Prosecutor* v. *Lubanga Dyilo*, ibid., para. 76 (emphasis in original).   [53] Ibid., para. 103.

[54] Ibid., paras. 130–57.

[55] See also on symbolic individual compensation the following two reparation orders, *The Prosecutor* v. *Germain Katanga* (ICC) (2017) and *The Prosecutor* v. *Ahmad Al Faqi Al Mahdi* (ICC) (2017) Appeal (2018), with particular reference to crimes against cultural heritage.

[56] *Prosecutor* v. *Lubanga Dyilo*, para. 184 (emphasis in original).

Lubanga case, this led the Appeals Chamber to exclude harm resulting from sexual violence from the scope of reparations as Lubanga had, controversially, not been charged with relevant crimes.

Only victims who suffer harm as a result of crimes for which a person has been convicted are eligible. Such harm includes material loss as well as physical and psychological suffering of direct and indirect victims. Importantly, if reparations are made to a 'community', the ICC must specify eligibility criteria so as not to exceed the scope of the convicted person's liability.[57]

Reparation under the ICC Rome Statute is owed by the individual and not the state or other entities, even though the latter may bear responsibility under international law. This may lead to the individualisation of reparation and result in discrepancies in cases where state responsibility cannot be established in other fora. It also presents considerable practical challenges for the Court, particularly on how to provide reparation to a large number of victims of the most serious crimes with limited means available. However, the challenges also bear considerable potential for the Court and the Trust Fund to develop the right to reparation in the context of international criminal law and thereby contribute to further cross-fertilisation in the broader international law context.[58]

15.6   THE RIGHT TO REPARATION AND VIOLATIONS BY NON-STATE ACTORS

As a general principle, a state is not responsible for violations by NSAs (who are themselves liable under national law or applicable legal regimes, such as international criminal law) unless it exercises effective control, colludes, acquiesces (in) or endorses such violations.[59] A state will, however, be responsible for a breach of its positive obligations in respect of acts committed by NSAs, for example failing to investigate violations such as enforced disappearance where the identity of the perpetrators is unknown.[60] None the less, there will be situations where NSAs, such as armed groups, have committed serious violations such as mass rape or killings, but the state concerned will not incur liability and nor will the victims be able to obtain reparation from the perpetrators. It is with this constellation in mind that the Basic Principles exhort states to 'endeavour to establish national

---

[57] Ibid., paras. 205–15.

[58] See further on relevant judicial developments on victim participation and reparation, I. Stegmiller, 'Legal Developments in Civil Party Participation at the Extraordinary Chambers in the Courts of Cambodia' (2014) 27 *Leiden Journal of International Law* 465.

[59] See in particular, arts. 4–11 ILC Articles on Responsibility of States for internationally wrongful acts (ARSIWA) and the provisions of human rights treaties, such as art. 1 CAT. Art. 10 ARSIWA provides for a further exception where insurgents become the new government or succeed in establishing a new state.

[60] *Velásquez Rodríguez* v. *Honduras* (IACtHR) (1988) paras. 172–7.

programmes for reparation and other assistance to victims in the event that the parties liable for the harm suffered are unable or unwilling to meet their obligations'.[61]

15.7   THE RIGHT TO REPARATION FOR HISTORICAL INJUSTICES AND VIOLATIONS

The fact that international crimes and human rights, including the right to reparation for their violation, are relatively speaking latecomers to international law has thrown up particular challenges in relation to past injustices. Claims for reparation have in this context in particular been made for slavery and colonialism either as unjust practices in their own right or in relation to specific incidents. Examples of the latter are the massacres of the Herero by Germany in the first decade of the twentieth century, and various violations attributed to the British forces in the context of the Mau Mau uprising in Kenya during the 1950s.[62] Although the documented facts of these cases appear to support reparation claims, there are a series of legal, policy, political and practical obstacles to be overcome. The acts committed were in many instances not recognised as international crimes or human rights violations at the time so that the law would have to be applied retroactively, unless national law provides otherwise.[63] Even where responsibility of a particular state can be established, difficulties abound, especially identifying the rights-holders (beneficiaries). This is important if states were to be designated as recipients of any compensation so as to ensure that the descendants of victims or a people as a whole were to benefit.[64] In a noteworthy development, the Caribbean Community (CARICOM), in March 2014, endorsed a ten-point action plan of the CARICOM Reparations Commission aimed at securing reparations for victims of genocide, slavery, slave trading and racial apartheid. The plan, directed at former slave-owning nations of

---

[61] See Chapter 19 for the responsibility of non-state actors.

[62] J. Sarkin, *Colonial Genocide and Reparations Claims in the 21st Century: The Socio-Legal Context of Claims under International Law by the Herero against Germany for Genocide in Namibia, 1904–1908* (Greenwood, 2009), and the Mau Mau reparations claims in the UK, see www.leighday.co.uk/International-and-group-claims/Kenya/The-Mau-Mau-claims.

[63] See for a discussion of the legal challenges posed by retroactivity, M. Bossuyt and S. Vandeginste, 'The Issue of Reparation for Slavery and Colonialism and the Durban World Conference against Racism' (2001) 22 *Human Rights Law Journal* 341.

[64] See for a discussion of appropriate forms of reparations, M. Du Plessis, 'Reparations and International Law: How are Reparations to be determined (Past Wrong or Current Effects), Against Whom, and What Form should they take?', in M. Du Plessis and S. Peté (eds.), *Repairing the Past? International Perspectives on Reparations for Gross Human Rights Abuses* (Intersentia, 2007) 147–77.

Europe, envisages a full formal apology, repatriation of 'descendants of stolen people', an indigenous peoples development programme, development of
cultural institutions, alleviating the public health crisis, illiteracy eradication,
carrying out an African knowledge programme, psychological rehabilitation,
technology transfer and debt cancellation.[65] The plan identifies important
components of reparations, such as the official recognition of the (historical)
wrong and financial support for initiatives to redress legacies of injustice. Its
broad reach reflects a holistic approach, but also illustrates the challenge of
establishing a sufficiently clear link between violations dating back a considerable time and the beneficiaries, as well as adequate forms of reparation.

The 2008 'deal' between Italy and Libya amply demonstrates the political
dimension of initiatives purporting to address past injuries. Italy's move to
pay Libya $5 billion and apologise for the damage inflicted during its colo-
nial rule was widely seen as an opportunity for Italy to strengthen its strategic relationship with Libya and for the latter to obtain some benefits and
enhance its international standing.[66] While remarkable, agreements of this
kind appear to turn colonialism or slavery into a pretext that masks cruder
current interests. It is indeed questionable to what degree, if at all, they
address the nature and legacy of violations and provide acknowledgement
and reparation to those whose ancestors suffered or who personally continue
to suffer from the long-term effects of past injustices.

QUESTIONS

1. In his critique of the findings of the International Commission of Inquiry on
    Darfur, Professor Christian Tomuschat argued that 'there is no customary
    international law rule governing individual reparation claims'.[67] What evidence is
    there to support or counter this assertion?
2. Do victims of violations have a right under international law to bring reparation
    claims in countries other than where the violation occurred?
3. Does state practice support the assertion that international law recognises the
    right to reparation for serious violations of international humanitarian law?
4. Can there be a right to reparation against the state where the violation has been
    committed by NSAs?
5. Does the current international legal framework provide an adequate basis for
    arguing reparation claims for slavery and colonialism?

[65] See www.leighday.co.uk/News/2014/March-2014/CARICOM-nations-unanimously-
    approve-10-point-plan.
[66] See Colonialism Reparation, *Italy-Libya* (undated), online at www.colonialism
    reparation.org/en/compensations/italy-libya.html.
[67] C. Tomuschat, 'Darfur: Compensation for the Victims' (2005) 3 *Journal of International
    Criminal Justice* 579.

15.8   THE NOTION AND LEGAL SIGNIFICANCE OF THE TERM 'VICTIM'

In legal terms, the status of 'victim' confers certain entitlements, namely the right to a remedy and reparation. It is also frequently equated with standing to bring claims and exercise procedural rights.[68] By that token it demarcates legal boundaries. The term 'victim' distinguishes between those whose suffering is recognised as giving rise to the right to reparation, for example where it results from arbitrary detention, and others whose suffering does not entail the same legal consequences, as would normally be the case with persons suffering harm due to economic misfortune or natural disasters. The notion of victim is associated with suffering and sacrifice. This understanding is reflected in legal definitions of 'victim', such as that found in the Basic Principles and the ICC Rules of Procedure and Evidence, which refers to persons who suffer harm as a result of a violation of his/her or their rights, or of having intervened to prevent victimisation (which is particularly important for human rights defenders).[69] Such harm may consist of 'physical or mental injury, emotional suffering, economic loss or substantial impairment of ... fundamental rights' (Basic Principles), which may have been suffered in an individual or collective capacity, as well as by natural and, to some extent, legal persons.[70]

QUESTIONS

1. What is the legal significance of the term 'victim'?
2. Does the determination of 'victim' status depend on subjective or objective criteria?

---

[68] See Chapter 7.2.1.1.

[69] Principle 8 of the Basic Principles: 'For purposes of the present document, victims are persons who individually or collectively suffered harm, including physical or mental injury, emotional suffering, economic loss or substantial impairment of their fundamental rights, through acts or omissions that constitute gross violations of international human rights law, or serious violations of international humanitarian law. Where appropriate, and in accordance with domestic law, the term "victim" also includes the immediate family or dependants of the direct victim and persons who have suffered harm in intervening to assist victims in distress or to prevent victimization.' Rule 85 of the 2002 ICC Rules of Procedure and Evidence: 'For the purposes of the Statute and the Rules of Procedure and Evidence: (a) "Victims" means natural persons who have suffered harm as a result of the commission of any crime within the jurisdiction of the Court; (b) Victims may include organizations or institutions that have sustained direct harm to any of their property which is dedicated to religion, education, art or science or charitable purposes, and to their historic monuments, hospitals and other places and objects for humanitarian purposes.'

[70] Ibid. and Chapter 7.2.1.1.

15.9 THE PROCEDURAL RIGHT TO AN EFFECTIVE REMEDY

15.9.1 Overview

The right to an effective remedy requires that victims, individually or collectively, are able to have recourse to avenues, be they judicial or otherwise, capable of redressing the alleged violation as a means of vindicating their rights. In cases of serious violations a remedy has to be of a judicial nature.[71] This requirement is of particular importance when designing reparation mechanisms that may restrict recourse to courts.[72]

Available remedies 'must be "effective" in practice as well as in law, in particular in the sense that [their] exercise must not be unjustifiably hindered by acts or omissions by the authorities of the respondent State'.[73] This formula opens the door for a host of measures that states need to take in order to ensure the effective exercise of the right to a remedy, a task that constitutes a challenge for any legal system. Besides granting the right to pursue claims for violations, states must guarantee and protect the administration of justice, including an independent judiciary, without which remedies will not be effective. Equally, it requires the absence of laws and/or jurisprudence that hinder the exercise of remedies, such as amnesties or immunities that bar the lodging of claims against the individual perpetrators or the state, or both.[74] In addition, statutes of limitation must not be unduly short as victims often experience displacement, financial hardship, trauma or other circumstances that prevent them from seeking timely recourse to available remedies.[75] An example of such an unduly short time limit is Nepal's Compensation of Torture Act, according to which victims need to bring a claim within thirty-five days.[76] Moreover, the administration of claims relating to alleged violations must not be subject to undue delays and the legal system must ensure enforcement of any awards or decisions made.[77] Beyond this, states should take a range of additional steps, as specified in the Basic Principles.

[71] *Bautista* v. *Colombia* (HRCtee) (1995) para. 8.2.

[72] This is particularly important in the transitional context, Office of the High Commissioner for Human Rights (OHCHR), *Rule-of-law Tools for Post Conflict States: Reparations Programmes* (UN, 2008) 34–6. See also CtAT, General Comment 3, para. 20: 'While collective reparation and administrative reparation programmes may be acceptable as a form of redress, such programmes may not render ineffective the individual right to a remedy and to obtain redress.'

[73] *Aksoy* v. *Turkey* (ECtHR) (1996) para. 95.

[74] HRCtee, General Comment 31, UN doc. CCPR/C/21/Rev.1/Add.13 (26 May 2004) para. 18; CtAT, General Comment 3, paras. 37–43.

[75] Ibid., HRCtee, General Comment 31, para. 18 and CtAT, General Comment 3, para. 40. See also *Mocanu and Others* v. *Romania* (ECtHR) (2014), particularly concurring opinion of Judge Pinto de Albuquerque, joined by Judge Vučinić.

[76] Art. 5(1) Compensation for Torture Act, 1996.

[77] See further HRCtee, General Comment 32: Article 14: Right to equality before courts and tribunals and to a fair trial, UN doc. CCPR/C/GC/32 (23 August 2007); REDRESS, *Waiting*

These involve disseminating information about available remedies and taking measures to minimise inconvenience and provide protection. They also encompass the provision of assistance and making available other legal, diplomatic and consular means, in case of foreign nationals and stateless persons, so that victims can have effective access to justice.[78] These measures are particularly important in respect of marginalised groups or victims such as women in cases of sexual violence, given that they are often unaware of their rights, impoverished, stigmatised, discriminated against and/or reluctant to exercise their rights in formal settings.[79]

The right to bring criminal complaints is an integral part of the right to an effective remedy. In practice, however, victims of human rights violations frequently encounter obstacles that hamper their right to pursue complaints effectively. To counter this, states have to put in place an effective legal and institutional framework with a view to investigating violations, which includes the establishment of effective oversight bodies. Conversely, states shall not take measures incompatible with their obligation to investigate serious violations effectively, such as amnesties, immunities and/or unreasonably short statutes of limitation.[80] There is often a close nexus between the two sets of remedies. The prospect of pursuing civil remedies and obtaining reparation is in many countries dependent on a criminal conviction, either by law or in practice. Where impunity is rife victims of violations are effectively deprived of any effective remedies. It is for this reason that victims should be able to pursue civil claims independently, and irrespective of the outcome of criminal proceedings, to ensure at least a measure of justice.

15.9.2   The Nexus between Civil and Criminal Proceedings: *Rajapakse* v. *Sri Lanka*

Mr Rajapakse, who claimed that he had suffered torture at the hands of the Sri Lankan police in April 2002, filed a fundamental rights petition before the Sri Lankan Supreme Court in May 2002.[81] The hearings before

---

for Justice: The Politics of Delays in the Administration of Justice in Torture Cases: Practice, Standards and Responses (2008).

[78] See in this regard in particular, *LaGrand (Germany* v. *United States of America)* (ICJ) (2001); case concerning *Avena and other Mexican Nationals (Mexico* v. *United States of America)* (ICJ) (2004); *The Right to Information on Consular Assistance in the Framework of the Guarantee of the Process of Law* (IACtHR) (1999). See also J. R. Dugard, Special Rapporteur, First Report on Diplomatic Protection, UN doc. A/CN.4/506 (7 March 2000), in particular comments on draft art. 4, paras. 75–93. His proposal that there should be a right to diplomatic protection in cases of violations of *jus cogens* rights has not been endorsed by states to date.

[79] Report of the Special Rapporteur on torture and other cruel, inhuman or degrading treatment or punishment, UN doc. A/HRC/7/3 (15 January 2008) paras. 61–2. See further CtEDAW, General Recommendation 33 on women's access to justice, UN doc. CEDAW/C/GC/33 (3 August 2015).

[80] HRCtee, General Comment 31, para. 18.   [81] *Rajapakse* v. *Sri Lanka* (HRCtee) (2006).

the Supreme Court had been repeatedly postponed up to the point when the HRCtee decided the case in March 2005:

The Committee observes that, as the delay in the author's fundamental rights application to the Supreme Court is dependent upon the determination of the High Court [criminal] case, the delay in determining the latter is relevant for its assessment of whether the author's rights under the Covenant were violated. It notes the State party's argument that the author is currently availing himself of domestic remedies. The Committee observes that the criminal investigation was not initiated by the Attorney-General until over three months after the incident, despite the fact that the author had to be hospitalised, was unconscious for 15 days, and had a medical report describing his injuries, which was presented to the Magistrates Court on 17 May 2002.[82]

The HRCtee went on to find a violation of article 2(3) in connection with article 7 ICCPR:

Under article 2, paragraph 3, the State party has an obligation to ensure that remedies are effective. Expedition and effectiveness are particularly important in the adjudication of cases involving torture. The general information provided by the State party on the workload of the domestic courts would appear to indicate that the High Court proceedings and, thus, the author's Supreme Court fundamental rights case will not be determined for some time. The Committee considers that the State party may not avoid its responsibilities under the Covenant with the argument that the domestic courts are dealing with the matter, when it is clear that the remedies relied upon by the State party have been prolonged and would appear to be ineffective.[83]

15.9.3 The Right to Property, and the Choice between Investment Arbitration and Human Rights Avenues

In some cases, the subject matter of a human rights violation may also be classified as a civil deprivation or breach of a contractual or other obligation. Both outcomes are unlawful and the entity deprived of its entitlement may seek reparation. Let us assume that a foreign company (an investor) has its assets expropriated in the host state, whether directly or indirectly (for example, through discriminatory, hostile, taxes), whose only purpose is to make its operations non-profitable. Such an outcome violates the investor's right to property and the prohibition against discrimination (human right violations), but at the same time it constitutes unlawful expropriation under international law. The investor may seek remedies on the basis of the customary nature of the prohibition against unlawful expropriation or as a result of a multilateral or bilateral treaty, but equally he or she may seek remedies arising from a pertinent human rights treaty (deprivation of the right to

---

[82] Ibid., para. 9.4.   [83] Ibid., para. 9.5.

property). Which is the more preferable option? Investment arbitration is more predictable because the various investor rights and guarantees are spelt out in detail in treaties, domestic laws and contracts and there is no need to exhaust local remedies.[84] Besides investment arbitration, such as under the International Centre for the Settlement of Investment Disputes (ICSID), expropriation claims have also been resolved by inter-state commissions, as is the case with the ongoing work of the Iran–US Claims Tribunal. In situations where the victim is not foreign, he or she has no access to investment arbitration, despite the fact that the same conduct would have amounted to a violation under international law if committed against a foreign investor. In the situation at hand, the victim may seek reparation through human rights or similar[85] mechanisms, after exhausting local remedies.

In the *Yukos* case tax assessments made against the company in 2004 for the year 2000 fell outside a three-year statutory time-bar set out in Article 113 of the Russian Tax Code,[86] but because the tax assessments for the year 2000 were subject to criminal proceedings a 14 July 2005 decision by Russia's Constitutional Court changed the interpretation of the rules on statutory time limits to tax assessments.[87] The Russian authorities made use of attachment, seizure and freezing orders for the enforcement of Yukos's tax debt,[88] leading to the auction of the company's main production unit (OAO Yuganskneftegaz (YNG)) in bankruptcy proceedings, ultimately sold at a low price to a sham bidder.[89] The ECtHR found that the Russian authorities lacked flexibility in their enforcement of the tax debt[90] and 'given the pace of the enforcement proceedings, the obligation to pay the full enforcement fee and the authorities' failure to take proper account of the consequences of their actions', it also held that that the 'domestic authorities failed to strike a fair balance between the legitimate aims sought and the measures employed'.[91] The ECtHR found a violation of article 6 ECHR (right to a fair trial) and article 1 of Protocol I (right to property). By mid-2015 Russia seemed intent on not satisfying the award of 1.8 billion euros awarded by the ECtHR.

Overall, foreign investors do not prefer human rights mechanisms over investment arbitration and find no compelling reason to employ human

---

[84] See Chapter 19.3.2 for a discussion of the human rights dimensions of foreign direct investment.

[85] By way of illustration, the Court of Justice of the European Union (CJEU) has been criticised for its failure to declare that juridical double taxation should be prohibited as discriminatory, especially as regards its judgments in *Damseaux* v. *Belgium* (CJEU) (2009), para. 27 and *Kerckhaert and Morres* (CJEU) (2006) paras. 19–24. The result in these cases is a violation of the right to property, enshrined in art. 17 of the EU Charter of Fundamental Rights, by reason of confiscatory double taxation to which the parties are subjected (in this case cross-border inheritance).

[86] *Yukos* v. *Russia* (ECtHR) (2012) paras. 561 and 564.   [87] Ibid., para. 565.

[88] Ibid., para. 646.   [89] Ibid., paras. 621 and 646.   [90] Ibid., para. 656.   [91] Ibid., para. 657.

rights arguments before investment tribunals.[92] This strategy is further justified by the fact that if human rights arguments are introduced by investors
they will equally have to be admitted for the host states, which possess a
much more compelling resonance, particularly as regards the obligation of
the state to uphold and protect socio-economic rights that are contrary to
their foreign direct investment (FDI) obligations.

QUESTION

1. **Why are non-judicial remedies considered inadequate in cases of serious
   violations of human rights?**

15.10   THE SUBSTANTIVE RIGHT TO REPARATION

15.10.1 State Responsibility

Under the rules of state responsibility states have a secondary duty in case of
a breach to cease the illegal conduct, offer assurances of non-repetition and
'to make full reparation for the injury caused by the internationally wrongful act'.[93] Such reparation 'shall take the form of restitution, compensation
and satisfaction, either singly or in combination'.[94] These rules provide the
broader legal framework within which the right to reparation for violations
of human rights and humanitarian law has developed.

15.10.2 Liability

In a typical case, violations are committed by individual officials acting
on behalf of the state (see 15.6 above for violations committed by NSAs).
This constellation gives rise to questions about the nature of liability of the
offending individual and the state and the relationship between the two.
Some legal systems provide for the primary if not sole liability of the individual official responsible.[95] This may be justified by arguing that the state
(and the taxpayer) should not be burdened with expenses incurred because
of the wrongdoing of its officials. The prospect of having to pay substantial
amounts of reparation personally can also act as a deterrent for individual

---

[92] The case before the ECtHR is exceptional. The claimants also pursued investment
proceedings and in *Yukos Universal Ltd (Isle of Man)* v. *Russia* (PCA) (2014), *Hulley
Enterprises Ltd (Cyprus)* v. *Russia* (PCA) (2014) and *Veteran Petroleum Ltd (Cyprus)* v.
Russia (PCA) (2014), Russia was ordered to pay over US $50 billion in compensation.
[93] Art. 31 ARSIWA.   [94] Art. 34 ARSIWA.
[95] See findings in the comparative study, REDRESS, *Reparation for Torture: A Survey of Law
and Practice in Thirty Selected Countries* (2003) 47–8.

officials and thus have a preventive effect. The rationale for such individual liability is sound. However, the rule is disadvantageous to victims claiming reparation because individual officials are often not in a position to pay substantial compensation or may evade personal responsibility. The focus on individual liability also obscures the ultimate responsibility of the state on whose behalf individual officials act. A system that provides for primary state liability or vicarious liability is therefore better suited to address these concerns as it enables a victim of a violation to have recourse against the state. At the same time, the state would be entitled to claim back any reparation made from the individual official(s) concerned.[96]

15.10.3 Standard of Reparation

The Basic Principles speak of 'full and effective' reparation. If read in the light of the qualifying clause 'as appropriate and proportional to the gravity of the violation and the circumstances of each case', it is clear that the standards provide states, adjudicative and other bodies with some latitude in determining reparation. This contextual nature of reparation is equally evident in the provisions vesting regional courts with discretionary power to award reparation.[97] The potential for arbitrariness of awards is in theory circumscribed by qualifying standards: reparation should as a general rule reflect the seriousness of the violation and be such that the violation is remedied as much as possible in the circumstances. They are also key principles safeguarding against inappropriate awards. Reparation should be victim-oriented and non-discriminatory, which has important implications for gender dimensions and reparation that need to be taken into consideration by courts and other bodies.[98]

15.10.4 Forms of Reparation

Reparation is often equated and confused with compensation. Such a narrow view is misleading notwithstanding the undeniable importance of compensation. It ignores the distinctive but interrelated functions that the various forms of reparation may serve. A victim of a violation will need the financial means and access to services to cope with the harm suffered. He, she or they will also seek to restore the dignity and integrity infringed by the violation,

---

[96] Principle 15 of the Basic Principles.
[97] See art. 41 ECHR, art. 63 ACHR and art. 27(1) of the ACHPR Protocol on the Establishment of an African Court on Human and Peoples' Rights, which stipulates that '[i]f the Court finds that there has been violation of a human or peoples' rights, it shall make appropriate orders to remedy the violation, including the payment of fair compensation or reparation.'
[98] A. Saris and K. Lofts, 'Reparation Programmes: A Gendered Perspective', in Ferstman et al., above note 11, 79–100.

which typically calls for acknowledgement of the wrongdoing and sanctions against the perpetrators.[99] Furthermore, victims and society as a whole have an interest in seeking prevention of similar violations, which requires measures aimed at non-repetition. The various forms of reparation can be distinguished into material and non-material (moral), remedial and preventive measures of an individual or collective nature. These distinctions can help to conceptualise the types and functions of reparation measures but should not distract from a broader understanding of reparation as a process and outcome that is both holistic and responsive to context. These considerations are reflected in the Basic Principles that recognise five forms of reparation, namely restitution, compensation, rehabilitation, satisfaction and guarantees of non-repetition.

15.10.5 Restitution

Restitution is the classic form of reparation. Where restitution is feasible, namely where the harm inflicted by the violation can still be reversed, it may be sufficient to remedy a violation, together with an acknowledgement of wrongdoing (and/or compensation for any irreversible harm suffered). Restitution may consist in particular of the following measures:

1. restoration of liberty (release): where individuals have been arbitrarily detained (or wrongfully convicted, in which case the appropriate remedy may be either release or a retrial), such as in the ECtHR landmark case of *Assanidze* v. *Georgia*[100] and in the IACtHR case of *Loayza Tamayo* v. *Peru*.[101] As states have a primary duty to cease ongoing violations, remedial measures taken in such instances may strictly speaking not be classified as reparation. However, measures taken to end ongoing violations such as arbitrary detention serve a dual purpose, namely cessation and undoing a wrong, and are for this reason frequently included as forms of reparation;

2. restoration of employment: where political opponents have been deprived of their employment rights, such as for example during the dictatorships in Argentina and Chile, or workers have been dismissed in violation of their rights, such as in *Baena Ricardo* v. *Panama*;[102]

3. restoration of identity and citizenship: where citizens have been expelled and/or stripped of their citizenship, for example in *Modise* v. *Botswana*;[103]

---

[99] See in this context, Y. Danieli, 'Massive Trauma and the Healing Role of Reparative Justice', in Ferstman et al., above note 11, 41–77.

[100] *Assanidze* v. *Georgia* (ECtHR) (2004) paras. 202–3.

[101] *Loayza Tamayo* v. *Peru* (IACtHR) (1997) para. 84.

[102] *Baena Ricardo* v. *Panama* (IACtHR) (2001) para. 203.   [103] See Case Study 6.1.

4. expunging of public records: where individuals have been convicted in violation of their rights, for example a journalist for defamation in *Tristán Donoso* v. *Panama*;[104]
5. return to one's place of residence: where individuals and groups of persons have been forcibly displaced, for example in Darfur, Sudan, since 2002;[105]
6. return of property: where property has been expropriated or seized, for example in *Papamichalopoulos* v. *Greece*.[106] Restitution and/or compensation – where return of property is not feasible – for violations of the right to property are particularly important in former communist countries, as evident in the cases of *Brumărescu* v. *Romania* and *Broniowski* v. *Poland*,[107] as well as in Bosnia and Herzegovina and Kosovo;[108]
7. guaranteeing indigenous peoples' ownership of their land, for example by return of the territory, protection and granting title in *Xákmok Kásek Indigenous Community* v. *Paraguay*.[109]

15.10.6 Compensation

Compensation is in practice one of the most important forms of reparation. It is often seemingly taken for granted that compensation is beneficial and in the interest of victims, particularly where it provides the means to address the adverse consequences of violations. In economic terms, compensation makes violations costly for the perpetrators and may have a deterrent effect. However, victims often see compensation as an insufficient form of reparation where it is not accompanied by acknowledgement and/or accountability. Moreover, even where compensation is paid, the amount of compensation is frequently contested and perceived to be inadequate.

15.10.7 Types of Damages

The components of compensation are similar to what is familiar in most domestic legal systems and can be said to constitute general principles of law. Compensation includes any economically assessable damages,

---

[104] *Tristán Donoso* v. *Panama* (IACtHR) (2009) paras. 193–5.
[105] Art. 21 of the Darfur Peace Agreement (5 May 2006): Urgent Programmes for Internally Displaced Persons (IDPs), Refugees and Other War-Affected Persons and Compensation for War Affected Persons; Chapter IV of the Doha Document for Peace in Darfur (14 July 2011).
[106] *Papamichalopoulos* v. *Greece* (ECtHR) (1996).
[107] *Brumărescu* v. *Romania* (ECtHR) (2001); *Broniowski* v. *Poland* (ECtHR) (2006).
[108] See in this context, C. Ferstman and S. P. Rosenberg, 'Reparations in Dayton's Bosnia and Herzegovina', in Ferstman et al., above note 11, 483–514.
[109] *Xákmok Kásek Indigenous Community* v. *Paraguay* (IACtHR) (2010) paras. 281–95.

comprising both material (pecuniary) and moral (non-pecuniary) damages. Material damages include, as specified in the Basic Principles: lost opportunities (including employment, education and social benefits); loss of earnings (including loss of earning potential); and costs required for legal or expert assistance, medicine and medical services, as well as psychological and social services. Non-material loss or moral damages are meant to compensate for harm, pain and suffering, including mental anguish, humiliation and a sense of injustice.

Punitive or exemplary damages known in particular in Anglo-American jurisprudence have not been expressly recognised by regional or international treaty bodies or courts.[110] Such damages, which go beyond compensating the actual damage caused, are meant to express the public condemnation of the violation and to have a punitive and deterrent effect. The award of such damages does not neatly fit into the paradigm of repairing the actual damage caused reflected in traditional notions of state responsibility.[111] In addition, if bodies were to openly follow such practice it could be expected to meet considerable resistance from states parties. None the less, as emphasised in the concurring opinion of Judge Pinto de Albuquerque, joined by Judge Vučinić in *Cyprus* v. *Turkey*, 'the existence of punitive or exemplary damages under the Convention is a fact in the Court's practice' and such damages 'are acknowledged in international practice and law'.[112] Clearly, punitive damages can be of symbolic and practical value as policy-oriented jurisprudence. In their concurring opinion, the two judges argued that such damages are essential under the ECHR 'in at least three cases: (1) gross violations of human rights ... (2) prolonged, deliberate non-compliance with a judgment of the Court ...; and (3) the severe curtailment, or threat thereof, of the applicant's human rights with the purpose of avoiding, impairing or restricting his or her access to the Court as well as the Court's access to the applicant.'[113]

The general principles governing the award of compensation are well-developed in national, regional and international jurisprudence. However, determining the amount of compensation is still fraught with difficulties. This amount is highly charged. As the 'bottom line' it expresses the adjudicative body's valuation of the violation. It quantifies the suffering of the victim(s) and specifies the sum payable by the state. The ECtHR, the IACtHR

---

[110] *Selçuk and Asker* v. *Turkey* (ECtHR) (1998) para. 119 and *Velásquez Rodríguez* v. *Honduras* (IACtHR) (1990) para. 38, but see also analysis of Judge Cançado Trindade in his 'reasoned' opinion, *Myrna Mack Chang* v. *Guatemala* (IACtHR) (2003).

[111] Although Rombouts, Sardaro and Vandeginste, above note 30, 390, rightly point out that 'the fact that human rights courts do take into account the gravity of the violation for quantifying the damages might suggest that damages have a purpose that is not merely reparative'.

[112] Concurring opinion of Judge Pinto de Albuquerque, joined by Judge Vučinić in *Cyprus* v. *Turkey*, paras. 12–13.

[113] Ibid., para. 18.

and the ACtHPR are the regional human rights courts that have awarded specific amounts of compensation for both pecuniary and non-pecuniary harm.[114] The ECtHR and IACtHR have awarded material damages on an equitable basis where the applicants provided sufficient proof that costs or losses had been, or would be, incurred as a result of the violation. Moral damages have been awarded in particular for serious violations in respect of which a presumption applies that they cause harm and suffering.[115] In determining quantum, courts have utilised factors such as the degree of suffering, the egregiousness of the violation(s), the number of violations, as well as the characteristics (for example, vulnerable children) and conduct of the parties concerned.[116]

It is difficult to quantify specific types of violations, but the awards rendered provide an indication of the amounts commonly granted.[117] The ICJ, in its first judgment of this kind, awarded compensation for material and non-material injury for arbitrary detention and unlawful expulsion in *Ahmadou Sadio Diallo (Republic of Guinea v. Democratic Republic of the Congo)*.[118] Treaty bodies such as the HRCtee have consistently held that respondent states parties responsible for violations should pay compensation without, however, specifying an amount.[119] Effectively, this practice refers the claimant back to the national system or a negotiated settlement, which has hampered enforcement of 'awards'.[120] For their part, most national legal

---

[114] In a noteworthy development, the ECOWAS CCJ has recently awarded specific amounts of compensation for human rights violations, namely in *Hadijatou Mani Koraou v. Niger* (ECOWAS CCJ) (2008), for violation of the prohibition of slavery. See also *Manneh v. Gambia* (ECOWAS CCJ) (2008), for violation of the right to liberty and security.

[115] *Caracazo v. Venezuela* (IACtHR) (2002) para. 50(e); the jurisprudence of the IACtHR is referred to and endorsed by the ACtHPR in *Nobert Zongo and Others v. Burkina Faso*, para. 55.

[116] See Shelton, above note 8, 343–8; Rombouts, Sardaro and Vandeginste, above note 30, 388–9.

[117] Non-pecuniary damages awarded by the IACtHR for violations such as arbitrary detention, torture, forced disappearances and extrajudicial killing may be a relatively paltry US$10,000, but may also amount to US$100,000 depending on circumstances. See C. Sandoval-Villalba, 'The Concepts of "Injured Party" and "Victim" of Gross Human Rights Violations in the Jurisprudence of the Inter-American Court of Human Rights: A Commentary on their Implications for Reparations', in Ferstman et al., above note 11, 243–82, at 258–71. The jurisprudence of the ECtHR also varies considerably. It has awarded significant amounts of non-pecuniary damages in instances of serious violations, such as torture, e.g. €120,000 in *Mikheyev v. Russia* (ECtHR) (2006) para. 163.

[118] *Ahmadou Sadio Diallo v. Democratic Republic of the Congo (Compensation)* (ICJ) (2012), US$85,000 for material injury and US$10,000 for non-material injury.

[119] See further D. Valeska, 'Reparations at the Human Rights Committee: Legal Basis, Practice and Challenges' (2017) 32 *Netherlands Quarterly of Human Rights* 8.

[120] See e.g., REDRESS, *Submission to the Human Rights Committee on Implementation of its Views in the Philippines* (December 2011).

systems and jurisprudence recognise at least some right of victims to claim compensation for human rights violations. However, practice differs widely. Deficient legislation, lack of compensation for non-pecuniary harm, small amounts of compensation and the difficulty of enforcement are some of the key challenges encountered by victims.[121]

15.10.8 *Proyecto de Vida*: *Loayza Tamayo* v. *Peru*

The case of *Loayza Tamayo* illustrates starkly the personal consequences of serious violations which led the IACtHR to develop 'loss of enjoyment of life' *(proyecto de vida* – 'life plan') as a further category of reparation:[122]

She [Loayza Tamayo] has degrees in education and in social work. Prior to her detention, she was a law student and had taken a number of academic courses and seminars. She was 36 years old at the time of her detention. At the time of her detention on February 6, 1993, she was living with her children ... [and] was working at José Gabriel Condorcanqui High School, where her area of specialization was history ... She was definitively removed from her post on May 29, 1993, on the grounds that she had abandoned her post without just cause. At the time of her detention, she was working at the National School of Dramatic Arts ...[and] at the School of Management of the Universidad de San Martín de Porres ... At the time she was detained she was in the process of building a house ... During her detention and up to the present, she has received a monthly pension from the Ministry of Health. During her incarceration, and as a consequence of the cruel, inhuman and degrading punishment to which she was subjected, she suffered serious health problems, treatment of which necessitated outlays of an unspecified amount, all paid by her next of kin. Her confinement brought on severe physical and psychological health disorders; some may be relieved with prolonged therapy, although others may be irreversible. [After her release] [s]he filed several of [sic] requests to be reinstated in her former posts ... The outcome of these requests is unknown. She now resides in the city of Santiago, Chile, is not working, and is undergoing medical treatment financed by 'FASIC.' The so-called 'life plan' deals with the full self-actualisation of the person concerned and takes account of her calling in life, her particular circumstances, her potentialities, and her ambitions, thus permitting her to set for herself, in a reasonable manner, specific goals, and to attain those goals.

The IACtHR found that the violations of Ms Loayza Tamayo's human rights caused grave damage to her 'life plan'. However, it concluded that:

neither case law nor doctrine has evolved to the point where acknowledgment of damage to a life plan can be translated into economic terms. Hence, the Court

---

[121] REDRESS, above note 95, 47–9.
[122] *Loayza Tamayo* v. *Peru* (IACtHR) (1998), particularly paras. 144–54.

is refraining from quantifying it. It notes, however, that the victim's recourse to international tribunals and issuance of the corresponding judgment constitute some measure of satisfaction for damages of these kinds.

The category of *proyecto de vida*, or life plan, which appears to have been conceived as being non-pecuniary in nature,[123] has attracted considerable interest but also reservations, as it is viewed as unduly broadening the reach of compensation.[124] The *proyecto de vida* certainly bears the potential to contribute to a more holistic understanding of the need to address the intangible long-term effects of harm caused by serious violations.[125]

POINTS TO CONSIDER

1. What role can the *proyecto de vida* play in developing the concept of reparation so as to be responsive to the nature of violations?

2. Can it be translated into something more tangible within the accepted legal framework of the elements of compensation?

15.10.9 Should Previous Conduct be Taken into Consideration when Awarding Compensation?

Individuals who become victims may, prior to the violation, have acted in a way seen as repugnant. This raises the vexing question whether such conduct justifies the denial of compensation. In *McCann* v. *United Kingdom*, for example, the ECtHR decided not to award compensation for a violation of the right to life to the relatives of three suspected IRA operatives who had planned a terrorist attack in Gibraltar but were confronted and killed by British forces.[126] National legal systems (in law, jurisprudence and compensation schemes) recognise that no one should benefit from a situation brought about by him- or herself.[127] This is reflected in article 8 of the European Convention on the Compensation of Victims of Violent Crimes,

---

[123] According to the IACtHR, ibid., para. 151: 'it [reparation for damages to the "life plan"] most closely approximates the ideal of *restitution in integrum*'. However, see *Cantoral Benavides* v. *Peru* (IACtHR) (2001) para. 60, funding scholarship for studies in respect of a violation of the right to liberty and security and freedom from torture which 'prevented the victim from fulfilling his vocation, aspirations and potential, particularly with regard to his preparation for his chosen career and his work as a professional'.

[124] Rombouts, Sardaro and Vandeginste, above note 30, 385, with further references.

[125] However, see note on the lack of consistent application of the concept in the jurisprudence of the IACtHR by T. M. Antkowiak, 'Remedial Approaches to Human Rights Violations: The Inter-American Court of Human Rights and Beyond' (2008) 46 *Columbia Journal of Transnational Law* 351, at 371, fn. 101.

[126] *McCann and Others* v. *United Kingdom* (ECtHR) (1996) para. 219.

[127] Critical in relation to the situation in the UK, Doak, above note 1, 228–9.

which stipulates that compensation may be reduced or refused on account of the victim's conduct, his or her involvement in violent or organised crimes or where it would be contrary to a sense of justice or to public policy.[128] However, there are no explicit provisions in any human rights treaties or instruments that rule out the award of compensation on account of previous conduct or public policy considerations. Not awarding compensation in such instances is problematic as it invokes the notion of an 'undeserving victim' and seems indirectly to validate a serious violation by not attaching pecuniary consequences to it. This is questionable from a policy perspective since the payment of compensation for human rights violations can also have a deterrent impact. Adjusting the amount of compensation may in exceptional circumstances be contemplated where the victim has directly contributed to a violation through his or her criminal and harmful conduct. However, this rationale should not be applicable in cases of absolute rights, such as the prohibition of torture, where no circumstances can justify a breach, and policy considerations weigh generally in favour of awarding adequate compensation for harm suffered.

15.10.10 Rehabilitation

The right to rehabilitation, which is recognised in several human rights treaties,[129] addresses the multifaceted rehabilitative needs of victims caused by violations. Rehabilitation, which should be holistic and victim-centred, 'seeks to enable the maximum possible self-sufficiency and function for the individual concerned, and may involve adjustments to the person's physical and social environment'.[130] Its aim is 'to restore, as far as possible, [the victim's] independence, physical, mental, social and vocational ability; and full inclusion and participation in society'.[131] According to the Basic Principles, '[r]ehabilitation should include medical and psychological care as well as legal and social services'. The state or others liable can provide such care and services either in kind or through money that enables victims to access rehabilitation. Rehabilitation appears to be most valuable if construed as an obligation of the state to establish and maintain a system that provides facilities and enables victims to access relevant services (on a priority basis where appropriate).[132] In national practice, provision and access to rehabilitation services are often either based on statutory schemes for victims of crimes or

---

[128] Council of Europe, European Convention on the Compensation of Victims of Violent Crimes, opened for signature by Member States of the Council of Europe on 24 November 1983 (1983) 22 ILM 1021.

[129] See e.g., art. 14 CAT; art. 39 CRC; art. 24 CPED.

[130] CtAT, General Comment 3, para. 11.   [131] Ibid.

[132] *Barrios Altos* v. *Peru* (IACtHR) (2001) para. 40; *Nineteen Tradesmen* v. *Colombia* (IACtHR) (2004) paras. 275–8; *'Juvenile Reeducation Institute'* v. *Paraguay* (IACtHR) (2004) paras.

have been part of efforts to address the legacy of violations in transitional justice contexts.[133] However, practice is largely ad hoc, which may also be attributed to the lack of attention to detail and effective implementation of the right to rehabilitation in the practice of treaty bodies and NGO advocacy. CtAT's General Comment on article 14 CAT provided an important opportunity to address the multiple questions surrounding the nature, content and implementation of the right to rehabilitation.[134]

15.10.11 Satisfaction

The term satisfaction encompasses a plethora of largely symbolic measures. It also includes key components of justice, such as public acknowledgement, truth and accountability. Satisfaction is a recognised term of art in the draft articles on state responsibility,[135] the ECHR, which may include compensation or simply consist of a declaratory judgment finding a breach,[136] and the Basic Principles, with the latter being broadest in scope.[137]

Cessation of violations denotes measures taken to stop ongoing violations, such as refraining from exposing a detainee to inhuman detention conditions. Such measures correspond to states' primary obligations to respect rights and prevent violations, which raises the question whether they can or should be classified as reparation.[138]

Acknowledgement denotes accepting responsibility for the wrong done, which can take various forms, such as a public statement, or a declaration, including in the course of judicial proceedings, as in several cases before the IACtHR.[139] The acceptance of responsibility should also be reflected in official accounts of events, including in schoolbooks where appropriate. Acknowledgement serves an important function in 'setting the public record straight', and thereby vindicating victims. It also acts as factual evidence that can be used to counter claims that certain violations never happened, for example the Holocaust.

318–20; CtAT, Conclusions and Recommendations: Zambia, UN doc. A/57/44 (SUPP) (25 September 2002) paras. 59–67, particularly at 66(g). See further REDRESS, *Rehabilitation as a Form of Reparation under International Law* (2009).

[133] Report of the Special Rapporteur, above note 11, paras. 35–7.

[134] CtAT, General Comment 3, paras. 11–15.

[135] Art. 37(2) ARSIWA: 'Satisfaction may consist in an acknowledgement of the breach, an expression of regret, a formal apology or another appropriate modality.'

[136] Art. 41 ECHR.   [137] Principle 22 of the Basic Principles.

[138] Shelton, above note 8, 149. Also, van Boven, above note 25, 25.

[139] See on this point in particular, the critical assessment of J. Cavallaro and S. E. Brewer, 'Reevaluating Regional Human Rights Litigation in the Twenty-First Century: The Case of the Inter-American Court' (2008) 102 *American Journal of International Law* 768, at 808–16.

Apologies are a related though conceptually distinct form of reparation.[140] They combine acknowledgement with an expression of remorse over someone's acts or omissions. Apologies have arguably been neglected as a form of reparation. This may be attributed to concerns over how genuine they are (although there are significant cultural differences – in Japan, for example, the inherent submission of making an apology may be considered sufficient, whereas in Western countries greater emphasis is placed on the correspondence of the expression with the thinking and feelings of the person making the apology). There is also concern over whether a person can be judicially forced to apologise. However, the IACtHR has developed a jurisprudence of ordering states to apologise for violations.[141] Apologies to victims have also featured in official responses to violations in times of or following political transition.[142] This is a welcome development as apologies can constitute an important symbolic measure for victims and serve goals of restorative justice.

Truth is an integral part of acknowledgement, but also a component of reparation in its own right. The IACtHR, as well as other international bodies and instruments, has recognised a distinctive right to truth, in particular in cases of enforced disappearances and extrajudicial killings.[143] The ECtHR has also referred to the right to truth in its recent jurisprudence.[144] This right entitles relatives to be informed about the fate and whereabouts of the victim(s), or their remains. It also encompasses access to factual and other relevant information concerning the violation, including archives.

Satisfaction comprises 'judicial and administrative sanctions against the persons liable for the violations'.[145] This category corresponds to the duty of states to investigate, prosecute and punish those responsible for serious

---

[140] See in particular, C. Jenkins, 'Taking Apology Seriously', in Du Plessis and Peté, above note 64, 53–81.

[141] See e.g., *Cantoral Benavides* v. *Peru*, para. 81; *Moiwana Village* v. *Suriname* (IACtHR) (2005) para. 216; *Gutiérrez Soler* v. *Colombia* (IACtHR) (2005) para. 59.

[142] Speech by Romania's President Traian Basecu in the Romanian Parliament (18 December 2006), online at www.icarfoundation.ro/index.php?option=com_content&task=view&id=29&Itemid=44.

[143] See *Rodríguez Vera et al. (The Disappeared from the Palace of Justice)* v. *Colombia* (IACtHR) (2014) paras. 508–11, and more broadly, IACHR, *The Right to Truth in the Americas*, OEA/Ser.L/V/II.152, doc. 2 (13 August 2014); *Selimovic and Others* v. *Republic Srpska* (Human Rights Chamber for Bosnia and Herzegovina) (2003) paras. 211–12; art. 24(2) CPED; principle 1 of the Updated Set of Principles for the Protection and Promotion of Human Rights through Action to Combat Impunity, UN Commission on Human Rights Resolution 2005/81 (21 April 2005); principle 22(b) and (c) of the Basic Principles.

[144] *El-Masri* v. *The Former Yugoslav Republic of Macedonia* (ECtHR) (2012) paras. 191–3, 175–9 (third-party interveners), as well as Joint Concurring Opinion of Judges Tulkens, Spielmann, Sicilianos and Keller and Joint Concurring Opinion of Judges Casadevall and López Guerra. See further J. A. Sweeney, 'The Elusive Right to Truth in Transnational Human Rights Jurisprudence' (2018) 67 *International & Comparative Law Quarterly* 353.

[145] Principle 22(f) of the Basic Principles.

violations.[146] Criminal accountability of the perpetrators is constitutive of adequate reparation, particularly in cases of gross violations.[147] Its opposite, i.e. impunity, leaves an important component of justice unaddressed and is prone to contribute to the perpetuation of violations.

Commemoration in the form of museums, plaques, naming streets after victims, ceremonies or educational materials combines elements of maintaining a public record of events with a recognition and restoration of the dignity of victims. Such symbolic measures form an integral part of the jurisprudence of the IACtHR.[148] They play an important role in affirming both the suffering and humanity of the victims and in empowering them to (re-)claim their place in society.

15.10.12 Guarantees of Non-repetition

Guarantees of non-repetition include measures such as protection, but largely denote a range of forward-looking measures that typically go beyond the individual case at hand and seek to prevent the recurrence of certain violations, particularly by bringing about systemic changes. The measures identified in the Basic Principles draw on rule of law components aimed at strengthening the independence of the judiciary as well as legislative and institutional reforms, especially of law-enforcement agencies, with a view to ensuring observance of international standards.

15.10.13 Reparation for the Violation of Collective Rights: *Saramaka People* v. *Suriname*

Providing compensation to groups of victims, be it for violations of collective rights or mass violations, presents a unique challenge for human rights treaty bodies. In cases of collective rights violations, such as the rights of indigenous peoples, the IACtHR has awarded collective damages in the form of a lump sum payable to a development fund for the benefit of the group concerned[149] or directly to the group.[150] It has also ordered other collective measures of reparation, such as a housing programme and development

---

[146] See Chapter 2.3.4.

[147] See e.g., *Miguel Castro-Castro Prison* v. *Peru* (IACtHR) (2006) paras. 436–41. See also the link between articles 12, 13 and 14 in the CtAT jurisprudence, e.g. *Ndagijimana* v. *Burundi* (CtAT) (2018) paras. 8.1–8.9.

[148] Antkowiak, above note 125, 381–2.

[149] *Aloeboetoe* v. *Suriname* (IACtHR) (1993) paras. 101–2. See also *Caracazo* v. *Venezuela*, para. 137; *Suárez Rosero* v. *Ecuador* (IACtHR) (1999) para. 107; '*White Van*' *(Paniagua Morales et al.)* v. *Guatemala* (IACtHR) (2001) para. 223; *Godínez Cruz* v. *Honduras* (IACtHR) (1990) para. 32.

[150] *Sarayaku* v. *Ecuador* (IACtHR) (2012) paras. 317 and 323.

programmes for communities whose members had been massacred.[151] Where a number of individuals have suffered similar violations, international compensation commissions, mass claims adjudication and the IACtHR have used categories of victims entitled to fixed amounts for certain types of violation.[152] The IACtHR has also awarded measures benefiting the members of targeted groups or communities in such cases.[153]

In *Saramaka People* v. *Suriname*,[154] the IACtHR found that Suriname had, by granting logging concessions to companies on Saramaka land, violated the rights of the Saramaka people, a tribal group, to judicial protection against violations of their right to property. The Court made a number of important findings on reparation: The group (Saramaka people) itself was entitled to compensation. The members of the community are the 'injured party' and 'beneficiaries of the collective forms of reparation'. Awards are for the benefit of the entire group. These include funds to provide 'educational, housing, agricultural, and health projects, as well as to provide electricity and drinking water' for the benefit of the community. Awards are made through trust funds. Three parties, namely representatives from each party and a third party agreed upon, are to decide about the use of the trust fund. This set-up was chosen to encourage parties to agree on the mode of implementation,[155] but was changed in later jurisprudence so as to provide a greater degree of autonomy to recipients.

POINTS TO CONSIDER

1. What are the challenges of poviding reparation for collective rights?

2. How satisfactorily has the IACtHR dealt with these challenges?

15.10.14 A Brief Assessment and Outlook

The adoption of the Basic Principles, the jurisprudence of national, regional and international bodies, particularly the IACtHR, as well as the work of individual experts, NGOs and victims movements worldwide have contributed to a better understanding of reparation and have strengthened the right of victims. However, several grey and under-developed areas remain. These apply in particular to adequate forms of reparation for violations of economic,

---

[151] *Plan de Sánchez Massacre* v. *Guatemala* (IACtHR) (2004) paras. 105–10.

[152] Holtzmann and Kristjánsdóttir, above note 34.

[153] *Massacres of El Mozote and Nearby Places* v. *El Salvador* (IACtHR) (2012) paras. 180–1, 208.

[154] *Saramaka People* v. *Suriname* (IACtHR) (2007).

[155] In *Sarayaku* v. *Ecuador*, para. 317, the Court ordered $90,000 to be paid to the Association of the Sarayaku People 'so that the People may decide, in accordance with its own decision-making mechanisms and institutions, how to invest the money ...'

social and cultural rights,[156] collective rights,[157] as well as a greater awareness of the gender dimensions of reparation.[158] One of the most serious challenges facing national systems as well as regional and international bodies is how to provide adequate reparation in instances of mass violations involving a large number of victims.[159]

QUESTIONS

1. Should the state be responsible for paying reparation for the criminal conduct (such as rape in custody) of its officials?

2. What understanding of reparation has motivated victims to reject compensation, particularly the offer of money to settle a case in return for dropping all claims and complaints?

3. How does reparation tackle impunity?

15.11   THE DOUBLE-EDGED SWORD OF VICTIMS' POLITICS

The status of 'victim' has gained prominence in political debates, where it has become a marker of identity and competing claims for public recognition and reparation.[160] The use of the term may in this context become a tactical weapon of choice, particularly to enhance the apparent legitimacy of claims. In this way, it puts the onus on governments or other entities to explain why they deny or neglect rights and/or contribute to 'victimisation'.

---

[156] There is a dearth of jurisprudence in this respect, particularly at the supranational level. See, however, *The Social and Economic Rights Action Centre (SERAC) and the Centre for Social and Economic Rights (CESR)* v. *Nigeria* (*Ogoniland* case) (ACmHPR) (2001), in which the ACmHPR recommended a range of remedial measures for violations of economic, social and cultural rights. This situation is set to change after the Optional Protocol to the ICESCR has become operational and the Committee develops its jurisprudence.

[157] See 15.10.10 and F. Lenzerini (ed.), *Reparations for Indigenous Peoples: International and Comparative Perspectives* (Oxford University Press, 2008).

[158] See in particular the Nairobi Declaration on Women's and Girls' Rights to a Remedy and Reparation (2007). See also Report of the Special Rapporteur on violence against women: its causes and consequences, Rashida Manjoo, UN doc. A/HRC/14/22 (23 April 2010) paras. 12–85.

[159] L. Oette, 'Bringing Justice to Victims? Responses of Regional and International Human Rights Courts and Treaty Bodies to Mass Violations', in Ferstman et al., above note 11, 217–42; Report of the Special Rapporteur, above note 11; and 'Redress Trust observations pursuant to Article 75 of the Statute', *In the Case of The Prosecutor* v. *Germain Katanga* (ICC) (15 May 2015).

[160] See in particular, in relation to violations related to World War II, J. Torpey, 'Victims and Citizens: The Discourse of Reparation(s) at the Dawn of the New Millennium', in De Feyter et al., above note 21, 41–5.

The importance of the status of victim, both in terms of being entitled to reparation and having one's suffering recognised by society, is particularly apparent where groups of victims are excluded altogether. For example, the victims of systemic injustices of a collective nature characteristic of the pervasive regime of apartheid were not recognised in South Africa's official dealing with the past, in contrast to (individualised) victims of discrete gross violations.[161] Exploitation and poverty are often not portrayed in terms of violations, victim status, rights and remedies, but characterised as economic or societal ills.[162] Such categorisation may result in charitable or humanitarian intervention that alleviates the suffering but will frequently have little effect on the status quo. Seizing victim status becomes, against this background, a highly politicised undertaking, with those who are able to influence the granting or denial of such status often acting as gatekeepers in public debates.

Referring to oneself or one's group as victims can be a means of staking claims in the course of debates about who should be entitled to reparation: 'I am/We are deserving of justice and reparation (but you/others aren't).' This may give rise to competition between victims of violations where one group of victims sees itself as more deserving than others (or the only group worthy of reparation). This applies in particular to those who suffered particularly egregious violations, such as torture, compared to, for example, 'mere' short-term wrongful imprisonment, and groups that have been specifically targeted. In the context of post-atrocity or conflict situations, such as in Rwanda or the Democratic Republic of the Congo, the public may find it difficult to understand why the legal status of victim attaches to certain 'violations' but not other forms of violence and/or hardship, as many people will have suffered and feel aggrieved in these circumstances.[163] Devising reparation programmes that do justice to the myriad forms of victimisation is therefore extremely challenging following a conflict or mass violations. In practice, this has often resulted in collective forms of reparation, such as building schools that may, however, be barely distinguishable from development measures and thereby defeat the purpose of reparation.[164]

The portrayal of suffering and representation of victims have raised concerns. The word 'victim' often carries negative connotations of passivity, helplessness and suffering. Describing someone as a victim or a group of

---

[161] See M. Mamdani, 'Amnesty or Impunity? A Preliminary Critique of the Report of the Truth and Reconciliation Commission of South Africa (TRC)', in Du Plessis and Peté, above note 64, 83–118.

[162] B. Hours, 'NGOs and the Victims Industry', *Le Monde Diplomatique*, English edition (November 2008).

[163] N. Roht-Arriaza, 'Reparations, Decisions and Dilemmas' (2004) 27 *Hastings International and Comparative Law Review* 157, at 188.

[164] Ibid., 186–92; Report of the Special Rapporteur, above note 11, paras. 38–42.

persons as victims can therefore be seen as a form of labelling, confining those concerned into a bounded and static societal straitjacket, which ignores individuality and agency.[165] Notably, individuals who have suffered violations such as torture often prefer to refer to themselves as survivors. The difference in meaning and in connotation of such a term is apparent. However, there are limitations to its use in all circumstances. The term survivor implies that the violation was life-threatening, either actually or symbolically (as a fundamental attack on the personality of the victim), which will not necessarily apply to all violations (such as forms of arbitrary arrest and detention). Moreover, some individuals will not survive violations, such as extrajudicial killings or enforced disappearance. As a legal category, it may therefore be preferable to retain the use of the term victim as shorthand for 'anyone who suffered harm as a result of a violation of his/her/their right(s)'. A plethora of people, in particular human rights defenders, speak about or on behalf of 'victims' and use the experience of suffering to pursue advocacy or other purposes. While this is often done with the best of intentions, the spectacle of suffering may easily be exploited. It also carries the risk of viewing and portraying victims as passive objects and of simultaneously appropriating their suffering and stifling their agency.[166] Such an approach has been criticised for overly focusing on protection, and the dependency it entails, instead of focusing on true democracy and freedom.[167] Victimisation rhetoric has been called a tragedy which resurrects the 'native' subject in international/post-colonial feminist legal politics that focus on violence against women.[168] Victims' advocacy is also bound to create an unequal power relationship between those claiming to be able to alleviate and/or help to remedy the suffering and the individuals or groups portrayed as victims.[169] However, this risk can be mitigated through the involvement of victims. Many human rights organisations or movements are founded or actively supported by individuals who have themselves suffered violations, and often engage them in their work. The degree to which any individual or organisation speaking

---

[165] See for a succinct overview of the debate with further references, M. Clapham and S. Marks, *International Human Rights Lexicon* (Oxford University Press, 2005) 404–5. See also chapter titled 'Trafficking in Hegemony' in C. Dauvergne, *Making People Illegal: What Globalization means for Migration and Law* (Cambridge University Press, 2008), particularly 69–83.

[166] See Dauvergne, ibid., on the United States' annual Trafficking in Persons report, and also in particular M. Mutua, *Human Rights: A Political and Cultural Critique* (University of Pennsylvania Press, 2002) 27–39.

[167] W. Brown, *States of Injury: Power and Freedom in Late Modernity* (Princeton University Press, 1995).

[168] For a post-colonial, feminist critique, see in particular R. Kapur, *Erotic Justice: Law and the New Politics of Postcolonialism* (Glass House Press, 2005) 95ff.

[169] Hours, above note 162.

on behalf of victims actually has such direct links and mutual channels of communication is therefore an important yardstick of legitimacy.

A highly problematic aspect of victims' politics is its use as licence to justify violations. Such charges have been levelled against Israel and Rwanda, for example, and are by necessity highly contentious and fraught with difficulties. The perception of one's own victim status may have two consequences in this context. It may underpin a collectively shared fear, whether objectively justified or not, that a repetition or similar violations as the ones which caused the original victimisation may recur. This may result in an uncompromising outlook, militarisation and the willingness to use excessive force or legitimise human rights violations.[170] The victim status may also become the founding myth, *raison d'être* and legitimising factor of a state or a regime. This may be used to enshrine the latter's pre-eminence in national politics and provide justification for repression. It may also serve as a tool for neutralising political opposition that is portrayed as pursuing the agenda of the erstwhile perpetrators even where it formulates legitimate demands or grievances.[171]

This brief review of the notion and broader debates surrounding the politics of victimhood demonstrates that the term 'victim' is by no means unproblematic. Using it requires awareness and caution, and its use in any given context should be subject to critical interrogation as to its appropriateness and the motives of the user(s) for doing so.

15.12   NEGOTIATING, LITIGATING AND ADMINISTERING REPARATIONS: EXPERIENCES FROM THE HOLOCAUST AND WORLD WAR II REPARATIONS

Reparation costs money. In instances of mass violations, the overall amount of compensation in question is by definition substantial. It is for this plain truth that states (and others) are frequently reluctant to provide reparation of their own will. The question of reparation becomes in these circumstances often a highly politicised process. It depends on the influence, standing and efficiency of victims, and/or their advocates, the availability of effective legal avenues or other mechanisms, and a variety of factors that may persuade the state or others concerned that providing reparation is the right thing to do and/or in their best interest.

---

[170] See also in this context, the controversial comparisons with and charges of colonialism and apartheid in Report of the Special Rapporteur on the situation of human rights in the Palestinian territories occupied since 1967, John Dugard, UN doc. A/HRC/4/17 (29 January 2007).

[171] See e.g., S. Newton, 'Law and Power in the Shadow of the Genocide' (2007) 2 *Journal of Comparative Law* 151.

The Holocaust and World War II reparations are arguably the most instructive example given their scope and time span. The question of payments for victims came to the fore in the late 1940s. Many Jewish organisations claimed compensation and restitution as 'a small measure of justice for Jewish victims of Nazi persecution'.[172] The Federal Republic of Germany, for its part, had a political interest in gaining legitimacy by showing its willingness to bear responsibility, which was viewed as a precondition for becoming accepted by other Western states and others. However, the proposals made led to fierce opposition in Israel. Compensation was seen as blood money that denigrates the suffering of the victims, the Holocaust being such an unimaginable crime that it could never be compensated for in monetary terms. Significantly, even those Jewish survivors in favour of compensation used the word *Shilumim*, i.e. recompense, instead of the term reparations (*Wiedergutmachung*) favoured by Germany. In the end, after intense negotiations, Israel and Germany reached an agreement in 1952 that paved the way for the payment of tens of billions of German marks over the next decades.[173] Since then, three important challenges have resurfaced frequently. Who should be covered by reparations? How should reparations be administered? And, can the forms of reparations available ever do justice to survivors and victims?

The official reparation schemes had significant omissions. One of the most glaring was the fact that many victims of slave labour and forced labour[174] had not received reparations and that some of the main beneficiaries thereof, in particular German companies, had not been held accountable. The victims of these violations and organisations working on their behalf, particularly the Conference on Jewish Material Claims Against Germany, employed a variety of strategies. They sought to negotiate terms with the German government and to persuade the relevant industries to provide compensation. This was complemented by resort to class action suits in the USA, i.e. legal action brought on behalf of a large number of victims who claim to have suffered common or similar harm, aimed at reaching a settlement for the benefit of all victims. In the Swiss settlement case,[175] '[Judge

---

[172] G. Taylor, G. Schneider and S. Kagan, 'The Claims Conference and the Historic Jewish Efforts for Holocaust-Related Compensation and Restitution', in Ferstman et al., above note 11, 103–14, at 103.

[173] See for a detailed account, A. Colonomos and A. Armstrong, 'German Reparations to the Jews after World War II: A Turning Point in the History of Reparations', in de Greiff, above note 10, 390–419.

[174] Slave labour referred to concentration camp labour whereas forced labour referred to other forms of labour, in particular for the German industry. The majority of survivors of slave labour were Jewish and of forced labour Eastern European.

[175] This concerned a lawsuit in which the plaintiffs alleged that the Swiss Banks in question had retained and concealed the assets of Holocaust victims, laundered Nazi loot and transacted in the profits of slave labour. See *In re Holocaust Victim Assets Litigation* (US) (2000).

Koman] encouraged and actively participated in settlement negotiations, thereby facilitating the historic agreement that resolved the lawsuits and created the $1.25 billion settlement'.[176] A combination of factors, including international advocacy, political developments in Germany, the USA and Eastern Europe in the 1990s, and the threat of adverse judgments and consequences for the German companies that had benefited from slave/forced labour, provided the impetus for negotiations that resulted in the setting up of a foundation to compensate the victims of these violations.[177] Importantly, the payment of compensation was accompanied by an official note of apology from the German President, thus making acknowledgement an integral part of the reparations programme.

The setting up of reparations schemes resulting from advocacy, litigation and negotiations constituted an important victory for the individuals and organisations involved. However, legal and practical challenges in administering these reparations abound. How is an eighty-year-old woman living in an isolated part of the Ukraine to find out about the forced labour reparations programme? How can she prove that she was subjected to forced labour if she lost all her documents in the aftermath of the war? How does one calculate adequate compensation for her, if she was not only forcibly made to perform factory work, but was also repeatedly raped by her 'employers'? Those responsible for administering reparation programmes tend to utilise a number of techniques to address these challenges. These include outreach, adequate time for submission of applications, relaxed standards of proof and standardised claims according to categories of violations. These techniques are used to enable as many genuine victims as possible to benefit from the scheme within a realistic time frame. By their nature, these techniques are developed and applied to respond to the exigencies of the situation concerned. This means that there is often an experimental element to their use. Nevertheless, over time, individuals and organisations have developed considerable expertise and means to administer reparation schemes that address some if not all of the challenges.[178]

Ultimately, a reparations scheme must go beyond efficient administration. Its success will in large part depend on its ability to provide reparation that is meaningful in a victim-oriented manner. This includes the role of the victim, the procedure applied and the form of reparation provided. All too often, victims have become disillusioned with bureaucratic schemes that are seen as insensitive to their experience. This is articulated in a lawyer's account of the administration of the German reparations laws of 1965:

[176] J. Gribetz and S. C. Reig, 'The Swiss Banks Holocaust Settlement', in Ferstman et al., above note 11, 115–42, at 118.

[177] J. Authers, 'Making Good Again: German Compensation for Forced and Slave Laborers', in de Greiff, above note 10, 420–48.

[178] Holtzmann and Kristjánsdóttir, above note 34.

No one bothered to restore the survivor's dignity. On the contrary, the procedures inherent in some of the paragraphs of the [German] Restitution Laws, inflict indignities upon the claimants while at the same time German authorities are elevated to the status of superior beings who adjudge the claimant's veracity and honesty and classify them in accordance with the degree of their damage ... To receive payments, often sorely needed, the applicants had to subject themselves to the most humiliating and degrading, seemingly very correct legal type of reparations.[179]

15.13 REPARATION IN ACTION: LITIGATING HUMAN RIGHTS CASES

15.13.1 Litigation Strategies

Human rights lawyers, victims' organisations and NGOs have been at the forefront of promoting victims' rights and pursuing claims on their behalf. Beyond seeking justice for individuals, human rights cases frequently serve broader objectives. This instrumental approach is known as strategic litigation. It seeks to identify cases that address key obstacles which, if successful, set a precedent that will benefit a large number of victims.[180] This may concern the recognition (and/or elaboration) of rights or fundamental principles, the availability of legal avenues and types of reparation. An example is the landmark case of *Hadijat Mani* v. *Niger*, in which the Economic Community of West African States Community Court of Justice (ECOWAS CCJ) ruled that Niger had to pay $19,000 compensation for failing to protect the applicant from slavery (which lasted over eight years).[181] This case resulted in the recognition of positive obligations on the part of the state to prevent slavery and set a regional precedent of awarding specific amounts of compensation.

Strategic litigation can be pursued before national, regional or international courts or bodies, or a combination thereof. It can take the form of representing claimants, public interest litigation or intervening as *amicus*, the so-called friend of the court where a third party is allowed to make submissions on legal issues if considered relevant to the case – this practice is increasingly utilised by NGOs, human rights law centres and others, often

---

[179] M. Kestenberg, 'Discriminatory Aspects of the German Restitution Law and Practice', quoted in Danieli, above note 99, at 57.

[180] The NGO Interights, e.g., was well-known for its strategic litigation programme. See European Roma Center, Interights and Migration Policy Group, 'Strategic Litigation of Race Discrimination in Europe: From Principles to Practice' (2004), online at www.migpolgroup.com/public/docs/57. StrategicLitigationofRaceDiscriminationinEuropefrom PrinciplestoPractice_2004.pdf and www.interights.org.

[181] *Hadijatou Koraou Mani* v. *Niger*.

working in collaboration, as a means of seeking to influence court decisions on legal principles and legal policy issues.[182]

Public interest litigation is a particular type of strategic litigation. It has been used, often effectively, in several countries, such as India, South Africa, the USA and elsewhere with a view to bringing about broader changes to strengthen rights protection and social justice.[183] Initially, efforts largely focused on violations of civil and political rights. More recently, there has been an increasing emphasis on litigating cases of violations of economic, social and political rights.[184] For example, in *People's Union for Civil Liberties* v. *Union of India and Others*,[185] the litigants successfully petitioned the Supreme Court of India to order the government of India to implement a series of food and benefit distribution schemes, as well as to provide access to information. Two of the lawyers involved in the case highlighted internal debates within the People's Union for Civil Liberties as to whether – given their policy nature – it would be worthwhile to pursue claims relating to the right to food before the Supreme Court. In the lawyers' analysis, the orders set an important precedent on the right to food and the entitlements flowing from it. They also point out the valuable lessons of how to break down broad economic, social and cultural rights into specific demands so as to turn them into claims which can be litigated and adjudicated upon.[186]

15.13.2 Pursuing Reparation Claims, with Particular Reference to Litigating Torture Cases

Individuals who suffer from serious violations such as torture frequently struggle to rebuild their lives as best as possible. As put in 2005 by Leopoldo García Lucero, a Chilean refugee who survived a sustained period of torture at the hands of the Pinochet regime in the 1970s:

---

[182] See e.g., Special Court of Sierra Leone in the Trial Chamber, *The Prosecutor against Morris Kallon*, *Amicus Curiae* Brief submitted by the Redress Trust, Lawyers Committee on Human Rights (now Human Rights First) and the International Commission of Jurists (on the legality of amnesties for international crimes) (24 October 2003), www. redress.org/case-docket/the-prosecutor-against-morris-kallon, and Brief of *Amici Curiae* International Human Rights Organizations Center for Constitutional Rights, Human Rights Watch and International Federation of Human Rights in support of petitioner, in the case of *Hamdan* v. *Rumsfeld* (concerning Guantánamo Bay and right of access to courts) (US) (6 January 2006), online at www.fidh.org/IMG/pdf/amicus012006a.pdf.

[183] See further C. R. Epp, *The Rights Revolution: Lawyers, Activists and Supreme Courts in Comparative Perspective* (University of Chicago Press, 1998); S. A. Scheingold, *The Politics of Rights: Lawyers, Public Policy and Political Change*, 2nd edn (University of Michigan Press, 2004).

[184] See V. Gauri and D. M. Brinks (eds.), *Courting Social Justice: Judicial Enforcement of Social and Economic Rights in the Developing World* (Cambridge University Press, 2010).

[185] *People's Union for Civil Liberties* v. *Union of India and Others* (India) (2003).

[186] See B. Guha-Khasnobis and S. Vivek, *Rights-based Approach to Development: Lessons from the Right to Food Movement in India*, WIDER Research Paper (January 2007), online at www.wider.unu.edu/sites/default/files/rp2007-04.pdf.

Now I am 73. I have been here [in the UK] for 30 years and every part of my body has problems. But my biggest problem is that my head injuries meant that I could never learn English. My three daughters have children but [when] they speak to me I can't understand what they are saying and I feel bad. If you cut a wound and you can't heal it, it gets bigger and bigger. That's what happened to me. Pinochet has never been put in prison so the wound gets bigger. I am not at peace. I want to go back to Chile, but it would be very difficult for me because they took everything ...[187]

Seeking reparation may be part of the process of trying to rebuild one's life. It is also frequently driven by a series of other factors and objectives. Survivors may need financial and other help to cope with the consequences of violations. They may want to find answers, have a desire for acknowledgement, and/or retribution, and a deep-rooted quest for justice. Some survivors become highly motivated to bring about changes to the system and to enhance the protection of human rights, for example by calling for public inquiries into violations. However, empirical research shows that survivors perceive reparation in different ways.[188] This means that it is difficult if not impossible to generalise in this respect – worse, generalising may ignore survivors' agency and fail to duly consider their needs and wishes. Whereas some survivors pursue reparation vigorously, even to the point that the process of so doing might become an end in itself, others prefer not to seek justice. This can be due to multiple factors. Survivors often have a high degree of traumatisation and fear of having to relive the trauma as part of an (alienating) legal procedure. Even where survivors decide to pursue reparation, it can be highly difficult because the process or outcome might not meet expectations or prove more strenuous than expected. These difficulties and challenges are often exacerbated where reparation is sought by a group of survivors. They have to agree on representation and strategies and will have to grapple with the inevitable group dynamics that such an undertaking entails. An example is the representation of victims of the Castro-Castro Prison massacre in Peru that ended in open disagreement before the IACtHR.[189]

Lawyers and others representing survivors of violations encounter different types of challenges. In many instances, it will take a considerable time for the full story to emerge, especially in relation to acts of sexual violence. Accounts of arrest, detention, torture and other violations may be patchy, and even seemingly contradictory, which can often be attributed to the disorientation caused by events or injuries. Survivors will also in many instances not have obtained other vital evidence in time, such as medico-legal reports,

---

[187] REDRESS, *Torture: Stories of Survival* (2005). See on his case, *García Lucero et al.* v. *Chile* (IACtHR) (2013).

[188] See e.g., REDRESS, *Torture Survivors' Perceptions of Reparation: Preliminary Survey* (2001).

[189] *Miguel Castro-Castro Prison* v. *Peru*, para. 40.

either because it was not feasible or because they did not have any or adequate legal representation or assistance at the time. Dealing with survivors therefore differs markedly from an ordinary lawyer–client relationship and requires a high degree of empathy and understanding of survivors' experiences, which have often been highly traumatic, and their consequences.

INTERVIEW 15.1

Litigation, Advocacy and Social Change

(Basil Fernando)

Basil Fernando is a Sri Lankan lawyer. He left Sri Lanka in 1989 when the country was in the grip of a state-sponsored campaign of enforced disappearances and extrajudicial killings. At the time, he became a target of the death squads on account of taking up cases against the police and some powerful persons, and his human rights activism. Subsequently, he worked for the UN in post-genocide Cambodia as a Senior UN Human Rights Officer, before becoming the director of the Hong Kong-based Asian Human Rights Commission (AHRC), one of the leading regional human rights organisations in Asia. Basil Fernando and the AHRC have championed a distinctive human rights approach with a strong focus on empowering people.[1] They have also worked vigorously towards strengthening the rule of law at all levels of society, particularly at the institutional level.[2]

What is distinctive about your approach to litigation?

We try to establish a different type of lawyer–client relationship than what usually exists in Sri Lanka. The reason for this is that torture victims and victims of human rights abuse in general come from socially extremely weak sections of society. They do not have the social skills of litigants who will approach lawyers in their chambers, adjust to the time schedules of lawyers, do the preliminary work of preparation such as finding documents and providing the lawyers with various materials and pay their fees. We have created a combination of a solidarity group consisting of people who are close to victims.

Another aspect we have to be careful of all the time is the protection of the victim and also the lawyers who work on these cases. Dangers are very real and there are some well-known cases where the victim has been assassinated or very seriously harassed. The lawyers themselves have faced serious

---

[1] In 2014, Basil Fernando won the prestigious Right Livelihood Award, see www.rightlivelihood.org/fernando.html.

[2] See www.basilfernando.net and www.ahrchk.net.

attacks, such as grenade attacks on their houses and arson in their offices. Further, there are peculiar difficulties in dealing with human rights-related cases. Often there are strong societal prejudices which need to be fought against slowly and attitude changes need to be brought about on issues such as the prevention of torture, extrajudicial killings and the like. In short, each case is not only a legal case but a discourse with society on vital issues. Secondly, unless those who are involved in the litigation are motivated by other factors than pure economic factors, as is often involved in normal litigation, the kind of litigation that we are involved in cannot be consistently and perseveringly carried out.

What are you seeking to achieve through your case work?

This is a very interesting question. If you look at this problem from purely the standards of developed countries, some may even perceive our work as an exercise in futility. When we undertake a case we are fully aware that if there is to be a positive outcome from a legal sense it will happen only many years later. The delay is so great that by the time a final outcome arrives it may have lost most of its social significance. Besides that, except in very rare instances, the actual award may be insignificant. For example, after a successful outcome in a fundamental rights case before the Supreme Court on issues such as torture the award may be a paltry sum. In cases of criminal charges on torture, extrajudicial killing and the like, the likelihood of a successful outcome is very low. In a very few cases where there had been some sentencing of perpetrators the lengths of proceedings, which may take ten years or more, virtually deprives them of significance. The real deterrence value as it is now is low and the risks such as bodily harm, various types of long psychological harassment, demoralisation among the victims themselves and financial difficulties are all real problems.

However, introducing human rights remedies to a legal system where such remedies have not been a part, this initial stage has to be faced at some point or another. In this process we have to condition the minds of lawyers, litigants, judges, prosecutors and also police investigators into a new kind of thinking and habits. The ultimate success of introducing human rights redresses lies with winning over public opinion in favour of such redress. For many reasons the old mentalities support various types of repression by the state either directly or indirectly. For example, the idea that torture by the police is a necessary condition for social security is a social prejudice that is quite inbuilt. Further, that torture victims are bad criminals is also a very hardened perception. We try to demonstrate that this kind of prejudice and perceptions are in fact contrary to reality, that law-enforcement without torture can create far better community spirit and that society benefits from a legal system where there are adequate remedies for violations.

That kind of social discourse cannot be carried out without practical participation in the litigation process. For example, by merely teaching human rights and law reform, it is not possible to introduce adequate remedies. The people have to go to court to demonstrate the difficulties involved in actually achieving these remedies. In this process many sectors of society and the state come to understand and appreciate the meaning of adequate remedies for human rights in terms of article 2 of the ICCPR.

Can you describe how you practically work on cases? How do you identify cases, who is involved, what are the challenges and how do you seek to address them?

In many of our cases torture victims or their relatives who have heard about the work of our groups approach them when they have a difficulty. Over many years these groups are now trained to interview victims in detail in order to record what they say and also to quickly get further information by way of verification and of gaining greater details about the actual incidents. With such information the victims are helped to make formal complaints to authorities about this incident.

For example a person may be still undergoing torture and illegal detention at the same time when a relative or a friend narrates the story. The group then immediately writes letters to the relevant authorities giving the details of the incident and seeking urgent intervention. The same material collected at the early stage of the incident is also used by the AHRC to create urgent appeals on behalf of the victims. These urgent appeals are sent to large networks and intervention is sought. Thereafter the lawyers associated with the groups interview the victims and witnesses, prepare the necessary papers and file applications for litigation. When finally the case comes to court, the lawyers appear for victims and where necessary also get the intervention of senior counsel. Such interventions go from the lower courts up to the Apex court. Meanwhile studies are conducted into the circumstances and the background of the case. A constant discourse is conducted in the media of the circumstances surrounding torture and related problems within the criminal justice system.

Where there are reasons to be dissatisfied with the local litigation process when the defects of litigation can amount to human rights violations, communications are also filed with the HRCtee. There have been some successful outcomes of such communications. Submissions are also made to the Human Rights Council (HRC), the CtAT and relevant UN rapporteurs on the basis of these cases. The intervention of all these agencies is sought in order to improve an adequate remedy for human rights violations.

The challenges are related to a slow legal process with enormous defects in the constitutional and criminal law, which constantly conflict with all attempts to find justice. The conflict between the defective legal system and frustrations relating to justice creates various types of mentalities which obstruct internal public opinion making progress to have changes. We try to counteract demoralising negative experiences by a regional organisation based outside the local context constantly being in support of the local effort. This includes publicity generation, training, legal advice, and finding some financial resources for the work to create a combination that can at least to some extent address these challenges. It is a unique process of collaboration of victims, local solidarity groups, lawyers and other local agents, together with people from outside who constantly back up the work of each other.

How does human rights litigation fit in with your advocacy work?

The litigation connects everyone who is involved into a very real legal and societal process where people find themselves as they seek an adequate remedy for human rights violations. It is the real world from which there is no escape. The advocacy based on the real information is powerful. It seems to be just generalisations on the basis of some accepted norms and standards. The application of international standards to real situations generates information which has a greater power to create strong impressions. A discourse based on such impressions has a greater impact. A judge who is made to see many gruesome cases of torture may begin to challenge his own prejudices and open his mind to the validity of the advocacy that demands a more comprehensive remedy for abuse of rights. This happens to others too. This happens also to the international community. One of the great problems of international advocacy is that those who live in societies where rule of law and democratic systems are well-established are unable to grasp the problems of countries with weak rule-of-law systems and various kinds of authoritarian political systems. When persons from such backgrounds are confronted with detailed information and analysis of this other situation, they too are likely to look into the advocacy into these problems in a different manner.

What has been the impact of your work?

I think the impact has been very significant. There is a widespread acknowledgement of serious defects of the constitutional and criminal law system that frustrates the rule of law. In fact, there is a new language when talking about these matters. No one will challenge when it is said today that the policing system in Sri Lanka has completely collapsed. At the time when our work started such a statement would have been considered an exaggeration. This is also the case on issues such as torture and the abuse of police powers of arrest and detention for purely corrupt purposes. Like this a vast list of matters relating to inadequate remedies for human rights violations can be mentioned. All this is today very much accepted and often even regarded as an understatement rather than an exaggeration. There is greater appreciation

of the problems at many levels. What prevents more rapid changes are political factors relating to the state which require a greater political will to deal
with. This is beyond the capacity of a human rights group or those involved
in human rights litigation alone. However, as and when these political problems are addressed, the issues of adequate remedies for human rights violations will not be lost in the debate. Sufficient public attention has been
paid to these issues and there are more people who are deeply committed to
pursuing this advocacy.

Can you think of any cases that stand out as a particular success or setback?

There are several cases which are simply unforgettable. Take the case of
Gerard Mervyn Perera. He was arrested on mistaken identity and beaten up
inside a police station to such an extent that he suffered renal failure. After
two weeks in a coma he recovered and later, with the help of our group, filed
a fundamental rights application at the Supreme Court. The case was heard
in a relatively short time and the judgment is a strong case on torture. The
three-bench court ordered the highest amount of compensation awarded up
to then and also made some significant recommendations for the prevention
of torture. After this award by the Supreme Court, the Attorney-General filed
a criminal action against several police officers under the CAT Act, no. 22 of
1994. The torture victim was to give evidence before the High Court in this
trial. After many warnings to alter his evidence or not to appear in court,
which the victim refused, he was fatally wounded while he was travelling to
work. Several years later at the High Court in the torture trial, the accused
were acquitted on the basis that the torture victim was not there to identify
the perpetrators. This judgment has since been appealed and the Court of
Appeal has given leave to proceed.[3] This case expresses all the contradictions of litigation relating to torture and other human rights violations in
Sri Lanka.

   Then there is the case of Sugath Nishantha Fernando. Mr Fernando was a
complainant in a bribery case and a torture case. Once the Commission for
Bribery and Corruption filed a case against a police officer attached to the
Negombo police station he received death threats demanding that he not give
evidence in court. When he refused to comply, about twenty officers sur-
rounded his house and attacked his wife, two children and himself. Later he
filed a fundamental rights case before the Supreme Court regarding the torture and was granted leave to proceed. In that case he named twelve officers
as respondents. Then he received death threats to withdraw the fundamental

---

[3] There had been a conviction in the murder trial; see Asian Human Rights Commission, 'Sri
   Lanka: Sub-Inspector and his Assistant Convicted, Sentenced to Death for Murder' (24 June
   2015), online at www.countercurrents.org/ahrc240615.htm.

rights application within twenty-four hours or he would be assassinated. He made complaints to the Inspector General of Police and all other authorities for protection. However, no protection was provided. Later he was assassinated in broad daylight by two unidentified persons. One year has passed after this incident and no one has been arrested for the murder. The family suspect the police officers who are respondents in the above-mentioned cases as having organised the murder. The widow and the two children have been receiving death threats ever since and are living in hiding, even having had to flee to a neighbouring country for some time. As the local system of litigation and protection has failed they filed a communication before the HRCtee, which admitted the communication and requested the Sri Lankan government to provide protection to the family. However, Sri Lanka has not complied with this recommendation.[4]

The case generated an enormous amount of publicity and discussion. However, within a political context where the criminal justice system has been suppressed, the case has manifested the enormous problems involved in the system to achieve an adequate remedy for human rights violations.

---

[4] See for the final views, *Pathmini Peiris* v. *Sri Lanka* (HRCtee) (2011), finding that Sri Lanka had breached a number of its obligations under the ICCPR.

POINTS TO CONSIDER

1. What are the most significant aspects of the recent phase of reparations for violations committed by Nazi Germany, and what are the strategies that have been used by claimants and Jewish organisations to seek and obtain reparation?

2. Consider the following fictional press release: 'The victims of industrial operations, pollution and land degradation committed by the company x with the support of government y in country z are many. They are faceless but real. These victims need our help to obtain justice. You can support our work to advocate victims' rights by donating $10 per month.' What concerns does it raise in terms of victims' politics?

3. Consider having to advise an individual claiming to have suffered prolonged arbitrary detention and ill-treatment in detention. The detention was justified by security legislation that allows detention without judicial review and access to a lawyer for ninety days. The individual is in financial difficulties and wonders whether to pursue a claim or to accept the settlement offered by the authorities on condition that he refrains from pursuing any civil claims, criminal complaints or other remedies in the matter. What is the dilemma posed, what are the criteria that should be taken into consideration, and what might be possible solutions?

FURTHER READING

Antkowiak, T., 'An Emerging Mandate for International Courts: Victim-Centered Remedies and Restorative Justice' (2011) 47 *Stanford Journal of International Law* 279.

Bassiouni, C. M., 'International Recognition of Victims' Rights' (2006) 6 *Human Rights Law Review* 203.

De Feyter, K., S. Parmentier, M. Bossuyt and P. Lemmens (eds.), *Out of the Ashes: Reparations for Gross Violations of Human Rights* (Intersentia, 2006).

De Greiff, P. (ed.), *The Handbook of Reparations* (Oxford University Press, 2006).

Doak, J., *Victims' Rights, Human Rights and Criminal Justice: Reconceiving the Role of Third Parties* (Hart, 2008).

Du Plessis, M., and S. Peté (eds.), *Repairing the Past? International Perspectives on Reparations for Gross Human Rights Abuses* (Intersentia, 2007).

Evans, C., *The Right to Reparation in International Law for Victims of Armed Conflict* (Cambridge University Press, 2012).

Ferstman, C., *International Organizations and the Fight for Accountability: The Remedies and Reparations Gap* (Oxford University Press, 2017).

Ferstman, C., M. Goetz and A. Stephens (eds.), *Reparations for Victims of Genocide, War Crimes and Crimes Against Humanity: Systems in Place and Systems in the Making* (Martinus Nijhoff, 2009).

Haldemann, F. and T. Unger (eds.), *The United Nations Principles to Combat Impunity: A Commentary* (Oxford University Press, 2018).

Lenzerini, F. (ed.), *Reparations for Indigenous Peoples: International and Comparative Perspectives* (Oxford University Press, 2008).

Letschert, R., and J. van Dijk (eds.), *The New Faces of Victimhood: Globalization, Transnational Crimes and Victim Rights* (Springer, 2011).

Moffett, L., *Justice for Victims before the International Criminal Court* (Routledge, 2014).

Randelzhofer, A., and C. Tomuschat (eds.), *Reparation in Instances of Grave Violations of Human Rights* (Kluwer Law International, 1999).

REDRESS, *Reaching for Justice: The Right to Reparation in the African Human Rights System* (2013).

REDRESS, TRIAL, FIDH, ECCHR, *Driving Forward Justice: Victims of Serious International Crimes in the EU* (2014).

'Reparation for Victims of Armed Conflict: Impulses from the Max Planck Trialogues' (2018) *Zeitschrift für ausländisches öffentliches Recht und Völkerrecht* 519.

Shelton, D., *Remedies in International Human Rights Law*, 3rd edn (Oxford University Press, 2015).

Wemmers, J.-A. M. (ed.), *Reparation for Victims of Crimes against Humanity: The Healing Role of Reparation* (Routledge, 2014).

Zegveld, L., 'Victims' Reparations Claims and International Criminal Courts: Incompatible Values' (2010) 8 *Journal of International Criminal Justice* 79.

Websites

International Centre for Transitional Justice: www.ictj.org

REDRESS: www.redress.org

Special Rapporteur on the promotion of truth, justice, reparation and guarantees of non-recurrence: www.ohchr.org/EN/Issues/TruthJusticeReparation/Pages/Index.aspx

16 The Application of Human Rights in Armed Conflict

CONTENTS

16.1   INTRODUCTION

This chapter discusses the development and application of international humanitarian law (IHL) and its interrelationship with human rights law. It further examines this special relationship, which is of particular importance for the protection of civilians, especially where the applicability of IHL is contested or where IHL constitutes an exception to certain rights, such as the right to life, or fails to prevent and/or provide effective remedies for violations. The chapter seeks to identify the scope of application of IHL and demonstrate the degree to which the two can be reconciled. Moreover, a special case is made for the law applicable in situations of military occupation whereby human rights are subordinate to IHL. Despite this subordination, in practice because international human rights tribunals are not mandated to apply humanitarian law they necessarily interpret and enforce the rights of the victims on the basis of the rights found in their respective statutes. As a result, the jurisprudence of human rights tribunals is not always consistent with IHL. Yet such tribunals are hard-pressed to accept jurisdiction over situations which would otherwise be resolved on the basis of IHL alone. This chapter therefore goes on to discuss the exercise of extraterritorial jurisdiction by human rights tribunals. This is particularly significant because European states involved in the occupation of Iraq or other territories generally argue that the European Convention on Human Rights (ECHR) is inapplicable. The European Court of Human Rights (ECtHR) has taken a different approach. The parameters and consequences of this approach will be highlighted.

16.2   THE FUNDAMENTAL PREMISES OF IHL

IHL is also known as *jus in bello* or laws of war (as opposed to the *jus ad bellum* which concerns the law relating to the use of armed force by states). Unlike human rights, which apply at all times, the application of IHL is dependent on the existence of an armed conflict. There are two types of armed conflict, international and non-international, to which distinct sets of rules apply, although in their majority they now converge. In accordance with common article 2 of the 1949 Geneva Conventions,[1] international armed conflicts are triggered either by the mere occurrence of armed hostilities between two nations, irrespective of their intensity; an effective occupation of foreign territory, even if it is not met with resistance; a declaration of war; or by the existence of armed violence in otherwise internal conflicts in which peoples are fighting against colonial, alien and racist regimes in their exercise of self-determination.[2] The following subsections examine the fundamental tenets of IHL.

16.2.1   Distinction between Combatants and Non-combatants

IHL distinguishes between combatants[3] and civilians, and between military and civilian objects, requiring that only combatants and military objects be made the subject of attack.[4] This is known as the rule of distinction and is the cornerstone of IHL. A military objective encompasses those objects which by their nature, location, purpose or use make an effective contribution to military

---

[1] Convention for the Amelioration of the Condition of the Wounded and Sick in Armed Forces in the Field (I), 75 UNTS 31; Convention for the Amelioration of the Condition of the Wounded, Sick, and Ship-wrecked Members of Armed Forces at Sea (II), 75 UNTS 85; Convention Relative to the Treatment of Prisoners of War (III), 75 UNTS 135; Convention Relative to the Protection of Civilian Persons in Time of War (IV), 75 UNTS 287.

[2] 977 Protocol I to the 1949 Geneva Conventions relative to the protection of victims in international armed conflicts (Protocol I), 1125 UNTS 3, art. 1(4).

[3] Although the use of this term in non-international armed conflicts is not without controversy.

[4] Art. 48 Protocol I; *Legality of the Threat or Use of Nuclear Weapons* (ICJ) (1996) para. 78.

action and whose total or partial destruction, capture or neutralisation, in the circumstances ruling at the time, offers a definite military advantage.[5]

The distinction between *combatants* and *non-combatants* is equally important. Combatant status not only allows a person to be lawfully targeted, it also confers significant entitlements. It grants a licence to lawfully kill other combatants and be afforded prisoner-of-war status (POW) upon capture. Persons who do not satisfy the criteria for combatant status, such as civilians who randomly and treacherously kill members of the occupying force, do not enjoy the entitlements of combatants or the immunities of civilians from attack and are criminally liable for killing enemy personnel. It is important, therefore, to define the relevant concepts. Combatants are persons taking a direct part in hostilities. This in itself, however, is not enough. IHL requires that conflicts are fought between organised groups, whether set up by the state or by private entities, such as militias, paramilitary groups and resistance movements. Only members of such groups are permitted to engage in actual combat operations. Moreover, the group itself must satisfy the conditions that: (1) it is structured under an authority of responsible command; (2) its members distinguish themselves from the civilian population through a distinct emblem or uniform; (3) arms are carried openly; (4) the group conducts its operation in accordance with the laws and customs of war.[6] The rationale behind these requirements is to promote discipline, responsibility and compliance with the laws of war in exchange for recognition of legitimate combatant status. By way of illustration, members of terrorist groups do not generally satisfy conditions (2) and (4) and although they may take a direct part in hostilities they are not considered combatants.

There is dissension among scholars as to whether a distinction can be made between lawful and unlawful combatants. Some contend that the only possible distinction is between combatants and civilians, there being no other categories. Others, however, argue that persons taking a direct part in hostilities without satisfying the four criteria set out in the Geneva Conventions are unlawful combatants and hence do not enjoy the rights and privileges

---

[5] Under art. 52(2) Protocol I, a 'military advantage' must be concrete, imminent and finite, and not merely hypothetical or applicable to the general armed conflict as a whole. As a result, it is limited in time and space and concerns only a particular military operation. See Y. Dinstein, *The Conduct of Hostilities and the Law of International Armed Conflict* (Cambridge University Press, 2010) 92–100.

[6] Art. 4(A)(1)–(3) and (6) of Geneva Convention II and art. 43 Protocol I. The same status is also enjoyed by persons falling under the category of *levée en masse*, which is described in art. 4(A)(6) of Geneva Convention III and art. 2 of the 1907 Hague Regulations Respecting the Laws and Customs of War on Land. The concept refers to the spontaneous taking of arms by inhabitants of a non-occupied territory at the approach of the enemy. In this case, although such persons would normally fail to satisfy the conditions of responsible command and of sufficient distinction, they still enjoy combatant status where they satisfy the remaining two criteria.

afforded to combatants.[7] The status of unlawful combatant was used by the Bush administration to deny relevant entitlements under IHL to members of the Taliban.[8] It has also been employed to deny combatant status to mercenaries, even if they satisfy all four criteria.[9]

16.2.2   Restricted Targeting of Military Objects

In the previous section we explained the basic rule whereby IHL distinguishes between combatants and non-combatants on the basis of active participation in hostilities and emphasised that only combatants may be targeted. In practice, more complex situations may arise where the status of certain persons is not wholly susceptible to such distinctions.

A civilian is any person who is not a member of the armed forces, a resistance movement or similar group. Taken together, all persons who are civilians constitute the civilian population.[10] On the basis of this definition the distinction between combatants and non-combatants should have been straightforward. Yet it is not, because it is disputed whether certain activities entail a direct part in hostilities. By way of illustration, it is not obvious whether civilian labourers working in a military factory should be considered legitimate targets on the basis that they contribute to their country's war effort. To take things a step further, should such labourers be targeted when out shopping with their families? Clearly, combatant status is less plausible in the second scenario. Both cases illustrate the pressing need for a boundary that avoids attributing each and every activity to the war effort, lest everyone be presumed to take a direct part in hostilities by reason of paying taxes which ultimately fuel the capacity of the state to wage war. Although there is no clear-cut answer to the question at hand, it seems fair to argue that civilian workers do not qualify as combatants, although a munitions factory is a legitimate military objective that can be attacked while it is operational.[11] This necessarily means that the workers cannot be individually targeted whether inside the factory or outside.[12] Expert meetings convened

---

[7] See K. Dörmann, 'The Legal Situation of Unlawful/Unprivileged Combatants' (2003) *International Review of the Red Cross* 45; J. Callen, 'Unlawful Combatants and the Geneva Conventions' (2004) 44 *Virginia Journal of International Law* 1026.

[8] See G. H. Aldrich, 'The Taliban, Al-Qaeda and the Determination of Illegal Combatants' (2002) 96 *American Journal of International Law* 893.

[9] Art. 47 Protocol I.

[10] Art. 50(2) Protocol I. In *ICTY Prosecutor* v. *Blaškić* (ICTY) (2000) para. 180, the International Criminal Tribunal for the former Yugoslavia (ICTY) also defined them as 'persons who are not, or no longer are, members of the armed forces'.

[11] D. Fleck (ed.), *The Handbook of Humanitarian Law in Armed Conflicts*, 3rd edn (Oxford University Press, 2014) 85–95.

[12] Certainly, a case can be made in favour of targeting those persons who possess exceptional technical skills capable of producing sophisticated weaponry, because their activities

by the International Committee of the Red Cross (ICRC) suggest that in order for particular conduct to qualify as direct participation (and hence a legitimate target):

1. The act must be likely to adversely affect the military operations or military capacity of a party to an armed conflict or, alternatively, to inflict death, injury, or destruction on persons or objects protected against direct attack (*threshold of harm*); and
2. There must be a direct causal link between the act and the harm likely to result either from that act, or from a coordinated military operation of which that act constitutes an integral part (*direct causation*); and
3. The act must be specifically designed to directly cause the required threshold of harm in support of a party to the conflict and to the detriment of another (*belligerent nexus*).[13]

This discussion is meant to highlight the fact that distinguishing between combatants and non-combatants is not always a straightforward exercise. The situation is even more complicated in the context of non-international armed conflicts. Broadly speaking, these involve armed confrontations of some intensity and duration – thus excluding isolated and sporadic acts of violence – between dissident groups and government forces within the territory of a single state. The international regulation of such internal conflicts has unsurprisingly been resisted by states. They have traditionally viewed any external intervention or regulation as an encroachment in their domestic affairs. It is for this reason that the 1949 Geneva Conventions contained only a single provision on non-international armed conflicts (article 3 common to all four conventions), as opposed to the elaborate body of law applicable to international armed conflicts. In 1977, Protocol II to the Geneva Conventions was adopted, which spelt out in more detail the rights and obligations of states in non-international armed conflicts and concretised the protection of civilian populations thereto.[14]

As a result of this uneven development of rules between the two types of armed conflict, IHL does not oblige states to recognise the rebels as legitimate combatants, even if they would otherwise qualify as such in the context of an international armed conflict. Thus, members of rebel entities, even if sufficiently organised and compliant with the *jus in*

---

contribute directly to the military superiority of the enemy. Yet this remains a grey area subject to the dubious legality of *targeted killings*, for which the reader is directed to Chapter 18.6.2.

[13] ICRC, *Interpretive Guidance on the Notion of Direct Participation in Hostilities* (ICRC, 2009) 46ff.

[14] Protocol Additional to the Geneva Convention of 1949 and Relating to the Protection of Victims of Non-International Armed Conflicts (Protocol II), 1125 UNTS 609.

bello, can be considered common criminals by the state and be liable for murder, treason and other offences under domestic law. In practice, this means that, unlike their counterparts in international armed conflicts, members of rebel groups engaged in non-international armed conflicts will not be granted a licence to kill government soldiers or enjoy POW status upon capture under the laws of the country wherein they operate.[15] Thus, whereas general international law and IHL impose human rights restrictions on the treatment of rebel personnel and civilians in internal armed conflicts, they none the less allow states to classify and regulate participation in rebel activities under their domestic law. This by no means implies that domestic law overrides international law in internal armed conflicts. On the contrary, it is now well accepted that all parties to internal armed conflicts must comply with IHL and that persons who commit any infractions incur international criminal liability, as opposed to liability under domestic law alone.[16] It is true to say that the largest part of IHL is now common to both international and internal armed conflicts.

16.2.3 Means and Methods of Warfare are Not Unlimited

The means and methods of injuring the enemy are not unlimited. This fundamental rule is expressly provided in articles 22 and 23 of the 1907 Hague Regulations and article 35 of Protocol I of 1977 and is predicated on humanitarian principles and good faith. Humanitarian principles generally prohibit killing or wounding the enemy who has laid down his or her arms or is no longer able to defend him or herself (when a person is incapacitated in this manner he is referred to as *hors de combat*). Humanitarian principles moreover prohibit refusal to provide quarter (essentially, to surrender) and the causing of superfluous injury or unnecessary suffering. This prohibition includes all those weapons whose direct, as opposed to incidental, use on the enemy would bring about this effect. Incendiary weapons would fall within this category. The rules on good faith prohibit killing or wounding the enemy treacherously, or deceiving him or her by the improper use of the flag of truce, of national emblems or by wearing enemy uniforms, as well as by the improper use of the Red Cross emblem.

---

[15] Although under art. 6(5) Protocol II, governments are urged to offer the widest possible range of amnesties to rebel groups after the end of hostilities to the extent that these are related to their participation in the armed conflict (i.e. they would not cover common crimes or war crimes).

[16] See particularly, *ICTY Prosecutor* v. *Tadić* (ICTY) (1995) paras. 116–17; ICC Statute, art. 8(2) (c)–(e).

16.3 RIGHTS AND OBLIGATIONS IN HUMANITARIAN LAW

The foundations of IHL are different from the body of law known as human rights. First, and most importantly, because of the armed conflict context IHL permits the parties to an armed conflict to target and kill persons taking a direct part in hostilities, whereas under international human rights law the right to life is non-derogable, despite a qualified and highly controversial set of exceptions (for example, abortion and the death penalty). Clearly, therefore, while one may speak of the positive obligation of the state to preserve the life of its citizens as a matter of human rights, IHL is premised on the right to kill. This approach is hardly an anachronism. The international community has long recognised that although recourse to armed force is, and must be, prohibited,[17] this fact alone does not necessarily guarantee the cessation of armed hostilities from the world stage. The prevalence of armed conflicts, whether large or small, short-lived or otherwise, has increased in the aftermath of the Cold War. Moreover, some conflicts are the direct result of causes unknown to past generations, such as disputes between pastoralist and farming communities in the developing world over access to valuable land and its natural resources.[18] The seeming inevitability of violence in human relations even up to this day has necessitated the formulation of binding regulations that are both realistic and acceptable within the current state-centric order. By way of example, states would find unacceptable a prohibition to kill enemy combatants on the battlefield as this would render redundant the relevant provisions of the United Nations (UN) Charter relating to self-defence and the responsibility to protect (R2P), not to mention the rationale for the formation of professional armies. With this in mind, it makes sense to 'humanise' the conduct of warfare by restricting the range of persons who can be lawfully targeted, particularly with a view to sparing the civilian population and those combatants who are no longer capable of threatening their adversaries. This 'humanisation' of war, although certainly influenced by human rights notions, should be distinguished from any discussion about rights. Indeed, the rationale for contemporary human rights

---

[17] Subject of course to the express exceptions permitted by the *jus ad bellum*, i.e. self-defence (art. 51 UN Charter) and UNSC authorisations (art. 42 UN Charter).

[18] UN Environment Programme (UNEP), 'Understanding Environment, Conflict and Cooperation', UNEP doc. DEW/0571/NA (2004). More specifically, see UNEP, 'Post-Conflict Environmental Assessment', UNEP doc. DEP/0816/GE (2007) 8–10, 83, which states that localised conflicts over land in Sudan have been prevalent since at least the 1930s, but these did not culminate in widespread hostilities until recently. In the Darfur conflict, some of the contributing – not root – causes have been competition over oil and gas reserves, water and timber, confrontations over the use of agricultural land, with particular emphasis on rangeland and rain-fed land, which is scarce in the mostly arid Darfur region. Such traditional conflicts have become large-scale because of the availability of weapons and the involvement of third parties.

is founded on the uneven distribution of power between the state and its citizens (and others falling within its jurisdiction), thus requiring the state to limit its power against the governed and provide the necessary conditions for the exercise of a range of freedoms. IHL, on the other hand, is concerned with the reciprocal expectations and obligations of equal sovereigns in respect of international conflicts. It is not founded on rights claims by the actors engaged in armed conflict (although human rights do play a residual role), but on reciprocal treatment and chivalry between the governments of the warring parties,[19] as well as self-interest.

Of course, this does not mean that IHL is simply contractual in nature. Rather, those engulfed by armed hostilities are protected by a plethora of rules. Yet it is not wise to compare these rules to, or conflate them with, the individual entitlements inherent in human rights law.[20] No doubt, IHL recognises a number of entitlements, such as those afforded to POWs in the Third Geneva Convention and these clearly mirror a species of human rights. At the same time, however, the prohibition against indiscriminate attacks on civilians or denial of quarter cannot neatly be described as individual rights because in practical terms they are not enforceable by the intended rights-holders in the midst of battle. It is for these reasons that IHL, instead of setting out lists of rights, emphasises the protection afforded to 'protected persons'. Thus, it is best to approach IHL not as a system of rights (despite the existence of numerous individual rights) but as a corpus of law, whose primary interest is to offer protection in a highly volatile situation.

Another difference between IHL and human rights relates to the notion of obligation. Whereas traditionally international human rights obligations are addressed to states, IHL obligations are incumbent on all parties to an armed conflict. This includes non-state actors (NSAs), such as rebel and paramilitary groups, mercenaries and private security firms. All of these entities have an obligation to respect the laws of war and may not use their inferior military power in relation to government forces as an excuse to violate IHL, such as by employing terror tactics against the civilian population.

Finally, unlike human rights treaty bodies vested with the adjudication of individual complaints, IHL treaties are not supported by predetermined international enforcement mechanisms, or an individual complaints system. Enforcement jurisdiction is assumed either by national courts or other ad hoc or hybrid international tribunals. In any event, the primary responsibility of the perpetrators is criminal,[21] unlike human rights tribunals, where

[19] C. Droege, 'Elective Affinities? Human Rights and Humanitarian Law' (2008) 9 *International Review of the Red Cross* 501, at 503–4.

[20] Ibid., at 503–7; M. Sassóli and A. A. Bouvier, *How Does Law Protect in War?* (ICRC, 1999) 265–7.

[21] The violation of IHL rules gives rise to war crimes or grave breaches and the perpetrator incurs liability under international law. See Chapter 17.3.

the liability sought is primarily of a civil, tort or similar nature. Despite the obvious and conflicting differences between human rights and IHL they are far from being characterised as wholly incompatible. The following section attempts to highlight where they meet and how they interact.

16.4   HUMANITARIAN LAW AS *LEX SPECIALIS* TO HUMAN RIGHTS LAW

Despite the horizontal relationship between the actors that promulgated the rules of IHL (i.e. states acting for the benefit of their armies), as well as the authority conferred upon combatants to employ lethal force against their adversaries, it is generally agreed that human rights play a distinct role in the operation of IHL. For one thing, the essence of IHL is not to legitimise violence in situations of armed conflict; rather, it is to limit the range of persons and objects against which armed force may be employed. It is no wonder, there-fore, that the fundamental rule of IHL permits only the targeting of combat-ants and military objects. If this protection were to be framed in human rights terms, it would encompass both an obligation on the state and an enforceable entitlement in favour of the (unlawfully) targeted person. In IHL the individual entitlement is missing and the state is responsible for educating, preventing and punishing its forces for any infractions of the *jus in bello*. Moreover, the perpetrators of IHL violations are criminally liable under domestic and inter-national law. Evidently, this is exclusively a state-centric process. It is also obvious that there is a practical dimension to the absence of rights in most fields of IHL. In the midst of combat operations it is futile to dispute one's combatant rights and all the individual entitlements that flow from this status.

Hence, the incorporation of a rights discourse in IHL must be couched in fundamentally other terms. It is obvious that IHL and human rights share the same subjects and converge in at least two respects. First, human rights law permits derogations in times of emergency, including during armed con-flict, in which case it would be lawful to kill an enemy combatant. This is consistent with the rationale of IHL. Secondly, both human rights law and IHL seek the minimisation of physical harm against combatants and other persons engaged in armed conflict when other means for neutralising them are available. While the International Court of Justice (ICJ) in its 1996 advi-sory opinion on the *Legality of the Threat or Use of Nuclear Weapons* vali-dated this convergence, it expressly recognised the underlying limitations by observing that:

the protection of the [International Covenant on Civil and Political Rights] ICCPR does not cease in times of war, except by operation of article 4 of the Covenant whereby certain provisions may be derogated from in a time of national emergency. Respect for the right to life is not, however, such a provision. In principle, the right to be deprived of one's life applies also in hostilities. The test of what is an arbitrary deprivation of life, however, then falls to be determined by the applicable *lex specialis*, namely, the law applicable in armed conflict which is designed to regulate the conduct of hostilities. Thus, whether a particular loss of life, through the use of a certain weapon in warfare, is to be considered an arbitrary deprivation of life contrary to article 6 of the Covenant, can only be decided by reference to the law applicable in armed conflict and not deduced from the terms of the Covenant itself.[22]

The ICJ's characterisation of IHL as *lex specialis* suggests that the legality of public or private conduct in armed conflict cannot ultimately be determined by reference to human rights rules but by IHL. In a subsequent advisory opinion on the *Legal Consequences of the Construction of a Wall in the Occupied Palestinian Territory* the Court elaborated that the interplay between the two bodies of law gives rise to three possible situations: that some matters may be exclusively regulated by IHL, others exclusively by human rights norms and yet others by a combination of both.[23] Although the ICJ has failed to specify in what manner the *jus in bello* operates as *lex specialis*, it is fair to argue that it is employed not as a tool of treaty interpretation but as a conflict of rules mechanism.[24] This means that where a rule of IHL is in direct conflict with a rule of human rights law – assuming the two are truly irreconcilable in particular cases – the former takes precedence.[25] We have already alluded to some situations involving the primacy of IHL (for example, the rights of combatants to kill other combatants), whereas in respect of others there is a clear synergy and compatibility between IHL and human rights. This is true, for example, in respect of fundamental guarantees afforded to civilian populations in situations of belligerent occupation. This solution offered by the Court is not without its critics, who generally argue that the ICJ artificially fragments the two bodies of law when it could just as well bring them together in harmony.[26] This position is also implicitly maintained by the UN Human Rights Committee (HRCtee), which noted that:

---

[22] *Legality of the Threat or Use of Nuclear Weapons*, para. 25.

[23] *Legal Consequences of the Construction of a Wall in the Occupied Palestinian Territory* (*Wall* case) (ICJ) (2004) para. 106.

[24] See W. Jenks, 'The Conflict of Law-Making Treaties' (1953) 30 *British Yearbook of International Law* 401, at 446, who stated that 'the clear applicability of [the *lex specialis* principle] ... is afforded by instruments relating to the laws of war which, in the absence of a contrary intention or other special circumstances, must clearly be regarded as a *leges speciales* in relation to instruments laying down peace-time norms concerning the same subjects'. See also M. Milanovic, 'The Lost Origins of Lex Specialis: Rethinking the Relationship between Human Rights and International Humanitarian Law', in J. Ohlin (ed.), *Theoretical Boundaries of Armed Conflict and Human Rights* (Cambridge University Press, 2015), who does not perceive the differences between the two regimes to be particularly significant.

[25] See also *Coard* v. *USA* (IACHR) (1999) para. 42, which iterated the ICJ's *lex specialis* argument.

[26] N. Prud'homme, 'Lex Specialis: Oversimplifying a More Complex and Multifaceted Relationship?' (2007) 40 *Israel Law Review* 536.

The Covenant applies also in situations of armed conflict to which the rules of international humanitarian law are applicable. While, in respect of certain Covenant rights, more specific rules of international humanitarian law may be specially relevant for the purposes of the interpretation of Covenant rights, both spheres of law are complementary, not mutually exclusive.[27]

The synergy and complementarity between IHL and human rights has been expressed in emphatic terms by the Inter-American Commission of Human Rights (IACHR). In defending its authority to entertain a case involving the application of IHL because of the existence of an armed conflict, it held that:

In common with other universal and regional human rights instruments, the American Convention and the 1949 Geneva Conventions share a common core of non-derogable rights and the mutual goal of protecting the physical integrity and dignity inherent in the human being ... The Inter-American Court has emphasized that 'there is a similarity between the content of article 3, common to the 1949 Geneva Conventions, and the provisions of the American Convention and other international instruments regarding non-derogable human rights (such as the right to life and the right not to be submitted to torture or cruel, inhuman or degrading treatment)' and repeated that 'the provisions relevant to the Geneva Conventions may be taken into account as interpretative elements for the American Convention itself' ... Due to their similarity and the fact that both norms are based on the same principles and values, international human rights law and IHL may influence and reinforce each other, following as an interpretative method enshrined in article 31(3)(c) of the Vienna Convention on the Law of Treaties, which establishes that in interpreting a norm 'any relevant rules of international law applicable in the relations between the parties' may be considered. The foregoing shows that international human rights law may be interpreted in the light of IHL and the latter may be interpreted in the light of international human rights law as required. ... In this way, although the *lex specialis* with respect to acts taking place in the context of an armed conflict is IHL, this does not mean that international human rights law is inapplicable. On the contrary, it means that when applying the law of human rights, in this case the American Convention, international humanitarian law, as the specific rule governing armed conflict, is resorted to for interpretation.[28]

16.5   WHY HUMAN RIGHTS BODIES FIND THE APPLICATION OF HUMANITARIAN LAW PROBLEMATIC

Because the founding premises of IHL and human rights are different, the two bodies of law do not always approach their subject matter in the same way. This of course has not stopped human rights treaty bodies applying human rights to situations of armed conflict without making use of the *lex*

---

[27] HRCtee, General Comment 31, UN doc. CCPR/C/21/Rev.1/Add.13 (2004) para. 11.
[28] *Franklin Guillermo Aisalla Molina (Ecuador v. Colombia)* (IACHR) (2010) paras. 117–22.

specialis principle. This approach is not justified as a matter of legal doctrine but by practical considerations. Human rights treaty bodies are only empowered to apply their respective treaties, none of which makes direct references to IHL. As a result, the only way such courts could legitimately employ IHL is by approximating and rendering it compatible with human rights law. Were human rights courts to follow the *lex specialis* approach of the ICJ they would be forced to admit the superiority of IHL over the provisions of their statutes in relevant situations, and thus either refuse to pass judgment or otherwise be forced to use rules found outside their statutes.

One should also note the lack of expertise of human rights treaty bodies with other specialist areas of international law which, coupled with their desire to promote protection, may allow them to render erroneous results.[29] There is the 'danger' that if treaty bodies apply IHL instruments they will necessarily be drawn into the relevant jurisprudence of international criminal tribunals with which they may be unfamiliar. Moreover, the jurisprudence may turn out to produce results that clash with the case law of treaty bodies, not to mention that by applying IHL instruments they risk being accused of acting ultra vires.[30]

The ECtHR has had the opportunity to deal with situations of internal armed conflict, in situations where it was claimed by the victims that government forces used excessive force against the civilian population. In the *Isayeva*, *Yusupova* and *Bazayeva* cases, Russian armed forces had launched a missile attack against a civilian convoy in their pursuit of Chechen rebels, which culminated in the death of the children of one of the claimants. The Court accepted that because of the insurgency the employment of lethal force was justified, but this was necessarily limited to legitimate targets, while at the same time the government was required to minimise any harm to civilians.[31] Upon finding that government forces had taken no such measures to make this distinction the Court upheld a violation of article 2 of the Convention that guarantees the right to life.[32] The language is reminiscent

---

[29] In *Medvedyev and Others* v. *France* (ECtHR) (2010), a French warship intercepted and arrested the crew of a Cambodian vessel transporting drugs. The ECtHR misconstrued the ambit of art. 110 of the UN Convention on the Law of the Sea (UNCLOS), by asserting that non-flag states do not require the consent of the flag state in order to search and seize foreign vessels in cases of piracy, slave trade, unauthorised broadcasting and in respect of stateless ships (para. 54).

[30] The practice of the IACHR seems to be exceptional. In the *Tablada* case (IACHR) (1997) paras. 157–64, the Commission held that it could validly apply IHL because Organization of American States (OAS) member states were parties to the Geneva Conventions, and also because since the American Convention did not provide for violations during armed conflict it would have to decline jurisdiction, which would have been absurd. See also *Democratic Republic of Congo* v. *Rwanda, Burundi, Uganda* (ACHPR) (2003).

[31] *Isayeva and Others* v. *Russia* (ECtHR) (2005) paras. 175–8.

[32] See equally, *Benzer and Others* v. *Turkey* (ECtHR) (2013) and *Meryem Celik and Others* v. *Turkey* (ECtHR) (2013), which concerned, among others, indiscriminate bombings and

of the obligation to take precautions in attack, which is inherent in IHL legal terminology.[33] In all the cases involving non-international armed conflicts the substantive and procedural (for example, access to the ECtHR or the IACHR) guarantees of human rights law are certainly far superior to those found in IHL. In the Chechen cases, the majority of which involve, among others, enforced disappearances and ineffective or non-existent investigations, the ECtHR has been able to confirm the existence of a 'systemic problem of non-investigation'.[34]

Although human rights courts cannot apply IHL over and above their founding instruments, they cannot lightly dismiss the reality of armed conflict and the rationale of IHL rules, to which, in any event, all states have subscribed by reason of treaty or customary international law. Hence, just like *Yusupova* and *Bazayeva*, the ECtHR in *Ergi* v. *Turkey* considered the right to life in the context of military operations in a non-international armed conflict from the point of view of necessity and proportionality. While it did not dispute the army's entitlement to attack rebel elements, it questioned its choice of 'feasible precautions' in order to 'minimise incidental loss to civilian life'.[35] Given that this is exactly what the relevant rules of IHL postulate it is easy to see that human rights courts are necessarily drawn into accepting and applying the fundamental guarantees of the *jus in bello* in situations of human rights violations in armed conflicts. As will be explained in the next section, the ECtHR in *Hassan* v. *UK* fused the obligations under IHL and human rights in order to interpret the occupying power's capture and detention of enemy combatants.[36] The obligation to take precautions in order to avoid civilian casualties is addressed to government forces, not rebels, unlike IHL where the relevant obligations are addressed equally to all warring parties. The rationale of the Court is that if rebel forces can be apprehended with minimal, non-lethal, force, then any disproportionate lethal force and the use of indiscriminate weapons is a violation of the right to life among others.[37]

Human rights courts have not, however, gone as far as saying that government forces must try to first arrest a combatant or rebel before opening fire against him or her or using other lethal force. None the less, they have distinguished armed conflicts from other situations involving lower-intensity

---

targeting of Kurdish villages by the Turkish army. The scale of the operation brings such operations within the realm of IHL; similarly, *Esmukhambetov* v. *Russia* (ECtHR) (2011) and *Abdulkhanov and Others* v. *Russia* (ECtHR) (2013), regarding Russian land and airstrikes on Chechen villages.

[33] Art. 57(2)(a)(ii) Protocol I.

[34] *Pitsayeva and Others* v. *Russia* (ECtHR) (2014) paras. 395 and 471.

[35] *Ergi* v. *Turkey* (ECtHR) (2001) para. 79.   [36] *Hassan* v. *UK* (ECtHR) (2014).

[37] *Hamiyet Kaplan* v. *Turkey* (ECtHR) (2005) paras. 51–5; *Isayeva and Others* v. *Russia*, para. 191; *Akhmadov* v. *Russia* (ECtHR) (2008) para. 99.

hostilities, such as terrorist operations, in respect of which they have asserted the obligation of the state to arrest the suspect, rather than kill, where this is feasible.

16.6   HUMAN RIGHTS IN SITUATIONS OF MILITARY OCCUPATION

In recent times occupations have arisen by unilateral military action, or as a result of coalition initiatives supported by the UN Security Council (UNSC), as was the case with the occupation of Iraq in 2003. Given that all types of military occupation involve the dissolution of sovereign powers, which are thereafter assumed by the occupier, it is only natural that international law imposes a set of strict obligations on the occupier, the purpose of which is to protect the rights of the occupied civilian population. Under article 42 of the 1907 Hague Regulations, a territory is considered occupied when it is actually placed under the authority of the occupying state. In this manner, the existence of occupation is a matter of fact, rather than a matter of law and exists irrespective of its recognition by the occupier. Moreover, the legal effects of occupation extend only to territories over which the occupying power exercises effective control. This observation is particularly important for the application of human rights, because under customary international law the occupier replaces the previous government in the territory concerned and must 'take all the measures in [its] power to restore, and ensure, as far as possible, public order and safety, while respecting, unless absolutely prevented, the laws in force in the country'.[38] This necessarily means that the occupier becomes the government responsible for the occupied territory and not merely an interim administrator stripped of responsibility.[39] If this were not so, there would exist no authority to protect the rights of civilian populations in occupied territories. IHL and general international law, simply put, do not accept that the occupying power can deny or relinquish its responsibility to protect the occupied population.[40]

In the previous section we discussed the clash in certain instances between human rights and humanitarian law in situations of armed conflict. The particular context of a military occupation lies somewhere between war and peace and is generally characterised by the cessation of armed hostilities

[38] Art. 43 Hague Regulations 1907; see also case concerning *Armed Activities on the Territory of the Congo* (*DRC* v. *Uganda*) (ICJ) (2005) paras. 172–5.

[39] See O. B. Naftali and Y. Shany, 'Living in Denial: The Application of Human Rights in the Occupied Territories' (2003–2004) 37 *Israel Law Review* 17, at 52–3, for an analysis of the objections of Israel and the USA on this matter.

[40] In *Varnava and Others* v. *Turkey* (ECtHR) (2009), the ECtHR found a continuing violation of the right to life by the occupier on account of its failure to conduct an effective investigation of persons gone missing as a direct result of the hostilities leading up to the occupation.

and the resumption of civilian life. Despite the absence of armed hostilities a military occupation is none the less chiefly regulated by IHL, not by human rights law, and thus the armoury of human rights is not automatically transplanted in the relationship between the occupier and the occupied population. There are some cogent reasons for this approach, particularly the possible existence of resistance movements and the resumption of armed confrontations by non-state actors against the occupier during the course of the occupation. However, unless civilians take up arms against the occupying forces in an organised manner or through the re-emergence of their national army, in which case the relevant entitlements of the *jus in bello* come into operation, the occupying power is not permitted to treat the civilian population as combatants or as otherwise lawful targets. Hence, if members of the occupied population are found to possess weapons in their homes it would be going too far to target them under the pretence that they are combatants, particularly if the local law prior to the occupation justified the possession of weapons. As a result, there is a need to determine the precise boundary between the obligation of the occupier to protect the civilian population from the entitlement under the laws of war to attack those civilians who take up arms against its authority.

This entitlement (for the occupier) only arises where the renewed levels of violence reach the threshold of an armed conflict. In all other cases, the protection owed to the civilian population is very much akin to human rights in times of (a strained) peace. Even so, the relevant *jus in bello* treaties (namely the 1907 Hague Regulations, Geneva Convention IV and Protocol I of 1977) treat the obligations of the occupier vis-à-vis the occupied population as 'guarantees', thus seemingly excluding the conferral of individual or collective rights.[41] Reason dictates that the *lex specialis* character of the law of belligerent occupation does not exclude the application of human rights to the occupied population, so long as such rights are not detrimental to law and order or violate the occupier's rights under international law.

Moreover, IHL has not developed an elaborate enough corpus of rules and jurisprudence to deal with the guarantees it provides. For example, if the occupier is permitted to suspend those laws that are deemed abusive, discriminatory or of a similar nature, under what legal criteria is this to be assessed and implemented? Clearly, the introduction of legislation against discrimination, universal schooling, social security, freedom of thought, conscience and religion, among others, can only be premised on human rights law.[42] In this sense, human rights law is deemed *lex generalis* and applies by reason of the fact that no special rules of IHL exist. While it is clear that in theory the *lex generalis* nature of human rights should ensure their

---

[41] See arts. 43–51 Hague Regulations 1907.

[42] See A. Roberts, 'Transformative Military Occupation: Applying the Laws of War and Human Rights' (2006) 100 *American Journal of International Law* 589, at 594.

application in military occupations, most occupying powers would disfavour such a wholesale and automatic importation because it would entail the wholesale application of their human rights legislation in the occupied territory; the latter would effectively become an extension of their own territory for the purpose of individual (and collective) rights. Such an eventuality brings with it a significant complication which the occupier would rather avoid. Whereas under the (IHL) law of occupation the occupier may derogate from certain rights in order to restore public order and safety, it would not be able to derogate from fundamental rights if the occupation was regulated by human rights law.[43] Hence, the potential of human rights law in military occupation is beyond gap-filling, but may indeed transform the obligations of the occupier.

No doubt, many states have resisted the notion that human rights law can dictate how the restoration of law and order should be assessed and whether the issue is even justiciable. None the less, the jurisprudence of the ICJ,[44] human rights treaty bodies[45] and UN institutions is unequivocal that human rights are an integral part of the international law of occupation – provided of course that they do not clash with a *lex specialis* rule of IHL. However, in the course of occupation no such clashes exist because public order can only be restored through police action and not military operations that would necessitate the derogation of rights.[46] By way of illustration, where an occupier finds itself in a law-enforcement situation and in a position to effectuate an arrest, it should comply with the requirements of human rights law and minimise his use of lethal force rather than kill the suspect. In theory, the very same result is warranted under IHL.[47] In *Hassan* v. *UK*, it was claimed that the applicant's brother had been unlawfully arrested and later detained in a British military facility by the British armed forces in Basra, Iraq. In an

---

[43] Derogations in times of war and military occupation are expressly provided in the major international human rights instruments (save for the International Covenant on Economic, Social and Cultural Rights (ICESCR)), in situations involving 'a public emergency threatening the life of the nation' (art. 4(1) ICCPR). The HRCtee has concluded as a result that military occupations justify only permissible derogations under the ICCPR. See Concluding Observations on Cyprus, UN doc. CCPR/C/79/Add.39 (21 September 1994) para. 3; Concluding Observations on Israel, UN doc. CCPR/CO/78/ISR (21 August 2003) para. 11.

[44] *Armed Activities on the Territory of the Congo* (New Application: 2002) (ICJ) (2006) para. 216; *Wall* case, paras. 107–12.

[45] *Loizidou* v. *Turkey* (ECtHR) (1997); *Cyprus* v. *Turkey* (ECtHR) (2002).

[46] M. Sassòli, 'Legislation and Maintenance of Public Order and Civil Life by Occupying Powers' (2005) 16 *European Journal of International Law* 661, at 665.

[47] N. Meltzer, *Targeted Killings* (Oxford University Press, 2007) 224–30. The so-called Martens clause, e.g., which is found in the preamble to Hague Convention IV of 1907, was intended to offer additional protection to victims of armed conflict in situations where IHL was silent or under-developed. The same result is also confirmed by art. 72 Protocol I, which stipulates that the provisions of section III thereof supplement Geneva Convention IV (the Civilians and Occupation Convention), as well as 'other applicable rules of international law relating to the protection of fundamental human rights during international armed conflict'.

exceptional foray into IHL, the ECtHR confirmed that the deceased was heavily armed and on the roof of his brother's house. It went on to emphasise that the application of the right to liberty and security in situations of armed conflict should be accommodated and construed within the POW regime and the attendant security risks to the occupier under the Third and Fourth Geneva Conventions. In fact, the British government had from the outset requested an interpretation of its obligations under article 5 ECHR that was consistent with its powers of detention under IHL. In the circumstances of the case, the Court held – albeit with a fair share of critical dissenting opinions – that the application of the occupier's screening and detention measures were in harmony with its obligation under article 5 ECHR.[48]

That human rights law applies in occupied territories – and by extension the international human rights obligations of the occupier – is necessitated by practical considerations. Occupations can drag on for decades in relative peace and order, so it is inconceivable that the occupier could suspend the enjoyment of rights to the civilian population indefinitely. This practical necessity was recognised by the UNSC in resolution 1483 which called on the Coalition Authority in occupied Iraq to cooperate with the UN 'in promoting the protection of human rights' in its process of governmental and judicial reform.[49] Furthermore, in respect of the West Bank and the Gaza strip, Israel has maintained that it is merely a temporary administrator for the former and that since 2005 it has had no authority over Gaza whatsoever, having withdrawn its troops from the area. In reality, Israel maintains a strong and effective military presence in the West Bank and an aerial, naval and land blockade in Gaza. Its denial of occupation is clearly aimed at avoiding the full gamut of obligations pertaining to occupying powers. Yet even the Israeli Supreme Court has held that the Fourth Geneva Convention and the 1907 Hague Regulations are part of customary international law and apply to Israeli 'occupied territories'.[50] This is a logical, yet bold, decision that denies the Israeli government the right to suspend international law from those territories.

16.6.1   The Extraterritorial Application of Human Rights in Occupied Territories

It has been established that the occupier cannot deny the applicability of its ordinary human rights obligations to the population of the occupied territory. This obligation is subject to two distinct practical limitations. First, the

---

[48] *Hassan* v. *UK.*

[49] UNSC resolution 1483 (22 May 2003) para. 8(c), (g), (i). See also UNSC resolution 1546 (8 June 2004), para. 7(b)(iii), which subsequently extended this mandate to another entity.

[50] *Beit Sourik Village Council* v. *The Government of Israel* (Israel) (2004) paras. 23–5. For a more comprehensive review readers should consult Y. Shany, 'Binary Law meets Complex Reality: The Occupation of Gaza Debate' (2008) 41 *Israel Law Review* 68.

territory in question must be actually occupied, thus excluding parts thereof that are controlled, or sufficiently resisted, by rebel movements. Secondly, the application of human rights by the occupier does not *ipso facto* entail access to its national courts, unless this possibility is expressly postulated.

The human rights obligations of a state are generally owed to all persons on its territory, both citizens and aliens; they are not owed to persons situated in other states. As a result, the ordinary operation of human rights is territorial, whereas the operation of humanitarian law is also extraterritorial, in the sense that it is applicable wherever a state is engaged in armed conflict, whether internally or abroad. We have already alluded to the fact that the extraterritorial application of human rights is exceptionally possible in situations of effective control of foreign territory. The *Al-Skeini* case is instructive of the problems inherent in the extraterritorial application of a state's human rights obligations in situations of military occupation. There, Baha Mousa, a man in the custody of British soldiers in the Iraqi city of Basra, died as a result of injuries inflicted following his arrest, and a further five civilians were randomly killed in the course of security operations. Although British forces were mandated to exercise occupation in the Al Basra and Maysan provinces, they had not put in place any executive, judicial or legislative authority in Basra City. The families of the deceased applied to British courts with a view to extending the application of the UK Human Rights Act to Iraq, which incorporates the ECHR. The majority of the Court of Appeals accepted that the lack of effective control precluded the application of the ECHR generally in Basra.[51] The Court of Appeals based this conclusion on the fact that the British contingent in Basra, although patrolling its streets and ensuring law and order in the city, had not set up any administrative or judicial structures such that would challenge local institutions.

This result is unconvincing because the primary reason for the presence of British troops in Basra was the occupation of Iraq, not a peacekeeping mandate.[52] The Grand Chamber of the ECtHR naturally disagreed with the

---

[51] *R* v. *The Secretary of State for Defence, ex parte Al-Skeini and Others* (UK) (2005) para. 124; sustained by the House of Lords in *R* v. *The Secretary of State for Defence, ex parte Al-Skeini and Others* (UK) (2008).

[52] In the subsequent case of *R (on the application of Al-Saadoon and Mufdhi)* v. *Secretary of State for Defence* (UK) (2009) paras. 32–3, the Court of Appeals held that the surrender of two Iraqis to the Iraqi authorities by British forces in Basra did not trigger the application of the Human Rights Act because from May 2006 onwards British forces were not authorised to carry out any military activities on Iraqi territory. At best, British forces were acting as an agent of the Iraqi courts when arresting persons accused of serious crimes. This line of reasoning was entrenched in the English Supreme Court, which dismissed an application by a soldier killed in Iraq. See *R (On the Application of Smith)* v. *Secretary of State for Defence et al.* (UK) (2010). The ECtHR avoided determination as to whether an occupation was in existence, accepting implicitly that the detention of the applicants by British forces sufficed to bring the situation within the jurisdiction of the Convention. *Al-Saadoon and Mufdhi* v. *UK* (ECtHR) (2010).

conclusion of the English court. It found that the UK itself declared to the UNSC its assumption of governmental powers after the fall of the Baath regime in Iraq and exercised effective control in the south-east corner of the country. As a result, the Convention was applicable to the events in question.[53]

Whereas occupying states have traditionally relied on the international law of occupation in order to avoid the application of human rights law,[54] the recent 'erosion' of this body of law by human rights courts has forced states to increasingly refute their exercise of occupation by relying on technicalities. Human rights courts have been able to expand the obligations of states beyond their territories not by enforcing the positive obligations owed by occupiers under IHL, but rather through a logical and purposive interpretation of the jurisdictional clauses contained in their statutes. Article 2(1) of the ICCPR confines a state's human rights obligations to persons 'within its territory and subject to its jurisdiction', while article 1 of the ECHR states that parties 'shall secure to everyone within their jurisdiction' the rights stipulated in the Convention. The jurisdictional clause of the ICCPR is a lot more restrictive than its ECHR counterpart, given that it seems to imply a cumulative application of both criteria. However, the HRCtee has refused to offer it such a narrow construction. Its rationale is that 'it would be unconscionable to so interpret the responsibility under article 2 of the Covenant as to permit a state party to perpetrate violations of the Covenant on the territory of another state, which violations it could not perpetrate on its own territory'.[55] Although this case concerned an extraterritorial kidnapping by state agents and not an armed conflict per se, we have already seen that the Committee has not hesitated to apply the Covenant to military occupations.[56]

16.6.2   The Effective Control Test

Following the invasion of Cyprus in 1974 by Turkish armed forces the island was effectively cut in the middle; the northern part was occupied by the Turkish military, whereas the southern part remained in the hands of its elected and universally recognised government, that of the Republic of Cyprus. Despite the claims of the occupier that the Turkish armed forces merely assisted the Turkish Cypriot community in the exercise of its right of self-determination, which led to the self-proclamation of the so-called Turkish Republic of Northern Cyprus (TRNC), no state has extended recognition to the TRNC. The

---

[53] See *Al-Skeini and Others* v. *UK* (ECtHR) (2011) paras. 143–50.

[54] See Droege, above note 19, at 511–13, who refers to the drafting history of art. 2(1) of the ICCPR, which originally read exactly like art. 1 ECHR. The US delegate was successful in inserting an amendment, which reflects its current wording, with the purpose of excluding the application of the Covenant in situations of military occupation.

[55] *Burgos* v. *Uruguay* (HRCtee) (1981) para. 12.3.   [56] HRCtee, General Comment 31.

aim of the occupier was clearly to refute any claims of occupation, arguing instead that a new nation had emerged which was not only a distinct entity from Turkey itself but a full sovereign. By doing so it also aimed to avoid all responsibility under general international law, IHL and human rights law. Within a few years of the separation of the island the Turkish government had resettled a significant number of persons from mainland Turkey with a view to altering the demographic status quo, and proceeded to abrogate the property rights of Greek Cypriots who had fled in fear of their lives.

The *Loizidou* case was the first to challenge Turkish assumptions about the legal status of the occupation. The applicant owned property in the occupied north prior to the invasion and was precluded by the authorities from peacefully enjoying her property rights. Turkey, on the other hand, argued that the territory of the TRNC, being an independent state, was outside its jurisdiction and hence outside the ambit of the ECHR. The central issue was therefore the precise meaning of 'jurisdiction' for the purposes of article 1 of the ECHR, with particular reference to situations in which a state party exercised some degree of control in the territory of a non-party state. The ECtHR iterated that the responsibility of a party may be invoked on account of: (1) acts of its authorities, whether performed within or outside national boundaries, which produce effects outside its own territory; as well as (2) 'when as a consequence of military action – whether lawful or unlawful – it exercises *effective control* of an area outside its national territory'.[57] Unlike other 'effective control' tests propounded for the determination of an agency relationship under general international law, for the purposes of the ECHR a detailed control over the policies and actions of the local authorities is not in fact required.[58] In the case at hand, the existence of large numbers of Turkish troops engaged in active duties in northern Cyprus was sufficient for a finding of effective overall control.[59]

Whereas Turkish military action best exemplifies a clear-cut case of belligerent occupation, there exist situations where armed violence is not followed by effective control, or where effective control is maintained only by instilling fear through the use of local agents. It is arguable whether in respect of any of these elements the ECHR may be triggered through the actions of the protagonist states. In the *Banković* case a NATO-led air force bombed the headquarters of Serbian radio and television, killing several employees in the process. The ECtHR contended that the aerial nature of the assault alone did not entail an effective control of Yugoslav territory and hence did not fall within the juridical space of the Convention.[60] Whereas some commentators may have characterised the *Banković* judgment as a regression in

---

[57] *Loizidou* v. *Turkey* (ECtHR) (1995) para. 62 (emphasis added).
[58] *Loizidou* v. *Turkey* (ECtHR) (1997) para. 56.   [59] Ibid.
[60] *Banković and Others* v. *Belgium and Others* (ECtHR) (2001) para. 75.

comparison to *Loizidou*, it in fact maintains the logical fault lines between IHL and human rights as identified above. Quite clearly, in *Banković* one cannot speak of an occupation but of an armed conflict in progress. It would be stretching the law of occupation and the meaning of 'effective overall control' to deem otherwise.

These situations should probably be contrasted with the Israeli control of Gaza, in respect of which Israel terminated its occupation in 2005, albeit maintaining full control over the largest part of the maritime and aerial entry point into Gaza. The Israeli Supreme Court has held that 'since 2005 Israel no longer has effective control over what happens in the Gaza strip'.[61] Although Israel's control of Gaza must certainly be distinguished from the Turkish occupation of Cyprus, it is undeniable that it exercises effective control over a strategic infrastructure directly affecting the people of Gaza. It should therefore bear responsibility for those rights which are directly affected by its maritime and naval blockade.

16.6.3   The Decisive Influence Test

The ECtHR has had the opportunity to deal with situations in which a third state was providing support to a separatist movement, without overtly employing armed force itself. In the *Ilaşcu* case the applicants were unlawfully arrested and detained by the breakaway authorities of the so-called Moldovan Republic of Transdniestria (MRT), which while claiming its unilateral independence, is in fact part of the Republic of Moldova. Yet because of Russian military and political assistance to Transdniestria and the presence of elements of the Russian army therein[62] – as part of military arrangements predating the independence of Moldova – the Moldovan government has been unable to quell the insurrection or use force against the separatist forces. The Court decided to dilute its effective overall control standard, without sufficient legal justification, stating that Russian jurisdiction and responsibility were triggered because the MRT 'remain[ed] under the effective authority, or at the very least under the decisive influence, of the Russian Federation, and in any event that it survives by virtue of the military, economic, financial and political support given to it by the Russian Federation'.[63] The Court did not view this case as exceptional, but as an alternative to situations of occupation proper entailing effective control. It was perhaps mindful that the exercise of 'decisive influence' and 'effective authority' would not be tantamount to a military occupation, while at the same time Russia was well capable of preventing the violations attributable to the separatist Transdniestrian regime on account of their agency relationship.[64]

---

[61] *Jaber Al-Bassiouni* v. *The Prime Minister of Israel* (Israel) (2008) para. 12.
[62] *Ilaşcu and Others* v. *Moldova and Russia* (ECtHR) (2005) para. 382.   [63] Ibid., para. 392.
[64] Ibid., para. 393.

The ICJ's determination of effective control by proxy is much more rigid, although in principle it is at par with the case law of the ECtHR. In the *Bosnian Genocide* case the ICJ refuted the claim that the Bosnian Serb army was an agent of the Federal Republic of Yugoslavia (FRY), irrespective of the fact that FRY paid the salaries of the army. Its rationale was predicated on the argument that an agency of this nature requires 'complete dependence' on the principal, which was missing in the present instance.[65] This responsibility of the principal in respect of acts of its agents is a significant feature of human rights law[66] – apart from the international law of state responsibility – because it serves to encompass the violations of the agent within the sphere of human rights obligations ordinarily applicable to the principal.

QUESTIONS

1. **What role does IHL play in the thinking and judgments of international human rights treaty bodies, particularly the ECtHR, the Inter-American Court of Human Rights (IACtHR), the IACHR and the HRCtee?**

2. **Does the *lex specialis* character of humanitarian law mean that human rights law is always subordinate?**

3. **What are the legal requirements for the application of humanitarian law and the law of belligerent occupation? What rights arise for the occupied civilian population as a result?**

4. **What justifies the legitimacy of certain killings in humanitarian law which would otherwise be unacceptable in human rights law?**

5. **Why is the application of human rights in armed conflicts important?**

16.7   THE RELEVANCE OF THE LAW TO BATTLEFIELD CONDITIONS

16.7.1   Human Physiology in Combat Situations

In assessing whether or not the laws of war are consistent with combat exigencies one must have recourse to factors that are external to law. Legislative drafting that is aimed at exacting conduct of a particular standard must be pitched at such a level that the conduct conforms to what may ordinarily be expected by the average person. If the required conduct were to exceed the ordinary capabilities of the average person, then the envisaged law would either fail or the authorities would be forced to punish the majority of the population; IHL is not excluded from this proposition. By way of illustration,

---

[65] *Application of the Convention on the Prevention and Punishment of Genocide* (*Bosnia and Herzegovina* v. *Serbia and Montenegro*) (ICJ) (2007) para. 392.

[66] *Issa and Others* v. *Turkey* (ECtHR) (2005) para. 71; *Cyprus* v. *Turkey*, para. 77.

it is reasonable to assume that the average person when faced with the threat of immediate and certain death would kill rather than be killed. If the law required that the threatened person should choose his or her death under such circumstances it would not only set an impossible standard for the average members of society (i.e. self-sacrifice), but it would moreover be absurd, since what future penalty could be worse had the threatened person decided to succumb to the threat?

In the *Erdemović* case the accused was an unwilling low-ranking conscript in the Bosnian Serb army, and in particular of a unit that had rounded up all Muslim males from the area of Srebrenica. When the prisoners were out of sight of the media and international peacekeepers, the leaders of the unit instructed the soldiers to open fire and kill everyone. A soldier who refused was himself immediately executed. As a result, Erdemović formed the opinion that any objection was pointless and felt compelled to execute the order, albeit under duress. Cassese J argued at the appeals level that society 'should not set intractable standards of behaviour which require mankind to perform acts of martyrdom and brand as criminal any behaviour falling below those standards'.[67] As a result, article 31(1)(d) of the International Criminal Court (ICC) Statute provides a full defence to situations of duress where the accused did not contribute to the harm and the threat was beyond the person's control.

On the face of it, IHL does not set intractable standards of behaviour to combatants. On the contrary, it would seem that obligations aimed to spare civilians, prisoners of war and wounded persons from harm, hardly place any suffering or stress on those engaged in armed conflict. Yet history shows that violations of IHL are a persistent factor in contemporary conflicts, and in many instances governments make every effort to conceal these from public scrutiny. How can this be explained? Although the authors of this book possess little expertise outside the realm of law to furnish specific solutions, the following discussion will set out some insights on the interplay between IHL and combat behaviour.

To begin this discussion we should first focus on the physiological strains of combat on the average combatant. The two strands of the human body's nervous system, the sympathetic (SNS) and the parasympathetic (PNS), ensure a healthy balance under ordinary circumstances. However, when stressors kick in, such as the prospect of lethal threat, conscious control is replaced by automation and in particular the SNS mobilises every atom in the human body as a reaction to the stressor. This is such an intense and automated process that the heart rate increases from seventy beats a minute to over two hundred beats a minute, while it has been reported that in the heat of deadly combat many soldiers find themselves unable to control their bladders or

---

[67] *ICTY Prosecutor v. Erdemović* (ICTY) (1997) Dissenting Opinion of Judge Cassese, para. 47.

sphincters.[68] A study carried out on the effects of heightened SNS as a result of combat stress demonstrates among others: diminished hearing (80 per cent), tunnel vision (80 per cent), slow motion time (65 per cent), intrusive destructive thoughts (26 per cent) and detachment (40 per cent).[69] These effects are induced by the secretion of hormones such as adrenaline, epinephrine and norepinephrine that dilate and constrict the body's bronchial tubes, vascular system and muscles during combat.[70] This automated process and its effects on physical and perceptual functions must return to some normality following the cessation of the stressful event; if SNS continues at peak level unabated the person will die. As a result, it is the PNS that ensures the body's return to the condition of homeostasis. The nervous system thus automatically operates as a thermostat to avoid overheating, so to speak. However, the parasympathetic descent to a state of relative calmness following an immediate stress upon the nervous system is not without consequences. The person generally feels weary, sleepy and exhausted. Whereas in ordinary situations the recuperative function of PNS will typically be followed by a significant and more or less permanent duration of normalcy, in the midst of combat the soldier and his or her superiors do not have this luxury. Hence, a weary combatant, who would otherwise need to rest in order to restore his physiological and mental faculties, will be forced to continue under arduous conditions. This is the norm in situations of continuous combat in which it is not unusual for troops to undergo numerous adrenaline surges followed by sharp PNS descents. This no doubt generates significant repercussions on the abilities of soldiers to operate not only in a combat environment but also in situations that do not trigger any significant stress, such as the handling of prisoners, interaction with civilians, conducting street patrols and others.

The general presumption, therefore, that soldiers perform better under combat pressure because their lives are in danger does not seem to be justified. On the contrary, it is probably discredited on the basis of the above.[71] In fact, in

---

[68] B. K. Siddle, *Sharpening the Warrior's Edge: The Psychology and Science of Training* (PPCT Research Publications, 1995); see also D. Grossman and L. Christensen, *On Combat: The Psychology and Physiology of Deadly Conflict in War and in Peace* (PPCT Research Publications, 2008) 30–1.

[69] Grossman and Christensen, above note 68, at 51–122.   [70] Ibid., 16–18.

[71] See S. L. A. Marshall, The Soldier's Load and the Mobility of a Nation (Marine Corps Association, 1980), who reached this conclusion. Some researchers have argued that frontline soldiers during the war of the trenches in World War I in fact took a distinct joy in killing because it served as an antidote to fear. The same researcher contended that the highest category of mental breakdown among troops consisted of those in combat support roles who did not have a chance to engage with the enemy. J. Bourke, *An Intimate History of Killing: Face to Face Killing in Twentieth Century Warfare* (Basic Books, 2000) 13 and 249. These theories have largely been rejected. See E. Jones, 'The Psychology of Killing: The Combat Experience of British Soldiers during the First World War' (2006) 41 *Journal of Contemporary History* 229, at 239–46.

a study completed at the close of World War II on United States (US) infantry who had fought in northern Europe, it was demonstrated that after a period of sixty days of continuous combat, 98 per cent of troops would suffer from a psychological condition, such as acute anxiety, combat exhaustion or depression, whereas the remaining 2 per cent developed an 'aggressive psychopathic personality' on the basis of which they could endure long periods of combat without any of the symptoms common to the majority of their comrades.[72]

This discussion was intended to shed some light on whether the obligations imposed by IHL on combatants are realistic in relation to the effects of combat stress. It is clear that IHL rules do not demand unrealistic conduct from their addressees. Professional armies, on the other hand, push their personnel to their limits and combat-weary soldiers are made to undertake sensitive duties, such as guarding prisoners or civilians, without having undergone sufficient psychological and physiological recovery. This does not of course absolve soldiers of any criminal responsibility for violating IHL under such circumstances, unless their state is such that they did not intend to commit the wrongful conduct, or lacked knowledge of it (lack of *mens rea*).[73] A soldier who commits a crime under immense stress but knowing full well and intending the consequence of his or her conduct is just as liable as a soldier under no stress whatsoever. It is obvious, however, that army leaders are responsible for their use of combat-weary soldiers in situations where their deployment raises alarm bells, or for failing to detect aggressive psychopathic personalities among their ranks. Thus, conformity with IHL is not only a matter of personal conduct, but more significantly it should also be a matter of adherence by army leaders to those rules of combat physiology that minimise the dangers of human frailty. It is right that the discussion on the application and enforcement of IHL should not focus on individual conduct alone, but should involve military policy more generally. This admonition is consistent with the introductory articles of the four Geneva Conventions under which 'the high contracting parties [not each soldier individually] undertake to respect and to ensure respect' for the conventions.

INTERVIEW 16.1

Battlefield Compliance

(Charles Garraway and Anon.)

Two senior military legal advisors were interviewed for the purpose of this section in 2010. The first is Colonel (retired) Charles Garraway (CG) of the

---

[72] R. L. Swank and W. E. Marchand, 'Combat Neuroses, Development of Combat Exhaustion' (1946) 55 *Archives of Neurology and Psychiatry* 236, at 244.
[73] See Chapter 17.3 on international criminal liability.

British Armed Forces. The second wished to remain anonymous and in 2010 was a legal advisor in the armed forces of a European nation, with deployment experience in both Bosnia and Afghanistan (Anon.).

In your opinion, for the soldier who is being deployed on a dangerous battlefield, what role does IHL play in the midst of life-threatening combat operations? Is the threat of sanctions a sufficient disincentive or is the instinct for survival stronger?

Anon.:   Assuming that your question relates to actual combat situations (so-called 'troops in contact'), a soldier will execute his drill in the midst of life-threatening combat operations. Rules of engagement (ROE)[1] and the principles of IHL are an inherent part of these drills. Soldiers are not compelled to apply IHL out of fear for the sanctions in case of non-compliance. I taught commanders and their subordinates that ROE and the principles of IHL are essential instruments at every level in the chain of command to ensure mission accomplishment. My motto is: a tactical success achieved by violating ROE and IHL will certainly create a strategic failure. If soldiers have to make decisions in a split second about defending themselves and afterwards it turns out that collateral damage has been caused, it does not necessarily follow that they will be prosecuted for violation of IHL or any other law.

CG: On the battlefield, the law plays a small part, as law. Life is instinctive and while in headquarters missions can be planned with careful weighing up of legal factors, the soldier on the front line does not have that luxury. Everything he does must be instinctive – or he is dead. It is thus more important to build an ethos than to rely on law. The soldier will not be thinking of sanctions on the battlefield. When I taught soldiers how to handle prisoners of war, my key point was to tell them that they were looking in a mirror. The soldier in front of them was themselves in a different uniform. Act to them as you would like them to act to you. And in 1990/91 that worked. During a Scud missile alert at our POW camp before the ground campaign started we had one prisoner brought back from a behind-the-lines operation. He was in a tent with a guard. As we pulled on our NBC kit,[2] the guard realised the prisoner did not have any and he began to give him some of his own. When I asked him why, he told me that it just seemed the right thing to do. He had understood. However, times have changed in the last twenty years and I am not sure that a scared young Iraqi can be compared to an Islamic fanatic. Nevertheless, I still feel that sanctions are an ineffective disincentive. It has got to be something deeper – honour, humanity, call it what you will. The survival instinct is strong but it can be controlled.

---

[1] The concept and significance of ROE are explained more fully in the next section.
[2] Nuclear, biological and chemical (NBC) first-aid kits.

> In the knowledge that the enemy has a complete disregard for IHL and will attempt to kill or maim you in every possible and treacherous way, what is the mentality of combat-weary troops?

Anon.: In general, they are aware that disregard for IHL as a result of the enemy's own disregard will negatively influence the operation. It is taken for granted that operations carried out in hostile environments raise the risk of blurring one's moral standards. Every soldier, and commanders in particular, must stay alert in anticipation of such blurring and be prepared to take firm action.

CG: A very good question. To be honest, I cannot comment from personal experience but I have noted an increased cynicism within the armed forces. I recently spoke at the Defence Medical Services Training Centre and was met with complete cynicism on the use of the emblem. I was told that whether or not the emblem is worn, the Taliban are deliberately targeting the medic on a patrol, identified by the different shape of his bergen.[3] The general view is that it is now better to rely on kinetic defence [i.e. use of active combat and force] rather than IHL and the emblem. This is worrying as one would expect medics more than any others to support IHL. This is precisely why trainers may have to change their approach to stress that this is a 'values' battle rather than a kinetic war.

> In your experience, irrespective of what their officers say, do combat-weary troops think that IHL is realistic and in touch with their particular exigencies?

Anon.: I instructed commanders (and sometimes also their subordinates) on ROE and IHL matters before their deployment to Afghanistan. If I would have asked them this question they probably would have said 'no, it is not'. In the deployment area I conducted ROE rehearsals with platoons and used real-life examples in which IHL would play an important role. Because of the discussions and answers to my questions I honestly believe that they would have answered this question in the affirmative. It is important that you translate IHL to concrete situations which they could be confronted with and then explain the 'do's' and 'don'ts' from an IHL (ROE) perspective and discuss possible consequences of their actions.

CG: My experience is of traditional wars where I found that one could persuade soldiers that IHL was realistic and in touch with their particular exigencies. I suspect that it is much harder now in current conflicts.

---

[3] Standard individual military backpack issued by armed forces.

It is rumoured that ROE in multinational combat operations in hot spots such as Iraq and Afghanistan are 'lighter' than current academic thinking on IHL. For example, street patrols, whether on foot or armoured vehicles, are given significant leeway in attacking persons who seem to be suicide bombers or in any way dangerous based on military briefings. In your experience, is this the case and is it perceived as a morale booster?

Anon.: No, that is not my experience. There were strict ROE and clear standing operational procedures regarding such situations.

CG: No. I have not seen the ROE and so cannot comment in detail. However, I am aware that ROE for pre-planned targeting operations require an assurance of zero collateral damage. This goes far beyond anything required by the laws of armed conflict and reduces the proportionality balance to nothing. This is certainly the cause of some frustration as soldiers do not necessarily appreciate that this is not a legal constraint but a policy constraint. I would suggest that, after the ICRC DPH paper,[4] 'current academic thinking on IHL' is anything but clear!

Given that soldiers on the battlefield are asked to risk their lives in a place far from home and under strong local hostility, in what way does the army depict the enemy and the local civilian population – particularly where the latter has ties with the enemy and may assist it – to its battle troops?

Anon.: Soldiers are taught the principles of counter-insurgency and the relationship between the enemy and the local population. They are being taught that local populations could pick up arms against our forces for many reasons. It is important that they are aware of this and are able to understand why this could happen. They are taught to be alert on this issue.

CG: I cannot talk about modern training. However, when I was teaching those soldiers who had to handle prisoners in 1990/91, I used to quote from Charles Kingsley and his character Mrs Doasyouwouldbedoneby. See the answer to the first question. One of the great dangers is to 'demonise' the enemy so that he is seen as 'subhuman' or 'different'. We were of course in those days 'liberators' of Kuwait and so the civilian population was not a problem.

Some of the responses referred to ROE and both interviewees were adamant that none of the ROE witnessed by them personally provided an explicit or implicit licence to violate IHL. This is certainly the case with most nations. Section 16.7.2 provides some examples that do not necessarily support this practice.

---

[4] ICRC, 'Direct Participation in Hostilities (DPH) Report' (2009).

16.7.2   The Dilution of Humanitarian Law and Problems in Ensuring Compliance

While it is true that compliance is to some degree predicated on personal traits, its general enforcement is dependent on a coherent system of discipline that allows for no deviation. This type of discipline is the hallmark of all professional armies, yet there exists a very real tension between armies and the executive branch of government. This tension arises from the fact that the gruesome, daily combat experience of the professional soldier is perceived as being inadequately communicated to the law-makers who make their decisions in the comfort of their office. At the same time, the law-maker is unable to communicate to the soldier the overarching political, military and economic aims of a military campaign, which are much broader than the calamities of the particular combat zone in which he or she is engaged. This tension surfaces even between senior military commanders and political leaders. By way of illustration, studies have shown that 'the perceived humanitarian bid by militaries may be overstated: commanders have little wish to see their forces lose basic war-fighting skills in the pursuit of other tasks, and in practical terms commitments in Afghanistan and Iraq have left major military actors overstretched'.[74]

More importantly, the military and the politicians cannot see eye to eye on the restrictions placed by the latter on the use of lethal force in combat and peacekeeping operations. Ordinarily, the use of lethal force would be circumscribed by the relevant rules of IHL as well as any particular mandate incumbent on the mission by the UNSC. In practice, however, this is not the case. When armies are sent to the battlefield or peacekeeping operations, depending on the projected intensity of resistance or other difficulties of the mission, they are issued with specific instructions regulating the circumstances under which they are allowed to employ lethal force. These regulations are termed ROE.[75] While no nation has ever claimed that its ROE were contrary to its obligations under IHL, none the less IHL is simply one of the factors in drafting ROE; others include the treachery of the enemy, the hostility of the civilian population, the terrain, as well as national policy.[76] It is no wonder therefore that mission-specific ROE are considered top secret, under the justification that it is tactically mistaken for the enemy to know how it is to be engaged. As correct as this may be, it leaves much to be desired in respect

---

[74] Humanitarian Policy Group (HPG), 'Resetting the Rules of Engagement: Trends and Issues in Military Humanitarian Relations' (HPG Report 21, March 2006) 2.

[75] The US Department of Defence Dictionary of Military and Associated Terms (US Government Printing Office, 1987) JCS Pub 1, 317, defines ROE as directives issued by competent military authority which circumscribe the circumstances and limitations under which US forces will initiate and/or continue combat with the enemy.

[76] See J. A. Roach, 'Rules of Engagement' (1983) 36 *Naval War College Review* 46, at 49.

of clandestine operations or combat-weary forces, or even with regard to armies that have a history of violating IHL.[77]

The secretive nature of ROE may moreover give rise to concerns for the conduct of private military companies whose operations fall within a grey zone of IHL. In general terms, mission-specific ROE are drafted by members of the senior military with policy input and approval by the executive. Although in their initial form they can be very elaborate, they distinguish between appropriate responses to 'hostile action' and 'hostile intent'. Hostile intent is certainly more difficult to substantiate, so troops are given some, but certainly limited, discretion in this regard.[78] ROE are not always static and they may change depending on the progress of the mission or the exigencies on the ground. Hence, a humanitarian mission, such as that of Somalia in 1991 (Operation Restore Hope), may escalate to a peace-enforcement operation. Accordingly, in such circumstances, the ROE must be amended; this process is known as 'mission creep'.

The intended addressees of ROE are combat personnel. Therefore, it is important that ROE are clear and simple, leaving no doubt as to their content.[79] It is taken for granted that military forces deployed in combat operations or other danger zones are well-versed in the fundamental principles of the *jus in bello*. Although this requirement seems self-evident for contemporary armies,[80] in fact the conduct of some professional armies has forced international human rights tribunals to demand that troops receive more stringent IHL education.[81] This is usually the case with armies that fail to invest in the development of their personnel and see little benefit in any comprehensive training that is not related to pure combat operations. It is also not uncommon for troops engaged in civil warfare, such as those that

---

[77] See P. Rowe, 'The Rules of Engagement in Occupied Territory: Should they be Published?' (2007) 8 *Melbourne Journal of International Law* 327, who argues that, at the very least, ROE in occupied territories should be published.

[78] *The San Remo Manual on Rules of Engagement* (International Humanitarian Law Institute, 2008) 22, defines hostile intent as 'the threat of imminent use of force. A determination of hostile intent is based on the existence of an identifiable threat recognisable on the basis of ... capability and intention ... Indicators of hostile intent [include]: (i) aiming or directing weapons; (ii) adopting an attack profile; (iii) closing within weapon release range; (iv) illuminating with radar or laser designators; (v) passing targeting information; (vi) laying or preparing to lay naval mines; (vii) failing to respond to proactive measures.'

[79] One of the deficiencies of the UN Somali (Restore Hope) ROE was the attempt by its drafters to insert a 'legislative approach', which made them indeterminate and unworkable in the life-and-death scenario of its intended addressees. See M. Martins, 'Rules of Engagement for Land Forces: A Matter of Training, not Lawyering' (1994) 143 *Military Law Review* 27, at 55.

[80] Art. 83 Protocol I.

[81] In *Mapiripán Massacre* v. *Colombia* (IACtHR) (2005) the IACtHR ordered Colombia, among other things, to create educational programmes on human rights and IHL for all its armed forces as a preventative measure.

make up the Colombian army and its paramilitary affiliates, to be afforded a significant degree of impunity as an incentive to persist under difficult and extremely dangerous combat situations.[82] If this impunity or lack of IHL training is further compounded by ROE that are inclined to abusive behaviour their addressees will feel no constraints in their treatment of the adversary or the civilian population.

Truth be said, the professional armies of developed nations are fluent in their knowledge of IHL, undergo extensive training and are subject to frequent psychometric tests and evaluations. These armies and their executives claim that they make every effort to prevent the perpetration of crimes, yet the practice of courts-martial against heinous behaviour on the battlefield or in occupied territories demonstrates a degree of leniency that would be unacceptable if the crimes under question had taken place during civilian life. The victims and families of such crimes understandably find this leniency hard to stomach.[83] Moreover, although we have generally little information about the content of ROE, it is presumed that the average soldier will be disinclined to exercise discretion in respect of an order which seems prima facie unjust. Disobedience is extremely exceptional as the following real-life scenario exemplifies. During the invasion of Iraq, Australian fighter pilots refused to comply with orders of US commanders to bomb particular targets because the intelligence given at pre-flight briefings and contained in their ROE did not match with the pilots' personal observations. Here is an extract from an interview by the squadron leader to the *Sydney Morning Herald* of 14 March 2004:

But it appears there were fundamental differences between the US-dominated headquarters and Australian pilots over what constituted a valid military target. Squadron leader Putney said under Australia's rules of engagement pilots had to ask themselves on each mission whether it was right to drop their bombs.

'Each guy would have made that decision once to half a dozen times in the conflict. It was presented as being just one pilot in the incident, but it was all of us several

---

[82] E.g., the UN Working Group on enforced and involuntary disappearances, Mission to Colombia, UN doc. E/CN.4/2006/56/Add.1 (2006), described in detail the culture of impunity associated with enforced disappearances by elements of the army and paramilitary groups.

[83] In *United States* v. *Steven Green* (US) (2011), the accused was sentenced to life imprisonment for the rape and murder of a fourteen-year-old Iraqi girl and the murder of her family. Despite the accused confessing to the murders the investigation in Iraq concluded that the crime had been committed by insurgents and Green was simply found to suffer from a personality disorder and given an honourable discharge. Military tribunals in past US wars were even more generous to persons accused of serious crimes. In the context of the My Lai massacre in Vietnam, the perpetrator, responsible for the murder of more than one hundred civilians, had his life sentence commuted and was later pardoned. See *Calley* v. *Calloway* (US) (1976). In the *Al-Skeini* case, it was the ceaseless efforts of the victim's family that led to the case being entertained and a subsequent inquiry launched.

times. We were providing an identification of targets in conjunction with ground forces and if we were not 100 per cent sure we were taking out a valid military target in accordance with our specifications we just did not drop.'

Squadron leader Putney said he could not comment on the reasons they aborted specific missions. But it seems that it was often to avoid the unnecessary killing of civilians. 'As we approached the target area we confirmed we had the right place. Then we'd run a check provided through our training that we were doing the right thing by our rules of engagement. We exercise those all the time. In Iraq it was a matter of the briefings we received prior in regard to our rules of engagement as to whether we thought this was a target we should be destroying. If it was not, then we decided not to deploy.' He said [continues the reporter] most decisions were made in the air, but some were command decisions.

This passage is a good indication of the effects of good IHL training and of responsible military personnel who are allowed to think for themselves, without blindly following orders. The situation would certainly have been different if the Australian ROE allowed no personal evaluation of the situation or where its pilots would have been subject to severe sanctions had they refused to follow orders given during their pre-mission briefing.

The dilution of IHL through secretive ROE has been demonstrated through a series of leaks concerning confidential documents that have come to light since 2007 in respect of the US-led war effort in Iraq. One of these documents is a US ROE addressed to its military personnel, which although generally consistent with IHL and while emphasising the importance of good conduct, contains none the less an injunction that is highly problematic. It elaborates on those targets that are deemed as being of 'high collateral damage' and in respect of which only the Secretary of Defense can authorise their destruction:

3.H(8) (S/REL). [High Collateral Damage Targets are those] that if struck, have a ten percent probability of causing collateral damage through blast debris and fragmentation and are estimated to result in significant collateral effects on non-combatant persons and structures, including: (A) Non-combatant casualties estimated at 30 or greater ... (C) In the case of dual-use facilities, effects that significantly impact the non-combatant population, including significant effects on the environment/facilities/infrastructure not related to an adversary's war making ability; or (D) Targets in close proximity to known human shields.[84]

Although, as has already been stated, the ROE were at pains to emphasise compliance with IHL, the risk to the civilian population from the operations described in the last section is very significant. It is difficult to justify the suggested casualty rate on the scale of military necessity, particularly given that the operations in Iraq did not involve a full-scale war, but were largely

---

[84] The document is entitled SECRET/REL TO USA, IRQ, MCFI/20151003. It is reproduced online at http://file.wikileaks.org/file/us-iraq-rules-of-engagement.pdf, at 25.

directed against insurgent attacks. It should be pointed out that the Obama administration subsequently proceeded to alter US ROE in Afghanistan and Iraq. This even led the military leadership of the campaign there to vociferously call for the 'easing of the rules of engagement', deeming the latest changes to be detrimental to the safety of troops and success of operations.[85]

FURTHER READING

Ben-Naftali, O., *International Humanitarian Law and International Human Rights* (Oxford University Press, 2011).

Bianci, A., and Y. Naqvi, *International Humanitarian Law and Terrorism* (Hart, 2011).

Cantor, D., and J. F. Durieux, *Refuge from Inhumanity? War Refugees and International Humanitarian Law* (Martinus Nijhoff, 2014).

Clapham, A., and P. Gaeta (eds.), *The Oxford Handbook of International Law in Armed Conflict* (Oxford University Press, 2014).

Darcy, S., *Judges, Law and War: The Judicial Development of International Humanitarian Law* (Cambridge University Press, 2014).

Dinstein, Y., *Non-International Armed Conflicts in International Law* (Cambridge University Press, 2014).

Forrest Martin, F., and S. J. Schnably, *International Human Rights and Humanitarian Law: Treaties, Cases and Analysis* (Cambridge University Press, 2011).

Fortin, K., *The Accountability of Armed Groups under Human Rights Law* (Oxford University Press, 2017).

Francioni, F., and N. Ronzitti, *War by Contract: Human Rights, Humanitarian Law and Private Contractors* (Oxford University Press, 2011).

Giacca, G., *Economic, Social and Cultural Rights in Armed Conflict* (Oxford University Press, 2014).

Kennedy, D., *Of War and Law* (Princeton University Press, 2006).

Kolb, R., *Advanced Introduction to International Humanitarian Law* (Edward Elgar, 2014).

Kolb, R., and G. Gaggioli (eds.), *Research Handbook on Human Rights and Humanitarian Law* (Edward Elgar, 2014).

Milanovic, M., *Extraterritorial Application of Human Rights Treaties: Law, Principles and Policy* (Oxford University Press, 2013).

Murray, D., et al. (eds.), *Practitioner's Guide to Human Rights Law in Armed Conflict* (Oxford University Press, 2016).

Ohlin, J. D., *Theoretical Boundaries of Armed Conflict and Human Rights* (Cambridge University Press, 2017).

Park, I., *The Right to Life in Armed Conflict* (Oxford University Press, 2018).

Provost, R., *International Human Rights and Humanitarian Law* (Cambridge University Press, 2005).

Rogers, A. P. V., *Law on the Battlefield*, 3rd edn (Manchester University Press, 2012).

Solis, G. D., *The Law of Armed Conflict: International Humanitarian Law in War* (Cambridge University Press, 2010).

Sriram, C. L., O. Martin-Ortega, and J. Herman, *War, Conflict and Human Rights* (Routledge, 2017).

Websites

ICRC: www.icrc.org/en

PRIO Data on armed conflict: www.prio.org/Data/Armed-Conflict/

Rule of Law in Armed Conflicts Project: www.geneva-academy.ch/RULAC/

Watchlist on Children and Armed Conflict: http://watchlist.org/

[85] E. Bumiller, 'Petraeus Pledges Look at Strikes in Afghanistan', *The New York Times* (29 June 2010).

17 Human Rights and International Criminal Justice

CONTENTS

17.1   INTRODUCTION

This chapter examines the criminal law dimension of human rights violations. International criminal law has evolved so much in the past two decades that it is now a structured sub-discipline of international law. It is beyond the purview of this book and this chapter to provide an overview of this sub-discipline and the reader will be directed at the end of this chapter to a more specialist bibliography. The focus here is on the international criminal dimension of human rights violations and the manner in which these are transformed into criminal rules and the criminal mechanisms through which they are enforced and implemented. Human rights, as is demonstrated throughout this book, are implemented through a variety of rules, including commercial and corporate (for example, for multinational companies) and a plethora of mechanisms (i.e. judicial and non-judicial). Their enforcement through criminal rules is therefore but one dimension of this process.

The chapter begins by explaining the complementary role of criminal law in the application of international human rights. It then goes on to analyse the function of the concept of individual criminal responsibility under international law and its relationship to human rights violations. Subsequently, we examine the processes and mechanisms for enforcement of criminal rules under international law with an emphasis on policy rather than the procedural rules underpinning jurisdiction. The 'peace versus justice' debate, namely whether international prosecution should sometimes be side-lined in favour of negotiated solutions to ongoing conflicts, is an integral part of this discussion. Finally, the chapter concludes with an analysis of the two core mass international crimes, namely genocide and crimes against humanity with a view to demonstrating that their formulation is largely based on human rights (i.e. rights of victims), rather than criminal law, considerations.

17.2   RELATIONSHIP BETWEEN INTERNATIONAL CRIMINAL LAW AND HUMAN RIGHTS

Human rights rules are multifaceted. The right to life, for example, encompasses not merely a negative obligation on the state to refrain from arbitrarily using lethal force, but also a positive obligation to prevent and punish those (including non-state actors) unlawfully taking the life of another.[1] This latter dimension of the right to life is, in addition to a positive obligation arising from human rights law, also a mandate upon domestic courts and prosecutors. This is so because domestic criminal law traditionally predates human rights and the positive obligations arising therefrom, albeit it does not always encompass all positive obligations under human rights law (for example, right to truth and effective investigation). Although domestic criminal law is not dependent on human rights norms in order to prosecute perpetrators of crimes – and hence its application and enforcement is distinct from human rights obligations – both are clearly mutually reinforcing. It is also evident that the tacit criminal dimension (i.e. the positive dimension) of human rights rules is insufficient to prescribe the objective (*actus reus*) and subjective (*mens rea*) elements in the definition of a criminal offence. For example, the right to life does not tell us with any degree of specificity when

---

[1] See Chapter 18.4 in relation to terrorism.

the taking of life amounts to a criminal offence,[2] including whether any defences (such as self-defence, acting under superior orders or coercion) may absolve or mitigate the liability of the accused. Of course, the reinforcing and supplementary role of human rights dictates and shapes the outer boundaries of the criminal justice process, from the right to a fair trial (as regards the rights of the accused) to the impermissibility of amnesties, the effect of which is to absolve an accused of criminal liability.

Where criminal conduct assumes an international character the substantive and procedural criminal law of a single state may not suffice to bring the perpetrator(s) to justice. In such situations the criminal conduct in question may be punishable only under the laws of a specific number of states (transnational crime) or be the subject matter of a global multilateral treaty or custom, in which case it is known as an international crime, or a crime under international law. In the first case, the conduct possesses an extra-territorial element (i.e. it was performed, or its effects materialised, in more than one state), whereas in the latter, besides a possible extraterritorial element, it is also of concern to the international community as a whole. It is clear that both extraterritorial and transnational crimes engage the criminal laws and criminal enforcement mechanisms of all concerned states. For the purpose of uniformity and legal certainty it makes sense for several types of criminal conduct with an extraterritorial element and of concern to the international community to undergo a process of international (as opposed to merely domestic) criminalisation. This is the case, for example, with genocide, crimes against humanity and torture.

There are, however, limits to the process of international criminalisation, chiefly because this lies at the discretion of states. Whereas some rights are enshrined in treaties (some sparsely ratified whereas others almost universally), others, particularly those in soft law instruments, are in a continuous tug-of-war between contesting states, and while their status is clear to some it is wholly refuted by others. What this means is that not every human rights violation corresponds to an international crime or even a transnational crime; although they may well give rise to criminal liability under domestic law. The right to development is an obvious contender, but even core socio-economic rights such as the right to education or the right to meaningful employment do not possess a criminal dimension under international law. In practice, evidence that a particular right corresponds to an international crime must be sought either through a discrete treaty (which criminalises the conduct) or a clear customary rule.

---

[2] Most criminal justice systems suggest that the appropriate *mens rea* for murder is direct intent or at least *dolus eventualis*, namely substantially high foreseeability and acceptance of the risk of death.

Unlike international humanitarian law (IHL), which constitutes a legal regime (because of the armed conflict dimension) that is distinct from (but certainly complementary to) the regime of international human rights and is therefore *lex specialis*,[3] international criminal law is not a distinct regime with rules potentially in conflict with international human rights. For practical purposes, this means that the prevention and punishment of international criminal conduct does not give rise to specialised or superior rules in relation to the pursuit of human rights objectives, as these are enshrined in treaties and custom by states. This is clearly understandable by the fact that a significant corpus of human rights rules and case law from international human rights tribunals concerns the criminal justice process. In equal measure, domestic and international criminal tribunals employ the full gamut of human rights law as this is expressly mandated in national constitutions and/or their founding treaties. The synergy between these two disciplines is further evidenced by the ever-increasing expansion of criminal liability upon non-state actors who, on account of not possessing human rights obligations, find themselves in an artificial zone of impunity. Multinational corporations and terrorist organisations, for example, are not burdened with human rights obligations as such (although they certainly carry other similar obligations),[4] yet it is well-documented that their conduct is otherwise criminal and has a significant negative impact on the lives of millions of people. Given the limited ambit of human rights rules against the conduct of these non-state actors, domestic and international criminal law has resolved that they can indeed incur liability (or responsibility) for international crimes.[5]

Human rights and international criminal law equally converge where the latter is employed to fulfil entitlements found in the former. The right to truth, for example, although usually discharged through non-punitive truth commissions, is also achieved through international trials, even if this is not a primary goal of international tribunals, as will be explored in Section 17.4 below. Other examples include the concerted prosecution of international crimes which has proven to facilitate the right to return of refugees and internally displaced persons.

While international criminal law and international human rights are clearly not in conflict, some of the policies associated with international criminal

---

[3] See Chapter 16.4.

[4] Under the doctrine of odious (sovereign) debt, a contractually (between a state and a private bank) incurred debt which knowingly violates the borrower state's human rights obligations and which is unconscionable is void and may be unilaterally repudiated by the state. The indirect human rights implications for the non-state actor in this scenario are arguably significant. See Chapter 14.6.

[5] See M. Pieth and R. Ivory, *Corporate Criminal Liability: Emergence, Convergence and Risk* (Springer, 2011); see also Chapter 19 on non-state actors.

justice may turn out to be in conflict with both disciplines. This observation, which is examined in Section 17.6, typically concerns diplomatic efforts to secure peace at the expense of dispensing criminal justice. However, it should be emphasised that this is not the result of a regime or rule-conflict, but an extra-normative deviation chosen by the relevant stakeholders.

17.3   INDIVIDUAL CRIMINAL LIABILITY UNDER INTERNATIONAL LAW

When a person engages in conduct that is unlawful in the state where the conduct takes place, two things happen simultaneously: (1) the elements of the crime are fulfilled; and (2) liability for the crime is attributed to the perpetrator. Liability, viewed through the lens of attribution, may entail that the conduct or its effects be attributable also to persons other than the direct perpetrator, such as accomplices and instigators. Liability is further conditioned by the existence of possible defences, such as duress, mental incapacity or coercion. Where a defence is sustained, a distinction should be made between the existence of the offence as such and the liability of the perpetrator, which may now become significantly limited or dissolved. This dichotomy between criminal *conduct and liability* should be highlighted.

Where the crime is of a purely domestic nature and concern, the accruing liability of the perpetrator(s) will arise under the domestic law of the territorial state (for example, burglary). If the crime, however, is of an international nature (a crime under international law), the attribution of liability will be determined by reference to international law, even if the crime in question took place solely on the territory of a single state. In this event, therefore, the criminal liability of the perpetrator is derived from international law, whereas in all other circumstances liability is derived solely from domestic law(s). This distinction is crucial because given the prevalence of international law over domestic law, any grounds offered in the latter which serve to mitigate or extinguish liability for an international crime are invalid. By way of illustration, the extermination, enforced disappearance or enforced racial segregation (apartheid) of one's political or other opponents in a widespread or systematic manner constitutes a crime against humanity. This is an international crime, prescribed by both treaty and customary international law. A crime against humanity arises even where the totality of the conduct and its effects have materialised on the territory of a single state, as was the case with the apartheid regime in South Africa and the heinous disappearance policies in Argentina and Chile in the 1970s and 1980s. If the governments of the concerned states (or others acting unilaterally) were to adopt amnesties or similar measures, the effect of which was to absolve the perpetrators from liability, these would be invalid under international law. The reason, of course, is that because crimes against humanity are crimes under international law, liability is equally derived from international law (international criminal liability), which trumps all grounds mitigating or extinguishing liability under domestic law.

This observation is significant because it suggests that the complementary relationship between international human rights and international criminal law cannot be superseded by a conflicting rule under domestic law. Going a step further, because the ambit of international criminal liability is circumscribed only by the pertinent processes of international law, there have been sweeping developments regarding the concept of international legal personality (ILP).[6]

ILP determines the range of rights and duties conferred on an entity under international law, including the capacity to enforce these for or against such entity (i.e. in a court, tribunal or through administrative means). Traditionally, as will be explained in Case Study 17.1, ILP was only confined to states and (certain activities of) international organisations. In recent years ILP has been extended to individuals in the field of human rights, international crimes, foreign investment[7] and numerous other arenas, but more significantly it is now well-stipulated in treaty law that ILP arises in respect of international crimes committed in a single state.[8] Hence, although domestic criminal law is important in order to enforce and prosecute international crimes, where domestic law confers amnesty or other impunity to perpetrators, as a matter of international law such amnesties are without merit.

CASE STUDY 17.1
International Criminal Liability at the Nuremberg Trial

The prosecution of the highest-ranking Nazi officials is considered the watershed for the extension of ILP to individuals and the creation of international criminal jurisdiction. In short, it is the foundation of modern international criminal law. The International Military Tribunal (IMT) at Nuremberg was established by the London Agreement of 8 August 1945 between the governments of Great Britain, the USA, France and the USSR,[1] to which the Tribunal's Charter was annexed. Article 6 of the Charter provided for the prosecution of

---

[1] 1945 Agreement for the Prosecution and Punishment of the Major War Criminals of the European Axis, 82 UNTS 279.

---

[6] See Chapter 2.3.

[7] Foreign investors, e.g., derive substantive and procedural rights against host states on the basis of bilateral investment treaties (BITs), contracts with host states and laws to this effect enacted by host states. See Chapter 19.3.1 and 19.3.2.

[8] In *ICTY Prosecutor* v. *Tadić* (ICTY) (1995) para. 134, it was unequivocally held that war crimes in non-international armed conflicts are international crimes. In equal measure, the ICC Statute renders war crimes in domestic conflicts and all situations of genocide or crimes against humanity international crimes.

offenders in respect of war crimes, crimes against humanity and crimes against peace. One of the principal challenges against the jurisdiction of the IMT was that the three crimes could not be attributable to them as physical persons, but to Germany, assuming that they constituted international crimes in the first place.[2] In this connection the defence asserted that individuals possessed no legal personality under international law and their conduct was subsumed by the state, and hence their criminal liability could only be assessed under the laws of Germany. Such a result, however, although consistent with the wholly artificial lack of international criminal liability in the pre-1939 era, was morally detestable. Given that the prevailing laws and mores during the reign of Hitler in Germany permitted or tolerated atrocities against vulnerable groups, the liability of the accused would have been seriously called into question.[3] The IMT was not overly troubled in applying the solution that best served the interests of legitimacy – although it was itself accused of victors' justice and selectivity – rather than the interests of strict legality. It took the position that despite the absence of express treaty references to personal criminal liability, the crimes encompassed within its Charter entailed such liability as a matter of customary international law and that in any event the accused clearly understood the gross criminal nature of their conduct.[4]

[2] With the exception of war crimes, which were contained in various multilateral treaties prior to 1939, crimes against peace and crimes against humanity lacked international codification and there is little evidence that they had crystallised as international crimes under customary international law. The IMT's approach to this question was that if a war of aggression is illegal in international law then it necessarily follows that those who plan and wage such a war are committing a crime. IMT judgment, reprinted in (1947) 41 *American Journal of International Law* 172, at 218.

[3] It should be pointed out that in 1946 the German jurist Gustav Radbruch, as a response to this situation, formulated a theory of justice versus formal law. He held that where a judge encounters a formal law whose application produces an unbearably unjust result, he or she should refuse enforcement or in any way consider it as valid law. This so-called Radbruch formula was subsequently applied by German courts in order to strike down Nazi legislation. See S. L. Paulson, 'Radbruch on Unjust Laws: Competing Earlier and Later Views?' (1995) 15 *Oxford Journal of Legal Studies* 489.

[4] IMT judgment, above note 2, at 218.

17.4   THE ENFORCEMENT OF INTERNATIONAL CRIMINAL LAW

International criminal law is primarily enforced by domestic mechanisms, such as courts, law-enforcement authorities and legislative bodies. These in turn correspond to the three branches of government and their respective powers (or jurisdiction), namely prescriptive (or legislative), judicial and enforcement. It is no wonder that, with few exceptions, the exclusive territorial jurisdiction of states with respect to all crimes (transnational and international) is prescribed in multilateral treaties and customary law. The jurisdiction of international criminal tribunals is an isolated exception to this rule, although the International Criminal Court's (ICC) jurisdiction is also founded on treaty. International tribunals simply do not have the capacity to deal with the plethora of international crimes, so ultimately they are forced to prosecute the most large-scale and heinous. The bulk of prosecutions naturally falls on national courts and institutions. The primary judicial, enforcement and prescriptive jurisdiction of states is reinforced by the residual jurisdiction of other states and exceptionally by international courts and tribunals. A radical feature of this residual mechanism is *universal jurisdiction*, which arises in respect of several international crimes (such as genocide and crimes against humanity), whereby any country may assume jurisdiction over pertinent offences irrespective of the absence of any link whatsoever with the offence, the offender or even the victims.

Besides unilateral action, however, states are increasingly resorting to bilateralism, as is the case with extradition and asset recovery, as well as multilateralism. Apart from formal multilateral agreements to criminalise conduct that was once tolerated, at best, such as transnational corruption, states are committing armed forces to engage with pirates on the high seas, in addition to contributing to multinational contingents to prevent and suppress gross human rights violations, including responsibility to protect (R2P).

However, the concept of 'enforcement' should not be understood as merely the meting out of punishment to the offenders. This is a rather narrow, offender-based understanding of enforcement. It is imperative that one identifies in advance the goals to be pursued by the operation of an international criminal justice mechanism; this is hardly self-evident. If the primary goal consists of general and special deterrence, incapacitation, rehabilitation or retribution, then the type of punishment meted out to the offender is clearly of paramount importance.[9] The pursuits and dynamics of criminal trials should not be confused or subsumed with the various manifestations and types of punishment. In the immediate aftermath of World War II the heads of Britain and the USSR, Churchill and Stalin, proposed the summary execution of Nazi leaders and their accomplices without the need for trials. They perceived this as a form of punishment. They could see little utility for trials in respect of mass criminality, because their apprehensions of martyrdom possibly claimed by the accused and their sympathisers, forced them to lose sight of the fact that the evidence of the atrocities would bury for ever any argument that the crimes in question had not taken place or that there was

---

[9] See M. Drumbl, *Atrocity, Punishment and International Law* (Cambridge University Press, 2007), for a thoughtful analysis of punishment theories in respect of international crimes.

something heroic about the Nazi leaders. Hence, even if the Nazi leaders had never been prosecuted but the trial had none the less taken place, the sheer weight of evidence would itself have made a profound impact.

It is not surprising, therefore, that the supporters of international trials attach great significance to the writing of a historical record and the need to provide a voice to the victims and their families, followed, where appropriate, by the secondary goal of reconciliation.[10] Indeed, for the European Jews of World War II or the Tutsi in Rwanda, the mere punishment or assassination of the genocidaires would not have satisfied the desire to record the atrocities, lest future generations forget or doubt their victimisation;[11] this was something that the assassination of the culprits could by no means have achieved. Trials also empower the victims, in the sense that they enable them to face up to their tormentors and through their personal account help to convict those responsible. Both of these processes may ultimately facilitate, to a larger or smaller degree, reconciliation between post-conflict communities. Finally, trials express and project the validity of international norms in a way that punishment alone cannot. They help to depoliticise acts of barbarity by turning them into legally enforceable criminal violations, making it clear that they do not belong outside the realm of law.[12]

Yet although the international community does not seem to possess a coherent plan of objectives in respect of international trials, it would be wrong to hold trials simply because of their record-writing capacity, or for the benefit of victims and any future goals of reconciliation. As laudable as these objectives are, they presume a priori that events happened in a particular way and place pressure on the prosecutor and judges to make convictions based on these presumptions. Such aspirations may be achieved through truth commissions. Any other result brings the independence and impartiality of international tribunals into question, and by implication the right to a fair trial. As a result, the primary objective of international trials should not be perceived as being different from their domestic counterparts. Rather, they should strive to enforce the law through fair judicial proceedings, following which they can then fulfil any of the aforementioned secondary aims

---

[10] See L. Douglas, *The Memory of Judgment: Making Law and History in the Trials of the Holocaust* (Yale University Press, 2001). In *ICTY Prosecutor* v. *Plavšić* (ICTY) (2003) paras. 79–81, the ICTY was at pains to argue that the admission of guilt by the accused contributed to the establishment of truth and was a significant effort towards the advancement of reconciliation, which was stated as one of the tribunal's primary aims.

[11] As a result, the vast majority of European nations have rendered Holocaust denial a criminal offence, against which the freedom of expression is generally inapplicable. See e.g., the French Gayssot Act 1990.

[12] R. A. Duff, *Trials and Punishments* (Cambridge University Press, 1986) 235ff., for an account of expressive theories of punishment in the domestic setting; D. Luban, *Fairness to Rightness: Jurisdiction, Legality and the Legitimacy of International Criminal Law*, Georgetown Public Law Research Paper no. 1154117 (July 2008) 10.

either directly[13] or indirectly. The fact that trials concerning mass atrocities may have a 'show trial' or meta-justice dimension, in that prosecution and punishment cannot even begin to encapsulate the horror of the conduct and the pain of the victims and their families,[14] should not lead to a broad dismissal of international trials. It is only natural that all those affected by the proceedings, from the accused to the victims, will seek to derive their own particular pursuits and objectives.

Fair trials in the manner described satisfy not only the requirement of legality in respect of the enforcement of international criminal law, but also that of legitimacy. What is important here is not so much *perceived* legitimacy (for example, outreach and history-writing) or even *normative* legitimacy, but rather *performance*-based legitimacy. Fair trials, even-handedness, objective application of human rights and acquittals in the interests of justice (even if politically sensitive) constitute robust performance indicators by which the legitimisation of international criminal tribunals will ultimately be assessed. Not surprisingly, *perceived* and *normative* legitimacy do not necessarily trickle down to their intended audiences.[15]

The first post-Nuremberg international tribunals were the ad hoc tribunals for the former Yugoslavia (ICTY) and Rwanda (ICTR). These two ad hoc tribunals were established by the United Nations (UN) Security Council (UNSC) in the form of subsidiary organs under article 29 of the UN Charter through two distinct resolutions.[16] An international tribunal predicated on a UNSC resolution rather than a treaty (and absent the consent of the territorial state) was a radical departure for the early 1990s,[17] but not by contemporary

---

[13] In recent years, states, sometimes through the assistance of international organisations, have resorted to truth commissions as a supplement to the operation of international criminal tribunals. Unlike the latter, truth commissions are best suited to directly serving truth-telling, reconciliation and victim participation.

[14] It is stated, e.g., that the prosecution of Eichmann was not so much about the person but about emphasising that Nazi crimes were committed against the Jewish people, a fact that was not highlighted during the Nuremberg proceedings. See M. Koskenniemi, 'Between Impunity and Show Trials' (2002) 6 *Max Planck Yearbook of UN Law* 1, at 3.

[15] In 2005 the UN Development Programme (UNDP) conducted a survey among the various ethnic groups in Bosnia and the people of Serbia. The survey showed that the majority of Bosnian Serbs and Serbs were in favour of criminal trials. However, for varying reasons that may no longer be relevant, 30 per cent of Serbs believed that the ICTY had not done a good job, but that its existence was none the less justified. See UNDP, 'Justice and Truth in BiH: Public perceptions' (2005) 15–16, online at www.undp.ba/upload/publications/JusticeoTruth%20in%20BH%20English.pdf.

[16] UNSC resolution 827 (25 May 1993) in respect of the ICTY and UNSC resolution 955 (8 November 1994) in respect of Rwanda.

[17] In fact, the *Tadić* (1995) Appeals jurisdiction decision, paras. 26ff., addressed this very issue, emphasising that the measures indicated in art. 41 UN Charter (which is the legal basis for the UNSC's authority to set up ad hoc tribunals) were merely indicative and by no means exhaustive.

standards. More importantly, the UNSC delegated significant powers to these tribunals, such as the authority to request and to compel the surrender of evidence, witnesses and accused persons from UN member states.[18] Thus, the ad hoc tribunals possessed primacy of jurisdiction over and above domestic courts, something missing in the ICC, which enjoys complementary jurisdiction, whereas the courts of member states enjoy primary jurisdiction. By the late 1990s the international political scene was generally ready to accept the creation of a permanent ICC, which came about through a treaty in 1998. Its statute was very much influenced by the then expanding jurisprudence of the ad hoc tribunals, and many issues that seemed insurmountable in the late 1980s (such as international criminal liability in internal armed conflicts) had by 1998 transformed into custom.[19]

17.5   UNIVERSAL JURISDICTION

All types of jurisdiction require some link to the forum state (territorial, victim-based, nationality-based or protective), but this is not the case with universal jurisdiction. The application of universal jurisdiction to a particular offence requires no link whatsoever, thus allowing prosecuting states to indict and prosecute offences subject to the universality principle.[20] Scholars generally distinguish between 'pure' or 'absolute' and 'conditional' universal jurisdiction. While neither requires a link with the prosecuting state, the former does not necessitate the presence of the accused there, whereas its conditional counterpart does.[21]

Due to the broad extraterritorial competence encompassed by the exercise of the universality principle, it is reasonable that it be confined to a limited number of offences. Crimes under international law have customarily

---

[18] Art. 29 ICTY Statute.

[19] Although established under different legal bases, besides the ICTY, ICTR and ICC, other international criminal tribunals include the SLSC; East Timor's Special Panel for Serious Crimes and Serious Crimes Unit; the so-called 'Regulation 64 Panels' in Kosovo; the War Crimes Chambers in the State Court of Bosnia and Herzegovina; the Extraordinary Chambers in the Courts of Cambodia (ECCC); the International Criminal Tribunal in Bangladesh; the Special Tribunal for Lebanon (STL); and Senegal's Extraordinary African Chambers.

[20] See K. Randal, 'Universal Jurisdiction under International Law' (1988) 66 *Texas Law Review* 785.

[21] Other more subtle categorisations have also been suggested in the scholarly literature. See L. Reydams, *Universal Jurisdiction: International and Municipal Legal Perspectives* (Oxford University Press, 2003) 28–42, who distinguishes between: (1) general cooperative universality, which applies to all serious offences recognised by nations, whether domestic or international; (2) limited cooperative universality, which applies only to international crimes; and (3) unilateral limited universality, which corresponds to the contemporary pure or conditional model.

attracted universal jurisdiction in two independent ways: (1) on the basis of the repugnant nature and scale of the conduct, as is the case with grave breaches of IHL[22] and crimes against humanity;[23] or (2) as a result of the inadequacy of domestic enforcement mechanisms over unlawful conduct committed in locations not subject to the authority of any state, such as the high seas. It cannot be over-emphasised that these two bases of universal jurisdiction are independent and conjunctive. The practical significance of this observation is that in order to discern whether or not an international crime is susceptible to universal jurisdiction, it must first be ascertained whether the nature and scale test or the *locus delicti commissi* principle is more appropriate, if any. In *Re Pinochet (No. 3)*, Lord Millet succinctly argued that international crimes attract universal jurisdiction where they violate *jus cogens*, the conduct is serious and perpetrated on such a large scale that they can be regarded as an attack against international legal order.[24] This statement makes ample sense, but if states decide by treaty to exclude the universality principle even in respect of offences that meet these criteria, national courts would have no power to exercise universal jurisdiction. Given also that the application of universality gives rise to political friction, one must seek the widest possible global consensus and support from pertinent treaties and customary international law in order to render universality a tool against impunity rather than a matter of sharp division and hostility. An example of treaty-based (and customary) universal jurisdiction is exemplified by article 105 of the UN Convention on the Law of the Sea (UNCLOS) in respect of piracy *jure gentium*. Customary universality is also recognised through consistent practice and this is true, at least, in the case of crimes against humanity, genocide and torture, among others.

Furthermore, in the absence of protest or an express prohibition, states may reasonably assume pure or conditional universal jurisdiction under their domestic laws. This should not be viewed as a unilateral act in all cases, but chiefly as an entitlement arising from treaties. By way of illustration, many crime-related treaties encourage parties to assert expansive forms of jurisdiction, very much akin to a universal model. Article 5(1) of the Convention against Torture and Other Cruel, Inhuman or Degrading Treatment or Punishment (CAT), for example, grants territorial, nationality and passive personality jurisdiction, while paragraph 2 of the same article stipulates further that:

---

[22] 1949 Geneva Conventions and both Additional Protocols 1977 to the 1949 Geneva Conventions.

[23] *Fédération Nationale de Déportés et Internés, Résistants et Patriotes and Others* v. *Barbie* (France) (1988) at 130. See also *Re Pinochet* (Belgium) (1999) at 702–3.

[24] *R* v. *Bow Street Metropolitan Stipendiary Magistrate and Others ex parte Pinochet Ugarte (No. 3)* (UK) (1999) at 177.

2) Each state party [shall] *take such measures as may be necessary to establish its jurisdiction* over such offences in cases where the alleged offender is present in any territory under its jurisdiction and it does not extradite him to any of the states mentioned in paragraph 1 of this article.

3) This Convention *does not exclude any criminal jurisdiction exercised in accordance with internal law* [emphasis added].

Article 5(2) and (3) thus indirectly permits the exercise of universal jurisdiction with respect to the incorporated domestic offence of torture. There is a further natural limitation to the universality in article 5(2) CAT that is not expressly encountered in piracy *jure gentium* or the grave breaches provisions of the Geneva Conventions. This is the requirement that the alleged offender actually be in the hands of the prosecuting state. The supporters of the conditional universality principle require the presence of the accused on the territory of the prosecuting state as a precondition for the exercise of universal jurisdiction.[25] A different conclusion, it is claimed, runs the risk of trials *in absentia* and violates the double jeopardy rule (i.e. that a person should not be tried twice under the same or similar charges). Yet both the pure and conditional universality schools of thought converge in the belief that preliminary investigations *in absentia* are welcome because they allow the collection and preservation of crucial evidence with a view to future trials.[26] Where the alleged offender is apprehended in a state unwilling to prosecute that state must extradite the accused – subject to bilateral or multilateral arrangements – to a country with a sufficiently close connection to the offence.[27]

There exists significant debate as to whether universal jurisdiction is an entitlement, an obligation, or both. State practice and pertinent treaties suggest that it is an entitlement, irrespective if its exercise gives rise to competing claims. In fact, this is most welcome because the multiplicity of claims satisfy the key aim of the principle, namely to combat impunity and extinguish all

---

[25] In *H* v. *Public Prosecutor* (*Afghan Asylum Seekers* case) (Netherlands) (2007), it was held that universal jurisdiction cannot be applied in absentia.

[26] See A. Poels, 'Universal Jurisdiction in Absentia' (2005) 23 *Netherlands Quarterly of Human Rights* 65. In the *Guatemalan Generals* (Spain) (2005) case, the Spanish Constitutional Tribunal (26 September 2005) emphasised that the Spanish law providing for universality over crimes such as genocide, torture and terrorism should be construed as permitting unconditional universal jurisdiction. Although Spanish law does not permit trials *in absentia* the Tribunal did not view this as a distinct ground of jurisdiction, thus paving the way for the permissibility of extradition requests in cases where the accused is not in Spanish territory. In 2014 the law, as pertains to universal jurisdiction, was abolished and was replaced by other jurisdiction bases. See R. A. A. Fernández, 'The 2014 Reform of Universal Jurisdiction in Spain: From All to Nothing' (2014) 13 *Zeitschrift für Internationale Strafrechtsdogmatik* 717.

[27] Art. 8(4) CAT.

safe havens. State practice is divisive as regards the obligatory character of universality. In the opinion of this author no such obligation exists and this is principally justified by the cautious and conservative approach of the vast majority of states in prosecuting crimes with which they have no link. Practical considerations further reinforce this view, especially given that a state may simply not have the resources to prosecute. A contrary conclusion would mean that following allegations of an international crime anywhere in the world every state would be obliged to issue an arrest warrant and pursue prosecution. None the less, the apprehending state is under an obligation to extradite persons accused of crimes subject to universal jurisdiction if it chooses not to prosecute. This conservatism in the recognition of a sovereign right to universal jurisdiction has manifested itself in the case law. A narrow view was confirmed by the International Court of Justice (ICJ) in the *Belgian Arrest Warrant* case. There, a Belgian investigating judge issued an international arrest warrant against the Congolese Foreign Minister, on the basis of a unique universal jurisdiction law enacted in Belgium in 1993. Congo brought legal proceedings against Belgium before the ICJ arguing that incumbent foreign ministers enjoy immunity from prosecution, even in respect of grave international crimes. The ICJ did not view universal jurisdiction as central to the issue at hand, but in his separate opinion, Judge Guillaume assumed a narrow conception of universality, finding it applicable in limited cases (absent a treaty stipulation) and certainly not *in absentia*.[28] Equally, in *Jones* v. *Ministry of Interior, Kingdom of Saudi Arabia*, the House of Lords held that no evidence exists whereby states recognise an international obligation to exercise universal jurisdiction over claims arising from breaches of *jus cogens*, and nor was there any compelling judicial practice that they should.[29]

A different stance was taken by the ICJ in the *Habre* case. As regards the obligation in article 6(2) of the Torture Convention, whereby a state party in whose territory a person alleged to have committed acts of torture is present must 'immediately make a preliminary inquiry into the facts', the Court observed that this must be done as soon as the suspect is identified in the territory of the state. With respect to the obligation to prosecute deriving from article 7(1) of the Torture Convention, the Court emphasised that it requires submission of the case to the competent authorities for the purpose of prosecution, irrespective of the existence of a prior request for the extradition of the suspect. While extradition was at the discretion of the requested state, prosecution was found to be an international obligation under the

---

[28] *Arrest Warrant of 11 April 2000 (Democratic Republic of Congo v. Belgium)* (ICJ) (2002), separate opinion of Judge Guillaume, para. 9.

[29] *Jones v. Ministry of Interior, Kingdom of Saudi Arabia* (UK) (2006), per Lord Bingham, para. 27.

Convention. Just like the *Pinochet* judgment, the ICJ was adamant that while the prohibition of torture was part of customary international law and had become part of *jus cogens*, the obligation to prosecute for torture applied only to facts having occurred after its entry into force for the state concerned.[30]

QUESTIONS

1. In what way is *legitimacy* different from *legality* in international criminal law?

2. What is the underlying rationale for the existence of many situation-specific international criminal tribunals when there is now a permanent international criminal court?

3. Is the application of universal jurisdiction viable only for rich, developed states or is it also (even potentially) an effective tool for less developed nations? Is it principally a matter of resources or political will?

4. Can multinational corporations (and other legal entities) incur international criminal liability for criminal conduct attributable to them? You should first read Chapter 19 on non-state actors and human rights.

17.6   PEACE VS INTERNATIONAL CRIMINAL JUSTICE

We have already seen that transitional (post-conflict/dictatorship) governments may be inclined towards amnesties, whether for truth-telling purposes or in order to terminate hostilities and restore peace. By doing so, they are making a choice for peace over criminal justice, without necessarily ignoring all the entitlements associated with victimhood. In theory at least, certain human rights may very well be achieved even in the absence of international criminal law enforcement, particularly if one views peace as a collective entitlement in its own right.[31] This section examines the arguments in favour and against this dilemma.

In their initial design, international criminal justice mechanisms were largely self-contained institutions that were unrelated to other parallel processes, particularly peace negotiations. They were set up because the

---

[30] *Belgium* v. *Senegal (Questions relating to the Obligation to Prosecute or Extradite)* (2012) (ICJ) paras. 71–117.

[31] The UN Millennium Development Declaration, sections II and VIII, explicitly recognised the links between peace, security, development and human rights; see also the UNGA Declaration on the Right of Peoples to Peace, resolution 39/11 (12 November 1984); see also Rio Declaration, principles 24 and 25; Beijing Platform for Action, UN doc. A/CONF.177/20 (1995) paras. 12 and 134; 1996 Habitat Agenda, para. 25.

international community reached a consensus that it could no longer tolerate particular instances of impunity and widespread human rights violations, and at the same time no other reaction was obvious to the international policy-makers of the day.[32] One may argue that this conclusion is flawed because one of the conditions of the Dayton Peace Accords of 1995, by which the belligerent parties agreed to end all hostilities in the former Yugoslavia, was that referrals of accused persons be made to the then fledgling ICTY.[33] As true as this may be, it is probably prudent to assume that the Council did not link its then ongoing peace efforts with the creation of the ICTY out of fear that this may have been perceived as hostile by some of the key players, who in turn may have been enticed to continue fighting.

In practice, the permanent members of the UNSC and their allies vigorously pursue peace or other similar deals with pertinent state and non-state actors, even alongside international criminal tribunals. Hence, it goes without saying that the Council in no way wishes to undermine its other peace and rule-of-law efforts by providing supreme judicial review powers to a court or tribunal. There is some evidence to suggest that some powerful nations in the UNSC regard peace deals with local warlords and states as the only viable mechanism (other than military subjugation) for the restoration of peace in beleaguered parts of the globe. In this light they are willing to offer considerable concessions to alleged criminals in exchange for their withdrawal from hostilities altogether.[34] Such an eventuality is even envisaged in article 53(2)(c) of the ICC Statute, which calls upon the Prosecutor to consider prior to the initiation of an investigation whether there does not in fact exist a sufficient basis for prosecution in cases where this would not be '*in the interests of justice*, taking into account all the circumstances, including the gravity of the crime, the interests of victims and the age or infirmity of the alleged perpetrator, and his or her role in the alleged crime'.

---

[32] Existing human rights mechanisms and bodies, whether regional or UN based, are not generally adapted to deal with urgent situations of mass crimes and their role is extremely limited in response to such events.

[33] General Framework Agreement for Peace in Bosnia and Herzegovina, (1996) 35 ILM 75, Annex 1(a), art. X; Annex 6, art. XIII(4).

[34] When the political leader of the Bosnian Serbs, Radovan Karadžić, was arrested in 2008 and brought before the ICTY, one of the first arguments he put forward was that he was entitled to immunity from prosecution by the ICTY because he had concluded a secret agreement on 18 and 19 July 1996 to that effect with US negotiator Richard Holbrooke following the Dayton Accords. This alleged agreement envisaged the accused's perpetual immunity if he agreed to disappear from public life from 1996 onwards. Karadžić further argued that Holbrooke brokered the agreement under actual or apparent authority from the UNSC; consequently, the legal and actual effect of the agreement was directly applicable to the Tribunal. The ICTY did not examine the veracity of these allegations because it found them of no legal significance given that the UNSC had not demanded that it refrain from prosecuting the accused. *ICTY Prosecutor* v. *Karadžić* (ICTY) (2009) paras. 1–19 and 33–7.

This is a radical provision that was never in the past imposed on the prosecutors of ad hoc or hybrid tribunals. Its scope is not clear and in any event the subjugation of criminal prosecutions to ongoing peace negotiations may not itself be in the interests of justice. It is also in direct conflict with the UN's understanding and application of the rule of law.[35] The ICC Office of the Prosecutor has attempted to de-politicise and downplay the exceptionalism personified by 'interests of justice' considerations by modelling a balancing test that takes into account the gravity of the crime, the interests of the victims and the particular circumstances of the accused.[36] Yet its policy paper on this matter is ambivalent and obscure, but it is clear that the Prosecutor is mandated to defer prosecution of a situation if requested to do so by the UNSC under article 16 ICC Statute. Such a deferral may well arise where a Council member is engaged in peace negotiations with the feuding parties. In the indictment of the then Sudanese President, Al-Bashir, however, despite Sudan rallying its allies to convince the UNSC to utilise its article 16 powers and defer the case, such an outcome never materialised.

There are mixed reactions about the peace versus accountability argument. On the one extreme, non-governmental organisation (NGO) campaigners take the view that the impact of justice mechanisms is often undervalued in resolving prolonged conflicts and that the supposed achievement of peace through impunity usually results in protracting conflicts.[37] This conclusion is also corroborated by some empirical data premised on case studies, which have shown, for example, that the warrants of arrest issued against members of the Lord's Resistance Army (LRA) in Uganda contributed to its isolation from its support base, further encouraging a new cycle of promising peace talks.[38]

On the other extreme, political analysts opine that in certain circumstances the arraignment of heads of state or prominent leaders does not necessarily lead to their isolation, whether internally or externally. The case of the then Sudanese President, Al-Bashir, is distinctly reflective of this tension. In July 2009 the United States (US) Special Envoy to Sudan, Scott Gration,

---

[35] Report of the UN Secretary-General, The Rule of Law and Transitional Justice in Conflict and Post-Conflict Societies, UN doc. S/2004/616 (23 August 2004) paras. 10 and 64. The Report does concede the limitations of international tribunals and supports alternative justice mechanisms and capacity building. It does not in any manner, however, sanction impunity regimes for the restoration of peace.

[36] ICC Office of the Prosecutor, 'Policy Paper on the Interests of Justice' (September 2007).

[37] Human Rights Watch, 'Selling Justice Short: Why Accountability Matters for Peace' (July 2009).

[38] P. Akhavan, 'The Lord's Resistance Army Case: Uganda's Submission of the First State Referral to the International Criminal Court' (2005) 99 *American Journal of International Law* 403, at 404. It should be noted, however, that while this holds true for the LRA operating in Uganda, during the same time the LRA continued to commit atrocities in other parts of the Great Lakes region.

stated that while the USA would engage with the Sudanese President, this 'does not mean that [Bashir] does not need to do what's right in terms of facing the International Criminal Court and those charges'.[39] Mixed signals were furthermore received from Sudan's domestic front. The Sudan People's Liberation Movement (SPLM), which at the time was fighting for the independence of South Sudan from the North, but which was also engaged in mediated efforts to bring the conflict to an end, was opposed to the indictment of the Sudanese President. The SPLM released a statement saying that 'Sudan should stand with Bashir at this hard time', and some of its officials were reportedly concerned that the indictment could have endangered the comprehensive peace talks on the political status of South Sudan – which ultimately did not come to pass, given that South Sudan became independent in early 2011.[40]

Equally, it has been claimed, and this is the fundamental premise against the justice argument, that those with the greatest responsibility for atrocities will not think twice about intensifying their criminal activity, let alone laying down their arms, if they believe or know that they are going to be prosecuted.[41] It is thus evident that the supporters of the peace argument are not exclusively political and military leaders who have a personal interest in ICC prosecutions; rather, the list also includes persons who are otherwise hostile to indicted leaders.

One of the contemplated potential impacts of ICC arrest warrants is that of 'marginalisation'. It is argued that a probable effect of an arrest warrant is that it weakens the negotiating power of the target party, decreases its popular base and by extension marginalises it both domestically and internationally. The test cases in support of this argument are the Darfur and LRA indictments. The former has been the subject of mixed reviews, some claiming a degree of marginalisation, whereas other circles, particularly from within the African Union (AU), seem to have rallied around the incumbent Sudanese President. The LRA case is interesting from the point of view of the target group, which is a rebel entity. The LRA is accused of widespread crimes over the course of the last decade in northern Uganda, and was until recently assisted by the current government of Sudan through some degree of financing and the provision of safe havens in southern Sudan as the base for their operations. The failure of the Ugandan government to successfully negotiate a peace settlement with the leaders of the LRA forced the Ugandan President, Yoweri Museveni, to refer the situation to the ICC, which proceeded

---

[39] US Congressional Research Service, 'International Criminal Court Cases in Africa: Status and Policy Issues', RI 34665 (14 July 2009) at 1.

[40] Ibid., at 14.

[41] A. Natsios, 'Beyond Darfur: Sudan's Slide Toward Civil War' (May/June 2008) 87 *Foreign Affairs* 77, at 82.

to unseal its arrest warrants in October 2005, although less than a year later, in July 2006, Museveni announced a complete amnesty for all LRA combatants under condition that they renounce terrorism and accept peace.[42] In response to the unsealing of the indictments and the active involvement of the ICC, severe criticism was voiced by all local actors, including the Acholi people, who were the subject of attacks and forced child recruitment, the Catholic Archbishop in Uganda, former and current mediators and many others.[43] Moreover, despite the stern position of the UNSC against impunity, it seems that those members of the international community involved in the ongoing peace process did not exactly herald the ICC indictments. They were generally viewed as untimely and not conducive to the peace negotiations. Some NGOs claim that in fact the indictments led the LRA to the negotiating table in the Juba talks between 2006 and 2008, and furthermore prompted Sudan to adopt a Protocol with Uganda which allowed the latter's armed forces to attack LRA camps in Southern Sudan.[44]

The successful marginalisation and de-legitimisation of former Liberian dictator, Charles Taylor, on the other hand, may to a large degree be attributed to his indictment by the Sierra Leone Special Court (SLSC), despite the ongoing peace process at the time. It is claimed that Liberians could not support a leader who was susceptible to arrest and prosecution every time he travelled abroad.[45] The better point of view seems to be that the marginalisation of Charles Taylor was exceptional because, unlike the LRA, he was a beleaguered leader with opposing rebel forces dangerously closing in on Monrovia, and being president he had nowhere to hide, as would be the case with a rebel entity intent on a protracted armed struggle. It is doubtful that an indictment would have prompted a premature departure had Taylor enjoyed full control over Liberian territory and appeased his neighbours. None the less, the Special Court indictment is an excellent example of how to put pressure on a beleaguered leader and speed up his deposition from power. The same outcome was also evident in the case of former Serbian President Milošević, whose arraignment, but especially his prosecution, by the ICTY culminated in the absence of domestic popular support. The absence of a prosecution is perhaps the reason why Al-Bashir and the LRA had not lost their popular support by their audiences.[46]

---

[42] See M. Ssenyonjo, 'The International Criminal Court and the Lord's Resistance Army Leaders: Prosecution or Amnesty?' (2007) 54 *Netherlands International Law Review* 51.

[43] Human Rights Watch, above note 37, at 29.

[44] Ibid., 31–3.   [45] Ibid., 22–3.

[46] See generally I. Bantekas, 'Sequencing Peace and Justice in Post-Conflict Africa: The ICC Perspective', in C. Jalloh and I. Bantekas (eds.), *The International Criminal Court and Africa* (Oxford University Press, 2017).

Some states, however, view judicial 'interference' in ongoing peace negotiations as part of the problem. The hostility of African nations and the AU, for example, to the issuance of arrest warrants by the ICC against African situations and African leaders, including the employment of universal jurisdiction by domestic courts in Europe, ultimately led to an impasse in the relations between Africa and the ICC. This outcome challenges the paradigm concerning the high levels of cooperation traditionally encountered in the practice of the ICTY, ICTR as well as hybrid tribunals. It demonstrates that a structured dialogue is clearly required between the ICC, the UNSC and like-minded/regional groupings. The majority position among African leaders has been that the indictment of African governmental leaders by international tribunals is not welcome where it endangers ongoing peace negotiations.[47] This position was echoed in the AU's condemnation of President al-Bashir's indictment by the ICC. Paragraph 4 of its Decision was adamant that no cooperation to the ICC was forthcoming because the indictment against him[48] was a publicity-seeking spectacle and the UNSC had refused to entertain the AU's request for deferral in order for an African solution to be negotiated. Paragraph 5, however, was much more to the point about the prevalence of peace over justice. It reads:

The decision bears testimony to the glaring reality that the situation in Darfur is too serious and complex an issue to be resolved without recourse to a harmonized approach to justice and peace, neither of which should be pursued at the expense of the other. Furthermore, the decision was taken after due evaluation of the situation in Darfur informed by the commitment of member states to finding a lasting solution to the problem in Darfur with a view to restoring peace, security and stability in the Sudan and the whole region and prevent further displacement and killings in that country.[49]

The AU-appointed High-level Panel on Darfur, which was headed by former South African President Thabo Mbeki (Mbeki Panel), saw the ICC indictment against Al-Bashir as a catalyst for justice,[50] but was reluctant to confirm the appropriateness of the ICC as a forum for resolving the Darfur crisis. The Report was careful to emphasise that:

---

[47] In fact, the AU seldom refers to the international criminal liability of perpetrators when addressing peace efforts. For example, the Declaration of the AU Assembly on the state of peace and security in Africa in 2006 omitted to mention the liability of those responsible for attacks against peacekeepers and only offered its sympathies to the victims and their families; AU doc. Assembly/AU/Decl.3 VI (2006).

[48] *ICC Prosecutor* v. *Al-Bashir* (ICC) (2009).

[49] AU Commission, Decision on the Meeting of African States Parties to the Rome Statute of the International Criminal Court (14 July 2009).

[50] Mbeki Panel Report, AU doc. PSC/AHG/2(CCVII) (29 October 2009) paras. 244–5.

Criminal justice will play an important role, but not an exclusive one, and must be underpinned by procedures that allow for meaningful participation of victims, as well as reparations and other acts of conciliation. Within the criminal justice system, the investigations, prosecutions, defence and judiciary must work in tandem, or in smooth sequence. Weaknesses in any one element of a criminal justice process would undermine the prospects of a successful outcome ... In order to respond effectively to the violations in Darfur, the system will need to draw upon Sudan's rich legal heritage, including Sharia (Islamic) law and practice, to the extent that Sharia emphasizes the participation of victims in proceedings and the making of reparations. Traditional justice models with their focus on conciliation and wider participation of the community also provide viable mechanisms for dealing with the past. Truth-telling and an independent and informed analysis of the past, in order to draw out the lessons of Darfur for Sudan, should also be given priority ...[51]

It was not a far leap on the basis of these conclusions for the Panel to suggest that the best possible mechanism was an independent *sui generis* hybrid tribunal.[52] The Mbeki Panel, without in any way dismissing the appropriateness of the ICC, noted that an entity enjoying local ownership and able to impose customary conciliatory mechanisms and operate as an equal partner with other Sudanese justice initiatives, including Sharia courts and customary courts dispensing blood money/*diya*, may be a more appropriate alternative.[53] The Panel was mindful not to state that ICC proceedings were injurious to the ongoing peace efforts in Sudan, but it is clear that it viewed its processes as far too rigid and remote for the exigencies of Darfur and the cultural experiences of its people. These developments in fact prompted the AU to suggest a third chamber to the African Court of Justice and Human Rights. The idea was that such a chamber would effectively try core international crimes perpetrated in Africa with a view to preventing the ICC from exercising its complementary jurisdiction. This was achieved through the adoption

---

[51] Ibid., para. 205.

[52] Ibid., paras. 252–4. See further L. Oette, 'The African Union High-level Panel on Darfur: A Precedent for Regional Solutions to the Challenges Facing International Criminal Justice?', in V. Nhemielle (ed.), *Africa and the Future of International Criminal Justice* (Eleven International Publishing, 2012) 353–74.

[53] The general concept of blood money predates Islam and was practised extensively in the Arabian Peninsula well before the advent of Prophet Mohammed. In most Muslim criminal justice systems the legislation on *diya* and *qisās* (essentially a claim for retaliation) is proceeded by a detailed annex specifying the monetary value of each human organ or limb in terms of retaliation. See Oman Royal Decree 118/2008 (7 November 2008), which provides for such an annex. It should be noted that *diya* is not a criminal punishment but merely civil compensation and belongs in the realm of private law, since in many cases it may be exacted from the perpetrator's male relatives. See R. Peters, *Crime and Punishment in Islamic Law: Theory and Practice from the Sixteenth to the Twenty-First Century* (Cambridge University Press, 2006) 7–8.

in 2014 of a subsequent Protocol amending the Protocol on the Statute of the African Court of Justice and Human Rights. Article 3(1) of this Protocol vests the Court with jurisdiction over international crimes.

INTERVIEW 17.1

Siri Frigaard: Former Chief Public Prosecutor and Director of the Norwegian National Authority for Prosecution of Organised and Other Serious Crime

What was the expectation of Norway regarding the prosecution of serious extraterritorial international crimes? Was it limited to persons already on Norwegian territory or was there an expectation of exercising universal jurisdiction against alleged offenders outside Norway and with no link to Norway? Were you constrained by budgetary considerations?

When the National Prosecution Authority for Organised and Other Serious Crimes was established in August 2005, it consisted of three prosecutors, including the director of the office. Today, six prosecutors, including the director, are employed. The task of the office is not limited to the prosecution of core international crimes, but also organised crime, computer crime, sexual abuse of children on the internet and terrorism. With respect to core international crimes, war crimes, crimes against humanity and genocide, the office has exclusive jurisdiction in Norway.

At the same time a police investigation section was established within the Norwegian National Investigation Service (Kripos). The section consists today of twelve persons, both investigators and police lawyers. The sole task of this section is to investigate core international crimes.

One of the arguments supporting the establishment of the prosecution office was that the authorities did not want Norway to be a 'safe haven' for alleged offenders of these most serious crimes. This implies that the expectation of the authorities was firstly to exercise universal jurisdiction against alleged offenders already on Norwegian territory.

However, the Norwegian authorities, accepting the international commitment to fight the impunity for these most serious crimes, adopted new regulations against war crimes, crimes against humanity and genocide, as well as a new regulation on universal jurisdiction for these crimes. These regulations came into effect on 8 March 2008, effectively meaning that Norway can prosecute alleged offenders for offences committed abroad by aliens even if they are outside Norway and the crime has no link to Norway.

Despite the fact that politicians provided the Authority with the tools to prosecute accused persons in and outside Norwegian territory (and with no link to Norway) the resources allocated indicate that the Authority must give priority to accused persons already in Norwegian territory.

The National Prosecution Authority for Organised and Other Serious Crimes has received several complaints against persons not present in Norway in respect of crimes against humanity. So far, none of these complaints has resulted in investigations due to lack of resources as priority must be given to those already in Norway. This is a fundamental criterion for the selection of a case and subsequent prosecution. As the criteria are flexible, the practice might change in the future, especially if more resources are allocated to the investigation and the prosecution units, or less complaints against persons already on Norwegian territory are received.

What in your opinion are the most serious impediments to fighting transnational and international crimes?

In order to successfully investigate and prosecute core international crimes it is important for all involved states to have sufficient resources, including the country where the offence was committed and the country where the alleged offenders might be present. This implies not only a sufficient number of investigators and prosecutors, but also requires appropriate competence and training. In turn, these prerequisites exist only if there is political will to fight transnational and international crimes.

Moreover, prosecutors are more likely to initiate an investigation in a case that will probably endure for several years if they know that they will be supported by the authorities. The investigation of transnational and international crimes is a long and costly process. For most countries, such as Norway, it is necessary for witnesses to provide their testimony directly to the court. This is not only an expensive process, but also a process that is difficult to manage, as it requires the issuance of passports, visas, air tickets, transport to and from the airfield, accommodation and so on. To be able to manage all this, one is dependent on other institutions, such as immigration authorities.

As war crimes, crimes against humanity and genocide are often committed in countries far away from the offender's country of nationality, and many of the potential witnesses are equally disbursed in different countries, legal aid is essential to a successful investigation. The absence of mutual legal assistance (MLA) treaties with some countries might also prove an impediment to the collection of evidence.

As I see it, the most important impediment is the lack of political will in some countries, not only the prosecuting one, but also those whose cooperation is crucial, as well as international political will. International pressure to fight these crimes is important, and today one might wonder if the fight against terrorism has been given priority over the fight against impunity for core international crimes.

Instead of creating expensive international tribunals with Western salaries do you consider that it would have been better for this money to have been invested by the international community in enhancing and empowering the criminal justice and rule of law system in developing countries?

After the World War II trials, there were several instances of prosecutions for core international crimes before international tribunals. The creation of international tribunals like the ICTY and the ICTR were therefore important because they gave the signal that the international community cared and moreover demonstrated that it was possible to investigate and prosecute those responsible for the most serious crimes. The disadvantage was that these tribunals were costly and prosecution was lengthy and took place far away from the actual crime scene where the victims were living.

In East Timor (Timor-Leste) a different system for offering justice to victims of serious crimes was created. A so-called hybrid court consisting of one local judge and two international judges was established, as well as an international serious crimes unit responsible for prosecution and investigation. The advantage with this system was that it helped the Timorese to rebuild their own justice system and to train their judges and prosecutors to a certain degree. Another advantage was that the trials took place in the country and it was thus easier for the victims to access the court and communicate with the prosecution authority. Moreover, offenders were convicted or acquitted by their own people.

This system had its disadvantages. For instance, when international lawyers are working with national lawyers and doing the same job, any sense of harmony is necessarily disrupted where the salaries of international personnel are much higher than those of their national counterparts. Another problem we were facing in East Timor was that the accused indicted with the most serious offences had left East Timor and were situated in neighbouring countries. As East Timor, a post-conflict country with a weak justice system, was not 'respected' by its bigger neighbouring countries, none of the absent indictees were extradited to East Timor. Even today, these offenders are at large and have not been prosecuted anywhere.

I find it difficult to say whether or not it is better to 'invest the money' in international tribunals or alternatively in developing countries. The situation will vary from one country to another. In respect of East Timor, its people have always wanted and still demand an international tribunal and cannot understand why they did not get one.

What lessons may be learned, in your opinion, from the Norwegian experience?

The most important lesson to be learned from the Norwegian experience is, in my opinion, that it is possible to prosecute and convict foreign offenders of the most serious international crimes if the will to do so is present. Even if the crimes were committed long ago and in countries far away, and despite the fact that all the evidence must be collected in countries with a different culture and justice system, it is possible to both collect enough evidence and to present this evidence in court, if gathered according to your own criminal procedure laws.

In my opinion, it is an advantage that special units for prosecution of these cases are established and given enough resources to be able to build up the expertise and knowledge that is vital in order to perform investigation and prosecution in a proper and expeditious manner.

When the two units were established in Norway, we had few resources, no proper regulation regarding the incorporation/implementation of international crimes in Norwegian law. We simply had Norwegian criminal law and little expertise of international law. But we had the will to do so. We had a slow start as at the same time that we started to investigate we had to train investigators and prosecutors, not only in international criminal law, but also in the cultural differences between countries. Knowledge, respect and appreciation of cultural differences are most important in order to succeed in this field. The work of the Norwegian special units for prosecution and investigation of core international crimes has so far resulted in the conviction of two perpetrators, one from the Balkans and one from Rwanda, as well as in the extradition of alleged perpetrators both to the Balkans and to Rwanda.

17.7   CORE INTERNATIONAL CRIMES

It is beyond the purview of this chapter to deal with the vast range of issues encompassed within the field of international criminal law. We shall deal here with two of the most heinous and large-scale (or mass) international offences which include within them most discrete international offences. These core crimes are genocide, crimes against humanity and grave breaches.[54] Although the first two could simply amount to a multiplicity of discrete offences, such as multiple murder, multiple rapes, multiple acts of torture, etc., their very existence is predicated on the desire to express in emphatic terms not simply the scale of the atrocity but also the plight of the victims. Hence the construction of these crimes is meant to emphasise the suffering of the particular victims, far more than the criminality of the person of the perpetrator(s). They may also be referred to as *label crimes*. This is a welcome synergy between criminal law and human rights, given that the pursuit of perpetrators alone is simply but one dimension of states' human rights obligations.

---

[54] Grave breaches are serious violations of the laws of war.

17.7.1 Genocide

The mass killing or other forms of extermination against a group of people enjoying particular characteristics (ethnic, religious or other) has been prevalent throughout history, and during the early part of the twentieth century there were at least two notable instances, namely the extermination of the Black Sea Greeks and the Armenians of the Ottoman Empire. It was not, however, until the Jewish Holocaust that the international community realised the need for (or was ready to accept) a global treaty against genocide. The Holocaust effectively encompassed a plan conceived by the Nazi regime, known as the Final Solution to the Jewish Problem, whereby it sought to exterminate the Jewish population of Europe. Although the crime of genocide overlaps to some degree with crimes against humanity and hence the former could have just as well been subsumed in the latter, the drafters of the Genocide Convention felt compelled to distinguish the two. They desired to emphasise the particular gravity of targeting members of a specific group (whereas the target of crimes against humanity is 'any civilian population') with a view to its intentional physical or biological destruction or extermination. Emphasis is therefore placed on the destruction of the group (group 'as such', article II of the Genocide Convention), whereas the victimisation of group members in their individual capacities takes second place.

It should be noted that the enforcement of the prohibition of genocide rests on two interrelated pillars. The first concerns suppression and prosecution at the domestic level by the territorial state,[55] or ultimately by any state given that genocide falls squarely under the rubric of universal jurisdiction.[56] The second pillar is a collective one. States acting collectively under chapter VII of the UN Charter and within the purview of the R2P doctrine may intervene militarily in a country where genocide is taking place with a view to protecting the targeted group.[57] In this respect, any state responsibility for

---

[55] Art. I Genocide Convention; equally, UNSC resolution 2171 (21 August 2014) preamble.

[56] Among other sources, art. 2(1) of the Princeton Principles of Universal Jurisdiction lists genocide as a universal jurisdiction crime.

[57] R2P was endorsed in the 2005 World Summit Outcome Document, adopted as UNGA resolution 60/1 (2005). It rests on three pillars: (1) every state has a primary responsibility to protect its people; (2) the international community is responsible for assisting states to protect their people; and (3) if the target state fails to protect its people, the international community is obliged to assume that role and may use force to do so, albeit only as a means of last resort. In the course of the 2011 Libyan uprising the UNSC adopted resolution 1973 (2011), which specifically invoked the principles underlying R2P. Art. 4(h) of the AU's Constitutive Act stipulates that the AU may intervene in a state in Africa pursuant to a decision of its Assembly 'in respect of grave circumstances, namely: genocide, war crimes and crimes against humanity'. This is an exceptional provision that is inconsistent with chapter VII UN Charter, but it is argued that it constitutes a reflection of

failure to prevent or punish genocide is independent, and additional, to the personal criminal liability of the perpetrators.[58]

The definition of genocide is found in article II of the 1948 Genocide Convention, which defines this offence as encompassing:

... any of the following acts committed with intent to destroy, in whole or in part, a national, ethnical, racial or religious group, as such:

a) killing members of the groups;
b) causing serious bodily harm or mental harm to members of the group;
c) deliberately inflicting on the group conditions of life calculated to bring about its physical destruction in whole or in part;
d) imposing measures intended to prevent births within the group;
e) forcibly transferring children of the group to another group.

The intent of the perpetrator to destroy the enumerated groups in whole or in part suggests the requirement of a special intent (*dolus specialis*) which is missing from the *mens rea* of other international crimes. The *dolus specialis* of genocide necessitates that the intention to commit genocide be formed prior to the execution of genocidal acts, although this requirement does not apply with respect to the individual offences that comprise genocide (for example killings, deportation, prevention of births etc.).[59] This requirement serves to exclude the possibility that genocide may ever occur by reason of spontaneous impulse. The execution of genocide involves two levels of intent: that of the criminal enterprise as a collective and that of the participating individuals. The next step is to establish whether the accused shared the intention that genocide be carried out.[60]

The 'in part' element does not characterise the destruction of the group, but refers instead to the intent of the perpetrator in destroying the group within the confines of a limited geographical area.[61] Thus, the crime of genocide does not require that the perpetrator must intend to kill each and every member of the group. Since genocide is a mass-victim offence, the part (of the group) targeted must consist of a substantial part of the group. In terms of victim numbers, the ICTY and ICTR suggest that the intent to destroy a part of the group must affect a considerable number of individuals that

---

the R2P principle in a regional context; see also Chapter 4.6 for an overview of collective security.

[58] In *Application of the Convention on the Prevention and Punishment of the Crime of Genocide (Bosnia and Herzegovina v. Serbia and Montenegro)* (ICJ) (2007) paras. 162–6, Serbia was found liable for its failure to punish genocide, particularly as regards its lack of cooperation with the ICTY.

[59] *ICTR Prosecutor v. Kaiyshema and Ruzindana* (ICTR) (1999) para. 91.

[60] *ICTY Prosecutor v. Krstić* (ICTY) (2001) para. 549.

[61] Ibid., paras. 582–4.

make up a 'substantial' part of that group.[62] In such cases, it must be proven that the perpetrators intended to destroy the targeted group in the particular geographical area, in addition to the intent to destroy a substantial part of that group as such.[63] The killing of at least 8,000 Muslim boys and men in Srebrenica by Bosnian Serb forces is emblematic of an intent to commit genocide by destroying a distinct part of the group (i.e. male members of a particular geographical location).

Article II of the Genocide Convention only penalises the destruction of four particular groups, namely, national, ethnic, racial and religious. The Convention is silent regarding admission (and acceptance) in a group. Equally, there is no guidance as to whether membership of a group should be viewed objectively or, alternatively, on the basis of subjective criteria, that is, exclusively through the perceptive lens of the perpetrator, irrespective if this contradicts objective standards. This issue became the make-or-break element in the first case before the ICTR. There, the Hutu (group), which was responsible for annihilating their rival Tutsi (group), could not be distinguished from the Tutsi under any of the four enumerated grounds. Their distinctiveness was lost in ancient African history and was engineered by Belgian colonisers as a form of social control, but equally, it should be noted, that contemporary Rwandese distinguish facial characteristics between Hutu and Tutsi which are not always evident to external observers. On the basis of this evidence, the ICTR Trial Chamber in the *Akayesu* case assessed group membership solely on subjective criteria,[64] which is methodologically consistent with the right to individual self-identification in human rights law.[65] The ICTR therefore constructed membership solely on the particular perception of the perpetrators, who considered themselves ethnically distinct from the members of the targeted group.[66]

Current practice clearly permits willing states to expand the range of targeted groups encompassed under the legal concept of genocide. This includes any 'stable' group, other than the four enumerated groups in the Genocide Convention. This is a matter of state practice, which may in fact be wider than a strict interpretation of the Genocide Convention; albeit there is no legitimate restriction to such expansive practice. In the *Jorgić* case

---

[62] Ibid., paras. 586–8; *ICTR Prosecutor v. Bagilishema* (ICTR) (2001) para. 64.

[63] *ICTY Prosecutor v. Sikirica* (ICTY) (2001) para. 61.

[64] At a collective level, when we talk about the mores and norms associated with a grouping of individuals (society or social system) what we are really investigating is the culture of the group. Culture is therefore a set of shared meanings communicated by language or other forms (e.g. symbols) between group members.

[65] *Lovelace v. Canada* (HRCtee) (1981).

[66] *ICTR Prosecutor v. Akayesu* (ICTR) (1998) para. 702.

the German Federal Constitutional Court accepted that article 220(a) of the Criminal Code in force in 1997 was consistent with international law, despite encompassing within its ambit of group destruction 'a group as a social unit in its distinctiveness and particularity and its feeling of belonging together'.[67] Several countries have taken up this mantle and have proceeded to prosecute for genocide in situations where the targeted group espoused a particular political ideology. Article 281 of the Ethiopian Penal Code includes political groups as possible targets of genocide and the country's former president was charged as such for his role in the so-called 'Red Terror' campaign between 1977 and 1978.[68]

17.7.2   Crimes against Humanity

Although references to 'laws of humanity' existed prior to World War II,[69] crimes against humanity as an international crime appeared in the aftermath of that war in article 6(c) of the Charter of the Nuremberg Tribunal of 1945. The rationale for formulating this particular offence was the absence in international law of an offence encompassing crimes against one's own population. As a result, Nazi atrocities against German Jews and other civilians could only be prosecuted as individual or collective offences under German criminal law. This outcome, however, would have been absurd given that the Holocaust was much more than simply the accumulation of multiple offences and could not in any way be left to the devices of ordinary criminal law.

Unlike genocide, which developed through a treaty, until the adoption of the ICC Statute in 1998, crimes against humanity were largely the product of customary international law. As a result, there are notable definitional discrepancies in the statutes of the Nuremberg, ICTY, ICTR and ICC tribunals. The majority of these are clearly contextual and nothing more than political compromises, but customary law in this field evolved so rapidly in the 1990s that by the end of that decade, and following the adoption of the ICC Statute, we now have a very clear idea of the elements of this international offence. For example, while a link to an armed conflict was required in the ICTY Statute, this is not the case under customary law. As a result, a crime against humanity may be defined as an attack against any civilian population, in

---

[67] The relevant passages are cited in *Jorgić* v. *Germany* (ECtHR) (2008) paras. 18, 23, 27, 36.

[68] *Special Prosecutor* v. *Mengistu Hailemariam and Others* (Ethiopia) (2006). See F. K. Tiba, 'The Mengistu Genocide Trial in Ethiopia' (2007) 5 *Journal of International Criminal Justice* 513.

[69] See I. Bantekas, *International Criminal Law*, 4th edn (Hart, 2010) 185–6.

situations where the attack is widespread or systematic and the perpetrator has knowledge of the attack.[70]

The concept of *attack* presupposes a number of underlying offences (killing, enforced disappearance, rapes etc.) which, taken as a whole, give form and existence to an organisational policy against a targeted civilian group. Whereas each underlying offence would individually amount to a war crime or other offence, taken cumulatively they give rise to an 'attack'. The various crimes which comprise the attack need not be perpetrated at the same time or place. An individual offence, irrespective of its gravity, does not amount to a crime against humanity if it is not connected to an ongoing 'attack' in the manner described. It is notable that serious human rights violations, such as enforced disappearance and rape (as a weapon of war) are now not only considered international crimes, but may constitute grounds for the existence of an 'attack'.[71]

The concept of 'civilian population' is much broader than the four groups enumerated in the Genocide Convention. It is even broader than the concept of civilian populations as these are understood in the 1949 Geneva Convention IV. It 'may also encompass situations of mistreatment of persons taking no active part in hostilities, such as those held in detention'.[72] The *Kunarac* Appeals judgment held that:

the use of the word 'population' does not mean that the entire population of the geographical entity in which the attack is taking place must have been subjected to that attack. It is sufficient to show that enough individuals were targeted in the course of the attack, or that they were targeted in such a way as to satisfy the Chamber that the attack was in fact directed against a civilian 'population', rather than against a limited and randomly selected number of individuals.[73]

Quite clearly, any group not encompassed under the Genocide Convention could be the subject of a crime against humanity. It is important that there is no need to demonstrate any particular group characteristics (unlike genocide) as long as the group enjoys civilian status.

The 'systematic' element of crimes against humanity does not require an expressly declared plan or an official state policy, and in any event it is now well-recognised that such crimes may be perpetrated by non-state entities.[74] The *Blaškić* Trial Chamber accepted that the term 'systematic' requires the

---

[70] Art. 7(1) ICC Statute.   [71] See art. 7(2)(i) and (1)(g) ICC Statute.

[72] *ICTY Prosecutor* v. *Kunarac and Others* (ICTY) (2001) para. 416.

[73] *ICTY Prosecutor* v. *Kunarac and Others* (ICTY) (2002) para. 63.

[74] *ICTR* v. *Kaiyshema and Ruzindana*, para. 125; *ICC Prosecutor* v. *Ruto and Others (Situation in the Republic of Kenya)* (ICC) (2012) paras. 184ff.

following ingredients: (1) the existence of a political objective, a plan pursuant to which the attack is perpetrated or an ideology that aims to destroy, persecute or weaken a community; (2) the perpetration of a crime on a large scale against a civilian group, or the repeated and continuous commission of inhumane acts linked to one another; (3) the perpetration and use of significant public or private resources, whether military or other; and (4) the implication of high-level political and/or military authorities in the definition and establishment of the plan.[75] The 'widespread' element is easier to substantiate as it refers to the scale of the crimes and the number of victims. The *Akayesu* judgment defined the widespread element as 'massive, frequent, large-scale action, carried out collectively with considerable seriousness and directed against a multiplicity of victims'.[76]

Individual liability for crimes against humanity arises not merely where a person commits crimes on a widespread or systematic scale. Rather, it is required that the perpetrator have knowledge of the 'overall context' within which an underlying crime is committed, combined with an intention to contribute to the overall context (i.e. the attack against a civilian population) through the underlying crime.

It is evident that the prosecution of crimes against humanity constitutes a mechanism that is complementary to existing non-punitive processes whose aim is to respond to massive human rights violations. A mechanism of this nature is the revamped ECOSOC 1503 procedure, which is examined elsewhere.[77] It should be noted that the International Law Commission (ILC) has appointed a Special Rapporteur in order to set out a comprehensive treaty on crimes against humanity.

QUESTIONS

1. What is the underlying rationale for the construction of genocide and crimes against humanity given that they ultimately encompass a number of other discrete international crimes?

2. What are the essential arguments in favour and against the peace argument which rejects the existence of parallel (and independent) prosecution of those involved in peace negotiations?

3. Why is the AU hostile to the application of universal jurisdiction against people for whom there exists clear evidence of gross human rights violations?

---

[75] *ICTY Prosecutor* v. *Blaškić* (ICTY) (2000) para. 580.
[76] *ICTR Prosecutor* v. *Akayesu*, para. 580.   [77] See Chapter 4.3.2.

17.8   THE PLACE OF IMMUNITIES IN HUMAN RIGHTS AND INTERNATIONAL CRIMINAL JUSTICE

Once an international crime is committed the perpetrator incurs international criminal liability. The courts will then assess whether any particular defences are applicable, such as duress or self-defence. If so, while the criminal conduct will still be attributable to the perpetrator, his or her liability will either be extinguished or mitigated (for ever). This is the legal effect of a valid defence. Where the perpetrator, however, invokes immunity, such a plea, if successful, does not serve to mitigate or extinguish liability. Rather, liability remains but is simply frozen in time until the perpetrator's immunity disappears or is otherwise revoked. An immunity plea is not therefore a defence but merely a procedural bar to the jurisdiction of the competent court(s). For the purposes of this chapter, two types of crime-related immunities are distinguished: (1) functional (*ratione materiae*), whose aim is to shield the particular (state) act and hence it is only coincidental that the physical perpetrator is also shielded; and (2) personal (*ratione personae*), whereby the immunity is afforded directly and specifically to the particular individual because of his or her person. Personal immunities are limited and pertain only to a small group of persons, namely serving heads of state, heads of government, foreign ministers and diplomats. In equal measure, functional immunities attach only to state (public) acts, thus excluding conduct personally attributable to the doer alone, such as rape.

Clearly, the privilege of immunity may well be abused by those in power, who view it as a tool for evading liability and living a life of impunity. On the other hand, it is undoubted that without the privilege of immunity state officials would be disinclined to travel abroad and conduct international relations if they feared arrest and prosecution by their enemies, or at the instigation of civil society. While immunities constitute a procedural bar to prosecution only before national courts – hence the creators of international tribunals typically remove immunities from their ambit – there is still some unease in respect of heinous criminal conduct and the reverential treatment afforded to the perpetrators on the basis of their immunity.

In the *Pinochet* case, the accused was a former dictator of Chile, whose brutal regime eliminated many of its political opponents through murders, torture and enforced disappearances. He resigned from power under condition that he not be prosecuted by the succeeding political powers of Chile. In the late 1990s he arrived in the UK for medical treatment and this sufficed for a Spanish prosecutor to request his extradition to Spain under several strands, one being that Pinochet had ordered the killing of a number of Spanish nationals during his presidency and the torture of political opponents. Hence Spain relied on passive personality-based and universal jurisdiction. In order for extradition to take place, however, the offences for which the request is made must concern prosecutable offences (of similar gravity) in both the requesting and requested states. The majority of the House of Lords took a very cautious approach to the issue of criminal liability, but its judgment is considered a referential affirmation on the status of immunities from criminal prosecution. It was held that torture under international law became a crime in the UK legal order in 1988 when CAT was incorporated by law. Hence Pinochet's liability for acts of torture, if any, would have to be assessed for conduct perpetrated from 1988 onwards. This limitation was unnecessarily strict, given that torture was already a crime under international law even before CAT came into force. Be that as it may, the real challenge for the House of Lords concerned the immunity of the accused. It correctly found that serving heads of state enjoy personal immunity (*ratione personae*) and may not be prosecuted before national courts while they are in office, irrespective of the gravity of the offence for which they are accused. When, however, they no longer occupy that office their immunity is lifted and they may be tried for crimes committed while they were in office as well as any other period before or after. As regards the crime of torture, Pinochet therefore could only be prosecuted for acts perpetrated after 1988. Ultimately, as a result of poor health it was decided that his extradition should be abandoned on humanitarian grounds.

One should contrast the *Pinochet* case with the indictment and prosecution of heads of state before international tribunals such as the ICTY and ICC. Immunities, both functional and personal, were developed to operate as procedural bars to prosecution before national courts. This means that states may through treaty or (subsequent) customary law remove immunities in other contexts or in ad hoc situations. A characteristic example of a treaty-based immunity waiver is article 27 of the Rome Statute of the ICC, which explicitly provides that the Statute applies equally to all persons without distinction based on their official capacity. Equally, the UNSC possesses power under chapter VII of the UN Charter (as a matter of treaty law) to suspend a person's immunities by conferring jurisdiction to an ad hoc tribunal (such as the ICTY) or the ICC. Many of the defendants in the ICTY held high-ranking military and political posts, and several heads of state were encompassed in situations referred to the ICC by the UNSC. As a result of resolution 1593, the ICC Prosecutor issued an indictment against the then Sudanese President, Al-Bashir, for his role in the Darfur crisis.[78] The fact that Sudan never ratified the ICC Statute is irrelevant, since the ICC Statute grants the Council authority to refer a situation (although the Council could just as well have created its own ad hoc tribunal, which would have equally removed all immunities from those indicted and prosecuted).

[78] UNSC resolution 1593 (31 March 2005).

FURTHER READING

Akande, D., 'The Legal Nature of Security Council Referrals to the ICC and its Impact on Al-Bashir's Immunities' (2009) 7 *Journal of International Criminal Justice* 333.

Bass, G. J., *Stay the Hand of Vengeance: The Politics of War Crimes Tribunals* (Princeton University Press, 2002).

Cassese, A., 'The Legitimacy of International Criminal Tribunals and the Current Prospects of International Criminal Justice' (2012) 25 *Leiden Journal of International Law* 491.

Cryer, R., D. Robinson and S. Vasiliev, *Introduction to International Criminal Law and Procedure*, 4th edn (Cambridge University Press, 2019).

Fichtelberg, A., 'Democratic Legitimacy and the International Criminal Court: A Liberal Defence' (2006) 4 *Journal of International Criminal Justice* 765.

Glasius, M., 'Do International Criminal Courts Require Democratic Legitimacy?' (2012) 23 *European Journal of International Law* 43.

Kersten, M., *Justice in Conflict: The Effects of the International Criminal Court's Interventions in Ending Wars and Building Peace* (Oxford University Press, 2016).

Langer, M., 'The Diplomacy of Universal Jurisdiction: The Political Branches and the Transnational Prosecution of International Crimes' (2011) 105 *American Journal of International Law* 1.

Minow, M., *Between Vengeance and Forgiveness: Facing History after Genocide and Mass Violence* (Beacon Press, 2000).

Nouwen, S. M., *Complementarity in the Line of Fire: The Catalyzing Effect of the International Criminal Court in Uganda and Sudan* (Cambridge University Press, 2013).

O'Keefe, R., *International Criminal Law*, 2nd edn (Oxford University Press, 2017).

Simpson, G. J., *Law, War and Crime: War Crimes Trials and the Reinvention of International Law* (Polity Press, 2007).

Sliedregt, E., and S. Vasiliev, *Pluralism in International Criminal Law* (Oxford University Press, 2014).

Websites

Impunity Watch: www.impunitywatch.org

International Criminal Court: www.icc-cpi.int/Pages/default.aspx

International Criminal Tribunal for the former Yugoslavia: www.icty.org/

Project on International Courts and Tribunals: www.pict-pcti.org/

Trial: Track Impunity Always: www.trial-ch.org/en/

UN Mechanism for International Criminal Tribunals: www.unmict.org/

18 Human Rights and Counter-terrorism

CONTENTS

18.1 INTRODUCTION

The purpose of this chapter is not to describe the terrorist phenomenon, but rather to analyse the range of responses to it and their compliance with human rights law. This analysis necessarily takes into consideration the legal nature of terrorism under international law and its rapid transformations in the aftermath of the terrorist attacks against the United States (US) on 11 September 2001 (9/11). It is as a direct result of this transformation that the international legal framework on terrorism gave way to a model whose chief proponents endeavoured to locate it as far as possible beyond the ambit of the rule of law and the reach of the judiciary. Although this position was essentially posited by the direct victim of the 9/11 attacks, the USA, it was also widely shared by other nations, democratic and otherwise. The subsequent practice of these nations has given rise to a barrage of litigation worldwide and the submission of reports by United Nations (UN) rapporteurs and non-governmental organisations (NGOs) condemning the limitation and outright violation of human rights under the guise of counter-terrorism. The essential nature of the argument between the two sides may be expressed with the following question. Does the real and imminent threat posed by terrorism justify exceptional measures the effect of which is to deny fundamental rights to suspected terrorists? The answer to this question is not a simple one. No doubt governments, whether unilaterally or jointly, must take appropriate intelligence and law-enforcement measures in order to protect their people.[1] The clandestine nature of terrorism renders this task all the more difficult. Yet if, in the name of counter-terrorism, states are allowed to violate fundamental human rights, such impunity can turn out to pose a larger risk for all peoples, especially long-term, than the terrorists themselves. Although the terrorist phenomenon is a real challenge to our established perceptions of justice and rights, one has to think of the adverse consequences to organised society of an exceptional deviation of the treatment that should otherwise be afforded to terrorist suspects. Will an executive accustomed to power abuse give up this arbitrary authority lightly? What guarantees are there that the pursuit of terrorists and the subsequent limitation to rights will not become a permanent feature of legal systems? How can one be sure that governments will not extend this authority over their personal enemies and against innocent persons?

This chapter seeks to demonstrate, among other things, that these dangers to personal liberty far outweigh the threats to human safety posed by serious 'terrorist' threats. The reader will acquire an appreciation of the obligation of states to protect their citizens from terrorism, including the debate as to whether terrorists possess human rights obligations. We shall then proceed to examine the most pertinent human rights violations in counter-terrorist operations. These include the application of the principle of legality to terrorist legislation, the permissibility of relevant derogations, the right to life and the practice of targeted killings, the various contours of unlawful detention against terrorist suspects, torture and ill-treatment in order

---

[1] In exceptional circumstances, nations may decide to negotiate with 'terrorist organisations' for the benefit of civilian populations. Following the failure of the Pakistan army to defeat an eighteen-month Taliban insurgency into the country's Swat valley, it signed a peace accord with the insurgents according to which the Taliban would be free to impose Islamic law in exchange for peace. Report of the Special Rapporteur on the promotion and protection of human rights and fundamental freedoms while countering terrorism, UN doc. A/64/211 (3 August 2009) para. 36.

to gather intelligence information and promote confessions, and finally the practice of abductions, unlawful extraditions and illegal rendition. To be sure, counter-terrorist operations have been found to infringe a range of other civil and political rights, such as the freedom of expression and the right to a fair trial.[2] In some instances, such operations have been deemed as compromising economic and social rights.[3] However, it would go beyond the purpose of this chapter to examine in detail all of these violations.

18.2   THE LEGAL NATURE OF TERRORISM

Two myths underpin the international legal framework on terrorism: the first is that as an international crime it lacks a globally agreed definition, while the second is that all counter-terrorist efforts have always been unconcerned with the underlying causes of terrorism. As to the former, it is true that international efforts to suppress terrorism from the early 1960s to the present day have focused on the elaboration of discrete anti-terrorist treaties, each dealing with a particular manifestation of this phenomenon. By way of illustration, the 1963 Tokyo Convention on Offences and Certain Other Acts Committed On Board Aircraft is concerned with conduct jeopardising the safety of aircraft and persons on board. In the same manner, the 1998 Convention for the Suppression of Terrorist Bombings, the 1999 Convention on the Financing of International Terrorism and the 2005 Convention on the Suppression of Acts of Nuclear Terrorism, among others, do not address terrorism holistically but deal with distinct thematic issues. The reason behind this thematic (or sectoral) approach is not that states fundamentally disagree on the range of criminal conduct that amounts to terrorism. Rather, intractable differences have always arisen in ascribing the terrorist designation to

---

[2] In *Kadi and Al Barakaat International Foundation* v. *Council of the European Union* (CJEU) (2008) paras. 335–7, at 349, the Court of Justice of the European Union (CJEU) held that the imposition of targeted sanctions (freezing orders in the case at hand) against a suspected terrorist by the European Union (EU), without any remedy whatsoever in the form of judicial review or a hearing, violated the right of effective judicial protection; equally, in *A and Others*, v. *HM Treasury* (UK) (2008).

[3] In another case, the EU had implemented a freezing order against the assets of the family of a listed terrorist, which included social security benefits intended solely for meeting the family's basic needs. The CJEU rejected the application of the freezing order to such payments simply because the spouse may have been able to use some of those payments and therefore gain some benefit: Case C-340/08, *M and Others* v. *HM Treasury* (CJEU) (2010). The ICJ equally confirmed in its *Legal Consequences of the Construction of a Wall in the Occupied Palestinian Territory* advisory opinion (ICJ) (2004) para. 134, that one of the side effects of the construction of the wall, even for alleged counter-terrorism purposes, was the violation of the economic rights of the Palestinians because they had no access to work.

national liberation movements and in describing state violence as terrorist, and therefore as criminal under international law. Although few, if any, states openly argue that national liberation movements fighting against alien domination and foreign occupation in their pursuit of self-determination are prevented under international law from employing violence, interested states generally refute the accusation that they are suppressing legitimate self-determination claims and therefore have no qualms about branding all pertinent violence as generally criminal or terrorist.[4] Equally, no government has ever admitted to being a state sponsor of clandestine acts of violence against its civilian population, yet many developed nations routinely engage in illicit practices such as administrative detention, kidnappings of suspects, illegal renditions to third countries, targeted killings, torture and other violations of human rights and humanitarian law. Clearly, although all of these practices are contrary to fundamental human rights, states are understandably reluctant to admit them, let alone describe the relevant conduct as criminal.

Despite deeply entrenched legal disagreements, which have precluded the conclusion of a comprehensive treaty definition of terrorism, there is broad consensus as to the constituent elements of this offence. While states largely converge on the elements of a definition, they are divided regarding the contextual issues identified above.[5] The essential elements of the offence were aptly described in the UN General Assembly's (UNGA) 1994 Declaration on Measures to Eliminate International Terrorism, as follows:

criminal acts intended or calculated to provoke a state of terror in the general public, a group of persons or particular persons for political purposes [and that such acts] are in any circumstances unjustifiable, whatever the considerations of a political, philosophical, ideological, racial, ethnic, religious or other nature that may be invoked to justify them.[6]

These three elements, namely (1) the perpetration of serious criminal acts; (2) the intention to inflict terror on civilian populations, with the further aim of (3) compelling governments to do or abstain from doing any act,

---

[4] See UN Report of the High-level Panel on threats, challenges and change, UN doc. A/59/565 (2 December 2004) paras. 159–60, which emphasises that the lack of a comprehensive definition has embarrassingly stumbled on the lack of regulation of states' use of force against civilians and on divergences as to whether the right to resistance against an occupying power should be overridden in the context of a possible definition of terrorism.

[5] See e.g., *Al-Sirri* v. *Secretary of State for the Home Dept* (UK) (2013) para. 37, admitting the absence of a definition of terrorism under international law; *R* v. *Gul* (*Appellant*) (UK) (2013) paras. 44ff., which argued that there is no concrete general understanding that terrorism does not extend to the acts of insurgents in non-international armed conflicts.

[6] UNGA resolution 49/60 (9 December 1994).

have been given universal acceptance by the UN Security Council (UNSC) in the aftermath of the 9/11 terrorist attacks against the USA.[7] This definition is consistent with relevant domestic legislation in most states and may therefore constitute a general principle of law.[8] In this sense, terrorism is an aggravated form of the principal offence (i.e. murder and grievous bodily harm) coupled with a further specific intent (i.e. to compel governments and to terrorise civilian populations).

18.3   THE DISCUSSION ON UNDERLYING OR ROOT CAUSES

By the early 1970s the UNGA had become dominated by former colonial entities and the Western bloc was no longer in the driving seat of developments. During this time it was common for the Assembly to demonise South Africa and Israel (for different reasons), at a time when the Palestinian cause and the Palestinian Liberation Organization (PLO) were exerting a significant degree of influence on the so-called non-aligned movement. The Assembly decided to examine the issue of terrorism more closely and appointed an ad hoc committee for this purpose,[9] which met three times between 1972 and 1979. During that time, developing nations argued that terrorism should be examined from its root causes, such as racism, colonialism, occupation and apartheid, and that it should not be differentiated from action undertaken by national liberation movements. A parallel development, largely sponsored by Arab and developing states between 1972 and 1989, was initiated by the then UN Secretary-General Kurt Waldheim, whereby terrorism was discussed on an annual basis. The unduly long title of this annual meeting was 'Measures to prevent international terrorism which endangers or takes innocent human lives or jeopardises fundamental freedoms, and study of the underlying causes of those forms of terrorism and acts of violence which lie in misery, frustration, grievance and despair and which cause some people to sacrifice human lives, including their own, in an attempt to effect radical

---

[7] UNSC resolution 1566 (8 October 2004); UNSC resolution 1624 (14 September 2005); High-level Panel Report, above note 4, para. 164. The Special Tribunal for Lebanon (STL) adopted an interlocutory decision on the *Applicable Law: Terrorism, Conspiracy, Homicide, Perpetration, Cumulative Charging* (STL) (2011) para. 85, which claimed that these elements constitute the customary definition of terrorism under international law. This decision has been fiercely criticised on several grounds. See B. Saul, 'Legislating from a Radical Hague: The United Nations Special Tribunal for Lebanon Invents an International Crime of Transnational Terrorism' (2011) 24 *Leiden Journal of International Law* 677.

[8] See *R* v. *F* (UK) (2007) paras. 26–7, 29; *Madan Singh* v. *State of Bihar* (UK) (2004).

[9] UNGA resolution 3034 (XXVII) (18 September 1972).

changes'.[10] Its sponsors were clearly of the opinion that terrorism did not comprise mere acts of random violence but was connected to other fundamental root causes. This, no doubt, is a divisive matter that until recently was largely rejected by nations in the developed world. As a result, all of the post-1990 anti-terrorist international instruments have denied the application of ideological justifications to any forms of terrorist violence. This development had the effect of obliterating the so-called political offence exception to terrorism – this refers to conduct that would otherwise give rise to criminal liability had it not been committed on political grounds – which was prevalent in the 1970s and 1980s.[11]

For good reason, terrorist discourse by the states that have been targeted most since 9/11 is outright hostile to the idea that terrorism is somehow sustained by particular 'root causes' associated with the foreign policy of the target nations. Yet the majority of the members making up the UN accept that the lack of democratic governance, the absence of human rights and the rule of law are conducive to the spread of terrorism.[12] The UN Global Counter-Terrorism strategy produces an indicative list of these conducive causes, emphasising, however, that none of these justifies or excuses terrorism:

prolonged unresolved conflicts, dehumanisation of victims of terrorism in all its forms and manifestations, lack of the rule of law and violations of human rights, ethnic, national and religious discrimination, political exclusion, socio-economic marginalisation and lack of good governance.[13]

The need to promote good governance and human rights by the target states, as a direct corollary to their counter-terrorism strategies, was strongly highlighted in the report of the UN High-level Panel, which suggested that sole reliance on military, police and intelligence measures serves to:

[10] See I. Bantekas, *International Criminal Law* (Hart, 2010) 263–4.
[11] See e.g., UNSC resolution 1373 (28 September 2001) para. 2(e); art. 4(2) of the 2003 US–UK Extradition Treaty; art. 6 of the 1999 International Convention for the Suppression of the Financing of Terrorism.
[12] See UNSC resolution 2178 (24 September 2014), which speaks of 'underlying factors', such as radicalisation to terrorism, extremism, intolerance, economic development, social cohesion and inclusion (preamble). See also operative paras. 15–16. The preamble further states that respect for human rights and the rule of law 'are complementary and mutually reinforcing with effective counter-terrorism measures'; UNSC resolution 2171 (21 August 2014) speaks of 'root causes' of armed conflicts, emphasising the role of terrorism.
[13] UNGA resolution 60/288 (20 September 2006) Annex, 'UN Global Counter-terrorism Strategy: Plan of Action', section I. The link to poverty is made explicit by the reference to the Millennium Development Goals (MDGs) and the reaffirmation to eradicate poverty, promote sustained economic growth, social exclusion agendas (particularly youth unemployment), reduce marginalisation and 'the subsequent sense of victimisation that propels extremism and the recruitment of terrorists'.

alienate large parts of the world's population and thereby weaken the potential for collective action against terrorism. The crucial need, in relation to the states in the regions from which terrorists originate, is to address not only their capacity but their will to fight terror. To develop that will – with states drawing support rather than opposition from their own publics – requires a broader-based approach.

A thread that runs through all such concerns is the imperative to develop a global strategy of fighting terrorism that addresses root causes and strengthens responsible states and the rule of law and fundamental human rights.[14]

There is clear consensus therefore that the most significant root cause of modern, mass-scale terrorism is the absence of the rule of law and good governance, as well as opportunities for all (women, children, the underprivileged) in certain parts of the world, in addition to the incompatibility of counter-terrorism strategies with the fundamental standards of human rights.[15] It is impossible to win the hearts and minds of terrorist sympathisers by stamping on the very same rights violated by terrorists. What is significant from this examination is that the UN and the vast majority of its members have begun to view terrorism as a holistic phenomenon that should not be divorced from the causes that feed and sustain it, while at the same time recognising their own particular obligations, the non-fulfilment of which may constitute contributory causes. This, of course, does not mean that global anti-terrorist policy should be devoid of an effective system of prevention, sanctions and prosecution and even the use of force against entities such as Islamic State (IS).[16] Any discussion on root causes should not be directed at absolving the perpetrators of their heinous crimes or in any other way justifying their conduct; rather, its aim should be to adopt appropriate preventive policies.

At the close of this section, it should be stated that the UN's Global Anti-Terrorism Strategy is based on four pillars, which require states to adopt measures to: (1) address the conditions conducive to the spread of terrorism; (2) prevent and combat terrorism; (3) build states' capacity to prevent and combat terrorism and to strengthen the role of the United Nations system in

---

[14] High-level Panel Report, above note 4, paras. 147–8. The same conclusions were adopted in the 2002 Organization for Security and Cooperation in Europe (OSCE) Charter on Preventing and Combating Terrorism, para. 20.

[15] See UNSC resolution 1624; UN Secretary-General Report, Uniting against Terrorism: Recommendations for a Global Counter-terrorism Strategy, UN doc. A/60/825 (2006); UNSC resolution 2195 (19 December 2014), which considers several contributing causes, including the violation of the rights of women and children, the links between terrorism and organised crime, lack of burden-sharing and others.

[16] See e.g., UNSC resolution 2199 (12 February 2015), which recognises the importance of financial sanctions and the 'need for a comprehensive approach ... that integrates multilateral strategies with unilateral action'.

this regard; and (4) ensure respect for human rights for all and the rule of law as the fundamental basis of the fight against terrorism. By 2017, the coordination of the anti-terrorism work undertaken by a plethora of UN agencies had become a major challenge. Following a report in early 2017 by the UN Secretary-General,[17] the General Assembly soon after decided to consolidate the work of most UN agencies and bodies (but not all) under the newly established Office of Counter-Terrorism.[18]

18.4   THE OBLIGATION OF STATES TO PROTECT THEIR POPULATIONS FROM TERRORISM

The place of human rights in terrorist discourse is not obvious from the outset. Terrorism is a crime committed by private entities, as a result of which the culprits incur criminal liability. Consequently, the victims of terrorism are victims of (non-state) crime and not the subjects of human rights violations, because human rights violations are typically committed by state agents or persons acting in their name or on their behalf. Therefore, technically speaking, terrorism only engages the application of criminal law. Although this conclusion is consistent with the fundamental premises of human rights, it does not sit well with certain states and UN human rights bodies. Since the latter cannot argue that non-state actors are incumbent with human rights obligations under the relevant treaties, they contend instead that terrorists are responsible for the 'destruction' of human rights, as opposed to their 'violation', a term typically reserved for human rights infractions committed by state actors.[19] The practical effect of this distinction is limited. Yet it sends out the wrong message that the obligation to protect and promote human rights from terrorism is somehow not fully within the material capability of states. Turkey, for example, has repeatedly stated before international fora that the obligations contained in human rights instruments are also addressed to individuals and that terrorists violate rights in the same way as states.[20] In

---

[17] 'Capability of the United Nations system to assist Member States in implementing the United Nations Global Counter- Terrorism Strategy: Report of the Secretary-General', UN doc. A/71/858 (3 April 2017) paras. 63ff.

[18] UNGA resolution 71/291 (19 June 2017).

[19] UNGA resolution 48/122 (20 December 1993); UNGA resolution 49/185 (23 December 1994); UNGA resolution 50/186 (22 December 1995); UNGA resolution 51/210 (17 December 1996); UNGA resolution 52/133 (27 February 1997). This phraseology is justified by its authors on account of art. 5(1) ICCPR and art. 30 Universal Declaration of Human Rights (UDHR).

[20] UN Secretary-General, 'Report on Human Rights and Terrorism', UN doc. A/58/533 (24 October 2003) paras. 4–5.

practice, this 'destruction' of human rights by non-state actors is countered through the application of domestic and international criminal law, not by human rights law.[21] The remit of international criminal law suffices in order to prevent, suppress and prosecute terrorist attacks. Yet the trend does give rise to some concern, since it is echoed in the work of few intergovernmental bodies. The now-defunct Commission on Human Rights went beyond the 'destruction' terminology by expressing concerns 'at the gross violations of human rights committed by terrorists'.[22]

Since the state is not accused of having committed, or assisted, in the perpetration of the terrorist act, it would ordinarily bear no responsibility in respect of it. Moreover, on the basis of the argument that terrorists violate or destroy human rights, the stage may be set for some states to contend that human rights law does not impose a positive burden upon them to avert terrorist attacks or prosecute the culprits, thus admitting only a negative obligation regarding the right to life. This is clearly wrong and should never be supported. It may well lead to a claim that in order for a positive obligation of this nature to be assumed it is essential that suspected terrorists be ultimately stripped of their human rights altogether; hence, it may be used to justify extrajudicial killings, among others.

This argument is flawed. The jurisprudence of international human rights treaty bodies suggests that states are under a positive obligation to protect their citizens' right to life when threatened by terrorist or other violence committed by private actors, as long as the risk is immediate and the authorities knew or ought to have known about it.[23]

This positive duty arising from the threat or infliction of serious crime, including terrorism, extends far beyond a mere obligation to protect one from a known imminent risk, encompassing moreover a duty to investigate, prosecute and provide remedies to the victims and their families.[24] It

---

[21] Report of the Special Rapporteur on the promotion and protection of human rights and fundamental freedoms while countering terrorism, UN doc. E/CN.4/2006/98 (28 December 2005) para. 69.

[22] Resolution 2004/44, preamble. It is a fallacy that the ECtHR supports this line of argument. In *A* v. *United Kingdom* (ECtHR) (1999) para. 22, it did not intimate that individuals could violate the rights enshrined in the Convention. Rather, it emphasised that states are under a duty to ensure that no one within their jurisdiction is subjected to ill-treatment by private individuals.

[23] See *Osman* v. *United Kingdom* (ECtHR) (1998) paras. 115–16; see also *Kiliç* v. *Turkey* (ECtHR) (2000) para. 62; *Neira Alegría* v. *Peru* (IACtHR) (1996) para. 75; HRCtee, General Comment 31, UN doc. CCPR/C/21/Rev.1/Add. 13 (26 March 2004) para. 8.

[24] See *Oliveira* v. *Brazil* (IACHR) (2010) paras. 82ff., where the IACHR held that Brazil had violated its obligation to protect the right to life by ignoring death threats against a journalist in Bahia, a region plagued by assassinations against people of that profession. This liability was further exacerbated by the lack of a thorough investigation.

is exactly because of this positive obligation that states have been granted exceptional powers in their struggle against international terrorism,[25] including the power to employ lethal force under certain circumstances.

CASE STUDY 18.1
Finogenov and *Chernetsova* v. *Russia*: European Court of Human Rights Admissibility Decision of 18 March 2010

On 23 October 2002 a group of Chechen terrorists took hold of the Dubrovka Theatre in Moscow and held more than 900 people captive and at gunpoint for three days. The terrorists had managed to booby-trap the building and moreover positioned eighteen suicide bombers among the hostages in order to prevent the authorities from staging a counter-attack. The terrorists demanded the withdrawal of Russian troops from Chechen territory and demonstrated their resolve by killing those hostages who resisted or attempted to escape. Three days later the Russian security forces mounted an armed operation, which involved pumping an unknown gas into the building's ventilation system which resulted in the loss of consciousness of both the terrorists and the hostages. Although the terrorist threat had seemingly been eliminated, it soon transpired that 129 hostages had also died as a result of the operation; 102 died on the spot because of the effects of the gas, including 3 who were shot, 21 died in the course of evacuation and transportation to hospital, while 6 people died subsequently in hospital. Two key questions arose in this connection: (1) whether Russia was responsible for not having foreseen the terrorist threat and subsequently for failing to take measures to protect the victims; and (2) whether the counter-terrorism operation in the theatre failed to respect the right to life of the hostages. The admissibility decision answered the first question in the negative, as follows:

173. The Court notes that, indeed, article 2(1) [right to life] enjoins the state not only to refrain from the intentional and unlawful taking of life, but also to take appropriate steps to safeguard the lives of those within its jurisdiction … However, this obligation is not unqualified. Thus, the first sentence of article 2 of the Convention, states that everyone's right to life 'shall be protected by law'. The applicants did not suggest that the state had not complied with its general duty to secure the right to life by putting in place criminal law provisions to deter the commission of terrorist acts, backed by law-enforcement machinery … As to more concrete measures which would possibly have prevented the hostage-taking, the Court reiterates that not every presumed threat to life obliges the authorities to

---

[25] Council of Europe (CoE), 'Guidelines on Human Rights and the Fight Against Terrorism' (11 July 2002) Guideline I.

take concrete measures to avoid the risk. A duty to take specific preventive action … arises only if the authorities knew or ought to have known at the time of the existence of a real and immediate risk to the life of an individual or individuals … This element is absent in the present case. There is no evidence that the authorities had any specific information about the hostage-taking being prepared.

The second question was answered in late 2011 by the Court. It held that given the seriousness of the situation at the time, the hardened resolve of the terrorists and the need for immediate action, the Russian authorities were justified in using force even though this was likely to culminate, and indeed did culminate, in civilian casualties.[1] Thus, the storming of the building itself did not violate the right to life of the hostages. Even the use of the lethal gas was not a disproportionate measure because the authorities intended the incapacitation of the terrorists, not the killing of hostages, despite some obvious risks to those with ill health.[2] In terms of the ensuing rescue and evacuation operation, however, the Court held that it was inadequately prepared, 'in particular because of the inadequate information exchange between various services, belated beginning of the evacuation, limited on-the-field coordination of various services, lack of appropriate medical treatment and equipment on the spot, and inadequate logistics'. These were found to have breached Russia's obligations under the right to life.[3] The ECtHR addressed the positive obligations of states in respect of mass terrorist operations, with Russia again as the focal point. In the Beslan incident, a school had been besieged by a group of 50 heavily armed terrorists. In the exchange of fire between security forces and the terrorists, over 330 people lost their lives, of which 180 were children. The Court held that Russian authorities failed in at least two respects. First, they had ample information of the impending attack and yet took no measures to adequately prevent it or alert the local population. Secondly, the use of force applied was grossly disproportionate, which included the use of tank cannons, grenade launchers and other heavy fire, which was a significant contributor to the many casualties.[4]

---

[1] *Finogenov and Others* v. *Russia* (ECtHR) (2011) paras. 213, 221, 226.
[2] Ibid., paras. 227–36.
[3] Ibid., paras. 263–6.
[4] *Tagayeva and Others* v. *Russia* (ECtHR) (2017).

QUESTIONS

1. If terrorists are capable of committing human rights violations by reason of acts that constitute terrorism, then the obligations addressed in human rights treaties are also addressed to them. Discuss.

2. A group uses violence even against civilians, claiming to reverse the acute and long-standing poverty of a population that has been financially exploited by a rich third nation under the corrupt acquiescence of the home state. Is violence justified in order to realise this cause? Are the 'root causes' of the violence significant in human rights and international law discourse and decision-making?

3. Under what circumstances does a state violate its human rights obligations by failing to prevent or punish those responsible for terrorist attacks?

4. In defusing serious terrorist threats states must sometimes accept heavy collateral civilian casualties in the course of their counter-terrorism operations. This is justified in order to save thousands of other lives. Discuss the moral and legal premise of this proposition.

18.5   HUMAN RIGHTS IN COUNTER-TERRORISM OPERATIONS

Given that states are responsible for protecting their populations from terrorist violence, they must necessarily enjoy the right to respond to such violence in an effective and deterrent manner. While it is true that terrorism poses a severe threat to human safety, the unchallenged authority of the state to employ armed force and limit civil liberties against those whom it deems terrorists in the name of counter-terrorism risks eroding the rights of terrorists and non-terrorists alike. For, if the state possesses the unilateral power to abrogate the rights of alleged terrorists, this very designation of 'terrorist' will soon become an instrument of oppression against all its perceived enemies. In the 'War on Terror',[26] initiated by the USA following the events of 9/11, there have been far too many cases of persons unconnected to terrorism being abducted and brutally tortured by security forces because

---

[26] This expression was deliberately coined in an address by US President G. W. Bush to a joint session of Congress and the American people on 20 September 2001, in which he declared that 'our war on terror begins with Al-Qaeda, but it does not end there. It will not end until every terrorist group of global reach has been found, stopped and defeated.' See online at www.theguardian.com/world/2001/sep/21/september11.usa13.

of suspicions or wrong information suggesting a terrorist link.[27] It is not only the 'innocent' that warrant protection from the excesses of government. Societies claiming to be grounded in the rule of law should not distinguish between the 'innocent' and the 'guilty' in order to assess whether a person deserves to enjoy human rights. Human rights pertain to all persons, irrespective of whether their conduct is reprehensible to the vast majority of society. Thus, the ill-treatment of suspected terrorists in secret detention merits an effective investigation in the same manner as if the ill-treatment was meted out to non-terrorists.[28] The observance of human rights and the rule of law against all persons not only ensures the objectivity of the application of law, but also diminishes any calls for the justification of terrorist violence by potential sympathisers and equally avoids the glorification of terrorists as martyrs.

During the 'War on Terror' many, if not most, participating states violated the rights of suspected terrorists in two ways: through clandestine acts, such as secret abductions and the use of secret torture locations; or by an intentionally erroneous interpretation of human rights law in order to suit their purposes, as was the case with the US denial of habeas corpus rights to Guantánamo detainees – or other US-held detainees around the world – on the basis that they were outside the ambit of US federal laws, in addition to being unlawful combatants.[29] It is evident, therefore, that states are prepared to overtly violate human rights in the face of extreme terrorist violence. In the aftermath of 9/11, the invasion of Afghanistan and Iraq and the incommunicado detention of large numbers of suspects gave rise to fears that the 'War on Terror' would be fought outside the international human rights framework.[30] This perception was soon quashed by the adoption of UNSC

---

[27] See *Al Rabiah* v. *United States* (US) (2009), where a Kuwaiti national was held at Guantánamo Bay by the US military under charges that he was an Al-Qaeda operative, despite the fact that the accused was quite obviously physically incapable of playing such a role. Under pressure from the weight of evidence the US government later dropped its case. The unauthorised and flawed nature of the CIA interrogation of alleged terrorists was also emphasised by the US Senate Select Committee on Intelligence, Study of the CIA Detention and Interrogation Program (2014) at 11. It found that its so-called enhanced interrogation techniques amounted to torture.

[28] *Extebarria Caballero* v. *Spain* (ECtHR) (2014).

[29] HRCtee, Concluding Observations on USA, UN doc. CCPR/C/USA/CO/3/Rev.1 (18 December 2006) para. 10, which criticised the USA's restrictive interpretation of its obligations under the ICCPR.

[30] The principal Council resolution related specifically to counter-terrorism in the aftermath of 9/11 was 1373. Although this did not make any reference to human rights, the HRCtee emphasised that resolution 1373 in no way justified human rights violations, including *refoulement* to countries where the accused risked being ill-treated. HRCtee, Concluding Observations on Lithuania, UN doc. CCPR/CO/80/LTU (4 May 2004) para. 7.

resolutions 1456[31] and 1624,[32] which stressed that any measure taken to combat terrorism must comply with international human rights law.[33]

The following sections will examine the limitations imposed by human rights law on select counter-terrorist operations.

18.5.1   Anti-terrorist Legislation and the Principle of Legality

The principle of legality is otherwise reflected in the Latin maxim *nullum crimen nulla poena sine lege scripta*. Although its original formulation was intended to prohibit retroactive criminal legislation, its contemporary meaning encompasses three other customary principles, which require: (1) the specificity of criminal rules; (2) the ban on analogy; and (3) interpretation of criminal rules in favour of the accused (when in doubt).[34] In the field of anti-terrorist legislation the lack of specificity is particularly acute. Specificity is generally satisfied 'where the individual can know from the wording of the relevant provision and, if need be, with the assistance of the court's interpretation of it, what acts and omissions will make him liable'.[35] This does not mean, however, that all criminal laws must explain in minute detail what conduct is expected. Legislative drafting of this nature would render criminal laws rigid and inflexible and incapable of responding to future social, economic and other developments. Moreover, if such rigid rules were construed restrictively, according to their letter alone, many forms of criminal conduct would escape liability because they would not exactly fit into the relevant definitions. At the other extreme, if criminal laws were excessively vague,[36] with a view to countering the problems of rigidity, they would afford great

---

[31] UNSC resolution 1456 (20 January 2003).

[32] UNSC resolution 1624 (14 September 2005); see also to the same effect, UNSC resolution 2178 (24 September 2014).

[33] Even as regards the listing of persons suspected of being associated with terrorism, the Council has adopted procedures whereby those believed to be erroneously listed can have recourse to grievance mechanisms. See UNSC resolution 1452 (20 December 2002) setting out humanitarian exemptions to freezing sanctions; UNSC 1904 (17 December 2009), establishing an ombudsperson; and UNSC resolution 2161 (17 June 2014) paras. 24ff., setting out the process for a fair and transparent listing and de-listing procedure.

[34] See Bantekas, above note 10, 21–8.

[35] *Kokkinakis* v. *Greece* (ECtHR) (1994) para. 52.

[36] In *Hashman and Harrup* v. *United Kingdom* (ECtHR) (2000), the applicants were activists who had disturbed a fox hunt and were subsequently handed with orders to keep the peace. The law upon which this penalty was imposed purported to criminalise behaviour that is 'wrong rather than right in the judgment of the majority of contemporary citizens'. In accepting that the applicants' freedom of expression had been violated the Court also ruled that this provision did not satisfy the standards set out by the rule of specificity.

latitude to judges and would ultimately offend the rule against the employment of analogies. Thus, a balance between the two extremes is necessary and legitimate.[37] A particular practice that has been found to violate legality is the issuance of post-sentence judicial determinations following the adoption of new case law, the effect of which is to prolong the convicted person's sentence or suspend his or her release.[38]

The Human Rights Committee (HRCtee) has routinely criticised numerous states for promulgating criminal legislation in which the definition of terrorism was deliberately vague or broad.[39] The purpose of such legislation (or its effect) is to permit unhindered recourse to emergency procedures, increase the risk of arbitrary detention and reduce the application of ordinary guarantees. In the case of Israeli anti-terrorist legislation the Committee was concerned that the law made no attempt to reduce delays before trial, remedy lack of access to legal counsel or reduce the possibility of judgments extending detention measures in the absence of the suspect.[40]

These vague and overly broad laws result in rendering terrorism a catch-all criminal offence that is subject to impermissible derogations by the state. Their nature allows the authorities to freely limit other economic and social rights that are seemingly unrelated to terrorism. In *Holder et al.* v. *Humanitarian Law Project et al.* the plaintiffs had sought to provide human rights training, advocacy and peacekeeping to the Kurdistan Workers' Party (PKK) in Turkey and the LTTE in Sri Lanka, both of which had already been designated terrorist organisations in the USA. Under a federal US statute it was a crime to 'knowingly provide material support or resources to a foreign terrorist organisation'.[41] The term 'material support' meant, among other things, 'training, expert advice or assistance'.[42] The US government construed the statute as prohibiting all types of training to designated terrorist organisations, including human rights training that is meant to promote non-violence within these organisations, the submission of an amicus brief in their favour by a lawyer, as well as helping a proscribed organisation to petition international bodies to end violent conflicts. The plaintiffs argued that

---

[37] *Kokkinakis* v. *Greece*, para. 40.

[38] *Del Rio Prada* v. *Spain* (ECtHR) (2013) paras. 51, 57, 59–64.

[39] See Concluding Observations on Israel, UN doc. CCPR/C/ISR/CO/3 (3 September 2010) para. 13; HRCtee, Concluding Observations on USA, para. 11, which noted that Executive Order 13224 (23 September 2001) – Blocking property and prohibiting transactions with persons who commit, threaten to commit, or support terrorism – extended the definition of terrorism to a broad range of conduct, including political dissent.

[40] Concluding Observations on Israel, ibid.; see also the HRCtee's Concluding Observations on the Russian Federation, UN doc. CCPR/C/RUS/CO/6 (24 November 2009) para. 7, which criticised the 2006 Terrorism Law on the same grounds, adding also that it places no limits on derogations and does not take into account the obligations imposed by art. 4 ICCPR.

[41] 18 USC §2339B(a)(1).   [42] Ibid., § 2339(B)(b)(1).

the statute was unnecessarily vague, thereby violating the Fifth Amendment to the US Constitution, which protects against abuse of government authority in a legal procedure. They also claimed a violation of the First Amendment, which protects the freedom of speech. The Supreme Court, however, with a majority of six to three, declared that the provision of intangibles such as human rights training allowed a proscribed organisation to free resources for other illegal purposes (fungibility), which it was in the interests of the executive to curtail. As a result, the prohibition of free speech was justified under the circumstances.[43]

This line of argumentation is certainly problematic, for it suggests that human rights are a weapon in the armoury of terrorists to which they should not have access. This reasoning is consistent with the US government's understanding of the concept of 'lawfare', which allows fringe groups to employ international law through local courts to discredit particular states. Human rights NGOs are at the centre of lawfare because it is believed that they do not simply provide human rights consultancy to proscribed organisations, but more significantly assist them in bringing lawsuits worldwide against government officials alleging the perpetration of international crimes.[44] A campaign by a number of NGOs is in place since 2002 to indict former US Secretary of Defense Donald Rumsfeld for torture inflicted against persons in the custody of the USA, following the revelation of the so-called torture memos in which he seems to have authorised illegal interrogation techniques. This campaign has been seeking Rumsfeld's criminal liability on the basis of universal jurisdiction through the courts of European states.[45]

18.5.2 Permissible Restrictions and Derogations Arising from Terrorist Threats

Every time an act of terrorism is perpetrated or a terrorist threat is revealed by the press or by a government, there is strong public demand to adopt timely and strict responses. It may be the case that a country's counter-terrorism legislation is inadequate to deal with the particularities of terrorist prosecution or that alternatively its intelligence has been poor and ineffective. Moreover, it may well transpire that certain modes of transport, such as air travel, have to be suspended in order to tighten controls over the imminent

---

[43] *Holder et al.* v. *Humanitarian Law Project et al.* (US) (2010).
[44] See T. Yin, 'Boumediene and Lawfare' (2009) 43 *University of Richmond Law Review* 865.
[45] K. Gallagher, 'Universal Jurisdiction in Practice: Efforts to Hold Donald Rumsfeld and Other High-level United States Officials Accountable for Torture' (2009) 7 *Journal of International Criminal Justice* 1087.

threat. Yet no matter what the terrorist threat may be, the ability of the state to suspend the application of human rights is certainly not unrestricted. Whereas states are permitted under particular circumstances to curtail the scope of particular rights, they are otherwise prohibited from suspending fundamental human rights, even in the face of an imminent emergency. Rights susceptible to such restrictions (otherwise known as qualified rights) include the freedom of expression[46] and the right of assembly[47] among others. Their restriction by the state is justified in those circumstances where their free exercise would be detrimental to the enjoyment of other rights.[48]

It may therefore make sense to prevent an organisation that supports terrorist causes from printing material that incites others to support such a cause, or exclude a political party that supports terrorism from enrolling in the political parties register, even if by doing so the right to freedom of expression and association are curtailed.[49] Equally, it is good law to restrict the circulation of pictures depicting the corpse of an assassinated politician, because the public interest in being informed does not, in the circumstances of the case, outweigh the emotional turbulence caused to the family of the deceased.[50] The state's ability to restrict this limited number of qualified rights further necessitates that any restriction conforms to the tests of legality, necessity, proportionality and non-discrimination. These concepts will be elaborated later in this chapter, but it suffices to say that what is necessary today may not be necessary tomorrow and that proportionality requires a delicate and objective balance of facts in any given case.

Human rights treaties further entitle states in times of emergency that threaten the life of a nation to suspend the application of certain rights altogether – and not simply to restrict them – through the process of *derogations*.[51] This, understandably, is an exceptional measure of last resort and is

---

[46] Art. 19(2) ICCPR.   [47] Art. 21 ICCPR.

[48] In *Öcalan* v. *Turkey (No. 2)* (ECtHR) (2014), the Court held that restrictions against the applicant's communication with the outside world were justified under art. 8 ECHR, considering the government's legitimate fear that such communication may become the platform for terrorist activity by the PKK; equally, in *Babar Ahmad and Others* v. *United Kingdom* (ECtHR) (2012) paras. 172–8 and 200ff., the ECtHR accepted that the surrender of several terrorist suspects to a super maximum security prison in the USA did not constitute inhuman and degrading treatment.

[49] *Herri Batasuna and Batasuna* v. *Spain* (ECtHR) (2009). The Court justified this restriction on the international desire to condemn the public defence of terrorism.

[50] *Hachette Filippachi Associés* v. *France* (ECtHR) (2009); even so, the wholesale suspension of an entire publication because it was alleged that it conducted propaganda in favour of a terror group, even briefly, was unjustifiable. See *Ürper and Others* v. *Turkey* (ECtHR) (2009).

inapplicable to fundamental rights, namely the right to life, protection from torture, inhuman and degrading treatment or punishment, protection from slavery and from retrospective criminal laws.[52] It would seem therefore that derogable rights can be suspended by the executive every time it declares a state of emergency; however, this is not the case. Although it is generally agreed that terrorism strains the capacity of the state to protect the right to life of its citizens and as a result specific limits on some guarantees are warranted, including those concerning detention and fair trial, this prerogative of the state is limited and should be narrowly construed.[53] Thus, the ability of a state to suspend particular rights depends on whether this is specifically permitted in a human rights treaty, as well as whether other rules of international law allow the suspension in question. By way of illustration, if a certain freedom is derogable under a human rights treaty, but the conduct implementing the derogation is considered an international crime, it is impermissible. The HRCtee, in its General Comment 29 (2001), provided the following illustrative examples:

(a) All persons deprived of their liberty shall be treated with humanity and with respect for the inherent dignity of the human person. Although this right, prescribed in article 10 ICCPR, is not separately mentioned in the list of non-derogable rights in article 4(2), the Committee believes that here the Covenant expresses a norm of general international law not subject to derogation. This is supported by the reference to the inherent dignity of the human person in the preamble to the Covenant and by the close connection between articles 7 and 10.

(b) The prohibitions against taking of hostages, abductions or unacknowledged detention are not subject to derogation. The absolute nature of these prohibitions, even in times of emergency, is justified by their status as norms of general international law.

...

(d) As confirmed by the Rome Statute of the International Criminal Court, the deportation or forcible transfer of a population without grounds permitted under international law, in the form of forced displacement by expulsion or other coercive means from the area in which the persons concerned are lawfully present, constitutes a crime against humanity.

---

[51] See R. Higgins, 'Derogations under Human Rights Treaties' (1976–1977) 48 *British Yearbook of International Law* 281, who argues that states enjoy a wide margin of appreciation in respect of characterising a situation as being one of emergency, whereas this discretion is narrow in relation to the applicable measures of necessity.

[52] Art. 4(2) ICCPR; art. 15(2) ECHR.

[53] Report of the UN Working Group on arbitrary detention, UN doc. E/CN.4/2004/3 (15 December 2003) para. 60.

> The legitimate right to derogate from article 12 of the Covenant during a state of emergency can never be accepted as justifying such measures.[54]

Much like the procedural guarantees required for the implementation of restrictions on rights, the same array of procedural safeguards must be put in place before a derogation issued by a state can take effect. The two most significant issues in counter-terrorist policies concern the verification and justification of the declared state of emergency and its adherence to general international law and human rights. In the *Lawless* case, the British government had set up a commission charged with special powers of arrest and detention against members of the outlawed Irish Republican Army (IRA) that was engaging in terrorist activities against British elements in Northern Ireland. The British government had duly notified the Council of Europe (CoE) of this exceptional measure, so when the accused was arrested and detained under powers of the commission it was questioned whether the derogation was actually necessary. The European Court of Human Rights (ECtHR) believed it to be necessary because under the circumstances at the time (i.e. late 1950s), the IRA and its splinter factions were operating throughout the country, were secretive and engaged in violent terrorist activities.[55] This public emergency justifying the imposition of a derogation need not necessarily materialise in the entirety of a country's territory; rather, as was evident in *Aksoy* v. *Turkey*, Turkey was able to substantiate the legality of restrictions against the right to liberty of alleged terrorists because of the extent and impact of PKK terrorist activity in south-east Turkey at the time of the complaint.[56]

What about the impact and duration of terrorism itself on the legitimacy of a derogation order? Unlike the parties to an armed conflict, the clash between a state and a terrorist organisation does not involve a constant, continuous, all-out war. In fact, the terrorists may just as well be satisfied if they are successful in instilling fear in the civilian population without any recourse to violence whatsoever, if in this manner many of their objectives are met. It is important therefore for a state to be able to take exceptional measures not only when a terrorist threat is present, but also when it is imminent.[57] Given that all the operations planned by organisations such as

---

[54] HRCtee, General Comment 29, UN doc. CCPR/C/21/Rev.1/Add.11 (31 August 2001) para. 13.

[55] *Lawless* v. *Ireland (No. 3)* (ECtHR) (1961) paras. 30–6.

[56] *Aksoy* v. *Turkey* (ECtHR) (1996) para. 70.

[57] *A and Others* v. *United Kingdom* (ECtHR) (2009) paras. 176–7. The Court noted that the requirement 'of imminence cannot be interpreted so narrowly as to require a state to wait for disaster to strike before taking measures to deal with it'; see E. Bates, 'A Public Emergency Threatening the Life of the Nation? The United Kingdom's Derogation of 18 December 2001 from the European Convention on Human Rights' (2005) 76 *British Yearbook of International Law* 245.

Al-Qaeda are part of a global network of terrorism that carries out violent activities when this is opportune, it may be said that as long as reliable intelligence is made available, a terrorist threat should be deemed to be imminent.

It has already been stated that the right to suspend particular rights should in no way be construed as providing a blank cheque to the executive. The exceptional measures taken in anticipation of a terrorist threat must be necessary, proportionate to the threat and consistent with general international law. In the *Aksoy* case the ECtHR was asked to assess whether the otherwise valid Turkish derogation against the prompt charging of detainees was lawful where the period of detention without judicial control was fourteen or more days. In an earlier judgment the Court had already observed that detention under these terms for a period of six days and four hours was unjustified because it left the accused not only vulnerable to arbitrary interference with his right to liberty, but also exposed him to torture.[58] Naturally, therefore, it was held that such a lengthy detention without recourse to judicial remedies was incompatible with the obligation of the state to prevent the infliction of torture and loss of the right to liberty.[59] States are not prevented from imposing lengthy detentions in pertinent circumstances. The ECtHR has consistently held that a lengthy detention imposed against a suspected terrorist is not indeterminate as long as a process of deportation has been put in place by the authorities; and therefore the accused has access to various remedies and the hope of ultimate release. As a result, a lengthy detention is arbitrary and therefore impermissible where its principal aim is simply to keep a dangerous suspect off the streets, and this is also true of the derogation that gives rise to it.[60] If the state considers someone as posing a terrorist threat it must compile the necessary evidence against that person before deciding to arrest and detain, provided of course that the evidence has not been procured by means of torture.[61]

18.6   THE RIGHT TO LIFE IN COUNTER-TERRORISM OPERATIONS

18.6.1   Situations when Lethal Force is Permissible

In late October 2010 confidential documents known as 'Iraq War Logs' were leaked by Wikileaks demonstrating that US military legal advisors in the Iraq campaign had advised aircrews that they were under no obligation to accept the surrender of enemy personnel (irrespective if they were designated

---

[58] *Brogan and Others* v. *United Kingdom* (ECtHR) (1988) para. 62.

[59] *Aksoy* v. *Turkey*, para. 78.

[60] *Chahal* v. *United Kingdom* (ECtHR) (1996) para. 113; *A and Others* v. *UK*, paras. 131 and 164ff.

[61] See *El Haski* v. *Belgium* (ECtHR) (2012).

terrorists or rebels). As a result, aircrews were at liberty to target and kill such persons. Despite the *lex specialis* character of international humanitarian law over human rights law,[62] there is nothing in that body of law that justifies the intentional killing of persons who are in the process of surrendering to their adversary. The rule against denial of quarter is absolute and the right to life guaranteed under this rule certainly cannot be construed narrowly on the basis of a technicality (i.e. the impractical dimension of surrender to an aircrew).[63] The matter is even more pertinent in the course of counter-terrorism, which does not involve a situation of armed conflict, and where therefore the absolute nature of the right to life should in theory be uncontested. It should be stated from the outset that it is false to assume that the positive obligation of the state to protect its citizens from the dangers of terrorism justifies in emergency situations the violation of rights, including the right to life.

If the right to life is absolute then any cases of lawful deprivation must apply to terrorists and non-terrorists alike. This suggests that irrespective of the security threat posed by suspected terrorists the authorities must first exhaust all means to arrest them before resorting to lethal force. This principle has been applied by the ECtHR since the McCann case[64] and also by the HRCtee. In *Guerrero* v. *Colombia* a guerrilla organisation had kidnapped a former ambassador who, according to intelligence reports, was kept at a house. Upon raiding the house and failing to retrieve the victim the security forces remained hidden in the house in wait for the occupants. When they eventually arrived they were shot at point-blank range although none of them was armed at the time. The Committee dismissed the government's argument that the taking of life was justified, arguing that:

the police action was apparently taken without warning to the victims and without giving them any opportunity to surrender to the police patrol or to offer any explanation of their presence or intentions. There is no evidence that the action of the police was necessary in their own defence or that of others, or that it was necessary to effect the arrest or prevent the escape of the persons concerned.[65]

Hence, when the authorities are capable of making an arrest, or otherwise incapacitating the accused, they are never justified in applying lethal force. Under

---

[62] See Chapter 16.4.

[63] Art. 23(d), Hague Regulations Respecting the Laws and Customs of War on Land 1907; art. 40 Protocol I (1977) to the 1949 Geneva Conventions; art. 8(2)(b)(xii) ICC Statute. In *Re Dostler* (WWII Military Commission) (1945) at 290, a US World War II military commission found that Hitler's Commando Order, which called for the extermination of all enemy commandos, was a war crime of this nature.

[64] *McCann and Others* v. *United Kingdom* (ECtHR) (1996) para. 200. For a fuller analysis see Chapter 8.2.4.

[65] *Camargo* v. *Colombia* (HRCtee) (1982) para. 14.3. The forensic reports showed that one of the female suspects was shot repeatedly after she had already died from a heart attack.

such circumstances the invocation of self-defence by the security forces is naturally implausible. In equal measure, when an arrest is impossible but the threat posed by the accused is not significant, the authorities are prohibited from violating the right to life because of its inherently disproportionate nature.[66]

Counter-terrorist operations may well involve situations where the suspected terrorists violently oppose their arrest. In such situations lethal force cannot be employed simply because the arrest is frustrated. Rather, suspects must be offered fair warning and ample opportunity to surrender before force can be used, and even so the force will be permissible only if the failure to arrest is absolutely necessary to avert the risk of terrorist killings. This test of absolute necessity is subject to a very high-threshold proportionality test. The European Commission of Human Rights deemed the test to have been satisfied in *Kelly* v. *United Kingdom*, which involved suspected IRA terrorists driving through a checkpoint without stopping, thus prompting the guards to shoot them. The Commission took into account the highly volatile climate in Northern Ireland at the time, holding that lethal force was justified because 'the kind of harm to be averted (as the soldiers reasonably thought) by preventing their escape was even greater, namely the freedom of terrorists to resume their dealing in death and destruction'.[67] This line of reasoning is somewhat problematic because it suggests that it is permissible to kill anyone suspected of being involved in terrorism who does not heed to a call for stop and search, on the vague ground that the suspect may or can commit terrorist acts in the future. Instead, it is better to argue that in exceptional cases of imminent terrorist threat the death of the suspect is permissible where he or she is in the process of avoiding arrest, if: (1) there is a very high likelihood that the suspect is about to engage in terrorist violence; or (2) where although the death caused was incidental to the force used (albeit probable under the circumstances), it was none the less justified because of the danger posed by the specific suspects.[68]

18.6.2   Targeted Killings and 'Shoot-to-kill' Strategies

The intentional killing of a suspected terrorist by secret agents would no doubt give rise to the liability of that state if arrest was in fact possible. What, however, if the suspect operates from the territory of a country that is

---

[66] See *Alejandre and Others* v. *Cuba (Brothers to the Rescue case)* (IACHR) (1999) paras. 37ff., which concerned the downing of a small civilian aircraft by Cuban authorities for allegedly having violated its airspace. See also *Nachova and Others* v. *Bulgaria* (ECtHR) (2006) para. 95, to the same effect.

[67] *Kelly* v. *UK* (ECtHR) (1993).

[68] See principle 9 of the UN Basic Principles on the use of force and firearms by law enforcement officials; UNGA resolution 45/166 (18 December 1999), which limits the

either supportive of terrorism, or which is otherwise reluctant to arrest and prosecute? In such situations the suspect poses a threat that is not susceptible to lawful arrest. The question then arises as to whether, since arrest is impossible, the authorities of the target state can lawfully kill the suspect in order to avert planned terrorist attacks on its territory. The USA and Israel have routinely resorted to such extrajudicial killings,[69] which do not differ in substance from assassinations orchestrated by various nations against political exiles, enemies of the state, spies and others living abroad. It is exactly because of this risk of arbitrariness that the HRCtee has objected to the practice of targeted killings of suspected terrorists, particularly where this is used as a substitute for arrest and prosecution and without first exhausting non-lethal means.[70]

One could well posit the argument that if a state is unable to arrest a terrorist suspect because of the intransigence or support of another nation then that state's need for security against an imminent terrorist threat can only be met by recourse to armed force against the supporting nation. The legality of such action, however, would be seriously contested. Therefore, the argument continues, targeted killings constitute the best possible alternative to the use of armed force by one state against another. This contention has been rejected by UN human rights bodies, largely because it undermines the essential foundations of human rights.[71] Moreover, the empirical evidence does not support the contention that targeted killings necessarily disable the resolve of terrorist organisations or decrease the loyalty of their sympathisers.[72]

The Israeli Supreme Court in the *Targeted Killings* case was charged with assessing this practice as applied against Palestinian members of alleged terrorist organisations. The Court dispensed the greater part of its analysis

---

use of force strictly to: 'self-defence or defence of others against the imminent threat of death or serious injury, to prevent the perpetration of a particularly serious crime involving grave threat to life, to arrest a person presenting such a danger and resisting their authority, or to prevent his or her escape, and only when less extreme means are insufficient to achieve these objectives'.

[69] See D. Kretzmer, 'Targeted Killing of Suspected Terrorists: Extra-judicial Executions or Legitimate Means of Defence?' (2005) 16 *European Journal of International Law* 171, who provides a general overview of the Israeli policy of targeted assassinations.

[70] HRCtee, Concluding Observations on Israel, UN doc. CCPR/CO/78/ISR (21 August 2003) para. 15.

[71] Report of the Special Rapporteur on extrajudicial, summary or arbitrary executions, UN doc. E/CN.4/2005/7 (22 December 2004) para. 41, who rejects the argument that targeting and eliminating known terrorists is more efficient and costs fewer lives than waging conventional war. He equally notes that this practice 'makes a mockery of whatever accountability mechanisms may have otherwise constrained or exposed such illegal action under either humanitarian or human rights law'.

[72] In a 2012 Pew Global survey on public opinion in Pakistan for drone attacks against terrorist targets in that country, 74 per cent strongly opposed them. See www.pewglobal.org/2012/06/27/pakistani-public-opinion-ever-more-critical-of-u-s/.

on the nature of the conflict and the status of the Palestinians therein, finding them not to be unlawful combatants and therefore enjoying the rights afforded under the *jus in bello* as long as they were taking a direct part in hostilities.[73] The Court accepted that targeted killings were possible so long as the information on the identity and activity of the suspects had been verified, no other means were available to the authorities and the risk of collateral damage to other civilians was not significant in relation to the military advantage anticipated.[74] This judgment cannot set a sound precedent for a very practical reason. The *jus in bello*, unlike human rights law, does not prevent states from killing enemy combatants irrespective of whether they can arrest or detain them, unless of course said combatants are *hors de combat* or have surrendered. The Supreme Court is here attempting to infuse human rights into its consideration of a situation that falls within the scope of the *jus in bello*.[75] Ordinarily, counter-terrorist operations involving targeted killings are perpetrated outside armed conflict situations and therefore the prohibition against targeted killings arising from the right to life is applicable.

Shoot-to-kill counter-terrorist policies are not targeted killings but do raise questions about the authority of the police to use lethal force against suspects who are in the process of committing a terrorist act. The Special Rapporteur on extrajudicial, summary or arbitrary executions, Philip Alston, has criticised shoot-to-kill policies quite aptly as follows:

The rhetoric of shoot-to-kill serves only to displace clear legal standards with a vaguely defined license to kill, risking confusion among law enforcement officers, endangering innocent persons and rationalizing mistakes, while avoiding the genuinely difficult challenges that are posed by the relevant threat.[76]

Some readers may find it odd that law-enforcement authorities are precluded from engaging in targeted killings and shoot-to-kill policies in respect of suicide bombers who detonate their explosive devices at the last minute. However, it should not be forgotten that the law as it stands does not exclude the employment of lethal force altogether. Rather, it requires that the authorities undertake such intelligence and surveillance operations as are necessary to avoid killing a terrorist suspect. Hence, a suicide bomber could just as well be arrested prior to carrying out the ultimate detonation (and ultimately charged with conspiracy to commit a terrorist offence, which may carry the

---

[73] See Chapter 16.2.1 on the meaning of combatant status and of 'taking a direct part in hostilities'.

[74] *Public Committee against Torture in Israel et al.* v. *The Government of Israel* (Israel) (2006) paras. 40–6.

[75] See also M. Milanovic, 'Lessons for Human Rights and Humanitarian Law in the War on Terror: Comparing Hamdan and Israeli Targeted Killings case' (2007) 89 *International Review of the Red Cross* 373, at 390.

[76] Report of the Special Rapporteur, UN doc. E/CN.4/2006/53 (8 March 2006) para. 45.

same sentence as a consummated terrorist act). If, however, despite all intelligence efforts suicide bombers cannot be arrested in advance, it would be far-fetched to argue that anyone resembling a suicide bomber should become a legitimate target of lethal force. The criticism against shoot-to-kill policies is that they legitimise arbitrariness and subsequently result in decreasing the quality of intelligence and investigations.

18.7   ATTEMPTS TO JUSTIFY ARBITRARY DETENTION

In the aftermath of the 9/11 attacks a number of countries, chief among them the USA, called into question the relevance of the international human rights regime in the face of this new type of terrorism. The kind of terrorism states were accustomed to until that time was organised around small groups, was secretive and sought to attract public sympathy and support for its ideology. Al-Qaeda, on the other hand, was not only unconcerned about receiving public sympathy from the Western population, but instead made it its primary target of violence in order to force Western governments to cease their presence in the Muslim world.[77] As a result, the US government in 2001 conceived the 'War on Terror' doctrine, through which it claimed that the threat posed by Islamic terrorism was not susceptible to the ordinary criminal law-enforcement and human rights rules, but was instead governed by the law of armed conflict. The term 'war' was thus not used as a mere metaphor, but as indicative of the new US position on how suspected terrorists should be treated.

The application of this new position soon materialised with the detention of suspected criminals at the US Army's Guantánamo Bay detention facility in Cuba. Those detained at Guantánamo had not only been transferred from Afghanistan and Iraq but also from other parts of the world; yet the common characteristic of the inmates was that none of them was officially charged and none had access to judicial remedies or to a lawyer. How was this possible? Even if these persons were to be classified as combatants, or worse, as unlawful combatants, their detention at the very least would have to be fully documented and they ought to have been provided with due process rights. The expectation of the US government at the time was that if the detainees were not physically held on US territory there would be no legal basis for granting them habeas corpus rights or any other access to judicial

---

[77] IS (and other similar groups such as Boko Haram) has taken this even further by its attacks against other Muslims (e.g. Kurds, Shi'ites) and its contempt of fundamental Muslim values. See M. Badar, 'The International Criminal Court and the Nigerian Crisis: An Inquiry into the Boko Haram Ideology and Practices from an Islamic Law Perspective' (2014) 3 *International Human Rights Law Review* 29.

remedies. In the same spirit, it was presumed that the full range of human rights granted to US citizens would not apply to these suspected terrorists. Moreover, the objective of subsuming counter-terrorist operations within the legal framework of the *jus in bello* was to render the targeting of suspects legitimate – whereas otherwise they would have had to be arrested and lawfully prosecuted.[78] Finally, the designation of suspected terrorists as unlawful combatants was meant to deprive them of even the most rudimentary rights under the *jus in bello*, despite the fact that there are no circumstances under customary international law that permit the deprivation of these fundamental guarantees to any person.[79]

The Guantánamo habeas corpus litigation first commenced with the petition brought in *Rasul* v. *Bush* on behalf of two British nationals and one Australian national before the District Court for the District of Columbia. When the petition finally reached the US Supreme Court its first task was to determine whether US courts lacked jurisdiction 'to consider challenges to the legality of the detention of foreign nationals captured abroad in connection with hostilities and incarcerated at Guantánamo Bay'.[80] The Court intimated that the petitioners were not nationals of countries at war with the USA and had moreover 'been imprisoned in territory over which the United States exercises exclusive jurisdiction and control'.[81] Consequently, it held that the habeas statute[82] conferred jurisdiction on federal courts. This led to a tug-of-war between the Court and Congress because soon afterwards Congress promulgated the Detainee Treatment Act of 2005 (DTA),[83] which attempted to strip federal courts of jurisdiction to entertain habeas petitions lodged by Guantánamo detainees. In response, the Supreme Court in *Hamdan* v. *Rumsfeld* held that the DTA could not apply retrospectively.[84] Congress, rather angrily, retorted by passing the Military Commissions Act of 2006,[85] effectively stripping federal courts of all jurisdiction over Guantánamo habeas claims, irrespective of when these were filed, and proceeded to reinstate the DTA. It became clear that the only way this dispute was going to be resolved once and for all was by judicial determination as to whether Guantánamo detainees possessed habeas claims before federal courts under

---

[78] Military Order of 13 November 2001, on detention, treatment and trial of certain noncitizens in the war against terrorism, F. Reg. 57833, vol. 66, no. 222, had the effect of subjecting the detainees to military commissions with unspecified habeas or other rights; in early 2015 Pakistan constitutional amendment 21 by which the Pakistan Army (Amendment) Act 2015 allows suspected terrorists to be tried by military courts, rather than civilian courts was adopted.

[79] Art. 75 Protocol I 1977.

[80] *Rasul* v. *Bush* (US) (2004) at 470; affirmed also in *Gherebi* v. *Rumsfeld* (US) (2003).

[81] *Rasul* v. *Bush*, at 476.   [82] 28 USC §2241ff.   [83] 119 Stat. 2742.

[84] *Hamdan* v. *Rumsfeld* (US) (2006) at 576ff.   [85] 28 USC §2241(e).

the US Constitution itself. The constitutional foundation of these habeas claims was confirmed by the Supreme Court in *Boumediene* v. *Bush*, which moreover held that the DTA review system was an inadequate substitute for habeas claims because it impeded the right to challenge one's charges, the right to collect and present evidence and because it did not provide sufficient review of the cause for detention, as well as the power to detain.[86] The result in *Boumediene* was subsequently ratified by the incoming administration[87] and entrenched as good law.[88]

By the time the effects of the *Boumediene* judgment were felt upon the counter-terrorist operations of the US military and its law-enforcement authorities a significant number of suspects had already spent years without recourse to judicial remedies or, in most cases, without their relatives or lawyers having even been informed of their detention. This type of deprivation of liberty is known as secret detention and is wholly unjustified under international law. Its nature as such is determined by its incommunicado character (i.e. no access to a lawyer) and lack of disclosure of the place of detention or lack of information about the fate of the detainee.[89] What then of the argument that some form of arbitrary detention may be necessary in order to counter the danger that terrorist suspects pose to national or international security, not to mention the need for protracted interrogations in order to secure vital intelligence that would otherwise be lost? Articles 9 and 5 of the International Covenant on Civil and Political Rights (ICCPR) and the European Convention on Human Rights (ECHR) respectively concur that the right to liberty and security of person is subject solely to the following limitations: (1) detention following conviction by a competent court; (2) detention upon reasonable suspicion that the accused has committed an offence or is about to commit one; and (3) detention aiming to prevent unauthorised entry into a country or in order to enforce a deportation or extradition order.[90] Both instruments, however, make it abundantly clear that these limitations must be prescribed by law and that once detained the accused must be promptly informed of the reason for the arrest and charges against him or her. Moreover, detainees must be given prompt access to

---

[86] *Boumediene* v. *Bush* (US) (2008) at 2266–70.

[87] Review and disposition of individuals detained at the Guantánamo Bay naval base and closure of detention facilities, Executive Order no. 13,492, 74 Fed. Reg. 4, 897 (27 January 2009).

[88] See also *Munaf* v. *Geren, Secretary of the Army et al.* (US) (2008), where the US Supreme Court acknowledged that persons detained in Iraq by US forces were entitled to habeas corpus, although jurisdiction for these claims lay with the Iraqi courts.

[89] See Joint Study on the Global Practices in Relation to Secret Detention in the Context of Countering Terrorism, UN doc. A/HRC/13/42 (19 February 2010) paras. 8–35.

[90] For a fuller analysis of the relevant ECHR provisions, see Chapter 8.4.

judicial remedies and a trial within reasonable time.[91] Persons deprived of their liberty by arrest or detention shall in all circumstances be entitled to due process rights before a court by which the lawfulness of their detention can be promptly decided. The intentional removal of a person from the protection of the law, which may well occur in respect of incommunicado detention, for a prolonged duration, constitutes (in addition) a denial of recognition as a person.[92] It is evident, therefore, that the conditions pertinent to the Guantánamo detentions rendered them entirely unlawful.[93] In cases of exceptionally serious and imminent threats to public safety, states have been given practical (sensible) latitude. In the course of the 2005 London public transport bombings the police arrested four persons but delayed their access to a lawyer while investigations were still ongoing. The ECtHR accepted that the terrorist threat provided compelling reasons for the delay.[94]

Although the law against unlawful detention seems fairly straightforward, there have been numerous attempts to bypass it under the guise of a seeming legality. Colombia's anti-terror legislation, for example, granted its armed forces the power ordinarily enjoyed by the judiciary, including the right to authorise detention and other measures without a prior order by regularly constituted courts.[95] The ECtHR has held that an otherwise lawful deprivation of liberty of a terrorist suspect had been rendered illegal by the fact that the authorities had failed to disclose that he was in the process of being extradited.[96] This element was particularly crucial under the facts of the case because of the frequency of torture and enforced disappearance inflicted on terrorist suspects by the requesting state.

By far the most common violation in European counter-terrorist operations has been the lengthy pre-trial detention of suspects under the guise of investigation or extradition/deportation proceedings, when in fact the aim of the authorities was to keep the accused detained as long as possible because of his or her perceived danger to the public. It is crucial in such cases to determine whether the government was in fact seriously trying to deport/extradite the suspect. In *A and Others* the ECtHR rejected the British derogation under the Convention that would have enabled it to indefinitely detain

---

[91] In *Berasategi* v. *France and Others* (ECtHR) (2012), a pre-trial detention of almost five years was deemed unreasonable, and on the basis of available evidence there was no particularly compelling reason for it.

[92] *Kroumi* v. *Algeria* (HRCtee) (2014) para. 8.9.

[93] Commission on Human Rights, Situation of Detainees at Guantánamo Bay, UN doc. E/CN.4/2006/120 (15 February 2006).

[94] *Ibrahim and Others* v. *United Kingdom* (ECtHR) (2014), as subsequently on appeal by the GC in the same case (2016); equally, *Sher and Others* v. *UK* (ECtHR) (2015).

[95] HRCtee, Concluding Observations on Colombia, UN doc. CCPR/CO/80/COL (26 May 2004) para. 9.

[96] *Shamayev and Others* v. *Georgia and Russia* (ECtHR) (2005) para. 425.

terrorist suspects under national security grounds.[97] Equally, the Court has held in a different case that a period of detention without judicial control for four days and six hours was contrary to the requirement that an accused be brought before a judge promptly.[98]

The lowest point in the recent history of unlawful pre-trial detention was the practice of secret detention centres on land as well as on board military aircraft. This practice was the direct and conscious product of collusion between the authorities of various nations. Initially, few believed the testimonies of those who had been held there, although not even the victims were fully aware of the countries in which they were held.[99] The plot came to light only after researchers discovered that flight plans from Iraq and Afghanistan had been falsified to avoid detection.[100] Unlawful detention has also had a negative spill-over as concerns organised criminal activity. UN Special Rapporteurs have reported an incident where elements of the Georgian mafia abducted an Algerian, thereafter selling him to the US Central Intelligence Agency (CIA), which then boarded him onto a plane towards Kabul.[101] The quality of the rule of law is in serious doubt where the authorities and organised crime collude and find common ground in justifying unlawful acts.

18.8   UNLAWFUL EXTRADITIONS AND ILLEGAL RENDITIONS OF SUSPECTED TERRORISTS

18.8.1   Washing One's Hands and Hiding Every Trace

We have already suggested that one aspect of the War on Terror was the war against human rights. This manifested itself in two ways: (1) as a struggle against the applicability of human rights and of the jurisdiction of ordinary courts, of which the Guantánamo paradigm is the most pertinent expression; and (2) by the conscious decision of some states that the use of legal

---

[97] *A and Others* v. *UK*, paras. 164ff. The ECtHR rejected it also because it found that it discriminated between nationals and non-nationals.

[98] *Brogan and Others* v. *United Kingdom* (ECtHR) (1988) para. 62; *Aksoy* v. *Turkey*, para. 66.

[99] Confirmed by the ECtHR in *El-Masri* v. *The Former Yugoslav Republic of Macedonia* (ECtHR) (2012) and *Al Nashiri* v. *Poland* (ECtHR) (2014), confirming that illegal detention by the CIA on these countries' territories with their consent and subsequent secret transfer to third nations violated the applicants' right to liberty of person and the right to be free from torture.

[100] Joint Study on Secret Detention, paras. 98–164, which provides a detailed account of such secret detention sites and the countries involved; see also Council of Europe Parliamentary Assembly, Alleged Secret Detentions and Unlawful Inter-state Transfers Involving Council of Europe Member States, CoE doc. 10977 (26 June 2006), and its follow-up, Secret Detentions and Illegal Transfers of Detainees Involving Council of Europe Member States: Second Report, CoE doc. 11302 Rev (11 June 2007) (so-called Marty report, after its author).

[101] Joint Study on Secret Detention, ibid., para. 134(b).

argumentation was inconvenient, cumbersome and ineffective and they thus felt compelled to operate outside the law altogether. As a result, they resorted to kidnappings, secret detention centres and surrender of persons to countries where it was expected that they would be tortured and perhaps killed. All of these unlawful activities typically took place outside the territory of the culprit states.

Before we go on to discuss the practice of illegal renditions per se, it is perhaps instructive to examine these attempts to bypass the legal requirements of extradition. States are generally free to extradite or expel aliens, or even their own nationals, to other countries, subject to certain human rights safeguards. Chief among these is that the offence in question be a crime of equal or similar gravity in both nations (double criminality rule); and that the accused will be prosecuted only for the offence for which extradition is agreed (speciality rule). Moreover, it is impermissible to try someone for the same conduct twice, even if under a different legal characterisation (double jeopardy rule). Finally, as a result of the prohibition of torture and ill-treatment under customary law, an additional rule has emerged whereby states are under an obligation not to extradite or expel aliens, including asylum seekers, to countries where they face a real risk of being subjected to torture or ill-treatment, or face the death penalty.[102]

The ECtHR has consistently applied this rule to the extradition of alleged terrorists as well as deportations.[103] The determination of the government's knowledge of circumstances giving rise to such risk is a subjective one. If it is demonstrated that at the time of extradition the serious likelihood of ill-treatment was 'known or ought to have been known' to the extraditing state, then it is wholly liable (or complicit) in the ill-treatment of the accused meted out by a third state.[104] The fact that the accused may be deemed dangerous and pose a serious threat to the community if not extradited in no way outweighs that person's right not to be subjected to a serious risk of ill-treatment.[105] In Europe, the courts' assessment of the risk of ill-treatment is adduced to a large degree from expert witnesses, as well as from NGO reports, based on expertise and field presence in the requesting states. The ECtHR is generally satisfied that the risk of ill-treatment has been adequately eliminated where the requested state's courts have weighed all the evidence and made a comprehensive assessment of the applicant's case.[106] This line of reasoning is

---

[102] See *Saidani* v. *Germany* (ECtHR) (2018), where it was held that the extradition of a terror suspect to Tunisia, which maintained the death penalty, was lawful because that country had imposed a moratorium on capital punishment.

[103] *Chahal* v. *United Kingdom*, paras. 73–4; *Cruz Varas and Others* v. *Sweden* (ECtHR) (1991) paras. 69–70; *HR* v. *France* (ECtHR) (2011).

[104] *Shamayev and Others* v. *Georgia and Russia*, para. 337.

[105] *Saadi* v. *Italy* (ECtHR) (2009) paras. 138–9; equally, *MA* v. *France* (EctHR) (2018).

[106] *X* v. *Germany* (ECtHR) (2017).

not, however, without its detractors. The Canadian Supreme Court in *Suresh* v. *Canada*, where a Sri Lankan refugee argued that his deportation to that country risked a substantial likelihood of torture, held that although torture was strictly prohibited under international law there did exist exceptional circumstances where its infliction as a result of deportation was justified on the basis of a balancing of competing interests. In the case at hand, such interests included the combating of terrorism and Canadian safety.[107]

In order to bypass this procedural safeguard, some states resorted to so-called diplomatic assurances during the peak of the War on Terror. These are bilateral agreements, whether formal or in the form of a memorandum of understanding (MoU), whereby the requesting state undertakes to uphold the rights of the accused and inform the extraditing nation of his or her where-abouts and physical condition. Subsequent cases unfortunately exposed the manipulation of such assurances, demonstrating that state officials of the requested state were not only aware but implicitly consented to the infliction of torture upon those extradited or deported.[108] In its particular examination of the practice of diplomatic assurances, the ECtHR held that it had found these to be wholly insufficient with respect to countries where ill-treatment was 'endemic and persistent'.[109] What is even more significant is that the Court has employed rule 39 of its Rules in order to adopt interim measures with regard to US extradition requests that would render extradited persons to US military commissions, despite the diplomatic assurances provided by the government of that country.[110] No doubt, where the Court is satisfied that particular risks have been adequately addressed in the assurances it will uphold them.[111] Exceptionally, the ECtHR has accepted that assurances against ill-treatment are consistent with the ECHR where their application is monitored by an independent human rights organisation with unlimited access to the extradited person in prison.[112]

---

[107] *Suresh* v. *Canada (Minister of Citizenship and Immigration)* (Canada) (2003).

[108] See *Agiza* v. *Sweden* (CtAT) (2005) para. 13.4 and *Youssef* v. *Home Office* (UK) (2004), both of which concerned the abuse by Egypt of diplomatic assurances. In the first case, the Committee against Torture (CtAT) found the Swedish government to have breached its international obligations by illicitly colluding with CIA agents to expel Agiza to Egypt, while 'it was known, or should have been known, to [Swedish] authorities at the time of the complainant's removal that Egypt resorted to consistent and widespread use of torture against detainees, and that the risk of such treatment was particularly high in the case of detainees held for political and security reasons'.

[109] *Ismoilov* v. *Russia and Others* (ECtHR) (2008) para. 127.

[110] *Mustafa Kamal Mustafa* (*Abu Hamza*) v. *United Kingdom* (ECtHR) (2008); in *Trabelsi* v. *Belgium* (ECtHR) (2014), Belgium's failure to observe the suspension of the extradition under rule 39 had irreversibly lowered the level of protection under art. 3 ECHR and had interfered with the applicant's right to individual petition.

[111] *Aswat* v. *UK* (ECtHR) (2015).

[112] *Othman (Abu Qatada)* v. *United Kingdom* (ECtHR) (2012).

18.8.2 From Arbitrary Detention and Unlawful Extradition the Road to Torture is Open ...

The inevitable consequence of arbitrary detention, particularly where it is incommunicado, is recourse to ill-treatment, torture and even death. Indeed, where law-enforcement authorities are ordered to kidnap and detain 'enemies of the state' at will, having received direct assurances of absolute impunity, while at the same time the state itself has distorted the boundaries of what constitutes lawful interrogation, it cannot but take the next step which is to inflict torture in order to elicit information. Human nature, under such unchecked and clandestine circumstances, can manifest its darkest side, especially where the interrogators are expected, if not mandated, to produce vital intelligence. Empirical evidence suggests that systematic ill-treatment and torture are the direct products of impunity and encouragement, even in countries otherwise premised on the rule of law. This is exemplified by the case of the Guantánamo detainees, those subject to illegal renditions and secret detention centres, as well as in respect of persons incarcerated in Iraq by coalition forces under conditions of secrecy.[113] The ECtHR has particularly highlighted the perils of the 'state secrecy' principle, which has been used to provide impunity to security forces to torture, hold persons in secret detention sites and illegally surrender them to authorities renowned for torture.[114]

In practice, although publicly denied, some states may earnestly believe that the infliction of torture is indispensable in the interrogation of terrorist suspects; no doubt, this is based on the perceived successes of this practice. It is probably also premised on the rationale that in order to counter an extreme form of criminal conduct, such as terrorism, extreme responses are required by the authorities, including torture. From the narrow point of view of one school of interrogators, it is probably true that ill-treatment ensures access to, at least some, immediate and crucial intelligence. However, there is no real empirical data suggesting unlawful forms of interrogation produce significant intelligence.[115]

Following the 9/11 terror attacks, the US Justice Department's Legal Counsel (OLC) was asked to provide advice on particular detention and interrogation policies and techniques against captured Al-Qaeda members. The OLC's first memo of 22 January 2002 argued that the country's treaty

---

[113] Human Rights Watch, Iraq: Wikileaks Documents Describe Torture of Detainees (23 October 2010), online at www.hrw.org/en/news/2010/10/24/iraq-wikileaks-documents-describe-torture-detainees.

[114] See *Nasr and Ghali* v. *Italy* (ECtHR) (2016).

[115] US Senate, Study of CIA Detention, above note 27, at 3, noting that the 'CIA's enhanced interrogation techniques were not an effective means of obtaining accurate information or gaining cooperation from detainees'.

obligations towards Afghanistan had been effectively suspended because the latter was a failed state, thus negating the protections offered by the Geneva Conventions and the Convention against Torture and other Cruel, Inhuman or Degrading Treatment or Punishment (CAT). This was followed by another memo of 1 August 2002 – now known as the Bybee torture memo, after its author – in which an attempt was made to redefine torture and the obligations of the USA. The redefinition of torture was arbitrarily premised on an augmentation of the permissible thresholds of physical and mental pain. Thus, interrogators were advised that physical pain 'must be equivalent in intensity to the pain accompanying serious physical injury, such as organ failure, impairment of bodily function, or even death'. Equally, the applicable threshold for mental pain was deemed to be severe and long-term psychological harm,[116] which is certainly far higher than the threshold required under CAT and customary international law.[117] As a result, the memo approved otherwise prohibited conduct, including hooding, water-boarding,[118] exploitation of phobias, stress positions, sleep deprivation and other treatment.[119] The Obama administration swiftly rescinded the orders approved by the Bybee torture memos.[120]

Of equally doubtful legality is the alleged exception to torture on the basis of the so-called ticking-bomb scenario, which envisages that in situations of extreme urgency a confirmed offender may be tortured in order to reveal the whereabouts of a time-bomb, or other imminent risk which poses an immediate threat to public safety. The Israeli Supreme Court, although ruling that brutal and inhuman interrogation techniques are prohibited at all times, did not definitively rule out the defence of necessity against the ticking-bomb scenario.[121]

One might assume that in the worst-case scenario the evidence seized from a suspected terrorist following torture or ill-treatment would be declared inadmissible either because it was unlawful per se or because the victim's right to a fair trial had been violated.[122] Yet if clandestine agencies enjoy

---

[116] Memorandum from Jay Bybee to Alberto R. Gonzales, counsel to the President, 'Standards of Conduct for Interrogation under 18 USC §§ 2340–2340A', online at www.washingtonpost.com/wp-srv/nation/documents/dojinterrogationmemo20020801.pdf.

[117] See Chapter 8.3 for a discussion of the right to be free from torture.

[118] Water-boarding consists of immobilising subjects while on their back and then pouring water over their face in order to cause the sensation of drowning.

[119] D. A. Wallace, 'Torture v. the Basic Principles of the US Military' (2008) 6 *Journal of International Criminal Justice* 309.

[120] Executive Order 13491, Ensuring Lawful Interrogations (22 January 2009).

[121] *Public Committee against Torture* v. *The State of Israel* (Israel) (1999).

[122] *Göçmen* v. *Turkey* (ECtHR) (2006) paras. 67–76; *A and Others* v. *Secretary of State for the Home Department* (UK) (2005).

impunity and are mandated to eliminate terrorism under any circumstances they are unlikely to have any desire to subject tortured suspects to trial. Knowing full well that any evidence will be treated as inadmissible the prospect of litigation is a disincentive. As a result, the suspect may, following ill-treatment, be eliminated, transferred to a country with an even more dire human rights record, or used as a decoy to lure other suspects. The situation is further exacerbated by the fact that in certain countries the law does not subject torturers to criminal liability because their conduct is deemed within the scope of their employment.[123] National courts are generally reluctant to compel disclosure in cases brought by abductees, the effect of which would be to stifle information-sharing between allied nations. This is also true in situations which may be perceived as prejudicial to national security, even if the evidence sought was obtained by torture or other illegal means.

This conclusion has not only been reached by US courts,[124] but has reluctantly been accepted by courts in the United Kingdom (UK) in their examination of allegations of torture against British nationals held at Guantánamo Bay.[125] A necessary by-product of this limitation has been the inability to claim compensation through the judiciary because a proper case cannot be made against the state for lack of evidence. Judges in the USA who have turned down similar applications deplore this failure of the legal system because it offers no protection to victims of illegal rendition or torture.[126] The Obama administration, shortly after taking up office, issued a memorandum through the Office of the Attorney-General, to the effect that the state's secret privilege should be invoked only to the extent necessary to protect against the risk of significant harm to national security. The privilege was inapplicable in order to:

---

[123] *Rasul* v. *Myers* (US) (2008) at 661; *In Re Iraq and Afghanistan Detainees Litigation* (US) (2007).

[124] *El Masri* v. *Tenet* (US) (2007); *Mohamed* v. *Jeppesen Dataplan Inc.* (US) (2008), at 1134. It should be mentioned that in subsequent phases of the latter case the Ninth Circuit took the view that an outright dismissal of a case on state secrets grounds should be disfavoured. See *Mohamed* v. *Jeppesen Dataplan Inc.* (US) (2009), at 1006. Eventually, sensitive information was not admitted at trial. Upheld finally in *Binyam Mohamed and Others* v. *Jeppesen Dataplan Inc.* (US) 2010.

[125] In *re Mohammed, Binyam* (UK) (2008) para. 105, the Queen's Bench Division of the Divisional Court held that the Foreign Office was under a duty to disclose classified information that was not only necessary but essential for the applicant's defence. It did, however, grant the government time to file a public interest immunity certificate, which it did, arguing that possible disclosure would hamper critical information-sharing with the USA and that such matters were best left to private discussions. The High Court eventually held that under the circumstances it would not compel disclosure, *Re Binyam Mohammed* (UK) (2009).

[126] In *Arar* v. *Ashcroft and Others* (US) (2009) the Court of Appeals held that as unfortunate as the situation was for the plaintiff, who had been rendered to Syria and tortured on

(i) conceal violations of the law, inefficiency, or administrative error; (ii) prevent embarrassment to a person, organisation or agency of the US government; (iii) restrain competition; or (iv) prevent or delay the release of information the release of which would not reasonably be expected to cause significant harm to national security.[127]

The memorandum is in fact quite narrow in scope. For one thing, it is not addressed to the courts, which must still submit filings to the National Security or Civil Division of the Department of Justice in order to assess whether the standard is satisfied. Secondly, it is not clear whether information which is reasonably expected to cause significant harm to national security can be released, even if it contains serious human rights violations. Finally, the memo itself is not a law, but a mere instrument of guidance and does not serve, in any event, to lift the impunity of those who have ill-treated suspected terrorists. In practice, its utility seems to be rather limited, as will be demonstrated in Section 18.9.3 on the basis of the litigation against a corporation that was alleged to have facilitated the logistics relating to illegal renditions.

CASE STUDY 18.2
Al-Rabiah v. USA

Al-Rabiah, a forty-three-year-old Kuwaiti, was seized by Afghan villagers in December 2001 as he was attempting to enter Pakistan unarmed, thereafter surrendering him to US forces.[1] They, in turn, moved him to Guantánamo Bay in May 2002. Although the accused insisted that he was in Afghanistan on a private charitable mission, the US authorities argued that he was a logistics advisor for Bin Laden and Al-Qaeda. At the time of his capture, Al-Rabiah was overweight at 240 lb, had long suffered a knee injury, possessed no previous military training – apart from a two-week course in the Kuwaiti army – and was the father of four. He had worked for Kuwait Airways for twenty years, having never missed a day at work and was credited with an exemplary record. He also had a long history of charitable work

---

[1] *Al-Rabiah* v. *USA* (US) (2009).

---

the basis of a collusion between US and Canadian secret services, the US Constitution did not offer an appropriate remedy. An exceptional remedy such as that created by the US Supreme Court in *Bivens* v. *Six Unknown Named Agents of the Federal Bureau of Narcotics* (US) (1971), in which a direct cause of action was allowed against the offending individuals (so-called *Bivens* action), was not possible under the circumstances.

[127] US Attorney-General, Memorandum for heads of executive departments or agencies (23 September 2009) s. 1(C).

with Muslim communities around the world, with volunteering activities in Bosnia, Kosovo, Bangladesh and Afghanistan, all of which were widely known to friends and family. In fact, Al-Rabiah had written numerous letters to his family about his aid work in Afghanistan and was on a two-week leave from his employer.[2]

The US federal court that heard the habeas corpus petition recounted that all witness testimony against him was hugely inconsistent and that some of the witnesses had previously made false statements against other persons. Eventually, Al-Rabiah, partly as a result of sleep deprivation, partly because he was threatened with perpetual incarceration at Guantánamo unless he confessed, entered a 'full' confession that seemed incredible even to his interrogators. He confessed, for example, that he had undertaken a leading role under Bin Laden in the Tora Bora mountains in Afghanistan, despite the fact that he was physically incapable and in any event was never in Afghanistan prior to 2001.[3] The court observed that:

the Government's simple explanation is that Al-Rabiah made confessions that the court should accept as true. The simple response is that the court does not accept confessions that even the Government's own interrogators did not believe.[4]

This case study exemplifies that unlawful detention and lack of fair trial with all due process guarantees necessarily leads to interrogational anarchy and abuse. The authorities became obsessed with the accused although it was clear even to them that he could not possibly have done the things that even he himself had confessed.

[2] Ibid., 20–34.   [3] Ibid.   [4] Ibid., 42.

QUESTIONS

1. What tangible benefits do secret services hope to gain from the infliction of torture and arbitrary detention against suspected terrorists?

2. Let us now examine the other side. What possible benefits for the prosecuting state and the international community can you see from the instigation of fair trial procedures against suspected terrorists? Think broadly and take into consideration the root causes of terrorism. Do these benefits outweigh those in question 1?

3. Many, but not all, of the persons detained at Guantánamo Bay freely admitted a smaller or larger connection with the activities of the Taliban and Al-Qaeda. This fact alone should serve to justify their prolonged detention on the ground that they pose a serious threat to security. Discuss.

4. The criminal conduct of secret agents, particularly torture, in the course of sensitive counter-terrorist operations should never be made public before the courts because of the risk to the agents themselves and national security. Discuss.

5. National security and human rights protection, even in the gravest of circumstances, are compatible. Discuss.

18.9 LEGAL AND OTHER STRATEGIES REGARDING DISAPPEARED TERRORIST SUSPECTS

18.9.1 The Potency of Advocacy and Outreach

So far we have discussed the range of rights pertinent to suspects in counter-terrorist operations, as well as certain unlawful practices undertaken by states in order to create *legal black holes* that would deprive suspects of their rights altogether.[128] While in the pre-9/11 era states stood to make significant political gains from publicly prosecuting alleged terrorists, this position has now drastically altered. Under this new paradigm the intelligence-gathering potential of detained suspects outweighs the benefits arising from their prosecution. Of course, this is not a novel idea, but in the age of the War on Terror its implementation has benefited from the secrecy of counter-terrorist operations in order to inflict torture and ill-treatment. However, governments are aware that in the current information era they cannot escape accusations of torture, nor can they expect to deter influential human rights NGOs from seeking judicial remedies in receptive fora. Moreover, the 'threat' from judicial activism is always far too great to ignore and was certainly a crucial factor, along with all the others, in the decision of the US government and of its secret services to resort to unlawful kidnappings, renditions and torture of suspected terrorists in secret locations throughout the world. The purpose of this section is to give some idea of the strategies pursued by the legal teams representing the families of missing persons. It should be stated from the outset that, with minor exceptions, detained persons were foreign nationals. In this section we will describe the plight of British detainees.

The approach of the legal teams was predicated on a variety of strategies, which can roughly be broken down into legal arguments and outreach/advocacy policy goals. The legal arguments can further be broken down into identification/tracing of missing persons, followed by the pursuit of release

---

[128] The term 'legal black hole' was probably first coined by Lord Steyn, in J. Steyn, 'Guantánamo Bay: The Legal Black Hole' (2004) 53 *International & Comparative Law Quarterly* 1.

remedies. The outreach dimension is simultaneous and inextricably linked to legal remedies and can only artificially be separated from these. Its various facets may be distinguished on the basis of their intended addressees, as follows: public policy-makers, public opinion and the courts.

18.9.2   Tracing Strategies and Release Arguments

The first stage in this process is ascertaining that the missing person has been abducted and held by government agents, as opposed to having voluntarily disappeared or been kidnapped for financial gain. In practice, as was the case with British abductees who went missing while outside the UK, the families suspected that their loved ones might have been caught up in clean-up operations and approached the UK authorities. The latter initially argued that they themselves had no information as to their whereabouts and that equally no information was available from the countries in which they were last sighted. It should be remembered that the practice of illegal abductions began as early as 2002, at which time even the existence of the Guantánamo Bay detention centre was unknown to the general public. It was only as a result of mounting newspaper stories, especially from *The Guardian*, the *Observer* and *The New York Times*, that the plot started to unravel.[129] Once this tentative link was established – in practice there were no doubt many others – the families could approach the UK authorities with more than a mere suspicion. But how could they be sure that their missing family member was in a secret detention centre and what avenues were open to the UK, which was not after all accused at that stage of being complicit? Feroz Abbasi and Shafiq Rasul, both British citizens, were arrested in Afghanistan in late 2001 in the aftermath of the coalition invasion of that country. They were soon after transferred to Guantánamo Bay and held in secret. It seems that the press tipped off the families of both men as to their whereabouts.[130]

With this information at hand the two respective legal teams set off on two distinct legal strategies. Abbasi's team focused on the diplomatic protection owed by Britain to its subjects, whereas the Rasul camp believed that it

---

[129] In *Abu Zubaydah* v. *Lithuania* (ECtHR) (2018), the family of a person detained at a CIA 'black site' was able to make an application to the ECtHR on the basis of information from a US Senate Committee report on CIA torture released in 2014, as well as witness testimony. The latter showed that Lithuania permitted the detainee to be transferred to another secret detention site in Afghanistan. The same transpired in *Al-Nashiri* v. *Romania* (ECtHR) (2018), where the ECtHR further held that Romania even hosted a secret CIA prison, code-named 'Detention Site Black', where the applicant had been detained for about eighteen months. Romania had also permitted him to be moved to another CIA detention site located either in Afghanistan (Detention Site Brown) or in Lithuania (Detention Site Violet), thus exposing him to further ill-treatment.

[130] G. Peirce, *Dispatches from the Darkside* (Verso, 2010) 18.

would stand a better chance by engaging the active protection of US courts. This required a firm finding of jurisdiction. Both strategies aimed at bringing detainees within the purview of a legal system and providing them with effective guarantees and protection. The diplomatic protection route presupposes that the incumbent government is either sympathetic to the particular claimant or his/her plight, or that it does not maintain the best of relations with the violating third state. None of these conditions prevailed under the circumstances at hand. The British government assured Parliament early on that despite the security situation all detainees were 'treated in accordance with humanitarian norms'.[131] As it later transpired, the British government was complicit in the ill-treatment – it is known at least that its agents were present and did not attempt to stop or mitigate it – so in hindsight diplomatic protection was hardly the most appropriate strategy. The government put forward the contention that diplomatic protection does not extend to acts, even torture, undertaken exclusively in a third country, since there exists no obligation to secure that third states acting within their own jurisdiction respect human rights. Of course, this was a narrow argument predicated solely on the territorial limitations of the ECHR.[132]

The *Abbasi* team did not press on with an *erga omnes* argument at this stage because given the security and political climate following 9/11 it would not have impressed English courts, which ultimately upheld the government's claims.[133] Although Abbasi himself was released a few years later on the strength of bilateral diplomacy, it was evident that the diplomatic protection strategy required a more potent and emotional legal argument. Quite clearly, the detainees' British nationality alone was insufficient to invoke the sympathy of the public and the judiciary. This sympathy was achieved by supplementing the nationality link with the horrendous treatment afforded to detainees. As will be observed in Section 18.9.3, the combined effect of press revelations, investigations by British parliamentary committees and international organisations, as well as the acknowledgement of arbitrary detention by US courts, assisted in transforming the arbitrary detention and torture card to a tool for political pressure as well as a legal argument aimed at the release of the detainees. As such, it was later employed in the *Al-Rawi* and *Mohamed* litigations, where the detainees were not British nationals but had been granted indefinite leave to stay in Britain.

The *Rasul* legal battle effectively took off upon receipt of information that the accused was held at Guantánamo. His family, via his legal team, instituted

---

[131] (2002) 378 Parliamentary Debates HC (6th Ser.) 623.
[132] In particular, in accordance with the judgment in *Bertrand Russell Peace Foundation* v. *United Kingdom* (UK) (1978) at 124.
[133] *R (Abbasi)* v. *Foreign Secretary and Home Secretary* (UK) (2002) para. 79.

proceedings in the USA with the hope of establishing that the courts of that country would accept jurisdiction over the illegality of his detention (habeas corpus claims). The relevant principles accepted by the US Supreme Court in that round of litigation have already been analysed in Section 18.7. It should be pointed out that there is no evidence of coordination between the detainees' legal teams in the USA and the UK. What is striking between the strategies pursued in both sets of cases is that the legal arguments by the *Rasul* and subsequent teams operating in the USA were by no means radical and did not challenge long-standing legal notions. Instead, they claimed the obvious: that fundamental constitutional guarantees serve to protect all persons in the custody of the state, irrespective of the location held. The *Abbasi* team could not raise this argument against the USA before English courts, and even the very plausible *erga omnes* claim would have constituted a radical departure for a national court to accept because it would have required the British government to take measures against the USA in case it failed to provide fair trial guarantees. Yet while the *Rasul* strategy managed to bring the detainees under the protection of the captor's Supreme Court, its *Abbasi* counterpart, while seemingly futile to start off with, ultimately culminated in diplomacy that led to the detainees' release.

With respect to the detainees who were long-term British residents, but not nationals, the failure of their direct diplomatic protection argument was only initially a setback – although of course it also served to prolong their detention. As it gradually became known that the UK had either been a passive participant in the brutal interrogation of persons with a British link, or had otherwise exchanged relevant intelligence with the USA,[134] the legal arguments necessarily changed. What was now crucial was to substantiate the complicity of the UK, at whatever level, which entailed full or partial disclosure of sensitive information. In national law this boils down to a judicial determination of whether particular information should be made available to a private party.[135] It is in essence a conflict between the right to a fair trial and legitimate national security concerns, including the deterioration of a country's diplomatic relations. Given that public and judicial opinion were turning in favour of the detainees, the British government persisted with its non-disclosure argument while at the same time made strenuous efforts to release the remaining British residents.[136] That judicial opinion had turned

---

[134] At some point a key witness from the UK security services testified under closed evidence that he was present during interrogation sessions and that the government was aware that the suspect was at times detained in Morocco and at others in the USA. *R (Mohamed)* v. *Secretary of State FCO* (UK) (2009) para. 88.

[135] In the case at hand it concerned the so-called public interest immunity (PII).

[136] The then Minister of State for the Foreign and Commonwealth Office (FCO) pointed out that the government was pressing 'for the release of Mr Mohamed's return from Guantánamo as vigorously as before'; (2009) 707 *Parliamentary Debates* HL (5th Ser.) 805.

to now favour the detainees was evident from the judgment of the Court of Appeals in a claim lodged by Binyam Mohamed after his release. The Court held that otherwise confidential information, which narrated acts of torture and which could not reveal any information of interest to terrorists, was indeed susceptible to public scrutiny.[137]

It is interesting to note in this respect the nature and tactics of the opponent, the Blair government, which was in office at the time. Although a significant amount of the intelligence requested to be made public had already been exposed in the course of litigation in the USA, or had otherwise been revealed, the legal team of the British government continued to resist its publication! By contrast, the Bush administration gradually conceded the ill-treatment as well as the illegal renditions and reacted only by changing its domestic law, crudely and in violation of its international obligations in order to suit its political and military objectives. The British government, up until the very end, never conceded any knowledge or involvement and decided to fight its corner.[138]

18.9.3 Advocacy Strategies

The powerful impact of advocacy strategies is evident in the case studies just described. Whether through habeas corpus litigation in the USA or feeble diplomatic protection claims against the British government, both culminated in the exertion of significant political pressure which resulted in the release of all known British detainees without even a criminal trial in the USA. We possess little or no evidence of the release attempts instigated by the governments of non-democratic states, but no doubt the lack of civil society mechanisms has precluded the exertion of adequate pressure. We have already emphasised that the litigation by and of itself was incapable of guaranteeing the release of the detainees. It is simply a weapon in the greater conflict between governments and the legal teams/civil society, which is to a large degree a war for the control of information. Peirce, a prominent British lawyer involved in the Guantánamo litigation, notes that the confidence of the British government's case lay 'in the extent to which the secret state believes it has consolidated and can control any mechanism that might allow discovery and challenge. It [relies] on its citizens never knowing properly, or

---

[137] *R (Mohamed)* v. *Secretary of State FCO* (UK) (2010) para. 52.
[138] The British Home Secretary defended the position that the secret services, and particularly MI5, had not been complicit in the torture of Mohamed, just days before the Court of Appeals judgment that declassified evidence showing the contrary and although in any event this was public knowledge. See *Sunday Times Online* (12 February 2010).

often not knowing at all.'[139] As a result, the ultimate purpose of legal arguments, including legal action, is to sensitise public opinion in such a way that: (1) the main issue becomes common and embedded knowledge; (2) it is sustained and reinforced by further official inquiries by public bodies and international organisations, as well as the press;[140] and (3) it places pressure on governments until their intransigence collapses, whether by judicial authority or policy concession, or a combination of both.

It is now widely accepted that the US government and its allies wished to conceal their arbitrary detention and illegal rendition programmes. The role of free press was paramount in exposing both of these at an early stage. Although details are not known, it is believed that the sources behind the revelations were of two types: the usual leaks from government agents with access to relevant information, as well as randomly from the general public, including plane spotters who noticed some very unusual air activity. The latter is particularly important, not only from the point of view of its effectiveness, but also because it demonstrates the interdependence between human rights protection and an open information society. Initially, the plane spotters simply took cognisance of what seemed to be government aircraft, or secretively operated aircraft, taking off and landing in remote airfields throughout Europe. This then caught the attention of the media and NGOs, which resulted in efforts to examine the flight records of these mysterious aircraft with a view to ascertaining their operators and whether their landing and take-off locations coincided with secret detention sites.

In the case of flights originating from the US military base of Diego Garcia, which constitutes British sovereign territory, it became apparent, for example, that the private firm Jeppesen was operating an aircraft registered as N379P. Its particular flight patterns immediately ignited suspicions that it was carrying detainees to locations around the world. Although unofficial evidence suggests that the aircraft's flight logs may have been falsified, or indeed destroyed, NGOs sought to find tangible links between the particular flights and complicit nations. An examination of records available for at least four suspected rendition flights by this aircraft reveals that it operated under various 'special status designators' which constitute privileges affordable only to aircraft at the highest echelons of governments, in this case, the governments of the UK and the USA.[141] A Jeppesen-operated aircraft most probably airlifted Binyam Mohamed to Guantánamo

---

[139] Peirce, above note 130, 8.

[140] For an account of the investigations carried out by British public bodies regarding the involvement of that country in torture and illegal rendition, see REDRESS, 'The United Kingdom, Torture and Anti-terrorism: Where the Problems Lie' (December 2008) 13–24.

[141] Reprieve, 'Ghost determination on Diego Garcia' (2009).

Bay, a fact which triggered a series of lawsuits against this company with a view to forcing it to release information about the rendition flights it had operated on behalf of the US government. With the intervention of the latter under a claim of national security privilege the action ultimately failed; yet the expression of concern by the Ninth Circuit should not be underestimated in terms of having won broad judicial favour. The majority thus stated:

We do not reach our decision lightly or without close and sceptical scrutiny of the record and the government's case for secrecy and dismissal. We expect our decision today to inform district courts that the [state secrets] privilege has its limits, that every effort should be made to parse claims to salvage a case like this [using the exclusion of privileged evidence rule], that the standards for peremptory dismissal are very high and it is the district court's role to use its fact-finding and other tools to full advantage before it concludes that the rare step of dismissal is justified ... We also acknowledge that this case presents a painful conflict between human rights and national security.[142]

By late 2010 the British government announced that it had come to a mediated settlement with all released detainees of British nationality and residency. Although the outcome of this process is confidential, a significant amount of compensation was paid to the victims, presumably in return for desisting with future claims and lawsuits on the complicity of the UK.[143]

18.9.4   Counter-terrorism: The Real Testing Ground for *Erga Omnes*

It has been explained elsewhere in this book that the obligation to protect fundamental human rights applies against all nations, and as a result every nation possesses legal standing (*locus standi*) to make relevant claims or bring suits before international and domestic fora. The rationale behind the *erga omnes* doctrine is that where the victims are unable to challenge their own state's violations, the international community has an interest in taking up the victims' plight. In some cases the *erga omnes* obligation may be dispensed with by publicly denouncing the relevant conduct or by openly refusing to give it approval, tacit or otherwise.

In the course of the *Al-Rawi* and *Mohamed* litigation the legal teams of the two men managed to bring into the public domain various paragraphs from classified documents. One of these, introduced as Exhibit LC7, was a report

---

[142] *Binyam Mohamed and Others v. Jeppesen Dataplan Inc.*
[143] (2010) 1116 *Parliamentary Debates* HC 753. In announcing the settlement the Justice Secretary, Kenneth Clarke, emphasised the obvious: 'No admissions of culpability have been made in settling those cases and nor have any of the claimants withdrawn their allegations.'

by the British Intelligence and Security Committee (ISC) on the 'handling of detainees by UK intelligence personnel in Afghanistan, Guantánamo Bay and Iraq'.[144] The report reproduced a guidance to address the concerns raised by a British secret service officer who had witnessed the infliction of torture by US operatives:

With regard to the status of the prisoners, under the various Geneva Conventions and protocols, however they are described [terror suspects] are entitled to the same levels of protection. You have commented on their treatment. It appears from your description that they may not be treated in accordance with the appropriate standards. Given that they are not within our custody or control, the law does not require you to intervene to prevent this. That said [the Government's] stated commitment to human rights makes it important that the Americans understand that we cannot be party to such ill-treatment nor can we be seen to condone it ... If circumstances allow, you should consider drawing this to the attention of a suitably senior US official locally.[145]

In other parts the guidance makes it clear that British personnel should under no circumstances engage in torture or other ill-treatment, lest they face criminal sanctions. It would seem therefore that on the face of it the British government is discharging its *erga omnes* obligations in arduous circumstances on the battlefield. A closer reading, however, demonstrates that the principal aim is to avoid possible complicity. As far as engaging with their US counterparts to persuade or chastise them to desist from employing torture there is only a very lukewarm instruction which, under the terms phrased, would carry no weight with its recipients. Rightly, therefore, the ISC report pointed out that:

These instructions did not go far enough. They should have required the [secret service] officer to report his concerns to the senior US official. They should also have required all officers to report any similar matters in the future to both the US authorities and to their respective headquarters in the UK. Furthermore, the Foreign Secretary should have been informed immediately that an officer had reported that a serious potential abuse by the US military had occurred [so that he can issue instructions].[146]

The *erga omnes* argument was only indirectly invoked in litigation in the UK and even then it was pegged to diplomatic protection and the legitimate expectations of Britons. The dilution of *erga omnes* in practice is manifest in the British government's admission that even its lukewarm application is conditioned by political expediency and the interests of diplomatic bargaining:

---

[144] Cm. 6469 (1 March 2005).   [145] Ibid., para. 47.   [146] Ibid., para. 50.

In deciding whether to make humanitarian representations in any case, the UK Government would have to take into account the extent to which it would have to expend significant political credit, and would have to risk losing a measure of credibility, with the state to whom the representations are made. This is so, irrespective of the context. It is particularly true in relation to *such highly controversial* and (especially from the US Government's point of view) sensitive matters as Guantánamo Bay and the circumstances and conditions of persons detained there [emphasis added].[147]

This is a low point for it suggests that human rights are but a costly, albeit certainly expendable, bargaining chip in the armoury of international politics. It also makes one sceptical about the true intentions behind state action, whether condemnatory, legal or forceful, taken against other nations accused of systematic human rights violations.

INTERVIEW 18.1
Legal Defender of Guantánamo Detainees
(Clive Stafford Smith)

Clive Stafford Smith is a British lawyer specialising in human rights and civil liberties and is the Legal Director of Reprieve UK.[1] He has defended numerous Guantánamo Bay detainees, among others.

A large segment of the general public does not understand on what grounds a lawyer would represent suspected terrorists. What is your personal position?

Being a lawyer means fighting for the rights of the powerless and those who cannot fight for themselves against government abuse. The majority of those seeking legal representation have sufficient access to justice, but those suspected of terrorism are denied all rights and are portrayed by the authorities in a manner that renders them undeserving of any legal protection.

Based on your litigation experience with suspected terrorists held abroad and the complicity of states in their illegal detention, what particular aspects of British law would you wish to see amended?

---

[1] The organisation's website is online at www.reprieve.org.uk.

---

[147] Reproduced in *R (Al-Rawi) and Others* v. *Secretary for Foreign and Commonwealth Affairs* (UK) (2006) para. 41.

Although the perpetration of torture is a horrendous act, by far the worst element in the war against terror is the attempt by the authorities to shroud the entire process with secrecy and to deter the public and the justice system from knowing what is taking place. Naturally, this has led to states covering up their covert illegal activities in order to avoid embarrassment, thus creating a vicious cycle from which it is hard to escape.

Successive British governments are in favour of secret courts and inquiries that are meant to avoid public scrutiny of their actions, and those of their agents and allies. Instead of amending this state of affairs, the Green Paper[2] recently circulated by the British government continues to place an emphasis on national security, thus perpetuating the culture of secrecy which has resulted in the violation of fundamental rights. This has got to stop.

If you could re-design counter-terrorist strategies following the 9/11 attacks, what type of actions would you recommend against suspected terrorists operating abroad?

I should recall that the first victim in the war against terror is human rights. The level of abuse perpetrated in Baghram airbase [in Iraq] is worse than Guantánamo Bay. It is essential, therefore, that fundamental rights be at the forefront of, and inform, all future anti-terrorist policies. The loss of civil liberties in the face of terrorism will inevitably lead to abuse. At present, the US government, in its attempt to circumvent relevant human rights issues, is employing unmanned drones whose aim is to kill without having to arrest and prosecute alleged terrorists. This is portrayed as a legitimate tool in the war against terror and as a way of avoiding further casualties. Yet these types of operations are an affront to the right to life and the right to a fair trial that are inherent in the operation of all democratic legal systems.

[2] Justice and Security Green Paper, Cm. 8194 (October 2011).

FURTHER READING

Ashby Wilson, R. (ed.), *Human Rights in the War on Terror* (Cambridge University Press, 2005).

Chakrabarti, S., *On Liberty* (Allen Lane, 2014).

Davis, F. F., *Critical Debates on Counter-Terrorism Judicial Review* (Cambridge University Press, 2016).

Doswald-Beck, L., *Human Rights in Times of Conflict and Terrorism* (Oxford University Press, 2011).

Duffy, H., *The War on Terror and the Framework of International Law*, 2nd edn (Cambridge University Press, 2015).

Giuffré, M., 'An Appraisal of Diplomatic Assurances One Year after *Othman (Abu Qatada) v. United Kingdom*' (2013) 2 *International Human Rights Law Review* 266.

Gunneflo, M., *Targeted Killing: A Legal and Political History* (Cambridge University Press, 2018).

Koh, H. H., 'The Case against Military Commissions' (2002) 96 *American Journal of International Law* 337.

De Londras, F., 'Can Counter-terrorist Internment ever be Legitimate?' (2011) 33 *Human Rights Quarterly* 593.

Detention in the War on Terror: Can Human Rights Fight Back? (Cambridge University Press, 2011).

Macken, C., *Counter-Terrorism and the Detention of Suspected Terrorists: Preventive Detention and International Human Rights Law* (Routledge, 2013).

Massferer, A., and C. Walker (eds.), *Counter-Terrorism, Human Rights and the Rule of Law: Crossing Legal Boundaries in Defence of the State* (Edward Elgar, 2013).

Meron, T., 'When do Acts of Terrorism Violate Human Rights?' (1989) 29 *Israel Yearbook of Human Rights* 271.

Moeckli, D., *Human Rights and Non-Discrimination on the War on Terror* (Oxford University Press, 2008).

Pejic, J., 'Terrorist Acts and Groups: A Role for International Law?' (2005) 75 *British Yearbook of International Law* 71.

Rehman, J., 'Islam, War on Terror and the Future of Muslim Communities in the United Kingdom: Dilemmas of Multiculturalism' (2007) 29 *Human Rights Quarterly* 831.

Saul, B., *Defining Terrorism in International Law* (Oxford University Press, 2008).

Stubbins-Bates, E. (ed.), *Terrorism and International Law: Accountability, Remedies and Reform* (Oxford University Press, 2011).

Tsang, S. (ed.), *Intelligence and Human Rights in the Era of Global Terrorism* (Stanford University Press, 2008).

Van de Herik, L., and N. Schrijver (eds.), *Counter-Terrorism Strategies in a Fragmented International Legal Order: Meeting the Challenges* (Cambridge University Press, 2014).

Waldron, J., *Torture, Terror and Trade-Offs: Philosophy for the White House* (Oxford University Press, 2012).

Warbrick, C., 'The European Response to Terrorism in an Age of Human Rights' (2004) 15 *European Journal of International Law* 989.

Websites

Liberty: www.liberty-human-rights.org.uk/

UN Office of Counter-Terrorism: www.un.org/en/counterterrorism/

UN Ombudsperson on terrorist listing: www.un.org/en/sc/ombudsperson/

UN Special Rapporteur on counter-terrorism and human rights: www.ohchr.org/EN/Issues/Terrorism/Pages/SRTerrorismIndex.aspx

19 Human Rights Obligations of Non-state Actors

CONTENTS

19.1   INTRODUCTION

In previous chapters we had a chance to examine the effect, both negative and positive, of non-state actors (NSAs) on human rights, particularly terrorist groups, non-governmental organisations (NGOs) and private companies, the latter in the context of economic and social rights. The present chapter sets out to explore the theoretical underpinnings of a much larger debate as to whether NSAs possess, or should possess, human rights obligations, much in the same way as states. This debate, as will be demonstrated, is not merely theoretical, because if one were to confer such obligations to actors other than states, then one must necessarily reconsider the entire architecture and rationale of the human rights system which has, for good reason, been founded on the idea that since states hold ultimate power over their people (police, fiscal, etc.) it is natural that only they owe human rights obligations. None the less, it is evident that NSAs have a significant impact on the enjoyment of human rights and that as a result some regulation and intervention is required; although framing the precise legal contours of such intervention is fraught with controversy.

The chapter sets off by examining the theoretical bases upon which an NSA may be deemed to possess human rights obligations, and critiques the various approaches put forward by states and the scholarly community. It then goes on to examine a variety of NSAs along with their own distinct position as regards their human rights role. Some NSAs, such as international financial institutions (IFIs), take a legalistic approach to the matter and are generally wary of accepting even the more fundamental obligations, whereas other actors are keen to achieve a broader human rights agenda and are thus willing to accept some human rights commitments. Besides intergovernmental organisations we shall also be focusing on multinational corporations (MNCs) and the way in which their operations have a significant impact on the rights of populations worldwide. It shall be demonstrated that while their human rights 'obligations', if any, have largely arisen as a result of voluntary undertakings, they are now entering a hybrid phase of limited regulation, or at least of an attempt at regulation. Finally, we shed some light on national liberation movements and rebel groups and their distinct responsibilities under international humanitarian law (IHL).

19.2   THE STATUS OF NSAS IN HUMAN RIGHTS LAW

NSA is a negative definition encompassing entities that do not exercise governmental functions or whose conduct cannot be described as possessing a public nature. In the field of human rights it mainly covers NGOs, paramilitary groups (including terrorist groups), national liberation movements and corporations, whether MNCs or domestic, as well as intergovernmental organisations, despite the fact that the latter are established by state entities. The definition also covers private actors generally, such as individuals or groups that commit crimes against women or other vulnerable groups.[1]

Traditionally, private persons were not considered as subjects of international law; that is, they were deprived of international legal personality and as such did not enjoy rights or bear obligations under international law. Rights and duties were only available under domestic law, while the interests of the person in the international sphere were assumed by the state as a matter of diplomatic protection.[2] The very subject matter of this book, and

---

[1] See Chapter 11 on women's rights.
[2] See Chapters 2.3.2, 17.2 and 17.3 for an analysis of the evolution of the principle of international legal personality.

indeed of this chapter, suggests that this traditional view no longer holds sway. Even so, while the available case law and treaties aptly confirm that private persons enjoy rights in their personal capacity, as opposed to enjoying them through their country of nationality, in addition to bearing liability for particular international crimes, such as war crimes, it is not also clear that private persons possess human rights obligations in the same manner as states, or in any other form for that matter. The purpose of this chapter is to assess whether such obligations in fact exist, and if so to determine their content.

Since the 1970s a debate has arisen as to whether this traditional conception should be adjusted so that NSAs may assume human rights obligations.[3] On the face of it this is an attractive proposition, especially considering that some NSAs are much wealthier than many states (for example MNCs), or possess military capacity of equal value, as is the case with certain paramilitary groups, private security firms and national liberation movements. If these NSAs possess the power and money to behave like states, it is argued that they should also bear the same obligations as states. It is not, of course, expected that NSAs should have a duty to provide the whole range of economic and social rights, as this would result in the wholesale substitution of the state – although their contribution is certainly important in countries where basic public services have been privatised.[4] Rather, the idea is that NSAs such as terrorist groups and private military companies may indeed violate entitlements such as the right to life by killing random civilians. However, if this proposition is accepted as legitimate then states may well deny the existence of their own positive duty concerning the right to life, predicated on the obligation to prevent terrorist attacks and punish offenders. In the end what remains is merely a negative obligation.[5] One should not go to the other extreme and contend that if a positive duty exists at all for states then suspected terrorists should be stripped of all their rights, something which is vehemently rejected under customary human rights law.[6] It is clearly obvious that the shifting of human rights obligations to outlawed, or unregulated, NSAs risks rendering states 'irresponsible' in respect of their own specific human rights duties.

There are other legal avenues for addressing 'violations' committed by terrorist and paramilitary groups. The application of criminal law is certainly far

---

[3] See A. Clapham, *Human Rights Obligations of Non-State Actors* (Oxford University Press, 2006) 29–56 and ch. 2, where he cites a number of legal arguments against the traditional dichotomy.

[4] See e.g., the discussion on the right to water and the right to health in Chapters 9.10 and 9.9 respectively.

[5] R. Provost, *International Human Rights and Humanitarian Law* (Cambridge University Press, 2002) 62ff.

[6] See Chapter 18.4 for a discussion of terrorists as human rights duty-holders.

more effective and lacks the risks identified above. Criminal law deals with such conduct far better through the process of criminal liability administered by an independent criminal justice system. This way, the positive obligation of the state to prevent and punish crime in order to uphold its human rights duties remains intact. In fact, international criminal law supplements the gaps in human rights law by expanding the ambit of actors subject to criminal liability. By way of illustration, international tribunals have accepted that war crimes committed in internal armed conflicts give rise to international criminal liability, rather than domestic liability,[7] and that mass offences, such as crimes against humanity, may indeed be planned and committed by NSAs, even though these offences were originally conceived as crimes requiring a state-like organisation on the part of the perpetrators.[8] Equally, although human rights law requires that in order to be an offence under law torture needs to be committed by agents of the state (or at least with their acquiescence under article 1 of the Convention against Torture (CAT)), this is no longer a requirement in humanitarian and international criminal law.[9] Herein lies the difference between international criminal tribunals and human rights treaty bodies in ascribing duties to NSAs. The former, in their effort to avoid offering impunity to those NSAs (and their individual members) that have clearly committed a heinous act, ascribe criminal liability to the conduct irrespective of the legal status of the offender. Human rights courts, on the other hand, are uneasy with bending the requirements found in the relevant instruments, albeit they generally recognise that criminal conduct may be ascribed to NSAs where there exists an element of state involvement.[10] In the case of torture, for example, they have emphasised that NSAs can commit the offence where states violate their obligation of *non-refoulement*, such as by sending detainees to be tortured by de facto entities.[11]

---

[7] Now firmly established in art. 8(2)(c) and (e) ICC Statute.

[8] ILC, Draft Code of Crimes Against the Peace and Security of Mankind, UN doc. A/51/10 (1996), Supp. 10, 94. See also *ICTY Prosecutor v. Karadžić and Mladić* (ICTY) (1996) paras. 60–4, where the ICTY admitted that a paramilitary group can commit crimes against humanity; *ICC Prosecutor v. Ruto and Others (Situation in the Republic of Kenya)* (ICC) (2012) paras. 184ff.

[9] *ICTY Prosecutor v. Kunarac* (ICTY) (2001) para. 495, where it was held that 'the characteristic trait of the offence … is to be found in the nature of the act committed rather than the status of the person who committed it'. Confirmed on appeal in *ICTY Prosecutor v. Kunarac* (ICTY) (2002) para. 148, noting that 'the public official requirement is not a requirement under customary international law in relation to the criminal responsibility of an individual for torture outside of the framework of the Torture Convention'. See also *ICTR Prosecutor v. Semanza* (ICTR) (2003) paras. 342–3.

[10] Exceptionally, as in *Kadic v. Karadžić* (US) (1995), the US second district court held that certain forms of conduct, particularly genocide and war crimes, violate the law of nations even if undertaken by NSAs in their private capacity.

[11] *Ahmed v. Austria* (ECtHR) (1997); *H. L. R. v. France* (ECtHR) (1998); *H.M.H.I. v. Australia* (CtAT) (2002).

This is not to say that the language of human rights obligations is inappropriate for all NSAs. Corporations, for example, are not illegal and their operations affect the lives of a large number of people, including their employees, customers and the local communities wherein they operate. Moreover, states use corporations in order to provide essential services to their people, such as a water supply, health care, pensions, running of correctional facilities and many others. Although in all of these cases the state continues to remain the primary duty bearer, it is fair to argue that the private party should possess a complementary duty to fulfil these entitlements, otherwise it will be free to treat relevant socio-economic rights through a strict business perspective that is predicated solely on financial considerations. Consider a situation where a poor country invites a foreign investor to construct a universal water supply system because it does not have the expertise or financial resources to do so itself. Although the country's water, as a public good, belongs to its people, the investor may refuse to supply those households that cannot afford to pay their water bills, thus depriving them of their right to water, an essential element for the preservation of life. Where the state does not possess the technical expertise to supply water and therefore to fulfil the right to water, the investor assumes that role through the agency created by the concession contract. If concessionaires were not mere agents of the state, then concessions could well terminate the human rights obligations of the state, without these being assumed by the concessionaire. This is clearly absurd. In the case at hand it could moreover be argued that the water, as a public good, does not belong to the investor who therefore cannot deprive its beneficiaries of it. The human rights duties of MNCs will be explored more fully in the following sections, but it suffices to say that, unlike criminal groups and organisations, MNCs must be deemed to possess particular human rights obligations (or obligations that produce several legal effects similar to those under human rights law) that are always complementary to those of the state.

The increased blurring of the private sphere, where human rights were traditionally inapplicable, with the public sphere is the reason why more and more NSA conduct is perceived as falling within the purview of human rights law.[12] The distinction is not always obvious and a fictitious case study is required to better illustrate the point. Following a natural disaster in country X a private charity makes a significant financial contribution through a trust fund set up by the government of X, which is vastly authoritarian. The trust deed contains a liability exclusion clause for the benefit of the charity, and the latter makes no further inquiry as to its use by the government, which then goes on to purchase arms in order to attack its political enemies and solidify its grip on power. Clearly, the charity directly contributed to the denial

---

[12] Clapham, above note 3, 1–25.

of fundamental rights, but is it fair justifying its negligence by reference to its benevolent intentions? Although the contribution was made in a private capacity its effect was to deny the enjoyment of rights, something relevant to the public sphere. Given the charity's intrusion into the public sphere it should at the very least be burdened with the duty to ensure that it does not contribute to human rights violations committed by governmental authorities.[13]

Several theories have been advanced to explain the application of positive duties on NSAs, mainly derived from the sphere of humanitarian law. It is first argued that members of non-state groups partaking in armed conflict are bound by treaties to which their state is a party because treaties apply to all persons in their territory and persons subject to their control.[14] Secondly, human rights and IHL treaties may directly impose obligations on individuals and groups, as is the case with common article 3 to the 1949 Geneva Conventions. Thirdly, in situations where a group is exercising functions that ordinarily pertain to a state it is generally viewed as possessing de facto governmental powers and is therefore liable in exactly the same manner as a state.[15] Paramilitaries acting under instructions of a state or de facto government entities cannot plausibly deny the administration of human rights to populations under their effective control given that the customary law of belligerent occupation – which applies *mutatis mutandis* in this case – obliges the occupier to protect and enforce the rights of the occupied/governed population. This result is usually also achieved through human rights obligations assumed by rebel groups/de facto governments on the basis of peace treaties and unilateral undertakings. Moreover, it is now firmly accepted under customary international law that the conduct of an insurrectional movement is considered an act of state when the movement succeeds to governmental power,[16] thereby conferring human rights obligations upon it. Alston has gone a step further and has tried to explain the applicability of human rights obligations, other than by relying on IHL or international criminal law. He argued in a report on the Tamil Tigers of Sri Lanka that human rights norms operate on three levels:

'As the rights of individuals, as obligations assumed by states and as legitimate expectations of the international community ... As a non-state actor, the [Tamil

---

[13] See I. Bantekas, *Trust Funds under International Law: Trustee Obligations of the UN and International Development Banks* (TMC Asser/Cambridge University Press, 2009) 190–6.

[14] Y. C. Sandoz, C. Swinarski and B. Zimmermann (eds.), *Commentary on the Additional Protocols of 8 June 1977 to the Geneva Conventions of 12 August 1949* (Martinus Nijhoff, 1987) para. 4444.

[15] See *Government of Spain* v. SS *Arantazu Mendi and Others* (UK) (1939), per Lord Atkin who defined them as exercising 'all the functions of a sovereign government in maintaining law and order'.

[16] See art. 10 of the ILC Articles on State Responsibility.

Tigers] do not have legal obligations under the [International Covenant on Civil and Political Rights] ICCPR, but remain subject to the demand of the international community, first expressed in the Universal Declaration of Human Rights, that every organ of society respect and promote human rights ... The Tamil Tigers and other armed groups must accept that insofar as they aspire to represent a people before the world, the international community will evaluate their conduct according to the Universal Declaration's 'common standard of achievement.'[17]

No doubt, the theoretical debate as to whether NSAs possess human rights obligations will intensify but will not be resolved quickly in favour of either camp. Rather, what this chapter aims to demonstrate is that whereas NSAs do not generally refuse to uphold human rights and humanitarian law, they do so through processes that are internal to them alone and not on the basis of accepted human rights standards. This cherry-picking of human rights breeds uncertainty, contributes to violations by NSAs and allows states to blur their own commitments.

19.3   MULTINATIONAL CORPORATIONS IN THE HUMAN RIGHTS ARCHITECTURE

19.3.1   MNCs as Foreign Investors

Companies cannot set up subsidiaries abroad because each country regulates the incorporation of companies in its legal order. Hence, in order for a foreign company to control affiliates established in more than one country it is necessary that the company and other affiliates incorporated elsewhere buy shares in each other (intra-shareholding) and appoint each affiliate's board of directors. This allows for a sufficient degree of control and coordination between the affiliates themselves and between the affiliates and the parent company without violating the incorporation rules of the territorial state.[18] This is a crude description of an MNC. Most MNCs never spell out the exact nature of this relationship and may in fact deny it in order to avoid tax liabilities and take advantage of preferential audit regimes.[19] The autonomy of the parent from its affiliate effectively means that whereas the affiliate may lawfully engage in conduct otherwise impermissible in the home state, it

---

[17] UN Special Rapporteur on extrajudicial, summary or arbitrary executions, UN doc. E/CN.4/ 2006/Add.5 (27 Mar 2006) paras. 25 and 27.

[18] E.g., see *OECD Guidelines for Multinational Enterprises* (2011) 17, online at www.oecd.org/ daf/inv/mne/48004323.pdf.

[19] A particularly troubling practice is 'transfer pricing', whereby entities operating under the umbrella of a parent company fix the price of goods or services that are sold or exchanged between them. Transfer pricing is commonly used by MNCs as a profit allocation mechanism whereby MNCs spread their net profits or losses (before being taxed) to their various subsidiaries in countries wherein these operate so as to minimise the existence

can engage in such conduct in the host state on account of its lax or weak regulatory framework.

Corporate entities, whether MNCs or other, are potent international actors requiring little diplomatic protection in disputes with foreign host states. Corporations satisfying the status of foreign investor because they operate in a state other than their own, are entitled to three layers of protection: (1) International law, chiefly through bilateral investment treaties (BITs) and multilateral ones, such as free trade agreements (e.g. the Energy Charter Treaty or NAFTA), as well as general international law, including customary law. Where a general right (such as the right against unlawful expropriation, whether direct or indirect) or an investment guarantee (e.g. most favoured nation, fair and equitable treatment, free repatriation of assets etc.) is found in a treaty or customary law it cannot be waived or restricted by domestic law or contract. More importantly, reference to investment or other arbitration under the BIT allows the investor to bypass the ordinary jurisdiction of the host state's (usually biased) local courts. (2) Domestic law: local investment laws typically set out investment incentives in the form of investment guarantees, which are binding on the host state. (3) Contract: there is no need for all investors to enter into a contract with the host state. Such contracts may overlap with the rights and guarantees under a BIT or customary law, but they may (and usually do) provide others and their governing law is the law of a state (e.g. English law). It has long been accepted that rights and guarantees in BITs, multilateral agreements and customary law are construed under international law and cannot be trumped by domestic law or contract.[20] All these layers of guarantees are intended to protect against interference with the investment (right to property), while at the same time reaping its developmental value (e.g. meaningful job creation, technology transfer etc.) for the host state, although there may of course exist some tension between the two.

Despite the conferral of rights and obligations in BITs and general international law, foreign investors (MNCs) have been allowed to cherry-pick legal regimes in a manner that affords them a great degree of self-regulation. By way of illustration, they are able to impose (or at least negotiate) stabilisation clauses in contracts with host states, whereby the latter agrees to freeze one

of taxable profits in a single jurisdiction. See Report of the UN Special Rapporteur on extreme poverty and human rights (Maria Sepulveda), UN doc. A/HR C/26/28 (22 May 2014), who noted that fiscal policies and unfair tax systems are among the major determinants in the enjoyment of human rights.

[20] In the eventuality of conflict between an investment treaty and the parties' contract, the tribunal will distinguish between disputes/violations arising from the treaty (and accordingly apply the governing law prescribed in the treaty) from disputes/violations arising from the contract (and accordingly apply the governing law prescribed there). *Wena Hotels Ltd* v. *Egypt* (ICSID) (2002) para. 36.

or more of its laws for a certain time against a particular investor. Despite the fact that stabilisation clauses fetter the authority of the state to legislate and obfuscate economic self-determination, their continuation demonstrates the power yielded by investors. In addition, the consistent practice of MNCs in particular cross-border industries creates rules recognised by courts and domestic laws as private custom. This rule-making capacity of corporate entities and MNCs is known as *lex mercatoria*,[21] and is part of a much larger process known as transnational law. Therefore, it is clear that MNCs not only enjoy a significant amount of international legal personality, but a large number of rights and guarantees as foreign investors.

Although MNCs enjoy a wide range of rights under international law, a rather different picture emerges as regards their respective obligations. While it is true that MNCs owe obligations to the host and home state under the terms of their concession and corporate laws respectively, three issues remain outstanding: (1) international treaties do not as a rule confer obligations on MNCs, subject to observations discussed in following sections; (2) the corporate and other laws of the home state do not as a rule apply to the operations of MNCs operating abroad through independent affiliates; and (3) the laws of the host state, particularly those that protect human rights and the environment, may be curtailed or stifled by the terms of the contract with the foreign MNC.

19.3.2   Human Rights and Foreign Direct Investment

In the last decade several model BITs have included provisions on human rights and environmental protection.[22] Even so, BITs are generally geared towards protecting the interests of investors from industrialised states, while at the same time developing host states are so eager to attract foreign direct investment (FDI) that they are willing to lower their human rights and environmental standards.[23] This process is aptly described as a 'race to the

---

[21] According to Teubner, the ultimate validation of *lex mercatoria* rests on the fact that not all legal orders are created by the nation state and accordingly that private orders of regulation can create law: G. Teubner, 'Global Bukowina: Legal Pluralism in the World Society', in G. Teubner (ed.), *Global Law Without a State* (Dartmouth, 1997) 15.

[22] Examples include the USA (arts. 8(3)(c)(i), 12 and 13), the Canadian FIPA (arts. 10(1), 11) and their Norwegian counterpart; indirectly, art. 5.5 of the Indian model BIT; art. 16 of the Brazilian Cooperation and Facilitation Investment Agreement (CFIA), which is effectively a model BIT/MIT.

[23] See e.g., K. J. Vandevelde, 'The Economics of Bilateral Investment Treaties' (2000) 41 *Harvard International Law Journal* 469, at 499, who argues that BITs 'seriously restrict the ability of host States to regulate foreign investment'. The US model BIT, e.g., prohibits performance obligations beyond what is established by international law, such as employability quotas of nationals of the host state; see also T. Gazzini, 'Bilateral Investment Treaties and Sustainable Development' (2014) 15 *Journal of World Investment* 936, who argues that the aim of sustainable growth is not directly measurable against the investor guarantees offered in BITs.

bottom'. It has to be said, however, that the persistent problem with invest-ment-related human rights is not so much the indifferent and/or abusive behaviour of foreign investors or their home states, but: (1) host states' poor domestication and monitoring of their human rights obligations,[24] which to some degree is predicated on the provision of investment guarantees that are detrimental to poor host states, and (2) the absence of a clear devel-opmental plan and objectives in the pursuit of FDI.[25] Indeed, in *Institute for Human Rights and Development* v. *DRC*, a relatively small Australian mining company operating in Kilwa, DRC, was found to have assisted the DRC army in the killing of more than seventy civilians and several other serious international crimes. The ACmHR identified the role of the mining company and recommended that the DRC government take specific measures to indemnify the victims and their families.[26] At the time of writing the DRC government had not taken any action. It is clear from this and similar situ-ations that foreign investors would not have acted in the way they did had it not been for the poor regulatory environment in the host state. No doubt, such an environment may well be a manifestation of the unequal power relationship between developing host states and foreign investors. A brief overview of developing states' investment-related human rights obligations demonstrates that these are weak, or vague, at best. Section 3 of the South African Protection of Investment Act 2015, which is among the very few with explicit reference to human rights treaties, reads:

This Act must be interpreted and applied in a manner that is consistent with:

a. its purposes as contemplated by section 4;
b. the Constitution, including:
    i. the interpretation of the Bill of Rights contemplated in section 39 of the Constitution;

---

[24] See CESCR, 'General Comment no 24 on state obligations under ICESCR in the context of business activities', UN doc E/C.12/GC/24 (10 August 2017) para. 13, which reads in part:

> States parties should identify any potential conflict between their obligations under the Covenant and under trade or investment treaties, and refrain from entering into such treaties where such conflicts are found to exist, as required under the principle of the binding character of treaties. The conclusion of such treaties should therefore be preceded by human rights impact assessments that take into account both the positive and negative human rights impacts of trade and investment treaties, including the contribution of such treaties to the realization of the right to development. ... The interpretation of trade and investment treaties currently in force should take into account the human rights obligations of the State ... States parties cannot derogate from the obligations under the Covenant in trade and investment treaties that they may conclude ...

[25] See I. Bantekas, 'The Linkages between Business and Human Rights and Their Underlying Causes', in I. Bantekas and M. A. Stein (eds.), *Cambridge Companion to Business and Human Rights* (Cambridge University Press, 2020) (forthcoming).

[26] *Institute for Human Rights and Development* v. *DRC* (ACmHPR) (2017).

ii. customary international law contemplated in section 232 of the Constitution; and

iii. international law contemplated in section 233 of the Constitution; and

c. any relevant convention or international agreement to which the Republic is or becomes a party.

The South African Act is exceptional, however. UNCTAD maintains an investment laws navigator[27] and it is disappointing to see that very few, if any, such laws make direct reference to human rights treaty obligations, as opposed to domestic law more generally, which may be overridden by BITs and (perhaps) contract.

Apart from poor domestication of international human rights law, a potent tension in foreign investment law is that (sometimes) the legitimate regulatory power of the host state may be curtailed by investment guarantees under a BIT, contract or host state laws. The *Tecmed* case is illustrative of this tension. It involved an investment agreement between Tecmed and Mexico with the purpose of constructing a landfill. Following the expiry of the first licence period the Mexican government refused to renew the licence, arguing correctly that the project caused adverse environmental and health effects on the local population. As a result, the investment was effectively terminated and the investor stood to suffer a financial loss. The investment tribunal to which the dispute was referred held that the 'government's intention [was] less important than the effects of the measures on the owner of the assets or on the benefits arising from such assets affected by the measure'.[28]

Despite the often-cited fragmentation of international investment law from general international law there are *some* signs of a human-centred investment architecture. Some model BITs are rendering human rights commitments an integral part of investment. The preamble to the 2015 Norwegian model BIT recognises that:

the promotion of sustainable investments is critical for the further development of national and global economies as well as for the pursuit of national and global objectives for sustainable development, and understanding that the promotion of such investments requires cooperative efforts of investors, host governments and home governments.

Moreover, in its definition of national treatment (i.e. that foreign investors shall be afforded the same treatment as the host state's nationals) in article 3(1), as well as most favoured nation (MFN) treatment, the BIT includes a very important footnote, which clarifies that:

---

[27] Available at: https://investmentpolicyhub.unctad.org/InvestmentLaws.

[28] *Técnicas Medioambientales Tecmed SA* v. *Mexico* (ICSID) (2003) para. 116; see also *Compãnia del Desarrollo de Santa Elena SA* v. *Costa Rica* (ICSID) (2000) para. 71.

a measure applied by a government in pursuance of legitimate policy objectives of public interest such as the protection of public health, human rights, labour rights, safety and the environment, although having a different effect on an investment or investor of another party, is not inconsistent with national treatment and most favoured nation treatment when justified by showing that it bears a reasonable relationship to rational policies not motivated by preference of domestic over foreign owned investment.

Even so, the problem with human rights stipulations in BITs is that they are meaningful only if they reinforce the human rights obligations of host states and in the process oblige investors to adhere to them. This is hardly the case. Powerful home states have demanded (through BITs and other agreements) that domestic host state laws, including human rights and environmental legislation, not be such as to effectively expropriate assets or strip foreign investors of legitimate investment guarantees. Although this seems common sense, situations may well arise where a host state's generous BIT or contractual obligations towards a foreign investor are in violation of its treaty-based human rights obligations. Investment treaties deal with such issues by prioritizing breaches of investor guarantees over and above other (including human rights-based) considerations. Exceptionally, such preferential treatment may be sidelined (or carved out) through general exception clauses in investment treaties, as is the case with article 10 of the Canadian Foreign Investment Promotion and Protection Agreements (FIPA). Article 11 of the FIPA goes on to say that host States must not lower domestic standards when attracting foreign direct investment. This 'principle' is accompanied by a consultation mechanism.

The Parties recognize that it is inappropriate to encourage investment by relaxing domestic health, safety or environmental measures. Accordingly, a Party should not waive or otherwise derogate from, or offer to waive or otherwise derogate from, such measures as an encouragement for the establishment, acquisition, expansion or retention in its territory of an investment of an investor. If a Party considers that the other Party has offered such an encouragement, it may request consultations with the other Party and the two Parties shall consult with a view to avoiding any such encouragement.

The last sentence of article 11 would otherwise be a wonderful display of international solidarity that places the international protection of human rights and the environment above the host state's endeavour to attract foreign investment.[29] However, the authors are not aware of a single instance where such consultations have taken place.[30]

[29] See also art. 11 Norwegian model BIT to the same effect; see also art. 1(6) of the French model BIT (2007), which states that: 'Nothing in this agreement shall be construed to prevent any contracting party from taking any measure to regulate investment of foreign companies and the conditions of activities of these companies in the framework of policies designed to preserve and promote cultural and linguistic diversity.'

[30] In *Hupacasath First Nation* v. *The Minister of Foreign Affairs of Canada and the Attorney-General of Canada* (Canada) (2015), the Court of Appeals upheld the judgment of the

Investment tribunals, with few exceptions,[31] are generally weary of allowing human rights claims by host states by which to override guarantees or rights owed to foreign investors.[32] Exceptionally, there is in practice a presumption in favour of tax sovereignty (and hence of fiscal self-determination) which renders expropriation claims almost redundant.[33] In the *Methanex* case, the tribunal held that the banning of a harmful gasoline additive was legitimate because it was not discriminatory and was undertaken within the scope of the host state's bona fide police powers.[34] The tribunal in *Saluka* fleshed out the competing tensions as follows:

It is now established in international law that states are not liable to pay compensation to a foreign investor when, in the normal exercise of their regulatory powers, they adopt in a non-discriminatory manner *bona fide* regulations that are aimed at the general welfare. [Given the absence of an appropriate international definition] it thus inevitably falls to the adjudicator to determine whether particular conduct by a state crosses the line that separates valid regulatory activity from expropriation.[35]

A similar approach was recently adopted in *Mamidoil* v. *Albania*, which concerned a fuel distributor's claim that reforms by Albania to its maritime transport sector in pursuit of an environmental policy amounted to creeping expropriation. The International Centre for the Settlement of Investment Disputes (ICSID) tribunal held that the claimant could not benefit from the BIT because the investment had been undertaken in violation of Albanian law and as a result no legitimate expectations could be lawfully anticipated. Moreover, the adoption of environmentally friendly laws were within the host state's 'legitimate policy choices' given that the only impact on the investment was a decrease in profits.[36] Regulatory sovereignty as a means

---

Federal Court (2013) FC 900, whereby the Canada/China BIT, which is similar to the FIPA, had not been proven to produce any appreciable and non-speculative effects on the rights and interests of the appellants.

[31] See *Urbaser S.A. and Consorcio de Aguas Bilbao Bizkaia* v. *Argentina* (ICSID) (2016).

[32] See B. Simma, 'Foreign Investment Arbitration: A Place for Human Rights?' (2011) 60 *International & Comparative Law Quarterly* 573; E. Guntrip, 'Self-determination and Foreign Direct Investment: Reimagining Sovereignty in International Investment Law' (2016) 65 *International & Comparative Law Quarterly* 829. See *CMS Gas Transmission Company* v. *Argentine Republic* (ICSID) (2005) para. 121, where the tribunal stated that 'there is no question of affecting fundamental human rights when considering the [application of the investment guarantees] contemplated by the parties'.

[33] The tribunal in *El Paso Energy International Company* v. *Argentine Republic* (ICSID) (2011) at para. 297, considered the export withholding taxes imposed on the investor to be 'reasonable governmental regulation within the context of the [Argentinian] crisis'. See A. Lazem and I. Bantekas, 'The Treatment of Tax as Expropriation in International Investor–State Arbitration' (2015) 30 *Arbitration International* 1–46.

[34] *Methanex Corp* v. *USA* (UNCITRAL) (2005) para. 7 of part IV.

[35] *Saluka Investments BV* v. *Czech Republic* (ICSID) (2006) paras. 262 and 264.

[36] *Mamidoil* v. *Albania* (ICSID) (2015).

of promoting and fulfilling fundamental socio-economic policies has been recognised by investment tribunals. In *Postova Banka AS and Istrokapital SE v. Greece*, an ICSID tribunal noted in respect of measures adopted by Greece following its debt crisis that '[i]n sum, sovereign debt is an instrument of government monetary and economic policy and its impact at the local and international levels makes it an important tool for the handling of social and economic policies of a State'.[37] The fact that host states possess authority to undertake regulatory actions in the pursuit of general welfare (i.e. for a public purpose) does not mean that they can directly or indirectly substantially deprive the enjoyment of the investment in an arbitrary and discriminatory manner. Meaningful investments are crucial to the economic development of states. But the stance of the tribunal in *Postova Banka* sadly seems to be unique.

From yet another perspective, economic self-determination clearly suggests that contracts and treaties which produce odious, illegitimate, illegal and unsustainable results and which are detrimental to the livelihood of the host state's population, albeit to the benefit of a few individuals or corporations, cannot remain intact simply by reason of the sanctity of contracts.[38] This is also evident and understandable from an economics approach and particularly the obsolescing bargain model. This is a model of interaction between a foreign investor/MNC and a host state, whereby although the initial bargain favours the MNC, as the MNC's fixed assets in the host state increase, so should the bargaining power of the host state. This has traditionally been one of the key requirements of foreign investment, namely the conferral of economic and developmental benefits to the host state.[39] One should by no means dismiss investment law and investor-state arbitration. In fact,

---

[37] *Postova Banka AS and Istrokapital SE v. Greece* (ICSID) (2015) para. 324.

[38] Among others, a study by the Netherlands Bureau for Economic Policy Analysis, Discussion Paper 298, entitled 'The Regional Impact of Bilateral Investment Treaties on Foreign Direct Investment' (2015) at 4, noted that although there was an average increase of 35 per cent of FDI flows as a result of the existence of a BIT, this outcome was only true in upper-middle-income countries, and that there was no increase in FDI flows in sub-Saharan Africa, South America and the Caribbean. See also the discussion in Chapter 13.6 on the impact of sovereign debt on human rights.

[39] See *Salini Construttori SpA Italstrade SpA v. Morocco* (ICSID) (2001) paras. 52–3. The *Salini* criteria required: (1) some degree of permanence; (2) assumption of risk; (3) contribution to the host state's development, as well as (4) substantial commitment, particularly through the infusion of capital and other assets. See also *Société Générale de Surveillance (SGS) v. Pakistan* (ICSID) (2003) para. 133; *Saipem v. Bangladesh* (ICSID) (2007) paras. 99–111; *Malaysian Historical Salvors v. Malaysia* (ICSID) (2009) paras. 57–81. Post-2008 non-binding accords adopted by the G20 and inter-governmental organisations clearly suggest that not all FDI is beneficial, but only that which qualifies as sustainable investment and aspires to inclusive growth. See para. v of the G20 Guiding Principles for Global Investment Policy Making.

because of the transparency of this judicial mechanism and its fairness,[40] despite some of its shortcomings identified above, it has been recommended by a high-level task force commissioned by the International Bar Association (IBA) as the best means of resolving issues of justice and human rights created by climate change.[41] That investor–state arbitration requires urgent and wholesale reform is in no doubt by all camps, however, particularly with a view to placating human rights and the environment therein.

19.3.3 Emerging Human Rights Obligations of MNCs in Multilateral Treaties and Soft Law

International treaties do not confer human rights obligations upon MNCs. Some, however, do so indirectly and this is achieved in two ways. The first comprises provisions that call on states parties to eliminate a prohibited conduct from corporate practice. Article 2(e) of CEDAW, for example, and article 2(1)(d) of ICERD require states to take all appropriate measures to eliminate discrimination by both public and private entities, thus implicitly encompassing corporations.

The second type of obligation arises from corporate criminal liability provisions in treaties, which suggest that corporations can and do bear criminal (and administrative) liability. This is true in respect of anti-corruption treaties, particularly articles 2 and 3(2) of the 1997 OECD Convention on Combating Bribery of Foreign Public Officials in International Business Transactions and article 26 of the 2003 UN Convention against Corruption, among others. It is assumed that because a corporation incurs criminal liability it is under an obligation not only to prevent the conduct in question but also to respect the underlying right or freedom. The right to be free from corruption encompasses numerous underlying entitlements that are not immediately clear. Given that it involves a country's resources and culminates in the deprivation of social welfare services and goods, corruption denies the right to economic self-determination, the right to food, water, health, social security, adequate standard of living and the overarching right to be free from poverty.

In fact, both treaty bodies and domestic courts have held in unequivocal terms that although human rights obligations are addressed to states, where their implementation is undertaken through the medium of corporate entities, the rights in question are also shouldered by the corporation in addition to the state. In *Etcheverry* v. *Omint* the applicant, who was an HIV sufferer, was provided by his employer with membership of a private health plan.

---

[40] It is instructive that almost 60 per cent of investment disputes have been resolved in favour of host states.

[41] IBA, 'Achieving Justice and Human Rights in an Era of Climate Change Disruption' (July 2014) 136–47.

When he was later made redundant he sought to continue his membership through private funds, but the insurance company refused. The Argentine Supreme Court held that private health providers were under a duty to protect the right to health of their customers and that their special relationship was not simply of a contractual nature.[42] Given the ever-growing privatisation of otherwise public social services, such as education, sanitation, water supply, utilities, health care and pensions, the obligations of corporate entities administering these services must be read in the light of duties to rights-bearers.[43]

Besides reading these human rights obligations in the relevant treaties, it is important to emphasise that in the early 1980s a movement began whose aim was to impose direct human rights obligations on MNCs. This started off as a standard-setting exercise in the form of non-binding guidelines issued by NGOs, business circles or intergovernmental organisations with the hope that MNCs would voluntarily adhere, whether by reason of commitment or reputational fear. Among the many hundreds of these instruments one may highlight Social Accountability (SA) 8000,[44] the Caux Principles for Business,[45] the Extractive Industries Transparency Initiative,[46] the UN Global Compact and the OECD Guidelines for Multinational Enterprises. The UN Global Compact, for example, is comprised of ten principles founded on the International Bill of Human Rights, the Rio Declaration on Environment and Development and anti-corruption treaties.[47] A large number of MNCs jumped enthusiastically on the bandwagon of these initiatives and despite their non-binding character many MNCs implemented them through the adoption of corporate policies. Moreover, the advancement of corporate social responsibility has given rise to a trend of voluntary social reporting which makes transparent the human rights and environmental record of MNCs, which in turn induces them to improve. The reporting of financial, social and environmental information within single or separate reports is known as 'triple bottom line'. An illustrative example is the Global Reporting Initiative (GRI). Its mission is to develop reporting and verification guidelines in respect of economic, environmental and social performance. The GRI guidelines serve as performance indicators for the corporations, as well as a measure of comparison within

---

[42] *Etcheverry* v. *Omint Sociedad Anónima y Servicios* (Argentina) (2001). In *Restrepo and López* v. *Salud Colmena* (Colombia) (2001), the Colombian Constitutional Court ordered a private hospital to carry out free HIV testing for indigent AIDS sufferers.

[43] CESCR, Statement on the obligations of states parties regarding the corporate sector and economic, social and cultural rights, UN doc. E/C.12/2011/1 (12 July 2011) para. 7; *I.D.G.* v. *Spain* (CESCR) (2015).

[44] Online at www.sa-intl.org/_data/n_0001/resources/live/2008StdEnglishFinal.pdf.

[45] Online at www.cauxroundtable.org/index.cfm?menuid=8.

[46] Online at https://eiti.org/eiti/principles.

[47] Available with commentary online at www.unglobalcompact.org/AboutTheGC/TheTenPrinciples/index.html.

a particular industry. Reports prepared on the basis of the GRI guidelines should be transparent, inclusive (i.e. involve the views of all stakeholders), auditable, complete, relevant, built within a sustainability context, accurate, neutral, comparable, clear and timely.

This euphoria that came with voluntary mechanisms was perceived by an expert subsidiary body of the UN Commission on Human Rights as a signal that MNCs were not wholly hostile towards the move from voluntary to more binding obligations. This perception was ultimately erroneous, culminating in the rejection by the business community of the more assertive Norms on Transnational Corporations and Other Business Enterprises with Regard to Human Rights.[48] The Norms sought to impose on MNCs the same range of human rights obligations under international law as those addressed to states, namely to promote, respect and fulfil human rights. The Norms' expansive approach linked corporate liability not only to the company's control over particular conduct, but also to its influence and benefit. The proposal created deep divisions between the business community and human rights advocates and was abandoned in favour of a special procedure that would undertake an assessment of MNCs' existing human rights obligations.

The UN Secretary-General's Special Representative on Business and Human Rights, John Ruggie, introduced three core principles on the basis of a differentiated yet complementary framework of responsibilities between MNCs and states. These consist of: (1) the state duty to protect against human rights abuses by third parties, including business; (2) the corporate responsibility to respect human rights; and (3) the need for more effective access to justice.[49] In 2011 these were formalised into a set of Guiding Principles on Business and Human Rights: Implementing the UN Protect, Respect and Remedy Framework, which were endorsed by the UN Human Rights Council.[50] Because the Special Representative had worked very closely with the business community for a period of six years and the Principles were realistic, they have very rapidly been accepted as an authoritative statement of MNCs' human rights responsibilities (as opposed to obligations).

At the heart of the Guiding Principles is the notion that states must protect against human rights abuses occurring on their territory by MNCs and other private entities. To this end they must undertake appropriate legislative and enforcement measures and should set out clearly the human rights responsibilities of MNCs and ensure among other things that laws pertinent to business enterprises, such as corporate law, enable business respect for human

---

[48] UN doc. E/CN.4/Sub.2/2003/12/Rev.2 (2003).

[49] See Report of the Special Representative, 'Protect, Respect and Remedy: A Framework for Business and Human Rights', UN doc. A/HRC/8/5 (7 April 2008).

[50] 'Guiding Principles on Business and Human Rights: Implementing the United Nations "Protect, Respect and Remedy" Framework', UN doc. A/HRC/17/31 (21 March 2011) Annex (Guiding Principles Commentary).

rights.[51] The dilemma about whether a state should choose to violate a treaty obligation rather than its human rights obligations should not arise in the first place, proclaims principle 9, and the growing investment jurisprudence on the sovereign regulatory authority of host states, as explored in the next section, confirms this principle.

Business and human rights soft law has become so extensive that some mechanisms even encompass an enforcement dimension. The OECD Guidelines on Multinational Enterprises, for example, although voluntary for businesses, requires adhering states to 'make a binding commitment to implement them'.[52] As a result, adhering states undertake to set up national contact points (NCPs) in order to 'further the effectiveness' of the Guidelines. Complainants, which could be anyone, may make a complaint alleging that businesses are in violation of the Guidelines and in turn seek some kind of resolution.[53] The 2011 revision of the Guidelines highlights the responsibility of business to respect rights, which itself arises from the UN Guiding Principles on Business and Human Rights.[54]

That states have a responsibility to regulate MNCs (and other private parties) in the discharge of their human rights duties has been highlighted manifold by treaty bodies.[55] The Human Rights Committee (HRCtee) emphasised in General Comment 31 that 'the positive obligations on states parties to ensure Covenant rights will only be fully discharged if individuals are protected by the state, not just against violations of Covenant rights by its agents, but also by acts committed by private persons or entities'.[56] In another section of this book this positive duty is explained in relation to terrorist acts endangering life and health.[57]

19.3.4   MNC Liability under Tort Law

The corporate responsibility to respect human rights is complementary to that of states. At the very least MNCs must respect domestic human rights law in their country of operation. This entails a duty to avoid infringing the

---

[51] Guiding Principles 1–3.

[52] OECD, 'Directorate for Financial and Enterprise Affairs, Guidelines for Multinational Enterprises' (2011) 13.

[53] Ibid., 71.   [54] Ibid., chapter IV.

[55] Committee on Economic, Social and Cultural Rights (CESCR), General Comment 18 (right to work), UN doc. E/C.12/GC/18 (6 February 2006) para. 35; CESCR, General Comment 15 (right to water), UN doc. E/C.12/2002/11 (20 January 2003) para. 23; Committee on the Rights of the Child (CtRC), General Comment 5 (persons with disabilities), UN doc. E/1995/22 (1995) para. 42; Committee on the Elimination of Discrimination against Women (CtEDAW), General Recommendation 25, paras. 7, 29, 31–2; CtEDAW, General Recommendation 24, paras. 14–17; HRCtee, General Comment 28, para. 31.

[56] HRCtee, General Comment 31, para. 8. In *Arenz et al.* v. *Germany* (HRCtee) (2004) para. 8.5 and *Cabal & Pasini Bertran* v. *Australia* (HRCtee) (2003) para. 7.2, the HRCtee discussed the admissibility of individual communications relating to abuse by private parties.

[57] See Chapter 18.4 and *Osman* v. *United Kingdom* (ECtHR) (1998) para. 115.

rights of others as well as addressing adverse human rights effects caused by their operations.[58] The Principles clearly suggest that where domestic law falls below fundamental human rights, MNCs should seek ways of honouring them.[59] Although MNCs are not the direct bearers of duties under international human rights law they are none the less obliged to respect human rights to the degree that these are prejudiced by their operations and as long as they have the capacity to take appropriate action. This obligation is premised on a threefold dimension. First, MNCs should adopt policy commitments upon which all future internal and external company dealings must be predicated. For example, a policy commitment to respect the right to water should be interpreted by the company's legal team and management board as prohibiting all contracts that infringe this right, including arbitral suits which, if successful, risk depriving a local population of its right to water.[60] Although consistent practice with respect to policy commitments does not exist it suffices to say that the public nature of these instruments is to make available all relevant company information to the company's stakeholders, including affected communities and consumers. In this manner a consumer could reasonably argue that the policy commitments had become an integral part of its agreement with the company through the so-called incorporation by reference doctrine, which is arguably a general principle of contract law.[61]

In any event, there are sensible restrictions to what a corporation can publicly claim, even if its statements are not viewed from the perspective of contract or tort.[62] In *Kasky* v. *Nike* an activist sued Nike Corporation, arguing that it had used false advertising in a publicity campaign to defend itself against accusations of engaging in manufacturing under inhuman manufacturing conditions in Asia. The California Supreme Court argued that since a company's public statements could conceivably persuade consumers to buy its products, such statements deserve only limited freedom of speech protection.[63]

---

[58] Guiding Principle 11.   [59] Guiding Principle 23(b).

[60] See 19.3.2, whereby the (state) parties, and by implication the private investors, are obliged to conform to international human rights and environmental treaties.

[61] Incorporation by reference means that reference in a contract to any policy, terms or other document, is binding on the parties, provided that the reference is such as to make that document part of the contract. It is generally accepted that the instrument incorporated by reference need not be an agreement previously concluded by the parties. It may just as well be one of the parties' standard terms or an instrument to which none of the parties has any other relationship. See *Thyssen Canada Ltd* v. *Mariana (The)* (Canada) (2000); *Fai Tak Engineering Co. Ltd* v. *Sui Chong Construction & Engineering Co. Ltd* (Hong Kong) (2009).

[62] In very general terms, a tort or delict is a civil wrong (and sometimes even a crime) which unfairly causes another person to suffer harm or loss and in respect of which the wrongdoer (tortfeasor) incurs civil (tort) liability, in addition to any criminal liability, if any.

[63] *Kasky* v. *Nike* (US) (2002), affirmed by the US Supreme Court in *Nike* v. *Kasky* (US) (2003).

The responsibility of MNCs to respect international human rights law in the course of their operations, especially extraterritorially, is not a mere theoretical construction. This has been enforced since World War II in cases where a number of senior industrialists were convicted for their role in accepting slave labour provided by the Nazis in their factories.[64] As far as the Guiding Principles are concerned the human rights responsibilities of MNCs and their corresponding liability are engaged in three situations: (1) by directly committing a violation; (2) by means of complicity; and (3) by failing to use leverage where the MNC has the 'ability to effect change in the wrongful practices of an entity that causes a harm'.[65] In *Doe* v. *Unocal*, a group of companies, including an American one, had undertaken the construction of a pipeline project in Myanmar. The regime of the country was notoriously brutal and autocratic, so it was no surprise that the government procured local workers under conditions of enforced labour. The same people endured acts of murder and rape by the government while working on the project. The plaintiffs relied on the US Aliens Tort Claims Act (ATCA), which confers federal jurisdiction over 'any civil action by an alien for a tort only, committed in violation of the law of nations or a treaty of the United States'.[66] When they filed a suit in the United States (USA) under the ATCA there was no contention that Unocal had orchestrated the violations, but it was clear that it had accepted the situation in full knowledge of the labourers' predicament. The California District Court held that MNCs may be held liable for violations of treaties and customary law independently of the actions of states, as well as for state-like acts or state-related conduct.[67] This ruling was in full conformity with the extraterritorial rationale of the ATCA, but has subsequently been eroded by the US Supreme Court.

In 2010, the Second Circuit Court of Appeals in *Kiobel* v. *Royal Dutch Petroleum Co.*[68] entertained a suit by Nigerian nationals alleging that various MNCs, including the sued oil giant, were complicit in human rights violations in Nigeria. The allegations were dismissed on the ground that the ATCA does not allow claims against corporations. Upon certiorari, the US Supreme Court affirmed the District Court's ruling against the extraterritorial presumption of claims under the ATCA, holding that: 'all the relevant conduct took place

---

[64] See *USA* v. *Carl Krauch et al. (IG Farben case)* (WWII Military Commission); *USA* v. *Flick* (WWII Military Commission) (1947); *USA* v. *Krupp* (WWII Military Commission) (1948).

[65] Guiding Principles Commentary, above note 50, at 17.

[66] 28 USC §1350.

[67] *Doe* v. *Unocal* (I) (US) (1997). None the less, in the instant case the district court held that although Unocal benefited from the abuses it was not proven that the company wanted to control, or that it in fact controlled, the Burmese military to perpetrate these acts. On appeal, the Court of Appeals for the ninth circuit reversed this decision, holding that plaintiffs need only demonstrate Unocal's assistance to the military: *Doe* v. *Unocal* (US) (2001).

[68] *Kiobel* v. *Royal Dutch Petroleum Co.* (US) (2010).

outside the United States. And even where the claims touch and concern the territory of the United States, they must do so with sufficient force to displace the presumption against extraterritorial application ... Corporations are often present in many countries, and it would reach too far to say that mere corporate presence suffices.'[69] The Supreme Court's opinion seems to exclude tort claims alleging violations of customary law based solely on conduct occurring abroad.[70] However, given that the Supreme Court never actually stated that corporations can never incur criminal liability, other district courts have taken the view that, although exceptional, corporations can indeed be found liable under the ATCA.

In *Re South Africa Apartheid Litigation*, an action in tort was brought against US corporations, such as Ford and IBM, alleging that they were complicit in violations during the apartheid era by manufacturing vehicles and computers for the then racist regime of South Africa. The court distinguished whether particular conduct violates a universal international norm, which is regulated by international law, and the question of who bears liability for the conduct, which is a matter for domestic law. The court had no problem finding that corporations can indeed incur liability in tort, rejecting the idea that a group of individuals could escape liability simply because they had incorporated into a legal person.[71]

Of equal importance are cases which the parties settle, even under strict confidentiality, because they demonstrate that the courts of the parent company are willing to entertain suits brought by foreign victims. In the *Trafigura* case, thirty-one Ivorians sued Trafigura, a Dutch company, in London for illegally dumping hundreds of tons of toxic waste in an area outside Abidjan, which ultimately had a serious health impact. Trafigura was reported as having agreed to a significant settlement with both the victims and the Ivorian government, the details of which were never officially disclosed.

In 2014, the Human Rights Council adopted Resolution 26/22,[72] requesting the OHCHR 'to facilitate the sharing and exploration of the full range of legal options and practical measures to improve access to remedy for victims of business-related human rights abuses'. The OHCHR had already set up its Accountability and Remedy Project,[73] and issued a comprehensive report in

---

[69] *Kiobel* v. *Royal Dutch Petroleum Co.* (US) (2013) at 1669.

[70] *Balintulo* v. *Daimler* AG (US) (2013) at 182.

[71] *Re South Africa Apartheid Litigation* (US) (2014); similarly, *Doe* v. *Nestle* (US) (2014), where it was held that allegations whereby the corporation was aware of child slavery among its supply chain, yet none the less retained these suppliers motivated by profit, was sufficient to establish the 'aiding and abetting' of child slavery under the ATCA.

[72] HRC resolution 26/22 (27 June 2014).

[73] Available at www.ohchr.org/EN/Issues/Business/Pages/ OHCHRaccountabilityandremedyproject.aspx.

2016. The report noted that poor access to judicial remedies was the result of 'fragmented, poorly designed or incomplete legal regimes; lack of legal development; lack of awareness of the scope and operation of regimes; structural complexities within business enterprises; problems in gaining access to sufficient funding for private law claims; and a lack of enforcement'.[74] While state-based judicial mechanisms were identified as key to accessing adequate remedies, the report highlighted the importance of state-based non-judicial mechanisms and non-state grievance mechanisms.[75] By way of illustration, there is proliferation of agreements between corporations and local communities, the purpose of which is to set up grievance mechanisms,[76] adequate consultation and disclosure. In 2011 the mining law committee of the IBA produced a model mining agreement for use by mining companies and mining communities known as the Model Mine Development Agreement (MMDA).[77] Although the MMDA recognises that mining projects must be financially viable it asks the parties to take a broader look at the social, natural and economic environments of their operations. The Agreement imposes human rights obligations on the parties,[78] the duty to negotiate community development agreements with the local population,[79] as well as a company grievance mechanism with access rights for the community.[80]

19.3.5   MNCs as Influencers and their Due Diligence Obligations

What is evident thus far is that despite the lack of direct obligations on MNCs in countries whose laws favour or turn a blind eye to human rights violations, MNCs can play a distinct role in protecting human rights. They can do this because of their asymmetric financial relationship with the host nation. Coca Cola Co., for example, declared a net profit of US$9.5 billion in 2010, while the gross domestic product (GDP) of Liberia during the same period was US$1 billion, that of Sierra Leone US$2 billion, US$5 billion for Malawi, US$4.5 billion for Guinea and a meagre US$800 million for Gambia. No doubt, this asymmetry, if coupled with a sincere corporate commitment to human rights, grants MNCs sufficient negotiating power vis-à-vis the host state to ensure compliance with human rights, particularly (but not

---

[74] OHCHR, 'Improving Accountability and Access to Remedy for Victims of Business-related Human Rights Abuse', UN doc. A/HRC/32/19 (10 May 2016) para. 4.

[75] Ibid., para. 3.

[76] In at least two countries there exists a statutory obligation to resolve such disputes involving a human rights element through arbitration. See Australia's Native Title Act 1993 and Canada's Yukon Oil and Gas Act, ch. 162.

[77] MMDA 1.0, online at www.mmdaproject.org/presentations/MMDA1_0_ 110404 Bookletv3.pdf.

[78] Ibid., s. 10.3.   [79] Ibid., s. 22.1.   [80] Ibid., s. 27.1.

exclusively) within the context of its operations, despite domestic laws and practices to the contrary. Although under no obligation, powerful MNCs can equally exert their influence on local governments to abstain from committing human rights violations.

MNCs have been criticized not only for failing to exert their influence over governments with which they are in close collaboration, but also for undermining the realization of rights and the environment by 'exerting undue influence over domestic and international decision-makers and public institutions'. This phenomenon is known as corporate capture.[81] No doubt, lobbying is a democratic right, but unchecked it risks corroding trust in public institutions.[82]

The exertion of influence and defiance of arbitrary laws and practices by MNCs has been found to give them a reputational advantage in the global consumer market, as the *Ogoniland* case aptly demonstrated. In 1995 the Abacha regime in Nigeria executed Ken Saro Wiwa and other activists who had fought a public campaign showing that the oil giant Shell had colluded with the authorities in oil-rich Ogoniland to expel the defiant local population. Moreover, it was demonstrated that both the government and Shell were responsible for polluting the water and other natural habitats to the detriment of the people's health.[83] Weeks prior to Wiwa's deplorable execution Shell was petitioned by NGOs worldwide to intervene and use its influence to avert the government's plan.[84] Shell adamantly refused to be dragged into local politics, but following Wiwa's execution the company's public image and finances suffered such a shock that it proceeded to change its official policy on human rights in 1997 through its General Business Principles. Consumer pressure is a significant aspect in the voluntary human rights policies and public pledges of MNCs and to a large degree has helped shape these policies.[85] It is no wonder that

---

[81] See www.escr-net.org/corporateaccountability/corporatecapture.

[82] See R. Chari, J. Hogan and G. Murphy, *Regulating Lobbying: A Global Comparison* (Manchester University Press, 2010).

[83] *Social and Economic Rights Action Center (SERAC) and Center for Economic and Social Rights (CESCR) v. Nigeria (Ogoniland case)* (ACmHPR) (2001).

[84] K. Tangen, K. Rudsar and H. O. Bergesen, 'Confronting the Ghost: Shell's Human Rights Strategy', in A. Eide, H. O. Bergesen and P. R. Goyer (eds.), *Human Rights and the Oil Industry* (Hart, 2000) 185.

[85] A study conducted in 2002 by Cone revealed that of US consumers aware of a corporation's negative corporate social responsibility (CSR) practice, 91 per cent would most probably prefer another firm, 85 per cent would disseminate this information to family or friends, 83 per cent would refuse to invest in that company, 80 per cent would refuse to work at that company and 76 per cent would boycott its products. Opinion Research Corporation International, *2002 Cone Corporate Citizenship Study.*

several models of corporate responsibility have been suggested by reference to corporate involvement in structural injustice. Iris Young's social
connection model of responsibility, for example, posits that all agents
who contribute by their actions to the structural processes that produce
injustice have responsibilities to work to remedy these injustices.[86] Readers
will readily combine these remarks with the use of advocacy as a potent
human rights tool.[87]

In between the responsibility to adopt corporate policies and prevent
human rights violations through non-complicity, including the use of adequate leverage, MNCs are under a duty to undertake human rights due diligence. Just like environmental impact assessment studies, which are now
mandatory in all projects, human rights due diligence aims to identify,
prevent, mitigate and account the adverse human rights effects of corporate operations.[88] This should be an ongoing process and must consider all
those factors where the MNC might cause or contribute to a negative impact
through its own activities, or by a direct link to its operations, products,
services or even by its business relationships.[89] By way of illustration, a gar-
ments producer setting up a production line in a developing country should
be alert to the following factors, among others, that can have a negative
human rights impact: whether its suppliers are employing children and if
they are in conformity with international labour standards;[90] whether the
authorities are discharging waste from the plant into potable reservoirs or
agricultural land; and whether its own workers are prevented by government orders from striking. Due diligence of this nature essentially ensures
that all of the corporation's departments and suppliers are in conformity
with human rights law.[91]

---

[86] See I. M. Young, 'Responsibility and Global Justice: A Social Connection Model' (2006) 23
Social Philosophy and Policy 102.

[87] See Chapter 3.9.4.

[88] In *Orlando José Morales Ramos* v. *Drummond Ltd* (Colombia) (2013), the Constitutional
Court held that the right to a healthy environment created an obligation on the operator
of a coal mine (especially in accordance with the protective and precautionary principles)
to take effective measures to prevent environmental degradation and health risks; equally,
Diaguita Community v. *Compañía Minera Nevada SpA (Pascua Lama case)* (Chile) (2013).

[89] Guiding Principle 17.

[90] See the Shell Supplier Principles, which place a heavy emphasis on human rights, online at
http://s01.static-shell.com/content/dam/shell/static/products-services/downloads/suppliers/
supplier-principles.pdf.

[91] E.g., following a devastating fire that caused loss of life to many Bangladeshi garment
labourers as a result of poor health and safety, a binding Accord on fire and building
safety was agreed to between brands and trade unions in Bangladesh. See http://
bangladeshaccord.org/.

CASE STUDY 19.1
Unilateral Repudiation of Arbitral Awards Violating Constitutional Guarantees

In a case entertained by the Caribbean Court of Justice (CCJ), a last instance court for Caribbean island-states, a newly elected Belize government repudiated a tax concession granted to a group of companies by means of a settlement deed negotiated by its predecessor government. The concession was adhered to by the parties for a period of two years, notwithstanding the fact that it had not been approved by the Belize legislature, was confidential (hence non-transparent) and was manifestly contrary to the country's tax laws. The successor government repudiated the concession and the private parties initiated arbitral proceedings which rendered an award for damages which they subsequently sought to enforce in Belize. The issue of enforcement ultimately reached the CCJ, which was asked to assess the government's claim that the violation of fundamental constitutional rules and the interests of the people of Belize dictated that the award in question violates Caribbean and international public policy.[1] The Court upheld these claims, arguing that public policy should be assessed by reference to 'the values, aspirations, mores, institutions and conception of cardinal principles of law of the people of Belize', as well as international public policy. The tax concession could only be considered illegal if it was found to breach 'fundamental principles of justice or the rule of law and represented an unacceptable violation of those principles'. The Court did not expressly say that such tax concessions were repugnant per se or that they gave rise to a legitimate human rights defence, but this was certainly implicit. What the Court did emphasise, however, is that tax concessions, even those subject to conduct-based estoppel such as the one at hand, are procedurally unfair or illegitimate because they violate fundamental principles of constitutional legal order and to 'disregard these values is to attack the foundations upon which the rule of law and democracy are constructed'.[2]

---

[1] Violation of public policy (both domestic and international) is one of the grounds under which an arbitral award may be refused enforcement under art. V of the 1958 New York Convention on the Recognition and Enforcement of Foreign Arbitral Awards.

[2] *BCB Holdings Ltd and Belize Bank Ltd* v. *Attorney-General of Belize* (CCJ) (2013). It should be noted that BCB and the Bank of Belize bypassed the CCJ by seeking to enforce the award in New York and ultimately succeeded. *Government of Belize* v. *Belize Social Development Ltd [formerly BCB]* (US) Ct Appeals judgment (13 May 2016), cert. den. US Supreme Court decision (12 January 2017).

QUESTIONS

1. What are the reasons inhibiting states from fully regulating the extraterritorial activities of MNCs?

2. One of the key debates in the discussion on the human rights obligations of MNCs is whether in the absence of a concrete legal regime the next best thing is to demand that MNCs undertake voluntary initiatives. Some of these are discussed in the following section. What are the benefits arising from voluntary initiatives and what possible drawbacks can you identify?

3. Can NSAs assume human rights obligations under international law? If so, is the obligation of the state primary or residual to that of NSAs?

4. In 2014 an idea was put forward for the creation of an international tribunal on business and human rights. It would have jurisdiction over corporate torts or delicts and the presumption is that corporations would provide their consent because of reputational factors, in addition to the tribunal's fair and expeditious proceedings.[92] What appeal do you think such a tribunal would have for corporations and even if it were to go ahead what pitfalls do you envisage for victims of transnational corporate violations?

19.4 HUMAN RIGHTS OBLIGATIONS OF INTERNATIONAL ORGANISATIONS

19.4.1 General Obligations

Intergovernmental organisations (IGOs) are set up by states with a view to accomplishing a variety of functions which no single country could undertake on its own.[93] As a result, they are founded on the principles of consent, cooperation and the pursuit of common aims and objectives. IGOs possess an international legal personality that is distinct from that of their member states, and their powers and functions are described in their founding instruments. Even so, IGOs possess additional 'implied' powers (i.e. not stipulated in their founding instruments) to the degree that these are essential for fulfilling the primary powers and functions entrusted to them.[94] This distinct

---

[92] See C. Cronstedt et al., 'An International Arbitration Tribunal on Business and Human Rights: Reshaping the Judiciary', online at http://business-humanrights.org/sites/default/files/media/documents/intl_arbitration_tribunal_version_3-23_june_2014.pdf.

[93] Art. 2(a) of the ILC Articles on the Responsibility of International Organisations (ARIO) (2011) defines an IGO as 'an organisation established by a treaty or other instrument governed by international law and possessing its own international legal personality. International organisations may include as members, in addition to states, other entities'.

[94] *Reparations for Injuries Suffered in the Service of the UN* (ICJ) (1949) at 198.

legal personality of IGOs means that they contract and assume liability independently of their member states, despite the fact that their member states act as their executive organs and adopt decisions that bind the legal person of the organisation.[95] Although this seems like a reasonable adaptation of the concept of legal personality found in domestic legal orders, it is not, because unlike domestic legal persons (for example, corporations), IGOs are established and operated by states but lack many of the liabilities and obligations associated with statehood, such as the duty to protect human rights for all persons under the state's authority. Hence, it is possible for a group of states to create an IGO in bad faith in order to achieve an illegitimate purpose, and therefore avoid liability, or with a view to bypassing obligations incumbent on states but not IGOs. With few exceptions, IGOs are not, and do not, become parties to human rights treaties, in contrast to their member states.[96] Hence, in theory, they are not bound by treaty-based human rights obligations, despite the fact that many of them have been set up to achieve broader human rights goals, such as the UN and the World Bank group (i.e. development and poverty alleviation). Only the European Union (EU) and its institutions are obliged to observe human rights, namely the EU Charter of Fundamental Rights, but only when implementing EU law.[97] As shall be explained subsequently in this section, states regularly abuse the international legal personality of IGOs to commit otherwise unlawful acts, as well as bypass the few human rights obligations of IGOs by acting in a private capacity.

The starting point of this discussion is that IGOs 'are bound by any obligations upon them under general rules of international law'.[98] Hence, although they are not bound by human rights treaties to which they are not parties, they are obliged to observe customary and *jus cogens* rules formulated by

---

[95] *J. H. Rayner (Mincing Lane) Ltd* v. *Department of Trade and Industry and Others and related appeals*; *MacLaine Watson & Co. Ltd* v. *Department of Trade and Industry*; *MacLaine Watson & Co. Ltd* v. *International Tin Council* (UK) (1989), per Lord Templeman, 678. These are collectively known as the Tin Council case.

[96] Exceptionally, under art. 6(2) of the 2007 Lisbon Treaty amending the Treaty of the European Union (TEU) (now art. 6 TEU), the EU shall accede to the ECHR. In its Opinion 2/13, *Re Accession to the ECHR* (CJEU) (2014), the CJEU was critical of the EU's draft accession agreement because, inter alia, it did not ensure the primacy of EU law in relation to the possibilities conferred by art. 53 of the EU Charter of Fundamental Rights as regards stronger fundamental rights in member states' constitutions. The EU is also a party to the UN Convention on the Rights of Persons with Disabilities (CRPD). In Case C-354/13, *Kaltoft* v. *Municipality of Billund* (CJEU) (2015), the CJEU was inspired by the wording of the CRPD in its assessment as to whether morbid obesity may amount to a 'disability' for the purposes of the Equal Treatment in Employment Directive.

[97] Art. 51 EU Charter of Fundamental Rights.

[98] *Interpretation of the Agreement of 25 March 1951 between the WHO and Egypt* (ICJ) (1980) para. 37; that IGOs must observe human rights is derived also from the CJEU's judgment in *Kadi and Al Barakaat International Foundation* v. *Council of the European Union* (CJEU) (2008).

states,[99] as well as general principles of law; although one may certainly question the basis of such an obligation upon IGOs. It would be absurd to argue otherwise, given that custom and *jus cogens* are not dependent on a contractual undertaking, nor the existence of statehood.[100] Moreover, states routinely perform several functions through IGOs without engaging their own responsibility, such as sovereign financing, in which case if the organisation is presumed to have no human rights duties towards the beneficiary/recipient state, then it would even be permitted to force the recipient state to abandon all its human rights obligations; this is clearly an untenable outcome. In addition, IGOs internalise/transform existing human rights norms into internal rules, although seldom by amendment to their founding instruments; the EU Treaty is an exceptional case. The UN, for example, has adopted a gender- and human rights-based approach to development cooperation,[101] and even the UN Security Council (UNSC), although a political organ, has set up an ombudsperson to deal with challenges against the imposition of targeted sanctions.[102] As far as the EU is concerned, the Court of Justice of the European Union (CJEU) has long postulated that fundamental rights are protected in the framework of the EU, but only as these are formulated and derived from the EU's internal order.[103] In order to avoid importing human rights obligations from the European Convention on Human Rights (ECHR) and the ICCPR, the CJEU went on to formulate so-called general principles of EU law. As these were to some degree structured around the EU's economic freedoms (for example, workers' freedom of movement and freedom of establishment for legal persons) as well as its member states' constitutional traditions, which in turn derived from their obligations under the ECHR, the relevant rights were not all that different from the jurisprudence of the European Court of Human Rights (ECtHR).[104] Some IGOs, particularly international financial institutions (IFIs) such as the World Bank group, undertake very little internalisation and in fact reject the notion that they are bound by any human rights obligations, chiefly because (as it turns out) their operations have a direct impact on economic and social rights

---

[99] See e.g., *Racke* v. *Hauptzollamt Mainz* (CJEU) (1998) para. 45.

[100] A. Reinisch, 'Developing Human Rights and Humanitarian Law Accountability of the Security Council for the Imposition of Economic Sanctions' (2001) 95 *American Journal of International Law* 851, at 858.

[101] See http://hrbaportal.org/the-human-rights-based-approach-to-development-cooperation-towards-a-common-understanding-among-un-agencies.

[102] UNSC resolutions 1904 (17 December 2009) and 1989 (17 June 2011), which extended the ombudsperson's powers.

[103] *Stauder* v. *City of Ulm* (CJEU) (1969) para. 7.

[104] See Case C-274/99, *Connolly* v. *Commission* (CJEU) (2001), freedom of expression; Case 130/ 75, *Prais* v. *Council* (CJEU) (1976), freedom of religion; *Booker Aquacultur Ltd and Hydro Seafood GSP Ltd* v. *The Scottish Ministers* (CJEU) (2003), right to property.

(for example, austerity measures imposed as part of structural adjustment conditionalities). The International Monetary Fund (IMF), for example, in justifying this position, relies on article IV(3)(b) of its Articles of Agreement, which obliges the Fund to respect the domestic social and political policies of members.[105] In recent years, both the International Bank for Reconstruction and Development (IBRD) and the IMF have adopted operational policies that in theory oblige themselves and their borrowers to respect particular rights, especially rights of indigenous peoples, and in the event of persistent breaches against such policies they undertake to cease any further funding.[106] These are at best selective (and very much watered-down) human rights commitments and this is plain to see in the quasi-judicial mechanisms set up by World Bank institutions, such as the Inspection Panel and the Multilateral Investment Guarantee Agency (MIGA) Ombudsman, which are only competent to hear complaints concerning violations of the Bank's internal rules, not violations of human rights law.[107]

Some, but certainly by no means all, IGOs oblige their organs and sub-entities to undertake human rights impact assessments (HRIA) through internalised guidelines. This is true, for example, in respect of the EU whenever its organs adopt legislation or enter into international agreements.[108] The CJEU has, in fact, emphasised the importance of such HRIAs in the adoption of primary and secondary EU legislation.[109] In one case, a complaint was made to the EU Ombudsman, arguing that in respect of the EU–Vietnam free trade agreement the EU Commission refused to prepare an HRIA, despite the fact that such agreements produce a significant impact on populations emerging from non-market economies, as is the case with Vietnam. The Ombudsman found such a failure to constitute an instance of maladministration.[110]

In addition to the above, IGOs are bound by IHL where they engage in armed hostilities or effectively occupy parts of a territory. Although it is true that the Geneva Conventions and general IHL were traditionally addressed to states, they are also applicable in situations of armed conflict where one of the parties comprises forces under the control of an international organisation.[111] Given that the UN exercises command and operational control over forces committed

---

[105] See S. Skogly, *The Human Rights Obligations of the World Bank and the International Monetary Fund* (Cavendish, 2001).

[106] Especially the IBRD's Operational Policy 4.10 on Indigenous Peoples (July 2005, as revised in April 2013).

[107] For an overview of the mandate and cases of the Inspection Panel, see http://ewebapps.worldbank.org/apps/ip/Pages/Home.aspx.

[108] EU Commission Working Paper Operational Guidance on taking account of fundamental rights in Commission impact assessments, SEC (2011) 567 Final (6 May 2011).

[109] *Schecke and Eifert* v. *Land Hessen* (CJEU) (2010).

[110] EU Ombudsman recommendation to complaint 1409/2014/JN (26 March 2015).

[111] The uncontested practice with respect to UN-mandated peacekeeping and peace-enforcement missions is that unlawful acts committed by national contingents

by member states for peacekeeping and peace-enforcement missions,[112] it would be absurd to exclude the application of IHL to such forces. The purpose of IHL is to render war more humane and to minimise its effects on the wounded and *hors de combat,* and as a result its application is triggered objectively by the existence of armed hostilities, not by the legal status of the parties to the conflict.[113] The obligation to abide with the laws of war is also acknowledged by the UN itself and the Secretary-General specifically issued a Bulletin in 1999, entitled 'Observance by United Nations Forces of International Humanitarian Law',[114] to make this point clear. The Bulletin, which is binding on all UN personnel, reflects fundamental principles of IHL, particularly protection of the civilian population, means and methods of combat, treatment of civilians, *hors de combat,* detained persons, the wounded, sick and medical personnel.

It is also indubitable that the UN and other organisations that have assumed the role of transitional administrators of territory that is not yet fully independent (or which is under effective occupation) are under an obligation to provide the full range of fundamental human rights to the population of the territory in question. Although this is generally stipulated in the mandate of the administering organisation, as was the case with the UN Mission in Kosovo (UNMIK),[115] given that IGOs supplement the authority of the state in the territory under consideration they are bound by the treaty law in force in the occupied territory, in addition to customary law and *jus cogens.* In Kosovo, UNMIK established a Human Rights Advisory Panel (HRAP)[116] in

---

participating in chapter VII action that are not constituted under a UN Force give rise to member state liability. On the other hand, the UN is liable for unlawful acts committed by national contingents that operate under a UN Force. See ILC Second Report on Responsibility of International Organisations, UN doc. A/CN.4/541 (2 April 2004), at 13–23. However, even in those cases where the national contingent is under a UN force but the retention of disciplinary power and criminal jurisdiction is vested exclusively in the contributing state, any unlawful act committed as a result engages the liability of the state and not the organisation. See *Attorney-General* v. *Nissan* (UK) (1969) at 646.

[112] Arts. 6–9 of the Model Agreement between the UN and member states contributing personnel and equipment to the UN peacekeeping operations, UN doc. A/46/185 (23 May 1991), Annex, stipulates that contributed forces come under exclusive UN control and serve UN interests, rather than national ones. None the less, criminal and disciplinary control is retained by national authorities.

[113] For a more thorough analysis of the aims and principles of IHL, see Chapter 16.2.

[114] UN doc. ST/SGB/1999/13 (6 August 1999). The UNSC has relied on the Bulletin to emphasise that UN forces must always comply with the laws of war. See UNSC resolution 1327 (13 November 2000).

[115] UNSC resolution 1244 (10 June 1999). This was further emphasised in the Report of the UN Secretary-General on the UN Interim Administration Mission in Kosovo, UN doc. S/1999/779 (12 July 1999) para. 42, stating that UNMIK will 'be guided by internationally recognised standards of human rights as the basis for the exercise of its authority in Kosovo'.

[116] UNMIK regulation 2006/12 (23 March 2006) on the Establishment of the Human Rights Advisory Panel.

order to implement its human rights responsibilities. In addition, a Human Rights Review Panel (HRRP) was established with similar tasks by the EU Rule of Law Mission in Kosovo (EULEX). The panels' decisions generally rely on the ECHR and have held the occupying IGOs to have violated the ECHR in several instances.[117] Although this development is unique to the administration of a territory by an IGO, it should be borne in mind that the recommendations of the panels are not binding on UNMIK and EULEX.

CASE STUDY 19.2
Non-consideration of Economic and Social Rights by the IMF in Tanzania

When Tanzania requested assistance from the IMF in 1985, the latter agreed to provide loans and assurances but conditioned them on the acceptance by the country of structural adjustment programmes (SAPs).[1] The measures imposed under the SAPs included the privatisation of Tanzania's mining industry, the adoption of trade liberalisation measures and the introduction of fees for health care and education, among others. Within a space of fifteen years the school enrolment rate dropped from 80 per cent to 66 per cent and the country's illiteracy rate rose to slightly above 50 per cent. The introduction of health care fees saw the AIDS rate rise to 8 per cent, and despite the deep austerity measures, which the IMF promised would reduce poverty and bring prosperity, per capita income was reduced from US $309 to US $210.

The IMF's contribution to the deterioration of economic and social rights is clearly direct because it was aware that Tanzania would agree to the conditions of the SAPs in order to secure the much-needed loan. The Fund was either aware or was grossly negligent about the failure of the programme and its consequences for the local population.

[1] For an analysis of the objective of SAPs and their potential impact on the enjoyment of human rights, see Case Study 14.1.

19.4.2   International Organisations as Violators of Human Rights: The Need for Dual Attribution

Clearly, the situation of human rights obligations of IGOs under international law is unsatisfactory and very much artificial. This is even more so given their direct impact on the enjoyment of rights. An illustration is instructive.

---

[117] In *Jocić* v. *UNMIK* (UNMIK HRAP) (2013), it was held that UNMIK had violated arts. 2 and 3 of the ECHR by failing to adequately investigate the disappearance of a Kosovo Serb.

A financing contract is agreed between developing country X and the World Bank for the construction of a dam. As it turns out the project is of little economic or investment value and results in the forceful eviction of the local population and the impairment of the natural environment, thus causing poor health and loss of lives. Moreover, because the agreement requires the dam and the attendant services to be privatised, the price of water and electricity for the poor of country X (which accounts for two-thirds of its population) becomes prohibitive. Had it not been for the positive conduct of the World Bank the adverse human rights effects would not have materialised. If one were to follow the legalistic argument that IGOs are not incumbent directly with human rights obligations under treaty law, or indeed indirectly by reason of human rights obligations of their members, a nonsensical void arises. Moreover, the victims in both cases would be unable to pursue legal action against the IGO as a matter of tort. They would, in addition, be unable to bring a claim against the states that are behind the IGO's executive decision because of their distinct legal personality from the IGO. If one further considers the extensive range of multilateral and bilateral immunities enjoyed by IGOs, it is evident that powerful states have every incentive to employ them as vehicles for violating human rights without incurring any liability whatsoever.

A particular example of an abusive IGO is the European Stability Mechanism (ESM),[118] established in the aftermath of the financial crisis in Europe by EU member states in the form of a distinct international organisation (which was, however, locally incorporated as a company). The aim of the ESM was to pool funds from wealthier EU states and disburse them as loans to countries in financial need. This 'bail-out' could not have been undertaken through the EU as such, because of the 'no bail-out' clause stipulated in article 125 of the Treaty on the Functioning of the European Union (TFEU), which prohibits the EU or its member states from becoming liable or assuming financial commitments of other member states. Any loan or other financial assistance originating from an EU institution would ordinarily be susceptible to the EU Charter of Fundamental Rights, but since the ESM was not an EU institution it was not bound to observe the Charter, article 51 of which reads:

The provisions of this Charter are addressed to the institutions, bodies, offices and agencies of the Union with due regard to the principle of subsidiarity and to the member states only when they are implementing Union law.

---

[118] ESM was established by EU Council Decision 2011/199/EU (25 March 2011), amending art. 136 TFEU. This Decision inserted a new paragraph 3 in art. 136 TFEU, which allowed the creation of ESM in order to safeguard the stability of the euro area. A subsequent treaty establishing the ESM was adopted in 2012 between all eurozone member states.

It is clear from this that all EU bodies are always bound by the Charter, whereas member states are bound only when implementing EU law. The applicant in the *Pringle* case, which was a referral from the Irish Supreme Court to the CJEU (with Ireland being a recipient of ESM funds), rightly argued that the establishment of ESM violated article 47 of the Charter, which guarantees to all the right to an effective remedy. In a judgment where the CJEU was aware of the politico-financial stakes, it held that the establishment of the ESM was lawful because the borrower remains responsible for its financial commitments towards the lenders, and in fact the purchase of sovereign bonds by the lender (where applicable) is subject to market prices; which clearly means that far from being a bail-out this is a profit-making activity for the sovereign lender. This astounding judgment suggests that EU member states can legitimately establish an IGO that bypasses all their human rights obligations, both collective and individual, and at the same time they are entitled to make a profit through such an IGO from the crisis of other EU member states.[119] The correct position as regards the application of the Charter of Fundamental Rights was stated by Advocate-General Kokott in the *Pringle* case, who emphasised that: 'the [EU] Commission remains, even when it acts within the framework of the ESM, an institution of the [European] Union and as such is bound by the full extent of EU law, including the Charter of Fundamental Rights'.[120]

Financing and aid mechanisms routinely make use of IGOs in order for states to escape subsequent liability or so that the undertakings be unsusceptible to human rights scrutiny. For example, the World Bank group and other IFIs have created *sui generis* trust vehicles through which wealthy states can dispense loans or aid to other states. The agreement between the funder and the trustee/IFIs stipulates that neither is liable to one another and certainly not to the third-party beneficiary. The assets of the trust are metamorphosed into a separate legal entity (for example, locally incorporated companies, trust accounts, even a new IGO) and hence, even in the unlikely event that the trustee is held liable or had its immunity lifted, the activities undertaken through the trust fund would be liable by its own assets and not the general assets of the IFI/trustee, and certainly not the participating/contributing state(s). Amazingly, even though the trust fund and its assets are locally incorporated and distinct from the assets of the IFI/trustee, the trust and its

---

[119] *Pringle* v. *Ireland* (CJEU) (2012). It was not a far leap for EU member states and the IMF to provide loans under private contract with English law as the choice of law – hence implicitly rejecting the application of human rights – in loan agreements with Greece, subject to conditionalities that violated fundamental human rights. Under pressure from creditors, including the ECB and ESM, as well as individual EU member states, Greece was effectively forced to bypass its constitutional procedures for ratification of treaties and hence none of its loan agreements was ever discussed or lawfully adopted by parliament.

[120] *Pringle* v. *Ireland*, view of A-G Kokott (26 October 2012) para. 176.

assets can, and in many cases do, enjoy the privileges and immunities of the trustee![121] Given that aid and financing arrangements constitute a source of neo-colonialism and encompass conditionalities that violate fundamental human rights, the existence of such mechanisms is an insult to the human rights obligations of their participants. In all these cases, at the very least, the contributing member states or states (non-parties as in the case of trust funds) using the IGO to achieve a self-serving aim while at the same time escaping liability should be held accountable for the conduct of IGOs.[122] Such conduct is clearly an internationally wrongful act committed through an agent.[123]

This line of thinking is certainly gaining ground, albeit with much resistance from powerful states. In *Nada* v. *Switzerland*, the Swiss authorities had implemented a UNSC freezing order against the applicant without scrutinising the human rights implications of that action, relying instead solely on the country's obligations under chapter VII of the UN Charter. The ECtHR did not limit its assessment to the hierarchical relationship between the ECHR and the UN Charter, but rather pointed to the fact that Switzerland had failed to take 'all possible measures to adapt the sanctions regime to the applicant's individual situation'.[124]

It is clear that if states are able to attribute otherwise personal action to IGOs to escape their human rights obligations, then in equal manner the states affected by the measures adopted by such IGOs can claim that they were required by treaty to adhere to them. In both cases there is an artificial absence of obligations and a corresponding absence of liability. Such a result is untenable and lacks legal foundation and has rightly been condemned by international and domestic courts, despite claims to the contrary by collaborating states. This type of liability is recognised in article 61 of the International Law Commission (ILC) Articles on the Responsibility of International Organisations (ARIO), which reads:

A State member of an international organization incurs international responsibility if, by taking advantage of the fact that the organization has competence in relation to the subject-matter of one of the State's international obligations, it circumvents that obligation by causing the organization to commit an act that, if committed by the state, would have constituted a breach of the obligation.

In *IKA-ETAM* v. *Greece*, Greece had argued that its withdrawal or slashing of pensioners' social security entitlements, which had led many to poverty, was

---

[121] See I. Bantekas, 'The Emergence of the Intergovernmental Trust in International Law' (2011) 81 *British Yearbook of International Law* 224, at 265–79.

[122] The ECtHR held in *T. I.* v. *UK* (ECtHR) (2000) that it would be incompatible with member states' obligations under the ECHR to absolve themselves from responsibility in respect of human rights violations committed by IGOs to which they were parties.

[123] Art. 8, ILC Articles on State Responsibility.

[124] *Nada* v. *Switzerland* (ECtHR) (2012) para. 196.

the direct result of its structural adjustment commitments to its bilateral and multilateral creditors, including the ESM, European Central Bank (ECB) and the IMF. Without the funds generated by IFIs, it was argued, the social security system would have collapsed and hence the restrictions to socio-economic rights were directly dictated in the form of conditionalities by these IGOs/IFIs. The European Committee of Social Rights (ECSR) was not impressed with this argument, nor indeed with the absence of even the most rudimentary of safety nets for the most vulnerable segments of society that were subject to unprecedented levels of poverty as a result of the measures adopted.[125] The same argument was sustained by the ECtHR with respect to similar conditionality demands by the IMF on Bulgaria. The Court held that 'the [Bulgarian] government's reliance on the alleged demands by the IMF to limit the courts' involvement in the closing of ailing banks was misplaced, because Bulgaria could not avoid its obligations under the Convention under the guise of complying with the recommendations of an international organisation'.[126] No doubt, the courts of states subject to unilateral coercive measures in the form of conditionalities in financing arrangements must be exceptionally bold to rebuke such arrangements as violating fundamental rights and domestic constitutional order.[127] The Latvian Constitutional Court in the *Latvian Pensions* case is a bright example of such a court. It emphasised that conditions laid down by loan agreements could not in any way replace the rights established by the Constitution, despite the difficulties such a result may have on the country's financing relations.[128] A noticeable outcome of the conditionalities in most contemporary financing arrangements concerns the dissolution of the borrower state's fiscal, economic and legislative sovereignty. In the case of Greece, for example, a delegation of its IGO creditors (the so-called troika) was effectively exercising sovereign powers in the country and no law could be adopted or public money spent without its prior approval.[129] In such situations it would be absurd not to extend *mutatis mutandis Loizidou* effective control considerations, given the existence of an effective fiscal and economic occupation.[130]

The immunities of IGOs are a further deterrent to their human rights accountability, as also are those of their member states. The functional

---

[125] *Federation of Employed Pensioners of Greece (IKA-ETAM)* v. *Greece* (ECSR) (2012) paras. 66–81; *Pensioners' Union of the Agricultural Bank of Greece (ATE)* v. *Greece* (ECSR) (2012) para. 48.

[126] *Capital Bank AD* v. *Bulgaria* (ECtHR) (2005) para. 90.

[127] The Greek Supreme Administrative Court (*Symvoulio Epikrateias*), e.g., upheld the constitutional nature of the measures (essentially) imposed upon the Greek government by its creditors on the rationale that otherwise the country would become insolvent! *Symvoulio Epikrateias* judgment no. 668/2012 (Greece) (2012).

[128] *Judgment no. 2009/4301 (Latvian Pensions case)* (Latvia) (2009).

[129] See M. Salomon, 'Of Austerity, Human Rights and International Institutions', LSE Working Paper 2/2015, at 9.

[130] *Loizidou* v. *Turkey* (ECtHR) (1995) para. 62.

immunities of natural persons for the purposes of criminal liability, as already discussed in Chapter 17.8, are much narrower than the extensive and very much absolute immunities afforded to IGOs, save for a limited number of contractual obligations.[131] This is because their immunities are conferred by general multilateral treaties,[132] the IGOs' own charters,[133] as well as headquarters agreements. Against this absolute immunity and the absence of concrete human rights commitments, it comes as no surprise that some IGOs, particularly IFIs, have imposed highly abusive clauses in loan or assurance agreements with borrower nations. By way of example, European Financial Stability Facility (EFSF) lending agreements stipulate that:

> The Borrower hereby irrevocably and unconditionally waives all immunity to which it is or may become entitled, in respect of itself or its assets, from legal proceedings in relation to this Agreement, including, without limitation, immunity from suit, judgment or other order, from attachment, arrest or injunction prior to judgment, and from execution and enforcement against its assets to the extent not prohibited by mandatory law.[134]

These wide and absolute immunities of IGOs have inhibited otherwise legitimate suits against them for actions or omissions that have caused significant and long-lasting harm to victims. In *Stichting Mothers of Srebrenica* v. *The Netherlands and the UN*, mothers of the deceased in the Srebrenica massacre sued the respondents in the Netherlands for their failure to prevent the massacre. In agreeing with the Dutch Supreme Court, the ECtHR held that 'the Convention cannot be interpreted in a manner which would subject the acts and omissions of the Security Council to domestic jurisdiction without the accord of the United Nations'.[135] In the European context, the ECtHR has held that in order to assess whether the interference of an immunity with the right to fair trial is proportionate, the applicants must have 'available to them reasonable alternative means to protect effectively their rights under

---

[131] *Lutcher SA e Papel Candor* v. *IDB* (US) (1967); but in *Scimet* v. *African Development Bank* (ADB) (Belgium) (1997) it was recognised that art. 50 of the African Development Bank's Articles of Agreement granted it immunity from jurisdiction in relation to all transactions, save those that arise from the exercise of its borrowing powers. The selective and arbitrary character of IFI immunities is best exemplified by the waiver of some immunities by the IBRD (art. VII(3) of its Articles of Agreement), contrary to the Articles of Agreement of other institutions in the World Bank group. The purpose of this 'concession' is finance-driven. The IBRD issues bonds from which it earns significant profit. Prospective buyers would be dissuaded if they had no legal recourse against the IBRD.

[132] E.g., 1946 Convention on Privileges and Immunities of the UN and 1947 Convention on the Privileges and Immunities of the Specialised Agencies.

[133] Art. VII(1)(4) IBRD Articles of Agreement.

[134] Art. 15(2) EFSF Framework Agreement, online at www.efsf.europa.eu/attachments/20111019_efsf_framework_agreement_en.pdf. This clause is used in the EFSF's lending agreements with borrowers.

[135] *Stichting Mothers of Srebrenica* v. *The Netherlands* (ECtHR) (2013).

the Convention.'[136] Although the ECtHR has effectively disregarded this rule in *Al-Adsani*,[137] other national courts have relied on it to highlight the obvious, namely, that the operation of immunity effectively precludes bona fide victims of IGOs from all remedies.[138] Given the aforementioned human rights violations through an abuse of the IGO vehicle by states and the IGO itself, it is evident that a universal recognition of *dual attribution* (i.e. to the IGO and pertinent states) is the only way of inducing responsibility and ascertaining liability in the fairest possible manner. This is exactly what the Dutch Supreme Court emphasised in finding that because Dutch forces exercised effective control in the Srebrenica enclave, the massacre could be attributed to both them and the UN as a matter of dual attribution.[139] National courts should not be afraid to lift the immunities of IGOs when it is clear that both they and their member states have acted illegally or in disregard of fundamental rights.

CASE STUDY 19.3
Complicity of States through/with IGOs

It is well documented that prior to the advent of decolonisation in the early 1960s, the World Bank group provided loans to colonial authorities in respect of projects which favoured almost exclusively the colonisers, as opposed to the colonised populations. In most cases the loans were spent on mining, agriculture and fuel projects, the raw material from which were transferred back to Europe for subsequent use in heavy industries or consumption. In the case of the Congo, the loans were spent by its Belgian colonisers to buy products exported by Belgium. Belgian Congo received loans amounting to US$120 million, of which US$105.4 million were spent in Belgium. Upon independence, Congo's leader, Patrice Lumumba, naturally denounced this debt, arguing that it burdened Belgium, not Congo. This stance infuriated Belgium, which with the assistance of the World Bank facilitated Mobutu's ascent to power (one of the most resilient and brutal dictators of Africa) and in the process hastened Lumumba's assassination. As it turned out, Mobutu repaid his sponsors' generosity by officially accepting the Belgian debts as Congolese debts and thus saddling the Congolese people with a debt that was not theirs and whose servicing required the violation of fundamental socio-economic rights, in addition

---

[136] *Beer and Regan* v. *Germany* (ECtHR) (1999) para. 58; *Waite and Kennedy* v. *Germany* (ECtHR) (2000) para. 95.

[137] *Al-Adsani* v. *United Kingdom* (ECtHR) (2001).

[138] *Western European Union* v. *Siedler* (Belgium) (2009).

[139] *Netherlands* v. *Nuhanović* (Netherlands) (2013).

to economic self-determination.[1] Moreover, in order to quell any opposition to such policies, Mobutu, with the indirect aid of other IFIs, engaged in the violation of all civil and political rights in his country.

[1] See E. Toussaint, *Banque Mondiale: Le Coup d'État Permanent. L'Agenda Caché du Consensus de Washington* (CADTM / Syllepse / CETIM, 2006). A summary in English is available online at http://cadtm.org/An-emblematic-IMF-and-World-Bank.

19.5 NATIONAL LIBERATION MOVEMENTS AND ARMED REBEL GROUPS

Unlike other NSAs, national liberation movements (NLMs) and armed rebel groups are specifically mentioned in IHL treaties. The obligations towards civilians, the wounded and sick and those rendered *hors de combat* in common article 3 to the 1949 Geneva Conventions, for example, are addressed to 'each party to the conflict' and therefore also to armed rebel groups. Protocol II of 1977 to the 1949 Geneva Conventions and relating to the protection of victims of non-international armed conflicts is equally addressed to all parties to a conflict, albeit requiring that the rebels exercise significant control over part of the embattled territory. Moreover, article 1(4) of Protocol I of 1977 to the 1949 Geneva Conventions, which regulates international armed conflicts, stipulates that 'armed conflicts in which peoples are fighting against colonial domination and alien occupation and against racist regimes in the exercise of their right to self-determination' are international conflicts. Such an outcome confers upon said armed groups international legal personality for the purpose of their armed struggle. Moreover, the legal effects arising from the conduct of an armed group continue especially if it accedes to power. Article 10(2) of the ILC Articles on State Responsibility state that '[t]he conduct of a movement, insurrectional or other, which succeeds in establishing a new state in part of the territory of a pre-existing state or in a new territory under its administration shall be considered an act of the new state under international law'. Many IHL treaties allow NLMs and rebel entities to make declarations of conformity with the relevant law.[140] This is more of a psychological inducement that gives the NLM a sense of external recognition while at the same time making it publicly accountable, given that NLMs incur specific obligations under the relevant treaties. It is also common for well-entrenched NLMs to enter into agreements with governmental forces, usually through a foreign mediator, in order to register their mutual intent to

[140] Art. 96(3) of Protocol I of 1977 and art. 7(4) of the 1980 Convention on Prohibitions or Restrictions on the Use of Certain Conventional Weapons.

comply with human rights and IHL. Again, although these agreements may seem legally superfluous[141] they render the parties more accountable and are therefore highly welcome. They are additionally significant to the degree that they 'humanise' the members of the rebel entity, especially since incumbent governments typically deny that NLMs are entitled to any privileges, particularly combatant status[142] and are treated as common criminals.

Whereas the application of obligations stemming from IHL are not contested as regards NLMs and rebel entities involved in armed conflict as a matter of customary law, the same is not necessarily true as regards human rights. From a practical point of view this question is moot because the laws of war, being moreover *lex specialis* as against human rights law, cover situations that would otherwise be regulated under human rights law.[143] Even so, certain scholars contend that rebel groups do not possess any human rights obligations, or at least those they are unlikely to be able to uphold, such as the obligation to offer due process rights because of their inability to administer a legal system.[144] This is probably true to some degree, but rebel entities are certainly in a position to guarantee fundamental human rights and should be held accountable for any failure in this regard, particularly in situations where they are in effective control of territory. Given that states are unable to positively protect human rights in territory they do not have any control over, it would render people living there devoid of any legal protection. The stipulation in article 10(2) of the ILC Articles on State Responsibility should also be read as conferring obligations (especially of a human rights nature) to rebel groups while these are not yet in power, subject to any subsequent liability once power is assumed. That rebel entities are subject to some human rights obligations is also confirmed by reference to several UNSC resolutions which consistently call directly on insurgents and rebels to comply with human rights and humanitarian law.[145]

None the less, humanitarian law is unable to cover all situations involving rebels and NLMs. This is particularly true in the absence of protracted armed conflict, in which case the laws of war are not triggered. In this type of scenario the rebels do not possess de facto authority over part of the territory and are not engaged in armed hostilities against the government. It is unlikely that under such circumstances, which are very much akin to the legal regime governing terrorist groups that the rebels are burdened with human rights obligations.

---

[141] See, however, C. Bell, 'Peace Agreements: Their Nature and Legal Status' (2006) 100 *American Journal of International Law* 373, who argues that they enjoy legal force.

[142] See *S* v. *Petane* (South Africa) (1988); *Military Prosecutor* v. *Kassem and Others* (Israel) (1971).

[143] For an analysis of their *lex specialis* character, see Chapter 16.4.

[144] L. Moir, *The Law of Internal Armed Conflict* (Cambridge University Press, 2002) 194.

[145] E.g., UNSC resolution 1193 (28 August 1998); UNSC resolution 1213 (3 December 1998); UNSC resolution 1572 (15 November 2004); UNSC resolution 1672 (25 April 2006).

19.5.1 'To Suffer thy Comrades': Responding to Human Rights Abuses by NSAs in the Philippines

The following is an excerpt from an introduction to a report on NSAs[146] written by Robert (Bobby) Francis B. Garcia, Secretary-General of PATH (Peace Advocates for Truth, Healing and Justice), and author of the book *To Suffer thy Comrades* (Manila: Anvil Publishing, 2001):

I used to be a 'non-state actor', having been a member of the Communist Party of the Philippines-New People's Army (CPP-NPA) during the 1980s, in the prime of my youth. I joined the guerrillas in the countryside and waged war against the state. Suffering torture, and perhaps a gruesome death, from government soldiers was something I dreaded but for which I somehow prepared. I never expected that the blows would come from my own comrades.

It was in 1988 when the anti-infiltration campaign called 'Oplan Missing Link' (OPML) happened. OPML would turn out to be just one of the numerous bloody campaigns undertaken by the [Communist Party of the Philippines – New People's Army] CPP-NPA to ferret out suspected 'deep-penetration agents' (DPAs) within its ranks. The pattern in all these anti-DPA campaigns was frighteningly similar: suspicion, arrest, interrogation, forced confession, detention, execution – a bloody domino effect that had bodies writhing, rolling and dying en masse. It was November 1988 when they arrested and tortured me and threw me along with fifty-six other chained guerrillas in the Sierra Madre mountain ranges. At that time, sixty-six suspects had already been executed. One of the worst punishments we endured was the denial of food. The torturers also experimented with various combinations of physical and psychological terror tactics. A female detainee was beaten up, hung on a tree and forced to watch how they beat up other victims. Then she was made to listen to the recorded voices of her children. Some were left dangling in trees for days. They slit the captives' skin with a knife or shaved off their eyebrows for fun. Captives' legs were forced apart and their thighs were sat upon. Their skin was seared with a lamp.

In its wake, I suffered a broken jaw, concussions on my head, wounds where the chains rubbed on the skin and a battered psyche that proved much harder to heal. The sheer brutality of the experience itself may have been one of the reasons why most of us refused to talk about it for a very long time. It was much easier to talk about military atrocities than the cruelty of one's own comrades. Thus the truth was buried for a very long time.

Talking about the experience was difficult enough as it were, finding legal redress was not even imagined. At least not until recently. In August 2003 we

---

[146] See REDRESS, 'Not Only the State: Torture by Non-state Actors' (REDRESS, 2006) 4–7.
[147] See also the discussion on de facto statehood and self-determination in Chapter 10.2.2.

brought together a group of people who were directly or indirectly victimised by the CPP-NPA's anti-infiltration campaigns – former comrades who survived the torture, families who lost a member or two, and compatriots who believe that the thousands of comrades who fell in the wake of these anti-infiltration campaigns must find their due. We formed the Peace Advocates for Truth, Healing and Justice (PATH). All of our members are involved in various other advocacies and campaigns, but find this particular one far harder and fraught with obstacles. Many of us are human rights workers who never tire of hollering against the state's abuses – work that is by no means easy, but pretty much cut and dried. It enjoys the luxury of certitude and 'political correctness'.

The issue of non-state-perpetrated violations, however, such as the Philippine communist purges, is much more complex and uncertain ... addressing the issue of past violations inevitably gets mired in political manoeuvrings. The government uses it as an effective propaganda ammunition against the rebels, while dispensing with counter-insurgency measures that fall way below human rights and international humanitarian law standards.

In addition to this, bringing up the issue remains a dangerous undertaking, simply because the CPP-NPA is still armed and active. They have also categorically dismissed any possibility of reopening the issue, claiming that it is already a closed book. The perpetrators, they say, have either fled the party or have been rightfully punished. The scores of victims' families who do not know what really happened and the thousands of dead and disappeared point to the contrary.

We at PATH have explored various legal options, one being the filing of individual criminal cases against identified lead perpetrators, such as those involved in the OPML in the province of Laguna. As expected, the wheels of justice grind almost to a standstill. Gathering evidence of a crime that happened more than a decade back poses a terrible challenge, including the lack of witnesses willing to testify and the blurring of memory through time.

The absence of an anti-torture law in the Philippines [note that this law has now been passed; see interview 19.1] also poses a limitation, thus the charges filed are limited to serious physical injuries and serious illegal detention. The case of Jesse Marlow Libre is a particular case in point. In November 2005, we at PATH, with the help of forensic scientists and volunteer experts, were able to exhume the remains of his parents, revolutionary couple Jesse and Nida Libre. They were falsely suspected as spies and killed by the CPP-NPA in Cebu on September 1985. The truth behind the disappearance of the young orphan's parents was withheld from him by the movement (they claimed the military killed them). It was only in 2005 that he learned the disconcerting reality upon seeing his parents' skeletons buried together in a mountain gravesite, bearing tell-tale signs of severe torture and violent death. Thus with the exhumation of truth comes the cry for justice.

What are the legal options available to him? We can barely find witnesses willing to testify. Who is responsible? A whole party organization was involved. What are the levels of accountability? It was a complex hierarchical set-up: there were onlookers, guards, interrogators, torturers, executioners, decision-makers and party directives. Truth and justice are simply lost in the labyrinth.

INTERVIEW 19.1

Judge and Activist on Philippines' Armed Groups

(Soliman M. Santos)

Soliman 'Sol' M. Santos, JR, is a municipal judge covering three rural towns in his home province of Camarines Sur in the Bicol Region of the Philippines. He has been a long-time non-governmental human rights and international humanitarian lawyer; peace advocate, researcher and writer; and the author and editor of several books, including on non-state armed groups. He has been among the international civil society pioneers in the theory and practice of constructive engagement with these groups, starting with the anti-landmines campaign in 1997.

What are your comments on Bobby Garcia's statement from the perspective of a lawyer seeking justice for violations by NSAs?

I fully understand the difficulties that Bobby speaks of in seeking justice for violations by NSAs, particularly armed groups. To start with, the Philippine criminal justice system has many inadequacies in general, including inadequate witness protection and forensic evidence-gathering technology. These general inadequacies are compounded considering the especially difficult and complex nature of dealing with the campaign of purges involving the CPP-NPA rebel group in the 1980s, given also the passage of more than thirty years. This particular event may already need a different, more effective approach or measure of redress than the usual mode of filing and prosecuting individual criminal cases. As for continuing and current incidents of violations by NSAs, these might be addressed more effectively by a purposive effort that engages the criminal justice system, including necessary law and justice reform and one that also explores and sets up alternative mechanisms outside that system, including the availing of relevant existing international mechanisms.

You were part of a campaign that actively lobbied for legislation that would criminalise torture and other violations by NSAs in the Philippines. What was the outcome, and what are your lessons from this experience?

The landmark Philippine Anti-Torture Law of 2009 emerged deliberately not covering non-state agent perpetrators of torture. The law's main sponsors in Congress (Parliament) and the main human rights groups campaigning for the law were largely responsible for this negative aspect of an otherwise positive outcome. On the other hand, our much smaller lobby for a definition of torture that is not limited to state agent perpetrators came into the picture, 'too little and too late', as they say. The first and main obstacle we encountered, both with fellow human rights advocates and with the main sponsors, was a traditionalist human rights paradigm that conceptually limits human rights violations to state/state agent violations. As they also say, 'old habits die hard'. The next arena for this engagement is the Anti-Enforced Disappearance Bill (which passed into law in 2012), and it looks like the same scenario of not covering state agent perpetrators will emerge, with hardly even any lobby effort on the non-state actor angle. Advocates of this angle must definitely regroup for more effective legislative intervention in the coming days and engagements.

Attempts have been made to forge an international South–South network addressing violations by NSAs. Why is there a need for such a network and what challenges does it face?

The problems involving non-state armed groups and the contexts they are in, that is armed conflicts, are largely found in the Global South or what used to be referred to as the Third World of Asia, Africa and Latin America. The purposive efforts to address this special kind of non-state problem, for which the existing largely state-oriented mechanisms are generally inadequate or inappropriate, should also come from this Global South, interlinked on a South–South basis. Being closer to the problem and its context allows for a perspective, a Southern perspective, that is more grounded and suited to addressing the problem. This importantly includes the perspectives of civil society and affected local communities, and situates and thus understands the armed conflicts in their respective political, economic, social, cultural, religious and ideological contexts and histories. This contrasts with the tendency of many Northern or Western approaches that tend to focus almost exclusively on the levels of violence but with inadequate understanding of the context. But an international South–South network necessarily has to relate to strategic partners, collaborators and cooperation points in the North, of course based on relations of equality and co-responsibility in the true spirit of internationalism. We envision the work as constructive engagement of non-state armed groups in a comprehensive range of fields and concerns affecting local communities, of which addressing their human rights violations is only one. The engagement is qualified as constructive, as opposed to destructive, as the latter kind of engagement is what states are mainly undertaking in their own approach to the problem.

The main need and challenge now is for an effective, viable and sustainable international South–South network for this comprehensive work. Our own particular attempt at this, the South–South Network (SSN) for Non-State Armed Group Engagement (www.southsouthnetwork.com) started in 2005, has unfortunately floundered and has not taken off mainly for lack of political, moral and funding support for what may be an unappreciated, controversial or even misunderstood area of work, as well due to certain organisational weaknesses.

From an international law perspective, what are the main changes needed to more effectively combat violations by NSAs?

The main changes required may be outlined on two levels which might be referred to broadly as internal and external. We already just mentioned the main change needed internally – breaking through on an effective, viable and sustainable international South–South network that can help comprehensively develop the work of constructive engagement of non-state armed groups, including addressing their human rights violations. Of course, the latter particular engagement can and should also be taken up by human rights groups and institutions in particular. The latter may be more disposed to criminal prosecution and other quasi-coercive or confrontational approaches, which are not mainly contemplated in constructive engagement by dialogue and persuasion to positively influence such armed groups.

But it is also with human rights groups and institutions where some external work by advocates of NSA engagement/accountability is needed for external changes. The main external change needed, as far as human rights groups and institutions are concerned, is one of attitude and/or orientation: a shift in the traditionalist human rights paradigm that conceptually limits human rights violations to state/state agent violations. For human rights groups and institutions to introduce or mainstream the non-state actor angle into their work on their particular human rights issue of concern like torture, even if still mainly addressing state/state agent violations, would already be a big step forward. The aforementioned breakthrough paradigm shift should/would be followed or accompanied by a breakthrough in another needed external change: developing at various levels what together might constitute a critical mass of appropriate and effective mechanisms, instruments, tools, frameworks, approaches, techniques and technology in seeking rebel accountability, including legal but not limited to it, for human rights violations.

QUESTIONS

1. The personnel of private security firms regularly engage in armed hostilities with guerrillas, rebels and paramilitaries, very often in occupied territory, as is the case with post-2003 Iraq. Do these persons and the firms that hire them assume obligations under IHL?

2. The World Bank Group facilitates loans to developing countries and countries facing illiquidity under condition of structural adjustments which generally require severe austerity measures by the borrowing nation. These measures are known to result in the elimination of many socio-economic rights, such as free education, welfare, pensions, health care and others. Who is, or should be, responsible for the violation of these rights, if at all?

3. International organisations do not assume human rights obligations under treaty law, but there is nothing preventing them from assuming said obligations as a matter of customary international law. Discuss with regard to the practical considerations of this statement.

4. There are at least two de facto states in the world today, Iraqi Kurdistan and Somaliland. Although they are not formally acknowledged as states they exercise functions and powers pertaining to states. Are they to be classified as NSAs for the purpose of attribution of human rights obligations, or are they to be assimilated to states?[147]

FURTHER READING

Alston, P. (ed.), *Non-State Actors and Human Rights* (Oxford University Press, 2005).

Amao, O., *Corporate Social Responsibility, Human Rights and the Law: Multinational Corporations in Developing Countries* (Routledge, 2011).

Baumann-Pauly, D., and J. Nolan, *Business and Human Rights: From Principles to Practice* (Routledge, 2016).

Clapham, A., *Human Rights Obligations of Non-state Actors* (Oxford University Press, 2006).

De Schutter, O., J. Swinnen and J. Wouters (eds.), *Foreign Direct Investment and Human Development: The Law and Economics of International Investment Agreements* (Routledge, 2012).

Deva, S., and D. Bilchitz (eds.), *Human Rights Obligations of Business* (Cambridge University Press, 2015).

Greathead, S., 'The Multinational and the "New Stakeholder": Examining the Business Case for

Human Rights' (2002) 35 *Vanderbilt Journal of Transnational Law* 719.

Jena, M., and K. E. Bravo, *The Business and Human Rights Landscape: Moving Forward Looking Back* (Cambridge University Press, 2015).

Joseph, S., *Corporations and Transnational Human Rights Litigation* (Hart, 2004).

Kamminga, M., and S. Zia-Zarifi (eds.), *Liability of Multinational Corporations under International Law* (Kluwer, 2005).

Karp, D. J., *Responsibility for Human Rights: Transnational Corporations in Imperfect States* (Cambridge University Press, 2014).

Kinley, D., and J. Tadaki, 'From Talk to Walk: The Emergence of Human Rights Responsibilities for Corporations at International Law' (2004) 44 *Virginia Journal of International Law* 931.

McCorquodale, R., and P. Simons, 'Responsibility Beyond Borders: State Responsibility for Extraterritorial Violations by Corporations of

International Human Rights Law' (2007) 70 *Modern Law Review* 598.

Muchlinski, P., *Multinational Enterprises and the Law* (Oxford University Press, 2007).

Mujih, E., *Regulating Multinationals in Developing Countries: A Conceptual and Legal Framework for Corporate Social Responsibility* (Edward Elgar, 2012).

Ratner, S., 'Corporations and Human Rights: A Theory of Legal Responsibility' (2001) 111 *Yale Law Journal* 443.

Rodriguez-Garavito, C. (ed.), *Business and Human Rights: Beyond the End of the Beginning* (Cambridge University Press, 2017).

Ruggie, J. G., 'Business and Human Rights: The Evolving International Agenda' (2008) 101 *American Journal of International Law* 819.

Ruggie, J. G., *Just Business: Multinational Corporations and Human Rights* (WW Norton, 2014).

Verbitsky, H., and J. P. Bohoslavsky (eds.), *The Economic Accomplices to the Argentine Dictatorship: Outstanding Debts* (Cambridge University Press, 2015).

Walker, C., and D. Whyte, 'Contracting Out War? Private Military Companies, Law and Regulation in the United Kingdom' (2005) 54 *International & Comparative Law Quarterly* 651.

Wouters, J., E. Brems and S. Smis (eds.), *Accountability for Human Rights Violations by International Organisations* (Intersentia, 2010).

Zegveld, L., *Accountability of Armed Opposition Groups in International Law* (Cambridge University Press, 2002).

Zerk, J. A., *Multinationals and Corporate Social Responsibility: Limitations and Opportunities in International Law* (Cambridge University Press, 2011).

Websites

Business and Human Rights Resource Centre: http://business-humanrights.org/en

Committee for the Abolition of Third World Debt: http://cadtm.org/

Corporate Responsibility Index: www.bitc.org.uk/services/benchmarking/cr-index

OHCHR, Business and Human Rights: www.ohchr.org/EN/Issues/Business/Pages/BusinessIndex.aspx

UN Global Compact: www.unglobalcompact.org/

UN Working Group on Human Rights and Transnational Corporations and other Business Enterprises: www.ohchr.org/EN/Issues/Business/Pages/WGHRandtransnationalcorporationsandotherbusiness.aspx

World Bank Inspection Panel: http://ewebapps.worldbank.org/apps/ip/Pages/Home.aspx

20 Globalisation and its Impact on Human Rights

CONTENTS

20.1   INTRODUCTION

This chapter is necessarily interrelated with the one concerning the right to development, but also informs all other chapters in one way or another. Globalisation is a topic that has been discussed from multiple perspectives, including the freedom offered to private actors by which to generate non-state sanctioned laws,[1] its traversal of traditional barriers through advanced technologies and communications and the fostering of better understanding among cultures. Although there are positive connotations to the term, it is generally viewed negatively because it is perceived as a process that was created by the rich and powerful and one which brings little or no benefit to the poor and vulnerable.

---

[1] See G. Teubner, 'Global Bukowina: Legal Pluralism in the World Society', in G. Teubner (ed.), *Global Law Without a State* (Dartmouth, 1996) 3.

This chapter attempts very briefly to sketch the economic rationale underpinning globalisation and explain in what manner its adherents envisaged a better world. Given that the subject matter is vast, the analysis is limited to three spheres which either drive the processes of globalisation, or upon which it produces a significant impact. We go on to explore the concept of trade liberalisation and whether its application has the potential to equitably distribute the financial benefits of a globalised marketplace. From there, we shall discuss the liberalisation of agricultural commodities with a view to ascertaining whether this is the right approach to food security in the developing world. A very particular aspect of the economic globalisation agenda is the protection of innovators and their patents. The chapter discusses the degree to which the protection of the intellectual property rights pertaining to pharmaceutical companies inhibits the right to health and in particular access to essential medicines for the impoverished. Intellectual property protection is an integral part of trade liberalisation and it is only natural that multinational corporations (MNCs) are eager to safeguard the fruits of their research as well as benefit from the competitive advantage of cheap labour offered by the plethora of poor nations vying for foreign investment. Although increased refugee and immigrant flows are not necessarily a cause of globalisation, they constitute an important dimension of this phenomenon and in this chapter a significant part is devoted to an examination of the protection of refugees and migrants under international law.

The chapter does not advocate that globalisation is inherently destructive or in conflict with human rights. Quite the contrary: trade liberalisation has the potential to provide the much-needed financial resources to fulfil states' human rights obligations. None the less, the means by which globalisation is pursued is inherently at odds with fundamental human rights. Its emphasis is on financial growth without any reference whatsoever to human well-being. Overall profits are viewed as more important than food security, equitable distribution of wealth and poverty reduction. Human rights play no part at all in the ebb and flow of international trade, or at least in the inception of this scheme, and it is for this reason that the United Nations (UN) and other intergovernmental organisations have begun to underline the importance of human rights linkages to trade.[2] As a result, one of the central ideas of globalisation, i.e. that governments, being ineffective actors, should not interfere in trade and services, is being discredited on the ground that privatisation of essential services (such as water, energy, education and pensions) leads in fact to the privatisation and irrelevance of human rights – an

---

[2] See e.g., UNGA resolution 62/151 (6 March 2008), which noted that globalisation 'should be guided by the fundamental principles that underpin the corpus of human rights'.

unacceptable outcome that is in stark conflict with the fundamental tenets of human rights.[3]

20.2   THE ORIGINS AND NATURE OF GLOBALISATION

Although globalisation is generally viewed as a complex, unavoidable[4] and multi-layered phenomenon, in reality it is neither complex, global nor a phenomenon. It is a wholly artificial construct that was purposely engineered by a handful of states in order to pursue a particular economic agenda.[5] Its theoretical underpinning is neo-liberal theory and particularly the so-called Washington Consensus which posits that free, unregulated, markets and trade liberalisation is the only way to spur financial growth. As a result, any governmental interference with market forces constitutes an impediment to growth and by extension to the potential for human well-being. This theory is largely discredited, not because increased trade and investment are inimical to human progress – quite the contrary; rather, it has been aptly demonstrated that economic and financial growth does not necessarily translate into human well-being, and nor is there any direct correlation between the two.[6] Neo-liberalism assumes that because the competitive forces inherent in markets drive competition and innovation to produce better and cheaper products and services, citing as examples the progress of industrialised nations, this model should be encouraged worldwide, particularly in developing nations. No doubt, inefficient and corrupt governments in the developing world have failed to make any tangible gains from the nationalisation of their natural resources and other industries and have instead accumulated significant debts. It was natural therefore for neo-liberal advocates to maintain that besides trade and financial liberalisation, states should accept deregulation,

---

[3] By way of illustration, in 1996 a World Bank report criticised water leakage levels between 1 and 5 per cent in Germany's public sector water operators for being too low. The principal author of the report, who went on to become head of the World Bank's water policy unit, noted that water should be allowed to leak if the cost of fixing the leak was greater than the profit that could be made if the water was sold! This is a clear example of a policy driven by profit considerations, not human welfare or rights concerns (i.e. the right to water for present and future generations). Quoted in M. Kothari, 'Privatising Human Rights: The Impact of Globalisation on Adequate Housing, Water and Sanitation', online at unpan1.un.org/intradoc/groups/public/documents/apcity/unpan010131.pdf, 3.

[4] R. Howard-Hassmann, 'The Second Great Transformation: Human Rights Leapfrogging in the Era of Globalisation' (2005) 27 *Human Rights Quarterly* 1.

[5] See particularly the forceful argument of P. O'Connell, 'On Reconciling Irreconcilables: Neo-liberal Globalisation and Human Rights' (2007) 7 *Human Rights Law Review* 483, at 489.

[6] See Chapter 14.2. Equally, UN Secretary-General Report, Globalisation and its Impact on the Full Enjoyment of All Human Rights, UN doc. A/55/342 (31 August 2000) para. 13.

privatisation, unhindered foreign direct investment (FDI) and competitive exchange rates in order to attract foreign capital. They also maintained that since the public sector generally tends to expand and become inefficient, governments should be flexible and downsized and subject to strict fiscal discipline.[7]

There are several deficiencies to this otherwise laudable agenda, most of which will be explored in subsequent sections. It suffices to note at this stage that none of the pursuits of neo-liberalism were directly geared towards alleviating poverty and joblessness, universal health care or other social goals. Privatisation, one of the mantras of neo-liberalism, is a good example. By way of illustration, although the privatisation of the health and water sectors may render the provision of these public goods cost-effective and efficient, private operators naturally deny them to those unable to afford them; yet the right to health and water are fundamental rights whose provision is incumbent on the state. As a result, privatisation that is unregulated and not subject to any social controls will be inclined towards deprivation and discrimination between the vulnerable and the wealthy.[8]

Equally, many forms of FDI produce no benefit to host states, with labour-unintensive industries being a prime example. The same is also true of investments in respect of which the investor is free to repatriate all profits without an obligation to re-invest in the host nation. Moreover, in a deregulated environment where the sole interest of businesses is the maximisation of profit and that of poor nations is the attraction of foreign capital, low salaries and weak labour rights are viewed as a competitive advantage. Thus, although foreign investors may not directly impose low wages or poor working conditions on host states, in most cases they would naturally favour those countries with the cheapest production costs for particular manufacturing activities. It is often argued that FDI of this type at least provides employment opportunities, even if poorly paid, allowing poor people to survive, albeit barely. This rationale, however, is antithetical to the UN Development Programme's (UNDP) assessment of human development, which is premised on the existence of longevity, knowledge and decent living standards.[9] Furthermore, it is contrary to the pursuit of national financial growth because poorly paid work does not contribute to the development of skilled labour, innovation, introduction of new technologies and empowerment, nor can it generate and finance other secondary sectors of the economy.

---

[7] W. K. Tabb, *Economic Governance in the Age of Globalisation* (Columbia University Press, 2005) 3.

[8] UN Commission on Human Rights, 'Report on Economic, Social and Cultural Rights: Liberalisation of Trade in Services and Human Rights', UN doc. E/CN.4/Sub.2/2002/9 (25 June 2002) paras. 44–5.

[9] See Chapter 14.2.

Two broad categories of globalisation are generally recognised. The first is the engineered model briefly described in the preceding paragraphs, which is centred around private profit maximisation, which we shall term economic globalisation.[10] The second is predicated on the advances in information and communications technologies which have resulted in the shrinking of time and space, the disappearance of borders, increased interaction between people and the development of mutual values and norms.[11] One dimension of this second category is so-called subaltern globalisation (also known as globalisation from below) which is driven by those opposed to the social injustices of economic globalisation, namely the marginalised and the excluded, with an emphasis on the democratisation of decision-making and the diffusion of power.[12] This movement is sometimes, but rather simplistically, referred to as anti-globalisation.

The paradox of economic globalisation is that it constitutes a policy by which to curtail public power and replace the state with private action under the banners of deregulation and privatisation. This is not merely a government-shrinking exercise but an affirmation that it is not only states that hinder good governance, international trade and prosperity, but that private actors are better off self-regulating their respective spheres of professional activity. Self-regulation may be achieved in the absence of formal laws (for example, MNCs in their dealings with external stakeholders and host governments) as well as in the process of implementing hard law (for example, implementation of anti-money laundering regulations by the banking sector). In every case, the chief aim of self-regulation is to replace the state in its public law-making function and pre-empt government action altogether. Although this idea is attractive because it minimises transaction costs and government bureaucracy, it also entails the privatisation of human rights since states are essentially absolved from many of their human rights obligations. It also has an impact on the payment of taxes by the wealthy, which in turn affects the enjoyment of socio-economic rights by the poor and the middle classes.

A pervasive side effect of economic globalisation and trade liberalisation is the integration of capital and trading markets. This means, for example, that agricultural and other commodities, such as sugar, grain and hydrocarbons, are bought and sold around the world at prices subject to external

---

[10] See W. T. Milner, 'Economic Globalisation and Rights: An Empirical Analysis', in
      A. Brysk (ed.), *Globalisation and Human Rights* (University of California Press, 2002)
      77, who defines economic globalisation as the integration of economies in institutional,
      commercial and financial terms.

[11] UNDP, *Human Development Report* (Oxford University Press, 1999) 1.

[12] O'Connell, above note 5, 493–4.

variables, such as global output in any particular year and artificial price fluctuations by traders intended to increase their revenues. In short, goods necessary for survival are subject to financial commodification. This is not necessarily a negative outcome because produce which would otherwise be bought cheaply can be traded at international prices, thus offering a higher income to least developed countries (LDCs) than if the same produce were traded locally. Attractive as this idea is, it is clearly not viable for small-scale farmers, or for countries with poor institutional capacities and weak trade deficits. This system does not allow individual producers or states to negotiate the price of their commodities, unless their production constitutes a significant bulk of global output. Given also that LDCs are by no means major trading players in international markets, the prices of basic foods for the sustenance of their people are dependent on the unregulated trading practices of several banks and trading companies operating under huge profits in the developed world.[13] This constitutes not only an elimination of economic sovereignty but an indirect denial of self-determination in respect of a country's natural resources. Consequently, if food production and trading are left to self-regulation alone, widespread poverty is the only natural outcome.

20.3   DOES THE EXISTING MODEL OF TRADE LIBERALISATION PROMOTE DEVELOPMENT AND ALLEVIATE POVERTY?

In the aftermath of World War II industrialised nations realised that if their production levels were to increase they would have to export their goods to even more countries in all continents. This ensured growth, investment in research, technological superiority and ample employment opportunities. The only problem was that although their products were competitive from a manufacturing point of view, they were rendered non-competitive or unattractive from a consumer standpoint the moment they entered the local market of the importing nation. This was because of the imposition of tariffs, which are essentially taxes on foreign goods entering a country

---

[13] Exogenous shocks to non-diversified economies are a major concern for LDCs. By way of illustration, with the urging and lending of the World Bank, Vietnam quickly rose to become the fourth largest coffee producer. As a result of increased output, global coffee prices were dramatically reduced and countries like Uganda, whose farming industry, both large- and small-scale, was based on coffee production, underwent a sharp decline in real income by the early 2000s. The erosion of LDCs' economic sovereignty by private banks and credit rating agencies is acknowledged by the International Labour Organization's (ILO) World Commission on the Social Dimension of Globalisation Report, entitled *A Fair Globalisation: Creating Opportunities for All* (2004) para. 163.

and which are directly payable to the government of that country.[14] Quite clearly, tariffs are discriminatory taxes on imported goods, the purpose of which is to favour a domestic product over a foreign import. As a result, because the domestic product is not subject to a tariff it is cheaper and thus more attractive than its foreign competitor. Low-income countries rely on tariffs not only to support their domestic industries but also because they generate significant income for the public purse. Yet if every country were to impose tariffs in this manner or subsidise its domestic industries, few exports would be financially viable and hence global production would significantly decrease and international trade would come to a standstill.

The only loser from tariff reduction/elimination seems to be the domestic industry for which the protectionist effect of tariffs was originally intended. Therefore, in order for developed countries to attract LDCs into the post-1945 world trading system, which was predicated on trade liberalisation (i.e. tariff and quota-free trade), they recognised the need for protection of certain LDC industries until such time as they could effectively compete with their foreign counterparts. This protectionism was hardly based on charity, but was the concerted result of an LDC coalition within the UN Conference on Trade and Development (UNCTAD), known as G77.[15] Article XVIII of the 1947 General Agreement on Tariffs and Trade (GATT)[16] offered LDCs exemptions from their commitments in order to 'grant the tariff protection required for the establishment of a particular industry'. The rationale was to promote certain industries through import substitution policies and thus restrict imports. In 1965, part IV of GATT, entitled 'Trade and Development', went even further and focused on expanding LDC access to the export markets of developed nations. The key to this expansion was the principle of special and differential treatment, through which developed nations were urged to make non-reciprocal tariff concessions to LDCs. As laudable as this was, the largest portion of part IV was not binding. In the 1970s developed countries were allowed to grant preferential tariffs to imports from LDCs, a system known as Generalised System of Preferences (GSP), which constituted an exception to the most favoured nation (MFN) principle, itself a cornerstone of GATT and later the World Trade Organization (WTO).[17] Many developed countries

---

[14] Trade liberalisation encompasses tariff barriers and non-tariff barriers. As far as the former is concerned, the term tariff is broad and includes practices such as duties, surcharges and export subsidies. Non-tariff barriers include licensing requirements, quotas and manufacturing standards, among others.

[15] S. E. Roland, 'Developing Countries Coalition at the WTO: In Search of Legal Support' (2007) 48 *Harvard International Law Journal* 487, at 488.

[16] 55 UNTS 194.

[17] This was formalised in 1979 through an instrument known as the Enabling Clause, arts. 1, 5, 7. See 'Differential and More Favourable Treatment Reciprocity and Fuller

went on to adopt GSP programmes that extended preferential terms of trade to LDCs.[18]

These exceptional concessions to LDCs seem like an ideal way of introducing them to the globalised trading system with a view to eventually rendering them equal trading partners. The first preambular paragraph to the 1994 WTO Agreement[19] even stresses that one of the principal goals of liberalised trade is to raise living standards and secure full employment on the basis of sustainable development. Although this echoes some of the essential underpinnings of the right to development, in fact the neo-liberal globalised trading system did not envisage any real linkages between human rights and trade, let alone the right to development. The application of the GSP device is certainly illustrative of the benefits it provides in many cases to developed nations and the subsequent harm it causes LDCs. GSP laws and agreements, at least those originating from the European Union (EU) and the USA, typically subject all the concessions offered to a range of conditionalities, some of which are human rights-based.[20] This is consistent with the vociferous support by developed nations of non-trade issues in the international trade agenda, particularly human rights, labour rights and environmental protection. LDCs have remained hostile to such linkages, for good reason.

Under the theory of comparative advantage, two or more countries with unequal industrial and financial development can still benefit from free trade between themselves by concentrating on the production of goods for which they enjoy the greatest comparative advantage, and import those products in respect of which they do not enjoy an advantage. One of the comparative advantages of LDCs is their availability of relatively cheap labour, which means that certain products that do not require skilled labour, particularly agricultural and textile-based, are cheaper to produce there. This, however, leads to a sharp decrease in core (and other local) labour standards, either

Participation of Developing Countries', Decision of 28 November 1979. This remains in force under art. 1(b)(iv) of the 1994 WTO Agreement.

[18] The USA, for example, enacted the Africa Growth and Opportunity Act, 19 USC §3721, whereas the EU entered into the Cotonou Agreement with LDCs from Africa, the Caribbean and the Pacific (ACP), which in turn spurred other initiatives, such as 'Everything But Arms' (EBA), through which all duties and quotas were eliminated for all products (save for arms) originating from LDCs.

[19] 1994 Marrakesh Agreement Establishing the World Trade Organization (WTO Agreement), 1867 UNTS 154.

[20] L. Bartels, *Human Rights Conditionality in the EU's International Agreements* (Oxford University Press, 2005) 68. EC Council Regulation 980/2005 (27 June 2005) on applying a scheme of generalised tariff preferences, OJ L 169/1, requires under its GSP Plus criteria that in order for a country to be eligible for preferential treatment, it 'must ratify and effectively implement' several international conventions dealing with human rights, labour laws, environmental protection, drugs and anti-corruption.

because their implementation entails a high cost for the investor or because other nations have lowered theirs in an attempt to become more attractive. This is known as the 'race to the bottom'. Empirical studies suggest an absence of a systematic relationship between a competitive advantage and diminished labour standards.[21] Even so, although low wages and poor labour conditions are not conducive to the full realisation of the right to development, at the very least one would have imagined that international trade liberalisation would allow cheaply made products to boost the economies of LDCs and improve their people's socio-economic status. Alas, this has not proven to be the case. The USA has consistently maintained that poor labour conditions, assessed on the basis of standards employed in developed nations and which include minimum wages and hours of work, justify the imposition of duties or trade sanctions against products originating from LDCs, thus denying them their only comparative advantage in US consumer markets.[22] This constitutes a clear form of protectionism in favour of domestic products and calls on LDCs to apply labour standards that are wholly unrealistic with their level of development.[23] Although they may be applied unilaterally, the USA has been very consistent in including employment standards in its free trade agreements with other nations.[24] The consequence of such measures is their immediate impact on vulnerable populations. In Bangladesh, for example, the mere consideration by the US Congress of banning products manufactured by child labour led to the dismissal of female children in the textiles industry, many of whom were forced into prostitution

[21] D. Rodrik, 'Labour Standards in International Trade: Do They Matter and What do we Know about Them?' in R. Lawrence, D. Rodrik and J. Whalley, *Emerging Agenda for Global Trade: High Stakes for Developing Countries* (Overseas Development Council, 1996) 35; Organisation for Economic Cooperation and Development (OECD), *International Trade and Core Labour Standards* (2000), which bases its empirical observations on the fact that sharp FDI increases have been observed in the service sectors, thus affecting employees with better-than-average working conditions.

[22] A related, highly controversial and largely unresolved issue concerns so-called social dumping. Art. 2 of the WTO Agreement on Implementation of art. VI of the General Agreement on Tariffs and Trade 1994 (Agreement on Dumping) prohibits the introduction of imports at a price which is less than the normal value of the import. Where such a product is none the less found to have been imported, the importing state may impose an anti-dumping duty in order to offset the dumping margin. Many developed nations argue that the use of cheap labour in LDCs renders products imported therefrom subject to dumping regulations. See OECD, 'Trade, Employment and Labour Standards: A Study of Core Workers' Rights and International Trade' (1996) 170–1, which does not endorse this view.

[23] No doubt, certain well-entrenched labour rights, such as collective bargaining, freedom of association and prohibition of forced labour, are not dependent on a country's level of development and do not require any additional resources. See J. Bhagwati, 'Afterword: The Question of Linkage' (2002) 96 *American Journal of International Law* 126.

[24] See e.g., chapter 18 of the 2004 US–Chile Free Trade Agreement.

by destitute parents.[25] Of course, we are not advocating the perpetuation of Dickensian child labour in the developing world. Rather, it is imperative that the issue be confronted holistically by the entirety of the international community, not by the type of shock treatment that is inherent in unilateral measures that produce such unintended consequences.

GSPs themselves appear to be discriminatory and arbitrary on many occasions, despite their intended goal of facilitating preferential LDC access into the international trading arena. It is reported, for example, that US domestic industries regularly lobby in favour of protectionist measures against LDC imports,[26] further aided by the fact that the executive's assessment of such measures is not subject to independent review.[27] Another protectionist US measure is the denial of GSP status to those LDC products that occupy a significant place in market percentage terms. Moreover, GSP status is denied in respect of those LDC products that are crucial in terms of their export capacity, such as agricultural goods, textiles and clothing, thus rendering these preferences more or less redundant.[28]

It is thus evident that LDCs have been exposed to a liberalised global trading system with little, or no, protection for the needs of their individual development, a system which allows rich nations to manipulate the few comparative advantages of LDCs while at the same time forcing them to reduce tariffs and non-tariff barriers to foreign imports. Although there is no doubt that international trade can benefit all countries, including LDCs, by providing them with the requisite resources for raising the living standards of their people and for meeting their human rights obligations, the impact of trade liberalisation on poverty is necessarily very country specific.[29] What works for one country, especially a developed one, need not benefit another, particularly given the heavy debt burden of LDCs, their exposure to international financial markets and currency fluctuations, their dependency on agriculture and thus lack of diversification, poor education and many other problems.

The principal impediment to poverty alleviation and development in the current scheme of international trade liberalisation is its focus on production volume rather than human development. Its adherents wrongly advocate (or at best presuppose) that the former guarantees the latter. The greatest

[25] Bhagwati, above note 23, 132.

[26] P. Alston, 'Labour Rights Provisions in US Trade Law: Aggressive Unilateralism?' in L. A. Compa and S. F. Diamond (eds.), *Human Rights, Labour Rights and International Trade* (University of Pennsylvania Press, 1996) 71, 84.

[27] *International Labour Rights Education and Research Fund v. Bush* (US) (1990).

[28] A. E. Cassimatis, *Human Rights Related Trade Measures under International Law* (Martinus Nijhoff, 2007) 411.

[29] C. Lumina, 'Free Trade or Just Trade? The World Trade Organisation, Human Rights and Development (Part 1)' (2008) 12 *Law, Democracy and Development* 20, at 25.

empirical proof that this is a fallacy is the fact that even those few countries that have seen a rapid growth to their trade output (for example, India), with the exception of China,[30] have made little progress in combating poverty overall. Other poor nations, especially those in Africa that relied almost exclusively on agriculture have even found themselves worse-off in terms of securing food for their people because their economies were not suited to trade liberalisation. In the absence of a true human rights-based approach to international trade none of the inherent pitfalls of liberalisation can be mitigated. Neo-liberalism is clearly inconsistent with the right to development, and the existing tentative human rights linkages to trade are not only inadequate but serve to mask the process of fragmentation between these two spheres, a development which is contrary to the human rights obligations of WTO member states. In 2016 the UN Independent Expert on the promotion of a democratic and equitable international order, Alfred de Zayas, issued a report[31] that was notable for several reasons. The report dismisses investor–state dispute settlement (ISDS) altogether and assumes that awards are always in favour of investors. Despite what are mainly the failings of ISDS, empirical evidence does not corroborate the report's assertion, and in any event investor protection is and should be an important dimension of international development law. The report does introduce the concept of R2A – responsibility to act in the public interest, on the basis of which all trade and investment treaties must be construed by tribunals and states in accordance with human rights.[32] The R2A idea is not in the least radical and helps dismiss the existing fragmentation of the various legal regimes (e.g. international trade, foreign investment and human rights). It also reinforces an existing constitutional obligation for all states, as well as a tool of human-centred treaty interpretation.

20.3.1   Liberalisation of Agriculture and its Impact on Food Security

The effects of liberalised trade on agricultural products must be assessed against global food security and individual well-being and not on whether global output has in fact increased. In short, its measure of success should reflect tangible benefits to an ever-increasing number of individual livelihoods. If this is not found to be the case then the current system must be deemed a failure. Let us look to numbers once again. In India 60 per cent

---

[30] China has, in fact, reduced its poverty levels (less than US$1 per day) from 85 per cent in 1981 to 16 per cent in 2005, although there are huge discrepancies, especially between the urban rich and the rural poor. In any event, it is unknown whether overall poverty levels will resume once the country's growth ultimately reaches its peak.

[31] 'Report: Note by the Secretariat', UN doc. A/HRC/33/40 (12 July 2016).

[32] Ibid., paras. 13ff.

of the population lives off agriculture, whereas in Nepal the same activity is carried out by a staggering 93 per cent of the population. This should be contrasted with 2.7 per cent in the USA and 1.7 per cent in the United Kingdom (UK).[33] Moreover, the vast majority of farmers in LDCs operate small-scale farms, whether family-owned or leased, while at the same time dependent family members usually have no other employment and are expected to assist the principal bread winner. In contrast, few farms in the developed world are independent, with large farming conglomerates controlling overall production and prices. The bigger a farming company becomes, the less it is reliant on subsidies and the more it becomes able to affect the cost of productivity globally. Even so, farming receives significant subsidies in the USA and the EU.

Small-scale farmers require subsidies not only to stay in business, but also in order to compete with their larger rivals who control the means of production and distribution and can thus outprice them. As a result, otherwise prohibited subsidies under the terms of the WTO's trade liberalisation are crucial for sustaining small-scale farming in LDCs, which remains by far the principal economic activity of the poor. Small-scale farming subsidies, however, are not only important because they provide employment, but also because the agricultural output of small-scale farming in the developing world is consumed locally, which in turn contributes to food security. If small-scale farmers could no longer afford the means to sow seeds and harvest their fields they would be forced to abandon farming altogether, thus leading to severe food shortages, which in turn would force the poor to buy their staple food from non-local markets, the prices of which are prohibitive. A similar outcome is guaranteed in situations where an LDC is eager to export its agricultural produce by reallocating land and resources from domestic food production without first securing adequate food supplies for its people.[34]

Non-governmental organisations (NGOs) correctly maintain that agricultural trade liberalisation is injurious in respect of job and food security of poor people in LDCs. Apart from the reasons already analysed, they add that there is no guarantee that LDC exports will be accepted in developed nations

---

[33] 3D, *Planting the Right Seed: A Human Rights Perspective on Agriculture Trade and the WTO* (March 2005) 1.

[34] The risks arising from export-oriented agriculture policies in LDCs were highlighted by the Special Rapporteur on the right to food in his report on Guatemala. He noted that this policy deepens extreme inequality in ownership of resources and must be replaced with a strategy that directly improves food security through implementation of agrarian reform and small-scale peasant agriculture. Report on Mission to Guatemala, UN doc. E/CN.4/2006/44/Add.1 (18 January 2006) para. 58; equally in respect of Bolivia, UN doc. A/HRC/7/5/Add.2 (30 January 2008) para. 59, and CESCR Concluding Observations on Paraguay, UN doc. E/C.12/PRY/CO/3 (4 January 2008) para. 31.

because of food safety and packaging requirements, which LDC farmers cannot possibly meet. Moreover, because LDCs must admit high levels of imports given that they are not allowed to set quota restrictions, MNCs have been able to sell their surpluses to LDCs at prices below the cost of production (dumping) at no loss, having maintained artificially high prices in global markets in previous years.[35] Finally, it is argued that real profit from agricultural produce is made by a handful of MNCs which control global production and which are in receipt of generous subsidies by developed nations, a fact which not only renders LDC exports uncompetitive abroad but also domestically.[36]

As a result, in the context of existing agricultural socio-economic relations, any benefits to LDCs from trade liberation – which is clearly asymmetrical and one-sided – are outweighed by their potentially detrimental effects on job and food security. The potential of even the slightest price volatility of staple commodities as a result of the uncontrolled and profit-driven financialisation of commodity futures trading is devastating for those who live at or below the poverty line.[37] The right to food, as this has been elaborated by the Committee on Economic, Social and Cultural Rights (CESCR),[38] must serve as the paramount criterion in any trading agenda concerning agricultural production, and LDCs should not be encouraged to export their agricultural produce, or to dismantle small-scale farming, if they have not first achieved sufficient food security for domestic consumption. No one should be denied access to food on the basis of financial or other criteria.

CASE STUDY 20.1
Liberalisation of Zambia's Maize Production

Until the early 1990s African governments typically controlled the prices, distribution, processing and marketing of most staple agricultural products, which was maize in the case of Zambia. The margin of loss between state-mandated

---

[35] The Special Rapporteur on the right to food, while encouraging public investment in India's smallholder agriculture, noted that 'greater liberalization of trade in basic staple foods should not be pursued as long as subsidies in developed countries keep international prices at artificially low levels, otherwise India will suffer from competition from dumped agricultural products that will undermine its own production, especially of rice and wheat'. Report on Mission to India, UN doc. E/CN.4/2006/44/Add.2 (20 March 2006) para. 48.

[36] See Lumina, above note 29, at 27, who narrates that in 2000 every cow in the EU was subsidised by US$913, whereas each person in sub-Saharan Africa received US$8 in EU aid.

[37] UN Secretary-General Report, 'Globalisation and its Impact on the Full Enjoyment of all Human Rights', UN doc. A/64/265 (7 August 2009) 10–11.

[38] See CESCR, General Comment 12: the right to adequate food, UN doc. E/C.12/1999/5 (1999).

purchase prices and selling prices as a result of the intervening marketing costs was offset by government subsidies and low-interest loans to the state cooperatives that ran the maize industry. The deficit quickly escalated and whereas in 1984 maize subsidies accounted for 5.5 per cent of the country's budget, by 1990 the figure had reached 13 per cent.[1] It should be noted that 67 per cent of Zambia's workforce is employed in small-scale agriculture, with 80 per cent of the country's agricultural produce consisting of maize. As a result of a heavy debt burden the government of Zambia was effectively driven to partly liberalise its maize production in 1990 with full liberalisation taking place in 1995.

Following liberalisation the price offered to producers declined whereas the market price of maize in Zambia increased. Although maize was the country's staple food, due to now higher prices local consumption naturally decreased among the rural, poor, population. Empirical evidence suggests that although production levels have increased, the emergence of a vibrant trading sector has been slow, and small-scale farmers continue to be plagued by inadequate finance, storage and transportation facilities. At the same time those unable to cope with the changes were driven out of the sector altogether, which in conjunction with succeeding droughts, caused widespread malnutrition and severe health problems, including a surge in child mortality.[2]

[1] A. Mwanaumo, W. A. Masters and P. V. Preckel, 'A Spatial Analysis of Maize Marketing Policy Reforms in Zambia' (1997) 79 *American Journal of Agricultural Economics* 514, at 514–15.

[2] See V. Seshamani, 'The Impact of Market Liberalisation on Food Security in Zambia' (1998) 23 *Food Policy* 539.

INTERVIEW 20.1

The Director of Food First

(Eric Holt-Giménez)

Dr Eric Holt-Giménez is Executive Director of the Institute for Food and Development Policy, otherwise known as 'Food First'. The mission of Food First is to end the injustices that cause hunger.

What would a fair, poverty-alleviation targeted international trade policy look like?

The main challenge to a fair international trade policy for poverty alleviation is to protect and improve the conditions of the 2 billion resource-poor, smallholder and subsistence farmers. The right to protect national markets from international dumping and to maintain local grain reserves (to protect against price volatility), needs to be a structural part of this policy. This probably implies taking agriculture out of the WTO and most of the bilateral free trade agreements. Tight regulation of foreign investment (trade in capital and capital goods) to protect rural communities from recent trends in land grabbing is also important.

What are the principal reasons, or actors, hindering developed states from adopting trade policies that ensure a dignified life for all people of the world?

For over two decades the trade policies of the USA and Europe have been driven by overproduction and cheap grain that is ultimately dumped abroad. The main winners in this strategy have been the international grain companies that bought grain at a deflated price. Now, grain prices are high and subject to extreme price swings. The oligopolies controlling the flow of grain and speculators in commodity investment funds (CIFs) have a financial stake in this volatility. These actors, land speculators and the seed and input monopolies now attempting to break into the markets at the 'base of the pyramid' are the main obstacles to a dignified life for the poorest of the poor. Global, unregulated markets and monopolies are incapable of resolving these problems – on the contrary they have brought them on.

In terms of actual finances and global resources, is it feasible to expect that the entirety of the world's population can enjoy a decent standard of living and eliminate poverty altogether?

The world already produces enough food to feed ten billion people. The problem is that over 40 per cent of the grain produced is converted into fuel or meat. We have the resources to eliminate poverty and hunger, but not the political will to control the markets and monopolies that produce poverty. Most of the billion hungry people in the world are resource-poor subsistence farmers. Sustainable rural livelihoods based on a fair social wage (health education and welfare), access to basic resources (like land, water, health services and education) and support to develop sustainable forms of agriculture will lay the basis for the rural and urban elimination of poverty and hunger.

Please provide a practical illustration of the relevance of human rights in designing a trade agenda.

The right to food is a human right and should be justiciably recognised in trade policy. Any trade policies that impede a person's right to food, such as dumping, land-grabbing investments, genetic contamination or international hoarding and speculation should be heavily sanctioned.

20.4 HOW INTELLECTUAL PROPERTY RIGHTS HINDER ACCESS TO ESSENTIAL MEDICINES FOR THE POOREST

One of the neo-liberal assumptions was that the liberalisation of trade would ultimately reduce costs related to bureaucracy, transactions and production. Moreover, because this process was calculated to distribute income to even greater masses of people as a result of new employment opportunities, it was thought that health care and medicines would become cheaper by reason of user volume alone. However, equitable income distribution from the fruits of trade liberalisation failed to materialise, and to make things worse LDCs were further burdened with heavy external debts which they were forced to service at the expense of economic, social and cultural rights, including universal health care. An additional obstacle in realising the right to health, particularly accessibility to affordable medicines, is the commercial value afforded to pharmaceutical patents over and above their potential to save lives. No doubt, the regime of intellectual property (IP), including patents, serves to incentivise innovators investing time and money on new discoveries by protecting their work against usurpers. Were it not for the benefits of IP protection, pharmaceutical companies investing billions of dollars into drug research would be exposed to parallel production by generic drug manufacturers once the drug went into circulation. As a result, the general application of IP law in the field of pharmaceuticals is to reward innovation by providing a commercial head start to the innovator with a view to cementing his position in the market, recouping research and manufacturing costs and making a profit. This IP regime, however, is clearly in conflict with the right of access to affordable medicines because pharmaceutical companies are naturally unwilling to slash their prices for the poor and the vulnerable, let alone allow generic manufacturers to produce and sell at low cost.[39] The CESCR has called on states to prevent unreasonably high medicine costs resulting from the protection of IP, emphasising that products should be denied patentability where 'commercialisation would jeopardise the full realisation' of other rights, particularly the right to health and adequate standard of living.[40]

Poor countries facing health epidemics are unable to pay the high prices demanded by pharmaceutical companies and thus desire the freedom to

---

[39] In a relatively recent test case the Egyptian Court of Administrative Justice dismissed a decree establishing a new pricing system for brand names and generic drugs, on the basis that it would render them far too expensive for the average Egyptian and would thus violate the right to obtain affordable medicines. *Egyptian Drug Pricing case* (Egypt) (2010).

[40] CESCR, General Comment 17: the right to moral and material interests from scientific, literary or artistic production, UN doc. E/C.12/GC/17 (12 January 2006) para. 35.

produce these drugs themselves.[41] The South African case study is instructive. In response to the country's HIV/AIDS epidemic a law was adopted that allowed the health minister to curtail the patent rights of pharmaceutical MNCs through parallel imports and compulsory licences.[42] Parallel imports refers to patented drugs already in circulation elsewhere and which are imported (at lower prices) without the patent-holder's consent, whereas compulsory licences allow generic manufacturers to cheaply produce a drug without the patent-holder's approval and in violation of his IP rights. Although both of these exceptions to the rights of patent-holders[43] clearly offend his or her rights, they are exceptionally permitted under article 8(1) of the WTO Agreement on Trade-Related Aspects of Intellectual Property Rights (TRIPS Agreement)[44] in order to 'protect public health and nutrition', among other things.[45] As a result, cheap anti-retroviral drugs were produced or imported and distributed free of charge to those who could not afford them. A group of thirty-nine pharmaceutical MNCs commenced legal proceedings for the violation of their IP rights. The government responded that it was under a constitutional duty to protect the health of its citizens.[46] It should be stated that although the case was settled through the adoption of a joint understanding between the USA and South Africa, for a while the US government partially withheld its GSP treatment of South Africa.[47]

Despite strong opposition from developed nations and part of the industry itself, it seems quite settled, as a result of the Doha Declaration and the TRIPS Agreement, that poor nations may validly substitute patented drugs with cheap generics in order to tackle acute health crises.[48] This view was further cemented in December 2005 by the General Council of the WTO.[49]

---

[41] Empirical studies have demonstrated that once drugs are patented their price increases by at least 100 per cent. See A. Subramanian, 'The AIDS Crisis, Differential Pricing of Drugs and the TRIPS Agreement: Two Proposals' (2001) 4 *Journal of World Intellectual Property* 323.

[42] 2002 Medicines and Related Substances Act Control Amendment Act.

[43] Arts. 30–2 of the TRIPS Agreement. These are technically known as TRIPS flexibilities.

[44] TRIPS Agreement, 1869 UNTS 299.

[45] These so-called flexibilities against the otherwise rights of the patent-holder were iterated in para. 5 of the 2001 Doha Ministerial Declaration on the TRIPS Agreement and Public Health, WTO Doc. WT/MIN(01)/DEC/2 (20 November 2001). Para. 4 of this Declaration very significantly emphasised that the TRIPS Agreement should not prevent countries from 'taking measures to protect public health and that the Agreement can and should be interpreted and implemented in a manner supportive of WTO members' right to protect public health and, in particular, to promote access to medicines for all'.

[46] *Pharmaceutical Manufacturers' Association of South Africa et al. v. President of the Republic of South Africa* (South Africa) (1998).

[47] See also Chapter 9.9 on the right to health.

[48] See *WTO Agreements and Public Health: A Joint Study by the WHO and WTO Secretariat* (2002) 38–47, 97–111.

[49] Amendment of the TRIPS Agreement, Decision of 6 December 2005, doc. WT/L/641 (8 December 2005).

Even so, some commentators point to attempts by certain countries to frustrate the Doha Declaration in practice, particularly through the proliferation of free trade agreements. These inhibit the use of TRIPS flexibilities by developing nations and impose on them high standards of IP protection, thus effectively precluding the manufacture or import of cheap generic drugs.[50] Recently, in response to Swiss trade agreements with LDCs that effectively negated the right to generic drugs guaranteed by the Doha Declaration, the CESCR admonished Switzerland to 'take into account its partner countries' obligations when negotiating and concluding trade and investment agreements [and] undertake an impact assessment to determine the possible consequences of its foreign trade policies and agreements on the enjoyment by the population of the state party's partner countries of their economic, social and cultural rights'.[51]

CASE STUDY 20.2
Biopiracy and the Mayocoba Bean

Mayocoba beans had been grown in Mexico for centuries and constituted a staple food for millions. Naturally, no Mexican farmer or the country's government ever thought of patenting what nature bountifully gave to the land. In 1994 a US national, Larry Proctor, purchased a bag of mayocoba beans in Mexico and planted them in his farm in Colorado, allowing them to self-pollinate. Of those grown he selected yellow beans from several generations, which he proceeded to name Enola (after his wife) and within two years he filed for an exclusive monopoly patent in the USA. Despite the fact that Proctor had not invented the bean itself nor engineered the variety he was granted the patent, which gave him the right to exclusively use the bean for twenty years! Once his patent was in place he brought suits against several Mexican companies on the ground

---

[50] C. Lumina, 'Free Trade or Just Trade? The World Trade Organisation, Human Rights and Development (Part 2)' (2010) 14 *Law Democracy and Development* 1, at 15. See also the CESCR's Concluding observations on Costa Rica, which noted with concern the impact from the coming into force of the Central American Free Trade Agreement on traditional agriculture, labour rights, access to generic medicines and biodiversity, among others. UN doc. E/C.12/CRI/CO/4 (4 January 2008) para. 27.

[51] CESCR, Concluding Observations on Switzerland, UN doc. E/C.12/CHE/CO/2–3 (26 November 2010) para. 24; in *Azanca Alheli Meza García* (Peru) (2004) the Peruvian Constitutional Tribunal held that the state was under an obligation to provide drugs to an HIV sufferer who could not afford them on the ground that the realisation of social rights of this nature should be a priority in the country's budget.

that they were in violation of his IP rights. Had Proctor moved for a worldwide patent on 'Enola', indigenous Mexican farmers would not have been able even to cultivate this indigenous crop variety in their own country. With respect to those exporting the bean to the USA, however, Proctor demanded (and received) a royalty of 6 cents per pound, irrespective of whether the grower/importer was indigenous. Not surprisingly, Mexican exports dropped as much as 90 per cent, causing significant financial loss to thousands of Mexican farmers.

The case would have received little attention had it not been for the civil society organisation International Centre for Tropical Agriculture (CIAT), which challenged the validity of the patent before US courts. The US Federal Court of Appeals ultimately affirmed the invalidity of the patent.[1] Even so, this tip-of-the-iceberg case is paradigmatic of law's manipulation by the rich against the destitute, and usurpation for purely financial gain of traditional knowledge.[2]

---

[1] In *re Pod-Ners LLC* (US) (2009).
[2] M. V. Gubarev, 'Misappropriation and Patenting of Traditional Ethnobotanical Knowledge and Genetic Resources' (2012) 8 *Journal of Food Law and Policy* 65.

20.5 THE *MCLIBEL* CASE: SALES GLOBALISATION AND ITS IMPACT ON RIGHTS

For the practical application of this closing chapter we could have chosen a case study closely associated with one of the themes explored in the preceding sections. None the less, we opted for something that on the surface only tangentially deals with the issues arising in the globalisation debate and which could also feature in the chapter dealing with non-state actors. In that chapter (Chapter 19) it was demonstrated that MNCs possess the privilege to choose where they will manufacture their products, with nations, especially poor ones, offering a plethora of incentives in order to secure much-needed capital investment. Whereas human rights-related globalisation is typically associated with the manufacturing and outsourcing dimension of MNC operations (i.e. low wages, poor labour conditions, corruption, environmental degradation, etc.), little attention has been paid to their sales capacity. This is because of the much-hailed assumption that sales are determined by market forces and consumer choice. It is therefore considered axiomatic that no one in their right mind would purchase an inferior product at a high price, especially when better and cheaper products are on offer. This assumption is logical but not always practical, because it fails to appreciate the immense power of advertising, the impact of media, the vastness of information and the pace of urban life which leave little, if any, time for informed consent on consumer choices.[52] In very simple terms, I would not buy a sweater in the knowledge that the seller or manufacturer had forced a five-year-old to knit it without pay or food. However, I would have few hesitations about eating a hamburger during a hungry lunch break if the seller's advertising campaign sheltered and cushioned me from information about cruelty to animals, low staff wages, the unhealthy nature of the food, the deliberate targeting of children as future consumers and the company's negative environmental impact.

The *McLibel* case is instructive of the way in which MNCs have assumed the mantle of making consumer choices for the public and globalised their products under the guise of 'culture'. In 1986 a little-known NGO, London Greenpeace, not to be confused with Greenpeace International, distributed a pamphlet entitled *What's Wrong with McDonald's: Everything They Don't Want you to Know*. Although this was a relatively small campaign, well before the internet era, with the aim of educating the public on the methods of the company's food production, the products' health hazards and the company's poor animal welfare, environmental and labour record, it caused McDonald's some concern. The NGO was infiltrated for a period of about eighteen months by persons covertly working for the corporate giant and pretending to support the NGO's original cause. In fact, McDonald's had employed two separate teams of informants, none of whom were aware of the others' existence! Once the informants had gathered ample material, some of which was outright stolen from the NGO's premises, the McDonald's legal team put together a case against five members of London Greenpeace, charging them with libel. McDonald's naturally assumed that the defendants would be an easy target, since prior to this litigation it had threatened major newspapers, broadcasting corporations and other smaller media outlets (including a student newspaper) with libel suits, all of which resulted in settlements and public apologies. In fact, under threat of action three of the original NGO defendants offered an apology, but Helen Steel and David Morris refused to cave in.

During the first hearing before the High Court the trial was clearly unfair.[53] The defendants were denied legal aid even though they were relatively poor,

---

[52] The issue of consumer rights has generally been ignored by human rights scholarship because of the classic assumption that the relations between consumer and seller are regulated predominantly by contract, whereas relations with the manufacturer are based on the law of tort. In this triangular relationship it is thought that the state plays no visible part and both seller and manufacturer owe no other obligations other than those already mentioned. This assumption is clearly problematic, as the *McLibel* case illustrates.

[53] It was not difficult for the ECtHR to reach the same conclusion. See *Steel and Morris v. United Kingdom* (ECtHR) (2005). Unfortunately, the burden of proof in defamation and libel laws have remained largely the same.

whereas McDonald's employed a large team of top lawyers. Moreover, under English law the burden of proof in libel cases at the time rested on the defendants, not on the plaintiffs. If that was not enough, at trial the judge somehow managed to determine that the issues in the case were too complex for lay jury members to comprehend (David Morris was a postman and Helen Steel a gardener, it should be noted) and so instructed that the case be heard by a single judge rather than a jury. Although the pair received some free legal advice from a human rights barrister, they defended themselves through the course of examinations and cross-examinations that lasted well over a year and on a daily basis. It is illustrative that at some point Morris was so worn out that her doctor prescribed some respite, which the court refused to provide! A year into proceedings McDonald's approached the pair for a settlement, having realised that Morris and Steel had nothing to lose personally and that the case had attracted serious negative media attention for the corporation. The trial and its outcome[54] ultimately turned out to be less important for the campaigners, as the publicity which attracted the proceedings was a public relations disaster for the corporation and provided the general public with a new awareness about the health risks associated with fast food. It also brought to light the atrocious means of production and advertisement. Ultimately, the process dragged on for an extraordinary nine years and six months, with the trial alone lasting two and a half years.

One of the important issues that emerged from the campaign through the course of the proceedings was that mega-corporations such as McDonald's were using the power of advertising to 'exploit' children's vulnerabilities. Advertising tried to portray the company's food as being nutritious, which is completely antithetical to what it really is. In equal measure, the company sought to groom younger generations into an addictive fast-food lifestyle knowing full well its hazardous health effects. This lifestyle is the product of a sales globalisation which MNCs are able to endorse worldwide with little hindrance, especially if no critical voices are raised. Defamation laws such as those of the UK are assisting them in their cause. The *McLibel* case demonstrates that negative rights-related sales globalisation may be overcome by active campaigning even against one of the biggest corporate giants. As Morris and Steel aptly put it: 'Who said ordinary people can't change the world?'[55]

---

[54] *McDonald's Corp* v. *Steel and Morris* (UK) (1997). Incidentally, although the judge found that some allegations were true, it was held that others had not been proven and thus found the defendants liable. On appeal, the Court of Appeals sustained the defendants' basic argument, among others, that a McDonald's diet increases the risk for heart disease as well as cancer, but ruled against them on other grounds.

[55] The two set up a new NGO, which also features an excellent documentary about the case, from which much information in this section was adapted. See www.mcspotlight.org/case/.

QUESTIONS

1. Is it at all possible to reconcile neo-liberal economic theories with the right to development?

2. The projected benefits to poverty alleviation promised by trade liberalisation are to a large degree predicated on the comparative advantages of even the poorest nations. What obstacles have developed nations posed to the comparative advantages of their developing counterparts?

3. It is not in the interests of developing nations to liberalise their agricultural sectors. Explain what the vulnerable and poor therein can expect to lose from this process and discuss the benefits that may accrue from public investment in small-scale farming.

4. Should trade liberalisation encompass the staple foods produced and consumed in developing countries? Explain.

5. The patent flexibilities of TRIPS have been extended by the Doha Declaration until 2016. What strategies would you recommend so that pharmaceutical companies can maintain their incentive for innovation through profit, while at the same time offering cheap drugs to those who need them most but cannot afford them?

6. Surely the proliferation of low-skilled jobs in poor nations is welcome because they spur growth, reduce unemployment and cater for large segments of the population, which is in any event unskilled. Low salaries are better than no salaries and poor labour conditions are a small price to pay. Do you agree? Discuss.

FURTHER READING

Bantekas, I., 'Wealth and Growth-based Policies Augment Global Poverty and Erode Human Rights: A Return to Human-centred Thinking' (2012) 1 *International Human Rights Law Review* 30.

Benedek, W., K. De Feyter and F. Marrella (eds.), *Economic Globalisation and Human Rights* (Cambridge University Press, 2007).

Choudhury, B., *Public Services and International Trade Liberalization: Human Rights and General Implications* (Cambridge University Press, 2014).

Cottier, T., J. Pauwelyn and E. Burgi (eds.), *Human Rights and International Trade* (Oxford University Press, 2005).

Cullet, P., 'Human Rights and Intellectual Property Protection in the TRIPS Era' (2007) 29 *Human Rights Quarterly* 403.

Drahos, P., *The Global Governance of Knowledge: Patent Offices and their Clients* (Cambridge University Press, 2010).

Fox, E. M., 'Globalisation and Human Rights: Looking out for the Welfare of the Worst' (2003) 35 *New York University Journal of International Law and Policy* 201.

Gött, H. (ed.), *Labour Standards in International Economic Law* (Springer 2019).

Harvey, D., *Neoliberalism: A Brief History* (Oxford University Press, 2005).

Ho, C. M., 'Biopiracy and Beyond: A Consideration of Socio-cultural Conflicts with Global Patent Policies' (2006) 39 *University of Michigan Journal of Law Reform* 433.

Mechlem, K., 'Harmonizing Trade in Agriculture and Human Rights: Options for the Integration of the Right to Food into the Agreement on Agriculture' (2006) 10 *Max Planck Yearbook of UN Law* 127.

Morjin, J., *Reframing Human Rights and Trade: Potential and Limits of a Human Rights Perspective of WTO Law on Cultural and Educational Goods and Services* (Hart, 2010).

Nowak, M., *Human Rights or Global Capital: The Limits of Privatization* (University of Pennsylvania Press, 2016).

Marcellin, S., *The Political Economy of Pharmaceutical Patents: US Sectional Interests and the African Group at the WTO* (Routledge, 2010).

Reid, E., *Balancing Human Rights, Environmental Protection and International Trade: Lessons from the EU Experience* (Hart, 2015).

Sibanda, O., 'A Human Rights Approach to World Trade Organisation Trade Policy: Another Medium for the Promotion of Human Rights in Africa' (2005) 5 *African Human Rights Law Journal* 387.

Wills, J., *Contesting World Order? Socioeconomic Rights and Global Justice Movements* (Cambridge University Press, 2018).

Websites

ATTAC: www.attac.org/

Corporate Europe Observatory: http://corporateeurope.org/

InterAction: www.interaction.org/

UN High-level Task Force on Global Food and Nutrition Security: www.un-foodsecurity.org/

UNCTAD: http://unctad.org

World Intellectual Property Organization (WIPO), Traditional Knowledge (section): www.wipo.int/tk/en/

WTO: www.wto.org/

INDEX